Contents

The Best of the Magazine Markets for Writers

A Directory of Publications That Buy Freelance Material

www.WritersInstitutePublications.com

edgments

rs of this market directory appreciate the generous contributions of our instructors udents and the cooperation of the magazine editors who made clear their policies d practices.

Susan Tierney, Editor
Sherri Keefe, Assistant Editor
Amy Berkun, Copy Editor

Listings Writers
Kristen Bishop
Sherry Gerstein
Dawn Handschuh
Susan Sulich

Cover Design and Production
Joanna Horvath

Cover image of *Asimov's Science Fiction* © 2012 by Penny Publications and reprinted with permission of the publisher. Cover image of *Scientific American* reproduced with permission, copyright © 2011 Scientific American, a division of Nature America, Inc. All rights reserved. Cover images of *Delicious Living*, *Sierra*, and *Yankee* reprinted with permission of the publishers.

International Standard Book Number 978-1-889715-69-8

1-800-443-6078 www.writersbookstore.com
email: services@writersbookstore.com

Printed and bound in Canada.

Contents (cont.)

Basics of Freelancing

Basics of Freelancing

What is your freelance writing strategy? Are you writing regularly? Are you marketing continuously? Charting a strategy is essential for freelance success. Your strategy for the next year should include a healthy dose of both writing *and* marketing, a delicate balance that has its challenges, especially in a time of questionable publishing budgets and many personnel changes.

Yet in today's transforming, fast-paced, new media marketplace, you will find more outlets than ever for your writing. Despite the still struggling economy, new print magazines are launching every day, many with online counterparts that feature additional content. Numerous online-only magazine start-ups are hungry for fresh material, as are an increasing number of media companies that create apps. With so many places to sell your writing, it is important to incorporate marketing efforts into each and every piece you write—even before you write it.

Most sales combine three elements: the writer's familiarity with a market and its readership; a well-developed idea that is appropriate for that readership; and a polished presentation of the idea, whether as a query letter or manuscript, to help an editor recognize its merits. Meeting these goals can be a challenge, but they are key to creating a marketable manuscript.

Targeting magazines in this way often requires as much imagination and perseverance as the writing itself. Many writers succeed in creating marketable manuscripts yet struggle when trying to find appropriate magazine markets for them. *Best of the Magazine Markets* is designed to link you with that information in an accessible way.

Finding the Best Opportunities

To help you locate the most viable freelance markets, the editors of the *Best of the Magazine Markets* annually evaluate thousands of magazines through encompassing research that includes coverage of dozens of trade sources, our own market questionnaires, and rounds of fact-checking—all to provide you with a comprehensive directory of publications that depend on freelance submissions.

Most longer listings feature magazines that:

- receive at least 25 percent of their published material from non-staff writers;
- publish at least 25 freelance submissions each year;
- have a circulation of at least 2,500;
- publish at least two issues a year.

Quarter-page listings also offer viable markets, often for other reasons. Although some of these publications met only two or three of the criteria above, or did not provide us with enough information to include them as half-page listings, you can still approach these markets confidently. They may represent a fresh fiction market, one open to new writers, or a segment of the magazine marketplace not filled by other publications.

You will also find in *Best of the Magazine Markets* a good number of publications that launched in the past year. The number and variety of these potential markets is encouraging. Mediafinder reports that 195 new print titles started up, an increase of 14 over the previous year. Knowing about those will help you see possible new directions for your ideas and queries, give you a handle on new directions in the market, and perhaps give you even more impetus to plan for the future.

To find the best outlets for your work, carefully consider your options. Look beyond the most obvious markets to find ones that may be lesser-known but more accessible. For example, if a publication you know and love is 55 percent written by nonstaff writers and publishes 30 freelance submissions yearly, you may be able to increase your chances of acceptance by targeting a similar market that is 95 percent written by freelancers and publishes 100 submissions yearly. On pages 40 and 41 you will find more explanations of how to interpret and use the information given for each magazine, along with a sample listing.

The Nature of Today's Market

The more than 20,000 magazines published in the U.S. are split into two general categories:

- Consumer and literary magazines
- Trade and professional magazines

Most consumer magazines cover topics of interest to the general public, although more special interest magazines are launched each year. These address a narrower range of subject matter, often with more in-depth articles in publications such as *Home Energy, Horticulture,* and *Hispanic Career World*. If you have expertise in a particular field, special interest magazines can be a good market for your writing.

Trade magazines publish material about specific professions and industries and their focus can vary widely, from publications like *Ski Area Management* to *Cloud Computing*.

For this edition alone, our research yielded 156 new markets for your work. We list 1,135 consumer and 322 trade publications that are nationally or regionally distributed. We also list 312 regional magazines targeting residents of particular cities, states, or regions.

Get to Know Your Readers

To target submissions successfully, it's important to identify the magazine readerships that will be interested in your topic. It could be a specific group, such as senior travelers, businesspeople, hobbyists, or young parents, or your idea may address a subject matter of interest to several overlapping groups.

Once you've identified your audience, look through the Category Index beginning on page 713, as well as other listings in this guide to find publications that may be interested. Make a list of all those that target your audience and are likely to run a piece on your topic.

Next, obtain several recent sample issues of a magazine, plus a copy of its writers' guidelines, if available. Increasingly, issues or sets of articles, and the submission guidelines are available online. As you look at sample issues, note the topics the magazine has covered recently, the age of the targeted audience, and the tone and writing style used. Would you describe the "personality" of the publication as straightforward and factual, warm and personal, or something else? Also note the experience level of the writers and watch for any distinctive characteristics in the content.

Beyond knowing that a magazine is published for expectant mothers, for example, you also want to understand the specific range and scope of the kinds of articles it runs, whether 150-word reviews of new products, 750-word personal experience essays, or 1,500-word health or how-to articles. Unless you take the time to do this

As part of your research on a publication's target audience, check out its media kit, or information for advertisers. These facts and figures often include a detailed analysis of audience age, gender, and interests, as well as an overall picture of the image the magazine wants to project. You may also be able to glean additional info about upcoming special issues.

Add-ons for the Web

The magazine market is wider and deeper these days with the addition of online content. Now more than ever, publishers are using the Web to enhance and promote their publications. Some magazines make limited use of the Web, while many offer online content only, or enhanced versions of articles from their print editions, as well as interactive features such as videos, slides, and podcasts.

The increasing importance of Web content means more—and different—opportunities for writers. Study both the print and online editions of your target publication; how is the website different than the print version? Is there additional content on the website that does not appear in print? If so, it is worth your time to consider ways to supplement your pitch with online-worthy content.

Editors will be attracted to a pitch that offers the "whole package," including unique elements for all of their magazine's formats. If you are willing to learn some basic techniques of video and photography, for example, your pitch becomes even more valuable to a busy editor searching for well-rounded content. Even something as simple as including Web references in your article might help an editor to better visualize how your idea could be used in more than one way.

research, you'll be submitting or querying without truly knowing a publication.

For fiction submissions, it's important to examine prospective magazines just as closely. With online publications expanding and increasing in number all the time, the fiction market is growing. Competition can still be strong however, and pay rates often lower than for nonfiction. Study magazines and their writers' guidelines to determine the specific genres they publish (science fiction, experimental, mainstream). If a magazine publishes only fantasy, it's not likely to buy a Western, no matter how well written.

After completing this important research, you'll have a stronger understanding of a magazine and its readers and can begin compiling a list of publications that seem most likely to acquire work like yours, creating a file for each (see sample below).

Analyze the publications in terms of what you've learned about them and how that can be applied to your manuscripts. If your idea and a certain magazine aren't a match right now, your search may still lead you to other ideas, angles, or markets. Periodically updating market files like these can also help generate ideas for future manuscripts.

Developing a Slant and Matching Readers' Needs

Generating an idea goes beyond simply selecting a subject. To hook an editor, who reviews hundreds of query letters, you'll need a very specific slant. A *subject* is a broad topic, while a *slant* is what gives an article its uniqueness. The slant is your chosen presentation of a topic, an angle that makes your article stand out. To find a slant, try focusing on specific elements of a larger topic, such as key people, places, or events.

You can also create several slants for your idea, resulting in a wider range of possible markets. An article on the historic Georgian Hotel in Santa Monica could be slanted for publication in *Fate Magazine* and *AARP the Magazine* simply by focusing on slightly different aspects of the subject. A description of the Georgian's haunted history would be perfect for *Fate Magazine*; a history of the hotel during its heydey in the mid-1900s is a nice fit for *AARP*. Take advantage of your research time and write multiple articles on a single subject.

After you've created your list of ideas, match your ideas with publications to come up with a final list of prospective magazines. Then use the listings to rank each publication.

Before you submit your manuscript or query, re-read several recent issues cover-to-cover and study the magazine's writers' guidelines to confirm that you've got a good match. If, in the past year, any of the magazines you're considering have published material similar to what you're proposing, you'll need to give your idea a significantly different slant from the one they've already used.

Name of Magazine: *Sport Fishing* **Managing Editor:** Stephanie Pancratz

Address: 460 North Orlando Ave., Suite 200, Winter Park, FL 32789 **Website:** www.fishchannel.com

Freelance Percentage: 40%

Description: What subjects does this magazine cover? Fishing in North America, science and conservation related to saltwater fishing.

Readership: Who are the magazine's typical readers? Serious fishermen.

Articles and Stories: What particular slants or distinctive characteristics do its articles or stories emphasize? How-to, where-to. Fresh, different angles to make readers say "I never knew that."

Potential Market: Is this magazine a potential market? Yes. I have a long history of sport fishing.

Ideas for Articles or Stories: What article, story, or department idea could be submitted? An article on the impact of superstorms like Sandy and hurricanes on sport fishing and related ecological issues.

Preparing to Submit a Manuscript

Your manuscript and submission package showcase both your writing skills and your professionalism. When preparing a cover letter to accompany an unsolicited manuscript:

- Provide a *brief*, clear description of the article and how it specifically relates to the magazine's needs. Include only the most essential information.
- List some of your publishing credits or personal qualifications relevant to the topic. If appropriate, note photos or other artwork you can provide to accompany the manuscript.
- If you're also sending the submission to other magazines, indicate this by noting at the end of your letter: "Thank you for your consideration of this manuscript, which is a simultaneous submission."

For a solicited manuscript:

- Indicate in your cover letter that the editor has asked to see the manuscript.
- Add a bibliography if requested.

Name
Address
Telephone Number
Email/Fax

Date

Ms. Nancy Clark
Family Circle
Gruner + Jahr USA Publishing
375 Lexington Avenue
New York, NY 10017-5514

Dear Ms. Clark:

Opener: Be clear and direct. Provide a brief introduction to the enclosed manuscript.

"Are they yours?" I have been on the receiving end of this question many times since the adoption of my two beautiful children from Baku, Azerbaijan, in January of 2001. As an adoptee who is now an adoptive parent, I assumed that I would be prepared to deal with adoption-related issues. I quickly discovered that even I was shocked at the boldness of strangers in asking about my children's personal history. Over the past few years, I have learned how to proactively deal with comments and questions in a way that best benefits my family.

Body: Describe how the story meets the magazine's editorial needs, including word length and other submission requirements. Note if it is a simultaneous submission.

With increasing diversity among today's families, it seems that everyone knows someone who has been adopted. According to the National Adoption Information Clearinghouse sponsored by the U.S. Department of Health and Human Services, American families completed more than 120,000 domestic and international adoptions each year for a decade. I have documented my family's experience in the attached 1,000-word essay, "Are They Yours?" I believe my essay would be a positive way for your Full Circle column to provide support and education for the increasing number of today's women who are touched by adoption through parenthood, friendship, or as members of a community.

Briefly cover any publishing credits.

I am the author of several adoption-related articles for *Baku Today* and *Azerbaijan International.*

Closing: Indicate if a SAS postcard or an SASE is enclosed.

Please consider the attached essay. I have enclosed an SASE for your reply. Thank you for your time.

Sincerely,

Kathleen Wilson Shryock

Enc.: Essay, clips, SASE

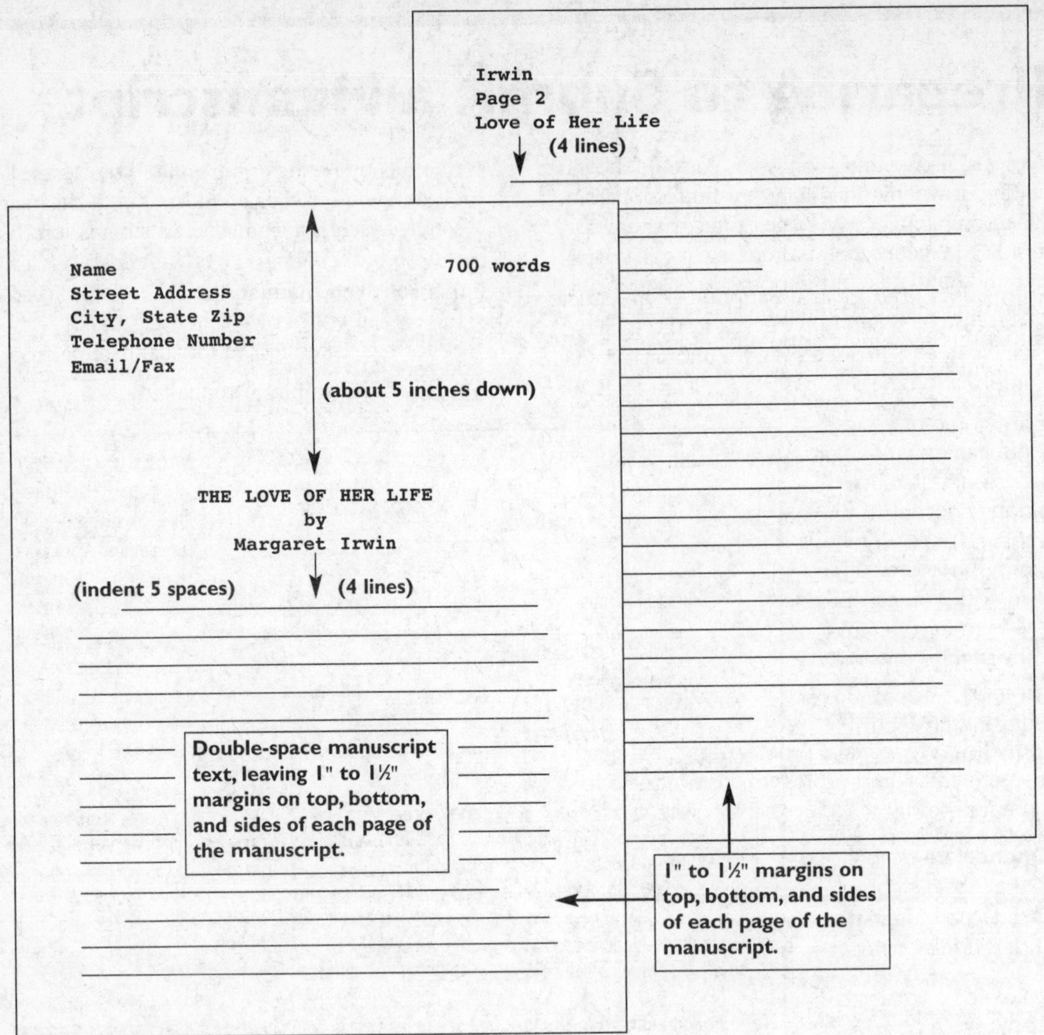

For all manuscripts, before mailing your submission package:

- Carefully follow the format above as you prepare the manuscript. Double-spacing your text, using wide margins all around, and leaving space at the top of the first page helps make reading easier for editors, who see thousands of such pages. It also allows room for the edits and notes they may need to make. It's essential to use this format if your submission is going to hold its own among the huge number of submissions that many editors receive.
- Follow the guidelines for length and preferred manuscript format that are specified in a magazine's listing or in its writers' guidelines.
- Carefully proofread the manuscript for typographical errors. Be sure the pages are clean and neat.
- If submitting by mail, you may enclose a self-addressed, stamped postcard for the editor to acknowledge receipt of the manuscript and a self-addressed envelope with sufficient postage for the return of the manuscript if it is not accepted.
- Increasingly, publications prefer to receive submissions by email. For some, attachments are acceptable in designated formats. Others prefer to receive submissions as text embedded within the message rather than as attachments. If magazine listings or guidelines don't indicate which method to use, email the editor to ask.

Keys to Writing a Query Letter

To most beginning writers, breaking into print seems harder than cracking the Kryptos. The idea of sending a one-page letter to an unknown editor who receives hundreds of queries every month sounds like an impossible route to success. What many writers don't realize, however, is that this seemingly impossible goal is actually well within their reach—as long as they've mastered the art of the query letter.

A query letter summarizes an article idea in a concise and appealing way, usually a page or less, and is intended to pique an editor's interest in the hope that he or she will request a copy of the complete article for review and possible publication. In effect, it is a 30-second sales pitch, the equivalent of an "elevator speech" in the marketing world.

The query letter highlights the subject of your proposed article, but it also does much more than that: It shows off your writing style and voice, credentials, proofreading skills, research skills, and professionalism. It also lets the editor know whether you've done your homework—is your article specifically targeted for the magazine's audience? If you can write a query that reflects favorably on all of the above, your chances for publication (or at least a request for review) just increased tenfold.

When magazine guidelines offer you the choice of submitting either a query or a complete manuscript, there are many reasons why a query is the best way to determine whether an editor is interested in your work:

- Editors tend to respond faster to queries than to manuscripts.
- Your chances of a sale and your efficiency in writing the piece are both enhanced because if interested, the editor can supply suggestions to help you tailor the article to the magazine's preferences.
- Receiving an editor's input in this way helps you direct and focus both your research and your writing.

Every query should include a title. A good title should be short and snappy—and clarify what the reader will "take away" from the experience.

Be Brief, Specific, and Polished

Your query is your sales pitch, and also provides a sample of your writing style and voice, so every word and sentence must count. You need to grab an editor's attention with the first sentence and keep him reading through the use of crisp, clear writing and a well-summarized idea.

To target a query letter toward a specific magazine, refine your idea based on what you learn from studying the magazine's content. If, for example, a magazine favors heavily researched articles with lots of quoted material from experts, you'll want to include in your query some relevant, persuasive facts about your topic and the names of expert sources you plan to interview.

Editors will find your query irresistible if you can demonstrate an ability to provide new knowledge in a way that is relevant to that publication's readers. Is your slant built around little-known facts? Does it include intriguing information that could only come from a personal interview? Your original take on the subject will attract attention and win writing assignments.

A strong and effective query summarizes what makes a particular topic worthy and appropriate for a magazine's readers, shows how you'll approach that topic, and includes a description of what the piece will include. It also specifies the article's proposed length, availability of photos and other supplementary material, and includes some background information about your writing experience, or why you're qualified to write on the topic. Highlight any unique marketing angles of the story *or* of yourself as the writer, such as unusual story elements, intriguing personal experiences, or writing awards.

Listed below are the steps required in composing a query letter. (For examples of query letters, see pages 13 and 16.) Depending on what magazine you query, you will need to include some or all of these steps:

- Read a few sample issues and review writers' guidelines.
- Verify that a query is the requested submission method.
- Address query to a specific editor by name.
- Begin with a strong lead paragraph that captures the editor's interest, conveys your angle, and reflects your knowledge of the magazine and the topic.
- Include a one- or two-line description of your article.
- Show how the idea meets the magazine's editorial goals and note if it fits a particular department or section.
- Indicate length.
- Provide details about the article's proposed content—quotes from experts, anecdotal material, case histories, etc.
- Cite sources, research resources, and interview sources you plan to include.
- Indicate number and type of photos or illustrations available.
- Include possible completion date.
- List your publishing credentials briefly and refer to any enclosed clips or writing samples. Mention any background information that especially qualifies you to address the topic.
- Close by thanking the editor for considering your query; mention if query is a simultaneous submission.
- Include your complete contact information.
- Proofread thoroughly to ensure query is free of typographical, spelling, and grammatical errors.

Keep in mind that queries are rejected by editors for many reasons. It may not be that your query wasn't good enough; the magazine may have published an article on a similar topic recently, or the topic may already be assigned to another writer. You can avoid some of these obstacles simply by doing your homework before querying, but don't be discouraged by rejection. Head back to the drawing board, tweak your idea, and send it out again. If you have your heart set on writing for a particular magazine, research other ways to forge a connection, such as fact checking or consulting as an expert on a subject. The editor may appreciate your efforts and open the door just wide enough for you to get a toehold in the market.

Email Queries

Many publishers now accept queries via email, which saves on postage, paper, and time. If you've checked the publisher's submission guidelines and this is the case, by all means take advantage of this policy.

In general, editors seem to prefer email queries to be shorter than traditional paper ones. One to three paragraphs is usually sufficient, starting with the pitch—what you have to offer—rather than the traditional "hook" designed to catch the editor's attention. The pitch should be followed by a more specific description of the article, including any subtopics that would be covered, and your credentials. End with a closing paragraph that reviews your article and invites the editor to contact you.

In an email query, your contact information should appear at the end of the letter, after your "signature." Unless the submission guidelines direct otherwise, use a subject header like "Query" or "Article Submission" to catch an editor's attention. Lastly, avoid adding any attachments to your email; many editors are wary of electronic viruses and will likely pass by those queries that rely on them. However, links to websites where your work is displayed are usually acceptable.

Query Letter Checklist

Name
Address
Telephone Number
Email/Fax

Date

K. C. Compton, Editor in Chief
Grit
1503 SW 42nd St.
Topeka, KS 66609-1265

Dear K.C. Compton:

Imagine sitting on your dad's shoulders while he zips along on a skateboard at 20 miles per hour! That's the feeling Jacques Graber gets when he's racing along on his bicycle. But not just any bicycle—one of his antique high wheels. "The view is wonderful," he says, "and the speed exhilarating."

There are more than 85 million bicycle riders in the United States. But few have experienced the thrill of riding a bicycle with a front wheel as high as their shoulder. Most that have are members of the Wheelmen—a national organization dedicated to keeping alive the heritage of American high wheels.

In my 932-word article, "Kings of the Road," readers learn about the early history of these high wheels and meet several members of the Wheelmen, including ten-year-old Joel Luciano, from Garden City, Kansas, whose family enjoys collecting and riding these antique bicycles. Would you like to take a look? I've enclosed a full list of my references, and have some great digital photographs to illustrate this piece if you're interested.

My nonfiction for kids has been published in many magazines such as *U*S* Kids, Child Life, ASPCA Animal Watch*, and *Guide*. Thanks very much for your time and consideration.

Truly yours,

Dianna Winget

Enc: SASE

❶ Make sure that you have designated the current editor and spelled the name correctly. Verify the magazine's name and current address.

❷ Lead with a paragraph that catches the editor's interest and reflects your writing style.

❸ Give examples of the article's content, and let the editor know if artwork or photographs are available.

❹ Mention your relevant publishing credits, if you have them. Do not tell the editor that you are unpublished.

❺ Mention word length, and tell the editor about interviews you have planned or any other unique material you may have uncovered.

❻ Keep the closing brief.

❼ Sign and send; don't forget to include an SASE.

Cover Letters

Cover letters are often part of a professional submission package. Some publishers prefer receiving a complete manuscript right from the start, an instance that calls for an accompanying cover letter. In other cases, you'll send a query first, and may need a cover letter only after you get a favorable response from an editor. No matter what the situation, a simple, professional cover letter reflects well on both you and your manuscript.

Cover Letter Tips

A cover letter is typically sent with a complete manuscript and includes title and word length, a brief description of the piece, and a short explanation of how it fits the editor's needs.

A cover letter also provides a separate record of your submission and your contact information, and offers an opportunity for you to provide additional information about the manuscript, for example, if you are submitting photographs or sidebars, or

Sample Cover Letter

Johnene Granger, Fiction Editor
Woman's World
Bauer Publishing Company
270 Sylvan Avenue
Englewood Cliffs, NJ 07632

Dear Ms. Granger:

Detective Joanna Weeks is presented with a tricky case: A wealthy man is murdered behind a locked door. The chief suspect is his ne'er-do-well half-brother, and yet, Mrs. Edwina Perkins, a very credible witness, insists the deed was committed by a stranger.

I offer you the enclosed 998-word story, "Stranger Danger?" as a possibility for your Solve-It-Yourself Mystery section of *Woman's World.*

I have enclosed a self-addressed, stamped envelope for your reply.

Sincerely,
Laura Gates-Lupton

Enc.: Manuscript, SASE

contact names and sources for fact checking. If you're sending a cover letter in response to an editor's request, it also acts as a reminder that he or she requested your manuscript.

Whatever information you include, always keep your cover letter short and to the point. Provide essential information only.

When sending your manuscript, make certain that it follows word lengths and format preferences indicated in the magazine's guidelines, or those that the editor has specified. If you are asked to submit the manuscript by computer disk, identify the word-processing program you've used and also send a paper or "hard" copy. If you'd like your manuscript returned, enclose a self-addressed, stamped envelope; if not, include a self-addressed, stamped postcard indicating your preference.

Sample Cover Letter

Ken Tate, Editor
Good Old Days
306 East Parr Road
Berne, IN 46711

Dear Mr. Tate:

The good old days are on the minds of many people these days. The words themselves mean different things to different people. The heartland, family, and traditions are words that describe my memories of the good old days. Most of my mother's family lives in the Midwest. My maternal grandparents were first-generation Americans, dedicated to this country, family, and hard work.

When I was a child, we went to visit them every summer for our family vacation. Landscapes, smells, and interactions with family members and family heirlooms are a vivid part of my memory of these wonderful times together. I have documented one area of my experiences in the attached 900-word article, "I Thought It Was the Ring." I believe my article will resonate with your readers who find comfort in reflecting on the past. I look into the past through the eyes of a child and reflect on the truth through the eyes of an adult.

I look forward to your response. I have enclosed an SASE for your convenience.

Sincerely,
Kelley Birch

Enc.: Essay, SASE

Sample Query Letter

Walter K. Lopez, Senior Editor
New Mexico Magazine
495 Old Santa Fe Trail
Santa Fe, NM 87501

Dear Mr. Lopez:

The plan was to spend Thanksgiving with our friends, Frank and Inez, but since their Oregon in November was about as raw as our Wyoming, we looked for a warmer site. After meeting at the Denver International Airport a few days before Thanksgiving, we headed south to Gila, New Mexico.

This was our first trip to the remote village nestled between the Gila River and the rugged southern border of the Gila Wilderness Area. We'd rented, sight unseen, an adobe house more than 100 years old that owner Emmanuel Stamler promised "had been lovingly restored." And indeed it had been. Now I'd like to tell the history of the River House and how, as a turn of the century, one-room homestead, it was saved from destruction to become one of the most interesting and charming guest houses we had ever spent time in.

I'm a full-time writer who has published more than 250 essays and articles. My work has appeared in magazines including *Newsweek*, *Reader's Digest*, *Field & Stream*, *Philadelphia Magazine*, and *Delaware Today*.

"River House Rendezvous" should run about 1,500 words and I can deliver it within 30 days. I have enclosed a self-addressed, stamped envelope for your reply.

Sincerely,
Bill Pippin

Enc: SASE

Other items to remember:

- Demonstrate that you are writing the piece specifically for this magazine.
- Tell the editor if this is a simultaneous submission.

Last but not least:

- Prepare your letter on bond paper.
- Use a letter-quality printout and be sure the type is dark.
- Proofread your letter for spelling and grammatical mistakes. Redo it if necessary to be sure it is neat, clean, and error-free.

Résumé

Several publications in this directory request that writers enclose a résumé or article outline with their query. Résumés show editors whether a prospective writer has the necessary experience to research and write material for their publication.

The résumé you submit to a magazine is different from what you would submit when applying for a job because it emphasizes writing experience, memberships in writing associations, and education. It doesn't need to list all of your work experience or every association to which you belong. Instead, it should emphasize those credentials that demonstrate experience related to the magazine's editorial needs and focus.

This résumé is one you might send to a magazine. Study this example closely as much for what is *not* included as for what is.

In addition to the traditional résumé, consider creating a website with your brief biography, areas of expertise, and current contact information. Online platforms such as these can easily be built up over time as your writing credits increase, and are accessible to editors.

Sample Résumé

Name
Address
Telephone Number
Email/Fax

Writing Experience

- Author of fiction and nonfiction articles and stories in national and regional publications: *Leading Edge Science Fiction and Fantasy, Dog Fancy, Faith & Family, L.A. Parent Magazine, The News Times, Parade,* and *Reptiles.*

Editing Experience

- Freelance editor for *The News Times,* a local Connecticut newspaper, June 2002–Present.

Professional Organizations

- Member of the Science Fiction Writers Association
- Member of the Connecticut Authors' and Publishers' Association

Education

- Bachelor of Arts degree, English, Western Connecticut State University, 2002
- Long Ridge Writers Group, Breaking into Print program, 2003

Article Outline

An outline should expand on the information that you provided about the article in your query letter. The format of the outline can vary from the traditional with Roman numerals to something like the one shown here.

Working title: "Hunting Down the 'Certified Paranormal Investigator'"

Type of Article: Informational

Headline: You may be an experienced paranormal investigator, but are you as qualified as the next guy? Find out why some organizations want to create official standards for the field.

Lead:

> Would you like to become a professional ghost hunter? Are you interested in learning more about how to conduct paranormal investigations? If so, sign up now and earn your official Ghost Researcher Certification.

Jack Keating, a paranormal investigator of 10 years, has tracked ghosts everywhere from important historical landmarks to old outhouses on the Great Plains, but nothing has proved to be as elusive as the term "Certified Paranormal Investigator." [Anecdote about Keating's run-in with an investigator who claimed to be certified but did more harm than good at one historic Pennsylvania location.]

Body of Article:

Main Points:

1. What do certification programs claim to teach? What are their goals? Includes a look at the curriculum of the Foundation for Paranormal Education and an interview with the founders.
2. An examination of the differences between how non-certified ghost hunters conduct their business in comparison with certified ghost hunters. Includes exclusive interviews with ghost hunters of both types, as well as with clients.
3. Analysis of the consumer perspective: What do clients look for in an investigator? Is this a needed standard in the field?

Sidebar:

1) Ways to improve your ghost-hunting expertise as suggested by experienced ghost hunters, including physics/history education and reading works by other experienced investigators. A list of recommended parapsychology titles is included.

Follow Up with the Editor

Waiting for responses to submissions can be one of the most challenging parts of freelancing. That's why it's good to keep creating and polishing more submission possibilities and getting them out into the marketplace.

While editors generally try to respond to submissions within the time period specified in their magazine's listing, many have desks that are swamped with work and submitted material. If you haven't heard from an editor after the stated response time elapses, wait at least three more weeks before following up with a brief, polite note. Inquire about the status of your submission, note when you sent it and the title used in your manuscript or query, and include your contact information. You might also use this opportunity to include additional material or information that shows that the topic is continuing to generate interest. Be sure to enclose another self-addressed, stamped envelope with this follow-up note.

An exception to this general rule is when you have already enclosed a postcard with your manuscript submission. Expect to receive this postcard about three weeks after mailing the manuscript. If you haven't received it by then, write to the editor to say that you previously sent a submission and want to confirm that it was received.

If you do not receive a satisfactory response after following up and want to send your manuscript elsewhere, send a certified letter to the editor withdrawing the work from consideration and requesting its return. You are then free to submit the work to another magazine.

What You Can Expect

The most common responses to submissions are: an impersonal rejection letter or form; a personalized rejection letter; an offer to look at your material on speculation (with no guarantee that the magazine will buy it); an assignment to write the article; or the magazine's offer to purchase your manuscript. If you receive one of these three positive responses, you'll either send your completed manuscript in the format the editor has requested, accept the assignment by replying to the editor and ensuring that you understand all of the assignment's particulars (what kind of contract you may need to sign, etc.), or acknowledge that you would like to sell the manuscript the editor has already seen for the terms and price offered.

If you receive an impersonal rejection notice, send your work to the next editor on your list. If you receive a personal rejection note, always send a thank-you note in reply.

Set Up a Tracking System

It's important to have a system for tracking the status of queries and manuscripts you've sent out in order to stay organized.

You can create such a system in a notebook, on your computer, or on file cards (see below). This will give you an easy-to-use record that shows how long you've worked on a manuscript, to which magazines you've submitted an idea, how many queries and manuscripts you've sent over a given period of time, and which editors you need to follow up with.

Submission Tracking

Develop a means, such as this form, to track the status of the articles and stories you send out.

Magazine	*Article/Story*	*Submitted*	*Status*	*Due*	*Publication*	*Payment*
American History	John Trumbull & CT history	2/25/12	accepted	submitted	May 2013	5/30/12
Fine Gardening	Aristaeus & beekeeping	4/1/12	revising	5/15/12		
CelticLife	Hurling, a Prehistoric Sport	4/6/12	rejected			
Ancient American	Hurling, a Prehistoric Sport	5/10/12	expanding bibliography	6/1/12		

Frequently Asked Questions

How can I review sample copies and writers' guidelines?

If a magazine has a website, it often includes sample articles or stories from recent issues as well as writers' guidelines and/or an editorial calendar with a list of upcoming themes. If the website does not include these items, you can always write a brief note to the magazine requesting that they be sent to you in the self-addressed, stamped envelope that you provide. If there is a cost for a sample copy, include this payment. If not, ask the publication to enclose an invoice for any charge.

Should I submit my query or manuscript via email, or send a hard copy?

Many magazines now accept queries through email, which can save writers time and money. However, it is essential that you check a magazine's submission guidelines before sending anything—via email or otherwise. Some publications accept submissions in numerous ways, while others want email or hard copy exclusively. Also, publishers dealing with email usually define specific formats and methods for sending items electronically.

I need to include a bibliography with my article proposal. How do I set one up?

The reference section of your local library can provide several sources that will help you set up a bibliography. A style manual such as the *Chicago Manual of Style* will show you the proper format for citing your sources, including unpublished material, interviews, and Internet material.

Can I query a publication that requests clips even if I have no publishing credits?

If you've never been published before, don't let that stop you from querying a magazine that requests clips (previously published writing). Personal experience related to your subject is often just as valuable to editors, as is access to experts in the field. Unpublished writing samples are also acceptable, but should not be referred to as clips. You need not make any reference to your unpublished status.

I don't need my manuscript returned. How do I indicate that to an editor?

Now that manuscripts can be stored electronically for future use, many writers keep postage costs down by enclosing a self-addressed, stamped postcard (SASP) saying: "No need to return the enclosed manuscript. Please use this postcard to advise of the status of my submission. Thank you."

What are simultaneous or multiple submissions, and when is it acceptable to make them?

Manuscripts or queries sent to more than one magazine at a time are known as multiple or simultaneous submissions. Since many magazines only want to purchase the rights to one-time use of a manuscript, as long as you are not also submitting it to any of their direct competitors, they don't mind receiving a simultaneous submission. However, most also like to be notified that you're doing this, which you can indicate by including a sentence at the end of your cover or query letter that informs them that it is a simultaneous submission. If a magazine's guidelines state that it doesn't accept simultaneous submissions, don't plan to submit your manuscript to any other publications until after you have heard whether or not this first magazine wishes to use it.

Copyright and Permissions

For every writing sale you make there are contract and copyright issues that are just as crucial—and sometimes just as challenging—as the writing itself. It's especially important for writers to understand these tools, which can have powerful effects on the relationship between publisher and writer. Taking some time to understand these business basics will go a long way toward building a successful freelance career.

In the literary field, a copyright is legal ownership of an original written work. The owner or writer has the legal right to decide how a work is reproduced, and, for certain works, how it is performed or displayed. According to the Copyright Act of 1976 (effective January 1, 1978), this protection exists from the moment the work is recorded in a tangible medium, such as a computer file or on paper, without any need for legal action or counsel.

As a result of the Copyright Term Extension Act of 1998, you now own all rights to work you created during or after 1978 for your lifetime plus 70 years, until you choose to sell all or part of the copyright for this work. But remember that it is only your unique combination of words—how you wrote something—that the law protects and considers copyrighted. Ideas or facts that are expressed in your work cannot be copyrighted.

Do You Need to Register Your Work?

Once your manuscript is completed, your work is protected by the current copyright laws. You don't need to register your work with the United States Copyright Office. Editors want to buy your work; they have no need to steal it. A copy of the manuscript and a dated record of your submission will provide proof of creation.

Editors view an author's copyright notice on manuscripts as a sign of amateurism, or a signal that the author doesn't trust the publication. However, if you decide to register your work, obtain an application form and directions on the correct way to file your copyright application. Write to the Library of Congress, Copyright Office, 101 Independence Ave. SE, Washington, DC 20559-6000. These forms and directions are also available online in Adobe Acrobat format at: www.copyright.gov/ forms. Copyright registration fees are currently $35–$65.

If you have registered your unpublished manuscript with the Library of Congress, notify your editor of that fact once it is accepted for publication.

Rights Purchased by Magazines

Magazines request and purchase certain rights to publish manuscripts. A publisher is restricted by an agreement with you on when, how, and where he or she may publish your manuscript. Below is a list of common rights that are purchased by magazines:

All World Rights: The publisher purchases all rights to publish your work anywhere in the world any number of times. This includes all forms of media (both current and those which may be developed later). The publisher also has the right to all future use of the work, including reprints, syndication, creation of derivative works, and use in databases. You no longer have the right to sell or reproduce the work, unless you can negotiate for the return of certain rights (for example, book rights).

In many cases, publishers are unlikely to need or use all of the rights they purchase. Keep in mind that negotiation is a key part of the contractual process; writers who know what to ask for will often come out ahead.

All World Serial Rights: The publisher purchases all rights to publish your work in newspapers, magazines, and other serial publications throughout the world any number of times. You retain all other rights, such as the right to use it as a chapter in a book.

First Rights: A publisher acquires the right to publish your work for the first time in any specified media. Electronic and nontraditional markets often seek these rights. All other rights, including reprint rights, belong to you.

Electronic Rights: Publishers use this as a catch-all for inclusion in any type of electronic publication, such as CD-ROMs, websites, ezines, or in electronic databases.

First North American Serial Rights: The publisher can publish your work for the first time in a U.S. or Canadian periodical. You retain the book and North American reprint rights, as well as first rights to a foreign market.

Second or Reprint Rights: This allows a publication non-exclusive rights to print the material for the second time. You may not authorize second publication to occur until after the work has appeared in print by the publisher who bought first rights.

One-time Rights: Often bought by regional publications, this means the publication has bought the right to use the material once. You may continue to sell the material elsewhere; however, you should inform the publisher if this work is being simultaneously considered for publication in a competing magazine.

Numerous ads try to recruit writers for Web content, but beware of payment policies and rights before signing on. Some sites offer a pay-per-click system, based on how many times a piece is viewed, while others pay a flat fee upon publication. In addition, some sites purchase all rights, leaving the writer with little to show for a lot of hard work.

You should be aware that an agreement may limit a publisher to the right to publish your work in certain media (e.g., magazines and other periodicals only) or the agreement may include wider-ranging rights (e.g., the right to publish the manuscript in a book or an audiocassette). The right may be limited to publishing within a specific geographic region or in a specific language. Any rights you retain allow you to resell the manuscript within the parameters of your agreement.

It is becoming increasingly common for magazines to purchase all rights, especially those that host Internet sites and make archives of previously published articles available to readers. Unless you have extensive publishing credentials, you may not want to jeopardize the opportunity to be published by insisting on selling limited rights.

Contracts and Agreements

Typically, when a publisher indicates an interest in your manuscript, he or she specifies what rights the publication will acquire. Then, usually, a publisher will send you a letter of agreement or a standard written contract spelling out the terms of the agreement.

If a publisher does not send you a written contract and appears to be relying on oral consent, you need to consider your options. While an oral agreement may be legally binding, it is not easy to enforce. To protect your interests, draft a letter outlining the terms as you understand them (e.g., a 500-word article without photos, first North American serial rights, paying on acceptance at $.05 a word). Send two copies of the letter to the editor (with a self-addressed, stamped envelope), asking him or her to sign one and return it to you if the terms are correct.

Work-for-Hire

Another term that is appearing more frequently in contracts is work-made-for-hire. As a freelance writer, most editors treat you as an independent contractor (not an employee) who writes articles for their publication. In this case, you usually retain the copyright to your article—unless you have specified otherwise in writing—and enter into an assignment of rights contract with the publisher, allowing the purchase of various rights relating to publication. Sometimes, however, magazine editors may assign or commission articles to freelancers as works-made-for-hire, making the finished article property of the publisher.

Under current copyright laws, only certain

types of commissioned works are considered works-made-for-hire, and only when both the publisher and the commissioned writer agree in writing. These works typically include items such as contributions to "collective works" such as magazines. A contract or agreement clearly stating that the material is a work-made-for-hire must be signed by both parties and be in place before the material is written. Once a writer agrees to these terms, he or she no longer has any rights to the work.

Note that a pre-existing piece, such as an unsolicited manuscript that is accepted for publication, is not considered a commissioned work.

Guidelines for Permission to Quote

When you want to quote another writer's words in a manuscript you're preparing, you must get that writer's permission. Sometimes this means contacting the permissions department of that writer's publisher. Without permission, you could be sued for copyright infringement.

Below are some copyright guidelines:

- Any writing published in the U.S. prior to 1923 is in the public domain, as are works created by the U.S. government. Such material may be quoted without permission, but the source should be cited.
- No specific limits are set as to the length of permitted quotations in your articles: different publishers have various requirements. Generally, if you quote more than a handful of words, you should seek permission. Always remember to credit your sources.
- The doctrine of "fair use" allows quoting portions of a copyrighted work for certain purposes, as in a review, news reporting, nonprofit educational uses, or research. Contrary to popular belief, there is no absolute word limit on fair use. But as a general rule, never quote more than a few successive paragraphs from a book or article and credit the source.
- If you're submitting a manuscript that contains quoted material, you'll need to obtain permission from the source to quote the material before it is published. If you're uncertain about what to do, your editor should be able to advise you.

It's important for freelance writers to be as knowledgeable about selling their work as they are about creating it. For real-world advice, check out writers' groups (such as the Authors Guild), which sometimes offer contract advice, sample contracts, and tips on contract negotiation.

Resources

Interested in finding out more about writers and their rights under the law? Check these sources for further information:

- The Publishing Law Center www.publaw.com/legal.html
- *The Copyright Handbook: What Every Writer Needs to Know,* 10th Edition by Attorney Stephen Fishman. Nolo, 2008.
- *The Writer's Legal Guide,* 3rd Edition by Tad Crawford and Kay Murray, Allworth Press, 2002.

Contracts, Payments, and Finances

This section outlines the variety of contracts, the pros and cons of different payment methods, and the need to keep track of expenses.

Contracts

When an editor indicates an interest in your manuscript, he or she specifies what rights the publication will acquire. Then, usually—but not always—an editor will send a letter of agreement or a standard written contract to you spelling out the terms of the agreement. Standard contracts, also known as boilerplate, can be negotiated if the terms are not acceptable to you. For example, the publisher may want all rights and you prefer not to sell them, or the payment rate may be lower than you wish. Once the terms are acceptable to both you and the publisher, you sign the letter or contract, keep a copy, and send the original back to the editor.

If an editor does not send you a contract and appears to be relying on a verbal agreement, you need to consider your options. While a verbal agreement is legally binding, it is not as easy to enforce as a written one, nor are memories always reliable. Therefore, you may want to draft a letter outlining the terms as you understand them (e.g., a 2,500-word article without photos, first North American serial rights, paying on acceptance at $.05 a word), then send two copies of the letter to the editor (with a self-addressed, stamped envelope), asking for a signature on one to be returned to you.

"On Spec"

Until you have accumulated a portfolio of published clips, you may decide to write "on spec." This refers to "on speculation," a common industry practice. When an editor reads a query and is interested in the idea, he or she requests a complete manuscript without the obligation to buy the piece if it turns out to be inappropriate for the magazine.

On occasion, editors ask writers who haven't published in the article's field (e.g., a travel article by a fiction writer) to write the proposed manuscript "on spec."

Payment Methods

The payment period can vary greatly (e.g., 30 days after acceptance or two months after publication); the most common payment times are either on publication or on acceptance.

Writers prefer payment on acceptance rather than on publication. If a magazine pays on publication and holds off a decision for months about whether or not to publish your manuscript, then ultimately decides not to publish the piece, your manuscript could be out-of-date. All the hard work you put into it may have been for naught. If a magazine pays on acceptance and never publishes the piece, you will have at least been paid.

Kill Fee

Many magazines pay a fee to a writer if an article has been assigned, but an editor later decides to "kill" or not print the article. The fee is a percentage (usually between 25 percent and 50 percent) of the agreed-upon payment for the article. This may not be your highest priority when targeting markets, yet if a magazine pays kill fees, at least you will receive some sort of payment in exchange for your work.

Expenses

Whether or not a magazine pays for expenses related to writing an article, keep records of your costs. If a magazine does pay some costs, have those expenses spelled out in the letter of agreement and submit an expense report with your bill, along with copies of the receipts. If not, keep records to deduct the expenses from your taxes.

Costs to consider include lodging, meals, mileage, tolls, parking, telephone service, and other expenses you incur while writing an article or story.

Taxes and Finances

As a freelance writer, you are the owner of a small business, and you are entitled to tax deductions and are required to file various tax forms.

Allowable expenses include dues for professional organizations, writing courses, a post office box, supplies such as business cards and letterhead, pertinent magazine subscriptions, equipment purchases and repairs, and a host of others. It is vital that you keep accurate records of all transactions, including contracts, payments, and expenses.

As a small business owner, file a form with the Internal Revenue Service quarterly estimating your income for the upcoming quarter.

These tax laws and forms are complicated, so you should consult an accountant for the current federal and state tax regulations.

Common Publishing Terms

All rights: Contractual agreement by which a publisher acquires the copyright and all use of author's material.

Assignment: Manuscript commissioned by an editor for a stated fee.

Byline: Author's name credited at the heading of an article.

Caption: Description or text accompanying an illustration or photograph.

CD-ROM: (compact disk read-only memory) Non-erasable compact disk containing data that can be read by a computer.

Clip: Sample of a writer's published work.

Column-inch: Text contained in one vertical inch of a typeset column.

Contributor's copies: Copies of the publication issue in which the writer's work appears.

Copyedit: To edit with close attention to style and mechanics.

Copyright: Legal rights that protect an author's work (see page 21).

Cover letter: Brief letter sent with a manuscript.

Disk submission: Manuscript that is submitted on computer disk.

Editorial calendar: List of topics, themes, or special sections that are planned for specific upcoming issues.

Electronic submission: Manuscript transmitted to an editor from one computer to another through a modem.

Email: (electronic mail) Messages sent from one computer to another via computer network or modem.

Experimental Fiction: Term used to describe fiction written without a traditional beginning, middle, and end and/or contains loosely connected events.

Filler: Short item that fills out a page (e.g., joke, light verse, or fun fact).

First serial rights: The right to publish a work for the first time in a periodical. Can be limited to a language or geographical region (see page 22).

Genre: Category of fiction characterized by a particular style, form, or content, such as mystery or fantasy.

Hard copy: Printed copy produced from the submitted computer disk.

In-house: See **Staff-written**.

International Reply Coupon (IRC): Coupon exchangeable in any foreign country for postage on a single-rate, surface-mailed letter.

Kill fee: Percentage of fee paid to a writer in the event an editor decides not to use a purchased manuscript.

Layout: Plan for the arrangement of text and artwork on a printed page.

Manuscript: A typewritten or computer-printed version of a document (as opposed to a published version).

Masthead: The printed matter in a newspaper or periodical that gives the title and pertinent details of ownership, staff, advertising rates, and subscription rates.

Modem: An internal device or a small electrical box that plugs into a computer, used to transmit data between computers, often via telephone lines.

Ms/mss: Manuscript/manuscripts.

One-time rights: The right to publish a piece once, often not the first time (see page 22).

On spec: Refers to writing "on speculation," without an editor's commitment to purchase the manuscript.

Outline: Summary of a manuscript's contents, usually nonfiction, organized under subheadings with descriptive sentences under each (see page 18).

Payment on acceptance: Author is paid following an editor's decision to accept a manuscript.

Payment on publication: Author is paid following the publication of the manuscript.

Pen name/pseudonym: Fictitious name used by an author.

Common Publishing Terms

Proofread: To read and mark errors, usually in printed text.

Query: Letter to an editor to promote interest in a manuscript or an idea (see pages 11–16).

Reprint: Another printing of an article or story; can be in different magazine format, such as an anthology.

Reprint rights: See **Second serial rights**.

Response time: Average length of time for an editor to accept or reject a submission and contact the writer with his or her decision.

Résumé: Account of one's qualifications, educational and professional background, and publishing credits (see page 17).

SAE: Self-addressed envelope (no postage).

SASE: Self-addressed, stamped envelope.

Second serial rights: The right to publish a manuscript that has appeared in another publication; known also as reprint rights (see page 22).

Serial: Term used when acquiring the right to publish a manuscript in a publication only; it means that a periodical appears "serially" (see page 21).

Sidebar: A short article that accompanies a feature article, and highlights one aspect of the feature's subject.

Simultaneous submission: Manuscript submitted to more than one publisher at the same time; also known as multiple submission.

Slant: Specific approach to a subject to appeal to a certain readership.

Slush pile: Term used within the publishing industry to describe unsolicited manuscripts.

Solicited manuscript: Manuscript that an editor has requested or agreed to consider.

Staff-written: Prepared by members of the magazine's staff. Also known as in-house.

Synopsis: Condensed description or summary of a manuscript.

Tear sheet: Page from a magazine containing author's printed work.

Trade magazines: Publications directed to professionals in a specific field.

Transparencies: Positive color images, such as 35mm slides; not color prints.

Unsolicited manuscript: Manuscript not specifically requested by an editor.

Work-Made-for-Hire: Work specifically ordered, commissioned, and owned by a publisher for its exclusive use (see page 22).

World rights: Contractual agreement whereby the publisher acquires the right to reproduce the work throughout the world.

Writers' guidelines: A publisher's editorial objectives or specifications, which usually include word length, slant, and subject matter.

Writing sample: Example of your writing style, tone, and skills; may be a published or an unpublished piece.

Market Articles

Story for Story's Sake
The World of Literary Magazines

By Katherine Swarts

Everyone loves a good story. Everyone has ideas on what makes a story good. Quality fiction of any kind has important commonalities, but commercial (sometimes called *genre*) fiction and literary fiction also have differences. While commercial fiction may get most of the attention in book publishing, literary holds the edge in magazines. And while literary magazines are often small, they are generally a strong and growing market today.

Melanie Ann Billings, Acquisitions Editor for Whiskey Creek Press, says, "I think literary magazines are on the upswing, with the explosion of social media and the recent focus on translating classical and modern literature to the big screen. Literary magazines are a really good fit for social media and newer developments in technology."

"Readers have never been so inundated with choices and pressed for the kind of time that reading asks for," says Sven Birkerts, Editor of Boston University's *AGNI Magazine*. "Yet there is also the sense that people are looking [at literary magazines], and that when the right note is struck, word gets out, the work gets circulated and read. Literary magazines are the place of first encounter, and the writers who change the way we think and experience late modernity—or whatever it is we are experiencing—always show up first in lit mags."

Defining *Literary*

Storytelling is a very human, universal art form, but the line between commercial and literary is frequently difficult to draw. To children, a good story is a good story, and trying to categorize it spoils the fun. Many college literature students, and more than a few mature readers, might well agree. For instance, was Charles Dickens a commercial writer or a literary one and in what way does it matter?

"From my perspective, borderline genre stories are the most popular" in the literary world, says C. Hope Clark, Editor of the ezine *FundsforWriters* and author of *Lowcountry Bribe: A Carolina Slade Mystery* (Bell Bridge Books). She says a borderline genre "serves as a bridge between cerebral and entertaining." Nonetheless, she continues, "There's still a them-or-us feeling in the *literary* world. When I see writing classes at conferences, the lessons are about pace, hook, and emotion. Slow down to dig into a character, and you're accused of slowing down the plot. Quite the opposite is taught in MFA [Master of Fine Arts] classes, where literary fiction is groomed. And as an entrepreneur, I see lit mags always falling short on the business side, not knowing how to advertise, market, and solicit new talent. I like diversity, but [literary magazines] need to get more business-minded and less artsy to succeed and grow."

Other professionals complain that *literary* connotes snobbishness, and starving-writer syndrome. "Some magazines use the term *literary* in their description when they are anything but," says Angela Hoy, Co-owner of marketing ezine *WritersWeekly.com* and Booklocker.com. "Others use that term as an excuse to pay low-ball wages."

In its better sense, the sense its fans appreciate, literary fiction has emotional and intellectual depth. "For me, there is a special feeling to a literary story," says Veronica Ross, Fiction Editor at *The Antigonish Review*. "It shines and glows, maybe even shakes. It is not just about plot. The use of language is superb; it has a distinctive voice. You remember the story and the characters. Everything comes together."

Susan Burmeister-Brown and Linda Swanson-Davies, Co-editors of the short story journal

Glimmer Train say, "Most literary magazines try to present work that has value beyond the moment, that will continue to be of interest and significance over time. Literary fiction tends not to depend heavily on big action. It is rare that plots include fist fights, sex scenes, apocalypse, lawsuits, murders, or supernatural happenings, though in fact all those things have appeared in our pages—not because the action was exciting, but because it revealed so much about how humans are moved by internal and external challenges, how we interpret and integrate expanded perspectives, how we cope and move forward. The stories we publish also tend to be multilayered, just like life, so characters often must sort through conflicting needs. In a time of relentless and consuming superficial connection, literary short fiction is uniquely built to remind us how deeply akin we are to one another, even when our external lives are vastly different. People yearn for reminders of that basic connection."

"It's less a question of genre than of the ambition of the work," notes Birkerts. "We take the idea of *literary* seriously, the idea of work that uses language with maximal inventiveness toward serious expressive ends." A literary story is marked by "deep and considered engagement with the resources—form and language, and the ambition to voice a true, and unique, understanding of character and situation."

"The works in a literary magazine reflect a love of language," says Julie Wakeman-Linn, Editor in Chief of *Potomac Review*.

The depth of literary writing extends to language choices and imagery. John W. Hathorn III, Vice President of the Houston Writers Guild, says, "Literary writing should use alliteration, similes, and metaphors to develop such a flow to the words that the reader gets enthralled. Just as in a beautiful song, the reader should not want the paragraph to end."

"There's a kind of poetry in literary prose writing," agrees Paulette Licitra, Publisher of *Alimentum: The Literature of Food*. "The writer is aware of words, not just reporting. You get the sense that this came from a deeper place. Literary writing connects matters of life with matters of the soul—I don't mean religion; I mean the soul of who we are."

How Not to Write a Literary Story

Getting down to soul level is tricky, and many attempts at literary fiction fail because the writer stayed so deep in his or her own psyche that no one else could identify with the result. Another common and equally self-centered mistake is assuming that literary equals snobbery or elitism, as in brandishing linguistic and grammatical knowledge at the expense of essential story elements. As Hathorn notes, "Some writers try to overwhelm the reader with vocabulary."

"A well-executed story written in simple, plain prose can be beautiful and powerfully affecting," say the *Glimmer Train* editors. While "a deep love of language and a drive to find exactly the right words is a big plus as long as the language serves the story," the plus becomes a minus when language becomes "just a platform for showing off."

Yet another common misconception about literary fiction is that it is invariably sad and grim or must include some other common aspect vaguely remembered from the high school literature anthology. The worst case is the writer who is too obsessed with formula to give her own unique voice a chance. "Write what you love in your own voice," says Ross. "Be yourself. Don't write like anyone else." And in fact, says Billings, "The most popular literary stories are those with happy endings."

To focus on questions of genre, happy or sad endings, settings, protagonist types, and the like, says Birkerts, "leaves out the main source of appeal, which is voice. Readers report back to us most often when they have been captivated by a new or commanding or irresistibly comical or heartbreaking authorial voice." Voice is rooted in one's own deepest feelings, strongest interests, and past experience. "Know your material inside and out before you start writing about it," says Billings.

One last mistake writers may make is to assume they can sell any literary story to any literary periodical. "No two are alike," says Clark. "As with any market, read previous issues. Do they like edgy, urban, soft? Are they setting-driven? Is there a theme? Do previous issues abound with MFA authors? Know to whom you are submitting."

"Every editorial board has a unique sensitivity," agrees Wakeman-Linn. "The writer needs to know the magazine to understand favorite choices in style, subject matter, and range of genre."

"Know your market," says Birkerts. "Everyone

always says this, but that's because it's true. When you find the ones that feel right, be courteous and persistent. So many writers make their way in on later attempts."

Billings notes one more essential: "Be sure to see what others have already written!" No magazine wants a virtual duplicate of a recently published piece.

Ultimately, submitting to a literary publication is no different than with any other market. Never neglect editing. "Polish every sentence in a story," says Wakeman-Linn, "before you send it to us."

"Read your own work aloud before sending it off," say Burmeister-Brown and Linda Swanson-Davies. "Have others read it aloud to you. It will give you a chance to hear rough spots, and also areas where you're so into the story that you've forgotten to provide necessary details."

"Be professional," says Hoy. "Provide an outstanding query letter with no mistakes, and show some humility. Writers who come across as overly confident or who request special favors are a huge turn-off. Being rude and issuing demands in an attempt to make editors think you're better than the rest is the wrong way to attempt publication."

One widespread element in literary writing is a humbling effect on the reader's spirit. That is an attitude every writer should take into their soul.

AN EDITOR'S PERSPECTIVE

Ralph Adamo, Editor of *Xavier Review,* discusses his views of literary journals:

"The content in most literary magazines—*Xavier Review* among them—includes poetry, reviews and sometimes scholarship, creative nonfiction, and frequently art of some kind, and also interviews, so there is more content than just fiction. That said, I think the essence of a literary magazine is that it treats literature and reading as serious undertakings, worthy of respectful forums and venues. On a more basic level, literary magazines exist to announce new voices to the reading public, to promote those voices as well as established ones, to rearrange—however minutely and incrementally—the landscape of literature.

"What makes a story literary to me is a level of seriousness of purpose, as well as success of execution. The former is unknowable on some level, and the latter is largely subjective. However, I would like to note that the division (promoted primarily by publishers and booksellers) between literary and other types of fiction seems bogus to me. I especially reject any classification of writers like Ruth Rendell, Charlie Huston, Mo Hayder, Henning Mankell, Patricia Highsmith, Jo Nesbo, etc., that demotes them to consideration as anything less than great and serious writers of significant literature. In that vein, I am especially proud to have published, in the first issue of *Xavier Review* I edited (Volume 31.1), a story by Tom Andes ("The Hit") that was subsequently reprinted in *The Best American Mystery Stories 2012*.

"Of course, there are *schools* and movements with their own journals, and perhaps the proliferation of venues makes it less likely that a single issue of something like the old *Paris Review* or even the old *Granta* will contain any sort of definitive look at the literature of the moment. The other and most significant new factor is, of course, the Internet, and the reality that publishing a hard copy of a journal is not even really necessary anymore, as desirable as it may still be, and as different as the world will be when we can't run into physical copies of old and powerful journals. (I have a copy of the first issue of *Genesis West*, for example, and holding it in my hand is an experience I do not expect the Internet—however eternal it makes everything—will be able to replicate.) Certainly we know there are more writers trying to publish than ever before, and it seems true that literary magazines of whatever sort are filling the need they always did fill: a place to publish your new work rather quickly, and a place for readers to see what is happening in the world of words.

"The obvious best advice is to know where you are sending your work—either to have seen a copy or to have a good sense of the proclivities and tastes of the editors. And to be patient with rejection, recognizing that the market is a wild and uneven and unfair place."

A History Lesson Worth Hearing: Markets Are Everywhere

By Michael L. Cooper

Just about everyone is interested in some aspect of the past, whether out of curiosity about personal ancestry, or a fascination with the American Civil War, Japan, Eastern European cooking, Renaissance art, or old fire engines. If you are an aspiring writer, and a lover of history, your choices of subjects and markets are myriad.

The markets range widely: prestigious, big-name history markets, like *American Heritage, American History,* and *Smithsonian*; specialized magazines, like *Air & Space Smithsonian* and *Preservation*; cultural magazines, like *IrishAmerica* and *Hadassah*; regional heritage magazines, such as *Alabama Heritage, Nebraska History,* and *Route 66;* regional travel magazines, including *Arizona Highways* and *Discover Maine*; art magazines, like *Antique Trader*; nostalgia magazines, such as *Capper's* and *Good Old Days*; and association publications, like *American Legion* and *Elks Magazine*.

People First

For many of us, selling a historical feature to *American Heritage, American History,* or *Smithsonian* is a distant goal. *American Heritage*'s list of contributors is a *Who's Who* of American historians. A roster of somewhat lesser stars fill the pages of *American History*, and the bylines of many recognizable writers and scholars appear in *Smithsonian* as well. Fortunately, for those of us who are not quite as well known but like to write about history, many other publications accept history submissions.

Air & Space Smithsonian is a magazine that is not so much about airplanes, rockets, and other technology as it is about the people involved with them.

"On history-related articles, we are looking for stories that are both original and compelling," says Executive Editor Paul Hoversten. "Too often, we are pitched ideas that have already appeared somewhere, either in print or on the web. Or, that are simply too broad to be covered in a 2,500- to 3,000-word feature. I once had a writer propose a story on aviation in the Marine Corps, which of course can—and does—fill books."

For the kinds of articles he likes, Hoversten suggests reading three *Air & Space* articles available online that "are well-written and tell a compelling story." Two are in the January 2012 issue. "A Pearl Harbor Mystery" follows a pilot who read about a woman flight instructor flying near Pearl Harbor on December 7, 1941; the pilot sets out 60 years later to find and restore the flight instructor's plane. "The Candle Lighters" is about the team that launched the Mercury-Redstone rocket carrying Alan Shepard, the first American in space. In the November 2011 *Air & Space*, "Mind If I Borrow It" tells the story of an Air Force mechanic in 1956 with little flight training, who nonetheless decided to take an F-86 fighter jet for a spin.

Profiles are not of interest to Hoversten. "We generally stay away from them since they are often difficult to do in the long-form narrative format that is the magazine's style. Many times, writers will pitch ideas for a profile without offering any new information on the person. And if it's a well-known person, which many of these are, there is generally a wealth of information out there already—another reason we often turn down pitches."

Anniversaries

An obvious news peg for historical articles is anniversaries, says Dennis Hockman, Editor of *Preservation*, published by the Trust for Historic Preservation in Washington, D. C.

During the 2012 sesquicentennial of the bloody Civil War engagement at Antietam, *Preservation* published a long article on the Antietam National Battlefield in northern Virginia, and a historian named Nicholas Redding who specializes in preserving Civil War sites. "It is always good to have a news hook," Hockman says. "Pitching anniversary ideas a year or more in advance is not uncommon. It is the only way we can get the timing right."

Hockman also places some limits on profiles. "We don't profile historical figures. We profile historic places that are important to our national identity and the modern day people who save them. Many of those historic places are attached to historical figures. So, if we did a story on Montpelier, for example, James Madison would be key to the story, but we would also be talking about the various preservation projects ongoing there today."

Preservation doesn't just publish articles on saving historical structures. "We also focus heavily on heritage travel—travel for people who like history," he says. "So, for example, if we did a story on a trip to Chattanooga, the recommendations for where to eat, what to do, and what accommodations to select would be related to the history that makes these places worth visiting."

What kinds of proposals does Hockman see too often? Writers often submit ideas about "this place was or needs to be saved. There are countless historic places that are being preserved or need to be. That, in and of itself, does not make a good story."

Advisories

Hockman has one complaint about submissions he receives that is nearly universal among magazine editors. Many writers do not bother "familiarizing themselves with the publication," he says. "The magazine is 60 years old and it has been through many changes." Do not assume "you can pitch a story based on what the magazine was doing five years ago. [In 2012, *Preservation*] did a complete redesign of the look and content to address our current and future readership. Our new tag line for the magazine is People Saving Places. We try to make sure that is always at the core of our stories. What readers are interested in are important historical places and compelling stories about the people who work tirelessly to save or protect them." He advises writers studying the magazine to focus on issues published in 2012 and later.

The most common mistake by writers submitting to *Air & Space,* Hoversten agrees, "is failing to read the magazine to study our style and the sorts of stories we publish before pitching an idea. Also important to remember: Don't think *subject*; think *story*, with a beginning, a middle, and an end. Take the time to find a new angle on what it is you're proposing. Then, we'll be much more receptive to your pitch."

Greg Lalire, Editor of *Wild West*, says too many of the 20 to 25 queries or submissions he receives monthly are "on the same subject as recent wild west books," and they are not coming from their authors. "We do articles adapted from books," he says, "but only written by the authors of those books."

The *Wild West* editor cites two other problems: the numerous proposals about well-known events, such as the Battle of the Little Bighorn and the shootout at the O.K. Corral, and too many submissions "based solely on basic online research." Lalire is looking for "articles involving original research from source material not available on the web" such as "diary or journal entries from the time."

Queries or manuscripts should "be colorful and entertaining," Lalire advises, while offering "something new about a familiar westerner or some person or event not well known." When submitting a proposal, list your sources and any photos or illustrations that could accompany the article. Please do not, Lalire says, send several proposals at once.

Department Break-ins

While it can be difficult to publish full-length features in the big-name magazines, it is not impossible to break in at some of them. *Smithsonian* is open to submissions to some of its departments and website.

The Phenomena & Curiosities department is open to pieces 1,000 to 1,500 words on subjects such as recent scientific discoveries, and on nature, especially peculiar flora or fauna. Points of Interest is a 1,200- to 1,750-word column focusing on Americana. The topics can be current or historical but tend to be unusual or quirky. One covered a 24-hour bird-watching marathon in New Jersey. Submissions about

HISTORY MARKETS

GENERAL INTEREST HISTORY
American Heritage
American History
Smithsonian

SPECIALTY
Air & Space
Archaeology
Aviation History
Early American Life
Good Old Boat
Military History
Muzzleloader
National Parks
Naval History
Nineteenth Century
Preservation
Sea History
Wild West

CULTURAL, ETHNIC
CelticLife
GermanLife
Hadassah
IrishAmerica
Italian America
ScottishLife

ART MAGAZINES
American Fine Art
Antique Trader
Treasures: Ancient to Modern

REGIONAL HERITAGE MAGAZINES
Alabama Heritage
Appalachian Heritage
California Territorial Quarterly
East Texas Historical Journal
Michigan History
Nebraska History
Pennsylvania Heritage
Route 66
South Carolina Historical
Southwestern Historical Quarterly

REGIONAL/TRAVEL MAGAZINES
Arizona Highways
Discover Maine
Georgia Backroads
Horizon Air

NOSTALGIA MAGAZINES
Capper's
Good Old Days

ASSOCIATIONS
American Legion Magazine
Elks Magazine
VFW Magazine

GENEALOGY
Family Tree

historical events need an angle and recent interviews. Presence of Mind only appears in *Smithsonian* a couple of times a year but consists of "reported essays" of 1,200 to 2,000 words, often about contrary historical arguments or points of view. For example, was the Lewis and Clark expedition actually important? Or, did the Founding Fathers' views on slavery detract from their accomplishments?

At *Air & Space* "there are a number of sections that are appropriate for history-related submissions," says Hoversten. "Our Cancelled series looks at airplane types that never made it past prototypes, or if they did, they didn't last long in production. Then there is Flights & Fancy, a whimsical, brief reflection that should leave the reader chuckling. Oldies and Oddities is a bit of funky, little-known history. And Above & Beyond is a first-person narrative of an adventure in air or space."

Lesser Known

Publications that might not be categorized immediately, or primarily, as history magazines also publish historical articles. One place to look is to service and fraternal organizations.

Elks Magazine is published 10 times a year for the nearly one million members of the Benevolent and Protective Order of Elks. The magazine buys 20 to 30 freelance articles a year.

Historical articles published in 2012 included: "Don't Tread on Me: How the Rattlesnake Became a Symbol of American Unity and Freedom;" "A Successful Failure: The U.S. Camel Corps;" and "The Age of the Steamboat in America." *Elks* accepts complete manuscripts of 1,200 to 2,000 words submitted either by mail or email. A response is promised within 30 days.

American Legion Magazine (www.legion.org/magazine) runs one or two historical articles a month. Recent articles have covered the Cuban missile crisis; the Grand Army of the Republic, an organization formed by white and African American Civil War veterans that became an organizational model for fraternal groups like the American Legion; and an atomic bomb that was lost after a mid-air collision between a B47 bomber and an F86 fighter jet near Savannah, Georgia in 1958.

Articles for the National Parks Conservation Association's *National Parks Magazine* may have historical components. Among those published recently was "Angel of the Battlefield," about Clara Barton's home in Glen Echo, Maryland; and a National Historic "On The Right Track" looked at the Pullman District, a residential neighborhood on Chicago's South Side where some 12,000 laborers for the Pullman Car Works once lived. A bill originally sponsored by Illinois Congressman Jesse Jackson Jr. would make the neighborhood Chicago's first national park.

Features for *National Parks* run from 1,800 to 2,000 words. News articles and department submissions are 500 to 1,200 words. Payment is 70¢ to $1 a word.

Whatever aspect of history interests you, you will find a market for related articles. You will just have to remember, and have your article put a new twist on, the famous George Santayana quote: "Those who cannot remember the past are condemned to repeat it."

Have Pen, Will Travel

By Christina Hamlett

Among the glamorous magazine gigs a person might land, writing travel features ranks high on the list. While the ultimate goal may be to find a premiere publication that will underwrite your expenses to exotic ports of call, more than enough print and online markets for travel articles exist to help defray at least some of the costs of vacations and earn you a living as a writer. If you are a truly zealous globetrotter, you might even compile enough material for a guidebook. You can develop the signature style of someone who is not just at home in the world, but can invite others to feel the same way.

Travel Writing 101

In addition to exceptional writing and good photography skills, three prerequisites are needed to crack this market. The first, and most obvious, is that you are well qualified to write about your chosen topics. You must have lived, studied, or worked in the fascinating locale that is your subject. You should also know what it is to spend time living out of a suitcase and be comfortably familiar with geography, history, foreign cuisine, customs, and the tourism industry.

"Get out there!" says *Outside Magazine* correspondent Tim Sohn who has done worldwide reporting for *Men's Journal, New York,* the *New York Times,* and the Travel Channel. "It's difficult to write interestingly about anything until you've seen some of the world, and this goes double for travel writing. Travel however you can. When I was starting out, I took random jobs in random places, betting that the experiences would help. And they do: Every trip makes you a more skilled traveler, a more nuanced observer, and better attuned to what makes a place potentially story-worthy."

A second prerequisite is a keen awareness of what travel niches are the best match for your talents (i.e., family-friendly vacations, eco-tours and campgrounds, resort destinations, budget travel). For Tracey Ceurvels, founder of *The Busy Hedonist* (thebusyhedonist.com), the door to becoming a regular correspondent for the *Boston Globe*'s travel section five years ago was opened by food. "I had written for the *Boston Globe* dining section a few times and thought it would be fun to write for the travel section since traveling is one of my favorite activities. I decided to pitch them an insider's guide to eating in Chinatown, the neighborhood where I lived in New York City. They bought the story and then I started pitching other ideas that they liked."

The third requirement is the ability to create a unique slant. For instance, some of the features I have written for *USA Today, Go World Travel, Travel Holiday,* and Local.com focused on topics, such as the best bookstores in Paris, what to do with kids on a rainy Manhattan day, quirky regional food festivals, and maximizing your wardrobe for a minimalist carry-on. Sohn says, "The beauty—and occasional terror—of travel writing is that everything is potential material and you're never off duty. You also need to remember that *exotic* is not the same as *interesting*. Not always at least. A good story could be down the block, across the river, or across an ocean, but it comes from hard work and research and knowing your craft and your sensibility, not from spinning the globe at random."

Wish You Were Here

"We view the world as one big backyard to explore, and we've covered destinations in more

RESOURCES

Books

- *Lonely Planet Travel Writing*, by Don George
- *Secrets of a Professional Travel Writer: A How-To Guide for Writers*, by Cindy Lou Dale
- *Travel Writer's Guide*, by Gordon Burgett
- *The Travel Writer's Handbook: How to Write and Sell Your Own Travel Experiences*, by Jacqueline Harmon Butler and Louise Purwin Zobel
- *Travel Writing: See the World, Sell the Story*, by L. Peat O'Neil

Organizations

- British Guild of Travel Writers: www.bgtw.org
- International Food, Wine & Travel Writers Association: ifwtwa.org
- Society of American Travel Writers: www.satw.org
- Travelwriters.com: www.travelwriters.com

than 90 countries," says Janna Graber, Editorial Director of *Go World Travel*, an online publication targeted to travel enthusiasts in the U.S., U.K., Canada, Australia, and New Zealand who travel internationally. "We offer an experiential look at a destination, from what it looks and sounds like to the people the author encountered. Our content is designed to 'take you there' and provide an inside glimpse at that destination."

For prospective writers, Graber emphasizes the importance of studying back issues and familiarizing yourself with the magazine's tone and voice. "We prefer first-person articles, but the piece should not be all about the author. It's about the destination as seen through the author's eyes. We also prefer to see finished submissions rather than queries. New coverage of the world's most popular destinations is always welcome, as well as continued coverage of off-the-beaten path destinations." Like any industry in today's economy, tourism has been hit hard, Graber says. "Since our site is online only, however, we can still offer our tourism partners an affordable and very effective way to reach our target market. GoWorldTravel.com is almost a decade old, and it's still going, so we must be doing something right!"

Have you published travel books in print or edited anthologies that are widely available? If so, *Perceptive Travel* may be your online market for stories and reviews that appeal to adventurous, intelligent, and curious international travelers. Editor Tim Leffel says, "If you're an experienced professional writer with a strong following, query with a good description of the angle and your credentials. Linking to a portfolio site should be a given, but no attachments. Sending the full manuscript is fine too, provided you've read the guidelines first and know it's a great match. We publish offbeat stories you won't find elsewhere and choose them based on how interesting they are, not on whether the destination is popular with vacationers right now. We also publish travel book reviews and world music reviews each issue."

Perceptive Travel, Leffel stresses, is not a market for beginning writers to pitch. "We want book authors with a strong following, based on book sales and social media/blog audiences, with an experienced and unique voice. We showcase the writers' book(s) prominently next to the story in return."

The Great Outdoors

For some travelers, it is the beauty, diversity, and simplicity of Mother Nature that trumps all the glitz and glam of man-made attractions. Where else can you put your workaday worries on hold, breathe fresh air, and be mesmerized by the fact that no two sunsets are exactly the same?

Annie Stoltie, Editor of *Adirondack Life*, says, "We are the only magazine in the Adirondacks that explores this state park's people, places, wildlife, history, and public issues, and gives readers inside tips on outdoor recreation as well as how to capture the region's signature style in their camps and homes." Stoltie is open to query letters with a pitch and directed at a specific department. "We encourage writers to check out our indexes to be sure we haven't already covered a topic." Region-specific photographs by freelancers are also welcome.

If a getaway vacation to the woods, beaches, mountains, or even junkets into cities includes the family dog, Publisher Susan Sims describes *FIDO Friendly* as "*Travel & Leisure* for the canine set." She explains, "We're the only magazine dedicated to the travel and lifestyle of consumers and their dogs." If you are well versed on pet-friendly hotels, dog spa resorts, and canine health and wellness tips for safe travels, Sims invites a query with a sample paragraph of your writing. On her wish list for 2013–14? "More economy travel pieces for our Bowser on a Budget column, adoption stories, and articles about people making a difference."

Luxury Getaways

Aruba, Jamaica, Bermuda, Bahamas, Key Largo, Montego: It is hard to get the Beach Boys' "Kokomo" lyrics out of your head when you are surfing the print and online pages of *Aruba Nights, Aruba Nights Hotel Edition, Bonaire Nights, Curaçao Nights, St. Maarten/St. Martin Nights,* and *Island Gourmet* (www.nightspublications.com). Editor Jennifer McMorran explains that these six publications are targeted to travelers who are in Aruba, Bonaire, Curaçao, and St. Martin, as well as cruise ship passengers to those destinations. "We're the premier travel and lifestyle magazines for these destinations and they're widely read by people who are already on the islands. For 2013–14, we're looking for query letters with pitches focused on great profile stories about local islanders; exciting stories about the things (culture, food, nightlife, geography, history) that set these destinations apart; and original, first-person accounts of interesting island experiences."

"Great stories that present local perspectives from all around the world" sums up what Julia Cosgrove, Vice President and Editor in Chief of *Afar* (www.afar.com), wants to see in submissions from freelancers. "Our target readers are affluent, well-educated, conscientious and passionate travelers interested in going beneath the surface of a place and having deeper, more meaningful travel experiences." For new contributors, she urges careful study of the magazine's guidelines. "Tailor your pitches very tightly and concisely." *Afar* is published in both print and online editions.

Road Trip

For travelers who prefer cars and motorcycles over planes, trains, and ships, there are multiple venues for kindred spirits to give them advice. One of them—*Road & Travel* —celebrates its twenty-fifth anniversary in 2013. "Through many ups and downs over those years, we've never given up, no matter how tough times have been," says Courtney Caldwell, the magazine's founder, CEO, Publisher, and Editor in Chief. "Our target readership is the everyday consumer, with a subtle slant towards women who are interested in travel tips, car buying tips, and personal safety on the road. In fact, *Road & Travel* is a pioneering publication in targeting the women's consumer market with information on car purchases and repairs."

Road & Travel has transitioned to an online publication. Caldwell encourages writers to review its editorial calendar prior to submitting content. "For 2013–14, I'd like to see new car reviews in a conversational and informative format, as well as travel reviews from firsthand experience written by professional writers."

"If you want to break into *Backroads Motorcycle Tourmagazine*," says Publisher Brian Rathjen Sr., "you have to be motorcyclecentric!" Published in print as well as digitally, Rathjen's target readers are motorcycle riders and travelers. "What distinguishes us is that we provide places to go and things to see on motorcycles. For new contributors, we like to see full articles along with high-resolution images; the latter, in fact, is a must." Columns that are open to freelancers include The Great All American Diner Run, Big City Getaway, Mysterious America, We're Outta Here, and Thoughts From the Road.

Final Notes

A diversified portfolio will carry you far on your journey to reach the top-paying slots with premier travel magazines and consumer guidebooks. Consider, for instance, blogging, publishing travel memoirs, contributing SEO content, designing promotional materials and newsletters for travel agencies, penning reviews on local

TRAVEL MARKETS

- *Adirondack Life:* www.adirondacklifemag.com
- *Afar:* www.afar.com
- *Aruba Nights, Bonaire Nights, Curaçao Nights, St. Martin Nights, Island Gourmet:* www.nightspublications.com
- *Fido Friendly:* www.fidofriendly.com
- *Go World Travel:* www.goworldtravel.com
- *Motorcycle Tourmagazine:* www.backroadsusa.com
- *Outside Magazine:* www.outsideonline.com
- *Perceptive Travel:* www.perceptivetravel.com
- *Road & Travel:* www.roadandtravel.com

attractions, and writing trip advisories for government agencies.

Want to increase your chances of being discovered? From Ceurvels comes the advice to hone your pitching skills. "A great pitch letter is your ticket into publishing your travel stories. You also need to research all the publications where you want to submit your stories so you can keep abreast of what locations they've covered and what kinds of stories they publish. Travel writing is a numbers game. Pitch five publications every week. With that kind of consistent goal, your odds of getting published are greatly increased."

Sohn advises, "Learn to edit your impulses. Learn what you're best at. Learn what editors want. Take notes relentlessly. If you don't have a notebook in your pocket, you're doing it wrong! The more details you record, the better. And don't forget to take down names and contact info for everyone interesting you meet: Not only will you need it for follow-up reporting and fact-checking, but it's always great to return somewhere you haven't been in years and call up the folks you previously met. Lastly, I realize you want to go to the Maldives on someone else's dime—we all do!—but it's not happening, especially not as a greenhorn. So buckle down, find your stories, and you might get there eventually."

Last but not least is the dual issue of professionalism and respect. Just because you are a travel writer with a camera does not grant you *carte blanche* to aim it at whatever you would like. It is critical to always carry photo release forms if your shots feature close-ups of individuals or private property. You should also always ask where it is permissible to take photos, especially in museums, places of worship, or venues where security is an issue.

Now get out of your chair and start traveling. *Bon voyage!*

Consumer Magazines

Guide to the Listings

The annotations on the sample listing (page 41) will help you understand the importance of each section.

Departments and Interests

Here you will find a description of the publication, its type (lifestyle, glossy, ezine, newsletter, etc.), the general subject matter, as well as information about mission, voice, and more. You will also find insights into how editors view their magazines, as well as information about current editorial needs.

Freelance Potential

Our Freelance Potential section helps writers judge a magazine's receptivity to freelance material. In addition to designating how much of the publication is written by nonstaff writers (also known as freelance writers), the section highlights a magazine's receptivity to unpublished writers or to previously published authors who are new to that magazine. For certain magazines, this section also notes how much material is written by writers who have expertise in a particular field or industry.

To find magazines most open to submissions by unpublished writers, turn to "Best for Unpublished Writers" on page 712. For a list of the magazines that are receptive to previously published authors who have not written for that magazine, turn to "Best for First-Time Writers" on page 710.

Submissions

While many publications accept unsolicited manuscripts, many others prefer writers to submit query letters or pitches. The Submissions section indicates whether a magazine editor accepts a query letter, complete manuscript, or some other form, and whether hard copy or electronic submissions are preferred. Increasingly, publications are using forms of submissions manager such as Submishmash, and that preference is included. The section indicates whether a publication accepts multiple or simultaneous submissions, and other information required, such as résumés, writing samples, or clips of published articles or stories. Be sure to follow the submission requirements exactly.

Rights and Payment

This section notes the rights the magazine usually acquires (see page 21 for more information on copyright) and payment rates for written material and artwork.

These and other factors reveal significant details about the magazines that you can use to your advantage. As you study the listings and sample issues of the magazines, realize that you have many choices and many potential directions to take with your writing. Depending on your personal goals, you may place a greater value on one publication over another.

Consumer vs. Trade

One way to distinguish consumer publications from trade periodicals is to examine distribution. Consumer periodicals are sold mainly on newsstands and through subscriptions. Some are distributed through *controlled* circulation. This means the magazine is not purchased but goes to an audience in a "controlled" manner—given out at select locations or to club members, for instance.

Because many trade periodicals are sold primarily through subscriptions or distributed through controlled circulation, you may need to acquire a sample issue from the publisher instead of purchasing one at a newsstand. Increasingly, however, sample issues or articles are available at magazine websites. For publications that are solely published online, we include hits per month.

Sample Consumer Listing

Desert Ashram

 New for 2013

Desert Ashram
3403 West Sweetwater Drive
Tucson, AZ 85745-9301

Submissions Editor: Marianne Martin — Whom to contact

Description and Interests
This magazine appeals to spiritual seekers—all those who are interested in a universal approach to spirituality, meditation, healing practices, personal growth, and the interface of science and spirituality. Articles are inspiring and uplifting in tone, never derogatory, with universal meanings or messages. Circ: 24,000.

Profiles the magazine, its interests, and readers; provides circulation.

Contents: 80% articles; 15% depts/columns; 5% fiction and poetry
Frequency: Quarterly
Website: www.light-of-consciousness.org

Breaks down contents and frequency to help define readership and editorial slant; gives website location.

Freelance Potential
85% written by nonstaff writers. Publishes 6–8 freelance submissions yearly; 10% by unpublished writers, 50% by authors who are new to the magazine. Receives 60 queries, 30+ unsolicited mss monthly.

Indicates openness to freelance submissions, including how many are published yearly and the percentage by unpublished writers, when provided by the publisher.

Submissions
Query or send complete ms via website (Word attachments). Accepts simultaneous submissions if notified. Responds in 1–2 months.

- Articles: 1,000–4,000 words. Informational, how-to, and personal experience. Topics include spiritual growth, meditation, spirituality, healing, the environment, nature, the arts, pilgrimages.
- Fiction: 1,000–3,000 words. Spiritual stories.
- Depts/columns: Staff-written.
- Other: Poetry; no line limits.

Provides guidelines for submitting material; lists word lengths and types of material accepted from freelance writers.

Sample Issue
64 pages. Advertising. Sample articles available. Guidelines and editorial calendar available at website.

- "Karma and the Voice of Conscience." Hearing what the voice of conscience is saying depends on one's inner state.
- "Prayer of the Heart." Entering the mystery of Divine Love through the spiritual practice of internal prayer.

Analyzes a recent issue, briefly describing selected articles, stories, departments, etc. Provides cost and postage information to obtain a sample copy and writers' guidelines.

Rights and Payment
One-time rights. No payment. Provides 1+ contributor's copies.

Lists types of rights acquired, payment rate, and number of copies provided to writers who are published.

Icon Key

 New Listing  Epublisher  Not currently accepting submissions

 Overseas Publisher  Fiction makes up at least 10% of magazine editorial content

AARP Bulletin

601 E Street NW
Washington, DC 20049

Editor: James Toedtman

Description and Interests

This newspaper for AARP members is a go-to source for news and information relevant to the over-50 population. Articles focus on health and health policy, Medicare, Social Security, independent living, and personal finance. Its readers are active and involved. Circ: 22 million.

Contents: 75% articles; 25% depts/columns
Frequency: 10 times a year
Website: www.aarp.org/bulletin

Freelance Potential

75% written by nonstaff writers. Publishes 75–80 freelance submissions yearly; 20% by authors who are new to the magazine, 30% by experts. Receives many queries monthly.

Submissions

Query. Accepts hard copy. SASE. Responds in 2 weeks.

- Articles: 600–2,500 words. Informational and how-to articles, profiles, interviews, personal experience pieces, creative nonfiction, humor, and new product information. Topics include personal finance, careers, current events, government issues, medical care, nutrition, the changing workplace, and social issues—all as they apply to seniors.
- Depts/columns: 600–1,500 words. Health updates, personal finance, expert tips, and opinion pieces.

Sample Issue

40 pages. Advertising. Sample copy available at website.

- "Tattoos for Medical Alerts: New Form of Medical ID is on the Rise." Pros and cons of getting tattoos to alert health care providers to medical conditions.
- Sample dept/column: Scam Alert gives six tips on how to avoid being scammed by a locksmith.

Rights and Payment

Rights vary. Written material, payment rates vary. Pays on publication. Provides contributor's copies.

AARP The Magazine

Editorial Submissions
601 E Street NW
Washington, DC 20049

Editor in Chief: Nancy Perry Graham

Description and Interests

AARP The Magazine is the world's largest circulation magazine and the lifestyle publication for AARP's nearly 40 million members. It features lifestyle topics and celebrity interviews, along with informative articles on health, aging, financial issues, and consumer topics. All material targets the AARP member demographic: those 50 years and older. It considers itself America's good-life guide for grown-ups, and all material should reflect that. It does not accept unsolicited submissions, but will entertain article ideas. Most material is generated in-house or through contract writers. Circ: 22 million.

Contents: Articles, depts/columns
Frequency: 6 times a year
Website: www.aarp.org/magazine

Freelance Potential Unavailable.

Submissions

Query with story idea, recent clips, an explanation of your angle or approach, and the target location in the magazine (feature or specific dept/column). Accepts hard copy and email to AARPMagazine@aarp.org (no attachments).

- Articles: Word lengths vary. Informational and how-to articles, profiles, and interviews. Topics include lifestyle, health and fitness, current events, financial issues, careers and retirement, travel, consumerism, relationships.
- Depts/columns: Word lengths vary. Money, health, food, media reviews.

Sample Issue

68 pages. Advertising. Sample copy and guidelines available at website.

- "Escape Your Comfort Zone." Taking risks and embarking on new adventures can make a person feel happier and more satisfied with life.
- "Diane Keaton: Here I Am." Oscar-winning actress tells about her successes and offers stay-young advice.

Rights and Payment

Buys first worldwide publication rights. Written material, payment rates vary; 25% kill fee. Pays on acceptance.

About.com

Editor

Description and Interests

About.com consists of a series of more than 900 guides that offer information, and often, solutions on a wide range of topics, from acne to adoption to ancient history to auto repair. Writers may become guides, or may apply to become topic writers, freelancers who write content on more specialized topics. Part of the New York Times Company, About.com regularly uses contributors who are experts in their fields. Visit the website to see which topics are in need of freelancers. Video producers are also needed. Hits per month: varies by topic and guide page.

Contents: Articles; depts/columns

Frequency: Ongoing
Website: www.beaguide.about.com

Freelance Potential

Publishes 7,000+ freelance submissions monthly.

Submissions

Check website for application to become a guide contributor or topic writer, and for a list of topics in need of writers.

- Articles: Word lengths vary. Informational and how-to articles. Topics are varied and numerous; they include entertaining, parenting, cooking, health and wellness, travel, animals, religion, finance, style, hobbies, pregnancy, and sports.

Sample Issue

Advertising. Online articles.

- "The Big College To-Do List." Article provides tips for buying, preparing, and packing for college.
- "Help Your Tween Make and Keep Friends." Article discusses how parents can help their kids make the rights choices.

Rights and Payment

Exclusive, perpetual online rights. Guides are guaranteed a per-article rate for a maximum number of articles (usually 8 per month), and also may receive payment based on hits, or page views.

Acoustic Guitar

P.O. Box 767
San Anselmo, CA 94979

Managing Editor: Mark Smith

Description and Interests

Offering something for every player in every style, *Acoustic Guitar* presents a mix of musician profiles, musical genre explorations, and step-by-step playing techniques. It is interested in any articles that help readers—which include beginners through performing professionals—learn guitar techniques and get to know the artists who created them. Circ: 70,000.

Contents: Articles; depts/columns
Frequency: Monthly
Website: www.acousticguitar.com

Freelance Potential

60% written by nonstaff writers. Publishes 100+ freelance submissions yearly; 10% by authors who are new to the magazine.

Submissions

Query with clips. Accepts hard copy and email queries to editors.ag@stringletter.com (no links to websites). SASE. Responds in 1 month.

- Articles: Word lengths vary. Informational and how-to articles, profiles, interviews, and new product information. Topics include all issues concerning acoustic guitars and acoustic guitar playing.
- Depts/columns: 600–1,000 words. Player profiles, stage and studio news, how-to's, shop talk, and new product information.

Sample Issue

98 pages. Advertising. Sample articles available to view at website.

- "Regal Flattops." A look at the instruments and history of the Regal Guitar Company.
- "Justin Townes Earle." Interview with this eclectic styled guitar player/songwriter and his rocky road to success.
- Sample dept/column: Instruction teaches readers the techniques of this roots/blues fingerpicking guitar style.

Rights and Payment

Rights vary. Written material, payment rates vary. Pays on publication.

Ad Astra

1155 15th Street NW, Suite 500
Washington, DC 20005

Assignment Editor: Katherine Brick

Description and Interests

This member magazine of the National Space Society combines the latest news in space exploration and aerospace science with stunning photography. Reaching a sophisticated audience of scientists, technologists, and avid space enthusiasts, it also includes book reviews. It seeks well-written articles that showcase professional expertise. Circ: 20,000.

Contents: Articles; depts/columns
Frequency: Quarterly
Website: www.nss.org/adastra

Freelance Potential

95% written by nonstaff writers. Publishes 50 freelance submissions yearly. Receives 5–6 queries, 5–6 unsolicited mss monthly.

Submissions

Prefers query with résumé; accepts complete ms with résumé. Writers interested in being considered for assignments can send résumé, areas of expertise, and publishing credits. Accepts email to adastra@nss.org. Response time varies.

- Articles: Features, 1,200–4,000 words; profiles, 600–750 words. Informational articles, profiles, and interviews. Topics include space, people, science, and technology related to space exploration and the aerospace industry.
- Depts/columns: 600–750 words. Book reviews and opinion pieces.
- Artwork: Color digital images at 300 dpi.

Sample Issue

64 pages. Advertising. Sample copy available. Sample articles available to view at website. Guidelines available at website.

- "The Development of Space: Opportunities to Improve Life on Earth." Ways to use space and space technology to better life both nationally and globally.
- Sample dept/column: Book Review of *The Space Shuttle: Celebrating Thirty Years of NASA's First Space Plane.*

Rights and Payment

First North American serial rights. Written material, $.25 per word. Artwork, payment rates negotiable. Payment policy varies. Provides 1 author's copy.

Adbusters

1243 West 7th Avenue
Vancouver, British Columbia V6H 1B7
Canada

Editor in Chief: Kalle Lasn

Description and Interests

Adbusters describes itself as an ecological magazine that examines the relationship between humans and their physical and mental environments. It features philosophical articles and activist commentaries on issues ranging from genetically modified foods to media concentration. It looks for articles that offer a fresh angle on the world; it could be political analysis, an activist victory, a new culture jam, or a short story illustrating the madness of the modern world. Circ: 120,000.

Contents: 75% articles; 20% depts/columns; 5% fiction
Frequency: 6 times each year
Website: www.adbusters.org

Freelance Potential

80–90% written by nonstaff writers. Publishes 40–80 freelance submissions yearly; 20% by unpublished writers, 15–30% by new authors. Receives 100 unsolicited mss monthly.

Submissions

Send complete ms. Accepts hard copy and email submissions to editor@adbusters.org. Material is not returned. Responds in several months.

- Articles: Word lengths vary. Informational articles, profiles, essays, interviews, personal experience pieces, and humor. Topics include advertising, the media, communications, consumer culture, and geopolitics.
- Depts/columns: 500–750 words. Media reviews and political analysis.
- Artwork: Prints; JPEGs at 72 dpi.

Sample Issue

100 pages. No advertising. Sample articles and guidelines available at website.

- "Logic Freaks." Essay explores how economics has become a theoretical rather than practical science.
- "Canada's Spiritual Quest." An assessment of half a century of effort to advance environmental causes and concerns.

Rights and Payment

All rights. Written material, payment rates vary. Pays on publication. Provides 1 contributor's copy.

Adoptive Families

39 West 37th Street, 15th Floor
New York, NY 10018

Submissions: Joanna Yeung

Description and Interests
Adoptive Families is a resource for advice, news, and practical information for all stages of the adoption process. It features personal stories, book reviews, and essays, as well as articles that cover the middle-school and teen years, adoptive parent support groups, and school issues. Circ: 40,000.

Contents: 70% articles; 30% depts/columns
Frequency: 6 times each year
Website: www.adoptivefamilies.com

Freelance Potential
75% written by nonstaff writers. Publishes 100 freelance submissions yearly; 20% by unpublished writers, 50% by new authors.

Submissions
Send complete ms for personal essays. For all other pieces, query with brief description or outline, intended section of the magazine, why you should write article, author bio, and recent clips. Prefers email to submissions@adoptivefamilies.com (Word attachments); will accept hard copy. SASE. Responds in 6–8 weeks.

- Articles: 500–1,800 words. Informational, self-help, and how-to articles; and personal experience pieces. Topics include preparing for adoption, health issues, birth families, and parenting and family issues.
- Depts/columns: 700–1,400 words. Legal and medical issues, growing up adopted, single parenting, interracial adoption, opinions, news, and gear.

Sample Issue
66 pages. Advertising. Sample articles and guidelines available at website.

- "Bringing Heritage Home." Ways to blend an adoptive child's background into everyday family life.
- "Adoption Through a Child's Eyes." By understanding how children of different ages see adoption, parents can more effectively communicate with them on the subject.

Rights and Payment
All rights. Personal essays, no payment but authors receive a 1-year subscription. Other material, payment rates vary. Pays on publication. Provides 2 contributor's copies.

Adventure Cyclist

Adventure Cycling Association
150 East Pine Street, P.O. Box 8308
Missoula, MT 59807

Editor: Michael Deme

Description and Interests
This publication from the Adventure Cycling Association inspires readers of all ages to explore on bicycle the landscape and history of America and places abroad. The majority of its content is destination pieces, but it also covers equipment, gear, technical advice, and association news. It is always interested in hearing about people involved in the cycling industry. Humorous essays are especially welcome. Photos are a must with touring pieces. Circ: 43,500.

Contents: 75% articles; 25% depts/columns
Frequency: 9 times each year
Website: www.adventurecycling.org/mag

Freelance Potential
75% written by nonstaff writers. Publishes 20–25 freelance submissions yearly; 25% by authors who are new to the magazine. Receives 50 queries monthly.

Submissions
Requires query prior to submission. Accepts email queries to mdeme@adventurecycling.org and simultaneous submissions if identified, during submission periods; see website for current schedule. Responds in 2–4 weeks.

- Articles: 2,000–3,500 words. Informational articles, profiles, humor. Topics include cycling destinations in the U.S. and abroad, personalities on bicycles and within the bicycle industry.
- Depts/columns: The Final Mile, essays less about locale than singular trip experience, 1,200–1,500 words. Other departments are staff-written.
- Artwork: 35mm color slides; digital images at 300 dpi.

Sample Issue
40 pages. Advertising. Guidelines and sample articles available at website.

- "Passing Down the Bike." Tips for encouraging kids to learn to love biking.
- "A World View with Spokes." Profile of David Mozer, founder of the International Bicycle Fund and Bicycle Africa.

Rights and Payment
First rights. Written material, \$.30–\$.50 per word. Pays on publication. Provides 1 contributor's copy.

The Advocate

P.O. Box 4371
Los Angeles, CA 90078

Associate Editor: Michelle Garcia

Description and Interests

The Advocate focuses on the news, not the lifestyle, affecting gays and lesbians. Instead of grooming tips, fitness articles, and fashion advice, readers will find articles on politics, arts and entertainment, and culture. It does not accept fiction and poetry and publishes one first-person guest columnist or essayist per issue. Circ: 150,000.

Contents: 90% articles; 10% depts/columns
Frequency: 10 times a year
Website: www.advocate.com

Freelance Potential

60% written by nonstaff writers. Publishes 50 freelance submissions yearly; 10% by unpublished writers, 15% by authors who are new to the magazine, 20% by experts. Receives 35 queries monthly.

Submissions

Query with detailed letter (500 words or less) and published clips or URLs to online work. Prefers email to newsroom@advocate.com; will accept hard copy. No SASE; materials not returned. Responds in 1 month via email only.

- Articles: Cover stories and features, 2,000 words. Shorter articles, 800–1,000 words. Informational articles, interviews, and profiles. Topics include career and employment issues, gay marriage, discrimination, legislation, social issues, and entertainment.
- Depts/columns: 200–750 words. Opinion pieces, news briefs, personal essays, Q&As, and media reviews.

Sample Issue

80 pages. Advertising. Guidelines available. Sample articles available for view at website.

- "The Contenders: Hot LGBT Prospects for Office." A rundown of LGBT candidates running for elected offices this year.
- "Scouts' Dishonor." Discusses the policy of the Boy Scouts of America with regard to homosexual leaders and members and what is being done to try to change it.

Rights and Payment

All rights. Written material, payment rates vary. Pays on publication. Provides 1 contributor's copy.

African American Career World

Equal Opportunity Publications, Inc.
445 Broad Hollow Road, Suite 425
Melville, NY 11747

Editor: James Schneider

Description and Interests

This magazine seeks to be the link between African American students and professionals and the companies looking to hire them. It covers career strategies, industry trends, and role-model profiles in all fields. Articles should relate to students and young professionals. Circ: 18,000.

Contents: Articles; depts/columns
Frequency: Twice each year
Website: www.eop.com/mags-AACW.php

Freelance Potential

50% written by nonstaff writers. Publishes 15 freelance submissions yearly; 25% by unpublished writers, 25% by authors who are new to the magazine, 50% by experts. Receives 10 queries, 5 unsolicited mss monthly.

Submissions

Query with outline for articles. Send complete ms for filler. Accepts hard copy, Macintosh disk submissions, and email to jschneider@eop.com. SASE. Responds in 1 month.

- Articles: 1,500 words. Informational and how-to articles, profiles, interviews, and personal experience pieces. Topics include business, career, and industry profiles as they relate to the African American community.
- Depts/columns: To 800 words. Career strategies and tools.

Sample Issue

46 pages. Advertising. Sample articles available at website.

- "Job References in the Social Media Age." Using social media sites to increase your visibility to prospective employers.
- "Dell—Changing the Marketplace." Profile of this corporation and professional opportunities offered for African Americans in the IT field.

Rights and Payment

First North American serial rights. Written material, $.10 per word. Pays on publication. Provides 1+ contributor's copies.

AGNI

Boston University
236 Bay State Road
Boston, MA 02215

Editor: Sven Birkerts

Description and Interests

Home to original works from both emerging and established writers, *AGNI* looks for poetry, fiction, and essays that possess passion and a unique vision. It has an ongoing interest in important cultural questions. Each issue includes approximately 40 writers and artists from around the globe. The magazine's website features additional work, including reviews and interviews. Considers book excerpts if they can stand alone. All submissions considered for both print and online. Circ: 3,000.

Contents: 35% fiction; 35% poetry; 30% essays
Frequency: Print, twice each year; online, twice each month
Website: www.agnimagazine.org; www.bu.edu/agni

Freelance Potential

95% written by nonstaff writers. Publishes 120 freelance submissions yearly; 10% by unpublished writers, 70% by authors who are new to the magazine, 30% by experts. Receives 1,000 unsolicited mss monthly.

Submissions

Send complete ms with cover letter between September 1 and May 31 only. Work must be unpublished. Accepts hard copy, submissions made via the website, and simultaneous submissions if identified. SASE. Responds in 2–4 months.

- Essays: No word limits. Creative nonfiction, personal experience, memoir; 1 per submission.
- Fiction: No word limits. Literary fiction; 1 per submission.
- Other: Poetry, to 5 poems per submission.

Sample Issue

248 pages. Little advertising. Sample stories available. Guidelines available at website.

- "Movie Nights in Rangoon." Story about a family in Burma who acquires a rare commodity for their time and place: a television.
- "Vertigo." Essay on the influence of author W.G. Sebald.

Rights and Payment

First North American serial rights (print magazine) and first worldwide serial rights (website). Prose, $10 per page; poetry, $20 per page; $150 maximum. Pays on publication. Provides 2 contributor's copies, a 1-year subscription, 4 gift copies.

Air & Space Smithsonian

P.O. Box 37012
MRC 513
Washington, DC 20013-7012

Executive Editor: Paul Hoversten

Description and Interests

This magazine targets readers who have an interest in aeronautics, space travel, and aircraft of all kinds. It encompasses every era and development in flight and space exploration and emphasizes the human stories more than the technology. First-time contributors will find the best chance for publication through a column or department. Circ: 240,000.

Contents: 80% articles; 20% depts/columns
Frequency: 6 times each year
Website: www.airspacemag.com

Freelance Potential

95% written by nonstaff writers. Publishes 45 freelance submissions yearly; 10% by unpublished writers, 20% by new authors. Receives 35 queries, 15 unsolicited mss monthly.

Submissions

Send complete ms for humor or first-person narratives. For all other material, query with clips and 1-page proposal introducing the article you envision, the sources, possible illustrations, and writer's credentials; or send complete ms. Accepts hard copy and email to editors@si.edu. SASE. Responds in 1 month.

- Articles: Word lengths vary. Informational and historical articles, and personal experience pieces. Topics include aviation, space technology, aircraft, history, and technology.
- Depts/columns: Reviews, 200–500 words. Soundings, Above & Beyond, Flights & Fancy, Oldies and Oddities, word lengths vary.

Sample Issue

80 pages. Advertising. Sample articles and guidelines available at website.

- "First Neighborhood on Mars." The creator of The Sims imagines what life will be like on the red planet.
- "Emissary." The potential scientific discoveries and possible pitfalls of the rover, Curiosity.

Rights and Payment

First North American serial rights. Written material, payment rates vary. Kill fee varies. Pays on acceptance. Provides 1 contributor's copy.

AKA Mom

H2O Print Media
16526 West 78th Street, #359
Eden Prairie, MN 55346-4302

Publisher: Sara Conners

Description and Interests

Created by moms for moms, this magazine appears in print, online, and even as an iPad app. It made its debut in the summer of 2011 and targets modern, fashion-savvy mothers. Besides advice on parenting and children's health, each issue offers articles that speak to the other roles of its readers: wife, lover, stylish woman, and career woman. Circ: 200,000.

Contents: Articles; depts/columns
Frequency: Quarterly
Website: www.akamommamagazine.com

Freelance Potential

Unavailable.

Submissions

Query. Send email queries to editorial@ akamommagazine.com. Response time varies.

- Articles: Word lengths vary. Informational articles, profiles, personal experience pieces, and how-to's. Topics include parenting issues, balancing work and home life, relationships, style and fashion, family travel, fitness, pregnancy, and careers.
- Dept/Columns: Word lengths vary. Fashion and beauty tips, new products, celebrity news.

Sample Issue

76 pages. Advertising. Sample copy available at website.

- "Can Your Hormones Decide Your Career?" Article discusses research that indicates the amount of male hormones women are exposed to in utero can determine interests later in life.
- "Stories of Motherhood." Article features an interview with Tori Spelling about her experiences with pregnancy and motherhood.
- Sample dept/column: Beauty suggests the best makeup products for the winter season.

Rights and Payment

Rights vary. Payment rates and policy vary.

AKC Family Dog

American Kennel Club
260 Madison Avenue
New York, NY 10016

Editorial Director: Erika Mansourian

Description and Interests

This publication from the American Kennel Club is focused on ways to care for and love purebred dogs. Its articles cover canine health, agility, training, behavior, and the histories of various breeds. It also profiles well-known or extraordinary dogs, including work dogs. Material should be current and come from reliable sources, and be written in a lively, conversational tone. Circ: 180,000.

Contents: 50% articles; 50% depts/columns
Frequency: 6 times each year
Website: www.akc.org/pubs/familydog

Freelance Potential

70% written by nonstaff writers. Publishes 30 freelance submissions yearly; 15% by authors new to the magazine, 85% by experts. Receives 5–10 queries monthly.

Submissions

Accepts queries and complete manuscripts to ejm@akc.org (Word attachments). Accepts simultaneous submissions if identified.

- Articles: 1,000–2,000 words. Informational and how-to articles, profiles, humor, and new product information. Topics include dog grooming, training, behavior, health, nutrition, pet therapy, breed history, current events involving canines, dog work, and travel with dogs.
- Depts/columns: Staff-written.

Sample Issue

54 pages. Advertising. Sample copy available at website. Guidelines available by emailing vxr@ akc.org.

- "Diners, Drive-ins, and Dogs." How to help dogs maintain healthy eating habits when traveling.
- "Pups and Preschoolers." Training tips to help facilitate a safe and happy relationship between dogs and young children.

Rights and Payment

First North American serial rights. Articles, $125–$500. Pays on acceptance. Provides 1 contributor's copy.

Alaska Airlines

2701 First Avenue, Suite 250
Seattle, WA 98121

Editor: Paul Frichtl

Description and Interests

Targeting business and leisure travelers, this magazine combines high-quality photography with entertaining editorial on a broad range of subjects, including travel, sports, popular culture, business, technology, and history. It is read by the passengers of Alaska Airlines. The best way for new writers to break in is by submitting something for a department or column. Features are usually assigned to experienced writers. Circ: 1.8 million.

Contents: 80% articles; 20% depts/columns
Frequency: Monthly
Website: www.alaskaairlinesmagazine.com

Freelance Potential

75% written by nonstaff writers. Publishes 150 freelance submissions yearly; 20% by authors who are new to the magazine. Receives 30–50 queries each month.

Submissions

Query with clips and sample lead that represents the direction, tone, and style proposed for the article. Accepts hard copy. SASE. Responds in 6 weeks.

- Articles: 2,000–2,500 words. Informational articles, profiles, and interviews. Topics include travel destinations, history, nature, entertainment, and consumer and business interests.
- Depts/columns: 300–1,600 words. Destinations, restaurant and lodging reviews, travel, business, personal finance, science and technology, sports, health and fitness, culture, and the arts.

Sample Issue

170 pages. Advertising. Sample copy, guidelines, and editorial calendar available at website.

- "Precious Medals." Roundup of Olympic hopefuls from the Pacific 12 college athletic conference.
- Sample dept/column: Great Escapes explores the vibrant city of Vancouver.

Rights and Payment

First North American serial rights with reprint rights. Articles, $700. Depts/columns, $150–$500. Kill fee, 33%. Pays within 30 days of publication. Provides 2 contributor's copies.

Alaska Quarterly Review

University of Alaska-Anchorage
3211 Providence Drive (ESH 208)
Anchorage, AK 99508

Editors

Description and Interests

A showplace for award-winning literature, this journal, now in its 30th year, is published by the University of Alaska-Anchorage. It features high-quality literary fiction, creative nonfiction, poetry, and plays, in both traditional and experimental forms. It welcomes new writers while continuing to publish established authors. Circ: 3,000.

Contents: 55% fiction; 25% articles; 20% other
Frequency: Twice each year
Website: www.uaa.alaska.edu/aqr

Freelance Potential

100% written by nonstaff writers. Publishes 60–80 freelance submissions yearly; 15% by unpublished writers, 80% by authors who are new to the magazine. Receives 500 unsolicited mss monthly.

Submissions

Send complete ms between August 15 and May 15 only. Accepts hard copy and simultaneous submissions if identified. SASE. Responds in 2–4 months.

- Articles: To 50 pages. Literary nonfiction. Topics include contemporary literature, multicultural issues, and the environment.
- Fiction: To 50 pages. Short stories and novel excerpts in traditional and experimental styles.
- Other: Plays, to 50 pages. Poetry, to 20 pages. Traditional and experimental styles (no light verse for poetry).

Sample Issue

234 pages. Sample copy available. Guidelines available at website.

- "The Dinner Party." Short story.
- "Good Neighbors." Short story.

Rights and Payment

First North American serial rights. Written material, payment rates vary. Pays on publication. Provides 1 contributor's copy.

Alive Now

The Upper Room
1908 Grand Avenue
P.O. Box 340004
Nashville, TN 37203-0004

Editor: Beth A. Richardson

Description and Interests

Through meditations, stories, poetry, and prayers, this devotional magazine explores how contemporary issues impact one's faith. Its audience includes both lay people and church professionals of all ages. Each issue is themed and submissions must match an upcoming theme to be accepted. Circ: 37,000.

Contents: 20% articles; 20% depts/columns; 20% poetry; 10% fiction; 30% other
Frequency: 6 times each year
Website: www.upperroom.org; http://alivenow.upperroom.org

Freelance Potential

90% written by nonstaff writers. Publishes 50–60 freelance submissions yearly; 15% by unpublished writers, 20% by authors new to the magazine, 70% by experts. Receives 100 mss monthly.

Submissions

Send complete ms with theme identified. Accepts up to 2 stories/articles or 6 poems/prayers per theme, per writer. Prefers email to alivenow@-upperroom.org (Word attachments). Accepts hard copy, SASE. Response time varies.

- Articles: 250–400 words. Devotionals and personal experience pieces. Topics include multicultural and ethnic issues, nature, religion, spirituality, and social issues.
- Depts/columns: Word lengths vary. Reflections on Bible readings.
- Fiction: 250–400 words. Meditations and inspirational stories.
- Other: Poetry and prayers, to 40 lines.

Sample Issue

48 pages. No advertising. Sample copy, guidelines, and theme list available at website.

- "Lenten Practices." Using silence and solitude as a way of drawing closer to God and to take care of spiritual "housecleaning."
- "In the Wilds." Poem expressing the need for God's care in times of temptation.

Rights and Payment

One-time, newspaper, periodical, and electronic rights. Written material, $35+. Pays on acceptance. Provides 10 contributor's copies.

Alternatives Journal

Faculty of Environmental Studies
University of Waterloo
200 University Avenue W
Waterloo, Ontario N2L 3G1
Canada

Editor: Eric Rumble

Description and Interests

As Canada's environmental magazine, *Alternatives Journal* explores how ideas and actions can turn into results. Each issue delivers information on Canadian and global environmental issues, news, and profiles of environmental leaders. Articles must meet the highest standards in terms of the analytical rigor and reliability of the information presented. All material will be blind-reviewed by experts in the topic. Circ: 3,200.

Contents: 70% articles; 30% depts/columns
Frequency: 6 times each year
Website: www.alternativesjournal.ca

Freelance Potential

95% written by nonstaff writers. Publishes 100 freelance submissions yearly; 40% by unpublished writers, 40% by authors who are new to the magazine, 60% by experts. Receives 30 queries monthly.

Submissions

Query with proposal (300 words maximum) conveying content, scope, approach, and style; list of potential sources; word count; and writing samples. Accepts email queries to editor@alternatives-journal.ca (text attachments). Responds in 1 month.

- Articles: Features, to 2,000 words. Reports, 500–1,200 words. Notes, to 500 words. Informational articles, profiles, interviews, and humor. Topics include the environment, conservation, social issues, economics initiatives, politics, and current events.
- Depts/columns: 600–750 words. News, book and media reviews, science updates, politics, opinion pieces.

Sample Issue

48 pages. Advertising. Guidelines, theme list, and sample articles available at website.

- "Northern Getaway." Ecotourism advocates weigh in on the plan to divide British Columbia with a pipeline.
- "The Unsinkable Scientist." An environmental scientist investigates the decline of sockeye salmon.

Rights and Payment

First North American serial rights. Written material, $.10 per word.

America

106 West 56th Street
New York, NY 10019-3803

Editor in Chief: Drew Christiansen, S.J.

Description and Interests

Offering ethical and theological reflection on contemporary issues facing the Catholic Church and the world, *America* has an audience of laypeople and clergy. It features articles, essays, and criticism in each issue. It welcomes articles written for a general audience on education, social issues, public affairs, politics, and the environment. Circ: 43,000.

Contents: Articles; depts/columns
Frequency: Weekly
Website: www.americamagazine.org

Freelance Potential

80% written by nonstaff writers. Publishes 35–50 freelance submissions yearly. Receives 75 unsolicited mss monthly.

Submissions

Send complete manuscript with author biography and credentials. Accepts email submissions to articles@americamagazine.org (Word or WordPerfect attachments). Send book reviews to reviews@americamagazine.org; send poetry via hard copy. No simultaneous submissions. SASE. Responds in 3 weeks.

- Articles: 1,500–2,000 words. Informational articles. Topics include religion, education, the environment, politics, public affairs, and social issues.
- Depts/columns: To 900 words. Faith in Focus, first-person account of faith; Of Other Things, commentary; book reviews.
- Other: Poetry, to 30 lines.

Sample Issue

38 pages. Advertising. Sample articles and guidelines available at website.

- "Heart and Soul." Spiritual conversation and the role it plays in pastoral care.
- Sample dept./column: Faith in Focus, a new mom tells why she chose to move home.

Rights and Payment

First and reprint rights. Written material, $200. Pays on acceptance. Provides 5 contributor's copies.

American Angler

735 Broad Street
Augusta, GA 30901

Editor: Steve Walburn

Description and Interests

American Angler is devoted exclusively to fly fishing. Articles cover every aspect of the sport, from technique to finding fish and tying flies. It also features new gear and accessories, as well as problem-solving pieces. Though it focuses mainly on coldwater fly fishing, it includes information on warm water and saltwater fly fishing as well. Circ: 40,000.

Contents: 70% articles; 25% depts/columns; 5% other
Frequency: 6 times each year
Website: www.americanangler.com

Freelance Potential

95% written by nonstaff writers. Publishes 60–80 freelance submissions yearly; 5% by unpublished writers, 30% by authors who are new to the magazine, 60% by experts. Receives 10–30 queries, 3–10 unsolicited mss monthly.

Submissions

Query with outline and availability of photos. Accepts hard copy and email submissions to steve.walburn@morris.com. SASE. Responds in 6–8 weeks.

- Articles: 800–2,200 words. Informational and how-to articles, and personal experience pieces. Topics include fly fishing and fly tying, angling techniques, destinations, fish behavior, tackle, entomology, and ecology.
- Depts/columns: 350–750 words. Warm-water fishing, tying flies, field notes, technique, and fishing history.

Sample Issue

72 pages. Sample copy available. Guidelines available at website.

- "Fly Fishing High Water." Tips and techniques for fly fishing in swollen rivers.
- "Tying the Shasta Shad." A do-it-yourself guide to striper fishing in Montauk.

Rights and Payment

First North American serial print, electronic, and in-house marketing rights. Written material, $200–$450. Pays on publication.

American Athlete

Submissions Editor

Description and Interests
This sports-focused ezine, launched in late 2011, bills itself as a different kind of sports magazine. It covers professional, college, and amateur athletes for a readership of athletic-minded adults. Its slant is the athlete's "inner life: mind, body, and spirit," publishing portraits of the athlete experience. It is also available as a mobile app, with full interactivity. Writers should go beyond routine event coverage, analysis, and statistics to show readers what it's like and what is required to compete at the most challenging levels. Hits per month: Unavailable.
Contents: Articles; depts/columns
Frequency: Updated regularly
Website: www.americanathletemag.com

Freelance Potential
Receives many freelance submissions monthly.

Submissions
Contact editor for submissions information and guidelines. Send email to info@americanathletemag.com.

- Articles: Word lengths vary. Informational and how-to articles and profiles. Topics include training, conditioning, nutrition, strength and endurance, and competition training.
- Depts/columns: Word lengths vary. Training tips, gear, health and nutrition.

Sample Issue
Sample articles available at website.

- "Why Isn't Your Performance Improving?" Article explains how to deal when progress gets derailed and what the body is trying to tell you.
- "Yoga in Mind." Article discusses ways in which yoga can help athletes-in-training.
- Sample dept/column: Sidelines profiles the first African-American Olympic medalist.

Rights and Payment
Rights vary. Payment rates and policy varies.

American Baby

375 Lexington Avenue, 10th Floor
New York, NY 10017

Editorial Assistant: Jessica Wohlgemuth

Description and Interests
Written for pregnant couples and new parents, this magazine offers easy-to-read, hands-on information that can be used right away. It also offers a balanced view of controversial parenting issues. With the idea that new parents don't have a lot of time to read, it looks for articles that are short and informative. Circ: 2 million.
Contents: Articles; depts/columns
Frequency: Monthly
Website: www.americanbaby.com

Freelance Potential
55% written by nonstaff writers. Publishes 24 freelance submissions yearly; 1% by unpublished writers, 1% by authors who are new to the magazine. Receives 83 queries and unsolicited mss each month.

Submissions
Query with clips or writing samples; or send complete ms. Accepts hard copy and simultaneous submissions if identified. SASE. Responds in 2 months.

- Articles: 1,000–2,000 words. Informational and how-to articles, profiles, interviews, humor, and personal experience pieces. Topics include pregnancy, child care, child development, health, fitness, nutrition, and travel.
- Depts/columns: 1,000 words. Health briefs, fitness, new products, and fashion.
- Other: Submit seasonal material 3 months in advance.

Sample Issue
72 pages. Advertising. Sample copy and guidelines available.

- "10 Truths About Baby Sleep." Understanding newborn sleep habits and how to get some rest for yourself.
- "Have a Better Bed Rest." Tips for getting through this stressful time.

Rights and Payment
First serial rights. Articles, to $1,000. Depts/columns, to $1,000. Kill fee, 25%. Pays on publication. Provides 5 contributor's copies.

American Book Review

School of Arts and Sciences
University of Houston–Victoria
3007 North Ben Wilson
Victoria, TX 77901

Managing Editor: Jeffrey A. Sartain

Description and Interests

American Book Review sees its primary role as reviewing books of fiction, nonfiction, and poetry from independent, university, and small presses. It also features literary and cultural criticism from small, regional, university, ethnic, avant-garde, and women's presses. It is edited by writers for writers and the general public. It does not review how-to or self-help books. Circ: 8,000.

Contents: 90% articles; 10% depts/columns
Frequency: 6 times each year
Website: www.americanbookreview.org

Freelance Potential

100% written by nonstaff writers. Publishes 170 freelance submissions yearly; 2% by unpublished writers, 10% by authors who are new to the magazine, 5% by experts. Receives 30 queries monthly.

Submissions

Query with CV and 2 writing samples, preferably book reviews, or the review you'd like to submit. Accepts email to americanbookreview@uhv.edu. Response time varies.

- Articles: 750–1,250 words. Informational articles, essays, and book reviews. Topics include fiction, literary criticism, biography, creative writing, and cultural studies.
- Depts/columns: Staff-written.

Sample Issue

32 pages. Little advertising. Sample copy and guidelines available.

- "Review." Daniel T. O'Hara reviews Frank Lentricchia's *The Sadness of Antonioni.*
- "Review." Eugene Wildman reviews Elizabeth Searle's *Girl Held in Home.*

Rights and Payment

First North American serial and international rights. No payment. Provides contributor's copies or a 1-year subscription.

American Car Collector 

P.O. Box 4797
Portland, OR 97208-4797

Editor: Jim Pickering

Description and Interests

From the publisher of *Sports Car Market* comes this new magazine geared to the avid collector of American cars. Each issue gives readers a detailed, insider's look at the growing American collector car market and provides car profiles, events, and other news. The audience consists of high-end collectors. Circ: Unavailable.

Contents: Articles; depts/columns
Frequency: 6 times each year
Website: www.americancarcollector.com

Freelance Potential

Receives several freelance submissions monthly.

Submissions

Query. Accepts hard copy. SASE. Response time varies.

- Articles: Word lengths vary. Informational articles and profiles. Topics include American cars, auctions, and car values.
- Depts/columns: Events calendar, news.

Sample Issue

Sample articles available at website.

- 1967 Chevrolet Corvette 427/435." Article describes the restoration of a convertible that was sold by a dealer in Lafayette, IN.
- "1972 Chevrolet K5 Blazer." Article showcases a car that has been restored and is up for sale.
- Sample dept/column: News discusses Vicari's plans to offer special Chevelles at an upcoming New Orleans auction.

Rights and Payment

Rights vary. Payment rates and policy vary.

American Fine Art 

International Artist Publishing
7530 East Main Street, Suite 105
Scottsdale, AZ 85251

Editor: Joshua Rose

Description and Interests

Dedicated entirely to the market for historic American art, this new magazine sets itself apart by previewing upcoming sales and auctions before they happen rather than reviewing once the show is over. Each issue also includes photo-essays of top collector homes, interviews with market personalities, and market insights from curators, dealers, conservators, and appraisers. Circ: Unavailable.

Contents: Articles; depts/columns
Frequency: 6 times each year
Website: www.americanfineartmagazine.com

Freelance Potential

Unavailable.

Submissions

Query Accepts email queries to editor@americanfineartmagazine.com. Response time varies.

- Articles: Word lengths vary. Informational and how-to articles, profiles, interviews, and photo-essays. Topics include American art auctions, collectors, and market reports
- Depts/columns: Word lengths vary. Market reports and industry news.

Sample Issue

Sample articles available at website.

- "Strive for Simplicity." Article features a profile on William Morris Hurst and the artistic legacy he left behind.
- Houses & History with Art Collector Frank Hayman." Article takes a visual tour of some historic homes.
- Sample dept/column: Gallery Preview discusses the upcoming Philadelphia Art Collectors of the Gilded Age gallery.

Rights and Payment

Rights vary. Payment rates and policy vary.

The American Gardener

7931 East Boulevard Drive
Alexandria, VA 22308

Editor: David J. Ellis

Description and Interests

The official publication of the American Horticultural Society, this magazine is read by experienced amateur gardeners, Master Gardeners, and professional horticulturists. It seeks to provide readers with the newest information on plants, landscape design, gardening techniques, trends, and influential personalities in the field. All articles stress use of environmentally responsible gardening practices. It is always in need of articles on landscape design and how to construct simple garden features. Circ: 25,000.

Contents: 60% articles; 40% depts/columns
Frequency: 6 times each year
Website: www.ahs.org/publications/the_american_gardener

Freelance Potential

60% written by nonstaff writers. Publishes 40 freelance submissions yearly; 15% by new authors, 60% by experts. Receives 25 queries monthly.

Submissions

Query with outline, description of topic, and why it is of interest to readers; include clips or writing samples and gardening expertise. Accepts email to editor@ahs.org and hard copy. No simultaneous submissions. SASE. Responds in 3 months.

- Articles: 1,500–2,500 words. Informational articles and profiles. Topics include plant groups, garden design, gardening techniques, heirloom gardening, horticultural history, and prominent horticulturists and gardeners.
- Depts/columns: Natural Connections, 750–1,000 words; Homegrown Harvest, 900–1,100 words; Plant in the Spotlight, 600 words.

Sample Issue

64 pages. Advertising. Sample copy available. Guidelines available at website.

- "Gardening in Jefferson's Footsteps." A profile of Monticello's head gardener, Pat Brodowski, who reveals how she is preserving Jefferson's horticutural legacy.
- Sample dept/column: Plant in the Spotlight features Sugar Tip Rose of Sharon.

Rights and Payment

Rights vary. Articles, $300–$500. Depts/columns, $100–$250. Kill fee, 25%. Pays on publication. Provides 3 contributor's copies.

American History

Weider History Group
19300 Promenade Drive
Leesburg, VA 20176-6500

Articles Editor: Sarah Richardson

Description and Interests

American History tells the stories of the people and events in U.S. history while providing insight into the cultural, political, military, and social forces that shaped the nation. It is written for a general audience. It looks for thoroughly researched stories with sound organization, a lively style, and a high level of human interest. Circ: 100,000.

Contents: 80% articles; 20% depts/columns
Frequency: 6 times each year
Website: http://www.historynet.com/american-history

Freelance Potential

75% written by nonstaff writers. Publishes 30 freelance submissions yearly; 40% by authors who are new to the magazine. Receives 40 queries monthly.

Submissions

Query with 1- to 2-page proposal. Accepts hard copy and email queries to americanhistory@weiderhistorygroup.com. SASE. Responds in 2 months.

- Articles: Features about events and people of national historical significance, 1,500–3,000 words. Human interest articles and pieces about historical sites, the recent past, and popular culture, 2,000–3,000 words.
- Depts/columns: Word lengths vary. Short biographies, Americana, and reviews.

Sample Issue

74 pages. Advertising. Sample articles and guidelines available at website.

- "Abraham Lincoln's Refuge." Reveals what life was like for the first family at Soldiers Home, a summer retreat where Lincoln worked on the Emancipation Proclamation.
- "American History Interviews Civil Engineer Henry Petroski." A look at the role of engineering in U.S. history and some of its greatest successes and failures.

Rights and Payment

All or first serial rights. Written material, payment rates vary. Pays on acceptance. Provides 2 contributor's copies.

American Hunter

National Rifle Association
11250 Waples Mill Road
Fairfax, VA 22030

Editor in Chief: J. Scott Olmsted

Description and Interests

This magazine for outdoorsmen/women is published by the National Rifle Association for its members. It offers information and advice on hunting all types of North American game, as well as articles on safety and gear. It welcomes articles for all levels of hunting expertise and is interested in personal experience hunting trips—the good *and* the bad. Circ: 1 million.

Contents: 78% articles; 22% depts/columns
Frequency: Monthly
Website: www.americanhunter.org

Freelance Potential

80% written by nonstaff writers. Publishes 50 freelance submissions yearly; 5% by authors who are new to the magazine. Receives 75 queries, 80 unsolicited mss monthly.

Submissions

Query with outline; or send complete manuscript. Accepts hard copy and email to publications@nrahq.org. No simultaneous submissions. Availability of artwork improves chance of acceptance. SASE. Responds in 3 months.

- Articles: 1,800–2,000 words. Informational and how-to articles, personal experience pieces, and humor. Topics include hunting, wildlife, firearms, optics, and ammunition.
- Depts/columns: 1,000–2,000 words. Hunting destinations, marksmanship, and first aid. Member's Hunt, 800 words.
- Artwork: 35mm color transparencies and color prints; digital images.

Sample Issue

96 pages. Sample articles available to view at website. Guidelines available.

- "From the Cookbook: Squirrel and Dumplings." How to prepare this game in a tasty way.
- "Hunting Sunburned Ducks." How hunters can protect themselves during sunny seasons.

Rights and Payment

First North American serial rights. Articles, to $1,500. Depts/columns, $500–$900. Pays on publication. Provides 2 contributor's copies.

The American Interest

1730 Rhode Island Avenue NW, Suite 617
Washington, DC 20036

Managing Editor: Daniel Kennelly

Description and Interests
Policy, politics, and culture are the mainstays of this magazine of sophisticated commentary and analysis. It provides a forum for ideas regarding the United States' activities in national and international affairs. Its readership is well educated and sophisticated and it prefers writers who have a professional or research background in the subject on which they are commenting. Circ: 18,000.

Contents: Articles; depts/columns
Frequency: 6 times each year
Website: www.the-american-interest.com

Freelance Potential
95% written by nonstaff writers. Publishes 90 freelance submissions yearly; 5% by unpublished writers, 50% by authors who are new to the magazine. Receives 10–15 queries, 10–15 unsolicited mss monthly.

Submissions
Query or send complete ms. Accepts hard copy and email to ai@the-american-interest.com (attach files). No simultaneous submissions. SASE. Responds in 2 weeks.

- Articles: To 6,000 words. Informational articles and opinion pieces. Topics include foreign affairs, international relations, politics, policy, culture, economics, and history.
- Depts/columns: Word lengths vary. Personal essays, notes, and reviews.

Sample Issue
148 pages: Advertising. Sample articles and guidelines available at website.

- "The Pak-Saudi Nuke, and How to Stop It." The impact on Pakistan and Saudi Arabia of Iran successfully developing nuclear weapons.
- "Beyond the Continental Divide." The negative consequences of the Obama administration's "pivot to Asia."

Rights and Payment
First rights. Written material, payment rates vary. Pays on publication.

The American Legion Magazine

700 North Pennsylvania Street
P.O. Box 1055
Indianapolis, IN 46206

Editor: Jeff Stoffer

Description and Interests
With a target audience of military veterans, this publication covers national defense, foreign affairs, and issues affecting active and retired military service personnel and their families. It is patriotic and value-oriented. Writers seeking to write for this publication should choose compelling issues in American society and have a firm understanding of the topic, as well as credible sources. Circ: 2.3 million.

Contents: 80% articles; 20% depts/columns
Frequency: Monthly
Website: www.legion.org/magazine

Freelance Potential
70% written by nonstaff writers. Publishes 35–40 freelance submissions yearly; 5% by unpublished writers, 5% by authors who are new to the magazine, 50% by experts. Receives 60 queries monthly.

Submissions
Query with outline and writing samples. Accepts hard copy and email to magazine@legion.org. SASE. Responds to queries in 4–6 weeks.

- Articles: 750–2,000 words. Informational articles. Topics include national security, foreign affairs, business trends, social issues, health, education, ethics, military history, and the arts.
- Depts/columns: Word lengths vary. American Legion news, health tips, current events, and veterans' affairs.

Sample Issue
64 pages. Advertising. Sample articles available at website. Guidelines available.

- "Unintended Consequences." A look at the impact on the economy of a weakened military.
- "The Last Battle." Examines the fight that ended the Vietnam War and how it reflected the rest of the conflict.

Rights and Payment
First North American serial rights. Written material, payment rates vary. Kill fee, 25–100%. Pays on acceptance. Provides 3 contributor's copies.

American Libraries

American Library Association
50 East Huron Street
Chicago, IL 60611

Editor/Publisher: Laurie Borman

Description and Interests
Written for members of the American Library Association, this publication offers diverse viewpoints and critical interpretations of industry concerns and developments. It also covers legislation and association news. It seeks articles that are informal and inviting, but informative and readable, with responsible industry research and interviews. *American Libraries* accepts submissions from both professional librarians and freelance writers with reporting experience. Circ: 65,000.

Contents: 50% articles; 50% depts/columns
Frequency: 6 times each year
Website: www.americanlibrariesmagazine.org

Freelance Potential
70% written by nonstaff writers. Publishes 30 freelance submissions yearly; 50% by authors who are new to the magazine. Receives 50 unsolicited mss monthly.

Submissions
Send complete ms. Prefers email to americanlibraries@ala.org (Word attachments); will accept hard copy. No simultaneous submissions. SASE. Responds in 4–8 weeks.

- Articles: 600–1,500 words. Informational articles, profiles, and interviews. Topics include ALA news, library-related legislation, professional concerns and developments, and libraries around the world.
- Depts/columns: Word lengths vary. Information technology, opinion pieces.

Sample Issue
72 pages. Advertising. Sample articles, editorial calendar, and guidelines available at website.

- "Removing Barriers to Access." How libraries are ensuring equal access of their resources to all segments of the community through bookmobiles, branches, and other options.
- "Building Tomorrow from the Ground Up." Explains how a grant is helping libraries reach the immigrant populations in their communities.

Rights and Payment
Exclusive North American rights for 3 months after publication and electronic rights. Written material, \$100–\$250. Pays on acceptance. Provides 1+ contributor's copies.

American Literary Review 

University of North Texas
English Department
P.O. Box 311307
Denton, TX 76203-1307

Editor: Ann McCutchan

Description and Interests
For more than 20 years, the University of North Texas has been accepting unpublished short stories and poetry for this literary review. It also considers memoirs, personal essays, and literary journalism and criticism. Distinctive, character-driven fiction has the best chance of being accepted. Poems can be in any form and on any subject matter. Circ: 1,000.

Contents: Fiction; poetry; creative nonfiction
Frequency: Twice each year
Website: www.engl.unt.edu/alr

Freelance Potential
100% written by nonstaff writers. Publishes 40–50 freelance submissions yearly; 90% by authors who are new to the magazine. Receives 300 unsolicited mss monthly.

Submissions
Send complete ms between October 1 and May 1 only. Accepts hard copy and simultaneous submissions if identified. Label submission as Fiction, Poetry, or Nonfiction. SASE; include self-addressed, stamped postcard for receipt notification. Responds in 3–5 months.

- Articles: To 6,500 words. Memoir, personal essays, literary journalism, and experimental nonfiction.
- Fiction: To 8,000 words. Literary and contemporary fiction.
- Other: Poetry, no line limits; to 5 poems per submission.

Sample Issue
212 pages. No advertising. Sample copy available. Guidelines available at website.

- "The Waiver." Nonfiction piece.
- "On Huron." Short story.

Rights and Payment
First North American serial rights. No payment. Provides 2 contributor's copies.

American Profile

341 Cool Springs Boulevard, Suite 400
Franklin, TN 37067

Features Editor: Stuart Englert

Description and Interests

Inserted into local newspapers throughout the U.S., *American Profile* publishes positive, uplifting articles that celebrate the people, places, and things that make each part of the country unique. It looks for articles that are personal, informative, concise, and filled with detail and color. Articles need to have a long shelf life but still be relevant. Circ: 11 million.

Contents: 70% articles; 30% depts/columns
Frequency: Weekly
Website: www.americanprofile.com

Freelance Potential

80% written by nonstaff writers. Publishes 75 freelance submissions yearly; 10% by authors who are new to the magazine, 10% by experts. Receives 20 queries monthly.

Submissions

Send 1-page query with résumé and clips. Accepts hard copy only. SASE. Responds in 1–2 months.

- Articles: 350–1,000 words. Informational and how-to articles, profiles, and interviews. Topics include artisans, celebrities, hometowns, hometown heroes, incredible kids, collections, jobs and careers, places.
- Depts/columns: Word lengths vary. Family matters, gardening, home projects, and personal finance.

Sample Issue

16 pages. Advertising. Sample articles and guidelines available at website.

- "Ronnie Milsap Sings Hymns." Profile of the country singer and a look back at the early part of this life, which inspired his gospel CD.
- "Deaf Bulldog Teaches Compassion to Kids." How a class pet helps young children learn about the art of caring.

Rights and Payment

First print and electronic rights for 6 months; nonexclusive rights thereafter. Written material, payment rates vary. Pays within 45 days of acceptance. Provides contributor's copies.

The American Quarter Horse Journal

1600 Quarter Horse Drive
Amarillo, TX 79104

Managing Editor: Becky Newell

Description and Interests

Owners, trainers, breeders, and exhibitors of American Quarter Horses read this magazine for its comprehensive coverage of training techniques, equine health, breeding, and AQHA-sponsored activities. It prefers submissions from industry insiders. Articles related to equine health are always of interest. Circ: 45,000.

Contents: 95% articles; 5% depts/columns
Frequency: Monthly
Website: www.aqha.com

Freelance Potential

20% written by nonstaff writers. Publishes 20 freelance submissions yearly; 3% by unpublished writers, 3% by experts. Receives 5 unsolicited mss each month.

Submissions

Send complete ms with writing samples. Accepts email submissions to bnewell@aqha.org. Responds in 1 month.

- Articles: 1,500–2,500 words. Informational and how-to articles, profiles, interviews, and new product information. Topics include American Quarter Horses, riding techniques, training techniques, horse farm management, and equine health and care.
- Depts/columns: 750 words. Association news, product and show reviews, and show results.

Sample Issue

304 pages. Advertising. Sample copy and guidelines available. Editorial calendar available at website.

- "Jockey Roy Brooks Riding High at 71." Profile of a well-known, veteran jockey.
- "Choose the Right Western Spurs for You and Your Horse." Tips on selecting appropriate spurs.

Rights and Payment

One-time and Internet rights. Articles, $50–$1,000. Depts/columns, $50–$250. Kill fee, $300. Pays on acceptance. Provides 5 contributor's copies.

American School & University

9800 Metcalf Avenue
Overland, KS 66212-2215

Executive Editor: Susan Lustig

Description and Interests

Targeting those who design, build, and maintain school facilities, this publication provides construction and design information. It covers green practices, technology, security, and cost-saving measures. Almost all of its writers are experts in the fields of construction, design, or outfitting educational facilities. It seeks to provide readers with solution-based articles that are well researched. Circ: 63,000.

Contents: 65% articles; 35% depts/columns
Frequency: Monthly
Website: www.asumag.com

Freelance Potential

35% written by nonstaff writers. Publishes 40 freelance submissions yearly; 50% by authors who are new to the magazine, 100% by industry experts. Receives 15 queries monthly.

Submissions

Query with outline and suggested title, or send complete article. Accepts email to slustig@-asumag.com. Responds in 3 weeks.

- Articles: 1,200 words. Informational and how-to articles. Topics include facility planning and management, construction, retrofit, maintenance, technology, security, HVAC, lighting, and furnishings.
- Depts/columns: Word lengths vary. Case studies, new products, Construction Zone.

Sample Issue

60 pages. Advertising. Sample copy, guidelines and editorial calendar available at website.

- "Emerging Technology for School Security." Explores how new technology is enabling smartphones to unlock doors, as well as do laundry, buy food on campus, and more.
- "Strategies for Success: School Roofing." Suggestions for preventive maintenance for roofs on school buildings.

Rights and Payment

Feature articles, first-time exclusive rights. Other material, rights vary. No payment. Provides 2 contributor's copies.

American Spirit

Hammock Publishing
3322 West End Avenue, Suite 700
Nashville, TN 37203

Managing Editor: Jamie Roberts

Description and Interests

As the publication for the Daughters of the American Revolution, *American Spirit* is interested in the people, places, and events of Early American history. Its content covers historic preservation, patriotism, genealogy, collectibles, and historic travel. The magazine also profiles current DAR members and provides organizations information. Its articles focus on the Colonial period with an emphasis on the American experience as it relates to women. Circ: 35,000.

Contents: 60% articles; 40% depts/columns
Frequency: 6 times each year
Website: www.dar.org/americanspirit

Freelance Potential

60% written by nonstaff writers. Of the freelance submissions published yearly; 20% are by authors who are new to the magazine. Receives 6 queries each month.

Submissions

Query with résumé and clips. Accepts hard copy and email queries to jroberts@hammock.com. SASE. To be considered for assignments, mail résumé and clips. Responds in 1 month.

- Articles: 1,500–2,000 words. Informational articles, profiles, and interviews. Topics include Early American history, genealogy, civics education, historic preservation, collectibles, women's history and bibliography, and historical travel and tourism.
- Depts/columns: 750–1,000 words. Historic homes, book reviews, and profiles.
- Artwork: 35mm slides, prints; digital images.

Sample Issue

48 pages. Little advertising. Sample articles and guidelines available at website.

- "Today's Daughters: Marathon Woman." Profile of Amanda Clark, a DAR member who is competing on the U.S. Olympic sailing team.
- "In the Land of Columbus." The historic legends and stories behind famous American figures.

Rights and Payment

First North American periodical and electronic rights. Written material, payment rates vary. Pays on acceptance.

Amethyst Arsenic 

Editor: Samantha Milowsky

Description and Interests

This literary journal was founded in 2011 with the goal of publishing the best poetry and art for the widest possible audience. It prefers well-crafted imagery, supported by a fresh use of language and perception. Special consideration is given to vignettes, moments, stories, and meditations on people, objects, and scenes. All poems submitted will be considered for several awards. *Amethyst Arsenic* also accepts music. Circ: Unavailable.

Contents: Poetry
Frequency: Twice each year
Website: www.amethystarsenic.com

Freelance Potential

Very open to freelance submissions from new and established writers.

Submissions

Send complete ms. Accepts electronic submissions via website submissions manager. Send 3–5 poems (Word or RTF document). Refer to the website for specific reading periods for each issue. Accepts simultaneous submissions; notify if submission is accepted elsewhere. Previously published poems are acceptable; include information on place of publication, date, and confirm that the publication is no longer available. Response time, 30 days.

- Poetry: No line limits. All forms of poetry.
- Artwork: All forms welcome.

Sample Issue

Sample poems and writers' guidelines available at website.

- "Instructions On How To Be Sad." Satirical poem discussing how to be successful at being sad.
- "Pippa Bacca." Poem tells the story of a stage artist who was killed in the Middle East.
- "Dualities." Poem about a family and a summer night when things went wrong.

Rights and Payment

First North American and online archival rights. Poems, $5; $50 for poems nominated for awards.

Amp It Up! 

1916 Redbud Valley Drive
Maryville, TN 37801

Editor in Chief: Rick Bowers

Description and Interests

This new magazine covers health and lifestyle topics for amputees who want to live life fully. Articles offer information on how to improve health and prevent secondary conditions, and discuss developments in the fields of medicine and prosthetics. *Amp It Up!* is distributed to health care practitioners and facilities, as well as subscribers. Circ: Unavailable.

Contents: 80% articles; 20% depts/columns
Frequency: 9 issues each year
Website: www.ampitupmag.com

Freelance Potential

Open to ideas for upcoming issues.

Submissions

Query or send complete ms. Accepts hard copy. SASE. Response time varies.

- Articles: Word lengths vary. Informational and how-to articles, and personal experience pieces. Topics include technology, medical treatments, insurance, products, health and wellness, sports and recreation, peer support, and tips for daily living.
- Depts/columns: Word lengths vary. Related events.

Sample Issue

32 pages. Advertising. Sample copy available at website.

- "Adjusting to My New Life." Personal experience piece by a recent amputee.
- "Making a Difference." Article describes a peer mentoring program available through Hanger Clinic's Amputee Empowerment Partners Program.
- "Physical Therapy." Article explains how to achieve the best outcomes for a residual limb after amputation.

Rights and Payment

Rights vary. Payment rates and policy vary.

Analog Science Fiction and Fact

Dell Magazines Fiction Group
267 Broadway, 4th Floor
New York, NY 10007-2352

Editor: Stanley Schmidt

Description and Interests

Designed for lovers of science fiction, this publication is filled with serials, novellas, short stories, and poems. Also included are some scientific articles with futuristic themes. It seeks excellent storytellers who have a solid science base to produce suspenseful yet plausible reads. Circ: 40,000.

Contents: 80% fiction; 10% articles; 10% depts/columns
Frequency: 10 times each year
Website: www.analogsf.com

Freelance Potential

100% written by nonstaff writers. Publishes 80–90 freelance submissions yearly; 10% by unpublished writers, 10% by authors who are new to the magazine, 10% by experts. Receives 500 unsolicited mss monthly.

Submissions

Send complete manuscript and cover letter with story length, publishing history, author info; include synopsis for serials. Prefers electronic submissions via online submissions system (Word attachments); will accept hard copy. No simultaneous submissions. SASE. Responds in 5–12 weeks.

- Articles: To 4,000 words. Informational articles. Topics include science and technology.
- Fiction: Short stories, 2,000–7,000 words. Novellas and novelettes, 10,000–20,000 words. Serials, 40,000–80,000 words. Science fiction.
- Depts/columns: Staff-written.
- Other: Poems.

Sample Issue

144 pages. Little advertising. Sample copy available. Guidelines available at website.

- "The Liars." Fiction.
- "Atlas' Apprentices: Amateur Contributions in Astronomy and Astrophysics." Examines important discoveries by amateur observers.

Rights and Payment

First North American serial and non-exclusive rights. Fiction: $.06–$.08 per word for stories up to 7,500 words; $450–$600 for stories 7,500–10,000 words; $.05–$.06 per word for longer stories. Articles, $.06 per word. Pays on acceptance. Provides 2 contributor's copies.

Angels on Earth

16 East 34th Street, 21st Floor
New York, NY 10016

Editor in Chief: Colleen Hughes

Description and Interests

Published by Guideposts, this digest-sized magazine is meant to inspire and comfort with its real-life stories of angels and the amazing ways they impact peoples' lives. Its pages are filled with first-person accounts of miraculous encounters and heartwarming stories of faith. Personal stories are welcome. It is also interested in articles about people in the community doing "angelic" deeds for others. Circ: 500,000.

Contents: 80% articles; 20% depts/columns
Frequency: 6 times each year
Website: www.angelsonearth.com

Freelance Potential

90% written by nonstaff writers. Publishes 100 freelance submissions yearly; 80% by unpublished writers, 80% by authors who are new to the magazine, 5% by experts. Receives 500 unsolicited mss monthly.

Submissions

Send complete ms. Accepts hard copy and electronic submissions via website. SASE. Responds in 2 months.

- Articles: To 1,500 words. Inspirational, personal experience, and confession. Topics include personal beliefs, faith, religion, angels, and altruism.
- Depts/columns: 50–250 words. Brief anecdotes, recipes, and book recommendations.

Sample Issue

76 pages. Little advertising. Sample articles available at website.

- "A Reminder of God's Love." On a day when she's feeling blue, a woman receives a comforting sign of divine love.
- "Just the Right Child." She had bought the Christmas toy everyone wanted, but she had no one to give it to.

Rights and Payment

All rights. Articles, $100–$500. Depts/columns, $25–$100. Pays on publication. Provides 10–15 contributor's copies and a 1-year subscription.

Annals of Improbable Research

P.O. Box 380853
Cambridge, MA 02238

Editor: Marc Abrahams

Description and Interests
This parody of scientific magazines includes humorous research reports, both real and imagined. It features weird, odd, and sometimes ridiculous studies—actual and fictitious. The purpose is to make readers laugh and think at the same time. It is available in print or as a downloadable PDF. It prefers reports about research *results* rather than suggestions. Circ: 10,000.

Contents: 40% articles; 30% depts/columns; 30% fiction
Frequency: 6 times each year
Website: www.improbable.com

Freelance Potential
70% written by nonstaff writers. Publishes 40 freelance submissions yearly; 70% by unpublished writers, 40% by authors who are new to the magazine, 75% by experts. Receives 100 unsolicited mss monthly.

Submissions
Send complete ms. Accepts email submissions to marca@chem2.harvard.edu (Word attachments); will accept hard copy. SASE. Responds in 1–2 months.

- Articles: 500–2,000 words. Informational, satirical, and humorous articles on scientific research. Topics include physics, chemistry, biology, anthropology, and psychology.
- Fiction: 500–2,000 words. Humor and satire pertaining to science; fictional research.
- Depts/columns: Word lengths vary. News.

Sample Issue
28 pages. No advertising. Sample copy and guidelines available at website.

- "Finding an Optimal Seating Chart." Tongue-in-cheek article suggesting a mathematical formula for devising a wedding reception seating chart.
- "The Basic Laws of Human Stupidity Suggest a Better Way to Choose Politicians." Explores random selection of candidates as a superior option to elections.

Rights and Payment
All rights. No payment. Provides 1 contributor's copy.

The Antioch Review

P.O. Box 148
Yellow Springs, OH 45387

Editor: Muriel Keyes

Description and Interests
Comprised of essays on the social sciences and humanities, short stories, and poetry, *The Antioch Review* publishes the work of new and established writers. It seeks compelling stories that appeal to the intelligent reader and are written with distinction. It only accepts submissions during set reading periods. Circ: 3,000.

Contents: 40% articles; 40% fiction; 20% poetry
Frequency: Quarterly
Website: www.antiochreview.org

Freelance Potential
100% written by nonstaff writers. Publishes 80–100 freelance submissions yearly; 5% by unpublished writers, 25% by authors who are new to the magazine. Receives 150 unsolicited mss monthly.

Submissions
Send complete ms with type of submission (essay, fiction, poetry) noted on envelope. Submit essays and fiction between September 2 and May 31 only. Submit poetry between September 2 and April 30 only. Accepts hard copy. No simultaneous submissions. SASE. Responds in 4–6 months.

- Articles: To 5,000 words. Essays and personal experience pieces. Topics include the social sciences and humanities.
- Fiction: To 5,000 words. Genres include contemporary and literary fiction.
- Depts/columns: Staff-written.
- Other: Poetry, no line limits; 3–6 poems per submission.

Sample Issue
206 pages. Little advertising. Sample copy available for a fee. Guidelines available at website.

- "My Father's FBI File." Essay.
- "Blue Men Inside My Head." Short story.

Rights and Payment
First North American serial rights. Written material, $15 per published page. Pays on publication. Provides 2 contributor's copies.

Antique Trader

700 East State Street
Iola, WI 54990-0001

Print Editor: Karen Knapstein

Description and Interests

Professional antique dealers and casual collectors alike turn to *Antique Trader* as a key source of up-to-date information on collectibles and antiques. Highlighted in this tabloid's pages are current shows and events, in-depth guides to collectibles, recent pricing, and auction sale statistics. It looks for stories that are broad in scope and offer at least one sidebar that will give the reader recent news or an additional resource for the featured collectible category. Circ: 35,000.

Contents: 50% articles; 50% depts/columns
Frequency: 26 times each year
Website: www.antiquetrader.com

Freelance Potential

75% written by nonstaff writers. Publishes 200 freelance submissions yearly; 25% by unpublished writers. Receives 4 unsolicited mss monthly.

Submissions

Send complete ms with artwork. Prefers email submissions to karen.knapstein@fwmedia.com; will accept hard copy and disk submissions (Word files). SASE. Responds in 1 month.

- Articles: 750–1,000 words. Informational articles and profiles. Topics include antiques, collectibles, and Americana.
- Depts/columns: Word lengths vary. News, show and auction previews, regional spotlights, and recent sales.
- Artwork: B/W or color prints, slides or transparencies; digital images at 300 dpi. Line art.

Sample Issue

44 pages. Advertising. Sample articles available at website. Guidelines available.

- "Furniture Detective: How Antique Furniture Pieces Get Their Names." A look back at where common furniture terms and name originated.
- "Behind the Gavel: Why Dead Inventory Can Kill Your Antique Business." Suggestions for dealers on how to profitably dispose of unsalable items.

Rights and Payment

All rights. Written material, $50–$250. Pays on publication. Provides 1+ contributor's copies.

Appaloosa Journal

2720 West Pullman Road
Moscow, ID 83843

Editor: Dana Russell

Description and Interests

This magazine is the official publication of the Appaloosa Horse Club. It serves as a directory of members and services and also offers articles on breeding, riding (competitively and for sport), and equine care. It is interested in consumer issues, artwork that feature the Appaloosa horse, and trail-riding destinations. Circ: 15,700.

Contents: 50% articles; 25% depts/columns; 25% other
Frequency: Monthly
Website: www.appaloosajournal.com

Freelance Potential

90–95% written by nonstaff writers. Publishes 25 freelance submissions yearly; 5% by experts. Receives 10 queries, 5 unsolicited mss monthly.

Submissions

Send complete ms. Accepts hard copy and email to editor@appaloosajournal.com (Word or text files). SASE. Response time varies.

- Articles: Feature articles, 1,500–1,800 words. Articles, 600–800 words. Informational and how-to articles, profiles, and interviews. Topics include breeding, trainers, training methods, influential horses, youth and nonprofessional competitors, breed history, trail riding, and artists who use Appaloosa horses as subjects.
- Depts/columns: Staff-written.

Sample Issue

140 pages. Advertising. Sample articles and guidelines available at website.

- "Artificial Lighting to Induce Estrus." Discusses artificial means of altering the gestation process.
- "Show Guide." A look at the World Show and attractions in Fort Worth, TX.

Rights and Payment

First North American serial and electronic rights. Written material, payment rates vary. Pays on publication.

Apple

AHS Communications
10101 Southport Road SW
Calgary, Alberta T2W 3N2
Canada

Editor & Project Manager: Terry Bullick

Description and Interests

Apple is a new magazine for people living in Alberta, Canada, who are interested in leading a healthy and balanced life. Sponsored by BlueCross, it covers common health problems, health myths, expert advice on parenting, caring for seniors, product reviews, child safety tips, and healthy recipes. Circ: 120,000.

Contents: 40% articles; 60% depts/columns
Frequency: 3 times each year
Website: www.applemag.ca

Freelance Potential

Freelance percentage unavailable.

Submissions

Send complete ms. Accepts hard copy. Response time varies.

- Articles: Word lengths vary. Informational and how-to articles. Health and wellness, child development, and relationships
- Depts/columns: Word lengths vary. General health, mental health, medical myths, recipes, medical news.

Sample Issue

72 pages. Advertising. Sample copy available at website.

- "The Power of Dads." Article explains the power-ful and positive influence fathers have on a child's development.
- "Along the Faultines: Reframing Our Understanding of Addictions." Articles relates new research that shows some brains are more vulnerable to addiction.
- Sample dept/column: Body Talk discusses how to overcome loneliness.

Rights and Payment

Rights vary. Payment rates and policy vary.

Aquarius

A Sign of the Times

1035 Green Street
Roswell, GA 30075

Editor: Gloria Parker

Description and Interests

Published in tabloid format, *Aquarius* focuses on exploring the paths to personal and spiritual growth and inner health. Metaphysical, spiritual, and holistic topics are covered here. It considers articles that relate to metaphysical topics, holistic health, and spiritual pathways. Circ: 40,000.

Contents: Articles; depts/columns
Frequency: Monthly
Website: www.aquarius-atlanta.com

Freelance Potential

70% written by nonstaff writers. Publishes 12 freelance submissions yearly; 20% by unpublished writers, 50% by authors who are new to the magazine, 60% by experts. Receives 15–20 unsolicited mss monthly.

Submissions

Send complete ms. Prefers email submissions to aquariusnews@mindspring.com; will accept Macintosh disk submissions and simultaneous submissions if identified. SASE. Response time varies.

- Articles: 850 words. Informational, self-help, and how-to articles; profiles; interviews; and personal experience and opinion pieces. Topics include health, fitness, consumer interest, religion, social issues, psychology, science, holistic medicine, astrology, numerology, psychic abilities, business, the arts, travel, and leisure—all from a New Age perspective.
- Depts/columns: Staff-written.

Sample Issue

36 pages. Advertising. Sample articles and guidelines available at website.

- "If You Can Feel You Can Heal." Examines the role of self-love in the healing process.
- "Mastering Life's Energies: Simple Steps to a Luminous Life at Work and Play." The art of living a truly fulfilling life based on discovery of what is most significant to an individual.

Rights and Payment

First rights. No payment. Provides 2 contributor's copies.

Arabian Horse Times

20276 Delaware Avenue
Jordan, MN 55352

Editor: Kevin Ludden

Description and Interests

Owners, trainers, breeders, riders, and lovers of Arabian horses turn to this publication for current news and information about bloodlines, stables, and showing this breed. Personality profiles and articles on equine care are also found in its pages. It welcomes story ideas from authors who have a passion for Arabian horses and are immersed in the horse world. It is looking to increase its coverage of the people who are directly connected to Arabian horses and the places that showcase them. Circ: 15,000.

Contents: 60% articles; 40% depts/columns
Frequency: Monthly
Website: www.ahtimes.com

Freelance Potential

80% written by nonstaff writers. Publishes 60 freelance submissions yearly; 10% by unpublished writers, 20% by authors who are new to the magazine, 35% by experts. Receives 5 queries monthly.

Submissions

Query with résumé listing writing credentials. Accepts hard copy. SASE. Responds in 1 week.

- Articles: Word lengths vary. Informational and how-to articles, profiles, interviews, and personal experience pieces. Topics include Arabian horses, pedigrees, bloodlines, horse shows, showmanship, horse owners, and riding.
- Depts/columns: Word lengths vary. Horse care, equine law, training tips, and news.

Sample Issue

302 pages. Advertising. Sample copy available at website. Writers' guidelines and editorial calendar available.

- "Leaders of the Times." Article profiles five-time National Champion Stallion, Vitorio TO.
- "In Memoriam: Mike Villasenor." Tribute to a well-known horse breeder and trainer.

Rights and Payment

All rights. Written material, payment rates vary. Pays on publication. Provides 1 author's copy.

Archaeology

36-36 33rd Street
Long Island City, NY 11106

Editor in Chief: Claudia Valentino

Description and Interests

The adventure, discovery, history, and culture of archaeology is captured in this magazine of the Archaeological Institute of America. It features articles by both professional journalists and professional archaeologists for a readership that includes the general public, archaeology enthusiasts, and scholars. It is interested in a diverse mix of topics on not just the digging, but also the adventure, culture, history, technology, and travel that will appeal to its audience of enthusiastic amateurs and field scholars. Circ: 225,000.

Contents: 80% articles; 20% depts/columns
Frequency: 6 times each year
Website: www.archaeology.org

Freelance Potential

55% written by nonstaff writers. Publishes 18 freelance submissions yearly; 20% by new authors. Receives 10 queries monthly.

Submissions

Send query (up to 500 words) containing author qualifications, with clips. Suggested illustrations appreciated. Accepts hard copy and email queries to editorial@archaeology.org. SASE. Responds in 6–8 weeks.

- Articles: Word lengths vary. Informational articles, profiles, and photo-essays. Topics include archaeological digs, ruins, history, ancient culture, relics, and scientists.
- Depts/columns: Insider, 2,500 words; Conversations, 1-page interviews; Letter From, personal experience pieces, 2,500–3,000 words; Artifact, interesting facts, 200 words; media and museum reviews, 250–500 words.

Sample Issue

68 pages. Advertising. Sample articles and guidelines available at website.

- "Final Resting Place of an Outlaw." How archaeological and forensic detective work helped find the remains of legendary Australian criminal, Ned Kelly.
- "The Unknown Temple." Uncovering a temple in Greece, archaeologists use clues to discover its god.

Rights and Payment

Exclusive worldwide rights. Written material, \$.50–\$1 per word. Kill fee, 25%. Pays on acceptance. Provides 10 contributor's copies.

Art & Antiques

447 West 24th Street
New York, NY 10011

Senior Editor: John Dorfman

Description and Interests

This publication provides sophisticated features on fine arts and antiques of all categories for collectors. It covers places to discover these treasures, unique ways to use them to enrich living spaces, and news about events and people in the art world. The content is tailored to readers who are actively involved in the international art market. Its readership consists of sophisticated, high-end collectors, so it expects writers to be well versed in their subjects. Circ: 28,000.

Contents: Articles; depts/columns
Frequency: 10 times each year
Website: www.artandantiquesmag.com

Freelance Potential

60% written by nonstaff writers. Publishes 100 freelance submissions yearly; 1% by unpublished writers, 30% by authors who are new to the magazine, 75% by experts. Receives 75–100 queries each month.

Submissions

Query with scouting shots. No unsolicited mss. Accepts hard copy and simultaneous submissions if identified. SASE. Responds in 2–4 weeks.

- Articles: 2,000–3,000 words. Informational and how-to articles, and profiles. Topics include collections, fine art, antiques, and interior design.
- Depts/columns: 250–750 words. Antiques and art news, artist profiles, collecting trends, exhibitions, museums, reproductions, and antiquing destinations.

Sample Issue

120 pages. Advertising. Sample articles available at website. Guidelines and theme list available.

- "Baseball Card Values: Collections at Auction Hit Record Sales." These pieces of Americana are fetching handsome sums from collectors.
- "Santa Fe Prepares for Summer Fairs and Exhibitions." A roundup of arts and antiques offerings coming to this city.

Rights and Payment

All rights. Written material, $1 per word. Pays on acceptance. Provides 1 contributor's copy for features; 1 tearsheet for depts/columns.

Arthritis Today

1330 West Peachtree Street, Suite 100
Atlanta, GA 30309

Publishing Assistant: Christie Jarrett

Description and Interests

With the goal of helping arthritis patients improve their health through self-education and self-help, this publication features news of treatments, as well as articles about coping with the disease. All informational articles should come from medical practitioners or researchers. It welcomes articles of inspiration from anyone whose life has been touched by arthritis. Circ: 715,000.

Contents: 60% articles; 40% depts/columns
Frequency: 6 times each year
Website: www.arthritistoday.org

Freelance Potential

60% written by nonstaff writers. Publishes 60 freelance submissions yearly; 1% by unpublished writers, 10% by authors who are new to the magazine, 1% by experts. Receives 40 queries monthly.

Submissions

Query with clips. Prefers email queries to contactus@arthritis.org; will accept hard copy. SASE. Responds in 2 months.

- Articles: 1,500–3,000 words. Investigative, informational, inspirational, and how-to articles; and personal experience pieces. Topics include arthritis research, advancements, treatment options, coping with physical and emotional challenges, and exercise
- Depts/columns: 200–500 words. Your Self, nutrition, fitness, and balance; Your Life, Your Health, medwatch, experts on call; Your Foundation, foundation news.

Sample Issue

84 pages. Advertising. Sample articles available at website. Guidelines available.

- "Rheumatoid Arthritis and Periodontal Disease." Discusses the connection between the two.
- "Linda Boyer: Harmony and Healing." How this composer's music is being used to ease pain.

Rights and Payment

First North American serial rights. Articles, $450–$3,000. Depts/columns, $150+. Pays on acceptance. Provides 2 contributor's copies.

Art Jewelry

21027 Crossroads Circle
P.O. Box 1612
Waukesha, WI 53186-1612

Editor: Hazel Wheaton

Description and Interests

Instructions and ideas for creating all kinds of handcrafted jewelry appear in this magazine. It strives to appeal to experienced craftsmen and beginners alike. *Art Jewelry*'s features and departments cover project designs, techniques, materials, and equipment. Projects for beginners are always welcome. Circ: 40,000.

Contents: Articles; depts/columns
Frequency: 6 times each year
Website: www.artjewelrymag.com

Freelance Potential

60% written by nonstaff writers. Publishes 50 freelance submissions yearly; 30% by unpublished writers, 50% by authors who are new to the magazine, 50% by experts. Receives 20–30 queries monthly.

Submissions

Query with photos or sketches of project (or actual pieces) and list of materials, tools, and supplies. Accepts hard copy, email queries to editor@artjewelrymag.com, or uploaded queries via www.contribute.kalmach.com. SASE. Response time varies.

- Articles: 500–3,000 words. Informational, how-to, and reference articles; and profiles. Topics include jewelry-making techniques, materials and tools, and marketing.
- Depts/columns: Word lengths vary. Book, media, and product reviews; news; business advice; technique; and Q&As.
- Artwork: Digital images (RAW, JPEG, TIFF).

Sample Issue

82 pages. Advertising. Sample articles and guidelines available at website.

- "Set Up Your Studio—Metals." Adapting home spaces to create a workspace for metal crafts.
- "Build a Wire Bangle with a Woven Zigzag Pattern." Demonstrates an entry-level technique that can yield sophisticated effects.

Rights and Payment

All rights. Written material, payment rates vary. Pays on acceptance. Provides 2 contributor's copies.

Art of the West

15612 Highway 7, Suite 235
Minnetonka, MN 55345

Editor: Vicki Stavig

Description and Interests

Showcasing contemporary and historical Western art, this magazine is read by novice and experienced collectors. All types of Western art from the past to the present are covered and include Native American and cowboy works, as well as Western landscapes. It does not publish writers' guidelines and suggests that new writers spend time reviewing past issues to get a good sense of what type of material it publishes. *Art of the West* is always interested in profiling unique and up-and-coming Western artists. Circ: 30,000.

Contents: 70% articles; 30% depts/columns
Frequency: 7 times each year
Website: www.aotw.com

Freelance Potential

75% written by nonstaff writers. Publishes 25 freelance submissions yearly; 10% by authors who are new to the magazine, 90% by experts. Receives 20 queries monthly.

Submissions

Query. Accepts hard copy. SASE. Response time varies.

- Articles: Word lengths vary. Profiles of artists whose work focuses on the land and people of the American West.
- Depts/columns: Word lengths vary. News, commentary, and legal issues regarding the art world.

Sample Issue

100 pages. Advertising. Sample articles available at website.

- "On His Way." A look at the work of an emerging wildlife painter, Dustin Van Wechel.
- "Payne's Power." Profile of one of California's most celebrated early plein air painters, Edgar Payne.
- "Spiritual Messenger." The art and life of sculptor Dave McGary, friend of the Native American.

Rights and Payment

All rights. Written material, payment rates vary. Pays on acceptance.

Art Papers

P.O. Box 5748
Atlanta, GA 31107

Interim Editor in Chief: Cinqué Hicks

Description and Interests

Art Papers seeks to present a unique global perspective on what shapes contemporary art and culture today. It features articles, essays, and exhibit reviews on current artists and explores trends across the world. Informed, assertive, authoritative, and accessible—that is how the magazine describes itself. Its aim is to be the essential, independent guide to contemporary art. Circ: 180,000.

Contents: 90% articles; 10% depts/columns
Frequency: 6 times each year
Website: www.artpapers.org

Freelance Potential

90% written by nonstaff writers. Publishes 100 freelance submissions yearly; 5% by unpublished writers, 30% by authors who are new to the magazine, 80% by experts. Receives 50 queries monthly.

Submissions

Query with brief proposal (125–250 for features; 50 for columns), author biography, and 2 writing samples of 1,000–2,000 words each. Accepts hard copy and email queries to editor@artpapers.org. Responds in 2 months.

- Articles: 2,400–2,700 words. Informational articles, profiles, and interviews. Topics include contemporary art, literature, artists, and modern culture.
- Depts/columns: Surviving, Readings, and Studio Visit, 1,000 words. Reviews of solo or group shows, 600–800 words.

Sample Issue

72 pages. Advertising. Sample articles and guidelines available at website.

- "Rita Ackermann and the Traumas of War." Explores the work of this painter of emotionally turbulent adolescence.
- "Radically Unbound: Catherine A. Hollingsworth in Conversation with Performa 11 Curator Mark Beasley." Interview with the curator of the multi-arts presentation, Performa 11, and what goes on behind the scenes.

Rights and Payment

First rights. Articles and depts/columns, payment rates vary. Reviews, $75. Pays 1 month after publication. Provides 1 contributor's copy.

Arts & Activities

12345 World Trade Drive
San Diego, CA 92128

Editor in Chief: Maryellen Bridge

Description and Interests

Arts & Activities serves as a forum for the exchange of ideas, advice, and lesson plans between visual art educators. It seeks informational and inspirational articles that are relevant to kindergarten through high school classrooms. It welcomes submissions from art teachers, kindergarten through high school. Quality photography is important. Circ: 20,000.

Contents: 85% articles; 15% depts/columns
Frequency: 10 times each year
Website: www.artsandactivities.com

Freelance Potential

95% written by nonstaff writers. Publishes 100 freelance submissions yearly; 50% by unpublished writers, 50% by authors who are new to the magazine, 25% by experts. Receives 20 unsolicited mss monthly.

Submissions

Send complete ms with artwork and cover sheet indicating author's professional position and school location. Accepts hard copy, disk submissions (Word files), and email to ed@artsandactivities.com. No simultaneous submissions. SASE. Responds in 6–9 months.

- Articles: 500–1,500 words. Informational and how-to articles, and personal experience pieces. Topics include teaching art, cross-curriculum projects, photography, painting, drawing, ceramics, and sculpture.
- Depts/columns: Mostly staff-written.
- Artwork: Color prints; digital images.

Sample Issue

48 pages. Advertising. Sample copy, guidelines, and editorial calendar available at website.

- "Art Educator's Questions for Peter Max." Art teachers ask artist Peter Max about his work and how to best teach art to students.
- "Artists Paint...Summer." How famous artists have depicted summer in their works of art.

Rights and Payment

First North American serial rights. Written material, payment rates vary. Publication period, 9 to 30 months. Pays on publication. Provides 3 contributor's copies.

Asimov's Science Fiction 

Dell Magazine Group
267 Broadway, 4th Floor
New York, NY 10007-2352

Editor: Sheila Williams

Description and Interests

This magazine publishes thoughtful and accessible science fiction and fantasy stories, novellas, and novelettes from writers of all levels of experience. It also accepts poetry and book reviews. It likes character-driven stories that illuminate some aspect of human existence. Humor pieces will be considered. Circ: 60,000.

Contents: 90% fiction; 9% depts/columns; 1% poetry
Frequency: 10 times each year
Website: www.asimovs.com

Freelance Potential

97% written by nonstaff writers. Publishes 85 freelance submissions yearly; 10% by unpublished writers, 30% by authors who are new to the magazine. Receives 700 unsolicited mss each month.

Submissions

Send complete ms. Accepts hard copy and submissions through online submissions system available at website. No simultaneous submissions. Responds in 5 weeks.

- Fiction: To 20,000 words. Genres include science fiction and "borderline" fantasy.
- Depts/columns: Word lengths vary. Book and website reviews.
- Other: Poetry, to 40 lines.

Sample Issue

112 pages. Advertising. Sample stories and guidelines available at website.

- "The Last Islander." Short story.
- Sample dept/column: On Books reviews Suzanne Collins latest Sci-Fi series.

Rights and Payment

First worldwide English-language serial rights. Fiction: stories to 7,500 words, \$.06–\$.08 per word; stories longer than 12,000 words, \$.06–\$.065 per word; \$450 for stories between those lengths. Poetry, \$1 per line. Depts/columns, payment rates vary. Pays on acceptance. Provides 2 contributor's copies.

AskMen  

4200 St-Laurent, Suite 801
Montreal Quebec H2W 2R2
Canada

Editor in Chief: James Bassil

Description and Interests

This lifestyle ezine aims to be "the greatest site known to men" by helping guys from 18- to 34-years-old become better men. It offers timely and relevant advice on fashion, grooming, relationships, health, and personal finance. Entertainment and sports news round out the editorial mix. While it already has a core group of contributors who are experts in their topics, *AskMen* seeks new writers who have expertise in careers, finance, health, diet, and nutrition. Circ: 16 million.

Contents: Articles; depts/columns
Frequency: Ongoing
Website: www.askmen.com

Freelance Potential

90% written by nonstaff writers.

Submissions

Query with bio and clips. Accepts email to jamesb@askmen.com. Response time varies.

- Articles: Word lengths vary. Informational and how-to articles and profiles. Topics include fashion, grooming, health and wellness, dating and sex, finance, careers, sports, travel, and entertainment.
- Depts/columns: Word lengths vary. New products, advice.

Sample Issue

Advertising. Sample copy available at website.

- "Andrew Luck on How He Learned to Eat Right." Article features an interview with Indianapolis Colts quarterback Andrew Luck on how he changed his eating habits to improve his health.
- "Time Management." Article provides tips to mastering the skill of time management.
- "Memphis." Article shares the highlights and attractions of this Tennessee city.

Rights and Payment

Rights vary. Payment rates and policy vary.

Astonish

P.O. Box 563
San Francisco, CA 94104

Editor in Chief: Forvana Etonne

Description and Interests

A new upscale fashion and art magazine that premiered in September 2011, *Astonish* appears in print and digital editions. It uses high-fashion editorial photo stories. Its mission is to be the "premier platform for emerging artists to showcase their talents in a global spotlight, a movement calling for creative freedom without inhibitions." Writers are encouraged to send boundary-pushing, thought-provoking, and visually driven content. Editorial decisions are based upon creativity, quality, professionalism, knowledge of fashion, and how well the submission agrees with the issue or magazine as a whole. Circ: 50,000.

Contents: Articles; depts/column
Frequency: Quarterly
Website: www.astonishworld.com

Freelance Potential

Receives several freelance submissions monthly.

Submissions

Accepts submissions from premier members only. Query or send complete ms. Accepts electronic submissions at website. Response time varies.

- Articles: Informational articles, profiles and photo-essays. Topics include fashion, art, and photography.

Sample Issue

114 pages. Advertising. Sample articles and guidelines available at website.

- "Interview with Brazilian Photographer Bruna Castanheira." Article discusses the photographer's inspirations, muses, and aesthetics.
- "A Prelude to Circus Stroke." Article discusses the up-and-coming trend of colorful hues.

Rights and Payment

Rights vary. Payment rates and policy vary.

At the Center

P.O. Box 309
Fleetwood, PA 19522

Publisher: Jerry Thacker

Description and Interests

This informational ezine for pregnancy center workers offers Christian-centered articles on ways to better minister to pregnant women in need. It tackles such issues as pregnancy and post-abortive counseling, center management, fundraising, and increasing volunteerism. It looks for authors who share its pro-life stance and have experience writing on ministry and counseling issues. The editorial tone it strives for is informational without being preachy. Hits per month: Unavailable.

Contents: 85% articles; 15% depts/columns
Frequency: Quarterly
Website: www.atcmag.com

Freelance Potential

90% written by nonstaff writers. Publishes 40 freelance submissions yearly; 30% by authors who are new to the magazine, 60% by experts. Receives 5 unsolicited mss monthly.

Submissions

Send complete ms with author biography. Prefers email to publications@rightideas.us or info@atcmag.com (Word attachments); will accept hard copy. SASE. Responds in 3 months.

- Articles: 800–1,000 words. Informational articles and personal experience pieces. Topics include pregnancy counseling; volunteer recruiting, training, and support; post-abortion counseling; teen and single-parent issues; adoption; and relevant legal issues.
- Depts/columns: Word lengths vary. Marketing, board issues, and fundraising.

Sample Issue

Sample copy available at website.

- "More Than Food Stamps." Reminds counselors to offer hope routed in the teachings of the Bible, not just material assistance.
- "Wandering in a Fund-Raising Desert." Tips for fundraisers in an economically depressed time.

Rights and Payment

First North American serial rights. Written material, $150. Pays on publication.

Austin Man 

1213 West 49th Street
Austin, TX 78756

Editor: Deborah Hamilton-Lynne

Description and Interests
This new lifestyle publication is the counterpart to the established *Austin Woman* magazine. Everything from business and travel to style and sports is covered in each issue, alongside profiles of notable Austin professionals and entrepreneurs. *Austin Man* aims to reflect the diverse interests of the city and accentuate the unique qualities that define and differentiate Austin men. Circ: 27,000.

Contents: Articles; depts/columns
Frequency: Quarterly
Website: www.atxman.com

Freelance Potential
"Always looking for great people to join our team as . . . freelance writers."

Submissions
Query or send complete ms. Accepts email related to freelance opportunities to editor@awmedia.com and submissions to submissions@awmedia.com. Response time varies.

- Articles: Word lengths vary. Informational and how-to articles, personal experience pieces, and profiles. Topics include local personalities, dining, style, technology, and sports.
- Depts/columns: Word lengths vary. Health and fitness, travel, new products, personal finance, relationships, and local news.

Sample Issue
84 pages. Advertising. Sample copy available at website.

- "A Few Good Men." Article profiles local men who are making a difference to improve the city.
- "The Perfect Pairing for Sushi." Personal experience piece demystifies the Japanese drink sake and discusses how best to experience it.
- Sample dept/column: The Buzz reports on changes coming to local radio station WKUT.

Rights and Payment
Rights vary. Payment rates and policy vary.

Autism Asperger's Digest

P.O. Box 2257
Burlington, NC 27216

Managing Editor: Kim Fields

Description and Interests
A mix of first-person experiences, expertly written informational articles, and book and product reviews appear in this magazine for parents and educators of children with autism spectrum disorders. It also covers related events and news updates. It seeks features that have a strong hands-on approach, rather than being a general overview of a topic. Circ: 5,000.

Contents: Articles; depts/columns
Frequency: 6 times each year
Website: www.autismdigest.com

Freelance Potential
90% written by nonstaff writers. Publishes 50–60 freelance submissions yearly; 25% by unpublished writers, 70% by authors who are new to the magazine, 30% by experts. Receives 20 queries and unsolicited mss monthly.

Submissions
Query or send complete ms. Accepts hard copy and email to kfields@autismdigest.com (Word attachments or pasted into body of email). SASE. Responds in 6 weeks.

- Articles: Informational articles, 1,200–2,000 words. First-person accounts, personal experience pieces, inspirational pieces; 1,000 words. Topics include family issues, parenting, education, social issues, health, and therapy; must be austism-focused.
- Depts/columns: What's New?, 250–350 words.

Sample Issue
52 pages. Advertising. Guidelines and sample articles available at website.

- "Better Diet, Happier Kids." Examines how food choices impact children's moods.
- "What a Barber Taught Me About Raising My Son." An autistic child's haircut with a kind and understanding barber provides lessons this Dad was able to put into practice in other areas of his son's life.

Rights and Payment
First rights. No payment. Provides contributors with a 1-year subscription.

Automobile Magazine

120 East Liberty Street, 2nd Floor
Ann Arbor, MI 48401-4193

Editor in Chief: Jean Jennings

Description and Interests
With a focus on high-end automobiles, this magazine offers a mix of industry news and car performance features, as well as reviews of current and upcoming cars. It also showcases prominent personalities in the auto world and provides collector information. The majority of the magazine is written by experts in the automotive field and it expects authors to have a thorough knowledge of cars in general and their chosen topic in particular. Circ: 575,000.

Contents: 65% articles; 35% depts/columns
Frequency: Monthly
Website: www.automobilemag.com

Freelance Potential
50% written by nonstaff writers. Publishes 60 freelance submissions yearly; 1% by unpublished writers, 1% by authors who are new to the magazine, 90% by experts. Receives 15–20 queries monthly.

Submissions
Query with writing samples. Accepts hard copy. SASE. Responds in 3–4 weeks.

- Articles: 800–2,500 words. Informational articles, profiles, interviews, and new product information. Topics include automobile design, performance, racing, driving, and collecting; environmentally friendly vehicles; sports cars; muscle cars; luxury cars; and exotic cars.
- Depts/columns: 50–800 words. News, design, opinions, car reviews, and auction reports.

Sample Issue
144 pages. Advertising. Guidelines and sample articles available at website.

- "American Ace: Joey Hand." A well-known race car driver talks about being in the German DTM series.
- "New Cars 2013." A roundup of all the newest makes and models and their most significant features coming out in the next year.

Rights and Payment
First North American serial rights. Written material, payment rates vary. Pays on publication. Provides 2 contributor's copies.

Aviation History

Weider History Group
19300 Promenade Drive
Leesburg, VA 20176-6500

Editor: Carl von Wodtke

Description and Interests
Aviation buffs are informed and entertained by the well-researched and engaging articles about aeronautical history, both civilian and military, from the beginning of flight right up through the space age, found in this magazine. Traditional, as well as unusual, aviation history subjects are always welcome. Circ: 40,000.

Contents: 60% articles; 40% depts/columns
Frequency: 6 times each year
Website: www.historynet.com/aviation-history

Freelance Potential
80% written by nonstaff writers. Publishes 60 freelance submissions yearly; 10% by unpublished writers, 30% by authors who are new to the magazine, 60% by experts. Receives 30 queries, 10 unsolicited mss monthly.

Submissions
Prefers query with sources, résumé, and illustration ideas; will accept complete ms. Accepts hard copy (with "Aviation History Article/Idea" on envelope), disk submissions with hard copy, and email to aviationhistory@weiderhistorygroup.com. Availability of artwork improves chance of acceptance. SASE. Responds to queries in 1–3 months, to mss in 3 months.

- Articles: 3,000–3,500 words. Informational articles, profiles, and interviews. Topics include aircraft and historic persons.
- Depts/columns: 800–1,500 words. Reviews, airplane remodeling, aviation art, and aircraft recovery and restoration.
- Artwork: B/W or color prints or transparencies.

Sample Issue
66 pages. Advertising. Sample articles, guidelines, and editorial calendar available at website.

- "Movie Stars with Wings." A look at unique aircraft used in movies before computer-generated images became the norm.
- "Across the Hypersonic Divide." The story of the North American X-15 that was able to travel at six times the speed of sound.

Rights and Payment
All rights. Articles, $300+. Depts/columns, $150+. Reviews, $50–$100. Artwork, payment rates vary. Pays on publication. Provides 2 author's copies.

Azizah

WOW Publishing
P.O. Box 43410
Atlanta, GA 30336-0410

Editor in Chief: Tayyibah Taylor

Description and Interests

This is a magazine for contemporary Muslim women. It serves as a source of information, inspiration, and ideas, and connects readers with other like-minded women. Articles should be written from a contemporary Muslim woman's perspective and should challenge readers to talk about the subject when they have finished reading it. Circ: 40,000.

Contents: Articles; depts/columns; fiction
Frequency: Quarterly
Website: www.azizahmagazine.com

Freelance Potential

80% written by nonstaff writers. Publishes 30–50 freelance submissions yearly; 10% by unpublished writers, 10% by new authors, 10% by experts. Receives 10–15 queries monthly.

Submissions

Send complete ms for fiction or poetry. Query, indicating the department or section of the magazine article is for; sources; author qualifications; and one or two clips for all nonfiction work. Accepts email only to articles@azizahmagazine.com (Word attachments). Responds in 5 weeks.

- Articles: 1,500–2,500 words. Informational articles, profiles, interviews, personal experience and opinion pieces, and media reviews. Topics include religion, multicultural and ethnic issues, social issues, relationships, food, house and home, health, fitness, nutrition, travel, and leisure.
- Fiction: 1,500–2,500 words. Inspirational and literary fiction. Poetry.
- Depts/columns: 1,700 words. Essays and opinion pieces.

Sample Issue

112 pages. Advertising. Sample articles and guidelines available.

- "By the Book." Examines a new development in publishing: books for and by Muslim women.
- "Betrayal." Investigates the alarming rise in the number of Muslim marriages ending in divorce because of an unfaithful spouse.

Rights and Payment

First rights. Written material, payment rates vary. No payment for poetry. Kill fee, 50%. Pays on acceptance. Provides 2 contributor's copies.

Babble.com

520 Broadway, 9th Floor
New York NY 10012

Co-founders: Rufus Griscom and Alisa Volkman

Description and Interests

Babble garnered multiple website awards after it made its appearance in 2006, and five years later was purchased by the Walt Disney Corporation. This ezine covers all aspects of parenting, from conception through the preteen years, as well as home, food, entertainment, and lifestyle topics. Hits per month: 5,000,000.

Contents: 80% articles; 20% depts/columns
Frequency: Updated regularly
Website: www.babble.com

Freelance Potential

10% written by nonstaff writers. Two percent by writers new to the magazine.

Submissions

Query with links to published articles, 2-line description, first paragraph, and outline; or send complete ms. Accepts email to appropriate editor: news and features, mom@babble.com; mom, celebrity, style, and food submissions, lifestyle@babble.com; pregnancy, pregnancy@babble.com; baby, toddler, kid, health, and beauty, email kids@babble.com. If sending complete submission, include as attachment. Responds if interested.

- Articles: Informational, self-help, and how-to articles, profiles, interviews, and reviews. Topics include products, food, home, family, babies, toddlers, dads, moms, pregnancy, kids, travel, celebrities, school, behavior, child development, and crafts.

Sample Issue

Advertising. Sample articles available at website.

- "When Men Become Fathers." Article explains how a father's brain chemistry changes after a child is born.
- "Better Late Than Never." A woman's lingering resentment toward her father dissipates after the birth of her child.

Rights and Payment

Rights vary. Payment rates and policy unavailable.

BackHome

P.O. Box 70
Hendersonville, NC 28793

Editor in Chief: Lorna Loveless

Description and Interests
BackHome bills itself as a down-home, how-to magazine that encourages sustainable living and helps readers enjoy a more healthy, comfortable, and less stressful environment. It welcomes submissions on "green" family activities, healthy recipes, and home businesses that don't require unusual skills. Circ: 34,000.

Contents: 75% articles; 25% depts/columns
Frequency: 6 times each year
Website: www.backhomemagazine.com

Freelance Potential
90% written by nonstaff writers. Publishes 150 freelance submissions yearly; 60% by unpublished writers, 30% by authors who are new to the magazine, 20% by experts. Receives 30 queries, 10 unsolicited mss monthly.

Submissions
Query or send complete ms. Accepts hard copy and email to info@backhomemagazine.com. SASE. Response time varies.

- Articles: 850–3,000 words. How-to and self-help articles, and personal experience pieces. Topics include organic gardening, home construction and repair, cooking, crafts, outdoor recreation, family activities, livestock, home businesses, alternative energy, fuel efficiency, and community action.
- Depts/columns: Word lengths vary. Equipment maintenance and solar energy.
- Artwork: Prefers digital images at 300 dpi; accepts color prints and transparencies.

Sample Issue
64 pages. Advertising. Sample issue and guidelines available at website.

- "Become a Rooster Whisperer." Tips for taming an overly aggressive rooster.
- "Revitalize Your Garden." Replenishing soil with vital necessary nutrients for increased production and healthier plant growth.

Rights and Payment
First North American serial rights. Written material, $35 per page. Artwork, payment rates vary. Kill fee, $25. Pays on publication. Provides 2 contributor's copies.

Backroads

P.O. Box 317
Branchville, NJ 07826

Publisher: Brian Rathjen

Description and Interests
Backroads shares the excitement of touring by motorcycle with its readers. It features profiles, destination pieces, and new product information. It is decidedly non-political and secular. The magazine is about getting out and riding, not being in a particular group; no "us vs. them" submissions. Circ: 40,000.

Contents: 50% depts/columns; 40% articles; 10% other
Frequency: Monthly
Website: www.backroadsusa.com

Freelance Potential
60% written by nonstaff writers. Publishes 100+ freelance submissions yearly; 15% by unpublished writers, 15% by authors who are new to the magazine, 15% by experts. Receives 5 queries monthly.

Submissions
Query with images. Accepts hard copy and email to editor@backroadsusa.com. No simultaneous submissions. SASE. Responds in 3 months.

- Articles: 500–750 words. Informational and how-to articles, destination pieces. Topics include the motorcycling lifestyle and motorcycle travel.
- Depts/columns: 400–750 words. Great American Diner Run, Big City Getaway, Mysterious America, We're Outta Here, Thoughts From the Road.
- Artwork: Digital images at 300 dpi.

Sample Issue
68 pages. Advertising. Sample articles and guidelines available at website.

- "The Alps." Travel feature recounts a high alpine motorcycle tour, complete with routes, sites, and accommodations.
- Sample dept/column: Mysterious America takes the reader to the Zippo Case Museum in Bradford, PA.

Rights and Payment
First North American serial rights. Written material, $75+. Pays 30 days after publication. Provides 1 contributor's copy.

Backstagemouse.com  

P.O. Box 123
Kissimee, FL 34567

Chief Mouse: Paul

Description and Interests

This start-up publication is an online resource for all things Disney (though it is unaffiliated with the Walt Disney Company), *Backstagemouse.com* will provide detailed and up-to-date information to people who are passionate about Disney theme parks, as well as to those who just visit occasionally. In 2012, the website advertised for writers who share the same passion and are knowledgeable about the parks. Circ: Unavailable.

Contents: Articles
Frequency: Monthly
Website: www.backstagemouse.com

Freelance Potential

In need of experienced writers.

Submissions

Query with résumé or short bio, writing samples, and a head shot. Accepts electronic queries via website. Response time varies.

- Articles: Word lengths vary. Blog posts. Topics include Disney parks, attractions, food, music, nostalgia, memorabilia, and news.

Sample Issue

Advertising. Sample copy available at website.

- "In the Know: Art of Animation." Article provides a detailed account of the new Art of Animation resort.
- "A Guide to Pin Trading." Article explains the rules of trading and the variety of pins available.
- "The Magic of Disney Weddings." Article discusses the options available to those who want to marry at Walt Disney World.

Rights and Payment

Rights vary. Payment rates and policy vary.

Backwoods Home Magazine

P.O. Box 712
Gold Beach, OR 97444

Publisher & Editor: Dave Duffy

Description and Interests

Backwoods Home is a country-oriented, how-to magazine that specializes in teaching people how to build their own home, grow their own food, and create an independent, self-reliant lifestyle. It prints first-person narratives and wants articles from people who have done the things about which they write. Circ: 40,000.

Contents: Articles; depts/columns
Frequency: 6 times each year
Website: www.backwoodshome.com

Freelance Potential

88% written by nonstaff writers. Publishes 60 freelance submissions yearly; 30% by unpublished writers, 60% by new authors, 10% by experts. Receives 10 unsolicited mss monthly.

Submissions

Send complete ms with artwork. Accepts hard copy, disk submissions (Word and WordPerfect files), and email to article-submission@backwoods-home.com (no attachments; include "Submission" in subject line). No simultaneous submissions. Availability of artwork improves chance of acceptance. SASE. Response time varies.

- Articles: Word lengths vary. Informational and how-to articles, and personal experience pieces. Topics include home building, energy production, farming, raising livestock, food preservation, recipes, country skills, homeschooling, arts and crafts, and book reviews.
- Depts/columns: Staff-written.
- Artwork: High-resolution digital images and drawings (TIFF, JPG, PNG, or GIF formats).

Sample Issue

96 pages. Advertising. Sample articles and guidelines available at website.

- "Prepper Power!" Knowing what electrical needs are essential and how to provide power during an electricity outage.
- "Easy Homemade Dairy Products." How to make basic dairy products and the benefits of doing so.

Rights and Payment

First and anthology rights. Articles, $30–$200. Artwork, payment rates vary. Pays on acceptance. Provides 1 contributor's copy.

The Backwoodsman

P.O. Box 1740
Fulton, TX 78358

Editor & Publisher: Charlie Richie, Sr.

Description and Interests

Celebrating more than 30 years in publication, this magazine provides readers with the history and know-how of frontiersmen. It promotes and preserves such skills as wilderness survival and primitive hunting and fishing with informational and how-to articles and projects. Circ: 207,000.

Contents: 90% articles; 10% depts/columns
Frequency: 6 times each year
Website: www.backwoodsmanmag.com

Freelance Potential

50% written by nonstaff writers. Publishes 280 freelance submissions yearly; 50% by unpublished writers, 30% by authors who are new to the magazine. Receives 25 unsolicited mss monthly.

Submissions

Send complete ms with artwork. Accepts hard copy and simultaneous submissions if identified. Availability of artwork improves chance of acceptance. SASE. Responds in 1 month.

- Articles: Word lengths vary. Informational and how-to articles, personal experience pieces, profiles, and interviews. Topics include primitive survival, muzzleloading guns and hunting, homesteading, American history, Native American culture, woods lore, and leathercraft.
- Depts/columns: Staff-written.
- Artwork: High-resolution JPEG images; 35mm prints. Line art.

Sample Issue

72 pages. Advertising. Sample articles and guidelines available at website.

- "Dugout Dick...A True American Legend." Profile of an Idaho hermit who lived for more than 60 years in a cave.
- "The Need for Heirloom Gardens." Examines the benefits to growing heirloom fruits and vegetables.

Rights and Payment

One-time rights. No payment. Provides a small display ad or a 2-year subscription.

Baggers

Source Interlink Media
1733 Alton Parkway
Irvine, CA 92606

Associate Editor: Toph Bocchiaro

Description and Interests

Affluent baby boomers with luxurious tastes that extend to touring motorcycles are the target audience of *Baggers*. It features bikes of all kinds, tech gear, events, and the people involved. Circ: Unavailable.

Contents: Articles; depts/columns
Frequency: Monthly
Website: www.baggersmag.com

Freelance Potential

Receives many freelance submissions monthly.

Submissions

Query. Accepts hard copy and email queries to baggersmag@sorc.com. Artwork increases the chance of acceptance. SASE. Response time varies.

- Articles: Word lengths vary. Informational articles and profiles. Topics include touring motorcycles, tech gear, and personalities.
- Depts/columns: Word lengths vary. Road trips, product review, events.

Sample Issue

Advertising. Sample articles and guidelines available at website.

- "The King and the Sideshack." Article reviews the new three-wheel bike from Southeast Custom Cycles.
- "Puttin' Around Arkansas." Article highlights a trip along Arkansas roads with stops at biker-friendly Best Western hotels.
- Sample dept/column: Road Trip takes readers cruising along Colorado's I-70.

Rights and Payment

Rights vary. Payment rates and policy vary.

Bamboo Magazine

Conscious Family Living

9012 Haskell Ave.
North Hills, CA 91343

Editors: Anni Daulter and Ashley Ess

Description and Interests

This digital magazine targets parents who wish to raise their families in an eco-friendly manner. It covers natural living, organic nutrition and health, pregnancy, peaceful parenting, gardening, the environment, crafting, and alternative education. Its vision is to communicate not only to those already in the holistic parenting community, but also to those who may be curious or even skeptical about it. Writers will have the opportunity to promote their own causes, businesses, books, and blogs. Circ: Unavailable.

Contents: Articles
Frequency: Quarterly
Website: www.bamboofamilymag.com

Freelance Potential

Receives many freelance submissions monthly.

Submissions

Query with writing samples. Accepts email to submissions@bamboofamilymag.com or electronic submissions via website. Response time varies.

- Articles: Word lengths vary. Informational and how-to articles, interviews, and personal experience pieces. Topics include parenting, pregnancy and birth, nutrition, natural home and living, and health.

Sample Issue

Sample articles, guidelines, and editorial calendar available at website.

- "Is My Baby Teething?" Article explains a baby's teething process and discusses homeopathic remedies to alleviate discomfort.
- "Conscious Close Up with Ina May Gaskin." Article features an interview with the mid-wife who founded The Farm, a training center for mid-wives.
- "It's Easy to Be Green." Article offers five easy laundry tips that are eco-friendly.

Rights and Payment

Rights revert back to author after 90 days. No payment.

Bards and Sages Quarterly

Editorial Director: Faith Carroll

Description and Interests

Bards and Sages Quarterly is a print and digital journal that specializes in short speculative fiction. Its science fiction, fantasy, and horror come from both new and established authors. The quarterly also publishes interviews, book reviews, articles, and art focused on speculative fiction. Tone and style of the stories vary from the lighthearted to the dark. Be careful to review the very specific guidelines: The publication rarely accepts first-person narratives, anthropomorphic characters, paranormal romances, or submissions containing sex or vulgarity. The editors do not want full-length fiction such as novels, novellas, or story collections. Circ: Unavailable.

Contents: 80% articles; 20% depts/columns
Frequency: Quarterly
Website: www.bardsandsages.com

Freelance Potential

Unavailable.

Submissions

Accepts queries and submissions to the Fiction Department at bardsandsagesquarterly@gmail.com. Submit short stories as a Word attachment or RTF, and flash fiction in the body of the email. Stories may also be submitted through Google Docs. Do not include a bio or publishing credits. Responds within 3 months.

- Articles: Word lengths vary. Interviews, book reviews, articles on speculative fiction.
- Fiction: Short stories, 500–5,000 words. Flash fiction, to 500 words. Genres include fantasy, horror, science fiction.

Sample Issue

Sample copy and guidelines available at website.

- "The Library of Unfinished Books." An institution whose primary purpose is to preserve the realm of the possible.
- "Not Your Type." A woman learns that sometimes finding the perfect match means looking in strange places.

Rights and Payment

First worldwide electronic and print rights. Payment for short stories, $15; flash fiction, $5. Payment via PayPal.

Bartleby Snopes 

Managing Editor: Nathaniel Tower

Description and Interests

Bartleby Snopes is an online literary magazine with a specific mission: to offer the best new fiction the editors can find, give as many writers an opportunity to publish their best work as possible, and inspire prospective writers to create great works of fiction. It publishes two new stories online each week, and a semiannual PDF magazine in January and July. The editors look for stories that maintain focus and forward momentum —"Poe's prescription of a single effect and Aristotle's criterion of a rising action." The magazine also holds a Story of the Month contest. Circ: Unavailable.

Contents: Fiction; flash fiction
Frequency: Updated weekly
Website: www.bartlebysnopes.com

Freelance Potential

Encouraging of new and established writers.

Submissions

Send complete ms. Accepts electronic submissions via website. Accepts simultaneous submissions; report immediately if accepted elsewhere. See website for a list of "don'ts." Responds in 1 week.

- Fiction: 1,000–3,000 words. Literary fiction.
- Flash Fiction: To 1,200 words.

Sample Issue

Sample articles and writers' guidelines available at website.

- "Annie's Morning." Story about an elderly woman with dementia packing up and leaving her home to live with her daughter.
- "A Ouija Board, A Divining Rod." Story tells of a group of longtime friends driving across the country.
- "Robbie." Story is about a mother's grief and guilt over her son's death many years earlier.

Rights and Payment

First rights. Payment rates vary.

Bassmaster Magazine

3500 Blue Lake Drive, Suite 330,
Birmingham, AL 35243

Editor: James Hall

Description and Interests

Bassmaster Magazine is devoted to helping beginner, intermediate, and advanced fishermen catch more and bigger bass. It focuses exclusively on freshwater bass species, with coverage of techniques, patterns, behavior, and conservation. *Bassmaster* is also the member magazine of the B.A.S.S. fishing organization. It is seeking informative and authoritative articles that quote at least two sources. It is also in need of destination stories for North America. Circ: 519,354.

Contents: 75% articles; 15% depts/columns; 10% other
Frequency: Monthly
Website: www.bassmaster.com

Freelance Potential

90% written by nonstaff writers. Publishes 75 freelance submissions yearly; 1% by unpublished writers, 5% by new authors, 5% by experts. Receives 25 queries monthly.

Submissions

Query with clips. Accepts hard copy and email queries to editorial@bassmaster.com. SASE. Responds in 2 months.

- Articles: 1,200–2,500 words. How-to articles, and new product information. Topics include bass fishing, nature, marine life, and outdoor recreation.
- Depts/columns: 10 Minute Angler; Triple Threat, (3 ways to handle common angler scenarios); Pattern of the Month; Destinations Quarterly; Short Casts, lighthearted stories, conservation news. Word lengths vary. Tips and techniques, new products, and tournaments.

Sample Issue

68 pages. Advertising. Sample articles and editorial calendar available at website. Writers' guidelines available.

- "6 Ways to Save on Fishing Tackle." Bargain shopping tips to help fishermen get more bang for their tackle buck.
- "Rainstorms Can Liven Up Your Fishing." How to take advantage of the increased feeding fish do before and after rain to increase your catch.

Rights and Payment

All North American serial rights. Written material, $.40 per word. Pays on acceptance. Provides 2 contributor's copies.

Bead & Button

21027 Crossroads Circle
P.O. Box 1612
Waukesha, WI 53187-1612

Editorial Assistant: Lora Groszkiewicz

Description and Interests

Chock-full of inspiring projects for the intermediate and advanced beading enthusiast, this magazine features instructional articles, along with educational pieces, on the history and culture of beading and profiles of accomplished beadmakers. The magazine welcomes submissions that will inspire and challenge its readers. Circ: 102,000.

Contents: 60% articles; 40% depts/columns
Frequency: 6 times each year
Website: www.beadandbutton.com

Freelance Potential

80% written by nonstaff writers. Publishes 120 freelance submissions yearly; 50% by unpublished writers, 30% by authors who are new to the magazine, 20% by experts. Receives 10 queries monthly.

Submissions

Query with prints or slides of the piece to be made or the work of the artist to be profiled. Accepts hard copy, email queries to editor@beadandbutton.com, and uploads via the website. SASE. Responds in 4–6 weeks.

- Articles: 1,000–1,200 words. Informational and how-to articles, profiles, and interviews. Topics include bead jewelry making, jewelry artists, techniques, and ethnic or historic beading.
- Depts/columns: Word lengths vary. Tips and Techniques, Patterns, Your Work, and Bead Soup.

Sample Issue

130 pages. Sample articles and guidelines available at website.

- "Mesmerizing Masonry." Using brick stitch to create a bracelet with a complex pattern.
- "From Shop Girl to Glass Girl." Profile of lampwork artist Jennifer Geldard.

Rights and Payment

All rights. Articles, $300–$400. Projects, $75–$300. Pays on acceptance.

Bee Culture

623 West Liberty Street
Medina, OH 44256

Editor: Kim Flottum

Description and Interests

The art of beekeeping—and all it entails—is explored in this magazine. Its articles cover beekeeping history, equipment used, garden and forest management with bees, pollination, honey plants, pesticides, and pests and predators. The publication is open to both new and experienced writers. Circ: 16,500.

Contents: 60% articles; 40% depts/columns
Frequency: Monthly
Website: www.beeculture.com

Freelance Potential

35% written by nonstaff writers. Publishes 30–40 freelance submissions yearly; 30% by unpublished writers, 10% by authors who are new to the magazine, 60% by experts. Receives 12–15 queries, 10+ unsolicited mss monthly.

Submissions

Query with outline, proposal (500 words max), and photos; or send complete ms with photos. Prefers email submissions to kim@beeculture.com (Word or RTF attachments; attach photos); will accept hard copy. No simultaneous submissions. SASE. Responds in 2 weeks.

- Articles: 800–2,000 words. Informational and how-to articles, profiles, humor, and new product information. Topics include beekeeping and beekeepers, pollination, harvesting, marketing, pests, and gardening.
- Depts/columns: Staff-written.
- Artwork: TIFF or JPEG images at 300 dpi; prints and color transparencies.

Sample Issue

80 pages. Advertising. Sample articles and guidelines available at website.

- "Using Bait Hives." Explains how to capture swarms using baited boxes.
- "Beenglish Dictionary." A glossary of terms that defines the jargon of beekeeping.

Rights and Payment

First North American serial rights. Articles, $150–$200. Pays on publication. Provides 1 contributor's copy.

Best in Travel Magazine

Momentum House,
Lower Road
London SE1 8SJ
England

Editor: Anton Strack

Description and Interests

Luxury travelers turn to this new ezine for the latest news and trends in travel around the globe. Created by the World Travel Awards organization, articles take readers on virtual journeys near and far and provide the inspiration to make them happen. In addition to the website, *Best in Travel* is available as an Android app. Hits per month: Unavailable.

Contents: Articles
Frequency: Monthly
Website: www.bestintravelmagazine.com

Freelance Potential

Percentage of freelance submissions unavailable.

Submissions

Query or send complete ms. Accepts email to editor@bestintravelmagazine.com. Response time varies.

- Articles: Word lengths vary. Informational articles and profiles. Topics include destinations, hotels, cruises, luxury travel, and luxury goods.

Sample Issue

Advertising. Sample copy available at website.

- "License to Chill." Article features the five most luxurious hotels from James Bond movies.
- "A Sweet Suite." Article describes the newest suite at New York's St. Regis, named for, and designed in the spirit of, the luxury car company Bentley.
- "Netjets Open Private Terminal." Article provides details on a new private airport terminal at Los Angeles Airport.

Rights and Payment

Rights vary. Payment rates and policy vary.

Better Homes & Gardens

1716 Locust Street
Des Moines, IA 50309-3023

Department Editor

Description and Interests

Well-known for its stylish coverage of decorating, gardening, and entertaining, *Better Homes & Gardens* also covers parenting, health, and fashion topics. Best chances for new writers to break in are in the areas of travel, health, parenting, and education. Circ: 7.6 million.

Contents: 98% articles; 1% depts/columns; 1% other
Frequency: Monthly
Website: www.bhg.com

Freelance Potential

10% written by nonstaff writers. Publishes 25–30 freelance submissions yearly; 25% by authors who are new to the magazine. Receives 240 queries each month.

Submissions

Query with résumé and clips or writing samples. Accepts hard copy. SASE. Responds in 1 month.

- Articles: Word lengths vary. Informational articles and new product information. Topics include audio, video, software, collecting, computers, consumer interests, hobbies, disabilities, electronics, entertainment, family, parenting, food, dining, gardening, health, fitness, house and home, medical services, multicultural issues, nutrition, diet, travel, and leisure.
- Depts/columns: Word lengths vary. Readers' recipes, new products, education, parenting.

Sample Issue

260 pages. Advertising. Sample copy and guidelines available.

- "Throw a Mexican Themed Party." Top Chef judge Hugh Acheson gives his tip on how to create a fiesta that's fun and relaxing for host and guests alike.
- "5 Must-Have Pieces for Fall." Style maker Heidi Klum reveals her top fashion picks for fall.

Rights and Payment

All rights. Written material, $1–$2 per word. Kill fee varies. Pays on acceptance. Provides 1 contributor's copy.

Bibliotheca Sacra

Dallas Theological Seminary
3909 Swiss Avenue
Dallas, TX 75204

Editor: Roy B. Zuck

Description and Interests

Bibliotheca Sacra publishes scholarly studies in theology, Bible exposition, ministry, and current social issues as a resource for serious Bible students. As a scholarly publication, it has stringent research and referencing requirements. The majority of its articles are authored by respected theologians to be read by other theologians and theology students. It is open to hearing from scholars on a multitude of theological topics. Circ: 5,000.

Contents: 80% articles; 20% depts/columns
Frequency: Quarterly
Website: www.dts.edu/publications/bibliothecasacra

Freelance Potential

70% written by nonstaff writers. Publishes 26 freelance submissions yearly; 30% by unpublished writers, 50% by authors who are new to the magazine, 20% by experts. Receives 8 unsolicited mss each month.

Submissions

Send complete ms. Accepts hard copy and email submissions to bibsac@dts.edu (Word attachments). SASE. Responds in 3–6 weeks.

- Articles: 5,000–5,500 words. Informational articles, essays, and reviews. Topics include theology, biblical studies, and ministry.
- Depts/columns: Staff-written.

Sample Issue

128 pages. No advertising. Sample copy available. Guidelines available at website.

- "Chronological Issues in the Book of Revelation." Article uncovers and analyzes chronological discrepancies in this section of the Bible.
- "Did Jesus' Disciples Fast?" Article provides scholarly research into this question.

Rights and Payment

All rights. Written material, $150. Pays on publication. Provides 2 contributor's copies.

Bird Watcher's Digest

149 Acme Street
P.O. Box 110
Marietta, OH 45750

Editor: William H. Thompson III

Description and Interests

This magazine's informative, entertaining, and practical articles are aimed at bird watchers and birders of all interest levels. Each issue is an easy-to-use bird-watching guide and writers should be experienced bird watchers. Circ: 70,000.

Contents: 50% articles; 45% depts/columns; 5% fiction
Frequency: 6 times each year
Website: www.birdwatchersdigest.com

Freelance Potential

65% written by nonstaff writers. Publishes 60–70 freelance submissions yearly; 10% by unpublished writers, 30% by authors who are new to the magazine, 60% by experts. Receives 250 unsolicited mss monthly.

Submissions

Query or send complete ms. Accepts hard copy and email to submissions@birdwatchersdigest.com (Word or RTF attachments; include "Submission" and topic in subject line). SASE. Responds in 10–12 weeks.

- Articles: 500–2,500 words. Informational, how-to, personal experience, humor. Topics include species profiles, feeding and attracting birds, housing birds, bird-watching expeditions.
- Depts/columns: Word lengths vary. My Way, up to 1,000 words; The Well-Equipped Birder, up to 750 words; Far Afield, 500–1,500 words; The Bird Gardener; The Backyard.
- Artwork: Color transparencies or digital images (JPEG or TIFF), 300 dpi.

Sample Issue

128 pages. Advertising. Sample articles and guidelines available at website.

- "Species Profile: Common Raven." Everything there is to know about this bird.
- "Bird Feeder Trends." The latest on the different varieties of feeders and their aesthetic qualities and practical pros and cons.

Rights and Payment

One-time rights. Written material, payment rates vary. Artwork, $75+. Pays on publication. Provides 2 contributor's copies.

BirdWatching

Madover Media
85 Quincy Avenue, Suite 2
Quincy, MA 02169

Managing Editor: Matt Mendenhall

Description and Interests

Purchased in the summer of 2012 by Madover Media, this magazine publishes articles and photographs that appeal to the casual, as well as serious birder. It features information on types of birds, bird behavior, and ways to attract and identify them. Its audience is well versed in bird watching and interested in learning new things about their feathered friends. Circ: 33,000.

Contents: 50% articles; 40% depts/columns; 10% other
Frequency: 6 times each year
Website: www.birdwatchingdaily.com

Freelance Potential

80% written by nonstaff writers. Publishes 25 freelance submissions yearly; 5% by unpublished writers, 10% by authors who are new to the magazine, 75% by experts. Receives 10–15 queries monthly.

Submissions

Prefers query with description of focus and sources, potential illustrations, author qualifications, and clips. Accepts hard copy and email to mail@birdwatchingdaily.com. SASE. Responds in 1–3 months.

- Articles: 1,750–2,250 words. Informational, profiles, personal experience. Topics include birding hotspots, species profiles, attracting and feeding birds, conservation, bird biology, bird-related history.
- Depts/columns: 700–900 words. Identification tips, short profiles of birders.

Sample Issue

58 pages. Advertising. Sample articles and guidelines available at website.

- "Birdbath Basics." How to choose and properly maintain a birdbath that will attract the maximum number and variety of birds.
- "ID Tips: Wilson's Plover." Learn how to identify a Plover and all about their behaviors, eating habits, and migration patterns.

Rights and Payment

First rights. Articles, $400. Depts/columns, payment rates vary. Pays on publication. Provides 2 contributor's copies.

Bitch Magazine

Feminist Response to Pop Culture

4930 NE 29th Avenue
Portland, OR 97211

Editorial Director: Andi Zeisler

Description and Interests

Critiques, essays, and articles examining pop culture from a feminist perspective are featured in this magazine. It aims to be a toolkit for analysis that promotes activism and impels social change. It seeks sharp-eyed perspectives on cultural attitudes, social trends, and the media, both negative and positive. Circ: 50,000.

Contents: 80% articles; 20% depts/columns
Frequency: Quarterly
Website: www.bitchmagazine.org

Freelance Potential

85% written by nonstaff writers. Publishes 30–50 freelance submissions yearly; 5% by unpublished writers, 70% by authors who are new to the magazine, 10% by experts. Receives 50 queries, 20 unsolicited mss monthly.

Submissions

Prefers query with cover letter, clips or writing samples; will accept complete ms. Prefers email to info@b-word.org or via website; will accept hard copy. Accepts simultaneous submissions if identified. SASE. Responds in 3–5 weeks.

- Articles: 2,000–4,000 words. Informational, profiles, interviews, critical essays. Topics include pop culture, social trends, personalities.
- Depts/columns: 100–1,500 words. Reviews, critical essays, Q&As, brief activist profiles. Love It/Shove It, analysis of culture/societal happenings that enrage or please you, up to 500 words; Bitch List, highlights the best of Pop Culture, 100 words.

Sample Issue

96 pages. Sample articles, guidelines, and editorial theme list available at website.

- "Life on Mars." An analysis of faith and feminism and how they don't mix in one of the country's fastest-growing megachurches.
- "Pinned Down." A look at the social network vehicle Pinterest and what its approach is to female users.

Rights and Payment

First North American serial rights. Articles, $100. Depts/columns, $25–$50. Payment policy varies.

Bleu

349 Fifth Ave, 4th Floor
New York, NY 10016

Editor in Chief: Rannon Ray

Description and Interests

Bleu is a magazine for multicultural urban men that aims to transcend stereotypes and embody urban culture. It covers entertainment, fashion, technology, relationships, fitness, travel, and lifestyle. Readers are ages 21 to 39, educated, and affluent. Its new sister publication is *Pynk*. Circ: 150,000.

Contents: Articles; depts/columns
Frequency: 6 times each year
Website: www.bleumagazine.com

Freelance Potential

Accepts many freelance submissions monthly.

Submissions

Query. Accepts email to info@bleumag.com. Response time varies.

- Articles: Word lengths vary. Informational and how-to articles and profiles. Topics include seasonal fashion, health and fitness, technology, personal finance, cars, relationships, the arts, and food.
- Depts/columns: Reviews, grooming, and gadgets.

Sample Issue

Advertising. Sample articles and editorial calendar available at website.

- "Top 5 Fashion Fails of the Last Decade." Article discusses the worst men's fashion offenders from the last 10 years.
- "From Homie to Hologram." Article provides tips for juggling a relationship while still finding time to be with friends.
- Sample dept/column: Bleu's Street Style interviews men on the street about what they are wearing.

Rights and Payment

Rights vary. Payment rates and policy vary.

The Bloomsbury Review

1553 Platte Street, Suite 206
Denver, CO 80202-1167

Publisher/Editor: Marilyn Auer

Description and Interests

Featuring book reviews, essays, and poetry, *The Bloomsbury Review* is a magazine about books. It covers fiction and nonfiction, all genres and styles. Author profiles and interviews are also presented. Writers and reviewers need to have a good working knowledge of the author or subject matter and be sure to review the author's ideas, not their own. Circ: 35,000.

Contents: 70% reviews; 15% depts/columns; 13% articles; 2% poetry
Frequency: Quarterly
Website: www.bloomsburyreview.com

Freelance Potential

55% written by nonstaff writers. Publishes 50 freelance submissions yearly; 10% by unpublished writers, 10% by authors who are new to the magazine, 5% by experts.

Submissions

Send complete ms with author bio. Accepts email queries to bloomsb@aol.com (Word or WordPerfect attachments). Discourages simultaneous submissions. SASE. Responds in 3 months.

- Articles: 100–1,000 words. Book reviews, essays, interviews. Topics include books, writing, authors.
- Depts/columns: Word lengths vary. Children's and young adult book reviews.

Sample Issue

24 pages. 40% advertising. 34 articles; 1 poem; 1 dept/column. Sample copy, $5. Guidelines and theme list available.

- "*MGM: Hollywood's Greatest Backlot*, by Steven Bing, et al." Review.
- "*To Die in Mexico: Dispatches From Inside the Drug War*, by John Gibler." Review.

Rights and Payment

First rights and non-exclusive electronic rights. Essays and interviews, $20–$50. Reviews, $10–$15. Poetry, $5–$10 per poem. Gift subscriptions available in the place of cash payment. Pays on publication. Provides 2 contributor's copies.

Blue Ridge Country

3424 Brambleton Avenue
Roanoke, VA 24018

Editor: Kurt Rheinheimer

Description and Interests
Blue Ridge Country embraces the traditions and spirit of the Blue Ridge region, from western Maryland through Virginia's Shenandoah Valley, Northern Georgia and Alabama, and regions within a day's drive of the Blue Ridge Parkway. It also includes parts of Kentucky, Maryland, West Virginia, Virginia, North Carolina, South Carolina, and Tennessee. Stories focus on recipes, animal husbandry, farming, bed-and-breakfasts, and places and things to see. Circ: 60,000.
Contents: 80% articles; 20% depts/columns
Frequency: 6 times each year
Website: www.blueridgecountry.com

Freelance Potential
90% written by nonstaff writers. Publishes 18–30 freelance submissions yearly; 10% by new authors. Receives 20 queries monthly.

Submissions
Query with cover letter and writing samples, preferably published clips. Accepts hard copy and email to krheinheimer@leisure-publishing.com. SASE. Response time varies.

- Articles: 750–2,000 words. Informational, personal experience, profiles. Topics include regional history, legends, natural history, wildlife, the environment, travel, outdoor recreation.
- Depts/columns: 100–400 words. Country Roads, travel/environmental news and book reviews; Inns & Getaways; Festivals & Events; On the Mountainside, outdoor recreation; and Blue Ridge People.
- Artwork: Color prints or transparencies; high-resolution JPEG or TIFF images, 300 dpi.

Sample Issue
66 pages. Advertising. Sample articles, guidelines, and editorial calendar available at website.

- "Blue Ridge Eateries, Part 2." A rundown of six must-stop eateries along the Virginia section of the Blue Ridge Parkway.
- "Mountaintop Cabin Rentals in Georgia." Luxury cabins in Blue Ridge.

Rights and Payment
First North American serial rights. Articles, to $250. Depts/columns, $25+. Artwork, $50 per published photo. Pays on publication. Provides 2 contributor's copies.

Bon Appétit

Condé Nast Publications
4 Times Square, 5th Floor
New York, NY 10036

Submissions: Peggy Kaplin

Description and Interests
Geared toward foodies of all experience levels, this magazine's editorial recipe is a healthy mix of cooking techniques, nutrition information, entertaining ideas, foodie destinations, reviews, and, of course, recipes. Its focus is on what's current and stylish, as well what will help cooks in their own kitchen. It is interested in new ideas, whether they be for theme dining, recipes, or adding something different to one's cooking style. All writers must have a background in food or cooking. Circ: 1.5 million.
Contents: 70% articles; 30% depts/columns
Frequency: Monthly
Website: www.bonappetit.com

Freelance Potential
80% written by nonstaff writers. Publishes 100 freelance submissions yearly; 20% by authors who are new to the magazine. Receives 80 queries monthly.

Submissions
Query with clips. Accepts hard copy and email queries to peggy_kaplin@condenast.com. SASE. Responds in 6 weeks.

- Articles: 1,500–2,000 words. Short features, 200–400 words. Informational, how-to, profiles. Topics include food preparation, entertaining, nutrition, menus, lifestyle, travel, and restaurants.
- Depts/columns: 500–1,250 words. Wine and spirits, recipes.

Sample Issue
162 pages. Advertising. Sample articles available at website. Guidelines available.

- "Home Entertaining 2012." The latest and greatest trends, ideas, and food for hosting great get-togethers at home.
- "Family Style Feasts." Comfort food updated and served up in a relaxed style that's enjoyable for hosts and guests alike.

Rights and Payment
All rights. Written material, payment rates vary. Pays on acceptance. Provides 1 contributor's copy.

Boulevard

6614 Clayton Road
Box 325
Richmond Heights, MO 63117

Editor: Richard Burgin

Description and Interests
This literary journal, published by St. Louis University, accepts a mix of essays, short stories, interviews, and poetry from established and emerging writers. It believes that a good literary magazine reflects the world, remembers the world, and in a way, foretells the world. It seeks to produce a journal that showcases new work by old masters and masterful work by new ones. Circ: 3,500.

Contents: 50% fiction; 50% other
Frequency: 3 times each year
Website: www.boulevardmagazine.org

Freelance Potential
98% written by nonstaff writers. Publishes 100 freelance submissions yearly; 10% by unpublished writers, 60% by authors who are new to the magazine. Receives 1,000 unsolicited mss each month.

Submissions
Send complete ms between October 1 and May 1. Prefers submissions via the website at http://boulevard.submishmash.com/submit ($3 fee per electronic submission); will accept hard copy and simultaneous submissions if identified. SASE. Response time varies.

- Articles: To 8,000 words. Interviews, profiles, literary, cultural, and confession pieces, personal essays.
- Fiction: To 8,000 words. Literary fiction. No science fiction, erotica, Westerns, horror, romance, or children's stories.
- Other: Poetry, to 200 lines; limit 5 poems per submission.

Sample Issue
264 pages. Little advertising. Excerpts available to view at website. Guidelines available at website.

- "A Fully Imagined World." Short story.
- "Balkan Express." Creative nonfiction piece about a man traveling from Zagreb to Sofia.

Rights and Payment
First North American serial rights. Articles, $50–$300. Fiction, $50–$500. Poetry, $25–$500. Pays on publication. Provides 1 contributor's copy.

Bow & Arrow Hunting

Beckett Media
2400 East Katella Avenue, Suite 300
Anaheim, CA 92806

Editor: Joe Bell

Description and Interests
This is one of the oldest magazines devoted to bow hunting and the outdoors. It offers a mix of expert hunting techniques, new gear spotlights, product reviews, and true stories of hunting adventure. Quality photos increase the chance of getting an article published. Circ: 60,000.

Contents: 75% articles; 25% depts/columns
Frequency: 9 times each year
Website: www.bowandarrowhunting.com

Freelance Potential
80% written by nonstaff writers. Publishes 60+ freelance submissions yearly; 10% by unpublished writers, 20–30% by authors who are new to the magazine, 80% by experts. Receives 15 queries each month.

Submissions
Query with sample paragraph or detailed article outline. Accepts email queries to editorial@-bowandarrowhunting.com. Responds in 6–8 weeks.

- Articles: 2,000–2,500 words. Informational, how-to, personal experience, creative nonfiction, new product information. Topics include bow and arrow hunting, equipment, techniques, tales of the hunt.
- Depts/columns: Word lengths vary. Essays and Q&As.
- Artwork: B/W or color prints or slides; digital images at 300 dpi or higher.

Sample Issue
80 pages. Advertising. Sample articles available at website. Guidelines available.

- "Bowhunting Fitness." Why staying in shape improves hunting and how to use cross-training to accomplish fitness goals.
- "Gray Ghost." Personal experience piece about hunting Coues deer in the Mexican desert.

Rights and Payment
All or first North American serial rights. Written material, $200–$450. Artwork, payment rates vary. Pays on publication. Provides contributor's copies.

Bowhunter

InterMedia Outdoors
P.O. Box 420235
Palm Coast, FL 32142-0235

Editor: Dwight Schuh

Description and Interests

Published for outdoorsmen and women in the U.S. and Canada who are committed to hunting with a bow and arrow, *Bowhunter* includes both adventure features and educational articles. It seeks to capture the simplicity, beauty, and thrill of stalking wild game. It also features articles on animal behavior and hunting strategies, as well as reviews of new gear. Circ: 126,480.

Contents: 63% articles; 35% depts/columns; 1% fiction; 1% other
Frequency: 10 times each year
Website: www.bowhunter.com

Freelance Potential

90% written by nonstaff writers. Publishes 80–100 freelance submissions yearly; 10% by unpublished writers, 10% by authors who are new to the magazine, 30% by experts. Receives 20 queries, 50 unsolicited mss monthly.

Submissions

Query with outline or send complete ms. Accepts hard copy and disk submissions. SASE. Responds to queries in 2 weeks, to ms in 1 month.

- Articles: To 2,000 words. Informational, how-to, profiles, interviews, personal experience. Topics include hunting techniques, hunting stories, ethics, safety, history, legislation as related to bow hunting.
- Depts/columns: To 1,000 words. Hunting tips, personal experience pieces, trip suggestions, new product reviews, news items.

Sample Issue

136 pages. Advertising. Sample articles and guidelines available.

- "Back for Seconds: Alaska Brown Bear Hunt Pays Off." Firsthand account of hunting brown bears in Alaska.
- "Climber Primer: 6 New Climbing Tree Stands." Reviews of new hunting platforms that are positioned up in trees.

Rights and Payment

First North American serial rights. Articles, $200–$500. Depts/columns, $150. Pays on acceptance. Provides 1 contributor's copy.

Brew Your Own

5515 Main Street
Manchester Center, VT 05255

Editor: Chris Colby

Description and Interests

Targeting the extract brewer, the all-grain brewer, and all home brewers in between, this magazine features practical information, helpful tips, and balanced evaluations in each issue. Its mission is to provide readers with accurate and entertaining information that will help them brew the best beer they can. It looks for articles that fall into one of the following categories: recipes, brewing techniques, brewing science, and equipment. Interviews, historical pieces, and trends are also of interest. Circ: 40,000.

Contents: 60% articles; 40% depts/columns
Frequency: 8 times each year
Website: www.byo.com

Freelance Potential

85% written by nonstaff writers. Publishes 100 freelance submissions yearly; 15% by unpublished writers, 25% by authors who are new to the magazine, 25% by experts. Receives 25 queries monthly.

Submissions

Query with proposal, article angle, intended sources, and clips; or send complete ms. Prefers email queries to edit@byo.com (Word attachments); will accept CD submissions with hard copy. Responds in 6 weeks.

- Articles: 1,500–3,000 words. Informational, how-to, interviews. Topics include recipes, history, equipment, tasting, marketing homemade beer.
- Depts/columns: "Homebrew Nation," first-person brewing stories and photos; word lengths vary. Last Call, personal essays; 600–750 words.

Sample Issue

72 pages. Advertising. Sample articles and guidelines available at website.

- "Robust Porter: Style Profile." What goes into making this hoppy, dark brew.
- Sample dept/column: "Last Call" relates the author and his brew partner's big win at the annual home brew contest at Tun Tavern in Atlantic City, New Jersey.

Rights and Payment

All rights. Written material, $25–$200. Pays on publication. Provides 2 contributor's copies.

Brick

A Literary Journal

Box 609, Stn P
Toronto, Ontario M5S 2Y4
Canada

Submissions Editor: Nadia Szilvassy

Description and Interests

Thought-provoking works of nonfiction appear in the pages of this magazine for an audience that appreciates literature, the arts, and culture. It also features interviews. *Brick* considers itself to be primarily a publication of literary nonfiction, and therefore the few pieces of fiction and poetry in the magazine are solicited by the editorial board; no unsolicited submissions are accepted for these categories. Circ: 3,000.

Contents: 90% articles; 10% fiction
Frequency: Twice each year
Website: www.brickmag.com

Freelance Potential

100% written by nonstaff writers. Publishes 30 freelance submissions yearly; 10% by unpublished writers, 30% by authors who are new to the magazine, 60% by experts. Receives 30 unsolicited mss monthly.

Submissions

Send complete ms only. No unsolicited works of fiction accepted. Accepts hard copy and simultaneous submissions. Include email address for response. SAE/IRC. Responds in 3–6 months.

- Articles: 600–1,800 words. Informational articles, profiles, interviews, opinion. Topics include social issues, government, economics, arts, current events.
- Fiction: Solicited works only.
- Depts/columns: Word lengths vary. Media reviews, opinion pieces, and news briefs.
- Artwork: Digital images at 300 dpi.

Sample Issue

178 pages. Little advertising. Sample articles and guidelines available at website.

- "An Interview with Wim Wenders." An interview with this filmmaker.
- "Remembering Applegarth Follies." A look back at his literary magazines from the '70s and the people behind it.

Rights and Payment

First serial rights. Written material, $100–$350. Pays on publication. Provides contributors with a 1-year subscription.

The Brooklyner

Editor

Description and Interests

A mix of literary fiction, nonfiction, and poetry are published in this ezine,which was established to preserve passionate storytelling. It also features reviews and commentary on relevant pop culture. *The Brooklyner Literary* is published as a quarterly print journal, and accepts original literature, poetry, and art. Circ: Unavailable.

Contents: Articles; fiction; poetry
Frequency: Updated regularly
Website: www.brooklyner.org

Freelance Potential

Receives many freelance submissions monthly.

Submissions

Send complete ms and author bio. For ezine, accepts email to webrooklyner@gmail.com (include genre and word count in subject line; no attachments). For *The Brooklyner Literary*, accepts electronic submissions via Submishmash submissions manager only. Response time varies.

- Articles: To 3,000 words. Flash writing, to 1,000 words. Essays and reviews. Topics include pop culture, food, culture, behavior.
- Fiction: To 3,000 words. Flash fiction, to 1,000 words. Literary fiction.
- Poetry: No line limits.

Sample Issue

Sample copy and guidelines available at website.

- "First Date." Essay is about a first date that ends quickly.
- "It's Darkness He Wants." Story about a suicidal man looking for someone to help him.
- "Good Times Down South." Essay compares the days of a stay-at-home mom to that of a typical New Zealand woman.

Rights and Payment

Rights vary. Prose, up to $75; poetry, $25. Payment policy varies.

Bull Spec

P.O. Box 13146
Durham, NC 27709

Publisher: Samuel Montgomery-Blinn

Description and Interests
Available in print and digital versions, *Bull Spec* is a journal of speculative fiction. While currently not accepting submissions, it prints short stories, poetry, interviews with authors, and book reviews. Though it focuses on fantasy and science fiction, it is open to many genres. Circ: 500.
Contents: Fiction
Frequency: Quarterly
Website: www.bullspec.com

Freelance Potential
90% written by nonstaff writers. Of the freelance submissions published yearly, 35% are by unpublished writers, 50% are by authors who are new to the magazine. Receives 50 unsolicited mss monthly.

Submissions
Currently closed to fiction and poetry submissions. Send complete ms with author's city and state, word count, and whether submission has been published before. For fiction, accepts email to submissions@bullspec.com or for poetry, poetry@bullspec.com (attach files), and simultaneous submissions if identified. Check website for submission periods. Responds in 3 months.

- Articles: Word lengths vary. Interviews and book reviews.
- Fiction: 1,000–8,000 words. Genres include fantasy and science fiction.
- Other: Poetry, to 3 poems per submission.

Sample Issue
68 pages. Little advertising. Sample copy available. Guidelines available at website.

- "The Gearaffe Who Didn't Tick." Short story.
- "Fish Eyes." Short story.

Rights and Payment
Rights vary. Fiction and poetry, $.05 per word ($5 minimum for poetry, $50 minimum for fiction). Reprints, $.01 per word ($1 and $10 minimums). Provides 1 contributor's copy.

Cabin Life

1001 East Ninth Street
Duluth, MN 55805

Editor in Chief: Mark Johnson

Description and Interests
Owners of cabins, cottages, and lake homes are the audience for this magazine that captures the essence of the vacation home lifestyle. It offers readers ideas, information, and inspiration for enjoying their vacation homes every day spent there. It hires freelancers for assignments and accepts article pitches. The magazine is both a home and a lifestyle publication that appeals to people of all ages. Circ: 85,000+.
Contents: 55% articles; 40% depts/columns; 5% other
Frequency: 8 times each year
Website: www.cabinlife.com

Freelance Potential
90% written by nonstaff writers. Publishes 100 freelance submissions yearly; 2% by unpublished writers, 20% by authors who are new to the magazine, 5% by experts. Receives 20–25 queries monthly.

Submissions
Prefers queries with outline, proposed sources, author résumé, and clips. Send résumé and clips to be considered for assignments. Prefers email to editor@cabinlife.com; accepts hard copy. SASE. Responds in 3 months.

- Articles: 1,000–3,000 words. Informational, how-to, and personal experience. Topics include home maintenance, improvement, homebuilding, decor, cooking, entertainment, financing, cabin lifestyle, and wildlife.
- Depts/columns: 400–800 words. Home products, Q&As, reader photos.
- Artwork: JPEG or TIFF images at 300 dpi; prints, slides, or transparencies.

Sample Issue
66 pages. Advertising. Sample articles and guidelines available at website.

- "The Ailing Cabin: Do You Renovate or Rebuild?" Industry experts tell what to consider when making this decision.
- "Passing Down the Beloved Family Retreat." Estate planning to enable children and grandchildren to inherit and share your cabin.

Rights and Payment
All rights. Written material, payment rates vary. Pays on acceptance. Provides 3 contributor's copies.

Calyx

A Journal of Art and Literature by Women

P.O. Box B
Corvallis, OR 97339

Senior Editor: Rebecca Olson

Description and Interests

Published for more than 30 years, this journal celebrates all female writers and is especially interested in emerging voices. *Calyx* is a forum for short fiction, poetry, visual art, essays, reviews, and interviews, and offers writing by women of color, lesbian and bisexual women, older women, young women, and women from unique backgrounds. Circ: 4,000.

Contents: 40% fiction and essays; 60% other
Frequency: Twice each year
Website: www.calyxpress.org

Freelance Potential

100% written by nonstaff writers. Publishes 100 freelance submissions yearly; 20% by unpublished writers, 80% by authors who are new to the magazine. Receives 1,000 queries and unsolicited mss each reading period.

Submissions

Send complete ms with brief author bio for fiction, essays, articles, and poetry through online submission manager. Query with résumé and clips for book reviews. Accepts electronic submissions and hard copy between October 1 and December 31 and simultaneous submissions. SASE. Responds in 6–8 months.

- Articles: Book reviews, to 1,000 words. Essays, to 5,000 words. Interviews, to 2,500 words. Topics include gender, identity narratives, female writers and artists.
- Fiction: To 5,000 words. Literary fiction.
- Other: Poetry, no line limits; limit 6 poems per submission.

Sample Issue

128 pages. Little advertising. Article and story excerpts and guidelines available at website.

- "The Story You Gave Me." Short story.
- "Family Fest." An account of a Smoky Mountain event, The Gaither Gospel Song Fest.

Rights and Payment

First rights. No payment. Provides 1–5 contributor's copies and a 1-volume subscription.

Canadian Home Workshop

54 St. Patrick Street
Toronto, Ontario M5T 1V1
Canada

Editor in Chief: Douglas Thomson

Description and Interests

Expert-written how-to articles on woodworking and home repair projects for homeowners are the mainstay of this magazine. It offers a wide variety of projects suited to skill levels from beginner to advanced. Product reviews are also featured. It seeks writers who have not only the know-how, but also the ability to show-how, and prefers do-it-yourself projects that are geared toward average homeowners rather than professionally trained craftsmen. Circ: 90,000.

Contents: 70% articles; 30% depts/columns
Frequency: 6 times each year
Website: www.canadianhomeworkshop.com

Freelance Potential

85% written by nonstaff writers. Publishes 20 freelance submissions yearly; 5% by unpublished writers, 10% by authors who are new to the magazine, 80% by experts. Receives 20 queries monthly.

Submissions

Query with photos. Accepts email queries to editorial@canadianhomeworkshop.com (Word attachments). Responds in 1 month.

- Articles: Word lengths vary. Informational, how-to, profiles, and interviews. Topics include woodworking skills and techniques, project ideas, home improvement, joinery, and finishing.
- Depts/columns: Staff-written.

Sample Issue

68 pages. Advertising. Sample articles and guidelines available at website.

- "A Head of the Game." How to build a headboard from wood, foam, and fabric that will give your bedroom an instant facelift.
- "Hand Saws Put to the Test." Reviews of four different hand saws by readers who actually tried them out.

Rights and Payment

First North American serial rights for 1 year and electronic rights. Written material, payment rates vary. Pays on acceptance. Provides 3 contributor's copies.

The Canadian Organic Grower

39 McArthur Avenue, Level 1–3
Ottawa, Ontario K1L 8L7
Canada

Editor: Beth McMahon

Description and Interests
This magazine strives to be Canada's voice for organic food and growing alternatives. It provides a variety of information for farmers, gardeners, and consumers, including research, techniques, personal experiences, and profiles. It seeks articles on innovative and creative ways to grow food organically, as well as profiles of interesting and successful Canadian organic farms. Circ: 2,500.

Contents: Articles; depts/columns
Frequency: 3 times each year
Website: www.cog.ca/our-services/magazine/cog-magazine

Freelance Potential
95% written by nonstaff writers. Publishes 25 freelance submissions yearly; 10% by unpublished writers, 10% by authors who are new to the magazine. Receives 8 queries monthly.

Submissions
Query. Accepts email submissions to editor@cog.ca. Books reviews, send email to library@cog.ca. Response time varies.

- Articles: 1,200–2,000 words. Informational, how-to, research, profiles, interviews, and personal experience. Topics includes organic gardening and farming, sustainable agriculture, research, Canadian organic growers, cooking organic food.
- Depts/columns: Book reviews.
- Art: High resolution digital images.

Sample Issue
66 pages. Sample articles and guidelines available at website.

- "Ground Cherries." Profile of this little-known vegetable and how to grow it.
- "Raising Pigs on Rotational Pastures." A primer for pig raising using the technique of keeping them in fields that are being rested from crop growing.

Rights and Payment
First North American serial rights. Articles, $100–$200. Opinion pieces and book reviews, no payment. Pays on publication.

Canadian Rodeo News

272245 RR 2
Airdrie, Alberta T4A 2L5
Canada

Editor: Jim Pippolo

Description and Interests
This official publication of the Canadian Professional Rodeo Association covers the news, history, and personalities of the sport. It also features competition results and tour information. Writers are encouraged to query first to ensure that a story is appropriate for the publication and that it is not already assigned. Circ: 2,000.

Contents: 30% articles; 20% depts/columns; 50% other
Frequency: Monthly
Website: www.rodeocanada.com

Freelance Potential
90% written by nonstaff writers. Publishes 80 freelance submissions yearly; 25% by unpublished writers, 5% by authors who are new to the magazine, 15% by experts. Receives 1 query monthly.

Submissions
Query or send complete ms. Accepts hard copy, email to editor@rodeocanada.com, and simultaneous submissions if identified. SAE/IRC. Responds in 1 month.

- Articles: 500–1,200 words. Informational, how-to, personal experience, and profiles. Topics include contestants, stock contractors, individual rodeos, rodeo heritage, and association news.
- Depts/columns: Staff-written.
- Artwork: 4x6 or larger B/W or color prints.

Sample Issue
32 pages. Advertising. Sample copy and guidelines available.

- "Get Smart Carries Another Bronc Rider to Top at Strathmore." Article reports on results at the Strathmore's saddle bronc riding event.
- "Lethbridge Whoop-Up Days Offers Something for Everyone." Article describes the activities at the annual Whoop-Up Days Pro Rodeo.

Rights and Payment
All rights. Articles, $30–$60 Canadian. Pays on publication. Provides 1 contributor's copy.

Canoe & Kayak Magazine

236 Avenida Fabricante, Suite 201
San Clemente, CA 92672

Managing Editor: Dave Shively

Description and Interests

Each issue of this magazine is packed with canoe and kayak destination pieces, the latest paddling techniques, expert reviews of paddle and camping gear, and family paddling tips. Writers must have experience canoeing, kayaking, and rafting. Circ: 50,000.

Contents: 60% articles; 30% depts/columns; 10% other
Frequency: 6 times each year
Website: www.canoekayak.com

Freelance Potential

90% written by nonstaff writers. Publishes 25 freelance submissions yearly; 5% by unpublished writers, 25% by authors who are new to the magazine, 90% by experts. Receives 10 queries monthly.

Submissions

Query with photo availability and writing experience. Accepts email queries to appropriate editor; see guidelines for breakdown. Responds in 6–8 weeks.

- Articles: 400–2,000 words. Informational, how-to, personal experience, and profiles. Topics include destinations, techniques, boat news and trends, retailer, outfitter, and manufacturer profiles.
- Depts/columns: 550–750 words. Personalities, adventures, trends, and gear updates.

Sample Issue

82 pages. Advertising. Sample articles and guidelines available at website.

- "The Wilderness Classroom." A couple's 11,700-mile North American paddle trip.
- "Stopping the Susitna." A proposal to dam Alaska's Susitna River is resurrected.

Rights and Payment

All rights. Written material, $.50 per word. Pays on publication. Provides 1 contributor's copy.

Capper's

1503 SW 42nd Street
Topeka, KS 66609-1265

Editor in Chief: Katherine Compton

Description and Interests

Capper's celebrates rural life with practical and inspirational features. It focuses on family gardening and farming, while also offering nostalgia pieces and reflections on the joys of country life. It does not publish fiction or poetry. Circ: 100,000.

Contents: 50% articles; 50% depts/columns
Frequency: 6 times each year
Website: www.cappers.com

Freelance Potential

90% written by nonstaff writers. Publishes 40–50 freelance submissions yearly; 50% by unpublished writers, 70% by authors who are new to the magazine. Receives 40 queries and unsolicited mss each month.

Submissions

All articles are assigned. Query via email to cregan@grit.com. Send complete manuscript for Heart of the Home column, attention Traci Smith or email to tsmith@ogdenpubs.com. Responds to queries in 1 month.

- Articles: 800–1,500 words. Informational, how-to, historical, inspirational, and nostalgia. Topics include rural living, farming, gardening, livestock, cooking, do-it-yourself, machinery, tools, community, and seasonal.
- Depts/columns: 500–1,500 words. Country Tech; Looking Back; In the Shop, farm items; Comfort Foods; Recipe Box; In the Wild, rural wildlife; Sow Hoe, Heart of the Home, humorous, heartwarming, reader-written stories, to 300 words.
- Artwork: Photos, JPEGs at 300 dpi.

Sample Issue

96 pages. Advertising. Sample articles available on website.

- "10 Easy Plants to Grow." Easy-to-grow plants for those who lack a green thumb.
- "A Bounty to Buzz About." The importance of pollinators for the home garden.

Rights and Payment

Shared rights. Written material, payment rates vary. Pays on publication. Provides 2 contributor's copies.

The Carousel News & Trader

11001 Peoria Street
Sun Valley, CA 91352

Editor: Roland Hopkins

Description and Interests

Carousels from the past and the present are featured in this magazine, along with artist and carver profiles, historical and restoration information, and lots of photography. It serves an international audience of carousel enthusiasts. It is interested in hearing about carousel events, historical facts, auction information, and any other happenings that are related to carousels. Circ: 2,500.

Contents: 80% articles; 20% depts/columns
Frequency: Monthly
Website: www.carouselnews.com

Freelance Potential

50% written by nonstaff writers. Publishes 25 freelance submissions yearly; 5% by unpublished writers, 10% by authors who are new to the magazine. Receives 2–5 queries and unsolicited mss each month.

Submissions

Query with bibliography; or send complete ms with artwork. Accepts hard copy and simultaneous submissions if identified. SASE. Responds in 1–2 months.

- Articles: Word lengths vary. Informational and profiles. Topics include carousels, band organs, amusement parks, history, collecting, carvers, art.
- Depts/columns: Staff-written.
- Artwork: 3x5 or 4x6 B/W or color prints.

Sample Issue

46 pages. Advertising. Sample articles available at website. Guidelines available.

- "Rich History at Hersheypark, PA and PTC #47." A look at the 1919 carousel in Hersheypark and the beautifully carved horses thought to be done by master carver, John Zalar.
- "Hawaii's 'Aloha Carousel' Project Underway." Details of a new carousel being built in Hawaii.

Rights and Payment

Rights negotiable. All material, payment rates vary. Pays on publication. Provides 1 contributor's copy.

Catholic Answers

2020 Gillespie Way
El Cajon, CA 92020-0407

Acquisitions Editor: Todd Aglialoro

Description and Interests

Formerly titled *This Rock*, this magazine of Catholic Apologetics and evangelization features articles that explore and support the teachings of the Catholic Church. It aims to give its readers the tools to defend the tenets of the Catholic faith, promote authentic teachings of the Church, and present ways to spread God's truth. Circ: 15,000.

Contents: 50% articles; 50% depts/columns
Frequency: 6 times each year
Website: www.catholic.com

Freelance Potential

50% written by nonstaff writers. Publishes 6–8 freelance submissions yearly; 5% by unpublished writers, 10% by authors who are new to the magazine, 80% by experts. Receives 1–2 unsolicited mss monthly.

Submissions

Send complete ms. Accepts email submissions to catholicanswersmagazine@catholic.com (include "Feature article" or "Conversion story" in subject field). Responds in 1 month.

- Articles: To 2,000 words. Informational, how-to, and personal experience. Topics include religion, church history, multicultural and ethnic issues, liturgical music, social issues, feminism, and education.
- Depts/columns: Word lengths vary. Personal stories of conversion to the Catholic faith.

Sample Issue

48 pages. Sample articles and guidelines available at website.

- "Contraception's Dark Fruits." Arguments to support the Catholic Church's position against birth control.
- "The Truth About 2012." Dispels the doom warnings that something significant is going to happen to the world on December 21, 2012.

Rights and Payment

First print and perpetual electronic rights. Damascus Road, $200. Pays on acceptance. Provides 2 contributor's copies.

Catholic Digest

P.O. Box 6015
New London, CT 06320

Assistant Editor: Kathryn Oates

Description and Interests

Since its beginning in 1936, *Catholic Digest* has used stories of real people to demonstrate that a life guided by faith can be exciting, enlivening, and joyous. Informational articles and personal stories of faith fill its pages, along with meaningful ways to connect faith with everyday life, and tips for strengthening family ties and friendships. Previously published professional writers may query with clips. Circ: 285,000..

Contents: 67% articles; 33% depts/columns
Frequency: 9 times each year
Website: www.catholicdigest.com

Freelance Potential

45% written by nonstaff writers. Publishes 100–200 freelance submissions yearly; 10–15% by authors new to the magazine. Receives 400 unsolicited mss monthly.

Submissions

Previously published writers may query with 1–2 published clips. Accepts email only to queries@-catholicdigest.com. Accepts complete manuscripts for Last Word and Open Door only to opendoor@-catholicdigest.com (no attachments). No simultaneous submissions. Responds if interested in 2–3 weeks.

- Articles: To 1,500 words. Informational, profiles, and personal experience pieces. Topics include marriage, practical spirituality, parish/work, parenting, grandparenting, homemaking, relationships, and good works.
- Depts/columns: Last Word, personal essay, 550–700 words; Open Door, true, personal experience pieces about converting to the Catholic faith or recovering faith that has been lost, 350–600 words.
- Artwork: JPEG files at 300 dpi.

Sample Issue

128 pages. Advertising. Sample articles and guidelines available at website.

- "Martyrs, Heroes, and Rebels: For Greater Glory." The story of the 1920s Cristero War as told in a new movie.
- "A Q&A with Bear Grylls, Adventurer." A conversation with this TV personality.

Rights and Payment

First rights. Articles, $500. Open Door, $100. Pays on publication. Provides 1 contributor's copy.

CCM Magazine

402 BNA Drive, Suite 400
Nashville, TN 37217

Editor: Caroline Lusk

Description and Interests

CCM stands for Christ, Community, Music, summing up what this publication is about. Readers of this ezine find information about all kinds of Christian music, from gospel and country to hip-hop and rock. The site profiles recording artists and reviews albums and events. It also features some articles on Christian culture. Real knowledge of Christian music is a must to write for this publication. Authors who have access to a Christian musician and are able to obtain an interview, should query. Hits per month: 1 million.

Contents: 60% articles; 40% depts/columns
Frequency: Daily
Website: www.ccmmagazine.com

Freelance Potential

90% written by nonstaff writers. Publishes 200 freelance submissions yearly; 5% by unpublished writers, 10% by authors who are new to the magazine, 75% by experts. Receives 8 queries monthly.

Submissions

Query. Accepts hard copy. SASE. Response time varies.

- Articles: 1,200–3,000 words. Informational, profiles, interviews, and new product information. Topics include Christian rock, hip-hop, hardcore, country, gospel, and other musical genres; and Christian musicians, songwriters, and producers.
- Depts/columns: 700–1,000 words. News, trends, personal essays. Music and book reviews, 300 words.

Sample Issue

70 pages. Advertising. Sample copy available at website.

- "Mark Schultz: Man on a Mission." Musician Mark Schultz talks about the birth of his own son and his work to help widows and orphans.
- "Getting to Know You." Profiles of the winners of the "Create New Artists Search 2012."

Rights and Payment

First and electronic rights. Articles, $100. Reviews, $40. Pays on publication.

CelticLife

P.O. Box 8805, Station A
Halifax, Novia Scotia B3K 5M4
Canada

Editor: Carol Moreira

Description and Interests

This magazine was created to celebrate the living culture of the Seven Celtic Nations. Written for international readers, its topics include Celtic history, language, culture, traditions, music, and folklore. It is always interested in hearing about the history and achievements of various Celtic people. Circ: 171,242.

Contents: Articles; depts/columns; other
Frequency: Quarterly
Website: www.celticlife.ca

Freelance Potential

40% written by nonstaff writers. Publishes 14–20 freelance submissions yearly; 20% by unpublished writers, 20% by authors who are new to the magazine, 40% by experts. Receives 20 queries monthly.

Submissions

Query. Accepts email queries to editor@-celticlife.ca (Word attachments). Responds in 1 month.

- Articles: 600–2,500 words. Informational, profiles, interviews, personal experience, and opinion. Topics include Celtic heritage, traditions, music, dance, history, travel, leisure, clans, and associations.
- Depts/columns: Word lengths vary. Reviews.

Sample Issue

92 pages. Advertising. Sample articles available at website. Guidelines available.

- "Celtic and Gaelic Studies." A high school teacher shares the surprisingly enthusiastic response she received from students in trying to form a Gaelic Society at her school.
- "True Colours." A look at early Celtic tattooing from the first to fourth centuries.

Rights and Payment

First North American serial rights. Payment varies. Pays on publication. Provides 1 contributor's copy.

Cessna Owner

N7450 Aanstad Road
P.O. Box 5000
Iola, WI 54945-5000

Editor: Keith Mathiowetz

Description and Interests

Filled with valuable information for anyone who owns a Cessna, this magazine focuses on aircraft maintenance, flying tips, storage advice, and destinations. Certified pilots and flight instructors supply the bulk of the freelance articles. Circ: 5,000.

Contents: 60% articles; 20% depts/columns; 20% other
Frequency: Monthly
Website: www.cessnaowner.org

Freelance Potential

80% written by nonstaff writers. Publishes 20–30 freelance submissions yearly; 10% by unpublished writers, 10% by authors who are new to the magazine, 80% by experts. Receives 15 queries monthly.

Submissions

Query. Prefers email queries to editor@cessnaowner.org (attach file); will accept hard copy. SASE. Responds in 2 months.

- Articles: 1,000–1,500 words. Informational, how-to, profiles, interviews, and personal experience. Topics include aircraft maintenance and technology, nostalgia, travel, and leisure.
- Depts/columns: 800–1,400 words. Opinion pieces, advice, aircraft- and air travel-related news, new product information.

Sample Issue

80 pages. Advertising. Sample copy and editorial calendar available at website. Guidelines available.

- "Fighting Rust and Corrosion." How to extend the life of an airplane by understanding and treating the various kinds of rust.
- "Shaking All Over." How to correct gear vibration and nose landing problems.

Rights and Payment

First rights. Written material, payment rates vary. Pays on publication. Provides 3–5 contributor's copies.

Chatelaine

1 Mount Pleasant Road
Toronto, Ontario M4Y 2Y5
Canada

Editor in Chief: Jane Francisco

Description and Interests
This magazine for Canadian women covers topics that run the gamut from investigative reports and controversial health stories to articles on work, women's issues, decor, fashion, and beauty. It features the works of many award-winning writers, but will also review submissions from new writers. Circ: 704,466.

Contents: Articles; depts/columns
Frequency: Monthly
Website: www.chatelaine.com

Freelance Potential
70% written by nonstaff writers. Publishes 350 freelance submissions yearly; 5% by authors who are new to the magazine. Receives 200 queries monthly.

Submissions
Query with 1–2 clips. Accepts email queries to storyideas@chatelaine.rogers.com (indicate in subject line whether query is for magazine or website). Responds in 1 month.

- Articles: Word lengths vary. Informational, self-help, how-to, profiles, interviews, and personal experience. Topics include health, fitness, beauty, fashion, nutrition, cooking, relationships, home decor, travel, and lifestyle issues.
- Depts/columns: Word lengths vary. Health updates, career profiles, expert advice, new product information, travel tips, and recipes.

Sample Issue
266 pages. Advertising. Sample articles and guidelines available at website.

- "Boost Your Mood and Improve Health with Seven Easy Tips." From dark chocolate to some time with a furry friend, simple acts to help you feel better instantly.
- "Modern Woman's Guide to Investing in the Stock Market." A beginner's guide to investing in the market presented in an entertaining and savvy manner.

Rights and Payment
First North American serial and website rights. Written material, payment rates vary. Payment policy varies.

Chess Life

United States Chess Foundation
P.O. Box 3967
Crossville, TN 38557

Editor: Daniel Lucas

Description and Interests
For more than 40 years, the U.S. Chess Federation has been publishing this magazine for players of all ages. Each issue includes instruction on playing strategies for novices through titled players, as well as reports on tournaments around the globe. It welcomes articles about chess in everyday life and player profiles. Circ: 80,000.

Contents: 66% articles; 34% depts/columns
Frequency: Monthly
Website: www.uschess.org

Freelance Potential
75% written by nonstaff writers. Publishes 30 freelance submissions yearly; 30% by unpublished writers, 15% by authors who are new to the magazine, 80% by experts. Receives 15–35 queries monthly.

Submissions
Query with clips or writing samples. Prefers email to dlucas@uschess.org; will accept hard copy. SASE. Responds in 2 weeks.

- Articles: 800–3,000 words. Informational, how-to, historical, profiles, humor, personal experience, and opinion. Topics include chess games and strategies, tournaments and events, and personalities in the game.
- Depts/columns: To 1,000 words. Profiles, how-to's, and reviews.
- Artwork: B/W or color prints.
- Other: Cartoons, puzzles, quizzes, and filler.

Sample Issue
72 pages. Advertising. Sample copy and guidelines available.

- "The April Check is in the Mail." Analysis of the tie reached in the 2011 Michigan State Championship.
- "Aloha Trophies: The 2012 Hawaii State Scholastics." Activities of the Hawaii Chess Federation.

Rights and Payment
All rights. Written material, $100 per published page. Artwork, $15–$100. Kill fee, 30%. Pays on publication. Provides 2 contributor's copies.

Children's Writer

Institute of Children's Literature
93 Long Ridge Road
West Redding, CT 06896-0811

Editor: Susan Tierney

Description and Interests

Children's Writer is a newsletter for writers, now available in an electronic edition, that reports on and analyzes trends in children's book and magazine publishing. It covers all categories, from picture books through novels, and magazines for all ages. The Marketplace section highlights news of the publishing industry and publisher needs. Other sections offer information on business issues, writing techniques, motivation, and research. Circ: 10,000.

Contents: 50% articles; 50% depts/columns
Frequency: Monthly
Website: www.childrenswriter.com

Freelance Potential

90% written by nonstaff writers. Publishes 75 freelance submissions yearly; 10% by unpublished writers, 15% by authors who are new to the magazine. Receives 5+ queries monthly.

Submissions

Query with detailed outline, potential length, potential sources, and proposed submission date. Prefers email query to cwtierney@ChildrensWriter.com, and attachments (Word). Accepts disk submissions with hard copy. Accepts simultaneous submissions if identified. SASE. Responds in 1 month.

- Articles: 1,700–2,000 words. Informational, analytical, how-to, and interviews. Topics include children's book and magazine publishing trends, new markets, genres, writing techniques and craft, and career.
- Depts/columns: To 750 words, plus 125-word sidebar. Writing techniques, business issues, commentary, technology, research strategies, motivation, and editor and publisher profiles.

Sample Issue

12 pages. No advertising. Sample copy available. Guidelines available at website.

- "Make Your Novel a Page-Turner." Ask the right questions to keep young readers intrigued.
- "It Sounds Like a Picture Book." The aural and lyrical qualities that make a picture book work.

Rights and Payment

First North American serial rights. Articles, $300. Depts/columns, $200. Pays on publication.

The Christian Century

104 South Michigan Avenue, Suite 1100
Chicago, IL 60603

Executive Editor: David Helm

Description and Interests

The Christian Century is a progressive, ecumenical magazine that explores what it means to believe in and live out the Christian faith in our time. It is read primarily by pastors and senior leaders of the church. It seeks articles that articulate the public meaning of faith, bringing the resources of religious tradition to bear on contemporary topics. Circ: 36,000.

Contents: 50% articles; 50% depts/columns
Frequency: 26 times each year
Website: www.christiancentury.org

Freelance Potential

70% written by nonstaff writers. Publishes 100 freelance submissions yearly; 10% by unpublished writers, 10% by authors who are new to the magazine.

Submissions

Query. Accepts email queries to submissions@christiancentury.org. Send poetry via email to poetry@christiancentury.org. Writers interested in writing book reviews can mail a résumé and list of subject interests (with "Attn: Book Reviews" on envelope). Responds in 4–6 weeks.

- Articles: 3,000 words. Informational, profiles, interviews, personal experience, opinion, and creative nonfiction. Topics include religion, faith, human rights, social justice, politics, current events, international relations, and popular culture.
- Depts/columns: Staff-written.
- Other: Poetry, to 20 lines.

Sample Issue

48 pages. Advertising. Sample articles and guidelines available at website.

- "Worship Without Walls." Explores the experience of worship by participating in liturgical services in public places.
- "Soup Night at the Bar." Chicago bar owner talks about the free community soup and bread meal she offers.

Rights and Payment

All rights. Articles, $150. Depts/columns, $75. Pays on publication. Provides 1 author's copy.

Christian Communicator

P.O. Box 110390
Nashville, TN 37222-0390

Managing Editor: Lin Johnson

Description and Interests

This magazine focuses on the how-to's of writing and speaking for those working in the Christian market. This includes writing in different genres, creativity, researching, and public speaking. It also features information on the writing market and reviews of books that pertain to writing and publishing. Circ: 3,000.

Contents: 50% articles; 50% depts/columns
Frequency: 11 times each year
Website: www.acwriters.com

Freelance Potential

50% written by nonstaff writers. Publishes 50–60 freelance submissions yearly; 1% by unpublished writers, 49% by authors who are new to the magazine, 50% by experts. Receives 10 queries, 20 unsolicited mss monthly.

Submissions

Query or send complete ms, with author bio. Accepts email to ljohnson@wordprocommunications.com. Responds in 3 months.

- Articles: 650–1,000 words. Informational, self-help, how-to, profiles, interviews. Topics include publishing, freelancing, creativity, research, genres, submissions procedures, editorial needs, marketing, public speaking, writers conferences.
- Depts/columns: 75–650 words. The Heart of a Communicator, first-person essays on spiritual struggles of the creative process; A Funny Thing Happened on the Way to Becoming a Communicator, reviews (query first).
- Other: Poetry, about writing/communicating, to 20 lines; submit via email to Sally Miller at sallymiller@ameritech.net.

Sample Issue

20 pages. Advertising. Guidelines available at website.

- "Writing With an International Flavor." Choosing words and illustrations that communicate across cultures and in foreign translations.
- "Citation Sightings." How to document your sources correctly.

Rights and Payment

First and reprint rights. Articles, $10. Book reviews, poetry, $5. Pays on publication. Provides 2 contributor's copies.

Christian Home & School

Christian Schools International
3350 East Paris Avenue SE
Grand Rapids, MI 49512

Managing Editor: Rachael Heyboer

Description and Interests

Christian parents read this magazine for articles on education, parenting, and matters related to Christian schooling. Articles must have real-world applications to education and offer a mature, biblical perspective. *Christian Home & School* is a publication of Christian Schools International. It plans to introduce an online format sometime in 2013. Refer to the editorial calendar for upcoming needs. Circ: 66,000.

Contents: Articles; depts/columns
Frequency: Twice each year, plus special high school issue
Website: www.csionline.org/chs

Freelance Potential

90% written by nonstaff writers. Publishes 12–15 freelance submissions yearly; 50–75% by unpublished writers, 10–25% by authors who are new to the magazine. Receives 25–50 queries, 1–10 unsolicited mss monthly.

Submissions

Send complete ms. Accepts hard copy or email to rheyboer@csionline.org (Word attachments). No simultaneous submissions. SASE. Responds in 4–6 weeks.

- Articles: 1,000–2,000 words. Informational, how-to, inspirational, and personal experience. Topics include education, parenting, life skills, decision-making, discipline, travel, faith, children's health, tutoring, learning difficulties, and standardized testing, all from a Christian perspective.
- Depts/columns: Parent Stuff, 100–250 words. Reviews and parenting tips.

Sample Issue

40 pages. Advertising. Sample copy, guidelines, and editorial calendar available at website.

- "When Perfection and Homework Collide." Changing the mindset of children with unrealistic expectations.
- "Celebrating Christian Education." The differences between Christian education and other forms of teaching.

Rights and Payment

First rights. Written material, $50–$300. Pays on publication. Provides 3 contributor's copies.

Christian Science Monitor

210 Massachusetts Avenue
Boston, MA 02115

Editor: John Yemma

Description and Interests

This newspaper covers national and international news and issues. It also offers personal stories and essays. Its modus operandi is to step back from a news story and analyze, sum up, and look ahead. It also accepts poetry for the Home Forum section. Circ: 80,000.

Contents: 65% articles; 20% depts/columns; 15% other
Frequency: Weekly
Website: www.csmonitor.com

Freelance Potential

35% written by nonstaff writers. Publishes 1,000 freelance submissions yearly; 40% by unpublished writers, 30% by authors who are new to the magazine, 30% by experts. Receives 50 queries, 50 unsolicited mss monthly.

Submissions

Query for new articles. Send complete ms for depts/columns. Accepts email submissions. See guidelines for appropriate editor's email address and specific submission requirements. Responds in 3–4 weeks if interested.

- Articles: 600–1,000 words. Informational articles, personal experience pieces, and humor. Topics include U.S. and international news, culture, nature, the environment, and family.
- Depts/columns: 400–1,000 words. Opinion, reviews, poems, and essays for Home Forum.

Sample Issue

20 pages. Advertising. Sample articles and guidelines available at website.

- "Why I Want to Retire to Smallville." The appeal of Superman's hometown as a retirement haven.
- Sample Dept/Column: One Minute Debate offers three opinions on whether states should legalize marijuana.

Rights and Payment

Worldwide exclusive and all newspaper rights. Articles, $200–$225. Depts/columns, payment varies. Home Forum, no payment. Kill fee, 50%. Pays on publication. Provides 1 author's copy.

The Chronicle of the Horse

P.O. Box 46
Middleburg, VA 20118

Editor: Beth Rasin

Description and Interests

Equestrian competitions, including dressage, hunters and jumpers, foxhunting, and steeplechase racing, are covered in detail here. The publication also offers features on grooming, equine health and riding techniques, along with horse and rider profiles. Circ: 16,000.

Contents: 80% articles; 20% depts/columns
Frequency: 40 times each year
Website: www.chronofhorse.com

Freelance Potential

80% written by nonstaff writers. Publishes 200 freelance submissions yearly; 10% by unpublished writers, 10% by authors who are new to the magazine, 50% by experts. Receives 10 queries, 5 unsolicited mss monthly.

Submissions

Query. Accepts email queries: news articles to results@chronofhorse.com; feature stories to bethr@chronofhorse.com. Responds in 1–2 months.

- Articles: 1,500–2,500 words. Informational, how-to, historical, profiles, interviews, humor, and personal experience. Topics include horse care, training, breeding, dressage, foxhunting, steeplechase racing, trail riding, equine activities for youth, horse shows and competitions, and personalities.
- Depts/columns: Staff-written.
- Artwork: Color prints; digital images at 300 dpi.

Sample Issue

116 pages. Sample copy available at website. Guidelines available.

- "Bandaging a Hoof Doesn't Have to Be Hard." Teaches and offers tips for this necessary but tricky job.
- "Olivier Philippaerts Becomes Youngest Winner of $1,021,711 CN International Grand Prix." The big news story from this horse show.

Rights and Payment

First North American serial rights. Articles, $150–$200. Pays on publication for news; on acceptance for features. Provides 1 author's copy.

Cigar Aficionado

387 Park Avenue
New York, NY 10016

Executive Editor: Gordon Mott

Description and Interests

Now celebrating its 20th anniversary, *Cigar Aficionado,* is a magazine for men who enjoy the best life has to offer. Despite its name, the magazine offers features on a wide variety of topics, including cigars, travel, entertainment, dining, and cars. Celebrity profiles are also included. New writers have the best chance with the Good Life Guide section. Circ: 300,000.

Contents: 60% articles; 40% depts/columns
Frequency: 6 times each year
Website: www.cigaraficionado.com

Freelance Potential

75% written by nonstaff writers. Publishes 80–100 freelance submissions yearly; 5–10% by unpublished writers, 20% by authors who are new to the magazine, 2% by experts. Receives 30 queries monthly.

Submissions

Query. Accepts hard copy. SASE. Responds in 6 weeks.

- Articles: 2,000 words. Informational, how-to, personal experience, profiles, and interviews. Topics include cigars, personalities, sports, gambling, fine automobiles, luxury goods, collectibles, drinks, fashion, travel, recreation, and lifestyles.
- Depts/columns: 1,000 words. Politics, culture, sports, investing.

Sample Issue

160 pages. Advertising. Sample articles available at website. Guidelines available.

- "Hawaiian Cigars?." Profile of Kauai cigar maker, Les Drent, the man who brought tobacco growing to Hawaii and details of the cigar he's attempting to create.
- "The Story Behind QB Ratings." Reports on the somewhat skewed system of ranking professional football players.
- Sample dept/column: Good Life Guide tells what it's like to have a celebrity chef in your kitchen.

Rights and Payment

World rights. Written material, payment rates vary. Kill fee, 25%. Pays 30 days after acceptance. Provides 2 contributor's copies.

Cigar & Spirits

Editorial Assistant: Audrey Abbott

Description and Interests

For the first time in the publishing industry, luxury cigars and spirits are covered under one title. This new magazine is tailored to the upscale man or woman who believes there is nothing in life like a great cigar, your spirit of choice, and good company. Reviews of top-of-the-line brands, industry news, and related lifestyle topics fill the magazine's pages. Circ: Unavailable.

Contents: Articles; depts/columns
Frequency: 6 times each year
Website: www.cigarandspirits.com

Freelance Potential

Receives many freelance submissions monthly.

Submissions

Query. Accepts email queries to audrey@cigarandspirits.com.

- Articles: Word lengths vary. Informational and how-to articles, and profiles. Topics include cigar brands, spirits, restaurants, nightlife, travel, and industry leaders.
- Depts/columns: Word lengths vary. Industry news, profiles, and luxury goods.

Sample Issue

Advertising. Sample copy available at website.

- "Charlie Sheen" Article features a profile of the actor and his tastes in cigars and spirits.
- "Ways to Season Your Humidor." Article includes tips for properly seasoning a humidor.
- "Sample dept/column: Spirits explains the Kentucky Derby traditional drink, Mint Julep.

Rights and Payment

Rights vary. Payment rates and policy vary.

Cineaste

243 Fifth Avenue, Suite 706
New York, NY 10016

Editor in Chief: Gary Crowdus

Description and Interests

Targeting sophisticated readers interested in art and politics, *Cineaste* offers a social, political, and esthetic perspective on cinema. Each issue includes features, interviews, and film and book reviews. It covers all areas of cinema, including old and current Hollywood, independent films, and the cinema of Europe and developing countries. Circ: 12,000.

Contents: 50% articles; 25% depts/columns; 25% other
Frequency: Quarterly
Website: www.cineaste.com

Freelance Potential

40% written by nonstaff writers. Publishes 50–60 freelance submissions yearly; 5% by authors who are new to the magazine. Receives 30 queries, 25 unsolicited mss monthly.

Submissions

Prefers query; will accept complete ms. Send submission with clips. Accepts hard copy and email submissions to cineaste@cineaste.com (Word attachments). No simultaneous submissions. SASE. Responds in 2–3 weeks.

- Articles: 3,000–4,000 words. Informational, profiles, interviews, opinions. Topics include film genres, theory, movements, production trends, career overviews, actors, directors, screenwriters.
- Depts/columns: 1,000–1,500 words. A Second Look, new take on a classic film; Lost and Found, review of films not likely to be seen in the U.S.; film reviews; book reviews, capsule reviews, 300–400 words.

Sample Issue

88 pages. Advertising. Sample articles and guidelines available at website.

- "The Invisible War Within the Military: An Interview with Kirby Dick." Interview with documentary filmmaker and his latest subject.
- "From 35mm to DCP: A Critical Symposium on the Changing Face of Motion Picture Exhibition." A look at the changes brought about by the advent of digital filming and its effect on cinema.

Rights and Payment

All rights. Articles, $100+. Depts/columns, $20–$50. Kill fee, 50%. Pays on publication. Provides 1 contributor's copy.

Classic Images

301 East Third Street
Muscatine, IA 52761

Editor: Bob King

Description and Interests

Classic Images caters to its audience of classic film buffs and collectors with the information they seek as part of their hobby, such as actor profiles, film history articles, and information on new video releases and film festivals. Writers should have a strong knowledge of the film industry. Circ: 7,000.

Contents: 80% articles; 20% depts/columns
Frequency: Monthly
Website: www.classicimages.com

Freelance Potential

100% written by nonstaff writers. Publishes 80 freelance submissions yearly; 10% by unpublished writers, 25% by authors who are new to the magazine, 15% by experts. Receives 15 queries monthly.

Submissions

Query. Prefers email queries to classicimages@classicimages.com; will accept hard copy. SASE. Responds in 2 months.

- Articles: 1,500–3,000 words. Informational, how-to, profiles, interviews, and media reviews. Topics include the film industry, classic films, screen legends, directors, producers, technicians, craftspeople, film history, and collector items.
- Depts/columns: 500–1,000 words. News, book and film reviews, movie history.

Sample Issue

84 pages. Advertising. Sample articles available at website.

- "50 Years of Classic Images." A look back at how the publication came to be and some of the many high points of the first 50 years.
- "Stage to Screen: The Making of Gregory La Cava's *Stage Door*." How the 1936 Broadway play became a film whose reputation only improves with age.

Rights and Payment

One-time and electronic rights. No payment. Provides 3 contributor's copies.

Classic Toy Trains

21027 Crossroads Circle
P.O. Box 1612
Waukesha, WI 53187-1612

Editor: Carl Swanson

Description and Interests

This photo-filled magazine is read by model train hobbyists for how-to articles and pieces on collecting and train history. It also publishes profiles of collectors. Of special interest are articles on wiring or scenery techniques, interesting layouts, historical toy trains or accessories, how to kitbash a structure or repair a locomotive. Circ: 55,000.

Contents: 67% articles; 33% depts/columns
Frequency: 9 times each year
Website: www.classictoytrains.com

Freelance Potential

20% written by nonstaff writers. Publishes 18 freelance submissions yearly; 50% by unpublished writers, 10% by authors who are new to the magazine, 50% by experts. Receives 4 queries, 2 unsolicited mss monthly.

Submissions

Prefers query with synopsis; will accept complete ms. Accepts disk submissions (Word or text files) with hard copy and email to manuscripts@classictoytrains.com (Word attachments). If sending hard copy, mark "Manuscript Enclosed" in lower left corner of envelope. No simultaneous submissions. SASE. Responds in 2–3 months.

- Articles: 500–5,000 words. Informational, how-to articles, profiles, and interviews. Topics include model train collecting, layouts, train history, wiring techniques, scenery building, kit modifications, and toy train repair.
- Depts/columns: Word lengths vary. Reviews, techniques, tips.
- Artwork: High-quality prints, digital images, color transparencies, glossy color prints, how-to illustrations, schematics, track plans.

Sample Issue

86 pages. Advertising. Sample articles and guidelines available at website.

- "Old Trains, New Technology." Pairing the latest Lionel electronics with classic toy trains.
- "6 Tips for Getting the Most from Your Motive Power Fleet." Learning to use your diesel locomotive fleet in novel ways.

Rights and Payment

All rights. Articles, $75 per published page. Pays on acceptance. Provides 1 contributor's copy.

Clay Times

P.O. Box 100
Hamilton, VA 20159

Editor & Publisher: Polly Beach

Description and Interests

Clay artists of all levels, teachers, students, and professionals, find information on trends, tools, and techniques in this magazine. Projects, profiles of artists, and articles on marketing strategies and running a studio are also featured here. The emphasis is on practical, hands-on information about all aspects of pottery and it appreciates submissions from writers with firsthand experience about their topic. Circ: 21,000.

Contents: 70% articles; 30% depts/columns
Frequency: Quarterly
Website: www.claytimes.com

Freelance Potential

80% written by nonstaff writers. Publishes 30 freelance submissions yearly; 5% by unpublished writers, 45% by authors who are new to the magazine, 30% by experts. Receives 6 queries and unsolicited mss monthly.

Submissions

Query with 2 clips or send complete ms. Accepts hard copy, disk submissions, and email to claytimes@gmail.com (Word files and attachments if using Mac, RTF files if using PC). Availability of artwork improves chance of acceptance. SASE. Responds in 1 month.

- Articles: 1,500–2,500 words. Informational, how-to, profiles. Topics include accomplished potters and their work, techniques, glazing, projects.
- Depts/columns: 500–1,000 words. Tips, classes, teaching techniques, tools, studio safety, media reviews, opinions.
- Artwork: Prints or slides; JPEG, TIFF, or PDF images at 300 dpi.

Sample Issue

50 pages. Advertising. Sample copy and guidelines available at website.

- "The Hare-Raising Secrets of Vince Sansone." A look at this artist's work and how his favorite subject has led him on different creative paths.
- Sample dept/column: "Studio Health and Safety" presents FAQ's on glaze.

Rights and Payment

All rights. Articles, $75. Depts/columns, payment rates vary. Artwork, $5–$12. Pays 45 days after publication. Provides 1 contributor's copy.

Clear

433 North Washington Avenue
Royal Oak, MI 48067

Creative Director/Editor: Emin Kadi

Description and Interests
Clear, a digital magazine available as an iPad app, describes itself as "the ultimate curator" of interesting items, objects, and ideas. Each themed issue presents the latest trends in fashion, design, art, and architecture to an upscale, sophisticated audience. It aims to appeal to all five of the reader's senses, while seamlessly bridging the gap between the indie and the classic publication. *Clear* wants articles that are intriguing to the individual who is looking for something different. It is open to material in a myriad of media. Circ: 110,000.

Contents: Articles; depts/columns
Frequency: Quarterly
Website: www.clearmag.com

Freelance Potential
60% written by nonstaff writers. Publishes 40 freelance submissions yearly; 5% by unpublished writers, 20% by authors who are new to the magazine. Receives 40 queries monthly.

Submissions
Query with relevant clips. Accepts email pitches to info@clearmag.com. Responds in 3 months.

- Articles: Word lengths vary. Informational, profiles, interviews, photo-essays, and new product information. Topics include the arts, architecture, home décor, fashion, and product and package design.
- Depts/columns: Word lengths vary. Product, media, and art reviews.

Sample Issue
138 pages. Advertising. Sample issues available on iTunes and guidelines available.

- "Banksy—Myths and Legends." Article discusses a book about the iconic street artist Banksy that is really a collection of stories blending facts, myths, and legends.
- "Daphne Guinness Exhibition Opening Next Month at the Museum at FIT." Article reports on the opening of an FIT exhibition on fashion icon Daphne Guinness.

Rights and Payment
All rights. Written material, payment rates vary. Payment policy varies.

Coastal Living

2100 Lakeshore Drive
Birmingham, AL 35209

Executive Editor: Jennifer Slaton

Description and Interests
Coastal Living showcases the homes, destinations, and people that are within sight, sound, taste, touch, or smell of saltwater. Its highly illustrated editorial covers home and design, cuisine, travel, environmental stewardship, and healthy living. It is interested in seeing more pieces on domestic travel, as well as family retreats at waterfront homes. Circ: 650,000.

Contents: 50% articles; 50% depts/columns
Frequency: 10 times each year
Website: www.coastalliving.com

Freelance Potential
50% written by nonstaff writers. Publishes few freelance submissions yearly; 1–2% by authors who are new to the magazine, 1–2% by experts. Receives 100 queries monthly.

Submissions
Query with clips; include photos for home and garden stories. Accepts hard copy and email to mamie_walling@timeinc.com. SASE. Response time varies.

- Articles: 500–1,000 words. Informational, how-to, profiles, and interviews. Topics include home decorating, organizing, building, renovation, gardening, landscaping, travel, outdoor recreation, lifestyles, dining, and entertaining.
- Depts/columns: Word lengths vary. Travel destinations, coastal homes, decorating tips, cooking and recipes, new products, and profiles.

Sample Issue
132 pages. Advertising. Sample articles available at website. Guidelines available.

- "Caribbean Colors." Ways to give your rooms new bounce with brightly colored accents that mimic turquoise waters, coral reefs, and other tropical sights.
- "Ask a Designer: Windsor Smith." California designer discusses everything about casual coastal design from colors to countertops.

Rights and Payment
All rights. Written material, $1 per word. Kill fee, 25%. Pays on acceptance.

Coast to Coast

Affinity Group, Inc.
2575 Vista Del Mar Drive
Ventura, CA 93001

Editor: Valerie Law

Description and Interests

This magazine is the membership publication for Coast to Coast Resorts. It is written for RV owners and offers articles on destinations, camping and RV resorts, recreation and leisure activities, and RV lifestyle and products. Editors are always in need of reviews of RV camping resorts for members. Read one of the current issues to see the details that are included. Circ: 60,000.

Contents: 75% articles; 25% depts/columns
Frequency: Quarterly
Website: www.coastresorts.com

Freelance Potential

80% written by nonstaff writers. Publishes 70 freelance submissions yearly; 20% by authors new to the magazine, 30% by experts. Receives 200 queries, 50 unsolicited mss monthly.

Submissions

Query with clips; or send complete ms. Accepts hard copy, disk submissions with hard copy, and email to editor@coastresorts.com. SASE. Responds in 1–2 months.

- Articles: 800–2,500 words. Informational and how-to articles, personal experience pieces, and profiles. Topics include recreational vehicles and equipment, travel destinations, and leisure activities.
- Depts/columns: 1,200–1,500 words. RV reviews, resort reports, and member news.

Sample Issue

26 pages. Advertising. Sample copy, guidelines, and theme list available.

- "Millwood Landing." Article details the offerings at this golf and RV resort located in central Arkansas.
- Sample dept/column: New & Notable reviews items to make the RVer's summer travel easier and more fun.

Rights and Payment

First North American serial rights. Articles, $75–$1,200. Depts/columns, $75–$150. Pays on acceptance. Provides contributor's copies upon request.

Collier's

1235 Westlakes Drive, Suite 320
Berwyn, PA 19312

Editor: John T. Elduff

Description and Interests

This once iconic general interest American weekly has recently been relaunched after a 55-year hiatus. Its template for engaging readers is health, wealth, and happiness. Readers will find stories on general health and well-being, advice on how to survive in the current economy, and original pieces of fiction and poetry. It welcomes submissions. Circ: Unavailable.

Contents: Articles; fiction; poems, depts/columns
Frequency: 6 times each year
Website: http://colliersmagazine.com

Freelance Potential

Freelance percentages not yet available.

Submissions

Accepts complete manuscripts via the online submission form, with author copyright release. Include a title page with article title, author name, any professional titles, and contact information; 100- to 200-word abstract; any acknowledgments; and works cited or references used (APA format). For submission-related queries, email the Editorial Director at editor@colliersmagazine.com. Submit cartoons and artwork in JPG format.

- Articles: word lengths vary. Infomational articles and reports, critical essays. Topics include culture, current events, health, the media, and economics.
- Fiction: Short shorts, to 1,000 words. Short stories, 1,000–10,000 words; longer stories may be accepted. Novels in serialized form.
- Poetry: Any length.
- Other: Cartoons, comic strips, of political or general interest.
- Artwork: Paintings, drawings, wtercolors, illutrations, photographs.

Sample Issue

Advertising. Sample issue available at website.

- "Bluster or Breakthrough." Is the medical report you heard about on TV this morning the result of a real breakthrough or a slow news day?
- "The Poetry of Nina Romano." Four poems by the two-time Pushcart Prize nominee.

Rights and Payment

Written material, payment rates vary. Pays on publication.

ColorLines

900 Alice Street, Suite 400
Oakland, CA 94607

Editorial Director: Kai Wright

Description and Interests
After years in print, *ColorLines* revamped itself as a digital magazine. Its primary goal is exposing racism through journalistic investigative reporting and news analysis and to seek solutions to it. It covers a broad range of issues, including politics, immigration reform, racial justice, and even pop culture. Hits per month: 30,000.

Contents: 65% articles; 35% depts/columns
Frequency: Updated regularly
Website: www.colorlines.com

Freelance Potential
80% written by nonstaff writers. Publishes many freelance submissions yearly; 20% by unpublished writers, 30% by authors who are new to the magazine, 50% by experts. Receives 20 queries monthly.

Submissions
Query explaining your article, why it is unique, and how it advances the discussion; include links to clips, if applicable. Accepts email queries to submissions@colorlines.com (no attachments; include "editorial query" in subject field). Responds in 3 weeks if interested.

- Articles: 1,500–2,000 words. Informational, profiles, interviews, opinion, and political commentary. Topics include social issues, current events, the arts, government, popular culture, and multicultural and ethnic issues.
- Depts/columns: To 1,500 words. Reviews, opinion pieces, news briefs, and humor.
- Artwork: Digital images at 300 dpi.

Sample Issue
Sample articles and guidelines available at website.

- "Hollywood Takes Up School Reform's Latest Agenda in 'Won't Back Down.'" A look at this film, the funding behind it, the cause and effect of its message.
- "Voting's Outcasts: Why One in Five Blacks in Kentucky Can't Cast a Ballot." How laws in this state regarding criminal records are prohibiting a segment of the population from voting.

Rights and Payment
First rights. Payment rates vary. Payment policy varies.

The Comics Journal

Fantagraphics Books, Inc.
7563 Lake City Way NE
Seattle, WA 98115

Editors: Timothy Hodler & Dan Nadel

Description and Interests
The Comics Journal, once a print magazine, has morphed into *TCJ.com*, a daily emagazine about comics. *The Comics Journal* continues to be published annually. They are both focused on the artists and impetus behind the comics. Esoteric and in-depth analysis of artists' motives and inspiration, as well as industry highlights, past and present, are featured. Hits per month: Unavailable. Print circulation: 7,000.

Contents: 30% articles; 20% depts/columns; 50% other
Frequency: Website, daily; print, annually
Website: www.tcj.com

Freelance Potential
70% written by nonstaff writers. Publishes 100 freelance submissions yearly; 5% by unpublished writers, 15% by authors who are new to the magazine, 20% by experts. Receives 50 queries, 10 unsolicited mss monthly.

Submissions
Query. Accepts email queries to editorial@tcj.com ("Submission Inquiry" in subject field). Response time varies.

- Articles: 1,000–8,750 words. Informational and profiles. Topics include successful or up-and-coming cartoonists, and all aspects of the comics industry.
- Depts/columns: 500–2,000 words. Reviews, industry news, interviews with artists, essays.

Sample Issue
208 pages. Advertising. Sample articles and guidelines available at website.

- "Before Barnaby: Crockett Johnson Grows Up and Turns Left." Traces back the life and artistic path of cartoonist David Johnson Leisk who later took the name of Crockett Johnson.
- "'I'm Trying to Be Someone Who Doesn't Understand What They're Doing': The Benjamin Marra Interview." A look at this comic artist and how his personality is inextricably and at times seemingly inexplicably bound up with his comics.

Rights and Payment
First rights. Articles and depts/columns, $.04 per word. Interviews, flat fee. Pays on publication.

Commonweal

475 Riverside Drive, Room 405
New York, NY 10115

Editor: Paul Baumann

Description and Interests
Commonweal presents itself as "a review of religion, politics, and culture." Published by Catholic laypeople, it runs features on current issues in the news, as well as media reviews, essays, and poetry. It looks for thoughtful and thought-provoking articles on topics of universal concern. Circ: 19,000.

Contents: 45% articles; 35% depts/columns; 20% other
Frequency: 22 times each year
Website: www.commonwealmagazine.org

Freelance Potential
65% written by nonstaff writers. Publishes 45 freelance submissions yearly; 5% by unpublished writers, 20% by authors who are new to the magazine, 45% by experts. Receives 20 queries monthly.

Submissions
Query with outline and résumé, or send complete ms. Accepts email submissions to editors@commonwealmagazine.org (Word attachments) and hard copy. For poetry, accepts hard copy only. SASE. No simultaneous submission. Responds in 4–6 weeks.

- Articles: 2,000–3,000 words. Informational, how-to, personal experience, and opinion. Topics include religion, politics, cultural and social issues, current events, civil liberties, and the environment.
- Depts/columns: Upfronts, interpretations of current news and headlines, 750–1,000 words. Last Word, personal essays or reflections on some aspect of the human condition, 750 words.
- Other: Poetry.

Sample Issue
38 pages. Little advertising. Guidelines and sample articles available at website. Sample copy available at newsstands.

- "Feeding the Beast." A look at how digital news transmission has transformed and even begun to shape political journalism in terms of subject matter and presentation.
- "Turning Point." Vatican II as remembered through the eyes of a theologian who participated as a young priest in 1965.

Rights and Payment
All rights. Written material, payment rates vary. Pays on publication. Provides 4 author's copies.

ComputorEdge

P.O. Box 83086
San Diego, CA 92138

Editor: Jack Dunning

Description and Interests
ComputorEdge is an online publication with both national and regional editions. It covers various informational aspects of computers, the Internet, and other digital technology. It also runs humor, fiction, and other genres with computer or Internet subjects. Feature articles must be relevant to the issue theme. It prefers a more relaxed style in writing tone. Hits per month: 120,000.

Contents: 50% articles; 50% depts/columns
Frequency: Weekly
Website: www.computoredge.com

Freelance Potential
80% written by nonstaff writers. Publishes 250 freelance submissions yearly; 10% by unpublished writers, 10% by authors who are new to the magazine, 70% by industry experts. Receives 25 queries monthly.

Submissions
Query with publishing credits and author bio. Accepts email to ceeditor@computoredge.com (include "Query" and target issue number in subject line). Responds if interested.

- Articles: 1,000–1,200 words. Informational, how-to, profiles, humor, and new product information. Topics include home computer networks, wireless access, the Internet, troubleshooting, software, hardware, operating systems, digital technology and products, and business issues.
- Depts/columns: 900 words. Mac Madness, The Linux Link.

Sample Issue
Sample copy, guidelines, and editorial calendar available at website.

- "Digital Cameras for the Neophyte Photographer." Choosing a digital camera has a lot to do with what you plan to do with the photos.
- "Windows Tips and Tricks: Disabling Annoying Windows Hotkeys." How to disable certain automatic keys to prevent unwanted actions.

Rights and Payment
Electronic publishing rights. Articles, $75. Depts/columns, $50. Pays 30 days after publication.

Confrontation

English Department
C.W. Post of Long Island University
Brookville, NY 11548

Editor in Chief: Jonna Semeiks

Description and Interests

Original works from new and established writers share the pages of this literary journal. It showcases the best in fiction, poetry, memoirs, and essays. It welcomes unique pieces from any writer, anywhere, on a variety of subjects. Circ: 2,000.

Contents: 60% fiction; 25% poetry; 15% articles
Frequency: Twice each year
Website: www.confrontationmagazine.org

Freelance Potential

85% written by nonstaff writers. Publishes 60 freelance submissions yearly; 40% by unpublished writers, 40% by authors who are new to the magazine, 20% by experts. Receives 75 queries, 300 unsolicited mss monthly.

Submissions

Send complete ms. Accepts hard copy between August 16 and May 15 only. Email submissions to confrontationmag@gmail.com accepted from writers living outside the U.S. only. Accepts simultaneous submissions if identified. SASE. Responds in 3–4 months.

- Articles: 1,000–3,000 words. Essays, opinion, and memoirs.
- Fiction: 3,000–5,000 words. Literary, contemporary, experimental, and mainstream.
- Depts/columns: Word lengths vary. Reviews.
- Other: Poetry and plays.

Sample Issue

330 pages. Little advertising. Sample copy available. Guidelines available at website.

- "Crazy for You." Short story.
- "Mufaro's Beautiful Daughter." Short story.
- "Forgive Us Our Skins: Reflections on Humanity, Mortality, and Small, Plastic Food-Storage Containers." Essay.

Rights and Payment

First North American serial rights. Written material, $25–$200. Pays on publication. Provides 1 contributor's copy.

Conscience

1436 U Street NW, Suite 301
Washington, DC 20009-3397

Editor: David J. Nolan

Description and Interests

Conscience is a news journal of Catholic opinion published by Catholics for Choice and focusing on reproductive rights, the roles of women, and policies affecting childbearing. It is read by policy makers, clergy, and lay people. Its goal is to promote ethical discussion for an audience which is educated and diverse professionally, culturally, and geographically. It does not shy away from issues of dissent in the church. Circ: 12,500.

Contents: 75% articles; 25% depts/columns
Frequency: Quarterly
Website: www.catholicsforchoice.org/conscience/default.asp

Freelance Potential

85% written by nonstaff writers. Publishes 40 freelance submissions yearly; 10% by unpublished writers, 50% by authors who are new to the magazine, 70% by experts. Receives 2 queries, 3 unsolicited mss monthly.

Submissions

Query or send complete ms. Prefers email to conscience@catholicsforchoice.org (Word attachments); will accept disk submissions. Accepts simultaneous submissions. SASE. Responds in 1–3 months.

- Articles: 1,200–2,500 words. Informational, profiles, interviews, personal experience, and opinion. Topics include church-state issues, reproductive issues, feminism, and the roles of women.
- Depts/columns: News briefs. Book reviews, 600–1,500 words.

Sample Issue

58 pages. No advertising. Sample articles available at website.

- "Papering Over the Differences." The current political climate has sparked an alliance between Evangelicals and the Catholic Right.
- "Religious Extremism Cloaked in Diplomacy." Revisiting the Holy See's claim to statehood and the impact that has on its role in the United Nations.

Rights and Payment

First international rights. Written material, $75–$200. Pays on publication. Provides 5–10 contributor's copies.

Conscious Dancer

Movement for a Better World

P.O. Box 2330
Berkeley, CA 94702

Editor: Mark Metz

Description and Interests

Conscious Dancer is an active lifestyle magazine that celebrates transformative dance, mind/body fitness, and the energy movement arts. It features articles on ecstatic movement, dance workshops, yoga, and holistic health. It encourages submissions from people who have been involved in ecstatic dance for years, as well as from those just discovering the rhythm in their soul. Circ: 40,000.

Contents: Articles; depts/columns
Frequency: Quarterly
Website: www.consciousdancer.com

Freelance Potential

50% written by nonstaff writers. Publishes 12 freelance submissions yearly; 25% by unpublished writers, 75% by authors who are new to the magazine.

Submissions

Query with clips or writing samples and outline; or send complete ms. Accepts email to mark@-consciousdancer.com (Word attachments). Response time varies.

- Articles: 1,500–2,000 words. Informational, how-to, profiles, and interviews. Topics include conscious dance, ecstatic movement, yoga, spirituality, meditation, holistic healing, the environment.
- Depts/columns: 100–250 words. Dance styles, apparel, nutrition, and instructor profiles.

Sample Issue

60 pages. Advertising. Sample copy available at website. Guidelines available.

- "Why I Teach: Vivid Existence Founder Leela Francis." Profile of this dance teacher and facilitator who offers events for women only to help them reclaim the healing art and empowerment found in dance.
- "Dance Train Station Belgium: 'Do-re-mi, The Sound of Music.'" A look at a flash mob dance scene that was a publicity stunt for a reality television show.

Rights and Payment

Rights vary. Written material, payment rates vary. Pays on publication. Provides 2+ contributor's copies.

Corporate Knights

147 Spadina Avenue, Suite 207
Toronto, Ontario M5V 2L7
Canada

Managing Editor: Jeremy Runnals

Description and Interests

This U.S. version of a Canadian magazine is an insert in the *Washington Post*. Its subtitle is "The Magazine for Clean Capitalism" and the mission is "to humanize the marketplace by providing the best tools to profit from clean capitalism." Circ: Unavailable.

Contents: Articles
Frequency: Quarterly
Website: www.corporateknights.ca, www.corporateknights.ca/category/ckusa

Freelance Potential

Receives several queries monthly.

Submissions

Query with key points, sources, author qualifications, résumé, and two clips. Accepts email to jeremy@corporateknights.com. No simultaneous submissions. Responds in 2+ months.

- Articles: Word lengths vary. Informational articles, essays, and profiles. Topics include the environmental and social impact of business decisions, leaders and innovators, economic and social issues.

Sample Issue

Advertising. Sample articles and guidelines available at website.

- "Workplace Environment." Article explores whether companies that contribute to the growing climate problem are more likely to have employees with mental health issues.
- "Eye Spy, Robots Don't Lie." Article discusses the increased use of robotic technology to monitor the deterioration of the world's oceans.
- "Too Much Carbon in Your Portfolio?" Article explains why capital spending on energy is heading in the wrong direction.

Rights and Payment

Rights vary. Payment rates and policy vary.

Cosmopolitan 

300 West 57th Street, 38th floor
New York, NY 10019-3299

Executive Editor: Nicole Beland

Description and Interests
Considered the "bible for fun, fearless women," this glossy monthly goes beyond fashion and beauty coverage to dig into relationships and help readers figure out men. The best query should have an attention-getting title and a short, snappy pitch that shows the writer understands the magazine's tone. While *Cosmopolitan* does not consider itself a good place for beginners, it does use freelance writers regularly. Circ: 3 million
Contents: Articles; depts/columns; product reviews
Frequency: Monthly
Website: http://www.cosmopolitan.com

Freelance Potential
10% written by nonstaff writers.

Submissions
Accepts queries and pitches to the Senior Articles Editor for the section being pitched; see the magazine masthead. Among the Senior Editors are Bethany Heitman, bheitman@hearst. com and Mina Azodi, mazodi@hearst.com.

- Articles: Word lengths vary. Health, crime, self-help. relationships, "as told to" stories.
- Depts/columns: Accepts first-person essays for The Naughtiest Thing I've Ever Done and Cosmo Confidential.

Sample Issue
Advertising.

- "Call Me Maybe: Carly Rae Jepsen." The secret bond she shares with Justin Bieber.
- Man Up and Brag a Little." Rave about your awesomeness without sounding obnoxious.

Rights and Payment
North American serial rights. Articles, $1.50–$2 a word. Kill fee, 15–20%. Pays on acceptance.

Cosmopolitan for Latinas 

300 West 57th Street, 38th floor
New York, NY 10019-3299

Editor in Chief: Michelle Herrera Mulligan

Description and Interests
The target audience for this semiannual offshoot of *Cosmopolitan* is the American Latina reader, particularly in Texas, California, Florida, and New York. The brand will have a content hub on Cosmopolitan.com for now, but it may eventually move to its own site. It looks for nonfiction articles on fashion, beauty, entertaining, family. Circ: 545,000
Contents: Articles; depts/columns; product reviews
Frequency: 2 times each year
Website: http://www.cosmopolitan.com/cosmo-latina/

Freelance Potential
Freelance percentages not yet available.

Submissions
Accepts queries with clips to youtellcosmo@hearst.com

- Articles/depts: word lengths vary. Topics include health, fashion, beauty, and in-depth culture articles that are specific to the Latina experience.

Sample Issue
Advertising. Sample articles available at website.

- "America Ferrera" Make way for "La Mala"
- "Your Perfect Color!"—Hair, Skin, Lips... *Everything*!

Rights and Payment
Written material, payment rates vary. Pays on publication.

The Country Connection

691 Pinecrest Road
Boulter, Ontario K0L 1G0
Canada

Editor: Gus Zylstra

Description and Interests

The Country Connection focuses on the restoration of the natural environment, preservation of heritage, and the celebration of nature-centered living. Articles, photography, and information on Ontario travel destinations are also included here, as well as cultural pieces on the arts, studio tours, and some fiction. It only works with Canadian authors. Specific needs for upcoming issues are posted in the guidelines. Circ: 4,000.

Contents: 90% articles; 5% depts/columns; 5% fiction
Frequency: Twice each year
Website: www.pinecone.on.ca

Freelance Potential

100% written by nonstaff writers. Publishes 40 freelance submissions yearly; 10% by unpublished writers, 25% by authors who are new to the magazine. Receives 20 queries monthly.

Submissions

Canadian authors only. Query with cover letter, summary, research sources, lead paragraph, and availability of artwork or send complete ms with cover letter, word count and available rights. Accepts email via website (Word attachments) and hard copy. SAE/IRC. No simultaneous submissions. Responds in 3 months.

- Articles: To 2,000 words. Informational, profiles, personal experience. Topics include wildlife, the environment, country living, nature, gardening, food, travel, the arts, culture, history, nostalgia.
- Depts/columns: Word lengths vary. News, reviews.
- Artwork: Prints; digital images, at least 300 dpi.
- Other: Poetry.

Sample Issue

46 pages. Advertising. Guidelines at website.

- "The Dirt on Dirt: Dumping Dirt Onto 'Protected' Watersheds." Discusses the ramifications of this practice.
- "The Life and Art of William Kurelek." Profile of this artist and a look at his work.

Rights and Payment

Rights vary. Written material, $.07–$.10 per word. Artwork, $10–$50. Poetry, $20. Pays within 90 days of publication. Provides 1 contributor's copy.

Country's Best Cabins

4125 Lafayette Center Drive, Suite 100
Chantilly, VA 20151

Editor: Whitney Richardson

Description and Interests

This magazine offers articles on the construction and preservation of cabins, as well as the lifestyle of those who live (or want to live) in them. It puts an emphasis on smaller homes and capturing the essence of cabin living. Its departments present the best opportunity for writers with construction or design expertise. Circ: 65,000+.

Contents: 55% articles; 45% depts/columns
Frequency: 6 times each year
Website: www.countrysbestcabins.com

Freelance Potential

40% written by nonstaff writers. Publishes 40 freelance submissions yearly; 2% by authors who are new to the magazine, 2% by experts. Receives 2 queries monthly.

Submissions

Query. Accepts email queries to wrichardson@homebuyerpubs.com (Word attachments). Responds in 1 month.

- Articles: 1,500 words. Informational and how-to. Topics include the design, construction, and maintenance of cabins; energy efficiency; home features; and new products.
- Depts/columns: 800 words. Decor, how-to's, landscaping, artist profiles, travel, recreation, leisure, and historical relevance.
- Artwork: Digital images at 300 dpi.

Sample Issue

Advertising. Sample articles at website. Guidelines available.

- "How to Live Harmoniously with Wildlife." Part of the charm and challenge of country living.
- "General Contracting: Can You Handle It?" How to decide if you're the right person for the job when it comes to overseeing renovations on your cabin.

Rights and Payment

First world, Internet, and reprint rights. Articles, $500. Depts/columns, $300. Artwork, payment rates vary for original illustrations or designs. Pays on acceptance. Provides 1 contributor's copy.

Cover of Darkness

Sam's Dot Publishing
P.O. Box 782
Cedar Rapids, IA 52406-0782

Editor: Herika Raymer

Description and Interests

An offshoot of *Aoife's Kiss*, which publishes science fiction and fantasy, *Cover of Darkness* is an e-digest that publishes horror and dark fantasy, nonfiction, and poetry. The editors look for engaging horror, including fantasy and the paranormal, that makes readers experience the protagonist's emotions. Stories should be original, eerie, dark, and create a strong connection between the characters and the audience. It is closed to submissions until April 2013. Check the website for updates. Circ: Unavailable.

Contents: Fiction; articles; reviews; poetry
Frequency: Quarterly
Website: www.samsdotpublishing.com

Freelance Potential

Receives several submissions monthly.

Submissions

Closed to submissions until April 2013. Send complete ms. Prefers email to coverdark2011@yahoo.com ("Submission" and title in subject line); will accept hard copy. No reprints. Response time varies.

- Nonfiction: 1,000–2,000 words. Articles, interviews, and reviews.
- Fiction: 2,000–8,000 words. Flash fiction, to 1,100 words. Genres include horror, fantasy, and paranormal.
- Other: Poetry, to 100 lines.

Sample Issue

Advertising. Sample copy available. Guidelines available at website.

- "Between Those Walls." Short story about a man trying to break from prison to see his dying wife.
- "A Time and Place for Darkness." Story about vampires, werewolves, and monsters during Herbert Hoover's 1930s Great Depression.

Rights and Payment

Rights vary. Fiction, $15; flash fiction; $5; nonfiction, $8; poetry, $4. Pays on publication. Provides 1 contributor's copy.

CQ Amateur Radio

25 Newbridge Road, Suite 309
Hicksville, NY 11801

Editor: Richard Moseson

Description and Interests

This magazine serves as an exchange of ideas for ham radio operators of all levels. Each issue features up-to-date information on equipment, technology, techniques, construction projects, and events. Amateur radio has a rich tradition of hams sharing their knowledge and experience with each other, both on air and through magazine pages. This publication welcomes personal experience pieces. Circ: 35,000.

Contents: 65% depts/columns; 33% articles; 1% fiction; 1% other
Frequency: Monthly
Website: www.cq-amateur-radio.com

Freelance Potential

95% written by nonstaff writers. Publishes 30–35 freelance submissions yearly; 15% by unpublished writers, 15% by authors who are new to the magazine, 5% by experts. Receives 5 queries monthly.

Submissions

Query with proposal and clips, if applicable. Prefers email queries to w2vu@cq-amateur-radio.com (Word attachments); accepts hard copy. SASE. Discourages simultaneous submissions. Responds in 1 month.

- Articles: 1,500–2,500 words. Informational, how-to, profiles, interviews, and personal experience. Topics include ham radio operation, technology, and events.
- Depts/columns: Staff-written.

Sample Issue

116 pages. Advertising. Sample copy available. Guidelines available at website.

- "Integrating Internet Technology with Amateur Radio for Public Service." A look at how the NYC-ARES used an APRS/AIS network to track the Staten Island Ferry.
- "Toyota Tacoma 'Truck-Tenna.'" How to adapt a military AT-1011/U antenna to use with a stationary vehicle for special events and emergencies.

Rights and Payment

First North American serial rights. Written material, payment rates vary. Pays on publication. Provides contributor's copies upon request.

Creations Magazine

P.O. Box 386
Northport, NY 11768

Publishers: Neil & Andrea Garvey

Description and Interests

This magazine "inspires the soul" through articles on personal and spiritual growth, alternative healing, nutrition, and holistic and sustainable living. It targets readers in New York City and Long Island, and it is distributed through health food stores, wellness centers, bookstores, and other venues. It serves the holistic-minded, health-conscious, spiritually centered, and creative communities. Articles should convey information and inspiration. Circ: 40,000.

Contents: 60% articles; 40% depts/columns
Frequency: 6 times each year
Website: www.creationsmagazine.com

Freelance Potential

80% written by nonstaff writers. Publishes 70 freelance submissions yearly; 30% by unpublished writers, 60% by authors who are new to the magazine, 50% by experts. Receives 25 unsolicited mss monthly.

Submissions

Send complete ms. Accepts email to neil@creationsmagazine.com. Responds in 3–4 weeks.

- Articles: To 850 words. Informational, self-help, personal experience, and book excerpts. Topics include creativity, prosperity, holistic health/nutrition, the environment, relationships, love, sex, death, recovery, men's/women's issues, yoga and meditation, and introspection.
- Depts/columns: Staff-written.
- Other: Poetry. Submit seasonal material 6 weeks in advance.

Sample Issue

28 pages. Advertising. Sample articles, guidelines, and editorial calendar available at website.

- "Who Am I Really? A Holistic Approach to Self Discovery." Author relays a long journey to understanding mind, emotions, and body for a total understanding of self.
- "The Obesity Time Bomb." The explosion of childhood obesity and why health-care professionals are extremely concerned about the future health of these children.

Rights and Payment

One-time rights. No payment. Provides 1 contributor's copy.

Creative Nonfiction

5501 Walnut Street, Suite 202
Pittsburgh, PA 15232

Editor: Lee Gutkind

Description and Interests

Featuring "true stories, well told," this literary magazine publishes compelling essays on various topics and articles about the genre that offers meaning, insight, and reflection. Most issues are themed, with specific calls for essays. It also accepts general submissions and material for its regular departments. Some of the themed calls include a cash award for the submission judged to be the best. Circ: 7,000.

Contents: Essays; depts/columns
Frequency: Quarterly
Website: www.creativenonfiction.org

Freelance Potential

95% written by nonstaff writers. Publishes 30 freelance submissions yearly; 10% by unpublished writers, 50% by authors who are new to the magazine. Receives 300 unsolicited mss each month.

Submissions

Send complete ms. Accepts hard copy for general submissions. To answer a specific call for themed manuscripts, follow guidelines. Query for regular departments. Accepts queries to queries@creativenonfiction.org and through website. Accepts simultaneous submissions if identified. Responds in 5 months.

- Articles: Word lengths vary. Literary journalism, narrative nonfiction, essays, and personal experience. Open to all topics for general submissions; other submissions must refer to the theme of the issue.
- Depts/columns: Word lengths vary. The writing process, specific subgenres, the business of writing, reading lists, literary timelines or comparisons of a genre's evolution, personal essays.

Sample Issue

80 pages. Little advertising. Sample copy available. Guidelines and theme list available at website.

- "Origami and the Art of Identity Folding." The author compares his experience of returning to jail to this ancient Oriental art form.
- Sample dept/column: Between the Lines discusses the ethics of writing about violence.

Rights and Payment

Rights vary. Written material, typically $50 acceptance fee, plus $10 per published page. Pays on publication. Provides 1 contributor's copy, plus extra copies at 50% discount.

Crochet World

DRG Publishing
306 East Parr Road
Berne, IN 46711

Editor: Carol Alexander

Description and Interests

This magazine offers a wide range of crochet projects for all levels of crafters. Emphasis is on homey, yet innovative designs and techniques. It also features interviews with designers and product and book reviews. Request an editorial calendar for a list of upcoming themes and design review deadlines. Circ: 110,000.

Contents: 80% projects; 15% depts/columns; 5% other
Frequency: 6 times each year
Website: www.crochet-world.com

Freelance Potential

90% written by nonstaff writers. Publishes 180 freelance submissions yearly; 10% by unpublished writers, 10% by authors who are new to the magazine, 80% by experts. Receives 20 queries monthly.

Submissions

Query. Prefers email to editor@crochet-world.com; accepts hard copy. No simultaneous submissions. SASE. Responds 2–4 weeks after scheduled project review (see editorial calendar).

- Articles: Informational, profiles, and how-to. Topics include crochet designers; new products; techniques; and projects for original crochet designs of afghans, baby gifts, clothing, toys, and household goods.
- Depts/columns: Staff-written.
- Other: Poetry, to 3 column inches.

Sample Issue

68 pages. Advertising. Sample copy and editorial calendar available. Guidelines available at website.

- "Beginner's Luck." How to crochet a goony bird tooth fairy pillow.
- "Celebrate Autumn: Just for Fun Wig." Crochet a funky long-haired wig that will make a trick-or-treater look like a rock star.

Rights and Payment

All rights. Written material, payment rates vary. Pays on acceptance. Provides 1 contributor's copy.

Cross Country Skier

P.O. Box 550
Cable, WI 54821

Editor & Publisher: Ron Bergin

Description and Interests

This magazine is for both recreational and competitive Nordic skiing enthusiasts who want practical and entertaining information on the training, destinations, events, and lifestyle of the sport. Equipment and techniques are also covered regularly. Most of the equipment coverage is handled in-house; however, the magazine invites queries from writers who have a special angle that is more than a test or review. Circ: 25,000.

Contents: 60% articles; 40% depts/columns
Frequency: 3 times each year
Website: www.crosscountryskier.com

Freelance Potential

60% written by nonstaff writers. Publishes 30–40 freelance submissions yearly; 10% by unpublished writers, 30% by authors who are new to the magazine, 20% by experts. Receives 5 queries monthly.

Submissions

Query with clips. Accepts email queries to ron@crosscountryskier.com. SASE. Responds in 6–8 weeks.

- Articles: Word lengths vary. Informational, how-to, profiles, interviews, and personal experience. Topics include Nordic skiing, ski destinations, hidden gems (smaller, out-of-the-way ski areas), interesting personalities in the sport, technique, equipment, and the outdoors.
- Depts/columns: Staff-written.
- Artwork: Digital files at 300 dpi.

Sample Issue

80 pages. Advertising. Sample copy and guidelines available at website.

- "Strike a Pose." Examines how yoga practice can help improve cross-country ski technique by increasing strength, flexibility, and focus.
- "Maine's Downeast Sunrise Trail." Destination piece describes the nearly 90 miles of skiing trails and accommodations in this northeastern state winter hotspot.

Rights and Payment

Rights vary. Written material, payment rates vary. Pays on publication. Provides 1 contributor's copy.

Crosswalk.com  

Editor

Description and Interests

This ezine is a destination for readers interested in all areas of Christian living—faith, family, fun, and community. Its mission is to provide compelling, biblically-based content that will aid Christians in their walk with Jesus. Bible studies, daily devotions, marriage and parenting advice, and media reviews are some of the categories covered. Hits per month: Unavailable.

Contents: Articles; depts/columns
Frequency: Updated regularly
Website: www.crosswalk.com

Freelance Potential

Freelance percentages not currently available.

Submissions

Query. Accepts electronic queries via www.crosswalk.com/feedback. Response time varies.

- Articles: Word lengths vary. Informational articles, personal experience pieces, devotionals, and interviews. Topics include Christianity as it relates to marriage, family, parenting, personal finance, careers, education, and leadership.
- Depts/columns: Word lengths vary. Book, music, and movie reviews; humor pieces; related news.

Sample Issue

Advertising. Sample copy available at website.

- "Do We Always Have To Be Content?" Article discusses how to talk with kids about contentment and what it really looks like in one's life.
- "How Did This Happen?" Essay looks at the current family crisis within society.
- "What is the Book of Job All About?" Article features an interview with a pastor about the meaning of the Old Testament's Book of Job.

Rights and Payment

Rights vary. Payment rates and policy vary.

Cruising World

55 Hammarlund Way
Middletown, RI 02842

Manuscript Editor

Description and Interests

Articles about cruising under sail, the boating lifestyle, and destinations are combined with how-to's on boat maintenance and gear in this magazine for those who love to take to their boats. It is always in need of articles about destinations and information that will help other sailors. Circ: 140,000.

Contents: 90% articles; 10% depts/columns
Frequency: Monthly
Website: www.cruisingworld.com

Freelance Potential

60% written by nonstaff writers. Publishes 200 freelance submissions yearly; 30% by unpublished writers, 15% by new authors, 30% by experts. Receives 100 unsolicited mss monthly.

Submissions

Send complete ms with artwork. Query for technical articles. Prefers email submissions to cw.manuscripts@gmail.com (Word or text file attachments) and disk submissions (Word or text files) with hard copy. No simultaneous submissions. SASE. Responds in 3 months.

- Articles: To 2,500 words. Informational, how-to, personal experience, profiles, and creative nonfiction. Topics include sailing small and medium-sized boats, maintenance, gear, and cruising destinations.
- Depts/columns: To 2,000 words. News, anecdotes, sailing lifestyles, maintenance tips, sailboat reviews, and profiles.
- Artwork: Color slides or transparencies; high-resolution digital images at 300 dpi (TIGG, JPEG formats).

Sample Issue

144 pages. Advertising. Sample articles, guidelines, and editorial calendar available at website.

- "Playing in Traffic." Five ways to avoid collision accidents when traveling in shipping channels.
- "Conch Charters at 25: The Dream Continues." A profile of this family-run British Virgin Islands company celebrating their silver anniversary.

Rights and Payment

First world rights. Articles, $25–$200 for short, news articles; $300–$1,000 for technical and feature articles. Artwork, $50–$600. Kill fee, $50. Pays on acceptance. Provides 1 contributor's copy.

Cultural Survival Quarterly

215 Prospect Street
Cambridge, MA 02139

Editor

Description and Interests

This magazine's mission is to bring attention to the culture and traditions of the indigenous peoples around the globe and the challenges they face in a modern world. A significant portion of the content is personal stories by indigenous writers. In addition to traditional reporting of an issue, it welcomes personal stories that put the issue in the context of and tell about a community. Circ: 7,000.

Contents: 80% articles; 20% depts/columns
Frequency: Quarterly
Website: www.culturalsurvival.org/publications/cultural-survival-quarterly

Freelance Potential

90% written by nonstaff writers. Publishes 20 freelance submissions yearly; 10% by unpublished writers, 80% by authors who are new to the magazine, 60% by experts. Receives 5 unsolicited mss monthly.

Submissions

Prefers query, will accept complete ms. Accepts disk submissions with hard copy and artwork and email to culturalsurvival@culturalsurvival.org. SASE. Responds in 6 weeks.

- Articles: 1,000–2,400 words. Informational, profiles, interviews, and personal experience. Topics include indigenous cultures, social issues, government, economics, and current events.
- Depts/columns: Word lengths vary. News items, reviews, notes from the field, and photo-essays.
- Artwork: B/W or color prints.

Sample Issue

32 pages. Little advertising. Sample copy and guidelines available at website.

- "When the Pen Is Mightier Than the Sword." A Shuar poet gives voice to the Ecuadorian Amazon people.
- "Confirming Rights." An Inter-American court ruling finds in favor of the Sarayaku people in defining free, prior, informed consent.

Rights and Payment

All rights. No payment. Provides 4 contributor's copies.

Curious Parents

2345 Bethel Avenue
Merchantville, NJ 08109-2715

Submissions: Jackie Piccone

Description and Interests

Parenting issues, as well as general topics that are of interest to parents, are covered in this family-oriented magazine. It is published in four local editions serving the Pennsylvania, New Jersey, and Delaware triangle. Parents also look to this publication for information about educational and recreational opportunities in their area. Circ: 375,000.

Contents: Articles; depts/columns
Frequency: Monthly
Website: www.curiousparents.com

Freelance Potential

80% written by nonstaff writers. Publishes 45 freelance submissions yearly; 60% by unpublished writers, 40% by authors who are new to the magazine, 30% by experts. Receives 10 unsolicited mss monthly.

Submissions

Send complete ms with brief description and author biography. Accepts email to editor@curiousparents.com (Word or text file attachments). Response time varies.

- Articles: Word lengths vary. Informational, how-to, self-help articles, profiles, interviews, and opinion pieces. Topics include crafts, hobbies, current events, recreation, regular and special education, college prep, safety, health, family entertainment, parenting, travel, camps, going green, seasonal fun, gardening, family finances.
- Depts/columns: Word lengths vary. Health, automobile safety, and book reviews.

Sample Issue

30 pages. Advertising. Sample copy and guidelines available at website.

- "Multilingual Families: How and Why Three Families Tackle Teaching Multiple Languages." Helping your child learn a second language.
- "Curacao: Caribbean Family Adventures." Profile of the outdoor adventure and family fun destination.

Rights and Payment

All rights. No payment. Provides 1 contributor's copy.

Curve

P.O. Box 467
New York, NY 10034

Managing Editor: Rachel Shatto

Description and Interests

For nearly 20 years, *Curve* has been serving its lesbian readers with smart, hip, irreverent, and hard-hitting articles. It combines interviews, reviews, reporting, celebrity news, fashion, and travel, with controversial topics. It is not limited to "lesbian-themed" topics, but all material must be relevant to or have a perspective that will appeal to lesbians. Circ: 250,000.

Contents: 50% articles; 40% depts/columns; 10% other
Frequency: 10 times each year
Website: www.curvemag.com

Freelance Potential

80–90% written by nonstaff writers. Publishes 10 freelance submissions yearly; 2% by unpublished writers, 60% by authors who are new to the magazine, 10% by experts. Receives 50 queries, 10 unsolicited mss monthly.

Submissions

Prefers query; will accept complete ms. Accepts email only to articles@curvemag.com (Word attachments). Also offers work-for-hire. Email résumé, clips, and letter with biographical information and topics of interest. No simultaneous submissions. SASE. Responds within 1 month.

- Articles: 200–2,500 words. Informational, profiles, and interviews. Topics include relationships, health, celebrities, pop culture, trends, fashion, lifestyle, and social and political issues—all as they relate to the lesbian community.
- Depts/columns: Staff-written.
- Artwork: Color and B/W digital images at 300 dpi.

Sample Issue

84 pages. Advertising. Sample articles and guidelines available at website.

- "Suze Orman: Finance Dynamo." Profile of this well-known personal finance expert.
- "Summer in the City." Explores what to do and where to stay in West Hollywood.

Rights and Payment

All rights. Written material, $40–$300. Pays on publication.

Dance International

Scotiabank Dance Centre
667 Davie Street, Level 6
Vancouver, British Columbia V6B 2G6
Canada

Managing Editor: Maureen Riches

Description and Interests

Dance International brings global coverage of both classical and contemporary dance to its readers. It offers reviews, criticism, profiles, and interviews. Writers are often dancers themselves, or they have extensive professional experience within the dance world. It covers contemporary dance and ballet companies from around the globe, and it is always in need of reviews of productions on foreign soil. Circ: 4,000.

Contents: Articles; depts/columns
Frequency: Quarterly
Website: www.danceinternational.org

Freelance Potential

85% written by nonstaff writers. Publishes 95 freelance submissions yearly; 9% by authors who are new to the magazine.

Submissions

Send complete ms. Prefers email submissions to danceint@direct.ca (RTF, Word, or WordPerfect attachments); will accept disk submissions (RTF files). SAE/IRC. Responds in 2 months.

- Articles: 1,500 words. Informational, opinion pieces, profiles, and interviews. Topics include classical and contemporary dance, dancers, performers, choreographers, companies, programs, performances, and competitions.
- Depts/columns: 1,000 words. Commentaries, book reviews, and performance reviews.
- Artwork: Prints; digital images at 300 dpi.

Sample Issue

62 pages. Advertising. Sample articles and guidelines available at website.

- "Dancing Don Q." Pacific Northwest Ballet choreographer's new take on the classic *Don Quixote*.
- "Touching Lives with Wheelchair Dancing." Learning wheelchair ballroom dancing.

Rights and Payment

First rights. Articles, $100–$150. Depts/columns, $100. Kill fee, 50%. Pays on publication. Provides 2 contributor's copies.

Dance Magazine

333 7th Avenue, 11th Floor
New York, NY 10001

Editor in Chief: Wendy Perron

Description and Interests

Dance students, teachers, and professionals read this magazine for articles that keep them abreast of what is going on in all disciplines of dance. It features techniques, training strategies, and profiles of dancers, companies, and productions. Writers should have a history with dance, either in performance, teaching, or critiquing. Though most of its coverage leans toward ballet and contemporary dance, it is open to pieces about any style. Circ: 50,000.

Contents: 75% articles; 25% depts/columns
Frequency: Monthly
Website: www.dancemagazine.com

Freelance Potential

80% written by nonstaff writers. Publishes 200 freelance submissions yearly; 5% by unpublished writers, 25% by authors who are new to the magazine. Receives 83 queries monthly.

Submissions

Query with clips. Accepts hard copy and email queries to wperron@dancemedia.com. SASE. Response time varies.

- Articles: To 1,500 words. Informational, profiles, and interviews. Topics include dance, dance instruction, choreography, the arts, family, and health concerns.
- Depts/columns: Word lengths vary. New product information, reviews, dance news, and instruction.

Sample Issue

138 pages. Advertising. Sample copy available at website.

- "Your Body: Nervous Energy." Examines how to leverage anxiety to improve performance.
- "Style Meets Substance." Profile of esteemed choreographer Annabelle Lopez Ochoa.

Rights and Payment

Rights vary. Written material, payment rates vary. Pays on publication. Provides 1 contributor's copy.

Dance Spirit

110 William Street, 23rd Floor
New York, NY 10038

Editor in Chief: Allison Feller

Description and Interests

By turns inspiring and instructional, this magazine is read by young dancers who are striving to break into the profession. It is always in need of submissions from writers who know the ropes and who can offer dancers accurate information that will help them hone their skills. The magazine offers features on competitions, trends, techniques, and fashion. Articles on tap and modern dance are especially sought. Circ: 100,000.

Contents: 35% articles; 40% depts/columns; 25% other
Frequency: 10 times each year
Website: www.dancespirit.com

Freelance Potential

50% written by nonstaff writers. Publishes 75 freelance submissions yearly; 10% by unpublished writers, 5% by authors who are new to the magazine, 85% by experts. Receives 10 queries monthly.

Submissions

Query with outline. Accepts email to afeller@dancemedia.com. Responds in 1 month.

- Articles: 800–1,200 words. Informational, instructional, how-to, profiles, interviews, and personal experience. Topics include dance careers, choreography, competitions and programs, and celebrity dancers.
- Depts/columns: 600 words. News briefs, competitions, conventions, advice, fitness, nutrition, beauty, costumes and gear, dance history, techniques, dance opportunities, profiles, and media reviews.

Sample Issue

176 pages. Advertising. Sample articles and editorial calendar available at website. Guidelines and theme list available.

- "The Best Competitions and Conventions to Attend This Year." A roundup of all the major dance events for the upcoming year.
- Sample dept/column: Martha Graham How-To gives walk-through instruction from the director of the Martha Graham School of Contemporary Dance on how to do an eight-count.

Rights and Payment

All rights. Articles, $100–$200. Depts/columns, $175–$250. Kill fee, 25%. Pays on publication. Provides 1 contributor's copy.

Deer & Deer Hunting

Krause Publications
700 East State Street
Iola, WI 54990

Editor: Daniel Schmidt

Description and Interests

White-tailed deer hunting by bow, gun, or camera is the focus of this magazine. Its comprehensive articles focus on deer behavior and habitat, management practices, hunting techniques, and hunting ethics. Articles dealing with deer biology or behavior should be documented by scientific research. Circ: 120,000.

Contents: 50% articles; 48% depts/columns; 2% fiction
Frequency: 10 times each year
Website: www.deeranddeerhunting.com

Freelance Potential

90% written by nonstaff writers. Publishes hundreds of freelance submissions yearly; 10% by unpublished writers, 75% by authors who are new to the magazine, 80% by experts. Receives 50 queries monthly.

Submissions

Prefers query with outline; will accept complete ms. Prefers email to dan.schmidt@fwpubs.com (Word or text attachments); will accept hard copy. SASE. Responds in 4–6 weeks.

- Articles: 1,000–2,000 words. Informational, how-to, and personal experience. Topics include white-tailed deer biology and behavior, management principles and practices, habitat, natural history, hunting techniques, and ethics.
- Fiction: Word lengths vary. Hunting stories.
- Depts/columns: Deer Browse, newsworthy briefs, deer observations; 200–500 words.
- Artwork: Digital JPEG or TIFF images.

Sample Issue

64 pages. Advertising. Sample copy available. Guidelines available at website.

- "How to Sharpen a Hunting Knife." A fast way to freehand sharpen a knife using a bench stone and the author's marker technique.
- "Deer Biologist Predicts Great Season." How a mild winter, optimal fawning conditions, and other factors all point to a good hunting in Vermont this year.

Rights and Payment

First North American serial and electronic rights. Articles, $150–$600. Deer Browse, $25–$250. Pays on acceptance. Provides 1 contributor's copy.

Delicious Living

1401 Pearl Street, Suite 200
Boulder, CO 80302

Editor in Chief: Radha Marcum

Description and Interests

With a focus on real food, natural health, and sustaining a green planet, *Delicious Living* publishes lifestyle, trend, and service-oriented articles on nutrition, organic family topics, health and wellness, natural beauty tips, and alternative medicine. Its readers are already interested in a natural and healthy lifestyle and are looking for tips, advice, and information to use in a practical way. Circ: 350,000.

Contents: 50% articles; 50% depts/columns
Frequency: Monthly
Website: www.deliciousliving.com

Freelance Potential

85% written by nonstaff writers. Publishes 90 freelance submissions yearly; 5% by unpublished writers, 10% by authors who are new to the magazine, 25% by experts. Receives 10 queries monthly.

Submissions

Query only with clips. Accepts hard copy and email queries to deliciousliving@newhope.com. SASE. Responds in 1 month.

- Articles: 1,000–1,200 words. Informational, how-to, profiles, interviews, and personal experience. Topics include health, nutrition, disease prevention, natural products, integrative medicine, healthy cooking, personal care, new products.
- Depts/columns: Fresh, news, research, the natural products industry, 50–250 words. Wellness, nutrition, supplements, natural parenting, beauty and body, quick and easy recipes, 600–800 words.

Sample Issue

66 pages. Advertising. Sample articles and guidelines available at website.

- "9 Tips to Eat Less Sugar." Three experts share their best suggestions for easy ways to cut back on sugar.
- "Natural Ways to Regulate Your Menstrual Cycle." Natural methods for correcting irregularities and discomfort of menstruation.

Rights and Payment

All rights. Written material, payment rates vary. Pays on publication. Provides 1 contributor's copy.

Democracy

A Journal of Ideas

818 18th Street NW, Suite 750
Washington, DC 20006

Managing Editor: Elbert Ventura

Description and Interests

This magazine seeks to be a true journal of ideas—where well thought-out observations and opinions about the way the world is working are celebrated. All topics relating to government and society are welcome here. It is strenuously nonpartisan in tone and is not interested in political positioning or electoral strategies of any party. It looks for pieces that are willing to confront big questions and boldly step outside the bounds of conventional wisdom. Circ: 5,000.

Contents: 50% articles; 50% other
Frequency: Quarterly
Website: www.democracyjournal.org

Freelance Potential

98% written by nonstaff writers. Publishes 45 freelance submissions yearly; 20% by unpublished writers, 80% by authors who are new to the magazine. Receives 20 queries and unsolicited mss each month.

Submissions

Query with detailed proposal; or send complete ms. Accepts email submissions to dajoi@democracyjournal.org. Responds in 2 weeks.

- Articles: 4,000–6,000 words. Informational and opinion. Topics include social issues, government, the economy, public and foreign affairs.
- Other: Book reviews, by assignment.

Sample Issue

120 pages. Little advertising. Sample articles and guidelines available at website.

- "The Long Term Is Now." Examines the financial and social costs of long-term care for an aging population and the feasibility of the current funding model.
- "The Forgotten 40 Percent." Discussion of the people in the bottom 40 percent of the economy and the ways in which they can build assets and savings.

Rights and Payment

Rights vary. Written material, payment rates vary. Payment policy varies.

Descant

P.O. Box 314, Station P
Toronto, Ontario M5S 2S8
Canada

Editor in Chief: Karen Mulhallen

Description and Interests

This literary journal, entering its fifth decade, is dedicated to presenting the rising stars of the writing world, along with established authors. It showcases contemporary fiction, creative nonfiction, plays, musical scores, and poetry, as well as visual presentations. *Descant* also offers themed issues that delve into cultural topics. It aspires to be a forum for expression and debate on social issues and norms, literature, and art, and is not afraid to publish something that pushes the creative envelope. Check guidelines for upcoming themes. Circ: 2,000.

Contents: 50% fiction; 40% poetry; 10% articles
Frequency: Quarterly
Website: www.descant.ca

Freelance Potential

90% written by nonstaff writers. Publishes 120 freelance submissions yearly; 5% by unpublished writers, 50% by authors who are new to the magazine, 10% by experts. Receives 1,000 unsolicited mss monthly.

Submissions

Accepts previously unpublished work only. Send complete ms. Accepts hard copy with type of submission noted on envelope and email to submit@-descant.ca (Word or PDF attacments). SAE/IRC. No simultaneous submissions. Response time varies.

- Articles: To 6,000 words. Creative nonfiction, memoir, essays, personal experience, opinion, and interviews. Topics include the arts and listed themes.
- Fiction: To 6,000 words. Novel excerpts, short stories, plays, musical scores. Genres: literary, contemporary, experimental, ethnic fiction.
- Other: Poetry, to 6 poems per submission.

Sample Issue

184 pages. Little advertising. Sample copy available. Guidelines, theme list available at website.

- "Nova Era." Creative nonfiction on the natural history of the author's basement using dirt as the context.
- "What I Said to Him in Bed After Moving My Dad's Dresser." Short story.

Rights and Payment

First rights. Written material, $100. Pays on publication. Provides 1 contributor's copy and a 1-year subscription.

Desert Ashram 

Desert Ashram
3403 West Sweetwater Drive
Tucson, AZ 85745-9301

Submissions Editor: Marianne Martin

Description and Interests

This magazine appeals to spiritual seekers—all those who are interested in a universal approach to spirituality, meditation, healing practices, personal growth, and the interface of science and spirituality. Articles are inspiring and uplifting in tone, never derogatory, and offer universal meaning or messages. Circ: 24,000.

Contents: 80% articles; 15% depts/columns; 5% fiction and poetry
Frequency: Quarterly
Website: www.light-of-consciousness.org

Freelance Potential

85% written by nonstaff writers. Publishes 6–8 freelance submissions yearly; 10% by unpublished writers, 50% by authors who are new to the magazine. Receives 60 queries, 30+ unsolicited mss monthly.

Submissions

Query or send complete ms via website (Word attachments). Accepts simultaneous submissions if notified. Responds in 1–2 months.

- Articles: 1,000–4,000 words. Informational, how-to, and personal experience. Topics include spiritual growth, meditation, spirituality, healing, the environment, nature, the arts, pilgrimages.
- Fiction: 1,000–3,000 words. Spiritual stories.
- Depts/columns: Staff-written.
- Other: Poetry; no line limits.

Sample Issue

64 pages. Advertising. Sample articles available. Guidelines and editorial calendar available at website.

- "Karma and the Voice of Conscience." Hearing what the voice of conscience is saying depends on one's inner state.
- "Prayer of the Heart." Entering the mystery of Divine Love through the spiritual practice of internal prayer.

Rights and Payment

One-time rights. No payment. Provides 1+ contributor's copies.

Devozine 

1908 Grand Avenue, P.O. Box 340004
Nashville, TN 37203-0004

Editor: Sandy Miller

Description and Interests

This devotional lifestyle magazine, written by teens and adults, helps Christian teens grow in their faith and discover how it relates to their daily lives. Each issue focuses on eight or nine themes with weekday meditations and a feature article for the weekend. The publication has expanded its online presence with a blog, website, and daily SMS text messages. Circ: 50,000.

Contents: 90% articles; 10% other
Frequency: 6 times each year
Website: www.devozine.org

Freelance Potential

100% written by nonstaff writers. Publishes 400 freelance submissions yearly; 50% by authors who are new to the magazine. Receives 18 queries, 150+ unsolicited mss monthly.

Submissions

Query for feature articles. Send complete manuscript for daily meditations. Accepts hard copy and online submissions at http://devozine.upperroom.org/write-for-us/submit-a-devo/. Also accepts email submissions to smiller@upperroom.org. SASE. Responds in 8–10 weeks.

- Articles: 500–600 words. Informational, devotional, profiles, personal experience, and reviews. Topics include faith, mentoring, independence, courage, teen parenting, creativity, social and teen issues, relationships, spiritual practices, health, media, self-image, technology.
- Depts/columns: 75–100 words. Reviews, new product information.
- Fiction: 150–250 words. Genres: adventure, historical, multicultural fiction.
- Other: Daily meditations, to 250 words. Prayers and poetry, 10–20 lines. Submit seasonal material 6–8 months in advance.

Sample Issue

64 pages. No advertising. Sample articles, guidelines, and theme list available at website.

- "Bullying and Depression." One girl's account of being bullied.
- "Friends Helping Friends." Sufferers of anxiety disorders and depression help each other.

Rights and Payment

First and second rights. Features, $100. Meditations, $25. Pays on acceptance.

Diabetes Forecast 

1701 North Beauregard Street
Alexandria, VA 22311

Editorial Director: Kelly Rawlings

Description and Interests
Subtitled "The Healthy Living Magazine," *Diabetes Forecast* is focused on self-care behaviors, physical activity, medication, monitoring, problem-solving, coping, and risk reduction for those living with diabetes. At this time, the magazine is accepting submissions for its Reflections column only. Circ: Unavailable.

Contents: Articles; depts/columns
Frequency: Monthly
Website: www.forecast.diabetes.org

Freelance Potential
Publishes 25% of unsolicited submissions received.

Submissions
Query with outline. Accepts hard copy and email to mailcall@diabetes.org. SASE. Response time varies.

- Articles: Word lengths vary. Informational and how-to articles. Topics include living and coping with diabetes, healthy cooking, health and fitness, and research.
- Depts/columns: 500 words. Reflections, personal experience piece focusing on some aspect of living with diabetes.

Sample Issue
Advertising. Sample copy and guidelines available at website.

- "Dating and Diabetes." Article discusses how to involve your significant other in the care of your disease.
- "Stressing Less." Article provides tips for dealing with stress the right way to protect your health.
- Sample dept/column: Reflections shares a woman's thoughts on her daily balance of food, insulin, and exercise.

Rights and Payment
All rights. No payment. Provides contributor's copies.

Diabetes Self-Management

150 West 22nd Street, Suite 800
New York, NY 10011

Editor: Ingrid Strauch

Description and Interests
A mix of informational, how-to, and self-help articles, all written with an upbeat tone, are found in this magazine. It focuses on nutrition, pharmacology, exercise, and medical advances, as well as the day-to-day and long-term concerns of those living with diabetes. Its readers have a range of knowledge of diabetes-related matters, but the publication is careful not to write down to them. It does not publish personal experience pieces, exposés, or research breakthroughs. Circ: 430,000.

Contents: 50% articles; 50% depts/columns
Frequency: 6 times each year
Website: www.diabetesselfmanagement.com

Freelance Potential
90% written by nonstaff writers. Publishes 70 freelance submissions yearly; 10% by authors who are new to the magazine, 90% by experts. Receives 5 queries monthly.

Submissions
Query with one-page rationale, outline, and clips or writing samples. Accepts email to editor@diabetes-self-mgmt.com. Responds in 6 weeks.

- Articles: 2,000–3,000 words. Informational, self-help, and how-to. Topics include pharmacology, nutrition, recipes, exercise, medical advances, travel, recreation, senior citizens with diabetes, psychology, and disabilities.
- Depts/columns: Staff-written.

Sample Issue
64 pages. Advertising. Sample copy available. Guidelines available at website.

- "High Blood Glucose: What's Behind the Symptoms." Why high blood glucose elicits certain body responses and reactions.
- "Foot Care Questions." An overview from foot experts on shoes, socks, insoles, orthotics, home remedies, and pedicures all for the diabetic patient.

Rights and Payment
All rights. Articles, payment rates vary. Kill fee, 20%. Pays on publication. Provides 3–5 contributor's copies.

Dirt

Straus News
20 West Avenue
Chester, NY 10918

Editor: Becca Tucker

Description and Interests

Subtitled "Healthy Living from the Ground Up," this natural lifestyle magazine, distributed throughout the New York-Pennsylvania-New Jersey borders, presents information on living sustainably, acting responsibly, and thinking locally. It covers farming, organic gardening, ecofashion, alternative lifestyles and energies, holistic health, education, parenting, and maintaining a green home. Material that has a local personality or angle is highly preferred. Circ: Unavailable.

Contents: Articles; depts/columns
Frequency: 6 times each year
Website: http://dirt-mag.com

Freelance Potential

Receives many queries monthly.

Submissions

Query. Accepts hard copy and email to editor.dirt@strausnews.com. Submissions are not returned.

- Articles: Word lengths vary. Informational articles, profiles, interviews, and personal experience pieces. Topics include organic gardening, holistic health, parenting, and green living.
- Depts/columns: Word lengths vary. Calendar, animals, regional travel, arts.

Sample Issue

Advertising. Sample articles available at website.

- "The Exaltation of a Shriveled Bean." Article discusses the health benefits and varied uses of the garbanzo bean.
- "Fracking's the Way Vs. No Fracking Way." Article explains why tapping into the shale gas supply could yield immense economic and environmental benefits.

Rights and Payment

Rights vary. Payment rates and policy vary.

Dirt Rag

3483 Saxonburg Boulevard
Pittsburgh, PA 15238

Editor in Chief: Mike Cushionbury

Description and Interests

This magazine covers all the terrain that mountain bikers do, from traveling to the best destinations to selecting and maintaining equipment. Event coverage and news items are also included. Passion for the sport is appreciated and should be evident in the articles, as well as experience and expertise in the subject matter. Circ: 50,000.

Contents: 60% articles; 30% depts/columns; 10% other
Frequency: 7 times each year
Website: www.dirtragmag.com

Freelance Potential

50% written by nonstaff writers. Publishes 25–40 freelance submissions yearly; 30% by unpublished writers, 20% by authors who are new to the magazine. Receives 50–70 unsolicited mss monthly.

Submissions

Query or send complete ms. Accepts email to editor@dirtragmag.com (Word or text file attachments) and simultaneous submissions if identified. Response time varies.

- Articles: 1,000–3,500 words. Informational, how-to, self-help, profiles, and interviews. Topics include biking, destinations, fitness, equipment, and travel.
- Depts/columns: To 1,000 words. Technical information and tips. Readings, short news bites; 100–500 words.
- Art: Digital images at 300 dpi (TIFF, JPEG, EPS, PDF files).

Sample Issue

100–120 pages. Advertising. Sample articles and guidelines available at website.

- "New Mountain Bike Shoes for Every Need." Roundup of new shoes that are available for bikers and the special features of each one.
- "Race Report: The Whole Enchilada Enduro, Moab." Destination piece reviewing the trails, accommodations, and other activities available in this western region.

Rights and Payment

All rights. Written material in print magazine, $.10 per word. No payment for articles used online. Pays on publication.

Dirt Toys Magazine

360 B Street
Idaho Falls, ID 83402

Editor

Description and Interests

Read by riders of ATVs, side-by-sides, and UTVs, this new magazine comes from Harris Publishing, whose other titles include *SnoWest* and *Sledheads*. *Dirt Toys* contains the latest information on summer motor sports—the machines, destinations, and riding tips. Rally coverage, industry news, and reviews of new models and products associated with motorsports are also included. Circ: Unavailable.

Contents: Articles; depts/columns
Frequency: Quarterly
Website: www.dirttoysmag.com

Freelance Potential

Freelance percentage not yet available.

Submissions

Query. Accepts electronic submissions via the website's Contact Us section. Response time varies.

- Articles: Word lengths vary. Informational and how-to articles, interviews, and reviews. Topics include new models, parts and accessories, destinations, travel, technical tips and installs, and industry news.
- Depts/columns: Word lengths vary. Product reviews, industry news, and personal experience pieces.

Sample Issue

Advertising. Sample copy and editorial calendar available at website.

- "Yamaha Sponsors Total Outdoorsman Challenge." Article describes a recent outdoor test of skill, nerve, strength, and agility with a Grizzly 4x4 ATV as the prize.
- "Dustin Nelson, Five-Time Champ, Prepares for Quad X Series." Article features an interview with the ATV racer.

Rights and Payment

Rights vary. Payment rates and policy vary.

Disciple Magazine

6815 Shallowford Road
Chattanooga, TN 37421

Editor: Justin Lonas

Description and Interests

This ezine targeting pastors and ministry leaders is an outreach of Advancing the Ministries of the Gospel (AMG) International. Its articles from pastors, theologians, and ministry leaders discuss Christian teachings; life; and ways to share the Gospel in one's own community, culture, or group. It seeks good, biblical exposition delivered in a readable format. Many of its writers are lay ministers or pastors. Hits per month: Unavailable.

Contents: 65% articles; 30% depts/columns; 5% other
Frequency: Updated 26 times each year
Website: www.disciplemagazine.com

Freelance Potential

85% written by nonstaff writers. Publishes 10–15 freelance submissions yearly; 60% by unpublished writers, 55% by authors who are new to the magazine, 5% by experts. Receives 1–2 unsolicited mss monthly.

Submissions

Send complete ms with author biography. Accepts Macintosh disk submissions and email submissions to justinl@amginternational.org. SASE. Responds in 4 months.

- Articles: 800–1,000 words. Inspirational articles, profiles, and interviews. Topics include spirituality, theology, ministry, leadership, the Gospel, Christian holidays, humanitarian outreach, and vacation Bible school.
- Depts/columns: 700 words. Sermon outlines, media reviews, news, missions.
- Other: Puzzles, cartoons, all related to church and the Bible.

Sample Issue

16 pages. Sample copy and guidelines available at website.

- "Care, Concern and Caution: More on Church Leadership." Looks at the third chapter of Paul's letter to Timothy, outlining the conduct and character of church leaders.
- "Church Builders." Profile of the late A.T. Robertson, a theologian, author, and professor at Southern Baptist Theological Seminary.

Rights and Payment

All rights. No payment.

Dog Fancy

BowTie Magazines
P.O. Box 6050
Mission Viejo, CA 92690-6050

Editor: Ernie Slone

Description and Interests

Dog Fancy is devoted to all dogs, whether purebred or mixed breed. It seeks articles that cover training, canine health and behavior, and living happily with a dog. It is accepting articles on holistic health for its new supplement, Natural Dog. New contributors with fresh ideas are welcome to query. Circ: 270,000.

Contents: Articles; depts/columns
Frequency: Monthly
Website: www.dogfancy.com

Freelance Potential

95% written by nonstaff writers. Publishes 20–25 freelance submissions yearly; 10% by authors who are new to the magazine, 40% by experts. Receives 45 queries monthly.

Submissions

Query with résumé, sources, and clips. Accepts email queries to barkback@dogfancy.com. Responds in 1 month.

- Articles: 850–1,200 words. Informational and how-to. Topics include canine health, nutrition, care, grooming, behavior and training, breed profiles, and legal issues.
- Depts/columns: 650 words. Dog news; traveling with dogs; natural therapies; health, grooming, and training tips; puppies; older dogs; canine luxury items; canine sports and exercise; home life; adoption; and rescue.
- Other: Children's puzzles and activities.

Sample Issue

96 pages. Advertising. Sample copy available. Guidelines available at website.

- "Ticked Off Dogs." Learning how the chemicals that deter ticks and fleas work.
- "Just Herdin' Around." Spotlight on the Welsh Corgi, a loyal companion.

Rights and Payment

First North American serial rights. Written material, payment rates vary. Pays on publication. Provides 2 contributor's copies.

Dog World

3 Burroughs
Irvine, CA 92618

Editor: Jackie Franza

Description and Interests

Aimed at breeders, exhibitors, groomers, and competitors, *Dog World* is committed to providing information on the breeds, behavior, and training of purebred dogs. It emphasizes practical information that readers can use in their work with dogs. It also features articles on its companion website. Authors need to have experience with purebred dogs. Circ: 50,000.

Contents: 50% articles; 30% depts/columns; 20% other
Frequency: Monthly
Website: www.dogworld.com

Freelance Potential

90% written by nonstaff writers. Publishes 60 freelance submissions yearly; 10% by authors who are new to the magazine, 80% by experts. Receives 5 queries monthly.

Submissions

Query. Accepts hard copy. SASE. Responds in 4–6 months.

- Articles: 1,300–2,000 words. Informational, how-to, profiles, interviews, and opinion. Topics include dog breeding, kennel operations, legislation, veterinary care, nutrition, grooming, animal welfare, showmanship, dog sports, breed spotlights, and obedience training.
- Depts/columns: Staff-written.
- Artwork: 35mm color prints and transparencies.

Sample Issue

72 pages. Advertising. Sample articles and guidelines available.

- "Very Vizsla." Profile of this Hungarian pointing breed recognized for its hunting skill and beautiful coat.
- "Secret Signs of Agility Injuries." Experts tell how to spot an injury that is impacting a dog's agility.

Rights and Payment

First North American serial rights. Written material, payment rates vary. Pays on publication. Provides 2 contributor's copies.

The Dollar Stretcher

P.O. Box 14160
Bradenton, FL 34280

Editor: Gary Foreman

Description and Interests

The Dollar Stretcher is actually a group of publications dedicated to "Living better . . . for less." It is a digest-sized magazine, a digital newsletter, and a website—each offering articles and tips designed to teach readers how to live a comfortable life while spending less. "How-to" is a common theme here. All articles must present practical information. Circ: 100,000.

Contents: 70% articles; 30% depts/columns
Frequency: Monthly, for print; 2 times each month, for digital newsletter
Website: www.stretcher.com

Freelance Potential

75% written by nonstaff writers. Publishes 100 freelance submissions yearly; 20% by unpublished writers, 70% by authors who are new to the magazine, 10% by experts. Receives 40 unsolicited mss monthly.

Submissions

Send complete ms. Accepts disk submissions and email to editor@stretcher.com (Word or text file attachments); indicate whether submission is for print or online. SASE. Responds in 2 months.

- Articles: To 500–700 words. Informational, how-to, profiles, interviews, and personal experience. Topics include creative ways to save on food, housing, cars, clothing, stage-of-life material, dealing with non-frugal family members.
- Depts/columns: Staff-written.

Sample Issue

32 pages. No advertising. Sample articles and guidelines available at website.

- "7 Tips for Picking an All-Inclusive Resort." Guide to comparing all-inclusive resorts and how to search out the best deal for your next vacation.
- "Tricks and Treats: What Not to Buy in October." A look at which items are likely to be a good buy during the month of October and which ones consumers will be paying top dollar for, as well as what drives the price points.

Rights and Payment

All rights. Written material, $.10 per word for print magazine; no payment for online use. Pays on acceptance. Provides 1 contributor's copy.

Dolls

Jones Publishing
N7528 Aanstad Road
P.O. Box 5000
Iola, WI 54945

Editor: Joyce Greenholdt

Description and Interests

Doll collectors turn to this magazine for its current and comprehensive coverage of other doll collectors and collections, as well as articles on doll history and doll making. Product reviews and current prices are also included, as well as features about doll events. Circ: 10,000.

Contents: 50% articles; 50% depts/columns
Frequency: Monthly
Website: www.dollsmagazine.com

Freelance Potential

75% written by nonstaff writers. Publishes 50 freelance submissions yearly; 10% by authors who are new to the magazine, 75% by experts. Receives 40 unsolicited mss monthly.

Submissions

Send complete ms. Accepts email submissions to carief@jonespublishing.com. Response time varies.

- Articles: 1,000–1,200 words. Informational, how-to, creative nonfiction, profiles, interviews, and new product information. Topics include doll collecting, history, events, museums, costumes, and artists.
- Depts/columns: Word lengths vary. Essays, doll restoration and repair, new dolls.
- Artwork: Color prints, slides, or transparencies; JPEG images at 300 dpi.

Sample Issue

50 pages. Advertising. Sample articles and editorial calendar available at website. Writers' guidelines available.

- "Bionic Glamour." Designer plans for the short-lived doll line modeled on the '70s television show, *The Bionic Woman*.
- "A Fairy-Tale Vocation: Nancy Wiley Combines Love of Dolls, Books." Profile of a children's book illustrator who also designs dolls.

Rights and Payment

Perpetual and assignable license. Written material, $200. Pays on publication.

The Drama Review

New York University, Tisch School of the Arts
665 Broadway, 6th Floor
New York, NY 10012-2331

Editor: Richard Schechner

Description and Interests

The Drama Review is about performance in any medium, setting, or culture with a focus on its social, economic, and political context. Articles cover theater, dance, music, performance art, rituals, entertainment, and sports. It puts an emphasis on experimental, avant garde, intercultural, and interdisciplinary performance. It publishes accounts of specific performances, theoretical articles, and reviews. Circ: 3,000.

Contents: 95% articles; 5% depts/columns
Frequency: Quarterly
Website: www.mitpressjournals.org/loi/dram

Freelance Potential

100% written by nonstaff writers. Publishes 45 freelance submissions yearly; 30% by unpublished writers, 60% by authors who are new to the magazine. Receives 5 unsolicited mss monthly.

Submissions

Send complete ms with 70- to 100-word abstract. Prefers email submissions to tdr@nyu.edu (Word attachments); will accept disk submissions (PC formatted, Word files) with hard copy. SASE. Responds in 3–6 months.

- Articles: Word lengths vary. Informational, profiles, interviews, essays, and reviews. Topics include theater, dance, music, film, video, rituals, plays, and sports.
- Depts/columns: Summaries of new books about performance theory, 100–150 words. Full book reviews, 750–2,000 words.
- Artwork: Prints or slides; TIFF or JPEG digital images; line art.

Sample Issue

212 pages. Little advertising. Sample articles and guidelines available at website.

- "The Pixelated Revolution." Analyzing the mobile phone images uploaded to the internet during the ongoing Syrian Revolution and what they mean in relation to the people.
- "Your Hero Is a Ghost." Review of this performance group and its exploration of relations of power as manifested in culture.

Rights and Payment

All rights. Written material, $.04 per word. Pays on publication. Provides 1 contributor's copy.

Dramatics

Education Theatre Association
2343 Auburn Avenue
Cincinnati, OH 45219-2815

Editor: Donald Corathers

Description and Interests

Written for theater students and teachers, *Dramatics* features informational articles on acting, directing, and set design. It also publishes profiles of theater professionals, reviews, and news. It focuses on all areas of the performing arts, including film and television. Submissions should engage an above-average high-school theater student and deepen his or her understanding and appreciation of theater. Circ: 40,000.

Contents: 70% articles; 20% depts/columns; 10% other
Frequency: 9 times each year
Website: http://schooltheatre.org/publications

Freelance Potential

80% written by nonstaff writers. Publishes 35–76 freelance submissions yearly; 10% by unpublished writers, 15% by authors new to the magazine. Receives 25 queries, 30–40 mss monthly.

Submissions

Prefers complete ms; will accept query. Accepts hard copy for ms; email queries to dcorathers@edta.org, and simultaneous submissions if identified. SASE. Responds in 6 weeks.

- Articles: Features, to 4,000 words. Shorter articles, 800–1,200 words. Informational, interviews, and book reviews. Topics include playwriting, musical theater, acting, auditions, stage makeup, set design, and theater production.
- Fiction: Word lengths vary. Full-length and one-act plays for high school audiences.
- Depts/columns: Word lengths vary. Industry news, acting techniques.
- Artwork: 5x7 or larger B/W prints; 35mm or larger color transparencies; high-resolution JPEGs or TIFFs. Line art.

Sample Issue

76 pages. Advertising. Sample articles and guidelines available at website.

- "Help! I Hate My Voice." Learn how to present your best speaking voice by relaxing and centering your speech.
- "Playing the Angles." Lighting angles and how to use them in designs.

Rights and Payment

First rights. Written material, $25–$400. Pays on acceptance. Provides 5 contributor's copies.

Dream Network Journal

1025 Kane Creek Boulevard
P.O. Box 1026
Moab, UT 84532

Editor/Publisher: H. Roberta Ossana

Description and Interests

This magazine strives to help readers improve their physical, psychological, and spiritual well-being through a better understanding of dreams in our lives and culture. Its writers and readers include lay persons, dreamworkers, and therapists. It explores what dreams reveal and encourages personal experience and sharing of dreams in articles, art, and poetry. Circ: 4,000.

Contents: 50% articles; 10% fiction; 20% depts/columns; 20% other
Frequency: Quarterly
Website: www.dreamnetwork.net

Freelance Potential

50% written by nonstaff writers. Publishes 22 freelance submissions yearly; 30% by unpublished writers, 30% by authors who are new to the magazine, 40% by experts. Receives 8 queries, 8 unsolicited mss monthly.

Submissions

Query or send complete ms with one-sentence author bio. Prefers email to publisher@dreamnetwork.net (Word attachment); will accept hard copy. SASE. Responds in 6–8 weeks.

- Articles: To 2,500 words. Informational, self-help, how-to, profiles, interviews, personal experience, and humor. Topics include dreams, psychology, myths, spirituality, and health.
- Fiction: Word lengths vary. Stories about myths and dreams.
- Depts/columns: Word lengths vary. Book and media reviews.
- Artwork: Prints; JPEG or TIFF files at 300 dpi.

Sample Issue

44 pages. Advertising. Sample articles and guidelines available at website.

- "Recurring Dreams: What Are They Saying?" Explores the significance of recurring dreams and how to figure out what they're saying.
- "The Gilgamesh Cantata." One person's exploration of the role of music in his dreams.

Rights and Payment

All rights. No payment. Provides 10+ contributor's copies and a 1-year subscription.

Earth Island Journal

2150 Allston Way, Suite 460
Berkeley, CA 94704

Editor: Jason Mark

Description and Interests

This magazine combines investigative journalism and thought-provoking essays that make subtle but profound connections between the environment and other contemporary issues. It is looking for articles that anticipate environmental concerns before they become pressing problems. *Earth Island Journal* also features stories of individuals and communities who are successfully defending and restoring the Earth. On-the-ground reports from outside North America are especially welcome. Circ: 12,000.

Contents: 90% articles; 10% depts/columns
Frequency: Quarterly
Website: www.earthisland.org/journal

Freelance Potential

80% written by nonstaff writers. Publishes 20 freelance submissions yearly; 5% by unpublished writers, 50% by authors who are new to the magazine, 5% by experts. Receives 15 queries monthly.

Submissions

Prefers detailed query. Accepts hard copy and email to jmark@earthisland.org. Does not return mss. Responds if interested.

- Articles: Investigative features, 2,500–3,000 words. Dispatches, 1,200–1,500. Informational, profiles, and personal experience. Topics include the environment, conservation, wildlife, global warming, and politics.
- Depts/columns: Word lengths vary. Environmental news, opinions, Q&As, media reviews.

Sample Issue

64 pages. Advertising. Sample issue and guidelines available at website.

- "Cash for Trash." Why the country's largest garbage company is trying to get state laws the boost composting repealed.
- "Hunt, Fish...and Save the Planet." A look at the role of hunters and anglers in an ethical ecology plan.

Rights and Payment

First serial print and electronic rights. Articles, $.20 per word. Payment policy varies. Provides 3 contributor's copies.

E: The Environmental Magazine

28 Knight Street
Norwalk, CT 06851

Editor: Brita Belli

Description and Interests
A clearinghouse of information and resources regarding environmental issues around the globe, this nonprofit magazine reaches people who are concerned about the environment and want to know what they can do to help. It prefers articles that, in addition to providing information, suggest ways readers can become involved in the issue at hand. Circ: 50,000.

Contents: 50% articles; 50% depts/columns
Frequency: 6 times each year
Website: www.emagazine.com

Freelance Potential
60% written by nonstaff writers. Publishes 200 freelance submissions yearly; 20% by unpublished writers, 30% by authors who are new to the magazine. Receives 200 queries monthly.

Submissions
Query with approximate length, intended section of the magazine, clips and photo availability. Prefers email queries to brita@emagazine.com. Responds in 2 months.

- Articles: 2,500–3,500 words. Informational. Topics include population growth, transportation, children's environmental health, biotechnology, environmental education, conservation, and energy.
- Depts/columns: 300–800 words. News, analysis, Q&As, eco-friendly finance, eco-tourism, green products, house and home, health, nutrition, eco style.

Sample Issue
62 pages. Advertising. Sample issue and guidelines available at website. Editorial calendar available.

- "The Book That Changed the World." A half a century after the publication of *Silent Spring,* what further measures are still necessary to protect the environment from harmful chemical contamination.
- "Green Job Hunting." Resources and opportunities for those looking to get a job that is environmentally oriented.

Rights and Payment
Rights vary. Written material, $.30 per word. Pays on publication.

Elk Hunter 

P.O. Box 11367j
Chandler, AZ 85248

Editor: Ryan Hatfield

Description and Interests
This new quarterly magazine is for the sportsman passionate about elk hunting. Each issue covers the tactics and techniques for ensuring success, as well as detailed information on the necessary gear. Personal experience pieces on hunting adventures round out the mix. Its sister publication is *Western Hunter.* Circ: Unavailable.

Contents: Articles; depts/columns
Frequency: Quarterly
Website: www.elkhuntermagazine.com

Freelance Potential
Freelance percentages not yet available.

Submissions
Query. Accepts hard copy and email queries to backcountryeditor@gmail.com. SASE. Response time varies.

- Articles: Word lengths vary. Informational and how-to articles and personal experience pieces. Topics include hunting tips, gear, tactics, adventures, and conservation.

Sample Issue
Advertising. Sample copy available.

- "The Peanut Gallery." Personal experience piece details a hunter's first trip to New Mexico.
- "Staying on Track in the Off-season." Personal experience piece discusses the author's success with Wilderness Athlete products in staying in shape.
- "5 Gift Ideas for Hunters." Article suggests holiday gift ideas for every budget.

Rights and Payment
Rights vary. Payment rates and policy vary.

The Elks Magazine

425 West Diversey Parkway
Chicago, IL 60614

Editor/Publisher: Cheryl T. Stachura

Description and Interests

As "the voice of the Elks," this magazine serves to promote activities of the organization across the country. In addition, it features fresh, thought-provoking articles on a wide variety of general interest topics, including science, technology, nature, Americana, leisure, sports, history, health, and personal finance. Its average reader is over 40, with some college education and an above-average income. It does not publish political or religious articles, or poetry and only rarely uses first-person pieces. Circ: 900,000+.

Contents: 30% articles; 5% depts/columns; 65% other
Frequency: 10 times each year
Website: www.elks.org/elksmag

Freelance Potential

45% written by nonstaff writers. Publishes 20–30 freelance submissions yearly; 50% by authors who are new to the magazine, 10% by experts. Receives 8 unsolicited mss monthly.

Submissions

Send complete ms. Accepts hard copy and email submissions to magnews@elks.org. SASE. Responds in one month.

- Articles: 1,200–2,000 words. Informational. Topics include science, technology, nature, Americana, sports, history, health, retirement, personal finance, leisure activities, and seasonal and holiday themes.
- Depts/columns: Staff-written.

Sample Issue

56 pages. Advertising. Sample copy and guidelines available at website.

- "Electoral College FAQs: A Presidential Election Primer." Explanation of this often misunderstood cornerstone of the American presidential process.
- "Elk Drug Awareness Program." Speaking tours and materials distributed as part of the Elks national program to fight drugs.

Rights and Payment

First North American serial rights. Written material, $.25 per word. Pays on acceptance. Provides 3 contributor's copies.

Entra

419 Larchmont Boulevard, #329
Los Angeles, CA 90004

Creative Director: Jeffrey Nemeroff

Description and Interests

Each issue of this new online magazine takes readers inside residences created by top international design professionals. *Entra* also features product design, architecture, antiques, and profiles of artist studios and design professionals. It is a collaboration between a photographer, an artist, and an electronic publisher. Hits per month: Unavailable.

Contents: Articles; depts/columns
Frequency: 6 times each year
Website: www.entramagazine.com

Freelance Potential

Freelance percentage not yet available.

Submissions

Query. Accepts email to editors@entramagazine.com. Response time varies.

- Articles: Word lengths vary. Photo-essays and profiles. Topics include designers, design studios, private homes, and decor.
- Depts/columns: Word lengths vary. Design solutions, and design showrooms.

Sample Issue

155 pages. Advertising. Sample copy available at website.

- "Renaissance Man." Photo essay showcases the house and garden of Thierry Bosquet, the renowned costume and scenery designer.
- "Labor of Love." Article details how Granada Tile was founded in order to replicate the tiles the owner was inspired by in his native country of Nicaragua
- Sample dept/column: Design Solutions offers wallpaper suggestions that will infuse a sense of summer into any space

Rights and Payment

Rights vary. Payment rates and policy vary.

Environment

Science and Policy for Sustainable Development

325 Chestnut Street, Suite 800
Philadelphia, PA 19106

Managing Editor: Margaret Benner

Description and Interests

This magazine analyzes the global issues, places, and people where environment and development come together. Each issue features peer-reviewed articles, essays, and reviews that are written by researchers and practitioners. Articles should be written so that someone who is interested in the topic, but may not know much about it, will find it easy to understand. It considers its readers talented generalists. Circ: 3,100.

Contents: 80% articles; 15% depts/columns; 5% other
Frequency: 6 times each year
Website: www.environmentmagazine.org

Freelance Potential

90% written by nonstaff writers. Publishes 25 freelance submissions yearly; 5% by authors who are new to the magazine, 100% by experts. Receives 10 queries monthly.

Submissions

Send complete ms and art when possible. Accepts submissions electronically only through ScholarOne Manuscripts at http://mc.manuscriptcentral.com/venv. Responds in 2 months.

- Articles: 3,500–5,000 words. Informational and critical analyses. Topics include the environment, sustainable development, science, public policy, and government.
- Depts/columns: 1,000–1,700 words. Education, institutions, policy. Report on Reports, 1,500–2,000. Commentary, 750 words. Books of Note, 200–400 words.

Sample Issue

60 pages. Advertising. Sample articles and guidelines available at website.

- "The Artic: Past or Prologue?" Investigation into the ecological, social, and economic factors that are changing in the Artic and the impact on climate and global environmental change.
- "Overcoming the Global Injustices of Energy Poverty." Discusses the inequity of access to energy services and the ramifications which are dependent on location.

Rights and Payment

First rights. No payment. Provides 4–10 contributor's copies.

Equestrian

4047 Iron Works Parkway
Lexington, KY 40511

Senior VP Marketing/Communication: Kathy Meyer

Description and Interests

The United States Equestrian Federation publishes this magazine for its members, offering comprehensive coverage of events, news, and competitions. It also features articles on equine health, breeding, and training. This magazine bills itself as "the official magazine of American equestrian sports" and has been published since 1937. Circ: 90,000.

Contents: 25% articles; 25% depts/columns; 50% other
Frequency: 6 times each year
Website: www.usef.org

Freelance Potential

50% written by nontariff writers. Publishes 50 freelance submissions yearly; 10% by authors who are new to the magazine, 90% by experts. Receives 17 queries monthly.

Submissions

Query with résumé and writing samples. Accepts email submissions to busboy@user.org. Responds in 1 week.

- Articles: 2,000–3,000 words. Informational, how-to, and profiles. Topics include equine health, breeding, training, USER competitions, clinics, and programs.
- Depts/columns: 500–1,000 words. News briefs, equine health and insurance, breed profiles, USER member profiles.

Sample Issue

56 pages. Advertising. Sample copy available at website.

- "The Yes Man." Actor and horseman William Shatner shares stories about his life and his love of horses.
- "Grand Oak." A look at Live Oak Stud, a horse farm in Florida.

Rights and Payment

First rights. Written material, payment rates vary. Kill fee, 50%. Pays on publication. Provides 1 contributor's copy.

Equine Journal

103 Roxbury Street
Keene, NH 03431

Editor: Kelly Ballou

Description and Interests

Equine Journal is read by horse professionals—such as breeders and trainers—as well as by amateur horse enthusiasts. For more than 20 years, it has covered all aspects of horse care in five regional editions. It offers features on breeds, riding styles, equine health, and competitions. It is open to any horse-related topic that would be of interest to riders, owners, breeders, trainers—or anyone who simply loves horses. Circ: 19,000.

Contents: 50% articles; 50% depts/columns
Frequency: Monthly
Website: www.equinejournal.com

Freelance Potential

95% written by nonstaff writers. Publishes 100 freelance submissions yearly; 10% by unpublished writers, 3% by authors who are new to the magazine, 20% by experts. Receives 1 unsolicited ms each month.

Submissions

Query with clips or send complete ms. Accepts hard copy and email submissions to editorial@equinejournal.com. Accepts simultaneous submissions if identified. SASE. Responds in 2 months.

- Articles: 1,800–2,000 words. Informational, how-to, profiles, interviews, and opinion pieces. Topics include breeds, riding tips, carriage driving, training, stabling, transportation, equine care, ranch management, equine insurance, nutrition, and regional equine news.
- Depts/columns: The Last Laugh, to 750 words. All others staff-written.

Sample Issue

260 pages. Advertising. Sample copy, guidelines, and editorial calendar available at website.

- "Horseplay Is Serious." Preview of an equine health and performance symposium.
- Sample dept/column: The Last Laugh takes a humorous look at one rider's attempts to learn to speak "horse."

Rights and Payment

First North American serial rights. Articles, $100–$225. The Last Laugh, $25–$75. Pays one month after acceptance. Provides 1 contributor's copy.

The Fader

71 West 23rd Street, Floor 13
New York, NY 10010

Editor in Chief: Matthew Schnipper

Description and Interests

The Fader magazine and its companion website focus on the latest music and associated lifestyles in New York City. Its authoritative, in-depth reporting and street sensibility alternate between the barely mainstream to deep underground. The website is continuously updated with online-only content on emerging music, styles, and pop culture. When submitting a query for an artist profile, be sure to focus on the angle of the story. It seeks stories that are hyperlocal and breaking. Issues are all themed. Circ: 97,500.

Contents: Articles; depts/columns
Frequency: 6 times each year
Website: http://www.thefader.com

Freelance Potential

50–60% written by nonstaff writers. 15–20% of queries accepted.

Submissions

All sections of the magazine and website are open to pitches. Prefers concise (500-word) but detailed email queries to editorial@thefader.com. Response time, 30 to 60 days.

- Articles: Word lengths vary. Interviews; event coverage; global field reportage; features. Topics: music, lifestyle, pop culture.
- Depts/columns: Word lengths vary.

Sample Issue

Advertising. Sample copy and editorial calendar available at website.

- "Usher: High Note," by Matthew Schnipper. An interview with the seven-time Grammy Award-winning musician.
- "Machel Montano: Delirious," by Nick Barat. A visit to Trinidad to meet the musician and his band, Xtatik.

Rights and Payment

Rights for one year. Payment, $.50–$1 a word, 60 days after invoice.

Faith Today

Box 5885, West Beaver Creek Post Office
Richmond Hill, Ontario L4B 088
Canada

Senior Editor: Bill Fledderus

Description and Interests

Faith Today provides connection and practical help to Evangelical Christians living in Canada. Read by ministers, church leaders, and lay people, it profiles Christians who put their faith to work, offers ministry ideas, and deals with social and political issues. It is interested in articles that provide analysis and interpretation, rather than straight reports. Circ: 20,000.

Contents: 60% articles; 40% depts/columns
Frequency: 6 times each year
Website: www.faithtoday.ca

Freelance Potential

60% written by nonstaff writers. Publishes 120 freelance submissions yearly; 1% by unpublished writers, 10% by authors who are new to the magazine. Receives 10 queries monthly.

Submissions

Query only with writing background and subject qualifications. Prefers email to editor@faithtoday.ca; will accept hard copy. SAE/IRC. Responds promptly.

- Articles: 800–2,000 words. Informational, inspirational, self-help, how-to, analysis, profiles, and slice-of-life pieces. Topics include Canadian trends, issues, and Evangelical ministries. Essays on spiritual and social issues, 650–1,200 words. News, 750 words.
- Depts/columns: Kingdom Matters, short items that reflect how God is at work in Canada; 50–350 words. Arts & Culture, reviews of works by Canadian authors; 300 words.

Sample Issue

64 pages. Advertising. Sample copy and guidelines available at website.

- "Why They're Leaving." Exploring why young adults are leaving, staying, or returning to the Evangelical Church.
- Sample dept/column: "Kingdom Matters" tells how five Canadian climbers staged a climb to raise funds to reduce human trafficking.

Rights and Payment

First North American serial rights and web rights. Features, $0.25 Canadian per word. Essays, $0.15 Canadian per word. Kingdom Matters and News, $0.20 Canadian per word. Kill fee, 30–50%. Pays on acceptance. Provides 2 contributor's copies.

Family Circle

Meredith Corporation
375 Lexington Avenue, 9th Floor
New York, NY 10017

Executive Editor: Darcy Jacobs

Description and Interests

Family Circle offers smart, practical advice on parenting issues, with an emphasis on concerns faced by mothers of tweens and teens. It also offers ideas for fun family activities, delivers the latest health news, and showcases projects to create a comfortable home. It is on the lookout for true stories about women making a difference in their communities and reports on social issues affecting American families. It welcomes new writers with national magazine experience. Circ: 3.8 million.

Contents: 65% articles; 35% depts/columns
Frequency: 15 times each year
Website: www.familycircle.com

Freelance Potential

80% written by nonstaff writers. Publishes hundreds of freelance submissions yearly. Receives hundreds of queries monthly.

Submissions

Query with clips (1 from a national magazine) and author bio. Accepts hard copy and email to fcfeedback@familycircle.com. No simultaneous submissions. SASE for response; materials are not returned. Responds in 6–8 weeks if interested.

- Articles: 1,000–2,000 words. Informational, inspirational, self-help, how-to, profiles, and personal experience. Topics include home, parenting, relationships, food, health, style, fashion, safety, and fitness.
- Depts/columns: 750 words. My Hometown, My Family Life, Good Works, recipes, beauty tips, shopping tips, fitness routines, advice.

Sample Issue

210 pages. Advertising. Sample copy available at website. Guidelines available.

- "Do Kids Really Need Homework?" A prominent educator claims there is no evidence that homework improves understanding or develops good work habits.
- "Tips for Relieving Allergy Symptoms." Suggestions for relieving seasonal symptoms.
- Sample dept/column: Kitchen Basics gives step-by-step steak searing instructions.

Rights and Payment

All rights. Written material, payment rates vary. Kill fee, 25%/ Pays on acceptance. Provides 1 contributor's copy.

FamilyFun

47 Pleasant Street
Northampton, MA 01060

Department Editor: Jonathan Adolph

Description and Interests

For the past 20 years, *FamilyFun* has been providing parents with ideas for having fun with their children. Original ideas for family projects and family-friendly travel destinations are always welcome. The emphasis is on activities and practical ways to build strong, healthy families that are family-tested, affordable, and easy. In 2012, the magazine was purchased by Meredith Corporation from Disney. Circ: 2 million+.

Contents: Articles; depts/columns
Frequency: 10 times each year
Website: www.parents.com/familyfun-magazine

Freelance Potential

80% written by nonstaff writers. Publishes 100+ freelance submissions yearly: 1% are by unpublished writers and 2% are by new authors. Receives 100+ queries and mss monthly.

Submissions

Query for features with content, structure, tone of article. Send complete ms for depts/columns. Include illustrations, if appropriate. Submit seasonal material 6 months in advance. Accepts hard copy and email queries to queries.familyfun@disney.com. SASE. Responds in 6–8 weeks.

- Articles: 850–3,000 words. Informational, how-to, personal experience pieces. Topics include food, crafts, parties, holidays, sports, games, creative solutions to common household problems and family challenges, educational projects, and home organizing and decorating.
- Depts/columns: 50–1,000 words. Let's Cook, Let's Party, Let's Go, Success Story, My Great Idea, Healthy Fun, Family Home, Our Favorite Things. See guidelines for details. Crafts, nature activities, recipes, family getaways and traditions, household hints, healthy fun, home decorating and gardening tips, and product reviews.

Sample Issue

120 pages. Advertising. Sample articles and writers' guidelines available at website.

- "Animal Attractions." Making jungle toy cards.
- Sample dept/column: "Let's Go" shares tips on Letterboxing, a modern-day treasure hunt.

Rights and Payment

First serial rights. Written material, payment rates vary. Pays on acceptance.

Family Motor Coaching

8291 Clough Pike
Cincinnati, OH 45244

Editor: Robbin Gould

Description and Interests

This magazine targets motor home owners and features destination pieces, as well as information on outfitting and maintaining motor homes. It is the member publication of the Family Motor Coach Association. The publication's emphasis is on the practical and it prefers to use writers who are technical experts and aficionados of the motor home lifestyle. Circ: 110,000.

Contents: 55% articles; 40% depts/columns; 5% other
Frequency: Monthly
Website: www.fmcmagazine.com

Freelance Potential

75% written by nonstaff writers. Publishes 50 freelance submissions yearly; 10% by unpublished writers, 10% by authors who are new to the magazine, 20% by experts. Receives 50 queries, 25 unsolicited mss monthly.

Submissions

Prefers query with résumé, outline, and clips; accepts complete ms with résumé. Author should provide photos to accompany article. Accepts hard copy and email queries to magazine@fmca.com. SASE. Responds in 3 months if interested.

- Articles: 1,500–2,000 words. Informational, how-to, profiles, interviews, humor, and personal experience. Topics include travel, equipment, maintenance, camping, the RV industry, and famous people with RV lifestyles.
- Depts/columns: 1,000 words. Travel tips, technical advice, cooking in a motor home, news, and new product information.
- Art: Digital photos, 300 dpi minimum, drawings.

Sample Issue

144 pages. Advertising. Sample articles available. Guidelines available via email request to magazine@fmca.com.

- "Memphis—Music and Much More." Destination piece on this home to the "King of Rock and Roll" and the civil rights attractions.
- Sample dept/column: Tech and Travel Tips offers clever solution for shoe storage at the door of the RV.

Rights and Payment

First North American serial and electronic rights. Written material, $50–$500. Pays on acceptance. Provides 1 contributor's copy.

Family Tree Magazine

10151 Carver Road
Cincinnati, OH 45242

Editorial Director: Allison Stacy

Description and Interests

This is the leading how-to publication for those who want to discover and celebrate their roots. It covers all areas of interest to family history enthusiasts, going beyond genealogy research. *Family Tree Magazine* provides engaging, easy-to-understand instructions that make genealogy a hobby anyone can do. It does not publish personal experience pieces. For writers new to the magazine, it is most open to short submissions for its departments and columns. Circ: 75,000.

Contents: 50% articles; 50% depts/columns
Frequency: 7 times each year
Website: www.familytreemagazine.com

Freelance Potential

75–100% written by nonstaff writers. Publishes 12–120 freelance submissions yearly: 10–25% developed from unsolicited submissions; 1–10% by authors new to the magazine; 1–10% by previously unpublished writers. Receives 25–50 queries, 25–50 manuscripts monthly.

Submissions

Query only with qualifications, clips, and suggestions for sidebars, tips, and resources. Prefers email queries to ftmedia@fwpubs.com. Accepts hard copy. No simultaneous submissions. SASE. Responds in 6–8 weeks.

- Articles: 2,000–3,500 words. Informational and how-to articles and new product information. Topics include genealogy, ethnic heritage, personal history, genealogy websites and software, photography, and photo preservation.
- Depts/columns: 300–1,000 words. Toolkit, technology resources; Branching Out, lively news bits; Everything's Relative, amusing stories of the lighter side of family history.

Sample Issue

76 pages. Advertising. Sample copy and guidelines available at website.

- "One in a Million." Eight steps to verifying your research findings.
- "Tips for Finding Clues in Family Photos." Confirming places, faces, and dates using old photos.

Rights and Payment

All rights. Written material, payment rates vary. Kill fee, 25%. Pays on acceptance. Provides 2 contributor's copies.

Fangoria

250 West 49th Street, Suite 304
New York, NY 10019

Editor in Chief: Chris Alexander

Description and Interests

Hard-core horror fans turn to this publication for the latest news and behind-the-scenes looks at various media. *Fangoria* features reviews of books, television shows, movies, and video games with horror themes. It also profiles actors and actresses, directors, game creators, and others involved in the production of any and all horror entertainment. The magazine is looking for writers with unique access to information or personalities relating to the horror genre. Articles need to give readers something they can't find online on their own. Circ: 260,000.

Contents: 70% articles; 30% depts/columns
Frequency: 10 times each year
Website: www.fangoria.com

Freelance Potential

95% written by nonstaff writers. Publishes 48 freelance submissions yearly; 1% by unpublished writers, 5% by authors who are new to the magazine, 95% by experts. Receives 10 queries monthly.

Submissions

Query. Accepts hard copy and email queries to info@fangoria.com. SASE. Responds in 3 months.

- Articles: 2,500–3,000 words. Informational, how-to, profiles, interviews, and media reviews. Topics include horror filmmaking, special effects, and thriller novelists.
- Depts/columns: 500–750 words. Book, film, video game, and DVD reviews.

Sample Issue

82 pages. Advertising. Sample articles available at website. Guidelines available.

- "The Making of *Silent Hill Revelation*." A behind-the-scenes look at this eagerly awaited 3D sequel, featuring interviews with director, Michael J. Bassett and monster maker, Paul Jones.
- "Hammer Horrors." Vintage interview with Hammer actresses Veronica Carlson and Virginia Wetherell.

Rights and Payment

All worldwide rights. Articles, $150–$250. Depts/columns, $75. Pays 1–3 months after publication. Provides 2 contributor's copies.

Fashion Etc.

155 East 55th Street, Suite 6H
New York, NY 10022

Editorial Director: Sonia Evers

Description and Interests

This online fashion and beauty publication offers original features, news, resources, and opinion for readers interested in trends related to fashion, style, and celebrities. It calls itself "the singular resource for the fashion-wise, beauty-driven" and provides direction for those interested in fashion. It was co-founded by the former CEO of *Women's Wear Daily* and *W,* Michael Coady. Circ: Unavailable.

Contents: Articles; depts/columns
Frequency: Updated regularly
Website: www.fashionetc.com

Freelance Potential

Receives several freelance submissions monthly.

Submissions

Query. Send email to fashionetcnews@fashionetc.com. Response time varies.

- Articles: Word lengths vary. Informational articles and profiles. Topics include fashion and beauty trends, shopping, entertainment, and designers.
- Dept/columns: Word lengths vary. New products, celebrities, fashion and retail news.

Sample Issue

Advertising. Sample articles available at website.

- "Kristen Stewart's *Twilight* Style Evolution." Article showcases the actress's change in style over the years as she rose to stardom.
- "Beauty Brands Going Fragance Free." Article discusses the trend in beauty products going fragance free due to skin irritations and allergies.
- Sample dept/column: Style Spotlight showcases Kate Moss's recent look at her book's launch party.

Rights and Payment

Rights vary. Payment rates and policy vary.

Fate

P.O. Box 460
Lakeville, MN 55044

Editor in Chief: Phyllis Galde

Description and Interests

This digest-sized magazine is filled with reports of strange occurrences, ancient mysteries, and paranormal activity. It also features readers' personal experiences. It is open to receiving any well-written, well-documented article on a wide variety of strange and unknown phenomena. *Fate*'s readers especially like reports of current investigations, experiments, theories, and experiences. Circ: 15,000.

Contents: 50% articles; 50% depts/columns
Frequency: 6 times each year
Website: www.fatemag.com

Freelance Potential

67% written by nonstaff writers. Publishes 120 freelance submissions yearly; 20% by unpublished writers, 50% by authors who are new to the magazine, 60% by experts. Receives 20 queries and unsolicited mss monthly.

Submissions

Query for articles. Send complete ms for depts/columns. Accepts email to fate@fatemag.com and disk submissions with hard copy. SASE. Responds in a few weeks.

- Articles: 1,500–3,000 words. Informational, how-to, profiles, interviews, and personal experience. Topics include psychic dreams, telekinesis, mysterious events, unexplained coincidences, mediums and spirit contact, astral travel, alternative healing and spirituality, UFOs, and ghosts.
- Depts/columns: True Mystic Experiences and My Proof of Survival, to 500 words.

Sample Issue

128 pages. Advertising. Sample articles and guidelines available at website.

- "The Magical Charm Gates in New Orleans." A lovely restaurant in the French Quarter of New Orleans is the setting for past-life encounters.
- "UFO Near Mars' Curiosity Rover?" Investigates a report regarding a UFO sighting over the Curiosity Rover.

Rights and Payment

All rights. Articles, $.05 per word. Depts/columns, $25. Pays 6 months after publication. Provides 1 contributor's copy.

Fellowship

Fellowship of Reconciliation
P.O. Box 271
Nyack, NY 10960

Editor: Ethan Vesely-Flad

Description and Interests

"A magazine of peacemaking," *Fellowship* helps people of faith commit themselves to a nonviolent world of justice, peace, and freedom. Articles, essays, and poems are all part of the editorial mix. It would like to see more submissions on the practical applications of active nonviolence in non-Western contexts. Circ: 5,500.

Contents: 50% articles; 35% depts/columns; 15% other
Frequency: Quarterly
Website: www.forusa.org

Freelance Potential

80% written by nonstaff writers. Publishes 10 freelance submissions yearly; 10% by unpublished writers, 20% by authors who are new to the magazine, 20% by experts. Receives 8 queries, 5 unsolicited mss monthly.

Submissions

Query or send complete ms. Accepts hard copy and email submissions to editor@forusa.org. SASE. Responds in 3 months.

- Articles: 700–2,000 words. Informational, how-to, profiles, and personal experience. Topics include activism, belief systems, religion, government, international relations, legal issues.
- Depts/columns: Word lengths vary. Opinion pieces, news, and book reviews.

Sample Issue

40 pages. Advertising. Sample copy available at website. Guidelines and theme list available.

- "Shackles and Sunlight." Cover story examines America's prison crisis and identifies ways to transform the system, as well as its inmates.
- Sample dept/column: Using Our Heads, Together discusses the importance of activism-oriented research.

Rights and Payment

First North American serial rights. No payment. Provides 3 contributor's copies and two 1-year subscriptions.

Feminist Studies 

0103 Taliaferro Hall
University of Maryland
College Park, MD 20742

Managing Editor: Karla Mantilla

Description and Interests

This scholarly journal features research, opinion, essays, fiction, and poetry that examine feminist issues, along with gender, racial identity, sexual orientation, economic means, geographical location, and physical ability. It is interested in social and political issues that affect women and men in the U.S. and around the world. Circ: 5,000.

Contents: 85% articles; 15% fiction
Frequency: 3 times each year
Website: www.feministstudies.org

Freelance Potential

98% written by nonstaff writers. Publishes 20 freelance submissions yearly; 15% by unpublished writers, 90% by authors who are new to the magazine, 100% by experts. Receives 12 unsolicited mss monthly.

Submissions

Send complete ms (include 200-word abstract for research and criticism pieces) with title page and cover letter. Must send hard copy and email (Word or WordPerfect attachments), or send disk submission with hard copy. See guidelines for addresses for specific submissions. Query with résumé and writing sample for review essays only. No simultaneous submissions. Materials not returned. Responds in 6 months.

- Articles: To 10,500 words. Research papers, criticism, essays, creative nonfiction, commentary, activist reports, political manifestos, and interviews. Topics include gender, social, political, racial, and economic issues.
- Fiction: To 25 pages. Contemporary and literary fiction.
- Other: Poetry, no line limit.

Sample Issue

248 pages. Advertising. Sample copy, guidelines, and upcoming needs available at website.

- "Mary E. Hutchinson, Intelligibility, and the Historical Limits of Agency." Analyzes the artist's paintings of couples.
- "Trafficking in Truth: Media, Sexuality, and Human Rights Evidence." Examines forced prostitution as portrayed in three films.

Rights and Payment

Rights negotiable. No payment. Provides 2 contributor's copies.

Fertility Today

P.O. Box 117
Laurel, MD 20725-0177

Editor: Diana Broomfield, M.D.

Description and Interests

Fertility Today serves as a comprehensive and up-to-date resource for all aspects of fertility and infertility. Nearly all articles are written by experts such as physicians, attorneys, third party reproduction organizations, complementary medicine advocates, mental health professionals, and patients who wish to share their experiences with others. Stories cover medical and legal issues, as well as the spiritual, emotional, and physical aspects of infertility. It strives to be the nation's leader in educating the public on reproductive health and features some personal experience pieces as well. Circ: 225,000.

Contents: 85% articles; 15% depts/columns
Frequency: Quarterly
Website: www.fertilitytoday.org

Freelance Potential

75% written by nonstaff writers. Publishes 150 freelance submissions yearly; 15% by new authors, 90% by experts. Receives 12 queries monthly.

Submissions

Send complete ms with résumé, bio, and address of practice. Accepts email submissions to articles@fertility-today.org or at the website. Responds in 2 months.

- Articles: 800–1,500 words. Informational, profiles, interviews, opinion, personal experience. Topics include fertility issues and treatments, male and female reproductive health, fertility drugs, assisted reproductive technology, third-party reproduction, genetics, recurrent pregnancy loss, high-risk obstetrics, alternative medicine.
- Depts/columns: 1,500 words. Exercise and Nutrition; Adoption/Child-Free Living; Mind, Body & Soul; My Story; Health Forum, written by physicians. Book reviews.

Sample Issue

96 pages. Advertising. Sample copy and guidelines available at website.

- "The Integrative Approach to Fertility." An acupuncturist and anti-aging expert on fertility.
- "Unexplained Infertility." A physician discusses laboratory tests and treatments recommended for this condition.

Rights and Payment

All rights. Written material, \$.50 per word. Pays on acceptance. Provides 3 contributor's copies.

Fibre Focus

Box 1444
Everett, Ontario LOM 1J0
Canada

Publisher: Graham McCracken

Description and Interests

The Ontario Handweavers and Spinners organization publishes this magazine for members and others who are weaving and spinning enthusiasts. It features organization news and articles on all aspects of the craft, including dyeing, knitting, basketry, feltmaking and papermaking, as well as craft supply and techniques. Also found on its pages are profiles of craftspeople, news items, and book reviews. Circ: 800.

Contents: Articles; depts/columns
Frequency: Quarterly
Website: www.ohs.on.ca/members/fibre-focus-magazine

Freelance Potential

65% written by nonstaff writers. Publishes 45 freelance submissions yearly; 50% by unpublished writers, 20% by authors who are new to the magazine, 30% by experts. Receives 2 queries monthly.

Submissions

Query or send complete ms with bio and artwork. Accepts email to ffpublisher@bell.net (Word, WordPerfect, or RTF attachments). Response time varies.

- Articles: Word lengths vary. Informational, how-to, profiles, and industry news. Topics include weaving, spinning, dyeing, knitting, basketry, feltmaking, papermaking, sheep-raising, craftspeople, and craft supply.
- Depts/columns: Staff-written.

Sample Issue

40 pages. Advertising. Sample articles and guidelines available at website.

- "Spinning, Dyeing, and Weaving a Book Cover: with Gerard Brender a Brandis." Replacing a hardcover book cover with this attractive woven cloth cover.
- "Fiber Optics Conference Preview." A sneak peak at who and what will be at this upcoming conference.

Rights and Payment

First-time rights. Articles, \$30 per page. Pays 1 month after publication. Provides 2 author's copies.

Fido Friendly

P.O. Box 160
Marsing, ID 83639

Submissions: Susan Sims

Description and Interests
This magazine is read by dog owners looking for information about pet-friendly travel destinations in the U.S. and Canada. Also published are articles on canine health and wellness, behavior and training, and even canine fashion. It provides readers with practical details, so destination pieces need to include a comprehensive list of site resources with addresses, phone numbers, and websites. Circ: 44,000.

Contents: 80% articles; 20% depts/columns
Frequency: Quarterly
Website: www.fidofriendly.com

Freelance Potential
75% written by nonstaff writers. Publishes 20 freelance submissions yearly; 10% by unpublished writers, 10% by authors who are new to the magazine. Receives 8 queries monthly.

Submissions
Query with sample paragraph. Accepts email queries to editorial@fidofriendly.com. Responds in 1 month.

- Articles: 800–1,200 words. Informational, how-to, and profiles. Topics include canine health, behavior, and training; travel; rescue; and celebrity dog owners.
- Depts/columns: Word lengths vary. Profiles, nutrition, health, training, adoptions, and gear.
- Artwork: TIFF images at 300 dpi.

Sample Issue
98 pages. Advertising. Sample articles available at website. Writers' guidelines available.

- "Day Trip: Taking the Fido Slopes by Snowstorm ala Skijoring and Snowshoeing." The growing popularity of dog-drawn sleds in Oregon.
- "Theater Capital Branson Entertains Canines." Canines can do some social networking at the Ozark's Hilton Branson Convention Center Hotel.

Rights and Payment
First rights. Written material, $.10 per word. Pays on publication. Provides 1 contributor's copy.

Field & Stream

2 Park Avenue, 9th Floor
New York, NY 10016

Editor in Chief: Anthony Licata

Description and Interests
This magazine is recognized as one of America's foremost consumer magazines for hunting and fishing information. It features how-to's, personal hunting tales, gear reviews, and articles on animal behavior and wildlife conservation. It is always in need of fresh material that will deliver something new to its readers. Circ: 1.2 million.

Contents: 60% articles; 40% depts/columns
Frequency: Monthly
Website: www.fieldandstream.com

Freelance Potential
85% written by nonstaff writers. Publishes 10–20 freelance submissions yearly; 2–3% by unpublished writers, 1–2% by authors who are new to the magazine. Receives 120 queries each month.

Submissions
Query with outline and availability of artwork. Accepts hard copy and email queries to fsletters@bonniercorp.com. SASE. Responds in 2 months.

- Articles: 500–1,500 words. Informational, how-to, profiles, humor, and nostalgia. Topics include hunting and fishing tactics, techniques, destinations, natural history, the environment, conservation, and the sportsman lifestyle.
- Depts/columns: 750–1,000 words. Sport shooting, hunting, fishing, waterfowl, game, recipes, and book reviews.

Sample Issue
104 pages. Advertising. Sample copy available at website.

- "Great Hunting, Fishing, and Camping Tips from the Readers of *Field & Stream*." Article offers readers' best tips from the field.
- "15 Reasons to Head to Michigan for Serious Flats Fishing." Article describes the state as a fisherman's paradise.

Rights and Payment
First North American serial rights. Written material, payment rates vary. Pays on acceptance.

Film Threat

Editor in Chief: Mark Bell

Description and Interests

Film Threat was a print magazine founded in the 1980s, retired in 1997, and now has returned to the scene digitally. It has had a renegade reputation for its film reviews, and its coverage of news, festivals, filmmakers, and the inspiration and process of filmmaking. New writers and reviewers are always needed, as well as information on film festivals and other film news. Circ: Unavailable.

Contents: Articles; depts/columns; reviews
Frequency: Updated regularly
Website: Website: www.filmthreat.com

Freelance Potential

Receives several queries monthly.

Submissions

Query. Accepts submissions via form at website. Response time varies.

- Articles: Word lengths vary. Informational articles and interviews. Topics include films, directors, filmmaking, and festivals.
- Depts/columns: Word lengths vary. Reviews and industry news.

Sample Issue

Advertising. Sample copy and guidelines available at website.

- "The Bootleg Files: Abraham Lincoln." Article discusses the recent Blu-ray release of a restored HD version of the 1930 feature film *Abraham Lincoln*.
- "Publishing His Luck." Article features an interview with filmmaker Luis Prieto about his new film *Pusher*.
- Sample dept/column: Review discusses the movie *Bert the Emotion Picture*.

Rights and Payment

Rights vary. No payment.

Fine Gardening

The Taunton Press
63 South Main Street
P.O. Box 5506
Newtown, CT 06470-5506

Editor: Steve Aitken

Description and Interests

Gardeners of all skill levels, from backyard flower enthusiasts to garden designers, read this magazine for ideas and information. All types of flower, fruit, and vegetable gardening are covered here. There are also articles on garden design elements, such as seating, trellises, and water features. Its readers are not experts, but they are well-versed in all aspects of gardening, and writers for this publication are expected to have a thorough knowledge of their subjects as well. Circ: 130,989.

Contents: 75% articles; 25% depts/columns
Frequency: 6 times each year
Website: www.finegardening.com

Freelance Potential

95% written by nonstaff writers. Publishes 60+ freelance submissions yearly; 15% by unpublished writers, 50% by authors who are new to the magazine, 65% by experts. Receives 50 queries, 20 unsolicited mss monthly.

Submissions

Query for features. Send complete ms for Tips and Last Word departments. Accepts hard copy and email to fg@taunton.com. Responds in 3 months.

- Articles: Word lengths vary. Informational, how-to, and personal experience. Topics include ornamental plants, flowers, vegetables, fruits, garden design, tools, pests, diseases, and garden structures.
- Depts/columns: To 800 words. Tips, techniques, plant selections, new products. Last Word, gardening-related essays.

Sample Issue

86 pages. Advertising. Sample articles and guidelines available.

- "Big Bloomers." Flower varieties with large, show-stopping blooms that have big impact in the garden.
- "A Big Garden on a Small Lot." How to pack a lot of plants into a small space for maximum beauty.

Rights and Payment

First rights. Written material, payment rates vary. Pays on acceptance. Provides 2 contributor's copies.

FineScale Modeler

21027 Crossroads Circle
PO Box 1612
Waukesha, WI 53187-1612

Editor: Matthew Usher

Description and Interests

This magazine is read for its detailed and well-illustrated how-to articles on scale modeling. Readers include beginners to the hobby, as well as advanced enthusiasts. Writers who are submitting to the magazine for the first time, or who are unpublished, will find a brief article on a popular subject, such as repairing and polishing clear parts, to be their best chance for acceptance. Circ: 60,000.

Contents: 30% articles; 30% depts/columns; 40% other
Frequency: 10 times each year
Website: www.finescale.com

Freelance Potential

85% written by nonstaff writers. Publishes 40 freelance submissions yearly; 20% by unpublished writers, 20% by authors who are new to the magazine, 10% by experts. Receives 17 queries, 15 unsolicited mss monthly.

Submissions

Prefers email query; include biography if first-time author. Accepts hard copy and disk submissions with hard copy, as well as submissions via website at www.contribute.Kalmbach.com. No simultaneous submissions. Availability of artwork improves chance of acceptance. SASE. Responds in 1–4 months.

- Articles: 750–2,500 words. Informational and how-to. Topics include modeling techniques; making, repairing, and polishing parts; painting; color schemes; displays and dioramas; and workshop techniques.
- Depts/columns: Staff-written.
- Artwork: Digital images; slides, prints. Scale drawings.

Sample Issue

74 pages. Advertising. Sample articles and guidelines available at website.

- "Airbrushing & Finishing: Quick, Easy Ship Weathering." Using toothpicks for this easy technique with sophisticated results.
- "Showcase: Super-Detailed Schnellboot." A fast boat that took a long time to construct.

Rights and Payment

All rights. All material, payment rates vary. Pays on acceptance. Provides 1 contributor's copy.

Fired Arts & Crafts

N7450 Aanstad Road
P.O Box 5000
Iola, WI 54945

Editor: Joyce Greenholdt

Description and Interests

Fired Arts & Crafts is like having your own personal fired arts instructor. Each issue provides readers with the latest techniques and a variety of do-it-yourself projects, from metal clay and wheel thrown pottery to glass and enamels. Contributors should start by sending snapshots of their creations. The magazine is always interested in hearing from writers who can share their techniques with its readers—novices, hobbyists, teachers, and business owners. Circ: 3,500.

Contents: Articles; depts/columns
Frequency: Monthly
Website: www.firedartsandcrafts.com

Freelance Potential

80% written by nonstaff writers. Publishes 90 freelance submissions yearly; 20% by authors who are new to the magazine.

Submissions

Query with photos of project. Accepts disk submissions and email to mikeh@jonespublishing.com. No simultaneous submissions. Responds in 1–3 months.

- Articles: Word lengths vary. Informational, how-to, and profiles. Topics include projects, all fired arts, firing techniques, teaching lessons, business issues, and new product information.
- Depts/columns: Word lengths vary. Projects, exhibition information.
- Artwork: High-resolution digital images at 300 dpi.

Sample Issue

52 pages. Sample copy and guidelines available at website.

- "Airbrushing & Fired Arts." How-to techniques for successful airbrushing of ceramics and safety precautions artists should take.
- "Discover the Versatility of Glass Painting." Explores the many possibilities of this art form, as well as techniques to produce beautiful pieces easily.

Rights and Payment

One-time rights. Written material, payment rates vary. Pays on publication. Provides 2 contributor's copies.

First Things

The Institute on Religion and Public Life
35 East 21st Street, 6th Floor
New York, NY 10010

Editor: R. R. Reno

Description and Interests

Published by the Institute on Religion and Public Life, this magazine features articles, essays, book reviews, and poetry about religion and contemporary society. Its slant is interreligious and nonpartisan. Circ: 33,000.

Contents: 60% articles; 20% depts/columns; 20% other
Frequency: 10 times each year
Website: www.firstthings.com

Freelance Potential

80% written by nonstaff writers. Publishes 80 freelance submissions yearly; 10% by unpublished writers, 20% by new authors. Receives 40 unsolicited mss monthly.

Submissions

Send complete ms. Prefers email submissions to ft@firstthings.com (Word attachments); will accept hard copy. Accepts poetry via hard copy only, attention "Poetry Editor." No simultaneous submissions. SASE. Responds in 2 months.

- Articles: 3,000–5,000 words. Informational, personal experience, creative nonfiction, theological essays, and review essays. Topics include religion and public affairs.
- Opinion pieces: 1,000–2,000 words. Topics include religion, social issues, philosophy, politics, science, technology, the arts, education, ethics, and current events.
- Depts/columns: 1,500–1,800 words. Book reviews.
- Other: Poetry, to 40 lines.

Sample Issue

80 pages. Advertising. Sample articles and guidelines available at website.

- "Thirteen Theses on Marriage." Scholars and writers respond to a variety of statements regarding sex, gender, and marriage in a religious and societal context.
- "A Mandate to Disobey." A look at the Affordable Care Act and the mandates being imposed on employers that violate their religious beliefs.

Rights and Payment

All rights. Written material, payment rates vary. Pays on publication. Provides 2 author's copies.

The Fiscal Times  

New York Office
712 Fifth Avenue, 47th Floor
New York, NY 10019

Editor in Chief: Jacqueline Leo

Description and Interests

The Fiscal Times is a digital news, opinion, and media service devoted to comprehensive quality reporting on vital fiscal, budgetary, health care, and economic issues. It strives to become one of the most trusted sources of news, opinion, and research on fiscal policy and its effects on the country at large, including businesses and consumers. Profiles of controversial political figures and business leaders and data-driven analyses of government reports are of particular interest. Hits per month: 12 million.

Contents: Articles; depts/columns
Frequency: Updated regularly
Website: www.thefiscaltimes.com

Freelance Potential

30% written by nonstaff writers. Always looking for new writers.

Submissions

Direct queries with bio and clips to appropriate editor: business or economy queries to yrosenberg@thefiscaltimes.com; personal finance to bbriody@thefiscaltimes.com; all other queries to info@thefiscaltimes.com.

- Articles: Word lengths vary. Informational articles, interviews; and opinion pieces.
- Depts/columns: Business & Economy and Life & Money are most open sections. Word lengths vary.

Sample Issue

Advertising. Sample articles available at website.

- "Obama Hits the Road for Michigan." The President travels to Michigan to continue campaigning for his tax policies.
- "Warren Buffet Bitch-Slaps the Billionaire Boys Club." A take on one of Buffet's op-ed pieces in the *New York Times*.

Rights and Payment

Writers retain right to reuse work in print (with permission and attribution) 6 months after publication. Payment, $.25–$.75 a word. Kill fee, 25%. Pays on publication.

Fitness 

805 Third Avenue
New York, NY 10022

Executive Editor: Pam O'Brien

Description and Interests

Fitness magazine and FitnessMagazine.com motivate women to move—for fun, for health, for life. With workouts and diet plans that get results, plus inspiring beauty and health tips, *Fitness* empowers women to be fierce about reaching for and achieving body success, however they define it. The editors look for creative, focused queries, especially based on recent research. A strong title and subtitle (dek) help. Circ: 1.5 million.

Contents: Articles; depts/columns
Frequency: 10 times each year
Website: www.fitnessmagazine.com/

Freelance Potential

Open to freelancers. Receives many queries monthly.

Submissions

Query to section editors, with a cover letter including bio, and clips. Direct queries with bio and clips to appropriate editor: health, mind/body articles to lisa.haney@meredith.com; fitness and exercise stories to jenna.autuori@meredith.com; news/reportage and lifestyle ideas to bethany.gumper@meredith.com; diet/nutrition/food stories to juno.demelo@meredith.com. Responds in 1–2 months.

- Articles: Word lengths vary. Informational and how-to articles, and interviews. Topics include health, fitness, workouts, and nutrition.
- Depts/columns: Word lengths vary.

Sample Issue

Advertising. Sample articles available at website

- "Drop 10 lbs This Month." Simple ways to get the body you've always wanted.
- "Stress Less Instantly." Suggestions for moves to undo all those kinks.

Rights and Payment

Buys licensing rights. Payment, $1+ per word. Kill fee, 25%. Pays on acceptance.

Fitness Rx for Men

21 Bennetts Road
Setauket, NY 11733

Publisher: Steve Blechman

Description and Interests

The editorial mission of *Fitness Rx for Men* is to provide its readers with the ultimate prescription for the perfect body. Its articles explore the proper exercise, training, nutrition, and supplements that can enhance men's appearance, performance, and sexual fitness. It prefers to hear from writers who are experts in fitness and performance-related fields. Circ: 300,000+.

Contents: 70% depts/columns; 30% articles
Frequency: 6 times each year
Website: www.fitnessrxformen.com

Freelance Potential

30% written by nonstaff writers. Publishes 30 freelance submissions yearly; 10% by authors who are new to the magazine, 40% by experts.

Submissions

Query or send complete ms. Accepts hard copy and email to editor@fitnessrxformen-mag.com. SASE. No response.

- Articles: 500–1,500 words. Informational, how-to, and profiles. Topics include fitness, bodybuilding, training, workouts, nutrition, supplements, health, and sex.
- Depts/columns: Staff-written.

Sample Issue

146 pages. Advertising. Sample articles available on website.

- "Kurt Angle: A Dream Revisited." Shows how this winner of a gold medal in the 1996 Summer Olympics is training to make a comeback in this year's Olympics.
- "Ripped on the Road!" Senior Event Manager with GNC shares how he stays in such hardcore shape with a schedule that requires large amounts of traveling for work.

Rights and Payment

All rights. Written material, payment rates vary. Pays on publication.

Fitness Rx for Women

21 Bennetts Road, Suite 101
Setauket, NY 11733

Publisher: Elyse Blechman

Description and Interests

This fitness magazine targets women who are already in shape and routinely working out, as well as women who are looking for the motivation to do so. It offers articles on nutrition, health and wellness, exercise, diet, and the fit lifestyle. Articles should supply inspiration and practical information that will help readers get or maintain their healthy lifestyle, but should not be preachy in any way. Authors with a professional background in nutrition, weight loss, or fitness training—and something new to offer—will be given preference. Circ: 317,000.

Contents: 70% articles; 30% depts/columns
Frequency: 6 times each year
Website: www.fitnessrxwomen.com

Freelance Potential

30% written by nonstaff writers. Publishes 30 freelance submissions yearly; 10% by authors who are new to the magazine, 40% by experts.

Submissions

Query or send complete ms. Accepts hard copy and email to editor@fitnessrxwomen-mag.com. SASE. Responds if interested.

- Articles: 500–1,500 words. Informational, how-to, and profiles. Topics include fitness, weight training, workouts, nutrition, supplements, health, pregnancy, beauty, sex, cosmetic enhancement, athletes, and celebrities.
- Depts/columns: Staff-written.

Sample Issue

132 pages. Advertising. Sample articles available at website.

- "Toning Without Bulk." While shot-putters and superstar actresses may both lift weights, the results are dramatically different. Learn how to use weights for strength and toning without the behemoth look.
- "Maintain the HARD Work." Five tips for maintaining once you've reached weight and fitness goals and how to prevent bad habits from creeping back in.

Rights and Payment

Rights vary. Written material, payment rates vary. Pays on publication.

FitPregnancy

21100 Erwin Street
Woodland Hills, CA 91367

Executive Editor: Sharon Cohen

Description and Interests

This magazine is a pregnant woman's guide to health, nutrition, exercise, and beauty. It also offers content on planning for birth, infant and baby care, as well as relationships and postpartum issues. It is interested in articles that have something new and fresh to offer, as well as personal experience pieces regarding pregnancy. Circ: 500,000.

Contents: 70% articles; 30% depts/columns
Frequency: 6 times each year
Website: www.fitpregnancy.com

Freelance Potential

40% written by nonstaff writers. Publishes 50 freelance submissions yearly; 3% by unpublished writers, 30% by authors who are new to the magazine, 3% by experts. Receives 30 queries monthly.

Submissions

Query with experts you plan to interview, your expertise, and clips. Accepts hard copy. Responds if interested.

- Articles: 1,000–1,800 words. Informational, profiles, and personal experience. Topics include pregnancy-safe workouts, postpartum issues, postpartum exercise stories, breast-feeding, prenatal nutrition, and prenatal or postpartum psychology/health issues.
- Depts/columns: 550–1,000 words. Essays by fathers, parenting and family issues, prenatal health, newborn health, psychology, childbirth, prenatal nutrition, recipes and meal plans, news briefs. Time Out, personal essay, 550 words.

Sample Issue

128 pages. Advertising. Sample articles, editorial calendar, and guidelines available at website.

- "Not to Worry." The four biggests pregnancy stresses and how to avoid them.
- "Baby Spice: How to Spice Up Your Own Homemade Purees." Simple spices can make baby food tastier when you add them to homemade purees.

Rights and Payment

Rights vary. Written material, payment rates vary. Pays on publication.

Flight Journal Magazine

88 Danbury Road
Wilton, CT 06897

Editor in Chief: Budd Davisson

Description and Interests

Aviation and military history buffs read this magazine for its focus on the role of aircraft in the past, as well as the future. Though it has an emphasis on military aircraft and missions from World War II, it also features articles on modern aircraft. It is not a general aviation magazine, and therefore not interested in flight destination or maintenance pieces, or anything to do with general aviation. It will run unusual or dangerous episode type stories, often with an "I was there" viewpoint. Circ: 65,000+.

Contents: Articles; depts/columns
Frequency: 6 times each year, plus special issues
Website: www.flightjournal.com

Freelance Potential

90% written by nonstaff writers. Publishes 40–50 freelance submissions yearly; 25% by authors who are new to the magazine. Receives 35 queries each month.

Submissions

Query with 1-page outline, clips, and available artwork. Accepts email to buddairbum@cox.net, hard copy with disk, and faxes to John Howell at 203-529-3010. SASE. Responds in 2–3 months.

- Articles: 2,500–3,000 words. Informational, historical, personal experience, profiles, and interviews. Topics include war stories, historical aircraft flights and missions, aviation, military aircraft, and new products.
- Depts/columns: Word lengths vary. News, flight gear, and reviews.

Sample Issue

68 pages. Advertising. Sample articles and guidelines available at website.

- "Footprint in the Dust: Armstrong Remembered." A look back at the life and distinguished aerospace career of Neil Armstrong.
- "Restored de Havilland Mosquito Flies Again." A Canadian-built fighter-bomber variant has recently taken to the skies—the first since the crash 15 years ago of the only other known airworthy example remaining of this type of plane.

Rights and Payment

All rights for 1 year. Articles, $600. Depts/columns, payment rates vary. Pays on publication. Provides 2 contributor's copies.

Florida Sportsman

2700 South Kanner Highway
Stuart, FL 34994

Executive Editor: Jeff Weakley

Description and Interests

The where-to's and how-to's of saltwater and freshwater fishing in Florida are the emphasis of this magazine, with occasional coverage of hunting, camping, and diving. Writers for this magazine should be knowledgeable about the state and able to write in a style that is entertaining and makes readers want to "go there and do that." Circ: 115,000.

Contents: 70% articles; 30% depts/columns
Frequency: Monthly
Website: www.floridasportsman.com

Freelance Potential

50% written by nonstaff writers. Publishes 60 freelance submissions yearly; 2% by unpublished writers, 5% by authors who are new to the magazine, 90% by experts. Receives 10 queries, 5 unsolicited mss monthly.

Submissions

Query with artwork; or send complete ms. Accepts hard copy, disk submissions, and email to jeff@floridasportsman.com. No simultaneous submissions. Responds in 1 month.

- Articles: 1,500–2,000 words. Informational, how-to, personal experience, and humor. Topics include fishing, boating, camping, hunting, conservation, the environment, and politics.
- Depts/columns: 800 words. New gear, food, outdoor events.
- Artwork: Color prints; high-resolution digital images.

Sample Issue

120 pages. Advertising. Sample articles on website. Guidelines available.

- "A Flash of Inspiration." Offers a new way to attract the popular Wahoo fish to a boat while drift fishing.
- Sample dept/column: The Sportman's Kitchen features directions on how to prepare Cajun-style redfish and beans.

Rights and Payment

First North American serial and non-exclusive additional rights. Articles, $475. Depts/columns and artwork, payment rates vary. Pays on acceptance. Provides 1 contributor's copy.

Fly Fisherman

InterMedia Outdoors Publications
P.O. Box 420245
Palm Coast, FL 32142-0235

Editor: Ross Purnell

Description and Interests

As a leading source of fly-fishing information, this sportsman's magazine is heavy on instructional pieces and technique. It covers gear and products, as well as articles on fish species, destinations, and conservation. It seeks articles that can speak to both beginners and to those who have been fly-fishing for years. Circ: 120,000.

Contents: 80% articles; 20% depts/columns
Frequency: 6 times each year
Website: www.flyfisherman.com

Freelance Potential

85% written by nonstaff writers. Publishes 30–40 freelance submissions yearly; 5% by unpublished writers, 15% by authors who are new to the magazine, 90% by experts. Receives 12 queries, 8 unsolicited mss monthly.

Submissions

Prefers query; will accept complete ms. Accepts hard copy and disk submissions (Word). SASE. Response time varies.

- Articles: Main features, 2,000–3,000 words. Short features, 750–1,500 words. Informational and how-to. Topics include fishing techniques, equipment, fishing destinations, and conservation.
- Depts/columns: Word lengths vary. News, gear, techniques, opinion pieces.
- Artwork: 35mm color slides or transparencies; B/W prints.

Sample Issue

64 pages. Advertising. Sample articles available at website. Guidelines available.

- "Western Spring Skwalas." Techniques and tips to maximize the catch in Montana when the Skwala bugs hatch, attracting large numbers of trout to the Bitterroot River.
- "Wading Boots." A roundup of the latest foot gear for fly-fishing and the key features for safety and comfort.

Rights and Payment

All rights. Written material, $100–$800. Artwork, $50–$500. Pays within 30 days of publication. Provides 2 contributor's copies.

Flyfishing & Tying Journal

P.O. Box 82112
Portland, OR 97282

Editor: Rob Crandall

Description and Interests

Fly-fishing techniques and destinations are the focus of this well-illustrated journal. The emphasis is on fishing for steelhead, salmon, and trout, rather than saltwater or warm water fishing. It is always in need of fresh new ideas for fly tying. Destination pieces should focus on a region with multiple fisheries and include sidebars. The magazine would love to see some hilarious essays on fly-fishing adventures and also seeks pieces that feature fly-casting tips. Circ: 60,000.

Contents: 70% articles; 30% depts/columns
Frequency: Quarterly
Website: www.amatobooks.com

Freelance Potential

80% written by nonstaff writers. Publishes 30 freelance submissions yearly; 20% by unpublished writers, 20% by authors who are new to the magazine, 60% by experts. Receives 30 queries monthly.

Submissions

Query. Accepts hard copy and email queries to rob@amatobooks.com. SASE. Responds in 2 months.

- Articles: 1,500–2,000 words. Informational, how-to, humor, personal experience, profiles, and interviews. Topics include fly-fishing techniques, equipment, technology, fishing destinations, and fish species.
- Depts/columns: Staff-written.

Sample Issue

78 pages. Advertising. Sample copy and guidelines available.

- "A Mid-Winter's Dream." Destination piece features fishing on the Yuba River.
- "2013 Sportsman's Shows." A roundup of upcoming sportman's shows and highlights of what to expect at each.

Rights and Payment

First North American serial rights. All material, payment rates vary. Pays on publication. Provides 1 contributor's copy.

Fly Rod & Reel

P.O. Box 370
Camden, ME 04843

Editor: Greg Thomas

Description and Interests

This fishing magazine presents a combination of how-to's and where-to's, along with articles about conservation, fish species and behavior, and fishing-themed fiction. It also includes information on the latest gear. It is always looking to offer its readers something new or thought-provoking. Circ: 50,000.

Contents: 50% articles; 30% depts/columns; 20% fiction
Frequency: 6 times each year
Website: www.flyrodreel.com

Freelance Potential

80% written by nonstaff writers. Publishes 20 freelance submissions yearly; 5% by unpublished writers, 20% by authors who are new to the magazine. Receives 15 queries, 25 unsolicited mss monthly.

Submissions

Query with outline and clips or writing samples; or send complete ms. Accepts hard copy and email to editor@flyrodreel.com. SASE. Response time varies.

- Articles: To 2,500 words. Informational, how-to, and profiles. Topics include equipment, fly-fishing techniques, new product information, conservation, and locales.
- Fiction: Word lengths vary. Fly-fishing stories.
- Depts/columns: 200–300 words. News briefs, travel, book reviews, conservation, interviews, fly-tying techniques.

Sample Issue

72 pages. Advertising. Sample articles available online.

- "Sensational Swimflies." The nuts and bolts of tying large swimflies with the idea that bigger flies catch bigger fish.
- "Best Jobs." So you think fishing every day would be the ideal career: here's how to turn the dream into a reality.

Rights and Payment

All or first rights. Articles, $400. Other material, payment rates vary. Pays on acceptance. Provides 1 contributor's copy.

Foreign Policy

11 Dupont Circle NW, Suite 600
Washington, DC 20036

Editor in Chief: Susan Glasser

Description and Interests

Foreign Policy is a magazine of global politics, economics, and ideas. It features news, analysis, and opinion from international journalists, professionals, and thinkers regarding global events, issues, and trends. Although its readers are well-informed, intelligent individuals, they are not all specialists in international affairs; material must be accessible. Circ: 110,000.

Contents: 66% articles; 34% depts/columns
Frequency: 7 times each year
Website: www.foreignpolicy.com

Freelance Potential

90% written by nonstaff writers. Publishes 25 freelance submissions yearly. Receives 60 queries monthly.

Submissions

Query with brief outline and contact details. Accepts email to editor@foreignpolicy.com. Responds in 1 month.

- Articles: 1,000–3,500 words. Informational, how-to, essays, and opinion pieces. Topics include current events, education, government, law, history, the media, the arts, multicultural and ethnic issues, politics, public affairs, science, nature, and social concerns.
- Depts/columns: 300–1,200 words. In Other Words, media reviews of books published outside the U.S.; Prime Numbers, data-intense graphics linked to text on one subject, news.

Sample Issue

104 pages. Advertising. Sample articles and guidelines available at website.

- "Who Broke the U.N.?" Experts and insiders reveal the U.N.'s biggest operating obstacles and discuss its role going forward.
- "Cities of the Future, Made in China." Urban innovations, including electric taxis and traffic-jumping buses being pioneered in China's cities.

Rights and Payment

Exclusive first serial rights. Written material, payment rates vary. Pays on acceptance. Provides 10 contributor's copies.

Foster Focus

608 Main Street
Watsontown, PA 17777

Publisher/Editor: Chris Chmielewski

Description and Interests

Foster Focus is a magazine that provides an in-depth look at the foster care industry for professionals, advocates, and clients. Its articles cover industry news, legislation, foster family relationships, family getaways, and careers within the industry. Each issue also offers a look at some of the children in the system who are eligible for adoption. Many of its writers work in the foster care system or have grown up in it. Circ: Unavailable.

Contents: Articles; depts/columns
Frequency: Monthly
Website: www.fosterfocusmag.com

Freelance Potential

Receives numerous queries monthly.

Submissions

Query. Accepts email to writers@FosterFocusMag.com.

- Articles: Word lengths vary. Informational articles, profiles, and personal experience pieces. Topics include the foster care system, living in foster care, and careers.
- Depts/columns: Word lengths vary. Q&As, essays, travel, profiles, and legal issues.

Sample Issue

Advertising. Sample articles available at website.

- "Dangers of Social Media & Care." Article discusses how social media can impact foster care.
- "Life Happens." Personal experience piece tells how a random advertisement found a boy the home of his dreams.
- Sample dept/column: Family Adventures offers ideas for a stay-cation.

Rights and Payment

Rights vary. Payment rates and policy vary.

Free Inquiry

P.O. Box 664
Amherst, NY 14226-0664

Editor: Thomas Flynn

Description and Interests

A publication of the Council for Secular Humanism, *Free Inquiry* publishes articles that explain the principles of secular humanism and support those living out its ideals. Submissions should have a journalistic tone and are judged on the basis of interest, clarity, significance, relevance, and authority. Circ: 30,000.

Contents: 60% articles; 40% depts/columns
Frequency: 6 times each year
Website: www.secularhumanism.org

Freelance Potential

75% written by nonstaff writers. Publishes 100 freelance submissions yearly; 20% by unpublished writers, 40% by authors who are new to the magazine, 50% by experts. Receives 40 unsolicited mss monthly.

Submissions

Send complete ms. Accepts CD or zip disk submissions with 3 hard copies. Send poetry to Austin MacRae. Accepts hard copy and email to amacrae@centerforinquiry.net (include poems in body of the email). No simultaneous submissions. SASE. Responds in 4 months.

- Articles: To 6,000 words. Informational, essays, opinion, and creative nonfiction. Topics include current events, secular living, ethics, humanism, the environment, the media, science, religion, social issues, history, public affairs, and government.
- Depts/columns: To 1,600 words. Opinions, media reviews, philosophy, church and state issues, ethics, science and religion, history, faith and reason, transnational humanism, Q&As.
- Other: Poetry, up to 3 poems per submission.

Sample Issue

62 pages. Advertising. Sample articles and guidelines available at website.

- "Saddle Up, Progressives!" Explanation as to why the secular humanists need to have a political identity and agenda.
- "Infighting or Healthy Debate?" Opinion piece on whether or not divisions and competing viewpoints among secular humanists are healthy or harmful.

Rights and Payment

All rights. No payment. Provides 2 contributor's copies.

Friction Zone 

44489 Town Center Way, Suite D497
Palm Desert, CA 92260

Editor: Amy Holland

Description and Interests
Friction Zone is a comprehensive resource for those who travel by motorcycle. It publishes separate editions for Eastern states and Western states. Both contain information about destinations, motorcycles and equipment, safety, and tips for making travel more enjoyable. It is the only motorcycle magazine that publishes motorcycle accident reports. New writers who want to break in to our magazine should consider the Discover section, which highlights motorcycle day trips in specific areas. Note, however, that it does not publish articles written in the first person. Circ: 30,000.
Contents: Articles; depts/columns
Frequency: Monthly
Website: www.friction-zone.com

Freelance Potential
Friction Zone is currently closed to freelance submissions, but hopes to open its submission desk presently. The editors advise checking the website.

Submissions
Check website for updates on submission policy.

- Articles: 1,000–2,000 words. Informational, how-to, profiles, interviews, and humor. Topics include motorcycles, travel routes and destinations, racing, touring, health, safety, motorcycle equipment, and new products.
- Depts/columns: To 2,000 words. Events, legal and insurance matters, product and media reviews.

Sample Issue
48 pages. Advertising. Sample articles available at website. Guidelines available at website.

- "The Deeley Motorcycle Exhibition." Details of motorcycle enthusiast Frederick Trevor Deeley and his private collection of motorcycles, the largest in Canada.
- Sample dept/column: Tech Tips provides how-to advice on buying the best GPS for motorcycle travel.

Rights and Payment
First North American serial rights. Written material, $.20 per word. Pays on publication.

Fried Fiction   

Editor: David Peters

Description and Interests
Fried Fiction is an online journal that welcomes all genres of serial fiction of unlimited length. Its goal is to promote talented writers and create an interactive forum. Stories are published in short episodes or scenes, with each story progressing at the author's desired pace. Episodes are written to leave the reader wanting more. Successful stories have a strong focus on characters and avoid excessive dialogue. Hits per month: Unavailable.
Contents: Serialized fiction
Frequency: Updated regularly
Website: www.friedfiction.com

Freelance Potential
Open to serial fiction.

Submissions
Send complete ms with 50-word bio, up to 1,000-word synopsis, and genre. Accepts email to submissions@friedfiction.com, with attached RTF or text (TXT) files, and "Fiction Submission" in the subject line. An online submissions form is being developed. Only the author's initial submission is required to pass through a selection process. Once approved, the author may add new episodes. Responds in 2–6 weeks.

- Fiction: To 1,000 words per episode. All genres except fan fiction and erotic fiction.

Sample Issue
No advertising. Sample copy and guidelines available at website.

- "Not that Kind of Witch." A woman posing as a witch imprisons a girl in her tower.
- "The Door in Roanoke." by Gretchen Tessmer. A savage winter approaches while men search for a child who is the key to opening an ancient door in the shadowlands of Roanoke.

Rights and Payment
$25 for first episode; no payment for subsequent episodes.

The Funny Times 

P.O. Box 18530
Cleveland Heights, OH 44118

Editors: Ray Lesser and Susan Wolpert

Description and Interests

"Humor, politics, and fun" is how this magazine describes its contents. Filled with interviews, stories, essays, satire, book reviews, and comics, *The Funny Times* puts no limit on the topics it covers, or the format, as long as its articles will make readers laugh. Everything it publishes must be funny. Circ: 70,000.

Contents: Articles; fiction; other
Frequency: Monthly
Website: www.funnytimes.com

Freelance Potential

95% written by nonstaff writers. Publishes 8–10 freelance submissions yearly; 10% by unpublished writers, 20% by authors who are new to the magazine. Receives 100–120 unsolicited mss monthly.

Submissions

Send complete ms. Accepts hard copy and simultaneous submissions if identified. SASE. Responds in 2–3 months.

- Articles: 500–700 words. Humorous and satirical. Topics include politics, contemporary issues, society, technology, relationships, pets, religion, business, current events, celebrities, health, science, and the human condition.
- Fiction: 500–700 words. Humorous fiction.
- Artwork: B/W cartoons.

Sample Issue

24 pages. No advertising. Sample articles and guidelines available at website.

- "Rock Star." A tongue-in-cheek look at middle-aged guys who still imagine they're going to be in a rock band some day.
- "Dave Barry Goes to the Olympics." This well-known humorist's take on the summer games.

Rights and Payment

One-time rights. Written material, $60. Artwork, $25–$40. Pays on publication. Provides 5 contributor's copies and a 1-year subscription.

Fur-Fish-Game

2878 East Main Street
Columbus, OH 43209

Editor: Mitch Cox

Description and Interests

Serious outdoorsmen read this magazine for the "how-to's" of hunting, fishing, and trapping, and for its first-person accounts of wilderness adventure and survival. Humor and human-interest articles are always welcome. It also offers gear pieces, both the latest and the greatest, as well as a look back at antique outdoorsmen equipment. Circ: 118,000.

Contents: 50% articles; 50% depts/columns
Frequency: Monthly
Website: www.furfishgame.com

Freelance Potential

67% written by nonstaff writers. Publishes 150 freelance submissions yearly; 10% by unpublished writers, 25% by new authors, 25% by experts. Receives 50 queries, 50 mss monthly.

Submissions

Prefers query; will accept complete ms. Accepts hard copy and email to ffgcox@ameritech.net. Availability of artwork improves chance of acceptance. SASE. Responds in two months.

- Articles: Informational, profiles, and interviews, 2,000–3,000 words. How-to's, 100–2,500 words. Personal experience and profiles, word lengths vary. Topics include hunting, trapping, freshwater fishing, predator calling, woodcrafting, camping, boating, and outdoor activities.
- Depts/columns: Staff-written.
- Artwork: High-resolution digital images; color slides; and B/W or color prints. Line art.

Sample Issue

64 pages. Advertising. Sample articles available at website. Guidelines and theme list available.

- "Rutting Buck Bow Trap." An on-the-ground hunting technique provides an alternative to spending days up in the trees.
- Sample dept/column: Fish and Tackle offers tips for hooking jumbo perch during their fall feeding spree.

Rights and Payment

First North American serial rights. Written material, $75–$250. Pays on acceptance. Provides 1 contributor's copy.

The Futurist

7910 Woodmont Avenue, Suite 450
Bethesda, MD 20814

Editor: Cynthia G. Wagner

Description and Interests

Published by the World Future Society, *The Futurist* features forward-looking articles on a plethora of subjects, including education, technology, society, and business. All articles should focus on the future, especially the period 5 to 50 years ahead. Circ: 12,000.

Contents: 80% articles; 20% depts/columns
Frequency: 6 times each year
Website: www.wfs.org

Freelance Potential

50% written by nonstaff writers. Publishes 30 freelance submissions yearly; 10% by unpublished writers, 10% by authors who are new to the magazine, 80% by experts. Receives 1,000 queries, 20 unsolicited mss monthly.

Submissions

Prefers ms with author biography; will accept query with detailed outline. Accepts email to cwagner@wfs.org (Word or RTF attachments) with "Article Submission" or "Query" in the subject line. Accepts simultaneous submissions if identified. Responds to queries in 3 weeks, to mss in 3 months.

- Articles: 1,000–4,000 words. Informational Topics include futurism, business careers, computers, conservation, education, government, public affairs, social issues, media, the environment, medical services, management, science, and technology.
- Depts/columns: To 1,000 words. Trends, book reviews. Future View, to 800 words.
- Artwork: Prints; high-resolution JPEG images. Line art.

Sample Issue

60 pages. Advertising. Sample copy and guidelines available at website.

- "Whatever Happened to Western Civilization? The Cultural Crisis, 20 Years Later." Revisits an article published in the magazine 20 years ago on cultural crisis—what's happened since and what the next 20 years might hold.
- Sample dept/columns: Tomorrow in Brief discusses threats to biodiversity in protected forests.

Rights and Payment

All rights. No payment. Provides 10 contributor's copies or a 1-year membership.

Game & Fish

2250 Newmarket Parkway, Suite 110
Marietta GA 30067

Editorial Director: Ken Dunwoody

Description and Interests

As its name implies, this magazine is for avid fishermen and hunters. It provides specific information on where and how to fish and hunt in each state or region. It is published in 28 state and regional editions with articles specific to those areas of the country. Where-to and how-to articles are the main editorial focus. Circ: 408,000.

Contents: 80% articles; 20% depts/columns
Frequency: Monthly
Website: www.gameandfishmag.com

Freelance Potential

80% written by nonstaff writers. Publishes 500 freelance submissions yearly; 2% by unpublished writers, 15–20% by authors who are new to the magazine. Receives 75 queries monthly.

Submissions

Query. Accepts email to ken.dunwoody@imoutdoors.com. Responds in 4 weeks.

- Articles: 1,500–2,500 words. Informational, how-to, and where-to. Topics include hunting, fishing, hunting and fishing destinations, firearms, and new products.
- Depts/columns: By assignment only.

Sample Issue

64 pages. Advertising. Sample articles available at website. Guidelines available.

- "10 Deer Hotspots." Tips for bow hunters for catching deer on public land.
- "Big Catfish Secrets." A fishing pro tells how to find and catch trophy fish.

Rights and Payment

First North American serial and non-exclusive rights. Written material, $150–$275 (photo payments extra). Pays 1 month prior to publication.

Games

6198 Butler Pike, Suite 200
Blue Bell, PA 19422-2600

Editor in Chief: R. Wayne Schmittberger

Description and Interests

Games presents a wide variety of quizzes, games, and brainteasers in each issue, along with board and electronic game reviews and event information. It also offers articles on the history of, and creative processes behind game and puzzle development. It welcomes ideas for feature articles about games, puzzles, wordplays, and the people who create them. Game reviews are by assignment only. Circ: 75,000.

Contents: 40% articles; 1% fiction; 59% other
Frequency: 10 times each year
Website: www.gamesmagazine-online.com

Freelance Potential

86% written by nonstaff writers. Publishes 200+ freelance submissions yearly; 10% by unpublished writers, 20% by authors who are new to the magazine. Receives 80 queries and unsolicited mss monthly.

Submissions

Prefers queries for articles; will accept complete ms. Send complete ms for short pieces. Accepts hard copy and email to wschmittberger@kappa-publishing.com. SASE. Responds in 6–8 weeks.

- Articles: 2,000–2,500 words. Informational, how-to, profiles, interviews, humor, and opinion. Topics include games, puzzles, magic, practical jokes, human ingenuity, and new product information.
- Fiction: Word lengths vary. Mystery and whodunits.
- Depts/columns: Staff-written.
- Other: Games, contests, quizzes, tests, visual puzzles.

Sample Issue

80 pages. Advertising. Sample articles and guidelines available at website.

- "Sherlock Holmes: Call Our Bluff." Which is the true story about the famous detective, and which is not?
- "It's a Pip!." Three puzzles that involve a double-18 set of dominoes.

Rights and Payment

All rights. Articles, $500–$1,000. Gamebits, $150–$250. Artwork, payment rates vary. Pays on publication. Provides 2 contributor's copies.

Garden Design

2 Park Avenue, 10th Floor
New York, NY 10016

Assistant Editor

Description and Interests

Garden Design targets an audience that is intensely interested in the aesthetics of gardening and the beauty and enjoyment of outdoor spaces. With compelling photography, it showcases innovative landscape design and stylish solutions for planting. It is always in need of fresh, unique stories that will inspire readers and offer useful information. Shorter pieces are always better, and the emphasis should be on the design side of gardening. Circ: 250,000.

Contents: 60% articles; 40% depts/columns
Frequency: 7 times each year
Website: www.gardendesign.com

Freelance Potential

60% written by nonstaff writers. Publishes 25 freelance submissions yearly; 10% by authors who are new to the magazine, 10% by experts. Receives 20 queries monthly.

Submissions

Query with résumé, clips, and up to 5 sample photos. Accepts hard copy. SASE. Responds only if interested.

- Articles: 800–1,200 words. Informational, how-to, and profiles. Topics include garden and landscape design, hardscapes, water features, plantings, lighting, topiary, outdoor furniture, and new product information.
- Depts/columns: 200–800 words. News, plants, exterior decorating, gardens around the world, advice, profiles of designers.
- Artwork: Low-resolution digital images.

Sample Issue

48 pages. Advertising. Sample copy available. Guidelines available at website.

- "Active Seats." Outdoor public garden seating ideas from two young designers, one in Korea and one in the Netherlands.
- "Landscaping Roof Terraces." Furniture, plantings, and design ideas to turn a roof into an extraordinary outdoor room.

Rights and Payment

First-time rights. Written material, payment rates vary. Pays on acceptance. Provides 1–2 contributor's copies.

Gardening How-To

P.O. Box 3401
Minnetonka, MN 55343

Editor: Kathy Childers

Description and Interests

"Bringing your garden to life" is the tagline for this colorful magazine from the National Home Gardening Club. Each issue offers timely and informative how-to articles that will inspire avid home gardeners in the U.S. and Canada. It offers features on a wide variety of flowers, trees, shrubs, and vegetables with an eye towards both the practical and the aesthetic. While most of its editorial content is written in-house or by writers who have a track record with the publication, it is open to queries from new writers. Circ: 4 million.

Contents: 55% articles; 45% depts/columns
Frequency: 5 times each year
Website: www.gardeningclub.com

Freelance Potential

65% written by nonstaff writers. Publishes 30–35 freelance submissions yearly; 1% by unpublished writers, 5% by authors who are new to the magazine. Receives 10 queries each month.

Submissions

Send complete ms. Accepts hard copy and email to kchilders@namginc.com. No simultaneous submissions. Responds only if interested.

- Articles: 500 words. Informational, how-to, and essays. Topics include gardening, landscaping, and horticulture.
- Depts/columns: Staff-written.

Sample Issue

64 pages. Advertising. Sample copy and guidelines available on website.

- "Amazing Amaranth." Discovering the beauty and technique for growing this colorful plant that is also edible and comes into its own when summer blooms are fading.
- "Get Your Sweet On!" Tips for growing and harvesting sweet potatoes in all climates.

Rights and Payment

First North American serial rights. Articles, $200 on acceptance. Provides 3 contributor's copies.

Gas Engine Magazine

1503 SW 42nd Street
Topeka, KS 66609-1265

Editor: Richard Backus

Description and Interests

Collectors and enthusiasts of tractor and stationary gas engines turn to this magazine for restoration articles, company histories, technical advice, and profiles of other collectors and hobbyists. Most of its writers are also fellow collectors, and submissions from gas engine hobbyists are encouraged. Circ: 23,000.

Contents: 86% articles; 14% depts/columns
Frequency: 6 times each year
Website: http://gasengine.farmcollector.com

Freelance Potential

80% written by nonstaff writers. Publishes 30 freelance submissions yearly; 70% by unpublished writers, 50% by authors who are new to the magazine, 15% by experts. Receives 5 unsolicited mss each month.

Submissions

Send complete ms with artwork. Prefers email to rbackus@ogdenpubs.com (Word attachments); will accept hard copy. SASE. Responds in 1 month.

- Articles: 500+ words. Informational, how-to, and personal experience. Topics include antiques, collecting, crafts, hobbies, history, and machining.
- Depts/columns: Word lengths vary. Restoration tips, modeling information.
- Artwork: B/W or color digital images at 300 dpi or larger.

Sample Issue

60 pages. Advertising. Sample copy available. Guidelines available at website.

- "How to Build a Metering Valve to Run Engines on Propane." Gives step-by-step instructions on how to make a modification to an engine so that it can run on propane.
- "Manitoba Engine Restoration: Crash Bang!" Restoring this engine proves more difficult than it first appears because of U.S. Standard/Metric bolt size confusion.

Rights and Payment

Rights vary. All material, payment rates vary. Payment policy varies. Provides 2–4 contributor's copies.

The Gay & Lesbian Review/Worldwide

P.O. Box 180300
Boston, MA 02118

Editor: Richard Schneider, Jr., Ph.D.

Description and Interests

Articles, essays, interviews, opinion, and media reviews that target a sophisticated gay and lesbian readership are found here. Its mission is to provide enlightened discussion of the issues and ideas of importance to the gay community. See website for upcoming issue themes. Book reviews are done on assignment. Writers can propose books they would like to review. Circ: 12,000.

Contents: 60% articles; 20% depts/columns; 20% other
Frequency: 6 times each year
Website: www.glreview.com

Freelance Potential

100% written by nonstaff writers. Publishes 130 freelance submissions yearly; 25% by authors who are new to the magazine. Receives 15 queries each month.

Submissions

Query (new writers should include writing sample) or send complete manuscript. Prefers email queries to hglr@aol.com; accepts hard copy. SASE. Responds in 1 week.

- Articles: 2,000–4,000 words. Informational, profiles, interviews, opinion. Topics include current events, history, politics, biography, social issues—all as they relate to gays and lesbians.
- Depts/columns: Media reviews, 600–1,200 words. Essays, word lengths vary.
- Other: Poetry, to 50 lines; limit 3 poems per submission.

Sample Issue

50 pages. Advertising. Sample articles and guidelines available at website. Theme list available in each issue and at website.

- "Reclaiming HIV as a 'Gay' Disease." Despite reports and investigations claiming otherwise, this disease still primarily affects the homosexual and bisexual communities.
- "Party Polarization Is Now Complete." Examines the Republican and Democratic party positions on homosexual and transgender issues.

Rights and Payment

Rights vary. Articles, $100 or 4 gift subscriptions. Book reviews, $50 or 4 gift subscriptions. Payment policy varies.

Generation Boom

P.O. Box 624
Derby, KS 67037

Creative Director: Kathryn Creel
Editor: Laurie L. Dove

Description and Interests

This magazine covers life after 40, including health, finance, and anything of interest to baby boomers. With a subtitle of "It's an Attitude," *Generation Boom* aims to redefine life, health, and finance after 40 with conversational and relevant articles that inspire, educate, and entertain. Circ: 15,000.

Contents: 40% articles; 60% depts/columns
Frequency: 6 times each year
Website: www.generationboom.com

Freelance Potential

Receives numerous queries each month.

Submissions

Query. Accepts email queries to editor@generationboom.com or submit via website. Response time varies.

- Articles: Word lengths vary. Informational and how-to articles and profiles. Topics include health and fitness, recreation, travel, inspiration, education, house and garden, business, and people.
- Depts/columns: Word lengths vary. Travel, legal advice, health and fitness, personal finance, and food.

Sample Issue

Advertising. Sample copy available at website.

- "Help for the Holidays." Article provides a list of tips to help survive the holidays.
- "Have Self, Will Travel." Article discusses the do's and don'ts for booking and taking a successful solo vacation.
- Sample dept/column: Body and Mind reveals the lastest information on breast cancer.

Rights and Payment

Rights vary. Payment rates and policy vary.

Georgia Review

320 South Jackson Street, Room 706
University of Georgia
Athens, GA 30602-9009

Editor: Stephen Corey

Description and Interests

Original works of fiction, nonfiction, and poetry fill the pages of this literary magazine from the University of Georgia. Accepting work from both new and established writers, it also publishes book reviews. It does not publish novel excerpts or translations. It welcomes informed essays that place their subject against a broad perspective. All submissions must be previously unpublished in any form. Circ: 3,000+.

Contents: 40% essays; 30% fiction; 20% poetry; 10% other
Frequency: Quarterly
Website: www.thegeorgiareview.com

Freelance Potential

99% written by nonstaff writers. Publishes 100 freelance submissions yearly; 5% by unpublished writers, 25% by new authors. Receives 30 queries, 1,000 unsolicited mss monthly.

Submissions

Send complete ms for fiction, essays, and poetry. Query for book reviews. Limit 1 story/essay, 3-5 poems. Accepts hard copy between August 16 and May 14 only. No simultaneous submissions. SASE. Responds in 2–3 months.

- Nonfiction: Word lengths vary. Essays and interviews. Topics include literature, the environment, history, the arts, and politics.
- Fiction: Word lengths vary. Contemporary, literary.
- Depts/columns: Word lengths vary. Book reviews.
- Other: Poetry, no line limits.

Sample Issue

200 pages. Little advertising. Issue excerpts and guidelines available at website.

- "Look at the World as It Is." An interview with Sir Salman Rushdie.
- "Out of the Mouths of Babes." Short story.

Rights and Payment

First North American serial rights. Fiction and nonfiction, $50 per published page. Poetry, $4 per line. Pays on publication. Provides 1 contributor's copy and a 1-year subscription.

German Life

1068 National Highway
LaVale, MD 21502

Editor: Mark Slider

Description and Interests

German Life is written for any reader interested in the diversity of German culture, past or present. It offers reporting on cultural and historical events, as well as lifestyle, business, and travel pieces. Because so many of its readers wish to visit (or revisit) Germany, it is always in need of travel pieces. Each issue is bound by the editorial calendar, so writers are advised to consult it before submitting. Circ: 40,000.

Contents: 80% articles; 20% depts/columns
Frequency: 6 times each year
Website: http://germanlife.com

Freelance Potential

90% written by nonstaff writers. Publishes 50 freelance submissions yearly; 50% by unpublished writers, 30% by authors who are new to the magazine, 30% by experts. Receives 40 queries, 20 unsolicited mss monthly.

Submissions

Query with clips; will accept complete ms. Accepts disk submissions (Word files) with hard copy or email. Does not accept simultaneous submissions. Responds in 2–8 weeks if interested.

- Articles: to 1,200 words. Informational, profiles. Topics include German history, culture, current events, travel, entertainment, and the arts.
- Depts/columns: 300 to 800 words. Travel information, history, food, family research. Book reviews, 250–300 words.
- Artwork: B/W or color prints or slides. Digital images at 300 dpi (TIFF or EPS files).

Sample Issue

64 pages. Advertising. Sample articles, guidelines, and editorial calendar available at website.

- "Ten Days on Remagen Bridge." A new museum in this city preserves its place in World War II military history as the access point for American troops to get across the river and possibly shorten the war.
- "Winter Travel to Germany? Why Not!" This off-peak travel time offers an opportunity to see a beautiful seasonal side to the country and enjoy great rates without the crowds.

Rights and Payment

First English/German language serial rights. Articles, $300–$500. Depts/columns, $80–$130. Pays on publication.

The Gettysburg Review

Gettysburg College
Gettysburg, PA 17325-1491

Editor: Peter Stitt

Description and Interests

Works from writers at all stages of their careers find a home within the pages of *The Gettysburg Review,* now in its 25th year of publishing. It accepts high-quality poetry, fiction, and essays on a variety of topics. Fiction is generally in the form of short stories, although lengthier pieces are sometimes accepted and serialized. Excerpts from novels have been published as well. Circ: 2,200.

Contents: 40% fiction; 30% essays; 30% poetry
Frequency: Quarterly
Website: www.gettysburgreview.com

Freelance Potential

98% written by nonstaff writers. Publishes 125 freelance submissions yearly; 20% by unpublished writers, 50% by authors who are new to the magazine. Receives 500–600 unsolicited mss monthly.

Submissions

Send complete ms between September 1 and May 31 only. Accepts hard copy and simultaneous submissions if identified. SASE. Responds in 3–5 months.

- Articles: 3,000–7,000 words. Literary reviews, essays, creative nonfiction, and memoir. Topics include literature, art, film, history, science, and contemporary thought.
- Fiction: 2,000–7,000 words. Literary short stories, novel excerpts, serialized stories.
- Other: Poetry, 1–5 poems, no line limits.

Sample Issue

164 pages. Little advertising. Sample articles and writers' guidelines available on website.

- "Blue Rain." Memoir of a songwriter musician by night who taught English to inner-city schoolchildren by day.
- "The Muskeg." Short Story.
- "The Way of Wood." Essay on acquiring an old loom and learning how to use it.

Rights and Payment

First serial rights. Articles and fiction, $30 per published page. Poetry, $2.50 per line. Pays on publication. Provides 1 contributor's copy and a 1-year subscription.

Gifted Education Press Quarterly

10201 Yuma Court
P.O. Box 1586
Manassas, VA 20109

Editor & Publisher: Maurice D. Fisher

Description and Interests

This newsletter, available online as well as in print, addresses issues related to educating gifted students. Written by leaders in the field, the articles and research studies target administrators, program coordinators, academics, and parents. It uses a scholarly tone and demands extensive research and references. Circ: 16,000.

Contents: 100% articles
Frequency: Quarterly
Website: www.giftededpress.com

Freelance Potential

75% written by nonstaff writers. Publishes 14 freelance submissions yearly; 67% by authors who are new to the magazine, 33% by experts. Receives 4 queries monthly.

Submissions

Query with writing sample. Accepts email queries to gifted@giftededpress.com. Responds in 1 week.

- Articles: 2,500–3,000 words. Informational, how-to, research, personal experience, profiles, interviews, and scholarly essays. Topics include gifted education; multicultural, ethnic, and social issues; homeschooling; multiple intelligences; parent advocates; academic subjects; the environment; and popular culture.

Sample Issue

14 pages. No advertising. Sample copy available at website.

- "Irving Berlin (1888-1989): The Giftedness of an American Icon and Musical Innovator." A profile of the famous composer and lyricist.
- "Inducing Critical and Creative Sets When Teaching Writing." Techniques for teaching writing to the gifted.

Rights and Payment

All rights. No payment. Provides a 1-year subscription.

Glamour

Condé Nast Publications
4 Times Square
New York, NY 10036

Editorial Development Director: Susan Goodall

Description and Interests

Published for more than 70 years, *Glamour* is a premier fashion and beauty magazine that brings young women the latest trends and expert advice. It also features investigative pieces on important social issues, celebrity profiles, and lifestyle articles on health, relationships, sex, and careers. It appreciates a writer with a strong viewpoint on a provocative, timely subject. Writers new to the magazine have the best shot with front of the book pitches. Circ: 2.3 million.

Contents: 60% articles; 40% depts/columns
Frequency: Monthly
Website: www.glamour.com

Freelance Potential

70% written by nonstaff writers. Publishes 25–50 freelance submissions yearly; 5% by unpublished writers, 10% by authors who are new to the magazine, 10% by experts. Receives 100+ queries monthly.

Submissions

Prefers query with outline; will accept complete ms. Send email to appropriate editor on masthead. Responds in 6 weeks.

- Articles: 2,500–3,000 words. Informational, how-to, self-help, profiles, and interviews. Topics include fashion, beauty, women's issues, careers, relationships, social issues, travel, food, health, fitness, and new products.
- Depts/columns: Word lengths vary. Fashion do's and don'ts, sexual health, media reviews.

Sample Issue

340 pages. Advertising. Sample articles available at website.

- "We Want Her Job." A peek into the life of Randi Zuckerberg who has a new company and a reality show on Bravo.
- "The Workout Every Woman Wants." A new exercise routine that does wonders for your rear view.

Rights and Payment

All rights. Articles, $2 per word. Depts/columns, payment rates vary. Kill fee, 25%. Pays on acceptance.

Glimmer Train 

4763 SW Maplewood
P.O. Box 80430
Portland, OR 97280-1430

Co-Editor: Susan Burmeister-Brown

Description and Interests

Both established and upcoming writers are encouraged to submit their work to this literary magazine. The editors look for well-written, emotionally engaging stories of all traditional genres. It also features interviews with writers on technique, but these are written by staff members. It does not accept novels, poetry, or stories written for children. Circ: 18,000.

Contents: 85% fiction; 15% articles
Frequency: Quarterly
Website: www.glimmertrain.org

Freelance Potential

Fiction, 100% written by nonstaff writers. Publishes 47 freelance submissions yearly; 80% by unpublished writers, 90% by authors who are new to the magazine. Receives 3,500 unsolicited mss each month.

Submissions

All submissions must be original and unpublished (online publication does not disqualify a piece). Send complete ms and reading fee if submitting for competition. See website for monthly categories and specific guidelines. Prefers submissions via website; will accept hard copy. Accepts simultaneous submissions if identified. Responds in 2 months.

- Articles: Staff-written.
- Fiction: Word lengths vary. All genres.

Sample Issue

220 pages. No advertising. Sample articles, stories, and guidelines available at website. Sample copy available.

- "Silenced Voices: Tashi Rabten." Profile of this Tibetan poet and his nonconformist viewpoint.
- "Fini." Short story of a couple who are trying to define their relationship and decide if it is a love story.
- "Charles Baxter." An interview of this writer reveals his belief that fiction is meant to bring out the hidden and repressed things in life.

Rights and Payment

First and one-time anthology rights. Written material, payment rates vary: $700 for standard story categories; more for competition winners. Pays on acceptance. Provides 10 contributor's copies.

Go For a Ride

14907 West Hardy Drive
Tampa, FL 33613

Editor: Michael Savidge

Description and Interests

Go For a Ride Magazine is designed to present a new perspective to the motorcycle community in central, southwestern, and western Florida. It offers family-friendly content on travel destinations, events, and industry news, and profiles of unique personalities. Each issue also includes a scenic ride map. It is always in need of motorcycle travel stories for its Travel Tales features. Circ: 8,000.

Contents: Articles; depts/columns
Frequency: Monthly
Website: www.gofarmag.com

Freelance Potential

50% written by nonstaff writers. Publishes 8 freelance submissions yearly. Receives 3 queries each month.

Submissions

Query. Accepts email to info@gofarmag.com. Responds in 2 months.

- Articles: 500–2,000 words. Informational, profiles, interviews, and personal experience. Topics include motorcycles, travel, safety, and new products.
- Depts/columns: Word lengths vary. News, veterans' information, road trips, motorcycle-related events, food, book reviews.

Sample Issue

44 pages. Advertising. Sample copy available at website.

- "Badlands and Good Times." One biker fulfills a bucket wish list and attends the Sturgis Motorcycle Rally out west.
- "Ride Smart: Phone Apps for Bikers." The most helpful apps to get for dedicated motorcycle riders and travelers.

Rights and Payment

First North American serial or reprint rights. Articles, $25. Depts/columns, payment rates vary. Pays on publication. Provides 2 contributor's copies.

Going Bonkers?

P.O. Box 7464
Hicksville, NY 11802

Editor in Chief: J. Carol Pereyra

Description and Interests

Going Bonkers? is all about "learning, laughing, and stress-free living." It is filled with self-help articles designed to help readers understand, manage, and overcome stress in all areas of their lives. Topics include personal growth, relationships, and mental and physical health. It strives to be educational, entertaining, and motivational while providing readers with useful solutions. It goes without saying that humor is always welcome. Circ: 100,000+.

Contents: 95% articles; 5% depts/columns
Frequency: Quarterly
Website: www.gbonkers.com

Freelance Potential

95% written by nonstaff writers. Publishes 200+ freelance submissions yearly; 20% by unpublished writers, 30% by authors who are new to the magazine, 50% by experts. Receives 100+ unsolicited mss monthly.

Submissions

Send complete ms with author biography. Accepts email submissions to Help@GBonkers.com (Word attachments; include "Article—subject matter" in subject line). Responds in up to several months if interested.

- Articles: 600–3,000 words. Informational, self-help, how-to, humor, and personal experience. Topics include health and fitness, family, medical services, psychology, success, motivation, self-improvement, and social issues.
- Depts/columns: 200–500 words. Humor, opinion, and short advice items.

Sample Issue

72 pages. Little advertising. Sample articles and guidelines available at website.

- "Mind Over Mattress: How to Become an Early Riser." Extols the many benefits of getting up early as opposed to flying out of the house every day in a frenzy caused by being late.
- "Beware the Underminer." Tips for recognizing and handling those family members, friends, and acquaintances who make us feel bad about ourselves.

Rights and Payment

Rights vary. No payment. Provides 1 contributor's copy.

Goldmine

700 East State Street
Iola, WI 54990-0001

Managing Editor: Susan Sliwicki

Description and Interests
This tabloid magazine serves as an information source and marketplace for collectible records, CDs, and music memorabilia. In addition to providing readers with current information on auctions, sales, and collecting, each issue features detailed reporting on some of the greatest bands, musicians, and record producers from rock, blues, country, folk, and jazz genres. Its readers are quite knowledgeable about music, as well as collecting, and the publication requires its writers to be similarly well versed. Circ: 15,000.

Contents: 75% articles; 25% depts/columns
Frequency: Monthly
Website: www.goldminemag.com

Freelance Potential
25% written by nonstaff writers. Publishes 300 freelance submissions yearly; 5% by unpublished writers, 10% by authors who are new to the magazine, 50% by experts. Receives 5 queries monthly.

Submissions
Query. Accepts email queries to susan.sliwicki@fwmedia.com (Word attachments). Responds in 3 weeks.

- Articles: 750 words. Informational, how-to, profiles, interviews, and personal experience. Topics include audio recordings, music history, trends, and collecting.
- Depts/columns: Word lengths vary. Recent auction results, interviews, reissues, new releases, music industry news.

Sample Issue
64 pages. Advertising. Sample articles available at website.

- "Get to Know the Rock Hall's 2013 Nominees." A look at the wide-ranging pool of candidates for possible inclusion in Rock Hall's Class of 2013 in blues, soul, rap, rock, and more.
- "Led Zeppelin's 'Celebration Day' is Aptly Named." Sneak preview of a new concert film of the band's 2007 reunion show.

Rights and Payment
All rights. Written material, $10–$300. Pays on publication.

Go Magazine

6600 AAA Drive
Charlotte, NC 28212

Associate Editor: Carol Gifford

Description and Interests
This AAA publication not only covers automotive and insurance issues, but also profiles international, national, and regional travel destinations. It is distributed to members in North and South Carolina. It is always in need of articles on insurance, car care, and local travel ideas in North and South Carolina and prefers lively, upbeat stories that appeal to a well-traveled, sophisticated audience. Circ: 1.7 million.

Contents: 50% articles; 50% depts/columns
Frequency: 6 times each year
Website: www.aaagomagazine.com

Freelance Potential
25% written by nonstaff writers. Publishes 15 freelance submissions yearly; 5% by authors who are new to the magazine, 5% by experts. Receives 5 queries monthly.

Submissions
Query with writing samples. Accepts email queries to cgifford@mailaaa.com. Will accept hard copy. Availability of art can increase chance of acceptance. Responds in 2 weeks.

- Articles: Up to 1,300 words. Informational. Topics include regional, domestic, and international travel; leisure; road safety; and automotive concerns. Only AAA-approved vendors may be mentioned in articles.
- Depts/columns: Word lengths vary. Association news, insurance, finances.
- Artwork: Digital images.

Sample Issue
48 pages. Advertising. Sample copy and guidelines available on website.

- "Disney Goes Hawaiian." Destination piece on a new Disney resort in Oahu that celebrates the art and cultural traditions of Hawaii.
- "AAA Car Care: A New Kind of Superhero Service." What AAA car care centers offer and how they differ from regular auto repair facilities.

Rights and Payment
One-time rights. Written material, $150. Pays on publication. Provides 2 contributor's copies.

Go Magazine

68 Jay Street, Suite 315
Brooklyn, NY 11201

Executive Editor: Jaime Lowe

Description and Interests

As AirTran Airway's in-flight publication, *Go Magazine* includes a mix of destination, celebrity, lifestyle, and business features that inform, entertain, and inspire readers. Each issue also includes a comprehensive city guide, as well as entertainment and new product information. It is looking for out-of-the-box approaches to the scenes and lifestyles of the destinations in AirTran's flight plans, as well as trends and interesting topics that will help the publication live up to its tagline: "There's no stopping you." Circ: 100,000+.

Contents: 80% articles; 20% depts/columns
Frequency: Monthly
Website: www.airtranmagazine.com

Freelance Potential

80% written by nonstaff writers. Publishes 100 freelance submissions yearly; 15% by authors who are new to the magazine, 50% by experts. Receives 100 queries monthly.

Submissions

Query only with clips and well-developed article idea. Accepts email to peter.koch@ink-global.com. Response time varies.

- Articles: 1,400–2,000 words. Informational, profiles, and interviews. Topics include destinations, lifestyle, travel, entertainment, and business-related subjects.
- Depts/columns: Staff-written.
- Artwork: Digital images at 300 dpi.

Sample Issue

162 pages. Advertising. Sample articles and guidelines available at website.

- "Saving the Shell Shocked." What the city of Pensacola is doing to save sea turtles, which have become threatened by pollution, tropical storms, and beach erosion.
- "Small Town Charm." A roundup of small towns in America that are rich in history and culture and bring true Americana to life.

Rights and Payment

First rights. Written material, payment rates vary. Artwork, payment rates vary. Kill fee, 50%. Pays on publication.

Good Old Boat

7340 Niagara Lane North
Maple Grove, MN 55311-2655

Editor: Karen Larson

Description and Interests

Emblazoned with the tagline, "The Sailing Magazine for the Rest of Us!" *Good Old Boat* is read by sailing enthusiasts who love older boats more than new ones. It is filled with information on sailboats that are from the 1950s–2000s, their maintenance, restoration techniques, and safe sailing tips. It welcomes articles about the pride of ownership, the technical elements of maintaining an older fiberglass sailboat, and reflections on sailing. It does not cover destinations or racing. Circ: 30,000.

Contents: 80% articles; 20% depts/columns
Frequency: 6 times each year
Website: www.goodoldboat.com

Freelance Potential

90% written by nonstaff writers. Publishes 30 freelance submissions yearly; 15% by unpublished writers, 25% by authors who are new to the magazine, 25% by experts. Receives 50 queries, 100 unsolicited mss monthly.

Submissions

Query or send complete ms. Accepts hard copy and email to karen@goodoldboat.com. SASE. Responds in 2–6 months.

- Articles: 1,500–5,000 words. Informational, how-to, technical, profiles, interviews, opinion, personal experience, and reviews. Topics include boat restoration and maintenance, boat owners, products, and history.
- Depts/columns: 300–2,500 words. How-to pieces, essays, book reviews.
- Artwork: Color slides or prints; digital images at 300 dpi (JPEG or TIFF format).

Sample Issue

76 pages. Advertising. Sample articles and guidelines available at website.

- "*Dalliance*, a Pacific Seacraft 34." A look at this vintage sailboat that has been lovingly cared for and maintained by her original owners.
- "Hot Water, Warm Boat." Addresses installing a hydronic system that extends sailing and showering season for boaters.

Rights and Payment

First serial rights. Written material, payment rates vary, $50–$700; photos, $50–$100. Pays 2 months before publication. Provides 2–3 contributor's copies.

Good Old Days

306 East Parr Road
Berne, IN 46711

Editor: Mary Beth Weisenburger

Description and Interests

Good Old Days recounts the best of times and features real stories of people who grew up from the 1930s through the mid-1960s. Stories involving childhood recollections of family life and other memories are contributed mainly by readers. The magazine accepts seasonal stories year-round, and humor is always a plus. Circ: 175,000.

Contents: 70% articles; 25% depts/columns; 5% poetry
Frequency: Twice each month
Website: www.goodolddaysmagazine.com

Freelance Potential

90% written by nonstaff writers. Publishes 575 freelance submissions yearly; 20% by unpublished writers, 20% by new authors. Receives 350 unsolicited mss each month.

Submissions

Send complete ms. Accepts hard copy and email to submissions to editor@goodolddaysonline.com. SASE. Artwork improves chance of acceptance. No simultaneous submissions. Responds in 2 months.

- Articles: 800–1,200 words. Conversational recollections, biographies, and humor. Topics include memorable events, fads, fashion, sports, music, literature, entertainment—all in the context of life in America between 1935 and 1965.
- Depts/columns: 500+ words. Good Old Days on Wheels, transportation-related stories; Good Old Days in the Kitchen, kitchen- and food-related; Looking Hollywood Way, classic actors/actresses of Hollywood's Golden Age.
- Artwork: Photographs, minimum 300 dpi resolution.
- Other: Poetry. Quizzes. Cartoons. Sheet music of old songs.

Sample Issue

82 pages. Advertising. Sample articles and guidelines available at website.

- "Daddy's Gift." A father encourages his daughter's love of music in 1940s Missouri.
- "Halloween in the Fifties." A look back at one of the most magical evenings of the year.

Rights and Payment

All rights. Payment rates vary. Pays on acceptance. Provides 2 contributor's copies.

GQ Magazine 

4 Times Square
New York, NY 10036

Editor in Chief: Jim Nelson

Description and Interests

GQ is the premier men's magazine, providing definitive coverage of style and culture for millions of men each month. The only publication that speaks to all sides of the male equation, *GQ* says it is simply sharper and smarter than other publications for this audience. When querying for the first time, freelancers should show knowledge of the magazine's sections and tone. Circ: 980,000.

Contents: Articles; depts/columns
Frequency: 12 times each year
Website: www.gq.com

Freelance Potential

Freelance percentage difficult to determine; GQ.com may offer more timely opportunities for writers.

Submissions

Queries on focused ideas, not broad features, are more likely to be of interest. Direct pitches, with bio and clips, to appropriate editors: feature pitches to donovan_hohn@condenast.com. Fashion queries to justin_doss@condenast.com or lance_lin@condenast.com. For other sections, see masthead at website for a senior editor.

- Articles: Word lengths vary. Topics include fashion, men's health/fitness; women; pop culture.
- Depts/Columns: Written by staff or regular contributors.

Sample Issue

Advertising. Sample articles and editorial calendar available on website.

- "Movie Star Channing Tatum: Workhorse Actor Turned A-list Darling." A profile of the actor, and how he is making it in Hollywood the "right" way.
- "Murder of an Idealist." How the murder of the U.S. ambassador to Libya has been politicized in Washington.

Rights and Payment

All rights. Payment, $2+ per word. Kill fee, 25%. Pays on acceptance.

Grandparents.com  

589 8th Avenue, 6th Floor
New York, NY 10018

Editor

Description and Interests

Grandparents.com serves as a hub of information for engaged and involved grandparents. Dedicated to fostering family connections, it offers a wide range of activities that grandparents and grandchildren can do together, as well as personal experience pieces that give insight into the unique grandparent/grandchild relationship. The editors are always looking for fresh, new story ideas and freelance writers to add to their editorial team. Hits per month: Unavailable.

Contents: 80% articles; 20% depts/columns
Frequency: Ongoing
Website: www.grandparents.com

Freelance Potential

75% written by nonstaff writers. Publishes 150 freelance submissions yearly; 20% by authors who are new to the magazine. Receives 30–50 queries each month.

Submissions

Query. Accepts email queries to contribute@grandparents.com. Responds if interested.

- Articles: Word lengths vary. Informational, how-to, essays, interviews. Topics: entertaining and educational activities, travel, lifestyle, real-life problems, social issues and skills, recipes, gifts.
- Depts/columns: Word lengths vary. Reviews. Topics: toys, games, books, gear, movies, and other family-friendly products.

Sample Issue

Advertising. Sample copy and guidelines available at website.

- "10 Tips to Promote Healthy Video Gaming." You know they're going to play them—here's how to cultivate good gaming habits.
- "3 Creative Cookie Recipes." Three special recipes from Stacy Adimando's The Cookiepedia.

Rights and Payment

Electronic rights. No payment.

Grantland Quarterly 

849 Valencia Street
San Francisco, CA 94110

Editor in Chief: Bill Simmons

Description and Interests

A collaboration between McSweeney's publishing house and the web magazine *Grantland*, this magazine publishes the best sports writing—fiction and nonfiction—and articles on pop culture. It regularly features work from well-known writers as Chuck Klosterman, Malcolm Gladwell, and Anna Clark. Circ: Unavailable.

Contents: Articles; fiction
Frequency: Quarterly
Website: www.grantland.com

Freelance Potential

Freelance percentages not yet available. Uses freelance contributors.

Submissions

Send complete ms. Accepts hard copy and electronic submissions via Submishmash submissions manager. SASE. Responds in 6 months.

- Articles: Word lengths vary. Informational articles and profiles. Topics include sports and personalities, events.
- Fiction: Word lengths vary. Sports.

Sample Issue

Advertising. Sample articles available at website.

- "Hoosier Daddy." Article discusses Indiana's undefeated basketball record to date and what the rest of the season may bring.
- "The Year of Living Cautiously." Articles looks back on some of the disappointments in this season in the NFL.

Rights and Payment

Rights vary. Payment rates vary. Pays on publication.

GreenPrints

P.O. Box 1355
Fairview, NC 28730

Editor: Pat Stone

Description and Interests

GreenPrints is a gardening magazine that isn't a magazine about gardening. Its articles celebrate the human side of gardening through personal essays, fiction, poetry, and drawings about the joy, humor, frustration, and heart in every garden (and gardener). It searches for pieces that will make readers laugh, cry, or nod sympathetically. Circ: 13,000.

Contents: 88% articles; 8% fiction; 4% poetry
Frequency: Quarterly
Website: www.greenprints.com

Freelance Potential

100% written by nonstaff writers. Publishes 45 freelance submissions yearly; 20% by unpublished writers, 60% by authors who are new to the magazine, 5% by experts. Receives 25 queries and unsolicited mss monthly.

Submissions

Query or send complete ms with cover letter. Prefers hard copy; will accept email submissions to pat@greenprints.com (include "Story Submission" in subject line) and simultaneous submissions if identified. SASE. Responds in 2 months.

- Articles: To 2,000 words. Essays and personal experience. Topics include gardens, gardening.
- Fiction: To 2,000 words. Gardening stories.
- Artwork: B/W prints. Line art.
- Other: Poetry, no line limits.

Sample Issue

94 pages. Advertising. Sample articles and guidelines available at website.

- "Sweet Violets." Essay relates how violet seeds transported the author back to a childhood gardening scene with her mother.
- "The Funny Bunny Year." Author tells about the abundance of rabbits in her garden and the rapport she has established with them.

Rights and Payment

First North American serial and reprint rights. Written material, to $150. Artwork, $75–$200. Poetry, $20. Pays on acceptance. Provides 2 contributor's copies.

Grit

1503 SW 42nd Street
Topeka, KS 66609-1265

Managing Editor: Caleb Regan

Description and Interests

Grit brings readers articles about living a self-sustaining life and raising a family on a farm, ranch, or another rural setting. It celebrates country lifestyles of all kinds and emphasizes the importance of community and stewardship. Its readers are well educated and are either already living a rural life or aspire to do so. Circ: 150,000.

Contents: 50% articles; 50% depts/columns
Frequency: 6 times each year
Website: www.grit.com

Freelance Potential

90% written by nonstaff writers. Publishes 80–90 freelance submissions yearly; 50% by authors who are new to the magazine. Receives 200 queries each month.

Submissions

Query only. Accepts email queries to cregan@grit.com (include "Query" and subject of query in subject line). Responds if interested.

- Articles: 800–1,500 words. Informational, how-to, humor, profiles, and personal experience. Topics include country living, land management, wildlife, pets, livestock, gardening, cooking, seasonal food, machinery and tools, do-it-yourself, and community.
- Depts/columns: 500–1,500 words. GRIT Gazette, news and quirky briefs of interest to farmers; Country Tech, farm equipment; Looking Back, nostalgic look at life on the farm; In the Shop, how-to for specialty farm items; Comfort Foods; Recipe Box; Wild GRIT; Sow Hoe, gardening.
- Artwork: Digital images.

Sample Issue

96 pages. Advertising. Sample articles and guidelines available at website.

- "10 Easy Crops to Grow." Low-maintenance, fast-growing plants.
- "Farm Restaurants Are All the Rage." Small-scale farmers are getting their produce to local eateries, and the public wants more.

Rights and Payment

Shared rights. Written material, photographs, payment rate varies. Pays on publication. Provides 2 contributor's copies.

Group

Simply Youth Ministry
1515 Cascade Avenue
Loveland, CO 80539

Associate Editor: Scott Firestone

Description and Interests

Group provides practical resources and inspiration for leaders of Christian youth groups. It focuses on strategies and ideas for effectively working with teens to encourage their spiritual development and enable them to do the work of ministry. It is an interdenominational publication and welcomes descriptions of successful youth ministry strategies, as well as articles about understanding kids and youth culture, recruiting and training adult leaders, and practical ideas for meetings and programs. Circ: 40,000.

Contents: 80% articles; 20% depts/columns
Frequency: 6 times each year
Website: http://groupmagazine.com/

Freelance Potential

60% written by nonstaff writers. Publishes 200 freelance submissions yearly; 50% by unpublished writers, 80% by authors who are new to the magazine, 80% by experts. Receives 25 unsolicited mss monthly.

Submissions

Send complete ms with brief cover letter that includes author information. Accepts email to puorgBus@group.com and hard copy. SASE. Responds in 8–10 weeks.

- Articles: 500–2,000 words. Informational, how-to. Topics include youth ministry strategies, recruiting and training adult leaders, understanding youth culture, professionalism, time management, leadership skills, and professional and spiritual growth of youth ministers.
- Depts/columns. Try This One, to 300 words; Hands-On Help, to 200 words.

Sample Issue

82 pages. Advertising. Sample articles and guidelines available at website.

- "So, a Jr. Higher Walks Into a Bar..." Setting the bar for spiritual growth.
- "Shattered: Entering Into Grief with Teenagers." Helping teens process grief in a Christ-centered environment.

Rights and Payment

All rights. Articles, $150–$350. Depts/columns, $50. Pays on acceptance.

Guideposts

16 East 34th Street, 21st Floor
New York, NY 10016

Editor in Chief: Edward Grinnan

Description and Interests

Guideposts offers hope, encouragement, and inspiration to its readers by telling the true stories of ordinary people with extraordinary life experiences. Founded by Dr. Norman Vincent Peale in 1945, the publication helps readers from around the globe assimilate their faith-filled values into their daily lives with dramatic stories of courage, strength, and positive attitudes. Circ: 2.5 million.

Contents: 90% articles; 10% depts/columns
Frequency: Monthly
Website: www.guideposts.com

Freelance Potential

80% written by nonstaff writers. Publishes 100 freelance submissions yearly; 15% by unpublished writers, 5% by authors who are new to the magazine, 2% by experts. Receives 4,000 unsolicited mss monthly.

Submissions

Send complete ms. Accepts submissions via website only. Responds in 2 months.

- Articles: 750–1,500 words. Personal experience and true stories. Topics include family and relationships, challenges, disabilities, careers, social issues, community service, and faith.
- Depts/columns: 250–750 words. Stories of good works, divine touch, the power of prayer, recipes.

Sample Issue

Sample copy, free. Sample articles and guidelines available at website.

- "Carried Home by a Heavenly Horse." A teen relies on divine guidance.
- "Hitting the Road to Honor Her Wayfaring Father." A trip to 19 lighthouses with memories of a departed dad.

Rights and Payment

All rights. Articles, $250–$500. Depts/columns, $50–$250. Kill fee, 25%. Pays on acceptance. Provides 5+ contributor's copies.

Guitar Aficionado

28 East 28th Street, 9th Floor
New York, NY 10016

Executive Editor: Brad Tolinski

Description and Interests

Guitar Aficionado is for passionate people who enjoy the guitar in all of its timelessness. Its readers are affluent people who respect a fine guitar the same way they respect a fine wine or a luxury automobile. Its articles include profiles of well-known people who are also guitar aficionados, as well as information on topics related to the luxury lifestyle. Writers who wish to contribute to this publication should know their way around a classic guitar. Circ: 100,000.

Contents: Articles; depts/columns
Frequency: 6 times each year
Website: www.guitaraficionado.com

Freelance Potential

75% written by nonstaff writers. Publishes 25 freelance submissions yearly; 5% by authors who are new to the magazine. Receives 20 queries, 20 unsolicited mss monthly.

Submissions

Query or send complete ms. Accepts email submissions to info@guitaraficionado.com. Response time varies.

- Articles: Word lengths vary. Informational, profiles, and interviews. Topics include guitars, guitar collecting, guitar designers, the luxury lifestyle, fine wine, travel, automobiles, jewelry.
- Depts/columns: Word lengths vary. New product reviews, guitar care, finance, sound systems, luxury trends.

Sample Issue

98 pages. Advertising. Sample articles available at website. Guidelines available.

- "Kevin Costner and Modern West." Feature on the band started by Kevin Costner just for fun that has resulted in four albums and tons of gigs.
- "The Collection." Whether playing solo or part of a band, Jakob Dylan's favorite guitars from his collection are the classically designed ones from the fifties and sixties.

Rights and Payment

First U.S. rights. Written material, payment rates vary. Pays on publication. Provides 2 contributor's copies.

Gulf Coast

English Department
University of Houston
Houston, TX 77204-3013

Fiction, Nonfiction, or Poetry Editor

Description and Interests

Published by the University of Houston, *Gulf Coast* is a journal of literary and fine arts. Each issue features a mix of short stories, essays, poems, interviews, and reviews. It only accepts previously unpublished works. It is student run and has an ever-expanding website to complement its print issues. Circ: 3,000.

Contents: 33% articles; 34% fiction; 33% poetry
Frequency: Twice each year
Website: www.gulfcoastmag.org

Freelance Potential

98% written by nonstaff writers. Publishes 135 freelance submissions yearly; 10% by unpublished writers, 50% by authors who are new to the magazine. Receives 500 unsolicited mss each month.

Submissions

Send complete ms between September 1 and March 1 only. Prefers email submissions through online submission manager at website; will accept hard copy addressed to appropriate editor and simultaneous submissions if identified. SASE. Responds in 4–6 months.

- Articles: To 7,000 words. Interviews, essays, personal experience pieces, and reviews.
- Fiction: To 7,000 words. Literary fiction.
- Other: Poetry; limit 5 poems per submission.

Sample Issue

250+ pages. No advertising. Article excerpts and guidelines available at website.

- "Grand Canyon II." Futuristic feature about returning to the Grand Canyon after a mining accident.
- "To Know Something Is to Kill It: Colin Cheney's *Here Be Monsters*." A review of this author's latest book of poetry.
- "Happy Birthday, Clementine." Short story about the dissolute and aimless life of a young party animal.

Rights and Payment

One-time rights. Fiction and articles, $20 per page; $150 maximum. Interviews, $100. Poetry, $30. Reviews, $50. Pays on publication. Provides 2 contributor's copies and a 1-year subscription.

Gumshoe

30 Deer Run Lane
Brick, NJ 08724

Senior Editor: Gayle Surrette

Description and Interests

Gumshoe is an ezine that seeks short original fiction and nonfiction essays that are of interest to readers, writers, and students of mysteries. The protagonist in its stories is usually an investigator, and the focus is on solving a crime, getting out of trouble, or seeking justice. Not of interest are character studies or mood pieces. Circ: Unavailable.

Contents: Fiction
Frequency: Monthly
Website: www.gumshoereview.com

Freelance Potential

Receives many freelance submissions monthly.

Submissions

Send complete ms with brief bio. Email fiction to editor@gumshoereview.com; include "Gumshoe Short Story Submission" in the subject line. Reviews, accepts hard copy (Attention: Sam Tomaino). SASE. Responds in 3 months.

- Articles: To 1,000 words. Essays. Topics should relate to the mystery genre.
- Fiction: To 1,000 words. Mysteries.
- Depts/columns: Staff-written.

Sample Issue

Advertising. Sample copy and guidelines available at website.

- "Bewitched, Bothered, and Biscotti: A Magical Bakery Mystery." Review of a new book written by Bailey Cates.
- "Christmas Crumble." Review of an electronic short story.

Rights and Payment

Rights vary. Written material, $.05 per word, to $50. Payment policy varies.

The G. W. Review

George Washington University
Box 20 The Marvin Center
800 21st Street NW
Washington, DC 20052

Fiction Editor: Nick Santangelo
Poetry Editor: Rosie Ebadat

Description and Interests

This magazine, George Washington University's international literary journal, publishes fiction, poetry, and two-dimensional art from writers throughout the world. It is proud to offer writers an international audience for their work and accepts submissions throughout the year. Circ: 2,000+.

Contents: 35% fiction; 65% other
Frequency: Twice each year
Website: www.gwreview.weebly.com

Freelance Potential

100% written by nonstaff writers. Publishes 28 freelance submissions yearly; 10% by unpublished writers, 70% by authors who are new to the magazine. Receives 60 unsolicited mss monthly.

Submissions

Send complete ms and cover letter with author bio. Accepts hard copy, disk submissions, and simultaneous submissions if identified. SASE. Responds in 3–4 months.

- Fiction: To 6,000 words. Contemporary, ethnic, experimental, humorous, mainstream, and literary fiction.
- Artwork: B/W prints. Line art.
- Other: Poetry, to 10 pages.

Sample Issue

80 pages. No advertising. Sample copy and guidelines available at website.

- "The Monster Business." Story describes a young boy's monster-hunting business.
- "Painting Desire." Story follows a middle-aged bachelor as he tries to connect with a Japanese art student.

Rights and Payment

First rights. No payment. Provides 2 contributor's copies.

Hadassah Magazine 

50 West 58th Street
New York, NY 10019

Associate Editor: Libby Goldberg Barnea

Description and Interests

For more than 25 years *Hadassah* has covered cultural, political, social, religious, and lifestyle trends from a Jewish point of view. It also presents stories—both fiction and nonfiction—on Jewish life in America, around the world, and in Israel. It prefers objective, lively writing with lots of quotes and without the author's voice intruding. Circ: 250,000.

Contents: 40% articles; 40% depts/columns; 10% fiction; 10% other
Frequency: Monthly
Website: www.hadassahmagazine.org

Freelance Potential

55% written by nonstaff writers. Of the freelance submissions published yearly, 10% are by unpublished writers, 10% are by authors who are new to the magazine, 10% are by experts. Receives 25 queries monthly.

Submissions

Query with writing samples. Accepts hard copy and email queries to lbarnea@hadassah.org. SASE. Responds in 1–2 months.

- Articles: 800–1,500 words. Creative nonfiction, profiles, interviews, reviews, personal experience, and opinion. Topics include social issues, food, arts, government, economics, current events—all from a Jewish perspective.
- Fiction: 1,000–3,000 words. Contemporary fiction and humorous stories related to Israel or Judaism.
- Depts/columns: Word lengths vary. Travel, reviews, profiles.

Sample Issue

88 pages. Advertising. Sample articles available at website. Guidelines available.

- "Candles in the Window: Where Memory Never Runs Out." Explains the ancient custom of observing *yortzeits* for the deceased and ways that the dead are remembered and honored today.
- "Old Values, New Blood: Hadassah 2.0." A look at the young women in Hadassah today.

Rights and Payment

Rights vary. Written material, payment rates vary. Kill fee, $250. Pays on acceptance. Provides 1 contributor's copy.

Harper's Magazine 

666 Broadway, 11th Floor
New York, NY 10012-2317

Editor: Ellen Rosenbush

Description and Interests

Launched in 1850 and revered by many as an American literary institution, *Harper's Magazine* publishes essays, opinion pieces, and news reports that reflect original thinking and foster an exchange of intellectual thought. The topics it covers range from social issues and economics to the arts and popular culture. It also publishes short fiction and reviews. Submissions to the Readings section are encouraged. Nonfiction submissions will not be considered unless they are preceded by a written query. Circ: 205,000.

Contents: 50% articles; 30% reviews; 10% fiction; 10% depts/columns
Frequency: Monthly
Website: www.harpers.org

Freelance Potential

50% written by nonstaff writers. Publishes 35 freelance submissions yearly. Receives 50 queries monthly.

Submissions

Query for nonfiction. Send ms for fiction only. Accepts hard copy. SASE. Responds in 3 months.

- Articles: Word lengths vary. Informational, essays, literary reviews, and memoirs. Topics include politics, society, the environment, culture.
- Fiction: Word lengths vary. Literary fiction.
- Depts/columns: Staff-written.

Sample Issue

80 pages. Advertising. Sample articles and guidelines available at website.

- "Why Vote? When Your Vote Counts for Nothing." Questions whether or not democracy really has an "infinite resilience" and makes the argument that it has actually been turned against society.
- "Contest of Words: High School Debate and the Demise of Public Speech." Changes in curriculum are creating a lack of knowledge on powerful and persuasive public speaking.

Rights and Payment

Rights vary. Written material, payment rates vary. Payment policy varies.

Harvard Magazine

7 Ware Street
Cambridge, MA 02138-4037

Editor: John S. Rosenberg

Description and Interests

This magazine has articles on university, student, and alumni news, but it also features pieces (with a Harvard angle) on education and business. It is open to a wide variety of subjects, as long as a Harvard connection or angle exists. Circ: 250,000.

Contents: 50% articles; 25% depts/columns; 25% other
Frequency: 6 times each year
Website: www.harvardmagazine.com

Freelance Potential

25% written by nonstaff writers. Publishes 20–30 freelance submissions yearly; 5–10% by authors who are new to the magazine. Receives 25–50 queries monthly.

Submissions

Query by email to john_rosenberg@harvard.edu. Accepts hard copy with clips. SASE. No simultaneous submissions. Responds in 1 week.

- Articles: 500–5,000 words. Informational and profiles. Topics include news, current events, research, and personalities—all as they relate to Harvard University and alumni.
- Depts/columns: 500–1,500 words. News, media reviews.

Sample Issue

76 pages. Advertising. Sample articles and guidelines available at website.

- "Architecture in Concert." A look at the unique designs of public spaces done by William Rawn (class of '69) and his company.
- "Can America Compete?" Report on the U.S. Competitiveness Project being developed by Harvard Business School Scholars, which is looking to devise strategies for a healthy U.S. economic future.

Rights and Payment

First and electronic rights. Articles, $200–$3,000. Depts/columns, $200–$500. Pays on publication. Provides contributor's copies upon request.

Healing Lifestyles & Spas

P.O. Box 271207
Louisville, CO 80027

Editorial Director: Melissa Williams

Description and Interests

This company publishes an annual directory of spas and renewal treatment information, with additional articles being posted online throughout the year. Helping its readers to feel better naturally is its editorial focus. Articles may address emotional, spiritual, or physical health. Circ: 100,000. Hits per month unknown.

Contents: Articles; depts/columns
Frequency: Annually
Website: www.healinglifestyles.com

Freelance Potential

85–90% written by nonstaff writers. Publishes 50+ freelance submissions yearly; 5% by unpublished writers, 10% by authors who are new to the magazine, 5% by experts. Receives 100 queries monthly.

Submissions

Query with résumé and clips. Accepts email queries to editorial@healinglifestyles.com. Response time varies.

- Articles: Word lengths vary. Informational and self-help. Topics include spirituality, mind-body practices, natural and alternative therapies, organic foods, nutrition, sustainability, ecotourism, and health spas.
- Depts/columns: Word lengths vary. Healing news, green products and practices, natural remedies, fitness routines, spa treatments, travel destinations, healthy cooking.

Sample Issue

88 pages. Advertising. Sample articles available at website.

- "Stress & the Havoc It Causes." You know it's bad for you, but did you know stress contributes to everything from sleeplessness to infertility to weakened immunity?
- "Guide to Nontoxic Skin-care." Decipher confusing skin-care terminology and claims with this showcase of products that contain no phthalates, parabens, or other known toxins.

Rights and Payment

First North American serial rights. Written material, payment rates vary. Pays on publication.

Health Magazine

2100 Lakeshore Drive
Birmingham, AL 35209

Editor in Chief: Amy O'Connor

Description and Interests

This magazine's emphasis is on the latest and most important developments in women's physical, emotional, and spiritual health. Regular features cover beauty, fitness, diet and nutrition, and lifestyle. It provides its readers with a dependable source of useful health information and a perspective on the rapidly changing face of personal health. Practical, service-oriented ideas presented in clear, jargon-free language are always welcome. Circ: 1.4 million.

Contents: 50% articles; 25% depts/columns; 25% other
Frequency: 10 times each year
Website: www.health.com

Freelance Potential

75% written by nonstaff writers. Publishes 25–30 freelance submissions yearly; 5% by unpublished writers, 15% by authors who are new to the magazine, 5% by experts. Receives 30–40 queries monthly.

Submissions

Query with résumé and writing samples. Accepts email queries to ask@health.com. Responds in 1–3 months.

- Articles: Word lengths vary. Informational, self-help, how-to, and profiles. Topics include health, fitness, weight loss, relationships, beauty, nutrition, mind/body issues, and alternative medicine.
- Depts/columns: 800 words. Beauty, exercise, nutrition, food.

Sample Issue

172 pages. Advertising. Sample articles available on website. Guidelines available.

- "Alternative Remedies That Actually Work." Cupping, acupuncture, and other perhaps wacky sounding treatments are becoming mainstream as physicians see that they work.
- "Healthy Soups to Master." One-pot wonders packed with nutritious ingredients and with the bonus benefit of suppressing appetite.

Rights and Payment

Rights vary. Written material, $1–$1.50 per word. Kill fee, 33%. Payment policy varies. Provides 2 contributor's copies.

Heart Insight

323 Norristown Road, Suite 200
Ambler, PA 19002

Managing Editor: Cynthia Laufenberg

Description and Interests

Heart Insight is a magazine for patients who have cardiovascular disease or related conditions, as well as their families and caregivers. It is published by the American Heart Association and offers information on managing and preventing heart-related disorders and strategies for improving heart health. It strives to give its readers practical advice on lifestyle changes and realistic goals against which to measure progress, but never using a preachy tone. Writers should be familiar with AHA treatment guidelines and Scientific Statements. Circ: 500,000.

Contents: 50% articles; 50% depts/columns
Frequency: Quarterly
Website: www.heartinsight.com

Freelance Potential

50% written by nonstaff writers. Publishes 24 freelance submissions yearly; 10% by authors who are new to the magazine. Receives 1–2 queries monthly.

Submissions

Query. Accepts email to cynthia.laufenberg@wolterskluwer.com. Responds in 2 weeks.

- Articles: 850–2,400 words. Informational, how-to, profiles, and interviews. Topics include heart health, general health and fitness, medical services and medical care, nutrition and diet, science, technology, and senior citizens.
- Depts/columns: Staff-written.

Sample Issue

24 pages. Advertising. Sample copy and guidelines available at website.

- "The Truth About Chocolate: Is it Really Good for You?" Everyone loves chocolate, but how much of a good thing is to our benefit and how much to our detriment?
- "Does Race and Ethnicity Play a Role in Heart Disease?" A look at how ethnic background affects the rate and risk of heart disease.

Rights and Payment

All rights. Written material, $.75 per word. Kill fee, 25%. Pays on acceptance. Provides 2 contributor's copies.

HeartLand Boating

319 North Fourth Street, Suite 650
St. Louis, MO 63102

Editor: Brad Kovach

Description and Interests

Focusing on the Heartland's freshwater inland rivers and lakes, this magazine covers all kinds of boating through middle America. Its articles reflect the lifestyle, challenges, and joys of life afloat. The magazine is written for boaters by boaters. It welcomes freelance submissions for the Marina Profiles and Heartland Haunts sections, as well as tech-related stories. Circ: 7,500.

Contents: 70% articles; 30% depts/columns
Frequency: 8 times each year
Website: www.heartlandboating.com

Freelance Potential

5% written by nonstaff writers. Publishes 110 freelance submissions yearly; 2% by unpublished authors; 10% by authors who are new to the magazine; 70% by experts. Receives 100+ unsolicited mss during submission period.

Submissions

Prefers query. Accepts complete ms, with word count. See website for specific editorial needs. Send submissions between May 1 and July 31 only. Accepts hard copy submissions. SASE. Responds in 6–12 weeks.

- Articles: 500–2,000 words. Informational, how-to, profiles, interviews, personal experience, opinion, and humor. Topics include inland boating, boat maintenance, marinas, recreation, and travel destinations.
- Depts/columns: 600–800 words. Nautical anecdotes, destinations, events, maritime law, reviews, news briefs.
- Artwork: JPEG or TIFF images; color prints.

Sample Issue

54 pages. Advertising. Sample articles and guidelines available at website.

- "Teach a Kid to Fish." What better way to celebrate National Fishing and Boating Week than by passing on this fun and useful skill.
- "Seven Days, Six States, 640 Miles." Recounts an epic boat journey on the waterways of middle America.

Rights and Payment

First and electronic rights. All material, payment rates vary. Pays on publication. Provides 2 contributor's copies.

Hemispheres

Ink Global
68 Jay Street, Suite 315
Brooklyn, NY 11201

Editor in Chief: Joe Keohane

Description and Interests

Hemispheres sees itself as not just another inflight magazine. It has high journalistic standards and while many of its features are naturally travel- or destination-related, it is seeking articles that would appear in a quality general interest publication. Writers with expert credentials and a strong narrative tone are encouraged in the exploration of places, people, and events with uniquely interesting slants. Circ: 12 million.

Contents: 80% articles; 20% depts/columns
Frequency: Monthly
Website: www.hemispheresmagazine.com

Freelance Potential

60% written by nonstaff writers.

Submissions

Query with clips and brief author bio. Prefers email queries to editorial@hemispheresmagazine.com. Response time varies.

- Articles: Informational articles; and profiles. Topics include travel destinations, culture, science, adventures, sports, well-known personalities, news.
- Depts/columns: 300 words. Destinations, short profiles, science and technology, sports, business, food, culture, and the arts.

Sample Issue

Advertising. Sample articles, guidelines and editorial calendar available at website.

- "Plunder Games." A professor turned explorer believes he has found the ship that Captain Morgan lost while sacking Panama City in 1671.
- Sample dept/column: Dispatches is a peek into the life of "Master Penman," Jake Weidmann, one of the world's best calligraphers.

Rights and Payment

Rights, 90 days exclusive. Written material, $1 a word. Kill fee, 50%. Pays on acceptance.

The Herb Quarterly

4075 Papazian Way, Suite 208
Fremont, CA 94538

Editor in Chief: Abbie Barrett

Description and Interests
This magazine is for people who are serious about herbs. It provides readers with information on the types of herbs and how to use them for physical and emotional healing, as well as illness prevention. For more than 30 years, it has been a definitive source for the cultivation, cooking, and medicinal use of herbs. It is always in need of recipes and other practical information for herbs' use. Circ: 56,000.

Contents: 60% articles; 40% depts/columns
Frequency: Quarterly
Website: www.herbquarterly.com

Freelance Potential
76–100% written by nonstaff writers. Publishes 30–40 freelance submissions yearly; 25% by authors who are new to the magazine. Receives 7 queries, 2 unsolicited mss monthly.

Submissions
Query with outline and résumé; or send complete ms with résumé and bibliography. Accepts hard copy and disk submissions. SASE. Responds in 2 months.

- Articles: 1,200–3,500 words. Informational, how-to, and personal experience. Topics include herbal lore and history, horticulture, recipes, medicines, types of herbs, gardening, and new products.
- Depts/columns: 500–2,000 words. Herbal medicine, book reviews, gardening tips, Q&As, herb-related briefs, and profiles.

Sample Issue
66 pages. Advertising. Sample copy and guidelines available.

- "Herbal Wines & Liqueurs." Article discusses how to infuse home-brewed refreshments with herbal flavors.
- "Going Up: 12 Flowering Vines for Your Garden." Article offers advice for growing a dozen different vines for outdoor color and indoor flavor.

Rights and Payment
First and second serial rights. Articles, $75–$200. Depts/columns, $50. Pays on publication. Provides 2 contributor's copies.

HGTV Magazine

300 West 57th Street, 12th Floor
New York, NY 10019

Editor in Chief: Sara Peterson

Description and Interests
This magazine, an offshoot of the popular Home and Garden Television channel, is produced by Hearst Communications and Scripps Networks. It aims to be fresh, fun, and focused on helping readers make small changes with a large impact. It is packed with tips and useful information on home makeovers, decorating, and gardening. Circ: Unavailable.

Contents: Articles
Frequency: 10 times each year
Website: www.hgtv.com/hgtv-magazine/package/index.html

Freelance Potential
Receives numerous submissions monthly.

Submissions
Query with clips. Accepts hard copy and email to speterson@hearst.com. SASE. Response time varies.

- Articles: Word lengths vary. Informational and how-to articles. Topics include decorating, entertaining, gardening, and renovations and makeovers.

Sample Issue
Advertising. Sample articles available at website.

- "Love Your Bed." Article provides 22 instant tricks to update or change one's bedroom style.
- "3 Amazing Family Kitchens." Article profiles three kitchens that underwent renovations to make them more family-friendly and functional.
- "Surprising Hues." Article discusses the best way to introduce black and white into the Christmas color palette.

Rights and Payment
Rights vary. Payment rates and policy vary.

High Country News

119 Grand Avenue
P.O. Box 1090
Paonia, CO 81428

Managing Editor: Jodi Peterson

Description and Interests

High Country News covers the important news and stories that define the American West. It strives to inform people through insightful, in-depth articles. Topics include the environment, culture, politics, and social issues. Stories that are well-researched and have significance across the 11-state region are preferred. Circ: 25,000.

Contents: 100% articles
Frequency: 22 times each year
Website: www.hcn.org

Freelance Potential

75% written by nonstaff writers. Publishes 50–70 freelance submissions yearly; 5% by unpublished writers, 30% by authors new to the magazine, 1% by experts. Receives 40 queries monthly.

Submissions

Query with résumé and clips. Accepts email queries to editor@hcn.org and include "Story Query" in subject line. Responds in 3 weeks.

- Articles: 1,600–10,000 words. Informational, profiles, and interviews. Topics include natural resources, the environment, culture, education, legislation, public access issues—all as they relate to the western region of the U.S.
- Depts/columns: 800–1,600 words. News, analysis, profiles, trends, reviews.
- Artwork: 8x10 B/W or color prints; 35mm negatives and slides; JPEG files at 300 dpi.

Sample Issue

28 pages. Advertising. Sample articles and guidelines available at website.

- "Can Pallis Sturgeon Hang on in the Overworked Missouri River." Scientists are studying these ancient fish and looking for signs that they will be able to continue to thrive in the Missouri.
- "The Politics of Public Health." Discussion of how environmental issues come to be political footballs kicked around by candidates during election years.

Rights and Payment

First North American serial and reprint rights. Written material, payment rates vary. Artwork, \$35–\$100. Pays on publication. Provides 1 contributor's copy.

Highways

P.O. Box 90017
Bowling Green, KY 42102-4265

Managing Editor: Cindy McCaleb

Description and Interests

The official publication of the Good Sam Club for recreational vehicle owners, *Highways* features destination pieces and information on owning, maintaining, buying, and selling an RV. It is looking for practical RV information, Good Sam Club-related stories, and well-written travel essays accompanied by high-quality photography. Circ: 1.3 million.

Contents: 50% articles; 50% depts/columns
Frequency: 5 times each year
Website: www.goodsamclub.com

Freelance Potential

25% written by nonstaff writers. Publishes 20 freelance submissions yearly; 10% by unpublished writers, 5% by authors who are new to the magazine, 50% by experts. Receives 50 queries monthly.

Submissions

Send complete ms for humor pieces. Query between April and June for all other material. Accepts email to comments@highwaysmag.com. Responds in 1 month.

- Articles: 1,000 words. Informational, how-to, and personal experience. Topics include RV travel and lifestyle, vehicle operation, safety, maintenance, new products, destinations, recreation, and hobbies.
- Depts/columns: Staff-written.
- Artwork: Color transparencies; high-resolution digital images.

Sample Issue

56 pages. Advertising. Sample articles available at website.

- "Reba McEntire, an American Icon." Q and A with the "Queen of Country" who discusses her career to date and the upcoming performance at the Daytona Rally.
- "Camping Under the Halo." Explains what the "Good Sam" rating system means and how to find an RV park that syncs up with the amenities and activities you are looking for.

Rights and Payment

First North American serial and electronic rights. Written material, payment rates vary. Pays on acceptance. Provides 2 contributor's copies.

Hippocampus Magazine

P.O. Box 411
Elizabethtown, PA 17022

.

Description and Interests

Launched in May 2011, *Hippocampus* is an online magazine of creative nonfiction. It aims to provide a forum for emerging writers and for established writers continuing to improve their craft. Memoirs, personal essays, interviews, and reviews are all enthusiastically accepted. It seeks pieces that are quirky, edgy, witty, smart, and those that will move the editors. Hits per month: Unavailable.

Contents: Articles; essays; interviews; reviews
Frequency: Monthly
Website: www.hippocampusmagazine.com

Freelance Potential

Receives numerous submissions monthly.

Submissions

Send complete ms. Accepts electronic submissions via website and simultaneous submissions. No multiple submissions. Responds in 3–4 months.

- Articles: To 3,500 words. How-to articles, interviews, reviews, memoirs, and personal essays.

Sample Issue

Sample articles and writers' guidelines available at website.

- "All's Well If It Ends Well." Article discusses the difficulty many writers have coming up with the right ending.
- "A Snip Decision." Essay tells of a man's thoughts while he prepares for a vasectomy.
- "Distant Relatives." Essay about a woman's encounter with several of her relatives at her grandfather's funeral.

Rights and Payment

One-time electronic rights. No payment.

Hispanic Career World

445 Broad Hollow Road, Suite 425
Melville, NY 11747

Director, Editorial & Production: James Schneider

Description and Interests

Hispanic college students and professionals who are actively seeking employment turn to this publication for career advice. It features the latest job market trends, networking, reviews of promising fields, profiles, and tips for maximizing hiring potential, all with an Hispanic slant. It sees itself as a recruitment link between prospective employees who are Hispanic and the employers that seek to hire them. Circ: 18,000.

Contents: Articles; depts/columns
Frequency: Twice each year
Website: www.eop.com

Freelance Potential

50% written by nonstaff writers. Publishes 15 freelance submissions yearly; 25% by unpublished writers, 25% by authors who are new to the magazine, 50% by experts. Receives 10 queries, 5 unsolicited mss monthly.

Submissions

Query with outline for articles. Send complete ms for filler. Accepts hard copy, Macintosh disk submissions, and email to jschneider@eop.com. SASE. Responds in 1 month.

- Articles: To 1,500 words. Informational, how-to, profiles, interviews, and personal experience. Topics include business, career, industry profiles—all as they relate to the Hispanic population.
- Depts/columns: To 800 words. Career strategies and tools.

Sample Issue

46 pages. Advertising. Sample articles and editorial calendar available at website.

- "Banking & Finance: A Wealth of Opportunities." An overview of the career opportunities in this field from a hispanic woman who has been in the business 14 years.
- "Good First Impression." 10 guidelines for job candidates to help them interview successfully and get the job.

Rights and Payment

First North American serial rights. Written material, $.10 per word. Pays on publication. Provides 1 contributor's copy.

The Hispanic Outlook in Higher Education

80 Route 4 East, Suite 203
Paramus, NJ 07652

Managing Editor: Suzanne Lopez-Isa

Description and Interests

Progressive articles on educational trends, issues, and experiences—and how they relate to Hispanic Americans—are highlighted in this magazine. It targets teachers, administrators, and students. Each issue is centered around a theme. Its aim is for the content of the publication to facilitate constructive discussion of issues faced by Hispanics and others on college campuses and in private industry. Circ: 28,000.

Contents: 50% articles; 50% depts/columns
Frequency: 23 times each year
Website: www.hispanicoutlook.com

Freelance Potential

40% written by nonstaff writers. Publishes 26 freelance submissions yearly; 5% by authors who are new to the magazine, 20% by experts. Receives 10 unsolicited mss monthly.

Submissions

Send complete ms with photos and author biography. Accepts disk submissions (WordPerfect 5.1) and email submissions to sloutlook@aol.com. SASE. Responds in 1 month.

- Articles: 2,000 words. Interviews, profiles, personal experience, and opinion. Topics include secondary education, government, educational law, scholastic sports, multicultural and ethnic issues, and politics.
- Depts/columns: 2,000 words. News, reviews.

Sample Issue

48 pages. Advertising. Sample articles available at website.

- "Debt Has Negative Impact on Enrollment in STEM for Latino Students." Examines the likelihood of more Latino students participating in STEM degree programs if the cost were reduced to lower the debt rate upon graduation.
- "Cloud Computing on Campus 101." A basic explanation of how storing data on "the cloud" can eliminate the need for students physically transporting files from one place to another.

Rights and Payment

All rights. Articles, $500. Depts/columns, $300. Pays on publication. Provides 2 contributor's copies.

Alfred Hitchcock's Mystery Magazine

267 Broadway, 4th Floor
New York, NY 10007-2352

Editor: Linda Landrigan

Description and Interests

For more than half a century, mystery lovers have subscribed to this digest to satisfy their appetites for stories of suspense, espionage, courtroom drama, and police procedurals. All of the stories it publishes are tied to a crime in some way. Reviews and puzzles are also included. If you can craft a mystery story that is fresh, well told, and absorbing, by all means, send it in. Do not send stories based on actual crimes or actual events. Circ: 75,000.

Contents: 95% stories; 5% depts/columns
Frequency: 10 times each year
Website: www.themysteryplace.com

Freelance Potential

98% written by nonstaff writers. Publishes 90–100 freelance submissions yearly; 5–10% by unpublished writers, 25–50% by authors who are new to the magazine. Receives 50–100 unsolicited mss monthly.

Submissions

Send complete ms. Accepts hard copy. No simultaneous submissions. SASE. Responds in 3–5 months.

- Fiction: To 12,000 words. Genres include classic crime mysteries, detective stories, suspense, private investigator tales, courtroom drama, and espionage.
- Depts/columns: Word lengths vary. Reviews, puzzles, profiles of bookstores.

Sample Issue

192 pages. Advertising. Sample excerpts, podcasts, and guidelines available at website.

- "Last Supper." Introduces a precocious teen sleuth.
- "The Sellout." A nameless accountant in a financial thriller.

Rights and Payment

First, serial, anthology, and foreign rights. Written material, payment rates vary. Pays on acceptance. Provides 2 contributor's copies.

HM Magazine

P.O. Box 4626
Lago Vista, TX 78645

Editor: Doug Van Pelt

Description and Interests
HM Magazine offers in-depth coverage and honest reviews of the Christian hard music scene, which includes punk, rock, metal, and alternative music. It is filled with artist interviews; event information; and music, DVD, and book reviews. Circ: 9,000.

Contents: Articles; depts/columns
Frequency: Monthly
Website: www.hmmag.com

Freelance Potential
50% written by nonstaff writers. Publishes 36–48 freelance submissions yearly; 3% by unpublished writers, 4% by authors who are new to the magazine, 5% by experts. Receives 6 queries, 2 unsolicited mss monthly.

Submissions
Query with 2 clips. Accepts email submissions to editor@hmmag.com.

- Articles: 400–2,000 words. Informational, profiles and interviews. Topics include the Christian hard music scene, artists, and recent releases.
- Depts/columns: 150–200 words. Music, DVD, book, and product reviews.

Sample Issue
58 pages. Advertising. Sample copy and guidelines available at website.

- "Jim Sonefield." Profile of this former member of Hootie and the Blowfish chronicling his descent into substance abuse and re-emergence with a new album with a Christian direction.
- "House of Heroes." A review of this group's latest record, *Cold Hard Want*, which features a new pop sensibility blended with their familiar signature song style.

Rights and Payment
All rights. Articles, $45–$100. Reviews, $15. Pays on publication.

Home Business

20711 Holt Avenue, #807
Lakeville, MN 55044

Editor in Chief: Stacy Ann Henderson

Description and Interests
Home Business reaches people who own or hope to own a home-based business. It provides success stories, information about getting started, and tips for growing a business. Articles should be practical and contain how-to information readers can use to generate income. Circ: 125,000+.

Contents: 50% articles; 50% depts/columns
Frequency: 6 times each year
Website: www.homebusinessmag.com

Freelance Potential
60% written by nonstaff writers. Publishes 100 freelance submissions yearly; 35% by unpublished writers, 33% by authors who are new to the magazine. Receives 600 unsolicited mss monthly.

Submissions
Query in bullet format; or send complete ms. Include résumé, clips, and article fee with submission. Accepts email submissions to editor@homebusinessmag.com. Responds if interested.

- Articles: 700–2,300 words, plus 10- to 50-word author's resource box. Informational, how-to, celebrity interviews, and personal experience. Topics include home-based businesses, telecommuting, sales, marketing, networking, and productivity.
- Depts/columns: Success stories, to 400 words. Marketing tips, business issues and opportunities, finance, news, reviews, 600–1,200 words.

Sample Issue
60 pages. Advertising. Sample copy, guidelines, and editorial calendar available at website.

- "The Cost-Cutter's Guide to Growth." Five low-budget tips for building a home business in a weak economy.
- "Home Office Setup Basic." How adjusting your chair to the proper height, seat, and back depth can make the difference between pain and productivity.

Rights and Payment
One-time and electronic rights. Written material, payment rates vary. Payment policy varies. Provides 1+ contributor's copies.

Home Education Magazine

Box 1083
Tonasket, WA 98855-1083

Editor: Mark Hegener

Description and Interests
This award-winning, recently redesigned magazine on homeschooling is written largely by those who are doing it. There is a heavy emphasis on practical techniques and first-person experiences that teach and encourage parents who homeschool. It also acts as a guide to resources on teaching topics. It is always in need of pieces on problem solving and tales of successful learning adventures. Circ: 110,000.
Contents: 50% articles; 50% depts/columns
Frequency: 6 times each year
Website: www.homeedmag.com

Freelance Potential
90% written by nonstaff writers. Publishes 35–40 freelance submissions yearly; 25% by unpublished writers, 40% by authors who are new to the magazine.

Submissions
Prefers complete ms. Will accept queries. Include 40- to 60-word author biography. Prefers email to articles@homeedmag.com (Word attachments; include author's last name, first name or initial, and title of article in subject line); will accept hard copy. SASE. Responds in 2 months.

- Articles: 900–1,700 words. Informational, how-to, interviews, opinion, and personal experience. Topics include homeschooling, activism, lessons, and parenting issues.
- Depts/columns: Word lengths vary. Q&As, essays, news items.
- Artwork: Color or B/W prints digital images at 200 dpi, 300 dpi for cover images.

Sample Issue
48 pages. Advertising. Sample copy and guidelines available at website.

- "Building Your Home Library: Picture Books." A roundup of books that are helpful for a homeschooling library.
- "Mailbox Travelers." A project that teaches children about other countries.

Rights and Payment
First North American serial print and electronic rights. Articles, $50–$100. Other material, payment rates vary. Payment policy varies. Provides 1+ contributor's copies.

Home School Enrichment Magazine ★

Editor: Jonathan Lewis

Description and Interests: Each issue of this magazine is designed to encourage and inspire Christian parents who homeschool their children. Most of its authors are homeschool parents themselves, so articles are filled with tried-and-true ideas that work for all ages in the real world of homeschooling. Also included are articles geared to children. Circ: Unavailable.
Contents: Articles; depts/columns
Frequency: 6 times each year
Website: www.homeschoolenrichment.com

Freelance Potential
Open to ideas and writing from homeschooling parents especially.

Submissions
Query. Accepts queries via website. Response time varies.

- Articles: Word lengths vary. Informational, inspirational, and how-to articles. Topics include enrichment activities, family life, teaching ideas, ages and stages, and special needs children.
- Depts/columns: Word lengths vary. Family matters, news and commentary, Unit studies, science projects, early learning, time management tips, children's activities.

Sample Issue
Advertising. Sample articles available at website.

- "How to Stay Inspired." Article offers innovative suggestions for keeping homeschooling on track.
- "34 Mommy Tips." Article provides tips for quick and easy ways to simplify one's life.
- "Developing a Philosophy of Education: How You Can and Why You Should." Essay gives encouraging words for how to make homeschooling work and the many benefits for everyone in the family.

Rights and Payment
Rights vary. Payment rates and policy vary.

Homeschooling Today

P.O. Box 244
Abingdon, VA 24212

Editor in Chief: Marilyn Rockett

Description and Interests
Presenting a mix of practical ideas and inspirational articles, this magazine is read by parents who seek information and support for their homeschooling activities. It reflects a Christian perspective and aims to bring the homeschool community useful information and resources. All material should be supported by a biblical conviction that God uses families to change the world. Circ: 25,000.

Contents: Articles; depts/columns
Frequency: Quarterly
Website: www.homeschoolingtoday.com

Freelance Potential
90% written by nonstaff writers. Publishes 60–70 freelance submissions yearly; 6% by unpublished writers, 14% by authors who are new to the magazine. Receives 5–10 unsolicited mss monthly.

Submissions
Send complete ms via email to editor@homeschoolingtoday.com (Word attachment). Accepts simultaneous submissions if identified. Responds in 6 months.

- Articles: 1,400–2,000 words. Informational, self-help, how-to, profiles, and personal experience. Topics include education, religion, music, technology, special education, the arts, history, mathematics, and science.
- Depts/columns: 500–920 words. Hearth and Homeschool, Father's Heart, and The First Year. Reviews, 150–475 words.

Sample Issue
68 pages. Advertising. Sample articles, guidelines, and theme list available at website.

- "Is Your Child a Struggling, Reluctant Reader?" Techniques for introducing the joy of reading to your child.
- "Do You Wish You Had More Time?" Creative ways to incorporate a lesson on leap year in your homeschool curriculum.

Rights and Payment
First North American serial rights. Written material, $.10 a word for print, $.08 a word for online publication, or a 100-word advertising bio in lieu of payment. Pays on publication. Provides 1 contributor's copy.

The Home Shop Machinist

P.O. Box 629
Traverse City, MI 49685

Editor: George Bulliss

Description and Interests
As the name implies, *The Home Shop Machinist* is for hobbyists who do metal work in their home shop. Its focus is on providing projects, guidance, tips, how-to information, and new product reviews to improve skills and enhance the shop environment. It is always in need of articles that feature practical (and safe) shortcuts and money-saving ideas for tools, materials, and projects. Circ: 34,000.

Contents: 85% articles; 15% depts/columns
Frequency: 6 times each year
Website: www.homeshopmachinist.net

Freelance Potential
90% written by nonstaff writers. Publishes 60 freelance submissions yearly; 20% by unpublished writers, 5% by authors who are new to the magazine, 20% by experts. Receives 15–20 queries, 10–12 unsolicited mss monthly.

Submissions
Query or send complete ms. Accepts hard copy and Macintosh disk submissions. SASE. Responds in 4–6 weeks.

- Articles: Word lengths vary. Informational, how-to, and personal experience. Topics include metalworking, tools, equipment, foundry work, and computers.
- Depts/columns: Word lengths vary. Project tips and new product information.
- Artwork: B/W or color prints. Line art.

Sample Issue
80 pages. Advertising. Sample articles available at website. Guidelines available.

- "Additions and Modifications to a Mini-lathe." Ways to augment this tool so it can be used for more and different tasks.
- "One Way to Make a Steam Ejector." Offers one method of creating a steam ejector.

Rights and Payment
First North American serial rights. Written material, $40 per published page. Artwork, $10–$30. Pays on publication. Provides 4 contributor's copies.

Hoof Beats

750 Michigan Avenue
Columbus, OH 43215

Executive Editor: T. J. Burkett

Description and Interests

Hoof Beats, the publication of the United States Trotting Association, features the horses, people, trends, issues, and races that make up the sport of harness racing. It also covers veterinary care of standardbreds. Unique horse stories, veterinary care news, and tips on equipment or feed innovations are always welcome. Circ: 13,500.

Contents: Articles; depts/columns
Frequency: Monthly
Website: www.hoofbeatsmagazine.com

Freelance Potential

70% written by nonstaff writers. Publishes 50 freelance submissions yearly; 20% by unpublished writers, 20% by authors who are new to the magazine, 20% by experts. Receives 10 queries monthly.

Submissions

Query with writing samples or send complete ms. Prefers email to tj.burkett@ustrotting.com (Word or Text attachments). Accepts hard copy submissions. Responds in 1 month.

- Articles: Word lengths vary. Informational, how-to, profiles, interviews, humor, and personal experience. Topics include harness racing, the history of the sport, trends, gambling, racing personalities, horses, equine care and medicine, and equipment or feed innovations.
- Depts/columns: 600–1,000 words. Association news, horse profiles.
- Artwork: Color slides or prints; digital images at 300 dpi or higher.

Sample Issue

116 pages. Advertising. Sample articles and guidelines available at website.

- "Quick Change." How shoe material and track makeup combine to help a horse do better in a race.
- Sample dept/column: Equine Clinic discusses a knee surgery done on the horse, Show Must Go On.

Rights and Payment

First North American serial rights and non-exclusive electronic rights. Articles, $500. Depts/columns, $100. Photo fees negotiated. Kill fee, 25%. Pays on publication. Provides 2 contributor's copies.

Horizon Air Magazine

2701 First Avenue, Suite 250
Seattle, WA 98121

Editor: Michele Andrus Dill

Description and Interests

This general interest magazine has a mission to inform, engage, and entertain passengers of Horizon Air. It specializes in articles about people and places in the airline's market—the Pacific Northwest of the U.S. and Canada. It accepts a broad range of topics. Articles should have a general appeal, focusing on business and travel. Circ: 574,000.

Contents: 80% articles; 20% depts/columns
Frequency: Monthly
Website: http://www.alaskaairlinesmagazine.com/horizonedition

Freelance Potential

80% written by nonstaff writers. Publishes 30–40 freelance submissions yearly; 20% by authors who are new to the magazine. Receives 30–50 queries monthly.

Submissions

Query with clips. Accepts hard copy only. Responds if interested.

- Articles: 2,000–2,500 words. Informational, profiles, interviews, travel stories, creative nonfiction, and humor. Topics include entertainment, history, sports, wildlife, consumer interests, science, technology, education, and careers.
- Depts/columns: 200–1,600 words. News analysis and corporate/industry, travel, community profiles from the Pacific Northwest.

Sample Issue

82 pages. Advertising. Sample copy, guidelines, and editorial calendar available at website.

- "Whatcom County Weekend." Scenic beauty create the perfect locale for birding, whale watching, and biking in the Bellingham area.
- "Majestic Mammoth." Snowboarding, skiing, and other fun winter activities to enjoy in the spectacular Eastern Sierra area.

Rights and Payment

First North American serial, digital/archival, and reprint rights. Written material: articles, $450+; departments, $100–$250+. Kill fee, 33%. Pays on publication. Provides 2 contributor's copies.

Horse Country

23-845 Dakota Street, Suite 203
Winnipeg, Manitoba R2M 5M3
Canada

Editor: Linda Hazelwood

Description and Interests
Riders of all levels seek the most up-to-date information on equine training, safety, and medical news in this magazine. Specific to the Canadian Prairie, it also features event news and profiles. It is always in need of solid equine training or health articles and is currently looking for audio or video interviews for its website, either as stand-alones or to complement print articles. Circ: 5,000.

Contents: 40% articles; 30% depts/columns; 30% other
Frequency: 8 times each year
Website: www.horsecountry.ca

Freelance Potential
10% written by nonstaff writers. Publishes 5 freelance submissions yearly; 1% by unpublished writers, 1% by authors who are new to the magazine, 3% by experts. Receives 5 queries monthly.

Submissions
Prefers email query with brief outline, approximate word count, type of article, fee, author qualifications, and clips to editor@horsecountry.ca (put "Editorial Submission" in subject line). Accepts hard copy. Responds in 2 months.

- Articles: 800–1,200 words. Informational, self-help, how-to, profiles, and interviews. Topics include horse breeding, training, showing, health, show jumping, dressage, new products—all with a Canadian Prairie focus.
- Depts/columns: 800 words. Equestrian events, competitions, profiles, book reviews.

Sample Issue
62 pages. Advertising. Sample articles and guidelines available at website.

- "Battle of the Sexes." A discussion regarding saddles and why men's saddles are not a good fit for women.
- "Identifying Lameness." How to uncover whether lameness is being caused by a bone or muscle issue and how to best treat it.

Rights and Payment
First North American and web rights (including archival). Payment negotiated. State expectation of compensation. Pays on publication. Provides 1 contributor's copy.

Horticulture

F+W Media
10151 Carver Road, Suite 200
Cincinnati, OH 45242

Executive Editor: Meghan Shinn

Description and Interests
Horticulture presents articles that instruct, as well as inspire experienced, hands-on gardeners. It is filled with information on designing and planting techniques and profiles of plants, gardens, and nurseries. It prefers articles written in a straightforward manner instead of an essay-like approach or a literary style. Circ: 207,000.

Contents: 70% articles; 30% depts/columns
Frequency: 8 times each year
Website: www.hortmag.com

Freelance Potential
90% written by nonstaff writers. Publishes 70 freelance submissions yearly; 1% by unpublished writers, 10% by authors who are new to the magazine, 90% by experts. Receives 23 queries monthly.

Submissions
Query or send complete ms. Accepts hard copy and email queries to edit@hortmag.com. SASE. Accepts simultaneous submissions. Responds in 4–6 weeks.

- Articles: 1,500–2,500 words. Informational, how-to, profiles, interviews, personal experience, and opinion. Topics include all aspects of planting and gardening.
- Poetry: To 42 lines. Maximum 3 per submission.
- Depts/columns: 200–1,500 words. Gardening tips, book reviews.

Sample Issue
104 pages. Advertising. Sample articles available at website. Guidelines available.

- "Learn the Proper Way to Divide Perennials from The New York Botanical Garden." This essential gardening skill is an easy way to propagate perennials, as well as being necessary for the survival of some varieties.
- "Frost-Tolerant Garden Vegetables." With the first frost on its way, which vegetables will survive and which should be picked beforehand.

Rights and Payment
Rights vary. Articles, $500–$800. Depts/columns, $50–$400. Pays on acceptance. Provides 2 contributor's copies.

Houseboat Magazine

360 B Street
Idaho Falls, ID 83402

Executive Editor: Brady L. Kay

Description and Interests

This family-oriented publication offers upbeat articles on the houseboat lifestyle, as well as information on the nuts and bolts of boat ownership. Fishing and water sports also are occasionally covered. It is always looking for fresh perspectives, new ideas, and timely topics that will inspire readers to enjoy their houseboats. Circ: 30,000.

Contents: Articles; depts/columns
Frequency: 8 times each year
Website: www.houseboatmagazine.com

Freelance Potential

10–30% written by nonstaff writers. Publishes 10 freelance submissions yearly; 5% by authors who are new to the magazine.

Submissions

Query. Prefers email queries to blk@harrispublishing.com (Word attachments); will accept hard copy. SASE. Responds in 1 month.

- Articles: 1,200–1,500 words. Informational, how-to, profiles, and interviews. Topics include boats, boat maintenance, operation, and safety, recreation and travel, health, marine life, the environment, and new products.
- Depts/columns: Word lengths vary. Industry news, events and shows, boat tests, and manufacturer profiles.
- Artwork: Color transparencies; TIFF images at 300 dpi or higher.

Sample Issue

54 pages. Advertising. Sample articles available at website.

- "Fall House (boat) Cleaning." A step-by-step primer on chores that are best done in the fall to keep a houseboat in top condition.
- "If I Can Draw It, I Can Build It." A self-employed remodeling contractor shows off his custom restoration of a 1972 Kingscraft.

Rights and Payment

First North American serial and electronic rights. Articles, $100–$400. Depts/columns, $50–$175. Artwork, payment rates vary. Kill fee, 25%. Pays on publication. Provides 1 contributor's copy.

The Humanist

1777 T Street NW
Washington, DC 20009-7125

Editor: Jennifer Bardi

Description and Interests

This nonprofit magazine is oriented toward articles and research on social issues. Its goal is to apply a naturalistic and progressive outlook informed by science and inspired by art to broad areas of social, political, and personal concern. Circ: 15,000.

Contents: 66% articles; 33% depts/columns; 1% fiction/poetry
Frequency: 6 times each year
Website: www.thehumanist.org

Freelance Potential

90% written by nonstaff writers. Publishes 80 freelance submissions yearly; 10% by unpublished writers, 50% by new authors, 25% by experts. Receives 40 unsolicited mss monthly.

Submissions

Query or send complete ms with author biography. Prefers email submissions to editor@thehumanist.org (Word attachments); will accept hard copy. SASE. Simultaneous submissions accepted. Responds in 1–6 months.

- Articles: 1,500–3,000 words. Informational, personal essays, and opinion. Topics include social issues, science and technology, current events, and politics.
- Other: Short fiction, to 1,500 words. Poetry.
- Depts/columns: News, personal experience pieces, essays, 700–1,400 words. Book and film reviews, 700–1,200 words. Opinion pieces, 500–1,500 words.

Sample Issue

48 pages. Advertising. Sample articles and guidelines available at website.

- "A Woman's Place? The Dearth of Women in the Secular Movement." An exploration into why there are so many fewer women than men in the secular and atheist movements.
- "Feminist, Author, Advocate." The magazine's interview with 2012 Humanist of the Year, the legendary feminist, Gloria Steinem.

Rights and Payment

First and online rights. Written material, payment rates vary. Pays on publication. Provides 10 contributor's copies for articles, 5 for depts/columns.

India Currents

1885 Lundy Avenue #220
San Jose, CA 95131

Managing Editor: Jaya Padmanabhan

Description and Interests

This publication is dedicated to the exploration of the heritage and culture of India as it exists in the United States. It covers a wide range of topics that are of interest to Indian Americans and Indophiles through articles, essays, profiles, and lifestyle pieces. Circ: 32,300.

Contents: 50% depts/columns; 30% articles; 10% fiction; 10% other
Frequency: Monthly
Website: www.indiacurrents.com

Freelance Potential

75% written by nonstaff writers. Publishes 200 freelance submissions yearly; 20% by unpublished writers, 25% by new authors. Receives 200 unsolicited mss monthly.

Submissions

Send complete ms with artwork. Accepts email submissions to editor@indiacurrents.com (Word attachments). Responds in 4–6 weeks.

- Articles: To 3,000 words. Informational, personal experience, and opinion. Topics include Indian culture and customs, current affairs, business, the arts, and entertainment.
- Fiction: 1,500–3,000 words. Literary, contemporary, historical, humor.
- Depts/columns: To 1,000 words. Recipes, lifestyle issues, media reviews.

Sample Issue

144 pages. Advertising. Sample articles available at website. Guidelines available.

- "On The American Story." Essay retelling one woman's mother's experience coming to America from India and making a life here.
- "A Clear Choice." An issue by issue comparison of where the two presidential candidates stand and what their plans and programs are for the future.

Rights and Payment

All rights. Written material, $50 per 1,000 words. Payment policy varies.

Insight

55 West Oak Ridge Drive
Hagerstown, MD 21740-7390

Editor: Dwain Neilson Esmond

Description and Interests

Insight's mission is to reach Seventh-day Adventist teens with articles that help them grow in friendship with God. It addresses topics such as friendship, social issues, faith, and serving one's community. Articles should discuss areas of interest to today's teens from a Christian perspective and have a biblical reference. Circ: 12,000.

Contents: 20% depts/columns; 5% articles; 75% other
Frequency: Weekly
Website: www.insightmagazine.org

Freelance Potential

50% written by nonstaff writers. Publishes 200–300 freelance submissions yearly; 50% by unpublished writers, 70% by authors who are new to the magazine. Receives 60 unsolicited mss monthly.

Submissions

Send complete ms. Accepts hard copy and email to insight@rhpa.org (Word attachments). SASE. Responds in 1–3 months.

- Articles: 500–1,200 words. Informational, profiles, biography, personal experience, and humor. Topics include faith, social issues, careers, Christian celebrities, and outstanding Seventh-day Adventist youths.
- Depts/columns: Word lengths vary. Bible lessons, relationship advice, true stories, personal experience.

Sample Issue

16 pages. Little advertising. Sample articles and guidelines available at website.

- "Evil Enticements." The story of King David and Bethsheba.
- "Deja Vu and a Divine View." Coming to terms with seizures and God's plan.

Rights and Payment

First rights. Written material, $60–$100. Reprints, $50. Pays on publication. Provides 5 contributor's copies.

The Intelligent Optimist

268 Bush Street, #4419
San Francisco, CA 94104

Editor: James Geary

Description and Interests

An independent international magazine that believes in progress, ongoing opportunities and the creativity of humankind, *The Intelligent Optimist* (originally titled *Ode*) and its companion website want to be the media space in which to read about good news rather than bad, solutions rather than problems, inspiration rather than desperation. The magazine seeks very original and creative ideas. Circ: 75,000.

Contents: Articles; depts/columns
Frequency: 6 times each year
Website: www.theoptimist.com

Freelance Potential

Looking for experienced, smart, optimistic writers.

Submissions

Query. Accepts email queries to support@theoptimist.com.

- Articles/depts: Word lengths vary. Topics include innovative technology, sustainability, health and spirituality, nutrition and personal growth.

Sample Issue

Advertising. Sample articles and guidelines available at website.

- "The Employee Always Knows Best." Why more and more companies are prioritizing staff over customers and shareholders.
- "Ideal Medical Practices." A small but growing group of physicians is committed to "ideal medical practices" that put the individual patient at the heart of health care.

Rights and Payment

Rights vary. Pay rate is negotiable. Kill fee: 50%. Pays after publication.

International Examiner

622 South Washington Street
Seattle, WA 98104

Editor in Chief: Diem Ly

Description and Interests

News, current events, and issues facing the Pacific Northwest's Asian American community are covered in this tabloid newspaper. It is interested in writers with experience as reporters and knowledge about the local, regional, national, and international issues facing the community to which its readers belong. Circ: 30,000.

Contents: 50% articles; 50% depts/columns
Frequency: 24 times each year
Website: www.iexaminer.org

Freelance Potential

50% written by nonstaff writers. Publishes 150 freelance submissions yearly; 25% by unpublished writers, 15% by authors who are new to the magazine, 10% by experts. Receives 5 queries, 10 unsolicited mss monthly.

Submissions

Query with résumé and 3 clips, or send complete ms. Accepts email to editor@iexaminer.org and hard copy. SASE.

- Articles: 500–700 words. Informational, profiles, interviews, and personal experience. Topics include the arts, social issues, education, multicultural and ethnic issues, and family and parenting concerns.
- Depts/columns: Word lengths vary. News briefs, media reviews.

Sample Issue

20 pages. Advertising. Sample copy and guidelines available at website.

- "Loving, Funny—THIS Is the Infamous Tiger Mother?" Profile of Amy Chua, the author of the controversial memoir, *The Battle Hymn of the Tiger Mother*.
- "Vietnamese Elders Struggle with Depression." A look at the above average rate of Vietnamese elderly suffering from depression and the cultural stigmas that make treatment challenging.

Rights and Payment

Rights vary. Written material, $25–$50+. Pays 30 days after publication.

The International Railway Traveler

2424 Frankfort Avenue, Suite 2
Louisville, KY 40206

Publisher & Editor: Owen C. Hardy

Description and Interests

The International Railway Traveler depicts the elegance and excitement of worldwide railway travel through lively feature articles and vivid photos. It is distributed to members of the Society of International Railway Travelers. Its articles emphasize railways, trains, and venues that are featured on the society's tour schedules. Superior color photos must accompany articles. Circ: 3,000.

Contents: 80% articles; 10% depts/columns; 10% other
Frequency: Occasionally
Website: www.irtsociety.com

Freelance Potential

90% written by nonstaff writers. Publishes 10 freelance submissions yearly; 5% by unpublished writers, 30% by authors who are new to the magazine. Receives 2 queries monthly.

Submissions

Query with clips or writing samples. Accepts email to ohardy@irtsociety.com (Word attachments). Responds in 1 month.

- Articles: 800–1,500 words. Informational and personal experience. Topics include railway travel and service, fares, routes, accommodations, and package tours.
- Depts/columns: To 100 words. News briefs about railway travel, book reviews.
- Artwork: 8x10 color prints or transparencies; JPEGs for Macintosh at 300 dpi.

Sample Issue

20 pages. Advertising. Sample copy available at website. Guidelines available.

- "Pride of Africa: Cape Town to Dar Es Salaam." Article profiles a luxury train, including its sleeping cars, dining options, and itinerary.
- "Glacier Express & Bernina Express: Switzerland's Classic Trains." Article describes this classic rail line and the spectacular Alpine scenery it traverses.

Rights and Payment

First North American serial rights. Written material, \$.03 per word. Artwork, \$10 per photo. Kill fee, 25%. Pays 1 month after publication. Provides 2 contributor's copies.

In These Times

2040 North Milwaukee Avenue
Chicago, IL 60647

Editor: Joel Bleifuss

Description and Interests

Investigative reports and news analysis are at the heart of this progressive current events magazine. National and international news, social issues, politics, and modern culture are examined through articles, essays, and even humor. It is particularly interested in covering issues and movements that have received little or no attention in the mainstream press. Circ: 20,000.

Contents: 50% articles; 50% depts/columns
Frequency: Monthly
Website: www.inthesetimes.com

Freelance Potential

85% written by nonstaff writers. Publishes 125 freelance submissions yearly; 5% by unpublished writers, 25% by authors who are new to the magazine, 10% by experts. Receives 50 queries monthly.

Submissions

Query with 2 or 3 clips. Accepts email queries only via website. Responds only if interested.

- Articles: 1,200–2,800 words. Informational, opinion, creative nonfiction, profiles, and interviews. Topics include current events, feminism, conservation, government, politics, public affairs, social concerns, multicultural and ethnic issues.
- Depts/columns: 400–1,285 words. News, book and media reviews, humor.

Sample Issue

36 pages. Advertising. Sample articles and guidelines available at website.

- "Big Money Can't Buy You Memes." Evaluating the various media from expensive paid advertising to homemade social media videos and quips to see what has the most effect on swaying voters.
- "After the Gold Rush." An artist makes a vacant house in her neighborhood into a confrontational sculptural object that has a message.

Rights and Payment

First and second serial rights. Written material, \$.12 per word. Kill fee, 50% for assigned stories. Pays 1 month after publication. Provides 3 contributor's copies.

The Iowa Review 

308 EPB
University of Iowa
Iowa City, IA 52242

Fiction, Poetry, or Nonfiction Editor

Description and Interests

While much of the fiction, creative nonfiction, poetry, and reviews that appear in *The Iowa Review* are written by established authors, the editors always welcome contributions from new talent. Published by the University of Iowa, it awards annual prizes for essays, fiction, and poetry. It is always searching for good, intriguing nonfiction. The publication will consider all topics and genres. Circ: 2,500.

Contents: 40% fiction; 40% poetry; 20% essays
Frequency: 3 times each year
Website: www.iowareview.org

Freelance Potential

100% written by nonstaff writers. Publishes 120 freelance submissions yearly; 20% by unpublished writers, 80% by authors who are new to the magazine. Receives 500 unsolicited mss monthly.

Submissions

Send complete ms between September 1 and November 31 only. It is not currently accepting interviews; check website for updates. Accepts hard copy, submissions via the website, and simultaneous submissions if identified. SASE. Responds in 1–4 months.

- Nonfiction: Word lengths vary. Creative nonfiction, autobiographies, essays, memoirs, book reviews, and interviews.
- Fiction: Word lengths vary. Literary fiction.
- Other: Poetry, no line limits.

Sample Issue

210 pages. Little advertising. Sample articles and guidelines available at website.

- "Norway." Futuristic short story of Black Americans who flee to Norway after some catastrophic war.
- "A Gift From the American People." Essay about Humanitarian Aid and how it is seen from the people who receive it.

Rights and Payment

First North American serial rights. Prose, $0.08 per word; $100 minimum. Poetry, $1.50 per line; $40 minimum. Interviews, $200 (published online only). Book reviews, $50. Pays on publication. Provides 2 contributor's copies.

Irish America

875 Sixth Avenue, Suite 201
New York, NY 10001

Editor in Chief: Patricia Harty

Description and Interests

This magazine features articles on noteworthy Irish Americans in entertainment, sports, and politics, along with news from Ireland and historical and cultural pieces. Articles should appeal to readers living in the U.S. Circ: 75,000.

Contents: Articles; depts/columns
Frequency: 6 times each year
Website: www.irishcentral.com/Irishamerica

Freelance Potential

50% written by nonstaff writers. Publishes 20–30 freelance submissions yearly; 5% by unpublished writers, 15% by authors who are new to the magazine, 30% by experts. Receives 20+ queries, 10 unsolicited mss monthly.

Submissions

Query with clips; or send complete ms. Accepts hard copy, email to pharty@irishamerica.com, and simultaneous submissions if identified. SASE. Responds in 2–3 months.

- Articles: 800–1,500 words. Informational, how-to, investigative, profiles, interviews, and personal experience. Topics include Irish American contributions, personalities, politics, social issues, history, sports, entertainment, Irish travel.
- Depts/columns: 600 words. Opinion pieces, media reviews, genealogy, news.

Sample Issue

82 pages. Advertising. Sample articles available at website. Guidelines available.

- "The Irish Coppers." How the image of the Irish-American policeman has evolved in real life and on screen.
- "Golfing the Emerald Isle." Destination piece tells about five days golfing on some of Ireland's best golf courses.

Rights and Payment

All rights. Written material, $.12 per word. Pays on publication. Provides up to 5 contributor's copies.

Island  

P.O. Box 210
Sandy Bay
Hobart, Tasmania 7006
Australia

Editorial Director: Dale Campisi

Description and Interests

Island explores important social, environmental, and cultural topics through the works of fiction, essays, poetry, and novel excerpts that it publishes. Book reviews also appear in each issue. It welcomes writers native to Australia, as well as those from around the world. *Island* often explores particular themes; watch the website for updates. Circ: 1,200.

Contents: 40% poetry and reviews; 30% articles; 30% fiction
Frequency: Quarterly
Website: www.islandmag.com

Freelance Potential

100% written by nonstaff writers. Publishes 120 freelance submissions yearly; 15% by unpublished writers, 60% by authors who are new to the magazine. Receives 70 unsolicited mss monthly.

Submissions

Accepts submissions with genre, word count, and short bio through website. Responds in 4 months.

- Articles: 2,500–5,000 words. Creative nonfiction and essays. Topics include the arts, conservation, feminism, history, nature, the environment, social issues, and writing.
- Fiction: 2,500–5,000 words. Contemporary and literary fiction.
- Other: Poetry, reviews, word lengths vary.

Sample Issue

144 pages. Little advertising. Sample copy available. Guidelines available at website.

- "Breath, Laughter, Creation: Launches, Reviews and Errata for Francis Webb's *Collected Poems*." Article reviews an edition of collected poems by the Australian poet.
- "A Trip to New Norfolk (In Memoriam)." Article talks of a trip to a closed institution for the mentally ill.

Rights and Payment

First rights. Payment rates vary (minimum $100). Pays on publication. Provides 1 contributor's copy and a 1-year subscription.

Jersey Devil Press  

Founding Editor/Publisher: Eirik Gumeny

Description and Interests

Published online, *Jersey Devil Press* features short fiction. It welcomes stories of all types, but humorous and offbeat stories are its specialty. Each year it publishes a print anthology of the best fiction that has appeared on its website in the previous year. Its tastes run toward funny, offbeat, and absurd, but it has been known to go for the occasional heartbreaking or thought-provoking piece, too. Looking for more strong female voices, lighthearted perspectives, and insane fiction, it will accept previously published work—as long as the piece isn't still available online or in print. All stories selected for online publication will automatically be considered for the yearly print anthology. Hits per month: Unavailable.

Contents: 100% fiction
Frequency: Monthly
Website: www.jerseydevilpress.com

Freelance Potential

95–100% written by nonstaff writers. Publishes 72–96 freelance submissions yearly; 10% by unpublished writers, 100% by authors who are new to the magazine.

Submissions

Accepts submissions with 100-word author bio via website. Accepts simultaneous submissions and reprints if identified. Response in 3 months.

- Fiction: To 4,200 words. Genres include contemporary, literary, mainstream, crime stories, mystery, and suspense.

Sample Issue

48 pages. No advertising. Sample copy and guidelines available at website.

- "Sum Quod Eris." Short story in which a late-night bistro worker encounters a ghost at the end of his shift.
- "Gate Night." Short story of a high school student stuck in a scary Halloween prank night turned real life.

Rights and Payment

Limited electronic rights. No payment.

Jewish Action

11 Broadway
New York, NY 10004

Editor: Nechama Carmel

Description and Interests
Jewish Action focuses on issues of Jewish life and experiences. It offers a mix of human-interest pieces, historical articles, poetry, and book reviews. Published by the Orthodox Union, it serves an international audience with the aim of "enlightening, educating, and inspiring" its readers. Circ: 40,000.

Contents: 50% articles; 40% depts/columns; 10% other
Frequency: Quarterly
Website: www.ou.org/jewish_action

Freelance Potential
80% written by nonstaff writers. Publishes 5–10 freelance submissions yearly; 10% by unpublished writers, 25% by authors who are new to the magazine; 10% by experts. Receives 15-20 unsolicited mss monthly.

Submissions
Send complete ms. Prefers email to ja@ou.org; will accept hard copy and fax submissions. SASE. Responds in 10–12 weeks.

- Articles: 1,000–3,000 words. Informational, profiles, interviews, personal experience, and humor. Topics include the arts, current events, religion, politics, science and technology, and multicultural issues.
- Depts/columns: 1,000 words. Book reviews, kosher cooking, opinion, poetry.

Sample Issue
72 pages. Advertising. Sample articles and guidelines available at website.

- "Why Is It So Hard to Change? The Six Obstacles to Teshuvah." A look at the repentant act of teshuvah and the many self-deceiving reasons practicing Jews don't do it.
- Dept/Column: kosher@work addresses the potential issues for a religious Jew who wishes to keep kosher in the workplace cafeteria.

Rights and Payment
First rights. Articles, $100–$400. Depts/columns, $100–$150. Pays on publication. Provides 2 contributor's copies.

Joy of Kosher with Jamie Geller

Managing Editor: Victoria Dwek

Description and Interests: This magazine aims to revolutionize the way people think about kosher cooking. Featuring famous chefs and Jewish food personalities, it offers tips, inspiration, and plenty of recipes to help readers succeed in the kitchen. It recently merged with *Bitayavon*, a magazine of upscale kosher cuisine. Jamie Keller is the author of the best-selling *Quick & Kosher Cookbook*. Circ: 70,000.

Contents: 50% articles; 50% depts/columns
Frequency: 6 times each year
Website: www.joyofkosher.com

Freelance Potential
Freelance percentage not yet available.

Submissions
Query. Accepts email to victoria@joyofkosher.com. Response time varies.

- Articles: Word lengths vary. Informational and how-to articles and recipes. Topics include kosher cooking, holidays, seasonal foods, entertaining, quick and easy recipes.
- Depts/columns: Word lengths vary. Menus, recipe remakes, product reviews.

Sample Issue
Advertising. Sample articles available at website.

- "From Humble Beginnings: A Haute Market in Jerusaelm." Article describes the history and offerings of Jerusalem's Machane Yehuda Market.
- "Cooking with Kids." Article provides an easy and fun recipe for making applesauce with kids.
- Sample dept/column: Kitchen Lab explains how to use xantham gum to make soups, sauces, and dressings.

Rights and Payment
Rights vary. Payment rates and policy vary.

The Kenyon Review 

Finn House
102 West Wiggin Street
Gambier, OH 43022-9623

Editor: David H. Lynn

Description and Interests

All types of literary material, including essays, fiction, reviews, plays, and poetry, are featured in this journal of Kenyon College. Its focus is on literature, culture, and the arts. It only accepts submissions during its reading period. Circ: 6,200.

Contents: 30% articles; 30% fiction; 30% poetry; 10% other
Frequency: Quarterly
Website: www.kenyonreview.org

Freelance Potential

100% written by nonstaff writers. Publishes 100–125 freelance submissions yearly; 5% by unpublished writers, 40% by authors who are new to the magazine. Receives 458–500 unsolicited mss monthly.

Submissions

Send complete ms between September 15 and January 15 only. Accepts submissions through website only. Accepts simultaneous submissions if identified. Response time varies.

- Articles: To 7,500 words. Informational, literary essays, criticism, interviews, and creative nonfiction. Topics include literature, popular culture, film, and theater.
- Fiction: To 7,500 words. Literary, contemporary.
- Other: Poetry, to 6 poems per submission. Plays and excerpts, to 30 pages.

Sample Issue

266 pages. Little advertising. Sample articles and guidelines available at website.

- "A Conversation with Anna Journey: Q&A with Davis McCombs's Graduate Poetry Course." An interview with famed poet Anna Journey about her poetry and the creative process.
- "Hurtling Along: on *Ennui Prophet* by Christopher Kennedy." A review of this fourth and latest collection of prose poems by Christopher Kennedy.

Rights and Payment

First North American serial rights. Fiction and articles, $30 per published page. Poetry, $40 per published page. Pays on publication. Provides 2 contributor's copies.

Knives Illustrated

4635 McEwen Road
Dallas, TX 75244

Managing Editor: Colleen Supan

Description and Interests

Knives, knife makers, and knife collectors are the focus of this photo-filled magazine. All kinds of knives, from hunting tools to kitchen cutlery to rare and collectible swords, are expertly covered. The readers of this publication are highly knowledgeable about knives, and so writers must be knife experts—whether aficionados, craftsmen, or collectors. Circ: 30,000.

Contents: 90% articles; 10% depts/columns
Frequency: 9 times each year
Website: www.knivesillustrated.com

Freelance Potential

90% written by nonstaff writers. Publishes 40 freelance submissions yearly; 5% by unpublished writers, 5% by authors who are new to the magazine, 90% by experts. Receives 15 queries, 10+ unsolicited mss monthly.

Submissions

Prefers query; will accept complete ms with artwork. Accepts hard copy and disk submissions. SASE. Responds in 2–3 weeks.

- Articles: Word lengths vary. Informational, how-to, profiles, and photo-essays. Topics include custom and high-tech knives, swords, equipment, materials, and knife making.
- Depts/columns: Word lengths vary. New product information, show coverage.
- Artwork: Color prints and slides; digital images.

Sample Issue

80 pages. Advertising. Sample copy available at website. Guidelines available.

- "Zac Brown's Baddest." A review of a folding knife that has some unique features.
- "Latest Knife Releases for 2012." A roundup of the latest and greatest knives of the year.

Rights and Payment

All or first rights. Articles, $200–$300. Depts/columns, payment rates vary. Pays on publication.

The Knot

195 Broadway, 25th Floor
New York, NY 10007

Assistant Editor: Amanda Black

Description and Interests

The Knot helps brides plan the weddings of their dreams. It is part of a three-tiered brand that also includes a popular website by the same name, and regional publications to help brides with their options close to home. The sections most open to new writers are the Real Weddings and Honeymoons features. The print quarterly is also available on tablets. Circ: 330,000.

Contents: Articles; depts/columns
Frequency: Quarterly
Website: www.theknot.com

Freelance Potential

Publishes 10% of freelance submissions received each year.

Submissions

Query with clips. Accepts email to ablack@theknot.com. Responds in 2 weeks.

- Articles: 1,200–1,400 words. Informational and how-to articles. Topics include all aspects of planning and preparing for a wedding and honeymoon.
- Depts/columns: Word lengths vary. New products, advice, and trends.

Sample Issue

Advertising. Sample copy available at website.

- "Life's A Beach." Article provides details on some honeymoon destinations that are postcard-perfect locales.
- "The Big White Dress." Article discusses the latest trend of adding a hint of color to the typical white wedding dress.
- Sample dept/column: "Color Report" depicts bridesmaid dress, cake design, and flower options in lavender.

Rights and Payment

First North American serial rights. Written material, $.50–$1 per word. Kill fee, 40%. Pays on acceptance.

Kronicle

60 Main Street, Suite 201
P.O. Box 190
Jeffersonville, VT 05464

Editor in Chief: Mike Horn

Description and Interests

This magazine and its readers are dedicated to backcountry snowboarding. Helping snowboarders get away from packed slopes and lines, *Kronicle* keeps fans in the know with informational articles, profiles, and snowboarders' own experiences. It also features gear and techniques. Circ: Unavailable.

Contents: Articles; depts/columns
Frequency: Quarterly
Website: www.kroniclemag.com

Freelance Potential

Receives several freelance submissions monthly.

Submissions

Query. Send email to mike@holpublications.com. Response time varies.

- Articles: Word lengths vary. Informational articles, profiles, interviews, and essays. Topics include backcountry snowboarding, locations, terrain, techniques, athletes, gear tests, snow skills, and safety.
- Depts/columns: Gear, travel, and essays.

Sample Issue

Advertising. Sample copy available.

- "Fast and Furious." Article features a profile on Xavier de le Rue, a French snowboarder.
- "Jewels of the Triple Crown." Article describes the three not-to-miss snowboard destinations in the Alps.
- Sample dept/column: Klassic Lines describes snowboarding in JC Couloir, Idaho.

Rights and Payment

Rights vary. Payment rates and policy vary.

Kung Fu Tai Chi

40748 Encyclopedia Circle
Fremont, CA 94538

Associate Publisher: Gene Ching

Description and Interests

Kung Fu Tai Chi is a magazine for martial arts enthusiasts. Its content features a blend of martial arts-related information and instruction, Chinese culture, and Eastern philosophy. It also profiles noted practitioners of the art form. It values articles about Chinese culture, as much as articles focusing on martial arts. Circ: 20,000.

Contents: 85% articles; 15% depts/columns
Frequency: 6 times each year
Website: www.kungfumagazine.com

Freelance Potential

70% written by nonstaff writers. Publishes 40 freelance submissions yearly; 5% by unpublished writers, 15% by authors who are new to the magazine, 70% by experts. Receives 20 queries monthly.

Submissions

Query with writing samples. Prefers email queries to gene@kungfumagazine.com. Accepts hard copy and email submissions to gene@kungfumagazine.com. No simultaneous submissions. Responds in 3 months.

- Articles: 1,500–2,500 words (no limit for Web edition). Informational, how-to, self-help, interviews, and personal experience. Topics include martial arts history, weapons, training tips and techniques, philosophy, and new products. At least 8 photos with captions (minimum 300 dpi) must accompany all articles.
- Depts/columns: Staff-written.

Sample Issue

98 pages. Advertising. Sample articles and guidelines available at website.

- "RZA on The Man with the Iron Fists." An interview with a famous martial arts expert.
- "Circles of Iron: Kung Fu's Training Rings." Using these training tools to increase strength and improve skills.

Rights and Payment

First rights. Articles, $125. Pays on publication. Provides 1 contributor's copy.

Kyria

465 Gundersen Drive
Carol Stream, IL 60188

Acquisitions Editor

Description and Interests

The former *Today's Christian Woman* has been revamped as this digizine. Published electronically, its articles offer in-depth biblical insight into topics of faith and ministry for mature Christian women. Articles should have a distinct Evangelical Christian perspective. It is published by Christianity Today International. Hits per month: Unavailable.

Contents: 60% articles; 40% depts/columns
Frequency: Monthly
Website: www.kyria.com

Freelance Potential

70% written by nonstaff writers. Publishes 30 freelance submissions yearly; 20% by unpublished writers, 20% by authors who are new to the magazine. Receives 30 queries monthly.

Submissions

Send query letter with article summary, purpose, and value to reader; author qualifications on topic; suggested length; and anticipated completion date. Accepts hard copy and electronic queries through the website. No simultaneous submissions. SASE. Responds in 2 months.

- Articles: 600–1,500 words. Informational, how-to, essays, interviews, and personal experience. Topics include women's ministry, family, marriage, church leadership, social issues, spiritual formation, Bible study, and devotionals—all with a Christian perspective.

Sample Issue

48 pages. Advertising. Sample copy, guidelines, and theme list available at website.

- "Pint-Sized Spirituality." Fostering your children's relationship with God.
- "Three Questions for... Ginny Owens." The Dove Award winner talks about her faith and music.

Rights and Payment

Exclusive online rights and non-exclusive rights. Articles, $50–$150. Pays on acceptance.

Lacrosse

113 West University Parkway
Baltimore, MD 21210

Editor: Paul Krome

Description and Interests

Lacrosse players, coaches, and fans read this magazine for athlete profiles, how-to articles on training and playing strategies, and collegiate team coverage. Product reviews and news from US Lacrosse, the sport's national governing body, appear as well. Circ: 400,000.

Contents: 60% articles; 40% depts/columns
Frequency: Monthly
Website: www.laxmagazine.com

Freelance Potential

30% written by nonstaff writers. Publishes 60 freelance submissions yearly; 5% by unpublished writers, 10% by authors who are new to the magazine, 85% by experts. Receives 5 queries monthly.

Submissions

Query. Accepts email to pkrome@uslacrosse.org (Word attachments). Artwork accepted via email or CD. Responds in 6 weeks.

- Articles: 800–1,000 words. Informational, how-to, and profiles. Topics include lacrosse training, playing strategies, athlete profiles, and collegiate team coverage.
- Depts/columns: 300 words. Product reviews, US Lacrosse news.

Sample Issue

72 pages. Advertising. Sample copy and guidelines available.

- "Halfpenny Has Notre Dame Running Full Speed." The new coach of the Fighting Irish makes changes on the field and ups the ante in intensive practice sessions.
- "Lifestyles: Actor-Model-Dancer Brian White." An interview with the former lacrosse and football player whose injury caused him to remake his career several times over.

Rights and Payment

Exclusive rights. Articles, $100–$300. Depts/columns, $100–$150. Pays on publication. Provides 1+ contributor's copies.

Ladies Home Journal 

Meredith Corporation
375 Lexington Avenue, 9th Floor
New York, NY 10017

Senior Articles Editor: Lorraine Glennon

Description and Interests

With the aim of helping women who want to "look good, do good, and feel great," *Ladies Home Journal* offers articles on every aspect of women's lives and relationships. Its readers are women, ages 35–50, who tend to be married, have older children, and are active in their communities. The magazine works with authors who have been previously published in national magazines. Circ: 3.2 million.

Frequency: 11 times a year
Website: www.lhj.com

Freelance Potential

15% written by nonstaff writers.

Submissions

Query with clips. Prefers one-page email directed to the appropriate editor for the queried topic. Check masthead for all section editors. News and general features, to lorraine.glennon@meredith.com. Senior articles to louise.sloan@meredith.com. Health, julie.bain@meredithcom. Fitness, jessica.brown@meredith.com. Responds in 2–4 weeks.

- Articles: Word lengths vary. Informational; how-to's; and profiles. Topics include health, food, fitness, relationships, money, psychology, parenting, community service, family, pets, home, and social issues.
- Depts/columns: Word lengths vary. Family Time; Animal Affairs; Do Good.

Sample Issue

Advertising. Sample articles and editorial calendar available at website.

- "A Non-Neurotic Guide to Germs." With thousands of viruses and bacteria swarming around us, what do we realistically have to be concerned about and where can we lighten up.
- "Surprising Secrets to an Always and Forever Marriage." A variety of relationship experts from therapists to bartenders ring in with their top advice for lasting marriages.

Rights and Payment

All rights. Written material, $1.50+ per word. Kill fee, 25%. Pays on acceptance.

Lakeland Boating

727 South Dearborn Street, Suite 812
Chicago, IL 60605

Editor: Lindsey Johnson

Description and Interests
Focusing on boating the Great Lakes and surrounding waterways, this magazine offers articles on the boating lifestyle, motorboats and sailboats, and ports of call. Maritime history and noteworthy current activities are also featured, as well as how-to tips for repair and maintenance, boat reviews, and new products of interest to boaters. In addition to solid writing, it seeks professional-quality photographs that will enhance the submission. Circ: 40,000.
Contents: 80% articles; 20% depts/columns
Frequency: 11 times each year
Website: www.lakelandboating.com

Freelance Potential
60% written by nonstaff writers. Publishes 60 freelance submissions yearly; 20% by authors who are new to the magazine. Receives 15 queries, 10 unsolicited mss monthly.

Submissions
Query with outline and clips; or send complete ms with artwork. Accepts email to staff@lakelandboating.com. Response time varies.

- Articles: 1,500–2,500 words. Informational, how-to, profiles, and interviews. Topics include cruising, destinations, boat charters, classic and antique boats, maintenance, navigation, and marine history.
- Depts/columns: 300–2,500 words. Regional boating news and events, boat tests, product reviews, marina profiles, lifestyle pieces.
- Artwork: B/W prints or 35mm color slides.

Sample Issue
52 pages. Advertising. Sample copy available at website. Guidelines available.

- "Great Lakes Inspiration." Jenn Gibbons shares the struggles and triumphs of her epic two-month, 1,500-mile journey rowing and biking the perimeter of Lake Michigan.
- "Boat Test: Carver 54 Voyager." An in-depth review of this vessel, examining all its features.

Rights and Payment
First North American serial rights. Articles, \$100–\$600. Depts/columns, \$50–\$200. Artwork, \$75–\$600. Pays 1 month after publication. Provides 1 contributor's copy.

The Land

418 South Second Street
P.O. Box 3169
Mankato, MN 56001

Editor: Kevin Schulz

Description and Interests
The Land is an agricultural magazine devoted to all types of farming and rural life in Minnesota and northern Iowa. Its tagline is "Where Farm and Family Meet," indicating its strong focus on the personal side of farming. It publishes separate editions for the northern and southern parts of the state. Purchased freelance articles will appear in both editions, on the website, and may appear in other CNHI newspapers. Circ: 30,813.
Contents: 70% articles; 30% depts/columns
Frequency: 26 times a year
Website: www.thelandonline.com

Freelance Potential
25% written by nonstaff writers. Publishes 70 freelance submissions yearly; 5% by authors who are new to the magazine, 5% by experts. Receives 2 queries monthly.

Submissions
Query. Prefers email queries to editor@thelandonline.com (no attachments); will accept hard copy. SASE. Responds in 1 month.

- Articles: To 500 words. Informational, how-to, self-help, profiles, and interviews. Topics include agriculture, legislation, equipment, livestock, farm maintenance, the environment, management, technology, and marketing.
- Depts/columns: Word lengths vary. Opinion, food, financing, business.
- Artwork: Color prints; digital images.

Sample Issue
64 pages. Advertising. Sample copy available at website. Guidelines and editorial calendar available.

- "Many Variations to Setting Up Flexible Lease Agreements." Discussion of several different constructs for those considering utilizing this farm management option.
- "Award-winning Pork Producers Focus on Stewardship." Profile of the Dahl family, winners of the 2012 Pork Industry Environmental Steward Award and their ethical practices with regard to hog farming and pork production.

Rights and Payment
First North American serial rights. Written material, \$40–\$70. Artwork, payment rates vary. Pays on acceptance. Provides 1 contributor's copy.

Latina Magazine

625 Madison Avenue, 3rd Floor
New York, NY 10022

Executive Editor: Lori Hoffman

Description and Interests

This publication's target audience is Hispanic women who live a bicultural life. It is a lifestyle magazine with an emphasis on fashion and beauty, relationships, and the world of Latino celebrities. It also covers social issues from a cultural perspective. Circ: 500,000.

Contents: 60% articles; 40% depts/columns
Frequency: 10 times each year
Website: www.latina.com

Freelance Potential

50% written by nonstaff writers. Publishes 150 freelance submissions yearly; 10% by authors who are new to the magazine. Receives 10–20 queries monthly.

Submissions

Query with résumé and clips. Accepts hard copy. SASE. Responds in 1–2 months.

- Articles: 1,500–2,500 words. Informational, self-help, how-to, confessional, personal experience, creative nonfiction, profiles, interviews, and humor. Topics include culture, careers, consumer issues, current events, entertainment, feminism, religion, health, fitness, music, nostalgia, lifestyles, celebrities, multicultural, ethnic, social, and relationships.
- Depts/columns: 600–800 words. Entertainment news, nutrition, finance, fashion, beauty and hair tips.

Sample Issue

152 pages. Advertising. Sample articles, editorial calendar, available at website.

- "In Search of God." Examines why more Latinos are leaving the Catholic Church for other religious and spiritual pursuits.
- "A Culinary Journey." Cuban chef Maricel Presilla's journey across Latin America and what she learned writing her book, *Gran Cocina Latina*.

Rights and Payment

World rights. Written material, $1–$2 per word. Kill fee, 25%. Pays on publication.

LIFE + DOG

1304 Malone Street
Houston, TX 77007

Editor in Chief: Ryan Rice

Description and Interests

This magazine premiered in 2011, serving dog owners in Texas with profiles, interviews, and lifestyle articles. It is also available by subscription nationally and is expanding its distribution areas. All submissions are reviewed by the editorial team to evaluate for inclusion in the publication or in one of the online components. Circ: 30,000.

Contents: Articles depts/columns
Frequency: 10 issues
Website: http://lifeanddog.com

Freelance Potential

Receives numerous queries monthly.

Submissions

Query. Accepts email to editor@lifeanddog.com. Response time varies.

- Articles: Informational and how-to articles, profiles, and essays. Topics include responsible pet ownership, travel with pets, animal advocacy, dog history, home decor, cooking, advice, and people making a difference in the community.
- Depts/columns: Word lengths vary. Profiles, interviews, travel with pets, health, and product reviews.

Sample Issue

Advertising. Sample articles and guidelines available at website.

- "Dialogue: Kathie Lee Gifford." Article features an interview with the *Today* show host about her life with her three dogs.
- "Dog Friendly Landscaping." Article offers tips on how to landscape a yard when there is a dog in the home.
- Sample dept/column: L&D Health tells which raw veggies are healthy dog snacks.

Rights and Payment

Rights vary. Payment rates and policy vary.

Lighthouse Digest

P.O. Box 250
East Machias, ME 04630

Editor: Tim Harrison

Description and Interests

Lighthouse enthusiasts and history buffs read this magazine for its articles on lighthouses, lighthouse keepers, and lighthouse history, including the men and women of the now defunct United States Lighthouse Service and the United States Life-Saving Service. Its articles also champion the efforts to conserve the country's remaining lighthouse properties. Its writers are often readers—people who love the beauty and nautical history of America's lighthouses. Circ: 18,000.

Contents: 98% articles; 1% fiction; 1% depts/columns
Frequency: 6 times each year
Website: www.lighthousedigest.com

Freelance Potential

10% written by nonstaff writers. Publishes 40 freelance submissions yearly; 5% by unpublished writers, 80% by authors who are new to the magazine, 5% by experts. Receives 10 queries monthly.

Submissions

Accepts complete ms. Prefers disk submission (text file or Word). SASE. Accepts email submissions to newstips@lighthousedigest.com. Artwork helps increase chance of acceptance. Responds in 2 weeks.

- Articles: 750–1,500+ words. Informational, profiles, interviews, creative nonfiction, personal experience, and opinion. Topics include lighthouses, antiques collecting, current events, history, nostalgia, and new products.
- Fiction: 750–1,500 words. Historical fiction.
- Depts/columns: 750 words. Nautical antiques, female lightkeepers, event news.
- Artwork: B/W or color prints, JPG or TIFF images at 300 dpi.

Sample Issue

38 pages. Little advertising. Sample articles and guidelines available at website.

- "Debunking a Lighthouse Myth." Tour guides tell tales of lighthouse keepers hauling gallons of oil to the top of the tower, but is it true?
- "Murder at Marshall Point Light." A lighthouse keeper may have had key evidence in a century-plus old murder mystery in Maine.

Rights and Payment

All rights. Written material, $75–$150. Pays on publication. Provides 2–5 contributor's copies.

Liguorian

1 Liguori Drive
Liguori, MD 63057-9999

Submissions: Patricia DeClue

Description and Interests

Liguorian is a general interest Catholic magazine founded by a Redemptorist priest in 1913. It publishes articles that inspire, motivate, and provide practical direction for adult Catholics in a rapidly changing world. It appreciates real-life examples and stories that will illustrate practical application. It also accepts fiction appropriate for a Catholic audience. Circ: 70,000+.

Contents: 60% articles; 30% depts/columns; 10% fiction
Frequency: 10 times each year
Website: www.liguorian.org

Freelance Potential

80% written by nonstaff writers. Publishes 30 freelance submissions yearly; 35% by authors who are new to the magazine, 20% by experts. Receives 75+ unsolicited mss monthly.

Submissions

Send complete ms. Accepts email submissions to liguorianeditor@liguori.org (Word attachments) or disk submissions. No simultaneous submissions. Responds in 8–12 weeks.

- Articles: 1,500–2,400 words. Informational and inspirational. Topics include spirituality, prayer, relationships, wellness, ethics, morality, saints.
- Fiction: 2,000 words. Stories with spiritual or inspirational themes.
- Depts/columns: Word lengths vary. Book reviews, essays, meditations.

Sample Issue

40 pages. Advertising. Sample articles and guidelines available at website.

- "Does Everything Happen for a Reason?" Discusses recognizing God's goodness and his presence in the midst of suffering.
- "As Chili Simmers, Add Grace." Short story about a young priest who is assigned to a small-town parish.

Rights and Payment

First rights. Written material, $.12–$.15 per word. Pays on acceptance. Provides 5 contributor's copies.

Lilith

250 West 57th Street, Suite 2432
New York, NY 10107

Editor in Chief: Susan Weidman Schneider

Description and Interests

Lilith describes itself as "independent, Jewish, and frankly feminist." Lively and inspiring works of nonfiction, fiction, and poetry on cultural, social, and political topics appear in each issue. It also offers investigative reports, new rituals and celebrations, historical and contemporary first-person accounts, and entertainment reviews. Circ: 8,000.

Contents: 70% articles; 25% depts/columns; 5% fiction
Frequency: Quarterly
Website: www.lilith.org

Freelance Potential

55% written by nonstaff writers. Publishes 30 freelance submissions yearly.

Submissions

Send complete ms with brief author bio. Prefers online submissions at website. Accepts hard copy. Accepts simultaneous submissions if identified. SASE. Responds in 8+ weeks.

- Articles: To 2,500 words. Informational, opinion, personal experience, profiles, and interviews. Topics include issues affecting Jewish women, literary criticism, grassroots projects, ceremonies and rituals, historical accounts and biographies, and events.
- Fiction: Word lengths vary. Contemporary stories with Jewish themes.
- Depts/columns: Word lengths vary. Reviews.
- Other: Poetry.

Sample Issue

48 pages. Advertising. Sample articles and guidelines available at website.

- "Consent and the Single Girl." When does seduction cross over to an act of violence and how can young women prepare ahead of time to not be ambushed in the murky waters.
- "Hybrid." A well-known fiction writer ponders how genes and culture will shape her Japanese-Jewish grandchild.

Rights and Payment

All rights. Written material, payment rates vary. Pays on publication. Provides 1 contributor's copy.

Linn's Stamp News

P.O. Box 926
911 South Vandemark Road
Sidney, OH 45365-0926

Editor: Michael Baadke

Description and Interests

Each issue of this magazine for philatelists provides a selection of facts, thoughts, and observations about stamps, postal markings, covers, and stamp-related subjects. It also includes club announcements and auction information. The ideal article has enough new information to instruct a specialist, but is written in a way to capture the attention of a novice collector. Circ: 29,000.

Contents: 50% articles; 45% depts/columns; 5% other
Frequency: Weekly
Website: www.linns.com

Freelance Potential

50% written by nonstaff writers. Publishes 20 freelance submissions yearly; 25% by unpublished writers, 25% by authors who are new to the magazine, 50% by experts. Receives 5 unsolicited mss monthly.

Submissions

Send complete ms with artwork. Accepts hard copy. SASE. Responds in 1 month.

- Articles: To 500 words. Informational and how-to. Topics include stamps, postal history, collecting, postal markings, and new product information.
- Depts/columns: By assignment.
- Artwork: 35mm color prints or slides; digital images at 300 dpi.

Sample Issue

54 pages. Advertising. Sample copy available at website. Guidelines available.

- "Characters from Forthcoming *Hobbit* Film Featured in New Zealand Stamp Set for Nov. 1." Behind-the-scenes look at a new, movie-inspired stamp soon to be released.
- "Canada Creates New Personalized Stamps." What's being offered are 12 new frame designs paying four rates.

Rights and Payment

First world serial rights. All material, payment rates vary. Pays on publication.

The Lion Magazine

300 West 22nd Street
Oak Brook, IL 60523-8842

Senior Editor: Jay Copp

Description and Interests

Written for and often by members of Lions Clubs, *The Lion Magazine* details service projects performed by members and chapters throughout the world. It also includes articles on community service, particularly to benefit the blind, the visually handicapped, and people in need. It rarely accepts general interest articles that are not directly related to Lions Clubs activities. Photos of members in action are always needed, but they should accompany stories that will be of interest to all readers, not strictly local social events, such as anniversaries or charter celebrations. Circ: 500,000.

Contents: 80% articles; 20% depts/columns
Frequency: 11 times each year
Website: www.lionsclubs.org

Freelance Potential

35% written by nonstaff writers. Publishes 25 freelance submissions yearly; 10% by authors who are new to the magazine. Receives 10 queries monthly.

Submissions

Prefers query or send complete ms. Accepts hard copy and email submissions to magazine@lionsclubs.org. SASE. Responds in 3 months.

- Articles: To 2,000 words. Informational, profiles, essays, and humor. Topics include member news and events, community service, consumer interest, medical services, and science—all as related to Lions projects.
- Depts/columns: Staff-written.
- Artwork: 5x7 color prints; JPEG, TIF or RAW images at least 300 dpi.

Sample Issue

60 pages. Little advertising. Sample copy and guidelines available at website.

- "SightFirst Has New Focus in China." An update of Lions work being done in China to help improve sight, including low-vision clinics and other medical vision care initiatives.
- "Lions' University." Campus Lions Clubs are a great opportunity for nurturing future Lions and community service givers.

Rights and Payment

All rights. Written material, $400–$1,000. Pays on acceptance. Provides 2–3 contributor's copies.

Literary Juice

Editor in Chief: Sara R. Rajan

Description and Interests: An online literary magazine produced from "100% pure originality," *Literary Juice* seeks original submissions that are bold, clever, and even a little bizarre. Creative nonfiction, poetry, fiction, and flash fiction are accepted year-round. Anotther of its categories is what the journal calls "pulp fiction"—a story in exactly 25 words. *Literary Juice* also sponsors an annual flash fiction contest. Circ: Unavailable.

Contents: Nonfiction; fiction; poetry
Frequency: 6 times each year
Website: www.literaryjuice.com

Freelance Potential

Freelance percentages not currently available.

Submissions

Send complete ms. Accepts submissions via online submissions manager, Submittable. Accepts multiple submissions. Include word count. No simultaneous submissions. No intense sexual content. Responds in 1–3 months.

- Articles: To 2,500 words. Factual narratives that read as fictional pieces.
- Fiction: To 2,500 words. All genres. Flash fiction, 100–600 words; stories should have a twist. Pulp fiction, 25 words, with a one-word title, and an element of surprise.
- Poetry: No line limits; up to 6 poems.

Sample Issue

Sample articles and guidelines available at website.

- "Social Sprawl." Story tells of a man's complicated social circle.
- "The Final Boxing Match." Story is about a boxing club under threat of closure.
- "Sorry." Pulp fiction about a dog, chocolate, and a tragic end.

Rights and Payment

Nonexclusive first world electronic rights. No payment.

Literary Laundry

Poetry or Fiction Editor

Description and Interests

Literary Laundry was established to promote masterful writing and discourse that continues in the light of the great literary and intellectual traditions—while engaging the complexities of the modern world. The online literary journal accepts poetry, prose fiction, one-act dramas, and critical reflections. Each issue is accompanied by a writing competition. Circ: Unavailable.

Contents: Fiction; poetry
Frequency: Updated regularly
Website: www.literarylaundry.com

Freelance Potential

Freelance percentages currently unavailable.

Submissions

Send complete ms with cover letter, including short author bio, and abstract of 1–2 paragraphs "explaining why the writing submitted is intellectually evocative or of interest to a contemporary audience." Accepts submissions via website. One work per category per review cycle accepted; multiple category submissions are allowed. Undergraduate submissions are given separate consideration. No simultaneous submissions. Response time varies.

- Articles: Word lengths vary. Critical reflections.
- Fiction: To 6,000 words. Prose fiction.
- Poetry: To 2 pages.

Sample Issue

Advertising. Sample articles available at website.

- "The Terrors of Choice." Essay discusses the importance of choosing a worldview even though the choice will prove imperfect.
- "Pitching Marilyn." Story is about a recently divorced man looking back on what went wrong.
- "White Girls Like to Party." Story tells of a girl who gets caught up in a gang and some drugs.

Rights and Payment

Author retains rights. All submissions are considered for Awards of Distinction; short story and poetry winners receive $500. Undergraduate contributors are eligble for a comparable award, with $250 for best short story and poem. Submissions also selected for *Literary Laundry*'s hard copy book collections receive $500 for publication.

Live

General Council of the Assemblies of God
1445 North Boonville Avenue
Springfield, MO 65802-1894

Editor: Richard Bennett

Description and Interests

This take-home paper for adult religious education classes publishes upbeat informational articles, true stories, and fiction that encourage Christian readers to apply biblical principles to everyday problems, including parenting and family relationships. True stories, nonfiction, how-to's, and fiction are accepted. Circ: 32,000.

Contents: 80% articles; 20% fiction
Frequency: Quarterly, in weekly sections
Website: www.gospelpublishing.com

Freelance Potential

75–100% written by nonstaff writers. Publishes 110 freelance submissions yearly; 25–50% by unpublished writers, 10–25% by authors who are new to the magazine. Receives 100–150 unsolicited mss monthly.

Submissions

Send complete manuscript. Prefers email submissions to rl-live@gph.org (Word attachments). Accepts hard copy with SASE. Accepts simultaneous submissions if identified. Responds in 1–6 weeks.

- Articles: 200–1,200 words. Informational, how-to, humor, inspirational, and personal experience. Topics include family issues, parenting, and general Christian living issues.
- Fiction: 300–1,100 words. Genres include inspirational and religious.
- Other: Poetry, 12–25 lines. Submit seasonal material 18 months in advance.

Sample Issue

8 pages. No advertising. Sample copy available. Guidelines available at website.

- "When Three Words Say a Lot." Three-word phrases that can be used every day to empathize, encourage, serve, and reconcile.
- "Encouraged by the Spirit." A man involved in missions work is encouraged as the Spirit guides a fellow believer to show him God's answer to his doubts from the Bible.

Rights and Payment

First and second, reprint rights. Written material, $.10 a word for first rights; $.07 a word for second rights. Poetry, $35–$60. Pays on acceptance. Provides 2 contributor's copies.

Live Steam & Outdoor Railroading

P.O. Box 1810
Traverse City, MI 49685-1810

Editor: Neil Knopf

Description and Interests
How-to articles, profiles and interviews, and product reviews are published in this magazine for hobbyists interested in metalworking and large-scale steam model railways. Subject matter includes destinations, building projects, and railroad events. It is always on the lookout for submissions from writers who share our readers' passion for large-scale outdoor model railroading. Circ: 10,000.

Contents: 75% articles; 25% depts/columns
Frequency: 6 times each year
Website: www.livesteam.net

Freelance Potential
95% written by nonstaff writers. Publishes 50 freelance submissions yearly; 25% by unpublished writers, 40% by authors who are new to the magazine, 50% by experts. Receives 10 queries, 7 unsolicited mss monthly.

Submissions
Query or send complete ms with artwork. Accepts hard copy, disk submissions, and email to nknopf@villagepress.com. SASE. Responds to queries in 1 month.

- Articles: Word lengths vary. Informational, how-to, profiles, and interviews. Topics include steam engines, large-scale railroading, and restoration and preservation projects.
- Depts/columns: Word lengths vary. News and reviews.
- Artwork: B/W or color prints. Line drawings.

Sample Issue
64 pages. Advertising. Sample copy and guidelines available.

- "A Tale of Three Locomotives." Article describes locomotive construction.
- "Gothic Beam Engine–Par 8." Article discusses stationary steam engines.

Rights and Payment
First rights. All material, payment rates vary. Pays on publication. Provides 4 contributor's copies.

Living Bird

159 Sapsucker Woods Road
Ithaca, NY 14850

Editor in Chief: Tim Gallagher

Description and Interests
Living Bird is published by the Cornell Lab of Ornithology, a nonprofit organization dedicated to informing and exciting the public about birds. Its editorial interests include bird behavior, habitat, scientific research, and conservation, as well as bird art. No bird-related subject will be considered off-limits, as long as it is informative, awe-inspiring, or otherwise brings the readership closer to the birds they love to watch. Articles that are of an educational nature should be impeccably researched. Circ: 32,000.

Contents: 60% articles; 40% depts/columns
Frequency: Quarterly
Website: www.allaboutbirds.org

Freelance Potential
80% written by nonstaff writers. Publishes 15 freelance submissions yearly; 20% by authors who are new to the magazine. Receives 30 queries monthly.

Submissions
Query with outline and artwork. Accepts email queries to livingbird@cornell.edu (attach file). Responds in 1–2 months.

- Articles: 2,000 words. Informational. Topics include bird physiology and behavior, habitat, conservation, research, and art.
- Depts/columns: Staff-written.
- Artwork: 35mm or larger color transparencies and 5x7 or 8x10 B/W prints.

Sample Issue
45 pages. Advertising. Sample articles available at website. Guidelines available.

- "Singing With His Wings." A look at the fascinating way that the Club-winged Mannakin makes birdsong with his wings.
- "By the Waters of Kariba." An exposé in words and photos of the many unique and colorful birds of all sizes and kinds that call this man-made African lake home.

Rights and Payment
One-time rights. Articles, $350. Artwork, payment rates vary. Pays on publication.

The Living Church

P.O. Box 514036
Milwaukee, WI 53203-3436

Managing Editor: John Schuessler

Description and Interests
Published by the Living Church Foundation, this magazine offers readers timely coverage of the Foundation's activities, news within the Episcopal Church, and personal opinion pieces, as well as devotions and reviews. Its mission is to promote and support Catholic Anglicanism within the Episcopal Church and the Anglican Communion. All submissions should be directed to the same end. Circ: 6,000.

Contents: 60% articles; 30% depts/columns; 10% other
Frequency: 26 times a year
Website: www.livingchurch.org

Freelance Potential
75% written by nonstaff writers. Publishes 10 freelance submissions yearly; 20% by authors who are new to the magazine, 40% by experts. Receives 3 unsolicited mss monthly.

Submissions
Send complete ms. Accepts hard copy. SASE. Responds in 3 months.

- Articles: To 2,000 words. Informational, how-to, profiles, interviews, opinion, and devotions. Topics include spirituality, Anglican heritage, theology, and current events as they pertain to Catholic Anglicanism and the Episcopal Church.
- Depts/columns: 600–700 words. News, Bible readings, book reviews.

Sample Issue
32 pages. Advertising. Sample copy and articles available at website. Guidelines available.

- "Walking Together in Haiti." Tells of a week that parishioners from a church in Delaware spent with a parish in Haiti, working side by side on the ministries of the area.
- "A Tale of Two Grandmothers." The prayers of the people during the Civil War and what the time period meant for faithful people on both sides of the conflict.

Rights and Payment
First North American serial rights. No payment. Provides 1 contributor's copy.

Living for the Whole Family

1251 Virginia Avenue
Harrisonburg, VA 22802

Editor: Melodie Davis

Description and Interests
This regional parenting and family magazine features helpful and positive articles on all topics relating to family, relationships, parenting, and childhood. Though published by an Evangelical Christian organization, it does not assume a Christian audience. Articles that embrace a positive outlook on the things that matter in life will get noticed. Circ: 125,000.

Contents: 90% articles; 10% depts/columns
Frequency: Quarterly
Website: www.livingforthewholefamily.com

Freelance Potential
85% written by nonstaff writers. Publishes 50 freelance submissions yearly; 20% by unpublished writers, 20% by authors who are new to the magazine. Receives 40 mss monthly.

Submissions
Send query or complete ms. Accepts hard copy, email submissions to melodiemillerdavis@gmail.com (put title of ms and "Submissions for Living" in subject line), reprints, and simultaneous submissions if identified. SASE. Responds in 3–4 months.

- Articles: 250–1,200 words. Informational, how-to, profiles, interviews, and personal experience. Topics include family issues, career, social issues, health and fitness, recreation, travel, parenting, religion, cultural issues, and education.
- Depts/columns: Staff-written.
- Other: Puzzles and activities.

Sample Issue
24 pages. Advertising. Sample articles and guidelines available at website.

- "Stop Sibling Bickering." An expert's suggestions for nipping this problem in the bud by laying out the ground rules when children are young.
- "Making Do with a 73-Year-Old Brain." Essay on the quirks of an aging brain, how to use it to its best advantage and accept its downfalls.

Rights and Payment
One-time and second rights. Written material, $35–$60. Photos, $10–$15. Pays 3 months after publication. Provides 1 contributor's copy.

Living ROOTS

1150 Hungryneck Boulevard., Suite C-351
Mount Pleasant, SC 29464

Publisher & Editor in Chief: Deona Smith

Description and Interests

Living ROOTS, subtitled "A Celebration of Southern Soul," concentrates on the Southern African American community's culture, history, and lifestyle. Covering everything from personal finance and health, to philanthropy, it especially highlights Lowcountry entrepreneurs, businesses, and people. Circ: Unavailable.

Contents: 30% articles; 70% depts/columns
Frequency: 6 times each year
Website: http://livingrootsmag.com

Freelance Potential

Receives numerous queries monthly.

Submissions

Query. Accepts email to deona@livingrootsmag.com. Response time varies.

- Articles: Informational articles and profiles. Topics include music, culture, fashion, local authors, personal finance, health, food, parenting, and community issues.
- Depts/columns: Weddings, local news, personal finance, giving, and style.

Sample Issue

42 pages. Advertising. Sample copy available at website.

- "The Soul of the South." Article features an interview with Grammy-nominated singer and songwriter Angie Stone.
- "African American Studies." Article describes the growing department of African American studies at the College of Charlestown.
- Sample dept/column: Style showcases the African jewelry collection of a local artist.

Rights and Payment

Rights vary. Payment rates and policy vary.

Log Home Living

4125 Lafayette Center Drive, Suite 100
Chantilly, VA 20151

Submissions Editor

Description and Interests

At 27 years old, *Log Home Living* is the oldest and most widely read publication for people who own or plan to build contemporary log homes. It features articles on the design and construction of log homes, as well as features about the log home lifestyle. How-to's on design and construction, along with technical articles, represent its biggest editorial needs. Circ: Unavailable.

Contents: Articles; depts/columns
Frequency: Monthly
Website: www.loghome.com/loghomeliving

Freelance Potential

Buys about 48 freelance features yearly. The editors welcome new talent and often develop long-term professional relationships with freelance contributors who consistently deliver quality work.

Submissions

Prefers query; will accept complete ms. Accepts hard copy and email submissions to editor@loghomeliving.com (Word attachments). SASE. Responds in 1 month.

- Articles: 1,500–2,000 words. Informational, how-to, and profiles. Topics include the design, construction, and maintenance of log homes; history; and the log home lifestyle.
- Depts/columns: Staff-written.
- Artwork: Color prints; digital images at 300 dpi.

Sample Issue

Advertising. Sample articles and guidelines available at website.

- "Mountain Retreat: A Guest-Friendly Log Home in Montana." Three generations enjoy this Big Sky country log home that takes advantage of scenic vistas and recreational opportunities.
- "Log-Cabin Wedding Venues: Goin' to the Chapel." Around the country, log cabin chapels are available for couples looking to get hitched surrounded by natural beauty.

Rights and Payment

First North American serial and non-exclusive reprint rights. Written material, payment rates vary. Kill fee, $100. Pays on acceptance. Provides 2 contributor copies.

The London Magazine

11 Queen's Gate
London SW7 5EL
United Kingdom

Editor: Steven O'Brien

Description and Interests

Having championed the works of Wordsworth, Lamb, De Quincy, and Clare in the past, *The London Magazine* is one of the United Kingdom's oldest and most celebrated literary journals. Published since the eighteenth century, it celebrates the works of writers from England and beyond. It seeks to publish the highest quality works of well-known writers, as well as emerging talents, and it is interested in writing that has a London focus, but not exclusively so. Circ: 1,200.

Contents: 25% articles; 25% fiction; 25% poetry; 25% reviews
Frequency: 6 times each year
Website: www.thelondonmagazine.org

Freelance Potential

100% written by nonstaff writers. Publishes 180 freelance submissions yearly; 25% by unpublished writers, 25% by authors who are new to the magazine. Receives 60 queries, 50 unsolicited mss monthly.

Submissions

Email complete ms to admin@thelondonmagazine.org; will accept hard copy. SASE/IRC. Response time varies.

- Articles: 800–2,000 words. Creative nonfiction, personal experience, memoirs, and humor. Reviews, to 2,000 words. Topics include arts and literature.
- Fiction: 1,000–4,000 words. Literary fiction. It does not normally publish science fiction, fantasy, or erotica.
- Other: Poetry, to 40 lines.

Sample Issue

144 pages. Little advertising. Guidelines available at website. Sample copy available.

- "Death and the Maiden." Short story.
- "Thomas Mann's *Disorder and Early Sorrow*: The Wounded Spirit." Delves into what was behind this particular work of Thomas Mann.

Rights and Payment

Rights vary. No payment. Provides 1 contributor's copy.

The Lookout

8805 Governor's Hill Drive, Suite 400
Cincinnati, OH 45249

Editor: Shawn McMullen

Description and Interests

Each themed issue of *The Lookout* deals with the needs of ordinary Christians who want to grow in their faith. A wide variety of topics are covered, including individual discipleship, family concerns, and social involvement from a "theologically conservative, nondenominational, and noncharismatic perspective." It typically publishes how-to articles that help readers apply Scripture to daily life, informational articles about current issues, and human interest stories that show God at work. Circ: 45,000.

Contents: 60% articles; 40% depts/columns
Frequency: Weekly
Website: www.lookoutmag.com

Freelance Potential

85% written by nonstaff writers. Publishes 175 freelance submissions yearly; 10% by unpublished writers, 20% by authors who are new to the magazine, 10% by experts. Receives 30 queries monthly.

Submissions

Query with résumé and outline or send complete ms with word count. Articles need to conform to theme list, available online or by request with SASE. Accepts hard copy, and email for queries only to lookout@standardpub.com, and simultaneous submissions. SASE. Responds in 2–3 months.

- Articles: 1,000–1,600 words. Informational, how-to, profiles, interviews, human interest, essays, and personal experience. Topics include Scripture, religion, social issues, and family life.
- Depts/columns: 500–800 words. Bible lessons, opinions, news, profiles.

Sample Issue

16 pages. Advertising. Guidelines, theme list, and sample articles available at website.

- "From Mount Carmel to a Cave." Offers practical advice on dealing with depression by way of looking at the prophet Elijah journeying from spiritual victory to depression and back.
- Sample dept/column: Where You Live offers personal counseling regarding anger with reference to Bible teaching.

Rights and Payment

First North American serial rights. Written material, \$.11–\$.17 per word. Pays on acceptance. Provides 4 contributor's copies.

Lost Treasure

P.O. Box 451589
Grove, OK 74345-1589

Managing Editor: Carla Banning

Description and Interests

This magazine is a "Treasure Hunter's Guide to Adventures and Fortune." Each issue is filled with personal stories and how-to articles of relic and cache hunting, as well as folklore and legends. Articles should coordinate with an issue's theme whenever possible. Circ: 50,000.

Contents: 50% articles; 20% depts/columns; 30% other
Frequency: Monthly
Website: www.losttreasure.com

Freelance Potential

96% written by nonstaff writers. Publishes 208 freelance submissions yearly; 20% by unpublished writers, 40% by authors who are new to the magazine, 40% by experts. Receives 25 unsolicited mss monthly.

Submissions

Send complete ms. Accepts disk submissions and email to managingeditor@losttreasure.com (Word attachments). SASE. Responds in 1 month.

- Articles: 500–1,500 words. Informational, how-to, personal experience, and folklore. Topics include treasure hunting, relic hunting, coinshooting, beachcombing, cache hunting, Western treasure, ghost towns, treasure values.
- Depts/columns: 1,500 words. News, product information, state treasures.
- Artwork: B/W or color prints.

Sample Issue

66 pages. Advertising. Sample articles available at website. Guidelines available.

- "The Viking Treasure of Bondi Bay." The search for Viking treasure in North America, specifically the vast forests and endless lakes of Muskoka, in Ontario, Canada.
- "The Bronze Age Shipwreck at Uluburun." An ancient disaster at sea leaves a cache of treasure on the floor of the Mediterranean Sea.

Rights and Payment

All rights. Written material, $.04 per word. Artwork, $5–$100. Pays on publication. Provides 1 contributor's copy.

Louisiana Kitchen & Culture

1450 Annunciation Street, Suite 2119
New Orleans, LA 70130

Editorial Director: Jyl Benson

Description and Interests

Launched in spring 2012, this magazine's goal is to celebrate Louisiana's rich cultural heritage and culinary traditions. Its audience is locals, visitors, and those who are fans of Louisiana fare. It seeks writers who are familiar with the state's culture and who are extremely knowledgeable about food and cooking. Circ: 75,000.

Contents: 80% articles; 20% depts/columns
Frequency: 6 times each year
Website: www.louisiana.kitchenandculture.com

Freelance Potential

Seeking writers knowledgeable about Louisiana culinary traditions and culture. Receives many queries monthly.

Submissions

Query with cover letter, résumé, and 3 clips. Explain your knowledge of Louisiana food. Accepts submissions via website and email submissions to jyl@kitchenandculture.com Responds if interested.

- Articles: Informational; how-to's; and profiles. Topics include Louisiana food, cooking, chefs, suppliers, and restaurants.

Sample Issue

Advertising. Sample articles, guidelines, and editorial calendar available at website.

- "An Afro Creole Thanksgiving." A look at what's on the menu, complete with recipes and traditions, for celebrating Bayou-style.
- "Giving Back at Cafe Reconcile." What one well-known New Orleans eatery is doing to share with the community.

Rights and Payment

First North American serial rights. Written material, payment varies depending on research and writer experience. Pays on publication.

Lucky Peach

849 Valencia Street
San Francisco, CA 94110

Editor

Description and Interests
Lucky Peach is a food and writing magazine from the publishers of McSweeney's Publishing. It was created by chef David Chang, writer Peter Meehan, and the producers of *Anthony Bourdain: No Reservations*. Each issue focuses on a single theme and explores that theme through essays, art, photography, and recipes. Travel, entertainment, and chefs are also covered. Editors are open to submissions outside of the themes. If the writing is superb, they will find a place for it. Circ: Unavailable.

Contents: Articles; depts/columns
Frequency: Quarterly
Website: www.mcsweeneys.net/luckypeach

Freelance Potential
Receives several submissions monthly.

Submissions
Send complete ms. Accepts electronic submissions via website and simultaneous submissions if identified. Responds in 8 weeks.

- Articles: Word lengths vary. Informational and how-to articles, profiles, personal experience pieces, and essays. Topics include food, travel, chefs, entertainment, and other food-related topics.
- Depts/columns: Word lengths vary. Reviews, recipes, essays, new products.

Sample Issue
Advertising. Sample articles available at website.

- "Chinatown: Real and Imagined." Article takes the reader on a visual culinary tour of Chinese neighborhoods around the world.
- "Take-Out Trifecta." Article discusses the history of the Asian condiment packets of soy sauce, duck sauce, and hot mustard.
- "Pro Choys." Article describes all of the greens that can be found in Chinese produce markets, as well as in many Asian recipes.

Rights and Payment
Rights vary. Payment rates and policy vary.

The Lutheran Digest

6160 Carmen Avenue East
Inver Grove Heights, MN 55076

Editor: Nicholas A. Skapyak

Description and Interests
Readers of this quarterly find stories of faith and articles on religious topics, along with some lighthearted fare. Though the material embraces Lutheran teachings, it can be enjoyed by Christians of all denominations. In true "digest" form, the majority of material is reprinted from other publications, with the balance coming from unsolicited material from freelance writers. It seeks articles about how God intervened in a person's life, seasonal material, and articles reflecting God's presence in nature. Circ: 70,000.

Contents: 90% articles; 10% other
Frequency: Quarterly
Website: www.lutherandigest.com

Freelance Potential
80% written by nonstaff writers. Publishes 80 freelance submissions yearly; 30% by authors who are new to the magazine. Receives 25 unsolicited mss monthly.

Submissions
Send complete ms with brief author biography. Prefers hard copy. Accepts email submissions to editor@lutherandigest.com (Word or PDF attachments). Accepts simultaneous submissions if identified. SASE. Responds in 2–3 months.

- Articles: To 7,000 characters. Informational, inspirational, and personal experience. Topics include spirituality, prayer, Bible lessons, and God's presence in everyday life and in nature.
- Other: Poetry, to 3 poems per submission. Filler, recipes, and jokes. Submit seasonal material at least 6 months in advance.

Sample Issue
64 pages. Little advertising. Sample copy available. Guidelines available at website.

- "Welcome to Old Age." A senior's prospective on aging: slowing down but never stopping.
- "Living With Less, Loving People More." Experiments with simplicity and learning to be content with what we have.

Rights and Payment
One-time and second rights. Articles, $35. Poetry and filler; no payment. Pays on publication. Provides 1 contributor's copy.

Macrobiotics Today

P.O. Box 3998
Chico, CA 95927-3998

Editor: Carl Ferré

Description and Interests
Representing diverse views in the macrobiotic community, this publication provides its readers with the latest information on macrobiotic education and physical, emotional, and spiritual health. Its articles, interviews, and reports combine contemporary thinking and scientific knowledge. It showcases the works of the leaders in the macrobiotic community and is interested in news on diet, health, and environmental consciousness. Circ: 5,000.
Contents: Articles; depts/columns
Frequency: 6 times each year
Website: www.ohsawamacrobiotics.com

Freelance Potential
80% written by nonstaff writers. Publishes 28 freelance submissions yearly; 5% by unpublished writers, 10% by authors who are new to the magazine, 95% by experts. Receives 3 queries, 1 unsolicited ms monthly.

Submissions
Query or send complete ms. Prefers email submissions to gomf@earthlink.net; will accept hard copy and disk submissions. SASE. Responds in 2–8 weeks.

- Articles: 1,000–2,500 words. Informational articles, profiles, interviews, and personal experience pieces. Topics include macrobiotics, diet, nutrition, cooking, health, green living, alternative energy, and social issues.
- Depts/columns: Staff-written.

Sample Issue
40 pages. Advertising. Sample articles available at website. Guidelines available.

- "Converting Your Friends." Article provides tips for introducing healthy eating to family and friends without alienating anyone.
- "Gluten-Free Breakfasts." Article shares recipes and ideas for a gluten-free meal.

Rights and Payment
All rights. Written material, $25–$50. Payment policy varies. Provides 5 contributor's copies.

The Magazine Antiques

575 Broadway, Fifth Floor
New York, NY 10012

Editor: Betsy Pochoda

Description and Interests
Antique furniture, artwork, and fine collectibles are presented in full-color, glossy format in this magazine. It has been covering exhibitions, collections, artists, and antiquing destinations for collectors and curators since 1922. Writers should capture the attention of its sophisticated readership of collectors and curators and have a deep knowledge of the world of antiques and fine arts contribute to this magazine. Circ: 5,300.
Contents: 80% articles; 20% depts/columns
Frequency: 6 times each year
Website: www.themagazineantiques.com

Freelance Potential
80% written by nonstaff writers. Publishes 50 freelance submissions yearly; 5% by authors who are new to the magazine, 95% by experts. Receives 10 unsolicited mss monthly.

Submissions
Send complete ms with artwork. Accepts hard copy. Availability of artwork improves chance of acceptance. SASE. Responds in 3–6 months.

- Articles: 3,000–3,500 words. Informational articles. Topics include antiques, fine art, artists, craftsmen, collecting, history, preservation, estates, design, and decorating.
- Depts/columns: Staff-written.
- Artwork: 8x10 B/W prints; 4x5 color transparencies; digital images at 300 dpi.

Sample Issue
104 pages. Advertising. Sample articles available at website. Guidelines available via email request to tmaedit@brantpub.com.

- "Right Place, Right Time: The Grigson-Didier House in New Orleans." Article describes the renovation of this antique home.
- "Beyond Moonlight and Magnolias." Article discusses the revitalization of the Museum of Early Southern Decorative Arts in North Carolina.

Rights and Payment
One-time rights. All material, payment rates vary. Pays on publication. Provides 2 contributor's copies.

Maine Home + Design

73 Market Street, Suite 203
Portland, ME 04101

Editor: Susan Kelley

Description and Interests
This magazine depicts the best home architecture and designs found in the state. *Maine Home + Design* has an upscale feel, with illustrated features on traditional and contemporary homes and the people who create and live in them. It is mainly interested in articles about exceptional Maine homes and profiles of individuals or businesses related to home design. Circ: 30,000+.

Contents: Articles; depts/columns
Frequency: 11 times each year
Website: www.mainehomedesign.com

Freelance Potential
50% written by nonstaff writers. Publishes 50 freelance submissions yearly; 10% by unpublished writers, 40% by authors who are new to the magazine, 50% by experts. Receives 12 queries monthly.

Submissions
Accepts queries with photos through the website only. Response time varies.

- Articles: 1,000–1,500 words. Informational articles, profiles, and interviews. Topics include architecture, interior design, remodeling, landscaping, art, antiques, and lifestyles.
- Depts/columns: 500–1,200 words. Essays, designer profiles, and reviews.

Sample Issue
112 pages. Advertising. Sample articles and guidelines available at website.

- "Opposite in Nature." Article details a road trip from Arizona to Maine taken by two designers in the middle of winter.
- "Scenic Overlook." Article showcases the design of a waterfront home in Rockport.
- "Blank Page." Article describes the building of a sustainable library on the Pemaquid Peninsula.

Rights and Payment
All rights. Written material, payment rates vary. Kill fee varies. Pays on publication. Provides 4 contributor's copies.

MASK
The Magazine

8937 East Bell Road, Suite 202
Scottsdale, AZ 85260

Editor in Chief: Michelle Jacoby

Description and Interests
MASK is the publication of the nonprofit organization Mothers Awareness on School-age Kids, founded by mothers who are concerned with the exposure of children to social, sexual, and substance abuse issues. Believing that communication between parents and kids is the best defense against destructive decisions, its articles—many written by experts in the field—provide awareness of issues, prevention tactics, and conversation starters for families. Its goal is to save children's lives by engaging, educating, and empowering families. All articles must tackle an issue of contemporary society that families are dealing with, or present inspiration and information on increasing honest dialogue among family members. Circ: 20,000.

Contents: Articles
Frequency: Quarterly
Website: www.maskmatters.org

Freelance Potential
35% written by nonstaff writers.

Submissions
Send complete ms. Accepts email submissions to info@maskmatters.org.

- Articles: Word lengths vary. Informational, personal experience, and how-to. Topics include substance abuse, parenting, education, self-esteem, bullying, health and fitness, and family relationships.

Sample Issue
Advertising. Sample articles available at website.

- "Making the Grade for High School." Easy access to prescription drugs is fueling a rise in prescription drug abuse among teens.
- "Facebook Frenemies." Advice for victims of social media attacks.

Rights and Payment
First rights. No payment; writers get a short biography at end.

Mature Living

Lifeway Christian Resources
One LifeWay Plaza
Nashville, TN 37234-0175

Content Editor: René Holt

Description and Interests

Geared to Christians over the age of 55, *Mature Living* features inspirational, educational human interest stories. Fiction and poetry are also found in each issue. It would like to see articles geared to the not-yet-retired group and pieces dealing with long-term marriage issues—how to keep the flame alive, for example. Circ: 318,000.

Contents: 61% articles; 25% depts/columns; 8% fiction; 6% other
Frequency: Monthly
Website: www.lifeway.com

Freelance Potential

95% written by nonstaff writers. Publishes 190 freelance submissions yearly; 15% by unpublished writers, 25% by authors who are new to the magazine, 10% by experts. Receives 60–70 unsolicited mss monthly.

Submissions

Send complete ms with word count. Accepts hard copy and email submissions to matureliving@lifeway.com. SASE. No simultaneous submissions. Responds in 2 months.

- Articles: 600–1,000 words. Informational and self-help articles, personal experience pieces, nostalgia, and humor. Topics include contemporary issues, family life, travel, history, and grandparenting.
- Fiction: 800–1,200 words. Stories that underscore a biblical truth.
- Depts/columns: 125–500 words. Gardening, crafts, health, finance, and travel.
- Other: Poetry, to 12 lines.

Sample Issue

58 pages. Advertising. Sample copy and guidelines available at website.

- "All God's Creatures." Article profiles a woman who shares the message of Jesus through the rehabilitation of wild animals.
- "Final Wishes." Article discusses the importance of having a will.

Rights and Payment

All rights. Written material, payment rates vary. Pays on acceptance. Provides 3 contributor's copies.

Mature Years

201 Eighth Avenue South
Nashville, TN 37202

Editor: Marvin W. Cropsey

Description and Interests

This Christian-themed magazine presents articles designed to help its readers capitalize on their faith and spirituality in order to get the most out of their post-55 years. The magazine is in large-print and features upbeat articles about mature adults and faith-filled advice, as well as Bible lessons and meditations. Circ: 50,000.

Contents: 70% articles; 25% depts/columns; 5% fiction
Frequency: Quarterly
Website: www.cokesbury.com

Freelance Potential

99% written by nonstaff writers. Publishes 60–70 freelance submissions yearly; 50% by authors who are new to the magazine. Receives 200 unsolicited mss monthly.

Submissions

Query or send complete ms. Prefers email submissions to matureyears@umpublishing.org (Word attachments); will accept hard copy. SASE. Responds in 2 months.

- Articles: To 2,000 words. Informational, how-to, essays, interviews, and personal experience that demonstrate faith in God as a life resource. Topics include health and fitness, housing, personal finances, social and emotional needs, security, family life, and self-help.
- Depts/columns: Daily Meditations and Bible Study; Fragments of Life, 250-600 words; Going Places, 1,000-1,500 words; Health Hints, 900-1,500 words; Media Shelf; Merry-Go-Round, cartoons, jokes, 4-6 line humorous verses; Modern Revelations, essays, advice for spiritual living, 900-1,500 words; Money Matters, 1,200-1,800 words; Puzzle Time; Social Security Q&A. Poetry, to 16 lines.
- Artwork: Color, b/w prints or transparencies.

Sample Issue

112 pages. Sample copy and guidelines available.

- "Retired Pastor Shares 13 Strategies for Retirement." Making the most of this time.
- "Seven Ways to Cut Expenses." Tips for frugal living.

Rights and Payment

One-time North American serial rights. Articles, $.05 a word; poetry, $1 per line; verse and fillers, $5 each; cartoons, $30. Pays on acceptance.

The Mennonite

3145 Benham Avenue, Suite 4
Elkhart, IN 46517

Associate Editor: Gordon Houser

Description and Interests

This magazine serves as a forum for the voices of Mennonite Church USA. It features articles about the church; religious faith; the Bible; and parenting, family, and contemporary issues from this church's perspective. It is especially interested in personal stories of Mennonites exercising their faith. Circ: 8,000.

Contents: 70% articles; 30% depts/columns
Frequency: Monthly
Website: www.themennonite.org

Freelance Potential

80% written by nonstaff writers. Publishes 75 freelance submissions yearly; 5% by unpublished writers, 5% by authors who are new to the magazine, 5% by experts. Receives 10 unsolicited mss monthly.

Submissions

Send complete ms. Prefers email submissions to gordonh@themennonite.org; will accept hard copy and simultaneous submissions if identified. SASE. Responds in 1 week.

- Articles: 1,200–1,500 words. Informational and how-to articles, profiles, interviews, creative nonfiction, and personal experience pieces. Topics include faith, Bible study, worship and prayer, the environment, aging, death, marriage, parenting, racism, peace, justice, health, and the arts.
- Depts/columns: 700 words. News, opinions.
- Artwork: Color prints. Line art, charts, graphs.

Sample Issue

56 pages. Advertising. Sample copy and guidelines available at website.

- "The Power of Story." Article relates the author's experiences of sharing stories to shape and transform people and communities.
- "Swords into Brooms." Article describes how one former gang member was able to turn his life around and follow Jesus.

Rights and Payment

Rights vary. No payment. Provides 1 contributor's copy.

MHQ

The Quarterly Journal of Military History

Weider History Group
19300 Promenade Drive
Leesburg, VA 20176-6500

Associate Editor: Nicholas Wood

Description and Interests

With content ranging from ancient and medieval warfare articles to military profiles and memoirs, this magazine informs and entertains avid enthusiasts of military history. The magazine rarely prints articles dealing with subjects it has already covered. Each issue contains a cumulative list of recently published article titles; writers should check it before submitting. Circ: 23,500.

Contents: 70% articles; 20% depts/columns; 10% other
Frequency: Quarterly
Website: www.historynet.com

Freelance Potential

95% written by nonstaff writers. Publishes 52 freelance submissions yearly; 5% by unpublished writers, 15% by authors who are new to the magazine, 80% by experts. Receives 15 queries, 6 unsolicited mss monthly.

Submissions

Query with information on prior writing experience. Send hard copy or email to mhq@weiderhistorygroup.com (Word attachments). Availability of artwork improves chance of acceptance. SASE. Responds in 1 year.

- Articles: 5,000–6,000 words. Informational articles and profiles. Topics include wars, battles, and military figures.
- Depts/columns: 1,500–2,500 words. Tactics, arms, strategy, and art. Reviews, to 800 words.
- Artwork: Illustrations with reprint permission.

Sample Issue

96 pages. Advertising. Sample articles and guidelines available at website.

- "The Spanish Road to the Netherlands." Article recounts the Duke of Alba's 700-mile march to the Netherlands in 1567 which marked a turning point in European history.
- "'Something Dark and Bloody': What Happened at My Lai?" Article details through interviews and research what led to the killing of 500 innocent Vietnamese civilians.

Rights and Payment

First serial rights. Articles, $800+. Depts/columns, $400+. Kill fee, 25%. Pays on publication. Provides 3 contributor's copies.

Michigan History

5815 Executive Drive
Lansing, MI 48911-5352

Editor

Description and Interests

Published by the Historical Society of Michigan, this magazine is written for history buffs, as well as history professionals. It features articles of all kinds about the state's colorful past, including its people, politics, shipwrecks, sports, industry, and arts heritage. It is not an academic journal, but writers shouldn't cut corners on research. It looks for interesting perspectives on the state's history that are accurate and well-written. Circ: 23,500.

Contents: 65% articles; 35% depts/columns
Frequency: 6 times each year
Website: www.hsmichigan.org/publications/michigan-history-magazine

Freelance Potential

90% written by nonstaff writers. Publishes 50 freelance submissions yearly; 10% by unpublished writers, 50% by authors who are new to the magazine, 50% by experts.

Submissions

Query with writing samples. Accepts hard copy and email to majher@hsmichigan.org. Responds in 6 months.

- Articles: 1,500–2,500 words. Informational articles, profiles, and interviews. Topics include Michigan history, natural history, lifestyles, personalities, and sports.
- Depts/columns: Staff written.

Sample Issue

64 pages. Advertising. Sample articles and guidelines available at website. Samply copy available by email request to mheditor@hsmichigan.org.

- "Remember the Time: An Old Fort Was Our Playground." Article traces the history of the author's childhood summer home which was located on a former fort.
- "Fuel-Efficient Fun! The Mobil Economy Run." Article describes the first of this popular event which began in 1967.

Rights and Payment

Reprint rights. Written material, $100–$400. Kill fee varies. Pays on publication. Provides 5 contributor's copies.

Midstream

633 Third Avenue, 21st Floor
New York, NY 10017-6706

Editor: Leo Haber

Description and Interests

Jewish people from all over the world look to this publication for articles on current events, history, politics, and social issues that affect them. *Midstream* also offers poetry, fiction, and essays with a Jewish slant. It strives to be the leading American Jewish Zionist intellectual journal. Circ: 10,000.

Contents: 50% articles; 30% depts/columns; 10% fiction; 10% other
Frequency: Quarterly
Website: www.midstreamthf.com

Freelance Potential

90% written by nonstaff writers. Publishes 60 freelance submissions yearly; 10% by unpublished writers, 15% by new authors, 25% by experts. Receives 60–120 mss monthly.

Submissions

Send complete ms. Accepts submissions to midstreamthf@aol.com (Word attachments). Responds in 3–6 months.

- Articles: 2,000–4,000 words. Informational articles, analytical and in-depth opinion pieces, profiles, interviews, personal experience pieces, literary criticism, and humor. Topics include Judaism, the Jewish experience, politics, education, world events, social issues, and multicultural and ethnic issues.
- Fiction: 2,000–5,000 words. Stories with a Jewish perspective.
- Other: Reviews, 1,000–2,000. Poetry with a Jewish perspective, to 3o lines.

Sample Issue

48 pages. Little advertising. Sample articles and guidelines available at website.

- "The Key to Imber." Article compares "The Star-Spangled Banner" and "Hatikvah."
- "In Defense of Jewish Nationalism." Article discusses the reasons behind the negative connotations of the term.

Rights and Payment

All rights. Articles and fiction, $.05 per word. Poetry, $25 per poem. Pays 2–3 months after publication. Provides 3 contributor's copies.

MidWest Outdoors

111 Shore Drive
Burr Ridge, IL 60527-5885

Publisher: Gene Laulunen

Description and Interests

To "help people enjoy the outdoors," *MidWest Outdoors* is full of positive articles on recreation, including fishing, hunting, and camping, within the region. Ideas for day and weekend trips are also featured. If a submission is not returned within 30 days, writers can assume the magazine will use it. However, it can be more than a year before a submission is published. Circ: 36,000.

Contents: 75% articles; 25% depts/columns
Frequency: Monthly
Website: www.midwestoutdoors.com

Freelance Potential

95% written by nonstaff writers. Publishes 3,000 freelance submissions yearly; 5% by unpublished writers, 10% by authors who are new to the magazine, 85% by experts. Receives 60 queries monthly.

Submissions

Query with clips or writing samples. Accepts email queries to info@midwestoutdoors.com. Responds in 2 weeks.

- Articles: 700–1,500 words. Informational, how-to, and where-to articles. Topics include camping, outdoor cooking, freshwater fishing, flyfishing, boat fishing, ice fishing, competitive fishing, powerboats and boating, canoes and paddling, hunting, hunting dogs, shooting, archery, and snowmobiling.
- Depts/columns: Staff-written.

Sample Issue

85 pages. Advertising. Sample copy available on website. Guidelines available.

- "Five Good Investment Tips to Stay Warm." Article discusses which clothing will keep a hunter warm and help avoid frostbite.
- "Introducing the Next Generation of Hunters." Article discusses the proper steps to take when introducing a child to hunting.

Rights and Payment

First regional exclusive rights. Written material, $30. Pays on publication. Provides contributor's copies upon request.

Military

2120 28th Street
Sacramento, CA 95818

Editor: John D. Shank

Description and Interests

Military aims to be a record of military history written by individuals who experienced it. It is written for and by veterans of all branches of the U.S. military, whether during war or peacetime. Relevant book reviews are also featured. It is interested only in nonfiction submissions of a military nature. Circ: 25,000.

Contents: 40% articles; 40% depts/columns; 20% other
Frequency: Monthly
Website: www.milmag.com

Freelance Potential

85% written by nonstaff writers. Publishes 80 freelance submissions yearly; 50% by unpublished writers, 20% by authors who are new to the magazine, 5% by experts. Receives 5 unsolicited mss monthly.

Submissions

Accepts submissions from subscribers only. Send complete ms with photos. Accepts hard copy, disk submissions, and email to editor@milmag.com. SASE. Responds in 1 month.

- Articles: 1,500+ words. Informational articles, personal experience pieces, and humor. Topics include the U.S. armed services, World War II, the Korean War, the Vietnam War, the Cold War, the Gulf Wars, and contemporary military issues.
- Depts/columns: 750–1,000 words. Opinions, news briefs, and book reviews.
- Encourages fillers of 150 to 300 words.

Sample Issue

40 pages. Advertising. Sample copy and guidelines available at website.

- "Honoring America's Fallen Warriors on Memorial Day." Article describes celebrations and memorials planned for veterans.
- Sample dept/column: Book Reviews discusses *The Third Reich at War*, by Richard J. Evans.

Rights and Payment

First North American serial rights. No payment. Provides 1+ contributor's copies.

Military Review

290 Stimson Avenue, Unit 2
Fort Leavenworth, KS 66027-1293

Director & Editor in Chief: COL John J. Smith

Description and Interests

Military Review provides a forum for the open exchange of ideas on military affairs. As the official publication of the United States Army, its articles analyze and debate concepts, doctrine, and warfighting at the tactical and operational levels of war. It is printed in English, Spanish, and Portuguese. Book reviews are by assignment only. Circ: 12,000.

Contents: 75% articles; 15% depts/columns; 10% book reviews
Frequency: 6 times each year
Website: http://usacac.army.mil/CAC2/MilitaryReview

Freelance Potential

100% written by nonstaff writers. Publishes 150 freelance submissions yearly; 60% by unpublished writers, 40% by experts. Receives 50–60 unsolicited mss monthly.

Submissions

Send complete ms. Accepts hard copy with disc and email submissions to usarmy.leavenworth.tradoc.mbx.military-review-public-em@mail.mil (Word attachments). Responds in 1 month.

- Articles: 3,500–3,500 words. Informational articles and opinion and personal experience pieces. Topics include military affairs, land warfare, combat studies, military history, government, and the media.
- Depts/columns: Reviews and opinions, 800–1,000 words. Book reviews, 300–500 words.
- Other: Poetry, to 30 lines.

Sample Issue

140 pages. No advertising. Sample copy, guidelines, and theme list available at website.

- "Just War Theory and Democratization by Force: Two Incompatible Agendas." Article examines whether minimum collateral damage is compatible with force.
- "Customary Law and Its Challenges to Afghan Statehood." Article discusses the importance of developing this country's judicial capabilities.

Rights and Payment

First rights. No payment. Provides 2 contributor's copies.

Ministry & Liturgy

Resource Publications
160 East Virginia Street, Suite 290
San Jose, CA 95112-5876

Publisher: William Burns

Description and Interests

Ministry & Liturgy seeks to provide practical resources and encourage creative dialogue for its audience of lay and ordained ministry leaders. All of its content supports the vision of the Second Vatican Council. It is looking for insight into the future of the evolving church and how it interacts with the world. New and published authors are welcome to send submissions. Circ: 20,000.

Contents: 50% articles; 50% depts/columns
Frequency: 10 times each year
Website: http://rpinet.com/ministry/

Freelance Potential

90% written by nonstaff writers. Publishes 40–50 freelance submissions yearly; 25% by unpublished writers, 25% by authors who are new to the magazine, 25% by experts. Receives 5–10 queries, 2–3 unsolicited mss monthly.

Submissions

Query. Prefers electronic submissions through website; will accept email to editor@rpinet.com. Responds in 2–6 weeks.

- Articles: 1,000–2,000 words. Informational and how-to articles, profiles, interviews, personal experience pieces, and humor. Topics include Roman Catholic liturgy, worship, multicultural issues, and church software.
- Depts/columns: Word lengths vary. Music, media reviews, and planning guides.

Sample Issue

30 pages. Advertising. Sample articles and guidelines available at website.

- "No Room at the Inn: Ministry to Homeless Families." Article shares examples of giving hope to those experiencing hard times.
- Sample dept/column: Moving Rite Along describes an "Aha!" moment.

Rights and Payment

First North American serial rights. Written material, $50–$100. Pays on publication. Provides 5 contributor's copies.

Mirror Moms

301 Cayuga Avenue
Altoona, PA 16602

Editor: Barbara Cowan

Description and Interests

Appearing as a print publication with an online presence, *Mirror Moms* is published by the *Altoona Mirror* daily newspaper. It is filled with news, features, and advice relevant to parents in central Pennsylvania. Features and columns cover family issues, education, and children's health and safety. Local authors and local sources are preferred. Blog opportunities are available. Circ: 30,000.

Contents: 50% articles, 50% depts/columns
Frequency: Quarterly
Website: www.mirrormoms.com

Freelance Potential

Freelance percentages not currently available.

Submissions

For submission information, send email to bcowan@altoonamirror.com.

- Articles: Word lengths vary. Informational, opinion, personal experience, profiles. Topics include parenting, family life, safety, health, education, and news relevant to local young people.
- Depts/columns: Health & Diet, Education, Tweens/Teens, Babies/Toddlers, Crafts & Recipes, Activities & Events.

Sample Issue

Advertising. Sample articles available at website.

- Get in the Mood for High School Musicals." Drama clubs at area high schools prepare for annual productions.
- "Prepare Your Kid to Get Creative with 10 Items that Should be in Every Craft Toolkit." Ten essential arts and crafts items to occupy your kids during spring break.

Rights and Payment

Rights and payment vary.

Model Railroader

Kalmbach Publishing
21027 Crossroads Circle
P.O. Box 1612
Waukesha, WI 53187-1612

Editor: Neil Besougloff

Description and Interests

This magazine shows and tells model railroad enthusiasts how to build and lay out the components of their track plans. Product reviews are also featured. Readers are looking for practical advice and detailed how-to instructions accompanied by ample, captioned illustrations to guide them. Circ: 182,000.

Contents: 60% articles; 40% depts/columns
Frequency: Monthly
Website: http://mrr.trains.com

Freelance Potential

80% written by nonstaff writers. Publishes 120 freelance submissions yearly; 20% by unpublished writers, 30% by authors who are new to the magazine. Receives 25 queries, 30 unsolicited mss monthly.

Submissions

Query with outline. Accepts hard copy and email to mrmag@mrmag.com. SASE. Responds to queries in 1 month, to mss in 2 months.

- Articles: To 2,000 words. Informational and how-to articles. Topics include model railway systems, displays, and crafting techniques.
- Depts/columns: Word lengths vary. Tips and techniques, new product information, and opinion pieces.
- Artwork: 5x7 or larger B/W or color prints and 35mm color slides; digital photos, 300 dpi, with printout.

Sample Issue

102 pages. Advertising. Sample articles and guidelines available at website.

- "Scratchbuilding Without Plans." Article offers construction tips for building a structure from prototype photos.
- Sample dept/column: Product Reviews discusses the Athearn Genesis series DDA40X.

Rights and Payment

All rights. Articles, $75–100 per printed page. Other material, payment rates vary. Pays on acceptance. Provides 1 contributor's copy.

Modern Drummer

12 Old Bridge Road
Cedar Grove, NJ 07009-1288

Editor: Adam Budofsky

Description and Interests

Avid drummers, whether garage band or professional musicians, seek out this magazine for the lowdown on the craft. How-to and feature articles offer information, while interviews and profiles offer inspiration. It is not a fan magazine. Instead it publishes material that will help readers hone their skills, select the best equipment, and develop a professional career if that is their goal. Circ: 100,000.

Contents: 85% articles; 15% depts/columns
Frequency: Monthly
Website: www.moderndrummer.com

Freelance Potential

80% written by nonstaff writers. Publishes 30–40 freelance submissions yearly; 20% by unpublished writers, 10% by authors who are new to the magazine, 70% by experts. Receives 5 queries monthly.

Submissions

Query to 200 words, with résumé and writing samples. Responds in 2 weeks. Educational columns and product review queries to Mike Dawson, miked@moderndrummer.com; all others to adamb@moderndrummer.com.

- Articles: 5,000–8,000 words. Informational and how-to articles, profiles, and interviews. Topics include music, professional and amateur drummers, equipment, and techniques.
- Depts/columns: Conceptual and technical pieces, 500–2,500 words. Profiles of up-and-coming drummers, 2,500–3,000 words. Reviews and short news pieces.

Sample Issue

152 pages. Advertising. Sample articles and guidelines available at website.

- "Discipline and Feel." Article profiles Doug Clifford and his rise to fame with Creedence Clearwater Revival.
- Sample dept/column: Product Close-up reviews the DW Black-Nickel Over Brass Snare.

Rights and Payment

All rights. Articles, $200–$500. Depts/columns, $50–$150. Pays on publication. Provides 1–3 contributor's copies.

Monitoring Times

7540 Highway 64 West
Brasstown, NC 28902

Editor: Ken Reitz

Description and Interests

Technical and feature articles, as well as product reviews, comprise the bulk of this magazine for radio monitoring enthusiasts. Topics include shortwave radios, scanners, satellites, and antique radios. Its readership is comprised of both advanced radio operators and novice hobbyists; all articles should inspire, as well as inform. New writers are welcome to send a query. Circ: 20,000.

Contents: 82% articles; 18% depts/columns
Frequency: Monthly
Website: www.monitoringtimes.com

Freelance Potential

15% written by nonstaff writers. Publishes 55 freelance submissions yearly; 18% by authors who are new to the magazine. Receives 4 queries, 4 unsolicited mss monthly.

Submissions

Query. Email to editor@monitoringtimes.com. Responds in 1–2 months.

- Articles: 2,000–3,000 words. Informational and how-to articles. Topics include audio, video, software, computers, hobbies, current events, entertainment, and science—all as they pertain to radio.
- Depts/columns: Word lengths vary. News, projects, ideas for beginners, and ham radio.

Sample Issue

76 pages. Advertising. Sample copy and guidelines available at website.

- "America's Voice for Asian Democracy." Article examines the role Radio Free Asia plays as a source of news and information.
- "Antennas for Shortwave Listening." Article explains what is required for the best possible shortwave reception at home.

Rights and Payment

First North American serial and reprint rights. Articles, $90–$100 per page. Depts/columns, payment rates vary. Pays on publication. Provides 1 contributor's copy.

More

125 Park Avenue
New York, NY 10017

Editor in Chief: Leslie Jane Seymour

Description and Interests

More is written "for women of style and substance" over the age of 40. Each issue focuses on beauty, style, personal finance, and mind and body, in addition to women who are making a difference. Queries should be brief, one to two pages, citing the lead and describing how the story will be researched and developed. The topic must involve and appeal to women ages 45–64. Circ: 1.3 million.

Contents: 75% articles; 25% depts/columns
Frequency: 10 times each year
Website: www.more.com

Freelance Potential

86% written by nonstaff writers. Publishes 100 freelance submissions yearly. Receives many queries monthly.

Submissions

Query with clips to appropriate editor on masthead. Accepts hard copy only. SASE. Responds in 3 months.

- Articles: Word lengths vary. Informational articles, personal experience pieces, profiles, interviews, and creative nonfiction. Topics include health, fitness, family, careers, consumer interest, entertainment, social issues, travel, and leisure.
- Depts/columns: Word lengths vary. Personal finance, health news, short profiles, and beauty updates.

Sample Issue

154 pages. Advertising. Sample articles and guidelines available at website.

- "A Breast Cancer You May Not Need to Treat." Article discusses whether Stage 0 cancer should be treated as aggressively as it has in the past.
- "Norma Kamali on Her Campaign to Empower Women." Article features interview with this fashion designer on her campaign to stop objectification of women.

Rights and Payment

All or first North American serial rights. Written material, payment rates vary. Kill fee, 25%. Pays on acceptance.

Mother Earth Living

1503 SW 42nd Street
Topeka, KS 66609-1265

Editor in Chief: Jessica Kellner

Description and Interests

In mid 2012, Ogden Publications merged *Natural Home & Garden* and *The Herb Companion,* to form *Mother Earth Living*. The new configuration bills itself as an authority on green lifestyle and design and offers advice on naturally healthy and nontoxic homes. It targets women, purchasers of organic foods and dietary supplments, and anyone interested in sustainable living. Regular topics include choosing natural remedies, practicing preventative medicine, cooking with nutritious and whole food, and gardening for food, wellness, and enjoyment. Ogden is also the publisher of *Mother Earth News.* Circ: 130,000.

Contents: Articles; depts/columns
Frequency: 6 times each year
Website: www.motherearthliving.com

Freelance Potential

Freelance potential not currently available.

Submissions

At writers' guidelines are available at *Mother Earth News* site; features written by contributing editors and freelance writers with knowledge of subject matter and writing experience. Query with one-page outline to letters. Accepts hard copy. SASE. Response time varies.

- Articles: Word lengths vary. Informational and how-to articles. Topics include health and wellness, green living, healthy cooking, and gardening.
- Depts/columns: Food and recipes.

Sample Issue

Advertising. Sample articles available at website.

- "Good Night Garden." Article provides a checklist for preparing a garden for the winter months and the spring ahead.
- "Brighter Living: A Healthy, Sunny Home in Ann Arbor, MI." Article showcases a home that combines efficient design and healthy living.
- "Plants for a Strong Immune System. Article discusses the best immune-boosting herbs, plant extracts, and supplements for keeping healthy.

Rights and Payment

Rights vary. Payment rates and policy vary.

Mother Jones

222 Sutter Street, Suite 600
San Francisco, CA 94108

Editors: Clara Jeffery & Monika Bauerlein

Description and Interests

Subtitled "Smart, Fearless Journalism," this magazine is known for its investigative reporting, often on provocative subjects. It focuses on national politics, environmental issues, corporate wrongdoing, human rights, and political influence. It relies on freelancers to fill the pages of the magazine with top-notch reporting on challenging topics, as well as thought-provoking and timely opinion pieces. Queries should include the author's qualifications and planned sources. The query should also convey the approach, style, and tone of the article. Circ: 240,000.

Contents: 90% articles; 10% depts/columns
Frequency: 6 times each year
Website: www.motherjones.com

Freelance Potential

98% written by nonstaff writers. Publishes 25 freelance submissions yearly; 30% by authors who are new to the magazine, 50% by experts. Receives 300 queries monthly.

Submissions

Query with summary, résumé, and clips or writing samples. Accepts hard copy and email queries to query@motherjones.com. SASE. Responds in 6–8 weeks if interested.

- Articles: 3,000–5,000 words. Informational articles, profiles, interviews, and investigative reports. Topics include cultural trends, consumer protection, the media, the environment, labor, and government.
- Depts/columns: Opinion pieces, 1,000–3,000 words. News items, 250–500 words.

Sample Issue

84 pages. Advertising. Sample copy and guidelines available on website.

- "Everything You've Heard About Failing Schools Is Wrong." Article describes the author's surprising experience of visiting a low-performing San Francisco school.
- "Dark Money's Top Target: Claire McCaskill." Article discusses Senator McCaskill's efforts to stop secret money used in politcal ads.

Rights and Payment

First serial rights. Written material, payment rates vary. Pays on acceptance.

MotorHome

2575 Vista del Mar Drive
Ventura, CA 93001

Editor in Chief: Eileen Hubbard

Description and Interests

MotorHome is an entertaining and informative magazine geared to motorized RV enthusiasts. All aspects of the motorhome lifestyle, from travel destinations and events to new products and service issues, are covered here. The best way for a new writer to get the editor's attention is to send a query on an interesting and tightly focused motorhome story. Circ: 128,000.

Contents: 70% articles; 30% depts/columns
Frequency: Monthly
Website: www.motorhomemagazine.com

Freelance Potential

60% written by nonstaff writers. Publishes more than 100 freelance articles yearly; 5% by authors who are new to the magazine, 50% by experts. Receives 18 queries monthly.

Submissions

Query with writing samples via email to info@motorhomemagazine.com. Accepts hard copy. SASE. No simultaneous submissions. Responds in 3 months.

- Articles: 1,200–1,800 words. Informational and how-to articles, profiles, interviews, new product information, and humor. Topics include RV travel, destinations, technical advice, current events, and personalities.
- Depts/columns: Escapes, 200 words. Lifestyle issues, tips, reviews, and news, word lengths vary.
- Artwork: 35mm slides; digital images at 300 dpi.

Sample Issue

66 pages. Advertising. Sample articles and guidelines available at website.

- "The Great Indoors." Article offers tips for selecting the proper TV products for an RV.
- "Campground Weddings." Article discusses options for destination weddings at campgrounds.

Rights and Payment

First North American serial and non-exclusive electronic rights. Articles, $400–$800. Depts/columns, $100–$400. Kill fee, 33%. Pays on acceptance. Provides 1 contributor's copy.

The Mountain Astrologer

P.O. Box 970
Cedar Ridge, CA 95924

Editor: Jan de Prosse

Description and Interests

Striving to be "the gateway to understanding the cosmos," *The Mountain Astrologer* is filled with information for aspiring and professional astrologers. Each issue contains a student section, articles on astrology's effect on world events, and a forecast section. It encourages suggestions for artwork or illustrations to enhance an article. Circ: 28,000.

Contents: 60% articles; 40% depts/columns
Frequency: 6 times each year
Website: www.mountainastrologer.com

Freelance Potential

95% written by nonstaff writers. Publishes 50 freelance submissions yearly; 20% by unpublished writers, 10% by authors who are new to the magazine, 60% by experts. Receives 20 queries monthly.

Submissions

Query with 1–3 page letter. Accepts hard copy or email to editorial@mountainastrologer.com ("TMA Query" in subject field). No multiple or simultaneous submissions. Responds in 2 months.

- Articles: Word lengths vary. Informational and how-to articles, profiles, interviews, and personal experience and opinion pieces. Topics include astrology, psychology, relationships, belief systems, health, spirituality, and computer software.
- Depts/columns: Word lengths vary. New product information; book, website, and media reviews; astrology news.

Sample Issue

112 pages. Advertising. Sample articles and guidelines available at website.

- "Cycles of Health." Article discusses astrological influences on one's health.
- "A Conversation with Alois Treindl." Article features an interview with the founder of www.astro.com.

Rights and Payment

First rights. Written material, $100–$400. Pays on publication. Provides 1–3 contributor's copies.

Movieguide

1151 Avenida Acaso
Camarillo, CA 93012

Editor: Dr. Tom Snyder

Description and Interests

The mission of this magazine is to provide church-going families with a tool they can use to choose movies and media entertainment. It offers a Christian-based analysis of entertainment content and messages. It also profiles entertainment personalities. Its reviews don't just offer an opinion—they consider the worldview, language, violence, sex, and alcohol use depicted in the entertainment. Circ: 5,000.

Contents: 30% articles; 20% depts/columns; 50% other
Frequency: 13 times each year
Website: www.movieguide.org

Freelance Potential

30% written by nonstaff writers. Publishes 72 freelance submissions yearly; 10% by unpublished writers, 10% by authors who are new to the magazine, 85% by experts. Receives 2 queries monthly.

Submissions

Query. Accepts hard copy and email queries to customerservice@movieguide.org. SASE. Responds in 2 months.

- Articles: 750–3,000 words. Informational articles, profiles, interviews, and opinion pieces. Topics include movies, TV, entertainment, popular culture, the arts, religion, history, education, and parenting.
- Depts/columns: Movie reviews, 500–700 words. News briefs, 300–1,200 words.

Sample Issue

46 pages. Little advertising. Sample articles available at website.

- "Exploring Tim Burton's Imagination." Article features an interview with the cast and crew of *Frankenweenie*.
- "Study Finds Family Content Helps Ad Success." Article discusses the success of advertising in family-friendly programming.

Rights and Payment

Second rights. Written material, payment rates vary. Payment policy varies. Provides 1 contributor's copy.

Mslexia

P.O. Box 656
Newcastle-Upon-Tyne NE99 1PZ
United Kingdom

Editorial Director: Debbie Taylor

Description and Interests

Mslexia is dedicated to encouraging, nurturing, and empowering women to write and get their work published. It features articles on writing, industry trends, and interviews with writers and publishers. It also accepts fiction and poetry for its New Writing section. Some of the sections have specific deadlines. Please see guidelines for information. Circ: 9,000.

Contents: Articles; depts/columns; poetry; fiction
Frequency: Quarterly
Website: www.mslexia.co.uk

Freelance Potential

60% written by nonstaff writers. Of the freelance submissions published yearly, 10% are by unpublished writers, 20% are by authors who are new to the magazine, 70% are by industry experts. Receives 24 queries monthly.

Submissions

Female writers only. Send complete ms for fiction and poetry. For all other material, query via email to submissions@mslexia.co.uk with synopsis and writing samples. Responds in 3 months.

- Articles: Word lengths vary. Informational, self-help, and how-to articles; profiles; interviews; and personal experience pieces. Topics include writing, creativity, and publishing.
- Fiction: To 2,200 words. Genres vary.
- Depts/columns: Word lengths vary. Book reviews and essays.
- Other: Poetry, to 40 lines, to 4 poems per submission. A Week of Tweets. Competitions with money prizes.

Sample Issue

74 pages. Advertising. Sample articles, guidelines, and theme list available at website.

- "Writer in the House." Article offers advice for seeking a writer-in-residence program.
- Sample dept/column: Mslexia Book Club reviews Hilary Mantel's *Bring Up the Bodies*.

Rights and Payment

Rights vary. Written material, payment rates vary. Payment policy varies

Muscle & Fitness

21100 Erwin Street
Woodland Hills, CA 91367

Editor

Description and Interests

Men and women who are serious about bodybuilding subscribe to *Muscle & Fitness*. The emphasis is on training techniques and proper nutrition to help readers reach their fitness goals. Its content fulfills two functions: information and entertainment, with special attention to how-to advice and accuracy. Queries should include a short summary of ideas, along with potential sources and author qualifications. The tone must be friendly, not academic. Circ: 400,000.

Contents: 75% articles; 25% depts/columns
Frequency: Monthly
Website: www.muscleandfitness.com

Freelance Potential

70% written by nonstaff writers. Publishes 60 freelance submissions yearly; 3% by unpublished writers, 5% by authors who are new to the magazine, 3% by experts. Receives 20 queries monthly.

Submissions

Query with clips. Accepts hard copy. SASE. Responds in 2 months.

- Articles: 800–1,800 words. Informational, self-help, and how-to articles; profiles; interviews; and humor. Topics include health, fitness, bodybuilding, injury prevention and treatment, exercise, and nutrition.
- Depts/columns: Staff-written.

Sample Issue

224 pages. Advertising. Sample copy and guidelines available.

- "Stretch Like the Pros of the NFL." Article shares the secrets of NFL players to increase flexibility.
- "M&F Iron Maiden: Natalie Pennington." Article features an interview with a bikini competitor.
- "Joe Weider Launches New Site." Article announces new site for nutrition tips, training, and bodybuilding news.

Rights and Payment

All rights. Articles, $400–$1,000. Pays on acceptance. Provides 1 contributor's copy.

MuscleMag International

400 Matheson Boulevard West
Mississauga, Ontario L5R 3M1
Canada

Editorial Director: Bill Geiger

Description and Interests

This magazine gives bodybuilders the information they need to be bigger, better, and healthier. It features articles on training techniques, diet, supplements, events, and profiles of bodybuilders. It does not shy away from the more controversial aspects of bodybuilding, such as steroid use and supplements. Health, as well as muscle growth, is emphasized. Circ: 390,000.

Contents: 50% articles; 50% depts/columns
Frequency: Monthly
Website: www.emusclemag.com

Freelance Potential

70% written by nonstaff writers. Publishes 40–50 freelance submissions yearly; 5% by authors who are new to the magazine, 95% by experts. Receives 40 queries, 5 unsolicited mss monthly.

Submissions

Prefers query; will accept complete ms with artwork (with written permission to use from photographers and models). Accepts email to editorial@musclemag.com (Word attachments). Responds in 1–2 months.

- Articles: 800–1,500 words. Informational and how-to articles, profiles, and humor. Topics include bodybuilding, strength training, health, nutrition, and fitness.
- Depts/columns: 600 words. New products, food, sexual advice, strength training tips, and gossip.
- Artwork: Digital high-resolution images.

Sample Issue

240 pages. Advertising. Sample copy available.

- "So You Think You've Got Abs?" Article features a six-week exercise guide for great abs.
- Sample dept/column: Exercise of the Month describes how to do the cable woodchop to build core strength.

Rights and Payment

All rights. Written material, payment rates vary. Artwork, $50–$400. Pays on publication.

Mushing

P.O. Box 1195
Willow, AK 99688

Publisher/Executive Editor: Greg Sellentin

Description and Interests

This magazine of "dog-powered adventure" shares the latest news on sled dog health, nutrition, behavior, and training, as well as musher profiles and interviews, trail tips, and race accounts. It considers personal experience pieces only when the experience illustrates information that is useful to mushers. Circ: 7,000.

Contents: 78% articles; 20% depts/columns; 2% fiction
Frequency: 6 times each year
Website: www.mushing.com

Freelance Potential

90% written by nonstaff writers. Publishes 60–75 freelance submissions yearly; 5% by unpublished writers, 30% by authors who are new to the magazine, 80% by experts. Receives 15 queries and unsolicited mss monthly.

Submissions

Prefers query with qualifications; will accept complete ms. Accepts hard copy, disk submissions, and email to editor@mushing.com. Responds in 2 weeks.

- Articles: 1,000–2,500 words. Informational and how-to articles, profiles, and interviews. Topics include trail tips, expeditions, races, and innovations; and sled dog history, health, behavior, and nutrition.
- Depts/columns: 500–1,000 words. News and business.
- Artwork: 8x10 B/W or color prints; 35mm or 120mm color slides; JPEG digital files.

Sample Issue

46 pages. Advertising. Sample copy, guidelines, and editorial calendar available at website.

- "The Cooks: A Family of Champions." Article profiles this family who has been breeding sled dogs for more than six decades.
- "Tolovana Roadhouse Lodge." Article shares the relaunch of historic roadhouse tours that celebrate pre-Iditarod days.

Rights and Payment

First North American serial rights. Written material, \$.08–\$.10 per word. Pays within 60 days of publication.

Mutineer Magazine

7510 Sunset Boulevard
Los Angeles, CA 90046

Editor in Chief: Brian Kropf

Description and Interests
This magazine reports on the world of fine beverages from a somewhat unconventional angle. Focusing on wine, beer, and spirits, it offers entertaining, offbeat writing about beverage products and the people who create and enjoy them. The magazine aims to be as informative as it is approachable and to have a focus on the history of beverages and their role in culture and society. Articles about food must have a tie-in to fine beverages. Circ: 25,000.

Contents: Articles; depts/columns
Frequency: 6 times each year
Website: www.mutineermagazine.com

Freelance Potential
40% written by nonstaff writers. Publishes 65 freelance submissions yearly; 21% by unpublished writers, 22% by authors who are new to the magazine, 87% by experts. Receives 20–30 queries monthly.

Submissions
Prefers query; accepts complete ms. Accepts email to editor@mutineermagazine.com. Response time varies.

- Articles: Word lengths vary. Informational and how-to articles, profiles, interviews, and new product information. Topics include beer, wine, and spirits and their history; and the role of fine beverages in society.
- Depts/columns: Word lengths vary. Opinion pieces and essays.

Sample Issue
84 pages. Sample articles available at website.

- "GABF Survival Guide." Article offers tips for making the most of one's time at the Great American Beer Festival.
- Sample dept/column: Mutineer Interview profiles the co-founders of The Alstrom Brothers.

Rights and Payment
Rights vary. Written material, $50. Pays on publication. Provides 2 contributor's copies.

Muzzle Blasts

National Muzzle Loading Rifle Association
P.O. Box 67
Friendship, IN 47021-0067

Editor: Eric A. Bye

Description and Interests
The era of muzzleloading firearms is covered in detail in this magazine for members of the National Muzzle Loading Rifle Association. It accepts historical pieces, as well as technical and instructional articles, and is always interested in submissions on hunting with traditional sidelock percussion and flintlock firearms. Simple and direct writing will appeal to the editors. How-to articles are always needed. Circ: 17,000.

Contents: 40% depts/columns; 35% articles; 5% fiction; 20% other
Frequency: Monthly
Website: www.nmlra.org

Freelance Potential
60% written by nonstaff writers. Publishes 50 freelance submissions yearly; 10% by unpublished writers, 10% by authors who are new to the magazine, 30% by experts. Receives 10 queries, 10 unsolicited mss monthly.

Submissions
Query or send complete ms. Accepts hard copy and email to nmlraweb@seidata.com. SASE. Responds in 10 days.

- Articles: 1,500 words. Informational and how-to articles, profiles, interviews, and personal experience pieces. Topics include muzzleloading firearms, history, hunting, gun-building, and rendezvous and primitive camping.
- Depts/columns: 850 words. Association news, legislative updates, product reviews.

Sample Issue
72 pages. Advertising. Sample copy, guidelines, and theme list available.

- "The Combination Gun in Pre-cartridge America."
- "Pre-1840 Folding Knives."
- "Grouseland Rifle Links Our Past and Present."

Rights and Payment
First rights. Articles, $100–$300. Depts/columns, $50–$150. Pays on publication. Provides 2 contributor's copies.

Muzzleloader

Scurlock Publishing Company
1293 Myrtle Springs Road
Texarkana, TX 75503-5006

Editor: Linda Scurlock

Description and Interests

Muzzleloader is devoted to celebrating the passion of traditional black powder shooting. In addition to firearm collecting and muzzleloading techniques, it offers articles on Early American history. Lack of proper documentation of references or illustrations are frequent reasons why it rejects manuscripts. Circ: 15,000.

Contents: 50% articles; 50% depts/columns
Frequency: 6 times each year
Website: www.muzzleloadermag.com

Freelance Potential

95% written by nonstaff writers. Publishes 48 freelance submissions yearly; 10% by unpublished writers, 20% by authors who are new to the magazine, 80% by experts. Receives 8 unsolicited mss monthly.

Submissions

Send complete ms with artwork if applicable. Accepts hard copy and disk submissions with hard copy. SASE. Responds in 6 months.

- Articles: Word lengths vary. Informational and how-to articles. Topics include black powder guns, shooting, hunting, and Early American history.
- Depts/columns: Word lengths vary. Book reviews, product information, and tips.
- Artwork: 5x7 or 8x10 B/W prints; JPEG or TIFF digital images. Line art; laser printouts.

Sample Issue

80 pages. Advertising. Sample copy and guidelines available.

- "Practical Methods for Problem Woods." Article offers tips for navigating unfamiliar woods.
- "Portals in Times." Article revisits the Lancaster rifle.

Rights and Payment

First North American serial rights. Written material, $25–$225. Pays on publication. Provides 2 contributor's copies.

Mystery Readers Journal

P.O. Box 8116
Berkeley, CA 94707

Editor: Janet A. Rudolph

Description and Interests

This publication features reviews, interviews, and essays about the genre of mystery writing. It does not publish fiction. Each issue has a theme and all articles are centered on that particular theme. Themes have included: Animal Mysteries; London Mysteries; and Hobbies, Crafts, & Special Interests. Writers need to consult the theme list on the website. It is not a scholarly publication. Writers striving for the publication's tone should think along the lines of talking to a friend about books. Circ: 2,500.

Contents: 80% articles; 20% depts/columns
Frequency: Quarterly
Website: www.mysteryreaders.org

Freelance Potential

90% written by nonstaff writers. Publishes 200 freelance submissions yearly; 5% by unpublished writers, 70% by authors who are new to the magazine, 20% by experts. Receives 20 queries monthly.

Submissions

Query or send complete ms. Accepts email queries to janet@mysteryreaders.org. Responds in 1 month.

- Articles: 1,000 words. Informational and how-to articles, profiles, interviews, and personal experience and opinion pieces. All topics relate to planned themes, each involving a different segment of the mystery genre.
- Depts/columns: 500 words. Reviews to 200 words.

Sample Issue

96 pages. No advertising. Sample articles, guidelines and theme list available at website.

- "The Curious Career of Martin H. Ehrengraf." Article tells of a novelist's experiences with researching this colorful lawyer's career.
- "For the Love of the Law." Article explains the author's love of writing and reading lawyer novels.

Rights and Payment

All North American serial rights. No payment. Provides 1 contributor's copy.

NACLA

Report on the Americas

38 Greene Street, 4th Floor
New York, NY 10013

Editor: Fred Rosen

Description and Interests

Politics, social issues, and current events, both national and international, relating to Latin America or Latin Americans in the United States are covered here. It is particularly interested in investigative articles on politics and economic developments, as well as on U.S. policy toward Latin America. Circ: 7,000.

Contents: Articles; depts/columns
Frequency: 6 times each year
Website: www.nacla.org

Freelance Potential

90% written by nonstaff writers. Publishes 60 freelance submissions yearly; 10% by unpublished writers, 20% by authors who are new to the magazine, 90% by experts. Receives 5 queries monthly.

Submissions

Query with outline and clips. Accepts email queries to fred@nacla.org (Word attachments). No simultaneous submissions. Responds in 2 weeks.

- Articles: 3,500–4,000 words. Shorter update or analysis pieces, 2,000 to 2,500 words. Topics include current events, social and political issues, education, feminism, history, and public affairs—all pertaining to Latin America and the Caribbean.
- Depts/columns: 650 or 1,300 words. News briefs, reviews, and activism reports.

Sample Issue

52 pages. Sample copy and guidelines available at website.

- "What Accounts for South America's Resilience?" Article explains why South American economies have shown a common resilience during the global economic crisis.
- Sample dept/column: Taking Note: A Rejuvenated Grassroots Movement in Columbia discusses the recent demonstrations that are leading to the new left movement in Columbia.

Rights and Payment

Reprint and electronic rights. Written material, $.12 per word. Pays on publication. Provides 5 contributor's copies.

National Enquirer

1000 American Media Way
Boca Raton, FL 33464

Editor

Description and Interests

Although it's best known for breaking news on celebrity, political, and crime scandals, *National Enquirer* also publishes articles about losing weight, consumer interests, and general interest topics. New writers shouldn't try their hand at celebrity-focused articles unless they can produce the goods from inside sources. The other topics are often a better fit when querying for the first time. Circ: 2.4 million.

Contents: 80% articles; 20% depts/columns
Frequency: Weekly
Website: www.nationalenquirer.com

Freelance Potential

30% written by nonstaff writers. Publishes 500 freelance submissions yearly; 5% by authors who are new to the magazine. Receives 500 queries monthly.

Submissions

Query with article summary and description of available artwork. Accepts email queries to letters@nationalenquirer.com. Responds in 2 weeks.

- Articles: Word lengths vary. Informational, self-help, and how-to articles; profiles; interviews; and confession and personal experience pieces. Topics include celebrities, popular culture, health, fashion, current events, and consumer interests.
- Depts/columns: Word lengths vary. Health issues, movie and television reviews, and personal stories from readers.

Sample Issue

60 pages. Advertising. Sample copy available.

- "Van Der Sloot: Reversal of Fortune?" Article provides an update of Joran Van Der Sloot's appeal trial.
- "Suri Wants to Be New Gabby." Article discusses Suri Cruise's passion for gymnastics after watching the Summer Olympics.

Rights and Payment

All North American serial rights. All material, payment rates vary. Pays on publication.

National Review

215 Lexington Avenue
New York, NY 10016

Editor: Richard Lowry

Description and Interests

This stalwart magazine for conservative politics features commentary, opinion, and analysis on current political, financial, and social issues. It's home to many conservative pundits, as well as emerging political voices. It encourages well thought-out positions and analysis and innovative writing. It is not bipartisan in its coverage, so writers should not try to "argue" for the liberal or Democratic perspective on issues. Circ: 150,000.

Contents: 70% articles; 30% depts/columns
Frequency: 24 times each year
Website: www.nationalreview.com

Freelance Potential

40% written by nonstaff writers. Publishes 200 freelance submissions yearly; 80% by experts. Receives 900 queries, 100 unsolicited mss each month.

Submissions

Query. Accepts email to submissions@nationalreview.com (no attachments). Responds in 10 days only if interested.

- Articles: Word lengths vary. Informational articles, analysis, and commentary. Topics include foreign affairs, domestic issues, social issues, politics, government, economics, and current events.
- Depts/columns: Word lengths vary. Opinion pieces, book reviews, and short news items.

Sample Issue

56 pages. Advertising. Sample article and guidelines available at website.

- "Bankrupt California." Article discusses reasonings behind high gas prices in that state.
- "A Likely List of Thursday's Debate Topics." Article reviews topics that will likely be part of the Vice Presidential debate.

Rights and Payment

All rights. Written material, $200 per printed page. Pays on publication. Provides 1+ contributor's copies.

Native Peoples

5333 North 7th Street, Suite C224
Phoenix, AZ 85014-2804

Editor: Daniel Gibson

Description and Interests

The diverse articles and photography in this magazine help foster understanding of Native American culture and its past, present, and future. Competition is stiff as the magazine receives many submissions. Writers with a unique approach to their subject are preferred. Circ: 35,000.

Contents: 40% articles; 60% depts/columns
Frequency: 6 times each year
Website: www.nativepeoples.com

Freelance Potential

95% written by nonstaff writers. Publishes 40 freelance submissions yearly; 5% by unpublished writers, 25% by authors who are new to the magazine, 70% by experts. Receives 20 queries, 2 unsolicited mss monthly.

Submissions

Prefers query; will accept complete ms. Availability of artwork improves chance of acceptance. Accepts email to editorial@nativepeoples.com. Responds in 2 months.

- Articles: 1,200–3,000 words. Informational articles and profiles. Topics include Native American art, culture, and history; current developments; people; and social issues.
- Depts/columns: Pathways, 700–1,500 words; Viewpoint, 800 words; History, 1,000–1,800 words.
- Artwork: Digital images at 300 dpi or higher. Slides, transparencies, or color prints.

Sample Issue

76 pages. Advertising. Sample copy available at website.

- "Native Couture." Article details the Indian country's fashion designers' move to the New York runway scene.
- "The New Frontier." Article discusses the proliferation of Native American-based websites.

Rights and Payment

First rights. Articles, $.25 per word. Depts/columns, payment rates vary. Pays on publication. Provides 1 contributor's copy.

Natural History

105 West Highway 54, Suite 265
Durham, NC 27713-6650

Editor in Chief: Vittorio Maestro

Description and Interests

All elements of the world's natural history are represented in this magazine, written for a general readership with an interest in the natural sciences. It features articles on prehistoric animals, evolution, society and culture, the universe, and wildlife species throughout the world. It primarily accepts work from scientists, science writers, and science journalists. Writers must be able to make thoroughly researched and documented scientific information appeal to readers. Circ: 200,000.

Contents: 50% articles; 50% depts/columns
Frequency: 10 times each year
Website: www.nhmag.com

Freelance Potential

90% written by nonstaff writers. Publishes 70 freelance submissions yearly. Receives 60 queries monthly.

Submissions

Query with writing samples. Accepts hard copy and email queries to nhmag@nhmag.com. SASE. Responds in 4–6 months.

- Articles: 1,400–2,500 words. Informational articles. Topics include archaeology, biological science, earth science, ecology, cultural and physical anthropology, and astronomy.
- Depts/columns: 800–1,500 words. Book reviews, new and ongoing research reports, astronomy, biomechanics, essays, and profiles.

Sample Issue

48 pages. Advertising. Guidelines available.

- "Red Wolf's Last Stand." Article explains how red wolves are near extinction and the process in one county to keep them alive.
- "Eat Dirt?" Article discusses connection between allergies, autoimmune diseases, and hygiene.
- Sample dept/column: Perspectives provides details on the efforts to restore alewife to the waters of Maine.

Rights and Payment

Rights vary. No payment. Provides contributor's copies upon request.

Natural Home & Garden

1503 SW 42nd Street
Topeka, KS 66609

Editor: Jessica Kellner

Description and Interests

The readers of *Natural Home & Garden* are looking to "go green" in all their living spaces. Articles feature ideas on building, furnishing, gardening, cooking, and other areas of lifestyle. Writers should think ecologically sound, sustainable, and beautiful when pitching ideas. Its readers are sophisticated and stylish, as well as "green" savvy. Circ: 157,500.

Contents: 50% articles; 50% depts/columns
Frequency: 6 times each year
Website: www.naturalhomeandgarden.com

Freelance Potential

70% written by nonstaff writers. Publishes 30–50 freelance submissions yearly; 5% by unpublished writers, 5–10% by authors who are new to the magazine, 10% by experts. Receives 50 queries monthly.

Submissions

Query. Accepts email queries to editor@naturalhomemagazine.com (Word attachments). Responds in 1–3 months.

- Articles: 1,000–2,000 words. Informational and how-to articles, profiles, interviews, and new product information. Topics include natural and sustainable building materials, alternative building systems, earth-friendly home decor and furnishings, gardening, and food.
- Depts/columns: 250–1,000 words. Natural cleaning products, energy conservation, advice on green living.

Sample Issue

96 pages. Advertising. Sample articles and guidelines available at website.

- "5 Hazardous Chemicals to Ban for a Healthy Kitchen." Article offers safer alternatives for cooking and food storage.
- "Maximize the Fall Harvest." Article explains how to extend one's growing season with a variety of flexible, inexpensive materials.

Rights and Payment

Shared non-exclusive rights. Written material, \$.33–\$.50 per word. Kill fee, 25%. Payment policy varies. Provides 2 contributor's copies.

Natural Life

P.O. Box 112
Niagara Falls, NY 14304

Editor: Wendy Priesnitz

Description and Interests

This magazine is written for an international audience of families who want progressive information about natural family living. It discusses sustainable practices and principles, and focuses especially on natural parenting, gardening, and housing. It looks for contributors who can write simply and clearly, in concise, nonacademic prose, not as professional "experts." The aim is for a style that is friendly, but not folksy. Circ: 35,000.

Contents: Articles; depts/columns
Frequency: 6 times each year
Website: www.naturallifemagazine.com

Freelance Potential

50% written by nonstaff writers. Publishes 40 freelance submissions yearly; 20% by unpublished writers, 20–30% by authors who are new to the magazine. Receives 15 queries monthly.

Submissions

Query with a detailed outline and a 50- to 200-word synopsis that highlights the article's main points, how it will benefit the reader, its timeliness and sources, and your qualifications to write it. Accepts email to editor@naturallifemagazine.com. Accepts simultaneous submissions if identified. Responds in 3–5 days.

- Articles: 1,500–2,500 words. Informational, how-to, profiles, interviews, and personal experience. Topics include green living, natural parenting, social issues, gardening, education, food and recipes, and sustainable housing.
- Depts/columns: Staff-written.
- Artwork: Color prints. High-resolution JPEG or TIFF images at 300 dpi.

Sample Issue

32 pages. Advertising. Sample copy and guidelines available at website.

- "Make Your Own Ginger Beer." Home-brewed drinks are fun, delicious, and healthy.
- "Growing Up in My Family." The author's fond memories of homeschooling and lots of pets.

Rights and Payment

Refer to the website. Receptive to bartering. Provides contributor's copies and subscription.

Naturally

P.O. Box 317
Newfoundland, NJ 07435-0317

Assistant Editor: Shem Bryant

Description and Interests

This magazine is about nude living and recreation. Each issue covers nudist destinations and resorts, personalities, and naturism news. It prefers submissions that speak to the "I can do that, I can go there" naturism attitude. Family-oriented articles are always welcome. Circ: 30,000.

Contents: 45% articles; 20% depts/columns; 35% other
Frequency: Quarterly
Website: www.internaturally.com

Freelance Potential

70% written by nonstaff writers. Publishes 40 freelance submissions yearly; 40% by unpublished writers, 40% by authors who are new to the magazine, 20% by experts. Receives 3 queries, 3 unsolicited mss each month.

Submissions

Query or send complete ms with artwork. Accepts hard copy, disk submissions, email to naturally@internaturally.com (Word attachments), and simultaneous submissions. SASE. Responds in 1–2 weeks.

- Articles: 2,000 words. Informational and how-to articles; personal experience pieces; media reviews; and new product information. Topics include naturist/nudist lifestyles, New Age issues, spiritual awareness, travel, and family.
- Depts/columns: 1,000 words. Art, news items, and travel.
- Artwork: B/W or color transparencies.

Sample Issue

58 pages. Advertising. Sample copy available. Guidelines available at website.

- "Fawlty Towers." Article reviews the new nudist hotel in Cocoa Beach.
- "Naked on Big Island, from Hiking Trails to Beaches." Article offers activity suggestions while vacationing on Hawaii's Big Island.

Rights and Payment

Assumes all rights. Pays 50% for previously published material. All material, $60 per page. Pays on publication. Provides 1 contributor's copy.

Naval History

U.S. Naval Institute
291 Wood Road
Annapolis, MD 21402-5034

Editor in Chief: Richard Latture

Description and Interests

American naval history buffs can find everything they seek in the pages of *Naval History*, from personal accounts of battles at sea to profiles of naval ships and the men who sailed them. Photo-essays and book reviews are commissioned by the magazine. The best way to break into *Naval History* is to identify a good story with drama, humor, irony, or emotion. Circ: 33,000.

Contents: 50% articles; 50% depts/columns
Frequency: 6 times each year
Website: www.usni.org

Freelance Potential

90% written by nonstaff writers. Publishes 40 freelance submissions yearly; 75% by authors who are new to the magazine. Receives 30–40 queries monthly.

Submissions

Prefers query with brief bio and clips; will accept complete ms with annotations, art suggestions, and author bio. Accepts disk submissions with hard copy and email to articlesubmissions@usni.org (attach files). For In Contact, accepts email to commentsanddiscussion@usni.org and faxes to 410-295-1049. Response time varies.

- Articles: To 3,500 words. Informational articles, essays, scholarly analyses, and personal experience pieces. Topics include U.S. naval and maritime history.
- Depts/columns: Word lengths vary. Book reviews, photo-essays, and anecdotes.

Sample Issue

76 pages. Advertising. Sample copy and guidelines available at website.

- "The Soviet Navy's Caribbean Outpost." Article reveals the lasting presence of Soviet forces in Cuba long after the Cuban Missile Crisis.
- Sample dept/column: Historic Aircraft profiles the Aeromarine's Model 39.

Rights and Payment

Rights vary. Articles, $60–$150 per 1,000 words. Book reviews, $75. Anecdotes, $25 each. Pays on publication.

The Neo-Independent 

400 CPW #2R
New York, NY 10025

Editor: Omar H. Ali

Description and Interests

Dedicated to covering the vision, history, issues, people, and politics of the independent voting movement and how it is reshaping American politics, this ezine features analysis, reporting, and opinion. Writers who have experience covering politics and who are familiar with the independent movement are needed. It is always looking for on-the-ground coverage of independents across the country and ways they are pushing state and local officials to advance the independent political reform agenda. Hits per month: 5,000.

Contents: 90% articles; 10% depts/columns
Frequency: 2–3 times each year
Website: www.neoindependent.com

Freelance Potential

20% written by nonstaff writers. Publishes several freelance submissions yearly; 5% by unpublished writers, 40% by authors who are new to the magazine, 90% by experts. Receives 1–2 queries monthly.

Submissions

Query. Accepts email to ohali@uncg.edu. Response time varies.

- Articles: 800–1,200 words. Informational and factual articles, and opinion pieces. Topics include politics, voting, American government, legislation, activism, and history.
- Depts/columns: Staff-written.

Sample Issue

No advertising. Sample issue available at website.

- "The Fight for Open Primaries in Kentucky." Article features an interview with Senator Jimmy Higdon on the fight for open primaries.
- "How to Turn Republicans and Democrats into Americans." Opinion piece about the changes to elections and government that will have people, not parties, in control of government.

Rights and Payment

Rights vary. Written material, payment rates vary. Payment policy varies.

Neurology Now

333 Seventh Avenue, 19th Floor
New York, NY 10001

Managing Editor: Michael Smolinsky

Description and Interests

Focusing its editorial on healthy living topics for neurology patients and their caregivers, *Neurology Now* also covers diseases and news of treatments. Its profiles spotlight patients who provide inspiration for living with a neurological disease. New writers have the best chance of acceptance with essays. Circ: 480,000.

Contents: 50% articles; 40% depts/columns; 10% other
Frequency: 6 times each year
Website: www.neurologynow.com

Freelance Potential

75% written by nonstaff writers. Of the freelance submissions published yearly; 2% are by unpublished writers, 5% are by authors who are new to the magazine, 5% are by experts. Receives 5 queries monthly.

Submissions

Query. Accepts email to mike.smolinsky@ wolterskluwer.com. Responds in 2 months.

- Articles: 600–1,500 words. Informational, self-help, and how-to articles; profiles; interviews; and personal experience pieces. Topics include living with, treatments for, and research into neurological disorders.
- Depts/columns: Word lengths vary. Living Well, Penny Wise, Eye on Therapy, New Frontiers, Waiting Room, and Speak Up.
- Other: Poetry.

Sample Issue

40 pages. Advertising. Sample copy and guidelines available at website.

- "One Precious Gift." Article discusses how brain donations can help answer questions, as well as help science.
- "Serious Laughs." Article features an interview with comedian Josh Blue about living with cerebral palsy.

Rights and Payment

All rights. Articles and depts/columns, $.75 per word. Poetry and essays, $100. Kill fee, 25%. Pays on acceptance. Provides 1 contributor's copy.

Nimrod International Journal

University of Tulsa
800 South Tucker Drive
Tulsa, OK 74104

Editor in Chief: Francine Ringold

Description and Interests

Dedicated to the discovery of new voices in literature, *Nimrod International Journal* publishes high quality fiction and poetry in each themed issue. It has been continuously published by the University of Tulsa since 1956. The mission is to discover and support new writing of vigor and quality. In each issue, the work of established writers appears alongside that of emerging writers of quality. Michael Blumenthal, Mark Doty, and Sue Monk Kidd are some of the authors whose work has appeared in *Nimrod*. Circ: 4,000.

Contents: 50% fiction; 50% poetry
Frequency: Twice each year
Website: www.utulsa.edu/nimrod

Freelance Potential

98% written by nonstaff writers. Publishes 125 freelance submissions yearly; 15% by unpublished writers, 70% by authors who are new to the magazine. Receives 250 unsolicited mss each month.

Submissions

Send complete ms between January 1 and November 30. Accepts hard copy and simultaneous submissions if identified. No email submissions. SASE. Responds in 1-3 months.

- Fiction: To 7,500 words. Literary, mainstream, and contemporary fiction.
- Poetry: 3–10 pages. All forms.

Sample Issue

200 pages. Little advertising. Sample copy and theme list available. Writer's guidelines available at website.

- "The Tarot of Lost Names." Story about a Romanian family fleeing poverty and disgrace for a new life in a new land.
- "Departures." Story follows a woman on her journey from Armenia to the prairie lands of Kansas.

Rights and Payment

First rights. No payment. Provides 2 contributor's copies.

North American Hunter

12301 Whitewater Drive
Minnetonka, MN 55343

Managing Editor: Dave Maas

Description and Interests

This official publication of the North American Hunting Club covers the "how-to's" and "where-to's" of hunting deer, moose, and turkeys in the U.S. and Canada. It also provides club news and new product information. Writers who are new have the best chance of acceptance with a query targeted to one of the member-focused sections. Please include high-quality slides or illustrations with a query letter. Circ: 850,000.

Contents: 60% articles; 40% depts/columns
Frequency: 8 times each year
Website: www.huntingclub.com

Freelance Potential

60% written by nonstaff writers.

Submissions

Query with artwork. Accepts email queries to dmaas@namginc.com. Response time varies.

- Articles: 2,000 words. Informational and how-to articles, profiles, interviews, and personal experience pieces. Topics include hunting, conservation, and wildlife.
- Depts/columns: Word lengths vary. New product information, gear reviews, member news, and opinion pieces.
- Artwork: Color slides; digital images at 300 dpi.

Sample Issue

124 pages. Advertising. Sample copy available at website. Writer's guidelines and editorial calendar available.

- "Metro Muleys." Article discusses the increasing occurrences of mule deers living in the middle of towns.
- "High Rollers." Article explains how moving higher up in altitude can result in more successful elk hunting.

Rights and Payment

First serial rights. Articles, $700. Depts/columns, $600. Artwork, payment rates vary. Pays on acceptance. Provides contributor's copies.

North American Whitetail

2250 Newmarket Parkway, Suite 110
Marietta, GA 30067

Editor: Patrick Hogan

Description and Interests

Written for the serious trophy deer hunter, this photo-filled magazine shares information on deer management, advanced hunting strategies, and world-class trophy hunts. It welcomes short nostalgic and humorous essays on whitetail hunting. Circ: 150,000.

Contents: 70% articles; 25% depts/columns; 5% fiction
Frequency: 8 times each year
Website: www.northamericanwhitetail.com

Freelance Potential

85% written by nonstaff writers. Publishes 40–50 freelance submissions yearly; 30% by unpublished writers, 30% by authors who are new to the magazine, 60% by experts. Receives 50 queries, 15 unsolicited mss monthly.

Submissions

Query or send complete ms with artwork. Accepts hard copy and email queries to whitetail@imoutdoors.com. SASE. Responds in 1 month.

- Articles: 1,500–2,300 words. Informational and how-to articles, profiles, interviews, and personal experience pieces. Topics include hunting tactics, trophy whitetails, wildlife management, firearms, and ammunition.
- Fiction: 1,000 words. Humorous hunting fiction.
- Depts/columns: Word lengths vary. News and essays.
- Artwork: Color prints or slides; JPEG or TIFF images at 300 dpi or higher.

Sample Issue

80 pages. Advertising. Sample articles and guidelines available at website. Guidelines available.

- "Best Deer Season Ever?" Personal experience piece about a bow hunter scoring two bucks in one season.
- "8 Tricky Deer Hunting Regulations." Article provides details on some of the stricter state regulations.

Rights and Payment

First North American serial rights. Written material, $200–$400. Kill fee varies. Pays 60 days before publication. Provides 1 contributor's copy.

Nostalgia Magazine

P.O. Box 8466
Spokane, WA 99203

Editor: Stephanie Regalado-Hertel

Description and Interests
Publishing ageless stories and photos that make the past come alive, *Nostalgia* recaptures life before the 1970s in Washington State and North Idaho. It's filled with stories and photography depicting experiences and memories of days gone by, including childhood and teen years. The journal includes personal remembrances and diaries and well-researched articles. Often, a treasured photo can be the start of a great story, whether that involves famous people you grew up with, interesting towns, or memorable events. Circ: 25,000.

Contents: Articles; depts/columns
Frequency: 6 times each year
Website: www.nostalgiamagazine.net

Freelance Potential
95% written by nonstaff writers. Publishes 80 freelance submissions yearly; 50% by unpublished writers, 90% by authors who are new to the magazine, 5% by experts. Receives 20 queries monthly.

Submissions
Accepts hard copy but prefers email submissions to editor@nostalgiamagazine.net. Include contact information, brief bio, and submission agreement downloaded from website. Include one photo for every 400 words of text. Availability of artwork improves chance of acceptance.

- Articles: 400–2,000 words. Informational, photo-essays, and personal experience pieces. Topics include nostalgia and lifestyles of the mid-twentieth century.
- Depts/columns: Yesterday's Kitchen and Love Stories, word lengths vary.
- Artwork: Photo originals will be scanned and returned. If sending on CD, scan at least 300 dpi resolution.

Sample Issue
48 pages. Little advertising. Sample copy available. Guidelines and submission agreement form available at website.

- "A Youthful Passion for Fun." Playing polo on Harleys in Spokane.
- "Simply Skating." Roller skating rinks in the 1950s.

Rights and Payment
Author retains rights. No payment. Provides 2 copies and bylined publication on website.

Nude & Natural

The Naturist Society
627 Bay Shore Drive, Suite 200
Oshkosh, WI 54901

Publisher: Nicky Hoffman Lee

Description and Interests
Published by the Naturist Society, this magazine focuses on destinations, activities, and lifestyle stories for nudists. While writers don't have to be a nudist to write for the magazine, they must be comfortable and familiar with the culture of nudity. Public land destination features are always needed. Circ: 20,000.

Contents: Articles; depts/columns
Frequency: Quarterly
Website: www.naturistsociety.com

Freelance Potential
50% written by nonstaff writers. Publishes 40+ freelance submissions yearly; 10% by unpublished writers, 10% by authors who are new to the magazine, 50% by experts. Receives 120 queries, 120 unsolicited mss yearly.

Submissions
Query or send complete ms with author bio. Prefers email to nickyh@naturistsociety.com (Word, RTF, or text attachments); will accept zip disk or CD submissions and simultaneous submissions if identified. Availability of artwork improves chance of acceptance. Materials are not returned. Responds in 1–2 months.

- Articles: 1,000–2,000 words. Informational articles, profiles, and personal experience pieces. Topics include travel, nudist venues and activities, pioneering naturists, and naturist philosophy.
- Depts/columns: Staff-written.
- Artwork: Digital images at 300 dpi or higher; color slides or prints. Line drawings.

Sample Issue
80 pages. Advertising. Sample articles and guidelines available at website.

- "Can't Wreck Her Beach." Article interviews Judy Williams, an activist who has fought to keep a popular beach natural and open to all.
- "Running in Circles Naked." Personal experience piece about author's first-ever naked 5K.

Rights and Payment
First serial rights. Written material, no payment. Artwork, $25–$250. Pays on publication. Provides 1 contributor's copy.

Ocean Magazine

P.O. Box 84
Rodanthe, NC 27968

Publisher: Diane Buccheri

Description and Interests

Ocean Magazine publishes articles and stories, essays, poems, and photography to celebrate and advocate the protection of the ocean. Pieces written with integrity and depth will get the editor's attention. Writers should become familiar with *Ocean* and its style before submitting manuscripts. Circ: 40,000.

Contents: 65% articles; 25% poetry;
Frequency: Quarterly
Website: www.oceanmagazine.org

Freelance Potential

75% written by nonstaff writers. Publishes 40–50 freelance submissions yearly; 10% by unpublished writers, 25% by authors who are new to the magazine, 50% by experts. Receives 100+ unsolicited mss monthly.

Submissions

Send complete ms with author bio. Accepts email to diane@oceanmagazine.org (no attachments) or via the website. Responds in 2 months.

- Articles: Word lengths vary. Informational articles, profiles, interviews, essays, and personal experience pieces. Topics include the ocean, marine life, conservation, current events, social issues, health, history, the environment, and recreation.
- Artwork: Digital images at 300 dpi.
- Other: Poetry.

Sample Issue

80 pages. Advertising. Sample copy available. Guidelines available at website.

- "Edge of the Eternal Sea." Article shares the contrast between the beauty of the Gulf of Mexico and the menacing oil rigs that loom there.
- "Tallulah." Article describes one of the unfortunate casualties of the BP oil spill.

Rights and Payment

One-time rights. All material, payment rates vary. Pays on publication. Provides 2 contributor's copies.

Ocean Navigator

58 Fore Street
Portland, ME 04101

Editor: Tim Queeney

Description and Interests

Marine navigation and ocean voyaging in sailboats and yachts are the focus of this magazine, read by experienced boaters. It covers boating news, racing events, navigation and boating techniques, and in-depth profiles of new boat designs. Articles should answer a question, provide valuable voyaging information, or share a voyaging experience that will teach and inspire readers. Circ: 41,000.

Contents: 50% articles; 15% depts/columns; 35% other
Frequency: 7 times each year
Website: www.oceannavigator.com

Freelance Potential

60% written by nonstaff writers. Publishes 100 freelance submissions yearly; 10% by unpublished writers, 20% by authors who are new to the magazine. Receives 18 queries, 12 unsolicited mss monthly.

Submissions

Query. Accepts hard copy, Macintosh disk submissions, email queries to tqueeney@oceannavigator.com, and simultaneous submissions. SASE. Responds in 1–2 months.

- Articles: 1,800+ words. Informational and how-to articles, personal experience pieces, and new product information. Topics include seamanship, marine issues, racing, yacht design, and ocean voyaging.
- Depts/columns: Word lengths vary. Maintenance tips, navigational topics, and news.

Sample Issue

56 pages. Advertising. Sample copy and guidelines available.

- "On Going Aground." Article shares what the author has learned living full-time aboard a 47-foot ketch.
- "A Hop, Skip, and a Jump to Panama." Article describes a late fall trip from the U.S. East Coast to Panama.

Rights and Payment

First North American serial rights. Written material, $.20–$.25 per word. Kill fee, $150–$200. Pays on publication.

Off Track Planet 

68 Jay Street, Suite 415
Brooklyn, NY 11201

Editor in Chief: Anna Starostinetskaya

Description and Interests

The concept for *Off Track Planet* was created by a group of travelers staying at a youth hostel. They decided to create a magazine, website, and social community where young people could share the wonders of traveling the globe. It works with young, professional travel writers as well as young folks who have experiences and advice on youth travel to share. *Off Track Planet*'s prime audience is college students and recent college grads and its tone is brash and edgy with tongue-in-cheek humor. Circ: 600,000.

Contents: Articles; depts/columns
Frequency: Quarterly
Website: www.offtrackplanet.com

Freelance Potential

Puts out calls for travel writers and contract freelancers.

Submissions

Query. Site requires registration. Accepts emails to contact@offtrackplanet.com.

- Articles: Word lengths vary. Topics include destinations, budget travel, culture, and events and festivals around the world.
- Depts/columns: Word lengths vary. Hostel reviews, advice, volunteer and study abroad.

Sample Issue

Sample articles available at website.

- "Getting Drunk with Locals: 10 Best Local Bars in Madrid." Article reports on the top hotspots in the city that are the favorites of locals.
- "10 Sexiest Germans of All Times." Article profiles the top 10 list which includes models, athletes, and other celebrities.
- "Carnivale It Up." Article describes the world-known festival in Rio de Janeiro.

Rights and Payment

All rights. Payment rates and policy vary.

OnEarth

Natural Resources Defense Council
40 West 20th Street
New York, NY 10011

Editor: Douglas Barasch

Description and Interests

A mix of investigative pieces, profiles, essays, poetry, and book reviews appear in this environmental magazine. It seeks to explore challenges and ultimately the solutions that will improve one's home, health, community, and future. The magazine prides itself on publishing some of the best environmental writers in the business. Circ: 175,000.

Contents: 80% articles; 20% depts/columns
Frequency: Quarterly
Website: www.onearth.org

Freelance Potential

98% written by nonstaff writers. Publishes 30 freelance submissions yearly; 10% by unpublished writers, 50% by authors who are new to the magazine, 30% by experts. Receives 9 queries monthly.

Submissions

Query up to 500 words, with clips or writing samples and résumé. Submit through contact form at website or email queries to onearth@nrdc.org. No simultaneous submissions. Responds in 2 months.

- Articles: 200–5,000 words. Informational and investigative articles, essays, profiles, interviews, and humor. Topics include environmental issues, politics, science, nature, wildlife, culture, and health.
- Depts/columns: Word lengths vary. News, reviews, and organization updates.

Sample Issue

64 pages. No advertising. Sample copy available at website. Guidelines and theme list available.

- "Can the Cruise Industry Clean Up Its Act?" Article reports on the environmental contradictions within the cruise industry.
- "How Cool Is That?" Article discusses Norway's plan to build an energy efficient data center underground.

Rights and Payment

First North American serial rights. Written material, payment rates vary. Pays on publication.

On Mission

4200 North Point Parkway
Alpharetta, GA 30022

Managing Editor: Joe Conway

Description and Interests

With a tight focus on missions and creative outreach ideas for churches, *On Mission* magazine is dedicated to helping church leaders and lay people share Christ in the real world. It counts on freelancers to bring interesting stories of faith and outreach. Circ: 200,000.

Contents: 58% articles; 31% depts/columns; 11% other
Frequency: Quarterly
Website: www.onmission.com

Freelance Potential

70% written by nonstaff writers. Publishes 15 freelance submissions yearly; 2% by unpublished writers, 30% by authors who are new to the magazine, 35% by experts. Receives 20 queries monthly.

Submissions

Query with résumé. Accepts email queries to onmission@namb.net. Responds in 1 month.

- Articles: 600–1,200 words. Informational and how-to articles, profiles, interviews, creative nonfiction, humor, and personal experience pieces. Topics include religion; spirituality; mission work; the arts; careers; entertainment; medical care; and multicultural, social, and ethnic issues.
- Depts/columns: Word lengths vary. Mission stories, Southern Baptist Convention news.
- Artwork: Digital images at 300 dpi.

Sample Issue

22 pages. Advertising. Sample copy and guidelines available at website.

- "Mobilize Me." Article explains how to get one's church involved in North American missions.
- "Called to Be Sent." Article describes how two couples came to a mission in the Northeast.
- Sample dept/column: The Pulse is a personal experience piece about relocating to another state to plant a church.

Rights and Payment

First North American serial rights. Written material, $.25 per word. Artwork, payment rates vary. Kill fee varies. Pays on acceptance. Provides 5 contributor's copies.

Ontario Out of Doors

4601 Guthrie Drive
P.O. Box 8500
Peterborough, Ontario K9J 0B4
Canada

Editor in Chief: Lezlie Goodwin

Description and Interests

Outdoor fun in the natural environs of Ontario is the focus of this magazine. It puts an emphasis on outdoor recreation as it relates to hunting and fishing. All topics related to these subjects and to wildlife are welcome, but articles must be related to the region. Circ: 90,000.

Contents: 60% articles; 40% depts/columns
Frequency: 10 times each year
Website: www.ontariooutofdoors.com

Freelance Potential

90% written by nonstaff writers. Of the freelance submissions published yearly; 5% are by authors who are new to the magazine, 95% are by established writers. Receives 14 queries monthly.

Submissions

Query. Prefers email queries to lezlie.goodwin@oodmag.com; will accept hard copy with disk submissions. SAE/IRC. Responds in 2–4 months.

- Articles: 1,000–2,400 words. Informational and how-to articles, profiles, and personal experience pieces. Topics include hunting, fishing, wildlife issues and management, camping, boating, and recreational vehicles.
- Depts/columns: News items, 50–250 words. Outdoor tips, 50–250 words.

Sample Issue

66 pages. Advertising. Sample copy, guidelines, and editorial calendar available.

- "Elk and Guinness Pie." Article shares a recipe for Guinness Pie using different types of game.
- "Beastie Bass (and more) of the East." Article profiles the fishing opportunities on Lake Erie.

Rights and Payment

First North American serial rights. Written material, approximately $.50 per word. Kill fee, varies. Pays on publication.

Orion

The Orion Society
187 Main Street
Great Barrington, MA 01230

Submissions Editor

Description and Interests
This magazine of "nature, culture, and place" accepts forward-thinking essays, photo-essays, and articles about the challenges and opportunities that lie ahead for people and nature. It only accepts submissions during reading periods specified at the website. Circ: 22,000.

Contents: 60% articles; 20% depts/columns; 20% other
Frequency: 6 times each year
Website: www.orionmagazine.org

Freelance Potential
95–100% written by nonstaff writers. Publishes 84 freelance submissions yearly; 5% by unpublished writers, 40% by authors who are new to the magazine. Receives 50 unsolicited mss each month.

Submissions
Accepts submissions 3 times a year during designated submission windows; only 1 submission per reading period. No unsolicited poetry. Prefers electronic submissions via website; will accept hard copy and simultaneous submissions. Availability of artwork improves chance of acceptance. Responds in 3 months.

- Articles: 1,500–6,000 words. Informational articles, essays, narrative nonfiction, profiles, interviews, and photo-essays. Topics include conservation, ecology, and wildlife.
- Depts/columns: 350–1,200 words. Eco news, opinions, sustainable living, essays, book reviews.
- Other: Poetry.
- Artwork: Digital images.

Sample Issue
80 pages. No advertising. Sample articles and guidelines available at website.

- "The Independent." Article features a profile of long-time Vermont Senator Bernie Sanders.
- Sample dept/column: The Wastelander is an essay about growing up in a small town on the Mississippi River.

Rights and Payment
First North American serial and electronic rights. Articles, $400–$1,000. Depts/columns, $50–$450. Artwork, payment rates vary. Pays on publication. Provides 2 contributor's copies.

Outdoor Canada

Quarto Communications
54 St. Patrick Street
Toronto, Ontario M5T 1V1
Canada

Submissions: Sandra Cheung

Description and Interests
Showcasing Canada's great outdoors, this magazine covers Canada's traditional outdoor sports of hunting and fishing. It also offers in-depth reporting on conservation issues. Service pieces must provide the latest, most reliable information; features should be well researched and original. Writers should be experts on their subjects, with queries relating to Canada only. Circ: 90,000.

Contents: 65% articles; 35% depts/columns
Frequency: 6 times each year
Website: www.outdoorcanada.ca

Freelance Potential
85% written by nonstaff writers. Publishes 20–30 freelance submissions yearly; 95% by experts.

Submissions
Query. Accepts hard copy. SAE/IRC. Responds in 3 months.

- Articles: 2,000–4,000 words. Informational and how-to articles, personal experience pieces, travelogues, and new product information. Topics include fishing, hunting, wildlife conservation, and Canada's natural heritage.
- Depts/columns: Word lengths vary. Primer, Sage Advice, and Field Guide, 500 words; Getaways, 50 words; Outdoor Smarts, 200 words; Fair Game and Waypoint, 700 words.
- Artwork: High-resolution digital files.

Sample Issue
84 pages. Advertising. Sample articles and guidelines available at website.

- "Where to Hunt Turkey in Ontario." Article provides details on the best places to hunt autumn turkeys.
- "8 Best Ice Fishing Tactics." Article offers tips for navigating ice to get more and bigger fish.

Rights and Payment
One-time rights. Written material, $.50+ per word; 10% more for non-exclusive rights for possible reuse across Quarto media properties. Pays on acceptance. Provides 2 contributor's copies.

Outside

400 Market Street
Santa Fe, NM 87501

Features Editor: Elizabeth Hightower

Description and Interests

The mission of *Outside* is to inspire active participation in adventure activities. It wants depth and range on articles from fitness and environmental activities to sports, recreation, environmental issues. science, and politics. The monthly also covers gear and apparel. Readers are as likely to be Northeasterners as Westerners. Circ: 675,000.

Contents: 80% articles; 20% depts/columns
Frequency: Monthly
Website: www.outsideonline.com

Freelance Potential

70% written by nonstaff writers. 15–20% of queries accepted.

Submissions

Query with clips and brief author bio. Departments offer the best opportunities for breaking in. All queries should inspire adventure. Accepts hard copy and email queries to ehightower@outsidemag.com. SASE. Responds in 6–8 weeks, for queries, 3 months for photos.

- Articles: 1,500–5,000 words. Informational and how-to articles; profiles; and interviews. Topics include outdoor activities, sports and adventure, travel, the environment, events, and seasonal activities.
- Depts/columns: 1,000–1,500 words. Dispatches and Bodywork are break-in departments.. News, short profiles, destinations, gear reviews.
- Photos: Original slides and prints, 35mm or larger by mail.

Sample Issue

Advertising. Sample articles and guidelines available at website.

- "Take Two Hours of Pine Forest and Call Me in the Morning." Researchers are finding that time outside can lower blood pressure, fight off depression, and even prevent cancer.
- Sample dept/column: Our Favorite Places explores the ocean town of Seaside, Oregon and the many outdoor activities it offers.

Rights and Payment

First North American serial and electronic rights. Written material, $1.50 per word. Kill fee, 25%. Pays on publication.

Oxygen

400 Matheson Boulevard West
Mississauga, Ontario L5R 3M1
Canada

Editor: Stacy Kennedy

Description and Interests

This publication's primary market is U.S. women ages 18–35 who are into intense physical fitness training. Its focus is weight lifting, cardio, and a strict eating regimen for weight loss and strength. Writers should read a complete issue, then query the appropriate editor with an idea. Circ: 360,000.

Contents: 50% articles; 50% depts/columns
Frequency: Monthly
Website: www.oxygenmag.com

Freelance Potential

75% written by nonstaff writers. Publishes 60 freelance submissions yearly; 5% by unpublished writers, 20% by authors who are new to the magazine, 30% by experts. Receives 60 queries monthly.

Submissions

Query with 1-page outline and 2 writing samples. Prefers email to editorial@oxygenmag.com; will accept hard copy. SAE/IRC. Response time varies.

- Articles: 1,200–2,000 words. Informational, self-help, and how-to articles, personal experience pieces, and profiles. Topics include health, fitness, sports, recreation, nutrition, weight loss, workout, routines, athletes, coaches, medical news, and fitness success stories.
- Depts/columns: Word lengths vary. Training tips, nutrition, health, fashion and beauty, product reviews, fitness news, motivation, and reader profiles.

Sample Issue

154 pages. Advertising. Sample articles available at website. Guidelines available.

- "Future of Fitness." Article profiles a former U.S. Army Sergeant and her secrets to staying fit and healthy.
- Sample dept/column: Health & Nutrition offers tips for slowing down one's eating.

Rights and Payment

First print and electronic rights. Written material, $.50 per word. Pays on acceptance. Provides 1 contributor's copy.

Pacific Standard  

804 Anacapa St.
Santa Barbara, CA 93102

Editor: Maria Streshinsky

Description and Interests
Pacific Standard is an online publisher that provides a research-driven, unique perspective into the social, political, and economic forces defining the world from the perspective of the Pacific, the U.S. and beyond. The emphasis is on fact-based, research-driven content, including articles on the global economy, environmental issues, education, and health care issues. Writers should combine great reportage and style. Circ: 115,000.

Contents: Articles; depts/columns
Frequency: 6 times each year
Website: http://www.psmag.com

Freelance Potential
75% witten by nonstaff writers.

Submissions
Accepts queries via email to editor@psmag.com. Journalistic skills are important to the website and the bimonthly print magazine.

- Articles:: Word lengths vary. Informational articles. Topics include global economy, social issues, health, and science, often with a focus on the Pacific Rim and the people who live there.

Sample Issue
Advertising. Sample articles and guidelines available at website.

- "How the U.S. Accidentally Helped China Get Ahead in Space." Now that America's space program is looking uncertain, China's is poised to take the lead.
- "The Music Man." Steven Angel uses drumming to teach literacy.

Rights and Payment
Purchases 120 days exclusive rights; rights are shared after that. Written material, $.50–$1.50 per word. Kill fee: 25%. Pays on acceptance.

Paint Horse Journal

P.O. Box 961023
Fort Worth, TX 76161-0023

Managing Editor: Jessica Hein

Description and Interests
Written for those who own, breed, race, or simply love Paint Horses, this magazine features articles about the breed, training, and showing. It also profiles the farms, racers, breeders, and competitions. It is the publication of the American Paint Horse Association. Long, rambling essays will be rejected, as will opinion pieces or articles that have not been carefully researched or that contain factual errors. Editors look for an accurate presentation of information written in an interesting manner. Circ: 20,000.

Contents: 60% articles; 40% depts/columns
Frequency: Monthly
Website: www.painthorsejournal.com

Freelance Potential
30% written by nonstaff writers. Publishes 12–14 freelance submissions yearly; 5% by unpublished writers, 2% by authors who are new to the magazine, 80% by experts. Receives 10 queries monthly.

Submissions
Query with availability of artwork. Accepts email to jhein@alpha.com. Response time varies.

- Articles: 1,000–2,000 words. Informational and how-to articles, profiles, and interviews. Topics include breeding, training, riding, showing, and caring for Paint Horses; breed history; equine health; and outdoor activities.
- Depts/columns: Staff-written.
- Artwork: 35mm color prints or slides; high-resolution digital images.

Sample Issue
232 pages. Advertising. Sample articles and guidelines available at website.

- "Learning Curve." Article explains how to lay a solid foundation for a young horse's future riding career.
- "A Legacy Honored." Article introduces the first 50 inductees into the APHA Hall of Fame.

Rights and Payment
First-time rights. Feature articles, $150–$500. Shorter articles, $35–$150. Pays on acceptance. Provides contributor's copies upon request.

Parabola

Society for the Study of Myth and Tradition
20 West 20th Street, 2nd Floor
New York, NY 10011

Managing Editor: Dale Fuller

Description and Interests

Parabola is a journal of articles and essays that explore the meaning of the world's myths, symbols, and rituals. Each issue is organized around a theme. It looks for lively material unencumbered by jargon or academic argument and prefers well-researched pieces that are grounded in one or more cultures or religions. Circ: 19,300.

Contents: 80% articles; 8% depts/columns; 12% other
Frequency: Quarterly
Website: www.parabola.org

Freelance Potential

80% written by nonstaff writers. Publishes 120 freelance submissions yearly; 20% by unpublished writers, 50% by authors who are new to the magazine, 70% by experts. Receives 25 queries monthly.

Submissions

Query with 1-page letter, author background, and publishing credits. Accepts email queries to editorial@parabola.org (no attachments). Response time varies.

- Articles: 1,000–3,000 words. Informational articles, essays, and translations. Topics include rites of passage, ceremonies, sacred space, humor, hospitality, ritual, prayer, and meditation.
- Depts/columns: 500–1,500 words, retelling of traditional stories. Book, performance, or media reviews, 500 words.
- Other: Poetry, to five poems. Accepts email only to poetry@parabola.org (Word, .txt, or RTF attachments).

Sample Issue

128 pages. Advertising. Sample articles, guidelines, and theme list available at website.

- "Seeing and the Yoga Sutra." Article discusses the meaning of the freedom of seeing in the Yoga Sutras.
- "Digging Deeper." Article offers an interview with writer Mark Boal.

Rights and Payment

Rights vary. Articles, \$150–\$400. Depts/columns, \$75. Pays on publication. Provides 2 contributor's copies.

Parade

711 Third Avenue, 7th Floor
New York, NY 10017

Articles Editor: Megan Brown

Description and Interests

Distributed nationwide as an insert in more than 600 Sunday newspapers, this magazine reaches a diverse audience with general interest articles and celebrity interviews. It accepts articles that will appeal to a broad audience, so the idea should have a perspective that will draw in the most readers. Circ: 32.2 million.

Contents: 50% articles; 50% depts/columns
Frequency: Weekly
Website: www.parade.com

Freelance Potential

90% written by nonstaff writers. Publishes 50 freelance submissions yearly; 20% by authors who are new to the magazine, 10% by experts. Receives 100 queries monthly.

Submissions

Query with source list, publishing credits, and writing samples. Accepts hard copy. SASE. Responds in 1 month.

- Articles: 1,200–1,500 words. Informational, how-to, and self-help articles; profiles; and interviews. Topics include celebrities, entertainment, relationships, family life, parenting, government, public affairs, current events, health, fitness, house and home, medicine, multicultural and ethnic issues, science, technology, recreation, travel, social issues, and education.
- Depts/columns: Staff-written.

Sample Issue

36 pages. Advertising. Sample articles available at website. Guidelines available.

- "Why So Many Parents Are Delaying or Skipping Vaccinations." Article reports on this growing trend and the sometimes tragic results.
- "Colin Powell: Kindness Works." Essay shares the former Secretary of State's views on passing along kindness.

Rights and Payment

First serial rights. Written material, payment rates vary. Pays on acceptance. Provides 2 contributor's copies.

Parameters

U.S. Army War College
Attn: Public Affairs Office
122 Forbes Avenue
Carlisle, PA 17013-5238

Editor: Col. Robert H. Taylor, USA Ret.

Description and Interests

Parameters is a referred journal of mature thought on the art and science of land warfare, military strategy, and national and international security affairs. Writers should avoid bureaucratic jargon. Dullness is not to be synonymous with learnedness; its readers appreciate lively and engaging writing. Circ: 14,500.

Contents: 80% articles; 20% depts/columns
Frequency: Quarterly
Website: www.carlisle.army.mil/usawc/parameters

Freelance Potential

89% written by nonstaff writers. Publishes 31 freelance submissions yearly; 65% by authors who are new to the magazine, 100% by experts. Receives 20 unsolicited mss monthly.

Submissions

Send complete ms with biography for articles. Prefers email submissions to usarmy.carlisle.awc.mbx.parameters@mail.mil (attach file); will accept hard copy with disk. No simultaneous submissions. SASE. Responds in 1–2 months.

- Articles: 4,500–5,000 words. Informational and analytical articles. Topics include military doctrine, operations, strategy, morality, leadership, weaponry, and specific wars.
- Depts/columns: Commentary on previously published articles, to 1,000 words. From the Archives, historical vignettes, 400 words. Book reviews and review essays, by assignment only.

Sample Issue

144 pages. No advertising. Sample articles and guidelines available at website.

- "The European Debt Crisis and American Security Policy." Article discusses the European Union's efforts to play a larger role in global security affairs.
- "Fear and Outrage as Terrorist Goals." Article examines the definition, diversity, and dynamics of terrorism.

Rights and Payment

One-time rights. Written material, payment rates vary. Pays on publication. Provides 2 contributor's copies.

Parenting

2 Park Avenue, 10th Floor
New York, NY 10016

Submissions Editor

Description and Interests

Parenting covers all stages of child development from infants through tweens. It also features articles on family matters, such as finances, nutrition, and mom and dad time. Its readers look to the publication as the authority on child health and development issues, so articles must be accurate and information backed up by respected experts. Departments represent the best opportunity for writers new to the publication. Circ: 2.2 million.

Contents: Articles; depts/columns
Frequency: 11 times each year
Website: www.parenting.com

Freelance Potential

80% written by nonstaff writers. Publishes 10–15 freelance submissions yearly; 5% by unpublished writers, 10% by authors who are new to the magazine. Receives 80+ queries monthly.

Submissions

Query with clips. Accepts hard copy. No simultaneous submissions. SASE. Responds in 2 months.

- Articles: 1,000–2,500 words. Informational, how-to, self-help, profiles, and personal experience. Topics include child development, behavior, health, pregnancy, family activities, and women's issues.
- Depts/columns: 100–500 words. Parenting tips by age range, personal experience pieces, kid-friendly recipes, beauty, health, fitness, relationships, safety tips, product reviews, expert advice, and humor.

Sample Issue

184 pages. Advertising. Sample copy available. Guidelines available at website.

- "Is One Child Enough?" Help in making the right choice on this mult-faceted issue.
- "Traveling While Pregnant." How to turn what seems like a daunting challenge into a unique opportunity to pamper yourself.

Rights and Payment

First world rights with 2 months' exclusivity. Written material, payment rates vary. Pays on acceptance. Provides 1 contributor's copy.

Parenting Children with Special Needs 

30905 East Stony Point School Road
Grain Valley, MO 64029

Editor: Kara Cowie

Description and Interests

Distributed in the Kansas City area through schools, hospitals, medical clinics, and businesses, this magazine is filled with practical articles for parents of special needs children. Each issue spotlights local resources, presents timely information from healthcare and other professionals, and offers poetry and personal experience pieces written by parents. Its mission is to offer support, understanding, encouragement, and guidance through the struggles and emotional turmoil parents face while raising a special needs child. Circ: 50,000.

Contents: 80% articles; 20% depts/columns
Frequency: 6 times a year
Website: www.pcwsn.com

Freelance Potential

Freelance percentage not currently available.

Submissions

Send complete ms. Accepts email submissions to kara@pcwsn.com. Response time varies.

- Articles: Word lengths vary. Informational and how-to articles, profiles, and personal experience pieces. Topics include special education, health, medical care, nutrition, social issues, and social skills.
- Depts/columns: Word lengths vary. Self-care for parents, educational programs, local resources, advice from healthcare and education professionals.
- Other: Poetry by parents, no line limits.

Sample Issue

No advertising. Sample copy available at website.

- "Our New Year's Inspirations." Inspiration from three special needs children and their families.
- Feeding Tube Diaries: A Lee's Summit Family's Struggles . . . and Ultimate Triumph." An infant with chronic lung and GI problems overcomes her challenges.

Rights and Payment

Rights vary. Written material, payment rates vary. Payment policy varies.

Pediatrics for Parents

P.O. Box 219
Gloucester, MA 01931

Editor: Richard J. Sagall, M.D.

Description and Interests

Known as the "Children's Medical Journal for Parents," this publication offers carefully researched information in language accessible to the lay reader. It will publish only material that is medically accurate, contains resource citations where applicable, and is useful to parents of children from prenatal to early teens. Submissions of previously published articles from medical and dental journals will be considered only if rewritten for a lay audience. The emphasis of this publication is on prevention. Circ: 250,000.

Contents: 100% articles
Frequency: 6 times each year
Website: www.pediatricsforparents.com

Freelance Potential

50% written by nonstaff writers. Publishes 30 freelance submissions yearly; 50% by unpublished writers, 50% by authors who are new to the magazine, 50% by experts. Receives 4–5 queries and unsolicited mss each month.

Submissions

Query or send complete manuscript with cover page. Prefers email submissions to submissions@pedsforparents.com (Word attachments). Response time varies.

- Articles: 750–1,500 words. Informational. Topics include prevention, fitness, medical advances, new treatment options, wellness, and pregnancy.
- Depts/columns: Word lengths vary. Article reprints, new product information.

Sample Issue

32 pages. Advertising. Sample copy and guidelines available at website.

- "Well-Child Visits." Are well-child visits long enough to answer parents' questions?
- "ADHD and Food Sensitivity." The possible connection between artificial food colors and ADHD.

Rights and Payment

First rights or reprint rights. Written material, to $25. Pays on publication. Provides 3 contributor's copies and a subscription.

Peloton

Move Press
636 Mission Street
South Pasadena, CA 91030

Editorial Director: Brad Roe

Description and Interests
Staffed by editors and writers who are self-professed "bike junkies," this magazine aims to share the many joys of cycling with readers, from the thrill of racing to the tranquility of peaceful rides. Articles cover the sport of cycling, the gear, the people, and the cycling lifestyle. Circ: Unavailable.

Contents: 80% articles; 20% depts/columns
Frequency: 9 times a year
Website: www.pelotonmagazine.com

Freelance Potential
Produced by a "collective" of writers, photographers and designers.

Submissions
For information on submissions, see editorial staff emails on the website, including Editorial Director Brad Roe, at brad@movepress.com.

- Articles: Word lengths vary. Informational, profiles, historical. Topics: bike technology, racers, manufacturers, race courses, cycling history.
- Depts/columns: Word lengths vary. Biking news, technology, products, photo-essays, race coverage.

Sample Issue
Advertising. Sample articles available at website.

- "Hilly Classics Shouldn't Be So Negative." Analysis of the Fleche Wallonne classic bike race.
- "The Capricious Speeds of Bike Racing." A look at the increase in bike racing speed and what's behind it.

Rights and Payment
Rights and payment information unavailable.

The Penn Stater

Pennsylvania State University
Hintz Family Alumni Center
University Park, PA 16802

Editor: Tina Hay

Description and Interests
This magazine is about the interesting people and events, past and present, that are part of Penn State University. It also covers campus news and developments. Information on national college trends is of interest, as long as they are examined from a Penn State perspective. Circ: 130,000.

Contents: 65% articles; 35% depts/columns
Frequency: 6 times each year
Website: www.pennstatermag.com

Freelance Potential
50% written by nonstaff writers. Publishes 12 freelance submissions yearly; 3% by unpublished writers, 5% by authors who are new to the magazine. Receives 10 queries monthly.

Submissions
Query with clips. Prefers email queries to pennstater@psu.edu; will accept hard copy. SASE. Responds in 4–6 weeks.

- Articles: 1,000–2,500 words. Informational articles, creative nonfiction, profiles, and interviews. Topics include Penn State alumni, students, and faculty; academic news; university sports; and campus activities.
- Depts/columns: 100–700 words. First-person pieces, profiles, news, and sports.

Sample Issue
88 pages. Advertising. Sample articles available at website. Guidelines available.

- "Behind the Scenes at *Sweeney Todd*." Article presents a preview of the latest theater production to hit Penn State.
- "A Good Night for Penn State Pride." Article discusses Penn State's commitment to complying with the Clery Act by hiring a compliance director.

Rights and Payment
First North American serial rights. Written material, $100–$3,000. Pays on acceptance. Provides 2 contributor's copies.

Persimmon Hill

National Cowboy & Western Heritage Museum
1700 NE 63rd Street
Oklahoma City, OK 73111

Editor: Judy Hilovsky

Description and Interests

The art, history, entertainment, travel, and personalities of the Western U.S. are featured in this magazine of the National Cowboy & Western Heritage Museum. Regional events are also covered. Stories that capture the spirit of individualism that typifies the Old West or reveal a facet of Western lifestyle in contemporary society will have the best chance at publication. Circ: 5,000.

Contents: 85% articles; 15% depts/columns
Frequency: Quarterly
Website: www.nationalcowboymuseum.org/involvement/PHillMagazine.aspx

Freelance Potential

70% written by nonstaff writers. Publishes 30–40 freelance submissions yearly; 10% by authors who are new to the magazine, 10% by experts. Receives 100 queries monthly.

Submissions

Query with clips or writing samples and availability of artwork. Prefers email to editor@nationalcowboymuseum.org; will accept hard copy. No simultaneous submissions. SASE. Responds in 6–10 weeks.

- Articles: To 1,500 words. Informational articles and profiles. Topics include cowboys, pioneers, rodeo, Western flora, animal life, and Western art.
- Depts/columns: To 1,000 words. Great Hotels of the West, historic lodgings; Western Entrepreneurs, traditional craftsmen; Western Personalities, people who are making a positive contribution to the Western lifestyle.
- Artwork: Color prints; B/W historical photographs; digital images at 300 dpi.

Sample Issue

62 pages. Sample copy available. Guidelines available at website.

- "Saving the Alamo—An Uphill Battle." Article discusses the efforts of a filmmaker trying to restore the 1960 epic movie, *The Alamo*.
- Sample dept/column: Digest profiles the band, Sons of the San Joaquin.

Rights and Payment

First North American serial rights. Written material, payment rates vary. Pays on publication.

Petersen's Bowhunting

P.O. Box 420235
Palm Coast, FL 32142

Editor: Christian Berg

Description and Interests

This magazine captures the adventure of bow hunting through articles on hunting techniques, strategies, gear, and set-up. It is always interested in fresh takes on these subjects. Circ: 155,000.

Contents: 45% articles; 45% depts/columns; 5% fiction; 5% other
Frequency: 10 times each year
Website: www.bowhuntingmag.com

Freelance Potential

90% written by nonstaff writers. Publishes 110 freelance submissions yearly; 5% by unpublished writers, 5% by authors who are new to the magazine, 95% by experts. Receives 12 queries, 5 mss monthly.

Submissions

Query or send complete ms with artwork. Accepts hard copy and disk submissions with hard copy (Word or text files). Availability of artwork improves chance of acceptance. SASE. Responds in 2 months.

- Articles: To 2,500 words. Informational and how-to articles, personal experience pieces, and new product information. Topics include bow hunting techniques, equipment, and destinations; wildlife; and conservation.
- Depts/columns: To 2,500 words. Bow hunting adventures, how-to's, and reviews.
- Artwork: High-resolution TIFF or JPEG files; 35mm slides or prints.

Sample Issue

88 pages. Advertising. Sample articles available at website.

- "Ground Attack: Bowhunting Whitetails without a Blind." Discusses a less popular but effective method for hunting deer.
- "Crossbows vs. Compounds: Comparing Apples to Apples." Reviews the speed, accuracy, and power of these two hunting weapons.

Rights and Payment

All rights for written material; one-time rights for artwork. Written material, $350–$600. Artwork, $100–$700. Pays on publication. Provides 2 contributor's copies.

Photo Technique

Preston Publications
6600 West Touhy Avenue
Niles, IL 60714-4516

Editor: Wendy Erickson

Description and Interests
photo technique explores the techniques used in creating photographs in the 21st century. It offers an eclectic mix of technique, commentary, inspiration, and history. The magazine's audience includes advanced amateurs and professional photographers interested in improving technique and sharing ideas. It seeks articles that inspire and provoke thought and lively discussion long after they are read. Queries unrelated to photography will not be answered. Circ: 20,000.

Contents: 95% articles; 5% depts/columns
Frequency: 6 times each year
Website: www.phototechmag.com

Freelance Potential
85% written by nonstaff writers. Publishes 6 freelance submissions yearly. Receives 10 queries, 3 unsolicited mss monthly.

Submissions
Query with description of the specific techniques the article will explain, artwork, and author bio and website link. Accepts email to wendy@phototechmag.com (Word or PDF attachments). Responds in 2 months.

- Articles: 800–1,200 words. Informational and how-to articles. Topics include traditional and digital photography, lighting, processing and printing, and technology.
- Depts/columns: Staff-written.
- Artwork: JPEG or PDF files labeled with author's Lastname_Firstname_Filename only.

Sample Issue
48 pages. Little advertising. Sample articles and guidelines available at website.

- "Determining Optimal Digital Camera Settings: No Light Meter Required?" Article explains how to manage digital image capture to achieve optimal dynamic range.
- "Scanning & Processing Recovered Fuji FP-100C Negatives." Article focuses on scanning and post processing negatives.

Rights and Payment
First North American serial rights. Written material, $200 per published page. Cover image, $350. Pays on publication. Provides 3 contributor's copies.

Pipers Magazine

Piper Owner Society
N7450 Aanstad Road
Iola, WI 54945

Editor: Keith Mathiowetz

Description and Interests
Written for owners of private Piper aircraft, this magazine combines articles on maintenance and technical issues with information on in-flight safety and interesting fly-in destinations. Writers familiar with Piper aircraft or flying in general are welcome to send their ideas. Circ: 6,000.

Contents: 60% articles; 20% depts/columns; 20% other
Frequency: Monthly
Website: www.piperowner.org

Freelance Potential
80% written by nonstaff writers. Publishes 20–30 freelance submissions yearly; 10% by unpublished writers, 10% by authors who are new to the magazine, 80% by experts. Receives 15 queries monthly.

Submissions
Query. Prefers email to editor@piperowner.org; will accept hard copy. SASE. Responds in 1 week.

- Articles: 1,000–1,500 words. Informational and how-to articles, profiles, interviews, personal experience pieces, and humor. Topics include aircraft maintenance and technology, nostalgia, travel, and leisure.
- Depts/columns: 800–1,400 words. Technical and financial advice, and news.
- Artwork: B/W or color transparencies; JPEGs at 300 dpi.

Sample Issue
72 pages. Advertising. Sample copy available at website. Guidelines available.

- "Naked as a Jay Bird." Personal experience piece about flying the original J-3.
- "Refurbishing a Lance II." Article describes the renovation of a Piper Lance/Saratoga.
- Sample dept/column: Under the Cowling explains how to correct nose landing gear vibration problems.

Rights and Payment
First rights. Written material, payment rates vary. Pays on publication. Provides 3–5 contributor's copies.

Plain Truth

Plain Truth Ministries
Pasadena, CA 91129

Managing Editor

Description and Interests

Plain Truth calls itself "a Christian magazine... without the religion." It offers a refreshing voice in the midst of traditional Christian journalism. It seeks to free Christians from the bonds of strict adherence to religious law through articles that focus on the issues of legalism. It seeks articles that show grace conquering legalism and personal stories of relationships over rituals. Circ: 15,000.

Contents: 70% articles; 10% depts/columns; 20% other
Frequency: Quarterly
Website: www.ptm.org

Freelance Potential

80% written by nonstaff writers. Publishes 50 freelance submissions yearly; 2% by unpublished writers, 10% by authors who are new to the magazine, 5% by experts. Receives 100 queries monthly.

Submissions

Query with outline, working title, and author profile outlining credentials to write the piece. Accepts hard copy and email to managing.editor@ptm.org. Accepts simultaneous submissions if identified. SASE. Response time varies.

- Articles: Word lengths vary. Informational articles, and personal experience and opinion pieces. Topics include Christianity, spirituality, biblical teachings, theology, faith, organized religion, current events, and social issues.
- Depts/columns: Staff-written.

Sample Issue

48 pages. Sample articles and guidelines available at website.

- "Christians & Politics." Article discusses the potential dangers when politics become too religious.
- "Who's Who in the Reformation?" Article profiles the men who challenged and repudiated Rome in the 13th and 14th centuries.

Rights and Payment

First North American serial and electronic or reprint rights. Articles, $.25 per word. Reprints, $.15 per word. Pays on publication. Provides 2 contributor's copies.

Ploughshares

Emerson College
120 Boylston Street
Boston, MA 02116-4624

Editor in Chief: Ladette Randolph

Description and Interests

Each issue of this literary journal is guest edited by a writer of prominence, with the guest editor soliciting up to half of the material for the issue. It primarily publishes short stories and poetry; however, it does feature an occasional essay or memoir. New this year is a digital-only series of individual stories, novels, or long essays that are up to 25,000 words. Circ: 6,000.

Contents: 45% fiction; 35% poetry; 15% depts/columns; 5% articles
Frequency: 3 times each year
Website: www.pshares.org

Freelance Potential

90% written by nonstaff writers. Publishes 60 freelance submissions yearly; 30% by unpublished writers, 50% by authors who are new to the magazine. Receives 1,200 unsolicited mss monthly.

Submissions

Send ms between June 1 and January 15. Send one submission at a time until the editors respond. Accepts hard copy, submissions through the website, and simultaneous submissions if identified. There is a $3 fee for online submissions. SASE. Responds in 3–5 months.

- Articles: To 6,000 words. Literary and personal essays and memoirs.
- Fiction: To 6,000 words. Self-contained novel excerpts, short stories, and literary fiction.
- Depts/columns: Staff-written.
- Poetry: 1–5 poems per submission.

Sample Issue

218 pages. Little advertising. Sample articles and guidelines available at website.

- "The Sinner." Short story.
- "Why I Play Golf." Essay about how golf would be the author's "Plan B" career, after being a writer.

Rights and Payment

First world serial rights. Written material, $50–$250. Pays on publication. Provides 2 contributor's copies and a 1-year subscription.

The Pointing Dog Journal

2779 Aero Park Drive
Traverse City, MI 49686

Managing Editor: Jason Smith

Description and Interests
This magazine is all about celebrating the relationship between man and hunting dog. For people who are truly passionate about the classic hunting dog experience, it offers articles about the sport. It looks for writers who are expert trainers, breeders, and wingshooters. Circ: Unavailable.
Contents: 80% articles; 20% depts/columns
Frequency: 6 times a year
Website: www.pointingdogjournal.com

Freelance Potential
Welcomes queries from writers experienced as dog owners and hunters.

Submissions
Query with proposed length and photo availability or send complete ms. Accepts email submissions to jake@villagepress.com and hard copy. SASE. Responds to queries in 3–4 weeks; manuscripts in 6–8 weeks.

- Articles: Informational and how-to articles and personal experience pieces. Topics include hunting techniques, adventures, dog care, and equipment.
- Depts/columns: Hunting equipment, training, techniques, and canine medical issues.

Sample Issue
Advertising. Sample articles and guidelines available at website. Detailed guidelines available from Jason Smith at jake@villagepress.com.

- "A Christmas Grouse." A veteran hunter fondly recalls his first grouse hunting experience.
- Sample dept/column: The Vet's Office discusses the symptoms and treatment of canine Pancreatitis.

Rights and Payment
Rights unknown. Written material, payment rates vary. Payment rates vary.

Pontoon & Deck Boat

360 B Street
Idaho Falls, ID 83402

Editor: Brady L. Kay

Description and Interests
Just about every topic of interest to pontoon and deck boat owners is covered in this magazine. Articles explore destinations, profile owners, and review new boat models. Writers knowledgeable about a topic that can be tied to boating have a good chance at publication here. Writing should have a light and fun tone. Circ: 82,000.
Contents: 70% articles; 30% depts/columns
Frequency: 11 times each year
Website: www.pdbmagazine.com

Freelance Potential
25% written by nonstaff writers. Publishes 40 freelance submissions yearly; 20% by unpublished writers, 5% by authors who are new to the magazine, 20% by experts. Receives 5 queries monthly.

Submissions
Query with one- or two-paragraph synopsis and author bio. Prefers email queries to blk@pdbmagazine.com (Word attachments); will accept hard copy. SASE. Responds in 6 weeks.

- Articles: 1,000–1,200 words. Informational and how-to articles, profiles, interviews, and new product information. Topics include pontoon and deck boats, equipment, events, and destinations.
- Depts/columns: Word lengths vary. Boating gear, fishing, and boating updates.
- Artwork: Color transparencies; digital images at 300 dpi.

Sample Issue
70 pages. Sample copy and guidelines available.

- "Winter Layup." Article discusses how to best prepare one's boat for a smooth spring launch.
- "PDB Spotlight." Article reviews the Veranda V 2075.
- Sample dept/column: Better Boater provides tips for winterizing gear.

Rights and Payment
First North American serial rights. Articles, $250–$400. Depts/columns, $50–$175. Pays on publication. Provides 3 contributor's copies.

Popular Woodworking

4700 East Galbraith Road
Cincinnati, OH 45236

Editor: Matthew Teague

Description and Interests
Woodworkers of all levels read this magazine to "learn how, discover why, and build better." Each issue is filled with in-depth projects, technique how-to's, and visual aids for both hand tool and power tool woodworking. Freelance writers do not need to be professional woodworkers to submit thoughts or tricks—just someone who loves it. Circ: 180,000.

Contents: 65% articles; 35% depts/columns
Frequency: 7 times each year
Website: www.popularwoodworking.com

Freelance Potential
70% written by nonstaff writers. Publishes 30 freelance submissions yearly; 5% by unpublished writers, 5% by authors who are new to the magazine, 90% by experts. Receives 30 queries, 25 unsolicited mss monthly.

Submissions
Send complete ms. Accepts hard copy and email submissions. Send End of Grain ms to megan.fitzpatrick@fwmedia.com. Send Tricks of the Trade to popwoodtricks@fwmedia.com. SASE. Responds in 2 months.

- Articles: Informational and how-to articles. Topics include all aspects of hand tool and power tool woodworking.
- Depts/columns: End Grain, humorous or serious essay about woodworking as a profession or hobby; 450 words. Tricks of the Trade, tips; word lengths vary.
- Artwork: Digital images. 3-view construction drawings.

Sample Issue
72 pages. Advertising. Sample copy available. Guidelines available at website.

- Sample dept/column: End Grain describes how the author's Asian upbringing has shaped his views on Japanese woodworking traditions.
- Sample dept/column: End Grain discusses modern technology.

Rights and Payment
All rights. Articles, payment rates vary. End Grain, $250+. Tricks of the Trade, $50–$100. Pays on acceptance. Provides 2 contributor's copies.

Prairie Schooner 

123 Andrews Hall
University of Nebraska
Lincoln, NE 68588-0334

Editor in Chief: Kwame Davis

Description and Interests
The University of Nebraska's literary journal features literature from some of the world's most renowned writers, as well as writing by newcomers with exceptional talent. Since 1926, it has been offering readers high-quality short stories, essays, interviews, poetry, and reviews. *Prairie Schooner* also awards annual writing prizes to authors of the work it publishes. It is always in need of book reviews of recent works. Writers are encouraged to read a few issues before submitting. Circ: 2,500.

Contents: 50% poetry; 25% fiction; 25% articles
Frequency: Quarterly
Website: http://prairieschooner.unl.edu

Freelance Potential
100% written by nonstaff writers. Publishes 150 freelance submissions yearly; 5% by unpublished writers, 25% by authors who are new to the magazine. Receives 800 unsolicited mss each month.

Submissions
Send complete ms between September 1 and May 1 only. Accepts hard copy and electronic submissions. No simultaneous submissions. SASE. Responds in 3–4 months.

- Articles: Word lengths vary. Essays, interviews, and book reviews.
- Fiction: Word lengths vary. Literary fiction.
- Other: Poetry; 5–7 poems per submission.

Sample Issue
192 pages. Little advertising. Sample articles and guidelines available at website.

- "The Canary Keeper." Short story about an out-of-work actor preparing for an audition.
- "Review." Review of *Engine Empire*, by Jeff Alessandrelli.

Rights and Payment
All rights. No payment. Provides 3 contributor's copies.

PRISM

P.O. Box 367
Wayne, PA 19087

Editor: Kristyn Komarnicki

Description and Interests

Subtitled "America's Alternative Evangelical Voice," *PRISM* seeks to challenge and equip its readers to follow Christ in both word and deed. It publishes articles on Christianity and how it relates to contemporary culture, social justice, holistic ministry profiles, and spiritual challenges. It is published by Evangelicals for Social Action. Fiction and poetry are not accepted. New writers should be willing to work on spec, as assignments are rarely given to new writers. Circ: 3,500.

Contents: 70% articles; 20% depts/columns; 10% other
Frequency: 6 times each year
Website: www.PRISMmagazine.org

Freelance Potential

90% written by nonstaff writers. Publishes 35 freelance submissions yearly; 50% by authors who are new to the magazine. Receives 10 queries and unsolicited mss monthly.

Submissions

Prefers complete ms; will accept query with clips. Accepts hard copy and email submissions to kkomarni@eastern.edu. Work-for-hire also available. Responds in 6–8 weeks.

- Articles: 800–3,000 words. Informational articles, profiles, and interviews. Topics include social issues, Christianity, holistic ministry, multicultural and ethnic issues, and spiritual challenges–all from a Christian perspective.
- Depts/columns: Word lengths vary. Media reviews, politics, legislation.
- Other: Submit seasonal material 6 months in advance.

Sample Issue

48 pages. Little advertising. Sample copy and guidelines available at website.

- "A War of Domination." Article reports on the crisis in Sudan.
- "Is It Hot in Here or Is It Just Me?" Article discusses the skepticism surrounding climate change.

Rights and Payment

All rights. Written material, $50 per printed page. Pays on publication. Provides contributor's copies and a 1-year subscription upon request.

The Progressive

409 East Main Street
Madison, WI 53703

Editor: Matthew Rothschild

Description and Interests

This left-leaning publication focuses on issues of social and economic justice, corporate and government wrongdoing, politics, and activism. It features investigative-style articles with in-depth reporting, interviews, reviews of books and music, and poetry. Detailed and fair reporting is valued and writers must use plenty of quotations in their pieces. It prefers a tone that is conversational and non-academic, and writing that is clear, thoughtful, and graceful. Circ: 55,000.

Contents: 75% articles; 25% depts/columns
Frequency: Monthly
Website: www.progressive.org

Freelance Potential

50% written by nonstaff writers. Publishes 36 freelance submissions yearly; 5% by authors who are new to the magazine. Receives 250 queries, 150 unsolicited mss monthly.

Submissions

Query or send complete ms. Accepts hard copy and email to editorial@progressive.org. No simultaneous submissions. SASE. Responds in 2–4 weeks.

- Articles: Word lengths vary. Investigative articles, profiles, interviews, and research pieces. Topics include social, economic, and political issues such as labor movements, civil liberties, and economic justice; foreign policy; activism; elections coverage.
- Depts/columns: Word lengths vary. On the Line, brief profiles of activists or activist groups.
- Other: Poetry that connects with political concerns.

Sample Issue

46 pages. Advertising. Sample articles and guidelines available at website.

- "Steve Earle." Article offers an interview with the musician and activist.
- "Inside the ALEC Dating Service." Article reports how corporations "hook up" with their state legislators.

Rights and Payment

All rights. Articles, $500–$1,300. On the Line, $50. Poetry, $150. Pays on publication. Provides contributor's copies upon request.

The Progressive Populist

P.O. Box 819
Manchaca, TX 78652

Editor: Jim Cullen

Description and Interests

This tabloid paper is the voice of the populist viewpoint on current issues in government, economics, farming, business, and society. It calls itself "A Journal From America's Heartland." Articles are well researched and contain specific facts and figures on topics currently in the news. Writers should use a journalistic style. While not strictly opinion pieces, all of the content has a populist slant. Circ: 15,000.

Contents: 80% articles; 20% depts/columns
Frequency: 22 times each year
Website: www.populist.com

Freelance Potential

95% written by nonstaff writers. Publishes 440 freelance submissions yearly; 5% by unpublished writers, 5% by authors who are new to the magazine, 20% by experts. Receives 12 queries, 60 unsolicited mss monthly.

Submissions

Query or send complete ms. Prefers email submissions to populist@usa.net; will accept hard copy. SASE. Responds in 2–4 weeks.

- Articles: 600–1,200 words. Informational articles, profiles, interviews, opinion pieces, and humor. Topics include politics, economics, social issues, corporations, rural issues, activism, the media, and public affairs.
- Depts/columns: 600–1,000 words. Opinions, media analysis, and book reviews.

Sample Issue

24 pages. Little advertising. Sample articles available at website. Guidelines and editorial calendar available.

- "Dixie Poverty and Politics." Article reports on the poverty figures among the southern states.
- "Forgotten and Invisible." Essay discusses the impact of poverty and the lower middle class on the presidential campaigns.

Rights and Payment

One-time rights. Written material, $25–$50. Depts/columns, $15–$50. Pays on publication. Provides contributor's copies upon request.

Psychology Today

115 East 23rd Street, 9th Floor
New York, NY 10010

Editor in Chief: Kaja Perina

Description and Interests

Tackling issues such as human behavior, personalities, relationships, and mental health, this popular consumer magazine covers psychology-related topics for a general readership. It looks for articles with an interesting angle or a unique spin on human behavior. Writers with a background in psychology are preferred. Circ: 300,000.

Contents: 40% articles; 40% depts/columns; 20% other
Frequency: 6 times each year
Website: www.psychologytoday.com

Freelance Potential

70% written by nonstaff writers. Publishes 20 freelance submissions yearly; 10% by unpublished writers, 60% by authors who are new to the magazine, 10% by experts. Receives 150 queries monthly.

Submissions

Query with 1-page letter explaining what you want to write, why you're the one to write about it, potential sources, and clips. Accepts hard copy and email to relevant editor (see masthead). Responds in 2 months.

- Articles: 500–3,000 words. Informational, self-help, and how-to articles; profiles; interviews; and personal experience pieces. Topics include psychology, relationships, mental health, and the psychology of marketing.
- Depts/columns: 350–800 words. Psychology briefs, profiles, global issues, beauty, sex, "quirky minds," health, relationships, and problem-solving.

Sample Issue

96 pages. Advertising. Sample articles and guidelines available at website.

- "Lessons for Living." Article suggests four principles for living, loving, and playing well with others.
- "Stealth Attack." Article examines new evidence that links pesticide exposure to health disorders in children.

Rights and Payment

First North American serial rights. Written material, $.75–$1 per word. Pays on publication. Provides 2 contributor's copies.

P31 Woman

616-G Matthew Mint Hill Road
Matthews, NC 28105

Assistant Editor: Janet Burke

Description and Interests

This magazine, geared to Christian women, encourages living in faith and applying godly principles, modeled in Proverbs 31, to all circumstances and relationships. Its features are written "woman to woman" and offer personal experience and practical advice. It is open to articles on just about any topic that applies to women today and the many roles they are called to fill. The tone is not "preachy" but rather gentle and personal. Check the website for suggested topics. Circ: 10,000.

Contents: 60% articles; 30% depts/columns; 10% other
Frequency: Monthly
Website: www.proverbs31.org

Freelance Potential

60% written by nonstaff writers. Publishes 60 freelance submissions yearly; 50% by authors who are new to the magazine, 20% by experts. Receives 20 unsolicited mss monthly.

Submissions

Send complete ms. Accepts email submissions to janet@proverbs31.org. Response time varies.

- Articles: 200–1,000 words. Informational and how-to articles, personal experience pieces, creative nonfiction, humor, interviews, devotions, and confession pieces. Topics include Christian parenting, family life, marriage, religion, spirituality, and relationships.
- Depts/columns: Staff-written.

Sample Issue

16 pages. Sample articles and guidelines available at website.

- "But I Really Don't Want To." Personal experience piece about a lesson learned while on a mission trip to El Salvador.
- "Surviving Mommy Stress." Article shares scriptures to deal with the stress of parenting.

Rights and Payment

Author retains rights. No payment. Provides 3 contributor's copies.

PTO Today

100 Stonewall Boulevard, Suite 3
Wrentham, MA 02093

Editor in Chief: Craig Bystrynski

Description and Interests

This magazine's mission is to serve as a resource to the leaders of parent groups in elementary and middle schools across the United States. The content specifically focuses on helping parent-teacher organizations be more effective and have a greater impact at their schools. Its aim is to assist volunteer leaders, who are mostly women ages 28–45, in managing their groups efficiently and supporting their schools effectively. It offers information on problem solving, fund-raising, running meetings, and enhancing the school experience. Circ: 80,000.

Contents: 60% articles; 40% depts/columns
Frequency: 6 times each year
Website: www.ptotoday.com

Freelance Potential

70% written by nonstaff writers. Publishes 15–20 freelance submissions yearly; 5% by unpublished writers, 15% by authors who are new to the magazine. Receives 8–10 queries monthly.

Submissions

Prefers queries with clips and cover letter that includes: subject, angle, possible interview sources, why the article will interest readers, and author's group leadership experience. Art suggestions to accompany article are appreciated. Prefers email queries to queries@ptotoday.com; accepts hard copy. Responds in 2 months.

- Articles: 800–1,500 words. Informational, how-to, and profiles. Topics include parent involvement, leadership, fund-raising, group organization, working with school staff, playgrounds, and the role of parent groups in education.
- Depts/columns: 300–800 words. News, opinions, profiles, leadership, advice, and event ideas.

Sample Issue

56 pages. Advertising. Sample copy and guidelines available at website.

- "Make Your Family Night a Winner." Ideas and tips for fun family nights.
- "Auctions: Make Them Fun and Festive." Boost profits from your next school auction event.

Rights and Payment

All rights. Articles, $200–$550. Depts/columns, $150–$300. Pays on acceptance. Provides 1 contributor's copy.

Purpose

616 Walnut Avenue
Scottsdale, PA 15683

Editor: Carol Duerksen

Description and Interests

This publication of the Mennonite Church provides inspiration through personal stories of action-oriented discipleship living. Poetry is also featured. Each issue is themed. Submissions related to the editorial theme list will have a better chance at publication. Check the website for the current list of themes. Circ: 9,000.

Contents: 75% articles and poetry; 25% depts/columns
Frequency: Monthly
Website: www.mpn.net

Freelance Potential

95% written by nonstaff writers. Publishes 150 freelance submissions yearly; 75% by unpublished writers, 15% by authors who are new to the magazine. Receives 200 unsolicited mss each month.

Submissions

Send complete ms. Accepts hard copy, email submissions to purposeeditor@mpn.net and simultaneous submissions if identified. SASE. Responds in 9 months.

- Articles: True, personal anecdotes, 400–600 words. Topics cover Christian faith and spirituality; check website or contact editor for current, specific themes.
- Depts/columns: Staff-written.
- Other: Poetry, to 12 lines.

Sample Issue

32 pages. No advertising. Sample articles, guidelines, and theme list available at website.

- "Celebrating Peace." Personal anecdote tells of the importance of compassion, caring, and empathy in one's daily life.
- "Yes! to Retirement." Personal story tells of woman who learns to accept her retirement when she loses her nursing job.

Rights and Payment

One-time rights. Articles, \$20–\$50. Poetry, \$7.50–\$20. Pays on acceptance. Provides 2 contributor's copies.

Pynk

349 Fifth Avenue, 4th Floor
New York, NY 10016

Editor in Chief: Shanel Odum

Description and Interests

Multicultural urban women are the target audience of *Pynk*. The demographic is ages 21 to 34, largely African American and Latina, and affluent. The angle is trendsetting. It is packed with stories, services, and products for and about multicultural women nationwide. It hopes to encourage readers to become more of who they really are, instead of dictating who they should aspire to become. *Pynk* is published by Bleu Life Media & Entertainment, which also publishes *Bleu*, a magazine for men. Circ: Unavailable.

Contents: Articles; depts/columns
Frequency: 6 times each year
Website: www.pynkmag.com

Freelance Potential

Recevies several freelance submissions monthly.

Submissions

Query. Accepts email to info@pynkmag.com. Response time varies.

- Articles: Word lengths vary. Informational and how-to articles and profiles. Topics include fashion, celebrities, style, beauty, career advice, and shopping,
- Depts/columns: Advice, music, arts, and gossip.

Sample Issue

Advertising. Sample articles available at website.

- "Watch Her Work." Article features a profile on Beverly Bond, a New York-based model turned disc jockey.
- "How to Surge Past the Fitness Plateau." Article discusses the importance of continuously adding new stimulus to a workout.
- "Health and Hobbies." Article includes a profile of lingerie football model Tanyka Renee.

Rights and Payment

Rights vary. Payment rates and policy vary.

Quaker Life

101 Quaker Hill Drive
Richmond, IN 47374

Editor: Katie Terrell Wonsik

Description and Interests

Quaker Life is a publication of the Ministry of Friends United Meeting that is meant to inform and equip Friends and help them become more involved in the activities of this faith. Articles describe some of the international ministries of the Quakers, as well as inspire readers to grow in the faith. It is always looking for personal experience pieces about participating in a specific mission project or true tales that reveal an opportunity for spiritual learning and growth. Circ: 3,000.

Contents: Articles; depts/columns
Frequency: 6 times each year
Website: www.fum.org

Freelance Potential

75% written by nonstaff writers. Publishes 15 freelance submissions yearly; 20% by unpublished writers, 75% by authors who are new to the magazine.

Submissions

Query or send complete ms with author biography. Prefers disk submissions (Word, RTF, or text files) or email to quakerlife@fum.org (attach file); will accept hard copy. SASE. Response time varies.

- Articles: 750–1,500 words. Informational articles, profiles, interviews, personal experience pieces, and essays. Topics include the Quaker faith and ministry, sacraments, and coping with daily life.
- Depts/columns: Reviews, 150–200 words. News, 50–200 words.

Sample Issue

46 pages. Sample articles and guidelines available at website. Theme list available by email request through website.

- "Faithful Prayers." Personal experience piece shares a moving experience that occurred at a prayer meeting.
- "Why Silent Worship Is Not Dying Soon." Articles discusses the benefits of praying in a silent environment.

Rights and Payment

First North American serial rights. No payment. Provides 3+ contributor's copies.

Queen's Alumni Review

Department of Marketing and Communications
Queen's University
Kingston, Ontario K7L 3N6
Canada

Editor: Ken Cuthbertson

Description and Interests

The people and current events of Queen's University and news of its alumni are the subjects of this publication. It also features interviews and profiles, as well as some essay and opinion pieces. Commentary and expert opinions on issues related to higher education that are consistent with the mandate of Queen's University are needed for the Viewpoint section. Circ: 125,000.

Contents: 65% articles; 35% depts/columns
Frequency: Quarterly
Website: www.alumnireview.queensu.ca

Freelance Potential

50% written by nonstaff writers. Publishes 20 freelance submissions yearly; 10% by unpublished writers, 25% by authors who are new to the magazine, 2% by experts. Receives 25 queries monthly.

Submissions

Query with 3–5 clips. Prefers email to review@queensu.ca; will accept hard copy. Responds in 1 week.

- Articles: 1,000–3,500 words. Informational articles, profiles, interviews, and opinion and personal experience pieces. Topics include all subjects related to Queen's University and alumni of the school.
- Depts/columns: 650–700 words. Campus and alumni news. "And Another Thing...", essay. Alumni spotlights.
- Artwork: B/W and color prints; digital images at 300 ppi.

Sample Issue

64 pages. Advertising. Sample copy and guidelines available at website.

- "A Passion for Sustainable Solutions." Article profiles four alumni who are building a new kind of engineering company.
- "Truly One of a Kind." Article profiles the late Ralfe Clench, a popular alumna and professor.

Rights and Payment

First world rights. Written material, $.50+ per word plus 10% rights fees. Pays on publication. Provides 3 contributor's copies.

Ellery Queen's Mystery Magazine

267 Broadway, 4th Floor
New York, NY 10007-2352

Editor: Janet Hutchings

Description and Interests

Lovers of the mystery genre read this digest-size publication for its top-notch fiction about crime and detection, psychological suspense tales, and private eye cases written by well-known and up-and-coming writers. It uses hard-boiled stories, as well as "cozies," but nothing with explicit sex or violence. Previously unpublished writers should send submissions to the Department of First Stories. Circ: 120,000.

Contents: 100% fiction
Frequency: 10 times each year
Website: www.themysteryplace.com

Freelance Potential

100% written by nonstaff writers. Publishes 120 freelance submissions yearly; 7% by unpublished writers, 25% by authors who are new to the magazine. Receives 200 unsolicited mss monthly.

Submissions

Send complete ms with cover letter stating story length and author publishing history. Accepts electronic submissions via online submission system at http://eqmm.magazinesubmissions.com (Word files only). Accepts hard copy only from established authors with no capability to submit electronically. Responds in 3 months.

- Fiction: Mysteries, psychological thrillers, crime stories, detective stories, and whodunits, Preferred length: 2,500–8,000 words. Short stories, 1,500–2,000 words. Minute mysteries, to 250 words. Novellas by established authors, to 20,000 words.
- Depts/columns: Staff-written.
- Other: Poetry.

Sample Issue

112 pages. Little advertising. Sample articles and guidelines available at website.

- "Mariel." Tale of a curiously threatening girl who frightens a neighborhood.
- "Old Man Gloom." Short story of a crime that takes the reader back to the WWII era.

Rights and Payment

First North American serial rights. Written material, \$.05–\$.08 per word. Pays on acceptance. Provides 3 contributor's copies.

Queen's Quarterly

Queen's University
144 Barrie Street
Kingston, Ontario K7L 3N6
Canada

Editor: Boris Castel
Fiction & Poetry Editor: Joan Harcourt

Description and Interests

Featuring a mix of articles, essays, short stories, and poetry, *Queen's Quarterly* is aimed at the general, educated reader who appreciates an intellectual overview of the world. Submissions should satisfy the curiosity of its readers, providing them with fresh, new ideas that will educate and entertain. Circ: 5,000.

Contents: 75% articles; 25% fiction
Frequency: Quarterly
Website: www.queensu.ca/quarterly

Freelance Potential

100% written by nonstaff writers. Publishes 60 freelance submissions yearly; 25% by unpublished writers, 25% by authors who are new to the magazine. Receives 100 unsolicited mss each month.

Submissions

Send complete ms. Prefers email submissions to queens.quarterly@queensu.ca (attach document); will accept hard copy and simultaneous submissions if identified. SAE/IRC. Responds in 4–8 weeks.

- Articles: To 3,000 words. Informational articles, profiles, media reviews, essays, and opinion pieces. Topics include public affairs, politics, psychology, music, history, government, and multicultural and social issues.
- Fiction: To 3,000 words; to 2 stories per submission. Literary, contemporary, and mainstream fiction.
- Other: Poetry, to 6 poems per submission.

Sample Issue

146 pages. No advertising. Sample articles and guidelines available at website.

- "Planetary Mood Pictures." Article discusses the use of Gustav Holst's *The Planets* in a multimedia extravaganza.
- "Architecture of Humanity." Article showcases the revolutionary projects designed by a Norwegian architectural firm.

Rights and Payment

First rights. Written material, payment rates vary. Pays on publication. Provides 2 contributor's copies.

Quill Magazine

3909 North Meridian Street
Indianapolis, IN 46208

Editor: Scott Leadingham

Description and Interests

Published by the Society of Professional Journalists, this magazine is known as the pulse of the industry and its practitioners. Its articles and essays focus on the challenges, opportunities, and responsibilities of journalism today. It prefers writers with a background in professional journalism. Well-written pieces about timely topics relevant to a wide range of journalists are most needed. Circ: 10,000.

Contents: 90% articles; 10% depts/columns
Frequency: 6 times each year
Website: www.spj.org/quill.asp

Freelance Potential

50% written by nonstaff writers. Publishes 10 freelance submissions yearly; 25% by authors who are new to the magazine, 25% by industry experts. Receives 20 unsolicited mss monthly.

Submissions

Send complete ms. Accepts hard copies, disk submissions, and email to sleadingham@spj.org (Word attachments). No SASE; materials not returned. Responds in 1 month.

- Articles: Word lengths vary. Informational and how-to articles, profiles, interviews, and media reviews. Topics include writing, digital media, ethics, global issues, politics, and public affairs—all as they relate to the field of journalism.
- Depts/columns: Word lengths vary. Essays, industry updates, interviews, education, and association news.

Sample Issue

40 pages. Little advertising. Sample articles, guidelines, and editorial calendar available at website.

- "Good Night, GRAMA." Article discusses the legislation attempting to change the open records law.
- "Profile: Utah State Ombudsman Rosemary Cundiff." Article features a profile on the training and complexities of Cundiff's job.

Rights and Payment

First non-exclusive rights. Written material, payment rates vary. Kill fee, 25%. Pays on publication. Provides 5 contributor's copies.

The Quilter Magazine

7 Waterloo Road
Stanhope, NJ 07874

Editor: Laurette Koserowski

Description and Interests

Quilting enthusiasts of all levels find a number of patterns and project ideas in each issue of this magazine. Quilter profiles, technique articles, and information on machine quilting round out the editorial content. Holiday items are always of special interest. Circ: 175,000.

Contents: 90% articles; 10% depts/columns
Frequency: 6 times each year
Website: www.thequiltermag.com

Freelance Potential

85% written by nonstaff writers. Publishes 160 freelance submissions yearly; 65% by unpublished writers, 25% by authors who are new to the magazine, 10% by experts. Receives 5 queries monthly.

Submissions

Query with artwork. Accepts hard copy and email queries to editors@thequiltermag.com. No simultaneous submissions. SASE. Responds in 6 weeks.

- Articles: 800–1,000 words. Informational and how-to articles, profiles, interviews, and new product information. Topics include quilting techniques, projects, and instructors; quilt designers; fabrics; equipment; and antique quilts.
- Depts/columns: Staff-written.
- Artwork: Digital images at 300 dpi or higher.

Sample Issue

114 pages. Advertising. Sample copy available. Guidelines available at website.

- "Quilt Minnesota: Sharing the Joy of Quilting." Article describes the events at the popular quilt Minnesota event.
- "Kathy McNeil's Inner Child." Article features a profile of this fabric artist.
- "Trading Butterflies." Article discusses the benefits of a quilt block exchange.

Rights and Payment

First North American serial rights. Written material, $150–$250. Projects, $175–$375. Pays on publication. Provides 2–4 contributor's copies.

Quilter's Newsletter

741 Corporate Circle, Suite A
Golden, CO 80401

Editor: Mary Kate Karr-Petras

Description and Interests

Deceptively named, this glossy, full-color magazine is packed with quilt patterns, techniques, and design trends. It also features profiles of quilters, personal stories from the crafters, and charity projects. The magazine's mission is to connect quilters through personal stories. Innovative and practical quilting applications are always welcome. Circ: 125,000.

Contents: 40% articles; 20% depts/columns; 20% patterns; 20% other
Frequency: 6 times each year
Website: www.quiltersnewsletter.com

Freelance Potential

50% written by nonstaff writers. Publishes 35–40 freelance submissions yearly; 10% by unpublished writers, 15% by authors new to the magazine, 75% by experts. Receives 25 unsolicited mss monthly.

Submissions

Send complete ms. Accepts email submissions for Quilter's Bee only to questions@qnm.com. All other submissions should be sent via postal mail. Availability of artwork improves chance of acceptance. No simultaneous submissions. SASE. Responds in 8–10 weeks.

- Articles: 1,000 words. Informational and how-to articles, profiles, personal experience pieces, and new product information. Topics include quilting techniques, studio space, projects, history, designers, and materials.
- Depts/columns: Word lengths vary. Photo Finish, Quilter's Bee, About Space.
- Artwork: Digital images at 300 dpi.

Sample Issue

90 pages. Advertising. Sample articles and guidelines available at website.

- "Experiencing the Civil War Through Quilts." Article shares highlights of a traveling exhibit at the American Textile History Museum.
- Sample dept/column: Photo Finish shows a quilt inspired by a photograph.

Rights and Payment

Limited exclusive rights. Written material, payment rates vary. Artwork, $20. Pays on publication. Provides 3 contributor's copies.

Rack

10350 Highway 80 East
Montgomery, AL 36117

Editor: Mike Handley

Description and Interests

Rack celebrates "adventures in trophy hunting," with detailed articles on taking trophy whitetails and other North American big game animals. It publishes only the stories behind the harvests of these world-class animals, so long as the animal qualifies for a major record book. Previously unpublished articles with at least two publishable photographs are preferred. It does not buy columns, how-to, where-to, or gear-related articles. Contact the magazine for its writers' guidelines. Circ: 70,000.

Contents: 100% articles
Frequency: 6 times each year
Website: www.buckmasters.com/top-stories/rack-magazine.aspx

Freelance Potential

85% written by nonstaff writers. Publishes 106 freelance submissions yearly; 68% by unpublished writers, 60% by authors who are new to the magazine, 1% by experts. Receives 5 queries, 1 unsolicited ms monthly.

Submissions

Query or send complete ms with artwork. Prefers email submissions to mhandley@buckmasters.com (Word or text attachments); will accept CD submissions. SASE. Responds in 1 month.

- Articles: 1,000 words. Personal experience pieces about big-game hunts.
- Depts/columns: Staff-written.
- Artwork: Prints; high-resolution JPEG images.

Sample Issue

72 pages. Advertising. Sample articles available at website. Guidelines available.

- "Illinois' New No. 3." Article describes a trip in which the hunter took down a 10-pointer.
- "Five Hundred Reasons." Personal experience piece about getting a giant buck that had eluded hunters for years.

Rights and Payment

First or second North American serial rights. Articles, $100–$325. Cover photo, $500. Pays on publication. Provides 2 contributor's copies.

Radish

1720 Fifth Avenue
Moline, IL 61265

Editor: Sarah J. Gardner

Description and Interests

Radish's goal is to improve readers' health through the natural foods, products, and services of western Illinois and eastern Iowa. It features articles on sustainable lifestyle choices, news and advice on diet, health and fitness, cooking, and local food and farmers' markets. Material must be well documented and tightly written. It will accept previously published material if it's specific to the region. Circ: 52,000.

Contents: 40% articles; 60% depts/columns;
Frequency: Monthly
Website: www.radishmagazine.com

Freelance Potential

75% written by nonstaff writers. Publishes 40–50 freelance submissions yearly; 10% by unpublished writers, 25% by authors who are new to the magazine. Receives 15 queries each month.

Submissions

Query with 1-page outline and clips. Accepts hard copy and email to editor@radishmagazine.com (Word attachments). Responds in 1 month.

- Articles: 750–1,100 words. Informational, how-to, and self-help articles; profiles; and personal experience pieces. Topics include the health opportunities specific to the region, local farms and farmers' markets, holistic medicine, self-renewal, and fitness.
- Depts/columns: 500–750 words. Healthy eating destinations, outdoor recreation, green living, health and fitness, alternative and integrative medicine practices, opinion pieces.

Sample Issue

32 pages. Sample copy and guidelines available at website.

- "The Right Brew for You." Article explains the different coffee labels available and their growing practices.
- Sample dept/column: Health & Fitness offers diet and exercise tips for optimal skeletal health.

Rights and Payment

Rights vary. Articles, $50–$150. Pays on publication. Provides 2 contributor's copies.

The Rag  

Editor: Seth Porter
Assistant Editor: Dan Reilly

Description and Interests

Launched in 2011, *The Rag* is an electronic literary magazine publishing short stories of all kinds. Its mission is to reinvigorate the short story form and present a literary magazine that is fun, entertaining, and thought-provoking. It plans to expand its scope to include poetry and novels. *The Rag* is available via subscription in electronic format and also via e-readers. Gritty stories, stories that are psychologically believable, and stories that have some humor in them, dark or otherwise are preferred. Circ: 70,000.

Contents: Fiction; poetry
Frequency: Quarterly
Website: http://raglitmag.com

Freelance Potential

As a new publication, the editors are actively seeking submissions from writers everywhere.

Submissions

Send complete ms. Accepts submissions via website or at http://raglitmag.submishmash.com/submit ($3 electronic submission fee). For those unable or unwilling to submit electronically, email dan@raglitmag.com for mail-in guidelines. Response time varies.

- Fiction: Word lengths vary. Short stories, flash fiction, novelettes.
- Other: Poetry, no line limits.

Sample Issue

62 pages. Sample work available at website ("Blog" section). Guidelines available at website.

- "Thirteen Units (According to Polish Logicians)." Short story about four college students and the different scenarios of how they spend their night.
- "Into the Light." Story about two co-workers beginning a relationship.
- "Kill Whitey." Story about a suspected thief and his encounter with a police officer.

Rights and Payment

First rights. Fiction, $150–$200. Poetry and flash fiction, $30–$50. Payment policy varies.

Range

106 East Adams Street, Suite 201
Carson City, NV 89706

Editor/Publisher: C. J. Hadley

Description and Interests

Range shares the stories, both good and bad, of farmers and ranchers in the American West, their land, and their way of life. It chronicles a land and a way of life in crisis. It wants clear-eyed reporting from people who are right where things are happening. Circ: 173,000.

Contents: 80% articles; 20% depts/columns
Frequency: Quarterly
Website: www.rangemagazine.com

Freelance Potential

75% written by nonstaff writers. Publishes 75 freelance submissions yearly; 30% by unpublished writers, 30% by authors who are new to the magazine, 5% by experts. Receives 50 queries, 40–50 unsolicited mss monthly.

Submissions

Query with 2-page writing sample, or send complete ms. Accepts disk submissions with hard copy and email to edit@rangemagazine.com (Word attachments). SASE. Responds in 3–4 months.

- Articles: 1,200–2,000 words. Mini-features, 600–1,200 words. Informational articles, interviews, and profiles. Topics include the people, cowboys, lifestyles, and wildlife of the American West; conservation; the environment; and politics.
- Depts/columns: 500–650 words. Essays. Confessions of Red Meat Survivors, nostalgia about people over 80.
- Artwork: TIFFs or JPEGs dropped on an FTP site or mailed on CD with color proofs sheet and captions; high-quality prints; 5mm slides.

Sample Issue

80 pages. Advertising. Sample copy and guidelines available at website.

- "Good-bye Property Rights." Article reports on sustainable development efforts that are affecting private property rights.
- "Buffaloed." Article reports on the politics behind the purchase of a Montana ranch.

Rights and Payment

First North American serial rights. Written material, $50–$500. Pays on publication. Provides 2 contributor's copies.

Real Simple

1271 Avenue of the Americas
New York, NY 10020

Deputy Editor: Noelle Howey

Description and Interests

As its title clearly states, the purpose of this publication is to provide practical ways for readers to simplify their lives. *Real Simple* covers a wide range of lifestyle topics, from health to finance to entertaining. The primary audience is women in their 20s to 60s. Health and money are the easiest areas to break into for new writers. Online writing opportunities are also available. Circ: 2 million+.

Contents: 80% articles; 20% depts/columns
Frequency: Monthly
Website: www.realsimple.com

Freelance Potential

30–40% written by nonstaff writers.

Submissions

Query with clips and author bio. Query should be written in the tone and style that will be used in the proposed article. Accepts email to Noelle_Howey@realsimple.com.

- Articles: 1,000–3,000 words. Informational articles; how-to's; profiles; and essays. Topics include health, finances, home, organization, entertaining, cooking, fashion and beauty, career, real women doing interesting things.
- Depts/columns: 100–1,000 words. News, service, how-to's. Topics include: health, fitness, nutrition, and personal finance.

Sample Issue

Advertising. Sample articles and editorial calendar available at website.

- "How to Correct 8 Common Beauty Mistakes." Easy ways to correct common makeup, hair, and skincare blunders.
- "How to Tell if Someone is Lying." Gives 5 tip offs that could indicate that a person isn't telling the truth.

Rights and Payment

All rights. Written material, $2 a word. Kill fee, 25%. Pays on acceptance.

Recreational Cheerleading

2319 FM 1794 W
Beckville, TX 75631

Editor: Valerie Ninemire

Description and Interests

Launched in late 2011 by Recreational Sports Media, *Recreational Cheerleading* is the only magazine dedicated solely to recreational cheerleaders, their coaches, and their parents. It reports on Pop Warner, scholastic, and all-star cheerleading throughout the country, and shares information on stunts, training, safety, coaching, and fundraising. Circ: Unavailable.

Contents: Articles; depts/columns
Frequency: Quarterly
Website: www.reccheermagazine.com

Freelance Potential

Receives many queries monthly.

Submissions

Query. Accepts email to valerie@recsportsmedia.com or submit via website. Response time varies.

- Articles: Word lengths vary. Informational and how-to articles and profiles. Topics include school and extracurricular cheerleading, coaching, training, techniques, stunting, fundraising, and safety.
- Depts/columns: Word lengths vary. Profiles, health, and fitness.

Sample Issue

Sample articles available at website.

- "Event Seeking Talented Leaders." Article discusses the details for the upcoming Champions Cup Cheer & Dance State Nationals.
- "'Get Psyched.'" Article announces the release of a new book series for young readers.
- Sample dept/column: News describes an iPhone-based cheerleading skills demonstration.

Rights and Payment

Rights vary. Payment rates and policy vary.

Redbook

300 W. 57th Street
New York, NY 10019

Editor: Jill Herzig

Description and Interests

Redbook embraces an audience of women in their 30s and 40s, especially those who are in the fullness of their family years. The monthly covers marriage, health, sex, beauty, fashion, finance, food, parenting, entertainment, and all subjects of interest to "real women," who are often profiled in its pages. Almost the entire magazine is open to pitches from seasoned freelancers. Ideas and angles for articles proposed to *Redbook* should be very focused, not generic. The website is written by staff and is not open to paid freelancers. Circ: 2.2 million.

Content: Articles; depts/columns
Frequency: 12 times each year
Website: www.redbookmag.com

Freelance Potential

60% written by nonstaff writers.

Submissions

Accepts queries via email to editors of appropriate departments. Check the masthead for section editors. For essays, general features, career, money, and advocacy, query jthompson@hearst.com. Send health pitches to mbertsos@hearst.com; relationship ideas to bburke@hearst.com; parenting pitches to jtung@hearst.com.

- Articles: Features, 200–2,000 words. Topics include relationships, health and nutrition, home, family care, money, beauty and fashion, entertainment, food, kids.
- Depts/columns: Be Part of the Solution, Family Secrets, Live Richly, Stuff My Kids Taught Me. Not open to freelancers are Inspiration Board and 50 Under 50.

Sample Issue

Advertising. Sample articles available at website.

- "Jennifer Hudson." How the singer/actress celebrates the holidays without putting on weight.
- "Love These Dresses!" Terrific clothes at amazing prices.

Rights and Payment

Rights vary. Pay rate: $1.50–$2 per word. Kill fee: 25%. Pays 10–12 weeks after acceptance.

Red Bulletin

RBNA Headquarters
1740 Stewart Street
Santa Monica, CA 90404

Deputy Editor: Ann Donahue

Description and Interests

In 2011, the makers of Red Bull energy drink launched this lifestyle magazine for young adults, primarily males 18 to 34. It covers sports, music, people, travel, arts, and culture. All content has a contemporary, pithy style. Inserted into major market newspapers and available at newsstands, *Red Bulletin* is also published in nine other countries and is available as an iPad app. Circ: 1.2 million.

Contents: Articles; depts/columns
Frequency: Monthly
Website: www.redbulletin.com

Freelance Potential

Receives numerous queries monthly.

Submissions

Query. Accepts email to ann.donahue@us.redbull.com. Response time varies.

- Articles: Word lengths vary. Informational articles, profiles, and interviews. Topics include celebrities, pop culture, sports, travel, food, music, and film.
- Depts/columns: Interesting news, products, and people around the world.

Sample Issue

Advertising. Sample articles available at website.

- "Heroes." Article profiles the latest and greatest names in music, sports, and art.
- "Action." Article showcases some of the more popular brass bands of New Orleans.
- Sample dept/colum: Bullevard interviews Paul Bonhomme, the latest winner of the Red Bull air race.

Rights and Payment

Rights vary. Payment rates and policy vary.

Reform Judaism

633 Third Avenue, 7th Floor
New York, NY 10017-6778

Managing Editor: Joy Weinberg

Description and Interests

As the official publication of the Union for Reform Judaism, this magazine covers news and developments within the movement, interprets world events, and celebrates the Jewish tradition. Articles are all written from a Reform perspective. Its articles are controversial and written to probe problems, explore solutions, teach, and inspire. Circ: 310,000.

Contents: 65% articles; 35% depts/columns
Frequency: Quarterly
Website: www.reformjudaismmag.org

Freelance Potential

70% written by nonstaff writers. Publishes 25 freelance submissions yearly; 10% by authors who are new to the magazine. Receives 50 unsolicited mss monthly.

Submissions

Query or send complete ms with cover letter and samples of published manuscripts, if applicable. Accepts hard copy. No SASE. To speed response, enclose postage-paid postcard with "Yes," "No," or "Maybe" boxes that we may check. Responds in 2 months.

- Articles: Cover stories, 2,500–3,500 words. Major features, 1,800–2,500 words. Secondary features, 1,200–2,000 words. Informational, investigative, and how-to articles, and personal experience pieces. Topics include Israel, religion, family life, history, heritage, archaeology, ethics, and social issues—all from a Reform perspective.
- Depts/columns: 1,200–1,500 words. Travel, *mitzvah*, and holidays.

Sample Issue

64 pages. Advertising. Sample articles and guidelines available at website.

- "Preparing for the New You." Article shares suggestions for taking stock of one's actions and preparing to change.
- "What Brought Me Back to Judaism." Article features two teens who found their way back to religion.

Rights and Payment

First North American serial rights. Written material, $.30 per word. Kill fee, 25%. Pays on publication. Provides 2+ contributor's copies.

Relish

341 Cool Springs Boulevard, Suite 400
Franklin, TN 37067

Editor in Chief: Jill Melton

Description and Interests

Targeting people who relish the thought of cooking family meals and learning more about nutrition and food, this magazine is distributed via newspapers throughout the country. Its articles cover food-related topics, dining out, and eating healthy. Most articles come complete with recipes. Articles should be topical, but have a long shelf life. Coverage of people and places must be enlightening, instructional, and have a broad national or regional relevance. Circ: Unavailable.

Contents: Articles; depts/columns
Frequency: Monthly
Website: www.relish.com

Freelance Potential

50% written by nonstaff writers. Publishes 30–50 freelance submissions yearly; 10–20% by authors who are new to the magazine.

Submissions

Query with 2–3 clips. Accepts queries through website only. Responds in 1–2 months.

- Articles: 200–500 words (not counting recipes). Informational and how-to articles, profiles, and new product information. Topics include food, dining, nutrition, and cooking.
- Depts/columns: Word lengths vary. News briefs, recipes.

Sample Issue

32 pages. Sample articles and editorial calendar available at website. Guidelines available.

- "Twist and Shout: Twist It Up Cookbook." Article profiles a young leukemia survivor who has a passion for cooking.
- "Care to Schnitzel?" Article shares two schnitzel recipes passed down from the author's Austrian father.
- "Sugarland: Vermont's Rustic Recipes." Article presents rustic recipes from a popular Vermont restaurant.

Rights and Payment

First-time print and electronic rights for 6 months; non-exclusive rights thereafter. Written material, payment rates vary. Pays within 45 days of publication. Provides 2 contributor's copies.

Reptiles

P.O. Box 6050
Mission Viejo, CA 92690-6050

Editor: Russ Case

Description and Interests

Targeting people who are just nuts over their pet reptiles and amphibians, *Reptiles* covers all aspects of owning such creatures. Information on proper care, species profiles, and breeding is offered here. The magazine is not for casual reptile enthusiasts. It seeks articles that give the kind of detailed information and tips that readers need to advance their hobby. Circ: 40,000.

Contents: 50% articles; 50% depts/columns
Frequency: Monthly
Website: www.reptilechannel.com

Freelance Potential

60% written by nonstaff writers. Publishes 55 freelance submissions yearly; 50% by unpublished writers, 40% by authors who are new to the magazine. Receives 20 queries monthly.

Submissions

Query with background information regarding reptile ownership or breeding. Accepts hard copy and email to reptiles@bowtieinc.com. SASE. No simultaneous submissions. Response time varies.

- Articles: To 3,000 words. Informational and how-to articles, interviews, personal experience pieces, and species profiles. Topics include reptile and amphibian health, nutrition, and breeding; news about reptiles and amphibians; field herping/travel; and trends in the hobby.
- Depts/columns: Staff-written.
- Artwork: 35mm slides; TIFF, JPEG, or EPS files at 300 dpi.

Sample Issue

68 pages. Advertising. Sample articles and guidelines available at website.

- "Amazon River Turtles in Danger." Article explains the need for more captive-breeding programs.
- "Keeled Box Turtle Breeding Program at Tennessee Aquarium Yields a Newly Hatched Turtle." Article discusses the first success in their breeding program.

Rights and Payment

First North American serial rights. Written material, $350–$500. Kill fee, 25%. Pays on publication. Provides 2 contributor's copies.

Response

United Methodist Women
475 Riverside Drive, Room 1501
New York, NY 10115

Editor: Yvette Moore

Description and Interests

Carrying the tag line "The Voice of Women in Mission," *Response* is read by Christian women who want to help create a more peaceful, just, and caring world. It profiles mission programs and the people who run them, as well as contemporary social issues. All articles must be about women's issues or programs, or be of special interest to women. Circ: 30,000.

Contents: 90% articles; 10% depts/columns
Frequency: 11 times each year
Website: www.umwmission.org

Freelance Potential

80% written by nonstaff writers. Publishes 150 freelance submissions yearly; 10% by unpublished writers, 50% by authors who are new to the magazine.

Submissions

Query. Accepts email queries to ymoore@unitedmethodistwomen.org. No simultaneous submissions. Responds in 1 month.

- Articles: Word lengths vary. Informational and how-to articles, profiles, interviews, and creative nonfiction. Topics include current events, family life, parenting, feminism, conspicuous consumerism, the environment, politics, public affairs, community activism, social issues, spirituality, youth ministry, and multicultural and ethnic issues.
- Depts/columns: Staff-written.

Sample Issue

48 pages. No advertising. Sample articles available at website.

- "Stumbling Over Reproductive Health." Article describes the lack of inadequate health care for women in developing countries.
- "A Life in Mission." Article features a profile of a nonagenarian who has committed her life to Christian mission.

Rights and Payment

All rights. Written material, payment rates vary. Pays on publication. Provides 3 contributor's copies.

Reunions

P.O. Box 11727
Milwaukee, WI 53211-0727

Publisher/Editor in Chief: Edith Wagner

Description and Interests

Contributors to this publication include individuals directly involved with planning family, military, class, and other reunions. Readers find ideas, inspiration, and resources for reunions and reunion planning. It considers only submissions directly related to reunions and particularly about planning them. Stories about successful reunions, accompanied by photographs that capture that success, are always welcome. Circ: 15,000.

Contents: 75% articles; 25% depts/columns
Frequency: Quarterly
Website: www.reunionsmag.com

Freelance Potential

75% written by nonstaff writers. Publishes 100 freelance submissions yearly; 60% by unpublished writers, 80% by authors who are new to the magazine, 5% by experts. Receives 50 queries, 25 unsolicited mss monthly.

Submissions

Query. Prefers email to editor@reunionsmag.com (Word attachments). Responds in up to 25 months.

- Articles: Word lengths vary. Informational, factual, how-to, profiles, and personal experience. Topics include organizing reunions, choosing locations, entertainment and activities, and genealogy.
- Depts/columns: 250–1,000 words. Opinion, personal experience, resource information, reviews.
- Artwork: Digital images at 300 dpi or higher.

Sample Issue

40 pages. Advertising. Sample copy and guidelines available at website.

- "Burges High School: Class of 1961, 50th Reunion." Report on an El Paso, Texas reunion that was just six months in the making.
- "Seize the Day!" High school graduations are a great venue for family reunions.

Rights and Payment

One-time and electronic rights. Written material, payment rates vary. Payment policy varies. Provides contributor's copies.

RoadBike

1010 Summer Street, 3rd Floor
Stamford, CT 06905

Editor: Steve Lita

Description and Interests

The joys of owning and riding a touring or cruising motorcycle are chronicled here. *RoadBike* publishes articles on destinations, bike and gear reviews, and personal experience tales of riding adventures. It covers all brands of road bikes and wants to hear from experienced riders. Writers should keep in mind that photos are the foundation of a great story. Check the website for specific photography guidelines. Circ: 50,000.

Contents: 80% articles; 15% depts/columns; 5% fiction
Frequency: 9 issues each year
Website: www.roadbikemag.com

Freelance Potential

50% written by nonstaff writers. Publishes 75 freelance submissions yearly; 25% by unpublished writers, 25% by authors who are new to the magazine, 25% by experts. Receives 4 unsolicited mss each month.

Submissions

Send complete ms with artwork. Accepts hard copy. Artwork increases chance of acceptance. Responds in 1–2 months.

- Articles: 1,200–1,500 words. Informational and how-to articles, profiles, interviews, and personal experience and opinion pieces. Topics include roadworthy metric motorcycles, machinery, maintenance, recreation, destinations, and collecting.
- Depts/columns: 400–500 words. Motorcycle event coverage, destination stories written in a condensed manner.
- Artwork: High-resolution digital images.

Sample Issue

82 pages. Advertising. Sample articles and guidelines available at website.

- "Oregon-Montana: Heaven to Hell." Article describes a road trip from Oregon to Montana.
- "Custom in Chrome." Article showcases the 2013 Harley-Davidson CVO Breakout.

Rights and Payment

Rights vary. All material, payment rates vary. Kill fee, 25%. Pays on publication. Provides 1 contributor's copy.

Robb Report

29160 Heathercliff Road, Suite 200
Malibu, CA 90265

Assistant Editor: Bailey S. Barnard

Description and Interests

Targeting affluent and stylish readers, *Robb Report* covers the luxury lifestyle, with articles on high-end automobiles, fashion, jewelry, real estate, and recreation, as well as financial and money management topics. Like its subject matter, its readers are sophisticated and well-educated. Writing must be able to get and keep their attention. Circ: 104,206.

Contents: 60% articles; 40% depts/columns
Frequency: Monthly
Website: www.robbreport.com

Freelance Potential

45% written by nonstaff writers. Publishes 200 freelance submissions yearly; 10% by authors who are new to the magazine. Receives 30 queries monthly.

Submissions

Query with clips. Accepts email queries to editorial@robbreport.com. Responds in 1 week.

- Articles: Word lengths vary. Informational and how-to articles, profiles, interviews, and new product information. Topics include automobiles, private aviation, yachting, real estate, fashion, jewelry, travel, golf, cuisine, wine, cigars, and finance.
- Depts/columns: Word lengths vary. Design, cars, travel, spas, sports, art, antiques, dining, wine and spirits, jewelry and watches, collectibles, home, and exclusive products.

Sample Issue

180 pages. Advertising. Sample articles available at website. Guidelines and editorial calendar available.

- "Culinary Masters Competition 2012: Rare Birds." Article features an interview with Japanese chef Masa Takayama.
- "Merchant of Venice." Destination article on things to do and see in this Italian city.

Rights and Payment

All or first North American serial rights. Written material, to $1 per word. Kill fee, 25%. Pays on acceptance. Provides 2–3 contributor's copies.

Rock & Gem

P.O. Box 6925
Ventura, CA 93006

Managing Editor: Lynn Varon

Description and Interests

This magazine is for rockhounding and lapidary hobbyists of all levels. It features articles on lapidary projects, specimen collecting field trips, gold prospecting, and lapidary skills. Articles that educate beginning rock collectors or lapidaries and promote active participation in the hobby are always welcome. Circ: 32,000.

Contents: 70% articles; 30% depts/columns
Frequency: Monthly
Website: www.rockngem.com

Freelance Potential

85% written by nonstaff writers. Publishes 50 freelance submissions yearly; 20% by unpublished writers, 20% by authors who are new to the magazine, 30% by experts. Receives 10 unsolicited mss monthly.

Submissions

Send complete ms with 8–15 photos and captions. Accepts CD or flash drive submissions with hard copy. No simultaneous submissions. SASE. Accepts email queries to editor@rockngem.com. Responds in 6 months.

- Articles: Features, 2,000–3,000 words. How-to articles, 800–1,000 words. Topics include minerals, geology, specimen collecting, step-by-step lapidary projects, hobby-related subjects. Field Trips, report of site dig and specimens recovered.
- Depts/columns: Staff-written.
- Artwork: Color prints; digital images at 300 dpi.
- Other: Submit material for theme issues at least 6 months in advance.

Sample Issue

76 pages. Advertising. Guidelines and theme list available at website.

- "Exotic Common Opals." Article showcases the colors and patterns commonly found in opals.
- "The Story of 'Big Red.'" Article describes how a rockhound discovered a jasper deposit.

Rights and Payment

First worldwide rights and unlimited, non-exclusive reprint rights (copyright remains with author/photographer). Written material, $100–$275. Full-length articles, plus photos $275. Pays on publication. Provides 5 contributor's copies.

Rolling Stone

Wenner Media
1290 Avenue of the Americas, 2nd Floor
New York, NY 10104-0298

Submissions Editor

Description and Interests

Rolling Stone is renowned for its cutting-edge articles and in-depth features on America's popular music and culture. It also offers reviews of movies and music, profiles of prominent personalities in the music industry, as well as insightful pieces on current events and politics. All of its writers are veteran reporters in the fields of entertainment and politics. The magazine rarely works with new freelancers and does not encourage submissions from them. Circ: 1.3 million.

Contents: 50% articles; 50% depts/columns
Frequency: 26 times each year
Website: www.rollingstone.com

Freelance Potential

50% written by nonstaff writers. Publishes 100+ freelance submissions yearly; 5% by unpublished writers, 10% by industry experts. Receives 100 queries monthly.

Submissions

Query with clips. Accepts email queries to rseditors@rollingstone.com and simultaneous submissions if identified. Responds in 6–8 weeks.

- Articles: To 3,000 words. Informational articles, profiles, interviews, and reviews. Topics include music, entertainment, popular culture, politics, youth issues, and current events.
- Depts/columns: To 1,000 words. Media reviews and entertainment news.

Sample Issue

126 pages. Advertising. Sample articles available at website.

- "Q&A: Pete Townshend." Interview with The Who guitarist about his five decades of music and new memoir.
- "Television: Spy Interrupted." Article discusses the popular Showtime series, *Homeland*.

Rights and Payment

First rights. Written material, $1 per word. Pays on publication. Provides 1 contributor's copy.

Rosebud

N3310 Asje Road
Cambridge, WI 53523

Managing Editor: Roderick Clark

Description and Interests

Rosebud is "the magazine for people who enjoy good writing." A mix of high-quality, vivid stories and poetry, along with a few essays, fill the pages of each issue. It is seeking submissions with more cultural diversity, varieties of subjects, and points of view. Due to the volume of submissions received and because it is a nonprofit organization staffed by volunteers, it uses Rosebud Fast-track Initiative (RFI) for submissions. Circ: 6,000.

Contents: 70% fiction and poetry; 20% depts/columns; 10% other
Frequency: 3 times each year
Website: www.rsbd.net

Freelance Potential

90% written by nonstaff writers. Publishes 45 freelance submissions yearly; 8% by unpublished writers, 60% by authors who are new to the magazine. Receives 100 unsolicited mss each month.

Submissions

For fiction and essays, send complete ms with $1 handling fee. Accepts hard copy (include the letters RFI on the envelope and circle them) and simultaneous submissions. Email poetry to John Smelcer at jesmelcer@aol.com. SASE. Responds in 45 days.

- Articles: Word lengths vary. Literary nonfiction and essays.
- Fiction: 1,000–3,000 words. Experimental, literary, and science fiction; and fantasy.
- Depts/columns: Staff-written.
- Other: Poetry, to 3 poems per submission.

Sample Issue

136 pages. Little advertising. Sample copy available. Guidelines available at website.

- "Chekhov in Love." Short story.
- "The Maxwell House Demon." Short story.

Rights and Payment

First serial and one-time rights. Prose, $30. Poetry, no payment. Pays on publication. Provides 3 contributor's copies.

The Rotarian

Rotary International
One Rotary Center
1560 Sherman Avenue
Evanston, IL 60201-3698

Editor in Chief: John Rezek

Description and Interests

This magazine puts a particular focus on the service aspects of Rotary Club membership, with profiles about the ways the organization helps people around the globe. Articles on topics of general interest to members, such as business management, world health, and the environment, are more likely to be accepted. Circ: 500,000.

Contents: 50% articles; 50% depts/columns
Frequency: Monthly
Website: www.rotary.org

Freelance Potential

40% written by nonstaff writers. Publishes 100 freelance submissions yearly; 10% by authors who are new to the magazine. Receives 50 queries monthly.

Submissions

Query with résumé, outline, and clips or writing samples. Accepts hard copy, email to rotarian@rotary.org, and simultaneous submissions if identified. SASE. Response time varies.

- Articles: To 1,500 words. Informational articles, profiles, interviews, opinion pieces, and new product information. Topics include association news, community concerns, education, global issues, business management, professional ethics, and the environment.
- Depts/columns: Word lengths vary. Book reviews, technology, news, and updates.
- Artwork: 5x7 JPEG photos at 300 dpi.

Sample Issue

80 pages. Advertising. Sample articles and guidelines available at website.

- "Polio's End Game." Article discusses what needs to be done to eradicate polio.
- "Side Trips from Lisbon." Article suggests day trips outside the city limits of Lisbon, which is the site of the 2013 RI Convention.

Rights and Payment

Rights vary. Written material, payment rates vary. Pays on acceptance. Provides 3 contributor's copies.

Route 66

P.O. Box 1129
Port Richey, FL 34673

Executive Editor

Description and Interests

Life and travel along America's storied Route 66, both past and present, are celebrated in this publication. It features lively and entertaining articles on the nostalgia, unusual events, and historical locations along the highway. It is always interested in backroad stories from all Route 66 states. Circ: 70,000.

Contents: 60% articles; 25% depts/columns; 15% other
Frequency: Quarterly
Website: www.route66magazine.com

Freelance Potential

75% written by nonstaff writers. Publishes 20 freelance submissions yearly; 25% by unpublished writers, 25% by authors who are new to the magazine, 50% by experts. Receives 10 unsolicited mss monthly.

Submissions

Send complete ms with artwork. Accepts hard copy, disk submissions (Word or Quark files), and email to route66magazine@yahoo.com. SASE. Responds in 1–2 months.

- Articles: 1,500–2,000 words. Informational articles, profiles, and interviews. Topics include history, travel, attractions, and culture—all as they relate to Route 66.
- Depts/columns: 300 words. Reviews, events, and museum reports.
- Artwork: Color prints or 35mm transparencies; JPEG or TIFF images at 300 dpi.

Sample Issue

64 pages. Advertising. Sample copy and guidelines available.

- "A Route 66 Adventure." Article provides details on an Illinois road trip from Joliet to Towanda.
- "Kingman Army Air Force Museum." Article profiles this museum in Arizona.

Rights and Payment

First North American serial rights. Articles, $60 per page. Other written material, payment rates vary. Pays 45 days after publication. Provides 2 contributor's copies.

Rugby Magazine 

11 Martine Avenue, 8th Floor
White Plains, NY 10606

Editor: Jackie Finlan

Description and Interests

The tradition, lifestyle, and game of rugby are explored in this magazine for fans and players alike. In late 2011, *Rugby Magazine* became an online-only publication. Its goal is to promote rugby, so it seeks submissions from writers who are as passionate and knowledgeable about the sport as its readers. Hits per month: Unavailable.

Contents: 50% articles; 50% depts/columns
Frequency: 6 times each year
Website: www.rugbymag.com

Freelance Potential

50% written by nonstaff writers. Publishes 400 freelance submissions yearly; 50% by unpublished writers, 50% by authors who are new to the magazine, 10% by experts. Receives 20 queries monthly.

Submissions

Query. Accepts email queries to scores@rugbymag.com. Responds in 1 month.

- Articles: Word lengths vary. Informational articles, profiles, interviews, personal experience pieces, and media reviews. Topics include rugby teams, competitions, training, and celebrities.
- Depts/columns: Word lengths vary. News briefs, tournament news, nutrition, refereeing, and player and coach profiles.

Sample Issue

64 pages. Advertising. Sample articles available at website. Guidelines available.

- "Coaching: Getting the Basics Down." Article discusses the importance of perfecting the basic skills before moving on to flashier plays.
- Sample dept/column: Op-Ed shares the factors, beyond game performances and championships, that make a rugby club a quality one.

Rights and Payment

One-time rights. Written material, payment rates vary. Pays on publication. Provides 5 contributor's copies.

Rug Hooking

5067 Ritter Road
Mechanicsburg, PA 17055

Editor: Debra Smith

Description and Interests

Rug hookers of all skill levels turn to this publication for patterns and inspiration. Interesting historical features on rug making and exhibit information round out the mix. Although the focus is on the craft of rug hooking and providing readers practical information and ideas, articles must also be well written and engaging. Circ: 20,000.

Contents: 40% articles; 50% depts/columns; 10% other
Frequency: 5 times each year
Website: www.rughookingmagazine.com

Freelance Potential

90% written by nonstaff writers. Publishes 65–75 freelance submissions yearly; 80% by unpublished writers, 40% by authors who are new to the magazine, 90% by experts. Receives 1-2 unsolicited mss monthly.

Submissions

Send complete ms with artwork and supporting material. Accepts hard copy. SASE. Response time varies.

- Articles: 1,800–3,200 words. Informational and how-to articles, profiles, interviews, personal experience pieces, and patterns. Topics include rug design, dyeing wool, and rug hooking events.
- Depts/columns: 1,000–2,000 words. Projects, short profiles, and techniques.
- Artwork: High-resolution digital images at 300 dpi.

Sample Issue

80 pages. Advertising. Sample articles and guidelines available at website.

- "Primitive Angels for Your Antique Baskets." Article provides instruction on finding baskets and hooking angels on top lid.
- "The Healing Side of Hooking." Article shares projects completed by dementia patients.

Rights and Payment

All rights. Written material, payment varies. Pays on publication. Provides 1 contributor's copy.

Rural Heritage

P.O. Box 2067
Cedar Rapids, IA 52406-2067

Editor: Joe Mischka

Description and Interests

Rural Heritage provides useful information for farmers and loggers who are enthusiasts of working with draft horses, mules, and oxen. It also publishes pieces about self-sufficient living and small diversified farming. Writers should be experienced teamsters, as readers are quick to notice errors in terminology, breed identification, and other details. Circ: 9,500.

Contents: 75% articles; 20% depts/columns; 5% other
Frequency: 6 times each year
Website: www.ruralheritage.com

Freelance Potential

95% written by nonstaff writers. Publishes 52 freelance submissions yearly; 20% by unpublished writers, 30% by authors who are new to the magazine, 40% by experts. Receives 12 queries, 6 unsolicited mss monthly.

Submissions

Query or send complete ms with author biography and qualifications. Accepts hard copy and email to info@ruralheritage.com (attach file). SASE. Response time varies.

- Articles: 650–1,500 words. Informational and how-to articles, and profiles. Topics include rural skills; draft animals; horse-drawn farm equipment; and specific farming, ranching, or logging options.
- Depts/columns: Word lengths vary. Book reviews, auction results, and humor.
- Artwork: 5x7 prints or color transparencies; high-resolution digital images. Line art.
- Other: Submit seasonal material 6 months in advance.

Sample Issue

114 pages. Advertising. Sample articles and guidelines available at website.

- "A View from Holmes County." Article provides an overview of the annual Horse Progress Days events.
- "The Masterson Method." Article introduces the philosophy, methods, and techniques of equine massages.

Rights and Payment

First rights. Written material, $.05 per word. Artwork, $10. Pays on publication. Provides 2 contributor's copies.

Ryse

2100 Lee Road, Suite D
Winter Park, FL 32789

Editor in Chief: J. Jackson, Sr.

Description and Interests

Targeting black business owners, entrepreneurs, managers, and executives, this magazine strives to be a meeting place and clearinghouse of information for Central Florida's young and rising business executives. The goals of *Ryse* are to motivate and educate by providing informational articles on careers and business, and to showcasing success area business people and their achievements. The target audience is aged 21 to 45. *Ryse* launched in the second half of 2011. Circ: Unavailable.

Contents: 80% articles; 20% depts/columns
Frequency: 6 times a year
Website: www.rysemagazine.com

Freelance Potential

Unavailable.

Submissions

Accepts submissions to submissions@rysemag.com.

- Articles: Informational, how-to, profiles, and interviews. Topics include business, careers, finance, arts, lifestyle, health and fitness, and travel.
- Depts/columns: Local business news, book reviews, dining, and lifestyle.

Sample Issue

68 pages. Advertising. Sample copy available at website.

- "Front and Center with Frontline Promotions." Profile of two businessmen partners and the very successful dining establishment they developed and run in Orlando, FL.
- "Tips for a Better Work Life Balance." Strategies for avoiding burnout and finding more opportunities to connect with loved ones in a businessperson's life.

Rights and Payment

Rights and payment vary.

Sacred Journey

The Journal of Fellowship in Prayer

291 Witherspoon Street
Princeton, NJ 08542

Editorial Projects Manager: Lisa M. Clayton

Description and Interests

This nondenominational magazine of Fellowship in Prayer presents religious practices and viewpoints meant to inspire a spiritual lifestyle. It publishes articles on spiritual experiences, prayer, meditation, and religious faiths, as well as book reviews and poems. Submissions should express an individual's personal experience while also conveying a deep, universally appealing spiritual message. Circ: 6,000.

Contents: 80% articles; 10% depts/columns; 10% poetry
Frequency: Quarterly
Website: www.fellowshipinprayer.org

Freelance Potential

90% written by nonstaff writers. Publishes 150+ freelance submissions yearly; 25% by unpublished writers, 50% by authors who are new to the magazine, 25% by experts. Receives 30 unsolicited mss monthly.

Submissions

Send complete ms with biography. Accepts hard copy and email submissions to submissions@sacredjourney.org. SASE. Responds in 2 months.

- Articles: 1,500 words. Personal experience pieces, profiles, and interviews. Topics include religion, faith, prayer, meditation, and spirituality.
- Depts/columns: Word lengths vary. Book reviews.
- Other: Poetry, to 35 lines; to 5 poems per submission. Submit seasonal material 4 months in advance.

Sample Issue

72 pages. No advertising. Sample articles and guidelines available at website.

- "Jewish Redemption." Article refers to two books that speak to being a partner in redemption with God.
- Sample dept/column: Reviews discusses the new book *Religion Gone Astray.*

Rights and Payment

Non-exclusive and electronic rights. No payment. Provides 5 contributor's copies and a 1-year subscription.

Safari

Safari Club International
4800 West Gates Pass Road
Tucson, AZ 85745

Editor: Stan Skinner

Description and Interests
The official publication of Safari Club International, this magazine focuses on big game hunting and conservation around the globe. Guns, animals, and hunting products are also covered. Writers must be an SCI member for submissions to be considered. Articles that deal with legally huntable big game of trophy in a natural setting are accepted. Accompanying photos must include the setting of the hunt, action shots of hunt party members, interesting gear, and the hunter with the trophy. Circ: 50,000.

Contents: 70% articles; 30% depts/columns
Frequency: 6 times each year
Website: www.scifirstforhunters.org

Freelance Potential
80% written by nonstaff writers. Publishes 70 freelance submissions yearly; 25% by unpublished writers, 30% by new authors, 20% by experts. Receives 10 unsolicited mss monthly.

Submissions
SCI members only. Send complete ms with artwork. Accepts disk submissions with hard copy (Word files). No simultaneous submissions. Availability of artwork improves chance of acceptance. SASE. Responds in 2 months.

- Articles: 2,000 words. Informational articles and personal experience pieces. Topics include ethnic and traditional hunts, game, weapons, hunting philosophy, and wildlife conservation and management.
- Depts/columns: Word lengths vary. Safari Club International news and events, new gear and equipment.
- Artwork: 5x7 and 8x10 B/W or color transparencies or color slides; digital images.

Sample Issue
176 pages. Advertising. Sample articles and guidelines available at website.

- "They Gave Us Ammo, Piece by Piece." Article details the history of factory loaded ammunition.
- "My Mexico Double." Article tells of a deer hunting trip in Mexico.

Rights and Payment
All rights. Professional writers, payment rates vary. Non-professional contributors receive honorarium of $25. Pays on publication.

SageWoman

P.O. Box 687
Forest Grove, OR 97116

Editor: Anne Newkirk Niven

Description and Interests
This magazine helps women explore their spiritual lives in a way that respects all persons, creatures, and the Earth. Each themed issue features positive essays, articles, and poetry that celebrate the goddess in every woman. It needs more first-person essays and writing from persons of color. It does not publish scholarly works or book excerpts. Circ: 15,000.

Contents: 55% articles; 45% depts/columns
Frequency: Quarterly
Website: www.sagewoman.com

Freelance Potential
90% written by nonstaff writers. Publishes 50 freelance submissions yearly; 20% by unpublished writers, 40% by authors who are new to the magazine. Receives 100 unsolicited mss monthly.

Submissions
Female writers only. Send complete ms. Prefers email submissions to editor2@bbimedia.com (Word attachments); will accept disk submissions with hard copy. SASE. Responds in 1 month.

- Articles: 800–5,000 words. Informational and self-help articles, personal experience pieces, and profiles. Topics include women's spirituality, green living, dance, prayer, sisterhood, alternative medicine, and health.
- Depts/columns: 1,000–2,000 words. Book reviews, new product reviews, celebrations, and ritual work.
- Other: Poetry.

Sample Issue
96 pages. Advertising. Sample articles, guidelines, and theme list available at website.

- "Secret Lives: Always Remember Who You Are." Article features an interview with the author of the new novel *Secret Lives*.
- "Embracing the Morrigan." Article describes how the goddess of hard truths helped the author seek change.

Rights and Payment
First worldwide serial rights. Written material, $.01 per word; $10 minimum. Pays on publication. Provides 1 contributor's copy and a 4-issue subscription for articles over 1,000 words.

Sail

125 East Main Street, P.O. Box 249
Port Washington, WI 53074

Editor in Chief: Peter Nielsen

Description and Interests

Sail seeks to provide its readers with entertaining, practical, and informational articles of coastal and blue-water sailing, cruising, and racing. It covers the sailing lifestyle, safety and seamanship, navigation, boat handling and maintenance, and the joys of boat ownership. Editorial needs include articles on sailing the waterways of America, as well as more exotic destinations. Circ: 103,348.

Contents: 75% articles; 25% depts/columns
Frequency: Monthly
Website: www.sailmagazine.com

Freelance Potential

50% written by nonstaff writers. Publishes 200 freelance submissions yearly; 10% by unpublished writers, 10% by authors who are new to the magazine, 60% by experts. Receives 20 queries, 20 unsolicited mss each month.

Submissions

Prefers query with sailing bio; will accept complete ms. Prefers email to editorial@sailmagazine.net; will accept disk submissions with hard copy. No simultaneous submissions. SASE. Responds in 2 months.

- Articles: 1,000–3,000 words. Informational articles, personal experience pieces, and essays. Topics include navigation, sail trim, seamanship, naval architecture and construction, sailing lifestyles, destinations, chartering, cruising, and racing.
- Depts/columns: How-to's, 1,000–2,000 words. Voice of Experience, 1,800 words. Sailing tips, news, book reviews, new product information, and Sailing Memories, word lengths vary.
- Artwork: Digital images; slides or prints.

Sample Issue

114 pages. Advertising. Sample articles and guidelines available at website.

- "The Mistress I Don't Mind." Article shares the details of a husband's mid-life crisis purchase of a Cape Dory Typhoon Weekender.
- Sample dept/column: Gear reports on the Forespar Tri-Reacher.

Rights and Payment

First North American serial rights. Written material and artwork, $50–$500. Pays on publication.

Sailing World

Bonnier Corporation
55 Hammarlund Way
Middletown, RI 02842

Editor: David Reed

Description and Interests

Sailing enthusiasts find up-to-date information on racing and performance sailing in each issue of this magazine. Techniques and strategies, as well as important events, are also featured. Its readers are educated about the sport. Unless dealing with a totally new aspect, discuss ideas on an advanced technical level. Circ: 50,000.

Contents: 50% articles; 50% depts/columns
Frequency: 9 times each year
Website: www.sailingworld.com

Freelance Potential

40% written by nonstaff writers. Publishes 50 freelance submissions yearly; 10% by unpublished writers, 10–15% by authors who are new to the magazine, 25% by experts. Receives 10 queries each month.

Submissions

Query. Accepts email to editor@sailingworld.com. Responds in 3 months.

- Articles: 2,000+ words. Informational and how-to articles, profiles, personal experience pieces, event coverage, and new product information. Topics include competitive sailing, racing strategies and techniques, boat design, and regattas.
- Depts/columns: Sailing news, 1,200 words. Race reports, 100 words.

Sample Issue

80 pages. Advertising. Sample articles and guidelines available at website.

- "Fresh Blood & Family Ties." Article reviews the latest in the Highlander class to hit the market.
- "The Brilliance of Bethwaite." Article presents a profile of the late Frank Bethwaite, an award-winning boat designer.
- Sample dept/column: Tech Review profiles the Emirates Team New Zealand.

Rights and Payment

First rights. Written material, $400+. Pays on publication. Provides 2 contributor's copies.

St. Anthony Messenger

Franciscan Friars of St. John the Baptist Province
28 West Liberty Street
Cincinnati, OH 45202-6498

Editor in Chief: John Feister

Description and Interests

With a mix of articles and poetry, *St. Anthony Messenger* addresses the teachings of the Catholic Church and how they apply to family life. Its mission is to help readers better understand the teachings of the gospel and the Catholic Church. Circ: 130,000.

Contents: Articles; depts/columns; fiction; poetry
Frequency: Monthly
Website: www.americancatholic.org

Freelance Potential

74% written by nonstaff writers. Publishes 57 freelance submissions yearly; 40% by authors who are new to the magazine. Receives 25 queries, 108 unsolicited mss monthly.

Submissions

Query with sources and author qualifications for articles. Send complete ms for fiction. Prefers email to stanthonymessenger.org; will accept hard copy. No simultaneous submissions. Responds in 2 months.

- Articles: To 2,500 words. Informational, inspirational, and how-to articles; personal experience pieces; profiles; and interviews. Topics include religion, the Catholic Church, marriage, parenting, family, and social issues.
- Depts/columns: Staff-written.
- Fiction: To 2,500 words. Inspirational fiction.
- Other: Poetry, to 25 lines. Submit seasonal material 1 year in advance.

Sample Issue

56 pages. Advertising. Sample articles, guidelines, and theme list available at website.

- "Catholic Culture; Native Roots." Article profiles the first Native American saint, St. Kateri.
- "Cardinal Dolan on the New Evangelization." Article presents an interview with the president of U.S. bishops.

Rights and Payment

First worldwide serial and electronic rights. Articles and fiction, $.20 per word. Poetry, $2 per line. Pays on acceptance. Provides 2 contributor's copies.

Sasee

P.O. Box 1389
Murrells Inlet, SC 29576

Editor: Leslie Moore

Description and Interests

Distributed in the Myrtle Beach community of South Carolina, *Sasee* appeals to women of all ages with inspirational and humorous essays, articles, and personal experience pieces on a variety of lifestyle topics. It seeks new, unpublished, first-person material that is about or for women. Diverse subjects that reflect all age groups and a variety of writing styles are invited. Circ: 25,000.

Contents: 90% articles; 10% depts/columns
Frequency: Monthly
Website: www.sasee.com

Freelance Potential

75% written by nonstaff writers. Publishes 108 freelance submissions yearly; 25% by unpublished writers, 25% by authors who are new to the magazine. Receives 100 unsolicited mss monthly.

Submissions

Send complete ms with brief author biography. Prefers email to editor@sasee.com (no attachments); will accept hard copy. Submissions will not be returned. Response time varies.

- Articles: 500–1,000 words. Informational articles, creative nonfiction, humor, and personal experience pieces. Topics include parenting, health, fitness, and social issues.
- Depts/columns: Word lengths vary. Local organization updates, profiles, and book reviews.

Sample Issue

42 pages. Advertising. Sample articles and guidelines available at website.

- "The Dance." Essay discusses the smaller-scale duties of a mother of the groom.
- "Who's the Fairest (Decorator) of Them All?" Article shares tips for decorating to one's own style.
- "Going Solo." Personal experience piece about a woman who realizes the gift of traveling alone.

Rights and Payment

First North American print and electronic rights. Written material, payment rates vary. Pays on publication. Provides 1 contributor's copy.

The Saturday Evening Post

1100 Waterway Boulevard
Indianapolis, IN 46202

Features Editor

Description and Interests
This family-oriented, general interest magazine has broadened its editorial focus to include well-researched and timely articles on finance, travel, health and wellness issues, home topics, entertainment, and personality profiles. It also publishes short fiction and how-to articles. For fiction, all genres are welcome—but if the story can make the editors laugh, chances are they will publish it. Circ: 350,000.

Contents: Articles; fiction; depts/columns
Frequency: 6 times each year
Website: www.saturdayeveningpost.com

Freelance Potential
50% written by nonstaff writers. Publishes 1,000 freelance submissions yearly; 10% by unpublished writers, 20% by authors who are new to the magazine, 10% by experts. Receives 100 queries, 200 unsolicited mss monthly.

Submissions
Query or send complete ms with author qualifications and clips. Accepts hard copy and simultaneous submissions if identified. SASE. Responds to queries in 3 weeks, to mss in 6 weeks.

- Articles: 1,000–2,000 words. Informational and how-to articles, profiles, essays, and humor. Topics include humor, finance, home improvement, personalities, entertainment, technology, collectibles, health, and fitness.
- Depts/columns: Word lengths vary. Health, food, technology, finance, and travel.
- Fiction: Word lengths vary.
- Other: Anecdotes, cartoons.

Sample Issue
96 pages. Sample articles and guidelines available at website.

- "America's Painful Divide." Article ponders what it will take to bring a polarized America back together.
- "Attack of the Killer Fees." Article presents tips on how to avoid the newest and most hidden banking charges.

Rights and Payment
All or first serial and electronic rights. Written material, $25–$400+. Payment policy varies.

Saudi Aramco World

Aramco Services Company
Mail Stop 546, Box 2106
Houston, TX 77252-2106

Managing Editor: Dick Doughty

Description and Interests
This magazine features positive and nonpolitical articles about aspects of the Arab and Muslim worlds, including their art, history, geography, and trends. Its audience ranges from people with little background in the subject matter to highly trained specialists. Poetry, memoirs, destination stories, and fiction are not accepted. Circ: 165,000.

Contents: 90% articles; 10% depts/columns
Frequency: 6 times each year
Website: www.saudiaramcoworld.com

Freelance Potential
95% written by nonstaff writers. Publishes 36 freelance submissions yearly; 2% by unpublished writers, 50% by authors who are new to the magazine, 65% by experts. Receives 50 queries monthly.

Submissions
Query with clips, author background and relevant experience, and photos or illustration ideas. Accepts hard copy and email to proposals@aramcoservices.com. SASE. Responds in 4 months.

- Articles: Word lengths vary. Informational articles, profiles, and interviews. Topics include the Middle East, languages, history, geography, multicultural and ethnic issues, the arts, cuisine, and cultural trends.
- Depts/columns: Staff-written.
- Artwork: 35mm or larger transparencies; digital images.

Sample Issue
48 pages. No advertising. Sample articles and guidelines available at website.

- "Hong Kong Day and Night." Article provides a sketchbook of the nationalities and origins that make up Hong Kong's history.
- "Mehter Music Echoes Down the Centuries." Article discusses the widespread influences this music from the Ottoman Empire had throughout the centuries.

Rights and Payment
All rights. Written material, $.50–$1.25 per word. Artwork, $70–$700. Kill fee, 30–75%. Pays on acceptance. Provides 6 contributor's copies.

Scale Auto

21027 Crossroads Circle
Waukesha, WI 53187

Editor: Jim Haught

Description and Interests

Scale automobile model builders, collectors, and enthusiasts use this magazine as a forum to share ideas and techniques. Well-illustrated, detailed how-to articles are featured prominently, as are reviews of models. Articles are evaluated based on the content of the how-to material, the quality of the accompanying photos and illustrations, and the writing style. Circ: 30,000.

Contents: 65% articles; 35% depts/columns
Frequency: 6 times each year
Website: www.scaleautomag.com

Freelance Potential

76% written by nonstaff writers. Publishes 35 freelance submissions yearly; 10% by unpublished writers, 10% by authors who are new to the magazine. Receives 4 queries, 1 unsolicited ms monthly.

Submissions

Send complete ms with artwork. Query for articles longer than 3,000 words. Prefers electronic submissions to www.contribute.kalmbach.com; will accept hard copy. Quality of artwork improves chance of acceptance. SASE. Response time varies.

- Articles: 750–3,000 words. Informational and how-to articles, profiles, and event reports. Topics include collecting and building scale model automobiles.
- Depts/columns: Word lengths vary. Reviews, new product information, and modeling tips.
- Artwork: High-quality digital images.

Sample Issue

58 pages. Advertising. Sample articles and guidelines available at website.

- "Builder's Guide to 1932-1934 Ford Kits." Article is a two-part series that reviews these kits.
- "Kitbash a 1971 Sox & Martin Hemi Cuda." Article explains how to convert Revell's street kit into a Pro Stock car.

Rights and Payment

All rights. Written material, payment rates vary. Pays on acceptance.

Science of Mind

United Church for Religious Science
United Centers for Spiritual Living
573 Park Point Drive
Golden, CO 80401-7042

Submissions: Claudia Abbott

Description and Interests

This digest-size magazine espouses principles of the Science of Mind philosophy. Its pages are filled with articles and interviews that offer spiritual guidance and advice for life-affirming spiritual practices, while also offering perspectives on current events. It seeks true stories about profound and life-changing events. Circ: 50,000.

Contents: 45% articles; 45% depts/columns; 10% other
Frequency: Monthly
Website: www.scienceofmind.com

Freelance Potential

90% written by nonstaff writers. Publishes 7 freelance submissions yearly; 15% by unpublished writers, 10% by authors who are new to the magazine, 75% by experts. Receives 20 queries monthly.

Submissions

Query with outline. Accepts hard copy and email queries to edit@scienceofmind.com. SASE. Responds if interested.

- Articles: 2,000–2,500 words. Inspirational, self-help, and how-to articles; profiles; interviews; and personal experience pieces. Topics include Science of Mind principles, spirituality, religion, metaphysics, the power of thought, the mind-body connection, spiritual leaders, and social action.
- Depts/columns: Your Space, 500 words. Personal experience pieces and media reviews, word lengths vary.

Sample Issue

112 pages. Little advertising. Sample copy available. Writer's guidelines and theme list available at website.

- "All You Need Is Love." Article ponders the power of love in spirituality.
- "Opening to Spirit Power." Article presents ways to open oneself up to spirituality.

Rights and Payment

First rights. Written material, payment rates vary. Pays on publication. Provides 5 contributor's copies.

Scientific American

Board of Editors
75 Varick Street, 9th Floor
New York, NY 10013-1917

Editorial Administrator: Avonelle Wing

Description and Interests
Written for a general readership with a keen interest in science, *Scientific American* is one of the oldest continuously published magazines in the country. Its articles report on groundbreaking events in science and technology and also pinpoint emerging trends. Its preferred authors have extensive firsthand knowledge of the field that they describe. Circ: 688,000.

Contents: 60% articles; 40% depts/columns
Frequency: Monthly
Website: www.scientificamerican.com

Freelance Potential
65% written by nonstaff writers. Publishes 80 freelance submissions yearly; most by unpublished writers and new authors.

Submissions
Query with 1- to 2-page proposal letter and author credentials. Accepts hard copy and email queries to editors@sciam.com (include author's last name and "Proposal" in the subject line). Materials not returned. Responds in 6–8 weeks.

- Articles: 2,500 words. Informational and factual articles, profiles, and interviews. Topics include archaeology, anthropology, astrophysics, biology, ecology, paleontology, physics, psychology, robotics, zoology, and science and technology issues.
- Depts/columns: Word lengths vary. Media reviews, opinion pieces, and Q&As.

Sample Issue
96 pages. Advertising. Sample articles and guidelines available at website.

- "Rising Energy Costs May Usher in U.S. Freight Rail Revival." Article discusses how high fuel prices are leading to a massive resurgence in freight rail.
- "Virtues of the American Autopsy." Article reports on the decline of standard autopsies in favor of virtual autopsies.

Rights and Payment
First worldwide rights. Written material, payment rates vary. Pays on acceptance.

Scientific American Mind

Board of Editors
75 Varick Street, 9th Floor
New York, NY 10013-1917

Editor in Chief: Mariette DiChristina

Description and Interests
Written for a general readership with a high interest in science and psychology, *Scientific American Mind* covers topics relating to psychology and neuroscience. Expert writers report on current events and breakthroughs and contribute articles on how the mind works. It is most interested in psychological topics that relate to a social trend or social issue that is at the forefront of our national conversation. Circ: 180,000.

Contents: 50% articles; 50% depts/columns
Frequency: 6 times each year
Website: www.scientificamerican.com/sciammind

Freelance Potential
80% written by nonstaff writers. Publishes 50 freelance submissions yearly; 50% by experts.

Submissions
Query. Accepts email queries to editors@sciammind.com. Responds in 1 month.

- Articles: 1,500–3,000 words. Informational and how-to articles, profiles, interviews, and new product information. Topics include psychology and counseling, medicine, brain anatomy, neuroscience, and social issues.
- Depts/columns: 150–300 words. News briefs, book reviews.

Sample Issue
76 pages: Sample articles and guidelines available at website.

- "Introducing the Genius Issue." Article reports on the information that can be gleaned from studying the minds of exceptionally creative people.
- "How to Spot Artistic Brilliance." Article presents details on extreme visual creativity as seen in some precocious young artists.

Rights and Payment
First worldwide and all language rights. Written material, payment rates vary. Kill fee, 25%. Pays on acceptance. Provides 5 contributor's copies.

Scouting

Boy Scouts of America
1325 West Walnut Hill Lane
P.O. Box 152079
Irving, TX 75015-2079

Managing Editor: John R. Clark

Description and Interests
Scouting is a publication for the adult leaders in the Boy Scouts of America, featuring articles that help them deliver a quality Scouting program to an increasing number of youth. It covers the full range of Scouting experiences, including strategies on character development, advancement, and outdoor skills to help boys become "Prepared. For Life." The best queries are ones that offer new ideas for programs or lessons. Circ: 1 million.

Contents: 30% articles; 70% depts/columns
Frequency: 5 times each year
Website: www.scoutingmagazine.org

Freelance Potential
50% written by nonstaff writers. Publishes about 8 freelance submissions yearly. 5% by authors new to the magazine. Receives 5–10 queries monthly.

Submissions
Query with outline. Accepts hard copy. SASE. Responds in 3 weeks.

- Articles: 500–1,200 words. Informational, how-to, experiential, and profiles. Topics include Boy Scout programs, activities, and events; leaders and leadership; volunteering and community service; outdoor activities; and nature.
- Depts/columns: 500–700 words. Outdoor activities, short profiles, Scout news. Issues associated with the Scouting program, including mentoring, advancement, health and physical fitness, and parenting.
- Other: Quizzes, puzzles, games.

Sample Issue
48 pages. Sample copy and guidelines available at website.

- "Hike This Way." Day hike tips from the world's best-known long distance hiker, Andrew Skurka.
- "Ethics in the Outdoors." Campsite etiquette shows respect for the environment and fellow Scouts.

Rights and Payment
First North American serial rights, to include online use. Written material, $1 a word. Pays on acceptance. Provides 2 contributor's copies.

Scrapbook Dimensions

1304 North Redwood Road, Suite 116
Sarasota Springs, UT 84045

Editor in Chief: Cindy Wycoff

Description and Interests
This online publication is updated regularly with plenty of ideas, tips, and projects for scrapbooking with paper crafts and computer software. *Scrapbook Dimensions* is available through subscription only. Writers should indicate in their submission which part uses traditional methods and which part uses a computer, even if it may seem obvious. Hits per month: Unavailable.

Contents: Articles; depts/columns
Frequency: Monthly
Website: www.scrapbookdimensions.com

Freelance Potential
90% written by nonstaff writers. Publishes 80 freelance submissions yearly; 25% by authors who are new to the magazine.

Submissions
Send complete ms with supply list and category of submission (see website). Accepts email to submissions@scrapbookdimensions.com. Responds in 6 weeks.

- Articles: Word lengths vary. Informational and how-to articles. Topics include scrapbook designs, techniques, projects, products, tools, software, and digital photography.
- Depts/columns: Word lengths vary. Product reviews, profiles of designers, and projects.
- Artwork: Digital images at 72 dpi.

Sample Issue
Sample copy available at website. Writers' guidelines available.

- "Silhouette Cameos." Article provides instructions for creating silhouette cameos.
- "Hybrid Ribbon Holder." Article provides creative ideas for organizing scrapbook supplies.
- "Color Palette Generator—Automatically From Any Photo." Article shares a website that automatically generates a color palette for an uploaded photo.

Rights and Payment
First and exclusive rights for 6 months. No payment.

Scuba Sport

2441 Cumberland Drive SE
Smyrna, GA 30080

Editor: Joe Froelich

Description and Interests

Positioning itself as a magazine strictly for recreational divers, *Scuba Sport* strives to inform and entertain. It offers information on diving destinations, technique, and equipment. It also features articles that focus on activities to engage non-divers, recognizing that many times divers have partners or families not diving but traveling with them. *Scuba Sport* launched in 2012. Circ: 15,000.

Contents: 80% articles; 20% depts/columns
Frequency: Bimonthly
Website: www.scubasportmag.com

Freelance Potential

Freelance percentage not yet available.

Submissions

Query or send complete ms. Prefers email submissions to joef@scubasportmag.com. Accepts simultaneous submissions if identified. Accompanying photos increase chance of acceptance.

- Articles: 1,200–2,500 words. Informational; how-to's; humor. Topics include dive destinations, techniques, equipment, activities for non-divers.

Sample Issue

52 pages. Advertising. Sample copy, guidelines and editorial calendar available at website.

- "Are You A Good Dive Buddy?" Explores the safety concerns of diving, the critical role of a dive buddy, and the qualifications for being a top-notch one.
- "What's Not to Like About Aruba." Explores what this destination has to offer divers under the water as well as land activities and attractions for post-diving.

Rights and Payment

First North American serial and digital rights. Written material and photographs, payment varies.

Sea Kayaker

P.O. Box 17029
Seattle, WA 98127-0729

Executive Editor: Angela Hyland

Description and Interests

Kayaking destinations, as well as techniques, gear, and safety, are covered in this magazine that helps readers "experience the world's waterways." It prefers to work with writers that are experienced sea kayakers, so that they can write from experience. Circ: 28,000.

Contents: 25% articles; 75% depts/columns
Frequency: 6 times each year
Website: www.seakayakermag.com

Freelance Potential

98% written by nonstaff writers. Publishes 30 freelance submissions yearly; 33% by unpublished writers, 33% by authors who are new to the magazine. Receives 30 queries, 20 unsolicited mss each month.

Submissions

Prefers query with outline and 300- to 500-word excerpt; will accept complete ms. Accepts disk submissions and email queries to editorial@seakayakermag.com (attach files). Response time varies.

- Articles: 2,500–4,000 words. Informational articles, personal experience pieces, and essays. Topics include kayaking, journeys, destinations, kayaking events, races, and history.
- Depts/columns: Word lengths vary. Short day trips, kayaking techniques, DIY projects, problem-solving tips, gear reviews, safety topics, paddler profiles.

Sample Issue

64 pages. Advertising. Sample articles and guidelines available at website.

- "Kayaking in the Australian Desert." Destination piece describes the solitude and wildlife found in Cooper Creek.
- "Fine-tuning Your Fitness." Article explains how to become stronger and more efficient with simple training tips.
- Sample dept/column: Gear Review takes a look at the Innova Swing II, a double inflatable kayak.

Rights and Payment

First North American serial rights. Written material, $.14 per word. Pays on publication. Provides 1 contributor's copy.

Sea Magazine

17782 Cowan, Suite C
Irvine, CA 92914

Managing Editor: Mike Werling

Description and Interests

Focusing on powerboating on the West Coast, *Sea Magazine* is filled with information on boats, destinations, equipment, safety, and gear. It is published with regional editions for California and the Pacific Northwest. The ideal writer is someone who knows powerboats. First-person destination stories, ideally with photos, as well as general boating features and in-depth refit pieces are always of interest. Circ: 50,000.

Contents: 60% articles; 40% depts/columns
Frequency: Monthly
Website: www.seamagazine.com

Freelance Potential

60% written by nonstaff writers. Publishes 80 freelance submissions yearly.

Submissions

Query or send complete ms with photos if applicable. Accepts hard copy and email queries to editorial@seamag.com. Responds in 3 months.

- Articles: 1,500–2,000 words. Informational and how-to articles, personal experience pieces, and new product information. Topics include West Coast powerboating, 30- to 80-foot boats, marine topics, safety, equipment, and boating destinations.
- Depts/columns: 1,200 words. Boat reviews, engines, electronics, sportfishing, gear, and reports from Mexico.

Sample Issue

104 pages. Advertising. Sample copy available.

- "Kadey-Krogen 52." Article provides an in-depth review of this new boat to hit the market.
- "Peace of Mind You Can Install." Article suggests three simple alarms to install that will alert boat owners to smoke, water, and overheating.
- Sample dept/column: Gear presents hydraulic autopilot, radar reflector, and voyage planner products.

Rights and Payment

First North American serial rights. Written material, payment rates vary. Pays on publication. Provides 1–2 contributor's copies.

The Secret Place

P.O. Box 851
Valley Forge, PA 19482-0851

Senior Editor: Evelyn Heck

Description and Interests

The Secret Place strives to draw Christians closer to God and one another by publishing spiritually insightful devotionals. It welcomes original, unpublished meditations, as well as devotionals that focus on one theme and encourage outreach, mission, and service. Of special interest are devotionals that address urban/suburban and rural/nature experiences, and those that appeal to all age groups. Circ: 16,000.

Contents: 95% articles; 5% depts/columns
Frequency: Quarterly
Website: www.judsonpress.com/catalog_secretplace.cfm

Freelance Potential

100% written by nonstaff writers. Publishes 365+ freelance submissions yearly; 25% by unpublished writers, 25% by authors who are new to the magazine. Receives 150 unsolicited mss monthly.

Submissions

Send complete ms. Prefers email submissions to thesecretplace@abc-usa.org; will accept hard copy. SASE. Responds in 6–8 months.

- Articles: 100–200 words. Meditations that include suggested scripture reading, "Thought for the Day," and concluding prayer. Topics include Christian living, faith, family, prayer, peace, justice, and contemporary social issues.
- Other: Submit seasonal material 9–12 months in advance.

Sample Issue

64 pages. Little advertising. Sample articles and guidelines available at website.

- "God Knows." Devotional speaks to God knowing when someone is in need and providing his followers through the help of each other.
- "Promises, Promises." Devotional discusses a parent's beliefs in the promises God makes when caring for his own.

Rights and Payment

First rights for print use, unlimited rights for use in related electronic material. Written material, $20. Pays on acceptance. Provides 1 contributor's copy.

Seek

8805 Governor's Hill Drive, Suite 400
Cincinnati, OH 45249

Editor: Margaret K. Williams

Description and Interests

Seek is a take-home paper designed to supplement religious education or Bible study lessons. It is directed at young adults and adults and contains inspirational stories and Bible lessons. Articles should encourage readers in their walk with Jesus Christ and help them apply biblical truths in their lives. Articles should be written for a specific theme; see website for theme list before submitting. Circ: 27,000.

Contents: 75% articles; 25% depts/columns
Frequency: Weekly material, published quarterly
Website: www.standardpub.com/view/seek_guidelines.aspx

Freelance Potential

85% written by nonstaff writers. Publishes 150–200 freelance submissions yearly.

Submissions

Send complete ms with targeted issue number and issue date. Accepts email submissions to seek@standardpub.com (Word or RTF attachments; include "Submission" and title of article in subject line). No simultaneous submissions. Response time varies.

- Articles: 850–1,000 words. Inspirational, devotionals, and personal experience. Topics include religious and contemporary issues, Christian living, coping with moral and ethical dilemmas, and controversial subjects.
- Depts/columns: Word lengths vary. Questions and activities for group discussion.

Sample Issue

8 pages. No advertising. Sample copy, guidelines, and theme list available at website.

- "Recipe for Worship." Having the proper spirit of worship compared to having the right ingredients to make a favorite dish.
- "Where You Live." An activity to supplement a church school lesson on 1 Timothy 2.

Rights and Payment

All rights. Written material, $.05–$.07 per word. Pays on acceptance. Provides 5 contributor's copies.

Self

Condé Nast Publishing
4 Times Square, 5th Floor
New York, NY 10036

Editorial Director: Carla Levy

Description and Interests

Women ages 22 to 45 are the target audience for this popular health and fitness magazine. With informational articles focusing on nutrition, beauty, fitness, relationships, careers, and style, its goal is to help women feel and be their best. It is interested in hearing about must-read news and surprising facts. *Self*'s tone is authoritative, but engaging. Writers with relevant consumer magazine experience or professional experience are encouraged to submit a query. Circ: 1.6 million.

Contents: Articles; depts/columns
Frequency: Monthly
Website: www.self.com

Freelance Potential

25% written by nonstaff writers. Publishes 70 freelance submissions yearly. Receives 50 queries monthly.

Submissions

Query with résumé and relevant clips. Accepts hard copy. SASE. Response time varies.

- Articles: Word lengths vary. Informational, self-help, and how-to articles; confession pieces; and personal experience pieces. Topics include health and fitness, nutrition, psychology, sex, relationships, self-help, careers, family and parenting issues, and social issues.
- Depts/columns: 100–300 words. New product information; and health, fashion, beauty, and fitness news.

Sample Issue

190 pages. Advertising. Sample articles available at website. Guidelines and editorial calendar available.

- "Nina Dobrev's Secrets to Getting Sexy." Article features a profile of *The Vampire Diaries* star and her style and fitness secrets.
- "Confessions of a Food Addict." Personal experience piece shares the steps the author took to overcome an unhealthy relationship with food.

Rights and Payment

Rights vary. Written material, payment rates vary. Payment policy varies.

Sewanee Review

University of the South
735 University Avenue
Sewanee, TN 37383-1000

Editor: George Core

Description and Interests

This literary journal features original fiction, poetry, and essays that represent depth of knowledge and skill of expression. It has published a mix of distinguished writers and talented newcomers in its 120-year history. It is old school in the best way possible, striving to be traditional—without being quaint—innovative, and mutinous. Humor pieces are always welcome. Please note that unsolicited reviews are very rarely accepted. Circ: 2,500.

Contents: 50% essays; 20% fiction; 20% depts/columns; 10% poetry
Frequency: Quarterly
Website: www.sewanee.edu/sewanee_review

Freelance Potential

99% written by nonstaff writers. Publishes 120 freelance submissions yearly; 1% by unpublished writers, 10% by authors who are new to the magazine. Receives 225 queries and unsolicited mss each month.

Submissions

Send complete ms between September 1 and May 30. Queries are suitable, though not preferred, for essays. Accepts hard copy. No simultaneous submissions. SASE. Responds in 6–8 weeks.

- Articles: To 7,500 words. Essays. Topics vary.
- Fiction: 3,500–7,500 words. All genres.
- Other: Poetry, to 40 lines; to 6 poems per submission.

Sample Issue

334 pages. Sample content and guidelines available at website.

- "Ode to My Son's Audiobooks." Essay discusses the merits of listening to literature.
- "Adventures with Friends of the Library." Essay recounts a couple's move back to their New Mexico hometown after 32 years.

Rights and Payment

First North American serial rights. Written material, payment rates vary. Pays on publication.

Sew News

741 Corporate Circle, Suite A
Golden, CO 80401

Editor: Ellen March

Description and Interests

Sew News inspires the enthusiastic and creative woman who loves to sew. It is filled with accurate, step-by-step information for creating original fashions, accessories, and home decor. Projects are geared to both beginning and advanced sewers. It is interested in hearing from new writers about innovative sewing projects and techniques. Hand weaving, hand needlecrafts, crochet, knitting, and macramé are generally not covered. Circ: 150,000.

Contents: 60% articles; 40% depts/columns
Frequency: 6 times each year
Website: www.sewnews.com

Freelance Potential

40% written by nonstaff writers. Publishes 72 freelance submissions yearly; 20% by unpublished writers, 15% by authors who are new to the magazine, 70% by experts. Receives 40 queries monthly.

Submissions

Query with outline, sketch or photo, list of illustrations, and author qualifications. Accepts hard copy and email to sewnews@sewnews.com. SASE. Responds in 3 months.

- Articles: Word lengths vary. Informational and how-to articles, profiles, interviews, product information, and projects. Topics include sewing techniques, machine embroidery, fitting, textiles, crafts, and industry trends.
- Depts/columns: Word lengths vary. Book reviews, sewing machines, and techniques.

Sample Issue

74 pages. Advertising. Sample copy available. Guidelines available at website.

- "Home-Dec Help." Article explains how to make a swag pattern to dress up windows.
- "Chiffon Chic." Article provides details for designing a chiffon blouse.
- "Fancy Flurries." Article offers step-by-step instructions for creating a clutch purse.

Rights and Payment

All rights. Written material, \$50–\$500 (new writers, generally \$50–\$150). Pays on publication. Provides 2 contributor's copies.

Sew Stylish

The Taunton Press
63 South Main Street
P.O. Box 5506
Newtown, CT 06470

Administrative Assistant: April Mohr

Description and Interests

Ideas and techniques for sewing the latest fashion trends are found in this magazine. Targeting beginning and intermediate sewers, it offers instructions for creating garments that are on the cutting edge of style, as well as how-to's on sewing basics. The goal is to give readers the tools they need to unleash their creativity. More articles that are focused on fashion-forward garment techniques are needed. Circ: Unavailable.

Contents: Articles; depts/columns
Frequency: Quarterly
Website: www.sewstylish.com

Freelance Potential

75% written by nonstaff writers. Publishes 25 freelance submissions yearly; 10% by unpublished writers, 20% by authors who are new to the magazine, 75% by experts. Receives 20 queries monthly.

Submissions

Query with 1- or 2-paragraph summary, outline, and sample photos of work illustrating the topic. Accepts hard copy and email queries to sewstylishletters@taunton.com. Responds in 6 months.

- Articles: Word lengths vary. Informational and how-to articles. Topics include fabrics, project preparation, notions, embellishments, couture tips, and quick projects.
- Depts/columns: Word lengths vary. Style guides and expert tips and techniques.

Sample Issue

98 pages. Advertising. Sample copy available. Guidelines available at www.threadsmagazine.com.

- "Zipper Exposé." Article provides instruction on transforming a basic closure into a decorative detail.
- "Snuggle Up Sweater Knits." Article offers tips for sewing chunky knit sweaters.

Rights and Payment

First and electronic rights. Written material, payment rates vary. Pays on publication. Provides 2 contributor's copies.

Shape

1 Park Avenue, 10th Floor
New York, NY 10016

Executive Editor: Trisha Calvo

Description and Interests

Shape hopes to create better lives and stimulate a deeper understanding of fitness for its audience of women, ages 18–34. Each issue is packed with valuable information and advice on exercise, nutrition, psychology, and beauty. Queries should be identified as either a feature or a column (and if for a column, which one). Circ: 1.7 million.

Contents: 50% articles; 50% depts/columns
Frequency: Monthly
Website: www.shape.com

Freelance Potential

75% written by nonstaff writers. Publishes 100 freelance submissions yearly. Receives 75 queries each month.

Submissions

Query with clips. Accepts hard copy and email queries to tcalvo@shape.com. SASE. Responds in 6 months.

- Articles: Word lengths vary. Informational, self-help, and how-to articles; personal experience pieces; and new product information. Topics include fitness, exercise, nutrition, health, beauty, fashion, and diet tips.
- Depts/columns: Word lengths vary. Fitness success stories, exercise routines, recipes, fashion trends, and beauty tips.

Sample Issue

250 pages. Advertising. Sample articles available at website. Guidelines available.

- "Nine Ways Being a Woman Affects Your Workout?" Article discusses common body issues that affect women in sports and exercise.
- "The Sad Truth About Bullying." Article profiles author Ilie Ruby and her work to combat teen bullying.
- "Seven Women Who Kept Their Weight-Loss Resolutions." Article shares tips from women who pledged to lose weight and succeeded.

Rights and Payment

All rights. Written material, $1 per word. Kill fee, 33%. Pays on acceptance. Provides 3 contributor's copies.

Sharing the Victory

8701 Leeds Road
Kansas City, MO 64129

Editor: Clay Meyer

Description and Interests

Exploring the relationship between faith and sports, *Sharing the Victory* is a ministry tool of the Fellowship of Christian Athletes. It is directed toward student and professional athletes and coaches, reminding them that they make an impact for Jesus Christ. Its articles, profiles, and first-person pieces are meant to inform and inspire readers. Profiles, interviews, and great photos are the best ways for freelancers to break into the magazine. All profile articles must contain an authentic spiritual angle depicting the person's struggles and successes, while including a strong tie to the FCA ministry. Circ: 75,000.

Contents: 60% articles; 40% depts/columns
Frequency: 6 times each year
Website: www.sharingthevictory.com

Freelance Potential

40% written by nonstaff writers. Publishes 20 freelance submissions yearly; 25% by unpublished writers, 10% by authors who are new to the magazine. Receives 4 queries and unsolicited mss monthly.

Submissions

Prefers query with outline and writing samples; will accept complete manuscript. Prefers email to stv@fca.org; will accept hard copy. Availability of artwork improves chance of acceptance. SASE. Response time varies.

- Articles: 1,000–2,000 words. Informational, profiles, interviews, and personal experience. Topics include sports, athletes, coaches, competition, training, focus, faith, missions, Christian education.
- Depts/columns: Staff-written.
- Artwork: Color prints; digital images at 300 dpi.
- Other: Submit seasonal material 3–4 months in advance.

Sample Issue

30 pages. Advertising. Guidelines available. Sample articles available at website.

- "Zeller Mania." It's all in the family for these Indiana basketball phenoms.
- "Touching Back." Faith and football go hand in hand for Tulsa's starting quarterback.

Rights and Payment

First serial rights. Articles, $150–$400. Pays on publication.

Shenandoah

The Washington and Lee University Review

Mattingly House
2 Lee Avenue
Washington and Lee University
Lexington, VA 24450

Editor: R. T. Smith

Description and Interests

After 60 years of publishing an award-winning print journal, *Shenandoah* has turned to a digital format. But it continues to publish quality writing from fledgling writers and established authors. It accepts short stories, short short stories, essays, interviews, reviews, and poetry. Please follow guidelines closely, as submission requirements have changed since going online. Hits per month: Unavailable.

Contents: 50% fiction; 25% nonfiction; 25% poetry
Frequency: Twice each year
Website: www.shenandoahliterary.org

Freelance Potential

100% written by nonstaff writers. Publishes 100 freelance submissions yearly; 5% by unpublished writers, 40% by authors who are new to the magazine. Receives 1,000 unsolicited mss monthly.

Submissions

Query for reviews and interviews. Send complete ms for all other material between September 15 and May 1 only. Accepts hard copy only for poetry; all other work can be submitted through website. Simultaneous submissions accepted if identified. SASE for poetry. Responds in 4–6 weeks.

- Articles: 3,000 words. Essays, interviews, and book reviews.
- Fiction: Word lengths vary. Literary fiction.
- Other: Poetry, 4–6 poems per submission.

Sample Issue

176 pages. Little advertising. Sample copy and guidelines available at website.

- "The Black Madonna." Essay recounts a trip visiting Orthodox churces in search of the Black Madonna.
- "Replacement Parts." Story tells of a teenaged girl who, after losing her mother, reconnects with her estranged father.

Rights and Payment

First North American serial rights. Payment rates vary. All submissions eligible for several annual contest prizes. Payment policy varies.

Shutterbug

1415 Chaffee Drive, Suite #10
Titusville, FL 32780

Editorial Director: George Schaub

Description and Interests

Everything relating to photography is covered in this magazine that targets both the professional and amateur photographer. Photography techniques, new technology, and product information are included in the editorial mix. It seeks articles that will help readers become better photographers. Circ: 115,000.

Contents: 60% articles; 40% depts/columns
Frequency: Monthly
Website: www.shutterbug.com

Freelance Potential

90% written by nonstaff writers. Publishes 50 freelance submissions yearly; 10% by unpublished writers, 20% by authors who are new to the magazine, 10% by experts. Receives 40 queries monthly.

Submissions

Query. Accepts email queries to editorial@shutterbug.com. Availability of artwork required for acceptance. Responds in 2 weeks.

- Articles: 1,000–2,000 words. Informational and how-to articles, profiles, interviews, and personal experience pieces. Topics include photography, digital imaging, equipment, business trends, technology, freelance photography, and techniques.
- Depts/columns: 1,000–1,500 words. Product reviews, news, and book reviews.
- Artwork: Digital images.

Sample Issue

186 pages. Advertising. Sample articles available at website. Guidelines and editorial calendar available.

- "Are Your Prints Too Dark? The Cause and the Cure." How-to article gives tips for avoiding photos that are too dark.
- "Interior Portraits Using Sunlight." Article explains how to master the technical and artistic principles of photographing human subjects.
- Sample dept/column: Equipment Reviews provides information on affordable digital SLRs.

Rights and Payment

First and second serial rights. All material, payment rates vary. Pays on publication. Provides 2 contributor's copies.

Sierra

Sierra Club
85 Second Street, 2nd Floor
San Francisco, CA 94105

Managing Editor

Description and Interests

With the motto "Explore, enjoy, and protect the planet," *Sierra* features articles about the natural world. It prefers to work with professional writers, ideally those who have covered environmental issues. Submissions should be well-researched and smartly written. Circ: 550,000.

Contents: 60% articles; 40% depts/columns
Frequency: 6 times each year
Website: www.sierraclub.org/sierra

Freelance Potential

45% written by nonstaff writers. Publishes 50 freelance submissions yearly; 10% by authors who are new to the magazine, 5% by experts. Receives 40–60 queries monthly.

Submissions

Query with clips or writing samples. Accepts email to submissions.sierra@sierraclub.org, and simultaneous submissions if identified. Responds in 2 months.

- Articles: 500–3,000 words. Informational, investigative, essays, personal experience, and opinion. Topics include environmental and conservation issues, adventure travel, nature, self-propelled sports, and trends in green living.
- Depts/columns: 50–1,500 words. Enjoy, upbeat look at green living; Explore, destinations; Grapple, environmental issues; Act, personality profiles; Comfort Zone, environmental design; Ponder, ruminative essay; Smile, humorous essay; Escape, eco-resort getaway; Survive, harrowing wilderness experience; Mixed Media, book and media reviews.

Sample Issue

76 pages. Advertising. Sample copy and guidelines available at website.

- "The Swamp Man." Louisiana activist fights to save wetland trees.
- "Keeping Bugs and Bears at Bay." Comparing natural and chemical repellants for safety and effectiveness.

Rights and Payment

First North American serial, reproduction, and archival rights. Articles, $.75 a word and up. Depts/columns, $50–$1,000. Pays on acceptance. Kill fee for assigned stories. Provides 2 contributor's copies.

Silent Sports

600 Industrial Drive
P.O. Box 620583
Middleton, WI 53562

Editor: Joel Patenaude

Description and Interests

Silent Sports is a regional magazine for the upper Midwest, with a focus on non-motorized aerobic sports. Its articles cover bicycling, cross country skiing, running, and kayaking, and range from how-to and destination pieces to personality profiles. Its readers are active in both competitive and noncompetitive events. Local writers are preferred, but material from writers outside of the region is accepted as long as it has a local angle. Circ: 10,000.

Contents: 65% articles; 15% depts/columns; 20% other
Frequency: Monthly
Website: www.silentsports.net

Freelance Potential

80% written by nonstaff writers. Publishes 125 freelance submissions yearly; 10% by unpublished writers, 25% by authors who are new to the magazine. Receives 15 queries monthly.

Submissions

Query. Accepts email queries to silentsports@gmail.com. Response time varies.

- Articles: To 1,200 words. Informational, how-to, and self-help articles; profiles; interviews; personal experience pieces; and product information. Topics include running, biking, kayaking, skiing, snowshoeing, skating, hiking, backpacking, training, safety, nutrition, and sports medicine.
- Depts/columns: Staff-written.

Sample Issue

72 pages. Advertising. Sample articles available at website. Guidelines available.

- "Ryan's Rules." Article presents a profile on the Green Bay Marathon and Door County Race director.
- "Extreme Skiing." Article describes the Arrowhead Ultra, a 135-mile winter sports race.

Rights and Payment

First serial rights. Written material, $40–$150. Pays on publication. Provides 1 contributor's copy.

S. I. Parent

Staten Island Parent Magazine

1200 South Avenue, Suite 202
Staten Island, NY 10314

Editor: Gerri Friscia

Description and Interests

Founded in 1989, *S. I. Parent* serves Staten Island families with information about parenting and education, child development topics, pregnancy issues, family fitness, and family-friendly recreation. It also features several calendar and community listings. Material with a local angle, sources, and resources is preferred. Circ: 60,000.

Contents: Articles; depts/columns
Frequency: Monthly
Website: www.siparent.com

Freelance Potential

10% written by nonstaff writers. Receives 60 mss monthly.

Submissions

Send complete ms and brief bio. Accepts email to editorial@siparent.com ("Editorial submission for *SI Parent*" in the subject line). Response time varies.

- Articles: 600–800 words. Informational and self-help articles, creative nonfiction, humor, personal experience pieces, and new product information. Topics include parenting issues, family relationships, house and home, recreation, sports, travel, seniors, pets, education, and disabilities.
- Depts/columns: Word lengths vary. Child development, health advice, humor, and media reviews.

Sample Issue

152 pages. Advertising. Sample articles and guidelines available at website.

- "Life Lessons from a Breastfeeding Mom." Personal experience piece shares a mom's trials and tribulations while nursing three children.
- "New Reason to Potty Train." Article discusses the harmful effects disposable diapers have on the environment.
- "Helping Kids Find the Right Extracurricular Activity." Article discusses which factors to consider when choosing an activity.

Rights and Payment

Regional exclusive rights. Articles, $.035 per word. Depts/columns, no payment. Pays on publication.

Skating

United States Figure Skating Association
20 First Street
Colorado Springs, CO 80906-3697

Editor: Troy Schwindt

Description and Interests
Figure skating and the personalities, programs, trends, and events that affect the sport are the focus of this magazine. It is written for members and fans of the United States Figure Skating Association. It looks to cover up-and-coming skaters from around the world, as well as coaches with interesting stories. Personalities or newsworthy items relating to figure skating in an author's local area are welcome. Circ: 42,000.

Contents: 80% articles; 10% depts/columns; 10% other
Frequency: 11 times each year
Website: www.usfigureskating.org

Freelance Potential
70% written by nonstaff writers. Publishes 15 freelance submissions yearly; 10% by unpublished writers, 20% by authors who are new to the magazine. Receives about 7 queries and unsolicited mss monthly.

Submissions
Query with résumé, clips, or writing samples, and photo ideas; or send complete ms. Accepts hard copy, disk submissions, and email queries to tschwindt@usfigureskating.org. SASE. Responds in 1 month.

- Articles: 750–2,000 words. Informational, how-to, profiles, and interviews. Topics include association news, competitions, techniques, personalities, and training.
- Depts/columns: 600–800 words. Competition results, profiles of skaters and coaches, sports medicine, fitness, technique tips.
- Artwork: B/W and color prints, slides, or transparencies; digital images at 300 dpi.

Sample Issue
76 pages. Advertising. Sample copy available at website. Guidelines available.

- "Partners in Life." Professional skaters are partners both on and off the ice.
- "Leading Lady." Ashley Wagner, a young skater from Virginia, battles injuries to become a leading figure skating contender.

Rights and Payment
First serial rights. Written material, $75–$150. Artwork, payment rates vary. Pays on publication. Provides 5–10 contributor's copies.

Skeet Shooting Review

5931 Roft Road
San Antonio, TX 78253

Editor: Susie Fluckiger

Description and Interests
This magazine covers competitions, techniques, and equipment for the sport of skeet shooting. It is the official publication of the National Skeet Shooting Association and covers news, events, and programs of the organization, as well as prominent practitioners of skeet shooting. Its readership is primarily men over the age of 40 who also enjoy hunting and outdoor activities in addition to skeet shooting. Articles are geared to all ability levels of the sport. Circ: 12,000.

Contents: 80% articles; 10% depts/columns; 10% other
Frequency: Monthly
Website: www.nssa-nsca.org

Freelance Potential
95% written by nonstaff writers. Publishes 60+ freelance submissions yearly; 50% by unpublished writers, 2% by authors who are new to the magazine, 90% by experts. Receives 3 unsolicited mss monthly.

Submissions
Send complete ms. Accepts disk submissions and email submissions to ssr@nssa-nsca.com. SASE. Response time varies.

- Articles: 500 words. Informational and how-to articles, profiles, interviews, and new product information. Topics include competitive and recreational skeet shooting.
- Depts/columns: 500 words. News and product reviews.

Sample Issue
78 pages. Advertising. Sample articles available at website. Theme list available.

- "Synchronize Gun with Target." Article offers tips for movement of the gun.
- "Traveling with Firearms." Article discusses how best to protect firearms while traveling.

Rights and Payment
All rights. Written material, payment rates vary. Pays on publication. Provides 3 contributor's copies.

Skeptical Inquirer

944 Deer Drive NE
Albuquerque, NM 87122

Editor: Kendrick Frazier

Description and Interests
Fringe science claims, paranormal activity, and unexplained phenomena are the subject material of this semi-scholarly journal. It seeks serious scientific evaluations followed by debate and discussion. *Skeptical Inquirer* also publishes book reviews and news stories. It has broadened the editorial scope to include a wide variety of scientific or investigative examinations of public issues that include biomedicine, education, technology, psychology, education, and social sciences. Circ: 40,000.

Contents: 75% articles; 25% depts/columns
Frequency: 6 times each year
Website: www.csicop.org

Freelance Potential
80% written by nonstaff writers. Publishes 30 freelance submissions yearly; 5% by unpublished writers, 10% by authors who are new to the magazine, 85% by experts. Receives 6 queries monthly.

Submissions
Query or send complete ms. Query for opinion pieces. Accepts hard copy and email submissions to kendrickfrazier@comcast.net. SASE. Response time varies.

- Articles: 2,000–3,200 words. Informational and research articles. Topics include paranormal events, the media, religion, communications, science, and technology.
- Depts/columns: Book reviews, 600–1,000 words. News and comment, 250–1,000 words. Opinion, to 1,200 words.

Sample Issue
78 pages. No advertising. Sample articles and guidelines available at website.

- "Neurologic Illness or Hysteria? A Mysterious Twitching Outbreak." Article examines a mysterious outbreak among teenaged girls in Western New York.
- "Enfield Poltergeist." Article describes strange happenings in an English home that required calling in a poltergeist.

Rights and Payment
All rights. No payment. Provides contributor's copies.

Skiing

5720 Flatiron Parkway
Boulder, CO 80301

Editor: Sam Bass

Description and Interests
The edgier side of skiing is the focus of this photo-filled magazine. It covers ski destinations, tips on techniques, profiles of skiers, and information on the latest gear. Its readers range in skill level from novice to experienced skiers, but they are always looking for their next big adventure and information about the latest trends in the sport. Circ: 300,000.

Contents: 70% articles; 30% depts/columns
Frequency: 4 times each year
Website: www.skiingmag.com

Freelance Potential
60% written by nonstaff writers. Publishes 50 freelance submissions yearly; 2% by unpublished writers, 5% by authors who are new to the magazine, 10% by experts. Receives 10–50 queries monthly.

Submissions
Query with clips or writing samples. Prefers email queries to editor@skiingmag.com; will accept hard copy. SASE. Responds in 2–4 months.

- Articles: To 2,000 words. Informational, how-to, profiles, interviews, humor, and adventure pieces. Topics include ski destinations, extreme skiing and adventures, personalities, techniques, and gear.
- Depts/columns: 100–500 words. Profiles, trends, travel, tricks, nutrition, training, gear, safety.

Sample Issue
164 pages. Advertising. Sample copy and guidelines available.

- "5 More Spring Flings." Best destinations for end-of-the-season competitions, parties, and pond skimming, from Oregon's Mt. Bachelor to Aleyeska, Alaska.
- "HBO Sports Sensationalizes Backcountry Skiing." A critique of a recent TV show about the sport on *Real Sports with Bryant Gumbel.*

Rights and Payment
First universal and all media rights. Written material, $1 a word. Pays on acceptance. Provides 2 contributor's copies.

Sky & Telescope

Sky Publishing
90 Sherman Street
Cambridge, MA 02140

Editor in Chief: Robert Naeye

Description and Interests

Sky & Telescope covers the latest news and leading-edge advances in the science and hobby of astronomy. Its articles and columns are written to appeal to everyone from amateur enthusiasts to professional astrophysicists. Because it caters to hobbyists, it looks for articles that are free of excessive technical jargon, but factually correct and written in a concise style. Circ: 100,000.

Contents: 50% articles; 50% depts/columns
Frequency: Monthly
Website: www.skyandtelescope.com

Freelance Potential

50% written by nonstaff writers. Publishes 25 freelance submissions yearly; 5% by unpublished writers, 20% by authors who are new to the magazine, 10% by experts. Receives 15 queries monthly.

Submissions

Query with outline. Prefers email to editor@skyandtelescope.com; will accept hard copy. No simultaneous submissions. Responds in 2–3 weeks.

- Articles: Feature articles 1,200–2,400 words. Articles, 800–1,200 words. Informational articles. Topics include astronomical research, technology, facilities, instruments, and advances in space science.
- Depts/columns: Focal Point, essays on contemporary issues in astronomy, 550 words. Celestial Calendar, upcoming astronomical events and tips for viewing, word lengths vary.
- Artwork: Color or B/W prints; high-resolution TIFF or JPEG digital images.

Sample Issue

86 pages. Advertising. Sample copy and guidelines available at website.

- "Touchdown on the Red Planet." Article discusses new discoveries about Mars' ability to support life.
- "The Evolving Eclipse Map." Article explains how today's eclipse maps can predict cosmic alignments with precision.

Rights and Payment

Rights vary. All material, payment rates vary. Pays on publication. Provides 2 contributor's copies.

Smithsonian

MRC 513
P.O. Box 37012
Washington, DC 20013-7012

Editor: Michael Caruso

Description and Interests

With an online presence, as well as a print edition, *Smithsonian* magazine brings readers a mix of history, archaeology, culture, science, arts, travel, and interesting profiles from around the world. Like the Institution and its many museums, this magazine has a far-reaching subject list. Prospective writers are given the opportunity to submit their work either to the print magazine or to the website. It is much easier to have an article published on the website. Circ: 2.1 million.

Contents: 85% articles; 15% depts/columns
Frequency: Monthly
Website: www.smithsonianmag.com

Freelance Potential

95% written by nonstaff writers. Publishes 100 freelance submissions yearly.

Submissions

Query with writing credentials. Accepts electronic queries sent via the "Contact Us" tab at website only. Responds in 3 weeks.

- Articles: 3,000–4,000 words. Informational articles, profiles, and interviews. Topics include history, nature, the environment, science, and the arts.
- Depts/columns: Phenomena & Curiosities, 1,000–1,500 words. Points of Interest, 1,250–1,750 words. Presence of Mind, 1,200–2,000 words.

Sample Issue

104 pages. Advertising. Sample copy and guidelines available at website.

- "Seoul of a New Machine." Article reports on Seoul's transformation from a third-world city into a tech-savvy mecca of artists and architects.
- "The Hunt for Ebola." Articles describes the CDC's race to find the origins of the deadly virus outbreak.
- "Breaking Point." Article discusses the clash between surfers, celebrities, and scientists over Malibu's coast.

Rights and Payment

First North American serial rights. Written material, payment rates vary. Kill fee varies. Pays on acceptance.

Social Justice Review

Catholic Central Verein of America
3835 Westminster Place
St. Louis, MO 63108

Editor: Rev. Edward Krause

Description and Interests
Founded by the Catholic Central Verein of America in 1908, *Social Justice Review* has a mission to advocate the Christian principles and social teachings of the popes. It publishes scholarly essays and opinion pieces, mostly on social topics, such as marriage, family, and humanity. It welcomes material on the history and principles of Catholic dogma, scholarly pieces on Catholicism and social justice, and articles about the works of the popes. All opinions and essays must be in keeping with the teachings of the Catholic Church. Circ: 3,500.

Contents: 80% articles; 20% depts/columns
Frequency: 6 times each year
Website: www.socialjusticereview.org

Freelance Potential
95% written by nonstaff writers. Publishes 45 freelance submissions yearly; 15% by unpublished writers, 20% by authors who are new to the magazine, 5% by experts. Receives 5 unsolicited mss monthly.

Submissions
Send complete ms. Accepts disk submissions with hard copy. SASE. Response time varies.

- Articles: To 3,000 words. Informational articles and essays. Topics include education, religion, politics, media issues, family life, cultural issues, human rights, theology, and social concerns.

Sample Issue
30 pages. No advertising. Sample articles available at website.

- "The For-Profit Social Welfare Policy Sector and End-of-Life Issues: A Troublesome Ethical Mixture." Essay discusses current factors that will increase ethical problems with end-of-life issues.
- "The Ongoing Identity Crisis on Campus." Article examines issues that arise when political correctness clashes with the Catholic faith on Catholic campuses.

Rights and Payment
First serial rights. Written material, $.02 per word. Pays on publication. Provides 2 contributor's copies.

The Social Media Monthly

Cool Blue Company, LLC
2100 M Street NW, Suite #170-242
Washington, DC 20037

Publisher and Editor: Robert Fine

Description and Interests
The Social Media Monthly reports on and analyzes developments in all the platforms of social media, and their impact on daily life around the world. The target audience is innovators, entrepreneurs, marketers, and analysts, as well as teachers, students, and everyone interested in social media beyond its mere use. It was recognized as one of the hottest launches of 2011 by *Min Online,* a publication on media. Circ: Unavailable.

Contents: Articles; depts/columns
Frequency: Monthly
Website: www.thesocialmediamonthly.com

Freelance Potential
Receives numerous queries monthly.

Submissions
Query. Accepts email queries to bob@thesocialmediamonthly.com. Response time varies.

- Articles: Word lengths vary. Informational and how-to articles, profiles, and interviews. Topics include social media apps, tablets, smart phones, photo sharing, business management of media, educational uses, and lifestyle trends.
- Depts/columns: Apps, trends, news.

Sample Issue
Advertising. Sample articles available at website.

- "Put Your Game Face On." Article discusses Facebook's new app, Bingo Friendzy, that allows users to play for real money.
- "The Wasted Opportunity: 2012, The Republicans and Social Media." Essay discusses why social media should be an integral part of a forward-looking campaign strategy.
- "A Big Bang: Notes from the First Foodservice Social Media Universe." Article provides highlights from the recent convention.

Rights and Payment
Rights vary. Payment rates and policy vary.

The Society Diaries 

M.M.G. Communications, Inc.
40 NE Loop 410, Suite 630
San Antonio, TX 78216

Editor in Chief: Lance Avery Morgan

Description and Interests

This newly launched magazine offers an insider view of *uber* luxurious lifestyles of the rich and famous in Central and South Texas. It covers high-profile events and fundraisers, people, parties, entertaining, charity, design, fashion, and travel. Circ: 10,000.

Contents: 80% articles; 20% depts/columns
Frequency: 6 times each year
Website: www.thesocietydiaries.com

Freelance Potential

75% written by nonstaff writers. Publishes 150 freelance submissions yearly; 20% by authors who are new to the magazine. Receives 30–50 queries each month.

Submissions

Query or send complete ms. Accepts email submissions to lance@thesocietydiaries.com.

- Articles: Word lengths vary. Informational articles and profiles. Topics include fashion, style, lifestyle, the arts, entertaining, charities, parties, events, relationships, travel, society.
- Depts/columns: Word lengths vary. Reviews, news, lifestyle.

Sample Issue

132 pages. Advertising. Sample copy available at website.

- "Art Collecting's New Realism." An inside look at one of the world's most exclusive art sales, just outside of Amsterdam.
- Sample dept/column: In Host department, a professional events planner offers tips for throwing a book launch party.

Rights and Payment

Rights unavailable. Written material, payment rates and policy unavailable.

Soft Dolls & Animals

Scott Publications
2145 West Sherman Boulevard
Muskegon, MI 49441

Editor: Kelly Koch

Description and Interests

Geared to beginner through advanced level sewers, this magazine features how-to articles, ideas, techniques, and patterns for making cloth dolls and animals. Profiles of well-known fabric craft artists are also regularly included. Editorial guidelines include detailed information about submitting a query for step-by-step projects. A written request should be included to have photos. Circ: 28,000.

Contents: Articles; depts/columns
Frequency: 6 times each year
Website: www.softdollsandanimals.com

Freelance Potential

100% written by nonstaff writers. Publishes 50 freelance submissions yearly; 50% by authors who are new to the magazine. Receives several queries monthly.

Submissions

Send complete ms with step-by-step instructions for projects, photos, author biography, and list of sources for materials. Accepts disk submissions with hard copy or email to kkoch@scottpublications.com. SASE. Response time varies.

- Articles: To 3,000 words. How-to projects for making cloth dolls and animals.
- Depts/columns: Word lengths vary. Patterns, new product information, events, Q&As, tips, techniques, and resources.

Sample Issue

66 pages. Little advertising. Sample copy available. Guidelines available at website.

- "Face Sculpting 101." Article explains a technique to create unique faces on existing patterns.
- "Pat and Gloria: Pregnant Friends." Article provides a pattern for a set of pregnant friends that have synthetic knit skin.
- "The Heart of the Doll." Article reports on a teddy bear design that made it to the big screen.

Rights and Payment

Rights vary. Written material, payment rates vary. Pays on publication.

The Southern Review

3990 West Lakeshore Drive
Baton Rouge, LA 70808

Fiction, Nonfiction, or Poetry Editor

Description and Interests

Established and emerging writers find a home here for their original works of fiction, poetry, creative nonfiction, and literary essays. Celebrating 75 years in publication, *The Southern Review* emphasizes contemporary literature in the U.S. and abroad. Poems and fiction are selected with careful attention to craftmanship and technique and to the seriousness of the subject matter. Although willing to publish experimental writing that appears to have a valid artistic purpose, the journal avoids extremism and sensationalism. Circ: 4,500.

Contents: 30% essays; 33% fiction; 33% poetry; 4% artwork
Frequency: Quarterly
Website: www.lsu.edu/tsr

Freelance Potential

100% written by nonstaff writers. Publishes 150 freelance submissions yearly; 50% by authors who are new to the magazine. Receives 600 unsolicited mss monthly.

Submissions

Send complete ms for nonfiction and fiction between September 1 and December 1; 1 submission each per reading period. Send complete ms for poetry between September 1 through February 1. Accepts hard copy and simultaneous submissions if identified. SASE. Responds in 6 months.

- Articles: 500–8,000 words. Creative nonfiction, essays, and literary criticism.
- Fiction: To 8,000 words. Literary fiction.
- Other: Poetry, to 5 poems per submission.

Sample Issue

192 pages. Little advertising. Sample copy available. Guidelines available at website.

- "Blood from a Stone." Play details the fraught relationships within a working-class family in Connecticut.
- "Swarm." Poem presents a visual and aural landscape about an invasion of ladybugs.

Rights and Payment

First North American serial rights. Written material, $25 per page, maximum payment of $200 for prose and $125 for poetry. Pays on publication. Provides 2 contributor's copies and a 1-year subscription.

Southwest Airlines Spirit

2811 McKinney Avenue
Dallas, TX 75204

Editor: Jay Heinrichs

Description and Interests

Southwest Airlines' inflight magazine, *Spirit,* explores a variety of general interest subjects, including pop culture, business, personal technology, sports, and health that appeal to the upscale consumer. It also publishes a small amount of fiction. Queries are only accepted for the magazine sections listed in the writer's guidelines. Circ: 3.4 million.

Contents: 55% articles; 45% depts/columns
Frequency: Monthly
Website: www.spiritmag.com

Freelance Potential

20–40% written by nonstaff writers. Publishes 50 freelance submissions yearly; 30% by authors who are new to the magazine, 5% by experts.

Submissions

Query with writing samples. Send complete ms for fiction. Accepts email to appropriate section editor, see guidelines for addresses. Responds in 2–3 months.

- Articles: Feature articles, to 5,000 words. Other articles, to 1,500 words. Informational, self-help, and how-to articles; profiles; and interviews. Topics include the arts, entertainment, software, business, careers, cars, computers, conservation, family, parenting, food, dining, health, fitness, recreation, travel, sports, and leisure.
- Fiction: To 1,500 words. All genres.
- Depts/columns: Business Idea, trends and entrepreneurial inspiration, to 1,500 words; The Numbers, interesting factoids, 120 words; Blessings Counted, word lengths vary.

Sample Issue

152 pages. Advertising. Sample articles and guidelines available at website.

- "Northwest Florida Beaches." Article offers a guide to the beaches, restaurants, and attractions in Northwest Florida.
- "A Story in Black and White." Essay discusses the prejudice and stigmatism against interracial couples in 1970s San Francisco.

Rights and Payment

First rights. Written material, $1 per word. Pays on acceptance. Provides 1 contributor's copy.

Southwest Review

Southern Methodist University
P.O. Box 750374
Dallas, TX 75275-0374

Fiction Editor: Jennifer Cranfill
Poetry/Nonfiction Editor: Wilard Spiegelman

Description and Interests

Short fiction and articles that address a broad spectrum of interests are found in this literary journal from Southern Methodist University. It also presents high-quality poetry in both experimental and traditional forms. For fiction, it prefers well-crafted stories that focus on character rather than plot. It is a good idea to read the magazine before submitting. Circ: 1,500.

Contents: 35% articles; 35% fiction; 30% poetry
Frequency: Quarterly
Website: www.smu.edu/southwestreview

Freelance Potential

100% written by nonstaff writers. Publishes 65–70 freelance submissions yearly; 80% by authors who are new to the magazine. Receives 200–300 unsolicited mss monthly.

Submissions

Send complete ms between September and May. Accepts hard copy and electronic submissions via the website ($2 fee for online). Prefers no simultaneous submissions. SASE. Responds in 3 months.

- Articles: 3,500–7,000 words. Informational articles, literary criticism, and essays. Topics include history, literature, folklore, current events, art, music, and theater.
- Fiction: 3,500–7,000 words. Literary fiction.
- Other: Poetry, no line limits, to 6 poems per submission.

Sample Issue

162 pages. Advertising. Sample copy available. Guidelines available at website.

- "Basement and Roof." Short story.
- "The Crystal Bridges Museum: American Art in the Heartland." Essay.

Rights and Payment

First North American serial rights. Written material, payment rates vary. Pays on publication. Provides 5 contributor's copies.

SpeciaLiving

P.O. Box 1000
Bloomington, IL 61702-1000

Editor: Betty Garee

Description and Interests

This digital magazine was created to help people with mobility impairments lead more active, fulfilling lives. Each issue offers information on services and products that facilitate more independent living. Travel stories and stories about personal success are needed. Everything must relate to improving life for the mobility-impaired. Hits per month: Unavailable.

Contents: 85% articles; 15% depts/columns
Frequency: Quarterly
Website: www.specialiving.com

Freelance Potential

90% written by nonstaff writers. Publishes 40 freelance submissions yearly; 20% by unpublished writers, 50% by authors who are new to the magazine, 10% by experts. Receives 20 queries monthly.

Submissions

Query stating availability of artwork. Accepts email queries to gareeb@aol.com. Responds in 1 week.

- Articles: To 800 words. Informational and how-to articles, personal experience pieces, profiles, interviews, and new product information. Topics include associations, careers, consumer interests, education, family, health, house and home, recreation, relationships, social issues, sports, and travel—all as related to mobility impairment.
- Depts/columns: Word lengths vary. Humor.
- Artwork: Color prints.

Sample Issue

68 pages. Advertising. Sample copy available at website.

- "Getting Back on the Road." Article discusses the factors which determine whether one is mobile enough to drive.
- "Meant for Motherhood." Personal experience piece tells of a new mother's struggle caring for her son with multiple sclerosis.

Rights and Payment

One-time rights. Written material, $.10 per word. Pays on publication. Provides 1 author's copy.

Speedway Illustrated

107 Elm Street
Salisbury, MA 01952

Editor: Karl Fredrickson

Description and Interests

Speedway Illustrated is written by racing enthusiasts for racing enthusiasts. Driver and car profiles, race information, and driving tips are all part of the mix. Its readers appreciate all levels of stock car racing, from local dirt tracks to NASCAR. Writers who have years of experience at the raceway or under the hoods of stock racing cars are preferred. Circ: 40,000.

Contents: 60% articles; 40% depts/columns
Frequency: Monthly
Website: www.speedwayillustrated.com

Freelance Potential

45% written by nonstaff writers. Publishes 50 freelance submissions yearly; 1% by unpublished writers, 10% by authors who are new to the magazine, 90% by experts. Receives 1 unsolicited ms monthly.

Submissions

Send complete ms with artwork. Accepts disk submissions and email submissions to editorial@speedwayillustrated.com. SASE. Responds in 1–2 months.

- Articles: 500–2,500 words. Informational and how-to articles, profiles, interviews, personal experience and opinion pieces, and new product information. Topics include stock car racing, events, and personalities; and car care accessories.
- Depts/columns: 500–800 words. Resources and racing photography.
- Artwork: High-resolution digital images.

Sample Issue

106 pages. Advertising. Sample copy available.

- "The Wall Broke, But the Driver Didn't." Article describes one of rookie Michael Welch's memorable races.
- "Madhouse: A Racer's Perspective." Article discusses whether Bowman Gray really is wild and crazy.

Rights and Payment

First rights. All material, payment rates vary. Pays on publication.

Spin

408 Broadway, 4th Floor
New York, NY 10013

Editor in Chief: Caryn Ganz

Description and Interests

For more than 25 years, *Spin* has celebrated the best of today's music as well as the music of years past. It chronicles the back stories behind today's most intriguing trends, scenes, and artists. *Spin* relies on solid reporting, but with an edge in perspective and voice. The magazine was acquired by digital network BuzzMedia in July 2012. Circ: 450,000.

Contents: 80% articles; 20% depts/columns
Frequency: 11 times a year
Website: www.spin.com

Freelance Potential: 70% written by nonstaff writers.

Submissions

Query with clips. Prefers email to cganz@spin.com.

- Articles: 1,000–4,000 words. Interviews, news features, criticism, event coverage, global field reportage, and blogs. Topics include music, people, scenes, culture, ranked lists of best albums, songs, reissues, videos, and books.
- Dept/columns: 100–450 words. News, concert and movie reviews.

Sample Issue

Advertising. Sample articles available at website.

- "Japandroids; Killing Yourself to Live." The Vancouver band prepares for its second release, *Celebration Rock*.
- "Rebooting Project Mersh: Hardcore Punks Threaten Indie Rock's Hold on the Cutting Edge." Hardcore punk bands that are pushing the envelope and redefining "cutting-edge."

Rights and Payment

First North American serial rights and web rights. Written material, payment rates vary. Kill fee, 25%. Pays within 30 days of publication.

Spirit of Change

P.O. Box 405
Uxbridge, MA 01569

Editor: Carol Bedrosian

Description and Interests

Holistic living and alternative health topics are the focus of this magazine. Regional in scope, it features articles on holistic health, spirituality, personal growth and psychology, and environmental awareness. It also reports on natural and holistic services and products available within the six New England states. While each issue centers around a theme, article submissions are not limited to them. It does not print articles that promote any one product, practitioner, event, or therapeutic modality. Circ: 55,000.

Contents: 55% articles; 45% depts/columns
Frequency: Quarterly
Website: www.spiritofchange.org

Freelance Potential

100% written by nonstaff writers. Publishes 50 freelance submissions yearly; 50% by authors who are new to the magazine.

Submissions

Send complete ms with author bio. Accepts hard copy. SASE. No electronic submissions. Response time varies.

- Articles: 500–5,000 words. Informational, inspirational, and how-to articles; profiles; and opinion pieces. Topics include holistic health, green living, and spirituality.
- Depts/columns: Word lengths vary. Interviews, music and book reviews, and recipes.

Sample Issue

68 pages. Sample copy, guidelines, and theme list available at website.

- "The Peace Abbey's Journey Continues." Article profiles this interfaith meeting place's commitment to social change.
- "1,000 Kisses Save Forgotten Dogs." Article describes seven extraordinary animal rescues.
- Sample dept/column: Healthy Cooking presents versatile recipes for fall vegetables.

Rights and Payment

All rights. No payment. Authors receive a bio and contact information at end of article.

Sport Fishing

460 North Orlando Avenue, Suite 200
Winter Park, FL 32789

Managing Editor: Stephanie Pancratz

Description and Interests

How-to, where-to, and science and conservation articles that relate to saltwater fishing are found in this magazine. Targeting an audience of serious fishermen, it focuses on North America, although other destinations are sometimes covered. It is only interested in ideas that are new, fresh, or different. Readers should say to themselves, "I never knew that." Circ: 120,000.

Contents: 60% articles; 40% depts/columns
Frequency: 9 times each year
Website: www.sportfishingmag.com

Freelance Potential

40% written by nonstaff writers. Publishes 20–25 freelance submissions yearly; 5% by unpublished writers, 5–20% by authors who are new to the magazine, 5–20% by experts. Receives 4 queries monthly.

Submissions

Prefers query; will accept complete ms. Accepts email to editor@sportfishingmag.com. Response time varies.

- Articles: Longer features, 1,700–2,200 words. Shorter features, 350–1,200 words. Informational and how-to articles. Topics include game fish; bluewater, reef, inlet, and inshore saltwater fishing; techniques; and equipment.
- Depts/columns: Game Plan features great ideas from sports professionals, 700–800 words.
- Artwork: Digital photos.

Sample Issue

82 pages. Advertising. Sample articles and guidelines available at website.

- "Fishing Hook Construction." Article explains how saltwater fishing hooks are made.
- "Fishing the Gulf's Open Waters." Article describes the best way to fish the open water structure of the Gulf.

Rights and Payment

All rights. Articles, $150–$750. Game Plan, $250. Artwork, payment rates vary. Pays on acceptance. Provides 1–3 contributor's copies.

Sports Afield

15621 Chemical Lane, Suite B
Huntington Beach, CA 92649-1506

Editor in Chief: Diana Rupp

Description and Interests

One of the oldest hunting magazines in the United States (founded in 1887), *Sports Afield* now focuses solely on big game hunting. It publishes articles about adventure hunts and destination pieces and also covers the latest guns and optical equipment necessary for such outings. It is not interested in mundane hunts or those that use questionable methods or ethics. Circ: 50,000.

Contents: 60% articles; 40% depts/columns
Frequency: 6 times each year
Website: www.sportsafield.com

Freelance Potential

85% written by nonstaff writers. Publishes 30 freelance submissions yearly; 10% by unpublished writers, 20% by new authors, 70% by experts. Receives 40 queries, 25 mss monthly.

Submissions

Prefers query with outline, photo availability, and author qualification; will accept complete ms. Accepts hard copy, disk submissions, and email to letters@sportsafield.com. SASE. Responds in 8 weeks.

- Articles: To 2,500 words. Informational articles, personal experience pieces, profiles, and interviews. Topics include big game safaris, weapons and equipment, and destinations.
- Depts/columns: 300–400 words. Short items on safari basics, conservation, shooting tips, world record animals.
- Artwork: Color slides or transparencies; high-resolution digital images.

Sample Issue

98 pages. Advertising. Sample articles and guidelines available at website.

- "Savage Lady Hunter." Article presents a new rifle specifically engineered for the serious female hunter.
- "Featured Destination: The Kalahari." Article discusses the abundance of game found in this African desert.

Rights and Payment

Articles, first North American serial rights. Depts/columns, all rights. All material, payment rates vary. Pays on acceptance.

Sportsnet

Rogers Sportsnet
One Mount Pleasant Road
Toronto, Ontario M4Y 3A1
Canada

Publisher & Editor in Chief: Steve Maich

Description and Interests

Sportsnet magazine was launched by Rogers Media, the same company that owns the Sportsnet television channels in Canada. The magazine and its companion website publish expert commentary and analysis of teams in the major professional leagues and premier amateur sporting events. Hockey, baseball, football, soccer, MMA—and the personalities behind them—are all covered. Circ: 100,000.

Contents: Articles; depts/columns
Frequency: 26 times each year
Website: www.sportsnet.ca

Freelance Potential

Receives several queries monthly.

Submissions

Query. Accepts email to rogersdigitalmedia@rci.rogers.com. Response time varies.

- Articles: Word lengths vary. Informational articles, profiles, interviews, and opinion pieces. Topics include major league sports, top amateur sports, athletes, coaches, programs, sports issues, and sporting events.
- Depts/columns: Word lengths vary. Sporting news.

Sample Issue

Advertising. Sample articles available at website.

- "I'm Scared." Article profiles mixed-martial artist Georges St-Pierre on the past year of training and injuries.
- "CFL Playoff Preview." Article discusses the season to date and the likely teams to make the playoffs.
- "Saint Lance." Article delves into the shocking details behind Lance Armstrong's downfall.

Rights and Payment

Rights vary. Payment rates and policy vary.

Sports Spectrum

P.O. Box 2037
Indian Trail, NC 28079

Managing Editor: Brett Honeycutt

Description and Interests

This is not just a sports magazine. *Sports Spectrum* is a Christian sports publication that seeks to reach Christians and non-Christians by focusing on key life issues through the experiences and testimonies of sports figures. The goal is to lead readers toward knowing and understanding the importance of faith in Christ. It welcomes submissions from Christian freelancers with experience in writing about sports who share the magazine's vision. Circ: 25,000.

Contents: 80% articles; 20% depts/columns
Frequency: Quarterly
Website: www.sportsspectrum.com

Freelance Potential

90–95% written by nonstaff writers. Publishes 30–40 freelance submissions yearly; 10% by unpublished writers. Receives 15 queries each month.

Submissions

Query with clips. Accepts email queries to editor@sportsspectrum.com. Responds in 1–2 weeks.

- Articles: 1,500–2,000 words. Informational articles, profiles, interviews, and creative nonfiction. Topics include faith and sports.
- Depts/columns: Staff-written.

Sample Issue

100 pages. Sample copy available. Guidelines available at website.

- "Russ Ortiz." Article profiles the MLB pitcher on how he meshes his two loves of baseball and Jesus.
- "Around the Net." Article discusses the influence Christian rapper Lecrae has had on Christian althetes in all sports.

Rights and Payment

All rights. Written material, $.21 per word. Kill fee, 50%. Pays on acceptance. Provides 5 contributor's copies.

Strange Horizons

Editor in Chief: Niall Harrison

Description and Interests

Strange Horizons is a magazine of and about speculative fiction, including science fiction, fantasy, horror, slipstream, and fantastika. Poetry, reviews, essays, and interviews also add to the editorial mix. Writers are encouraged to review its detailed guidelines available on the website. Circ: Unavailable.

Contents: Articles; fiction
Frequency: Weekly
Website: www.strangehorizons.com

Freelance Potential

Receives many freelance submissions monthly.

Submissions

Query or send complete ms for nonfiction. Send complete ms for fiction and poetry. Accepts email to appropriate department (see guidelines for contact information; include "Query," "Submission," "Poetry," or "Review" in subject line). No simultaneous submissions. Response time varies.

- Articles: 2,000–5,000 words. Informational articles, essays, reviews, and interviews. Topics include science, technology, history, culture, authors of speculative fiction, media reviews.
- Fiction: To 9,000 words. Science fiction, fantasy, horror, slipstream, and fantastika.
- Other: Poetry, to 100 lines. Reviews, 1,000–2,000 words.

Sample Issue

Advertising. Sample copy and guidelines available at website.

- "Steven Spielberg's Early Television Genre Works." Article examines the director's early television works to determine how his filmmaking career remains successful and relevant.
- "He Reminds Us." Story is about a guide who takes a reowned artist on his last tour.
- "*Channel Sk1n.*" Review looks at this new science fiction title by Jeff Noon.

Rights and Payment

Articles and reviews, ongoing nonexclusive electronic rights; payment rates vary. Fiction and poetry, first-printing world-exclusive English-language rights; payment rates vary.

Strategy Magazine

2625 Piedmont Road, Suite 56–370
Atlanta, GA 30324

Editor in Chief: Mavian Arocha-Rowe

Description and Interests

Businesspeople rely on *Strategy Magazine* for advice and information on what it takes to succeed. It covers the current economic climate and its impact on the business environment, while also offering strategies for improving sales and developing effective marketing, financial, and management plans. Writers should first review the magazine's departments and send a clear and concise query targeting one of them. Most writers have significant business experience. Circ: 25,000.

Contents: 60% articles; 40% depts/columns
Frequency: 6 times each year
Website: www.strategymagazine.com

Freelance Potential

50% written by nonstaff writers. Publishes 20 freelance submissions yearly; 5% by authors who are new to the magazine, 50% by experts.

Submissions

Query with clips or send complete ms. Accepts email to editor@strategymagazine.com. Responds in 2 weeks.

- Articles: 2,000 words. How-to and instructional articles, profiles, interviews, personal experience pieces, and new product information. Topics include business, management, the economy, science, and technology.
- Depts/columns: 500 words. Finance, management, business strategies, lifestyle, leadership development, and marketing.

Sample Issue

98 pages. Sample articles available at website.

- "Why Service Is the Answer." Article discusses how those stuck in a neutral job can strengthen skills and expand interests by working with nonprofits.
- "She's a Darn Good Thing." Article features a profile on Cynthia Good, the CEO of Little PINK Book.
- Sample dept/column: Personal Finance offers do's and don'ts when dining with one's boss.

Rights and Payment

Rights vary. Written material, payment rates vary. Pays on publication.

Style at Home

25 Sheppard Avenue West, Suite 100
Toronto, Ontario M2N 6S7
Canada

Editor in Chief: Erin McLaughlin

Description and Interests

Interior design, home styles, and decorating tips are the editorial focus of this Canadian magazine. It covers everything from emerging design trends and renovation projects to ideas for stylish entertaining at home. While many of the topics are universal in appeal, any profiled home, designer, product, or shopping destination must be located in Canada. Material that offers readers inspiration and solutions is always needed. Circ: 235,000.

Contents: 60% articles; 40% depts/columns
Frequency: Monthly
Website: www.styleathome.com

Freelance Potential

80% written by nonstaff writers. Publishes 130 freelance submissions yearly; 1% by unpublished writers, 10% by authors who are new to the magazine, 25% by experts. Receives 20 queries monthly.

Submissions

Query. Accepts email queries to letters@styleathome.com. Responds in 1 month.

- Articles: 500–1,000 words. Informational articles, profiles, and new product information. Topics include interior design and decorating, collecting, antiques, gardening, entertaining, food, and dining.
- Depts/columns: 300–700 words. Entertaining, design tips, designs for small spaces, and designs on a budget.

Sample Issue

186 pages. Advertising. Sample articles available at website. Guidelines available.

- "Something Old, Something New." Article showcases the home of a decorating guru that features a formal nature theme.
- "Lasting Impressions." Article provides ideas for incorporating artificial greenery into one's holiday decorating.

Rights and Payment

First rights. Written material, payment rates vary. Kill fee, 50%. Pays on acceptance. Provides 1 contributor's copy.

sub-Terrain

P.O. Box 3008, MPO
Vancouver, British Columbia V6B 3X5
Canada

Editor: Brian Kaufman

Description and Interests

The editors of *sub-Terrain* tend to favor writing that is edgy and provocative—the kind of writing that may not be found in more mainstream literary journals. It publishes creative nonfiction, commentary, fiction, poetry, reviews, and author profiles with excerpts. It no longer accepts general submissions of poetry; all poems must relate to one of the themes. It is interested in seeing more environmental journalism. Circ: 4,000.

Contents: 40% fiction; 30% articles; 10% depts/columns; 20% other
Frequency: 3 times each year
Website: www.subterrain.ca

Freelance Potential

90% written by nonstaff writers. Publishes 40–50 freelance submissions yearly; 30% by unpublished writers, 50% by new authors. Receives 100 unsolicited mss monthly.

Submissions

Send complete ms. Accepts hard copy (identify theme for which you are submitting). SAE/IRC. Response time varies.

- Articles: To 4,000 words. Creative nonfiction, commentary, opinion pieces, profiles, and interviews. Topics include politics, public affairs, social issues, and literature.
- Fiction: To 3,000 words. Literary fiction.
- Depts/columns: 500–700 words. Reviews and profiles of authors.
- Other: Poetry, must be related to theme.

Sample Issue

124 pages. Advertising. Sample copy, guidelines, and theme list available at website.

- "Carcass." Story tells of a deer carcass found along the side of the road.
- "Pretty on the Outside." Essay bemuses the author's obsession with makeup.

Rights and Payment

Rights vary. Fiction and nonfiction, $25 per page. Poetry, $25 per poem. Pays on publication. Provides 5 contributor's copies.

The Sun

107 North Roberson Street
Chapel Hill, NC 27516

Editor: Sy Safransky

Description and Interests

The Sun is an independent literary journal. For more than 30 years, it has published writing conveying the joy, heartache, and confusion that comes with being human. Fiction, poetry, essays, and interviews are published here. It favors personal writing, but is also interested in thoughtful essays on political, cultural, and philosophical themes. Circ: 70,000.

Contents: 50% articles; 30% depts/columns; 15% fiction; 5% poetry
Frequency: Monthly
Website: www.thesunmagazine.org

Freelance Potential

90% written by nonstaff writers. Publishes 100 freelance submissions yearly; 5% by unpublished writers, 30% by authors who are new to the magazine. Receives 10 queries, 700 unsolicited mss monthly.

Submissions

Query for interviews. Send complete ms for all other material. Accepts hard copy. SASE. Responds in 3–6 months.

- Articles: To 7,000 words. Interviews and essays. Topics include social issues, politics, economics, and current events.
- Fiction: To 7,000 words. Literary fiction.
- Other: Poetry.

Sample Issue

48 pages. No advertising. Sample article and guidelines available at website.

- "The First Year." Essay describes a couple's move to the suburbs as they expect their first child.
- "It's Hard to Know What You Need." Story is about a woman's conflicted feelings at her estranged mother's funeral.

Rights and Payment

One-time rights. Essays and interviews, $300–$2,000. Fiction, $300–$1,500. Poetry, $100–$500. Pays on publication. Provides 2 contributor's copies and a 1-year subscription.

T'ai Chi

P.O. Box 39938
Los Angeles, CA 90039

Editor: Marvin Smalheiser

Description and Interests
This magazine features articles that explore new developments, skills, and techniques in the world of martial arts. It also includes interviews with well-known tai chi experts in the T'ai Chi Ch'uan, internal martial arts, qigong, and traditional Chinese medicine disciplines. Circ: 50,000.

Contents: 95% articles; 5% depts/columns
Frequency: Quarterly
Website: www.tai-chi.com

Freelance Potential
95% written by nonstaff writers. Publishes 100 freelance submissions yearly; 35% by new authors, 65% by experts. Receives 10–12 queries, 8–12 unsolicited mss monthly.

Submissions
Query or send complete ms. Accepts hard copy and email to taichi@tai-chi.com (Word attachments). No simultaneous submissions. SASE. Responds in 2–3 weeks.

- Articles: 500–3,500 words. Informational and self-help articles, profiles, interviews, and personal experience pieces. Topics include t'ai chi ch'uan, qigong, Chinese traditional medicine, Chinese culture and philosophy, health, and training methods.
- Depts/columns: Staff-written.
- Artwork: Glossy B/W prints or slides; digital images at 300 dpi.

Sample Issue
68 pages. Advertising. Sample copy available. Guidelines available at website.

- "Value of Chinese Herbs." Article explains how herbs can balance the energies of the body.
- "How to Select a Good Video/DVD for Your Needs." Article discusses factors to consider when choosing a DVD about T'ai Chi Ch'uan or qigong.

Rights and Payment
First North American serial rights. Written material, $75–$500. Pays on publication. Provides 2 contributor's copies.

Tathaastu

25 South Main Street, Suite 2
Edison, NJ 08837

Editor in Chief: Georgy Bhaala

Description and Interests
Offering Eastern wisdom for the mind, body, and soul, *Tathaastu* seeks to be an informative guide to a happier and more peaceful life. It offers articles on yoga and fitness, alternative therapies, holistic medicine, and Eastern spirituality. Writers from all walks of life who understand the inner serenity that yoga, meditation, and holistic living can bring are welcome to send submissions. Most writers, however, are people who are practitioners, teachers, or speakers within these fields. It is not accepting submissions for its departments and columns at this time. Circ: 25,000.

Contents: Articles; depts/columns
Frequency: 6 times each year
Website: www.tathaastumag.com

Freelance Potential
60% written by nonstaff writers. Publishes many freelance submissions yearly.

Submissions
Send complete ms. Accepts email submissions to editor@tathaastumag.com. Response time varies.

- Articles: 700–1,400 words. Informational and how-to articles, and interviews. Topics include spirituality, Eastern philosophies, alternative health and remedies, holistic medicine, meditation, and yoga.
- Depts/columns: Not accepting at this time.

Sample Issue
104 pages. Advertising. Sample articles and guidelines available at website.

- "Coffee: Nature's Surprising Superfood." Article discusses health benefits found in coffee.
- "Yoga for Anxiety." Article explains how yoga therapy is a useful tool in managing anxiety.
- "Beauty Is in the Soul." Article describes how powerful potent energies such as trust, faith, and acceptance help guide one's life the right way.

Rights and Payment
Print and electronic rights. Written material, payment rates vary. Payment policy varies.

Tea

A Magazine

1000 Germantown Pike, Suite F-2
Plymouth Meeting, PA 19462-2486

Editor: Dan Bolton

Description and Interests

Anything and everything about tea is covered in this magazine for tea lovers around the world. Articles on its history, culture, and health benefits, including recipes, are found in each issue. There are no limits on word counts for articles. Writers that have an idea that will interest tea enthusiasts are encouraged to submit an article. Circ: 5,000.

Contents: Articles; depts/columns
Frequency: 6 times each year
Website: www.teamag.com

Freelance Potential

75% written by nonstaff writers. Publishes 20 freelance submissions yearly; 10% by unpublished writers, 60% by authors who are new to the magazine, 30% by experts. Receives 6 unsolicited mss monthly.

Submissions

Send complete ms. Accepts hard copy, disk submissions (Word), and email submissions to teamag@teamag.com. SASE. Response time varies.

- Articles: No word limits. Informational articles and new product information. Topics include health, fitness, nutrition, and history.
- Depts/columns: Word lengths vary. Collectibles, personal essays, tea recipes, and book reviews.
- Artwork: JPEG or TIFF files at 300 dpi.

Sample Issue

48 pages. Sample articles available at website. Guidelines available.

- "Healthy Herbals." Article takes a look at the health benefits of herbal infusions.
- "Sommelier Secrets: Matcha Demystified." Article provides information on the history and uses of this Japanese green tea.

Rights and Payment

All rights. Articles, $50–$200. Pays on publication. Provides 10 contributor's copies.

Tea Party Review

1101 Highland, Suite 201
P.O. Box 101688
Arlington, VA 22201

Editor: Steven Allen
Online Editor: Cheryl Chumley

Description and Interests

The *Tea Party Review* was launched at the Conservative Political Action Conference in Washington, DC, in 2011, and covers the presidential and other campaigns. Its stated mission is to be a place where Tea Partiers trade ideas, resolve disputes, find news of other activists, and move the goals of the party forward. Circ: Unavailable.

Contents: Articles
Frequency: Updated regularly
Website: www.teapartyreview.com

Freelance Potential

Receives numerous queries monthly.

Submissions

Query. Accepts email to editor@teapartyreview.com. Response time varies.

- Articles: Word lengths vary. Informational articles, news reports and analysis, opinion pieces, and satire. Topics include campaign coverage, candidates, Tea Party supporters, political corruption, family in America, big business, American politics, and the media.

Sample Issue

Advertising. Sample articles available at website.

- "Ted Cruz Comments on Supreme Court Ruling." Article includes the response of U.S. Senate candidate Ted Cruz on the U.S. Supreme Court decision on Arizona's immigration law.
- "The Osama Killing Versus the American Revolution." Opinion piece compares the differences of the killing of Osama bin Laden with the American Revolution.
- "Keep Moving, Tea Party!" Opinion piece is a rallying call for tea partiers to get involved.

Rights and Payment

Rights vary. Payment rates and policy vary.

Teddy Bear and Friends

Madavor Media LLC
85 Quincy Avenue, Suite B
Quincy, MA 02169

Editor: Joyce Greenholdt

Description and Interests

Teddy Bear and Friends has merged with its sister publication *Teddy Bear Review*. It continues to provide complete coverage of the teddy bear and plush collectibles markets for adults. Artists, manufacturers, retailers, and conventions are featured, along with how-to craft articles. The history of teddy bears has been thoroughly covered. Writers must have a remarkably different story to warrant publication. Circ: 10,000.

Contents: 70% articles; 30% depts/columns
Frequency: 6 times each year
Website: www.teddybearandfriends.com

Freelance Potential

90% written by nonstaff writers. Publishes 24 freelance submissions yearly; 10% by unpublished writers, 10–20% by authors who are new to the magazine, 20% by experts. Receives 8 queries, 3 unsolicited mss monthly.

Submissions

Query with résumé, writing samples, and photos; or send complete ms. Accepts hard copy. SASE. Responds in 2–3 months.

- Articles: 750–1,500 words. Informational and how-to articles, profiles, and interviews. Topics include collectible teddy bear and other plush toys, teddy bear figurines, artisans, manufacturers, suppliers, retailers, collectors, and conventions.
- Depts/columns: Word lengths vary. News, antique bears, and collecting updates.

Sample Issue

64 pages. Advertising. Sample articles available at website. Guidelines available.

- "Basel Toy Museum Announces Upcoming Exhibits." Article provides a glimpse of two exhibits opening in time for the holiday season.
- "An Artist's Insight: Taking Part in Online Shows." Article discusses how to maximize exposure when participating in an online show.

Rights and Payment

All rights. Written material, \$.30–\$.35 per word. Pays on publication. Provides 2+ contributor's copies.

Texas Runner & Triathlete

P.O. Box 19909
Houston, TX 77224

Editor: Lance Phegley

Description and Interests

Texas Runner & Triathlete was borne from the merger of *Inside Texas Running* and *Runner Triathlete News*. It is filled with information about marathons, half marathons, major road races, triathlons, duathlons, and cycling and adventure racing in the southwest. It also features articles on training, nutrition, runner profiles, product reviews, and news from the running community. It welcomes writers who can provide race coverage and running profiles. Circ: 13,000.

Contents: 25% articles; 25% depts/columns; 50% other
Frequency: Monthly
Website: www.texasrunnertriathlete.com

Freelance Potential

80% written by nonstaff writers. Publishes 60 freelance submissions yearly; 50% by unpublished writers, 30% by authors who are new to the magazine. Receives 3 unsolicited mss each month.

Submissions

Send complete ms. Accepts email submissions to lance@runningmags.com. Responds in 1–2 months.

- Articles: 800–1,000 words. Informational and how-to articles, profiles, interviews, humor, and opinion pieces. Topics include running, cycling, swimming, health, fitness, nutrition, and events coverage.
- Depts/columns: 800 words. News, equipment reviews, and event information.

Sample Issue

48 pages. Advertising. Sample copy and editorial calendar available.

- "Going for Gold in Golden Years." Article profiles a cancer-surviving senior couple who are competing in their second triathlon.
- Sample dept/column: Triathlete Notepad includes a calendar of upcoming events.

Rights and Payment

Rights vary. Written material, payment rates vary. Pays on publication. Provides 2 contributor's copies.

Third Coast

English Department
Western Michigan University
1903 West Michigan Avenue
Kalamazoo, MI 49008-5331

The Editors

Description and Interests

Showcasing quality writing in four genres, *Third Coast* is a literary magazine that welcomes submissions from student writers, as well as established authors. It publishes fiction (traditional, experimental, shorts, and novel excerpts), poetry, creative nonfiction, and drama. It is particularly interested in 10-minute plays that have had readings or productions, but have not received publication. Circ: 1,000.

Contents: 30% fiction; 30% poetry; 40% other
Frequency: Twice each year
Website: www.thirdcoastmagazine.com

Freelance Potential

95% written by nonstaff writers. Publishes 60–80 freelance submissions yearly; 20% by unpublished writers, 75% by new authors. Receives 300 queries and unsolicited mss monthly.

Submissions

Send complete ms between September 15 and March 31. Query with writing samples for interviews and book reviews. Accepts submissions via website form only (Word or RTF attachments only). Accepts simultaneous submissions if identified. Responds in 5 months.

- Nonfiction: To 6,000 words. Creative nonfiction, articles, memoirs. Essays, 700–2,000 words. Interviews and book reviews, word lengths vary.
- Fiction: To 7,500 words. Short stories, novel excerpts, and translations. Traditional and experimental fiction. Plays, up to 20 pages (one-acts).
- Other: Poetry, to 5 poems or 15 pages.

Sample Issue

184 pages. Little advertising. Sample copy, $8. Guidelines available at website.

- "Handsome Pair of Sunday Walkers." Fiction.
- "Demons by Other Means." Play.

Rights and Payment

First North American serial rights. No payment. Provides 2 contributor's copies and a subscription.

Threads

The Taunton Press, Inc.
63 South Main Street
P.O. Box 5506
Newtown, CT 06470-5506

Administrative Assistant: April Mohr

Description and Interests

Sewing, dressmaking, patternmaking, and embroidery make up the editorial focus of this magazine. Informational articles, how-to's, and sewing projects for people of all skill and interest levels are covered in detail. It works only with freelancers who have extensive sewing expertise. Circ: 150,000.

Contents: 60% articles; 40% depts/columns
Frequency: 6 times each year
Website: www.threadsmagazine.com

Freelance Potential

75% written by nonstaff writers. Publishes 50 freelance submissions yearly; 30% by unpublished writers, 50% by authors who are new to the magazine, 90% by experts. Receives 30 queries monthly.

Submissions

Query with 1- or 2-paragraph summary, detailed outline, and photos of the work. Accepts hard copy and email queries to th@taunton.com. Responds in 6 months.

- Articles: Word lengths vary. Informational and how-to articles, profiles, interviews, personal experience pieces, creative nonfiction, humor, and new product information. Topics include sewing techniques, patterns, designs, styles, garments, and tools.
- Depts/columns: Word lengths vary. News and reviews of sewing equipment and patterns, and sewing tips. Closures, humorous human-interest pieces, 400–600 words.

Sample Issue

90 pages. Advertising. Sample copy available. Guidelines available at website.

- "Just Add Sleeves." Article provides instructions for three sleeve options.
- Sample dept/column: Teach Yourself to Sew explains the basic kick pleat.

Rights and Payment

Exclusive rights. Written material, payment rates vary. Pays on publication. Provides 2 contributor's copies.

The Threepenny Review

P.O. Box 9131
Berkeley, CA 94709

The Editors

Description and Interests

Celebrating 30 years in publication, *The Threepenny Review* tackles current events, social issues, literature, and the arts, with its diverse mix of critical essays, memoirs, fiction, and poetry. It welcomes submissions from writers of all levels of experience. New writers have the best chance of acceptance with a review. Circ: 8,000.

Contents: 40% articles; 25% fiction; 25% poetry; 10% depts/columns
Frequency: Quarterly
Website: www.threepennyreview.com

Freelance Potential

100% written by nonstaff writers. Publishes 90–100 freelance submissions yearly; 15% by authors who are new to the magazine. Receives 400 unsolicited mss monthly.

Submissions

Send complete ms between January and June only. Accepts hard copy and electronic submissions via the website (Word attachments). No simultaneous submissions. SASE. Responds in 2 months.

- Articles: Memoirs, to 4,000 words. Critical essays on culture, literature, current events, and politics, 1,200–2,500 words.
- Fiction: To 4,000 words. Literary fiction.
- Depts/columns: 500–1,000 words. Table Talk uses first-person essays. Reviews.
- Other: Poetry, to 100 lines, 5 poems per submission.

Sample Issue

32 pages. Little advertising. Sample articles and guidelines available at website.

- "On Psychoanalysis." Essay ponders how psychoanalytic treatment works.
- "Villas of the Mysteries, Pompeii." Essay describes a William Lamson photograph.

Rights and Payment

First North American serial rights. Articles and fiction, $400. Table Talk, $200. Poetry, $200 per poem. Pays on acceptance. Provides contributor's copies and a 1-year subscription.

Thriving Family

Focus on the Family
8605 Explorer Drive
Colorado Springs, CO 80920

Editorial Director: Sheila Seifert

Description and Interests

This publication from Focus on the Family features articles on marriage and parenting from a biblical perspective. It looks for practical solutions based on true-life experiences. Profiles of well-known people in the Christian world are also found on its pages. Writers will find an issue-specific theme list and additional calls for submissions on the website. Circ: 300,000

Contents: 60% articles; 40% depts/columns
Frequency: 6 times each year
Website: www.thrivingfamily.com

Freelance Potential

Puts out regular calls for submissions.

Submissions

Query or send complete ms, depending on section (see guidelines for specifics). Accepts hard copy and email to thrivingfamilysubmissions@family.org.

- Articles: 1,200–1,500 words. Informational and how-to, articles, personal experience pieces, and profiles. Topics include faith issues relevant to family and parenting, well-known Christians, solutions to parenting and marital problems.
- Depts/columns: 50–450 words. Family Stages, age-appropriate parenting tips; For Her; For Him; Blended Family; Single Parent; Adoption/Special Needs.

Sample Issue

52 pages. Advertising. Sample articles, guidelines, theme list, current editorial needs available at website.

- "Growing Closer by Serving Together." Shows how couples can find opportunities to minister together in a way that serves God and strengthens their marriages.
- Sample dept/column: Single Parent suggests ways to simplify the Christmas season to reduce stress.

Rights and Payment

Rights, unknown. Written material, $.25 a word. Pays on acceptance.

Tidings

414-5165 Sherbrooke Street West
Montreal, Quebec H4A 1T6
Canada

Editor in Chief: Aldo Parise

Description and Interests

Read by a Canadian audience of gourmet food lovers and wine connoisseurs, *Tidings* includes recipes, reports on dining destinations around the world, and reviews of fine wines and spirits. It caters to somewhat affluent and sophisticated subscribers. Please keep in mind that most of the articles published have a Canadian angle, with travel pieces perhaps being the exception to that rule. Circ: 35,000.

Contents: 70% articles; 30% depts/columns
Frequency: 8 times each year
Website: www.tidingsmag.com

Freelance Potential

80% written by nonstaff writers. Publishes 20 freelance submissions yearly; 10% by unpublished writers, 30% by authors who are new to the magazine, 60% by experts. Receives 10 queries monthly.

Submissions

Query. Accepts email queries to editor@tidingsmag.com. Responds in 1 month.

- Articles: 700–1,400 words. Informational and how-to articles, profiles, interviews, and personal experience pieces. Topics include wine and spirits, fine dining, specialty foods, luxury items, and culinary-focused travel.
- Depts/columns: Word lengths vary. Recipes, new product reviews, books, libations, travel, and opinion pieces.

Sample Issue

66 pages. Advertising. Sample articles available at website. Editorial calendar available.

- "Restaurant Secrets." Article discusses key techniques for creating restaurant-quality meals.
- "The Point of the Sommelier." Article shares some tips for wine and food pairings

Rights and Payment

All rights. Written material, payment rates vary. Payment policy varies.

Tikkun Magazine

2342 Shattuck Avenue, Suite 1200
Berkeley, CA 94704

Editor: Michael Lerner

Description and Interests

Tikkun Magazine focuses on politics, spirituality, and culture with the intent of promoting social justice and "the repair of the world." Although it was born of the Jewish tradition, it has a political perspective that attracts a broader readership. Its print publication has become a quarterly, and its Web magazine has become more active. It prefers to work with writers who can apply a spiritual progressive worldview to their topic—whether it's recent movies, the West Bank, global warming, or gay rights. It will soon accept fiction submissions for the website. Check the website for updates. Circ: 50,000.

Contents: Articles; depts/columns
Frequency: Quarterly
Website: www.tikkun.org

Freelance Potential

80–90% written by nonstaff writers. Publishes 90 freelance submissions yearly; 10% by unpublished writers, 50–60% by authors who are new to the magazine.

Submissions

Send complete ms. Accepts electronic submissions via website link only (Microsoft Word attachments). Responds if interested.

- Articles: 800–2,400 words. Informational articles and opinion pieces. Topics include spirituality, politics, social issues, foreign affairs, and popular culture.
- Depts/columns: Word lengths vary. Religion, finance, and interviews. Book reviews, 500–800 words.
- Other: Poetry.

Sample Issue

80 pages. Sample articles and guidelines available at website.

- "A Red Letter Christian Speaks to the Palestinian Church." Opinion piece sharing an Evangelical minister's vision of healing the divide between Jewish Israelis and Palestinian Muslims.
- "Sabbath Practice as Political Resistance: Building the Religious Counterculture." Article examines the role religion has played in increasing equality and respect for humans.

Rights and Payment

Rights vary. No payment. Provides a 1-year subscription.

Timeline

The Ohio Historical Society
800 East 17th Avenue
Columbus, OH 43211

Editor: David A. Simmons

Description and Interests

This magazine, published by the Ohio Historical Society, embraces the history, prehistory, and natural sciences of Ohio. Lively and well-illustrated articles and photo-essays are featured in each issue. It would like to see more interpretive articles in the 500- to 1,000-word range. Photography should be included in the submission whenever possible. Circ: 10,000.

Contents: 92% articles; 8% depts/columns
Frequency: Quarterly
Website: www.ohiohistory.org/publications

Freelance Potential

95% written by nonstaff writers. Publishes 15 freelance submissions yearly; 5% by unpublished writers, 40% by authors who are new to the magazine, 75% by experts. Receives 10 queries, 8 unsolicited mss monthly.

Submissions

Query or send complete ms. Accepts hard copy. SASE. Responds to queries in 2 weeks, to mss in 4–5 weeks.

- Articles: 1,200–4,000 words. Informational articles, biographies, and photo-essays. Topics include Ohio's culture, geography, fine arts, society, politics, economics, natural history, environment, archaeology, cultural history, architecture, and personalities.
- Depts/columns: Staff-written.
- Artwork: 35mm B/W or color prints or transparencies.

Sample Issue

56 pages. Little advertising. Sample copy available. Guidelines available at website.

- "The Many and Pleasant Entertainments." Article presents a history of the Taft White House.
- "Battle of the Blizzard." Article revisits the infamous 1950 Thanksgiving snowstorm.

Rights and Payment

First North American serial rights. All material, payment rates vary. Pays on acceptance. Provides 12 contributor's copies.

Today's Pentecostal Evangel

1445 North Boonville Avenue
Springfield, MO 65802

Editor: Ken Horn

Description and Interests

Articles that focus on Christian living, especially understanding the Bible and developing a rich prayer life, are found in *Today's Pentecostal Evangel*. As the Voice of the Assemblies of God, it uses testimonies and other inspirational features to impel Christian missions. Though it accepts few unsolicited submissions, it is interested in reports about major events connected with the Assemblies of God. Circ: 150,000.

Contents: 90% articles; 5% depts/columns; 5% other
Frequency: Weekly
Website: www.pe.ag.org

Freelance Potential

30% written by nonstaff writers. Publishes 40 freelance submissions yearly; 5% by unpublished writers. Receives 50+ unsolicited mss each month.

Submissions

Send complete ms. Prefers email submissions to pe@ag.org (attach document); will accept hard copy. Responds in 1–2 months.

- Articles: 500–1,200 words. Informational articles, profiles, and interviews. Testimonies, 200–300 words. Topics include Christian living, salvation, contemporary issues, family life, parenting, and social issues.
- Depts/columns: Word lengths vary. News, Bible teachings, devotionals.

Sample Issue

32 pages. Sample articles and guidelines available at website.

- "Forgiveness." Article explains why forgiveness is the necessary twin of faith.
- "Sparking Students' Fervor for Missions." Article presents an interview with the district youth director for the Minnesota District Council of the Assemblies of God.

Rights and Payment

First or second rights. Written material, $.06 per word. Pays on acceptance. Provides 5 contributor's copies.

Touchstone

A Journal of Mere Christianity

P.O. Box 410788
Chicago, IL 60641-0788

Executive Editor: James M. Kushiner

Description and Interests

Touchstone is a conservative Christian journal, with a readership that includes Protestant, Catholic, and Orthodox believers. It provides a forum for Christian analysis, reporting, and opinion on current affairs. All article submissions are evaluated by a group of reviewers, a process that may take up to six weeks. Material is closely edited, so writers must be willing to work with editors to create an article in the magazine's style and to its standards. Circ: 10,750.

Contents: 70% articles; 30% depts/columns
Frequency: 6 times each year
Website: www.touchstonemag.com

Freelance Potential

70% written by nonstaff writers. Publishes 50–60 freelance submissions yearly; 10% by unpublished writers, 10% by authors who are new to the magazine. Receives 30+ queries and unsolicited mss monthly.

Submissions

Query or send complete ms with 40- to 50-word author bio. For queries, send email to editor@touchstonemag.com; for complete ms, email to submissions@touchstonemag.com (Word attachments). No simultaneous submissions. Responds in 1 month.

- Articles: 3,000–5,000 words. Informational articles, profiles, interviews, and personal experience pieces. Topics include religion, public affairs, education, and history.
- Depts/columns: 1,000–2,500 words. Opinion pieces and book reviews.

Sample Issue

48 pages. Little advertising. Sample articles and guidelines available at website.

- "Square None." Article discusses the danger of politicizing religion.
- "Moynihan's Family Arc." Opinion piece discusses whether the modern liberal approach to improving citizens' lives with the creation of government jobs is workable.

Rights and Payment

First and reprint rights. Written material, $125 per published page. Book reviews, no payment. Pays on publication. Provides 1 contributor's copy.

Toy Farmer

7496 106th Street SE
LaMoure, ND 58458-9404

Editorial Assistant: Cheryl Hegvik

Description and Interests

Toy Farmer offers avid collectors and enthusiasts informative articles on farm toy history, collecting, and pricing. It profiles collectors and collections, as well as manufacturers and new products. Two issues of the year feature custom/scratch projects from readers' stores. Show coverage is also included in each issue. Circ: 15,500.

Contents: 40% articles; 30% depts/columns; 30% other
Frequency: Monthly
Website: www.toyfarmer.com

Freelance Potential

100% written by nonstaff writers. Publishes 9 freelance submissions yearly; 40% by unpublished writers, 10% by authors who are new to the magazine, 50% by experts. Receives 1 query monthly.

Submissions

Query with writing samples. Accepts hard copy. SASE. Responds in 1 month.

- Articles: 1,500–2,000 words. Informational, how-to, and profiles. Topics include farm toy history, collectors and collecting, pricing, and manufacturers.
- Depts/columns: 1,300 words. Events, new products.

Sample Issue

78 pages. Advertising. Sample articles available at website. Guidelines and editorial calendar available.

- "2012 National Farm Toy Show Tractor." Tells the history of the four-wheel drive tractor.
- "Aumann Auctions, Inc,'s New Toy Listing." Details on a three-day room-trading, showroom and auction event.

Rights and Payment

First North American serial rights. Written material, $.10 per word. Pays on publication. Provides 2 contributor's copies.

TQR

Editor in Chief: Theodore Rorschalk

Description and Interests

TQR, or *Total Quality Reading,* is a new digital publication that accepts all genres of fiction, from romance to speculative. It sets itself apart from other publications by offering a "transparent editorial process–in other words, writers will be able to read the editors' comments on their work at the website as the submission makes its way through the editorial process. There are reading periods for each of the four editions. Circ: Unavailable.

Contents: Fiction
Frequency: Quarterly
Website: www.tqrstories.com

Freelance Potential

Receiving submissions is core to the operations of the publication and its editorial process.

Submissions

Accepts submissions October 15–November 15; January 15–February 15; and July 15–August 15. Send complete ms. Accepts email submissions to tgrstories@gmail.com (attach document; include "Submission: Title, Author name, word count in subject line). No simultaneous submissions.

- Fiction: 4,000–12,000 words. All genres of fiction accepted.

Sample Issue

Sample articles and guidelines available at website.

- Three of a Kind." Story tells of a mother and daughter new to town who are striking up their own friendships.
- "Radiation." Story is about Christian monks settling in Japan during World War II.

Rights and Payment

First electronic and nonexclusive archival rights. No payment.

Trailer Life

2575 Vista Del Mar Drive
Ventura, CA 93001

Editor: Kristopher Bunker

Description and Interests

Travel features appear in this magazine, along with technical and do-it-yourself information that will enhance the enjoyment of the RV lifestyle. It also publishes articles that address issues and legislation affecting RV owners. Humor pieces are welcome. Circ: 196,000.

Contents: 80% articles; 20% depts/columns
Frequency: Monthly
Website: www.trailerlife.com

Freelance Potential

60% written by nonstaff writers. Publishes 60–70 freelance submissions yearly; 5% by unpublished writers, 5% by authors who are new to the magazine, 20% by experts. Receives 30 queries, 10 unsolicited mss monthly.

Submissions

Prefers query with clips; will accept complete ms. Availability of artwork improves chance of acceptance. Accepts hard copy and CD submissions. No simultaneous submissions. SASE. Responds in 1 month.

- Articles: 1,000–1,800 words. Informational and how-to articles, personal experience pieces, profiles, interviews, and new product information. Topics include recreational vehicles, the RV lifestyle, travel, and leisure.
- Depts/columns: 50–200 words. Destinations, campgrounds, and RV maintenance.
- Artwork: Transparencies; digital images at 300 dpi.

Sample Issue

66 pages. Advertising. Sample articles and guidelines available at website.

- "Oysters and Seafood in Eastpoint, Florida." Travel article about the Florida town from where 90% of Florida's oysters come.
- Sample dept/column: 10-Minute Tech tells how to fix cap cracks.

Rights and Payment

First North American serial rights. Articles, $200–$700. Depts/columns, $100. Artwork, $75–$600. Kill fee, 30%. Pays on acceptance. Provides 1 contributor's copy.

Trail Runner

2567 Dolores Way
Carbondale, CO 81623

Editor: Michael Benge
Associate Editor: Ashley Arnold

Description and Interests

Off-road running enthusiasts read this magazine for information that will help them improve their health and fitness, while enjoying the outdoors. Queries should present a clear, original, and provocative story angle and should reflect the writer's knowledge of the magazine's content, style, and tone. Circ: 29,000.

Contents: 60% articles; 35% depts/columns; 5% other
Frequency: 8 times each year
Website: www.trailrunnermag.com

Freelance Potential

70% written by nonstaff writers. Publishes 50 freelance submissions yearly; 10% by unpublished writers, 25% by new authors, 80% by experts. Receives 30 queries monthly.

Submissions

Query with clips. Accepts hard copy and email to mbenge@bigstonepub.com or aarnold@bigstonepub.com. SASE. Responds in 2 months if interested.

- Articles: 2,000–3,000 words. Informational articles, profiles, interviews, personal experience pieces, and humor. Topics include top trail running destinations, race reports, current issues, and personalities.
- Depts/columns: 800–1,200 words. First-person adventures, travel destinations, runner profiles, race previews, training tips, health, injury prevention and treatment, nutrition, news, and Q&As.

Sample Issue

54 pages. Advertising. Sample copy, guidelines, and theme list available at website.

- "The Toughest Race You've Never Heard Of." Article discusses the new film *The Mountain Runners,* which tells of the turn-of-the-century Mount Baker Marathon.
- Sample dept/column: Take Your Mark discusses the increased popularity of winter uphill races.

Rights and Payment

First North American serial rights. Written material, $.25 per word. Pays 30 days after publication. Provides 1 contributor's copy.

Trains

The Magazine of Railroading

21027 Crossroads Circle
P.O. Box 1612
Waukesha, WI 53187-1612

Editor: Jim Wrinn

Description and Interests

News stories, feature articles, and personal recollections make up the bulk of this magazine for train buffs of all ages. All types of trains are covered, past and present, in entertaining and edifying articles. Material on trains of the eastern and southern U.S. is of particular interest. Circ: 95,000.

Contents: Articles; depts/columns
Frequency: Monthly
Website: www.trainsmag.com

Freelance Potential

65% written by nonstaff writers. Publishes 300–400 freelance submissions yearly; 25% by unpublished writers, 25% by authors who are new to the magazine, 25% by experts. Receives 25 queries monthly.

Submissions

Query first. Accepts email to editor@trainsmag.com. Send submissions via email and supporting material on disk via regular mail. SASE. Responds in 3 months.

- Articles: Word lengths vary. Informational, personal experience, and profiles. Topics include railroad companies, industry trends, train history, and industry personalities.
- Depts/columns: Word lengths vary. Railroad news, technology, train preservation, Q&As.
- Artwork: Digital images at 300 dpi; color transparencies.

Sample Issue

74 pages. Sample copy available. Guidelines available at website.

- "Locomotives for Little Guys." Short line and regional locomotives through the years.
- "The Kaolin Road." A look at the Sandersville Railroad in east-central Georgia.

Rights and Payment

Exclusive rights. Written material, $.10+ per word. Pays on acceptance. Provides 2 contributor's copies.

TransWorld Snowboarding

2052 Corte del Nogal, Suite 100
Carlsbad, CA 92011

Associate Editor: Ben Gavelda

Description and Interests
The oldest snowboarding publication, *TransWorld Snowboarding* appeals to enthusiasts of the sport, with engaging articles and compelling photography. The very best of snowboarding is celebrated in this publication. It profiles the raddest boarders and the best snowboarding destinations in the world, covers the latest gear, reports on competitions, and provides insight into the sharpest tricks. It is also available digitally and as an iPad app. Articles should be written with a pro-athlete insight and perspective. Circ: 1.4 million.

Contents: Articles; depts/columns
Frequency: 8 times each year
Website: www.snowboarding.transworld.net

Freelance Potential
10% written by nonstaff writers. Publishes 10 freelance submissions yearly; 2% by unpublished writers, 5% by authors who are new to the magazine, 96% by experts. Receives 10 queries monthly.

Submissions
Query. Accepts email queries to snowmail@transworld.net (Word attachments). Responds in 1 month.

- Articles: To 1,600 words. Informational, how-to, profiles, and photo-essays. Topics include snowboarding personalities, destinations, events, and news.
- Depts/columns: 300 words. News, Q&As, techniques, music, fashion, gear, and short destination pieces.

Sample Issue
228 pages. Advertising. Sample articles available at website. Guidelines and theme list available.

- "How To: Build a Snow Shelter." Creating an emergency shelter for overnight protection.
- "How To: Live in Your Whip." Outfitting a mobile home.

Rights and Payment
Rights vary. Written material, $.35 a word. Pays on publication. Provides 2 contributor's copies.

Travel + Leisure

American Express Publishing Company
1120 Avenue of the Americas
New York, NY 10036

Executive Editor: Jennifer Barr

Description and Interests
With a subscriber base that includes both business and leisure travelers, this magazine covers interesting destinations and provides useful travel advice and tips. Its goal is to help readers have a more enjoyable and hassle-free travel experience. Destination pieces must offer information on how to get there, where to stay, where to eat, and what to see and do. Readers must be able to follow in the author's footsteps. New writers have the best shot at publication with the front-of-the-book departments. Circ: 950,000.

Contents: 50% articles; 50% depts/columns
Frequency: Monthly
Website: www.travelandleisure.com

Freelance Potential
95% written by nonstaff writers. Publishes 150–200 freelance submissions yearly; 25% by authors who are new to the magazine, 20% by experts. Receives 200 queries monthly.

Submissions
Query with outline and clips. Accepts hard copy and electronic queries via website. Response time varies.

- Articles: 2,000–4,000 words. Informational, service, and how-to articles; essays; and narratives. Topics include worldwide travel destinations, lodging, airfare, and cruises.
- Depts/columns: To 1,200 words. Travel deals; hotel, spa, restaurant, bar, and club spotlights; fashion; shopping; art; wine; cruises; road trips; and travel technology.

Sample Issue
220 pages. Advertising. Sample articles and guidelines available at website.

- "City Getaways Ultimate Bucket List." Article shares a list of the must-see cities and the must-do attractions once you are there.
- "How to Get a Better Airline Seat." Article offers tips for getting the ideal airline seat.

Rights and Payment
First North American serial rights. All material, $100. Pays on acceptance. Provides 2 contributor's copies.

TravelSmart

P.O. Box 397
Dobbs Ferry, NY 10522

Publisher & Editor: Nancy Dunnan

Description and Interests
This travel newsletter, in its 35th year, provides insider advice and information to business and leisure travelers. Regional and international destinations are covered, as well as information on packaged deals; lodging; and train, bus, and air transportation. It also specializes in travel safety and how to save money and avoid scams. No first-person pieces, anecdotes, or photos. What it does want are short, pithy, fact-filled articles that will help readers travel better for less. This includes business travel articles, destination pieces, and service articles. Circ: Unavailable.
Contents: Articles; depts/columns
Frequency: Monthly
Website: www.travelsmartnewsletter.com

Freelance Potential
30% written by nonstaff writers. Publishes 50 freelance submissions yearly. Receives 30 queries monthly.

Submissions
Query. Accepts hard copy and email queries to ndunnan@aol.com or TravelSmartNow@aol.com. SASE. Responds in 1 month.

- Articles: 800–1,000 words. Informational and how-to articles. Topics include package tours, lodging, airfare, car rentals, trip insurance, safety, and travel gear.
- Depts/columns: Staff-written.

Sample Issue
12 pages. No advertising. Sample articles available at website. Guidelines and editorial calendar available.

- "Keeping Up with the Technology Curve." Article suggests the best smart phone applications for travel.
- "City Insider Report: Baltimore, MD." Article profiles the city and suggests the best value-added hotels and attractions.

Rights and Payment
All rights. Written material, $50–$150. Pays on publication.

Treasures
Antique to Modern Collecting

316 Fifth Street
Waterloo, IA 50701

Editor: Linda Kruger

Description and Interests
This is a new magazine formed by a merger of *Collectors News* and *Antiques & Collecting Magazine*. Antique lovers and collecting enthusiasts turn to this magazine to gain the tools to find, value, buy and sell, identify, and care for their discoveries. Circ: 8,100.
Contents: 60% articles; 40% depts/columns
Frequency: Monthly
Website: www.collectors-news.com; www.treasuresmagazine.com

Freelance Potential
90% written by nonstaff writers. Publishes 60 freelance submissions yearly; 10% by unpublished writers, 20% by authors who are new to the magazine, 60% by experts. Receives 10 mss monthly.

Submissions
Send complete ms. Accepts email only to lkruger@pioneermagazines.com. Responds in 2 months.

- Articles: 1,000 words. Informational and how-to articles, profiles, and historical pieces. Topics include finding, caring for, and displaying antiques and collectibles; specific collections; coins; stamps; furniture; housewares; textiles; toys; and memorabilia.
- Depts/columns: Word lengths vary. Market analysis, price index, reference book reviews, restoration and identification advice.
- Artwork: Word lengths vary. Digital high-resolution images at 300 dpi.
- Other: Query for seasonal material 3 months in advance.

Sample Issue
60 pages. Advertising. Sample articles available at website.

- "20th Century American Pewter." Surveys various styles and artists of decorative pewter.
- "Fragility Forever." Profiles Texas glass collector Nancy Norman who has spent four decades researching and collecting glass.

Rights and Payment
First serial rights for 1 year. Payment rates vary. Pays on publication. Provides 1 contributor's copy.

Tricycle

The Buddhist Review

1115 Broadway, Suite 1113
New York, NY 10010

Managing Editor: Rachel Hiles

Description and Interests

Founded in 1991, *Tricycle* presents Buddhist perspectives, practices, and values to a general audience. It publishes articles, essays, and opinion pieces about contemporary topics from a Buddhist perspective, as well as pieces about Tibet, spirituality, and open inquiry. It seeks work that reflects the writer's knowledge and interests, rather than trying to anticipate the magazine's needs. Circ: 60,000.

Contents: 80% articles; 20% depts/columns
Frequency: Quarterly
Website: www.tricycle.com

Freelance Potential

85% written by nonstaff writers. Publishes 50 freelance submissions yearly; 15% by unpublished writers, 20% by authors who are new to the magazine, 40% by experts. Receives 60 queries monthly.

Submissions

Query with author bio and Buddhist background, clips or writing samples, and manuscript word count. Prefers email to editorial@tricycle.com; will accept hard copy. SASE. Responds in 1 month.

- Articles: 2,000–3,000 words. Personal experience pieces, creative nonfiction, profiles, and interviews. Topics include current events, history, politics, family life, and social issues—all as they relate to Buddhism.
- Depts/columns: 750 words. Book reviews, news items, gardening, and relationships.

Sample Issue

120 pages. Advertising. Sample articles and guidelines available at website.

- "The Seeds of Life." Article features an interview with Trinlay Tulku Rinpoche, a Western-born tulku.
- "What's at Stake as the Dharma Goes Modern." Article explores the assumptions of modern age and the unique challenges they present.

Rights and Payment

Exclusive print and electronic rights for 18 months. Written material, payment rates vary. Kill fee, 25%. Pays on publication. Provides 2 contributor's copies.

True West

P.O. Box 8008
Cave Creek, AZ 85327

Editor in Chief: Meghan Saar

Description and Interests

True West has an editorial mission of keeping the spirit of the American West alive. Its specialty is its ability to tie the history and heritage of the Old West (between 1800 and 1910) to the modern Western lifestyle. It actively seeks creative writers who can infuse their articles with personality and humor. Circ: 200,000.

Contents: 60% articles; 40% depts/columns
Frequency: Monthly
Website: www.twmag.com

Freelance Potential

30% written by nonstaff writers. Publishes 100 freelance submissions yearly; 25% by authors who are new to the magazine, 75% by experts. Receives 25 queries monthly.

Submissions

Query with source list and artwork. Accepts hard copy. Availability of artwork improves chance of acceptance. SASE. Responds in 3 months.

- Articles: Feature articles, 1,500 words. Other articles, 250–500 words. Informational articles, humor, and profiles. Topics include Western history, ranching pioneers, the military, and Native Americans.
- Depts/columns: Word lengths vary. Historical events, book reviews, and military topics.
- Artwork: B/W or color slides or negatives; digital images at 300 dpi.

Sample Issue

80 pages. Advertising. Sample articles and guidelines available at website.

- "Wild Bill Says 'Muzzle Up.'" Article details the mountain man's journey from St. Louis to Wyoming's Wind River Country.
- "10 for 10: Dodge City, Kansas." Article describes 10 not-to-miss attractions in this city.

Rights and Payment

First North American serial and archival rights. Written material, $.25 per word. Artwork, $20. Kill fee, 50%. Pays on publication. Provides 4 contributor's copies.

Turkey Country

770 Augusta Road
P.O. Box 530
Edgefield, SC 29824

Editor: Karen Lee

Description and Interests

Turkey Country is the membership publication of the National Wild Turkey Federation. It features articles on techniques and destinations for sport hunting of turkey and other game. Conservation, habitat preservation, and wildlife education are part of its editorial mix, as is news of membership programs. Articles must appeal to a national readership and be meticulously researched. Limited use of personal experience is acceptable, but do include expert advice and anecdotes from others. Circ: 180,000.

Contents: 55% articles; 45% depts/columns
Frequency: 6 times each year
Website: www.turkeycountrymagazine.com

Freelance Potential

47% written by nonstaff writers. Publishes 180 freelance submissions yearly; 3% by unpublished writers, 10% by authors who are new to the magazine, 80% by experts. Receives 40 queries monthly.

Submissions

Query with graphic aid and sidebar ideas. Accepts email to klee@nwtf.net. Responds in 2 months.

- Articles: 1,000–1,200 words. Informational and how-to articles, profiles, interviews, and opinion and personal experience pieces. Topics include hunting, history, restoration, management, biology, and distribution of the North American wild turkey.
- Depts/columns: 500–1,000 words. Short how-to's, profiles, conservation, and biology.

Sample Issue

144 pages. Advertising. Sample articles and guidelines available at website.

- "Tree Talk." Article explains which plantings help wildlife survive the winter seasons.
- Sample dept/column: Shooting Savvy explains the benefits of using a single-shot shotgun.

Rights and Payment

First North American serial and electronic rights. Articles, $350–$550. Depts/columns, $250–$350. Pays on acceptance. Provides 1 contributor's copy.

Turning the Tide

Journal of Anti-Racist Action, Research & Education

P.O. Box 1055
Culver City, CA 90232

Editor: Michael Novick

Description and Interests

This tabloid focuses its articles, essays, and poetry on bringing acts of racism, sexism, police brutality, and oppression to the public eye. It embraces progressive politics and solutions to social injustice. Unapologetic in its stance against oppression of all kinds, the publication likes to hear from writers who share its mission. Circ: 8,000.

Contents: 80% articles; 5% fiction; 15% other
Frequency: Quarterly
Website: www.antiracist.org

Freelance Potential

80% written by nonstaff writers. Publishes 8–10 freelance submissions yearly; 20% by unpublished writers, 32% by authors who are new to the magazine, 60% by experts. Receives 2 queries, 5 unsolicited mss monthly.

Submissions

Query or send complete ms. Prefers email to la@antiracistcction.org (Word attachments). Responds in 2 months.

- Articles: To 2,000 words. Informational articles, profiles, interviews, and personal experience and opinion pieces. Topics include racism, sexism, homophobia, white supremacy, morality, and neo-Nazi activities.
- Fiction: Word lengths vary. Very short stories with anti-racism themes.
- Other: Poetry, no line limit. Cartoons.

Sample Issue

8 pages. No advertising. Sample copy available at website. Guidelines available.

- "Attica: 41 Years Later." Article reports on the conditions of Attica, which have not improved since the early seventies.
- "A Virtual Pilgrimage Regarding Racism." Essay tells how the author made virtual visits to areas of racism from the past by researching on Google Earth.

Rights and Payment

One-time rights. No payment. Provides 5 contributor's copies.

Turning Wheel

Buddhist Peace Fellowship
P.O. Box 3470
Berkeley, CA 94703-9906

Submissions

Description and Interests

Turning Wheel publishes material that promotes peace, social justice, environmental awareness, and social activism. Originally a print magazine, it is now a downloadable electronic publication. Of special interest are articles that explore the ways Buddhist practice informs compassionate action. It is also moving toward an emphasis on analysis of racism, gender and sexuality, ableism, capitalism, and internationalism. Circ: 10,000.

Contents: 60% articles; 25% depts/columns; 15% other
Frequency: Twice each year
Website: www.turningwheelmedia.org

Freelance Potential

85% written by nonstaff writers. Publishes 40 freelance submissions yearly; 20% by unpublished writers, 20% by authors who are new to the magazine. Receives 10 queries, 25 mss monthly.

Submissions

Query for book reviews. Send complete ms for other material. Accepts hard copy and email to everett@turningwheelmedia.org (Word attachments). Responds if interested.

- Articles: 800–2,000 words. Informational articles, personal essays, interviews, and opinion pieces. Topics include Buddhism, social justice, and the environment.
- Fiction: Short fiction that promotes peace and/or Buddhist principles.
- Depts/columns: Book reviews, 400–850 words.
- Artwork: B/W photos, 300 dpi or higher.
- Other: Poetry.

Sample Issue

48 pages. Little advertising. Sample copy and guidelines available at website.

- "End State Murder? Not So Simple." Article explains why the passing of California's Prop 34 is not a sure thing.
- "Action Alert: Facing Execution for Killing His Abusers." Article tells the story of Terry Williams who is set to be executed for killing the man who sexually abused him.

Rights and Payment

One-time rights. No payment. Provides 2 contributor's copies.

Twins Magazine

30799 Pinetree Road, #256
Cleveland, OH 44124

Editor in Chief: Christa D. Reed

Description and Interests

The goal of this digital magazine is to provide specific parenting resources that inform and inspire parents with twins, triplets, and higher order multiples. Feature articles and regular columns share the joys and challenges of parenting multiples, often with a double dose of humor. It is interested in new research specific to twins and multiples, as well as personal experience pieces about growing up as a twin. Circ: 40,000.

Contents: 40% articles; 40% depts/columns; 20% other
Frequency: 6 times each year
Website: www.twinsmagazine.com

Freelance Potential

50% written by nonstaff writers. Publishes 10–12 freelance submissions yearly. Receives 20 queries each month.

Submissions

Query or send complete ms with brief author biography and head shot image. Accepts email queries to twinseditor@twinsmagazine.com (Word or pdf attachments). Responds in 3 months.

- Articles: To 1,000 words. Informational, how-to, profiles, and personal experience. Topics include parenting, family life, health, fitness, education, music, the arts, the home, nutrition, diet, sports, social issues, crafts, and hobbies.
- Depts/columns: To 800 words. Mom-2-Mom, A Word from Dad, Family Health, LOL, Research Column, Resource Round Up, Tales from Twins, Twin Star Spotlight, news, new product information, opinion pieces, short items on child development.

Sample Issue

56 pages. Advertising. Sample articles and guidelines available at website.

- "When Parents Have a Favorite Twin." The dangers of playing favorites.
- "Great Birthday Gift Ideas & Party Favors." Tips for celebrating in a big way.

Rights and Payment

All rights. Written material, $50–$100. Pays on publication. Provides 2 contributor's copies.

UMM

Urban Male Magazine

300-131 Bank Street
Ottawa, Ontario K1P 5N7
Canada

Editor in Chief: Abbis Mahmoud

Description and Interests

A magazine strictly for Canadian guys, *UMM* covers everything from bars to bands, as well as travel, technology, fashion, relationships, and health topics. Its editorial content has a distinctly Canadian voice, therefore it works only with Canadian writers. It seeks articles that are fresh, hip, and entertaining, as well as informative. Circ: 95,000.

Contents: 60% articles; 40% depts/columns
Frequency: Quarterly
Website: www.umm.ca

Freelance Potential

80% written by nonstaff writers. Publishes 100+ freelance submissions yearly; 50% by authors who are new to the magazine.

Submissions

Canadian authors only. Prefers query; will accept complete ms. Accepts email to editor@umm.ca and simultaneous submissions if identified. Responds in 6 weeks.

- Articles: 1,200–3,500 words. Informational and how-to articles, profiles, interviews, and new product information. Topics include sports, health, fitness, entertainment, technology, equipment, travel, adventure, and fashion.
- Depts/columns: 100–150 words. Entertainment updates, fashion, travel, and new product information.
- Other: Filler.

Sample Issue

130 pages. Advertising. Sample articles available at website. Guidelines and theme list available.

- "Motor Dreamin': Wally Hermes Yachts." Article describes the latest luxury motor yacht to hit the market.
- "Closer to a Cure?" Article reports on the latest research for an HIV cure.

Rights and Payment

First North American serial rights. Articles, $100–$400. Depts/columns, $50–$150. Payment policy varies. Provides 1 contributor's copy.

The Upper Room

Daily Devotional Guide

1908 Grand Avenue
P.O. Box 340004
Nashville, TN 37203-0004

Managing Editor: Lindsay Gray

Description and Interests

With an international, interracial, and interdenominational audience, *The Upper Room* features meditations that focus on deepening readers' Christian commitment and nurturing their spiritual growth. A postcard will be sent to those writers whose work it is considering for publication. Unfortunately the magazine is unable to give updates on the status of submissions or to offer critiques. Circ: 2.75 million.

Contents: 100% meditations
Frequency: 6 times each year
Website: www.upperroom.org

Freelance Potential

95% written by nonstaff writers. Publishes 360 freelance submissions yearly; 50% by authors who are new to the magazine. Receives 350 unsolicited mss monthly.

Submissions

Send complete ms. Accepts hard copy, electronic submissions through the website, and email to theupperroommagazine@upperroom.org (no attachments). SASE for response. Responds in 6 weeks.

- Articles: To 250 words. Daily meditations that include: Bible reading, scripture verse, personal witness or reflection on scripture or prayer, and a thought for the day. Topics include religion, God, faith, and life issues.

Sample Issue

78 pages. Little advertising. Sample copy, guidelines, and editorial calendar available at website.

- "Worthy." Meditation is a reminder that God's children remain worthy even with sins.
- "Living Alone." Meditation is about a recent widower learning to live alone again.
- "God's Colorful Creation." Meditation is a reminder to appreciate diversity.

Rights and Payment

One-time rights. Meditations, $25. Pays on publication. Provides 5 contributor's copies and a 1-year subscription.

U.S. Catholic

205 West Monroe Street
Chicago, IL 60606

Submissions

Description and Interests
Devoted to the Catholic lifestyle and mores, this magazine features articles on Catholicism, issues facing the Church, morality, spirituality, prayer, and faith. It also publishes inspirational fiction. Few unsolicited articles and ideas are accepted, but writers are still welcome to submit. Circ: 41,000.

Contents: 20% articles; 70% depts/columns; 5% fiction; 5% other
Frequency: Monthly
Website: www.uscatholic.org

Freelance Potential
5% written by nonstaff writers. Publishes 120 freelance submissions yearly; 5% by unpublished writers, 20% by authors who are new to the magazine, 5% by experts.

Submissions
Query with clips or writing samples. Accepts hard copy and email queries to submissions@uscatholic.org; for poetry and fiction, email literaryeditor@uscatholic.org. SASE. Responds in 6 weeks. Response to fiction and poetry may take longer.

- Articles: 2,500–3,200 words. Informational articles, interviews, and personal experience pieces. Topics include marriage, prayer, parish life, and the sacraments. Essays, 700–1,800 words.
- Fiction: To 2,500 words. Inspirational fiction.
- Depts/columns: 450–900 words. Profiles, Catholic traditions, spirituality, and meditations. Sounding Board, opinion, 1,100–1,300 words. Reviews, 350 words.
- Other: Poetry, 3-5 poems.

Sample Issue
50 pages. Little advertising. Sample copy and guidelines available at website.

- "So Help Me God: Faith and the American Presidency." Article discusses how faith has played an important role historically in the Oval Office.
- "Returning Vets: Nobody Knows the Trouble I've Seen." Article discusses the uphill battle many veterans find when returning home from war.

Rights and Payment
First North American serial rights. Written material, payment rates vary. Pays on publication. Provides 2 contributor's copies upon request.

Venture Inward

Association for Research and Enlightenment
215 67th Street
Virginia Beach, VA 23451

Editor: Susan Lendvay

Description and Interests
This membership magazine of Edgar Cayce's Association for Research and Enlightenment, a nonprofit organization, is filled with articles on ancient mysteries, personal spirituality, holistic health, intuition, reincarnation, and dreams and dream interpretation. It accepts material only from writers who are familiar with the teachings and research of Edgar Cayce and experts who are on A.R.E.'s conference schedule. Circ: 30,000.

Contents: Articles; depts/columns
Frequency: Quarterly
Website: www.edgarcayce.org

Freelance Potential
50% written by nonstaff writers. Publishes 5–8 freelance submissions yearly; 10% by unpublished writers, 20% by authors who are new to the magazine, 50% by experts. Receives 10 unsolicited mss monthly.

Submissions
Send complete ms (include address, short bio, and links to website or blog, if applicable). Accepts email submissions to letters@edgarcayce.org. SASE. Response time varies.

- Articles: To 1,500 words. Informational articles, profiles, interviews, and personal experience pieces. Topics include the work of Edgar Cayce, personal spirituality, holistic health, ancient mysteries, and intuition.
- Depts/columns: Staff-written.

Sample Issue
50 pages. Sample articles available at website. Guidelines available.

- "Learning to 'Walk': My Struggle with ADD." Personal experience piece about a lifelong handicap and the treatment that finally worked.
- Sample dept/column: PSI Research shares the latest research on the health benefits of coffee and the use of a food diary to lose more weight.

Rights and Payment
One-time print and electronic archival rights. Written material, $25–$150. Pays on publication. Provides 2 contributor's copies.

VFW Magazine

Veterans of Foreign Wars
406 West 34th Street
Kansas City, MO 64111

Senior Editor: Tim Dyhouse

Description and Interests

Read by war veterans from World War II through Iraq and Afghanistan, this magazine seeks to pay tribute to military personnel and veterans. In addition, it offers articles on foreign policy, international events affecting national security, and veterans' concerns. Topics that coincide with an anniversary should be submitted at least six months in advance. When writing about military history, please take a fresh approach. Circ: 1.3 million.

Contents: 80% articles; 20% depts/columns
Frequency: 10 times each year
Website: www.vfwmagazine.org

Freelance Potential

10% written by nonstaff writers. Publishes 10 freelance submissions yearly; 4% by authors who are new to the magazine, 4% by experts. Receives 10 queries monthly.

Submissions

Prefers query with outline, résumé, and clips or writing samples. Accepts hard copy and email submissions to magazine@vfw.org. No simultaneous submissions. SASE. Responds in 1 month.

- Articles: 1,000 words. Informational articles. Topics include veterans' issues, foreign policy, defense, patriotism, and military history.
- Depts/columns: Staff-written.

Sample Issue

56 pages. Advertising. Sample articles and guidelines available at website.

- "Obama and Romney Square Off on Key Issues." Article reports on the key topics discussed at the presidential debates.
- "Korea's DMZ: Hostile Actions, 1945–49 and 1954–94." Article details events that occurred during these time frames.

Rights and Payment

First rights. Articles, payment rates vary. Kill fee varies. Pays on acceptance. Provides 3 contributor's copies.

Vibrant Life

55 West Oak Ridge Drive
Hagerstown, MD 21740

Editor: Heather Quintana

Description and Interests

Vibrant Life focuses on helping readers get and stay fit in mind, body, and spirit. Employing a Christian and spiritual tone, the articles cover such topics as cost-saving but healthy food, simple exercises to do at home, and the spiritual benefits of a restful (and prayerful) Sabbath. Its readers expect practical, affordable suggestions that fit into their demanding schedules, while helping them prevent and fight disease. The magazine is in need of material that addresses the whole family's health needs with a spiritual approach. Circ: 21,711.

Contents: 50% articles; 25% depts/columns; 25% other
Frequency: 6 times each year
Website: www.vibrantlife.com

Freelance Potential

95% written by nonstaff writers. Publishes 25 freelance submissions yearly; 30% by unpublished writers, 60% by authors who are new to the magazine, 35% by experts. Receives 25 queries and 12 unsolicited mss monthly.

Submissions

Send complete ms. Accepts hard copy, email to vibrantlife@rhpa.org (Word attachments), and simultaneous submissions if identified. SASE. Responds in 2 months.

- Articles: 450–1,000 words. Informational, how-to, self-help, profiles, and interviews. Topics include health, fitness, nutrition, family, spiritual balance, challenges and triumphs, safety, and environmental stewardship.
- Depts/columns: Word lengths vary. Health news, medical advice, green living, spiritual guidance, family life, recipes.

Sample Issue

32 pages. Advertising. Sample copy and guidelines available at website.

- "No-Meat Athletes." Eating less meat, and more plant-based foods, for energy.
- "6 Ways to Relieve Pain Naturally." Drug-free ways to deal with pain and illness.

Rights and Payment

First world serial rights, *Vibrant Life* reprint and website rights. Written material, $100–$300. Pays on publication. Provides 3 contributor's copies.

Videomaker

P.O. Box 4591
Chico, CA 95927

Query Editor

Description and Interests
Targeted toward video enthusiasts who seek the latest information on new products, technologies, and techniques, *Videomaker* serves the hobbyist and semi-professional videographer alike with ideas, information, and tips for creating—and publishing—great video. The ideal writer is one who is an expert in the field, but can write for video enthusiasts at all skill levels. Circ: 62,311.

Contents: 63% depts/columns; 36% articles; 1% other
Frequency: Monthly
Website: www.videomaker.com

Freelance Potential
60% written by nonstaff writers. Publishes 95 freelance submissions yearly; 2% by unpublished writers, 15% by authors who are new to the magazine, 60% by experts. Receives 10 queries monthly.

Submissions
Prefers query with résumé and clips; will accept complete ms. Prefers email submissions to editor@videomaker.com; will accept hard copy. No simultaneous submissions. Responds in 1–2 months.

- Articles: 1,200 words. Informational and how-to articles, and new product information. Topics include audio, video, software, electronics, and Web technology.
- Depts/columns: 800 words. Reader tips, new product tests, and industry news.

Sample Issue
64 pages. Advertising. Sample articles and guidelines available at website.

- "Recording in Public Places and Your First Amendment Rights." Article discusses what can be recorded while in public.
- "13 Keys to Successful Event Video." Article provides tips for shooting everything from a tax seminar to a wedding.
- "What to Charge—Freelance Video Hourly Rate Calculator." Article provides details to consider when determining shooting and editing rates.

Rights and Payment
All rights. Written material, $200. Pays on publication. Provides 1 contributor's copy.

Viking

Sons of Norway
1455 West Lake Street
Minneapolis, MN 55408

Editor: Amy Boxrud

Description and Interests
Viking magazine is sent to the members of the Sons of Norway, the largest Scandinavian American organization in the world. It keeps Norwegian heritage going strong with articles on history, culture, people, events, travel, and food. The publication also publishes news about its members and programs. The mission is to promote and preserve the culture of Norway and to encourage those of Norwegian descent to visit their homeland. Circ: 42,000.

Contents: 60% articles; 25% depts/columns; 5% fiction; 10% other
Frequency: Monthly
Website: www.sofn.com/norwegian_culture/viking_index.jsp

Freelance Potential
70% written by nonstaff writers. Publishes 35 freelance submissions yearly; 5% by unpublished writers, 15% by authors who are new to the magazine. Receives 5–10 queries monthly.

Submissions
Query. Accepts email queries to aboxrud@mspmag.com. Responds in 1 month.

- Articles: 400–1,200 words. Informational, how-to, and historical articles; profiles; interviews; and personal experience and opinion pieces. Topics include the arts, cuisine, customs, crafts and hobbies, social issues, sports, travel, leisure, and ethnic issues—all as they relate to Norway.
- Fiction: 400–1,200 words. Ethnic, historical, and humorous fiction.
- Depts/columns: 125–350 words. Member news, financial planning, and interviews.

Sample Issue
38 pages. Advertising. Sample copy and theme list available.

- "Handcrafted for the Holidays." Article shares gift ideas that are artisan-made.
- "Oral History How-to." Article provides tips for preserving one's family stories.

Rights and Payment
All rights for 60 days. Written material, $180–$400+. Pays on acceptance.

The Virginia Quarterly Review

University of Virginia
P.O. Box 400223
Charlottesville, VA 22904-4223

Associate Editor: Paul Reyes

Description and Interests

This journal seeks to publish the freshest, most accomplished writing available on topics of serious cultural significance. Its focus is wide-ranging and includes essays, fiction, and poetry from writers around the world. In short, it seeks nonfiction that looks out on the world, not within itself. Writers are encouraged to read several issues of the magazine; the majority of submissions received are not the right fit. Circ: 6,000+.

Contents: 50% articles; 40% fiction; 10% poetry
Frequency: Quarterly
Website: www.vqronline.org

Freelance Potential

100% written by nonstaff writers. Publishes 60 freelance submissions yearly; 10% by unpublished writers, 25% by authors who are new to the magazine. Receives 1,000–2,000 unsolicited mss each month.

Submissions

Send complete ms. Accepts submissions via website only between September 1 and May 31. No simultaneous submissions. Responds in 3+ months.

- Articles: 5,000–10,000 words. Informational articles, personal experience and opinion pieces, and book reviews. Topics include writing, history, current events, psychology, travel, social issues, and religion.
- Fiction: 2,000–8,000 words. Literary fiction.
- Other: Poetry, no line limits.

Sample Issue

216 pages. Little advertising. Sample articles and guidelines available at website.

- "Is There Such a Thing as the Female Conscience." Article takes a look at its history, from Plato to the current day.
- "A Book of Martyrs." Story tells of a young woman's visit to an abortion clinic.

Rights and Payment

First North American print rights and non-exclusive online rights. Articles and fiction, $.15–$.20 per word. Poetry, $5 per line; minimum $200. Pays on publication. Provides 1 author's copy.

Vista

P.O. Box 50434
Indianapolis, IN 46250

Editor: Jim Watkins

Description and Interests

This theme-based Christian take-home newsletter features articles and stories about holy living that appeal to all ages and stages of life—adults, families, teens, and empty nesters. Inspirational fiction and nonfiction, how-to articles, and humor pieces are included in the mix. It seeks pieces that support Christians in living as God's devoted disciples. Circ: 9,000.

Contents: 25% articles; 25% depts/columns; 25% fiction; 25% other
Frequency: Weekly
Website: www.wesleyan.org/wg

Freelance Potential

60% written by nonstaff writers. Publishes 250 freelance submissions yearly; 50% by unpublished writers, 40% by authors who are new to the magazine, 10% by experts. Receives 60 unsolicited mss monthly.

Submissions

Send complete ms. Accepts email submissions to vista@wesleyan.org (no attachments; write "Vista Submission" and genre in subject line). Response time varies.

- Articles: 500–550 words. Creative nonfiction; informational and how-to articles; and personal experience and humor pieces. Topics include spiritual growth, evangelism, family issues, parenting, seniors, and relationships.
- Fiction: 500–550 words. Inspirational fiction and stories with Christian themes.
- Other: Humor, 250–300 words. Filler, 100 words.

Sample Issue

8 pages. No advertising. Sample copy and guidelines available at website.

- "A Blessing for Sarah." Article is a reminder of how God's love enables us to help others in need.
- "Work Is a Four-Letter Word." Personal experience piece is a humorous look at a stay-at-home mother re-entering the workforce.

Rights and Payment

First rights. Written material, $15–$35. Pays on publication. Provides 1 contributor's copy.

The War Cry

Salvation Army National Headquarters
615 Slaters Lane
Alexandria, VA 22313

Editor in Chief: Major Ed Forster

Description and Interests

This magazine explores Christian growth, spirituality, and evangelism through its mix of insightful and inspirational stories, profiles, and interviews. Its mission is to preach the Gospel of Jesus Christ and meet human needs in his name, without discrimination. Each issue is theme-based; please check the website for a list. Circ: 300,000.

Contents: 65% articles; 35% depts/columns
Frequency: 26 times each year
Website: www.salvationarmyusa.org

Freelance Potential

50% written by nonstaff writers. Publishes 65 freelance submissions yearly; 10% by unpublished writers, 10% by authors who are new to the magazine. Receives 60 unsolicited mss each month.

Submissions

Send complete ms. Accepts email to war_cry@usn.salvationarmy.org. Artwork increases chance of acceptance. No simultaneous submissions. Responds in 3–4 weeks.

- Articles: To 1,200 words. Informational and self-help articles, profiles, interviews, and personal experience pieces. Topics include biblical perspectives on modern issues, stories of salvation, Salvation Army history, and spiritual beliefs.
- Depts/columns: Word lengths vary. Book reviews, news briefs, personal essays, and Bible studies.
- Artwork: Color slides or prints; digital images at 300 dpi.

Sample Issue

22 pages. No advertising. Sample articles and guidelines available at website.

- "The End of the World." Article discusses the speculation of the apocalypse and how best to respond.
- "In God's Hands." Personal experience piece shares a man's coping with a diagnosis of a rare cancer.

Rights and Payment

First rights. Articles, $.15 per word. Depts/columns, payment rates vary. Pays on acceptance.

The Washington Pastime

Editor in Chief: Michael Vidafar

Description and Interests

This online magazine was founded to fill a void in the literary journal market in Washington, DC. Its aim is to publish the best in literary and genre fiction, push boundaries, and revisit traditional perspectives. The editors are especially interested in humor, historical, and western submissions. Work that is chosen for publication will be considered for *The Washington Pastime Collections* series. Circ: 1,000+.

Contents: Articles; fiction
Frequency: Monthly
Website: www.washingtonpastime.com

Freelance Potential

Receives numerous queries monthly.

Submissions

Query with approximate word count. Accepts email to submissions@washingtonpastime.com and simultaneous submissions. Responds in 3 weeks.

- Articles: Word lengths vary. Informational and how-to articles on the writing industry.
- Fiction: 500–3,000 words. All genres including adventure, fantasy, horor, humor, science fiction, mystery, romance, and thriller.

Sample Issue

Sample articles and writer's guidelines available at website.

- "That Chocolate You Love." Story tells of a woman's guilt with spending time with her mother in a nursing home.
- "The Ties That Bind." Story is about a young girl coping with her mother's illness.

Rights and Payment

First world electronic rights, first print rights, and non-exclusive anthology rights. Payment rates and policy vary.

Washington Square

Creative Writing Program
New York University
58 West 10th Street
New York, NY 10011

Editor in Chief: Martin Rock

Description and Interests

Washington Square is a nationally distributed literary journal featuring a wide variety of traditional and experimental forms of fiction and poetry. Also included in its mix are essays and author interviews. A writing contest is offered once each year. It likes new and established writers who are not afraid to take creative risks. Circ: 2,000.

Contents: Articles; fiction; poetry
Frequency: Twice each year
Website: www.washingtonsquarereview.com

Freelance Potential

100% written by nonstaff writers. Publishes 50–60 freelance submissions yearly; 50% by unpublished writers, 75% by authors who are new to the magazine. Receives 350 unsolicited mss monthly.

Submissions

Send complete ms with dated cover letter and brief bio during two submissions windows: August 1–October 15, and December 15–February 1. Prefers electronic submissions; will accept hard copy and simultaneous submissions if identified. SASE for response only; mss are not returned. Submit to appropriate editor. Responds in 2–4 months during reading period.

- Fiction: To 20 pages. Short prose, 1 piece per submission. Contemporary, literary, experimental, and mainstream fiction; humor.
- Other: Poetry, to 10 pages; 3–5 poems per submission. Translation, same page limits, including original text.

Sample Issue

176 pages. Little advertising. Sample copy available. Guidelines available in each issue and at website.

- "Here Comes Your Man." Story.
- "Finnish Ride." Poem translation.
- "Interview." Interview with Sharon Olds.

Rights and Payment

First rights. No payment. Provides 2 contributor's copies.

Weird Tales

P.O. Box 38190
Tallahassee, FL 32315

Editor: Marvin Kaye

Description and Interests

Weird Tales is where speculative and alternative storytelling meet. In each themed issue, science fiction, fantasy, mystery, and other "weird" tales are published, along with articles, author profiles, and reviews. It is temporarily closed to fiction and poetry submissions; it is only accepting nonfiction submissions. Please continue to check the website for changes. Circ: 5,000.

Contents: 90% fiction; 10% depts/columns
Frequency: Quarterly
Website: http://weirdtalesmagazine.com

Freelance Potential

90% written by nonstaff writers. Publishes 40–50 freelance submissions yearly; 10% by unpublished writers, 30% by authors who are new to the magazine. Receives 50 queries, 1,500 unsolicited mss monthly.

Submissions

Only accepting nonfiction submissions at this time. Send query to weirdportal@gmail.com.

- Articles: Word lengths vary. Profiles of and interviews with writers.
- Fiction: To 8,000 words. Genres include fantasy, horror, and fantasy-based science fiction.

Sample Issue

96 pages. Little advertising. Sample copy available.

- "Secretario." Story features detectives, devils, and the dead.
- "Mr. Nine and the Gentleman Ghost." Story tells of a young woman summoned to join a mysterious ladies' society.

Rights and Payment

First North American serial rights. Written material, $.05 per word, $20 per poem. Pays on acceptance. Provides 2 contributor's copies.

Western & Eastern Treasures

P.O. Box 219
San Anselmo, CA 94979

Managing Editor: Rosemary Anderson

Description and Interests

Each themed issue of this magazine provides recreational treasure hunters with plenty of tips, advice, and—of course—news of exciting finds. New writers are encouraged to send their how-to tips and stories of good finds. Circ: 60,000.

Contents: Articles; depts/columns
Frequency: Monthly
Website: www.wetreasures.com

Freelance Potential

100% written by nonstaff writers. Publishes 156 freelance submissions yearly; 25% by unpublished writers, 25% by authors who are new to the magazine, 30% by experts. Receives 50+ unsolicited mss monthly.

Submissions

Send complete ms with artwork and 30-word biography. Accepts email submissions to treasurenet@prodigy.net. No simultaneous submissions. Response time varies.

- Articles: 1,250–1,750 words. Informational and how-to articles, profiles, interviews, and personal experience pieces. Topics include metal detecting, coin shooting, coins and tokens, silver and gold, relics and historical research, urban and indoor treasure hunting, beachcombing, and ghost towns.
- Depts/columns: Word lengths vary. News, history, and events.
- Artwork: Color prints or slides; color TIFF images at 300 dpi (with captions).

Sample Issue

60 pages. Advertising. Sample articles available at website. Guidelines available.

- "Follow the Straight and Narrow." Article discusses the discoveries one can usually find along sidewalks and parking strips.
- "Relics with a Special Message." Article describes the historical importance of axe heads.

Rights and Payment

All rights. Written material, \$.03 per word. Artwork, payment rates vary. Pays on publication. Provides 1 contributor's copy.

Western Horseman

2112 Montgomery Street
Fort Worth, TX 76107

Editor: Ross Hecox

Description and Interests

This magazine showcases the traditional western lifestyle with stories of modern-day cowboys (and cowgirls), rodeos, and horse breeding. Ranching and horsemanship are also featured on its pages. Queries should be geared to subjects suitable for both noncompetitive and competitive horsemen. Circ: 162,000.

Contents: 80% articles; 20% depts/columns
Frequency: Monthly
Website: www.westernhorseman.com

Freelance Potential

50% written by nonstaff writers. Publishes 30 freelance submissions yearly; 10% by authors who are new to the magazine. Receives 125 queries monthly.

Submissions

Query. Prefers email queries to edit@westernhorseman.com ("Freelance" in the subject line); will accept hard copy. Availability of artwork improves chance of acceptance. SASE. Responds in 1 month.

- Articles: 1,000 to 5,000 words. Informational and how-to articles, profiles, and interviews. Topics include horse breeds, training, ranching, gear, apparel, rodeos, and equine health.
- Depts/columns: Word lengths vary. Horsewomen and children, rodeos, horse shows, ranching, trail riding, and cowboy culture.
- Artwork: Color slides or B/W or color prints.

Sample Issue

176 pages. Advertising. Sample articles and guidelines available at website.

- "Cowboys & Cartels." Article discusses the dangers ranchers face along the violent Mexican border.
- "The Home Stretch." Profile features Mary Walker, the National Finals Rodeo barrel racing qualifier.

Rights and Payment

First rights. Articles, \$25–\$600. Depts/columns and artwork, payment rates vary. Pays on publication.

Wildfowl

7819 Highland Scenic Road
Baxter, MN 56425

Editor: Skip Knowles

Description and Interests

This magazine's audience is made up of hard-core waterfowlers who want to be entertained by detailed accounts of specific hunts in specific locales. Gear and gadgets are also covered. It is interested in submissions detailing the tools, techniques, and adventures indigenous to hunting waterfowl. Circ: Unavailable.

Contents: 45% articles; 45% depts/columns; 10% other
Frequency: 7 times each year
Website: www.wildfowlmag.com

Freelance Potential

75% written by nonstaff writers. Publishes 110 freelance submissions yearly; 5% by unpublished writers, 5% by authors who are new to the magazine, 90% by experts. Receives 5 queries, 8 unsolicited mss monthly.

Submissions

Query or send complete ms with artwork. Accepts hard copy for queries; disk with hard copy for mss (Word or text files). Availability of artwork improves chance of acceptance. SASE. Responds in 2 months.

- Articles: To 2,500 words. Informational articles and personal experience pieces. Topics include waterfowl hunting and conservation, hunting gear, and canine retrievers.
- Depts/columns: Staff-written.
- Artwork: Color transparencies; high-resolution color TIFF or JPEG images (with captions). Charts, graphs, and line art.

Sample Issue

96 pages. Advertising. Sample copy and guidelines available.

- "Splendid Specks: How to Decoy Specklebellies." Article explains how to decoy specklebellies.
- "Return of the King." Article discusses the rebounding population of canvasback.

Rights and Payment

All rights. Articles, $300–$600. Artwork, $75–$500. Pays on acceptance for articles, on publication for artwork. Provides 12 contributor's copies.

WineMaker

5515 Main Street
Manchester Center, VT 05255

Editor: Chris Colby

Description and Interests

WineMaker helps readers create their own great wines at home, with a combination of expert advice, award-winning recipes, technique tips, and how-to projects. Its goal is to provide valuable information in a fun and entertaining format. It looks for straightforward and well-researched articles that will help home winemakers produce the best wine, whether they use kits, concentrates, juices, non-grape fruits, or fresh grapes. Circ: 35,000.

Contents: 50% articles; 50% depts/columns
Frequency: 6 times each year
Website: www.winemakermag.com

Freelance Potential

80% written by nonstaff writers. Publishes 50 freelance submissions yearly; 20% by unpublished writers, 25% by authors who are new to the magazine, 25% by experts.

Submissions

Query with story angle, interview sources, and writing samples. Prefers email to edit@wine (attach document); will accept hard copy. SASE. Responds in 6 weeks.

- Articles: 1,000–3,000 words. Informational and how-to articles. Topics include grapes, wines, and winemaking as a hobby.
- Depts/columns: Word lengths vary. Instructional articles, new product information.
- Artwork: Digital images.

Sample Issue

80 pages. Advertising. Sample articles and guidelines available at website.

- "Making the Most of Your Winery Visit." Article provides tips for preparing and planning for a winery visit to make the most of the experience.
- "Italian Red Varietals." Article discusses the top 10 Italian red wine styles and how best to make them at home.

Rights and Payment

All rights. Articles, $200. Depts/columns, $150. Pays on publication. Provides 2 contributor's copies.

Wine Spectator

M. Shanken Communications
387 Park Avenue South
New York, NY 10016

Executive Editor: Thomas Matthews

Description and Interests

For true wine lovers with a sophisticated palate and an upscale pocketbook, *Wine Spectator* is a comprehensive resource about all things pertaining to the grape. Each tabloid-style issue features hundreds of wine ratings, suggestions for pairing food and wine, tasting and collecting tips, and even wine-themed trips and travel destinations. All of its writers are experts in the wine field and its readers already possess a high level of knowledge about wine and are refined in their other lifestyle choices as well. Circ: 375,000.

Contents: 80% articles; 20% depts/columns
Frequency: 15 times each year
Website: www.winespectator.com

Freelance Potential

20% written by nonstaff writers. Publishes 30–40 freelance submissions yearly; 2% by authors who are new to the magazine, 100% by experts. Receives 30 queries monthly.

Submissions

Query. Accepts hard copy. SASE. Responds in 3 months.

- Articles: 100–2,000 words. Informational and how-to articles, profiles, and interviews. Topics include wine vintages, tasting, and collecting; cooking with wine; successful vintners; and lifestyles.
- Depts/columns: Word lengths vary. Collecting and buying wine, industry news, winemaking, and new product information.

Sample Issue

168 pages. Advertising. Sample copy and guidelines available.

- "King of the Hill." Article includes a profile of winemaker Michel Chapoutier who oversees a growing collection of wineries in the Northern Rhone Valley.
- "Best of Miami Beach." Article describes the varied dining options in this city, everything from cosmopolitan cuisine to casual dining.

Rights and Payment

All rights. Written material, $100–$1,500. Pays on publication. Provides 1 contributor's copy.

Women's Running

1499 Beach Drive SE, Suite B
St. Petersburg, FL 33701

Editor in Chief: Jessica Sebor

Description and Interests

This magazine—written for smart and successful women who use running to balance and enrich their lives—covers health, fitness, sports, nutrition, travel, and beauty. It also offers profiles of inspirational female runners. It seeks well-researched and intelligent articles that are written in a lively voice. There is little interest in first-person, general articles about running and fitness, as well as race reports. New writers have the best chance of breaking in through the departments or feature profiles. Circ: 100,000.

Contents: 90% articles; 10% depts/columns
Frequency: 6 times each year
Website: www.womensrunning.com

Freelance Potential

80% written by nonstaff writers. Publishes 40 freelance submissions yearly; 5% by unpublished writers, 20% by authors who are new to the magazine, 80% by experts. Receives 40 queries monthly.

Submissions

Query with 2–3 relevant writing samples. Accepts email queries to editorial@womensrunningmag.com (attach document). Responds in 6+ weeks.

- Articles: 1,000-1,500 words. Informational and how-to articles, profiles, interviews, and new product information. Topics include running, health and fitness, nutrition, sports, and travel and leisure.
- Depts/columns: 1,000–1,500 words. Running techniques, training, nutrition, and beauty.

Sample Issue

74 pages. Advertising. Sample articles and guidelines available at website.

- "Running for Coverage During an Election Year." Article features a profile of Fox News reporter Shannon Bream.
- "Hydrate Right." Article provides nutritionist tips for fueling during and after a workout.

Rights and Payment

All rights. Written material, payment rates vary. Kill fee, 50%. Pays on publication. Provides 1 contributor's copy.

WoodenBoat

P.O. Box 78
Brooklin, ME 04616-0078

Editor: Matthew P. Murphy

Description and Interests

Owners, builders, and designers of wooden boats are the readers of this publication. It features in-depth articles about boatbuilding, design, repair, nautical history, woodworking, seamanship, and travel. Also included in the editorial mix are some first-person adventure stories. *WoodenBoat* readers are serious wooden boat enthusiasts who are well versed on these crafts. Writers must have a thorough knowledge of boating and boatbuilding to write for it. Circ: 65,000.

Contents: 75% articles; 25% depts/columns
Frequency: 6 times each year
Website: www.woodenboat.com

Freelance Potential

90% written by nonstaff writers. Publishes 60 freelance submissions yearly; 40% by unpublished writers, 50% by authors who are new to the magazine, 100% by experts. Receives 35 queries, 17 unsolicited mss monthly.

Submissions

Prefers query with outline and artwork; will accept complete ms. Prefers electronic submission; will accept hard copy. SASE. Responds in 8 weeks.

- Articles: 1,000–4,000 words. Informational, historical, and how-to articles; profiles; interviews; and new product information. Topics include commercial, sail, power, and pleasure boats.
- Depts/columns: Word lengths vary. How-to's, boat designs, technology, and reviews.

Sample Issue

144 pages. Advertising. Sample copy, guidelines, and editorial calendar available at website.

- "Building *Charlotte*." Article profiles Gannon & Benjamin co-founder Nat Benjamin and his company's new 50' schooner.
- "The Tour Boats of Glacier National Park." Article discusses the history of the fleet of wooden tour boats that were built starting in the late 1800s.

Rights and Payment

First world rights. Written material, payment rates vary. Pays on publication. Provides 1 contributor's copy.

World War II

Weider History Group
19300 Promenade Drive
Leesburg, VA 20176

Associate Editor: Caitlin Newman

Description and Interests

World War II buffs read this publication to revisit and learn more about this historic period. In-depth exploration of battles, weapons, and strategies on all fronts of the war fill its pages, along with real soldiers' first-person accounts. The best opportunity for freelance writers to break in to this magazine is the Time Travel column. First-person accounts are welcome. Circ: 91,000.

Contents: 50% articles; 50% depts/columns
Frequency: 6 times each year
Website: http://www.historynet.com/worldwar2

Freelance Potential

95% written by nonstaff writers. Publishes 50 freelance submissions yearly; 5% by unpublished writers, 15% by authors who are new to the magazine, 1% by experts. Receives 20 queries monthly.

Submissions

Query only with outline, writing credentials, and background. Accepts hard copy and email to worldwar2@weiderhistorygroup.com (Word attachments). No simultaneous submissions. SASE. Response time varies.

- Articles: 3,500–4,000 words. Informational articles, profiles, interviews, and personal experience pieces. Topics include World War II military strategy, arms, tactics, equipment, and military operations.
- Depts/columns: To 2,000 words. Profiles, reviews, and commentary.

Sample Issue

80 pages. Advertising. Guidelines, sample articles, and editorial calendar available at website.

- "Private Wojtek, Reporting for Duty." Tells about the mascot of the Polish II Corps's 22nd Artillery Supply Company, a 6-foot tall, fully grown brown bear.
- "From D-Day to Paris: The Story of a Lifetime." The story of the storytellers: three legendary World War II correspondents—Robert Capa, Ernie Pyle, and Ernest Hemingway.

Rights and Payment

All rights. Articles, $500+. Depts/columns, $300+. Pays on publication.

The Writer's Chronicle

AWP
George Mason University
4400 University Drive
MSN 1E3
Fairfax, VA 22030-4444

Editor: Supriya Bhatnagar

Description and Interests

The Writer's Chronicle is an educational resource for writers and teachers of writing. It presents essays on the craft of writing, career advice, and timely information about publishing opportunities. Articles should show a love for and command of literature. Circ: 39,000.

Contents: 70% articles; 10% depts/columns; 20% other
Frequency: 6 times each year
Website: www.awpwriter.org

Freelance Potential

100% written by nonstaff writers. Publishes 50 freelance submissions yearly; 10% by unpublished writers, 90% by authors who are new to the magazine, 100% by experts. Receives 10 queries, 25 unsolicited mss monthly.

Submissions

Query or send complete ms with clips between February 1 and August 31. Accepts complete ms only in hard copy. SASE. Use email for queries only: chronicle@awpwriter.org. No simultaneous submissions. Responds to queries in 1 week, to mss in 3 months.

- Articles: To 7,000 words. Informational and how-to articles, interviews, media reviews, essays, and personal experience and opinion pieces. Topics include literature, writing, the arts, and public affairs.
- Depts/columns: Word lengths vary. News, grants, awards, calls for submissions, conferences, and writers' colonies and centers.

Sample Issue

124 pages. Advertising. Sample copy available. Guidelines available at website.

- "The Book of Ruth." Article profiles Ruth Forman, an American poet.
- "In the Beginning: Creating Dynamic, Meaningful, and Compelling Openings." Article explains the importance of a strong opening and offers tips.

Rights and Payment

First serial and electronic rights. Written material, $.14 per 100 words. Pays on publication. Provides 5 contributor's copies.

WTOnline Webzine

General Council of the Assemblies of God
1445 North Boonville Avenue
Springfield, MO 65802-1894

Editor: Arlene Allen

Description and Interests

Christian women turn to this online publication to read about all aspects of life from a faith-based viewpoint. Articles are meant to inspire and help in practical ways on issues of home, work, and ministry. It also features personality profiles of born-again women who are leaders in their fields. Prospective writers should read currently posted material to get a feel for the style and the types of articles. A list of available photographs should accompany the proposed article, but do not send them. Hits per month: 3,000+.

Contents: 60% articles; 30% depts/columns; 10% other
Frequency: Updated weekly
Website: www.wtonline.ag.org

Freelance Potential

80% written by nonstaff writers. Publishes 30 freelance submissions yearly; 20% by unpublished writers, 30% by authors who are new to the magazine, 5% by experts. Receives 40 queries and unsolicited mss monthly.

Submissions

Query or send complete ms. Prefers email submissions to wtonline@ag.org; will accept hard copy. SASE. Responds if interested.

- Articles: 500–800 words. Informational and self-help articles, profiles, interviews, personal experience pieces, and humor. Topics include faith, spirituality, family life, ministry, forgiveness, and witnessing.
- Depts/columns: 50–250 words. Food, book reviews, and family issues.
- Other: Submit seasonal material 9–12 months in advance.

Sample Issue

Guidelines and editorial calendar available on website.

- "Book Club in Alaska." Article tells of a monthly book club that was started in Eagle River, Alaska.
- "Understanding 1 Timothy 2." Article explains why the meaning of this passage should not be taken literally.

Rights and Payment

One-time and electronic rights. No payment.

Yes!

Building a Just and Sustainable World

284 Madrona Way NE, Suite 116
Bainbridge Island, WA 98110-2870

Senior Editor: Madeline Ostrander

Description and Interests

This magazine aims to bring attention to global issues and offer solutions that will foster justice and sustain the Earth's living systems. It also profiles people who are making a difference. It is especially interested in authentic stories of positive change from the grassroots that can serve as models and inspiration for others. Circ: 50,000.

Contents: 55% articles; 40% depts/columns; 5% other
Frequency: Quarterly
Website: www.yesmagazine.org

Freelance Potential

60% written by nonstaff writers. Publishes 40 freelance submissions yearly; 25% by unpublished writers, 25% by authors who are new to the magazine. Receives 40 queries monthly.

Submissions

Query with clips. Send email queries to submissions@yesmagazine.org (attach document). Responds in 3 months.

- Articles: 1,000–2,500 words. Informational and how-to articles, profiles, and interviews. Topics include living in sustainable communities, new approaches to business and economics, social justice, democracy, changes in global relationships, standards of ethical behavior, the environment, science, technology, arts, and the media.
- Depts/columns: 100-1,000 words. News, opinion, and reviews.

Sample Issue

64 pages. No advertising. Sample articles and guidelines available at website.

- "Why Your Health Is Bigger Than Your Body." Article discusses new science that explains how politics, economics, and ecology affect one's body.
- "The Good Food Cure." Article takes a look at the transformation in Detriot as the city adopts a grow-your-own-food concept.

Rights and Payment

All rights. Written material, payment rates vary. Pays on publication. Provides 2 contributor's copies.

Yoga Journal

475 Sansome Street, Suite 850
San Francisco, CA 94111

Editor in Chief: Kaitlin Quistgaard

Description and Interests

This magazine explores yoga and its varied forms and practices. The emphasis is on integrating yoga philosophy into relationships, career, environment, and other aspects of everyday life. Also featured are articles on spiritual practices and practitioners, health, nutrition, exercise, and ideas that broaden the understanding of self and others. It defines yoga broadly to encompass practices that aspire to union or communion with some higher power or deeper source of wisdom, as well as practices that increase harmony of body, mind, and spirit. Circ: 350,000.

Contents: 50% articles; 50% depts/columns
Frequency: 9 times each year
Website: www.yogajournal.com

Freelance Potential

95% written by nonstaff writers. Publishes 50–60 freelance submissions yearly; 10% by unpublished writers, 10% by new authors, 80% by experts. Receives 100 queries monthly.

Submissions

Send complete ms for Yoga Diary to diary@-yjmag.com; query with approximate word count, sources, and brief bio for all other departments to queries@yjmag.com. Responds if interested in 6 weeks.

- Articles: To 1,400 words. Informational articles, profiles, interviews, and personal experience pieces. Topics include yoga disciplines, health and healing, fitness, nutrition, meditation, spirituality, home, work, nature, relationships, and instructors.
- Depts/columns: Word lengths vary. Interviews, media reviews, news, and trends. Yoga Diary, 250 words.

Sample Issue

148 pages. Advertising. Sample copy available. Guidelines available at website.

- "Meet Mark Gonzales." Article explores the yoga practice of this teacher.
- "Calm Interior." Article explains how to do a forward-folding practice that draws one's attention inward.

Rights and Payment

Rights vary. Written material, $50–$2,000. Pays on publication. Provides 3 contributor's copies.

Zoetrope: All Story

916 Kearny Street
San Francisco, CA 94113

Managing Editor: Derek Fagerstrom

Description and Interests

Short fiction and one-act plays comprise this literary magazine, founded by Francis Ford Coppola. It is dedicated to bringing the best of emerging writers to a sophisticated readership, while also publishing new works from established writers. It is unwavering in its desire to publish short fiction and one-act plays exclusively. Excerpts from larger works, screenplays, treatments, and poetry will be returned unread. Writers are welcome to take advantage of the free online writers' workshop. Circ: 25,000.

Contents: 85% fiction; 15% other
Frequency: Quarterly
Website: www.all-story.com

Freelance Potential

100% written by nonstaff writers. Publishes 28 freelance submissions yearly; 5% by unpublished writers, 75% by authors who are new to the magazine. Receives 12,000 mss annually.

Submissions

Send complete ms between January 1 and August 31 only. Accepts hard copy and simultaneous submissions if identified. Limit submissions to 2 annually. SASE. Responds in 7 months.

- Fiction: To 7,000 words. Literary and mainstream short stories and one-act plays. No excerpts.

Sample Issue

94 pages. Little advertising. Sample copy available. Guidelines available at website.

- "A Dream of Being Sufficient." Story is about an elderly woman and her home health-care workers.
- "Once There Was a Hushpuppy: On the Origins of Beasts of the Southern Wild." Story about turning a play into a feature film.

Rights and Payment

First North American serial rights and 1-year film option. Written material, $1,000. Pays on publication. Provides 10+ contributor's copies.

Additional Consumer Magazines

Art Times

Digital Publication

P.O. Box 730
Mount Marion, NY 12456-0730

Editor: Raymond Steiner — Whom to contact

Description and Interests: Works of fiction and poetry appear alongside articles and essays on film, theater, dance, and fine arts in this newsletter. Published six times each year, *Art Times* seeks high-quality short stories and poems pertaining to artists and the art world. Nonfiction is not accepted from freelance writers. Circ: 28,000.
Website: www.arttimesjournal.com

Gives brief characterization of the magazine, its frequency, the types and topics of articles and stories it publishes and needs, and its readers; gives website address.

Freelance Potential: 20% written by nonstaff writers. Publishes 40 freelance submissions yearly. Receives 50 unsolicited mss monthly.

Indicates openness to freelance submissions, including how many are published yearly and the percentage by unpublished writers, when provided by the publisher.

Submissions and Payment: Sample copy and guidelines available. Send complete ms. Accepts hard copy and simultaneous submissions if identified. SASE. Responds in 6 months. First North American serial rights. Fiction, 1,500 words; $25. Poetry, to 20 lines; no payment. Pays on acceptance. Provides 6 contributor's copies, plus one-year subscription.

Provides guidelines for submitting material; indicates typical rights and payment.

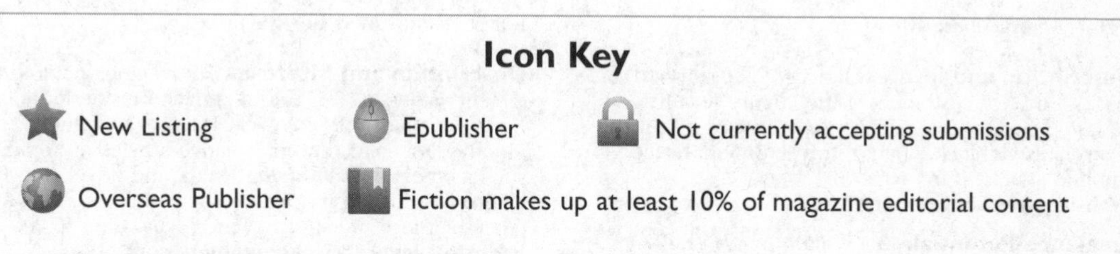

Icon Key
New Listing
Epublisher
Not currently accepting submissions
Overseas Publisher
Fiction makes up at least 10% of magazine editorial content

Able Newspaper

P.O. Box 395
Old Bethpage, NY 11804

Publisher/Editor: Angela Melledy

Description and Interests: Published for more than two decades, *Able Newspaper* is written for people with disabilities. The monthly informs readers about technologies that can improve their lifestyle and provides updates on legislation that may affect the disabled. It includes profiles and media reviews. Circ: 30,000.
Website: www.ablenews.com

Freelance Potential: 75% written by nonstaff writers. Publishes 60 freelance submissions yearly; 20% by authors who are new to the magazine, 60% by experts. Receives 5 queries monthly.

Submissions and Payment: Sample copy and editorial calendar available. Guidelines available via email request to abledeb@aol.com. Query with clips. Accepts hard copy. SASE. Responds in 1 month. First rights. Articles and depts/columns, 500 words; $40. Pays on publication.

Absinthe

P.O. Box 2297
Farmington Hills, MI 48333

Editor: Dwayne D. Hayes

Description and Interests: New European writing appears in this journal, published twice each year. *Absinthe* features poetry, fiction, essays, interviews, and book reviews. It is currently closed to submissions; check website for updates. Circ: 500.
Website: www.absinthenew.com

Freelance Potential: 98% written by nonstaff writers. Publishes 100 freelance submissions yearly; 95% by authors who are new to the magazine. Receives 15 unsolicited mss monthly.

Submissions and Payment: Guidelines and sample stories available at website. Send complete ms. Accepts hard copy and email submissions to dhayes@absinthenew.com (RTF attachments). No simultaneous submissions. SASE. Response time varies. First North American serial rights. Articles and fiction, to 6,000 words. Poetry, to 5 poems per submission. No payment. Provides 1 contributor's copy.

Accent

1384 Broadway, 11th Floor
New York, NY 10018

Editor: Karen Alberg-Grossman

Description and Interests: *Accent* is published twice yearly for customers of the Luxury Jewelry Resource Group stores. Its content focuses on the luxury lifestyle, including art, travel, dining, fashion, and fine jewelry. Circ: 600,000.
Website: www.busjour.com

Freelance Potential: 40% written by nonstaff writers. Publishes 10–20 freelance submissions yearly; 5–10% by unpublished writers, 10–20% by authors who are new to the magazine, 40% by experts. Receives 10–20 queries monthly.

Submissions and Payment: Sample copy available. Query with article angle and author bio. Accepts email to karena@busjour.com and simultaneous submissions if identified. Responds in 2–10 days. All rights. Articles, 600–1,500 words; $300–$500. Depts/columns, 600–800 words; $300. Kill fee, 50%. Pays on publication. Provides 2–4 contributor's copies.

Active Aging

125 South West Street, Suite 105
Wichita, KS 67213

Editor & Publisher: Becky Funke

Description and Interests: This regional tabloid targets readers age 55 and older who reside in the Kansas counties of Sedgwick, Harvey, and Butler. Monthly issues feature informative articles on topics such as the senior lifestyle, health, and travel, as well as profiles, interviews, and nostalgia pieces. All content has a local perspective and focus. Circ: 55,000.
Website: www.activeagingonline.com

Freelance Potential: 90% written by nonstaff writers. Publishes several freelance submissions yearly; 5% by authors who are new to the magazine. Receives 2 queries monthly.

Submissions and Payment: Sample copy available. Query. Accepts email queries to bfunke@activeagingonline.com. Responds in 1 month. First rights. Articles, 750–1,000 words; $100. JPEG files. Kill fee, $25. Pays on publication. Provides 2 contributor's copies.

ADDitude

39 West 37th Street, 15th Floor
New York, NY 10018

Editorial Assistant: Caitlin Ford

Description and Interests: In addition to articles written by mental health professionals and other experts, *ADDitude* features first-person pieces by parents and others who have personal experience with attention deficit disorder. It also hires bloggers. It appears five times a year. Circ: 40,000.
Website: www.additudemag.com

Freelance Potential: 80% written by nonstaff writers. Publishes 15–20 freelance submissions yearly; 30% by unpublished writers, 30% by new authors, 80% by experts. Receives 8 queries monthly.

Submissions and Payment: Sample copy available. Guidelines available at website. Query with outline and clips. Prefers email to submissions@additudemag.com (attachment files); will accept hard copy. Responds in 6–8 weeks. First rights. Articles, to 2,000 words. Depts/columns, word lengths vary. Written material, payment rates vary. Kill fee, $75. Pays on publication. Provides a 1-year subscription.

Adoptalk

970 Raymond Avenue, Suite 106
St. Paul, MN 55114

Communication Specialist: Diane Riggs

Description and Interests: The North American Council on Adoptable Children reaches child welfare professionals, foster and adoptive parents, and child advocates through this quarterly newsletter, with a focus on special needs adoptions. It publishes articles on parenting, North American adoption and foster care programs, and child welfare news. Circ: 2,500.
Website: www.nacac.org

Freelance Potential: 25–50% written by nonstaff writers. Publishes 2–4 freelance submissions yearly; 1–10% by unpublished writers, 1–10% by authors who are new to the magazine. Receives 1–5 queries and unsolicited mss each month.

Submissions and Payment: Sample copy and guidelines available. Query with article proposal or outline. Accepts email queries to dianeriggs@nacac.org. Responds in 1–3 weeks. Rights vary. Articles, 700–2,200 words. Depts/columns, word lengths vary. No payment. Provides 5 contributor's copies.

Adornment

Association for the Study of Jewelry & Related Arts
246 North Regent Street
Port Chester, NY 10573

Editor in Chief: Elyse Zorn Karlin

Description and Interests: Dedicated to the discussion of jewelry throughout the ages, *Adornment* features in-depth articles, artisan profiles and interviews, and reviews in each quarterly issue. It seeks more submissions on costume jewelry. Circ: 1,000+.
Website: www.jewelryandrelatedarts.com

Freelance Potential: 40% written by nonstaff writers. Publishes 6–7 freelance submissions yearly; 20% by authors who are new to the magazine. Receives 2 queries monthly.

Submissions and Payment: Sample copy available for $10. Guidelines available. Query. Accepts hard copy and email queries to ekarlin@usa.net. SASE. Responds in 1–2 weeks. First North American serial rights. Articles, 1,000–3,000 words. Written material, to $150 for assigned articles; no payment for unsolicited articles. Pays on publication. Provides 1 contributor's copy.

Aesthetica

P.O. Box 371
York Y023 1WL
United Kingdom

Marketing Officer: Helena Culliney

Description and Interests: This magazine, published six times each year, has an international audience that appreciates art and culture. It accepts freelance submissions of fiction and poetry for its annual Creative Works Competition only. Circ: 60,000.
Website: www.aestheticamagazine.com

Freelance Potential: 10% written by nonstaff writers. Publishes 10 freelance submissions yearly; 10% by authors who are new to the magazine, 90% by industry experts. Receives 25 unsolicited mss monthly.

Submissions and Payment: For Creative Works Competition: Guidelines available at website. Send complete ms. Accepts email to writing@aestheticamagazine.com. Response time varies. Author retains copyright. Fiction, to 2,000 words. Poetry, to 40 lines. Limit 2 works per entry. Entry fee, £10 per entry; multiple entries allowed. Award payment varies.

Aethlon

The Journal of Sport Literature

East Tennessee University
P.O. Box 70270
Johnson City, TN 37614-0270

Editor in Chief: Joyce Duncan

Description and Interests: Twice each year, this literary journal offers fiction, creative nonfiction, poetry, book reviews, drama, and essays—all with a sports theme. Circ: 1,000.
Website: www.uta.edu/english/sla/aethlon.html

Freelance Potential: 100% written by nonstaff writers. Publishes 20 freelance submissions yearly; 25% by unpublished writers, 50% by authors who are new to the magazine. Receives 3–5 unsolicited mss each month.

Submissions and Payment: Sample copy available. Guidelines available at website. Send complete ms to editor in charge of dept (check site for contacts). Prefers email submissions; will accept hard copy. SASE. No simultaneous submissions. Responds in 6–9 months. First North American serial rights. Written material, word lengths vary. No payment. Provides 1 contributor's copy.

African American Golfer's Digest

80 Wall Street, Suite 720
New York, NY 10005

Editor: Debert Cook

Description and Interests: Appearing quarterly, this magazine focuses on the African American golfer and golfing lifestyle. It includes sport tips, athlete interviews and profiles, and reviews of resorts and courses. Circ: 20,000.
Website: www.africanamericangolfersdigest.com

Freelance Potential: 95% written by nonstaff writers. Publishes 200 freelance submissions yearly; 10% by unpublished writers, 60% by authors who are new to the magazine, 30% by experts. Receives 20 queries, 5 unsolicited mss each month.

Submissions and Payment: Sample copy and guidelines available. Query or send complete ms. Accepts submissions via website and email to editors@africanamericangolfersdigest.com. Response time varies. All rights. Articles and depts/columns, word lengths vary. No payment.

Afar

40 Gold Street
San Francisco, CA 94133

Editor in Chief: Julia Cosgrove

Description and Interests: *Afar* is written for travelers who want to get to know the people and deeply experience the cultures of the destinations they are exploring. Appearing seven times each year, it targets educated travelers in their 30s, 40s, and 50s. Circ: Unavailable.
Website: www.afar.com

Freelance Potential: 30% written by nonstaff writers. Publishes 20–30 freelance submissions yearly; 25% by authors who are new to the magazine.

Submissions and Payment: Sample articles and guidelines available at website. Query. Accepts email queries for features to editorial@afar.com. Check website for depts/columns contacts. Response time varies. Rights vary. Articles, 400–4,000 words. Depts/columns, word lengths vary. Written material, payment rates vary. Pays on publication.

African American Review

Saint Louis University, Adorjan Hall 317
3800 Lindell Boulevard
St. Louis, MO 63108

Editor: Nathan Grant

Description and Interests: In addition to poetry and fiction, this quarterly literary journal from Saint Louis University presents essays on African American literature, theater, film, art, and culture. Circ: 2,000.
Website: http://aar.slu.edu

Freelance Potential: 100% written by nonstaff writers. Publishes 50 freelance submissions yearly; 5% by unpublished writers, 10% by new authors. Receives 50 unsolicited mss monthly.

Submissions and Payment: Sample copy, guidelines, and theme list available. Send complete ms with author bio. Accepts submissions via http://aar.expressacademic.org. Responds in 4–6 months. Author retains rights. Articles, 6,000–8,500 words. Fiction, to 3,500 words. Book reviews, word lengths vary. Poetry, no line limits; to 6 poems per submission. No payment. Provides 1 contributor's copy and 5 offprints.

African Violet Magazine

2375 North Street
Beaumont, TX 77702

Editor: Ruth Rumsey

Description and Interests: The African Violet Society of America publishes this magazine six times each year. People who are passionate about growing these plants find all the information they need to cultivate award-winning African violets, as well as updates on society news and members. Circ: 7,500.
Website: www.avsa.org

Freelance Potential: 70% written by nonstaff writers. Publishes 130+ freelance submissions yearly; 50% by unpublished writers, 30% by authors who are new to the magazine, 20% by experts. Receives 5 queries monthly.

Submissions and Payment: Sample copy and guidelines available. Query. Accepts email queries to rrumsey@earthlink.net. Responds in 2 weeks. All rights. Articles, 700 words. Depts/columns, 700–1,000 words. No payment. Provides 5 contributor's copies.

Airforce

P.O. Box 2460, Station "D"
Ottawa, Ontario K1P 5W6
Canada

Editor: Vic Johnson

Description and Interests: Known as "Canada's Air Force Heritage Voice," this quarterly magazine publishes articles that advocate for Canada's Air Force and commemorate the notable achievements of Canadian military aviators. Circ: 16,000.
Website: www.airforce.ca

Freelance Potential: 5% written by nonstaff writers. Publishes 15–25 freelance submissions yearly; 10% by unpublished writers. Receives 10 queries and unsolicited mss monthly.

Submissions and Payment: Editorial calendar available at website. Query or send complete ms. Accepts hard copy and email to vjohnson@airforce.ca. SAE/IRC. Responds in 2 weeks. Rights vary. Articles, 1,500–3,500 words. Depts/columns, word lengths vary. Written material, payment rates vary. Pays on publication. Provides 1 contributor's copy.

Alimentum

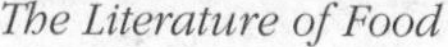
The Literature of Food

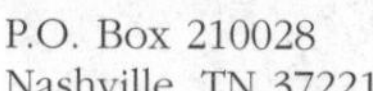
P.O. Box 210028
Nashville, TN 37221

Co-Editors: Paulette Licitra & Peter Selgin

Description and Interests: Food and food-related themes are the focus of the fiction, creative nonfiction, and poetry appearing in this literary journal. It plans to become an online journal in 2012 and will be updated frequently. Hits per month: Unavailable.
Website: www.alimentumjournal.com

Freelance Potential: 100% written by nonstaff writers. Of the freelance submissions published yearly, 5% are by unpublished writers, 85% are by authors who are new to the magazine. Receives 100 unsolicited mss monthly.

Submissions and Payment: Sample stories and guidelines available at website. Send complete ms during reading periods outlined in the guidelines. Accepts hard copy and simultaneous submissions if identified. SASE. Responds in 1–3 months. First North American serial rights. Articles and fiction, under 2,000 words. Poetry, to 5 poems per submission. No payment.

The Allegheny Review

Allegheny College
P.O. Box 32
Meadville, PA 16335

Senior Editor

Description and Interests: Fiction, creative nonfiction, and poetry by American undergraduate students are showcased in this annual journal. Creative nonfiction is especially sought. Circ: 1,000.
Website: www.alleghenyreview.wordpress.com

Freelance Potential: 99% written by nonstaff writers. Publishes 30 freelance submissions yearly; 90% by unpublished writers. Receives 40 unsolicited mss monthly.

Submissions and Payment: Sample copy available. Guidelines available at website. Post complete ms to website. No longer accepts submissions by mail or email. Responds in 5 months. All rights. Fiction and nonfiction, to 20 pages. Poetry, to 5 poems per submission. Written material, payment rates vary. Payment policy varies. Provides 1 contributor's copy.

Allergic Living

P.O. Box 1042
Niagara Falls, NY 14304

Editor: Gwen Smith

Description and Interests: The more recent American edition of this eight-year-old Canadian quarterly addresses readers who want to live healthy lives despite allergies and asthma. Circ: American circulation unavailable.
Website: www.allergicliving.com

Freelance Potential: Uses freelance writers and experts.

Submissions and Payment: Topics include strategies for allergy sufferers, including prevention, gluten-free food, vaccines, and specific conditions like celiac disease and asthma. Recent topics included a worry-free party, a stylish healthy home, research into "safe" levels of peanuts in food, a dietitian's nutritional analysis of pasta brands, dental defects and celiac disease, and keeping kids safe at extended family gatherings. Contact the magazine's founder and editor Gwen Smith at editor@allergicliving.com.

All You

Time Inc.
1271 Avenue of the Americas
New York, NY 10020

Publisher: Diane Oshin

Description and Interests: Published by the Time Inc. Lifestyle Group, along with *Cooking Light*, *Food & Wine*, *Coastal Living*, *Southern Living*, and others, *All You* is a monthly distributed exclusively in Walmart. In the current economy, the retailer's budget-driven audience has been expanding dramatically. *All You* aims at "value-conscious women" who are living busy lives. Circ: 1.5 million.
Website: www.allyou.com

Freelance Potential: Parent company Time Inc. does use freelancers, but is very competitive.

Submissions and Payment: Categories of interest are home, food, style, crafts, health, community, the seasons, money, shopping, and pets. Query before submitting. Send editorial queries to realitycheckers@allyou.com.

The Almanac for Farmers & City Folk

840 South Rancho Drive, Suite 4
P.O. Box 319
Las Vegas, NV 89106

Editor in Chief: Lucas McFadden

Description and Interests: Readers enjoy informative articles on a variety of topics that are never controversial nor purely anecdotal. Gardening, building, and crafting how-to's and humorous pieces are featured in this annual publication. Circ: 250,000.
Website: www.thealmanac.com

Freelance Potential: 70% written by nonstaff writers. Publishes 35–40 freelance submissions yearly; 30% by new authors. Receives 5 mss monthly.

Submissions and Payment: Sample copy available. Send complete ms by March 31 to be considered for publication in the upcoming edition. Accepts hard copy. SASE. Response time varies. Rights vary. Articles, to 1,200 words. Depts/columns, word lengths vary. Written material, $45 per page. Pays on publication. Provides 1 contributor's copy.

Alternative Harmonies

1830 Marvel Road
Brierfield, AL 35035

Editor: Jerri Hardesty

Description and Interests: The editors of this literary quarterly will consider fiction in all genres, creative nonfiction, and poetry. It includes work by new voices and established authors, as well as photography and illustrations. Circ: 350.
Website: www.newdawnunlimited.com

Freelance Potential: 100% written by nonstaff writers. Publishes 60–80 freelance submissions yearly; 50% by unpublished writers, 60% by authors who are new to the magazine. Receives 15–20 queries, 20–30 unsolicited mss monthly.

Submissions and Payment: Sample copy, guidelines, and theme list available. Query or send complete ms. Accepts hard copy. SASE. Responds to queries in 1 month, to mss in 3–6 months. One-time rights. Writing, word lengths vary. B/W prints or line art. No payment. Provides 1 contributor's copy.

Ambassador Magazine

National Italian American Foundation
1860 19th Street NW
Washington, DC 20009

Editor: Don Oldenburg

Description and Interests: Three times each year, *Ambassador Magazine* provides information and features about all things Italian American. It covers Italian American personalities, food, film, and culture, while also offering travel pieces about Italy and other destinations. Circ: 25,000.
Website: www.niaf.org

Freelance Potential: 70% written by nonstaff writers. Publishes 15 freelance submissions yearly. Receives 20 queries monthly.

Submissions and Payment: Sample copy available at website. Guidelines and editorial calendar available. Query with clips. Accepts email to don@niaf.org (Word attachments). Artwork improves chance of acceptance. Responds if interested. First rights. Articles, 1,000–1,500 words. Color JPEGs or TIFFs. All material, $300, plus $50 for photos that are used. Pays on publication. Provides contributor's copies.

American Archaeology

5301 Central Avenue NE, Suite 902
Albuquerque, NM 87108

Editor: Michael Bawaya

Description and Interests: Devoted exclusively to the field of North American archaeology, this quarterly looks for writers who have an ability to make long-dead civilizations come to life on the page. Read by professionals and non-professionals alike, it emphasizes the conservation of endangered archaeological sites. Circ: 30,000.
Website: www.americanarchaeology.com

Freelance Potential: 60% written by nonstaff writers. Publishes 20 freelance submissions yearly. Receives 10 queries monthly.

Submissions and Payment: Sample articles available at website. Guidelines available. Query with résumé and sources. Accepts hard copy. SASE. Responds in 2 months. First serial rights. Articles, 1,500–3,000 words; $700–$1,500. 35mm color slides; $50–$100. Kill fee, 20%. Pays on acceptance. Provides 4 contributor's copies.

American Artist

133 West 19th Street, 7th Floor
New York, NY 10011

Editorial Director: Michael Gormley

Description and Interests: This magazine was created for professional and advanced amateur artists who want to learn from other artists. It is filled with profiles of artists and detailed information about their techniques. Published nine times each year, it also reports on recent exhibitions and the business side of being a working artist. Circ: 50,000.
Website: www.artistdaily.com

Freelance Potential: 50% written by nonstaff writers. Publishes 60 freelance submissions yearly; 25% by unpublished writers, 15% by authors who are new to the magazine. Receives 10 queries monthly.

Submissions and Payment: Guidelines available at website. Accepts query with résumé, clips, and digital images. Accepts hard copy. Responds in 6–8 weeks. All rights. Articles, 1,500–2,000 words; $500. Pays on publication.

American Careers

Career Communications, Inc.
6701 West 64th Street, Suite 210
Overland Park, KS 66202

Editor in Chief: Mary Pitchford

Description and Interests: Articles on career and industry clusters appear in this annual publication, which has separate high school, middle school, and parent editions. Other topics include career development and education. It is distributed through schools. Articles should be written at a seventh- to tenth-grade reading level. Circ: 350,000.
Website: www.carcom.com

Freelance Potential: 5% written by nonstaff writers. Publishes 5 freelance submissions yearly; 1–2% by authors who are new to the magazine, 1–2% by experts. Receives 10 queries monthly.

Submissions and Payment: Sample copy, guidelines, and theme list/editorial calendar available. Query with résumé and clips. Accepts hard copy. SASE. Responds in 1 month. All rights. Articles, 300–750 words, payment rates vary. Pays within 1 month of acceptance. Provides 2 contributor's copies.

The American Dissident

217 Commerce Road
Barnstable, MA 02630

Editor: G. Tod Slone

Description and Interests: Poetry, short fiction, essays, and reviews by activists who dare to express their dissidence with the status quo find a place in this publication. Personal experience pieces are also welcome. *The American Dissident* appears twice each year. Circ: 200.
Website: www.theamericandissident.org

Freelance Potential: 85% written by nonstaff writers. Publishes 25 freelance submissions yearly; 25% by unpublished writers, 35% by authors who are new to the magazine. Receives 35 mss monthly.

Submissions and Payment: Sample copy and guidelines available at website. Send complete ms with bio. Accepts email, from subscribers only, to todslone@yahoo.com; accepts hard copy from non-subscribers. SASE. Responds in 3 weeks. First serial rights. Articles, 250–500 words; $5. Payment policy varies. Provides 1 contributor's copy.

American Entertainment

15420 Newberry Road
Blair, SC 29015

Submissions: W. C. Kirby

Description and Interests: This magazine, published six times each year, covers the entertainment market that performs for corporate conferences and other functions. It seeks profiles of artists with specialty causes. Circ: 14,000.
www.americanentertainmentmagazine.com

Freelance Potential: 40% written by nonstaff writers. Publishes 20 freelance submissions yearly; 15% by unpublished writers, 20% by new authors, 10% by experts. Receives 10 queries monthly.

Submissions and Payment: Guidelines and editorial calendar available on a per story basis. Sample copy available at website. Query. Accepts email queries to cameopublishing@earthlink.net. Responds in 1 month. All rights. Articles, 1,200–2,000 words; payment rates vary. Kill fee, 35%. Pays on publication. Provides 2 contributor's copies.

American Forests

734 15th Street NW, Suite 800
Washington, DC 20005

Editor: Lea Sloan, Vice President of Communications

Description and Interests: This quarterly covers issues related to trees and forests, from scientific discoveries to forest management and policies, to recreation. The editors suggest reviewing past issues of the publication before querying to get a better idea of its content. Circ: 25,000.
Website: www.americanforests.org

Freelance Potential: 85% written by nonstaff writers. Publishes 24 freelance submissions yearly; 20% by authors who are new to the magazine, 20% by experts. Receives 15 queries monthly.

Submissions and Payment: Sample copy available at website. Guidelines available. Query with clips. Accepts email to magazine@americanforests.org. Responds in 8–10 weeks. First North American serial rights. Articles, 750–2,000 words. Depts/columns, word lengths vary. Written material, payment rates vary. Pays on publication. Provides 3 contributor's copies.

American Indian Art Magazine

7314 East Osborn Drive
Scottsdale, AZ 85251

Editor: Tobi Taylor

Description and Interests: Well-illustrated articles on Native American art appear in this quarterly. It is read by art collectors, dealers, scholars, and students. Circ: 16,000.
Website: www.aiamagazine.com

Freelance Potential: 100% written by nonstaff writers. Publishes 16 freelance submissions yearly; 30–40% by unpublished writers, 20% by new authors, 70% by experts. Receives 20 queries monthly.

Submissions and Payment: Sample copy and guidelines available at website. Send complete ms with list of illustrations. Accepts email to editorial@aiamagazine.com, or CD submissions (Word documents). SASE. Responds in 3–4 months. One-time rights. Articles, 6,000–7,000 words; $200–$400. B/W or color prints, slides, or transparencies; payment rates vary. Payment policy varies. Provides 5 contributor's copies.

American Legion Auxiliary

8945 North Meridian Street, 2nd Floor
Indianapolis, IN 46260

Senior Editor: Stephanie L. Holloway

Description and Interests: This quarterly, the official publication of the American Legion Auxiliary, is dedicated to supporting the country's servicemen, veterans, and communities. It features news of the service programs sponsored by local units and salutes members' activities. Circ: 750,000.
Website: www.alaforveterans.org

Freelance Potential: 25% written by nonstaff writers. Publishes 10 freelance submissions yearly; 80% by unpublished writers, 20% by authors who are new to the magazine. Receives 5 queries monthly.

Submissions and Payment: Sample copy and guidelines available at website. Send complete ms. Accepts email to alamagazine@ALAforVeterans.org (Word attachments). Response time varies. Rights vary. Written material, word lengths and payment rates vary. Artwork, JPEG files. Pays on publication.

American Miniaturist

68132 250th Avenue
Kasson, MN 55944

Editor: Traci Nigon

Description and Interests: Miniatures of all kinds—from dollhouse furniture to figurines and their clothing—are featured in this full-color, digest-size publication. Each monthly issue includes how-to's for hobbyists, profiles of artisans, and updates on upcoming miniature shows being held across the country. Circ: Unavailable.
Website: www.americanminiaturist.com

Freelance Potential: 75% written by nonstaff writers. Publishes 80 freelance submissions yearly; 25% by authors who are new to the magazine.

Submissions and Payment: Guidelines and editorial calendar available. Send complete ms. Accepts email submissions to traci@ashdown.co.uk or melissa@ashdown.co.uk. Responds in 1 week. Publisher assumes all rights worldwide in all media. Articles and depts/columns, word lengths and payment rates vary. Payment policy varies.

American Snowmobiler

P.O. Box 1612
Waukesha, WI 53187-1612

Editor: Mark Savage

Description and Interests: This magazine captures the world of snowmobiling in six issues a year, all of which are published during the winter months. Avid snowmobilers turn to it for the latest news on sleds and technology, information about destinations, and racing reports. Every issue includes illustrated articles on new snowmobile models, as well as product tests and comparisons. Circ: 55,000.
Website: www.amsnow.com

Freelance Potential: 30% written by nonstaff writers. Publishes 10 freelance submissions yearly.

Submissions and Payment: Sample copy and guidelines available at website. Query. Accepts email queries to editor@amsnow.com (Word attachments). Responds in 1 month. Exclusive industry rights. Articles, 500–1,200 words. Color prints or JPEG images. Payment rates vary. Pays on acceptance.

American Spectator

1611 North Kent Street, Suite 901
Arlington, VA 22209

Managing Editor: Kyle Peterson

Description and Interests:
A voice for conservatives and libertarians, *American Spectator* provides commentary on and analysis of politics, social issues, the economy, and business. Published 10 times each year, it features well-known commentators, but editors are willing to consider the work of new writers. Circ: 50,000.
Website: www.spectator.org

Freelance Potential: 70% written by nonstaff writers. Of the freelance submissions published yearly, 5% are by unpublished writers, 20% are by authors who are new to the magazine, 15% are by experts. Receives 50 queries monthly.

Submissions and Payment: Sample copy and guidelines available at website. Send complete ms. Accepts email submissions to editor@spectator.org. Responds in 1 month if interested. Rights vary. Articles, 700–1,000 words. Depts/columns, 1,000 words. Payment rates and policy vary.

American Style

3000 Chestnut Avenue, Suite 300
Baltimore, MD 21211

Editor in Chief: Hope Daniels

Description and Interests: This magazine is designed for collectors of contemporary crafts. Published quarterly, it features information on American crafts in all media, collector profiles, and museum events. Circ: 125,000.
Website: www.americanstyle.com

Freelance Potential: 70% written by nonstaff writers. Publishes 5 freelance submissions yearly; 10% by unpublished writers, 10% by authors who are new to the magazine, 30% by experts. Receives 10 queries monthly.

Submissions and Payment: Sample copy and guidelines available at website. Query with sources and word count. Accepts email queries to hoped@rosengrp.com. Responds in 8–10 weeks. First North American serial rights. Articles, 1,000–1,200 words; $700. Depts/columns, 500–800 words; $400–$600. Pays on publication. Provides 1 contributor's copy.

America's Civil War

Weider History Group
19300 Promenade Drive
Leesburg, VA 20176-6500

Editor: Tamela Baker

Description and Interests: This magazine covers the American Civil War through illustrated articles on the people, issues, and combat that shaped that era. Published six times each year, it looks for well-researched pieces that history buffs will enjoy. Circ: 60,000.
Website: www.thehistorynet.com

Freelance Potential: 80% written by nonstaff writers. Publishes 30 freelance submissions yearly; most by established writers. Receives 60 queries monthly.

Submissions and Payment: Sample articles available at website; guidelines available upon request. Query with outline and writing experience. Accepts hard copy and email to acw@weiderhistorygroup.com. SASE. Responds in 6 months. All rights. Article to 3,000 words. Minimum payment $250. Pays on publication.

AMIT

817 Broadway
New York, NY 10003

Editor in Chief: Robert E. Sutton

Description and Interests: "Building Israel, One Child at a Time" is the goal of this quarterly, which publishes articles on education, traditional religious values, and Zionism. AMIT is an organization that nurtures and educates children in Israel. Circ: 45,000.
Website: www.amitchildren.org

Freelance Potential: 50% written by nonstaff writers. Publishes 8–10 freelance submissions yearly; 25% by authors who are new to the magazine. Receives 10 queries monthly.

Submissions and Payment: Sample copy available at website. Prefers query; will accept complete ms. Accepts hard copy and email to info@amitchildren.org (include "AMIT Children" in subject line), and simultaneous submissions if identified. SASE. Responds in 1 month. All rights. Articles, 750–1,000 words. Depts/columns, lengths vary. Payment rates vary. Pays on publication. Kill fee, $50. Provides 2 contributor's copies.

Amoskeag

Southern New Hampshire University
2500 North River Road
Manchester, NH 03106-1045

Editor: Michael Brien

Description and Interests: Published annually, this literary journal publishes short stories, essays, poetry, and artwork that address a variety of subjects. Circ: 1,500.
Website: www.amoskeagjournal.com

Freelance Potential: 99% written by nonstaff writers. Publishes 40 freelance submissions yearly; 20% by unpublished writers, 50% by authors who are new to the magazine. Receives 100 mss monthly.

Submissions and Payment: Sample articles and guidelines available at website. Send complete ms between August 1 and November 1. Accepts hard copy and simultaneous submissions. SASE. Response time varies. Rights vary. Creative nonfiction and fiction, to 2,500 words. Poetry, to 4 poems per submission. B/W prints; JPEG files. Line art. No payment. Provides 2 contributor's copies.

Ancient American

P.O. Box 370
Colfax, WI 54730

Editor: Lawrence Gallan

Description and Interests: *Ancient American* is a quarterly for enthusiasts and experts to express views and share research on the prehistory of the Americas. Its stance is that pre-Columbian travelers came to the Americas from Europe, Africa, the Near East, Asia, and the Western Pacific, and contributed to their civilizations in ways that traditional academic research does not yet acknowledge. Circ: Unavailable
Website: http://ancientamerican.com

Freelance Potential: Encourages freelance article submissions.

Submissions and Payment: Articles offer news on discoveries, original perspectives, or analyses of material that challenge entrenched perspectives. Mail or email complete ms to wayne@ancient-american.com, or contact for more information. Articles, to 3,000 words; must be accompanied by photos or illustrations. No first person articles. Payment, 5 contributor's copies; possible monetary payment. Guidelines available at the website.

The Anglican Journal

80 Hayden Street
Toronto, Ontario M4Y 3G2
Canada

Editor: Kristin Jenkins

Description and Interests: A national newspaper of the Anglican Church of Canada, this monthly covers events and issues relating to the church within Canada and around the world. Discussions of social and ethical issues, spirituality, and theology are presented. It also publishes book reviews, and occasionally film, music, and theater reviews. Circ: 170,000.
Website: www.anglicanjournal.com

Freelance Potential: 5% written by nonstaff writers. Publishes 10 freelance submissions yearly.

Submissions and Payment: Sample copy and guidelines available at website. Query. Accepts disk submissions and email to editor@national.anglican.ca. SAE/IRC. Responds in 2 months. All rights. Articles, to 1,000 words; $.25 Canadian per word. Depts/columns and reviews, $150. Prints and JPEG files at 300 dpi; payment rates vary. Pays on publication.

Animal Fair

545 Eighth Avenue, Suite 401
New York, NY 10018

Editorial Director: Wendy Diamond

Description and Interests: This magazine for pet lovers includes articles on everything from pet health and fitness to how to take photos at pet weddings. Each quarterly issue includes inspiring stories about pet ownership, new product information, advice from veterinarians, and profiles featuring celebrities and their pets. Circ: 200,000.
Website: www.animalfair.com

Freelance Potential: 25% written by nonstaff writers. Publishes 10–20 freelance submissions yearly.

Submissions and Payment: Sample articles, guidelines, and editorial calendar available at website. Query or send complete ms. Accepts email submissions to editor@animalfair.com. Responds in 2 months. Rights vary. Written material, word lengths vary. No payment. Provides 10 contributor's copies.

Animal Sheltering Magazine

2100 L Street NW
Washington, DC 20037

Editor: Carrie Allan

Description and Interests: Written for animal care professionals and volunteers, this magazine aims to help and inspire animal welfare organizations to work better, smarter, and happier. Published six times each year, it rarely accepts unsolicited work. Circ: 8,000.
Website: www.animalsheltering.org

Freelance Potential: 20% written by nonstaff writers. Publishes 6–10 freelance submissions yearly; 50% by authors who are new to the magazine, 10% by experts. Receives 50 queries, 5–10 mss monthly.

Submissions and Payment: Sample articles available at website. Guidelines available. Query or send complete ms. Accepts email submissions to asm@humanesociety.org. Response time varies. Rights vary. Written material, word lengths and payment rates vary. Artwork, $75–$150. Pays on publication.

The Annals of St. Anne de Beaupré

9795 St. Anne Boulevard
St. Anne de Beaupré, Quebec G0A 3C0
Canada

Editor: Fr. Guy Pilote, C.Ss.R.

Description and Interests: Six times each year, this Catholic magazine focuses on the Shrine of St. Anne de Beaupré with inspiring articles. Only Canadian writers are published. Circ: 26,000.
Website: http://annalsofsaintanne.ca

Freelance Potential: 70% written by nonstaff writers. Publishes 90 freelance submissions yearly; 20% by unpublished writers, 5% by authors who are new to the magazine. Receives 5 mss monthly.

Submissions and Payment: Canadian writers only. Sample articles and guidelines available at website. Send complete ms with word count, résumé, and clips. Accepts hard copy; send email to drsa@revuesainteanne.ca. No simultaneous submissions. SAE/IRC. Responds in 6 weeks. First serial rights. Articles, to 675 words; $70 Canadian. Pays on acceptance. Provides 3 contributor's copies.

Anotherealm

Senior Editor: Gary A. Markette

Description and Interests: Since its beginning in 1995, this speculative fiction ezine has been a forum for new writers to showcase their work and receive constructive comments. Stories include fantasy, science fiction, and horror. The site also offers a Flash Fiction section where writing skills can be polished. Hits per month: Unavailable
Website: http://anotherealm.com

Freelance Potential: Open to freelance submissions and runs ongoing contests.

Submissions and Payment: Guidelines available at website. Email manuscripts to editor@anotherealm.com with contact info and word count (no attachments). Accepts submissions anytime, but reviews only during an October-November reading period. See website for details about contest story submissions; contests run every 2 months. Stories, to 5,000 words. Contests, to 1,000 words. Recent contest topics have included bureaucracy, tourists on an unexpected journey, and moving. First worldwide electronic and anthology rights. Stories, $25. Pays on publication. Contests, publication in the ezine.

The Antigonish Review

P.O. Box 5000, St. Francis Xavier University
Antigonish, Nova Scotia B2G 2W5
Canada

Submissions: Bonnie McIsaac

Description and Interests: This quarterly publishes high-quality fiction, poetry, essays, and book reviews from talented new writers. Circ: 800.
Website: www.antigonishreview.com

Freelance Potential: 100% written by nonstaff writers. Publishes 1,250 freelance submissions yearly; 20% by unpublished writers, 30% by authors who are new to the magazine. Receives 75 mss monthly.

Submissions and Payment: Sample copy available. Guidelines at website. Send complete ms. Fiction accepted from October 1–May 31. Accepts hard copy; email to TAR@stfx.ca. No simultaneous submissions. Responds in 3–4 months. Rights vary. Fiction, to 3,000 words; $50. Articles and essays, 1,000–4,000 words; $50. Poetry, limit 6–8 poems per submission; $10 per page ($50 maximum). Book reviews, $50. Payment policy varies. Provides 2 contributor's copies.

Antiques & Fine Art

125 Walnut Street
Watertown, MA 02472

Editor in Chief: Johanna McBrien

Description and Interests: Targeting a sophisticated audience, this magazine showcases fine art and antiques through the twentieth century. Appearing six times each year, it also covers market trends and investing. Circ: 35,000.
Website: www.antiquesandfineart.com

Freelance Potential: 90% written by nonstaff writers. Publishes 10 freelance submissions yearly; 5% by unpublished writers, 60% by authors who are new to the magazine, 35% by experts. Receives 200 queries monthly.

Submissions and Payment: Sample articles available at website. Guidelines available. Query. Accepts email queries to johanna@antiquesandfineart.com. Responds in 1 month. All rights. Articles, 600–2,000 words. Depts/columns, 200–600 words. Digital images, transparencies, and 8x10 prints. All material, payment rates vary. Pays on publication. Provides up to 10 contributor's copies.

Aoife's Kiss

P.O. Box 782
Cedar Rapids, IA 52406-0782

Editor: Tyree Campbell

Description and Interests: This quarterly journal features fantasy and science fiction, as well as articles about the genres. It is no longer accepting horror submissions. Circ: 175.
Website: www.samsdotpublishing.com

Freelance Potential: 90% written by nonstaff writers. Publishes 80–100 freelance submissions yearly; 25% by unpublished writers, 25% by authors new to the magazine. Receives 50–60 mss monthly.

Submissions and Payment: Sample articles and guidelines available at website. Send complete ms. Accepts hard copy and email submissions to aoifeskiss@yahoo.com (Word or RTF attachments). No simultaneous submissions. Responds in 2–3 months. First North American serial rights. Articles, 2,000 words; $10. Fiction, to 10,000 words; $15. Reviews, to 2,000 words; $7. Poetry, to 100 lines; payment rates vary. Pays on publication. Provides 1 contributor's copy.

Apogee Photo Magazine

11121 Wolf Way
Westminster, CO 80031

Sales and Editorial Director: Marla Meier

Description and Interests: Amateur and professional photographers read this ezine for its in-depth product reviews, camera club news and events, and articles on the artistic and business aspects of photography. It is updated regularly. Hits per month: 350,000.
Website: www.apogeephoto.com

Freelance Potential: 80% written by nonstaff writers. Publishes 50 freelance submissions yearly; 50% by authors who are new to the magazine. Receives 5 queries and unsolicited mss monthly.

Submissions and Payment: Sample copy and guidelines available at website. Query with outline and artwork. Accepts email queries to editor.sales@apogeephoto.com (include "Subject: Editorial content" in subject field). Response time varies. One-time rights. Articles, to 2,000 words; to $.10 per word. Reprints, $.03 per word. Pays on publication.

Army Times

6883 Commercial Drive
Springfield, VA 22159

Managing Editor: Richard Sandza

Description and Interests: *Army Times* is an independent source of news and information for members of the military community. Published weekly, it features articles on military news and issues, education, and benefits, as well as general topics, such as entertainment. Circ: 250,000.
Website: www.armytimes.com

Freelance Potential: 20% written by nonstaff writers. Publishes 64 freelance submissions yearly; 1% by unpublished writers, 5% by authors who are new to the magazine, 1% by experts. Receives 10 queries monthly.

Submissions and Payment: Sample copy and guidelines available at website. Query with writing credits; or send complete ms. Accepts email queries to features@atpco.com. Response time varies. First rights. Articles, 500–1,200 words. Depts/columns, 350–500 words. Written material, $100–$500. Pays on publication. Provides 1 contributor's copy.

Artful Dodge

English Department
The College of Wooster
Wooster, OH 44691

Editor: Daniel Bourne

Description and Interests: This annual literary journal is interested in works that expand—or at least bend—the traditional definitions of American literature. It accepts American works of fiction, creative nonfiction, and poetry, as well as translations of literature and poetry from around the world. Circ: 1,000.
Website: www.wooster.edu/artfuldodge

Freelance Potential: 90% written by nonstaff writers. Publishes 40 freelance submissions yearly; 5% by unpublished writers, 50% by authors who are new to the magazine. Receives 100 unsolicited mss monthly.

Submissions and Payment: Sample copy and editorial calendar available. Guidelines available at website. Send complete ms. Accepts hard copy and simultaneous submissions. SASE. Responds in 6 months. First rights. Fiction and nonfiction, to 30 pages. Poetry, to 6 poems per submission. Payment rates vary. Pays on publication. Provides 2 contributor's copies.

The Artilleryman

234 Monarch Hill Road
Tunbridge, VT 05077

Editor & Publisher: Kay Jorgensen

Description and Interests: *The Artilleryman* is a quarterly magazine read by people interested in collecting and shooting artillery made in the period between 1750 and 1900. It is dedicated to the advancement of safety and skill in the shooting of muzzle loading cannon and mortar for exhibition and competition. Writers familiar with military history and ordnance are encouraged to submit pieces about places to visit. Circ: 1,400.
Website: www.artillerymanmagazine.com

Freelance Potential: 75% written by nonstaff writers. Publishes 20 freelance submissions yearly. Receives 1 query monthly.

Submissions and Payment: Sample articles available at website. Guidelines available. Query. Accepts disk submissions and email to mail@artilleryman-magazine.com. Responds in 1 week. First rights. Articles, to 4,000 words; $50–$100. Pays on publication. Provides 3 contributor's copies.

Arts & Crafts Homes and the Revival

10 Harbor Road
Gloucester, MA 01930

Editor in Chief: Patricia Poore

Description and Interests: Renovators and restorers of Arts and Crafts style homes turn to this magazine for information and inspiration. Quarterly issues offer profiles and interviews, how-to articles, and product information. Circ: 75,000.
Website: www.artsandcraftshomes.com

Freelance Potential: 25% written by nonstaff writers. Publishes 6 freelance submissions yearly; 5% by authors who are new to the magazine, 5% by experts. Receives 5 queries monthly.

Submissions and Payment: Sample articles available at website. Guidelines available. Query. Accepts submissions via website. Responds in 2–3 months. First rights. Articles, 750–1,200 words. Depts/columns, 800–1,500 words. Written material, $100–$200 per page. Pays on publication. Provides 3–5 contributor's copies.

Art Times

P.O. Box 730
Mount Marion, NY 12456-0730

Editor: Raymond Steiner

Description and Interests: Works of fiction and poetry appear alongside articles and essays on film, theater, dance, and fine arts in this newsletter. Published six times each year, *Art Times* seeks high-quality short stories and poems pertaining to artists and the art world. Nonfiction is not accepted from freelance writers. Circ: 28,000.
Website: www.arttimesjournal.com

Freelance Potential: 20% written by nonstaff writers. Publishes 40 freelance submissions yearly. Receives 50 unsolicited mss monthly.

Submissions and Payment: Sample copy and guidelines available. Send complete ms. Accepts hard copy and simultaneous submissions if identified. SASE. Responds in 6 months. First North American serial rights. Fiction, 1,500 words; $25. Poetry, to 20 lines; no payment. Pays on acceptance. Provides 6 contributor's copies, plus one-year subscription.

Ascent Aspirations Magazine

1560 Arbutus Drive
Nanoose Bay, British Columbia V9P 9C8
Canada

Editor: David Fraser

Description and Interests: *Ascent Aspirations* presents a spectrum of literary work in its monthly online publication. It also publishes one annual print publication anthology. Fiction, poetry, essays, and reviews are included. Hits per month: 5,000.
Website: www.ascentaspirations.ca

Freelance Potential: 98% written by nonstaff writers. Publishes 250 freelance submissions yearly; 5% by unpublished writers, 50% by authors who are new to the magazine. Receives 200 queries monthly.

Submissions and Payment: Sample copy and guidelines available at website. Send complete ms. Accepts email to ascentaspirations@shaw.ca (Word attachments; include type of submission in subject field). SAE/IRC. Response time varies. One-time rights. Fiction/nonfiction, to 1,000 words. Poetry, to 1 page. No payment. Provides 1 contributor's copy.

Athlon Sports

2451 Atrium Way, Building 2, Suite 320
Nashville, TN 37214

Editorial Director: Charlie Miller

Description and Interests: A product of media giant Athlon Sports Communications, *Athlon Sports* is inserted monthly into some of the largest circulation daily newspapers in the country. It covers all major professional, college, and youth sports, as well as the Olympics. Its articles, profiles, interviews, opinion pieces, and essays offer unique perspectives and analysis of the sports, athletes, teams, and coaches. Circ: 9 million.
Website: www.athlonsports.com

Freelance Potential: Open to freelance submissions.

Submissions and Payment: Sample articles available at website. Query. Accepts email queries to charlie.miller@athlonsports.com or athlonmedia3@athlonsports.com. Response time, rights, and payment rates vary.

Atlantic Salmon Journal

P.O. Box 5200
St. Andrews, New Brunswick E5B 3S8
Canada

Editor: Martin Silverstone

Description and Interests: This quarterly publication is written for the conservation-minded angler. Published by the Atlantic Salmon Federation since 1952, it features articles on fly-fishing for salmon, profiles, destination pieces, and information on protecting the species. Circ: 8,500.
Website: www.asf.ca

Freelance Potential: 70% written by nonstaff writers. Publishes 14 freelance submissions yearly; 20% by unpublished writers, 30% by authors new to the magazine. Receives 10 queries and mss monthly.

Submissions and Payment: Sample articles available at website. Guidelines available. Query or send complete ms. Prefers email to martinsilverstone@videotron.ca; will accept hard copy. SAE/IRC. Response time varies. First rights. Articles, to 2,200 words; $100–$600. Pays on publication. Provides 2 contributor's copies.

Australian Arabian Horse News

P.O. Box 8369
Woolloongabba, Queensland 4102
Australia

Editor: Sharon Meyers

Description and Interests: This magazine is delivered to every member of the Arabian Horse Society of Australia. It features historical and veterinary articles related to Arabian horses, as well as reports from major horse shows around Australia and New Zealand. Published quarterly, it covers horse health, breeding, and showing; provides information specific to Arabian horses; and presents profiles of horse owners. Circ: 10,000.
Website: www.arabianhorse.com.au

Freelance Potential: 75% written by nonstaff writers.

Submissions and Payment: Sample copy available at website. Query. Accepts email queries to sharon@vinkpub.com. Response time varies. One-time rights. Written material, word lengths vary; payment rates vary. Pays on publication.

Australian Photography + Digital

117-21 Bellevue Street
Surry Hills, New South Wales 2010
Australia

Editor: Robert Keeley

Description and Interests: This monthly, now merged with *Digital Photography + Design,* provides Australian photography enthusiasts with the information they need to take better pictures. It also caters to advanced hobbyists seeking information on new technology. Circ: 8,000–9,000.
Website: www.yaffa.com.au

Freelance Potential: 80% written by nonstaff writers. Receives 10–12 queries, 8–10 unsolicited mss monthly.

Submissions and Payment: Sample copy and guidelines available. Query or send complete ms. Accepts hard copy, disk submissions (Word attachments) with hard copy, and email followed by hard copy to yaffa@flex.com.au. SAE/IRC. Responds in 1 month. Rights vary. Articles and depts/columns, word lengths vary. Digital images at 300 dpi, A4 size. All material, payment rates vary. Payment policy varies.

Babysue

P.O. Box 15749
Chattanooga, TN 37415

Editor: Don W. Seven

Description and Interests: Satire and dark humor with a contemporary, cutting edge are featured in this monthly magazine. It publishes fiction, poetry, and music and entertainment reviews, in addition to cartoons. Work on almost any topic is considered. Circ: 50,000.
Website: www.babysue.com; www.lmnop.com

Freelance Potential: 10% written by nonstaff writers. Publishes 15–25 freelance submissions yearly; 15% by unpublished writers, 25% by authors who are new to the magazine. Receives 20 queries, 30 unsolicited mss monthly.

Submissions and Payment: Sample articles available at website. Guidelines available. Prefers complete ms; will accept queries. Accepts hard copy. SASE. Response time varies. One-time rights. All material, word lengths vary. No payment. Provides 5 contributor's copies.

Backyard Friends

6641 County Road B
Pittsville, WI 54466-9791

Editor: Cynthia Ruchti

Description and Interests: Personal experience pieces, essays, and Christ-based articles fill this magazine, published twice each year by the Heartbeat of the Home radio ministry. It also features news of how God is at work through the ministry. Circ: 5,000.
Website: www.heartbeatofthehome.org

Freelance Potential: 30% written by nonstaff writers. Publishes 4 freelance submissions yearly; 10% by unpublished writers, 10% by authors who are new to the magazine, 10% by experts. Receives 6 queries, 4 unsolicited mss monthly.

Submissions and Payment: Sample copy and guidelines available at website. Query or send complete ms. Accepts email submissions only to heartbeatofthehome@gmail.com (Word attachments). Responds in 4–6 weeks. First rights. Written material, 350–1,200 words. No payment.

Barbaric Yawp

BoneWorld Publishing
3700 County Route 24
Russell, NY 13684-3198

Fiction Editor: Nancy Berbrich

Description and Interests: A small, free-wielding literary journal, *Barbaric Yawp* has been publishing since 1997. Its title is taken from Walt Whitman's *Leaves of Grass*. It publishes experimental fiction, adventure, fantasy, historical fiction, horror, literary, mainstream, paranormal, regional, religious, science fiction, and suspense. No pornography or gratuitous violence. The quarterly also publishes literary essays, criticism, and poetry. Circ: 120.
Website: www.boneworldpublishing.com

Freelance Potential: Accepts 10–12 mss each issue, 40–48 mss yearly. Publishes 4-6 new writers yearly. Receives 30–40 unsolicited mss monthly.

Submissions and Payment: Query or mail complete ms with SASE. Responds in 2–8 weeks. Stories, to 1,500 words. Acquires one-time rights. No payment. Provides 1 contributor's copy.

Bass Player

1111 Bayhill Drive, #125
San Bruno, CA 94066

Editor: Brian Fox

Description and Interests: This magazine is read by electric and acoustic bass guitar enthusiasts of all playing levels. Each month, its pages are filled with profiles of professional bass guitar players, teachers, and instrument makers, as well as articles on playing techniques and reviews of gear and recordings. Also included are some historical features. The magazine is interested in practical "in-the-trenches" pieces on performing and recording. Circ: 30,000.
Website: www.bassplayer.com

Freelance Potential: 40% written by nonstaff writers. Receives 5–10 queries monthly.

Submissions and Payment: Sample copy and guidelines available. Query. Accepts email queries to bfox@musicplayer.com. Responds in 1 month. Rights vary. Articles, 500+ words; $200–$350. Pays on publication. Provides contributor's copies.

Bay Windows

28 Damrell Street, Suite 204
Boston, MA 02127

Editor in Chief: Sue O'Connell

Description and Interests: This weekly regional publication covers news, events, trends, and social issues for its gay, lesbian, bisexual, and transgendered readers. While not afraid to tackle hard-hitting issues, it also includes lighthearted fare that makes readers laugh. Circ: 21,000.
Website: www.baywindows.com

Freelance Potential: 10% written by nonstaff writers. Publishes 500 freelance submissions yearly; 10% by authors who are new to the magazine. Receives 10 queries monthly.

Submissions and Payment: Sample copy available at website. Guidelines available. Query. Accepts email queries to soconnell@baywindows.com. Responds in 1 month. One-time rights. Articles, 700–900 words; $40. Interviews, word lengths vary; $75. Depts/columns, 900 words; $40. Payment policy varies. Provides 1 contributor's copy.

Bead Trends

Northridge Publishing
P.O. Box 1670
Orem, UT 84059

Submissions

Description and Interests: This publication features creative bead projects, from jewelry to home design items, for crafters at all levels. It offers step-by-step directions, different techniques, and material suggestions to its readers. Northridge offers similar publications for other crafts, including scrapbooking and card-making. Circ: Unknown.
Website: www.northridgepublishing.com

Freelance Potential: Makes regular calls for submissions. Reads all submissions.

Submissions and Payment: Sample copy available. Specific submission calls on website. Accepts submissions of projects with description and photos, up to 2MB, via form on website. Rights, unavailable. Payment rates and policy, unavailable.

The Bear Deluxe

810 SE Belmont, Studio 5
Portland, OR 97214

Editor: Tom Webb

Description and Interests: *The Bear Deluxe* is an environmental magazine with a strong focus on the literary and visual arts. It is published twice each year. Circ: 44,000.
Website: www.orlo.org

Freelance Potential: 50% written by nonstaff writers. Publishes 20 freelance submissions yearly; 20% by authors who are new to the magazine. Receives 20 queries and unsolicited mss monthly.

Submissions and Payment: Sample articles and guidelines available at website. Query for nonfiction. Send complete ms for fiction and poetry. Accepts hard copy. SASE. Responds in 3–6 months. First, one-time, and web publishing rights for one year. Articles and depts/columns, word lengths vary. Fiction, 750–4,000 words. Poetry, to 50 lines; 3–5 poems per submission. Payment rates vary. Pays on publication. Provides contributor's copies and a 1-year subscription.

Bella

7247 Amboy Road
Staten Island, NY 10307

Editor in Chief: Courtenay C. Hall

Description and Interests: With a tagline of "beauty as defined by you," *Bella* focuses on health, beauty, and fitness topics, but also offers articles on philosophy; mind, body, and soul; and humor. Embracing the concept that beauty means different things to different people, the editors look for articles that encourage readers to discover and embody their ideal of beauty. Celebrity profiles and makeovers are also part of the editorial mix. *Bella* is published six times each year. Circ: 70,000.
Website: www.bellanyc.com

Freelance Potential: Accepts freelance submissions.

Submissions and Payment: Sample articles available at website. Query for submissions information. Accepts email inquiries to info@bellanyc.com. Response time varies. Payment information unavailable.

Bellingham Review

MS 9053, Western Washington University
Bellingham, WA 98225

Editor in Chief: Brenda Miller

Description and Interests: Fiction, poetry, and creative nonfiction that either nudge the limits of form or execute traditional forms exquisitely are welcome in this annual literary journal. Circ: 2,000.
Website: www.wwu.edu/bhreview

Freelance Potential: 100% written by nonstaff writers. Publishes 60 freelance submissions yearly; 10% by unpublished writers, 80% by authors who are new to the magazine. Receives 200 mss monthly.

Submissions and Payment: Sample copy and guidelines available at website. Send complete ms with word count between September 15 and December 1. Prefers submissions via website; will accept hard copy and simultaneous submissions if identified. SASE. Responds in 1–6 months. First serial rights. Fiction and prose, to 6,000 words. Poetry, 3 poems per submission. Payment rates vary. Pays on publication. Provides 1 contributor's copy and a gift subscription.

Beloit Fiction Journal

Box 11, Beloit College
700 College Street
Beloit, WI 53511

Editor in Chief: Chris Fink

Description and Interests: Established in 1985, this annual literary journal prides itself in publishing the best in contemporary short fiction. It welcomes new writers as enthusiastically as it does published authors. It is open to all subjects and themes, but avoids genre fiction, pornography, or political writing. Circ: Unavailable.
Website: www.beloitfictionjournal.wordpress.com/

Freelance Potential: 100% written by nonstaff writers. Publishes 20 submissions yearly.

Submissions and Payment: Sample copy available. Guidelines available at website. Send complete ms between August 1 and December 1 only. Hard copy only; accepts simultaneous submissions. SASE. Responds in 2 months. First North American serial rights. Fiction, to 60 pages; limit one story per submission. No payment. Provides contributor's copies.

Berkeley Fiction Review

University of California, Berkeley
10B Eshleman Hall
Berkeley, CA 94720-4500

Managing Editor: Brighton Earley

Description and Interests: This undergraduate journal looks for short fiction that plays with form and content, as well as stories with fresh voices and ideas. It is published annually. Circ: 400.
Website: www.ocf.berkeley.edu/~bfr

Freelance Potential: 100% written by nonstaff writers. Publishes 10–15 freelance submissions yearly; 30% by unpublished writers, 95% by new authors. Receives 100 unsolicited mss monthly.

Submissions and Payment: Guidelines available at website. Send complete ms with cover letter from May 1 to September 1. Accepts email only to bfictionreview@yahoo.com (Word or PDF attachments; include "Submission: Name, Title" in subject line). Accepts simultaneous submissions if identified. Responds in 1–6 months. Rights vary. Fiction, to 25 pages. B/W or color slides. No payment. Provides 1 contributor's copy.

Best New Writing

P.O. Box 11
Titusville, NJ 08560

Executive Editor: Christopher Klim

Description and Interests: Fiction and creative nonfiction are published in this annual anthology of original unpublished work by talented writers. It also features the winner of the Eric Hoffer Prose Award and the Gover Prize for short-short writing (less than 500 words). Circ: 1,500.
Website: www.bestnewwriting.com

Freelance Potential: 100% written by nonstaff writers. Publishes 20 freelance submissions yearly; 70% by unpublished writers, 100% by authors who are new to the magazine. Receives 200 unsolicited mss monthly.

Submissions and Payment: Guidelines available at website. Send complete ms. Accepts previously unpublished work only, submitted via website. No simultaneous submissions. Response time varies. First publication and one-time anthology rights. Written material, to 10,000 words. Pays $250, on publication, to each prizewinner. Provides 1 contributor's copy.

Bible Advocate

P.O. Box 33677
Denver, CO 80233

Associate Editor: Sherri Langton

Description and Interests: Published six times each year, *Bible Advocate* features articles on the Bible, Christian living, and social and religious issues, as well as personal experience pieces. Though it publishes poetry, it is not accepting poetry submissions until 2014. Circ: 13,000.
Website: www.baonline.org

Freelance Potential: 25% written by nonstaff writers. Publishes 5–10 freelance submissions yearly; 5% by unpublished writers, 10% by authors who are new to the magazine. Receives 10–15 mss monthly.

Submissions and Payment: Sample copy, guidelines, and theme list available at website. Send complete ms. Prefers email submissions to bibleadvocate@cog7.org (attachments OK); will accept hard copy. Accepts simultaneous submissions if identified. SASE. Responds in 1–3 months. First, or one-time and electronic rights. Articles, word lengths and payment rates vary. Pays on publication. Provides 2 contributor's copies.

Big World

55 Washington Street, Suite 460
Brooklyn, NY 11201

Editor in Chief: Mary D'Ambrosio

Description and Interests: This online multimedia magazine celebrates the many corners of the world, the people who live there, and the culture that thrives within them. It seeks articles from anyone who has traveled a road, fueled by curiosity, and returned home a changed person. It is updated weekly. Hits per month: 40,000.
Website: www.bigworldmagazine.com

Freelance Potential: 100% written by nonstaff writers. Publishes 50 freelance submissions yearly; 50% by authors who are new to the magazine.

Submissions and Payment: Sample copy and guidelines available at website. Send complete ms. Accepts submissions via website. Response time varies. Author retains rights. Articles, 500–2,000 words. Essays, to 1,500 words. No payment. Author gets 50% of any syndication fees.

Bike Magazine

P.O. Box 1028
Dana Point, CA 92629

Editor: Joe Parkin

Description and Interests: *Bike Magazine* is the publication to which expert level mountain bike enthusiasts turn to get news on riding spots, techniques, the best gear, and notable riders. It appears eight times each year. Circ: 45,300.
Website: www.bikemag.com

Freelance Potential: 40% written by nonstaff writers. Publishes 15 freelance submissions yearly; 5% by unpublished writers, 2% by authors who are new to the magazine. Receives 50 queries, 60 unsolicited mss monthly.

Submissions and Payment: Sample copy and guidelines available. Query or send complete ms. Accepts hard copy and email to bikemag@sorc.com SASE. Responds in 2 months. First North American serial rights. Articles, 1,000–2,000 words. Depts/columns, 600–700 words. Written material, payment rates vary. Pays on publication. Provides 1 contributor's copy.

The Bitter Oleander

4983 Tall Oaks Drive
Fayetteville, NY 13066-9776

Editor & Publisher: Paul B. Roth

Description and Interests: Published twice each year, *The Bitter Oleander* is a magazine of contemporary international poetry and short fiction. The editors are interested in serious writing only and seek more translations of contemporary poetry. Circ: 2,000.
Website: www.bitteroleander.com

Freelance Potential: 100% written by nonstaff writers. Publishes 80 freelance submissions yearly; 5% by unpublished writers, 40% by authors who are new to the magazine. Receives 200+ unsolicited mss each month.

Submissions and Payment: Guidelines available at website. Send complete ms. Prefers submissions through website, but accepts email attachments to info@bitteroleander.com. Responds in 1 month. First rights. Fiction, to 2,500 words. Poetry, no line limit; to 8 poems per submission. No payment. Provides 1 contributor's copy.

Blackbird  

Virginia Commonwealth University
Department of English
P.O. Box 843082
Richmond, VA 23284-3082

Senior Online Editor: M. A. Keller

Description and Interests: Published twice each year by Virginia Commonwealth University and New Virginia Review, this online magazine presents nonfiction, short stories, poetry, and essays. Check current issue for any guidelines changes. Hits per month: 30,000.
Website: www.blackbird.vcu.edu

Freelance Potential: 90% written by nonstaff writers. Publishes 100–150 freelance submissions yearly; 20% by unpublished writers, 60% by new authors. Receives 750 unsolicited mss monthly.

Submissions and Payment: Sample copy and guidelines available at website. Send complete ms from November 1–April 15 only. Prefers submissions via website; will accept hard copy. SASE. Responds in 5 months. First serial rights. Prose, to 8,000 words. Poetry, to 10 pages; 2–6 poems per submission. Payment rates vary. Pays on publication.

BlackFlash

P.O. Box 7381, Station Main
Saskatoon, Saskatchewan S7K 4J3
Canada

Managing Editor: John Shelling

Description and Interests: *BlackFlash* focuses on contemporary photographic and new media art in Canada. It appears three times each year and is read by artists, curators, and art enthusiasts. Circ: 1,500.
Website: www.blackflash.ca

Freelance Potential: 100% written by nonstaff writers. Publishes 12 freelance submissions yearly; 10% by unpublished writers, 60% by authors who are new to the magazine, 30% by experts. Receives 20 queries monthly.

Submissions and Payment: Guidelines available at website. Sample copy available. Query with outline, images, and 1–2 clips. Accepts hard copy. SASE. Responds in 6–8 weeks. Rights vary. Articles, 2,000–4,000 words. Reviews, 500–1,000 words. Interviews, 1,000–2,000 words. Written material, $.15 per published word. Pays on publication. Provides 2 contributor's copies.

Black Warrior Review

P.O. Box 862936
Tuscaloosa, AL 35486-0027

Editor: Emma Sovich

Description and Interests: The University of Alabama publishes this literary journal twice each year. Readers are offered a mix of fiction, creative nonfiction, and poetry written by award-winning authors, as well as emerging voices. Circ: 5,000.
Website: www.bwr.ua.edu

Freelance Potential: 100% written by nonstaff writers. Publishes 50+ freelance submissions yearly; 10% by unpublished writers, 75% by new authors Receives 250 unsolicited mss monthly.

Submissions and Payment: Sample copy available. Guidelines available at website. Send complete ms. Query for nonfiction over 7,500 words. Accepts electronic submissions via http://bwrsubmissions.ua.edu only. Responds in 3–5 months. One-time rights. Fiction, to 7,000 words. Nonfiction, to 7,500 words. Poetry, to 10 pages; to 5 poems per submission. Payment rates vary. Payment policy varies.

Blade

700 East State Street
Iola, WI 54990-0001

Managing Editor: Joe Kertzman

Description and Interests: Published monthly, *Blade* serves knife enthusiasts with articles about interesting collections, new designs and materials, and knives being used for interesting purposes. It does not cover knives used for combat or self-defense. Circ: 23,000.
Website: www.blademag.com

Freelance Potential: 90% written by nonstaff writers. Publishes 60 freelance submissions yearly; 2% by authors new to the magazine.

Submissions and Payment: Guidelines available at website. Query. Accepts hard copy and email queries to joe.kertzman@fwmedia.com (Word documents). Availability of artwork improves chance of acceptance. SASE. Response time varies. All rights. Articles, 500–1,700 words; $150–$300. Prints, slides, transparencies, or high-resolution digital images. Pays on publication.

Blitz

Australasian Martial Arts Magazine

1 Miles Street
P.O. Box 4075
Mulgrave, Victoria 3170
Australia

Editor: Ben Stone

Description and Interests: Filled with articles on all styles of martial arts and combat sports, *Blitz* is considered to be Australia's foremost magazine on these topics. Published monthly, it includes coverage of local full-contact fight news while also delivering information on combat psychology, self-defense strategies, and health and fitness tips. Profiles of martial artists and combat sports personalities are also offered. Circ: 31,000.
Website: www.blitzmag.net

Freelance Potential: 70% written by nonstaff writers.

Submissions and Payment: Guidelines available at website. Send complete ms. Accepts electronic submissions via website or email to ben@blitzmag.com.au. Response time varies. Rights vary. Articles and depts/columns, word lengths and payment rates vary. Payment policy varies.

Blue Mesa Review

Department of English
University of New Mexico
MCS 03-2170
Albuquerque, NM 87131-0001

Editor: Suzanne Richardson

Description and Interests: This annual literary journal seeks strong writers with a command of their craft. It accepts fiction, poetry, reviews, and interviews. Circ: 1,000.
Website: www.unm.edu/~bluemesa

Freelance Potential: 98% written by nonstaff writers. Publishes 50 freelance submissions yearly; 20% by unpublished writers, 85% by new authors. Receives 250 unsolicited mss monthly.

Submissions and Payment: Sample copy available. Guidelines available at website. Send complete ms between September 1 and May 31. Electronic submissions only, via http://bluemesareview.submishmash.com/submit. Responds in 2–6 months. First North American serial rights. Fiction and nonfiction, to 30 pages or 7,500 words. Poetry, to 6 double-spaced pages; limit 3–5 poems per submission. No payment. Provides 2 contributor's copies.

Bluestem

Eastern Illinois University
English Department
600 Lincoln Avenue
Charleston, IL 61920

Editor: Olga Abella

Description and Interests: Formerly titled *Karamu*, this literary journal publishes high-quality fiction, creative nonfiction, essays, and poetry once each year. It also publishes an online issue quarterly. Circ: 500.
Website: www.bluestemmagazine.com

Freelance Potential: 100% written by nonstaff writers. Publishes 70–80 freelance submissions yearly; 10% by unpublished writers, 90% by authors who are new to the magazine. Receives 150 unsolicited mss each month.

Submissions and Payment: Sample copy and guidelines available at website. Send complete ms and 100-word bio. Accepts electronic submissions via website and simultaneous submissions. Responds in 1–2 months. One-time rights. Prose, to 5,000 words; 1 story per submission. Poetry, no line limits; to 5 poems per submission. No payment. Provides 1 contributor's copy.

Boating

460 North Orlando Avenue, Suite 200
Winter Park, FL 32789

Editor in Chief: Randy Vance

Description and Interests: Articles on the power boating lifestyle and the nuts and bolts of boat ownership appear side by side in this photo-filled magazine. It is read by recreational boaters for its expert advice provided in 10 issues each year. Circ: 160,000.
Website: www.boatingmag.com

Freelance Potential: 50% written by nonstaff writers. Publishes 10 freelance submissions yearly; 5% by authors who are new to the magazine, 95% by experts. Receives 10 queries each month.

Submissions and Payment: Sample copy available. Query with writing samples. Accepts email queries to editor@boatingmag.com. Responds in 1 month. Rights vary. Articles and depts/columns, word lengths and payment rates vary. Pays on acceptance. Provides 1–10 contributor's copies.

Boating Sportsman

360 B Street
Idaho Falls, ID 83402

Editor: Brady Kay

Description and Interests: This sportsman's magazine, published six times a year, targets owners of aluminum boats. It features articles about the benefits of aluminum hulls, boat maintenance and equipment, plus hunting and fishing information. Circ: 55,000.
Website: www.boatingsportsman.com

Freelance Potential: 10% written by nonstaff writers. Publishes 5 freelance submissions yearly; 10% by unpublished writers, 5% by authors who are new to the magazine, 30% by experts. Receives 4–6 queries monthly.

Submissions and Payment: Sample copy, guidelines, and editorial calendar available. Query. Accepts email to blk@harrispublishing.com. Responds in 2 weeks. First serial rights. Articles, 800–1,500 words. Depts/columns, 700–800 words. Written material, $250–$350. Digital images, payment rates vary. Kill fee, 50%. Payment policy varies. Provides up to 5 contributor's copies.

Boating World

17782 Cowan, Suite A
Irvine, CA 92614

Managing Editor: Mike Werling

Description and Interests: *Boating World* is a family boating lifestyle magazine that features articles on boating, fishing, destinations, watersports, and cruising, as well as information on safety, maintenance, and trailering. Published nine times each year, it also offers reviews and engine test results. Writers knowledgeable about boats and marine engines are welcome to query. Circ: 80,060.
Website: www.boatingworld.com

Freelance Potential: 30% written by nonstaff writers. Publishes 20 freelance submissions yearly; 5% by unpublished writers, 100% by experts. Receives 3 queries monthly.

Submissions and Payment: Sample articles available at website. Query. Accepts hard copy. SASE. Response time varies. Rights vary. Articles, 1,000 words. Depts/columns, 600 words. Written material, payment rates vary. Kill fee, 25%. Pays on publication.

Bogg

A Journal of Contemporary Writing

422 North Cleveland Street
Arlington, VA 22201

Editor: John Elsberg

Description and Interests: This literary journal offers innovative writing that has a clear, distinctive voice. It accepts short experimental fiction, all forms of poetry, essays, reviews, and an occasional interview. *Bogg* is published irregularly. Circ: 850.
Website: www.depoetry.com/yymisc/bogg.html

Freelance Potential: 95% written by nonstaff writers. Publishes 100+ freelance submissions yearly; 50% by authors who are new to the magazine. Receives 10+ queries and 125 unsolicited mss monthly.

Submissions and Payment: Sample copy and guidelines available. Query with résumé for reviews. Send complete ms for all other material. Accepts hard copy. No simultaneous submissions. SASE. Responds in 1 week. First or one-time rights. Articles, 500–1,000 words. Fiction, 500 words. Poetry, no line limits. No payment. Provides 2 contributor's copies.

BootsnAll

237 NE Chkalov Drive, Suite 210
Vancouver, WA 98684

Online Managing Editor: Bob Kellett

Description and Interests: This is an online platform for travel writers, run by a travel company. The BootsnAll travel writers program looks for excellent articles that cover a subject thoroughly and have broad relevance for readers planning trips. It has a Feature Articles Program and an Expert Travel Articles program. It also hosts travel blogs. Hits per month: Unavailable
Website: www.bootsnall.com

Freelance Potential: Open to various freelance possibilities or an option for acquiring clips.

Submissions and Payment: Sample articles, guidelines, and editorial calendar available at website. Recent topics on the calendar were travel planning, travel tech, wine and beer, and North American cities. Pitch an article via form at website. Articles, 1,200–2,000 words; with photos. Features, $50. Expert articles, $30. Travel essays, $20–$40. Buys all rights; will accept articles to publish without payment in which the writer retains all rights.

Boston Review

P.O. Box 425786
Cambridge, MA 02142

Managing Editor: Simon Waxman

Description and Interests: A glossy, full-color magazine of ideas and opinion in myriad forms, including political essays, book reviews, fiction, poetry, and essays, *Boston Review* is published six times each year. Circ: 10,000.
Website: www.bostonreview.net

Freelance Potential: 95% written by nonstaff writers. Publishes 120 freelance submissions yearly; 10% by unpublished writers, 40% by authors who are new to the magazine. Receives 40 queries, 300 unsolicited mss monthly.

Submissions and Payment: Guidelines available at website. Query or send complete ms for nonfiction. Send complete ms for fiction and poetry. Accepts submissions via the website and simultaneous submissions if identified. Responds in 2–4 months. Rights vary. Nonfiction, to 5,000 words. Fiction, to 4,000 words. Payment rates vary. Payment policy varies.

The Briar Cliff Review

Briar Cliff University
3303 Rebecca Street
P.O. Box 2100
Sioux City, IA 51104-2100

Editor: Tricia Currans-Sheehan

Description and Interests: Published annually, this eclectic literary and culture magazine focuses on Siouxland writers and subjects. It seeks fiction, poetry, humor, and thoughtful nonfiction. Circ: 1,000.
Website: www.briarcliff.edu/bcreview

Freelance Potential: 95% written by nonstaff writers. Publishes 60 freelance submissions yearly; 10% by unpublished writers, 50% by authors new to the magazine. Receives 150 unsolicited mss monthly.

Submissions and Payment: Sample copy and guidelines available at website. Send complete ms with cover letter and short bio. Accepts hard copy and simultaneous submissions if identified. SASE. Responds in 6 months. First serial rights. Fiction and articles, to 6,000 words. Poetry, no line limits. No payment. Provides 2 contributor's copies.

Briarpatch

2138 McIntyre Street
Regina, Saskatchewan S4P 2R7
Canada

Editors/Publishers: Rebecca Granovsky-Larsen & Valerie Zink

Description and Interests: Appearing six times each year, *Briarpatch* features articles on topics that are relevant to grassroots movements for social and environmental justice. Circ: 2,500.
Website: www.briarpatchmagazine.com

Freelance Potential: 97% written by nonstaff writers. Publishes 100 freelance submissions yearly; 75% by authors who are new to the magazine, 10% by experts. Receives 20 queries, 5–10 unsolicited mss each month.

Submissions and Payment: Sample copy and guidelines available at website. Query with word count, publishing credits, and writing sample. Check website for specific issue deadlines. Accepts email to editor@briarpatchmagazine.com. Response time varies. All rights. Articles, to 2,500 words. Reviews, 300–1,000 words. Written material, $50–$150. Payment policy varies. Provides 2 contributor's copies.

The Bridge Bulletin

6575 Windchase Boulevard
Horn Lake, MS 38637-1523

Editor: Brent Manley

Description and Interests: Available exclusively to members of the American Contract Bridge League, this monthly magazine features articles for players at all skill levels. It serves as a source of information on strategy, bidding treatments, rules, tournaments, and profiles of notable bridge players (past and present). Authors must be well versed in the game. Circ: 150,000.
Website: www.acbl.org

Freelance Potential: 70% written by nonstaff writers. Publishes 50 freelance submissions yearly; 10% by unpublished writers, 20% by authors who are new to the magazine, 60% by experts. Receives 3 queries monthly.

Submissions and Payment: Query. Accepts email queries to editor@acbl.org. Response time varies. One-time rights. Articles, 500–2,000 words. Depts/columns, word lengths vary. Written material, payment rates vary. Pays on publication.

Button

P.O. Box 77
Westminster, MA 01473

Senior Editor: Sally Cragin

Description and Interests: *Button* may be small in size, but it is filled with fiction, poetry, and essays from novice writers and those who have been widely published. Appearing annually, it welcomes all voices. Circ: 1,200.
Website: www.moonsigns.net

Freelance Potential: 30–50% written by nonstaff writers. Publishes 5–8 freelance submissions yearly; 10% by unpublished writers, 100% by authors who are new to the magazine. Receives 50+ unsolicited mss monthly.

Submissions and Payment: Sample copy available at website. Guidelines available. Send complete ms. Accepts hard copy. SASE. Response time varies. First North American serial rights. Articles, to 2,000 words. Poetry, no line limit; 1–3 poems per submission. Small honorarium. Pays on publication.

Cadence

P.O. Box 282
Richland, OR 97870

Coordinating Editor: David Haney

Description and Interests: *Cadence* provides complete coverage of jazz, blues, and other improvised music through interviews and oral histories about the music and the musicians, as well as music and book reviews. It is published in one print edition and four digital versions each year. Circ: 10,000.
Website: www.cadencejazzmagazine.com

Freelance Potential: 10% written by nonstaff writers. Publishes 5 freelance submissions yearly; 30% by unpublished writers, 5% by authors who are new to the magazine. Receives 1 unsolicited ms monthly.

Submissions and Payment: Sample copy available. Send complete ms. Accepts hard copy, disk submissions, and email to cadencemagazine@gmail.com. SASE. Responds in 2 weeks. Shared rights. Q&A interviews, to 100,000 words. Depts/columns, 1,000 words. Written material, payment rates vary. Payment policy varies. Provides 2 contributor's copies.

Callaloo

4212 TAMU
Texas A&M University
College Station, TX 77843-4212

Editor: Charles H. Rowell

Description and Interests: This quarterly art and literary journal features the original work of black artists and writers based on themes related to the African Diaspora. In addition to fiction and poetry, it also publishes essays, interviews, drama, and book reviews. Circ: 600–800.
Website: http://callaloo.tamu.edu

Freelance Potential: 99% written by nonstaff writers. Publishes 300–500 freelance submissions yearly; 20% by unpublished writers, 95% by authors who are new to the magazine. Receives 50 unsolicited mss monthly.

Submissions and Payment: Sample copy available. Guidelines available at website. Accepts submissions to: http://callaloo.expressacademic.org/login.php. No simultaneous submissions. Responds in 1–6 months. Rights vary. Articles and fiction, to 10,000 words. Poetry, to 5 poems per submission. No payment.

Camping Today

Family Campers & RVers,
4804 Transit Road, Building 2
DePew, NY 14043

Editor: DeWayne Johnston

Description and Interests: *Camping Today*, published six times each year by the Family Campers & RVers Association, offers articles on family camping and the outdoors. Topics include road safety, wildlife, and destinations. Pieces written from personal experience that include the author's opinions and impressions are welcome. Circ: 10,000.
Website: www.fcrv.org

Freelance Potential: 40% written by nonstaff writers. Publishes 10 freelance submissions yearly; 10% by unpublished writers. Receives 2 unsolicited mss monthly.

Submissions and Payment: Sample copy, guidelines, and theme list available at website. Send complete ms with artwork. Accepts hard copy. SASE. Responds in 2 months. One-time rights. Articles, 1,000–3,000 words. Written material, $35–$150. JPEG images. Pays on publication. Provides 1+ contributor's copies.

Campus Activities

15420 Newberry Road
Blair, SC 29015

Editorial Director: Ian Kirby

Description and Interests: Nine times each year, this magazine presents articles on entertainers, speakers, and ideas for campus functions. It's currently interested in events and activities that support specific causes. Circ: 4,500.
Website: www.campusactivitiesmagazine.com

Freelance Potential: 25% written by nonstaff writers. Publishes 12 freelance submissions yearly; 10% by unpublished writers, 10% by authors who are new to the magazine, 5% by experts. Receives 10 queries monthly.

Submissions and Payment: Sample copy available. Guidelines provided upon assignment. Query. Accepts email to cameopublishing@earthlink.net. Responds in 1 month. All rights. Articles, 1,200–2,000 words; payment rates vary. Kill fee, $35. Pays on publication. Provides 2 contributor's copies.

Canadian Family

111 Queen Street East, Suite 320
Toronto, Ontario M5C 1S2
Canada

Editor in Chief: Jennifer Reynolds

Description and Interests: *Canadian Family* has been serving moms and dads for over 16 years with information on pregnancy, children's health issues, education, parenting guidance, reviews of baby and kid products, food and recipes, fashion, décor, travel, finance, book reviews, and crafts. It has a companion website. It prefers Canadian journalists who use Canadian sources. It is published eight times a year, plus two special issues. Circ: Unavailable
Website: www.canadianfamily.ca

Freelance Potential: Rarely accepts unsolicited submissions. Uses freelance writers who have a degree in journalism. Receives hundreds of queries monthly, but prefers to assign stories to reflect each issue's themes and communication goals.

Submissions and Payment: Sample copy available at website. Submit story pitches only to editor@canadianfamily.com. Rights and payment vary.

Canadian Gardening

25 Sheppard Avenue West, Suite 100
Toronto, Ontario M2N 6S7
Canada

Editor in Chief: Erin McLaughlin

Description and Interests: *Canadian Gardening* offers a mix of practical, how-to, and profile pieces seven times each year. It welcomes articles that address and solve a design challenge for city, country, indoor, or rooftop gardens. Circ: 100,017.
Website: www.canadiangardening.com

Freelance Potential: 85% written by nonstaff writers. Publishes 100 freelance submissions yearly; 1% by unpublished writers, 5% by new authors, 94% by experts. Receives 20 queries monthly.

Submissions and Payment: Sample copy available. Guidelines available at website. Query with writing samples and short bio detailing writing and gardening experience. Accepts hard copy. SAE/IRC. Responds in 3–4 months. Rights vary. Features, 500–2,000 words; $350+. How-to articles and depts/columns, 200–400 words; $125+. Kill fee, 25–50%. Pays on acceptance. Provides 1 contributor's copy.

Canadian Living

TC Media
25 Sheppard Avenue West, Suite 100
Toronto, ON M2N 6S7
Canada

Editor in Chief: Susan Antonacci

Description and Interests: A national family lifestyle monthly, *Canadian Living* targets primarily women, offering "inspiring ideas for everyday living." Categories of interest are family, career, finances, food, health, relationships, style, green living, travel, pets, and crafts. TC Media publications emphasize practical solutions and resources. Among the parent company's other magazines are *Elle Canada, Homemakers, More,* and the new *Fresh Juice*. Circ: 511,516.
Website: www.canadianliving.com

Freelance Potential: Open to freelancers.

Submissions and Payment: Sample copy available. Publishes general interest, how-to's, interviews, practical advice, profiles, crafts, and recipes. Query by mail, via the website form, or to letters@canadianliving.com, ATTN: Submissions Editor. Articles, 750–2,500 words. Payment varies.

Canadian Wildlife

350 Michael Cowpland Drive
Kanata, Ontario K2M 2W1
Canada

Editor: Cooper Langford

Description and Interests: Appearing six times each year and aimed at both teen and adult readers, this is the official publication of the Canadian Wildlife Federation. In addition to publishing information about Federation activities, it features carefully researched articles on Canadian wildlife and habitats, as well as first-person accounts of wildlife encounters. Circ: 4,000.
Website: www.cwf-fcf.org

Freelance Potential: Publishes several freelance submissions yearly.

Submissions and Payment: Guidelines available. Query with outline and writing samples. Accepts hard copy and email queries to editorial@cwf-fcf.org. SAE/IRC. Responds in 3 months. First North American serial rights. Articles, 1,200–2,500 words; $600–$1,200. Depts/columns, 750–1,400 words; $300–$600. Kill fee varies. Pays on acceptance.

Canadian Woodworking & Home Improvement

RR#3
Burford, Ontario N0E 1A0
Canada

Editor: Rob Brown

Description and Interests: Woodworking and home improvement are the focus of this specialty magazine for amateurs and professionals alike. In its six issues each year, readers can find articles on woodworking techniques, expert tips, product reviews, and step-by-step instructions for projects suitable for all skill levels. Circ: 112,000.
Website: www.canadianwoodworking.com

Freelance Potential: 60% written by nonstaff writers. Publishes 24 freelance submissions yearly; 25% by unpublished writers, 50% by authors who are new to the magazine. Receives 2–6 queries monthly.

Submissions and Payment: Query via email to fulcher@canadianwoodworking.com. Accepts hard copy. SAE/IRC. Response time varies. Rights vary. Written material, word lengths and payment rates vary. Pays on publication. Provides 2 contributor's copies.

Canteen Magazine

96 Pierrepont Street, #4
Brooklyn, NY 11201

Publisher: Stephen Pierson

Description and Interests: Appearing twice each year, *Canteen* offers readers original prose and poetry on all themes and in all genres. It is particularly interested in fiction and nonfiction material about the creative process. Circ: 4,000.
Website: www.canteenmag.com

Freelance Potential: 100% written by nonstaff writers. Of the freelance submissions published yearly, 20% are by unpublished writers, 100% are by authors who are new to the magazine. Receives 100 unsolicited mss monthly.

Submissions and Payment: Sample articles and guidelines available at website. Send complete ms. Accepts electronic submissions via website and simultaneous submissions. Responds in 3 months. Exclusive rights for 1 year. Fiction and nonfiction, to 4,000 words. Poetry, no line limits. Art, link to online portfolio. No payment. Provides 3 contributor's copies.

The Capilano Review

2055 Purcell Way
North Vancouver, British Columbia V7J 3H5
Canada

Managing Editor: Tamara Lee

Description and Interests: Dedicated to cutting-edge prose and poetry, *The Capilano Review* offers the finest work of new and established writers from all over the world. It appears three times each year. Circ: 800.
Website: www.thecapilanoreview.ca

Freelance Potential: 100% written by nonstaff writers. Publishes 60 freelance submissions yearly; 5% by unpublished writers, 30% by new authors. Receives 100 unsolicited mss monthly.

Submissions and Payment: Sample copy available. Guidelines available at website. Send complete ms. Accepts hard copy. No simultaneous submissions. SAE/IRC (SASE for Canadian submissions). Responds in 4–6 months. First North American serial rights. Fiction, to 6,000 words. Drama, to 15 pages. Poetry, to 8 pages. Written material, $50–$300. Pays on publication.

Careers & the Disabled

445 Broad Hollow Road, Suite 425
Melville, NY 11747

Director: Editorial & Production: James Schneider

Description and Interests: *Careers & the Disabled* offers individuals with disabilities informational articles on attaining employment and building careers. Inspiring stories of successful students and working professionals are also featured. This magazine is published six times each year. Circ: 10,500.
Website: www.eop.com

Freelance Potential: 60% written by nonstaff writers. Publishes 20 freelance submissions yearly; 10% by unpublished writers, 20% by authors who are new to the magazine, 25% by experts. Receives 10 queries monthly.

Submissions and Payment: Sample articles available at website. Guidelines and editorial calendar available. Query. Accepts email to jschneider@eop.com. Response time varies. First rights. Articles, 1,500 words; $.10 per word. Pays on publication. Provides 2 contributor's copies.

The Caribbean Writer 

University of the Virgin Islands
RR 1 Box 10,000
Kingshill, St. Croix, USVI 00850

Editor: Tregenza A. Roach

Description and Interests: This annual literary journal focuses on Caribbean writers and themes in the form of fiction, creative nonfiction, one-act plays, poetry, and book reviews. Circ: 1,200.
Website: www.thecaribbeanwriter.org

Freelance Potential: 100% written by nonstaff writers. Publishes 60–70 freelance submissions yearly; 25% by unpublished writers. Receives 83 mss monthly.

Submissions and Payment: Sample copy available. Guidelines available at website. Send complete ms with brief bio of writing experience and Caribbean connection. Prefers email to submit@thecaribbeanwriter.org (Word or RTF documents) or online submissions; will accept hard copy. Accepts simultaneous submissions. SASE. Responds in 3 months. One-time rights. Fiction/nonfiction, to 3,500 words or 10 pages. Poetry, no line limits. No payment. Provides 2 contributor's copies.

Carolina Quarterly 

CB#3520 Greenlaw Hall
University of North Carolina
Chapel Hill, NC 27599-3520

Editor in Chief: Matthew Hotham

Description and Interests: Published three times each year by the University of North Carolina, this literary journal seeks the best short stories, poetry, essays, and memoirs. Circ: 1,000.
Website: www.thecarolinaquarterly.com

Freelance Potential: 95% written by nonstaff writers. Publishes about 70 freelance submissions yearly; 30% by unpublished writers, 60% by new authors. Receives 600 unsolicited mss monthly.

Submissions and Payment: Sample copy and guidelines available at website. Send complete ms. Accepts electronic submissions via website year-round, or hard copy between September and April. Accepts simultaneous submissions. Only 1 genre per submission. SASE. Responds in 4–6 months. First serial rights. Prose, to 25 pages. Poetry, to 6 poems per submission. No payment. Provides 2 contributor's copies.

Catamaran Literary Reader 

1050 River Street, #113
Santa Cruz, CA 95060

Founding Editor: Catherine Segurson

Description and Interests: This quarterly literary journal features fiction, poetry, creative nonfiction, and art. Its goal is to "capture the vibrant creative spirit of California in writing and art from around the world." Themes include personal freedom, innovation, and environmentalism. Circ: Unknown.
Website: http://catamaranliteraryreader.com

Freelance Potential: 100% written by nonstaff writers.

Submissions and Payment: Excerpts and guidelines available at website. Send complete ms for fiction and nonfiction; up to 5 poems. Accepts submissions and reader fee via form on website. For questions, email: editor@calit.com. Rights, unavailable. Payment rates and payment policy, unavailable.

Catamaran Sailor

P.O. Box 2060
Key Largo, FL 33037

Editor: Rick White

Description and Interests: Published eight times each year for sailors of catamarans and tri-hulled boats, this news magazine is filled with extensive coverage of races around the world and exciting stories about the captains and crews. Also found in its pages are how-to tips and gear reviews. Some interactive pages and puzzles for young sailors are also included. Circ: 1,800.
Website: www.catsailor.com

Freelance Potential: 30% written by nonstaff writers. Publishes 25 freelance submissions yearly; 10% by authors who are new to the magazine, 10% by experts.

Submissions and Payment: Sample copy available. Query. Prefers email queries to rick@catsailor.com; will accept hard copy. SASE. Response time varies. Rights vary. Written material, word lengths vary. No payment.

Cathedral Age

3101 Wisconsin Avenue NW
Washington, DC 20016

Editor: Craig Stapert

Description and Interests: The National Cathedral in Washington, D.C., is the focus of this quarterly. Read by friends, supporters, and people of all faiths, it covers news and events specific to the cathedral, as well as religion and public affairs. Circ: 12,000.
Website: www.nationalcathedral.org

Freelance Potential: 60% written by nonstaff writers. Publishes 12 freelance submissions yearly; 10% by unpublished writers, 10% by authors who are new to the magazine. Receives 2 queries monthly.

Submissions and Payment: Sample copy available. Query. Accepts hard copy and email queries to cstapert@cathedral.org. SASE. Responds in 1–2 months. All rights. Articles, 1,200–1,600 words; $600–$750. Depts/columns, 50–1,000 words; $350. Pays on publication. Provides 6 contributor's copies.

Catholic Forester

Catholic Order of Foresters
355 Shuman Boulevard
P.O. Box 3012
Naperville, IL 60566-7012

Associate Editor: Patricia Baron

Description and Interests: Published quarterly for members of a fraternal insurance society, *Catholic Forester* features both practical and inspirational articles on a broad range of topics. Circ: 87,000.
Website: www.catholicforester.org

Freelance Potential: 20% written by nonstaff writers. Publishes 4–8 freelance submissions yearly; 20% by authors who are new to the magazine. Receives 20 unsolicited mss monthly.

Submissions and Payment: Sample copy and guidelines available at website. Send complete ms. Accepts hard copy and simultaneous submissions if identified. SASE. Responds in 3–4 months. One-time rights. Articles and fiction, 500 to 1,000 words. Written material, $.50 per word. Pays on acceptance. Provides 3+ contributor's copies.

Cent$

4333 Amon Carter Boulevard, MD 5374
Fort Worth, TX 76155

Editor in Chief: Jennifer Norris

Description and Interests: *Cent$* is the publication that services current and potential members of the American Airlines Federal Credit Union. Published quarterly, it provides the latest information on the credit union's programs, as well as easy-to-read features on topics like family and personal finances, savings plans, investment options, and consumer spending. Circ: 140,000.
Website: www.centsmagazine.com

Freelance Potential: 90% written by nonstaff writers. Publishes 8–10 freelance submissions yearly; 10% by authors who are new to the magazine.

Submissions and Payment: Sample copy available at website. Query or send complete ms. Accepts email to jennifer.norris@aa.com. Response time varies. First rights. Written material, word lengths vary; $1 per word. Pays on acceptance. Provides 1 contributor's copy.

Ceramics Monthly

600 North Cleveland Avenue, Suite 210
Westerville, OH 43082

Editor: Sherman Hall

Description and Interests: This magazine presents every aspect of the craft of ceramics to potters and collectors alike. Interested in both traditional and contemporary approaches, its articles offer how-to instruction, artist profiles, exhibitions, contest and event news, and book reviews. It is published 10 times each year. Circ: 23,000.
Website: www.ceramicsmonthly.org

Freelance Potential: 70% written by nonstaff writers. Publishes 100 freelance submissions yearly.

Submissions and Payment: Guidelines available at website. Send complete ms. Accepts disk submissions with hard copy and email submissions to editorial@ceramicsmonthly.org. Include images of work. SASE. Responds in 2 months. Exclusive rights. Articles, 750–1,500 words. Depts/columns, word lengths vary. Payment rates vary. Pays on publication. Provides 2 contributor's copies.

The Chaffin Journal

Case Annex 467
Eastern Kentucky University
Richmond, KY 40475-3102

Editor: Robert W. Witt

Description and Interests: Produced annually by Eastern Kentucky University, *The Chaffin Journal* publishes only fiction and poetry. It does not accept essays, creative nonfiction, or memoirs. Circ: 300.
Website: www.english.eku.edu/ chaffin_journal

Freelance Potential: 100% written by nonstaff writers. Publishes 60 freelance submissions yearly; 10% by unpublished writers, 60% by authors who are new to the magazine.

Submissions and Payment: Sample copy available. Guidelines available at website. Send complete ms with cover letter and bio between June 1 and October 1 only. Accepts hard copy and simultaneous submissions if identified. SASE. Responds in 3 months. First serial rights. Fiction, to 10,000 words. Poetry, line lengths vary; 3–5 poems per submission. No payment. Provides 1 contributor's copy.

Charisma

600 Rinehart Road
Lake Mary, FL 32746

Editor: Marcus Yoars

Description and Interests: Most of the readers of this monthly publication belong to Pentecostal churches or engage in charismatic practices. Formerly titled *Charisma & Christian Life*, it offers information and inspiration through personality profiles, stories of healings, and seasonal material. It also welcomes brief Christian news and trends stories. Circ: 110,000.
Website: www.charismamag.com

Freelance Potential: 80% written by nonstaff writers. Publishes about 40 freelance assignments yearly.

Submissions and Payment: Sample copy available. Guidelines available at website. Query with outline and clips. Accepts hard copy and email queries to charisma@charismamedia.com. SASE. Response time varies. All rights. Articles, 1,800–2,500 words. Depts/columns, word lengths vary. Payment rates vary. Pays on publication. Provides 2 contributor's copies.

Chattahoochee Review

Georgia Perimeter College
555 North Indian Creek Drive
Clarkston, GA 30021

Editor: Anna Schachner

Description and Interests: This publication, published three times each year, seeks literary fiction, poetry, personal essays, and author interviews. It is particularly interested in writing that challenges the traditional definition of "Southern." Circ: 1,500.
Website: www.chattahoochee-review.org

Freelance Potential: 100% written by nonstaff writers. Publishes 80 freelance submissions yearly; 50% by unpublished writers, 50% by new authors. Receives 250+ unsolicited mss monthly.

Submissions and Payment: Sample articles and guidelines available at website. Send complete ms with short bio. Accepts hard copy and simultaneous submissions if identified. SASE. Responds in 2–3 months. First serial rights. Fiction, to 6,000 words, $25 per page. Poetry, 3–5 poems per submission, $50. Other material, word lengths and payment rates vary. Payment policy varies.

Christian*New Age Quarterly

P.O. Box 276
Clifton, NJ 07015-0276

Editor: Catherine Groves

Description and Interests: Subtitled "A Bridge Supporting Dialog," this quarterly magazine encompasses diverse viewpoints with the goal of fostering communication between Christians and those with alternative spiritualities. It publishes thoughtful, well-crafted essays that respect all views. New writers are welcome. Circ: Unavailable.
Website: www.christiannewage.com

Freelance Potential: 50% written by nonstaff writers. Publishes 2–4 freelance submissions yearly; 20% by authors who are new to the magazine, 90% by experts. Receives 1 query, 1 unsolicited ms monthly.

Submissions and Payment: Sample copy available. Guidelines available at website. Query or send complete ms. Accepts hard copy. SASE. No simultaneous submissions. Responds in 1 month. First rights. Articles, 400–1,500 words. No payment. Provides a 4-issue subscription.

Christian Renewal

P.O. Box 770
Lewiston, NY 14092

Submissions Editor: John Van Dyk

Description and Interests: Published every three weeks, *Christian Renewal* is read by confessionally reformed Christians for articles on ecumenical issues, religion, politics, and education. It also publishes worldwide member church news. Circ: 3,200.
Website: www.crmag.com

Freelance Potential: 20% written by nonstaff writers. Publishes 10 freelance submissions yearly; 1% by unpublished writers, 5% by authors who are new to the magazine, 4% by experts. Receives 5 unsolicited mss monthly.

Submissions and Payment: Sample copy available. Query or send complete ms. Accepts email submissions to jvandyk@aol.com. Responds in 2 months. Rights vary. Articles, 1,000 words. Depts/columns, 500 words. Written material, $30–$150. Pays on publication. Provides 2 contributor's copies.

Christian Work at Home Moms

P.O. Box 974
Bellevue, NE 68123

Editor: Jill Hart

Description and Interests: This online magazine offers Christian moms advice and inspiration for building a home-based business. Articles cover a range of topics, including marketing, time management, ad writing, blogging, and website design, along with success stories and a dose of humor. *Christian Work at Home Moms* is updated weekly. Hits per month: 1.5 million.
Website: www.cwahm.com

Freelance Potential: 75% written by nonstaff writers. Publishes 50–100 freelance submissions yearly; 20% by unpublished writers, 20% by authors who are new to the magazine, 60% by experts.

Submissions and Payment: Sample copy available at website. Guidelines available. Send complete ms with author bio. Accepts email submissions through website. Response time varies. Electronic rights. Articles, 600–800 words. No payment.

Chronicle

5815 Executive Drive
Lansing, MI 48911

Executive Editor: Larry Wagenaar

Description and Interests: *Chronicle*, the membership publication of the Historical Society of Michigan, is a colorful compendium of informative articles, book reviews, educational resources, and member news. Quarterly issues cover a wide range of historical topics, including customs, industry, the military, and Michigan's natural wonders. Circ: 4,500.
Website: www.hsmichigan.org

Freelance Potential: 50% written by nonstaff writers. Publishes 10–15 freelance submissions yearly.

Submissions and Payment: Sample articles and guidelines available at website. Query with artwork ideas. Accepts email submissions to hsm@hsmichigan.org. Responds in 1–2 months. Rights vary. Articles, 1,500–4,000 words; $25–$100. Payment policy varies. Provides 5–10 contributor's copies.

Chrysalis Reader

Swedenborg Foundation
1745 Gravel Hill Road
Dillwyn, VA 23936

Co-Editor: Carol S. Lawson

Description and Interests: Each annual issue of this journal focuses on a meaningful theme that inspires essays, fiction, and poetry from many traditions and experiences. Circ: 2,000.
Website: www.swedenborg.com/chrysalis

Freelance Potential: 95% written by nonstaff writers. Publishes 30–40 freelance submissions yearly; 15% by unpublished writers, 80% by authors who are new to the magazine. Receives 75 unsolicited mss monthly.

Submissions and Payment: Sample articles, guidelines, and theme list available at website. Send complete ms. Accepts hard copy and email submissions to chrysalis@hovac.com (attach file). SASE. Responds in 6 months. One-time rights. Prose, to 3,000 words; payment rates vary. Poetry, to 5 poems per submission. Pays on publication. Provides 5 contributor's copies.

The Church Herald and Holiness Banner

7415 Metcalf Avenue
Overland Park, KS 66204

Editor: Mark Avery

Description and Interests: This official magazine of the Church of God (Holiness) deals with Christian issues and doctrine. It also offers reports of activities of local churches, mission programs, and Bible schools. It is published monthly. Circ: 900.
Website: www.heraldandbannerbooks.com

Freelance Potential: 95% written by nonstaff writers. Publishes 12 freelance submissions yearly; 2% by unpublished writers, 20% by authors who are new to the magazine, 2% by experts. Receives 3–5 unsolicited mss monthly.

Submissions and Payment: Sample copy and editorial calendar available. Send complete ms. Accepts email submissions to hbeditor@yahoo.com. Responds in 1–3 months. First and reprint rights. Articles, 500–1,200 words. No payment. Provides 1 contributor's copy.

The Cincinnati Review

P.O. Box 210069
Cincinnati, OH 45221-0069

Editor: Don Bogen

Description and Interests: Published twice each year, this journal seeks fiction, poetry, book reviews, and creative nonfiction from emerging and established writers. Circ: 500.
Website: www.cincinnatireview.com

Freelance Potential: 100% written by nonstaff writers. Publishes 88 freelance submissions yearly; 5% by unpublished writers, 75% by new authors. Receives 800 unsolicited mss monthly.

Submissions and Payment: Sample copy available. Guidelines available at website. Send complete ms between August 15 and April 15. Accepts hard copy and electronic submissions via website. SASE. Responds in 3–4 months. First serial and electronic rights. Fiction and creative nonfiction, to 40 pages; $25 per page. Book reviews, 1,500 words; payment rates vary. Poetry, to 10 pages; $30 per page. Pays on publication. Provides 2 contributor's copies.

City Journal

Manhattan Institute
52 Vanderbilt Avenue, 3rd Floor
New York, NY 10017

Editor: Brian C. Anderson

Description and Interests: Although some articles are set in specific cities, the focus of this quarterly publication is on issues that have a universal impact on urban settings. Topics covered include public policy, safety, social issues, crime, and education. Circ: 800,000.
Website: www.city-journal.org

Freelance Potential: 30% written by nonstaff writers. Publishes 20 freelance submissions yearly; 5% by authors who are new to the magazine. Receives 5+ queries, 2+ unsolicited mss monthly.

Submissions and Payment: Sample copy available at website. Query with outline, résumé, and clips or writing samples; or send complete ms. Accepts hard copy. SASE. Responds in 2 months. First or all rights. Articles, 2,000–5,000 words. Depts/columns, 700–4,000 words. Written material, $.30 per word. Pays on publication. Provides 3 contributor's copies.

CKI Magazine

3636 Woodview Trace
Indianapolis, IN 46268

Executive Editor: Amberly Peterson

Description and Interests: This online publication is written for service-minded college students. Articles cover current trends, leadership and career development, self-help, and community involvement. It is updated twice each year. Circ: 10,000.
Website: www.circleK.org

Freelance Potential: 20% written by nonstaff writers. Publishes 2–4 freelance submissions yearly; 5% by authors who are new to the magazine, 10% by experts. Receives 10 queries each month.

Submissions and Payment: Sample copy available at website. Query. Accepts email to ckimagazine@kiwanis.org. Responds in 1–3 months. First North American serial rights. Articles, 1,000–1,500 words; $150–$400. B/W or color prints. Pays on acceptance. Provides 3 contributor's copies.

Clarkesworld

P.O. Box 172
Stirling, NJ 07980

Publisher and Editor: Neil Clarke

Description and Interests: A Hugo Award-winning online science fiction and fantasy magazine with fiction, nonfiction, interviews, podcasts, and original art, *Clarkesworld* is updated monthly. Its original fiction is gathered into chapbooks and an anthology annually. Unique visitors per month: 30,000.
Website: http://clarkesworldmagazine.com

Freelance Potential: Not available.

Submissions and Payment: Sample copy and guidelines available at website. Send complete ms for fiction via the online submissions system with story title, word count, and author's publishing history. Query for nonfiction. Accept email queries to nonfiction@clarkesworldmagazine.com (include "Nonfiction Query: Title or Concept" in subject line). No simultaneous submissions. Response time varies. First world electronic rights for text and audio; first print rights; and non-exclusive anthology rights. Fiction, 1,000–8,000 words. Articles, to 2,500 words. Written material, payment rates vary. Payment policy varies.

Clavier Companion

Hugh Hodgson School of Music
250 River Road
Athens, GA 30602

Editor in Chief: Pete Jutras

Description and Interests: Appearing six times each year, *Clavier Companion* offers piano teachers, students, and enthusiasts alike informative articles on topics such as technique, performance, and methods of study. It also publishes reviews of new music and related materials. Circ: 9,000.
Website: www.claviercompanion.com

Freelance Potential: 60% written by nonstaff writers. Publishes 10–12 freelance submissions yearly; 20% by unpublished writers, 50% by authors who are new to the magazine. Receives 25 queries and unsolicited mss monthly.

Submissions and Payment: Sample copy available at website. Query or send complete ms. Accepts email submissions to editor@claviercompanion.com. Response time varies. All rights. Articles, 2,500–3,000 words; to $250. Pays on publication. Provides 2 contributor's copies.

Clutch

Editor: Zettler Clay

Description and Interests: *Clutch* is a digital magazine, now updated daily, whose target audience is urban women of color. It covers news, style, beauty, health, fitness, relationships, entertainment, gossip, education, career, and opinion. It also uses blog writers.
Website: www.clutchmagonline.com

Freelance Potential: Open to freelance writers.

Submissions and Payment: Recent articles have featured cross-dressing, women that overcome, fixing your finances, and many news items on celebrities. Has put out calls for submissions; visit www.pitchclutch.com for guidelines. Pitch to pitches@pitchclutch.com; describe yourself, your writing history, and include 2–3 pitches. Study *Clutch*'s content, voice, and audience first. Payment, $10–$15 for 200–400 words.

Coast & Kayak Magazine

PO Box 24 Station A
Nanaimo, British Columbia V9R 5K4
Canada

Editor: John Kimantas

Description and Interests: This photo-filled publication, formerly known as *WaveLength Magazine*, is dedicated to kayakers, particularly those who want to discover the Pacific Coast. In addition to destination pieces, quarterly issues also offer product reviews and event news. Circ: 22,000.
Website: www.coastandkayak.com

Freelance Potential: 90% written by nonstaff writers. Publishes 25 freelance submissions yearly; 10% by authors who are new to the magazine, 50% by experts. Receives 5 queries monthly.

Submissions and Payment: Sample copy available at website. Query. Prefers email to kayak@coastandkayak.com (no attachments). Accepts hard copy. SAE/IRC. Responds in 2 months. First North American serial and electronic rights. Articles, 1,000–1,500 words; $100–$200. JPEG images, $25–$100. Pays on publication. Provides 2 contributor's copies and a 1-year subscription.

Coins

Krause Publication
700 East State Street
Iola, WI 54990

Editor: Robert Van Ryzin

Description and Interests: Each monthly issue of this magazine covers important and timely information on coin, medal, and token collecting for both novice and expert collectors. Along with value guides and an event calendar, it features a mix of profiles, how-to pieces, and personal experience pieces. It has been published since 1955. Circ: 60,000.
Website: www.coinsmagazine.net

Freelance Potential: 40% written by nonstaff writers. Publishes 70 freelance submissions yearly; 5% by authors who are new to the magazine. Receives 3–5 queries monthly.

Submissions and Payment: Sample copy available at website. Guidelines available. Query. Accepts hard copy. SASE. Responds to queries in 1–2 months. Rights vary. Articles, 1,500–2,000 words. Written material, $.04 per word. Pays on publication. Provides contributor's copies upon request.

College News Magazine

730 North Franklin Street, Suite 604
Chicago, IL 60654

Editor: David Batka

Description and Interests: Written for and mainly by college students and recent grads, *College News* is a quarterly print magazine complemented by an active website updated regularly. It features news, reviews, opinion pieces, and lifestyle features on topics ranging from sex and campus life to careers. It is published quarterly. Circ: Unavailable.
Website: www.collegenews.com

Freelance Potential: 50% written by nonstaff writers. Its new website design allows freelancers to submit as often as they wish without having to be approved by an editor. Freelancers may submit to the website or the magazine.

Submissions and Payment: Digital copy available at website. Guidelines available. Query. Accepts email queries to janellev@bostonhannah.com or via www.collegenews.com/wcp/register. Responds immediately. All rights. Articles, word lengths vary. No payment. Provides 5 contributor's copies.

Colorado Review

9105 Campus Delivery
Colorado State University
Fort Collins, CO 80523-9105

Editor: Stephanie G'Schwind

Description and Interests: This national literary review features contemporary fiction, poetry, nonfiction, and book reviews. It is published three times each year. Circ: 1,100.
Website: http://coloradoreview.colostate.edu

Freelance Potential: 100% written by nonstaff writers. Publishes 100–150 freelance submissions yearly; 10% by unpublished writers, 60% by authors who are new to the magazine. Receives 1,000 mss monthly.

Submissions and Payment: Sample articles and guidelines available at website. Fiction and poetry, send ms between August 1 and April 30; nonfiction, send ms year-round. Reviews, send query to creview@colostate.edu. Accepts hard copy, submissions via website, and simultaneous submissions. SASE. Responds in 6–8 weeks. First serial rights. Prose, 15–25 pages. Poetry, to 5 poems per submission. Written material, $25 or $5 per page. Pays on publication. Provides 2 contributor's copies and a 1-year subscription.

Columbia: A Journal

Columbia University, 415 Dodge Hall
2960 Broadway
New York, NY 10027

Managing Editor: Jaime Green

Description and Interests: Edited by the students in Columbia University's graduate writing program, this literary journal offers top-notch original prose and poetry. It appears annually. Circ: 1,900.
Website: www.columbiajournal.org

Freelance Potential: 100% written by nonstaff writers. Publishes 40 freelance submissions yearly; 85% by unpublished writers, 85% by authors who are new to the magazine. Receives 200 mss monthly.

Submissions and Payment: Sample copy and guidelines available at website. Send complete ms between September 1 and May 1 only. Accepts electronic submissions via website. Responds in 4 months. First serial rights. Fiction, to 20 double-spaced pages. Poetry, to 5 poems per submission. No payment. Provides 2 contributor's copies.

Companion Parrot Quarterly

P.O. Box 812
Loveland, CO 80539

Editor: Sally Blanchard

Description and Interests: By turns entertaining and informative, this online publication explores the bird/human relationship through articles and personal experience pieces. Updated six times each year, it also covers topics such as parrot health, rescue, rehabilitation, breeding, and behavior. Hits per month: 8,000.
Website: www.companionparrotonline.com

Freelance Potential: 60% written by nonstaff writers. Publishes 15 freelance submissions yearly; 25% by unpublished writers, 25% by authors who are new to the magazine, 50% by experts. Receives 5 unsolicited mss monthly.

Submissions and Payment: Sample articles available at website. Send complete ms. Accepts email to staff@companionparrot.com (Word attachments). Responds in 1 month. Exclusive rights for 4 months. Written material, word lengths and payment rates vary. Pays on publication.

Conceit Magazine

P.O. Box 884223
San Francisco, CA 94188-4223

Editor: Perry Terrell

Description and Interests: Talented new writers are a mainstay of this monthly literary magazine, which offers poetry, short fiction, articles, and essays. Circ: 150.
Website: https://sites.google/site/conceitmagazine/

Freelance Potential: 99% written by nonstaff writers. Publishes 240 freelance submissions yearly; 50% by unpublished writers, 50% by authors who are new to the magazine. Receives 85 queries, 40 unsolicited mss monthly.

Submissions and Payment: Sample copy available. Guidelines available at website. Query or send complete ms with author bio. Accepts hard copy, email to conceitmagazine2007@yahoo.com, and simultaneous submissions if identified. SASE. Responds in 1 month. One-time rights. Written material, word lengths and payment rates vary. Payment policy varies. Provides 1 contributor's copy.

Concho River Review

Angelo State University
P.O. Box 10894 ASU Station
San Angelo, TX 76909-0894

Editor: Erin Ashworth-King

Description and Interests: Hoping to give its readers "escape, insight, laughter, and inspiration," this literary journal appears twice each year with fiction, essays, poetry, and book reviews. Its editors at Angelo State University seek traditional stories with a strong sense of conflict. Circ: 300.
Website: www.angelo.edu/dept/english

Freelance Potential: 100% written by nonstaff writers. Publishes 76 freelance submissions yearly; 35% by unpublished writers, 50% by authors who are new to the magazine. Receives 20 unsolicited mss monthly.

Submissions and Payment: Sample copy available. Guidelines available at website. Send complete ms with cover letter. Query for reviews. Accepts hard copy and email to appropriate editor (check website for contact information). SASE. Responds in 1–6 months. First rights. Fiction and nonfiction, 1,500–5,000 words. Poetry, 3–5 poems per submission. Book reviews, 500–1,000 words. No payment. Provides 1 contributor's copy.

Conduit

788 Osceola Avenue
St. Paul, MN 55105

Editor: William D. Waltz

Description and Interests: This art and literary magazine features work that demonstrates originality, humanity, and courage. Twice each year, it publishes poetry, fiction, creative nonfiction, translations, and artwork of new and established writers and artists. Circ: 1,000.
Website: www.conduit.org

Freelance Potential: 95% written by nonstaff writers. Publishes 60 freelance submissions yearly; 20% by unpublished writers, 70% by authors who are new to the magazine. Receives 200 unsolicited mss each month.

Submissions and Payment: Sample articles and guidelines available at website. Send complete ms. Accepts hard copy. SASE. Responds in 6 months. First rights. Articles and fiction, to 3,500 words. Poetry, no line limit; 3–5 poems per submission. B/W line art. No payment. Provides 4 contributor's copies.

Connecting

Solo Travel Network

689 Park Road, Unit 6
Gibsons, British Columbia VON 1V7
Canada

Editor: Diane Redfern

Description and Interests: Everything single travelers want to know is the key focus of this company. They publish articles in their periodicals and on the website that examine many aspects of solo travel with the goal of finding ways of making it comfortable and affordable both for those who wish to travel alone and solos seeking company. Circ: Unknown.
Website: www.cstn.org

Freelance Potential: Accepts multiple freelance submissions annually.

Submissions and Payment: Sample articles and guidelines available at website. Query or send complete ms through form at website. Rights vary. Articles, 1,500–2,500 words. Dept/columns include Reader Report, Travel Tale, Day Trips; 800–1,000 words. Article payment and rates vary. Dept/columns, $25–$35. Pays on publication.

Conservative Speculator

5 Savage Court
Bluffton, SC 29910

Editor: Lawrence C. Oakley

Description and Interests: This ezine covers financial news and investing trends to help keep readers abreast of the fluctuating markets. Updated constantly, it seeks writers who can prepare research reports on publicly traded corporations. Assignments are also available. Hits per month: 120,000+.
Website: www.wallstreetcorner.com

Freelance Potential: 10% written by nonstaff writers. Publishes 10 freelance submissions yearly; 5% by unpublished writers, 5% by authors who are new to the magazine, 5% by industry experts.

Submissions and Payment: Sample copy available at website. Query. Prefers calls to editor at 843-645-2729; will accept email queries to up415@aol.com (Word attachments). Responds in 1 month. All rights. Assigned articles, to 5 pages; payment rates vary. Unsolicited work, no payment. Pays on acceptance.

Continental Newstime

501 West Broadway, Plaza A, PMB #265
San Diego, CA 92101

Editor in Chief: Gary P. Salamone

Description and Interests: This general interest magazine seeks articles on topics that are underreported or unreported by most other media. It offers news and current affairs from around the globe, and commentary and analysis on economic, social, and other public policy issues. Features on the entertainment industry and travel are also regularly published. Appearing 26 times each year, it doubles as the newspaper feature catalog of Continental Features/Continental News Service in marketing to U.S. and foreign newspaper editors. Circ: Unavailable.
Website: http://continentalnewsservice.com

Freelance Potential: Publishes some freelance submissions yearly.

Submissions and Payment: Query with clips. Accepts email to continentalnewsservice@yahoo.com (no attachments) and hard copy. SASE. If no SASE, responds if interested. Rights vary. Articles, 700–800 words; payment rates vary. Payment policy varies.

Converge Point

Mail Code 200
11002 Lake Hart Road
Orlando, FL 32832

Editor: Bob Putman

Description and Interests: God-centered articles and news are published in this quarterly publication of Converge Worldwide (The Baptist General Conference). Circ: 43,000.
Website: www.convergeworldwide.org

Freelance Potential: 20% written by nonstaff writers. Publishes 8–10 freelance submissions yearly; 5% by unpublished writers, 5% by authors who are new to the magazine. Receives 20 queries monthly.

Submissions and Payment: Sample copy and guidelines available. Query with clips. Accepts hard copy and email to bob.putman@convergeww.org (Word attachments). SASE. Responds in 2 months. First serial rights. Articles, 600–1,500 words. Depts/columns, 200–750 words. Written material, payment rates vary. Kill fee, 50%. Pays on publication. Provides 6 contributor's copies.

Cooking Wild

P.O. Box 2474
Livermore, CA 94551-2474

Publisher: April Donald

Description and Interests: Created to "bridge the gap from field to the table," *Cooking Wild* is read by food-focused hunters, anglers, and foragers, as well as foodies who appreciate "wild" cooking. Its articles feature tips and techniques from experts, as well as recipes. It appears quarterly. Launched in 2010, *Cooking Wild* was named one of that year's best magazines by *Library Journal*. Circ: Unavailable.
Website: www.cookingwildmagazine.com

Freelance Potential: Open to freelance submissions. Potential topics include butchering, smoking game, hunting and food preparation experiences, and food storage methods.

Submissions and Payment: Sample articles available at website. For submission information or to submit a query, contact the publisher at april@cookingwildmagazine.com or via the contact form at website.

Coonhound Bloodlines

100 East Kilgore Road
Kalamazoo, MI 49002-5584

Editor: Vicki Rand

Description and Interests: People who own, breed, and hunt with coonhounds read this United Kennel Club publication to stay up to date on information that pertains to the breed. Appearing monthly, it features product reviews, interviews with and profiles of owners, and timely information on UKC-licensed events. Circ: 16,500.
Website: www.ukcdogs.com

Freelance Potential: 75% written by nonstaff writers. Publishes 100–200 freelance submissions yearly; 50% by unpublished writers, 20% by authors who are new to the magazine. Receives 5–10 queries monthly.

Submissions and Payment: Sample articles and guidelines available at website. Send complete ms. Accepts hard copy and email queries to vrand@ukcdogs.com. SASE. Response time varies. First North American serial rights. Articles and depts/columns, word lengths vary. Payment rates vary. Pays on publication.

Coping with Cancer

P.O. Box 682268
Franklin, TN 37068

Editor: Laura Shipp

Description and Interests: Six times each year, this magazine offers cancer patients and their families knowledge, hope, and inspiration. Most articles fall in the categories of survivor stories, professional advice, reflections, and support. Poetry is also featured. Circ: 90,000.
Website: www.copingmag.com

Freelance Potential: 90% written by nonstaff writers. Publishes 25 freelance submissions yearly; 20% by unpublished writers, 80% by authors who are new to the magazine, 80% by experts. Receives 10 unsolicited mss monthly.

Submissions and Payment: Guidelines available at website. Send complete ms. Accepts email to submissions@copingmag.com (must fill out form on website). Responds in 1–2 months. First serial rights. Written material, to 775 words. Poetry, to 50 lines. No payment. Provides 1 contributor's copy.

Cosign Magazine 

CEO/Founder: Kurtis "KG" Graham

Description and Interests: This magazine, which started out in digital form and has moved to print, strives to inspire and support the fresh, young, talented artists and entrepreneurs of today. Each issue covers the entertainment industry in detail with profiles of artists, producers, models, clothing designers, athletes, and other professionals. It is published six times each year. Circ: Unavailable.
Website: www.cosignmag.com

Freelance Potential: Receives many queries monthly.

Submissions and Payment: Sample articles at website. Query. Accepts email to info@cosignmag.com. Rights vary. Payment rates and policy vary.

The Covenant Companion

Evangelical Covenant Church
8303 West Higgins Road
Chicago, IL 60631

Features Editor: Cathy Norman Peterson

Description and Interests: This monthly strives to stimulate thought and tackle issues affecting the Evangelical Covenant Church and its members. Circ: 13,000.
Website: www.covchurch.org

Freelance Potential: 60% written by nonstaff writers. Publishes 15 freelance submissions yearly; 5% by unpublished writers, 15% by authors who are new to the magazine, 80% by experts. Receives 50 queries and mss monthly.

Submissions and Payment: Sample articles, guidelines available at website. Send ms with bio and church affiliation. Accepts hard copy and email to communications@covchurch.org. SASE. Responds in 1–3 months. All or first rights. Articles, to 1,800 words; $35–$100. B/W or color prints, illustrations, or color slides; $25. Pays on publication. Provides 3 contributor's copies.

Cowgirl

2660 NE Highway, Suite 112
Bend, OR 97701

Editor

Description and Interests: This magazine focuses on women who live in the contemporary west—women who are proud of their horse and cowgirl skills and also appreciate an elegant western design sense. Its subjects range from horses, tack, and shooting skills to fashion, contemporary western design trends, and decor. Profiles of country celebrities are also featured. It is published six times each year. Circ: Unavailable.
Website: www.cowgirlmagazine.com

Freelance Potential: Accepts freelance submissions. Writers should be familiar with the western lifestyle, equestrian subjects, or design.

Submissions and Payment: Sample articles available at website. Prefers query; will accept complete ms. Accepts hard copy and email to editor@cowgirlmagazine. SASE. Response time, word lengths, and payment rates vary. Payment policy varies.

Crab Orchard Review 

English Department
Southern Illinois University
1000 Faner Drive
Carbondale, IL 62901-4503

Managing Editor: Jon C. Tribble

Description and Interests: Each themed issue of this journal features creative nonfiction, fiction, interviews, and poetry. It is published twice each year. Circ: 3,000.
Website: www.craborchardreview.siuc.edu

Freelance Potential: 98% written by nonstaff writers. Publishes 80–120 freelance submissions yearly; 2% by unpublished writers, 60% by new authors. Receives 900–1,200 unsolicited mss monthly.

Submissions and Payment: Guidelines and theme list available at website. Send complete ms between February 15–April 30 or August 27–November 3 only. Accepts hard copy and simultaneous submissions. SASE. Responds in 5 months. First North American serial rights. Articles and fiction, to 25 pages. Poetry, to 6 poems per submission. Written material, $20 per published page. Pays on publication. Provides 2 contributor's copies.

Crafts 'n Things

P.O. Box 1009
Oak Park, IL 60304

Editor: Anne Niemiec

Description and Interests: This bimonthly from Amos Press covers a wide range of crafts, from knitting and crochet to paper crafts and floral arranging. Its editors like projects that mix traditional country with classic, contemporary, vintage, and French country styles. Proposed projects should have limited supply lists and easy directions for intermediate to advanced crafters; include photos when possible. Open to sewing, needlework, paper crafts, rubber stamping, floral arranging, beading, painting and clay, and other recent crafting trends. Circ: Unavailable.
Website: www.craftsnthings.com

Freelance Potential: Open to receiving craft projects of many kinds.

Submissions and Payment: Sample copy and guidelines available. Accepts hard copy to Attn: Submissions, or email to aniemiec@amoscraft.com. Rights and payment policy vary. Responds in 4 weeks.

The Crafts Report

P.O. Box 5000
Iola, WI 54945-5000

Editor: Dennis Piotrowski

Description and Interests: Subtitled "The Business Resource for Artists and Retailers," *The Crafts Report* aims to inform, instruct, and inspire both the beginning and established professional craftsperson and retailer. It offers how-to articles, industry news updates, and current trend information in each of its monthly issues. Circ: 6,000.
Website: www.craftsreport.com

Freelance Potential: 80% written by nonstaff writers. Publishes 100 freelance submissions yearly; 10% by authors who are new to the magazine.

Submissions and Payment: Sample copy available at website. Query. Accepts hard copy. SASE. Response time varies. All rights. Articles and depts/columns, word lengths and payment rates vary. Pays on publication. Provides 3–5 contributor's copies.

The Cream City Review

P.O. Box 413
University of Wisconsin-Milwaukee
Milwaukee, WI 53201

Editor in Chief: Ching-In Chen

Description and Interests: Featuring a mix of short stories, poetry, essays, book reviews, and interviews, *The Cream City Review* is a literary magazine published twice each year. Circ: 1,000.
Website: www.creamcityreview.org

Freelance Potential: 95% written by nonstaff writers. Publishes 100 freelance submissions yearly; 10% by unpublished writers, 75% by authors who are new to the magazine. Receives 300 unsolicited mss monthly.

Submissions and Payment: Sample copy and guidelines available at website. Send complete ms between August 1–November 1 and January 1–April 1. Accepts submissions via website only and simultaneous submissions if identified. Responds in 2–8 months. First North American serial rights. Prose, to 20 pages. Poetry, to 5 poems per submission. No payment. Provides a 1-year subscription.

Creating Keepsakes

741 Corporate Circle, Suite A
Golden, CO 80401

Managing Editor: Kerri Miller

Description and Interests: This magazine publishes original and creative ideas that will excite, motivate, teach, help, and inspire scrapbooking enthusiasts of all levels. It is published monthly. Circ: 300,000.
Website: www.creatingkeepsakes.com

Freelance Potential: 10% written by nonstaff writers. Publishes 10 freelance submissions yearly; 55% by unpublished writers, 2% by authors who are new to the magazine, 30% by experts. Receives 10 queries monthly.

Submissions and Payment: Sample copy, guidelines, and editorial calendar available at website. Query. Accepts email queries to editorial@creatingkeepsakes.com. Responds in 4–6 weeks. International rights. Articles, 700–1,200 words; $350–$600. Kill fee, 50%. Pays on publication. Provides 1 contributor's copy.

Creative With Words 

P.O. Box 223226
Carmel, CA 93922

Editor: Brigitta Geltrich

Description and Interests: Folklore for families is the focus of this literary magazine. Issues published twice each year feature poetry and prose, often with a sense of humor. Circ: Unavailable.
Website: http://members.tripod.com/creativewithwords

Freelance Potential: 99% written by nonstaff writers. Publishes 280–300 freelance submissions yearly; 50% by unpublished writers, 50% by authors who are new to the magazine. Receives 25–50 queries monthly.

Submissions and Payment: Sample copy available. Guidelines and theme list available at website. Prefers query, will accept complete ms. Accepts hard copy and email to geltrich@mbay.net. SASE. Responds to queries in 2 weeks, to mss in 1–2 months. First rights. Prose to 800 words. Poetry, to 20 lines; to 3 poems per submission. No payment. Provides contributor's copies at discounted rate.

Cross Currents 

475 Riverside Drive, Suite 1945
New York, NY 10115

Executive Editor: Charles Henderson

Description and Interests: *Cross Currents* is a quarterly journal of essays, fiction, poetry, and scholarly articles that relate religion to contemporary intellectual, political, and cultural ideas. Most material is written by theologians and scholars, but it welcomes fresh voices. Circ: 3,500.
Website: www.crosscurrents.org

Freelance Potential: 80% written by nonstaff writers. Publishes 30 freelance submissions yearly; 10% by authors who are new to the magazine. Receives 20 unsolicited mss monthly.

Submissions and Payment: Sample copy and guidelines available at website. Send complete ms. Accepts hard copy and email submissions to cph@crosscurrents.org. No simultaneous submissions. SASE. Responds in 2 months. First serial rights. Articles, 3,000-8,000 words. Depts/columns, word lengths vary. Poetry, no line limits. No payment. Provides 5 contributor's copies.

Cuban Affairs 

Institute for Cuban and Cuban-American Studies
1531 Brescia Avenue
Coral Gables, FL 33124

Assistant to the Editor: Susel Pérez

Description and Interests: *Cuban Affairs* is a digital publication that represents a variety of viewpoints on contemporary Cuba and the Cuban American community. Topics include economic, political, and social issues. Updated quarterly, it seeks dynamic and informative articles, as well as book reviews. Hits per month: Unavailable.
Website: www.cubanaffairsjournal.org

Freelance Potential: 90% written by nonstaff writers. Of the freelance submissions published yearly; 10% are by unpublished writers, 10% are by authors who are new to the magazine, 80% are by experts. Receives 2 unsolicited mss monthly.

Submissions and Payment: Sample copy and guidelines available at website. Send complete ms. Accepts hard copy and email to cubanaffairs@miami.edu. Responds in 1 month. Rights vary. Articles, 10–15 pages double-spaced. No payment.

Culinary Trends

503 Vista Bella, Suite 216
P.O. Box 2239
Oceanside, CA 92057

Founding Editor: Linda Mensinga

Description and Interests: Professional chefs are the main audience for this magazine, published six times each year. Each issue shares information on industry trends, original recipes, and profiles of chefs and restaurants. Circ: 10,000.
Website: www.culinarytrends.net

Freelance Potential: 50% written by nonstaff writers. Publishes 15–20 freelance submissions yearly; 10% by authors who are new to the magazine. Receives 1–2 queries monthly.

Submissions and Payment: Sample copy at website. Guidelines available. Query with artwork. Accepts email queries to editor@culinarytrends.net. Responds in 2 weeks. All rights. Articles, 1,500–2,000 words, plus recipes. Depts/columns, 700–1,000 words. Digital images at 300 dpi. All material, payment rates vary. Pays on publication. Provides 1 contributor's copy.

Culture

P.O. Box 1064
Lynnfield, MA 01940

Editor in Chief: Elaine Khosrova

Description and Interests: "The Word on Cheese" is the subtitle of this quarterly on all things cheese and cheese making. It is distributed nationally via supermarkets, specialty stores, box stores, and bookstores. Topics extend to profiles, travel, other food and drinks, business development, and entertaining. Circ: Unavailable
Website: www.culturecheesemag.com

Freelance Potential: Open to editorial inquiries.

Submissions and Payment: Sample articles available at website. A recent issue included articles on cheese recipes from America's best new chefs, British hard cheeses, the effects of seasonal changes on cheese making, dry Irish stouts, travel pieces on Los Angeles and Catalonia, and charities that support dairies around the world. Query to Editor in Chief Elaine Khosrova at editor@culturecheesemag.com.

CutBank

Department of English, LA 133
University of Montana
Missoula, MT 59812

Editor in Chief: Andrew Martin

Description and Interests: Appearing twice each year, *CutBank* offers top-notch prose and poetry that is global in scope, but with a regional bias. Emerging and established writers alike are featured. Circ: 1,000.
Website: www.cutbankonline.org

Freelance Potential: 90% written by nonstaff writers. Publishes 40 freelance submissions yearly; 30% by unpublished writers, 60% by new authors. Receives 70 unsolicited mss monthly.

Submissions and Payment: Sample material and guidelines available at website. Send complete ms with cover letter and author bio between October 1 and February 15 only. Accepts online submissions via website and simultaneous submissions if identified. Responds in 2–4 months. First North American serial and electronic rights. Prose, to 10,000 words. Poetry, to 5 poems per submission. Digital images at 300 dpi. No payment. Provides 2 contributor's copies.

Daily Science Fiction

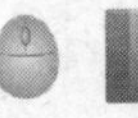

Editor: Jonathan Laden

Description and Interests: Speculative fiction is the specialty of this online publication. Updated regularly, it publishes science fiction, fantasy, slipstream, dark fantasy, and other subgenres. It is particularly looking for flash fiction. No horror or erotica. Publication is by email, on the website, via RSS, and through Kindle, iPhone, and iPad. Circ: Unavailable
Website: www.dailysciencefiction.com

Freelance Potential: Not available.

Submissions and Payment: Sample articles and guidelines available at website. Send complete ms. Accepts submissions via website. No multiple or simultaneous submissions. First worldwide rights and non-exclusive reprint rights for story anthologies. Fiction, to 10,000 words. Payment, $.08 per word. Anthologies payment, $.05 per word. Payment policy varies. Responds in 3 weeks.

Decline

25006 Avenue Kearny
Valencia, CA 91355

Editor: Alan Davis

Description and Interests: First published in 2003 and appearing 10 times each year, *Decline* is a lifestyle magazine for mountain bikers. It provides well-illustrated coverage of biking destinations and events, as well as mountain bike reviews and profiles of bikers. Circ: 40,000+.
Website: www.declinemagazine.com

Freelance Potential: 50–70% written by nonstaff writers. Of the freelance submissions published yearly, 20% are by unpublished writers, 20% are by authors who are new to the magazine, and 60% are by experts. Receives 10–20 queries each month.

Submissions and Payment: Sample copy available at website. Guidelines available. Send complete ms. Accepts disk submissions with 2 hard copies. Response time varies. All rights. Articles and depts/columns, word lengths and payment rates vary. Digital photos at 300 dpi. Payment policy varies. Provides 1 contributor's copy.

Denver Quarterly

University of Denver
Department of English
2000 East Asbury
Denver, CO 80208

Editor: Bin Ramke

Description and Interests: This quarterly literary journal publishes poetry and short fiction. It also features interviews with writers and nonfiction articles about the craft and process of writing. Circ: 2,000.
Website: www.denverquarterly.com

Freelance Potential: 100% written by nonstaff writers. Publishes 150 freelance submissions yearly; 5% by unpublished writers, 20% by authors who are new to the magazine. Receives 50 queries, 100 unsolicited mss monthly.

Submissions and Payment: Sample copy available. Guidelines available at website. Send complete ms between September 15 and May 15. Accepts hard copy. SASE. Responds in 2–8 weeks. First rights. Articles and fiction, to 15 pages. Poetry, no line limits; 3–5 poems per submission. Written material, $10 per published page. Pays on publication. Provides 2 contributor's copies.

Diabetes Health

365 Bel Marin Keys Boulevard, Suite 100
Novato, CA 94949

Editor in Chief: Nadia Al-Samarrie

Description and Interests: Information on the latest diabetes research, as well as stories about diabetics successfully managing their condition, combine to meet this publication's goal to "investigate, inform, and inspire." *Diabetes Health* appears six times each year. Circ: 125,000.
Website: www.diabeteshealth.com

Freelance Potential: 25% written by nonstaff writers. Publishes 10 freelance submissions yearly; 5% by unpublished writers, 10% by authors who are new to the magazine, 85% by experts. Receives 3 unsolicited mss monthly.

Submissions and Payment: Sample articles and guidelines available at website. Send complete ms. Accepts email to editor@diabeteshealth.com (Word attachments). Responds in 1 month. Rights vary. Articles, to 1,500 words; payment rates vary. Payment policy varies. Provides 2 contributor's copies.

Dialogue

P.O. Box 5181
Salem, OR 97304-0181

Editor: B. T. Kimbrough

Description and Interests: Created for the blind and visually impaired, this quarterly (published in large-print, braille, audio cassette, and electronic formats) features practical pieces and personality profiles. It is seeking articles from deaf/blind authors and parents of visually impaired children. Circ: 1,000.
Website: www.blindskills.com

Freelance Potential: 80% written by nonstaff writers. Publishes 60 freelance submissions yearly; 20% by unpublished writers, 15% by authors who are new to the magazine, 30% by experts. Receives 20 queries, 5 mss monthly.

Submissions and Payment: Sample articles and guidelines available at website. Editorial calendar available. Prefers query; will accept complete ms. Prefers email to magazine@blindskills.com; will accept hard copy. SASE. Responds if interested. First North American serial rights. Articles, to 1,000 words; $15–$35. Pays on publication. Provides 1 contributor's copy.

Dimensions

DECA, Inc.
1908 Association Drive
Reston, VA 20191

Editor: Christopher Young

Description and Interests: *Dimensions* is a quarterly educational journal for high school DECA students. It has the appeal of a commercial magazine for teens with editorial content that has educational substance. Topics include personal finance, marketing, sales, and business. Circ: 176,000.
Website: www.deca.org

Freelance Potential: 25% written by nonstaff writers. Publishes 6–8 freelance submissions yearly; 50–75% by authors who are new to the magazine.

Submissions and Payment: Sample copy available. Editorial calendar available at website. Query or send complete ms. Accepts hard copy, Macintosh disk submissions, and email to deca_dimensions@deca.org. SASE. Response time varies. First North American serial rights. Articles, 800–1,200 words. Depts/columns, 400–600 words. Written material, payment rates vary. Pays on publication.

Dimensions of Early Childhood

Southern Early Childhood Association
P.O. Box 55930
Little Rock, AR 77215-5930

Editor: Janet Brown

Description and Interests: This refereed professional journal focuses on early childhood issues, including infant, toddler, and school-aged programs; classroom practices; and education-related public policy. It is published three times each year for members of the Southern Early Childhood Association. Circ: 19,000.
Website: www.southernearlychildhood.org

Freelance Potential: 99% written by nonstaff writers. Publishes 40 freelance submissions yearly; 90% by unpublished writers, 80% by authors who are new to the magazine. Receives 3–4 mss monthly.

Submissions and Payment: Guidelines available at website. Send complete ms. Accepts email to editor@southernearlychildhood.org (attach file). No simultaneous submissions. Responds in 3–4 months. All rights. Articles, 5–16 pages. No payment. Provides 2 contributor's copies.

Dirt Rider

1733 Alton Parkway, Suite 100
Irvine, CA 92606

Editor: Jimmy Lewis

Description and Interests: The world of dirt bikes and dirt bike racing is covered in its entirety in this monthly magazine. It features articles about riding techniques, tips from the pros, reviews on new bikes, and coverage from competitions and other events across the country. In addition, it features interviews with professional and up-and-coming riders, and profiles of major races and tracks. Event coverage is a good way to get your foot in the door here. Circ: 121,000.
Website: www.dirtrider.com

Freelance Potential: 10% written by nonstaff writers. Publishes 20 freelance submissions yearly.

Submissions and Payment: Guidelines available. Query. Accepts hard copy. SASE. Response time varies. Rights vary. Articles, word lengths vary. 5x5 JPEG images at 300 dpi. All material, payment rates vary. Pays on publication. Provides 1 contributor's copy.

Diversity Employers

140 Carondelet Street
New Orleans, LA 70130

Editor: Stewart Ikeda

Description and Interests: This publication, a career and self-development magazine for those looking for employers recruiting a diverse workforce, represents a new name and new editorial direction for the former *Black Collegian* magazine. Published twice each year, it includes information on job opportunities, potential employers, and interviewing skills. Circ: 121,000.
Website: www.diversityemployers.com

Freelance Potential: 95% written by nonstaff writers. Publishes 20 freelance submissions yearly; 1% by unpublished writers, 33% by authors who are new to the magazine. Receives 5 queries monthly.

Submissions and Payment: Sample copy available at website. Send complete ms. Accepts electronic submissions via www.imdiversity.com. Response time varies. One-time rights. Written material, word lengths and payment rates vary Pays on publication. Provides contributor's copies.

Dossier

673 St. John's Place
Brooklyn, NY 11216

Editor: Katherine Krause

Description and Interests: Published twice each year, *Dossier* is a journal of arts and culture that accepts fiction, poetry, fashion, art, interviews, and even articles on culinary pursuits. It has no themes or guidelines, preferring instead to reflect the talents of its contributors. Circ: 10,000.
Website: www.dossierjournal.com

Freelance Potential: 90% written by nonstaff writers. Publishes 20–25 freelance submissions yearly; 60% by authors who are new to the magazine. Receives 5 unsolicited mss monthly.

Submissions and Payment: Sample copy available at website. Send complete ms. Accepts email submissions to submissions@dossierjournal.com. Responds in 4–6 weeks. All rights. Articles, fiction, and depts/columns; word lengths and payment rates vary. Payment policy varies.

Double Dealer Redux 

624 Pirate's Alley
New Orleans, LA 70116

Editor: Rosemary James

Description and Interests: Published by the Pirate's Alley Faulkner Society, this annual journal features literary work by developing and established writers. Published to coincide with the group's Words and Music Festival, it accepts poetry, short stories, and essays. Winners and finalists of its writing competition are given priority for publication. Circ: 7,500.
Website: www.wordsandmusic.org

Freelance Potential: 100% written by nonstaff writers. Publishes 50 freelance submissions yearly; 25% by unpublished writers, 25% by authors who are new to the magazine.

Submissions and Payment: Sample copy available. Send complete ms. Accepts email queries to info@wordsandmusic.org. Response time varies. One-time rights. Fiction, to 2,500 words. No payment. Provides 25 contributor's copies.

Downstate Story 

1825 Maple Ridge
Peoria, IL 61614

Publisher/Fiction Editor: Elaine Hopkins

Description and Interests: This regionally focused literary journal spotlights the finest work of writers and artists living in Illinois and the Midwest. Annual issues offer short fiction and narratives with a Midwestern perspective. Circ: 250.
Website: www.wiu.edu/users/mfgeh/dss

Freelance Potential: 100% written by nonstaff writers. Publishes 10 freelance submissions yearly; 50% by unpublished writers, 80% by authors who are new to the magazine. Receives 13–16 unsolicited mss each month.

Submissions and Payment: Sample copy available. Guidelines available at website. Send complete ms before June 30. Accepts hard copy and simultaneous submissions if identified. SASE. Responds in the fall of each year. First rights. Fiction, to 2,000 words; $50. Pays on acceptance.

Draft Magazine

300 W. Clarendon Avenue, Suite 155
Phoenix, AZ 85013

Managing Editor: Jessica Daynor

Description and Interests: *Draft Magazine* provides current, accurate, and creative coverage of beer and other areas of life six times each year. Enjoyed by mostly male readers, it features articles on beer/brewery trends, beer and food pairings, travel, sports, and leisure. All published reviews of beer are written in-house. Circ: 275,000.
Website: www.draftmag.com

Freelance Potential: 60% written by nonstaff writers. Publishes 80 freelance submissions yearly.

Submissions and Payment: Sample copy available. Guidelines available at website. Query with outline, sources, and two published clips (PDF files). Accepts email queries to jessica.daynor@draftmag.com. Responds in 1 month. All or first and electronic rights. Articles, 250–2,500 words; $.50–$.90 per word. Depts/columns, 350–950 words; $.50–$.80 per word. Pays on publication.

Dressage Today

656 Quince Orchard Road, Suite 600
Gaithersburg, MD 20878

Editor: Patricia Lasko

Description and Interests: Equine enthusiasts interested in the sport of dressage turn to this magazine for training tips, competition techniques, and profiles of the people and horses that make dressage exciting. *Dressage Today* is published monthly. Circ: 45,000.
Website: www.equisearch.com/magazines/dressage-today/

Freelance Potential: 30% written by nonstaff writers. Publishes 30 freelance submissions yearly; 1% by unpublished writers, 1% by authors new to the magazine, 98% by experts.

Submissions and Payment: Sample copy and guidelines available. Query or send complete ms. Accepts hard copy and email submissions to dressage.today@equinetwork.com. SASE. Responds in 2–4 months. All rights. Articles, to 2,500 words. Depts/columns, 900 words. Written material, payment rates vary. Provides 2 contributor's copies, plus tearsheets.

The Driver

4936 Yonge Street, Suite 509
Toronto, Ontario M2N 6S3
Canada

Editor: Paul Johnson Byrne

Description and Interests: *The Driver* is Canada's foremost automotive lifestyle magazine. It is published six times each year and specializes in car reviews, events, and one-on-one interviews with leading figures in the automotive industry. Circ: 38,500.
Website: www.thedriver.ca

Freelance Potential: 80% written by nonstaff writers. Publishes 50 freelance submissions yearly; 6% by unpublished writers, 12% by authors who are new to the magazine, 70% by experts. Receives 8 queries monthly.

Submissions and Payment: Sample copy and guidelines available. Query. Accepts email queries via website. Responds in 1 week. First rights. Articles, 700–2,000 words. Depts/columns, 1,000 words. Written material, $.20 per word. Pays on publication.

Ducks Unlimited

1 Waterfowl Way
Memphis, TN 38120-2351

Editor in Chief: Matt Young

Description and Interests: Directed at both wetlands conservationists and duck and goose hunters, this magazine offers a mix of reports on waterfowl habitat preservation and hunting tips, techniques, and stories. It appears six times each year. Circ: 600,000.
Website: www.ducks.org

Freelance Potential: 20% written by nonstaff writers. Publishes 15 freelance submissions yearly; 5% by unpublished writers, 5% by authors who are new to the magazine, 5% by experts. Receives 4–5 queries monthly.

Submissions and Payment: Sample articles available at website. Query. Accepts email queries to adelaurier@ducks.org. Responds in 4–6 weeks. First North American serial rights. Features, to 2,500 words; $800. News briefs, 50–200 words; $150+. Kill fee, 50%. Pays on publication. Provides 2 contributor's copies.

Early American Life

P.O. Box 221228
Shaker Heights, OH 44122-0996

Executive Editor: Jeanmarie Andrews

Description and Interests: This magazine focuses on American history, from the nation's founding to its antebellum years, with an emphasis on decorative arts. Carefully researched, informative articles explore topics, including home furnishings, antiques, architecture, and studio crafts. It also features travel pieces. *Early American Life* appears seven times each year. Circ: 100,000.
Website: www.earlyamericanlife.com

Freelance Potential: 70% written by nonstaff writers. Publishes 25 freelance submissions yearly; 10% by authors who are new to the magazine.

Submissions and Payment: Guidelines available at website. Query. Accepts hard copy (mark "Editorial Query" on envelope) and email to queries@firelandsmedia.com. Response time varies. Exclusive rights for 6 months. Articles, 750–2,500 words; $500+. Kill fee. Pays on acceptance.

East End Lights

11-4040 Creditview Road
P.O. Box 188
Mississauga, Ontario L5C 3Y8
Canada

Publisher: Kevin Bell

Description and Interests: This magazine is published quarterly, with insider information for Elton John fans. It highlights current tour information, news items, and recording release dates. Circ: 1,500.
Website: www.eastendlightsmagazine.com

Freelance Potential: 60% written by nonstaff writers. Publishes 10 freelance submissions yearly; 20% by unpublished writers, 20% by authors who are new to the magazine, 20% by experts. Receives 20 queries, 2 unsolicited mss monthly.

Submissions and Payment: Guidelines available. Query or send complete ms. Accepts hard copy and email to editor@eastendlightsmagazine.com. SAE/IRC. Responds in 2 months. First rights. Articles, 400–1,000 words; $20–$250. Depts/columns, word lengths vary; $20–$50. Pays 1 month after acceptance. Provides contributor's copies upon request.

Eastern Woods & Waters

30 Damascus Road, Suite 209
Bedford, Nova Scotia B4A 0C1
Canada

Editor and Publisher: Jim Gourlay

Description and Interests: *Eastern Woods & Waters* is a magazine in which expert fishermen, hunters, writers, and photographers present information about eastern Canada's outdoors. Published quarterly, it features informative and entertaining articles about the region's outdoor pursuits. Circ: 21,500.
Website: www.easternwoodsandwaters.ca

Freelance Potential: 85% written by nonstaff writers. Publishes 60 freelance submissions yearly; 15% by authors who are new to the magazine.

Submissions and Payment: Sample copy and guidelines available. Query with résumé, clips, and biographical note. Accepts email to editor@saltscapes.com. Responds in 1 month. First North American serial rights. Articles, 1,200–2,500 words. Depts/columns, 400 words. Written material, $.30–$.40 per word. Pays on publication.

Eating Well

Meredith Corporation
375 Lexington Avenue, 9th Floor
New York, NY 10017

Editorial Director: Lisa Gosselin
Nutrition Editor: Brierley Wright

Description and Interests: *Eating Well* is a glossy bimonthly now owned by Meredith Corporation. It covers healthy eating, cooking, nutrition science, food origins, and social issues, culture, and tradition related to food. It is journalistic in approach and emphasizes a base in science. Circ: 350,000.
Website: www.eatingwell.com

Freelance Potential: Welcomes ideas from new writers.

Submissions and Payment: Sample copy available. Detailed guidelines are available at the website, noting departments and sections that are particularly open, with editor emails. Send pitches via email to the appropriate editor. Describe your idea in 2–3 paragraphs, explaining why it is appropriate for the magazine; indicate your experience and topics that interest you. Do not send clips until requested. Responds in 1 month. Buys all rights. Payment, to $1 a word.

Ebony

Johnson Publishing Company
820 South Michigan Avenue
Chicago, IL 60605

Editor in Chief: Amy DuBois Barnett

Description and Interests: Published since 1945, today's *Ebony* covers music, culture, entertainment, style, health and fitness, sports, lifestyle, politics, current events, history, and issues of particular relevance to the African American community. Recent issues included articles on Black cancer-death disparities, a profile of entrepreneur Lisa Price, and how to retire young and rich. This African American general interest monthly has just undergone a redesign. Its companion publication is the *Jet*. Circ: 1.25 million.
Website: www.ebonyjet.com

Freelance Potential: Updating and redesigning indicate a vital, growing market.

Submissions and Payment: Sample copy available. Query. Accepts email to editors@ebony.com. Rights, payment rate, and payment policy, unknown.

Echo Ink Review

Fiction Editor: Don Balch
Poetry Editor: Maghan Lusk

Description and Interests: A small, independent journal, *Echo Ink Review* encourages up-and-coming writers. It looks for "surprising, precise language and dynamic character arcs and character-driven plots that resonate." The journal is looking for new and moderately established writers especially.
Website: www.echoinkreview.com

Freelance Potential: Publishes 20–25 mss a year. Receives 1,500 mss annually.

Submissions and Payment: Sample copy available. Guidelines available at website. Short fiction, 2,500–10,000 words. Flash fiction, 350–2,500 words. Poetry, 3–5 poems per submission. Reads and reviews submissions for free within 4 months, but also has expedited reading options for fees of $7.50 for a 30-day response, and $10 for 5 days. Submit via Submishmash, through the *Echo Ink Review* website. Accepts simultaneous submissions. Payment, $25 per accepted ms.

Eclectica Magazine

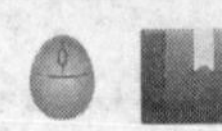

Editor: Tom Dooley

Description and Interests: Literary and genre works appear side by side in this online journal devoted to bringing the best writing to the Internet. Updated quarterly, *Eclectica* features fiction, creative nonfiction, poetry, interviews, reviews, humor, and drama. Hits per year: 4 million.
Website: www.eclectica.org

Freelance Potential: 95% written by nonstaff writers. Publishes 150–200 freelance submissions yearly; 40% by authors who are new to the magazine.

Submissions and Payment: Sample copy and guidelines available at website. Send complete ms. Accepts email submissions to submissions@eclectica.org (Word attachments). No simultaneous submissions except for poetry, interviews, and reviews. Response time varies. First North American serial and non-exclusive electronic rights. Written material, word lengths vary. Poetry, to 5 poems per submission. No payment.

Edible Communities

Founders: Tracey Ryder and Carole Topalian

Description and Interests: *Edible Communities* is a network of local food publications and websites across the U.S. and Canada. Its various locally owned publications share some articles and recipes, but also have distinct material as well, some by freelance writers. The focal point and commonality about the publications and websites is the local foods movement. Its magazines include *Edible Blue Ridge, Edible Boston, Edible Indy, Edible Nutmeg, Edible East Bay, Edible Hawaiian Islands,* and many more. Circ: Unavailable.
Website: www.ediblecommunities.com

Freelance Potential: Local magazines and sites through the communities use freelance material, varying by publication.

Submissions and Payment: Typical topics include profiles of local chefs or producers, and information about where certain foods are produced and how. See each individual *Edible* magazine website for contact and other information.

EFCA Today

418 Fourth Street NE
Charlottesville, VA 22902

Editor: Diane McDougall

Description and Interests: Now an online publication, *EFCA Today* aims to unify church leaders around the overall mission of the EFCA by bringing its stories and vision to life and generating conversations on topics pertinent to faith and contemporary life. Read by church lay leaders and pastors, it is updated weekly. Hits per month: Unavailable.
Website: www.efcatoday.org

Freelance Potential: 80% written by nonstaff writers. Publishes 40 freelance submissions yearly; 60% by unpublished writers, 40% by new authors, 5% by experts. Receives 20 queries monthly.

Submissions and Payment: Sample articles and guidelines available at website. Query with photo availability and sources. Accepts hard copy and email to editor@efca.org. SASE. Responds in 6 weeks. First and limited subsidiary rights. Articles, 300–800 words; $.23 per word. Kill fee, 50%. Pays on acceptance.

ELECTRICity

P.O. Box 43039
Philadelphia, PA 19129

Editor in Chief: Harry Jay Katz

Description and Interests: *ELECTRICity* is an online entertainment and leisure paper that is published weekly by National News Bureau. Each issue focuses on travel, beauty, fashion, theater, music, and food and wine. Hits per month: 60,000.
Website: www.nationalnewsbureau.com

Freelance Potential: 60% written by nonstaff writers. Publishes 100 freelance submissions yearly; 40% by unpublished writers, 10% by authors who are new to the magazine, 20% by experts. Receives 100 queries, 100 unsolicited mss each month.

Submissions and Payment: Guidelines available at website. Query. Accepts hard copy and email to nnbfeature@aol.com. SASE. Response time varies. All rights. Articles, and depts/columns, 1,500–2,500 words. Color or B/W images. Written material, payment rates vary. Pays on acceptance.

Ellipsis . . . Literature and Art

Westminster College
1840 South 1300 East
Salt Lake City, UT 84105

Poetry/Prose Editor

Description and Interests: The literary work of well-known, up-and-coming, and unpublished writers appears in this annual journal from Westminster College. It welcomes poetry, fiction, and creative nonfiction. Circ: Unavailable.
Website: www.westminstercollege.edu/ellipsis

Freelance Potential: 95% written by nonstaff writers. Publishes 65 freelance submissions yearly; 50% by unpublished writers, 90% by authors who are new to the magazine. Receives 250 mss monthly.

Submissions and Payment: Sample copy and guidelines available at website. Send complete ms with cover letter and brief bio between August 1 and November 1. Accepts submissions via website and simultaneous submissions. Response time varies. First serial rights. Prose, to 6,000 words; $50. Poetry, to 5 poems; $10. Pays on publication. Provides 2 contributor's copies.

Epoch

Cornell University
251 Goldwin Smith Hall
Ithaca, NY 14853

Editor: Michael Koch

Description and Interests: Published three times each year by the Department of English at Cornell University, this literary journal offers a mix of fiction, essays, and poetry on a wide range of themes. It steers clear of literary criticism in favor of creative expression. Personal essays continue to be the best opportunity for new authors. Circ: 1,500.
Website: www.arts.cornell.edu/english/publications/epoch/

Freelance Potential: 100% written by nonstaff writers. Publishes 45–50 freelance submissions yearly. Receives 1,000 unsolicited mss monthly.

Submissions and Payment: Sample copy and guidelines available. Send complete ms between September 15 and April 15 only. Accepts hard copy. No simultaneous submissions. SASE. Responds in 1 month. First North American serial rights. Word lengths vary. Payment, $5–$40 per printed page. Pays on publication.

Equal Opportunity

The Career Magazine for Minority Graduates

445 Broad Hollow Road, Suite 425
Melville, NY 11747

Editor: James Schneider

Description and Interests: *Equal Opportunity* is a career guidance magazine for minority graduates. Each of its three yearly issues is filled with information to help advance the professional interests of African Americans, Hispanics, Asian Americans, and Native Americans. Circ: 10,000.
Website: www.eop.com

Freelance Potential: 60% written by nonstaff writers. Publishes 20 freelance submissions yearly; 10% by unpublished writers, 20% by authors who are new to the magazine, 25% by experts. Receives 10 queries monthly.

Submissions and Payment: Sample articles and editorial calendar available at website. Guidelines available. Query with outline. Accepts email queries to jschneider@eop.com. Responds in 2 weeks. First rights. Articles, 1,000–2,000 words. Depts/columns, 500 words. Written material, $.10 per word. Pays on publication.

Equus

656 Quince Orchard Road, Suite 600
Gaithersburg, MD 20878

Editorial Director: Cathy Laws

Description and Interests: *Equus* magazine is a layman's publication focusing on equine health care, behavior, training techniques, veterinary breakthroughs, and exercise physiology. It appears monthly. Circ: 132,000.
Website: www.equisearch.com/magazines/equus/

Freelance Potential: 30% written by nonstaff writers. Publishes 24 freelance submissions yearly; 2% by unpublished writers, 10% by authors who are new to the magazine, 10% by experts. Receives 15 queries monthly.

Submissions and Payment: Sample copy available. Guidelines available at website. Send complete ms. Accepts hard copy and email submissions to EQletters@equinetwork.com. SASE. No simultaneous submissions. Responds in 3–6 months. All rights. Articles, 1,600–3,000 words. Depts/columns, 100–2,500 words. Written material, payment rates vary. Pays on acceptance. Provides 1 contributor's copy.

Espace

4888 Rue Saint-Denis
Montreal, Quebec H2J 2L6
Canada

Editor: Serge Fisette

Description and Interests: Understanding and appreciation of contemporary sculpture are fostered by *Espace,* Canada's only sculpture magazine. It provides readers with in-depth articles on artists and exhibitions, published in both English and French. It is produced quarterly. Circ: 1,400.
Website: www.espace-sculpture.com

Freelance Potential: 90% written by nonstaff writers. Publishes 40 freelance submissions yearly; 50% by unpublished writers, 50% by authors who are new to the magazine.

Submissions and Payment: Guidelines available at website. Send complete ms. Accepts email submissions to espace@espace-sculpture.com. Responds in 1 month. Rights vary. Articles, 1,000 words; $65 Canadian per page. B/W or color prints. Pays on publication. Provides 1 contributor's copy.

ESPN The Magazine 

ESPN Plaza
Bristol, CT 06010

Editor: Ryan Canner-O'Mealy

Description and Interests: ESPN The Magazine is for young men who want to stay on top of the athletes, team, topics, and upcoming events in their own sports world. It celebrates not only sports but the cultures and lifestyles that are an integral part of them. It is published twice each month. Circ: 2,059,269.
Website: www.espn.go.com/espnmag

Freelance Potential: Receives many queries monthly.

Submissions and Payment: Sample articles and editorial calendar available at website. Query. Accepts email to rcomealy@risemag.com. Response time varies. Written material, word lengths vary. Rights vary. Payment rates and policy vary.

Esquire

Hearst Magazines
300 West 57th Street
New York, NY 10019

Editor in Chief: David Granger

Description and Interests: *Esquire* is a monthly magazine for men who are interested in more than just photos of women. It is filled with articles on politics, culture, men's fashion, money management, and sports, as well as some articles on "hot" female celebrities. Circ: 700,000+.
Website: www.esquire.com

Freelance Potential: 30% written by nonstaff writers. Publishes 10–15 freelance submissions yearly; 5% by unpublished writers, 5% by new authors. Receives 300 queries, 300 unsolicited mss monthly.

Submissions and Payment: Sample copy available. Query with clips for nonfiction. Send complete ms for fiction. Accepts hard copy. SASE. Responds in 6 weeks. First North American serial rights. Articles and fiction, word lengths vary. Depts/columns, 2,000 words. Written material, $1.50–$2.50 per word. Pays on acceptance.

Essence

135 West 50th Street
New York, NY 10020

Editor in Chief: Constance White

Description and Interests: *Essence* is a monthly lifestyle magazine for African American women. Fashion, beauty, health, fitness, and relationships are among the topics covered. Circ: 1.2 million.
Website: www.essence.com

Freelance Potential: 30% written by nonstaff writers. Publishes 40 freelance submissions yearly; 1% by unpublished writers, 10% by authors who are new to the magazine, 2% by experts.

Submissions and Payment: Sample copy available. Guidelines and editorial calendar available at website. Query with concept and proposed length to appropriate section editor (listed at website). Accepts hard copy. SASE. Responds in 6–8 weeks. Internet and promotional rights. Articles, 1,200-3,000 words. Depts/columns, 600-800 words. Written material, $2 per word. Kill fee, 25%. Pays on acceptance. Provides 2 contributor's copies.

Ethical Living  

5 Losecoat Close
Stamford, Lincolnshire PE9 1DU
United Kingdom

Editor: Kim Marks

Description and Interests: An eco-friendly approach to women's issues is found in *Ethical Living*. This online publication covers the types of topics typically found in women's magazines—fashion, beauty, health, fitness, relationships, home decorating, and travel—but from an environmentally sustainable perspective. It also addresses social topics and issues related to fair trade. Hits per month: Unavailable.
Website: www.ethical-living.org

Freelance Potential: 70% written by nonstaff writers. Publishes 48 freelance submissions yearly; 20% by authors who are new to the magazine.

Submissions and Payment: Sample articles available at website. Query. Accepts email queries to hello@ethical-living.org. Response time varies. One-time rights. Written material, word lengths and payment rates vary. Pays on publication.

Euphony Journal 

5706 South University Avenue, Room 001
Chicago, IL 60637

Fiction or Poetry Editor

Description and Interests: The University of Chicago's literary journal presents poems, short stories, creative nonfiction, and essays that are crafted by writers with all levels of experience. It is published twice each year and accepts traditional and experimental forms. Circ: 700–1,000.
Website: www.euphonyjournal.com

Freelance Potential: 95% written by nonstaff writers. Publishes 60 freelance submissions yearly; 25% by unpublished writers, 80% by authors who are new to the magazine. Receives 20 unsolicited mss each month.

Submissions and Payment: Sample articles and guidelines available at website. Send complete ms. Accepts email submissions (Word attachments; check website for email address) and simultaneous submissions if identified. Responds in 3 months. Rights vary. Written material, word lengths vary. No payment. Provides 2 contributor's copies.

Evansville Review 

University of Evansville
Creative Writing Department
1800 Lincoln Avenue
Evansville, IN 47722

Editor in Chief: James Drury

Description and Interests: This annual journal from the University of Evansville offers literature in a broad range of styles on diverse topics. Short fiction, creative nonfiction, poetry, and short drama are accepted. Circ: 1,000.
Website: http://evansvillereview.evansville.edu

Freelance Potential: 99% written by nonstaff writers. Publishes 60 freelance submissions yearly; 5% by unpublished writers, 90% by authors new to the magazine. Receives 150 mss monthly.

Submissions and Payment: Sample copy available. Guidelines available at website. Send complete ms with brief author bio between September 1 and December 1 only. Accepts hard copy. SASE. Response time varies. Rights vary. Articles and fiction, to 10,000 words. Poetry, to 5 poems per submission. No payment. Provides 2 contributor's copies.

Event 

P.O. Box 2503
New Westminster, British Columbia V3L 5B2
Canada

Editor: Elizabeth Bachinsky

Description and Interests: The finest work of emerging and established writers appears in this literary journal. Fiction, creative nonfiction, poetry, and book reviews are offered in issues published three times each year. Circ: 1,100.
Website: http://eventmags.com

Freelance Potential: 100% written by nonstaff writers. Publishes 72–95 freelance submissions yearly; 25% by unpublished writers. Receives 150 unsolicited mss monthly.

Submissions and Payment: Guidelines available at website. Send complete ms with publishing credits. Query for book reviews. Accepts hard copy. SAE/IRC. Responds in 1–6 months. First North American serial and limited, non-exclusive digital rights. Fiction, to 5,000 words; to 2 stories per submission. Poetry, 3–8 poems per submission. Written material, $25+ per printed page. Pays on publication.

Ever

Rive Gauche Media Inc.
60 Bloor Street West, Suite 1106
Toronto, ON M4W 3B8

Publisher/Editor in Chief: Olivier Felicio

Description and Interests: Consumers with an interest in jewelry and fashion read this magazine for the latest in buying information, trends, and designs. Published six times each year, it features articles on the history, culture, and designers of jewelry. Circ: 42,500.
Website: www.evermagazine.ca

Freelance Potential: Receives many queries monthly.

Submissions and Payment: Sample copy available at website. Query. Accepts hard copy. Written material, word lengths vary. Rights vary. Payment rates and policy vary.

Farm and Ranch Living

5925 Country Lane
Greendale, WI 53129

Editor: Robin Hoffman

Description and Interests: Packed with photo-illustrated articles about present-day farm and ranch families, this magazine is written for and read by an audience that reads it not for profit, but for pure pleasure. Published six times each year, it seeks first-person narratives. Circ: 250,000.
Website: www.farmandranchliving.com

Freelance Potential: 90% written by nonstaff writers. Publishes 36 freelance submissions yearly; 50% by unpublished writers, 50% by authors who are new to the magazine. Receives 120 queries and mss monthly.

Submissions and Payment: Sample copy available. Guidelines available at website. Query or send complete ms. Accepts hard copy and email submissions to editors@farmandranchliving.com. SASE. Responds in 6 weeks. One-time rights. Articles, 1,500 words; $150–$300. Depts/columns, 350 words; $10–$75. Color prints or digital images at 300 dpi. Pays on publication. Provides 1 contributor's copy.

FellowScript

1301-2365 Lam Circle
Victoria, British Columbia V8N 6K8
Canada

Editor: Bonnie Way

Description and Interests: Articles that provide support, inspiration, and instruction to members of the InScribe Christian Writers' Fellowship are found in *FellowScript*. It is published quarterly. Circ: 200.
Website: www.inscribe.org

Freelance Potential: 100% written by nonstaff writers. Publishes 70 freelance submissions yearly; 2% by unpublished writers, 17% by authors who are new to the magazine, 1% by experts. Receives 4 unsolicited mss monthly.

Submissions and Payment: Sample copy available. Guidelines available at website. Send complete ms with word count. Accepts email submissions to fellowscript@gmail.com (Word attachments). Response time varies. First or one-time rights. Articles, 750–1,300 words; payment rates vary. Pays on publication.

The Fiddlehead

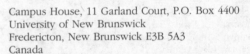

Campus House, 11 Garland Court, P.O. Box 4400
University of New Brunswick
Fredericton, New Brunswick E3B 5A3
Canada

Editor: Ross Leckie

Description and Interests: *The Fiddlehead* is Canada's longest living literary journal. It is published quarterly with short stories, poems, book reviews, and a small number of personal essays. Circ: 1,200.
Website: www.thefiddlehead.ca

Freelance Potential: The editors are open to submissions in English from throughout the world. Unsolicited submissions of fiction and poetry are especially welcome.

Submissions and Payment: Sample copy available. Send complete ms with cover letter, stated genre, and a 1- to 3-line bio about your writing career. Accepts hard copy. SAE/IRC. Responds in 3–9 months. First serial rights. Fiction, to 6,000 words; 1 submission at a time. Poetry, no line limit; 3–5 poems per submission. Written material, $40 Canadian per published page. Payment policy varies. Provides 2 contributor's copies.

Fiddler Magazine

P.O. Box 125
Los Altos, CA 94023

Editor: Mary Larsen

Description and Interests: Traditional and jazz fiddling are the focus of this quarterly magazine. Read by fiddlers of all levels, it addresses fiddling techniques and presents profiles of outstanding musicians. Circ: 2,500.
Website: www.fiddle.com

Freelance Potential: 100% written by nonstaff writers. Of the freelance submissions published yearly; 5% are by unpublished writers, 10% are by authors who are new to the magazine, and 80% are by experts. Receives 3–5 queries monthly.

Submissions and Payment: Sample articles available at website. Guidelines available. Query with writing samples. Accepts email queries to mary@fiddle.com (Word attachments). Responds in 1–2 weeks. First North American serial rights. Articles, 500–3,000 words. Fiction, 500–1,000 words. Written material, $50–$100. Pays on publication. Provides 3–5 contributor's copies.

Fifth Wednesday Journal

P.O. Box 4033
Lisle, IL 60532-9033

Editor: Vern Miller

Description and Interests: Original fiction, creative nonfiction, poetry, interviews, book reviews, and photography are offered in this literary journal, which appears twice each year. Circ: 600+.
Website: www.fifthwednesdayjournal.com

Freelance Potential: 100% written by nonstaff writers. Publishes 50+ freelance submissions yearly; 10% by unpublished writers, 80% by authors who are new to the magazine. Receives 300–350 mss monthly.

Submissions and Payment: Sample articles and guidelines available at website. Send complete ms between August and December, or between March and May. Accepts electronic submissions via website and simultaneous submissions if identified. Responds in 6 months. First North American serial rights. Fiction and nonfiction, 1,000–12,000 words. Poetry, no line limits; to 5 poems per submission. No payment. Provides 2 contributor's copies and a 1-year subscription.

Financial History

48 Wall Street
New York, NY 10005

Editor: Kristin Aguilera

Description and Interests: The Museum of American Finance publishes this quarterly magazine for its members. Articles focus on the financial history of the United States. Book reviews and profiles are also featured. Circ: 6,000.
Website: www.moaf.org

Freelance Potential: 90% written by nonstaff writers. Publishes 20 freelance submissions yearly; 10% by unpublished writers, 60% by authors who are new to the magazine, 80% by experts. Receives 10 queries monthly.

Submissions and Payment: Sample copy available. Guidelines provided upon query acceptance. Query. Accepts email queries to editor@moaf.org. Responds in 2 months. Worldwide rights. Articles, 2,500 words. Book reviews, 500 words. B/W or color JPEG or TIFF images at 300 dpi. Written material, $250. Pays on publication. Provides 10 contributor's copies.

Fine Tool Journal

P.O. Box 737, 9325 Dwight Boyer Road
Watervliet, MI 49098

Editor: Jim Gehring

Description and Interests: Collectors of antique hand tools are the niche market for this quarterly magazine. Each issue features pictures and descriptions of a variety of collectibles, while also providing articles on collecting, pricing, and upcoming auctions. Circ: 3,000.
Website: www.finetoolj.com

Freelance Potential: 75% written by nonstaff writers. Publishes 20 freelance submissions yearly; 20% by unpublished writers, 20% by authors who are new to the magazine. Receives 2 queries monthly.

Submissions and Payment: Sample copy and guidelines available. Query. Accepts hard copy. SASE. Responds in 2–4 months. First rights. Articles, 1,500–2,000 words; $100–$300. Depts/columns, 500 words; payment rates vary. Kill fee, $50. Payment policy varies. Provides 3 contributor's copies.

The First Line

Blue Cubicle Press
P.O. Box 250382
Plano, TX 75025-0382

Manuscript Coordinator: Robin LaBounty

Description and Interests: This quarterly literary journal demands one thing of all its submissions: they each begin with a specific opening line. It invites writers to explore where one simple sentence can take them. Circ: 2,000.
Website: www.thefirstline.com

Freelance Potential: 95% written by nonstaff writers. Publishes 40 freelance submissions yearly; 10% by unpublished writers, 75% by authors who are new to the magazine. Receives 200 unsolicited mss monthly.

Submissions and Payment: Sample copy available. Guidelines and opening lines available at website. Send complete ms with 2-sentence bio. Prefers email to submission@thefirstline.com; will accept hard copy. SASE. Response time varies. Rights negotiable. Articles, 500–800 words; $20. Fiction, 300–3,000 words; $30. Pays on publication. Provides 1 contributor's copy.

Flint Hills Review

Department of English, Box 4019
Emporia State University, 1200 Commercial Street
Emporia, KS 66801-5087

Editor: Kevin Rabas

Description and Interests: Quality short fiction, drama, and poetry are selected for this annual literary journal from Emporia State University. The editors are particularly seeking short plays and flash fiction. Circ: 350.
Website: www.emporia.edu/fhr

Freelance Potential: 90% written by nonstaff writers. Publishes 60 freelance submissions yearly; 15% by unpublished writers, 60% by new authors. Receives 25 queries, 25 unsolicited mss monthly.

Submissions and Payment: Guidelines available at website. Send complete ms. Accepts hard copy and simultaneous submissions if identified. SASE. Reads between January and March, responds in November. First North American serial rights. Fiction and nonfiction, to 25 pages. Poetry, 3–6 poems per submission. Short plays, to 10 minutes. B/W prints. No payment. Provides 1 contributor's copy.

The Florida Review

University of Central Florida, Department of English
P.O. Box 161346
Orlando, FL 32816

Editor: Jocelyn Bartkevicius

Description and Interests: In addition to poetry, fiction, and essays, this literary journal accepts interviews and book reviews. It is published twice each year. Circ: 1,000.
Website: www.floridareview.cah.ucf.edu/

Freelance Potential: 97% written by nonstaff writers. Publishes 1,000+ freelance submissions yearly; 10% by unpublished writers, 60% by authors who are new to the magazine. Receives 300 unsolicited mss each month.

Submissions and Payment: Guidelines available at website. Send complete ms between August and May. Accepts hard copy, submissions via website, and simultaneous submissions if identified. SASE. Responds in 3 months. First rights. Essays and fiction, to 25 pages. Poetry, 5 poems per submission. Book reviews and comics, word lengths vary. No payment. Provides 2 contributor's copies.

Flower Magazine

P.O. Box 530645
Birmingham, AL 35253

Editor: Margot Shaw

Description and Interests: This quarterly seeks to inspire and enrich its audience through the beauty of flowers. It is looking for contributions to its new Outside In department, which focuses on interior design. Circ: 27,000.
Website: www.flowermag.com

Freelance Potential: 85% written by nonstaff writers. Publishes 60 freelance submissions yearly; 5% by unpublished writers, 10% by authors who are new to the magazine. Receives 12 queries monthly.

Submissions and Payment: Sample copy available. Query with clips. Accepts email queries to editorial@flowermag.com. Responds in 1–2 months. First North American serial and electronic rights. Articles, 1,000–1,200 words; $400. Depts/columns, 600–900 words; $150–$300. JPEG images at 300 dpi. Kill fee, 20%. Pays on publication. Provides 2 contributor's copies.

Folio

Department of Literature
American University
4400 Massachusetts Avenue NW
Washington, DC 20016-8047

Administrative Coordinator: Catherine A. Johnson

Description and Interests: This literary journal, published by the College of Arts and Sciences at American University, accepts poetry, creative nonfiction, fiction, and art in all forms and genres. It appears annually. Circ: 500.
Website: www.american.edu/cas/literature/folio

Freelance Potential: 100% written by nonstaff writers. Publishes 20 freelance submissions yearly; 30% by unpublished writers, 90% by authors who are new to the magazine. Receives 100 mss monthly.

Submissions and Payment: Guidelines available at website. Submit complete ms via website with brief bio between August 10 and March 5. Accepts simultaneous submissions if identified. Responds in 2–6 months. First rights. Prose, to 5,000 words. Poetry, to 5 poems per submission. B/W prints or color slides. No payment. Provides 2 contributor's copies.

For Every Woman

General Council of the Assemblies of God
1445 North Boonville Avenue
Springfield, MO 65802

Editor: D. Hampton

Description and Interests: Christian-themed articles about issues affecting women of all ages are the focus of this online publication. Each month's articles center around a particular theme, such as careers, marriage, ministry, health, and volunteerism. Inspirational and motivational articles are welcome. Hits per month: 83,000.
Website: www.women.ag.org

Freelance Potential: 50% written by nonstaff writers. Of the freelance submissions published yearly, 80% are by unpublished writers, 10% are by authors who are new to the magazine. Receives 20–30 queries and mss monthly.

Submissions and Payment: Guidelines available. Query or send complete ms. Accepts email to dhampton@ag.org (Word attachments). Response time varies. One-time rights. Articles, 500–800 words. No payment.

Forge

1610 South 22nd Street
Lincoln, NE 68502

Editors: Leif Milliken and Melissa Wolfe

Description and Interests: Four online issues of *Forge* appear each year. It features short fiction, graphic novels, poetry, and music and media reviews. Art and illuminated letters are also covered. Hits per month: Approximately 200 unique views.
Website: www.forgejournal.com

Freelance Potential: 100% written by nonstaff writers. Publishes 80 freelance submissions yearly; 5–10% by unpublished writers, 80% by authors who are new to the magazine, 5% by experts. Receives 30–40 unsolicited mss monthly.

Submissions and Payment: Sample copy and guidelines, available at website. Send complete ms. Accepts email to forgejournal@gmail.com (with "Attention General Editor" or "Attention Poetry Editor" in subject line; attach file) and simultaneous submissions if identified. Responds in 3–4 months. Rights vary. Written material, word lengths vary. No payment.

Forward in Christ

2929 North Mayfair Road
Milwaukee, WI 53222

Executive Editor: Rev. John A. Braun

Description and Interests: The Wisconsin Evangelical Lutheran Synod publishes this monthly magazine for its members, although nonmember Christians are part of its readership. *Forward in Christ* offers articles on Christian living and the Bible, personal experience pieces, profiles, and interviews, as well as news on the activities of the Synod. Circ: 47,000.
Website: www.wels.net/forwardinchrist

Freelance Potential: 50% written by nonstaff writers. Publishes 150 freelance submissions yearly.

Submissions and Payment: Sample copy and guidelines available. Send complete ms. Accepts electronic submissions via website. No simultaneous submissions. Responds in 2 months. First print and electronic rights. Articles, 600–1,200 words; $75–$125. Pays on publication.

Foursquare.org

1910 West Sunset Boulevard, Suite 200
P.O. Box 26902
Los Angeles, CA 90026-0176

Editorial Director: Marcia Graham

Description and Interests: This ezine is published for members of the International Church of the Foursquare Gospel. Updated weekly, it offers news from Foursquare Churches and profiles of pastors. The purpose is to promote Christian values while bringing readers closer to God. Hits per month: Unavailable.
Website: www.foursquare.org

Freelance Potential: 50% written by nonstaff writers. Publishes 25 freelance submissions yearly; 5% by authors who are new to the magazine, 80% by experts. Receives 20 queries each month.

Submissions and Payment: Sample articles available at website. Query. Accepts hard copy and email queries to comm@foursquare.org. SASE. Responds in 1 month. All rights. Articles and depts/columns, word lengths and payment rates vary. Pays on publication.

Fourteen Hills: The SFSU Review

SFSU Creative Writing Department
1600 Holloway Avenue
San Francisco, CA 94132-1722

Fiction or Poetry Editor

Description and Interests: Twice each year, this journal from San Francisco State University publishes poetry, short stories, flash fiction, and experimental literature. It rarely publishes nonfiction. Circ: 1,500.
Website: www.14hills.net

Freelance Potential: 100% written by nonstaff writers. Publishes 50 freelance submissions yearly; 30% by unpublished writers, 80% by new authors. Receives 100 unsolicited mss monthly.

Submissions and Payment: Guidelines available at website. Send complete ms between February 1 and July 1 or September 1 and January 1. Accepts electronic submissions via website and simultaneous submissions. Responds in 5 months. First rights. Fiction, to 25 pages. Poetry, 3–5 poems per submission. No payment. Provides 1 contributor's copy.

4 Wheel Drive & Sport Utility Magazine

1733 Alton Parkway
Irvine, CA 92606

Editor in Chief: Phil Howell

Description and Interests: People who like off-road adventures and exploring the backcountry in their vehicles subscribe to this publication. It includes destination pieces, how-to's on vehicle maintenance, new product information, and updates about four-wheel drive clubs and their events. Circ: 25,733.
Website: www.4wdandsportutility.com

Freelance Potential: 30% written by nonstaff writers. Publishes 40–50 freelance submissions yearly; 50% by unpublished writers, 10% by authors who are new to the magazine.

Submissions and Payment: Guidelines provided upon acceptance of query. Query. Accepts hard copy. SASE. Response time varies. All North American serial and electronic rights. Articles and depts/columns, word lengths and payment rates vary. Pays on publication.

FreeFall

922 9 Avenue SE
Calgary, Alberta T2G 0S4
Canada

Editor: Micheline Maylor

Description and Interests: Calling itself "Canada's Magazine of Exquisite Writing," *FreeFall* is published twice each year by the FreeFall Literary Society of Calgary. It features fiction, poetry, creative nonfiction, author interviews, and reviews. Circ: Unavailable.
Website: www.freefallmagazine.ca

Freelance Potential: Open to submissions from throughout the world, but maintains an 85% commitment to Canadian content.

Submissions and Payment: Sample copy available. Guidelines available at website. Send complete ms for fiction and poetry. Query for interviews, book reviews, and essays. Deadlines: April 30 and August 31. All submissions must be accompanied by cover letter and 50-word author bio. Accepts hard copy and email to freefallmagazine@yahoo.ca. Response time varies. Rights vary. Prose, to 4,000 words; $10 per page, $100 maximum. Poetry, to 2–5 poems; $25 per poem. Pays on publication. Provides 1 contributor's copy.

The Free Press

Speaking Truth to Power

1021 East Broad Street
Columbus, OH 43205

Editor: Bob Fitrakis

Description and Interests: Sponsored by the Columbus Institute for Contemporary Journalism, *The Free Press* is an online forum for commentary, investigative reports, and news analysis from a progressive viewpoint. It is updated regularly. Hits per month: Unavailable.
Website: www.freepress.org

Freelance Potential: 100% written by nonstaff writers. Publishes 100+ freelance submissions yearly; 50% by unpublished writers, 20% by authors who are new to the magazine, 30% by experts. Receives 75 queries monthly.

Submissions and Payment: Writers' guidelines available at website. Send complete ms with brief author bio. Accepts email queries to submissions@freepress.org (Word attachments). Responds in 2–3 days if interested. Rights vary. Articles, 500–1,500 words. No payment.

Frigg

A Magazine of Fiction and Poetry

9036 Evanston Avenue North
Seattle, WA 98103

Editor: Ellen Parker

Description and Interests: Updated quarterly, this online literary magazine features cutting-edge, thought-provoking fiction and poetry. Hits per month: 8,000.
Website: www.friggmagazine.com

Freelance Potential: 100% written by nonstaff writers. Publishes 50 freelance submissions yearly; 10% by unpublished writers, 80% by authors who are new to the magazine. Receives 500 unsolicited mss each month.

Submissions and Payment: Sample copy and guidelines available at website. Send complete ms. Accepts email to webmaster@friggmagazine.com (indicate Fiction or Poetry Editor in subject line) and simultaneous submissions if identified. Responds in 2–12 weeks. One-time electronic rights. Fiction, to 8,000 words. Flash fiction, to 1,000 words. Poetry, to 5 poems per submission. No payment.

Garage Style Magazine

P.O. Box 812
La Habra, CA 90633-0812

Editor/Publisher: Don Weberg

Description and Interests: Automobile collectors and enthusiasts who want to house their cars in style are the target audience for this quarterly magazine. It depicts creative ways to shelter and showcase vintage and late-model cars. Profiles of car owners and product reviews are also part of the mix. The magazine is now beginning to cover automotive and transportation-themed office spaces. Circ: 10,000.
Website: www.garagestylemagazine.com

Freelance Potential: 10% written by nonstaff writers. Publishes 5 freelance submissions yearly; 5% by unpublished writers, 5% by authors who are new to the magazine, 5% by experts.

Submissions and Payment: Sample copy available. Query. Accepts email queries to don@garagestylemagazine.com. Response time varies. All rights. Articles and depts/columns, word lengths and payment rates vary. Pays on publication.

A Gathering of the Tribes

P.O. Box 20693, Tompkins Square Station
New York, NY 10009

Executive Director: Steve Cannon

Description and Interests: This literary journal publishes poetry, fiction, creative nonfiction, and occasional essays with an emphasis on multiculturalism and alternative viewpoints. *A Gathering of the Tribes* appears annually. Circ: 2,500.
Website: www.tribes.org

Freelance Potential: 100% written by nonstaff writers. Publishes 80–100 freelance submissions yearly; 15% by unpublished writers, 90% by new authors. Receives 200 unsolicited mss monthly.

Submissions and Payment: Guidelines available at website. Send complete ms. Accepts hard copy and email to tribes.editor@gmail.com (include "Submission" in subject line). SASE. Responds if interested. One-time rights. Poetry, to 5 poems. Prose, to 5,000 words, double spaced. Provides 1 contributor's copy and/or an honorarium.

Georgetown Review 

400 East College Street
Box 227
Georgetown, KY 40324

Prose or Poetry Editor

Description and Interests: This annual literary journal accepts fiction, creative nonfiction, and poetry, with no restrictions on style, content, or form. Circ: 2,200.
Website: http://georgetownreview.georgetowncollege.edu

Freelance Potential: 100% written by nonstaff writers. Publishes 15–20 freelance submissions yearly; 10% by unpublished writers, 100% by authors who are new to the magazine. Receives 400 unsolicited mss monthly.

Submissions and Payment: Sample articles and guidelines available at website. Send complete ms between September 1 and December 31 only. Accepts hard copy and simultaneous submissions if identified. SASE. Responds in 3 months. First North American serial rights. Articles and fiction, word lengths vary. Poetry, to 20 pages. No payment. Provides 2 contributor's copies.

The Golfer

59 East 72nd Street
New York, NY 10021

Associate Editor: Loren Zhimanskova

Description and Interests: Passionate golfers are the target audience for this upscale magazine. Published six times a year, it focuses not only on the game of golf, but also on the lifestyle that goes along with it. *The Golfer* covers equipment, courses and destinations, resorts, and living the good life. Circ: 250,000.
Website: www.thegolfermag.com

Freelance Potential: 70% written by nonstaff writers. Publishes 15 freelance submissions yearly; 15% by unpublished writers, 25% by authors who are new to the magazine.

Submissions and Payment: Sample copy available. Query or send complete ms. Accepts email submissions to loren@thegolfermag.com. Response time varies. All rights. Written material, word lengths and payment rates vary. Payment policy varies. Provides contributor's copies upon request.

GolfNews Magazine

P.O. Box 1040
Rancho Mirage, CA 92274

Editor in Chief: Dan Poppers

Description and Interests: All aspects of golf are covered in *GolfNews*, but its editors place a premium on high-quality, creative writing and welcome essays and other creative works. It is published nine times each year. Circ: 14,000.
Website: www.golfnewsmag.com

Freelance Potential: 45% written by nonstaff writers. Publishes 10 freelance submissions yearly; 10% by unpublished writers, 10% by authors who are new to the magazine, 80% by experts. Receives 8–10 queries; 3–5 unsolicited mss monthly.

Submissions and Payment: Sample copy available at website. Query or send complete ms. Accepts hard copy and email to danpoppers@aol.com. SASE. Responds in 1–2 weeks. First North American rights. Written material, word lengths and payment rates vary. High-resolution, color digital images. Pays on acceptance. Provides contributor's copies.

Good Life Living Green Magazine

#317-1489 Marine Drive
West Vancouver, British Columbia V7T 1B8
Canada

Editor: Connie Ekelund

Description and Interests: Distributed free with national daily papers across Canada, this magazine offers ideas, information, and inspiration for living an eco-friendly, sustainable lifestyle. Published quarterly, it focuses on green consumer products and environmentally friendly industries and businesses. Circ: 100,000.
Website: www.goodlifelivinggreen.com

Freelance Potential: 95% written by nonstaff writers. Publishes 100–200 freelance submissions yearly; 50% by authors who are new to the magazine.

Submissions and Payment: Sample copy available at website. Query with clips; or send complete ms. Accepts hard copy and email to info@fusionpublishing-inc.com. SASE. Response time varies. First rights. Articles and depts/columns, word lengths and payment rates vary. Payment policy varies.

Good Times

Transcontinental Media Inc.
25 Sheppard Avenue West, Suite 100
Toronto, Ontario M2N 6S7
Canada

Editor in Chief: Murray Lewis

Description and Interests: "Canada's Lifestyle Magazine for Successful Retirement" is published 11 times each year with articles designed to help readers plan for and make the most of their retirement. A mix of financial management, health, home and garden, and travel destination articles are published here. Circ: 160,000.
Website: www.goodtimes.ca/

Freelance Potential: Open to freelance submissions. Material that has Canadian content and a positive tone is given preference.

Submissions and Payment: Sample copy available. Guidelines available at website. Query with explanation of article focus, outline, and potential sources. Accepts hard copy and email to editor@goodtimes.ca. Response time varies. Articles and depts/columns, 750–2,500 words. Payment information unavailable.

Grain

P.O. Box 67
Saskatoon, Saskatchewan S7K 3K1
Canada

Editor: Rilla Friesen

Description and Interests: Canadian and international writers find a home for their work in this quarterly journal of eclectic writing. Submissions should be engaging, surprising, and challenging. Circ: 1,100.
Website: www.grainmagazine.ca

Freelance Potential: 98% written by nonstaff writers. Publishes 120 freelance submissions yearly; 60% by unpublished writers, 75% by authors who are new to the magazine. Receives 15 queries, 250 unsolicited mss monthly.

Submissions and Payment: Sample copy available. Guidelines available at website. Query or send complete ms between September 1 and May 31. Accepts hard copy. SAE/IRC. Responds in 3–6 months. First Canadian serial rights. Fiction, to 5,000 words; limit 2 stories per submission. Literary nonfiction, to 5,000 words. Poetry, to 12 pages per submission. Written material, $50–$225 Canadian. Pays on publication. Provides 2 contributor's copies.

Grand Magazine

4791 Baywood Point Drive South
St. Petersburg, FL 33711

Publisher: Christine Crosby

Description and Interests: Described as "the online magazine for grandparents," *Grand Magazine* reports on a wide range of topics, including the role of grandparents, raising grandchildren, relationships, intergenerational travel, and health. Interviews with celebrities, as well as profiles of notable grandparents, are also regularly featured. The ezine appears six times each year. Hits per month: Unavailable.
Website: www.grandmagazine.com

Freelance Potential: 60% written by nonstaff writers. Receives 100 queries monthly.

Submissions and Payment: Guidelines available at website. Query. Accepts email to ccrosby@grandmagazine.com. Response time 48 hours. Rights vary. Written material, word lengths and payment rates vary. Kill fee, 20%. Pays on acceptance.

Grasslimb

P.O. Box 420816
San Diego, CA 92142

Editor: Valerie Polichar

Description and Interests: This international journal of art and literature publishes poetry, prose, artwork, and book and music reviews. It is published in tabloid format twice each year. Circ: 200.
Website: www.grasslimb.com/journal/

Freelance Potential: Open to submissions on all topics, though material regarding romance, sex, aging, and children is less likely to be selected. Fiction in an avant-garde or experimental mode is favored over a traditional story.

Submissions and Payment: Sample articles and guidelines available at website. Send complete ms. Accepts hard copy, email to editor@grasslimb.com (text, Word, RTF, or AppleWorks attachments), and simultaneous submissions if identified. Responds in 4 months. First print serial rights. Prose, to 2,500 words; $10–$70. Reviews, 500–1,000 words; $15–$25. Poetry, no line limit, to 4–6 poems per submission; $5–$20 per poem. Pays on acceptance. Provides 2 contributor's copies.

Gray Areas

5838 West Olive Avenue, C-105
PMB 624
Glendale, AZ 85302

Editor in Chief: Netta Gilboa

Description and Interests: Founded on the belief that in life there is no black and white, only gray areas, this magazine publishes articles and essays on controversial subjects. It appears sporadically, but aims for a quarterly publication schedule. Circ: 10,000.
Website: www.grayarea.com

Freelance Potential: 80% written by nonstaff writers. Publishes 60–75 freelance submissions yearly; 30% by unpublished writers, 60% by authors who are new to the magazine, 10% by experts. Receives 100 queries, 50 unsolicited mss monthly.

Submissions and Payment: Sample copy available. Guidelines available at website. Query or send complete ms. Prefers disk submissions with hard copy; will accept hard copy and simultaneous submissions if identified. SASE. Responds in 1 week. One-time rights. Written material, word lengths vary. No payment. Provides 5 contributor's copies.

Great American Patriot

7405 Greenback Lane, #129
Citrus Heights, CA 95610

Publisher: Rev. Paul V. Scholl

Description and Interests: Published online exclusively, *Great American Patriot* offers a conservative perspective on current affairs, politics, and history. It puts a strong emphasis on patriotism, religious values, and military service. In addition to opinion pieces, profiles, interviews, and informative features, it presents short fiction that is inspirational, historical, or humorous. Hits per month: 30,000.
Website: www.greatamericanpatriot.com

Freelance Potential: 90% written by nonstaff writers.

Submissions and Payment: Guidelines available. Send complete ms. Accepts email submissions to publisher@greatamericanpatriot.com (Word attachments). Responds in 1 month. Rights vary. Articles and depts/columns, 500–750 words. No payment.

Greatest Uncommon Denominator

GUD Publishing
P.O. Box 1537
Laconia, NH 03247

Editor: Kaolin Fire

Description and Interests: High-quality writing and content that pushes the envelope characterize the fiction and poetry in this literary magazine. It also features interviews and well-researched reports on topical issues. *GUD* appears twice each year. Circ: 400.
Website: www.gudmagazine.com

Freelance Potential: 100% written by nonstaff writers. Publishes 50 freelance submissions yearly; 50% by unpublished writers, 90% by new authors. Receives 500 unsolicited mss monthly.

Submissions and Payment: Guidelines available at website. Send complete ms via website. Response time varies. First world print and electronic rights. Articles and fiction, to 15,000 words. Poetry, 1 poem per submission. Payment rates vary. Pays on publication.

The Green Hills Literary Lantern

English Department, McClain Hall
Truman State University
Kirksville, MO 63501

Fiction: Jack Smith; Poetry: Joe Benevento
Nonfiction: Adam Brooke Davis

Description and Interests: *The Green Hills Literary Lantern* showcases poetry; fiction; and creative nonfiction, including essays, memoirs, and travel pieces. Published and unpublished writers are encouraged to submit. Hits per month: Unavailable.
Website: http://ghll.truman.edu

Freelance Potential: 100% written by nonstaff writers. Publishes 75 freelance submissions yearly; 5% by unpublished writers, 70% by authors new to the magazine. Receives 80 unsolicited mss monthly.

Submissions and Payment: Guidelines available at website. Send complete ms with author biography. Accepts hard copy. SASE. Digital submissions to ids@truman.edu. Responds in 3–4 months. One-time rights. Fiction and nonfiction, to 7,000 words. Poetry, to 7 poems per submission. No payment.

Green Mountains Review

337 College Hill
Johnson, VT 05656

Editor/Poetry Editor: Elizabeth Powell

Description and Interests: Literary writing in a wide range of styles appears in this twice-yearly journal, including fiction, creative nonfiction, and poetry. Circ: 1,500.
Website: http://greenmountainsreview.com/

Freelance Potential: 100% written by nonstaff writers. Publishes 80 freelance submissions yearly; 10% by unpublished writers, 60% by authors who are new to the magazine. Receives 250 unsolicited mss each month.

Submissions and Payment: Guidelines available at website. Submit from September 1 to March 1. Send complete ms. Accepts hard copy and electronic submissions. SASE. Responds in 3–6 months. First serial rights. Fiction, 200–1,000 words. Poetry, no line limits. Written material, $25. Pays on publication. Provides 2 contributor's copies and a 1-year subscription.

The Greensboro Review

MFA Writing Program at UNC Greensboro
3302 HHRA Building
Greensboro, NC 27402-6170

Editor: Jim Clark

Description and Interests: Fiction and poetry in all styles and on all subjects can be found in this journal. Published twice each year, it welcomes literary work created by new and unpublished writers. Circ: 1,000.
Website: www.greensbororeview.org

Freelance Potential: 100% written by nonstaff writers. Of the freelance submissions published yearly; 10% are by unpublished writers and 90% are by new authors. Receives 150 unsolicited mss monthly.

Submissions and Payment: Sample articles and guidelines available at website. Send complete ms by September 15 or February 15. Accepts hard copy and electronic submissions via website. No simultaneous submissions. SASE. Responds in 3 months. First serial rights. Fiction, to 7,500 words. Poetry, no line limits, 5–7 poems per submission. No payment. Provides 3 contributor's copies.

Guitar World

28 East 28th Street, 12th floor
New York, NY 10016

Managing Editor: Jeff Kitts

Description and Interests: *Guitar World* has long been the go-to source for information and inspiration for professional guitar players and serious amateurs. It has recently revamped both its print edition and website, with a goal of making them both easier to use. The editorial content continues to focus on contemporary music artists—with artist profiles, playing tips, music and performance reviews, and information on guitars and equipment. Circ: 150,000.
Website: www.guitarworld.com

Freelance Potential: Query for current freelance needs. May use some submissions on its website.

Submissions and Payment: Sample articles available at website. For submission information, query to Managing Editor at jeffkitts@aol.com. Written material, word lengths and payment rates vary. Payment policy varies.

Gulf Stream

English Department
Florida International University
3000 NE 151st Street
North Miami, FL 33181-3000

Editor: James Elens

Description and Interests: Produced twice each year by the Creative Writing Program at FIU, this journal features an array of fiction, poetry, essays, book reviews, and interviews. Circ: 200.
Website: www.gulfstreamlitmag.com

Freelance Potential: 100% written by nonstaff writers. Publishes 36 freelance submissions yearly; 5% by unpublished writers, 90% by authors who are new to the magazine. Receives 100 mss monthly.

Submissions and Payment: Sample copy and guidelines available at website. Send complete ms with bio between September 15 and November 15, or January 15 and March 15. Accepts submissions via website and simultaneous submissions. Responds in 3–6 months. First serial rights. Prose, to 10,000 words. Poetry, to 5 poems per submission. No payment. Provides 2 contributor's copies and a 1-year subscription.

Hand/Eye Magazine

P.O. Box 921
Shelter Island, NY 11964

Editor: Keith Recker

Description and Interests: This magazine explores design and creativity from a perspective of cultural, commercial, and environmental ethics. Its articles cover design as a tool for creative expression and income generation, but also as a platform for environmental, ethical, and social progress. Profiles of artists, exhibitions, and "inspired" retailers are also offered. It appears quarterly. Circ: Unavailable.
Website: www.handeyemagazine.com

Freelance Potential: Editors report they are eager to expand the magazine's network of correspondents. A list of story ideas they would like to see developed can be found at the website.

Submissions and Payment: Sample articles and editorial calendar available at website. Send ms; or query with detailed summary and writing samples. Accepts email to editor@handeyemagazine.com. Response time varies. Word lengths vary. No payment at this time, but it plans to become a paying market in the future.

Hanging Loose

231 Wyckoff Street
Brooklyn, NY 11217

Editor: Robert Hershon

Description and Interests: Contemporary, literary, and experimental fiction can be found in *Hanging Loose*, one of the nation's oldest continuously published literary journals. It also features poetry and includes a section that highlights the work of high school students. It appears twice each year. Circ: 2,000.
Website: www.hangingloosepress.com

Freelance Potential: 100% written by nonstaff writers. Publishes 60 freelance submissions yearly; 20% by unpublished writers, 50% by authors who are new to the magazine.

Submissions and Payment: Sample copy available. Guidelines available at website. Send complete ms. Accepts hard copy. No simultaneous submissions. SASE. Responds in 3 months. Rights vary. Poetry, to 6 poems per submission. Written material, payment rates vary. Pays on acceptance. Provides 2 contributor's copies.

Hardboiled

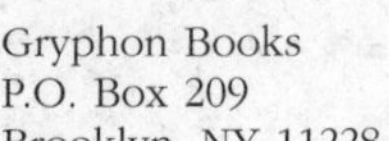

Gryphon Books
P.O. Box 209
Brooklyn, NY 11228

Editor: Gary Lovisi

Description and Interests: Writers of cutting-edge crime fiction may find a home for their work in *Hardboiled,* which appears two times each year. Short crime stories with shock endings are sought for this magazine, which also offers reviews and articles about real-life mysteries. Circ: 1,000.
Website: www.gryphonbooks.com

Freelance Potential: 95% written by nonstaff writers. Publishes 10–30 freelance submissions yearly; 10% by unpublished writers, 50% by new authors. Receives 30 queries, 100 mss monthly.

Submissions and Payment: Sample copy and guidelines available. Query for nonfiction. Send complete ms for fiction. Accepts hard copy. SASE. Responds to queries in 1 month, to mss in 2 months. All rights. Articles, word lengths vary. Fiction, 500–5,000 words. Written material, $5–$50. Pays on publication. Provides 2 contributor's copies.

Harpur Palate

English Department
Binghamton University
P.O. Box 6000
Binghamton, NY 13902-6000

Fiction, Nonfiction, or Poetry Editor

Description and Interests: For more than 10 years, this journal has offered fiction, poetry, and creative nonfiction to a readership interested in fine literature. The editors would like to review more flash fiction. It is published twice a year. Circ: 750.
Website: http://harpurpalate.binghamton.edu

Freelance Potential: 100% written by nonstaff writers. Publishes 90–120 freelance submissions yearly; 5–10% by unpublished writers, 60% by authors who are new to the magazine. Receives 200 mss each month.

Submissions and Payment: Sample copy available. Guidelines available at website. Send complete ms. Prefers submissions via website; will accept hard copy and simultaneous submissions if identified. SASE. Responds in 4–8 months. First North American serial and electronic rights. Prose, to 8,000 words. Poetry, to 10 pages. No payment. Provides 2 contributor's copies.

Hawai'i Review

2445 Campus Road, Hemenway Hall 107
Honolulu, HI 96822

Editor in Chief: Rachel Wolf

Description and Interests: Students of the University of Hawaii at Manoa comprise the staff of this literary journal, published twice a year. While some of its content focuses on Hawaii and the Pacific, it offers a variety of themes and welcomes submissions from around the world. Circ: 500.
Website: www.kaleo.org/hawaii_review/

Freelance Potential: 100% written by nonstaff writers. Publishes 35–50 freelance submissions yearly; 50% by unpublished writers, 95% by authors who are new to the magazine. Receives 30 mss monthly.

Submissions and Payment: Sample copy available. Guidelines available at website. Send complete ms. Accepts hard copy and email to hawaiireview@gmail.com (Word attachments). SASE. Responds in 4–6 months. First North American serial rights. Interviews and reviews to 10,000 words. Fiction and nonfiction, to 9,000 words. Poetry, to 6 poems. No payment. Provides 1 contributor's copy.

Hayden's Ferry Review

Arizona State University
P.O. Box 875002
Tempe, AZ 85287-5002

Prose or Poetry Editor

Description and Interests: Short stories, novel excerpts, nonfiction, poetry, and translations are found in this literary journal, published twice yearly by Arizona State University. Circ: 1,400.
Website: www.asu.edu/piper/publications/haydensferryreview/

Freelance Potential: 98% written by nonstaff writers. Publishes 75 freelance submissions yearly; 20% by unpublished writers, 70% by authors new to the magazine. Receives 600 mss monthly.

Submissions and Payment: Articles and guidelines available at website. Send complete ms. Accepts electronic submissions via website and simultaneous submissions if identified. Responds in 3–4 months. First serial rights. Articles and fiction, word lengths vary. Poetry, to 6 poems per submission. No payment. Provides 2 contributor's copies and 1-year subscription.

HBCU Connect On Campus

750 Cross Pointe Road, Suite Q
Gahanna, OH 43230

Editor: Elynor Moss

Description and Interests: Targeting students and alumni of historically black colleges and universities, this publication serves as a social network and offers readers comprehensive career information for a number of fields, including technology, public affairs, the arts, and education. It is published twice each year. Circ: 100,000.
Website: www.hbcuconnect.com

Freelance Potential: 80% written by nonstaff writers. Publishes 10 freelance submissions yearly; 5% by unpublished writers, 80% by authors who are new to the magazine, 15% by experts.

Submissions and Payment: Sample copy and guidelines available. Send complete ms. Accepts email to oncampus@hbcuconnect.com. Responds in 1 day. All rights. Written material, word lengths and payment rates vary. Pays on publication. Provides several contributor's copies.

The Health Wyze Report

142 Redwood Drive
Mocksville, NC 27028

Editor: Thomas Corriher

Description and Interests: *The Health Wyze Report* covers alternative health issues from the standpoint that God has provided, in nature, all that is necessary for a long and healthy life, and that pharmaceuticals cause more harm than good. An ezine, it also posts inspirational stories that appeal to its primary readership of Christian women, ages 19–40. It is updated on an irregular basis. Hits per month: 4,960,000.
Website: http://healthwyze.org

Freelance Potential: 10% written by nonstaff writers. Publishes 25 freelance submissions yearly. Receives 4 unsolicited mss monthly.

Submissions and Payment: Sample copy and guidelines available at website. Send complete ms. Accepts email submissions to sarah@healthwyze.org. Response time varies. Non-exclusive reprint rights.

Heroes & Heartbreakers

Submissions

Description and Interests: This website, run by romance publisher Heroes and Heartbreakers, is home to original short romance stories in all subgenres, including contemporary, paranormal/urban fantasy, women's fiction, historical, and romantic suspense. Hits per month: Unavailable.
Website: www.heroesandheartbreakers.com

Freelance Potential: The editors welcome submissions of romance stories in all subgenres, but they are not interested in true confessions or other nonfiction material. Opportunities also exist for writers wishing to blog on the site; query with your writing interests to blogging@heroesandheartbreakers.com.

Submissions and Payment: Sample stories and guidelines available at website. Send complete ms with cover letter explaining subgenre of story and writing experience. Accepts email to submissions@heroesandheartbreakers.com and simultaneous submissions. Response time varies. Rights vary. Fiction, 6,000–15,000; $1,000 against a 25% royalty (for downloadable versions). Payment policy varies.

Hobby Farms

P.O. Box 8237
Lexington, KY 40533

Editor: Stephanie Staton

Description and Interests: Articles of interest to people who live on small and hobby farms appear in this magazine, published six times each year. It focuses on rural lifestyle issues, such as small farm equipment and country cooking, as well as on raising livestock. Circ: 110,000.
Website: www.hobbyfarms.com

Freelance Potential: 75% written by nonstaff writers. Publishes 40 freelance submissions yearly; 10% by new authors.

Submissions and Payment: Sample copy and guidelines available at website. Query with writing samples between January 1 and April 1. Accepts hard copy and email to hobbyfarms@bowtieinc.com. No simultaneous submissions. SASE. Responds in 6–8 weeks. First North American serial rights. Articles, 2,000–2,500 words; $300+. Happenings, to 500 words; $50–$75. Color slides and digital images, payment rates vary. Pays on publication.

Hogan's Alley

P.O. Box 47684
Atlanta, GA 30362

Editor: Tom Heintjes

Description and Interests: Appearing annually in print, but updated regularly online, *Hogan's Alley* pays homage to the cartoon arts through articles on everything from the art of editorial cartooning to the historical strips that paved the way for modern artists. It publishes interviews with and articles about cartoonists and currently seeks biographical pieces. Circ: 5,000.
Website: http://cartoonician.com

Freelance Potential: 80% written by nonstaff writers. Publishes 4 freelance submissions yearly; 20% by authors who are new to the magazine, 80% by experts. Receives 5 queries monthly.

Submissions and Payment: Sample copy available. Query with outline. Accepts email queries to hoganmag@gmail.com. Responds in 1 month. First North American serial and electronic rights. Articles and depts/columns, word lengths and payment rates vary. Pays on publication. Provides 3 contributor's copies.

Home Planet News

P.O. Box 455
High Falls, NY 12440

Editor: Donald Lev

Description and Interests: Published up to three times a year, this journal targets independent-minded readers who love books, poetry, and small presses. It publishes short fiction, poetry, and book reviews. Circ: 1,000.
Website: www.homeplanetnews.org

Freelance Potential: 90% written by nonstaff writers. Publishes 90 freelance submissions yearly; 5% by unpublished writers, 25% by authors who are new to the magazine. Receives 2 queries, 40 mss monthly.

Submissions and Payment: Guidelines available at website. Send complete ms. No simultaneous submissions. Accepts hard copy. SASE. Responds in 4 months. First rights. Articles, 5,000 words. Fiction, 3,000 words. Poetry, no line limits. No payment. Provides 3 contributor's copies and a 1-year subscription.

Home Times Family Newspaper

P.O. Box 22547
West Palm Beach, FL 33416

Editor: Dennis Lombard

Description and Interests: This bimonthly covers current events, such as science, sports, entertainment, and education, all from a positive, biblical perspective that reflects traditional American values. Fiction and short poetry are sometimes featured. It especially seeks humorous takes on history and politics. Circ: 4,000.
Website: www.hometimes.org

Freelance Potential: 50% written by nonstaff writers. Publishes 10–12 freelance submissions yearly; 10% by authors who are new to the magazine, 30% by experts. Receives 5–10 unsolicited mss monthly.

Submissions and Payment: Sample copy and guidelines available. Send complete ms. Accepts hard copy, reprints, and simultaneous submissions if identified. SASE. Responds in 1 month. One-time and electronic rights. Articles and depts/columns, 500–1,000 words. Fiction, 500–1,200 words. Written material, payment rates vary. Pays on publication.

The Hopkins Review 

Johns Hopkins University
3400 North Charles Street
Baltimore, MD 21218

Editor: John T. Irwin

Description and Interests: *The Hopkins Review* offers a balanced mix of poetry, short fiction, essays on literature, and memoirs. This quarterly also publishes reviews of books, performances, and exhibits. Circ: Unavailable.
Website: www.press.jhu.edu/journals/the_hopkins_review/

Freelance Potential: 80% written by nonstaff writers. Publishes 8–10 freelance submissions yearly; 5% by unpublished writers, 15% by authors who are new to the magazine. Receives 50 unsolicited mss monthly.

Submissions and Payment: Sample articles and guidelines available at website. Send complete ms between September and April; indicate genre. Accepts hard copy. No simultaneous submissions. SASE. Responds in 1–4 months. First and electronic rights. Articles, to 30 pages. Fiction, to 40 pages. Poetry, to 5 poems per submission. Payment rates and policy vary. Provides 1 contributor's copy.

Horizons

100 Witherspoon Street
Louisville, KY 40202-1396

Assistant Editor: Yvonne Hileman

Description and Interests: Issues of interest to Presbyterian women are covered in this magazine, appearing six times each year. Designed to both inform and inspire, it is published in thematic issues. Circ: 25,000.
Website: www.pcusa.org/horizons

Freelance Potential: 80% written by nonstaff writers. Publishes 1–2 freelance submissions yearly; 15% by new authors. Receives 10 queries, 20 unsolicited mss monthly.

Submissions and Payment: Sample copy, guidelines, and editorial calendar available at website. Send complete ms. Accepts hard copy, email to yvonne.hileman@pcusa.org, or faxes to 502-569-8085. Responds in 3 months. All rights. Written material, 600–1,800 words; $50+ per page. Kill fee, 50%. Pays on publication. Provides 2 contributor's copies.

The Horn Book Magazine

56 Roland Street, Suite 200
Boston, MA 02129

Editor in Chief: Roger Sutton

Description and Interests: Six times each year, *The Horn Book Magazine* provides insight into children's book publishing with reviews, opinions, and articles on writing. It also features commentaries, poetry, sketches, and comics. Circ: 8,000.
Website: www.hbook.com

Freelance Potential: 70% written by nonstaff writers. Publishes 12–15 freelance submissions yearly; 10% by unpublished writers, 30% by authors who are new to the magazine, 90% by experts. Receives 12 unsolicited mss monthly.

Submissions and Payment: Sample copy and guidelines available at website. Send complete ms. Accepts hard copy and email to magazine@hbook.com (include "Article Submission" in subject line). SASE. Responds in 3 months. One-time rights. Articles, to 2,500 words. Payment rates vary. Pays on publication. Provides 3 contributor's copies.

Horse & Rider

2520 South 55th Street, Suite 210
Boulder, CO 80301

Managing Editor: Jennifer Paulson

Description and Interests: This monthly magazine is read by Western riders and trainers for its expertly written articles. It covers topics, such as equine health, behavior, and breeding. It also features interviews with notable men and women in the field. Circ: 160,020.
Website: www.horseandrider.com

Freelance Potential: 15% written by nonstaff writers. Publishes 20–30 freelance submissions yearly; 3% by unpublished writers, 1% by authors who are new to the magazine, 80% by experts. Receives 10 queries monthly.

Submissions and Payment: Guidelines available at website. Query with outline. Accepts disk submissions and email queries to jpaulson@aimmedia.com. No simultaneous submissions. SASE. Responds in 3 months. All rights. Articles, 600–1,200 words. Depts/columns, to 900 words. Written material, $25–$400. Payment policy varies. Provides 1 contributor's copy.

Horse Illustrated

P.O. Box 8237
Lexington, KY 40533

Editor: Elizabeth Moyer

Description and Interests: *Horse Illustrated* promotes responsible horse ownership through in-depth articles on topics ranging from equine health to training tips for riders. Both English and Western disciplines are covered in this photo-filled monthly magazine. Most columns and breed profiles are assigned to established writers. Circ: 161,613.
Website: www.horsechannel.com

Freelance Potential: 80% written by nonstaff writers. Publishes 50 freelance submissions yearly. Receives 10 queries, 5 unsolicited mss each month.

Submissions and Payment: Guidelines available at website. Prefers complete ms with digital images; will accept query with detailed outline, sample paragraphs, and clips. Accepts hard copy. No simultaneous submissions. SASE. Responds in 2–3 months. First serial rights. Articles, to 2,000 words. Depts/columns, 200–1,400 words. Written material, $50–$425. Pays on publication. Provides 2 contributor's copies.

Hot Rod

831 South Douglas Street
El Segundo, CA 90245

Editor: David Freiburger

Description and Interests: *Hot Rod* appeals to the car enthusiast with its in-depth coverage of high-performance cars and trucks. This includes technical tips, racing news, event coverage, new product information, and driver profiles. Published monthly, it accepts submissions from writers with extensive knowledge of hot rods and the race circuit. Circ: 654,000.
Website: www.hotrod.com

Freelance Potential: 15% written by nonstaff writers. Publishes 24 freelance submissions yearly. Receives 20 queries monthly.

Submissions and Payment: Guidelines available at website. Query. Accepts hard copy. SASE. Responds in 1 week. All rights. Articles and depts/columns, word lengths vary. B/W or color prints or 35mm color transparencies. All material, payment rates vary. Pays on publication. Provides 3 contributor's copies.

Hunger Mountain

Vermont College of Fine Arts
36 College Street
Montpelier, VT 05602

Editor: Miciah Bay Gault

Description and Interests: Once each year, the Vermont College of Fine Arts presents *Hunger Mountain*, a collection of poetry, literary fiction, nonfiction, and reproductions of a wide variety of artwork. Circ: 1,000.
Website: www.hungermtn.org

Freelance Potential: 100% written by nonstaff writers. Publishes 30 freelance submissions yearly; 10–15% by unpublished writers, 80% by authors who are new to the magazine. Receives 200 unsolicited mss monthly.

Submissions and Payment: Guidelines available at website. Send complete ms. Accepts submissions via website and simultaneous submissions. Responds in 4 months. First worldwide serial rights. Fiction and nonfiction, to 10,000 words; $5 per page, $30 minimum. Poetry, to 3–10 poems; payment rates vary. Pays on publication. Provides 2 contributor's copies.

IAE Magazine (I Am Entertainment)

P.O. Box 440232
Kennesaw, GA 30160

Editor in Chief: Shaine Freeman

Description and Interests: Published six times each year, *I Am Entertainment* was established in 2009 as an ezine and moved into print in 2011. It provides informational and educational articles to aspiring entertainment industry professionals in the fields of film, music, TV, gaming, and sports. Its content focuses on industry news and what it takes to succeed in "the biz," plus profiles of successful performers and other professionals who have made it big. Circ: 100,000 print and digital.
Website: www.iaemagazine.com/magazine.html

Freelance Potential: Very open to submissions by writers familiar with the film, TV, music, gaming, or sports industries.

Submissions and Payment: Sample copy available at website. Send complete ms. Accepts email submissions to info@iaemagazine.com. Response time varies. Payment information unknown.

ID: Ideas and Discoveries

Bauer Publishing Group
270 Sylvan Avenue
Englewood Cliffs, NJ 07632

Editor: Sebastian Raatz

Description and Interests: Based on the successful German magazine titled *Welt De Wunder*, this magazine approaches the science and technology magazine category with an editorial balance of contemporary science, nature, the human body, psychology, history, and current events. It is published six times each year and plans to become a monthly. Circ: Unavailable.
Website: www.ideasanddiscoveries.com

Freelance Potential: The magazine looks for articles that offer a unique approach to the topics at hand.

Submissions and Payment: Sample articles available at website. For submission information, send email to questions@ideasanddiscoveries.com.

Illuminations

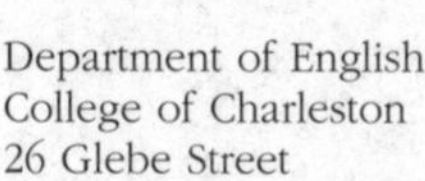

Department of English
College of Charleston
26 Glebe Street
Charleston, SC 29424

Editor: Meg Scott-Copses

Description and Interests: This international magazine of contemporary writing, published annually, features original fiction of many styles and forms, creative nonfiction, and poetry. Circ: 500.
Website: www.cofc.edu/illuminations

Freelance Potential: 100% written by nonstaff writers. Receives about 1,600 submissions of poetry and fiction yearly.

Submissions and Payment: Sample copy available. Guidelines available at website. Accepts hard copy and email to scottcopsesm@cofc.edu. Poetry, to 6 poems at a time; include name and contact information with each poem. Also accepts fiction and, occasionally, short prose. No simultaneous submissions. SASE. Response time varies. One-time rights; pays in contributor's copies.

Image

Art, Faith, Mystery

3307 Third Avenue West
Seattle, WA 98119

Editor in Chief: Gregory Wolfe

Description and Interests: The fiction, essays, reviews, and poetry that appear in this quarterly literary journal examine the relationship between religious and contemporary art and literature. The editors are interested in seeing more writing about film, theater, dance, and visual arts. Translations are also welcome. Circ: 4,500.
Website: www.imagejournal.org

Freelance Potential: 95% written by nonstaff writers. Publishes 75 freelance submissions yearly; 8% by unpublished writers, 50% by authors who are new to the magazine. Receives 100 unsolicited mss monthly.

Submissions and Payment: Guidelines available at website. Query or send complete ms. Accepts hard copy. SASE. Responds in 6 months. First serial rights. Written material, to 6,000 words; payment rates vary. Pays on acceptance. Provides 4 contributor's copies.

Indiana Review

Indiana University
Ballantine Hall 465
1020 East Kirkwood Avenue
Bloomington, IN 47405-7103

Fiction, Poetry, or Nonfiction Editor

Description and Interests: *Indiana Review* seeks well-crafted literary works that "have consequences beyond the world of their speakers or narrators." It offers fiction, nonfiction, poetry, and book reviews twice each year. Circ: 3,500.
Website: www.indianareview.org

Freelance Potential: 95% written by nonstaff writers. Publishes 50 freelance submissions yearly; 50% by unpublished writers, 80% by new authors. Receives 600 unsolicited mss monthly.

Submissions and Payment: Guidelines available at website. Send ms with short bio. Accepts hard copy, submissions via website, and simultaneous submissions if identified. SASE. Responds in 2–4 months. First rights. Prose to 8,000 words. Reviews, 500–800 words. Poetry, to 6 poems/12 pages. Written material, $5 per published page. Pays on publication. Provides 2 contributor's copies.

Indian Life Newspaper

P.O. Box 3765, Redwood Post Office
Winnipeg, Manitoba R2W 3R6
Canada

Editor: Jim Uttley

Description and Interests: Intertribal Christian Communications publishes this newspaper six times each year. It covers the social, spiritual, and cultural issues that affect members of the North American Indian Church. Native North American writers are preferred. Circ: 18,000.
Website: www.indianlife.org

Freelance Potential: 80% written by nonstaff writers. Publishes 40 freelance submissions yearly; 10% by unpublished writers, 40% by authors who are new to the magazine, 5% by experts. Receives 20 queries and unsolicited mss monthly.

Submissions and Payment: Sample copy and guidelines available at website. Prefers query; will accept complete ms. Accepts hard copy and email to ilmeditor@indianlife.org. SAE/IRC. Responds in 6 weeks. First rights. Articles, 250–2,000 words; $.15 per word. Pays on publication. Provides 3 contributor's copies.

Inkwell

Manhattanville College
2900 Purchase Street
Purchase, NY 10577

Poetry, Fiction, or Nonfiction Editor

Description and Interests: This literary journal appears twice each year, offering top-drawer writing, as well as artwork. Interviews of prominent literary figures are welcome. Circ: 500.
Website: www.inkwelljournal.org

Freelance Potential: 100% written by nonstaff writers. Publishes 44 freelance submissions yearly; 75% by unpublished writers, 15% by new authors. Receives hundreds of unsolicited mss monthly.

Submissions and Payment: Sample articles and guidelines available at website. Send complete ms with word count. Accepts hard copy (indicate genre and target issue) and electronic submissions via website. SASE for response only. Responds in 3–6 months. First North American serial rights. Prose, to 5,000 words. Poetry, to 70 lines; to 5 poems per submission. 4x6 B/W or color JPEGS. Written material, $10 per page. Pays on acceptance. Provides 2 contributor's copies.

Inns Magazine

P.O. Box 998
Guelph, Ontario N1H 6N1
Canada

Editor: Mary Hughes

Description and Interests: Inns, bed-and-breakfasts, and country resorts throughout North America are the focus of this travel and leisure magazine (formerly titled *North American Inns Magazine*). It is designed to give readers a resource for making their travel, wedding, or spa get-away plans. Each of its quarterly issues adhere to an individual theme. Writers who are able to offer a well-researched profile will be well received here. Circ: 21,000.
Website: www.innsmagazine.com

Freelance Potential: 15% written by nonstaff writers. Publishes 12 freelance submissions yearly; 60% by authors who are new to the magazine.

Submissions and Payment: Query. Accepts email to editor@harworthpublishing.com (Word attachments). Response time varies. First and electronic rights. Written material, 300–600 words; $50–$200. Pays on publication.

Instinct Magazine

303 North Glenoaks Boulevard, Suite L-120
Burbank, CA 91502

Editor in Chief: Mike Wood

Description and Interests: *Instinct Magazine* is written exclusively for gay men. Published monthly, it offers profiles and articles on relationships, health, and travel, as well as lifestyle features and reviews. Circ: 112,000.
Website: www.instinctmagazine.com

Freelance Potential: 25% written by nonstaff writers. Publishes 2 freelance submissions yearly; 30% by unpublished writers, 10% by authors who are new to the magazine, 60% by experts. Receives 50 unsolicited mss monthly.

Submissions and Payment: Sample copy available. Guidelines available. Send complete ms with clips. Accepts hard copy and simultaneous submissions if identified. SASE. Responds in 1 month. First and 90-day rights. Articles, 2,100–2,800; $50–$300. Kill fee, 20%. Pays on publication. Provides 1+ contributor's copies.

International Figure Skating

85 Quincy Avenue, Suite 2
Quincy, MA 02169

Executive Editor: Susan D. Russell

Description and Interests: Comprehensive coverage of the world of figure skating is found in this magazine, published six times each year. It provides news on skating personalities, as well as practical information for improving techniques. Circ: 40,000.
Website: www.ifsmagazine.com

Freelance Potential: 40–50% written by nonstaff writers. Publishes 180 freelance submissions yearly; 5% by authors who are new to the magazine, 5% by experts.

Submissions and Payment: Sample articles available at website. Guidelines available. Query with outline and word count. Accepts email queries to srussell@madavor.com. Response time varies. All rights. Articles, 1,200–1,500 words. Depts/columns, 200–400 words. Written material, $75 per published page. Pays on publication. Provides 1 contributor's copy.

International Gymnast

3214 Bart Conner Drive
Norman, OK 73072

Editor: Dwight Normile

Description and Interests: Published 10 times each year, this magazine spotlights worldwide professional and college-level gymnasts and tournaments. It also has training tips, product information, and a kids page. Circ: 12,000.
Website: www.intlgymnast.com

Freelance Potential: 10% written by nonstaff writers. Publishes 5 freelance submissions yearly; 50% by unpublished writers, 50% by authors who are new to the magazine. Receives 1 unsolicited ms monthly.

Submissions and Payment: Sample copy available. Send complete ms. Accepts hard copy and simultaneous submissions if identified. SASE. Responds in 1 month. All rights. Articles, 1,000–2,250 words. Depts/columns, 700–1,000 words. Fiction, to 1,500 words. Written material, $15–$25. Pays on publication. Provides 1 contributor's copy.

In the Wind

P.O. Box 3000
Agoura Hills, CA 91376-3000

Editor: Kim Peterson

Description and Interests: This distinctly adult magazine provides quarterly coverage of the motorcycle lifestyle—including bike events, parties, and women. It seeks event coverage that is both accurate and humorous. Circ: 52,300.
Website: www.easyriders–magazine.com

Freelance Potential: 25% written by nonstaff writers. Publishes 4 freelance submissions yearly; 85% by unpublished writers, 10% by authors who are new to the magazine, 50% by experts. Receives 50 queries, 30 mss monthly.

Submissions and Payment: Sample copy and guidelines available. Prefers query; will accept complete ms. Accepts email submissions to kpeterson@easyriders.net. Responds to queries in 3–6 weeks, to mss in 2 months. All rights. Articles and depts/columns, to 750 words; $100–$600. B/W and color slides and digital images; $30–$500. Pays on publication.

iPhone Life

Mango Life Media
110 North Court
Fairfield, IA 52556

Editor in Chief: Alex Cequa

Description and Interests: Written for users of iPhones, iPod Touches, and iPads, this magazine aims to help readers get the most from their devices. Its articles offer information, interviews, how-to's, and reviews regarding the devices, operating systems, and applications. It is published six times each year in print and a digital edition. Circ: 150,000.
Website: www.iphonelife.com

Freelance Potential: Very open to working with freelancers. Queries from iPhone enthusiasts who can give readers useful information are welcome.

Submissions and Payment: Sample articles and guidelines available at website. Query. Accepts queries via online form and email to alex@iphonelife.com. Response time varies. Articles, 600–1,200 words. Depts/columns, word lengths vary. No payment. Publishes author bio.

Irreantum

P.O. Box 581422
Salt Lake City, UT 84158

Editors: Jack Harrell & Josh Allen

Description and Interests: Literary and informative work exploring the Mormon experience is published here twice each year. It accepts articles, essays, fiction, poetry, and reviews. Circ: 300.
Website: www.irreantum.mormonletters.org

Freelance Potential: 90% written by nonstaff writers. Publishes 20–30 freelance submissions yearly; 25% by unpublished writers, 75% by new authors. Receives 10–20 mss monthly.

Submissions and Payment: Sample copy available. Guidelines available at website. Send complete ms. Articles and fiction are reviewed January 1 through May 31, and poetry, reviews, and critical essays are accepted year-round. Accepts email submissions only; check website for contact information (Word or RTF attachments; include genre in subject line). Responds in 2 months. One-time rights. Articles, to 5,000 words. Fiction, to 7,500 words. Depts/columns, 2,000 words. Poetry, to 100 lines. No payment. Provides 1 contributor's copy.

Irish Connections

305 Madison Avenue, Suite 1462
New York, NY 10165

Editor: Grahame Curtis

Description and Interests: This quarterly publication is for people of Irish descent with a strong attachment to their heritage. Its pages are filled with news and personalities centered on Irish business, entertainment, travel, and music. Also featured are historic articles of Irish interest. Circ: 35,000.
Website: www.irishconnectionsmagazine.com

Freelance Potential: 30% written by nonstaff writers. Publishes 5 freelance submissions yearly; 30% by unpublished writers. Receives 10 unsolicited mss monthly.

Submissions and Payment: Sample copy available at website. Send complete ms. Accepts hard copy and email to editorial@irishconnectionsmagazine.com. SASE. Response time varies. Rights vary. Articles and fiction, 1,500–2,500 words. Depts/columns, 1,000 words. Written material, $.10 per word. Pays on publication.

Italian America

219 E Street NE
Washington, DC 20002

Editor in Chief: Dona DeSanctis

Description and Interests: Produced by the Order Sons of Italy in America, this quarterly is dedicated to presenting Italian culture and history in America. It likes to see features on Italian American personalities from the past and present and reports on little-known chapters in Italian American history. Circ: 65,000.
Website: www.osia.org

Freelance Potential: 25% written by nonstaff writers. Publishes 12–15 freelance submissions yearly; 10% by unpublished writers, 10% by authors who are new to the magazine. Receives 10 queries monthly.

Submissions and Payment: Sample articles and guidelines available at website. Query (to 300 words). Accepts hard copy and email queries to ddesanctis@osia.org. SASE. Responds in 2 months. Worldwide non-exclusive rights. Articles, 750–1,000 words; $100–$250. Digital images at 300 dpi. Pays on acceptance. Provides 2 contributor's copies.

Italian Americana

University of Rhode Island-Providence
80 Washington Street
Providence, RI 02903-1803

Editor in Chief: Carol Bonomo Albright

Description and Interests: An international, peer-reviewed journal, *Italian Americana* publishes historical articles, fiction, creative nonfiction, and poetry that capture the Italian experience in the New World. It is printed twice each year. Circ: 1,000.
Website: www.italianamericana.com

Freelance Potential: 100% written by nonstaff writers. Publishes 10 freelance submissions yearly; 30% by unpublished writers, 80% by authors who are new to the magazine. Receives 5 unsolicited mss each month.

Submissions and Payment: Sample copy available. Guidelines available at website. Send 2 copies of complete ms; include email address. Accepts hard copy and email submissions to it.americana@yahoo.com. SASE. Responds in 4–6 weeks. First North American serial rights. Articles and fiction, to 20 double-spaced pages. No payment. Provides 1 contributor's copy.

Jabberwock Review

Department of English, Drawer E
Mississippi State University
Mississippi State, MS 39762

Fiction, Nonfiction, or Poetry Editor

Description and Interests: Published twice each year by the students and faculty of Mississippi State University, *Jabberwock Review* features the finest poetry and prose of all forms and styles. Circ: 1,000.
Website: www.jabberwock.org.msstate.edu/

Freelance Potential: 100% written by nonstaff writers. Publishes 30 freelance submissions yearly; 5–10% by unpublished writers, 50% by authors who are new to the magazine. Receives 120 unsolicited mss monthly.

Submissions and Payment: Guidelines available at website. Send complete ms with bio between August 15–October 20 or January 15–March 15. Accepts hard copy, electronic submissions, and simultaneous submissions. SASE. Responds in 3 months. First serial rights. Articles and fiction, word lengths vary. Poetry, to 5 poems. No payment. Provides 2 contributor's copies.

Jet

Johnson Publishing
820 South Michigan Avenue
Chicago, IL 60605

Editor in Chief: Mitzi Miller

Description and Interests: Both informative and entertaining, *Jet* magazine has been serving a loyal audience of African Americans since 1951. Entertainment, current events, sports, relationships, fashion, and culture are regularly covered here. It is published six times each year. When crafting a pitch, writers should detail why the story should be written now and why it would interest *Jet* readers. Circ: 700,000.
Website: www.jetmag.com

Freelance Potential: 55-60% written by nonstaff writers. Receives many freelance submissions monthly.

Submissions and Payment: Sample articles available at website. Send query with related clips. Accepts email to appropriate editor. Response time varies. Written material, word lengths vary. Universal rights. Payment rates vary. Pays on publication.

Jewish Currents

P.O. Box 111
Accord, NY 12404

Editor: Lawrence Bush

Description and Interests: Appearing quarterly with holiday supplements, this magazine carries on the insurgent tradition of the Jewish left through independent journalism, political commentary, and a countercultural approach to Jewish arts and literature. Circ: 4,000.
Website: http://jewishcurrents.org

Freelance Potential: 50% written by nonstaff writers. Publishes 8–12 freelance submissions yearly; 10% by unpublished writers, 30% by authors who are new to the magazine, 10% by experts. Receives 5 queries, 10 unsolicited mss monthly.

Submissions and Payment: Sample copy and guidelines available. Query or send complete ms. Accepts hard copy. SASE. Responds in 2 months. Rights negotiable. Articles, to 3,000 words. Depts/columns, word lengths vary. No payment. Provides 6 contributor's copies and a 1-year subscription.

J Journal

New Writing on Justice

John Jay College of Criminal Justice, Dept. of English
524 West 59th Street, 7th Floor
New York, NY 10019

Co-Editors: Adam Berlin & Jeffrey Heiman

Description and Interests: *J Journal* seeks fiction, personal essays, first person narratives, and poems that examine questions of justice. Though most pieces published relate tangentially to the justice theme, it also accepts work that speaks directly of crime, criminal justice, law, and law enforcement. It appears twice each year. Circ: 1,200.
Website: http://jjournal.org

Freelance Potential: 100% written by nonstaff writers. Publishes 50 freelance submissions yearly; 5% by unpublished writers, 80% by authors who are new to the magazine. Receives 50 unsolicited mss monthly.

Submissions and Payment: Guidelines available at website. Send complete ms. Accepts hard copy. Provide email address for reply. Response time varies. First serial rights. Fiction/nonfiction, to 6,000 words. Poetry, to 3 poems. No payment. Provides 2 contributor's copies.

Jones Magazine

321 West 44th Street, Suite 203
New York, NY 10036

Editor in Chief: Tracey M. Ferguson

Description and Interests: This quarterly magazine calls itself a "shopping guide for women who know better." Its target audience is affluent African American women with a love for the latest new looks in fashion and beauty. Each issue reveals hidden shopping treasures and informs readers on where to find the best of everything for themselves and their homes. Circ: 125,000.
Website: www.jonesmagazine.com

Freelance Potential: 40% written by nonstaff writers. Publishes 20 freelance submissions yearly; 35% by authors who are new to the magazine. Receives several queries monthly.

Submissions and Payment: Sample copy available at website. Query. Accepts email queries via website. Response time varies. Rights vary. Written material, word lengths vary. No payment. Provides 2 contributor's copies.

The Journal

Department of English
Ohio State University
164 West 17th Avenue
Columbus, OH 43210

Fiction, Poetry, or Nonfiction Editor

Description and Interests: This literary journal seeks quality fiction, poetry, and nonfiction of any type and of any length. It is published quarterly (two print issues and two digital issues) and also accepts reviews of new books of poetry. Circ: 1,500.
Website: http://thejournalmag.org

Freelance Potential: 99% written by nonstaff writers. Publishes 80 freelance submissions yearly; 50% by unpublished writers, 80% by authors who are new to the magazine. Receives 350 queries, 400 unsolicited mss monthly.

Submissions and Payment: Sample copy and guidelines available at website. Send complete ms. Accepts electronic submissions via website and simultaneous submissions if identified. Responds in 3–4 months. First rights. Prose, word lengths vary. Poetry, 3–6 poems per submission. No payment. Provides 2 contributor's copies and a 1-year subscription.

The Journal of Adventist Education

12501 Old Columbia Pike
Silver Spring, MD 20904-6600

Editor: Beverly Robinson-Rumble

Description and Interests: Seventh-day Adventist teachers and educational administrators around the world read this journal, which is published five times a year. It prefers articles that offer a call for action on a problem and suggestions for how to solve that problem. Circ: 22,000.
Website: http://jae.adventist.org

Freelance Potential: 85% written by nonstaff writers. Publishes 40 freelance submissions yearly. Receives 3–5 queries monthly.

Submissions and Payment: Guidelines available at website. Send complete ms with affiliation and author photo. Accepts disk submissions and email to rubleb@gc.adventist.org (Word or RTF attachments). Responds in 1–3 months. First North American serial rights. Articles, to 10 pages, 2,000 words. Digital images (JPEGs or TIFFs), prints or slides. Payment rates vary. Pays on publication. Provides 2 contributor's copies.

The Journey

5 Meadowlawn Drive, #3
Mentor, OH 44060

Editor: Clyde Chafer

Description and Interests: *The Journey* is a magazine of articles, resources, and essays relating to metaphysical and holistic topics. It seeks articles that are written from the author's own life experiences, as well as interviews, profiles, and media reviews. Each of its six issues each year is themed. Circ: 35,000.
Website: www.thejourneymag.com

Freelance Potential: 80% written by nonstaff writers. Publishes 55 freelance submissions yearly; 25% by authors who are new to the magazine.

Submissions and Payment: Guidelines and theme list available at website. Send complete ms with optional 75-word bio and photo. Accepts email to submissions@thejourneymag.com (Word attachments). Response time varies. All rights. Articles, 700–1,200 words. B/W or color digital images at 300 dpi. No payment.

Kaleidoscope

Exploring the Experience of Disability Through Literature and the Fine Arts

701 South Main Street
Akron, OH 44311-1019

Editor in Chief: Gail Willmott

Description and Interests: Twice each year, *Kaleidoscope* presents fiction, nonfiction, and poetry that examine the experience of living with a disability. It seeks writing that finds the good in adversity while avoiding stereotyping and sentimental attitudes. Humor is especially needed at this time. Circ: 1,000.
Website: www.udsakron.com

Freelance Potential: 90% written by nonstaff writers. Publishes 40 freelance submissions yearly; 10% by unpublished writers, 75% by authors who are new to the magazine. Receives 30 unsolicited mss monthly.

Submissions and Payment: Sample copy available. Guidelines available at website. Send complete ms. Accepts hard copy and simultaneous submissions. SASE. Submission deadlines, March 1 and August 1. Responds in 6 months. First North American serial rights. Written material, to 5,000 words; $10–125. Pays on publication. Provides 2 contributor's copies.

The Keeper's Log

9005 Point No Point Road NE
Hansville, WA 98340

Executive Director: Jeff Gales

Description and Interests: A quarterly publication for members of the United States Lighthouse Society, *The Keeper's Log* combines well-researched historical articles regarding U.S. and foreign lighthouses with human-interest pieces about lighthouse keepers, their families, or restoration projects. It also publishes pieces on lighthouse associations, tours, and even the occasional lighthouse sale. It looks for writers who love lighthouses as much as its readers do. Circ: Unavailable.
Website: www.uslhs.org

Freelance Potential: Publishes 50 freelance submissions yearly.

Submissions and Payment: Sample copy available. Send complete ms. Accepts email submissions to info@uslhs.org. Response time varies. First North American serial rights. Articles and depts/columns, word lengths and payment rates vary. Payment policy varies.

Kelsey Review

Mercer County Community College
P.O. Box B
Trenton, NJ 08690

Editor: Edward Carmien

Description and Interests: This is a regional literary journal that puts the spotlight on writers from the Mercer County area region. It accepts short fiction, creative nonfiction, and poetry from students of the college, as well as other writers. It is published annually. Circ: 2,000.
Website: www.mccc.edu/community_kelsey-review.shtml

Freelance Potential: 100% written by nonstaff writers. Publishes 25 freelance submissions yearly; 75% by unpublished writers, 50% by authors who are new to the magazine. Receives 12 unsolicited mss each month.

Submissions and Payment: Send complete ms with cover letter by May 15. Accepts hard copy. No simultaneous submissions. SASE. Responds in August. Rights vary. Prose, to 5,000 words. Poetry, to 6 poems per submission. No payment. Provides 4 contributor's copies.

Kerem

3035 Porter Street NW
Washington, DC 20008

Co-Editors: Gilah Langner & Sara R. Horowitz

Description and Interests: This literary journal, published occasionally, is dedicated to presenting a collection of fine writing on Jewish matters. It seeks poetry and fiction, as well as articles, reflections, and text studies. Circ: 1,500.
Website: www.kerem.org

Freelance Potential: 90% written by nonstaff writers. Publishes 10–15 freelance submissions yearly; 25% by unpublished writers, 75% by authors who are new to the magazine. Receives 5 unsolicited mss monthly.

Submissions and Payment: Sample copy and guidelines available at website. Send complete ms. Prefers email to langner@erols.com or to kerem@sympatico.ca; will accept two hard copies (three copies for poetry). SASE. Responds in 3–5 months. First rights. Articles and fiction, to 20,000 words. No payment. Provides 2–5 contributor's copies.

Kestrel

A Journal of Literature and Art

Fairmont State University
1201 Locust Avenue
Fairmont, WV 26554

Fiction, Poetry, or Nonfiction Editor

Description and Interests: *Kestrel* is a twice yearly literary journal of poetry, fiction, creative nonfiction, translations, and artwork. Its editors encourage submissions from West Virginian and Appalachian writers. Circ: 500.
Website: www.fairmontstate.edu/publications/kestrel/default.asp

Freelance Potential: 100% written by nonstaff writers. Publishes 40 freelance submissions yearly; 30% by unpublished writers, 60% by authors who are new to the magazine. Receives 75–100 mss monthly.

Submissions and Payment: Sample copy available. Guidelines available at website. Send complete ms between May 1 and July 31 or November 1 and January 31. Accepts hard copy. SASE. Responds in 3 months. First serial rights. Fiction, to 5,000 words. Nonfiction, word lengths vary. Poetry, 3–5 poems per submission. No payment. Provides 2 contributor's copies.

Kittens USA

P.O. Box 6050
Mission Viejo, CA 92690-6050

Managing Editor: Lisa King

Description and Interests: *Kittens USA* is filled with information for those who are considering adopting a purebred or a mixed-breed kitten. Its editorial mix includes how to choose a kitten and get your home ready, and articles on kitten health and behavior, and kitten breeds. It is published annually. Circ: 78,350.
Website: www.catchannel.com

Freelance Potential: 80% written by nonstaff writers. Publishes 10–12 freelance submissions yearly; 10–20% by authors who are new to the magazine.

Submissions and Payment: Sample copy and guidelines available at website. Query between January 1 and May 1 (queries for trend pieces accepted year-round). Accepts hard copy. Response time varies. First North American serial rights. Articles and depts/columns, word lengths and payment rates vary. Payment policy varies. Provides 2 contributor's copies.

Krave Magazine

2700 Canton Street, #412
Dallas, TX 75226

Editor in Chief: Dorian Willis

Description and Interests: Published quarterly, *Krave Magazine* is a fashion, lifestyle, and entertainment publication designed to address the needs and interests of urban men of color. It caters to a professional, worldly, cutting-edge, and open-minded audience. In addition to articles on music, the arts, menswear, and fitness, it presents profiles of successful black and Latino men. Circ: 162,000.
Website: www.kravemagazine.net

Freelance Potential: 90% written by nonstaff writers. Publishes 20+ freelance submissions yearly; 50% by authors who are new to the magazine.

Submissions and Payment: Sample copy available. Query or send complete ms. Accepts hard copy. SASE. Response time varies. Rights vary. Articles and depts/columns, word lengths vary. No payment.

Lapham's Quarterly

33 Irving Place, 8th Floor
New York, NY 10003

Editor: Lewis H. Lapham

Description and Interests: History and literature are woven together in *Lapham's Quarterly*. Each issue explores a single theme—for example, medicine, war, or nature—and includes commentary and criticism from contemporary scholars and writers that draw on the annals and archives of the past. It does not accept unsolicited original work, but seeks interesting or unusual historical documents and articles. Circ: 20,000.
Website: www.laphamsquarterly.org

Freelance Potential: 20% written by nonstaff writers. Publishes 4–8 freelance submissions yearly; 10% by unpublished writers, 75% by authors who are new to the magazine.

Submissions and Payment: Guidelines available at website. Send complete historical documents. No unsolicited submissions. Accepts hard copy and email to editorial@laphamsquarterly.org. SASE. Response time varies. No payment.

Laptop Magazine

150 Fifth Avenue, 9th floor
New York, NY 10011

Managing Editor: Anna Attkisson

Description and Interests: Subtitled "The Pulse of Mobile Tech," this monthly focuses on the technology needed to thrive in the wireless world. Reviews, news, tips, and tricks for using wireless products fill its pages. Writers must be knowledgeable about the mobile technology market. Circ: 90,000.
Website: www.laptopmag.com

Freelance Potential: 10% written by nonstaff writers. Publishes 10 freelance submissions yearly; 1% by authors who are new to the magazine, 5% by experts. Receives 2 queries each month.

Submissions and Payment: Sample copy and editorial calendar available at website. Query with résumé and clips. Accepts email queries to aattkisson@laptopmag.com. Responds in 1 month. All rights. Articles, 600–2,500 words. Depts/columns, 600–1,000 words. Written material, $.50+ per word. Pays on publication. Provides 1 contributor's copy.

Latina Style

106B East Broad Street
Falls Church, VA 22046

Managing Editor: Gloria Romano

Description and Interests: Addressing the concerns of the Latina professional woman, this magazine appears six times each year. It focuses on Latina achievement in business, science, civic affairs, and education. Circ: 150,000.
Website: www.latinastyle.com

Freelance Potential: 60% written by nonstaff writers. Publishes 20–24 freelance submissions yearly; 10% by authors who are new to the magazine, 50% by experts. Receives 40–50 queries, 20 unsolicited mss monthly.

Submissions and Payment: Sample copy, guidelines, and editorial calendar available. Query or send complete ms. Accepts email to gloria@latinastyle.com. Response time varies. Rights vary. Articles, 1,300–1,500 words. Depts/columns, 700 words. Color digital images at 300 dpi. All material, payment rates vary. Kill fee, 25%. Pays 1 month after publication.

Latin Beat

14752 Crenshaw Boulevard, Suite 223
Gardena, CA 90249

Publisher/Editor: Rudy Mangual

Description and Interests: Dedicated to Latin pop and jazz, salsa, and Afro-world music, this magazine pumps up fans with profiles of musicians and groups; features on instruments, music, and events; and reviews. It is published 10 times each year. Circ: 50,000.
Website: www.latinbeatmagazine.com

Freelance Potential: 20% written by nonstaff writers. Publishes 10–12 freelance submissions yearly; 10% by unpublished writers, 20% by authors who are new to the magazine, 70% by experts. Receives 3 queries monthly.

Submissions and Payment: Sample articles available at website. Theme list/editorial calendar available. Query. Accepts email queries to info@latinbeatmagazine.com. Responds in 6 weeks. All rights. Articles, 1,500–2,000 words. Fiction, 1,000–1,500 words. Depts/columns, 1,000–1,200 words. No payment. Provides 6 contributor's copies.

Lava Magazine

514 Via de la Valle, Suite 300
Solana Beach, CA 92075

Editor in Chief: Brad Culp

Description and Interests: This sports magazine targets triathlon athletes and delivers solid information on training, competition readiness, new gear, racing strategies, and the multi-sport lifestyle. It also offers news on athletes and competitions throughout the country. It appears nine times each year and is available as a print magazine, ezine, or iPhone/iPad app. Circ: 63,000 (print and digital).
Website: www.lavamagazine.com

Freelance Potential: Submissions welcome. Writers should be well-versed in Ironman or multi-sport competition. It is specifically interested in race coverage, training tips, and human interest articles.

Submissions and Payment: Sample copy available at website. Query for submission information. Accepts email to bradculp@ironman.com. Response time varies.

Leading Edge Magazine

4087 JKB
Provo, UT 84602

Fiction or Poetry Director

Description and Interests: This literary journal features fantasy and science fiction, as well as poetry. All new contributors will receive a critique from two editors, whether the work is published or not. It appears twice each year. Circ: 200.
Website: www.leadingedgemagazine.com

Freelance Potential: 95% written by nonstaff writers. Publishes 18 freelance submissions yearly; 70% by unpublished writers, 70% by new authors. Receives 30 unsolicited mss monthly.

Submissions and Payment: Sample copy available. Guidelines available at website. Send complete ms with cover letter listing publishing credits. Accepts hard copy. No simultaneous submissions. SASE. Responds in 4–6 months. First North American serial rights. Fiction, to 15,000 words; $.01 per word, $50 maximum. Poetry, no line limits; $10. Pays on publication. Provides electronic copy to contributors.

Leben

2150 River Plaza Drive, Suite 150
Sacramento, CA 95833

Editor: Wayne Johnson

Description and Interests: *Leben* reveals the stories of the lesser-known "sons and daughters" of the Protestant Reformation. Carefully researched and compelling historical biographies are published in each quarterly issue. Articles focusing on lesser-known events or people are preferred. Circ: 5,000.
Website: www.leben.us

Freelance Potential: 40% written by nonstaff writers. Publishes 5 freelance submissions yearly; 20% by unpublished writers, 20% by authors who are new to the magazine. Receives 2 unsolicited mss monthly.

Submissions and Payment: Sample copy and guidelines available at website. Query. Accepts email submissions to editor@leben.us (Microsoft Word attachments). Responds in 1 week. First North American serial and electronic rights. Articles, 500–2,500 words, $.05 per word. Pays on acceptance. Provides 2 contributor's copies on request.

Left Curve

P.O. Box 472
Oakland, CA 94604-0472

Editor: Csaba Polony

Description and Interests: Traditional and experimental fiction, critical essays, reviews, journalistic articles, and poetry fill the pages of this annual, artist-produced literary journal. It seeks submissions that address the problems of cultural forms. Circ: 2,000.
Website: www.leftcurve.org

Freelance Potential: 90% written by nonstaff writers. Publishes 30 freelance submissions yearly; 5% by unpublished writers, 20% by authors who are new to the magazine. Receives 50 queries, 100 unsolicited mss monthly.

Submissions and Payment: Sample articles and guidelines available at website. Send complete ms. Accepts hard copy and email to editor@leftcurve.org. SASE. Responds in 3+ months. Rights vary. Articles and fiction, 2,500–5,000 words. Poetry, to 8 pages. No payment. Provides 3–5 contributor's copies.

Liberty Magazine

12501 Old Columbia Pike
Silver Spring, MD 20904

Editor: Lincoln Steed

Description and Interests: The articles found in *Liberty Magazine* explore the separation of church and state. Each of the six issues published each year includes opinion pieces on current events, government, politics, and religious liberty. Circ: 200,000.
Website: www.libertymagazine.org

Freelance Potential: 80% written by nonstaff writers. Publishes 30 freelance submissions yearly; 10% by unpublished writers, 20% by authors who are new to the magazine, 20% by experts. Receives 10 unsolicited mss monthly.

Submissions and Payment: Sample articles available at website. Send complete ms. Accepts hard copy and email submissions to lincoln.steed@nad.adventist.org. SASE. Response time varies. Rights vary. Articles, 1,900 words; payment rates vary. Pays on publication. Provides 5–6 contributor's copies.

Lightspeed

Editor in Chief: John Joseph Adams

Description and Interests: An online magazine focusing exclusively on science fiction and fantasy, *Lightspeed* offers a mix of original work and reprints from bestselling authors. Each monthly issue also offers author interviews and spotlights. Hits per month: Unavailable.
Website: www.lightspeedmagazine.com

Freelance Potential: Open to submissions; no topics are off-limits. Accepts fantasy, as well as science fiction, now that sister publication *Fantasy* is fully integrated into *Lightspeed*. Not currently accepting nonfiction. Check website for submission updates.

Submissions and Payment: Sample articles and guidelines available at website. Send complete ms. Accepts submissions at http://lightspeed.sendsubmission.com. Responds in 2 weeks. Rights vary. Fiction, to 7,500 words; $.05 per word. Pays on acceptance.

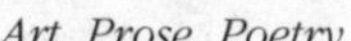

Limestone

Art. Prose. Poetry.

1215 Patterson Office Tower
Department of English
University of Kentucky
Lexington, KY 40506

Fiction or Poetry Editor

Description and Interests: This annual literary journal is published by graduate students of the English Department of the University of Kentucky. It showcases fiction, poetry, and art with the goal of publishing established talent alongside newer artists. Circ: 500.
Website: www.limestonejournal.com

Freelance Potential: 100% written by nonstaff writers. Publishes 30–35 freelance submissions yearly; 80% by authors who are new to the magazine. Receives 40 unsolicited mss monthly.

Submissions and Payment: Sample copy available. Guidelines available at website. Send complete ms. Accepts hard copy and simultaneous submissions if identified. SASE. Response time varies. All rights. Fiction, to 30 pages. Poetry, to 5 poems per submission. No payment. Provides 1 contributor's copy.

Literal

770 South Post Oak Lane, Suite 530
Houston, TX 77056

Director: Rose Mary Salum

Description and Interests: This journal of "Latin American Voices" features essays about current events, as well as short stories, poetry, personal essays, and book reviews. It is published quarterly. Circ: 10,000.
Website: www.literalmagazine.com

Freelance Potential: 10% written by nonstaff writers. Publishes 8–10 freelance submissions yearly; 10% by unpublished writers, 10% by authors who are new to the magazine. Receives 4 queries, 8 unsolicited mss monthly.

Submissions and Payment: Sample copy available at website. Guidelines and theme list available. Query or send complete ms with résumé. Accepts email to info@literalmagazine.com. Responds in 6 months. One-year rights. Articles and depts/columns, 1,600+ words. Fiction, to 2,400 words. Poetry, to 40 verses. No payment. Provides 5 contributor's copies.

Literary Mama

Fiction, Poetry, or Nonfiction Editor

Description and Interests: This ezine focuses on fiction, essays, and poetry by mothers about motherhood. The editors encourage submissions from nontraditional mothers. It is updated monthly. Hits per month: 55,000.
Website: www.literarymama.com

Freelance Potential: 78% written by nonstaff writers. Publishes 120 freelance submissions yearly; 20% by unpublished writers, 80% by new authors. Receives 100 unsolicited mss monthly.

Submissions and Payment: Sample copy and guidelines available at website. Query for profiles and reviews. Send complete ms and cover letter for all other work. Accepts email submissions (see guidelines for department heads and addresses; include "Submission" in subject line), and simultaneous submissions. Responds in 1–6 months. Nonexclusive rights. Fiction, to 5,000 words. Nonfiction, 500–7,000 words. Poetry, no line limit, to 4 poems. No payment.

The Literary Review

Fairleigh Dickinson University
285 Madison Avenue
Madison, NJ 07940

Editor: Minna Proctor

Description and Interests: This international journal of contemporary writing is published quarterly, featuring poetry, prose, and reviews from literary artists around the world. Each issue addresses a theme. Circ: 2,000.
Website: www.theliteraryreview.org

Freelance Potential: 97% written by nonstaff writers. Publishes 100 freelance submissions yearly; 45% by unpublished writers, 45% by authors who are new to the magazine. Receives 100 unsolicited mss monthly.

Submissions and Payment: Guidelines and theme list available at website. Send complete ms. Accepts electronic submissions via website and simultaneous submissions. Responds in 3–12 months. One-time rights. Poetry, 3–7 poems per submission. No payment. Provides 2 contributor's copies and a 1-year subscription.

Livestrong Quarterly

210 Central Park South, Suite 5C
New York, NY 10019

Editor: Curtis Pesmen

Description and Interests: Sponsored by the Lance Armstrong Foundation, *Livestrong Quarterly* has a mission to make cancer a global priority through raising awareness and sharing compelling stories of survivors and advocates. Its content offers a mix of cancer-related subjects, including health, wellness, and body advocacy. It publishes profiles, articles on medical advancements, and inspirational pieces. It is available in print and digital editions, as well as print-on-demand. Circ: 1.15 million (print and digital).
Website: www.livestrongmagazine.com

Freelance Potential: This is a custom publication created by SpotOn Media. Query for information.

Submissions and Payment: Sample articles and guidelines available at website. Query for submission information. Accepts email to info@spotonmedia.com.

Living Blues

1111 Jackson Avenue West
P.O. Box 1848
University, MS 38677

Editor: Brett Bonner

Description and Interests: Afficionados of American blues subscribe to this magazine for information on new artists and releases, as well as historical and retrospective pieces about this musical genre. Published six times each year, it includes interviews with music legends and musicians on the rise. Circ: 20,000+.
Website: www.livingblues.com

Freelance Potential: 50% written by nonstaff writers. Publishes 380+ freelance submissions yearly; 5% by unpublished writers, 25% by authors who are new to the magazine. Receives 50 queries monthly.

Submissions and Payment: Sample copy and guidelines available. Query. Accepts email queries to brett@livingblues.com. Responds in 2 months. First rights. Articles, word lengths vary; $250–$500. Pays on publication. Provides 3 contributor's copies.

Living the Country Life

1716 Locust Street, LS265
Des Moines, IA 50309-3023

Editor in Chief: Betsy Freese

Description and Interests: Narrowly focused on the demographic of rural homeowners on large properties, *Living the Country Life* offers practical and lifestyle features on a wide variety of topics, including gardening, livestock, equipment, and property enhancement. It appears six times each year. Circ: 200,000.
Website: www.livingthecountrylife.com

Freelance Potential: 10% written by nonstaff writers. Of the freelance submissions published yearly, 10% are by authors who are new to the magazine.

Submissions and Payment: Sample copy and guidelines available. Query. Accepts email queries to betsy.freese@meredith.com. Response time varies. All rights. Articles and depts/columns, word lengths vary. Written material, $1 per word. Pays on acceptance. Provides contributor's copies upon request.

Living Light News

5306 89th Street, #200
Edmonton, Alberta T6E 5P9
Canada

Editor: Jeff Caporale

Description and Interests: Published by an evangelical Christian ministry, this tabloid offers stories and personal testimonies that present the gospel message in a powerful, contemporary way. Appearing every other month, it seeks profiles of prominent Christians, news, and family-focused articles that will improve readers' lives. Circ: 75,000.
Website: www.livinglightnews.org

Freelance Potential: 100% written by nonstaff writers. Publishes 50 freelance submissions yearly.

Submissions and Payment: Sample copy available. Guidelines available at website. Query with word count, plan for images, and anticipated timeline. Accepts email queries to shine@livinglightnews.org. Response time varies. First North American serial rights. Written material, word lengths vary; $.08 per word. Pays on publication.

The Long Story 

18 Eaton Street
Lawrence, MA 01843

Editor: R. P. Burnham

Description and Interests: Published once each year, this independent literary journal presents fiction between 8,000 and 20,000 words to a serious, educated readership. It looks for authors who write about what they can imagine, not just what they know. Circ: 500.
Website: www.longstorylitmag.com

Freelance Potential: 95% written by nonstaff writers. Publishes 7–8 freelance submissions yearly; 10% by unpublished writers, 50–75% by new authors. Receives 50 unsolicited mss monthly.

Submissions and Payment: Sample copy available. Guidelines available at website. Send complete ms between January and June or September and December. Accepts hard copy and simultaneous submissions. SASE. Responds in 2 months. First North American serial rights. Fiction, 8,000–20,000 words. No payment. Provides 2 contributor's copies.

The Louisville Review 

Spalding University
851 South Fourth Street
Louisville, KY 40203

Prose or Poetry Editor

Description and Interests: Submissions of short fiction, creative nonfiction, poetry, and drama are accepted by *The Louisville Review*. Published twice each year, it also showcases the best literary work of elementary and high school students. Circ: 1,000.
Website: www.louisvillereview.org

Freelance Potential: 90% written by nonstaff writers. Publishes 90 freelance submissions yearly; 80–90% by authors who are new to the magazine. Receives 700 unsolicited mss monthly.

Submissions and Payment: Sample copy available. Guidelines available at website. Send complete ms. Prefers electronic submissions; will accept hard copy and simultaneous submissions if identified. SASE for reply only. Responds in 4–6 months. One-time rights. Fiction, word lengths vary. Poetry, to 5 poems per submission. No payment. Provides 2 contributor's copies.

Loving Out Loud

7405 Greenback Lane
Citrus Heights, CA 95610

Publisher: Rev. Paul V. Scholl

Description and Interests: A newsletter-style publication, *Loving Out Loud* offers its readers spiritual insight, encouragement, and inspiration. It is published quarterly and features how-to and personal experience pieces, fiction, poetry, and humor centered on faith, love, and God's presence in people's lives. Circ: 1,000.
Website: www.lovingoutloud.com

Freelance Potential: 25% written by nonstaff writers. Publishes 10–15 freelance submissions yearly.

Submissions and Payment: Sample articles available at website. Send complete ms. Accepts email submissions to go2dlyt@aol.com (Word attachments) and simultaneous submissions if identified. Responds in 1 month. Rights vary. Articles and depts/columns, 500–750 words. Fiction, word lengths vary. No payment. Provides 6 contributor's copies.

Loyola Magazine

4501 North Charles Street
Baltimore, MD 21210-2699

Managing Editor: Rita Buettner

Description and Interests: Feature articles and updates about current happenings at Loyola University Maryland are found in this publication, written for alumni and current and future students. Profiles of people who teach at the university or have attended the school fill many of its pages. It is published three times each year. Circ: 54,000.
Website: www.loyola.edu/magazine

Freelance Potential: 5% written by nonstaff writers. Publishes 6–7 freelance submissions yearly; 5% by authors who are new to the magazine, 5% by experts. Receives 3 queries each month.

Submissions and Payment: Sample copy and guidelines available. Query with résumé and 3 writing samples; or send complete ms. Accepts hard copy. SASE. Responds in 1 month. First rights. Articles, 500-2,000 words; payment rates vary. Kill fee, 50%. Pays on acceptance. Provides 2 contributor's copies.

Lullwater Review

Emory University
P.O. Box 122036
Atlanta, GA 30322

Editor in Chief: Laura Kochman

Description and Interests: Continually seeking fresh aesthetic perspectives from new and established authors and artists, *Lullwater Review* publishes poetry, prose, and artwork. It appears two times each year. Circ: 2,500+.
Website: www.lullwaterreview.com

Freelance Potential: 100% written by nonstaff writers. Publishes 25–30 freelance submissions yearly; 90% by authors who are new to the magazine. Receives 100 unsolicited mss monthly.

Submissions and Payment: Sample copy available. Guidelines available at website. Send complete ms with cover letter. Accepts hard copy and simultaneous submissions if identified. SASE. Responds in 3–4 months. First serial rights. Fiction, to 5,000 words. Poetry, no line limit; to 5 poems per submission. JPEG or PDF images on Macintosh disk; to 10 images. No payment. Provides 3 contributor's copies.

The MacGuffin

Schoolcraft College
18600 Haggerty Road
Livonia, MI 48152-2696

Managing Editor: Gordon Krupsky

Description and Interests: Founded in 1984, this literary journal publishes poetry, short fiction, and creative nonfiction. It appears three times each year. Circ: 500.
Website: www.schoolcraft.edu/macguffin

Freelance Potential: 100% written by nonstaff writers. Publishes 130 freelance submissions yearly; 35% by unpublished writers, 45% by authors who are new to the magazine. Receives 200 unsolicited mss monthly.

Submissions and Payment: Sample copy available. Guidelines available at website. Send complete ms. Accepts hard copy, email to macguffin@schoolcraft.edu (Word attachments), and simultaneous submissions if identified. SASE for reply only. Responds in 2–4 months. First serial rights. Fiction and nonfiction, to 5,000 words. Poetry, to 400 lines; to 5 poems per submission. No payment. Provides 2 contributor's copies.

The Madison Review 

University of Wisconsin
6193 Helen C. White Hall
600 North Park Street
Madison, WI 53706

Fiction or Poetry Editor

Description and Interests: Edited by students at the University of Wisconsin, this twice-yearly literary journal presents a broad range of fiction and poetry. Contributors include celebrated authors, as well as unknowns. There is a small fee for each submission. Circ: 750.
Website: www.english.wisc.edu/madisonreview

Freelance Potential: 100% written by nonstaff writers. Publishes 40–50 freelance submissions yearly; 15% by unpublished writers, 85% by new authors. Receives 200 unsolicited mss monthly.

Submissions and Payment: Sample copy available. Guidelines available at website. Send complete ms. Accepts electronic submissions via website and simultaneous submissions if identified. Responds in 4–5 months. Rights vary. Fiction, to 30 pages. Poetry, to 3 pages; to 5 poems per submission. No payment. Provides 2 contributor's copies.

The Magazine of Fantasy & Science Fiction 

P.O. Box 3447
Hoboken, NJ 07030

Editor: Gordon Van Gelder

Description and Interests: Six times each year, this digest offers a full menu of science fiction and fantasy novelettes and short stories. More science fiction and humor submissions are sought. Circ: 45,000.
Website: www.fandsf.com

Freelance Potential: 98% written by nonstaff writers. Publishes 60–80 freelance submissions yearly; 5% by unpublished writers, 10% by authors who are new to the magazine. Receives 600 unsolicited mss monthly.

Submissions and Payment: Sample copy available. Guidelines available at website. Send complete ms. Accepts hard copy. No simultaneous submissions. SASE. Responds in 2 months. First North American and foreign serial rights; option on anthology rights. Fiction, to 25,000 words; $.06–$.09 per word. Pays on acceptance. Provides 2 contributor's copies.

Make

1005 Gravenstein Highway North
Sebastopol, CA 95472

Editor in Chief: Mark Frauenfelder

Description and Interests: *Make* describes itself as a do-it-yourself technology magazine. Published quarterly, it features project ideas, reviews of gadgets and technology-related media, and profiles of inventors. Circ: 110,000.
Website: www.makezine.com

Freelance Potential: 75% written by nonstaff writers. Publishes 100 freelance submissions yearly; 25% by unpublished writers, 50% by authors who are new to the magazine, 5% by experts. Receives 200 queries monthly.

Submissions and Payment: Sample copy available. Guidelines available at website. Query. Accepts queries via website. Responds in 2 weeks. Rights vary. Articles, 600–1,000 words. DIY projects, 200–750 words. Reviews, 200 words, $25–$100. Other written material, payment rates vary. Kill fee, 33%. Pays on acceptance. Provides 2 contributor's copies.

Makeshift 

2075 Vine Drive
Merrick, NY 11566

Editor in Chief: Steve Danielas

Description and Interests: Global creativity and grassroots ingenuity is the focus of this quarterly publication. From the *favelas* of Rio to the alleys of Delhi, it showcases inventions, innovations, and solutions devised in environments where resources are very limited but resourcefulness and self-expression shine. Circ: Unknown.
Website: www.mkshft.org

Freelance Potential: Open to inquiries from contributing writers.

Submissions and Payment: Sample articles available at website. Query to editor@mkshft.org. Rights, unknown. Written material, payment rate and payment policy, unknown.

Make/Shift

P.O. Box 27506
Los Angeles, CA 90027

Editors: Jessica Hoffmann & Daria Yudacufski

Description and Interests: This magazine creates, documents, and engages with contemporary feminist culture and activism. It is published twice each year. Refer to the website's guidelines for specific needs for each issue. Circ: 1,500.
Website: www.makeshiftmag.com

Freelance Potential: 100% written by nonstaff writers. Publishes 40 freelance submissions yearly; 20% by unpublished writers, 25% by authors who are new to the magazine. Receives 20 queries, 10 unsolicited mss monthly.

Submissions and Payment: Sample copy available. Guidelines available at website. Query or send complete ms. Accepts email to info@makeshiftmag.com. Responds in several months. First serial rights. Articles, 300–3,000 words. Fiction, 500–3,000 words. Depts/columns, 800–1,000 words. Poetry, to 3 poems per submission. Written material, $.02 per word. Pays on publication. Provides 2 contributor's copies.

The Malahat Review

University of Victoria
P.O. Box 1700, STN CSC
Victoria, British Columbia V8W 2Y2
Canada

Editor: John Barton

Description and Interests: This quarterly literary review features short stories, poetry, creative nonfiction, interviews, and reviews. Circ: 5,000.
Website: www.malahatreview.ca

Freelance Potential: 95% written by nonstaff writers. Publishes 110 freelance submissions yearly; 5% by unpublished writers, 30% by new authors. Receives 250–300 queries and unsolicited mss monthly.

Submissions and Payment: Guidelines available at website. Send complete ms with short bio. Query for reviews and interviews only. Accepts hard copy. SAE/IRC. Responds in 1–9 months. First world serial rights. Fiction, 1,200–8,000 words. Creative nonfiction, 1,000–3,500 words. Poetry, 5–10 poems per submission. Reviews, 800–1,000 words. Written material, $35 Canadian per page. Pays on acceptance. Provides 2 contributor's copies and a 1-year subscription.

Marian Helper

Eden Hill
Stockbridge, MA 01263

Executive Editor: David Came

Description and Interests: A source of information about the mission and current works of the Marians, this magazine also seeks to provide spiritual nourishment and education about the Catholic faith. It is published quarterly by the Congregation of Marians of the Immaculate Conception. Circ: 400,000.
Website: www.marian.org

Freelance Potential: 15% written by nonstaff writers. Publishes 10–12 freelance submissions yearly; 10% by unpublished writers, 50% by experts. Receives 50 queries monthly.

Submissions and Payment: Sample copy available at website. Query. Accepts hard copy and email queries to editorial@marian.org. SASE. Responds in 6 weeks. One-time rights. Articles, 500–1,000 words; $250. Kill fee, 30%. Pays on publication. Provides 10 contributor's copies.

Marlin

Bonnier Corporation
460 North Orlando Avenue, Suite 200
Winter Park, FL 32789

Editor: Dave Ferrell

Description and Interests: Offshore sportfishing enthusiasts read this magazine for the latest information on destinations, techniques, gear, and boats. It appears eight times each year. Circ: 40,000.
Website: www.marlinmag.com

Freelance Potential: 60% written by nonstaff writers. Publishes 25 freelance submissions yearly; 10% by unpublished writers, 50% by experts. Receives 3 queries, 1 ms monthly.

Submissions and Payment: Sample copy and guidelines available. Query or send complete ms. Accepts email to editor@marlinmag.com. Responds in 1 month. First serial rights. Articles, 1,500–3,000 words; $300–$500. Depts/columns, 250–1,500 words; $100–$200. Color slides and transparencies; $50–$1,200. Kill fee, 33%. Pays on publication. Provides 2 contributor's copies.

Massachusetts Review 

South College
University of Massachusetts
Amherst, MA 01003

Editor: Jim Hicks

Description and Interests: An independent quarterly of literature, the arts, and public affairs, *Massachusetts Review* offers poetry and stories, personal witness pieces, and incisive social and historical commentary. It caters to readers who care both about literature and the wider world. Circ: 2,000.
Website: www.massreview.org

Freelance Potential: 99% written by nonstaff writers. Publishes 50 freelance submissions yearly; 99% by new authors. Receives 500 mss monthly.

Submissions and Payment: Guidelines available at website. Send complete ms between October 1 through May 1. Accepts hard copy and electronic submissions via website. SASE. Responds in 6–12 weeks. All North American rights. Articles and fiction, 30 pages or 8,000 words; $50. Poetry, to 100 lines, to 6 poems per submission; $.50 per line. Pays on publication. Provides 2 contributor's copies.

Maxim

415 Madison Avenue
New York, NY 10017

Managing Editor: Yeun Littlefield

Description and Interests: This lifestyle magazine for men ages 18 to 40 covers the topics this demographic wants to read and see—mainly sex, women, and sports. A mix of how-to, informational, self-help, and personal experience pieces appear within its pages. Published monthly, it also features articles on fashion, music, entertainment, health, and celebrity profiles. Circ: 2 million+.
Website: www.maximonline.com

Freelance Potential: 40% written by nonstaff writers. Publishes 30 freelance submissions yearly. Receives 50 queries monthly.

Submissions and Payment: Sample copy and editorial calendar available. Query. Accepts hard copy. SASE. Responds in 6 months. All rights. Written material, word lengths and payment rates vary. Pays on publication.

Maximum Tech

4000 Shoreline Court, Suite 400
South San Francisco, CA 94080

Editor in Chief: Katherine Stevenson

Description and Interests: *Maximum Tech* is written for the technology consumers who are usually the first to adopt new products. Published six times each year, it provides complete coverage and reviews of the newest smartphones, tablets, apps, and video/audio equipment. It also offers lifestyle articles for the tech-focused reader, including such topics as cars, gaming, green living, and health and fitness. A companion, interactive website is available, offering editorial. Circ: Unavailable.
Website: www.maximumtech.com

Freelance Potential: Writers must be at the cutting-edge of consumer technology to be considered.

Submissions and Payment: Sample articles available at website. Query for submission information. See www.maximumtech.com for a complete list of editors, the categories they cover, and their individual contact information. Response varies. Written material, word lengths vary. Payment information unknown.

The Maynard  

3-1252 King Street West
Toronto, Ontario M6K 1G5
Canada

Editor: Moss Whelan

Description and Interests: Published online six times each year, *The Maynard* features the very best prose and poetry of both new and experienced writers. A variety of topics, themes, genres, and forms is included in every issue. Hits per month: 2,000.
Website: www.themaynard.org

Freelance Potential: 100% written by nonstaff writers. Publishes 80 freelance submissions yearly; 50% by unpublished writers, 75% by authors who are new to the magazine.

Submissions and Payment: Sample copy available. Send complete ms with 50-word author bio. Accepts email submissions to fiction@themaynard.org, nonfiction@themaynard.org, or poetry@themaynard.org. Accepts simultaneous submissions if identified. Responds in 6 weeks. Rights vary. Articles and fiction, 5,000 words. Poetry, to 5 poems per submission. No payment.

McSweeney's Quarterly Concern

849 Valencia Street
San Francisco, CA 94110

Editor

Description and Interests: *McSweeney's Quarterly Concern* began in 1998 as a literary journal with a mission to publish only works that were rejected by other magazines. Today, the quarterly magazine regularly attracts some of the finest authors in the country, while still being a home for new and unpublished writers. Circ: Unavailable.
Website: www.mcsweeneys.net

Freelance Potential: It encourages new writers and reports it is "committed to publishing exciting fiction regardless of pedigree." Submissions for the website are also accepted; see guidelines for details.

Submissions and Payment: Guidelines available at website. Send ms with cover letter. Accepts hard copy and electronic submissions through Submishmash link on website (Word attachments). SASE. Responds in 9 months. Rights vary. Word lengths and payment rates vary. Pays on publication.

Memoir Journal

1316 67th Street #8
Emeryville, CA 94608

Submissions Editor

Description and Interests: No submission is too unusual or too traditional for this journal that is published twice each year. It features memoirs in a variety of forms, including prose, poetry, and narrative photography. Refer to the website for specific deadlines for each issue. Circ: 2,000.
Website: www.memoirjournal.com

Freelance Potential: 100% written by nonstaff writers. Publishes 75 freelance submissions yearly; 10% by unpublished writers, 95% by new authors. Receives 500 unsolicited mss monthly.

Submissions and Payment: Sample copy and guidelines available at website. Send complete ms. Prefers electronic submissions via website; will accept hard copy and simultaneous submissions. Responds in 4 months. One-time rights. Prose, to 10,000 words. Poetry, to 5 poems per submission. B/W TIFF and EPS images. No payment. Provides 3 contributor's copies and a 1-year subscription.

Men's Health

33 East Minor Street
Emmaus, PA 18098

Editor: Peter Moore

Description and Interests: Breaking news and in-depth coverage of men's health issues are the prime directive here. Published 10 times each year, it looks for expert, insider information on fitness, nutrition, and medicine, as well as new takes on evergreen topics like sex and relationships. Celebrity profiles are also part of the mix. Circ: 1.9 million.
Website: www.menshealth.com

Freelance Potential: 60% written by nonstaff writers.

Submissions and Payment: Sample articles available at website. Email queries with relevant clips to the editor of the section your idea is for: health and sex to julie.stewart@rodale.com; food and nutrition, paul.kita@rodale.com; technology, eric.adams@rodale.com. All rights. Written material, $1.00–$3.00 a word. Kill fee, 25%. Pays on acceptance.

Message

55 West Oak Ridge Drive
Hagerstown, MD 21740

Editor in Chief: Carmela Monk Crawford

Description and Interests: Providing a contemporary Christian perspective for the urban-minded reader, *Message* is a publication of the Seventh-day Adventist Church. It appears six times each year, offering inspirational and informational articles about faith and other issues dealing with daily living. Circ: 60,000.
Website: www.messagemagazine.org

Freelance Potential: 75% written by nonstaff writers. Publishes 12–15 freelance submissions yearly.

Submissions and Payment: Sample copy available. Guidelines available. Query or send complete ms with 1- to 2-sentence bio. Accepts email to ccrawford@rhpa.org; will accept hard copy. SASE. Response time varies. First North American serial rights. Articles, 600–800 words, including 1- to 2-line author bio. Written material, payment rates vary. Pays on publication. Provides 3 contributor's copies.

Message of the Open Bible

2020 Bell Avenue
Des Moines, IA 50315-1096

Managing Editor: Andrea Johnson

Description and Interests: Written by and for members of the Open Bible family, this publication, appearing six times each year, seeks to inform, inspire, and unify. Circ: 2,500.
Website: www.openbible.org

Freelance Potential: 55% written by nonstaff writers. Publishes 2 freelance submissions yearly; 5% by unpublished writers, 5% by authors who are new to the magazine, 90% by experts. Receives 4 queries, 1 unsolicited ms monthly.

Submissions and Payment: Sample articles available at website. Guidelines and theme list available. Query with writing samples; or send complete ms with brief author bio and photo. Accepts email to message@openbible.org. Responds to queries in 1 week; to mss in 1 month. Writers retain rights. Articles, 700 words. No payment. Provides 5–10 contributor's copies.

Michigan Quarterly Review

0576 Rackham Building
915 East Washington Street
Ann Arbor, MI 48109-1070

Editor: Jonathan Freedman

Description and Interests: This academic journal sets high standards for the articles, essays, short stories, and poetry it selects. Published quarterly by the University of Michigan, it prefers serious fiction and scholarly articles on a variety of topics. Circ: 1,000.
Website: www.michiganquarterlyreview.com/

Freelance Potential: 95% written by nonstaff writers. Publishes 70 freelance submissions yearly; 5% by unpublished writers, 40% by authors who are new to the magazine. Receives 400 unsolicited mss monthly.

Submissions and Payment: Sample copy and guidelines available at website. Send complete ms. Accepts hard copy and simultaneous submissions if identified. SASE. Responds in 6 weeks. First rights. Articles and fiction, 1,500–7,000 words. Poetry, 8–12 pages. Written material, $10 per published page. Pays on publication.

Mid-American Review

English Department
Bowling Green State University
Bowling Green, OH 43403

Fiction, Nonfiction, or Poetry Editor

Description and Interests: Poetry and prose in traditional and experimental forms, as well as reviews, are found in the *Mid-American Review*. It is published twice each year. Circ: 2,500.
Website: www.bgsu.edu/midamericanreview

Freelance Potential: 98% written by nonstaff writers. Publishes 50–60 freelance submissions yearly; 25% by unpublished writers, 75% by new authors. Receives 600 unsolicited mss monthly.

Submissions and Payment: Sample copy available. Guidelines available at website. Send complete ms. Accepts electronic submissions via website and simultaneous submissions. SASE. Responds in 1–5 months. First rights. Articles and fiction, to 6,000 words. Poetry, no line limit; to 6 poems per submission. Reviews, 400 words. No payment. Provides 2 contributor's copies.

Military Heritage

Military Heritage Submissions
6731 Whittier Avenue
McLean, VA 22101

Editor: Roy Morris

Description and Interests: *Military Heritage* publishes high-quality, well-researched military history articles. Its arena is ancient to contemporary history, anywhere on the globe: the Napoleonic wars, the Boer War, the American Civil War, the Indian Wars, and even the Cold War. Circ: Unavailable.
Website: www.militaryheritagemagazine.com

Freelance Potential: Unavailable.

Submissions and Payment: Sample copy available. Guidelines available at the website. Query or send complete manuscript. Accepts hard copy and email queries only to editor@militaryheritagemagazine.com; do not send unsolicited manuscripts by email. Features, 1,500–7,000 words. Departments, 2,000–3,000 words. Include suggestions or sources for illustrations. Payment rates vary; pays on acceptance.

Military History

19300 Promenade Drive
Leesburg, VA 20176

Editor: Michael Robbins

Description and Interests: *Military History* provides its readers with well-researched, engaging articles that educate as they entertain. The magazine, published six times each year, covers the world's pivotal wars, battles, and warriors, and puts a premium on quality writing. Circ: 61,000.
Website: www.militaryhistory.com

Freelance Potential: 90% written by nonstaff writers. Publishes 60 freelance submissions yearly; 70% by unpublished writers, 30% by new authors, 20% by experts. Receives 30 queries monthly.

Submissions and Payment: Sample copy available. Guidelines available at website. Query with cover letter outlining writing experience. Accepts hard copy and email to militaryhistory@weiderhistorygroup.com. SASE. Responds in 6 months. All rights. Articles, 3,500–4,000 words; $400. Depts/columns, 2,000 words; $200. Pays on acceptance. Provides 2 contributor's copies.

Miniature Donkey Talk

P.O. Box 982
Cripple Creek, CO 80813

Editor: Mike and Bonnie Gross

Description and Interests: As the "talk of the donkey world," this magazine covers every aspect of owning and caring for miniature donkeys. In addition to articles on breeding, training, and health care, it features breeder profiles and event coverage. It is published quarterly. Circ: Unavailable.
Website: www.miniaturedonkeytalk.com

Freelance Potential: 50% written by nonstaff writers. Publishes 50 freelance submissions yearly; 25% by unpublished writers, 25% by authors who are new to the magazine, 50% by experts. Receives 5 unsolicited mss monthly.

Submissions and Payment: Sample articles available at website. Guidelines and editorial calendar available. Send complete ms. Accepts email submissions to mike@donkeytalk.info. Responds in 1 week. First rights. Written material, word lengths vary; $30–$125. Pays on acceptance. Provides 1 contributor's copy.

Miniature Horse World

5601 South I-35W
Alvarado, TX 76009

Editor: Melissa Powell

Description and Interests: The world of miniature horses is explored in this magazine for members of the American Miniature Horse Association. It offers articles on topics ranging from the breed's history to animal care and health. It covers association activities and features profiles of its members. *Miniature Horse World* is published six times each year. Circ: 7,000.
Website: www.amha.org

Freelance Potential: 20% written by nonstaff writers. Publishes 5 freelance submissions yearly; 10% by unpublished writers, 85% by authors who are new to the magazine, 95% by experts. Receives 2 queries monthly.

Submissions and Payment: Sample copy and guidelines available. Query. Accepts email queries to editor@amha.org. Response time varies. Rights vary. Articles, word lengths vary. B/W or color digital images. No payment.

The Minnesota Review

905 W. Main St., Suite 18B
Durham, NC 27701

Editor: Janell Watson

Description and Interests: Now published by Duke University Press, this journal of creative and critical writing offers contemporary poetry and fiction, as well as interviews, essays, and reviews on themes of interest to the critical humanities. Issues appear twice each year. Circ: 1,000.
Website: www.dukeupress.edu/

Freelance Potential: 90% written by nonstaff writers. Publishes 30 freelance submissions yearly; 5% by unpublished writers, 50% by authors who are new to the magazine. Receives 100 mss monthly.

Submissions and Payment: Sample copy available. Guidelines available at website. Query or send complete ms. Accepts online submissions and email to submissions@theminnesotareview.org. Response time varies. First serial rights. Nonfiction, to 10,000 words. Fiction, to 10,000 words. Reviews, to 5,000 words. No payment. Provides 2 contributor's copies.

Mississippi Review

The University of Southern Mississippi
Box 5144, 118 College Drive
Hattiesburg, MS 39406-0001

Editor: Andrew Milward

Description and Interests: This literary journal appears twice each year. One issue contains submissions that have been awarded the Mississippi Review Prize, while the other is built largely around solicited work. Fiction and poetry are the mainstay of both issues. Circ: 2,000.
Website: www.usm.edu/mississippi-review

Freelance Potential: 100% written by nonstaff writers. Publishes 40 freelance submissions yearly; 5% by unpublished writers, 40% by authors who are new to the magazine.

Submissions and Payment: Sample copy available. Guidelines available at website. Send complete ms. Accepts hard copy. Mss are not returned. Response time varies. First serial rights. Fiction, 1,000–8,000 words. Poetry, to 10 pages; limit 3 poems per submission. Fee, $15 per entry. Payment of $1,000 for prize winners only. Provides 2 contributor's copies. All entrants receive a copy of the prize issue.

M Magazine

Conde Nast Traveler
4 Times Square
New York, NY 10036

Editorial Director: Peter Kaplan

Description and Interests: *M Magazine* has been relaunched after it folded in the 1990s. An upscale men's magazine, it plays on men's desires to "look under the hood" featuring the brands, products, and trailblazers that are making an impact in the world of style today. Each of its quarterly issues is themed. Circ: 75,000.
Website: www.condenast.com

Freelance Potential: Receives many freelance submissions monthly.

Submissions and Payment: Query. Accepts phone calls to 212-630-3500. Response time varies. Written material, word lengths vary. Rights vary. Payment rates and policy vary.

Mobius

The Journal of Social Change

505 Christianson Street
Madison, WI 53714

Fiction Editor: Fred Schepartz
Poetry Editor: F. J. Bergman

Description and Interests: *Mobius* blends art and politics in the forms of prose and poetry, offering social commentary from a nonpartisan perspective. An online publication, it is updated quarterly. Hits per month: 1,500.
Website: http://mobiusmagazine.com

Freelance Potential: 95% written by nonstaff writers. Publishes 20 freelance submissions yearly; 30% by unpublished writers, 90% by authors who are new to the magazine. Receives 10 unsolicited mss monthly.

Submissions and Payment: Sample copy and guidelines available at website. Send complete ms. For prose, prefers email to fmschep@charter.net, accepts hard copy. No simultaneous submissions SASE. Responds in 1–4 weeks. For poetry, email submissions only to demiurge@fibitz.com. Responds in 1 week. One-time and electronic rights. Fiction, to 5,000 words. Poetry, 3–5 poems. No payment.

Model Airplane News

Air Age Publishing
88 Danbury Road, Route 7
Wilton, CT 06897

Executive Editor: Debra Cleghorn

Description and Interests: Anything and everything that is related to the collecting, building, and flying of RC model airplanes is found in this monthly magazine. Written by enthusiasts who really know their stuff, its articles include information on specific models, aftermarket customization, and flying competitions. Circ: 95,000.
Website: www.modelairplanenews.com

Freelance Potential: 80% written by nonstaff writers. Publishes 100+ freelance submissions yearly; 33% by authors who are new to the magazine. Receives 12–15 queries monthly.

Submissions and Payment: Sample articles available at website. Query with outline and bio. Accepts hard copy. SASE. Responds in 6 weeks. North American serial rights. Articles, 1,700–2,000 words. Depts/columns, word lengths vary. Written material, $175–$600. Pays on publication. Provides up to 6 contributor's copies.

Modern Haiku

P.O. Box 33077
Santa Fe, NM 87594-3077

Editor: Charles Trumbull

Description and Interests: Original haiku, senryu, haibun, and haiga fill the pages of this independent journal. Also offered are essays on the haiku genre, as well as reviews of haiku collections and studies. *Modern Haiku* is published three times each year. Circ: 600.
Website: www.modernhaiku.org

Freelance Potential: 85% written by nonstaff writers. Publishes 1,000 freelance submissions yearly; 15% by new authors. Receives 500 mss monthly.

Submissions and Payment: Sample articles and guidelines available at website. Query for essays and reviews. Send complete ms for haiku. Accepts hard copy and email to modernhaiku@gmail.com. SASE. Responds in 4–6 weeks. International serial rights, electronic rights, and limited reprint rights. Essays and reviews, word lengths vary; $5 per page. Haiga; $10. Haiku, 5–15 per submission, 2 submissions per issue; $1 each. Halibun, $2 each. Pays on acceptance.

Modernism

199 George Street
Lambertville, NJ 08530

Editor in Chief: Andrea Truppin

Description and Interests: *Modernism* is a quarterly magazine dedicated to twentieth-century modernist architecture, design, and decorative arts. Its readership includes collectors, dealers, and design professionals. Articles cover topics, such as furnishings, graphic design, textiles, and lighting. Profiles of designers and decorative artists, as well as interviews with collectors, are also published. Circ: 30,000.
Website: www.modernismmagazine.com

Freelance Potential: 75% written by nonstaff writers. Publishes 16 freelance submissions yearly; 75% by authors who are new to the magazine.

Submissions and Payment: Guidelines available at website. Query with résumé and two samples of previously published writing and one unpublished. Accepts email queries to andrea@modernism-magazine.com. Response time varies. All rights. Articles, 1,000–2,500 words; $600. Payment policy varies.

Moment Magazine

4115 Wisconsin Avenue NW, Suite 102
Washington, DC 20016

Editor in Chief: Nadine Epstein

Description and Interests: *Moment* is an independent, general-interest magazine offering a fresh perspective on the North American Jewish community and Israel. It publishes in-depth journalistic articles that address cultural, political, historical, and religious issues, as well as first-person and humorous pieces on Jewish life. It is published six times each year. Circ: 100,000.
Website: www.momentmag.com

Freelance Potential: 30% written by nonstaff writers. Publishes 20 freelance submissions yearly. Receives 200 queries monthly.

Submissions and Payment: Guidelines available at website. Query. Accepts email queries to editor@momentmag.com. Responds if interested. All rights. Articles, 900–6,000 words. Depts/columns, word lengths vary. Written material, payment rates vary. Pays on publication.

Mom Magazine

2532 Santiam Highway SE, #102
Albany, OR 97322

Editor: Krista Klinkhammer

Description and Interests: Motherhood is celebrated in this upbeat magazine written by and for moms. Topics covered include everything moms do, from planning birthday parties to balancing career and family. It is published six times each year. Circ: 60,000.
Website: www.mommag.com

Freelance Potential: 85% written by nonstaff writers. Publishes 50 freelance submissions yearly; 50% by unpublished writers, 50% by authors who are new to the magazine. Receives 20 queries, 10 unsolicited mss monthly.

Submissions and Payment: Sample articles and guidelines available at website. Query or send complete ms. Accepts email submissions to krista@mommag.com (Word attachments). Response time varies. Reprint rights. Articles, 500 words. Depts/columns, word lengths vary. No payment. Provides 2 contributor's copies.

The Monthly Aspectarian

P.O. Box 1342
Morton Grove, IL 60053

Editors: James Loftus and Jeanne Spiro

Description and Interests: With a focus on holistic, New Age, and spiritual healing and growth, this monthly publication offers articles, book reviews, resources, and event listings. Also included are personal opinion pieces. Appearing both in print and as a digital magazine, its target audience is the greater Chicago area. Circ: 40,000.
Website: www.monthlyaspectarian.com

Freelance Potential: 80% written by nonstaff writers. Publishes 10 freelance submissions yearly; 40% by authors who are new to the magazine, 60% by experts.

Submissions and Payment: Sample copy and guidelines availabe at website. Send complete ms. Accepts email to walter@monthlyaspectarian.com (Word or text file attachments; "Attn: Aspectarian Editor" in subject line). Responds in 1 month. One-time rights. Articles, 800–1,500 words. No payment. Provides 3 contributor's copies.

More

Transcontinental Media Inc.
25 Sheppard Avenue West, Suite 100
Toronto, Ontario M2N 6S7
Canada

Editor in Chief: Linda Lewis

Description and Interests: *More* presents articles that celebrate the fabulousness of women over 40, while giving them the information and inspiration that fit their needs. Features on health and beauty, body and mind, relationships, travel and adventure, style, family, and career appear alongside inspiring profiles of celebrities and other successful women. It is published six times each year. Circ: Unavailable.
Website: www.more.ca

Freelance Potential: Open to submissions; prefers work that has a Canadian subject or angle. The editors also accept work for the website.

Submissions and Payment: Sample articles available at website. Guidelines available. Query, with clips. Accepts hard copy and electronic queries via the website. SASE. Responds in 8 weeks. Rights vary. Articles and depts/columns, 1,000–2,500 words; payment rates vary. Pays 30 days after acceptance.

Mountain Record

The Zen Practitioner's Journal

P.O. Box 156
831 Plank Road
Mt. Tremper, NY 12457

Managing Editor: Vanessa Goddard

Description and Interests: *Mountain Record* is a quarterly journal with a mission to present to people of all faiths a strong, authentic example of spiritual practice in the midst of everyday life. Much of it is written by Zen experts, but it accepts essays and poetry about life philosophies and book reviews from non-experts. Circ: 5,000.
Website: http://dharma.net/mountainrecord

Freelance Potential: 50% written by nonstaff writers. Of the freelance submissions published yearly, 5% are by unpublished writers, 5% are by authors who are new to the magazine, 80% are by experts. Receives 3 unsolicited mss monthly.

Submissions and Payment: Sample copy and guidelines available. Send complete ms. Accepts hard copy. SASE. Responds in 1 month. One-time print and electronic rights. Articles, 5,000 words. No payment. Provides 2 contributor's copies.

Ms. Fitness

P.O. Box 2490
White City, OR 97503

Editor: Greta Blackburn

Description and Interests: Women seeking information and tips for a healthy, active lifestyle turn to this quarterly publication. It is filled with articles on fitness training, exercise, nutrition, and celebrity workouts and diets. Circ: 90,000.
Website: www.msfitness.com

Freelance Potential: 50% written by nonstaff writers. Publishes 40 freelance submissions yearly; 60% by unpublished writers, 50% by authors who are new to the magazine, 60% by experts. Receives 5 queries, 5 unsolicited mss each month.

Submissions and Payment: Sample copy available, guidelines and editorial calendar available. Query or send complete ms. Accepts hard copy, disk submissions, and simultaneous submissions if identified. SASE. Responds in 2–3 months. Rights vary. Written material, word lengths vary. No payment. Provides 1 contributor's copy.

Ms. Magazine

433 South Beverly Drive
Beverly Hills, CA 90212

Senior Editor: Michele Kort

Description and Interests: *Ms. Magazine* offers informative articles, contemporary fiction, and investigative reports from a feminist viewpoint. It is published quarterly. Circ: 110,000.
Website: www.msmagazine.com

Freelance Potential: 85% written by nonstaff writers. Publishes 4 freelance submissions yearly; 5% by unpublished writers, 30% by authors who are new to the magazine, 30% by experts. Receives 60 queries, 50 unsolicited mss monthly.

Submissions and Payment: Sample articles and guidelines available at website. Query with brief bio and clips; or send complete ms with cover letter. Accepts hard copy and email to mkort@msmagazine.com. SASE. Responds in 3 months. First North American serial rights. Articles and fiction, 1,500–3,000 words. Depts/columns, 600–1,200 words. Written material, payment rates vary. Kill fee, 25%. Pays on publication. Provides 2 contributor's copies.

My Home My Style

August Home Publishing
2200 Grand Avenue
Des Moines, IA 50312

Managing Editor: Dave Stone

Description and Interests: This magazine for creative do-it-yourselfers focuses on creating a home that reflects the owner's personality and lifestyle. Ideas, practical tips, and affordable design options are covered. Each article includes information on how readers can replicate a project in their own homes—and alter it to fit their own styles. It accepts no advertising. Circ: Unavailable.
Website: www.augusthome.com/brands/myhomemystyle/

Freelance Potential: Material should be written in a friendly, personal style, as if at work in the workshop. Contributors should be well-informed on the topics about which they write.

Submissions and Payment: Sample articles available at website. To submit ideas or query about freelance opportunities, contact the editor via the form at website. Response time varies.

Na'amat Woman

505 Eighth Avenue, Suite 2302
New York, NY 10018

Editor: Judith A. Sokoloff

Description and Interests: NA'AMAT USA publishes this quarterly magazine to inform members about its worldwide activities. Its articles cover topics from a Jewish perspective, such as women's rights, arts and literature, and the relationship between the U.S. and Israel. Circ: 10,000.
Website: www.naamat.org

Freelance Potential: 70% written by nonstaff writers. Publishes 20–25 freelance submissions yearly; 10% by authors who are new to the magazine. Receives 5 queries, 10 unsolicited mss each month.

Submissions and Payment: Sample copy available at website. Guidelines available. Query or send complete ms with clips. Accepts hard copy. SASE. Responds in 1 month. First North American serial rights. Articles and fiction, 2,000–3,000 words; $.10–$.15 per word. Pays on publication. Provides 2 contributor's copies.

Nano Fiction 

P.O. Box 2188
Tuscaloosa, AL 35402

Editor: Kirby Johnson

Description and Interests: This literary magazine features flash fiction of 300 words or fewer. Writers from across the country, at all levels of their careers, are represented. *NANO Fiction* appears twice each year. Circ: 500.
Website: www.nanofiction.org

Freelance Potential: 100% written by nonstaff writers. Publishes 40 freelance submissions yearly; 60% by unpublished writers, 95% by authors who are new to the magazine.

Submissions and Payment: Guidelines available at website. Send complete ms. Accepts submissions through website only. Response time varies. Exclusive print and electronic rights for 3 months; non–exclusive rights, indefinitely. Written material, to 300 words; limit 5 pieces. No payment. Provides 1 contributor's copy.

Narrative

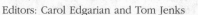

Editors: Carol Edgarian and Tom Jenks

Description and Interests: This digital publication offers a vehicle for bringing new literature by celebrated authors as well as new and emerging writers to readers everywhere free of charge. It accepts poetry; fiction, including short stories, novel excerpts, and novellas; and creative nonfiction, including essays, humor, memoirs, commentary, and reportage. *Narrative* also offers many contests. Circ: Unknown.
Website: www.narrativemagazine.com

Freelance Potential: Publishes many freelance submissions each year..

Submissions and Payment: Sample articles available at website. Send complete ms, author bio, and submission fee. Accepts submissions through website and simultaneous submissions. Responds in 4–12 weeks. Rights, unknown. Fiction and nonfiction, 500–2,500 words, $150–$300; 2,000–15,000 words, $350–$1,000; book-length work, rates vary; poetry, up to 5 poems per submisission; $50 minimum per poem. Payment policy, unknown.

The Nation

33 Irving Place, 8th Floor
New York, NY 10003

Editor: Katrina vanden Heuvel

Description and Interests: *The Nation* covers national and international affairs and the arts through journalistic articles, essays, and commentary—all from a left wing/liberal perspective. It is published weekly. Circ: 185,000.
Website: www.thenation.com

Freelance Potential: 70% written by nonstaff writers. Publishes 10 freelance submissions yearly; 10% by unpublished writers, 40% by authors who are new to the magazine. Receives 100 queries monthly.

Submissions and Payment: Sample articles and guidelines available at website. Query. Prefers query via website; will accept hard copy. SASE. Responds in 1 month. First rights. Articles, 1,500–2,500 words; $350–$500. Commentary, 750 words; $150. Depts/columns and poetry, word lengths and payment rates vary. Kill fee, 33%. Pays on publication. Provides 2 contributor's copies.

National Masters News

P.O. Box 1117
Orangevale, CA 95662

Publisher: Randell Sturgeon

Description and Interests: Dedicated to track and field, long-distance running, and racewalking for men and women over the age of 30, *National Masters News* provides detailed coverage of all masters division events throughout the United States. Published monthly, it also features training tips and athlete profiles. Circ: 5,000.
Website: www.nationalmastersnews.com

Freelance Potential: 90% written by nonstaff writers. Publishes 64 freelance submissions yearly; 10% by unpublished writers, 10% by authors who are new to the magazine. Receives 4 queries, 6 unsolicited mss monthly.

Submissions and Payment: Sample copy and guidelines available. Query or send complete ms. Accepts hard copy and simultaneous submissions if identified. SASE. Responds in 2 weeks. One-time rights. Written material, 750-1,500 words. No payment. Provides contributor's copies upon request.

Natural Bridge

University of Missouri-St. Louis English Department
1 University Boulevard
St. Louis, MO 63121

Managing Editor: Lauren Wiser

Description and Interests: Twice each year, this literary journal publishes high-quality short fiction, poetry, and creative nonfiction. It welcomes work from new, as well as established authors. Circ: 5,000+.
Website: www.umsl.edu/~natural

Freelance Potential: 100% written by nonstaff writers. Publishes 60 freelance submissions yearly; 20% by unpublished writers, 80% by authors who are new to the magazine. Receives 200 unsolicited mss monthly.

Submissions and Payment: Sample copy and guidelines available at website. Send complete ms year round (will not be read between May 1 and August 1). Accepts online submissions through website, hard copy and simultaneous submissions if identified. SASE. Responds in 6 months. Rights vary. Fiction, personal essays, and translations, to 30 pages. Poetry, no line limit; to 6 poems per submission. Submit to only one genre per reading period. No payment. Provides 2 contributor's copies and a 1-year subscription.

Nebo

A Literary Journal

English Department, Witherspoon 141
Arkansas Tech University
Russellville, AR 72801

Nebo Editor

Description and Interests: Appearing twice each year, *Nebo* features fiction, poetry, and art that is technically and creatively exceptional. It publishes emerging, as well as well-known writers. Circ: Unavailable.
Website: www.atu.edu/worldlanguages/Nebo.shtml

Freelance Potential: 80% written by nonstaff writers. Publishes 25 freelance submissions yearly; 25% by unpublished writers, 40% by authors who are new to the magazine. Receives 30–40 queries and unsolicited mss monthly.

Submissions and Payment: Sample copy available. Guidelines available at website. Send complete ms with cover letter, bio, credits, and mailing address between August 15 and January 31. Accepts hard copy and email to nebo@atu.edu. SASE. Responds in 2–4 months. Rights vary. Fiction, 2,000 words. Poetry, to 5 poems. No payment. Provides 2 contributor's copies.

Necrology Shorts

P.O. Box 510232
St. Louis, MO 63151

Editor

Description and Interests: This ezine features horror, science fiction, and fantasy in the style of Lovecraft and Howard—that is, dark and suspenseful. It publishes fiction, poetry, book and movie reviews, photography, and cartoons from first-time writers, as well as professional authors. Hits per month: 25,000–30,000.
Website: www.necrologyshorts.com

Freelance Potential: 99% written by nonstaff writers. Publishes 300 freelance submissions yearly; 20% by unpublished writers, 60% by authors who are new to the magazine. Receives 2,000 unsolicited mss each month.

Submissions and Payment: Sample copy and guidelines available at website. Send complete ms. Accepts email to submit@necrologyshorts.com (Word, PDF, text files, JPEG, GIF, or Photoshop attachments). Responds in 2 weeks. Online rights; option on anthology rights. Fiction, at least 2,000 words. Reviews, 1,000–2,000 words. Poetry, to 5 poems per submission. No payment.

Neo-opsis Science Fiction Magazine

4129 Carey Road
Victoria, British Columbia V8Z 4G5, Canada

Editor: Karl Johanson

Description and Interests: This magazine is published up to three times each year, filled with science fiction and fantasy short stories, poetry, reviews, science fiction news, and informative articles. It opens and closes submissions for each issue; check website for current dates. Circ: 580.
Website: www.neo-opsis.ca

Freelance Potential: 78% written by nonstaff writers. Publishes 24 freelance submissions yearly; 5% by unpublished writers, 90% by authors who are new to the magazine. Receives 250 unsolicited mss monthly.

Submissions and Payment: Guidelines available at website. Send complete ms. Accepts hard copy and email to neoopsis@shaw.ca (Word or RTF attachments; include submission, title, and word count in subject line). No simultaneous submissions. SAE/IRC. Responds in 2 months. First serial rights. Articles and fiction, to 6,000 words. Written material, $.025 per word; $125 maximum. Pays on publication. Provides 1–2 copies.

The New Centennial Review

Department of English, 17-A Morrill Hall
Michigan State University
East Lansing, MI 48824-1036

Editors: Scott Michaelsen & David Johnson

Description and Interests: This scholarly journal is devoted to comparative studies of the Americas that suggest possibilities for a different future. It is published three times each year. Circ: 1,000.
Website: www.msupress.msu.edu/journals/cr//

Freelance Potential: 100% written by nonstaff writers. Publishes 30 freelance submissions yearly; 5% by unpublished writers, 40% by authors who are new to the magazine. Receives 20 queries, 30 unsolicited mss monthly.

Submissions and Payment: Sample copy and editorial calendar available. Guidelines available at website. Query or send complete ms. Accepts hard copy. SASE. Responds to queries in 2 weeks, to mss in 2–3 months. All rights. Written material, word lengths vary. No payment. Provides 2 contributor's copies.

New Delta Review  

15 Allen Hall, Department of English
Louisiana State University
Baton Rouge, LA 70803–5001

Editor: Becky Kaiser

Description and Interests: Produced by students in the MFA program at Louisiana State University, *NDR* encourages new and unpublished writers to submit their work for publication in its online format. Two issues are produced each year and include fiction, nonfiction, and poetry, as well as interviews, reviews, and artwork. Hits per month: Unavailable.
Website: http://ndrmag.org

Freelance Potential: 90% written by nonstaff writers. Publishes 40 freelance submissions yearly; 20% by unpublished writers, 65% by authors who are new to the magazine. Receives 80 mss monthly.

Submissions and Payment: Sample copy available. Guidelines available at website. Send complete ms. Accepts hard copy and online submissions; simultaneous submissions permitted if identified. SASE. Responds in 6 months. First North American serial rights. Fiction, to 6,000 words. Poetry, to 5 poems per submission. No payment.

New Letters 

University of Missouri-Kansas City
University House
5101 Rockhill Road
Kansas City, MO 64110–2499

Editor in Chief: Robert Stewart

Description and Interests: This literary magazine showcases the finest work of today's authors. Quarterly issues offer original fiction, poetry, and creative nonfiction covering a wide range of genres, styles, and subject matter. Circ: 3,000.
Website: www.newletters.org

Freelance Potential: 99% written by nonstaff writers. Publishes 100 freelance submissions yearly; 20% by unpublished writers, 30% by authors who are new to the magazine. Receives 250 unsolicited mss monthly.

Submissions and Payment: Sample copy available. Guidelines available at website. Send complete ms between October 2 and April 30. Accepts hard copy only. SASE. Responds in 5 months. First North American serial rights. Prose, 3,000–5,000 words. Poetry, to 6 poems. Payment rates vary. Pays on acceptance. Provides 2 contributor's copies.

New Orleans Review 

Loyola University, Box 195
6363 St. Charles Avenue
New Orleans, LA 70118

Editor: Mark Yakich

Description and Interests: Published twice each year, this international literary journal features original fiction, poetry, creative nonfiction, translations, book reviews, and interviews. Circ: 1,400.
Website: http://neworleansreview.org

Freelance Potential: 99% written by nonstaff writers. Publishes 100 freelance submissions yearly; 5% by unpublished writers, 80% by authors who are new to the magazine. Receives 250 unsolicited mss each month.

Submissions and Payment: Sample copy available. Send complete ms between August 15 and May 15. Accepts submissions via website only; $3 submission fee. Accepts simultaneous submissions if identified. Responds in 3–4 months. First North American serial rights. Needs and requirements vary per issue; check website. No payment. Provides 2 contributor's copies.

The New Orphic Review 

706 Mill Street
Nelson, British Columbia V1L 4S5
Canada

Editor in Chief: Ernest Hekkanen

Description and Interests: Published twice each year, this literary journal offers fiction, poetry, and articles on a wide range of topics and themes. Circ: 250.
Website: www3.telus.net/neworphicpublishers-hekkanen

Freelance Potential: 99% written by nonstaff writers. Publishes 20–25 freelance submissions yearly; 60% by unpublished writers, 80% by authors who are new to the magazine. Receives 35 unsolicited mss each month.

Submissions and Payment: Sample copy and guidelines available. Send complete ms. Accepts hard copy and simultaneous submissions if identified. SAE/IRC. Responds in 3 months. First North American serial rights. Articles and fiction, to 10,000 words. Depts/columns, 1,000 words. Poetry, no line limit. No payment. Provides 1 contributor's copy.

The New Quarterly 

St. Jerome's University
290 Westmount Road North
Waterloo, Ontario, Canada N2L 3G3

Editor: Pamela Mulloy

Description and Interests: Both new and established Canadian writers find a home for their work in this quarterly journal. It features fiction, nonfiction, and poetry. Circ: 3,500.
Website: www.tnq.ca

Freelance Potential: 90% written by nonstaff writers. Publishes 72 freelance submissions yearly; 25% by authors who are new to the magazine. Receives hundreds of queries and unsolicited mss monthly.

Submissions and Payment: Canadian writers only. Sample copy available. Guidelines available at website. Query to editor@tnq.ca for nonfiction. Send complete ms for fiction and poetry with cover sheet from website. Reading periods, September to December and March to June. One submission in each genre per year. Accepts hard copy and simultaneous submissions if identified. SASE. Responds in 4 months. First Canadian rights. Fiction and essays, word lengths vary; $250. Poetry, $40. Pays on publication.

The New Renaissance 

26 Heath Road, #11
Arlington, MA 02474-3645

Senior Editor: Michal Anne Kucharski

Description and Interests: This highly selective literary magazine publishes well-crafted, thought-provoking essays and fiction twice each year. All fiction and poetry submissions are entered into the magazine's awards program. Circ: 1,200.
Website: www.tnrlitmag.org

Freelance Potential: 90–95% written by nonstaff writers. Publishes 60–70 freelance submissions yearly; 15% by unpublished writers, 25–50% by authors who are new to the magazine. Receives 5–10 queries, 130–170 mss monthly.

Submissions and Payment: Guidelines available at website. Send complete ms for fiction, poetry, and essays; January to June and September to October only. Accepts hard copy. SASE. Submission fee: $17.50 ($22 foreign) for nonsubscribers; $14.75 ($18 foreign) for subscribers. Responds in 5–8 months. First rights. Fiction and nonfiction, 300–10,000 words; payment rates vary. Pays after publication. Provides 2 contributor's copies.

NewsUSA

2841 Hartland Road, Suite 301
Falls Church, VA 22043

Managing Editor: Jake Maurer

Description and Interests: This placement service provides newspaper features and filler that inform and educate readers about a number of consumer issues related to finance, health, safety, home, and travel. It is published 24 times each year. All work must follow the AP style of writing. Circ: 10,000.
Website: www.newsusa.com

Freelance Potential: 10% written by nonstaff writers. Publishes 60 freelance submissions yearly; 50% by authors who are new to the magazine. Receives 5 queries monthly.

Submissions and Payment: Sample copy and guidelines available. Query. Accepts email queries to jmaurer@newsusa.com. Response time varies. All rights. Articles, 350–400 words. Depts/columns, word lengths vary. Written material, $50. Pays on acceptance.

The Newtowner 

P.O. Box 456
Newtown, CT 06470

Editor in Chief: Georgia Monaghan

Description and Interests: *The Newtowner* is a local quarterly arts and literary magazine that features fiction, memoirs, essays, and poetry, as well as articles that profile local writers and visual and performing artists. Its mission is to celebrate and showcase new and established writers and artists. It also offers a section of writing by youths. Circ: Unavailable.
Website: www.thenewtownermagazine.com

Freelance Potential: It is mostly written by nonstaff writers. Accepts freelance submissions in all categories.

Submissions and Payment: Sample copy available. Send complete ms. Accepts electronic submissions via website. Responds in 2–3 months if interested. Fiction, to 4,000 words. Poetry, to 35 lines; to 3 poems per submission. Creative nonfiction, to 3,000 words. First North American serial rights. No payment. Provides 2 contributor's copies.

Nineteenth Century

The Victorian Society in America
P.O. Box 403
Stony Brook, NY 11790-0403

Editor: William Ayres

Description and Interests: As the official publication of the Victorian Society in America, *Nineteenth Century* provides readers with a glimpse of what life was like in the Victorian era. Articles cover lifestyle, arts, architecture, fashion, and the social climate. It is published twice each year. Circ: 28,000.
Website: www.victoriansociety.org

Freelance Potential: 100% written by nonstaff writers. Publishes 8–10 freelance submissions yearly; 50% by authors who are new to the magazine, 50% by experts. Receives 4 queries, 4 unsolicited mss monthly.

Submissions and Payment: Sample copy available. Guidelines available at website. Query with biography; or send complete ms. Accepts hard copy. SASE. Responds in 2–3 weeks. First rights. Articles, 3,000–5,000 words. B/W prints. No payment. Provides 5 contributor's copies.

North American Review 

University of Northern Iowa
1222 West 27th Street
Cedar Falls, IA 50614-0516

Fiction, Poetry, or Nonfiction Editor

Description and Interests: High-quality poetry, fiction, and nonfiction are published here quarterly. It will review all submissions, but prefers pieces on the environment, gender, race, and class. Circ: 2,500.
Website: www.NorthAmericanReview.org

Freelance Potential: 98% written by nonstaff writers. Publishes 240 freelance submissions yearly; 6% by unpublished writers, 7% by authors who are new to the magazine. Receives 595 unsolicited mss monthly.

Submissions and Payment: Sample copy available. Guidelines available at website. Send complete ms. Accepts electronic submissions via website. Responds in 5 months. First North American serial rights. Poetry, to 6 poems. Fiction, to 1 short story or 2 short-short stories. Nonfiction, to one article or essay. Written material, word lengths vary; $20–$100. Pays on publication. Provides 2 contributor's copies.

North Atlantic Review 

15 Arbutus Lane
Stony Brook, NY 11790-1408

Editor: John E. Gill

Description and Interests: This annual literary journal is an eclectic mix of short stories, poetry, humor, nonfiction, essays, and satire. It also features special sections on cultural and social issues. Specific calls for submissions for the special sections will be posted on the website. Circ: 500.
Website: www.northeaglecorp.com/nar.html

Freelance Potential: 90% written by nonstaff writers. Publishes 25 freelance submissions yearly; 20% by unpublished writers, 70% by authors who are new to the magazine. Receives 50 queries and unsolicited mss monthly.

Submissions and Payment: Sample copy available. Guidelines available at website. Send complete ms. Accepts hard copy, email to johnedwardgill@cs.com, and simultaneous submissions if identified. SASE. Responds in 5–6 months. First rights. Fiction, to 6,000 words; poetry, to 1,000 words. No payment. Provides contributor's copies.

North Carolina Literary Review 

Department of English, East Carolina University
Mailstop 555 English
Greenville, NC 27858-4353

Editor: Margaret Bauer

Description and Interests: Each annual issue of *NCLR* centers on the state's writers and literature. Articles cover literary history and culture. Prose, poetry, reviews, and essays are also published. Circ: 750.
Website: www.nclr.ecu.edu

Freelance Potential: 80% written by nonstaff writers. Publishes 25 freelance submissions yearly; 25% by unpublished writers, 75% by authors who are new to the magazine.

Submissions and Payment: Sample copy available. Guidelines and theme list available at website. Query or send complete ms. Fiction and poetry accepted only through contests (see guidelines for information). Accepts electronic submissions via website. Reading periods vary. Responds in 1–3 months. All rights. Poetry, to 5 pages. Other written material, word lengths vary. Payment policy varies. Provides 2 contributor's copies.

North Dakota Quarterly

University of North Dakota
Merrifield Hall Room 15
276 Centennial Drive Stop 7209
Grand Forks, ND 58202-7209

Editor: Robert W. Lewis

Description and Interests: This literary journal from the University of North Dakota offers the work of new and established writers. It offers fiction, poetry, and essays, and often features articles on Northern Plains culture and American Indian studies. Circ: 700.
Website: www.und.edu/org/ndq

Freelance Potential: 99% written by nonstaff writers. Publishes 80 freelance submissions yearly; 5% by unpublished writers, 30% by authors who are new to the magazine. Receives 125 unsolicited mss monthly.

Submissions and Payment: Sample copy available. Guidelines available at website. Send complete ms. Accepts hard copy. Accepts simultaneous submissions for fiction and essays only. SASE. Responds in 3 months. First serial rights. Written material, word length varies. No payment. Provides contributor's copies.

Notre Dame Review

840 Flanner Hall
University of Notre Dame
Notre Dame, IN 46556

Managing Editor

Description and Interests: This literary journal features American and international fiction, poetry, and criticism in each of its two issues published every year. There is also an online companion to the print version, which offers additional material. Circ: 1,500.
Website: http://ndreview.nd.edu

Freelance Potential: 100% written by nonstaff writers. Publishes 100 freelance submissions yearly; 20% by unpublished writers, 50% by authors who are new to the magazine. Receives 200 unsolicited mss monthly.

Submissions and Payment: Sample copy available. Guidelines available at website. Send complete ms from September to November or January to March. Accepts hard copy and simultaneous submissions if identified. SASE. Responds in 3–12 months. First North American serial and anthology rights. Fiction and essays, to 5,000 words. Poetry, word lengths vary. Small honorarium paid on publication. Provides 1 contributor's copy.

Now What?

P.O. Box 33677
Denver, CO 80233

Associate Editor: Sherri Langton

Description and Interests: This monthly ezine focuses on the "felt needs" of people, such as grief, depression, unemployment, and sickness. The writing describes personal struggles that led the authors to faith in Christ or deepened their walk with God. It is a publication of the General Conference of the Church of God (Seventh Day). Hits per month: Unavailable.
Website: http://nowwhat.cog7.org

Freelance Potential: 100% written by nonstaff writers. Publishes 12–20 freelance submissions yearly. Receives 20 unsolicited mss monthly.

Submissions and Payment: Sample copy and guidelines available at website. Send complete ms. Prefers email submissions to bibleadvocate@cog7.org; will accept hard copy, simultaneous submissions, and reprints. SASE. Responds in 1–2 months. First, electronic, and reprint rights. Articles, to 1,500 words; $25–$55. Pays on publication.

Obsidian

North Carolina State University
English Department Box 8105
Raleigh, NC 27695-8105

Editor in Chief: Sheila Smith McKoy

Description and Interests: This literary magazine, published twice a year, features prose and poetry about the African Diaspora. It also publishes interviews, essays, and book reviews. Circ: 500.
Website: http://english.chass.nscu.edu/obsidian

Freelance Potential: 100% written by nonstaff writers. Publishes 40 freelance submissions yearly; 50% by unpublished writers, 50% by authors who are new to the magazine. Receives 20 unsolicited mss monthly.

Submissions and Payment: Sample copy available. Guidelines and theme list available at website. Send complete ms. Accepts submissions online only (in Word). SASE. Responds in 3 months. All rights. Articles and fiction, 20 pages. Poetry, to 8 pages; to 5 poems per submission. No payment.

OK! Weekly

4 New York Plaza
New York, NY 10004

Editor in Chief: Ryan Pienciak

Description and Interests: This popular checkout aisle weekly is filled with all the latest buzz on America's movie, television, and music celebrities. It also features entertainment reviews and articles on fashion, relationships, and health. This publication is a market for experienced writers; beginner writers may find it difficult to break into. Circ: 400,000.
Website: www.okmagazine.com

Freelance Potential: 10% written by nonstaff writers. Publishes 50–70 freelance submissions yearly; 5% by authors who are new to the magazine, 10% by experts. Receives 3 queries each month.

Submissions and Payment: Sample copy available at newsstands. Guidelines available. Query. Accepts hard copy. SASE. Response time varies. All rights. Articles, 200–800 words; payment rates vary. Pays on publication. Provides 1 contributor's copy.

Old Cars Weekly News & Marketplace

700 East State Street
Iola, WI 54990-0001

Editor: Angelo Van Bogart

Description and Interests: This tabloid provides a comprehensive view of the world of vintage automobiles for collectors, dealers, and enthusiasts. Appearing weekly, it features articles on buying, selling, and appreciating older cars, as well as reports on notable events and auctions. Circ: 70,000.
Website: www.oldcarsweekly.com

Freelance Potential: 30–40% written by nonstaff writers. Publishes 1,500 freelance submissions yearly; 10% by unpublished writers, 10% by authors who are new to the magazine, 80% by experts. Receives 200 unsolicited mss monthly.

Submissions and Payment: Sample copy and guidelines available. Send complete ms. Accepts email submissions to angelo.vanbogart@fwmedia.com. Response time varies. All rights. Written material, word lengths vary; $.05 per word. Pays after publication.

Old-House Interiors

108 East Main Street
Gloucester, MA 01930

Editor in Chief: Patricia Poore

Description and Interests: This magazine of "period-inspired home design" showcases the best of today's period rooms, both historical and interpretive. Published six times each year, it offers expert advice on finishing, decorating, and furnishing period homes. Circ: 120,000.
Website: www.oldhouseonline.com

Freelance Potential: 25% written by nonstaff writers. Publishes 6 freelance submissions yearly; 5% by authors who are new to the magazine, 5% by experts. Receives 5 queries monthly.

Submissions and Payment: Sample copy and guidelines available. Editorial calendar available at website. Query with scouting shots. Accepts hard copy. SASE. Responds in 2–3 months. First rights. Articles, 750–1,200 words. Depts/columns, 800–1,500 words. Written material, $100–$200 per page. Transparencies; payment rates vary. Pays on publication. Provides 3–5 contributor's copies.

The Oldie

65 Newman Street
London W1T 3EG
England

Features Editor: Jeremy Lewis

Description and Interests: *The Oldie* publishes a mix of profiles, interviews, essays, and articles. While the topics it covers may vary, all articles are written with humor. Published 13 times a year, it is most interested in receiving pieces for its I Once Met and Rant sections. Circ: 36,000.
Website: www.theoldie.co.uk

Freelance Potential: 90% written by nonstaff writers. Publishes 20 freelance submissions yearly; 10% by unpublished writers, 20% by authors who are new to the magazine. Receives 60–100 unsolicited mss monthly.

Submissions and Payment: Sample copy available. Guidelines available at website. Send complete ms. Accepts hard copy and email submissions to jeremylewis@theoldie.co.uk (Word attachments). SAE/IRC. Responds in 1 month. Rights vary. Articles, to 1,300 words; £100 per published page. Pays on publication. Provides 1 contributor's copy.

One

CNEWA
1011 First Avenue
New York, NY 10022-4195

Executive Editor: Michael La Civita

Description and Interests: *One* is the publication of the Catholic Near East Welfare Association. Published six times each year, it focuses on humanitarian needs in the Near East and the Middle East and on issues affecting the Orthodox and Catholic union. Circ: 67,000.
Website: www.cnewa.org

Freelance Potential: 80% written by nonstaff writers. Publishes 20 freelance submissions yearly; 3% by unpublished writers, 30% by authors who are new to the magazine, 30% by experts. Receives 5 queries monthly.

Submissions and Payment: Sample copy available at website. Guidelines available. Query with résumé and clips or writing samples. Accepts hard copy. SASE. Responds in 1 month. All rights. Articles, to 2,500 words. Written material, payment rates vary. Pays on publication. Provides 5 contributor's copies.

One Story

232 Third Street, #E106
Brooklyn, NY 11215

Editor: Hannah Tinti

Description and Interests: Believing that short stories are best read alone, *One Story* offers readers an alternative to the usual literary journal that is packed with stories and poetry. Published 18 times each year, *One Story* contains just one short story—but a great one—per issue. It welcomes new and established authors. Circ: 6,000.
Website: www.one-story.com

Freelance Potential: 100% written by nonstaff writers. Publishes 18 freelance submissions yearly; 100% by authors who are new to the magazine. Receives 600 unsolicited mss monthly.

Submissions and Payment: Guidelines available at website. Send complete ms between September 1 and May 31. Accepts electronic submissions through website only (RTF files) and simultaneous submissions. Responds in 1–3 months. First North American serial rights. Fiction, 3,000–8,000 words; $250. Pays on publication. Provides 25 contributor's copies.

On the Premises

Chief Editor: Tarl Roger Kudrick

Description and Interests: *On the Premises* is an online literary journal that has been featuring short fiction since 2006. Stories in a variety of genres are welcome. A new issue is posted three times each year. Awards for first, second, and third prize are presented to the best stories in each issue. Hits per month: 5,000.
Website: www.onthepremises.com

Freelance Potential: 98% written by nonstaff writers. Publishes 15–18 freelance submissions yearly; 20% by unpublished writers, 80% by authors who are new to the magazine. Receives 50–100 unsolicited mss monthly.

Submissions and Payment: Sample copy, guidelines, and topics available at website. Send complete ms. Accepts entries online via website (Word, RTF, plain text, and OpenOffice formats). Response time varies. HTML and PDF rights. Fiction, 1,000–5,000 words. Payment to contest winners only, to $180.

On Spec

Box 4727
Edmonton, Alberta T6E 5G6
Canada

Managing Editor: Diane Walton

Description and Interests: *On Spec* is a quarterly magazine of speculative writing. It showcases original works of fiction and contemporary poetry written predominantly by Canadian writers and artists. It seeks the highest quality fantasy, science fiction, horror, ghost and fairy stories, and magic realism. It does not accept nonfiction. Circ: 1,000.
Website: www.onspec.ca

Freelance Potential: 95% written by nonstaff writers. Publishes 40 freelance submissions yearly.

Submissions and Payment: Sample copy, guidelines, and editorial calendar available at website. Send complete ms with brief author biography; check website for reading periods. Fiction may be mailed or emailed to onspecmag@gmail.com. Poetry must be mailed. SASE/IRC. Responds in 4–6 months. First North American serial rights. Short fiction to 1,000 words; $50. Fiction, to 6,000 words; $125–$200 and a 1-year subscription. Poetry, 4–100 lines; $50. Pays on acceptance.

Open Minds

3116 South Mill Avenue, #153
Tempe, AZ 85282

Editor: Jason McClellan

Description and Interests: Aliens and UFOs are the subjects of this magazine, published six times each year in print and a digital edition. It focuses on exploring the nature of the UFO phenomenon, its history, evidence, and sociopolitical ramifications. Topics include UFO sightings, alien abductions, interplanetary missions, and "far out" scientific advances and discoveries. Circ: Unavailable.
Website: www.openminds.tv/magazine

Freelance Potential: Open to submissions for the magazine and the website. Submissions must include credible witnesses, substantiated claims, good scientific evidence, and "more information than opinion."

Submissions and Payment: Sample articles and guidelines available at website. Send complete ms. Accepts hard copy and email submissions to contact@openminds.tv. SASE. Response time varies. Rights vary. Articles, 6,000–15,000 characters (spaces included); word lengths vary. Payment policy varies.

Opera News

Metropolitan Opera Guild
70 Lincoln Center Plaza, 6th Floor
New York, NY 10023-6593

Features Editor: Kitty March

Description and Interests: Opera buffs read this monthly magazine for its celebrity profiles and interviews, as well as news and reviews of the upcoming opera seasons, both in the U.S. and abroad. Circ: 101,000.
Website: www.operanews.com

Freelance Potential: 85% written by nonstaff writers. Publishes 5–10 freelance submissions yearly; 10% by authors who are new to the magazine, 90% by experts. Receives 10 queries, 5 unsolicited mss monthly.

Submissions and Payment: Sample articles, editorial calendar, and guidelines available at website. Query or send complete ms with published clips. Accepts hard copy and email to info@operanews.com. SASE. Responds to queries in 2 weeks, to mss in 2 months. All rights. Articles, 1,800–2,500 words. Depts/columns, 500–800 words. Written material, $450–$1,000. Pays on publication. Provides 2 contributor's copies.

Outdoor America

707 Conservation Lane
Gaithersburg, MD 20878-2983

Editor: Dawn Merritt

Description and Interests: This quarterly membership magazine of the Izaak Walton League focuses on environmental and conservation issues. Each issue also shares news and updates on members, activities, and policies. Circ: 40,000.
Website: www.iwla.org

Freelance Potential: 20% written by nonstaff writers. Publishes 16 freelance submissions yearly; 5% by experts. Receives 4 queries, 2 unsolicited mss monthly.

Submissions and Payment: Sample articles available at website. Guidelines available. Query or send complete ms. Prefers email to oa@iwla.org; will accept disk submissions (Word files). SASE. Responds in 2 months. First North American serial rights. Articles, 2,000–3,000 words; $.50 per word. Kill fee, varies. Pays on acceptance. Provides 3 conributor's copies.

Outlooks Magazine

542 Parliament Street
Toronto, Ontario M4X 1P5
Canada

Editor in Chief: Jim Brosseau

Description and Interests: This Canadian magazine targets young, educated, affluent professionals interested in GLBT issues. Published 10 times each year, it needs more articles on lifestyle and social issues. Circ: 40,000.
Website: www.outlooks.ca

Freelance Potential: 95% written by nonstaff writers. Of the freelance submissions published yearly, 20% are by unpublished writers, 30% are by authors who are new to the magazine, 50% are by experts.

Submissions and Payment: Sample copy available at website. Query. Accepts hard copy and email queries to editor@outlooks.ca. SAE/IRC. Responds in 1 month. Rights vary. Articles, 750–2,200 words. Depts/columns, 600–700 words. Written material, payment rates vary. Kill fee, $75 Canadian. Pays on publication. Provides 1 contributor's copy.

Oxford Magazine  

356 Bachelor Hall, Miami University
Oxford, OH 45056

Editor in Chief: Tony Ramstetter

Description and Interests: Produced by graduate students at Miami University and appearing two times a year, *Oxford Magazine* is a Web-based journal featuring the best in fiction, poetry, essays, creative nonfiction, and the occasional literary interview. Hits per month: Unavailable.
Website: www.orgs.muohio.edu/oxmag

Freelance Potential: 100% written by nonstaff writers. Publishes many freelance submissions yearly. Receives 20–50 mss monthly.

Submissions and Payment: Sample copy and guidelines available at website. Send complete ms. Accepts email submissions; essays to oxmagessayseditor@muohio.edu; fiction to oxmagfictioneditor@muohio.edu; and poetry to oxmagpoetryeditor@muohio.edu (Word or RTF attachments; include name and genre in subject line). Accepts simultaneous submissions if identified. Responds in 12 weeks. First North American serial, one-time anthology, and online serial rights. Written material, to 3,000 words. No payment.

Painted Bride Quarterly 

Drexel University, Departments of English & Philosophy
3141 Chestnut Street
Philadelphia, PA 19104

Editor: Kathleen Volk Miller

Description and Interests: Fiction, poetry, essays, and reviews appear in this literary magazine. A print edition is published annually, but work is posted to the website on a quarterly basis. Hits per month: 18,000–30,000. Circ: 2,500.
Website: www.pbq.drexel.edu

Freelance Potential: 99% written by nonstaff writers. Publishes 120 freelance submissions yearly; 20% by unpublished writers, 20% by authors who are new to the magazine. Receives 200 unsolicited mss monthly.

Submissions and Payment: Sample copy, guidelines, and theme list available at website. Send complete ms with author bio. Accepts submissions via website. Responds in 3–6 months. First rights. Fiction, to 5,000 words. Essays and reviews, to 3,000 words. Poetry, to 5 poems per submission. Written material, payment rates vary. Payment policy varies.

Palate Press  

The Online Wine Magazine

9425 Meridian #201
Indianapolis, IN 46260

Managing Editor: Ryan Reichert

Description and Interests: This contemporary ezine aims to demystify the wine industry and make it accessible for wine lovers everywhere. It covers everything from how to buy a good wine, to wine pairing, to the science behind wine making, and varietals. Profiles of wineries, vintners, and wines are also featured. Hits per month: Unavailable.
Website: www.palatepress.com

Freelance Potential: Open to freelance writers, especially new writers. Knowledge of wine is a must. In addition to articles for the site, opportunities exist for on-the-scene reporters at wine-related events.

Submissions and Payment: Sample articles and guidelines available at website. Query with suggested title, proposed lede, 2-sentence article description, and links to author website or published writing samples. Accepts electronic queries via website. Response time varies. Rights vary. Features, 1,000–2,000 words; $150. Shorter articles, 500 words, $25. Payment policy varies.

ParentingHumor.com 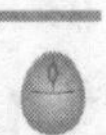

P.O. Box 2128
Weaverville, NC 28787

Editor in Chief: Sharon Byrer

Description and Interests: This weekly online magazine offers a humorous take on the serious job of parenting. Topics range from waiting for the baby to arrive to waiting up for the teenager to get home. It also offers activities for shared time and recipes. Experienced as well as talented new writers are welcome. Hits per month: Unavailable.
Website: www.parentinghumor.com

Freelance Potential: 98% written by nonstaff writers. Publishes 100 freelance submissions yearly. Receives 50 queries monthly.

Submissions and Payment: Sample copy and guidelines available at website. Query. Accepts queries via online submission form only. Response time varies. One-time, non–exclusive electronic rights. Articles, word lengths vary. No payment. Offers an author bio and a link to the author's website.

The Paris Review

62 White Street
New York, NY 10013

Fiction or Poetry Editor

Description and Interests: Founded in 1953, *The Paris Review* has forever since been welcoming good writers and good poets to its pages, published quarterly. Short stories, poetry, essays, and interviews are accepted by new, as well as established and well-known writers. Circ: 17,000.
Website: www.theparisreview.org

Freelance Potential: 100% written by nonstaff writers. Publishes 35 freelance submissions yearly. Receives 1,000 unsolicited mss monthly.

Submissions and Payment: Sample articles and guidelines available at website. Send complete ms. Accepts hard copy and simultaneous submissions if identified. SASE. Responds in 4 months. First North American serial rights. Articles and fiction, word lengths and payment rates vary. Poetry, no line limits, to 6 poems per submission; payment rates vary. Pays on publication. Provides 2 contributor's copies.

Parting Gifts

3413 Wilshire Drive
Greensboro, NC 27408

Editor: Robert Bixby

Description and Interests: *Parting Gifts* is always interested in finding the very best poetry and short fiction from writers both established and unpublished. It seeks tightly written stories with strong plots and poems that do not rely heavily on rhyme or meter. Appearing twice each year, this literary journal also accepts memoirs. Circ: Unavailable.
Website: www.marchstreetpress.com

Freelance Potential: 96% written by nonstaff writers. Publishes 200+ freelance submissions yearly; 5% by unpublished writers, 10% by authors who are new to the magazine. Receives 100 unsolicited mss each month.

Submissions and Payment: Sample copy and guidelines available at website. Send complete ms. Accepts hard copy. SASE. Responds in 1 week. First North American serial rights. Fiction, to 1,000 words. Poetry, to 2 pages. No payment. Provides 1 contributor's copy.

Passager

University of Baltimore, 1420 North Charles Street
Baltimore, MD 21201-5779

Editors: Mary Azrael & Kendra Kopelke

Description and Interests: Writers over the age of 50 can find a home for their work in *Passager*. It publishes two issues each year: one is a poetry contest issue and the other is an open issue. Exceptional literature in the form of fiction, memoir, and poetry is accepted for publication. Circ: 1,500.
Website: http://www.passagerbooks.com/

Freelance Potential: 99% written by nonstaff writers. Publishes 80 freelance submissions yearly; 33% by unpublished writers, 33% by authors who are new to the magazine. Receives 25 unsolicited mss monthly.

Submissions and Payment: Sample articles and guidelines available at website. Send complete ms with cover letter, author bio, (and $20 reading fee for contest issue). Accepts hard copy and simultaneous submissions if identified. SASE. Responds in 6–12 months. First North American serial rights. Articles and fiction, to 4,000 words. Poetry, to 50 lines; to 5 poems per submission. Cash prize for poetry issue; no payment for open issue. Provides 1 contributor's copy.

Passages North

Department of English
Northern Michigan University, Gries Hall
1401 Presque Isle Avenue
Marquette, MI 49855

Editor in Chief: Kate Myers Hanson

Description and Interests: *Passages North* is the annual literary journal sponsored by Northern Michigan University. It publishes high-quality short fiction, creative nonfiction, poetry, and spoken-word poetry. Circ: 1,500.
Website: http://myweb.nmu.edu/~passages

Freelance Potential: 100% written by nonstaff writers. Publishes 100 freelance submissions yearly; 25% by unpublished writers, 95% by authors who are new to the magazine. Receives 150 unsolicited mss monthly.

Submissions and Payment: Sample copy available. Send complete ms with cover letter between September 1 and April 15. Accepts hard copy only; simultaneous submissions if identified. SASE. Responds in 6–8 weeks. All rights. Essays and fiction, one piece to 7,500 words or 3 short-shorts. Poetry, to 100 lines; to 5 poems per submission. No payment. Provides 2 contributor's copies.

Paterson Literary Review

Passaic County Community College, Poetry Center
1 College Boulevard
Paterson, NJ 07505-1179

Executive Director: Maria Mazziotti Gillan

Description and Interests: High-quality short stories and poetry are found in each issue of this journal, published annually. Writing that is direct and accessible will get the editor's attention. Circ: 1,000.
Website: www.pccc.edu/home/cultural-affairs

Freelance Potential: 100% written by nonstaff writers. Publishes 350 freelance submissions yearly; 5% by unpublished writers, 35% by authors who are new to the magazine. Receives 1,000 unsolicited mss monthly.

Submissions and Payment: Sample articles and guidelines, available at website. Send complete ms between December 1 and March 31. Accepts hard copy and simultaneous submissions if identified. SASE. Responds in 6 months. First North American serial rights. Fiction, to 1,500 words. Poetry, to 2 pages; to 5 poems per submission. No payment. Provides 1 contributor's copy.

Pathfinders Travel

6325 Germantown Avenue
Philadelphia, PA 19144

Editor in Chief: Pamela J. Thomas

Description and Interests: Written for an affluent audience of African Americans and other minorities, this magazine seeks fresh ideas about domestic and international travel. It is published quarterly. Circ: 100,000.
Website: http://pathfinderstravel.com

Freelance Potential: 60% written by nonstaff writers. Publishes 10 freelance submissions yearly; 10% by authors who are new to the magazine. Receives 10–15 unsolicited mss monthly.

Submissions and Payment: Sample articles available at website. Guidelines and editorial calendar available. Send complete ms with artwork. Accepts hard copy and email submissions to pjthomas@pathfinderstravel.com (text-only attachments). Availability of artwork improves chance of acceptance. SASE. Responds in 1 month. Rights vary. Articles, 1,000-1,200 words; $150. Depts/columns, 500-600 words; $100. Artwork, $25–$50. Pays on publication.

Paved

236 Avenida Fabricante
San Clemente, CA 92672

Editor: Joe Parkin

Description and Interests: This is a "skinny tire" sister magazine from the editors of *Bike*, covering the road cycling sport. Published by the Grind Media division of Source Interlink Media, it is a photo-rich magazine that provides coverage of street cycling and racing, product reviews, training tips, and profiles of riders. It appears quarterly. Circ: Unavailable.
Website: www.pavedmag.com

Freelance Potential: Contributors must be avid cyclists. Topics include bike reviews, techniques, training how-to's, and personal experience pieces regarding races or multi-day cycling excursions.

Submissions and Payment: Sample articles available at website. Query for submissions information. Contact via hard copy or through contact form found at website.

Pearl

3030 East Second Street
Long Beach, CA 90803

Editor: Marilyn Johnson

Description and Interests: This literary journal publishes two annual issues—one each for poetry and short fiction. All works are finely crafted, original pieces, whether light and humorous or serious and ironic. Much of *Pearl*'s content speaks particularly to women. Circ: 600.
Website: www.pearlmag.com

Freelance Potential: 100% written by nonstaff writers. Publishes 150 freelance submissions yearly; 10% by unpublished writers, 50% by authors who are new to the magazine. Receives 100 unsolicited mss monthly.

Submissions and Payment: Sample copy available. Send complete ms between January and June. Accepts hard copy and simultaneous submissions if identified. SASE. Responds in 6–8 weeks. First North American serial rights. Fiction, to 1,200 words. Poetry, to 40 lines. No payment. Provides 1 contributor's copy.

Perdido

2081 Calistoga Drive, Suite 2N
New Lenox, IL 60451

Editor: Mary Rundell-Holmes

Description and Interests: Published quarterly, *Perdido*'s goal is to inspire "leadership with a conscience." Through features, profiles, and reviews, it offers innovative and positive suggestions for today's managers and executives. Circ: 2,200.
Website: http://perdidomagazine.com

Freelance Potential: 55% written by nonstaff writers. Publishes 16 freelance submissions yearly; 20% by unpublished writers, 30% by authors who are new to the magazine, 30% by experts. Receives 5–10 queries, 5–10 unsolicited mss monthly.

Submissions and Payment: Sample copy and guidelines available at website. Editorial calendar available. Query or send complete ms. Accepts hard copy and disk submissions. SASE. Responds to queries in 2 months, to mss in 1–2 months. First North American serial rights. Articles, 1,500–3,000 words. Depts/columns, 1,000 words. Written material, $.05–$.07 per word. Pays on publication. Provides 2 contributor's copies.

Peregrine

Amherst Writers & Artists
P.O. Box 1076
Amherst, MA 01004

Editor: Nancy Rose

Description and Interests: *Peregrine* is an annual literary magazine that features poetry and fiction. It seeks exceptional work that reflects diversity and is unpretentious and memorable. Circ: 600–800.
Website: http://amherstwriters.com

Freelance Potential: 100% written by nonstaff writers. Publishes 40–50 freelance submissions yearly; 5% by unpublished writers, 80% by authors who are new to the magazine. Receives 150 unsolicited mss each month.

Submissions and Payment: Sample copy available. Guidelines at website. Send complete ms (see website for submission dates). Accepts hard copy and simultaneous submissions if identified. SASE. Responds in 3–6 months after submissions deadline. First North American rights. Fiction, to 3,000 words. Poetry, to 40 lines (and spaces); 3–5 poems per submission. No payment. Provides 2 contributor's copies.

Personal Finance

7600A Leesburg Pike
West Building, Suite 300
Falls Church, VA 22043

Editor: Elliott Gue

Description and Interests: *Personal Finance* is a newsletter, published 24 times each year, that provides personal investors with information on the financial markets and investing. Market trends, investment strategies, and portfolio management are among its topics. It seeks professional analysts who can supply timely, accurate, and unbiased information. Circ: 70,000.
Website: www.pfnewsletter.com

Freelance Potential: 95% written by nonstaff writers. Publishes 3–5 freelance submissions yearly; 5% by unpublished writers, 10% by new authors who are new to the magazine, 90% by experts. Receives 20–30 queries monthly.

Submissions and Payment: Sample copy available at website. Query. Accepts hard copy. SASE. Responds in 2 weeks. All rights. Articles, 1,000–1,100 words; payment rates vary. Pays on publication.

Phoebe

A Journal of Literature and Art

George Mason University, MSN 2D6
4400 University Drive
Fairfax, VA 22030-4444

Poetry, Fiction or Nonfiction Editor

Description and Interests: *Phoebe* seeks high-quality fiction and poetry that go beyond the conventions of genre and dare something new. Published twice each year from George Mason University, it showcases new and established writers. Circ: 1,200.
Website: www.phoebejournal.com

Freelance Potential: 89% written by nonstaff writers. Publishes 68 freelance submissions yearly; 50% by unpublished writers, 90% by authors who are new to the magazine. Receives 80 unsolicited mss monthly.

Submissions and Payment: Sample articles and guidelines available at website. Send complete ms between August 15 and April 15. Accepts hard copy, electronic submissions at the website, and simultaneous submissions if identified. SASE. Responds in 4–6 months. All rights. Fiction, to 4,000 words. Prose, to 4,000 words. Poetry, 3–5 poems per submission. No payment. Provides 2 contributor's copies.

Pilot Getaways

P.O. Box 550
Glendale, CA 91209–0550

Editor: John Kounis

Description and Interests:
Private pilots read this publication to find fly-in destinations for leisure travel. Published six times each year, it also offers technical and how-to articles and aviation event information. Circ: 25,000.
Website: www.pilotgetaways.com

Freelance Potential: 20% written by nonstaff writers. Publishes 6–10 freelance submissions yearly; 5% by unpublished writers, 5% by authors who are new to the magazine, 90% by experts. Receives 20 queries monthly.

Submissions and Payment: Sample copy and guidelines available. Query. Accepts email queries to editor@pilotgetaways.com. Responds in 1 month. First serial rights. Articles, 2,200–4,000 words. Depts/columns, 700–1,000 words. Written material, $.10 per word. Digital images at 300 dpi, $25. Pays on publication. Provides 5 contributor's copies.

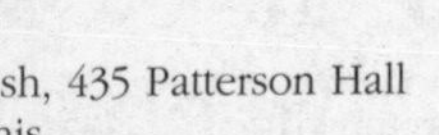

The Pinch

Department of English, 435 Patterson Hall
University of Memphis
Memphis, TN 38152–6176

Poetry, Nonfiction, or Fiction Editor

Description and Interests: A literary journal published twice each year, *The Pinch* accepts fiction, creative nonfiction, poetry, and visual art. It seeks more submissions of flash fiction and creative nonfiction. Circ: 3,000.
Website: www.thepinchjournal.com

Freelance Potential: 100% written by nonstaff writers. Publishes 50 freelance submissions yearly; 40% by unpublished writers, 30% by authors who are new to the magazine. Receives 150-200 unsolicited mss monthly.

Submissions and Payment: Sample copy available. Guidelines available at website. Send complete ms between August 15 and March 15. Accepts hard copy, electronic submissions via website, and simultaneous submissions. SASE. Responds in 3 months. First North American serial rights. Articles and fiction, to 5,000 words. Poetry, to 5 poems per submission. Digital images. No payment. Provides 2 contributor's copies.

The Pink Chameleon

Editor/Publisher: Dorothy Paula Freda

Description and Interests: This family-oriented ezine, updated annually, presents fiction, poetry, and nonfiction that lift the spirit and touch the heart. Humor and suspense are currently sought. New writers are encouraged to submit. Hits per month: 100.
Website: www.thepinkchameleon.com

Freelance Potential: 100% written by nonstaff writers. Of the freelance submissions published yearly, 50% are by unpublished writers, 50% are by new authors. Receives 40 mss monthly.

Submissions and Payment: Sample copy and guidelines available at website. Send complete ms January 1 to April 30 or September 1 to October 31 only. Accepts email submissions to dpfreda@juno.com (no attachments). No simultaneous submissions. Responds in one month. One-year electronic rights. Prose, to 2,500 words. Poetry, to 36 lines. No payment.

Plain Spoke

6199 Steubenville Road SE
Amsterdam, OH 43903

Editor: Cindy Kelly

Description and Interests: As its name implies, this quarterly literary publication looks for writing that is "plain spoken." It features fiction and poetry that has a strong sense of clarity and is wise and true. Circ: 400.
Website: http://plainspoke.net

Freelance Potential: 100% written by nonstaff writers. Publishes 80–100 freelance submissions yearly; 10% by unpublished writers, 90% by authors who are new to the magazine. Receives 100–150 unsolicited mss monthly.

Submissions and Payment: Guidelines available at website. Send complete ms with brief author bio. Prefers email submissions to plainspoke@gmail.com (Word or RTF attachments); will accept hard copy. Accepts simultaneous submissions. SASE. Responds in 1–3 months. First North American serial rights. Fiction, to 5,000 words. Poetry, to 30 lines. Provides 1 contributor's copy and discount on additional copies.

Plane and Pilot

Werner Publishing Corporation
12121 Wilshire Boulevard, 12th Floor
Los Angeles, CA 90025-1176

Editor: Jessica Ambats

Description and Interests: This magazine, published 11 times a year, offers how-to and personal experience pieces for pilots, instructors, mechanics, technicians, and other aviation enthusiasts. Topics include pilot proficiency and travel. Circ: 150,000.
Website: www.planeandpilotmag.com

Freelance Potential: 80% written by nonstaff writers. Publishes 75–85 freelance submissions yearly.

Submissions and Payment: Sample articles and guidelines available at website. Query for articles. Send complete ms for depts/columns. Accepts hard copy and email to editor@planeandpilotmag.com. SASE. Responds in 4 months. All rights. Articles, to 1,200 words. Depts/columns, 900–1,000 words. Written material, $200–$500. Kill fee varies. Pays on publication. Provides 1 contributor's copy.

Planet

The Welsh Internationalist

P.O. Box 44, Aberystwyth
Ceredigion SY23 3ZZ
Wales

Editor: Emily Trahair

Description and Interests: This quarterly features articles, essays, fiction, and poetry about Welsh politics, culture, and art. It is particularly interested in politics and news. Circ: 1,400.
Website: www.planetmagazine.org.uk

Freelance Potential: 95% written by nonstaff writers. Publishes 132 freelance submissions yearly; 10% by unpublished writers, 20% by authors who are new to the magazine; 70% by experts. Receives 30 queries monthly.

Submissions and Payment: Sample copy available. Query with synopsis. Accepts hard copy and email to planet.enquiries@planetmagazine.org.uk. SAE/IRC. Responds in 3 months. First British serial rights. Articles, 1,700–3,500 words. Fiction, to 4,000 words. Depts/columns, 400–800 words. Poetry, 4–6 poems per submission. Payment rates vary. Pays on publication. Provides 1 contributor's copy.

Pleiades

Department of English, Martin 336
University of Central Missouri
Warrensburg, MO 64093

Fiction, Nonfiction, or Poetry Editor

Description and Interests: Published twice each year, this literary journal accepts fiction, essays, interviews, poetry, and book reviews. It welcomes the work of new writers. Circ: 3,000.
Website: www.ucmo.edu/pleiades

Freelance Potential: 95% written by nonstaff writers. Publishes 80 freelance submissions yearly; 5% by unpublished writers, 50% by authors who are new to the magazine. Receives 50 queries, 1,000 unsolicited mss monthly.

Submissions and Payment: Sample copy and guidelines available at website. Query with clips for book reviews. Send complete ms for other material. Online submissions via website; accepts hard copy and simultaneous submissions if identified. SASE. Responds in 1–4 months. First serial rights. Fiction and nonfiction, word lengths vary. Poetry, no line limits; 4–5 poems per submission. Written material, payment rates vary. Pays on publication.

Plus

The Power of Faith

Peale Center for Christian Living
66 East Main Street
Pawling, NY 12564

Editors: Mary Lou Carney & Mimi Hedwig

Description and Interests: Published six times each year, *Plus* is a pocket-sized magazine filled with inspirational stories of faith and perseverance. It also offers profiles of people who have lived a life close to God. Circ: 71,000.
Website: www.guidepostsfoundation.org

Freelance Potential: 75% written by nonstaff writers. Publishes 12–16 freelance submissions yearly; 25% by unpublished writers, 25% by authors who are new to the magazine, 50% by experts. Receives 20 unsolicited mss monthly.

Submissions and Payment: Sample copy available. Send complete ms. Accepts hard copy and email submissions to mhedwig@guideposts.org. SASE. Responds in 1 month. All rights. Articles, to 2,000 words; $75 per published page for original stories, $25 per page for reprints. Pays on publication. Provides 5 contributor's copies.

Pointe

333 Seventh Avenue, #11
New York, NY 10001

Managing Editor: Carol Rubin

Description and Interests: This magazine is for those who love to watch and perform ballet and those hoping to make it a career. Published six times each year, it contains articles on well-known dance troupes, profiles, how-to's, and production reviews. Circ: 40,000.
Website: www.pointemagazine.com

Freelance Potential: 75% written by nonstaff writers. Publishes 1–2 freelance submissions yearly; 25% by authors who are new to the magazine, 10% by experts. Receives 2 queries monthly.

Submissions and Payment: Sample copy available. Query with writing samples. Accepts email queries to janderson@pointemagazine.com. Response time varies. Rights vary. Articles, 1,200 words; $400. Reviews, 500 words; $125. Depts/columns, word lengths vary; $200. Kill fee, 25%. Pays on acceptance. Provides 1 contributor's copy.

Pointed Circle

Portland Community College/SC 206
705 North Killingsworth Street
Portland, OR 97217

Editorial Advisor: Wendy Bourgeois

Description and Interests: *Pointed Circle* is a student-edited literary journal that seeks fiction, nonfiction, and poetry on a variety of topics. Original artwork is also accepted. It is published annually by Portland Community College. Circ: 350.
Website: www.pcc.edu

Freelance Potential: 30% written by nonstaff writers. Publishes 10 freelance submissions yearly; 79% by unpublished writers, 20% by authors who are new to the magazine. Receives 10 unsolicited mss monthly.

Submissions and Payment: Send complete ms with 25-word author bio between October 1 and March 11; email wendy.bourgeo@pcc.edu for official submission form. Accepts hard copy. Responds in 6 months. Rights vary. Prose, to 3,000 words. Poetry, to 6 pages. B/W photos; line art. No payment. Provides 2 contributor's copies.

Popular Anthropology

Southern Illinois University-Carbondale
1000 Faner Drive, Room 3525-MC 4502
Carbondale, IL 62901

Submissions: Dawn C. Stricklin

Description and Interests: *Popular Anthropology* is an online magazine dedicated to fostering a much-needed dialogue between anthropologists and the public. It seeks to bring anthropological research to a readership that includes students, scholars, and the general public. It accepts research papers, interviews, scholarly reviews, and informational articles in all disciplines of anthropology. Hits per month: Unavailable.
Website: www.popanthro.com

Freelance Potential: Very open to submissions. It is looking for original, scientifically accurate, and interesting articles.

Submissions and Payment: Sample copy and guidelines available at website. Send complete ms. Accepts email to dstricklin@popanthro.com (Word attachments). Response time varies. Author retains copyright. Articles, 500–20,000 words. No payment.

Porchlight

A Literary Magazine

25 Colonel Robert Magaw Place, #5E
New York, NY 10033

Editor: L. J. Moore

Description and Interests: *Porchlight* is an online literary magazine that seeks uncommon work that engages the minds and hearts of its readers. Updated quarterly, it publishes creative nonfiction, fiction, and poetry. *Porchlight* is not accepting submissions at this time. Check the website for changes. Hits per month: 1,500.
Website: http://porchlightzine.wordpress.com

Freelance Potential: 100% written by nonstaff writers. Publishes 30–36 freelance submissions yearly; 20% by unpublished writers, 100% by authors who are new to the magazine. Receives 2 queries, 100 unsolicited mss monthly.

Submissions and Payment: Sample copy and guidelines available at website. Query for nonfiction and memoirs. Send complete ms for fiction and poetry. Accepts email submissions to porchlightzine@gmail.com (Word attachments). Response time varies. First rights. Written material, to 4,000 words. No payment.

Portland Review

Portland State University
P.O. Box 347
Portland, OR 97207-0347

Editor in Chief: Sarah Marshall

Description and Interests: Original short prose and poetry from new and established writers all over the world appear in this literary journal. Published three times each year by Portland State University, it also seeks reviews of small press books. Online publishing opportunities exist on its website. Circ: 500.
Website: http://theportlandreview.com

Freelance Potential: 99% written by nonstaff writers. Publishes 60 freelance submissions yearly; 5–10% by unpublished writers, 80–90% by authors who are new to the magazine. Receives 1,000 unsolicited mss monthly.

Submissions and Payment: Sample copy available. Guidelines available at website. Send complete ms; see website for calendar. Accepts submissions via website and simultaneous submissions. Responds in 5–6 months. First serial rights. Prose, to 6,250 words. Poetry, to 10 poems per submission. No payment. Provides 2 contributor's copies.

Potomac Review

Montgomery College
51 Mannakee Street, MT/212
Rockville, MD 20850

Editor in Chief: Professor Julie Wakeman-Linn

Description and Interests: *Potomac Review* is an annual literary journal that features fiction, creative nonfiction, essays, and poetry. Material should conform to one of the upcoming issues' themes. Circ: 1,000.
Website: www.montgomerycollege.edu/potomacreview

Freelance Potential: 100% written by nonstaff writers. Publishes 60–80 freelance submissions yearly; 30% by unpublished writers, 35% by authors who are new to the magazine. Receives 100 queries, 100 unsolicited mss monthly.

Submissions and Payment: Sample copy available. Guidelines and theme list available at website. Send complete ms with brief author bio between September 1 and May 1. Accepts electronic submissions via the website and simultaneous submissions. Responds in 6 months. First serial rights. Articles and fiction, to 5,000 words. Poetry, to 3 poems or 5 pages. No payment. Provides 2 contributor's copies.

Power Boating Canada

1121 Invicta Drive, Unit 2
Oakville, Ontario L6H 2R2
Canada

Editor: Bill Taylor

Description and Interests: This magazine for owners of power boats and personal watercraft is published seven times each year. It features reviews of new boats and equipment, destinations, and how-to tips for boaters. Circ: 40,000.
Website: www.powerboating.com

Freelance Potential: 60% written by nonstaff writers. Publishes 30 freelance submissions yearly; 5% by unpublished writers, 5% by authors who are new to the magazine, 20% by experts. Receives 20 queries monthly.

Submissions and Payment: Sample copy available. Query. Prefers email to editor@powerboating.com; will accept hard copy. SAE/IRC. Responds in 2–4 weeks. First North American serial rights. Articles, 1,000–1,800 words. Depts/columns, word lengths vary. Written material, payment rates vary. Pays on publication. Provides 2 contributor's copies.

Power & Motoryacht

10 Bokum Road
Essex, CT 06426

Editor in Chief: Capt. George Sass

Description and Interests: Published monthly, *Power & Motoryacht* offers its readers information on the newest boats and accessories, as well as spectacular destinations. While the focus is on "escape," it also offers practical material and yachting lifestyle pieces. Circ: 156,859.
Website: www.powerandmotoryacht.com

Freelance Potential: 20% written by nonstaff writers. Publishes 10–12 freelance submissions yearly; 15% by authors who are new to the magazine, 85% by industry experts. Receives 2 queries monthly.

Submissions and Payment: Sample copy and guidelines available. Query with publishing credits. Accepts hard copy and email queries to richard.thiel@pmymag.com SASE. Responds in 1–2 months. All rights. Articles, 1,000–1,500 words; $500–$1,200. Kill fee, 33%. Pays on acceptance. Provides 2 contributor's copies.

Prairie Journal

28 Crowfoot Terrace NW
P.O. Box 68073
Calgary, Alberta T3G 3N8
Canada

Editor: Anne Burke

Description and Interests: Original poetry, short fiction, plays, and essays fill the pages of *Prairie Journal,* which is published twice each year. All topics are welcome. It also accepts interviews and book reviews. Circ: 1,300.
Website: www.prairiejournal.org

Freelance Potential: 100% written by nonstaff writers. Publishes 25 freelance submissions yearly; 75% by authors who are new to the magazine. Receives 25 queries each month.

Submissions and Payment: Sample copy available. Guidelines available at website. Query with clips or writing samples. Accepts hard copy. No simultaneous submissions. SAE/IRC. Responds in 2–6 months. First North American serial rights. Written material, word lengths and payment rates vary. Pays on publication. Provides 1 contributor's copy.

Praxis

Gender & Cultural Critiques

Women's & Gender Studies Department
State University of New York-Oneonta
Oneonta, NY 13820

Executive Editor: Kathleen O'Mara

Description and Interests: This biannual journal, formerly *Phoebe* and now renamed *Praxis,* publishes research, criticism, and theory focused on gender, sexuality, and women's lives in the U.S. and globally. It also publishes short fiction and poetry. Circ: 100.
Website: http://www.oneonta.edu/academics/praxis/

Freelance Potential: 95% written by nonstaff writers. Publishes 58 freelance submissions yearly; 20% by unpublished writers, 90% by new authors. Receives 10 unsolicited mss monthly.

Submissions and Payment: Sample copy available. Guidelines available at website. Send complete ms. Accepts 2 hard copies and email to praxis@oneonta.edu. SASE. Responds in 3–6 months. All rights. Articles, 5,000–7,000 words. Creative work, any length. No payment. Provides 2 contributor's copies for essays, 1 copy for short stories and poetry.

Presbyterian Record

50 Wynford Drive
Toronto, Ontario M3C 1J7
Canada

Editor: David Harris

Description and Interests: This magazine is published by the Presbyterian Church of Canada 11 times each year. It features profiles and articles on worship, mission work, popular culture, and spirituality, as well as book reviews and church news items. Circ: 30,000.
Website: www.presbyterianrecord.ca

Freelance Potential: 50% written by nonstaff writers. Publishes 36 freelance submissions yearly; 20% by authors who are new to the magazine. Receives 60 queries monthly.

Submissions and Payment: Sample copy available at website. Query with 150-word summary. Accepts email queries to dharris@presbyterian.ca. Responds if interested. First rights and perpetual electronic rights. Articles, 500–750 words. Depts/columns, word lengths vary. Written material, $.15 per word. Pays on publication. Provides 2 contributor's copies.

Presbyterians Today

100 Witherspoon Street
Louisville, KY 40202–1396

Editor: Eva Stimson

Description and Interests: Written for members of the Presbyterian Church (U.S.), this magazine offers spiritual guidance and information about mission activities of the Presbyterian Church (U.S.). Appearing 10 times each year, it also covers current societal issues from the church's perspective. Circ: 40,000.
Website: www.pcusa.org/today

Freelance Potential: 10% written by nonstaff writers. Publishes 10 freelance submissions yearly; 2% by unpublished writers, 10% by authors who are new to the magazine, 60% by experts. Receives 10 queries monthly.

Submissions and Payment: Sample copy, guidelines, and editorial calendar available at website. Query. Accepts hard copy and email queries to today@pcusa.org. SASE. Responds in 1 month. All rights. Articles, 1,500 words; payment rates vary. Pays on acceptance. Provides 2 contributor's copies.

Prims

Art Inspired by a Bygone Era

22992 Mill Creek Drive
Laguna Hills, CA 92953

Editor: Jennifer Jackson Taylor

Description and Interests: This hobby magazine covers the rustic elegance of primitive, folk, historic, and early Americana-style handcrafted art. In 2012, it moved to a thrice-yearly publication schedule. Its articles deal with the art, collecting, and creation of dolls, teddy bears, paintings, and mixed-media artwork. Artist profiles are also included. Circ: Unavailable.
Website: www.stampington.com/prims

Freelance Potential: Accepts freelance submissions from artisans, collectors, and writers familiar with primitive folk art. Articles about specific projects should be accompanied by instruction.

Submissions and Payment: Sample articles, guidelines, and deadlines available at website. Specific calls for submissions are listed in the magazine. Query with letter and samples (or photos) of work. Accepts hard copy and email to prims@stampington.com. SASE. Response time varies. Rights vary. Word lengths and payment rates vary. Payment policy varies.

Prism International

University of British Columbia
Buchanan E-462, 1866 Main Mall
Vancouver, British Columbia V6T 1Z1, Canada

Editors: Anna Ling Kaye & Leah Horlick

Description and Interests: *Prism International* is a quarterly journal best known for offering offbeat fiction and poetry. It also publishes creative nonfiction and drama. Circ: 1,500.
Website: www.prismmagazine.ca

Freelance Potential: 100% written by nonstaff writers. Publishes 50 freelance submissions yearly; 10% by unpublished writers, 70% by authors who are new to the magazine. Receives 200–300 unsolicited mss monthly.

Submissions and Payment: Sample articles and guidelines available at website. Send complete ms. Accepts hard copy and online submissions, and simultaneous submissions if identified. SAE/IRC. Responds in 2–6 months. First rights. Articles and fiction, to 25 pages; $20 per printed page. Poetry, to 7 poems or 25 pages; $40 per printed page. Electronic rights, $10 per page. Pays on acceptance. Provides a 1-year subscription.

Privacy Journal

P.O. Box 28577
Providence, RI 02908

Publisher: Robert Ellis Smith

Description and Interests: This monthly newsletter reports on the latest technological advances that can protect—or threaten—privacy. Both personal and business issues are examined with an emphasis on news, recent legislation, and court cases pertaining to privacy. It also features excerpts and book reviews. Circ: 20,000.
Website: www.privacyjournal.net

Freelance Potential: 40% written by nonstaff writers. Publishes 10 freelance submissions yearly; 10% by unpublished writers, 5% by authors who are new to the magazine, 50% by experts. Receives 1 query monthly.

Submissions and Payment: Sample copy available. Query. Accepts hard copy and email queries to orders@privacyjournal.net. SASE. Response time varies. Rights are negotiable. Articles, 1,200 words. Payment rates vary. Pays on acceptance.

Prologue

Quarterly of the National Archives and Records Administration

700 Pennsylvania Avenue NW, Room 400
Washington, DC 20408-0001

Managing Editor: Mary Ryan

Description and Interests: This quarterly publication gives insight into the past through the detailed information contained in the National Archives. Articles should fascinate history buffs, as well as a general readership. Circ: 2,600.
Website: www.archives.gov/publications/prologue

Freelance Potential: 30% written by nonstaff writers. Publishes 10 freelance submissions yearly; 2% by unpublished writers, 40% by authors who are new to the magazine, 85% by experts.

Submissions and Payment: Sample copy and guidelines available. Query with detailed summary. Accepts email queries to prologue@nara.gov (Word attachments). Responds in 1 week. Author retains rights. Articles, 3,000–5,000 words. Depts/columns, 600–1,200 words. JPEG or TIFF files at 300 dpi. No payment. Provides 10 contributor's copies.

Quarterly West

255 South Central Campus Drive, Room 3500
University of Utah
Salt Lake City, UT 84112-0494

Co-Editors: C.A. Schaefer & Sadie Hoagland

Description and Interests: This literary journal is comprised of high-quality fiction, creative nonfiction, poetry, and reviews submitted by writers from all over the country. It is published twice each year. Circ: 1,700.
Website: www.quarterlywest.utah.edu

Freelance Potential: 99% written by nonstaff writers. Publishes 105 freelance submissions yearly; 10% by unpublished writers, 40% by new authors. Receives 400–500 mss monthly.

Submissions and Payment: Sample copy available. Guidelines available at website. Send complete ms between September 1 and April 30. Accepts submissions through website only. Responds in 3–6 months. First North American serial rights. Prose, to 5,000 words; flash fiction to 1,000 words. Poetry, 3–5 poems per submission. Pays honorarium when able. Provides 2 contributor's copies.

Quest

The History of Spaceflight

P.O. Box 5752
Bethesda, MD 20824-5752

Editor: Dr. David Arnold

Description and Interests: This quarterly magazine focuses on the people, projects, programs, and policies that have been instrumental in the history of civil, military, commercial, and international space activities. Readers include former space professionals, space historians, teachers, and others interested in the history of science and technology. Circ: 1,000.
Website: www.spacehistory101.com

Freelance Potential: 100% written by nonstaff writers. Publishes 25–30 freelance submissions yearly; 75% by authors who are new to the magazine.

Submissions and Payment: Sample articles and guidelines available at website. Query. Accepts email to historyofspace@aol.com. Response time varies. All rights. Feature articles and depts/columns, 3,000–10,000 words. Interviews, 1,000–10,000+ words. No payment. Provides 1 digital copy and 5 print copies to contributors.

Quilter's World

House of White Birches
306 East Parr Road
Berne, IN 46711-1138

Editor: Carolyn Vagts

Description and Interests: Six times each year, this magazine offers profiles of quilters, new products, techniques, and a variety of patterns for all skill levels. Circ: 110,000.
Website: www.quiltersworld.com

Freelance Potential: 10% written by nonstaff writers. Publishes 72 freelance submissions yearly; 10% by unpublished writers. Receives 40 queries, 15 unsolicited mss monthly.

Submissions and Payment: Sample copy and editorial calendar available. Guidelines available at website. Query with clips; or send complete ms. Prefers email queries to Editor@QuiltersWorld.com; will accept hard copy. SASE. Responds in 2 months. All rights. Articles, 1,000–2,000 words. Depts/columns, word lengths vary. Written material, $100–$500. Pays on publication. Provides 1 contributor's copy.

The Quilt Life

P.O. Box 3290
Paducah, KY 42002-3290

Editor in Chief: Jan Magee

Description and Interests: From the American Quilter's Society comes this quilting magazine, published six times each year. Because there is more to quilting than making quilts, this magazine strives to go beyond patterns to cover "the quilting life," including learning new techniques, planning your day to allow time for quilting, quilt trends, and expressing yourself through quilts. Circ: Unavailable.
Website: www.americanquilter.com/quilt_life/

Freelance Potential: Very open to submissions that are "quilt-centric" on one or more of the topics outlined in the submission guidelines.

Submissions and Payment: Sample articles and guidelines available at website. Query or send complete ms. Accepts hard copy and email to submissions@thequiltlife.com (mss) or info@thequiltlife.com (queries). SASE. Response time varies. Articles, 500–2,000 words. Written material, payment rates vary. Pays on publication.

Radio Control Car Action

Air Age Publishing
88 Danbury Road, Route 7
Wilton, CT 06897

Senior Editor: Kevin Hetmanski

Description and Interests: All aspects of radio controlled cars are covered in this monthly magazine for hobbyists. It presents product reviews and event coverage, in addition to articles on painting and detailing, conversion kits, and scratch-built projects. Circ: 140,000.
Website: www.rccaraction.com

Freelance Potential: 30% written by nonstaff writers. Publishes 50 freelance submissions yearly. Receives 30+ queries and unsolicited mss monthly.

Submissions and Payment: Sample articles available at website. Query or send complete ms. Accepts hard copy, disk submissions, submissions via website, and email queries to rcca@airage.com. SASE. Response time varies. All North American serial rights. Written material, word lengths and payment rates vary. Pays on acceptance. Provides 2 contributor's copies.

Railroad Evangelist

P.O. Box 5026
Vancouver, WA 98668

Editor: Joe Spooner

Description and Interests: Published three times each year by the Railroad Evangelistic Association, this magazine seeks to promote mutual Christian fellowship among people in the railroad industry, as well as model railroad hobbyists. It features a mix of articles, fiction, and poetry. Be sure to query only on topics of specific interest to this publication; the editor is receiving too many unrelated queries. Circ: 2,400.
Website: http://railroadevangelist.com

Freelance Potential: 90% written by nonstaff writers. Publishes 10 freelance submissions yearly; 80% by unpublished writers, 20% by authors who are new to the magazine. Receives 1 query monthly.

Submissions and Payment: Sample copy and guidelines available at website. Query. Accepts email to rrjoe@comcast.net (Word attachments). Response time varies. All rights. Articles and fiction, 300–800 words. Poetry. B/W prints. No payment. Provides contributor's copies.

Rambunctious Review 

1221 West Pratt Boulevard
Chicago, IL 60626

Editors: N. Lennon & E. Hausler

Description and Interests: This annual journal seeks out the new (but does not scoff at the timeless), the insightful, the visionary, and the funny in fiction, poetry, and art. It also sponsors poetry, fiction, graphic arts, and photography contests with cash prizes. Circ: 450.
Website: www.rambunctiousreview.org

Freelance Potential: 100% written by nonstaff writers. Publishes 35 freelance submissions yearly; 30% by unpublished writers, 50% by authors who are new to the magazine. Receives 25 unsolicited mss monthly.

Submissions and Payment: Sample copy and theme list available. Guidelines available at website. Send complete ms between September and May. Accepts hard copy. SASE. Responds in 6–12 months. First North American serial rights. Fiction and humor, to 12 pages. Poetry, to 3 pages. No payment. Provides 2 contributor's copies.

Rampike 

University of Windsor, Department of English
401 Sunset Avenue
Windsor, Ontario N9B 3P4
Canada

Editor/Publisher: Karl Jirgens

Description and Interests: Examples of postmodern fiction and poetry appear in each themed, twice-yearly issue. *Rampike* also publishes reviews and interviews with artists. Most of the material is solicited, but unsolicited material may be submitted if writers consult with the editors in advance. Circ: 2,000.
Website: http://web4.uwindsor.ca/rampike

Freelance Potential: 80% written by nonstaff writers. Publishes 80 freelance submissions yearly; 25% by unpublished writers, 25% by new authors. Receives 25 queries, 25 unsolicited mss monthly.

Submissions and Payment: Excerpts and guidelines available at website. Query. Accepts hard copy and email to jirgens@uwindsor.ca. SAE/IRC. Responds in 3 months. First North American serial rights. Articles, 500–1,000 words. Fiction, 500–2,000 words. Poetry, no line limits. No payment for unsolicited works. Provides 2 contributor's copies.

Raven Chronicles

12346 Sand Point Way NE
Seattle, WA 98125

Managing Editor: Phoebe Bosché

Description and Interests: Appearing twice each year, *Raven Chronicles* seeks uncommon fiction, poetry, essays, articles, reviews, and talk art/spoken word. It targets an audience that is hip, literate, funny, and has a multicultural sensibility.
Circ: 3,000+.
Website: http://ravenchronicles.org

Freelance Potential: 95% written by nonstaff writers. Publishes 90–100 freelance submissions yearly; 10% by unpublished writers, 50% by authors who are new to the magazine. Receives 50 unsolicited mss monthly.

Submissions and Payment: Sample copy available. Guidelines available at website. Send complete ms. Accepts hard copy. SASE. Responds in 3 months. One-time rights. Articles and fiction, 10–12 double-spaced pages. Poetry, to 3 poems per submission. Written material, payment rates vary. Pays on publication. Provides 2 contributor's copies.

Reason

5737 Mesmer Avenue
Los Angeles, CA 90230

Senior Editor: Brian Doherty

Description and Interests: Published 11 times each year, *Reason* offers informative articles, news reports, essays, and commentary on current events and issues. Its viewpoint is always nonpartisan and thought-provoking. Circ: 55,000.
Website: http://reason.com

Freelance Potential: 30% written by nonstaff writers. Publishes 50–60 freelance submissions yearly.

Submissions and Payment: Sample copy available. Guidelines available at website. Prefers query with clips; will accept complete ms. Prefers email to bdoherty@reason.com. Accepts hard copy. SASE. Responds to queries in 6 weeks; to mss in 2 months. First North American serial rights. Articles, 850–5,000 words; $300–$2,000. Pays on publication. Provides 3 contributor's copies.

Red Cedar Review

Department of English
Michigan State University
1405 South Harrison
25 Manly Miles Building
East Lansing, MI 48823-5245

Managing Editor: Shelby Dosser

Description and Interests: Original works of fiction, creative nonfiction, and poetry are found on the pages of this literary journal. Accepting work from undergraduate writers of all levels, it is published annually by Michigan State University. Circ: Unavailable.
Website: http://msupress.msu.edu/rcrorg

Freelance Potential: 100% written by nonstaff writers. Publishes 20–30 freelance submissions yearly; 70% by unpublished writers, 90% by authors who are new to the magazine. Receives 25 unsolicited mss monthly.

Submissions and Payment: Sample copy available. Guidelines and submission calendar available at website. Accepts hard copy. No simultaneous submissions. SASE. Responds in 4–6 weeks. First rights. All genres, to 20 pages. No payment. Provides 2 contributor's copies.

Red Rock Review

English Department, J2A
Community College of Southern Nevada
3200 East Cheyenne Avenue
North Las Vegas, NV 89030

Editor in Chief: Dr. Richard Logsdon

Description and Interests: Twice each year, *Red Rock Review* offers the finest fiction, poetry, and creative nonfiction from both established and emerging writers. Circ: 1,000.
Website: http://sites.csn.edu/english/redrockreview

Freelance Potential: 98% written by nonstaff writers. Publishes 60 freelance submissions yearly; 2% by unpublished writers, 60% by authors who are new to the magazine. Receives 200 unsolicited mss monthly.

Submissions and Payment: Sample copy available. Guidelines and submission calendar available at website. Accepts email to RedRockReview@csn.edu (Word, RTF, or PDF attachments). Responds in 3 months. First North American serial rights. Essays, to 5,000 words. Fiction, to 7,500 words. Poetry, to 80 lines. No payment. Provides 2 contributor's copies.

Red Wheelbarrow 

De Anza College
21250 Stevens Creek Boulevard
Cupertino, CA 95104–5702

Editor: Ken Weisner

Description and Interests: With an eye for the unpretentious, this annual literary journal offers fiction, creative nonfiction, and poetry. It seeks an artistically and culturally diverse range of voices from around the world. Circ: 500.
Website: www.deanza.edu/redwheelbarrow

Freelance Potential: 100% written by nonstaff writers. Publishes 50 freelance submissions yearly; 2% by unpublished writers, 85% by authors who are new to the magazine. Receives 50–100 unsolicited mss monthly.

Submissions and Payment: Sample copy available. Guidelines available at website. Send complete ms with author bio between September 1 and January 31. Accepts hard copy and email to weisnerken@fhda.edu. SASE. Responds in 2–6 months. First North American serial rights. Fiction and nonfiction, to 4,000 words. Poetry, to 5 poems. Prints and slides; line art. No payment. Provides 1 contributor's copy.

Reed Magazine 

Department of English
San Jose State University
One Washington Square
San Jose, CA 95192-0090

Faculty Advisor: Nick Taylor

Description and Interests: Published annually, this literary journal showcases fiction and nonfiction, as well as poetry and essays. It also features works of art. Circ: 4,000.
Website: www.reedmag.org

Freelance Potential: 100% written by nonstaff writers. Publishes 20 freelance submissions yearly; 40% by unpublished writers, 60% by authors who are new to the magazine. Receives 110 unsolicited mss monthly.

Submissions and Payment: Sample copy available. Guidelines and contest information available at website. Send complete ms via website from June 1 to November 1. Accepts simultaneous submissions. Responds in 2 months. First North American serial rights. Fiction, to 6,000 words. Nonfiction, to 3,000 words. Poetry, to 5 poems per submission. No payment. Provides contributor's copies.

Relix Magazine

104 West 29th Street, 11th Floor
New York, NY 10001

Editor: Josh Baron

Description and Interests: This magazine, appearing eight times each year, covers non-mainstream music, including blues, jam bands, jazz, reggae, and early rock and roll. It reports on the entire music scene from concerts and recording reviews to news, profiles, and features on social and political issues with a music slant. Circ: 102,000.
Website: www.relix.com

Freelance Potential: 60% written by nonstaff writers. Publishes 400 freelance submissions yearly; 100% by experts. Receives 5 unsolicited mss monthly.

Submissions and Payment: Sample copy available. Query or send complete ms. Accepts hard copy, disk submissions, and email queries to editors@relix.com. SASE. Responds in 6 months. First rights. Articles and depts/columns, word lengths and payment rates vary. Pays on publication. Provides 1–2 contributor's copies.

Review 

Literature & Arts of the Americas

Americas Society
680 Park Avenue
New York, NY 10065

Editor: Daniel Shapiro

Description and Interests: This twice-yearly literary review publishes the creative work of writers from North, Central, and South America. It seeks pieces of far-ranging and illuminating prose, particularly from writers in Colombia, the Southern Cone, and Central America. Circ: 10,000.
Website: www.americas-society.org

Freelance Potential: 90% written by nonstaff writers. Publishes 10–15 freelance submissions yearly; 25% by unpublished writers, 50% by authors who are new to the magazine, 25% by experts. Receives 5–10 queries monthly.

Submissions and Payment: Sample copy available. Query with short writing sample. Accepts hard copy and email queries to dshapiro@as-coa.org. SASE. Responds in 2 months. All rights. Written material, 2,000 words; $250. Pays on publication. Provides 1 contributor's copy.

Revolver

406 Wacouta Street, #106
St. Paul, MN 55101

Editor: Alexander Helmke

Description and Interests: *Revolver* is an arts and cultural magazine that publishes writing that "hits the brain like a bullet." It doesn't divide the publication into traditional genre categories—poetry, fiction, and essays—but rather based on word count. The magazine appears twice a year. Circ: Unavailable.
Website: www.around-around.com

Freelance Potential: Receives many freelance submissions monthly.

Submissions and Payment: Sample articles at website. Send complete ms. Accepts electronic submissions at website. Responds in 1 month. Written material, to 1,000 words or 1,001–5,000 words. Rights vary. Payment rates and policy vary.

RGS

The Ruffed Grouse Society Magazine

451 McCormick Road
Coraopolis, PA 15108

Editor: Anna Stubna

Description and Interests: Sport bird hunting and maintaining and improving woodland habitats are the main topics of this magazine. It is published four times each year and contains how-to and informational articles. Circ: 16,000.
Website: www.ruffedgrousesociety.org

Freelance Potential: 70% written by nonstaff writers. Publishes 20 freelance submissions yearly; 10% by experts. Receives 1–2 queries, 5 unsolicited mss monthly.

Submissions and Payment: Sample copy and guidelines available. Query or send complete ms. Accepts hard copy and email submissions to annas@ruffedgrousesociety.org. SASE. Responds in 2–3 months. One-time rights. Articles and depts/columns, 1,200 words; payment rates vary. Pays on acceptance. Provides 1 contributor's copy.

Rider

2575 Vista Del Mar Drive
Ventura, CA 93001

Editor: Mark Tuttle

Description and Interests: *Rider* delivers features on motorcycle touring, travel, and adventure for motorcycle enthusiasts. Published monthly, it is interested in short and full-length tour and travel features. It covers street cycling only—no racing or dirt bikes. Circ: 140,000.
Website: http://ridermagazine.com

Freelance Potential: 30% written by nonstaff writers. Publishes 25–50 freelance submissions yearly; 3% by unpublished writers, 5% by authors who are new to the magazine, 85% by experts. Receives 12 queries, 15 unsolicited mss monthly.

Submissions and Payment: Sample copy available. Guidelines available at website. Query. Accepts hard copy. No simultaneous submissions. SASE. Responds in 2–3 months. Exclusive first North American serial and online rights. Articles, 1,000–1,800 words; payment rates vary. Pays on publication. Provides contributor's copies upon request.

RiverSedge

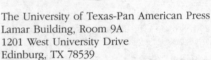

The University of Texas-Pan American Press
Lamar Building, Room 9A
1201 West University Drive
Edinburg, TX 78539

General Editor: Dr. Douglas LaPrade

Description and Interests: Published twice yearly, this literary journal publishes poetry, short stories, essays, and artwork. Though it accepts work from new and established artists everywhere, it puts an emphasis on those from the southwestern U.S. Circ: 400.
Website: http://portal.utpa.edu/utpa_main/daa_home/ogs_home/utpress_home/journals

Freelance Potential: 90% written by nonstaff writers. Publishes 400 freelance submissions yearly; 30% by unpublished writers, 50% by authors who are new to the magazine. Receives 70 unsolicited mss monthly.

Submissions and Payment: Sample copy available. Send complete ms with bio. Accepts hard copy and email to bookworm@utpa.edu. SASE. Responds in 3–6 months. First rights. Fiction, to 3,000 words. Poetry, to 25 lines. B/W prints and illustrations. No payment. Provides 2 contributor's copies.

River Styx

3547 Olive Street, Suite 107
St. Louis, MO 63103-1002

Editor: Richard Newman

Description and Interests: Three times a year, *River Styx* publishes poetry, short fiction, essays, and art selected for their originality, energy, and craftsmanship. New and established writers are encouraged to submit their work. Circ: 2,000.
Website: http://riverstyx.org

Freelance Potential: 100% written by nonstaff writers. Publishes 80 freelance submissions yearly; 10% by unpublished writers, 30% by authors who are new to the magazine. Receives 20 queries, 1,000 unsolicited mss monthly.

Submissions and Payment: Sample copy available. Guidelines available at website. Query or send complete ms between May and November only. Accepts hard copy. SASE. Responds in 3–5 months. One-time rights. Articles and fiction, 10–35 double-spaced pages. Poetry, 3–5 poems per submission. Written material, $8 per published page. Pays on publication. Written material, amount varies. Provides 2 contributor's copies and a subscription.

Road

25006 Avenue Kearney
Valencia, CA 91355

Submissions: Dillon Clapp

Description and Interests: This magazine is all about road cycling and the cycling lifestyle. Each of its 11 issues includes race reports, new product information, opinion pieces, and cycling tips. Circ: 40,000.
Website: www.roadmagazine.net

Freelance Potential: 20–50% written by nonstaff writers. Publishes numerous freelance submissions yearly; 20% by unpublished writers, 20% by authors who are new to the magazine, 60% by experts. Receives 10–20 queries monthly.

Submissions and Payment: Sample copy and guidelines available at website. Query with event stories. Accepts hard copy. SASE. Response time varies. Rights vary. Written material, word lengths and payment rates vary. Payment policy varies. Provides 1 contributor's copy.

Road & Travel Magazine

3228 Patriot Way
West Greenwich, RI 02817

Editor: Courtney Caldwell

Description and Interests: Updated 26 times each year and geared mostly toward women, this online magazine offers articles on automobile buying, travel, and safety. It also features hotel, spa, and resort reviews. Hits per month: Unavailable.
Website: www.roadandtravel.com

Freelance Potential: 50% written by nonstaff writers. Publishes 20+ freelance submissions yearly; 10% by unpublished writers, 10% by authors who are new to the magazine, 10% by experts. Receives 20 unsolicited mss monthly.

Submissions and Payment: Sample copy and guidelines available at website. Query or send complete ms with signed guidelines. Accepts email submissions via website only. Responds in 3 months if interested. First and second serial rights. Articles, 1,000–1,200 words. Columns, 500 words. Blog articles, 200–300 words. Payment rates vary.

Roanoke Review

Roanoke College
221 College Lane
Salem, VA 24153

Editor: Paul Hanstedt

Description and Interests: Fiction, creative nonfiction, and poetry fill the pages of this annual literary journal. New writers and experienced authors are equally encouraged to submit material. Circ: 500.
Website: http://roanokereview.wordpress.com

Freelance Potential: 100% written by nonstaff writers. Publishes 30–40 freelance submissions yearly; 15% by unpublished writers, 98% by new authors. Receives 300 unsolicited mss monthly.

Submissions and Payment: Sample copy available. Guidelines available at website. Send complete ms between September 1 and January 31. Accepts hard copy, simultaneous submissions, and email to review@roanoke.edu. SASE. Responds in 6 months. All rights. Fiction, to 5,000 words. Creative nonfiction, to 5,000 words. Poetry, to 100 lines; to 5 poems per submission. Written material, payment rates vary. Payment policy varies. Provides 2 contributor's copies.

Rockford Review

Rockford Writers' Guild
P.O. Box 858
Rockford, IL 61105

Editor: Connie Kuntz

Description and Interests: Twice each year, this literary magazine features eclectic prose and poetry that expresses fresh insight into the human condition. While themes are varied, sexist, pornographic, or supremacist content will not be considered. A national editorial board selects all material. Circ: 500.
Website: www.rockfordwritersguild.com

Freelance Potential: 100% written by nonstaff writers. Publishes 125 freelance submissions yearly; 25% by unpublished writers, 50% by authors who are new to the magazine. Receives 15–20 queries, 75–100 unsolicited mss monthly.

Submissions and Payment: Sample copy available. Guidelines and deadlines available at website. Send complete ms with brief author bio. Accepts hard copy or email to editor@rockfordwritersguild.com. SASE. Response time varies. First rights. Prose, to 1,300 words. Poetry, to 50 lines. Written material, $5 per published piece. Provides 1 contributor's copy.

Room

P.O. Box 46160, Station D
Vancouver, British Columbia V6J 5G5
Canada

Submissions Editor

Description and Interests: This quarterly literary magazine publishes top-notch prose, poetry, and creative nonfiction for, by, and about women. It also features interviews, reviews, and art. Circ: 1,000.
Website: http://roommagazine.com

Freelance Potential: 90–95% written by nonstaff writers. Publishes 100 freelance submissions yearly; many by new authors. Receives 60–100 unsolicited mss monthly.

Submissions and Payment: Sample copy available. Guidelines available at website. Send complete ms. Accepts online submissions via website. Responds in 6 months via email. First North American serial rights. Fiction and creative nonfiction, to 3,500 words. Poetry, to 5 poems per submission. Honorarium. Provides 2 contributor's copies and a 1-year subscription.

Rose & Thorn Journal

4705 Inniswold Road
Baton Rouge, LA 70809-2626

Editors: Kathryn Magendie & Angie Ledbetter

Description and Interests: Emerging and established writers contribute to this quarterly online literary journal. It accepts original poetry, fiction, and creative nonfiction that reflect a diversity of style and content. Hits per month: 3,500.
Website: www.roseandthornjournal.com

Freelance Potential: 97% written by nonstaff writers. Publishes 70+ freelance submissions yearly; 40% by unpublished writers, 80% by authors who are new to the magazine. Receives 100+ unsolicited mss monthly.

Submissions and Payment: Sample copy and guidelines available at website. Send ms with brief author bio. Accepts email to prose@roseandthornjournal.com (include "Submission" and word count in subject line) and poetry@roseandthornjournal.com; (no attachments). Responds in 2 weeks. First rights. Articles and fiction, to 3,000 words. Poetry, to 3 poems. No payment.

Rosicrucian Digest

1342 Naglee Avenue
San Jose, CA 95191

Editor

Description and Interests: Published by the Worldwide Rosicrucian Order, this magazine explores spirituality, science, history, philosophy, mysticism, and the arts. Appearing twice each year, it includes essays, poetry, book reviews, and informative articles. Its readership includes members of the Order, as well as the general public. Circ: 10,000.
Website: www.rosicrucian.org

Freelance Potential: 50% written by nonstaff writers. Publishes 5–6 freelance submissions yearly; 25% by authors who are new to the magazine. Receives 20 queries monthly.

Submissions and Payment: Sample copy and guidelines available at website. Query. Accepts email submissions to editorinchief@rosicrucian.org (Word or RTF attachments). SASE. Responds in 2–3 months. First North American serial rights. Articles, 1,000–2,000 words; $.06 per word. Pays on acceptance. Provides 2 contributor's copies.

Runway

Celebrity Collections Fashion Magazine

4413 North Saddlebag Trail, #1
Scottsdale, AZ 85251

Submissions: Megan Accordino

Description and Interests: *Runway* takes a modern approach to fashion, covering all aspects from the beauty salon to the red carpet. Published bimonthly, it is filled with celebrity interviews, designer profiles, and expert shopping and beauty tips. Circ: 120,000.
Website: www.runwaylive.com

Freelance Potential: 95% written by nonstaff writers. Publishes 105 freelance submissions yearly; 5% by unpublished writers, 20% by authors who are new to the magazine, 75% by experts. Receives 9 unsolicited mss monthly.

Submissions and Payment: Sample copy, guidelines, and theme list/editorial calendar available. Send complete ms. Accepts email submissions to info@runwaybeauty.com. Responds in 2 weeks. Temporary rights. Articles, 500+ words; $.02–$.40 per word. Pays on publication. Provides 1 contributor's copy.

Russian Life

P.O. Box 567
Montpelier, VT 05601-0567

Editor: Paul Richardson

Description and Interests: This magazine captures all aspects of life in Russia for an American readership. Published six times each year, it covers everything from Russian politics and history to culture, entertainment, travel, and food. Circ: 20,000.
Website: www.russianlife.com

Freelance Potential: 80% written by nonstaff writers. Publishes 6–12 freelance submissions yearly; 10% by unpublished writers, 25% by authors who are new to the magazine, 10% by experts. Receives 5 queries monthly.

Submissions and Payment: Sample copy available. Guidelines available at website. Query. Accepts email queries to editors@russianlife.com. Responds in 1 week. First serial and non-exclusive electronic rights. Articles, 2,000–5,000 words; $100–$300. Pays on publication. Provides 4 contributor's copies.

RV Lifestyle Magazine

1121 Invicta Drive, Unit 2
Oakville, Ontario L6H 2R2
Canada

Editorial Director: Norm Rosen

Description and Interests: Canadian families who enjoy the recreational vehicle lifestyle turn to this magazine for information about destinations and campgrounds, RV maintenance and care, and other topics that enhance the RV experience. It is published seven times each year in English and four times each year in French (titled *Vie en Plein Air*). Circ: 42,000.
Website: http://rvlifemag.com

Freelance Potential: 15% written by nonstaff writers. Publishes 10 freelance submissions yearly; 3% by unpublished writers, 10% by authors who are new to the magazine.

Submissions and Payment: Sample copy available at website. Query. Accepts email queries to nrosen@rvlifemag.com. Response time varies. First Canadian rights. Written material, word lengths and payment rates vary. Payment policy varies.

Sabbath School Toolbox

55 West Oak Ridge Drive
Hagerstown, MD 21740

Editor: James W. Zackrison

Description and Interests: This publication, which has replaced *LEAD* magazine, is a resource digest for pastors and Sabbath School leaders of the Seventh-day Adventist Church. Quarterly issues include articles on the four purposes of Sabbath School, as well as study guide highlights and creative teaching approaches. Circ: 4,000.
Website: www.sabbathschooltoolbox.org

Freelance Potential: 10% written by nonstaff writers. Publishes 3 freelance submissions yearly; 2% by new authors, 98% by experts.

Submissions and Payment: Since the content of this publication is very specialized, query first. Accepts email queries to sabbathschooltoolbox@rhpa.org (Word attachments). Response time varies. First rights. Articles, 700–750 words. Payment rates vary. Pays on acceptance. Provides 1 contributor's copy.

Sacred Fire

3010 12th Avenue NE
Olympia, WA 98506

Managing Editor: Sharon Brown

Description and Interests: This quarterly magazine offers non-denominational spiritual content on all aspects of life and nature. It features articles, essays, fiction, and poetry. Circ: 5,000.
Website: http://sacredfiremagazine.com

Freelance Potential: 70% written by nonstaff writers. Publishes 30 freelance submissions yearly; 40% by unpublished writers, 70% by authors who are new to the magazine, 60% by experts. Receives 4 queries monthly.

Submissions and Payment: Guidelines available at website. Query or send complete ms. Accepts hard copy and email submissions to submissions@ sacredfiremagazine.com. Responds in 3 months. One-time print and electronic rights. Articles, 1,200–3,500 words. Short pieces, 50–500 words. Fiction, to 3,000 words. Poetry, to 50 lines; 3 poems per submission. Written material, payment rates vary. Payment policy varies.

The Saint Ann's Review

Saint Ann's School
129 Pierrepont Street
Brooklyn, NY 11201

Editor: Beth Bosworth

Description and Interests: Accepting fiction, poetry, reviews, plays, and excerpts, *The Saint Ann's Review* is published twice each year. Circ: 2,000.
Website: http://saintannsreview.com

Freelance Potential: 90% written by nonstaff writers. Publishes 70+ freelance submissions yearly.

Submissions and Payment: Sample copy available. Guidelines available at website. Query or send complete ms September through July. Prefers online submissions via website; will accept hard copy and simultaneous submissions if identified. SASE. Responds to queries in 1 month, to mss in 4 months. First North American serial rights. Fiction and nonfiction, to 6,000 words. Poetry, to 10 pages. Plays and excerpts, to 25 pages. No payment. Provides 2 contributor's copies.

Salt Hill

English Department
Syracuse University
Syracuse, NY 13244-1170

Fiction, Poetry, or Nonfiction Editor

Description and Interests: Featuring a mix of poetry, prose, translations, reviews, and interviews, *Salt Hill* is published twice each year by Syracuse University's English Department. Circ: 1,000.
Website: www.salthilljournal.net

Freelance Potential: 90% written by nonstaff writers. Publishes 80–100 freelance submissions yearly; 25% by unpublished writers, 75% by authors who are new to the magazine. Receives 200 unsolicited mss monthly.

Submissions and Payment: Sample copy available. Guidelines available at website. Send complete ms with a cover letter between August 1 and April 1. Accepts online submissions only through Submismash and simultaneous submissions if identified. Responds in 2–6 months. First rights. Fiction and nonfiction, to 30 pages. Poetry, to 5 poems per submission. No payment. Provides 2 author's copies.

Salt Water Sportsman

460 North Orlando Avenue
Winter Park, FL 32789

Editor in Chief: John Brownlee

Description and Interests: Published 10 times a year, this magazine offers expert-written articles on the techniques and equipment that will help saltwater anglers hook the best catch. Circ: 135,000.
Website: www.saltwatersportsman.com

Freelance Potential: 90% written by nonstaff writers. Publishes 15–20 freelance submissions yearly; 10% by unpublished writers, 5% by authors who are new to the magazine, 100% by experts. Receives 5 queries monthly.

Submissions and Payment: Sample copy available. Editorial calendar available at website. Query. Accepts email queries to editor@ saltwatersportsman.com. Responds in 2 months. First North American serial rights. Articles, 1,000–2,000 words. Depts/columns, 800–1,500 words. Written material, payment rates vary. Pays on acceptance. Provides up to 6 contributor's copies.

Salvo Magazine

P.O. Box 410788
Chicago, IL 60641

Senior Editor: Bobby Maddex

Description and Interests: *Salvo* targets young adults with content that "deconstructs societal myths" by offering an alternative viewpoint to the mainstream media on society, science, and sex. Investigative journalism pieces are especially sought. It appears quarterly. Circ: 3,200.
Website: www.salvomag.com

Freelance Potential: 50% written by nonstaff writers. Publishes 50 freelance submissions yearly; 50% by authors who are new to the magazine. Receives 20 queries monthly.

Submissions and Payment: Sample copy available. Query with writing samples. Accepts email queries to editor@salvomag.com. Responds in 1 month. All rights. Articles, 600–2,500 words. Depts/columns, 800–1,200 words. Written material, $.20 per word. Kill fee, $100. Pays on publication. Provides 1 contributor's copy.

Sanskrit

University of North Carolina-Charlotte
Student Union Room 045
9201 University City Boulevard
Charlotte, NC 28223

Submissions Editor

Description and Interests: The University of North Carolina publishes this annual literary magazine filled with original essays, fiction, poetry, and artwork. Circ: 3,000.
Website: http://sanskrit.uncc.edu/

Freelance Potential: 98% written by nonstaff writers. Publishes 34 freelance submissions yearly; 90% by unpublished writers, 90% by new authors. Receives 15 unsolicited mss monthly.

Submissions and Payment: Sample copy available. Guidelines available at website. Send complete ms with author biography and word count; see website for current deadline. Accepts email to sanskrit@uncc.edu. Response time varies. One-time rights. Fiction and essays, to 3,500 words; to 5 entries per submission. Poetry, to 15 poems per submission. No payment. Provides 1 contributor's copy.

The Savage Kick

Murder Slim Press
29 Alpha Road
Gorleston, Norfolk NR31 0LQ
United Kingdom

Editors: Steve Hussy & Richard White

Description and Interests: This adult-content literary magazine is published annually. In the editors' own words, "sleazy and confessional tales form the basis of its content." When it comes to topics, anything goes, but genres are limited to confessional/memoir tales or distinctive crime/war stories. Circ: 400.
Website: http://murderslim.com

Freelance Potential: 90% written by nonstaff writers. Publishes 8 freelance submissions yearly; 20% by unpublished writers, 50% by new authors . Receives 10–20 queries monthly.

Submissions and Payment: Excerpts and guidelines available at website. Send complete ms with bio. Accepts hard copy and email submissions to slim@murderslim.com (Word or RTF attachments). Responds in 1 month. First print, electronic rights. Articles/fiction, 1,000–8,000 words; $25–$35. Pays on acceptance.

Scandinavian Review

58 Park Avenue
New York, NY 10016

Editor: Richard Litell

Description and Interests: You won't find travel articles in this magazine. Instead, *Scandinavian Review*, published three times each year, focuses on the region's culture, business, politics, and arts. It is available to members of the American–Scandinavian Foundation and by subscription. Circ: 6,000.
Website: www.amscan.org

Freelance Potential: 99% written by nonstaff writers. Publishes 30 freelance submissions yearly; 50% by authors who are new to the magazine.

Submissions and Payment: Sample copy and guidelines available. Query with résumé and clips or writing samples; or send complete ms. Accepts hard copy and email to rjlitell@gmail.com. SASE. Responds in 1–3 weeks. First North American serial rights. Articles, 1,500–2,000 words; $200+. Prints to 11x14 and color slides; payment rates vary. Pays on publication. Provides 2 contributor's copies.

Sculpture Review

75 Varick Street, 11th Floor
New York, NY 10013

Managing Editor: Germana Pucci

Description and Interests: *Sculpture Review* is a quarterly publication for those who love and admire figurative sculpture as collectors, viewers, and creators. Its pages are filled with photographs and in-depth features on technique, history, and appreciation of the art form. Circ: 7,000.
Website: http://sculpturereview.com

Freelance Potential: 70% written by nonstaff writers. Publishes 20 freelance submissions yearly; 30% by unpublished writers, 30% by authors who are new to the magazine. Receives 2 queries monthly.

Submissions and Payment: Sample copy and guidelines available. Query with samples of related articles. Accepts hard copy. SASE. Responds in 6 months. All rights. Articles, 500–1,500 words; $.30–$.50 per word. 8x10 B/W prints or 5x7 color transparencies. Pays on publication. Provides 2 contributor's copies.

Sea History

National Maritime Historical Society
5 John Walsh Boulevard
P.O. Box 68
Peekskill, NY 10566

Editor: Deirdre O'Regan

Description and Interests: All aspects of maritime history—primarily U.S., but also international—are covered in this quarterly publication, including heritage, education, and preservation. Writing should appeal to a general audience. Circ: 25,000.
Website: http://seahistory.org

Freelance Potential: 90% written by nonstaff writers. Publishes 10 freelance submissions yearly; 50% by authors new to the magazine, 75% by experts. Receives 10 queries monthly.

Submissions and Payment: Sample copy available. Guidelines available at website. Query with outline or send complete ms with brief author bio. Prefers email queries to editorial@seahistory.org (Word attachments); will accept hard copy. SASE. Responds in 6–8 weeks. First rights. Articles, 1,200–3,000 words. Depts/columns, word lengths vary. No payment. Provides 4 contributor's copies.

The Seattle Review 

University of Washington
P.O. Box 354330
Seattle, WA 98195-4330

Fiction, Nonfiction, or Poetry Editor

Description and Interests: *The Seattle Review* publishes poetry, fiction, and nonfiction twice each year. Daring and diverse topics from new and established writers are encouraged. Circ: 1,000.
Website: http://depts.washington.edu/seaview

Freelance Potential: 100% written by nonstaff writers. Publishes 50 freelance submissions yearly; 10% by unpublished writers, 40% by new authors. Receives 100 unsolicited mss monthly.

Submissions and Payment: Sample copy available. Guidelines available at website. Send complete ms. Accepts hard copy between October 1 and May 31 and electronic submissions year round through submissions manager at website. No simultaneous submissions. SASE. Responds in 1–4 months. First rights. Prose, 40–90 pages. Poetry, 10–30 pages; to 5 poems per submission. Written material, payment rates vary. Payment policy varies. Provides 4 contributor's copies.

Seeing the Everyday

P.O. Box 380038
Cambridge, MA 02238

Editors: Ami Frost & Sara Thomas

Description and Interests: True, personal stories fill each quarterly issue of this family-oriented magazine. These stories document the profound, yet simple experiences of parents and children. A selected submission offers a meaningful and uplifting message to readers, showing how the experience shaped the writer's attitude and development. Circ: 7,000.
Website: http://seeingtheeveryday.com

Freelance Potential: 90% written by nonstaff writers. Publishes 80 freelance submissions yearly; 75% by unpublished writers, 65% by authors who are new to the magazine.

Submissions and Payment: Sample articles and guidelines available at website. Send complete ms. Accepts email to stories@seeingtheeveryday.com. Response time varies. Rights vary. Articles, to 750 words. No payment.

SFRevu  

30 Deer Run Lane
Brick, NJ 08724

Senior Editor: Gayle Surrette

Description and Interests: An ezine of fantasy and science fiction, *SFRevu* features literary criticism, book reviews, and author interviews related to the genre. It is published monthly. Circ: Unavailable.
Website: http://sfrevu.com

Freelance Potential: Receives many freelance submissions monthly.

Submissions and Payment: Sample copy at website. Query. Accepts email to editor@sfrevu.com. Response time varies. Written material, word lengths vary. Rights vary. Payment rates and policy vary.

Shelf Unbound  

Shelf Media Group
3322 Greenview Drive
Garland, TX 75044

Publisher: Margaret Brown

Description and Interests: This digital magazine strives to bring the best books of the small and independent presses and self-published books to its readers. It offers book reviews, author interviews, excerpts, and photo essays. Because it is digital, readers are also able to link to additional info and a purchasing source for the books. Circ: 100,000+.
Website: www.shelfmediagroup.com

Freelance Potential: Unavailable.

Submissions and Payment: Sample copy and guidelines available at website. Currently only accepting courtesy essays and reviews, up to 1,500 words. Send complete ms with blog or website link to margaret@shelfmediagroup.com. Rights, unknown. No payment.

Single Again 

7405 Greenback Lane, #129
Citrus Heights, CA 95610–5603

Publisher: Paul V. Scholl

Description and Interests: Newly divorced, separated, and widowed readers find advice and support here to "Make the Rest of Your Life the Best of Your Life." This ezine publishes interviews and articles by writers who know what it's like to be single again. Hits per month: 105,000.
Website: www.singleagain.com

Freelance Potential: 80% written by nonstaff writers. Publishes 75 freelance submissions yearly; 10% by unpublished writers, 80% by authors who are new to the magazine, 10% by experts. Receives 15–20 queries monthly.

Submissions and Payment: Query or send complete ms. Accepts hard copy and email to publisher@singleagain.com (must include "Submission from Long Ridge" in subject line). SASE. Responds in 4–6 weeks. First rights. Written material, word lengths vary. No payment. Provides 1 live link to author's website and/or email address.

Sinister Wisdom 

6910 Wells Parkway
University Park, MD 20782

Editors: Julie R. Enszer & Merry Gangemi

Description and Interests: Literature and art reflecting the multicultural, multi-class, lesbian community are featured in this journal of essays, fiction, poetry, and humor. *Sinister Wisdom* only publishes work by lesbians. It appears three times each year. Circ: 1,000.
Website: www.sinisterwisdom.org

Freelance Potential: 95% written by nonstaff writers. Publishes 150 freelance submissions yearly; 95% by unpublished writers, 75% by authors who are new to the magazine.

Submissions and Payment: Sample copy available. Guidelines available at website. Send complete ms. Prefers online submissions via website; will accept hard copy. SASE. Responds to queries in 1 month, to mss in 6–8 months. First rights. Articles and fiction, up to 2 short pieces or one longer to 5,000 words. Poetry, to 5 poems per submission. No payment. Provides a 1-year subscription.

Ski Magazine

5720 Flatiron Parkway
Boulder, CO 80301

Editor: Greg Ditrinco

Description and Interests: Expert-written articles are a main feature of this photo-filled publication for skiers. Articles cover all aspects of the sport, from gear and techniques to destinations and the skiing lifestyle. The concerns and interests of skiers of all levels of experience are addressed in this magazine, which appears six times each year. Circ: 450,000.
Website: www.skinet.com

Freelance Potential: 70% written by nonstaff writers. Publishes 25–30 freelance submissions yearly; 3% by unpublished writers, 72% by experts. Receives 80 queries monthly.

Submissions and Payment: Sample copy available. Query with résumé and writing samples. Accepts hard copy. SASE. Responds in 3 weeks. First North American serial rights. Articles, 1,000–2,000 words. Depts/columns, 1,000 words. Written material, $300–$1,000. Pays on acceptance.

Ski Racing

P.O. Box 1467
Ketchum, ID 83340

Editor in Chief: Sarah Tuff

Description and Interests: *Ski Racing* is "the journal of snowsport competition." Published monthly, it covers competitions, personalities, and equipment. Circ: 25,000.
Website: www.skiracing.com

Freelance Potential: 30% written by nonstaff writers. Publishes 20 freelance submissions yearly; 30% by authors who are new to the magazine, 100% by experts. Receives 20 queries monthly.

Submissions and Payment: Sample copy available at website. Guidelines and editorial calendar available. Query with outline. Accepts hard copy and email queries to stuff@skiracing.com. SASE. Responds in 1 month. First North American serial rights. Articles, 1,000 words. Depts/columns, 500 words. Digital images at 150 dpi or higher. All material, payment rates vary. Pays 60 days after publication.

Skirt!

725 Broad Street
Augusta, GA 30901

Editor

Description and Interests: With both a print magazine and website, *Skirt!* addresses all issues of interest to women. Personal essays and features on work, families, relationships, style, creativity, health, finance, and much more make up its very accessible content. It appreciates attitude and point of view from its writers. Circ: Unknown.
Website: www.skirt.com

Freelance Potential: Open to contributing writers for articles, blogs, and essays.

Submissions and Payment: Sample articles, guidelines, and theme list available at website. Send complete ms with word count. Prefers email to submissions@skirt.com; accepts hard copy. SASE. Responds if interested in 6–8 weeks. Rights, unknown. Written material, payment rates vary. Payment policy, unavailable.

Slap

High Speed Productions
1303 Underwood Avenue
San Francisco, CA 94124

Editor: Nick Lattner

Description and Interests: The world of skateboarding, from techniques and terrain to culture and lifestyle, is the focus of this online publication. Updated daily, *SLAP* is an acronym for Skateboarding, Life, Art, and Progression. Hits per month: 200,000.
Website: http://slapmagazine.com

Freelance Potential: 40% written by nonstaff writers. Publishes 24 freelance submissions yearly; 20% by unpublished writers.

Submissions and Payment: Send complete ms. Prefers email to info@slapmagazine.com. Accepts hard copy, disk submissions, and simultaneous submissions if identified. Availability of artwork improves chance of acceptance. SASE. Responds in 2 months. All rights. Articles and depts/columns, word lengths and payment rates vary. Pays on publication.

Slate & Style 

National Federation of the Blind—Writer's Division
504 South 57th Street
Omaha, NE 68106–3216

Editor: Robert Lesley Newman

Description and Interests: *Slate & Style* publishes articles that help blind writers market and publish their work. Published quarterly in braille, audio, and large-print editions by the National Federation of the Blind, it also features fiction and poetry. Circ: 200.
Website: www.nfb-writers-division.net/slate_style

Freelance Potential: 50% written by nonstaff writers. Publishes 10–15 freelance submissions yearly; 10% by unpublished writers, 25% by authors who are new to the magazine, 65% by experts. Receives 2 unsolicited mss monthly.

Submissions and Payment: Sample copy and guidelines available. Send complete ms. Accepts hard copy and email submissions to newmanrl@cox.net (no attachments). SASE. Responds in 3 months. First rights. Articles, 1,000 words. Fiction, 2,000 words. Poetry, to 36 lines. No payment. Provides 1 contributor's copy.

Small Boats

P.O. Box 78
48 WoodenBoat Lane
Brooklin, ME 04616-0078

Editor: Matthew P. Murphy

Description and Interests: Articles written by experts only are what make *Small Boats,* the annual special publication of *Wooden Boat* magazine, the authoritative voice on towable watercraft. Profiles and reviews are also featured in each photo-filled issue. Circ: Unavailable.
Website: http://woodenboat.com

Freelance Potential: 90% written by nonstaff writers. Publishes 25 freelance submissions yearly; 40% by unpublished writers, 50% by authors who are new to the magazine, 100% by experts. Receives 35 queries, 17 unsolicited mss monthly.

Submissions and Payment: Sample copy available. Guidelines and editorial calendar available at website. Query with 1-page letter and illustration samples; or send complete ms. Accepts hard copy and disk submissions. SASE. Response time varies. First world rights. Articles, word lengths vary; $.30 per word. Pays on publication. Provides 1 contributor's copy.

Small Farm Canada

4623 William Head Road
Victoria, British Columbia V9C 3Y7
Canada

Editor: Tom Henry

Description and Interests: Small and hobby farmers find useful tips and practical information in this magazine. It is published six times each year. Circ: 17,000.
Website: http://smallfarmcanada.ca

Freelance Potential: 80% written by nonstaff writers. Publishes 40 freelance submissions yearly; 20% by authors who are new to the magazine, 20% by experts. Receives 10 unsolicited mss monthly.

Submissions and Payment: Sample copy, editorial calendar and guidelines available. Send complete ms. Accepts email to tomhenry@smallfarmcanada.ca (attach file). Responds in 3 months. One-time print and electronic rights. Articles, 900–1,500 words. Depts/columns, 550 words. Written material, $.30 per word. Kill fee, negotiable. Pays on publication. Provides 2 contributor's copies.

Smithsonian Zoogoer

Friends of the National Zoo
P.O. Box 37012, MRC 5516
Washington, DC 20013-7012

Editor: Peter Winkler

Description and Interests: Published six times each year for Friends of the National Zoo members, this magazine explores topics relating to the animals and staff of the zoo, in addition to wildlife conservation and current scientific research. Circ: 40,000.
Website: http://nationalzoo.si.edu/Publications/ZooGoer

Freelance Potential: 15% written by nonstaff writers. Publishes 8–10 freelance submissions yearly; 5% by authors who are new to the magazine. Receives 60 queries yearly.

Submissions and Payment: Sample articles available at website. Guidelines available. Query. Accepts hard copy and email queries to zoogoer@si.edu (Word or plain text attachments). SASE. Responds in 1 month. First print and electronic rights. Articles, 2,000 words. Depts/columns, 800–1,500 words. Written material, $.80 per word. Pays on publication. Provides 5 contributor's copies.

SnoWest

360 B Street
Idaho Falls, ID 83402

Editor: Lane Lindstrom

Description and Interests: Snowmobiling and other winter motorized recreational activities are covered in this magazine, which focuses on the western U.S. and Canada. Published six times each year, it includes test reports, travel pieces, and technical advice. Circ: 102,000+.
Website: www.snowest.com

Freelance Potential: 10% written by nonstaff writers. Publishes 1–3 freelance submissions yearly; 1% by unpublished writers, 9% by authors who are new to the magazine, 90% by experts. Receives 5 queries monthly.

Submissions and Payment: Sample copy and guidelines available. Query. Accepts email queries to lindstrm@snowest.com. Responds in 1–2 weeks. First North American serial rights. Articles, to 2,000 words. Depts/columns, 500–1,500 words. Written material, payment rates vary. Pays on publication. Provides 2 contributor's copies.

Snowy Egret

P.O. Box 9265
Terre Haute, IN 47808

The Editors

Description and Interests: This journal of nature writing examines the psychological and poetic responses to the natural world. Published twice each year, it accepts creative nonfiction, fiction, and poetry. Circ: 400.
Website: http://snowyegret.net

Freelance Potential: 100% written by nonstaff writers. Publishes 40 freelance submissions yearly; 25% by unpublished writers, 80% by authors who are new to the magazine. Receives 80 unsolicited mss monthly.

Submissions and Payment: Sample copy available. Guidelines available at website. Send complete ms. Accepts hard copy. SASE. Responds in 1 month. First North American serial rights. Articles and fiction, to 10,000 words; $2 per page. Poetry, $4 per page. Pays on publication. Provides 2 contributor's copies.

SN Review

197 Fairchild Avenue
Fairfield, CT 06825

Editor: Joseph Conlin

Description and Interests: A mix of non-genre literary fiction, creative nonfiction, essays, and poetry submitted by writers from all walks of life appear in this online publication. Updated quarterly, *SN Review* seeks original, engaging works that have interesting plots, characters, themes, writing styles, and points of view. Hits per month: 15,000.
Website: www.snreview.org

Freelance Potential: 100% written by nonstaff writers. Publishes 150 freelance submissions yearly; 80% by authors who are new to the magazine.

Submissions and Payment: Sample copy and guidelines available at website. Send complete ms. Accepts email submissions to editor@snreview.org (no attachments). Responds in 6 months. First rights. Fiction and nonfiction, to 7,000 words. Poetry, to 200 words. No payment.

Social Forces

The University of North Carolina Press
Box 2288
Chapel Hill, NC 27515

Editor: Arne L. Kalleberg

Description and Interests: *Social Forces* is an international journal of social research that publishes articles on social psychology, anthropology, history, political science, and economics. It appears quarterly. Circ: 2,500.
Website: http://sf.oxfordjournals.org/

Freelance Potential: 100% written by nonstaff writers. Publishes 70 freelance submissions yearly; 3% by unpublished writers, 65% by authors who are new to the magazine, 95% by experts. Receives 30 unsolicited mss monthly.

Submissions and Payment: Sample copy available. Guidelines available at website. Send complete ms with $50 submission fee. Accepts submissions through website. No simultaneous submissions. Responds in 4 months. All rights. Articles, to 9,000 words, including references and endnotes. Book reviews, to 800 words. No payment.

So to Speak

George Mason University
4400 University Drive, MSN 2C5
Fairfax, VA 22030-4444

Managing Editor: Mike Stein

Description and Interests: Founded by an editorial collective of women at George Mason University, this feminist journal looks for fiction, poetry, and nonfiction that address issues of significance to women's lives. It is published twice a year in print, and once a year online. Circ: 1,300.
Website: http://sotospeakjournal.org/submit

Freelance Potential: 100% written by nonstaff writers. Publishes 40 freelance submissions yearly; 15% by unpublished writers, 80% by authors who are new to the magazine. Receives 81 unsolicited mss monthly.

Submissions and Payment: Sample copy available. Guidelines available at website. Send complete ms with author bio August 1–October 15 and January 1–March 15. Accepts submissions through Submishmash and simultaneous submissions. Responds in 1–4 months. First rights. Articles, to 4,500 words. Fiction, to 4,500 words. Poetry, to 5 poems, 10 pages total. No payment. Provides 2 contributor's copies.

South American Explorers

126 Indian Creek Road
Ithaca, NY 14850

Managing Editor: Lucy E. Cousins

Description and Interests: In-depth, highly readable travel articles that touch on a wide range of topics, including history, conservation, archaeology, and culture, are offered in this quarterly magazine. Circ: 14,000.
Website: www.saexplorers.org

Freelance Potential: 85% written by nonstaff writers. Publishes 20 freelance submissions yearly; 80% by unpublished writers, 70% by authors who are new to the magazine. Receives 4–5 queries monthly.

Submissions and Payment: Sample copy and guidelines available at website. Query to 500 words. Accepts hard copy, email to magazine@saexplorers.org, and simultaneous submissions if identified. SASE. Responds in 2 months. First North American serial rights. Articles, 800–3,000 words. Depts/columns, word lengths vary. Filler, 500–1,500 words. Written material, $50–$300. Pays on publication. Provides contributor's copies and a 1-year subscription.

The South Carolina Review

Center for Electronic & Digital Publishing
Clemson University, Strode Tower, Room 611
Box 340522
Clemson, SC 29634-0522

Editor: Wayne Chapman

Description and Interests: First published in 1968, Clemson University's literary journal publishes writers from the U.S., Great Britain, and Ireland, but it has a distinctive southern edge. Published twice each year, it accepts fiction, poetry, interviews, and essays. Circ: 400.
Website: www.clemson.edu/cedp/cudp/scr/about.htm

Freelance Potential: 95% written by nonstaff writers. Publishes 110 freelance submissions yearly; 70% by authors who are new to the magazine. Receives 100 unsolicited mss monthly.

Submissions and Payment: Sample copy available. Guidelines available at website. Send complete ms. Accepts hard copy. SASE. Responds in 1–3 months. First rights. Written material, word lengths vary. No payment. Provides 2 contributor's copies.

South Dakota Review

University of South Dakota
Department of English
414 East Clark Street
Vermillion, SD 57069

Editor: Brian Bedard

Description and Interests: This quarterly literary journal contains works that have a western regional emphasis, although selection is based on the quality of the work rather than on subject matter. It accepts fiction, nonfiction, essays, and poetry. Circ: 500.
Website: http://orgs.usd.edu/sdreview

Freelance Potential: 95% written by nonstaff writers. Publishes 100 freelance submissions yearly; 10% by unpublished writers, 20% by authors who are new to the magazine. Receives 100 unsolicited mss monthly.

Submissions and Payment: Sample copy available. Guidelines available at website. Send complete ms with brief author bio. Accepts hard copy and online submissions via website. SASE. Responds in 8–10 weeks. First North American serial and electronic rights. Fiction and nonfiction, 1,000–6,000 words. Poetry, no line limits; to 5 poems per submission. No payment. Provides 2 contributor's copies and a 1-year subscription.

The Southeast Review 

Florida State University, Department of English
Tallahassee, FL 32306

Editor: Katie Cortese

Description and Interests: Published twice each year by the English Department at FSU, this literary journal features short fiction, nonfiction, book reviews, interviews, and poetry. Circ: 1,200.
Website: www.southeastreview.org

Freelance Potential: 95% written by nonstaff writers. Publishes 70 freelance submissions yearly; 20% by unpublished writers, 75% by authors who are new to the magazine. Receives 300 unsolicited mss monthly.

Submissions and Payment: Sample copy available. Guidelines available at website. Query for interviews only by email to southeastreview@gmail.com. Send complete ms for all other work. Accepts submissions via website and simultaneous submissions. Hard copy submissions will not be read unless they are contest submissions. Responds in 2–4 months. First North American serial rights. Fiction and nonfiction, to 7,500 words. Poetry, to 5 poems, to 15 pages total. Book reviews, 800–1,000 words. No payment. Provides 2 contributor's copies.

Southern California Review 

3501 Trousdale Parkway
Taper Hall THH 355J
University of Southern California
Los Angeles, CA 90089-0355

Fiction, Poetry, or Nonfiction Editor

Description and Interests: This student-run literary journal is published annually. It accepts fiction, poetry, creative nonfiction, interviews, and one-act stage plays and screenplays. Circ: 1,000.
Website: http://dornsife.usc.edu/mpw

Freelance Potential: 90% written by nonstaff writers. Publishes 30 freelance submissions yearly; 25% by unpublished writers, 25% by authors who are new to the magazine. Receives 40 unsolicited mss monthly.

Submissions and Payment: Sample copy available. Guidelines available at website. Send complete ms with cover letter. Accepts hard copy and online submissions; simultaneous submissions if identified. SASE. Responds in 3–6 months. One-time rights. Prose, to 7,000 words. Poetry, 1 poem per page; to 3 poems per submission. No payment. Provides 2 contributor's copies.

Southern Humanities Review

9088 Haley Center, Auburn University
Auburn, AL 36849–5202

Editor: Chantel Acevedo

Description and Interests: With a mission to rediscover and revisit our cultural heritage, this quarterly journal publishes fiction, poetry, personal and critical essays, cultural studies, book and art reviews, and historical studies. Circ: 700.
Website: www.cla.auburn.edu/shr

Freelance Potential: 100% written by nonstaff writers. Publishes 60–75 freelance submissions yearly; 50% by authors who are new to the magazine. Receives 1–2 queries, 300–400 unsolicited mss monthly.

Submissions and Payment: Sample copy available. Guidelines available at website. Query or send complete ms. Accepts hard copy, email to shrsubmissions@auburn.edu, and simultaneous submissions. SASE. Responds in 1–3 months. First rights. Prose, 3,500–15,000 words. Book reviews, to 1,200 words. Poetry, to 2 pages; 3–5 poems per submission. No payment. Provides 2 contributor's copies.

South Loop Review

Columbia College Chicago, English Department
600 South Michigan Avenue
Chicago, IL 60605

Editors: Rose Blouin & Josalyn Knapic

Description and Interests: This annual journal publishes essays and memoir, lyric and experimental forms, non-linear narratives, blended genre, photography, and art. *SLR* looks for personal essays and memoirs with fresh voices and new takes on presentation and form. In addition, *SLR* looks for photography and art that creates a strong resonance. Circ: 1,500.
Website: http://cms.colum.edu/southloopreview

Freelance Potential: 90% written by nonstaff writers. Publishes 30 freelance submissions yearly; 10% by unpublished writers, 99% by authors who are new to the magazine. Receives 50 unsolicited mss monthly.

Submissions and Payment: Query or send complete ms. Accepts hard copy, email submissions via the literary journals website Tell It Slant (www.tellitslant.com), and simultaneous submissions. Responds in 6 months. First rights. Written material, 8–12 pages. No payment. Provides 2 contributor's copies.

Specialty Travel Index

P.O. Box 458
San Anselmo, CA 94979

Publisher: Andy Alpine

Description and Interests: Read by travelers and travel agents, *Specialty Travel Index* is a resource for those looking for special interest and adventure vacations worldwide. Appearing twice each year, the magazine usually offers six destination articles, as well as an activity and geographical index that travelers can use to plan the exact type of trip in the region of the world they wish to visit. Circ: 20,000.
Website: www.specialtytravel.com

Freelance Potential: 70% written by nonstaff writers. Publishes 10 freelance submissions yearly; 30% by authors who are new to the magazine. Receives 40 queries monthly.

Submissions and Payment: Sample copy and guidelines available. Query. Accepts email queries to info@specialtytravel.com. Responds in 1–2 months. One-time rights. Articles, 1,200 words; $300. Pays on acceptance. Provides 1 contributor's copy.

Spin-Off

201 East 4th Street
Loveland, CO 80537

Editor: Amy Clarke Moore

Description and Interests: Handspinners—those who make yarn by hand—are inspired and challenged with techniques and projects in this quarterly publication. Circ: 26,280.
Website: www.spinningdaily.com

Freelance Potential: 90% written by nonstaff writers. Publishes 50 freelance submissions yearly; 80% by unpublished writers, 80% by authors who are new to the magazine, 5% by experts. Receives 5 queries each month.

Submissions and Payment: Sample copy available. Guidelines available at website. Query with artwork and spinning details; or send complete ms. Accepts hard copy, disk submissions, and email to spinoff@interweave.com. No simultaneous submissions. Responds in 6 months. First North American serial and non–exclusive electronic and reprint rights. Articles, 250–2,700 words; $50 per published page. Artwork, $10 per photo. Kill fee, 25%. Pays on publication. Provides 1 contributor's copy.

Spirituality & Health

107 Cass Street, Suite C
Traverse City, MI 49684

Managing Editor: Ilima Loomis

Description and Interests: The connection between physical and mental health and spirituality is the primary focus of this magazine. Published six times each year, it features informational and how-to articles, opinion pieces, essays, book and music reviews, and poetry. A news brief for its Updates & Observations section gives new writers the best chance at acceptance. Circ: 65,000.
Website: www.spiritualityhealth.com

Freelance Potential: 20% written by nonstaff writers. Publishes 10 freelance submissions yearly.

Submissions and Payment: Sample copy and guidelines available at website. Prefers query. Accepts email to editors@spiritualityhealth.com. Response time varies. World print and electronic rights. Articles, 800–2,500 words; $300–$1,000. News briefs, 50–400 words; $50–$200. Pays 3 months after acceptance.

Spitball

The Literary Baseball Magazine

5560 Fox Road
Cincinnati, OH 45239

Editor in Chief: Mike Shannon

Description and Interests: This publication celebrates America's favorite pastime with original fiction, poetry, nonfiction, and baseball book reviews twice each year. It has updated its website to include a Poem of the Month. Circ: 2,000.
Website: www.spitballmag.com

Freelance Potential: 80% written by nonstaff writers. Publishes 40 freelance submissions yearly; 20% by unpublished writers, 40% by new authors, 40% by experts. Receives 20 unsolicited mss monthly.

Submissions and Payment: Sample copy available. New writers must purchase sample copy before sending submission. Guidelines available at website. Send complete ms with bio. Accepts hard copy. No simultaneous submissions. SASE. Responds in 1–2 months. First North American serial rights. Written material, word lengths vary. B/W prints. No payment. Provides 2 contributor's copies.

The Splinter Generation

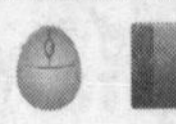 

Editor: Seth Fischer

Description and Interests: A very specific group of writers, those born between 1973 and 1993, are invited to submit work to this online literary journal. It is looking for the very best poetry, fiction, and creative nonfiction of the "splinter generation." The site is updated weekly. Hits per month: Unavailable.
Website: www.splintergeneration.com

Freelance Potential: 100% written by nonstaff writers. Publishes 40 freelance submissions yearly; 40% by unpublished writers, 100% by authors who are new to the magazine. Receives 15–100 unsolicited mss monthly.

Submissions and Payment: Guidelines available at website. Send complete ms during reading periods, listed at website. Accepts email submissions to splinterfiction, splintercnf, or splinterpoetry@gmail.com. Response time varies. First North American serial rights. Articles and fiction, to 3,000 words. Poetry, to 3 poems, no more than 5 pages total. No payment.

Sporting Classics

P.O. Box 23707
Columbia, SC 29224

Editor: Chuck Wechsler

Description and Interests: Those who are passionate about sport hunting are the audience of this magazine, published six times each year. Its editorial mix includes not only hunting advice, true-life adventures, and equipment, but also fiction and art with hunting themes. Circ: 40,000.
Website: www.sportingclassics.com

Freelance Potential: 51% written by nonstaff writers. Publishes 70 freelance submissions yearly; 5% by authors who are new to the magazine. Receives 15 unsolicited mss monthly.

Submissions and Payment: Sample copy and guidelines available. Query or send complete ms. Prefers email submissions to matt@sportingclassic.com. Responds in 2 months if interested. One-time rights. Articles, to 2,500 words; $300–$700. Fiction, 1,500–3,000 words; $300–$800. Depts/columns, 800–1,200 words; $250–$750. B/W prints and color slides; $50–$250. Pays on publication. Provides 2–5 contributor's copies.

Spotlight on Recovery

9602 Glenwood Road, #140
Brooklyn, NY 11236

Editor/Publisher: Robin Graham

Description and Interests: This quarterly, now in its 10th year, provides a dialogue on recovery by sharing personal stories on domestic violence, drug abuse, children at risk, and more. Circ: 3,000+.
Website: http://spotlightonrecovery.com

Freelance Potential: 99% written by nonstaff writers. Publishes 70 freelance submissions yearly; 35% by unpublished writers, 40% by authors who are new to the magazine, 25% by experts. Receives 12 queries monthly.

Submissions and Payment: Sample copy, guidelines, and theme list/editorial calendar available. Query with clips. Accepts email queries to rgrham_100@msn.com (Word attachments). Responds in 1 week. Rights vary. Articles and depts/columns, to 1,500 words. Poetry, to 700 words. Written material, $.05 per word. Pays on publication. Provides 5 contributor's copies.

Spry

341 Cool Springs Boulevard, Suite 400
Franklin, TN 37067

Editor in Chief: Lisa Delaney

Description and Interests: *Spry* is a monthly health and wellness magazine distributed in daily newspapers throughout the country. It seeks inspiring stories of people who define the word "spry"; advice; and articles on nutrition, healthy living, and fitness. Circ: Unavailable.
Website: www.spryliving.com

Freelance Potential: 50% written by nonstaff writers. Publishes 30–50 freelance submissions yearly; 10–20% by authors who are new to the magazine.

Submissions and Payment: Sample articles available at website. Guidelines available. Query with 2–3 clips. Accepts hard copy. SASE. Responds in 1–2 months. First-time print and electronic rights for 6 months; non-exclusive rights thereafter. Articles, 450–1,200 words. Depts/columns, word lengths vary. Written material, payment rates vary. Pays within 45 days of publication. Provides 2 contributor's copies.

Standard

2923 Troost Avenue
Kansas City, MO 64109

Submissions: Charlie L. Yourdon

Description and Interests: Inspirational Christian writing is found in each weekly edition of *Standard.* It no longer reviews unsolicited manuscripts, but will accept queries from experienced Christian writers. Circ: 100,000.
Website: www.wordaction.com

Freelance Potential: 35% written by nonstaff writers. Of the freelance submissions published yearly, 15% are by unpublished writers, 15% are by authors who are new to the magazine, 25% are by experts. Receives 12 queries monthly.

Submissions and Payment: Sample copy available. Query. Accepts queries from experienced Christian writers only. Responds in 3 months. First or reprint rights. Articles and fiction, 1,200 words; $.035 per word. Poetry, to 30 lines; $.25 per line (minimum $5). Pays on acceptance. Provides 3 contributor's copies.

Stand Magazine

Department of English
Virginia Commonwealth University
Richmond, VA 23284-2005

Associate Editor: David Latané

Description and Interests: Started 60 years ago, *Stand Magazine* is a literary magazine that believes the arts can and should play a role in the fight against injustice and oppression. It accepts the highest quality short fiction, poetry, translations, and criticisms and is always in search of inventive, radical, or experimental works. It is published quarterly. Circ: 1,000.
Website: www.people.vcu.edu/~dlatane/stand-maga

Freelance Potential: 98% written by nonstaff writers. Of the freelance submissions published yearly, 70% are by authors who are new to the magazine.

Submissions and Payment: Sample copy available. Guidelines available at website. Send complete ms. Accepts hard copy. SASE. Response time varies. First serial and electronic rights. Fiction, to 3,000 words. Poetry, word lengths vary. Written material, payment rates vary. Pays on publication.

StarDate

1 University Station
A2100
University of Texas at Austin
Austin, TX 78712

Editor: Rebecca Johnson

Description and Interests: *StarDate* covers a wide range of topics related to astronomy, space exploration, sky lore, and sky watching. Published six times each year, it includes articles about recent scientific discoveries or missions, as well as the history and future of astronomy. Circ: 9,000.
Website: http://stardate.org

Freelance Potential: 50% written by nonstaff writers. Publishes 8 freelance submissions yearly; 50% by authors who are new to the magazine, 50% by experts. Receives 5 queries monthly.

Submissions and Payment: Sample copy and guidelines available. Query. Accepts hard copy and email queries to rjohnson@stardate.org. SASE. Responds in 6 weeks. First North American serial rights. Articles, 1,800–2,500 words; payment rates vary. Kill fee, 25%. Pays 2 months after acceptance. Provides 3 contributor's copies.

Stone's Throw Magazine

Editor: Tami Haaland

Description and Interests: Updated two to three times each year, this web-based literary journal features writers from around the world. It welcomes submissions of fiction, essays, reviews, interviews, and poetry, as well as brief accounts of daily life from around the world. Hits per month: Unavailable.
Website: http://stonesthrowmagazine.com

Freelance Potential: 95% written by nonstaff writers. Publishes 150+ freelance submissions yearly; 90% by authors who are new to the magazine. Receives 50–100 mss monthly.

Submissions and Payment: Guidelines available at website. Send complete ms. Accepts electronic submissions through website only. Response time varies. Author retains rights. Articles and fiction, to 5,000 words. Reviews and interviews, to 1,500 words. Poetry, 3–5 poems per submission. No payment.

Story Quarterly

English Department
Rutgers University
311 North Fifth Street, Armitage 481
Camden, NJ 08102

Editor: J. T. Barbarese

Description and Interests: This journal publishes literary fiction in print on an annual basis and maintains an online presence to showcase work year-round. It publishes emerging and established writers. Circ: 6,000.
Website: www.camden.rutgers.edu/storyquarterly

Freelance Potential: 99% written by nonstaff writers. Publishes 35–50 freelance submissions yearly; 10% by unpublished writers, 88% by new authors. Receives 2,000 mss monthly.

Submissions and Payment: Sample stories and guidelines available at website. Send complete ms. Accepts electronic submissions via website and simultaneous submissions. Responds in 2–4 months. First North American serial rights. Fiction, 1,000–7,500 words. Written material, $150–$200. Payment policy varies. Provides 10 contributor's copies and a lifetime subscription.

The Storyteller

2441 Washington Road
Maynard, AR 72444

Editor: Regina Williams

Description and Interests: This quarterly magazine welcomes the work of new writers. It accepts fiction, essays, and poetry. Circ: 700.
Website: www.thestorytellermagazine.com

Freelance Potential: 90% written by nonstaff writers. Publishes 250 freelance submissions yearly; 40% by unpublished writers, 60% by authors who are new to the magazine. Receives 500 unsolicited mss monthly.

Submissions and Payment: Sample stories and guidelines available at website. Send complete ms with cover letter and word count. Accepts hard copy and simultaneous submissions if identified. SASE. Responds in 1–2 weeks. First North American serial rights. Fiction and nonfiction, to 2,500 words. Poetry, to 40 lines, up to 3 poems per submission. No payment at the current time; check the website for updates to this policy.

Subtropics

P.O. Box 112075, 4008 Turlington Hall
University of Florida
Gainesville, FL 32611-2075

Editor: David Leavitt

Description and Interests: Published three times each year, *Subtropics* celebrates the original work of new authors and established writers and seeks fiction, essays, and poetry. Much of what it receives is written in first-person present tense; it is eager to see work from a new perspective. Circ: Unavailable.
Website: www.english.ufl.edu/subtropics

Freelance Potential: 100% written by nonstaff writers. Publishes 30–35 freelance submissions yearly.

Submissions and Payment: Sample stories and guidelines available at website. Send complete ms with cover letter between September 15 and April 15. Accepts online submissions only (see website for link); accepts simultaneous submissions for prose only. Responds in 1 month. First North American serial or one-time rights. Articles and fiction, word lengths vary; $1,000. Short-shorts, 250 words; $500. Poetry, to 5 poems per submission; $100. Pays on acceptance. Provides 1 contributor's copy.

Sunshine Artist

Palm House Publishing
4075 L. B. McLeod Road, Suite E
Orlando, FL 32811

Editor: Nicole Sirdoreus

Description and Interests: *Sunshine Artist* keeps show exhibitors, promoters, and patrons informed on all aspects of art shows and festivals around the country. Each monthly issue lists and reviews upcoming events and provides information on trends, sales, artist amenities, and booth fees. Circ: 30,000.
Website: www.sunshineartist.com

Freelance Potential: 80% written by nonstaff writers. Publishes 20+ freelance submissions yearly; 5% by authors who are new to the magazine.

Submissions and Payment: Sample copy, editorial calendar, and guidelines available. Query with résumé. Accepts hard copy and email queries to editor@sunshineartist.com. SASE. Response time varies. All rights. Articles, 1,500–2,000 words; $100–$250. Show reviews, word lengths vary; $30. Pays on publication. Provides 2 contributor's copies.

Supermodels Unlimited

155 Industrial Drive
Northhampton, MA 01060

Editor: Kimberly Lawrence

Description and Interests: Young women ages 16 to 26 are the target audience of this magazine, published six times each year. Featured on its pages are beauty, fashion, and fitness tips for aspiring models and pageant competitors. It offers interviews and profiles of supermodels, as well as coverage of the entertainment world and celebrities. Circ: 269,000.
Website: www.supermodelsunlimited.com

Freelance Potential: 40% written by nonstaff writers. Publishes 20+ freelance submissions yearly; 10% by unpublished writers, 10% by authors who are new to the magazine, 20% by experts. Receives 8–10 queries monthly.

Submissions and Payment: Sample copy and guidelines available. Query. Accepts hard copy. SASE. Response time varies. First rights. Articles and depts/columns, word lengths and payment rates vary. Pays on publication. Provides 1 contributor's copy.

Survive Parenting

P.O. Box 1120
Vancouver, British Columbia
Canada

Managing Editor: Jesse Yardley

Description and Interests: This is an online magazine for people who don't want to "sugar coat" parenting. It offers real information and venting from real parents who know that sometimes parenting—and other parents—can drive you crazy. Most material is delivered with a dose of humor and attitude. Hits per month: Unavailable.
Website: http://survivemag.com/

Freelance Potential: Freelance submissions welcome. It prefers a "quirky" attitude and a writing style that matches the magazine. It is most open to submissions on technology, how-to's, and parenting tricks.

Submissions and Payment: Sample articles and guidelines available at website. Send complete ms. Accepts email to editorial@survivemag.com. Responds in 1 month if interested. Author retains copyright. Articles, 400–800 words. No payment. Authors receive link to their website or blog.

Switchback

University of San Francisco, MFA Writing Program
2130 Fulton Street
San Francisco, CA 94117

Managing Editor: Keith J. Powell

Description and Interests: Read by the University of San Francisco's MFA community, *Switchback* welcomes fiction, poetry, flash work, and literary reviews from writers of all experience levels. Two issues per year; flash work is published monthly. Hits per month: 2,000+.
Website: www.swback.com

Freelance Potential: 100% written by nonstaff writers. Publishes 44+ freelance submissions yearly; 95% by authors who are new to the magazine. Receives 50 unsolicited mss monthly.

Submissions and Payment: Guidelines and deadlines available at website. Send complete ms. Accepts electronic submissions via Submishmash link at website. Response time varies. Electronic rights. Literary reviews, 500–1,500 words. Prose, 2,000–7,500 words. Flash fiction, to 500 words. Poetry, no line limits; to 3 poems. No payment.

Sycamore Review

Department of English
Purdue University
500 Oval Drive
West Lafayette, IN 47907-2038

Poetry, Fiction, or Nonfiction Editor

Description and Interests: This journal for the arts is published twice each year by Purdue University's Department of English. It seeks original poetry, fiction, creative nonfiction, and artwork. Circ: 1,000.
Website: www.sycamorereview.com

Freelance Potential: 90% written by nonstaff writers. Publishes 40 freelance submissions yearly; 15% by unpublished writers, 50–80% by authors who are new to the magazine. Receives 800 unsolicited mss monthly.

Submissions and Payment: Sample copy available. Guidelines available at website. Send complete ms with cover letter between August 1 and March 31. Accepts electronic submissions via website and simultaneous submissions if identified. Responds in 3–4 months. First North American serial rights and electronic rights. Articles, word lengths vary; $50. Fiction, to 10,000 words; $50. Poetry, 3–5 pages; $25. Provides 2 contributor's copies.

Tales of the Talisman

Hadrosaur Productions
P.O. Box 2194
Mesilla Park, NM 88047-2194

Editor: David Lee Summers

Description and Interests: Science fiction, fantasy, horror stories, and poetry appear in this quarterly literary journal. Victorian-era speculative fiction is especially sought. Circ: 150.
Website: www.talesofthetalisman.com

Freelance Potential: 99% written by nonstaff writers. Publishes 50 freelance submissions yearly; 10% by unpublished writers, 33% by authors who are new to the magazine. Receives 5 queries, 50 unsolicited mss monthly.

Submissions and Payment: Sample copy available. Guidelines available at website. Send complete ms. Accepts hard copy and email to hadrosaur@zianet.com (RTF attachments). Reading periods begin January 1 and July 1. No simultaneous submissions. SASE. Response time varies. One-time rights. Fiction, to 6,000 words; $10. Poetry, to 50 lines, to 5 poems; $4 per poem. Payment policy varies. Provides 1 contributor's copy.

Tampa Review

401 West Kennedy Boulevard
Tampa, FL 33606–1490

Editor: Richard Matthews

Description and Interests: Twice each year, this literary review spotlights the best in fiction, poetry, and creative nonfiction from new voices, as well as established authors. Circ: 1,000.
Website: www.ut.edu/tampareview

Freelance Potential: 100% written by nonstaff writers. Publishes 40 freelance submissions yearly; 10% by unpublished writers, 70% by new authors. Receives 500 unsolicited mss monthly.

Submissions and Payment: Sample copy available. Guidelines available at website. Send complete ms between September 1 and November 30. Accepts hard copy, disk submissions, and electronic submissions via the website. No simultaneous submissions. SASE. Responds in 3–4 months. First North American serial rights. Articles, to 5,000 words. Fiction, to 5,000 words. Poetry, 3–6 poems, no line limit. Written material, $10 per page. Pays on publication. Provides 1 contributor's copy.

Teaching Tolerance

Southern Poverty Law Center
400 Washington Avenue
Montgomery, AL 36104

Managing Editor

Description and Interests: *Teaching Tolerance* publishes articles that present innovative and thoughtful ideas and programs to promote diversity and equity in school communities. It appears twice each year. Circ: 400,000.
Website: www.tolerance.org

Freelance Potential: 50% written by nonstaff writers. Publishes 12–14 freelance submissions yearly; 20% by unpublished writers, 20% by authors who are new to the magazine, 20% by experts. Receives 90 queries monthly.

Submissions and Payment: Sample copy and guidelines available at website. Query with clips or writing samples. Accepts email queries to editor@teachingtolerance.org. Responds if interested. All rights. Articles, 800–2,000 words. Depts/columns, 400–800 words. Written material, $.25–$1 per word. Pays on acceptance. Provides 2 contributor's copies.

TechRevu

30 Deer Run Lane
Brick, NJ 08724

Editor: Ernest Lilley

Description and Interests: *TechRevu* is an online publication that covers the worlds of science and technology, with an eye towards how our increasing knowledge of the world and the tools we create can help both individuals and communities flourish. It features news, articles, essays, and interviews. Circ: Unavailable.
Website: www.techrevu.com

Freelance Potential: Receives many freelance submissions monthly.

Submissions and Payment: Sample copy at website. Query. Accepts email to editor@techrevu.com. Response time varies. Written material, word lengths vary. Rights vary. Payment rates and policy vary.

Telemark Skier

3485 S West Temple
Salt Lake City, UT 84115

Editor: Tony Gill

Description and Interests: The sport of telemark (freeheel) skiing and the lifestyle of the telemark skier are the focus of this quarterly publication. Techniques, equipment, safety, and destinations are covered in detail. Circ: 20,000.
Website: http://telemarkskier.com

Freelance Potential: 60% written by nonstaff writers. Publishes 12 freelance submissions yearly; 15% by unpublished writers, 50% by authors who are new to the magazine, 75% by experts. Receives 50 queries monthly.

Submissions and Payment: Sample copy and guidelines available. Query with clips. Accepts email queries via website. Response time varies. First North American serial rights. Articles and depts/columns, word lengths and payment rates vary. Pays 2 months after publication.

Tell Magazine

1500 Spring Garden Street
Center City, PA 19130

Publisher: Rick Albuck

Description and Interests: Formerly known as *e-Gear Magazine, Tell Magazine* covers consumer electronics and entertainment, including movies, music, and television. It appears six times each year. Writers well versed in consumer electronics, with a colorful writing style, are needed for blogging. Check the Jobs page on the website for more information. Circ: 700,000.
Website: www.technologytell.com

Freelance Potential: Receives many freelance submissions monthly.

Submissions and Payment: Sample copy at website. Query with résumé, author bio, and 3 sample articles. Accepts email to rickalbuck@napco.com (include "TechnologyTell.com Blogger" in subject line). Articles, 200–400 words. Response time varies. Rights vary. Payment rates and policy vary.

Tennis Now

200 West 39th Street, Suite #11
New York, NY 10018

Editor in Chief: Theodore LePak

Description and Interests: *Tennis Now,* formerly *Tennis Week*, is now an online publication. Lovers of the sport read it for breaking news, tournament updates, gear reviews, training tips, and gossip. It welcomes queries from knowledgeable writers. Weekly ezine readers: 80,000.
Website: www.tennisnow.com

Freelance Potential: 60% written by nonstaff writers. Publishes 40 freelance submissions yearly; 5% by unpublished writers, 10% by authors who are new to the magazine, 100% by experts. Receives 10 queries monthly.

Submissions and Payment: Query with 50- to 60-word summary. Email queries to Media@TennisNow.com. Responds only if interested. Electronic rights. Articles and depts/columns, word lengths and payment rates vary; to $300. Pays on publication.

Testimony Magazine

2450 Milltower Court
Mississauga, Ontario L5N 5Z6
Canada

Editor: Stephen Kennedy

Description and Interests: Published by the Pentecostal Assemblies of Canada, *Testimony Magazine* is a monthly that offers the Christian perspective on a wide range of social issues. It also updates readers on PAOC activities. Circ: 8,000.
Website: www.testimonymag.ca

Freelance Potential: 80% written by nonstaff writers. Publishes 55 freelance submissions yearly; 10–15% by unpublished writers, 10–15% by authors who are new to the magazine, 10–15% by experts. Receives 10 queries monthly.

Submissions and Payment: Sample articles, guidelines, and theme list available at website. Query. Accepts email queries to testimony@paoc.org. Responds in 2 weeks. Rights vary. Articles, 800–1,000 words. Color prints, JPEG images at 300 dpi. Honorarium paid on publication. Provides contributor's copies.

The Texas Review

Department of English and Foreign Language
Sam Houston State University
P.O. Box 2146
Huntsville, TX 77341-2146

Editor: Dr. Paul Ruffin

Description and Interests: Original works of fiction, poetry, and creative nonfiction fill the pages of this literary review, published twice each year. Though published by Sam Houston State University, it welcomes work from writers throughout the country. Circ: 1,250.
Website: www.shsu.edu/~www_trp/

Freelance Potential: 95% written by nonstaff writers. Publishes 120 freelance submissions yearly; 5% by unpublished writers, 40% by authors who are new to the magazine.

Submissions and Payment: Sample copy available. Guidelines available at website. Send complete ms with cover letter from September through April. Accepts hard copy. No simultaneous submissions. SASE. Responds in 1–6 months. First North American serial rights. Fiction, 20–30 pages. Poetry, limit 2 poems per submission. No payment. Provides 1 contributor's copy and a 1-year subscription.

TheatreForum

University of California, San Diego
9500 Gilman Drive, 0344
La Jolla, CA 92093-0344

Editors: Jim Carmody, John Rouse, Adele Shank, & Ted Shank

Description and Interests: This international theater journal from the University of California, San Diego, features articles pertaining to the global, contemporary theater, as well as artist interviews and original scripts. It is published twice each year. Circ: 500+.
Website: www.theatreforum.org

Freelance Potential: 100% written by nonstaff writers. Publishes 12 freelance submissions yearly; 70% by authors who are new to the magazine.

Submissions and Payment: Sample copy available. Guidelines available at website. Query. Accepts email queries to TheatreForum@ucsd.edu or through the website. Response time varies. Rights vary. Articles, 1,000–4,000 words; $.05 per word; $150 maximum. Plays, word lengths vary; $300. B/W and color digital images at 300 dpi. Payment policy varies.

Thema

Box 8747
Metairie, LA 70011-8747

Fiction Editor: Virginia Howard
Poetry Editor: Gail Howard

Description and Interests: Short stories with clever plot twists and thoughtfully constructed poetry will get the attention of the editors of this literary journal. Themed issues appear three times each year. Circ: 300.
Website: http://themaliterarysociety.com/

Freelance Potential: 99% written by nonstaff writers. Publishes 55 freelance submissions yearly; 10% by unpublished writers, 50% by authors who are new to the magazine. Receives 50 unsolicited mss monthly.

Submissions and Payment: Sample copy available. Guidelines and theme list available at website. Send complete ms with target theme indicated. Accepts hard copy. SASE. Responds in 4 months. One-time rights. Fiction, to 20 double-spaced pages; $10–$25. Poetry, to 3 pages; $10. B/W prints and line art; $10–$25. Pays on acceptance. Provides 1 contributor's copy.

Thoroughbred Times

P.O. Box 8237
Lexington, KY 40533

Managing Editor: Tom Law

Description and Interests: This is a biweekly newsmagazine of thoroughbred racing for trainers, breeders, managers, and buyers. All newsworthy developments and events are covered, in addition to articles that convey the traditions and history of the sport. Circ: 18,000.
Website: www.thoroughbredtimes.com/

Freelance Potential: 52% written by nonstaff writers. Publishes several freelance submissions yearly; 2% by authors who are new to the magazine, 5% by experts. Receives 2 queries each month.

Submissions and Payment: Sample copy available. Query with résumé. Accepts email queries to letters@thoroughbredtimes.com (Word attachments). Responds in 1 month. First rights. Articles, 1,200–2,000 words. Depts/columns, 1,200 words. Written material, $.15 per word. Kill fee, 50%. Pays on publication.

ThoughtsAbout God.com

27062 26A Avenue
Vancouver, BC V6C 2X3
Canada

Directors: Katherine J. Kehler & Marvin Kehler

Description and Interests: The goal of this ezine is to help Christians grow in their relationship with God. It offers its international audience true-life stories; inspirational articles; how-to features on prayer, Bible study, and Christian living; and even humor and poetry. Freelancers should review the Statement of Faith on the website before submitting. Hits per month: 68,000+.
Website: www.thoughts–about–god.com

Freelance Potential: 99% written by nonstaff writers. Publishes 600+ freelance submissions yearly; 40% by authors who are new to the magazine.

Submissions and Payment: Guidelines available at website. Accepts email submissions to katherine.kehler@shaw.ca. Responds in 2 weeks if interested. First or reprint rights. Articles, 500–700 words. No payment.

Tiferet

A Journal of Spiritual Literature

211 Dryden Road
Bernardsville, NJ 07924

Editor in Chief: Diane Bonavist

Description and Interests: *Tiferet* is a literary journal with an annual print issue, as well as a digital edition that appears five times a year. It is also a writing community that is dedicated to revealing the Spirit through the written word. It is a multi-faith publication that features works of fiction, creative nonfiction, and poetry. Circ: 500.
Website: www.tiferetjournal.com

Freelance Potential: 95% written by nonstaff writers. Publishes 100 freelance submissions yearly; 20% by unpublished writers, 40% by authors who are new to the magazine. Receives 50 unsolicited mss monthly.

Submissions and Payment: Sample copy available. Guidelines available at website. Send complete ms. Accepts email submissions through the website only (Word attachments). Responds in 3 months. First North American serial, electronic, and one-time anthology rights. Written material, word lengths vary. No payment. Provides 1 contributor's copy.

Timber Home Living

4125 Lafayette Center Drive, Suite 100
Chantilly, VA 20151

Editorial Director: Sara Brown

Description and Interests: *Timber Home Living* provides information about planning, designing, building, and furnishing timber homes. Appearing seven times each year, it also profiles homeowners and includes articles about historical timber homes. Circ: 50,000.
Website: www.timberhomeliving.com

Freelance Potential: 75% written by nonstaff writers. Publishes 48 freelance submissions yearly; 2% by unpublished writers, 50% by new authors, 2% by experts. Receives 3 queries monthly.

Submissions and Payment: Sample copy available. Guidelines and theme list/editorial calendar available at website. Query and include SASE. Email submissions to editor@timberhomeliving.com. First and Internet rights. Articles, 1,500 words. Depts/columns, 700 words. High-resolution digital images. Written material, payment rates vary. Pays on publication. Provides 2 contributor's copies.

Tin House

P.O. Box 10500
Portland, OR 97210

Editor: Rob Spillman

Description and Interests: New and established writers are published in this quarterly journal of both a literary and political bent. It features fiction, nonfiction, poetry, and interviews. Circ: 12,000.
Website: www.tinhouse.com

Freelance Potential: 95% written by nonstaff writers. Of the freelance submissions published yearly, 10% are by unpublished writers, 50% are by authors who are new to the magazine. Receives 1,000 unsolicited mss monthly.

Submissions and Payment: Sample copy available. Guidelines available at website. Send complete ms with cover letter September 1 to May 31. Accepts hard copy, electronic submissions through website, and simultaneous submissions. SASE. Responds in 3 months. All rights. Articles, fiction, to 10,000 words. Poetry, to 5 poems. Depts/columns, 500 words. Written material, payment rates vary. Kill fee varies. Pays on acceptance.

Today's Parent

1 Mount Pleasant Road, 8th floor,
Toronto, Ontario M4Y 2Y5
Canada

Managing Editor: Katie Dupuis

Description and Interests: *Today's Parent* is Canada's number one parenting magazine and website. The print edition provides information on a range of parenting issues, from children's health and development to family fun each month. Material should be grounded in the reality of Canadian family life and strike a balance between the practical and the reflective. Circ: 165,000.
Website: www.todaysparent.com

Freelance Potential: Though open to all writers, Canadian writers are favored.

Submissions and Payment: Sample copy available. Guidelines available at website. Send complete manuscript for Your Turn column only. Query with detailed proposal, writing samples, and proposed length for all other material. Accepts hard copy and email to editors@todaysparent.com. Responds in 6 weeks. Buys all rights. Payment rates vary. Pays 30 days after acceptance.

Tor.com

Submissions Editors

Description and Interests: This website is for readers interested in science fiction and fantasy. It publishes original short fiction, commentary on the genre, and articles on related subjects. It is updated regularly. Hits per month: Unavailable.
Website: www.tor.com

Freelance Potential: Open to submissions of original, speculative fiction and poetry. Its definition of speculative fiction is broad; it also accepts horror, alternate history, and related genres. Nothing over 17,500 words will be read.

Submissions and Payment: Sample stories and guidelines available at http://www.tor.com/page/submissions-guidelines. Send complete ms. Accepts email to tordotcomsubs@gmail.com (.doc, RTF, or text attachments) and simultaneous submissions. Responds in about 6 months. Buys exclusive rights for a year; retains non-exclusive rights after that. Fiction, to 17,500 (to 12,000 is preferred); $.25 per word for the first 5,000 words, $.15 per word for the next 5,000 words, and $.10 per word after that.

Tots to Teens

& In B-Tween

P.O. Box 1233
Plainfield, IL 60586

Editor in Chief: Phyllis Pometta

Description and Interests: This digital magazine targets parents of children ranging in age from toddlers to tweens and teens. Published quarterly, it offers articles on parenthood, family life, money management, technology, organic cooking, celebrity moms, balancing work and family, and school issues. It also tackles the subjects of education, child development, and behavior from various age perspectives. Hits per month: Unavailable.
Website: www.totstoteensmagazine.com

Freelance Potential: Open to pitches on all parenting topics. Also accepts pitches regarding products or services that should be profiled.

Submissions and Payment: Sample copy and editorial calendar available at website. Query with detailed article pitch. Accepts email to editor@totstoteensmagazine.com. Response time varies. Written material, word lengths vary.

Toward Freedom

A Progressive Perspective on World Events

300 Maple Street
Burlington, VT 05401

Editor: Ben Dangl

Description and Interests: This online magazine features articles on national and international topics, including politics, labor, women's rights, health, and the environment. All material has a progressive perspective. It is updated four times each week. Hits per month: 60,000.
Website: www.towardfreedom.com

Freelance Potential: 95% written by nonstaff writers. Publishes 180 freelance submissions yearly; 25% by unpublished writers, 50% by authors who are new to the magazine, 5% by experts. Receives 20–30 queries, 30–50 unsolicited mss monthly.

Submissions and Payment: Prefers complete ms; will accept query with writing samples. Accepts email submissions to ben@towardfreedom.com (put "Submission" in subject line). Responds in 2 weeks. Rights vary. Articles, to 3,000 words; payment rates vary. Pays on publication.

Toy Trucker & Contractor

7496 106th Avenue SE
LaMoure, ND 58458-9404

Editorial Assistant: Kathy Heckbet

Description and Interests: Articles and photography that showcase die-cast toy replicas of trucks and construction equipment appear in this monthly. Written for collectors, it includes profiles, interviews, new product information, and personal experiences. Circ: 8,000.
Website: www.toytrucker.com

Freelance Potential: 100% written by nonstaff writers. Of the freelance submissions published yearly, 10% are by unpublished writers, 20% are by authors who are new to the magazine, 70% are by experts. Receives 1 query monthly.

Submissions and Payment: Sample copy and guidelines available. Query with artwork. Accepts hard copy. SASE. Responds in 1 week. Exclusive rights for 60 days. Articles, 1,500–2,000 words. Depts/columns, 1,500 words. Digital images at 300 dpi. Written material, $.10 per word. Pays on publication. Provides 2 contributor's copies.

Triathlete Magazine

10179 Huennekens, Suite 100
San Diego, CA 92121

Editor in Chief: Julia Beeson Polloreno

Description and Interests: *Triathlete Magazine* is read by amateur and professional triathlon competitors alike. It appears monthly and offers athlete profiles and articles on training, nutrition, and gear. Circ: 97,000.
Website: http://triathlon.competitor.com

Freelance Potential: 50% written by nonstaff writers. Publishes 100 freelance submissions yearly; 5% by unpublished writers, 10% by authors who are new to the magazine, 85% by experts. Receives 15 queries monthly.

Submissions and Payment: Sample copy available. Guidelines and editorial calendar available at website. Query. Accepts email queries to JPolloreno@competitorgroup.com. Responds in 6–8 weeks. All rights. Articles, 800–1,200 words. Depts/columns, 250–1,000 words. Written material, $.20 per word. Kill fee, $100. Pays on publication.

TriQuarterly

Northwestern University
School of Continuing Studies
339 East Chicago Avenue
Chicago, IL 60611–3008

Managing Editor: Lydia Pudzianowski

Description and Interests: This online journal seeks literature that embraces the world and continues the ongoing global conversation about culture and society. It welcomes fiction, creative nonfiction, poetry, short drama, and hybrid work, as well as short-short prose. Hits per month: Unavailable.
Website: www.triquarterly.org

Freelance Potential: 100% written by nonstaff writers. Publishes 30–50 freelance submissions yearly; 10% by unpublished writers, 20% by new authors. Receives 200 queries monthly.

Submissions and Payment: Submit online to http://submissions.triquarterly.org/ between October 16 and July 15. Responds in 3–4 months. First North American serial rights. Fiction, to 3,500 words; $5 per page, $50 minimum. Poetry, to 6 poems; $.50 per line, $50 minimum. Slides, prints, transparencies; payment rates vary. Pays on publication.

Tropical Fish Hobbyist

One T.F.H. Plaza
Third and Union Avenues
Neptune City, NJ 07753

Editorial Department

Description and Interests: Written for aquarium hobbyists, this magazine covers marine life, fish varieties, fish care, and garden ponds. Each issue is filled with tips, techniques, and photography that will educate and entertain readers. It is published monthly. Circ: 40,000.
Website: www.tfhmagazine.com

Freelance Potential: 95% written by nonstaff writers. Publishes 100 freelance submissions yearly; 50% by unpublished writers, 60% by authors who are new to the magazine.

Submissions and Payment: Sample copy available. Guidelines available at website. Send complete ms with artwork. Accepts hard copy and email to associateeditor@tfh.com. SASE. Responds in 1–3 months. All rights. Written material, word lengths vary; $100–$250. Pays on acceptance. Provides 3 contributor's copies.

Truck Trend

831 South Douglas Street
El Segundo, CA 90245

Editor: Allyson Harwood

Description and Interests: Catering to readers who love trucks and sport utility vehicles, this magazine covers new models, how-to articles related to maintenance and customization, and design trends. Personal experience pieces are also featured in issues that appear six times each year. Circ: 73,000.
Website: www.trucktrend.com

Freelance Potential: 80% written by nonstaff writers. Publishes 20 freelance submissions yearly; 10% by unpublished writers, 10% by authors who are new to the magazine, 80% by experts. Receives 5 queries monthly.

Submissions and Payment: Sample copy available. Query. Accepts hard copy. SASE. Responds in 1 month. All rights. Written material, word lengths vary; payment varies. Pays on publication. Provides 1 contributor's copy.

True Blue Trucks

P.O. Box 30806
Knoxville, TN 37930-0806

Publisher: John Goethert

Description and Interests: Ford trucks are the focus of this quarterly (although soon to be biweekly) publication. *True Blue Trucks* relies on reader submissions to fill its pages. Technical pieces are among its current needs. Circ: 15,000.
Website: http://truebluetrucks.com

Freelance Potential: 75% written by nonstaff writers. Publishes 50–75 freelance submissions yearly; 20% by unpublished writers, 15% by authors who are new to the magazine, 50% by experts. Receives 3 queries monthly.

Submissions and Payment: Sample copy available. Query or send complete ms. Accepts hard copy and email queries to info@truebluetrucks.com (Word or .doc attachments). SASE. Responds in 2 months. All rights. Articles, word lengths and payment rates vary. Pays on acceptance. Provides 5 contributor's copies.

Unity Magazine

1901 NW Blue Parkway
Unity Village, MO 64065-0001

Editor: Toni M. Lapp

Description and Interests: The Unity organization is the publisher of this magazine, which appears six times each year. Its focus is on helping people of all faiths put positive spiritual practices to work in their daily lives. Circ: 25,000.
Website: www.unitymagazine.org

Freelance Potential: 75% written by nonstaff writers. Publishes 25 freelance submissions yearly; 10% by unpublished writers, 20% by authors who are new to the magazine, 80% by experts. Receives 250–300 queries monthly.

Submissions and Payment: Sample copy available. Guidelines available at website. Query with author bio and writing credits. Accepts hard copy and email queries to lapptm@unityonline.org. SASE. Responds in 2 months. First North American serial rights. Written material, 900–2,200 words; payment rates vary. Pays on acceptance. Provides 4 contributor's copies.

USA Today

7950 Jones Branch Drive
McLean, VA 22108

Op-Ed Page Editor: Glen Nishimura

Description and Interests: The only section of this national daily newspaper open to freelance writers is the Op-Ed page. *USA Today* looks for pieces that focus on issues currently in the news that will have national appeal. Op-Eds must be well written, with a clear, fresh viewpoint. Please request writers' guidelines before submitting. Circ: 1.7 million.
Website: www.usatoday.com

Freelance Potential: Op-Eds: 100% written by nonstaff writers. Publishes 400 freelance submissions yearly. Receives several hundred unsolicited mss monthly.

Submissions and Payment: Sample copy available. Guidelines available. Send complete ms. Accepts email submissions to theforum@usatoday.com (no attachments). Responds in 1 week. Rights vary. Articles, 700–800 words; $250+. Kill fee, 50%. Pays on publication.

USHospice.com

1237 Crescendo Drive
Roseville, CA 95678

Publisher: Rev. Paul V. Scholl

Description and Interests: This website is designed to provide in-depth and timely information about hospice services, care, and issues on both a local and national level. Updated frequently, it includes how-to and informational articles, a comprehensive resources section, profiles, and both humorous and inspirational fiction, as well as poetry. Hits per month: 18,000.
Website: www.ushospice.com

Freelance Potential: 90% written by nonstaff writers.

Submissions and Payment: Send complete ms. Accepts email submissions to go2dlyt@aol.com (Word attachments) and simultaneous submissions if identified. Responds in 1 month. Rights vary. Articles and depts/columns, 500–1,000 words. Fiction, word lengths vary. No payment.

Vegetarian Journal

P.O. Box 1463
Baltimore, MD 21203

Managing Editor: Debra Wasserman

Description and Interests: This quarterly magazine's mission is to educate its readers about vegetarian and vegan diets and the interrelated issues of health, nutrition, ecology, ethics, and world hunger. Published by the Vegetarian Resource Group, it features practical and scientific articles, many written by registered dietitians or medical doctors. Circ: 20,000.
Website: www.vrg.org

Freelance Potential: 65% written by nonstaff writers. Publishes 8 freelance submissions yearly; 25% by unpublished writers, 10% by authors who are new to the magazine, 75% by experts. Receives 8 queries monthly.

Submissions and Payment: Sample articles and guidelines available at website. Query. Accepts hard copy. SASE. Responds in 2 months. All rights. Articles and depts/columns, word lengths vary; $100–$200. Pays on acceptance.

Verbatim

The Language Quarterly

4907 North Washtenaw Avenue
Chicago, IL 60625

Editor: Erin McKean

Description and Interests: All aspects of language are explored in this quarterly magazine. It seeks illuminating, moving, and fascinating articles that will interest academicians, as well as those with an interest in language and linguistics. It is currently closed to submissions; check website for updates. Circ: 1,200.
Website: www.verbatimmag.com

Freelance Potential: 90% written by nonstaff writers. Publishes 32 freelance submissions yearly; 60% by authors who are new to the magazine, 15% by experts. Receives 15–25 queries each month.

Submissions and Payment: Sample copy and guidelines available at website. Query or send complete ms. Prefers email queries to editor@verbatimmag.com; will accept complete ms through website. Responds in 4–6 weeks. All rights. Articles, to 3,000 words; $25–$500. Pays on publication.

Vermont Ink

P.O. Box 3297
Burlington, VT 05408–3297

Editor: Donna J. Leach

Description and Interests: This quarterly literary journal publishes poems and short stories. It accepts G-rated adventure, fantasy, historical fiction, humor, mystery/suspense, romance, science fiction, and westerns. Circ: 500.
Website: www.vermontink.com

Freelance Potential: 100% written by nonstaff writers. Publishes 70–80 freelance submissions yearly; 33% by unpublished writers, 67% by authors who are new to the magazine. Receives 200 unsolicited mss monthly.

Submissions and Payment: Sample copy and guidelines available. Send complete ms with cover letter and brief author bio. Accepts hard copy and email to vermontink@aol.com (no attachments). SASE. Responds in 3–4 months. One-time rights. Fiction, 2,000–3,000 words; $.025–$.050 per word. Poetry, 4–20 lines; to $5. Pays on acceptance.

Vestal Review 

2609 Dartmouth Drive
Vestal, NY 13850

Editors: Mark Budman & Susan O'Neill

Description and Interests: Appearing twice each year, *Vestal Review* features flash fiction in a variety of genres. Its readers are discerning and relish humor. Circ: Unavailable.
Website: www.vestalreview.net

Freelance Potential: 100% written by nonstaff writers. Publishes 20–30 freelance submissions yearly; 5% by unpublished writers, 80% by authors who are new to the magazine. Receives 200 unsolicited mss monthly.

Submissions and Payment: Sample copy available. Guidelines available at website. Send complete ms with cover letter and brief author bio. Accepts submissions through submissions manager at website from February to May and August to November. Responds in 4 months. First North American serial and electronic rights. Fiction, to 500 words; $.03–$.10 per word. Pays on publication. Provides 1 contributor's copy.

Vette

Source Interlink Media
9036 Brittany Way
Tampa, FL 33619

Editor: Jay Heath

Description and Interests: Written for Corvette fans, this monthly has recently folded *Corvette Fever* into its pages. It covers the spectrum of Corvette topics, from performance, restoration, and how-to articles to news and car-related events. Circ: 35,563.
Website: www.vetteweb.com

Freelance Potential: 50% written by nonstaff writers. Publishes 100+ freelance submissions yearly; 5% by authors who are new to the magazine, 30% by experts. Receives 1–2 queries each month.

Submissions and Payment: Sample copy available. Guidelines and editorial calendar available through website. Query. Accepts hard copy. SASE. Responds in 6 months. All rights. Articles, 1,000–2,000 words. Depts/columns, 2,500 words. Written material, payment rates vary. Pays on publication. Provides 1 contributor's copy.

Vietnam

19300 Promenade Drive
Leesburg, VA 20176-6500

Editor: Roger L. Vance

Description and Interests: Six times each year, this history magazine presents articles about the Vietnam War, including profiles of, and interviews with, those who served. Circ: 90,000.
Website: www.historynet.com/magazines/vietnam

Freelance Potential: 98% written by nonstaff writers. Publishes 50 freelance submissions yearly; 10% by unpublished writers, 50% by authors who are new to the magazine, 20% by experts.

Submissions and Payment: Sample copy available. Guidelines available at website. Query or send complete ms. Accepts email to vietnam@weiderhistorygroup.com. Responds in 3 months. All rights for 6 months and second rights. Articles, 3,000–4,000 words; $300. Depts/columns, to 1,800 words; $150. Pays on publication. Provides 2 contributor's copies.

Vim & Vigor

1010 East Missouri Avenue
Phoenix, AZ 85014

Editor in Chief: Beth Tomkiw

Description and Interests: *Vim & Vigor* is Community Healthcare System's quarterly family health magazine featuring informational articles about health issues, including nutrition, exercise, heart disease, sports injuries, and surgery. It highlights services of Community Healthcare Systems and also features profiles of celebrities in relation to health topics. It prefers to work with experts in the health industry. Circ: 1.4 million.
Website: www.comhs.org/vim_vigor

Freelance Potential: 90% written by nonstaff writers. Publishes 32 freelance submissions yearly; 5% by unpublished writers, 80% by experts.

Submissions and Payment: Sample copy available at website. Guidelines and editorial calendar available. All articles are assigned. Send résumé and clips. Accepts hard copy. SASE. Response time varies. All rights. Articles, 500–1,400 words; $.25–$.75 per word. Pays on acceptance.

Vogue

Condé Nast Publications
4 Times Square, 12th Floor
New York, NY 10036

Submissions: Molly Creeden

Description and Interests: The latest and greatest in fashion, style, and beauty are covered in each issue of this popular monthly. Entertainment, dining, the arts, and health and fitness round out the editorial mix. Circ: 1.2 million.
Website: www.vogue.com

Freelance Potential: 70% written by nonstaff writers. Publishes 100–150 freelance submissions yearly; 2% by unpublished writers, 10–15% by authors who are new to the magazine. Receives 60 queries monthly.

Submissions and Payment: Sample copy and guidelines available. Query with clips or writing samples. Accepts hard copy and email to molly_creeden@condenast.com. SASE. Responds in 3 months. Rights negotiable. Articles, 500–2,500 words. Depts/columns, word lengths vary. Written material, $1–$2 per word. Pays on acceptance.

Vogue Knitting International

161 Sixth Avenue, Suite 1301
New York, NY 10013

Editor: Trisha Malcolm

Description and Interests: Using the art of knitting to create highly fashionable items is the focus of this quarterly publication. It includes techniques, trends, and step-by-step instructions and patterns. Circ: 200,000.
Website: www.vogueknitting.com

Freelance Potential: 25% written by nonstaff writers. Publishes 12 freelance submissions yearly; 25% by authors who are new to the magazine, 100% by experts. Receives 10 queries monthly.

Submissions and Payment: Sample copy and guidelines available. Query with clips or writing samples. Accepts hard copy, email to editors@sohopublishing.com, and simultaneous submissions if identified. SASE. Responds in 1–2 months. All rights. Articles and depts/columns, word lengths vary. JPEG and TIFF images at 300 dpi. All material, payment rates vary. Pays on acceptance.

The Way of St. Francis

The Way of St. Francis
1112 26th Street
Sacramento, CA 94816–5610

Editor: Jeff Shackleton, OFM

Description and Interests: Six times each year, *The Way of St. Francis* reveals to readers the Franciscan worldview in the form of essays, stories, and poetry. Circ: 5,000.
Website: http://sbfranciscans.org/theway

Freelance Potential: 95% written by nonstaff writers. Publishes 20 freelance submissions yearly; 20% by unpublished writers, 10% by authors who are new to the magazine, 20% by experts. Receives 8 unsolicited mss monthly.

Submissions and Payment: Sample copy and theme list available. Guidelines available at website. Query or send complete ms. Prefers email to ofmcaway@att.net (Word attachments); will accept hard copy. SASE. Responds in 8 weeks. First rights. Articles and fiction, to 2,000 words. Depts/columns, 900–1,000 words. Written material and cover art, $50. Pays on publication. Provides 2 contributor's copies.

Weave Magazine 

7 Germania Street
San Francisco, CA 94117

Editor: Laura Davis

Description and Interests: This annual literary magazine seeks to publish the finest prose and poetry of writers from all walks of life, both novice and established. Please check the website for current submission guidelines and for information on writers' workshops. Circ: 300.
Website: www.weavemagazine.net

Freelance Potential: 100% written by nonstaff writers. Publishes 70–80 freelance submissions yearly; 29% by unpublished writers. Receives 75 unsolicited mss monthly.

Submissions and Payment: Sample stories available at website. Guidelines available at website. Send ms. Accepts electronic submissions through website. Response time varies. First North American serial rights. Fiction and nonfiction, 3,000 words. Flash fiction, to 1,000 words, to 3 pieces. Poetry, 3–5 poems. No payment. Provides 1 contributor's copy.

Weavings

Weavings Editorial Office
1908 Grand Avenue
P.O. Box 340004
Nashville, TN 37203

Editor: Lynne M. Deming

Description and Interests: Appearing six times each year, *Weavings* speaks to Christian clergy, lay leaders, and others who wish to engage in the contemplative life. Its prose and poetry are thought-provoking but not scholarly. Circ: 18,000.
Website: www.weavings.upperroom.org

Freelance Potential: 90% written by nonstaff writers. Publishes 30–40 freelance submissions yearly; 10% by authors who are new to the magazine.

Submissions and Payment: Sample copy available. Guidelines and theme list available at website. Query or send complete ms. Accepts hard copy and email to weavings@upperroom.org (Word attachments). SASE. Responds in 3 months. Rights vary. Articles, 1,000–2,000 words. Fiction, sermons, book reviews, poetry, and reports; word lengths vary. Written material, payment rates vary. Payment policy varies. Provides 2 contributor's copies.

West Branch

Bucknell Hall
Bucknell University
Lewisburg, PA 17837

Editor: G. C. Waldrep

Description and Interests: Bucknell University's Stadler Center for Poetry publishes this literary magazine three times each year. It includes the very best in prose and poetry by new and established writers alike. Circ: 1,200.
Website: www.bucknell.edu/westbranch

Freelance Potential: 100% written by nonstaff writers. Publishes 60 freelance submissions yearly; 5% by unpublished writers, 60% by authors who are new to the magazine. Receives 350 unsolicited mss monthly.

Submissions and Payment: Sample works and guidelines available at website. Send complete ms between August 15 and April 1. Accepts submissions via website. Response time varies. First North American serial rights. Prose, to 30 pages; $30–$100. Poetry, to 6 poems; $20 per poem. Pays on publication. Provides 2 contributor's copies and a 1-year subscription.

The Western Historical Quarterly

Utah State University
0740 Old Main Hill
Logan, UT 84322-0740

Editor: David Rich Lewis

Description and Interests: This quarterly promotes the study of the North American West by offering articles on the history, cultures, colonization, and expansion of this part of the globe. Circ: 2,500.
Website: www.usu.edu/whq

Freelance Potential: 100% written by nonstaff writers. Publishes 16 freelance submissions yearly; 25% by unpublished writers, 95% by authors who are new to the magazine, 100% by experts. Receives 5–6 unsolicited mss monthly.

Submissions and Payment: Sample copy available. Guidelines available at website. Send 2 copies of complete ms. Accepts hard copy. No simultaneous submissions. SASE. Responds in 3 months. All rights. Articles, to 10,000 words (including endnotes). 8x10 B/W prints and negatives. No payment. Provides 5 contributor's copies.

Western Humanities Review

University of Utah English Department
255 South Central Campus Drive, LNC 3500
Salt Lake City, UT 84112-0494

Managing Editor: Nate Liederbach

Description and Interests: Now appearing three times each year—the newest edition being an issue of hybrid and collaborative work—this literary journal continues to publish fiction, nonfiction, and poetry. Circ: 1,000.
Website: www.hum.utah.edu/whr

Freelance Potential: 100% written by nonstaff writers. Publishes 60 freelance submissions yearly; 2% by unpublished writers, 18% by authors who are new to the magazine. Receives 400 unsolicited mss monthly.

Submissions and Payment: Sample copy available. Guidelines available at website. Send complete ms via online submissions manager. Accepts simultaneous submissions. Responds in 3–5 months. First North American serial rights. Articles, 10,000 words. Fiction, 7,000–8,000 words. Written material, $5 per printed page. Pays on publication. Provides 2 contributor's copies.

Western Hunter 

P.O. Box 11367
Chandler, AZ 8524

Editor: Ryan Hatfield

Description and Interests: *Western Hunter* is a resource for hunting all western species, including elk, deer, antelope, bighorn sheep, and moose. Articles cover hunting gear, tips and tactics, field judging trophies, and adventures. It is the sister publication to *Elk Hunter Magazine*. Circ: Unavailable.
Website: www.westernhuntermagazine.net

Freelance Potential: Receives many freelance submissions monthly.

Submissions and Payment: Sample articles available at website. Query. Accepts email queries to backcountryeditor@gmail.com. Response time varies. Written material, word lengths vary. Rights vary. Payment rates and policies vary.

Westview

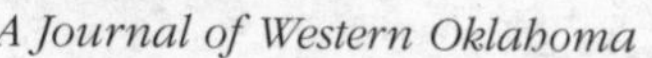

A Journal of Western Oklahoma

Southwestern Oklahoma State University
100 Campus Drive
Weatherford, OK 73096

Editor: Dr. James Silver

Description and Interests: *Westview* now includes writers from outside the Southwest; however, it still seeks only the finest fiction, nonfiction, drama, and poetry for issues appearing twice each year. Circ: 250.
Website: www.swosu.edu/academics/langarts/westview

Freelance Potential: 97% written by nonstaff writers. Publishes 50–60 freelance submissions yearly; 60% by new authors. Receives 20–30 unsolicited mss monthly.

Submissions and Payment: Sample copy available. Guidelines available at website. Send complete ms with brief biography. Prefers hard copy; will accept email submissions to james.silver@swosu.edu. SASE. Responds in 3–4 months. First rights. Articles and fiction, 10–15 double-spaced pages. Poetry, no line limits. B/W prints or slides. No payment. Provides 1 contributor's copy.

Where Women Cook 

22992 Mill Creek, Suite B
Laguna Hills, CA 92653

Managing Editor

Description and Interests: Women who are passionate about food are the common denominator of the articles in this magazine, published by Stampington & Co. Recipes, entertaining, and kitchen design are all featured. Its aim is to inspire its readers in the kitchen. Circ: Unknown.
Website: www.wherewomencook.com

Freelance Potential: Parent company Stampington & Co. is open to submissions.

Submissions and Payment: Sample articles available at website. Accepts email to us@wherewomencreate.com. Written material, payment rates vary. Rights, payment policy, unknown.

Where Women Create

22992 Mill Creek, Suite B
Laguna Hills, CA 92653

Editor in Chief: Jo Packham

Description and Interests: *Where Women Create* features extraordinary women and the inspiring workspaces they have designed for their creative activities. Each article is filled with beautiful photography that showcases women's workspaces and the unique expression of their creative spirit. The magazine is published quarterly. Circ: 70,000.
Website: www.stampington.com

Freelance Potential: 75% written by nonstaff writers. Publishes 48 freelance submissions yearly; 70% by authors who are new to the magazine.

Submissions and Payment: Sample copy and guidelines available. Query with 5–6 photos of creative space(s). Accepts hard copy and email queries to jo@wherewomencreate.com. Response time varies. All rights. Articles and depts/columns, word lengths vary. Digital images at 300 dpi. All material, payment rates vary. Payment policy varies.

Whiskey Island Magazine

Department of English
Cleveland State University
Cleveland, OH 44115-2214

Genre Editor

Description and Interests: *Whiskey Island Magazine* is a literary journal published twice each year. It accepts innovative works of fiction, creative nonfiction, and poetry. Circ: 1,200.
Website: www.csuohio.edu/class/english/whiskey_island/

Freelance Potential: 100% written by nonstaff writers. Publishes 100 freelance submissions yearly; 5% by unpublished writers, 95% by authors who are new to the magazine. Receives 100 unsolicited mss monthly.

Submissions and Payment: Sample copy and guidelines available. Send complete ms with brief author bio. Accepts electronic submissions via website and simultaneous submissions if identified. Responds in 3 months. First rights. Prose, to 5,000 words. Poetry, 3–5 poems per submission. No payment. Provides 2 contributor's copies.

Whispering Wind

P.O. Box 1390 (Department 3)
Folsom, LA 70437-1390

Editor: Jack Heriard

Description and Interests: Appearing six times each year, this magazine celebrates American Indian material culture, arts and crafts, and modern-day powwow wear. Book and music reviews are also featured. Circ: 21,000.
Website: www.whisperingwind.com

Freelance Potential: 100% written by nonstaff writers. Publishes 15–20 freelance submissions yearly; 50% by unpublished writers.

Submissions and Payment: Sample copy available. Guidelines available at website. Query or send complete ms with bibliography and author bio. Accepts email to jack@writtenheritage.com and hard copy. SASE. Response time varies. All rights. Articles, word lengths vary. Depts/columns, 450–600 words. Prefers B/W and color digital images at 300 dpi (email 72 dpi for review); will accept prints in duplicate. No payment. Provides 6 contributor's copies and a 1-year subscription.

Whitefish Review

708 Lupfer Avenue
Whitefish, MT 59937

Editor: Brian Schott

Description and Interests: This literary review, published twice each year, looks for original fiction, creative nonfiction, poetry, and interviews—all with a slant toward mountain culture. Circ: 2,000.
Website: http://whitefishreview.org

Freelance Potential: 99% written by nonstaff writers. Publishes 40 freelance submissions yearly; 25% by unpublished writers, 99% by authors who are new to the magazine. Receives 100 unsolicited mss monthly.

Submissions and Payment: Sample copy available. Guidelines available at website. Send complete ms. Accepts electronic submissions through website during reading periods outlined at website. Limit 1 submission per reading period. Response time varies. One-time rights. Fiction and nonfiction, to 5,000 words. Poetry, to 3 poems. Written material, $25–$50. Pays on publication. Provides 2 contributor's copies.

Whitetails Unlimited Magazine

2100 Michigan Street, P.O. Box 720
Sturgeon Bay, WI 54235

Editor: Jeff Davis

Description and Interests: Hunting enthusiasts read this quarterly for articles on hunting techniques, gear, personal experience pieces, and wildlife management. Circ: 90,000.
Website: www.whitetailsunlimited.com

Freelance Potential: 75% written by nonstaff writers. Publishes 24 freelance submissions yearly; 10% by unpublished writers, 25% by authors who are new to the magazine, 65% by experts. Receives 10 queries monthly.

Submissions and Payment: Sample copy and guidelines available at website. Prefers query or send complete ms with photo descriptions (do not send photos unless requested). Accepts hard copy. SASE. Responds in 4–6 weeks. First North American serial and electronic rights. Articles, 1,500–2,500 words. Written material, $100–$350. Pays on publication. Provides 6 contributor's copies.

The Wild Foods Forum

P.O. Box 61413
Virginia Beach, VA 23466-1413

Editor: Vickie Shufer

Description and Interests: Informative articles on how to identify edible and medicinal wild plants are the mainstay of this specialty publication. This quarterly newsletter also includes tips on preparing plants for use. Circ: 500.
Website: www.ecoimages-us.com

Freelance Potential: 70% written by nonstaff writers. Publishes 4–6 freelance submissions yearly; 5% by unpublished writers, 10% by authors who are new to the magazine, 50% by experts. Receives 2 unsolicited mss monthly.

Submissions and Payment: Sample copy and guidelines available. Send complete ms with artwork. Accepts email submissions to wildfood@cox.net (text files). Responds in 2 months. All rights. Articles, 100–500 words. Depts/columns, 50–100 words. Color or B/W prints; line art. All material, payment rates vary. Payment policy varies. Provides a 1-year subscription.

Wild West

19300 Promenade Drive
Leesburg, VA 20176–6500

Editor: Greg Lalire

Description and Interests: *Wild West* features carefully researched articles about the people, places, and events that make up the history of the American frontier. It appears in six photo-filled issues each year. Circ: 50,000.
Website: www.thehistorynet.com/magazines/wild_west

Freelance Potential: 80% written by nonstaff writers. Publishes 60 freelance submissions yearly; 10% by unpublished writers, 20% by new authors, 60% by experts. Receives 30 queries, 10 unsolicited mss monthly.

Submissions and Payment: Sample copy available. Guidelines available at website. Query or send complete ms. Accepts disk submissions with hard copy and email submissions to greg.lalire@weiderhistorygroup.com. SASE. Responds to queries in 4–6 months, to mss in 3 months. All rights. Articles, 3,500 words; $300. Depts/columns, 1,200 words; $150. Pays on publication.

The William and Mary Review

Campus Center
P.O. Box 8795
Williamsburg, VA 23187-8795

Prose or Poetry Editor

Description and Interests: *The William and Mary Review* is a literary and art magazine that features a mix of original poetry, fiction, nonfiction, and visual art. It is published annually. Circ: 1,600.
Website: http://wmpeople.wm.edu/

Freelance Potential: 100% written by nonstaff writers. Publishes 15–18 freelance submissions yearly; 25% by unpublished writers, 75% by authors who are new to the magazine. Receives 200 unsolicited mss monthly.

Submissions and Payment: Sample copy available. Send complete ms with cover letter and brief author bio between September and February 1. Accepts hard copy and simultaneous submissions if identified. SASE. Responds in 3–5 months. First North American serial rights. Articles and fiction, to 7,000 words. Poetry, to 6 poems per submission. No payment. Provides 5 contributor's copies.

Willow Review

College of Lake County
19351 West Washington Street
Grayslake, IL 60030-1198

Editor: Michael Latza

Description and Interests: The literary works of authors from the midwest are presented in *Willow Review*. Published annually, it accepts fiction, nonfiction, and poetry. It also publishes reviews of books written by midwestern writers. Circ: 1,000.
Website: www.clcillinois.edu/community/willowreview.asp

Freelance Potential: 99% written by nonstaff writers. Publishes 30–40 freelance submissions yearly; 2% by unpublished writers, 80% by authors who are new to the magazine. Receives 300 unsolicited mss monthly.

Submissions and Payment: Sample copy available. Guidelines available at website. Send complete ms and cover letter between September 1 and May 1. Accepts hard copy and simultaneous submissions if identified. SASE. Responds in 6–8 weeks. First serial rights. Fiction and nonfiction, to 7,000 words. Poetry, no line limit; to 5 poems per submission. No payment. Provides 2 contributor's copies.

Willow Springs

Eastern Washington University
501 North Riverpoint Boulevard, Suite 425
Spokane, WA 99202

Editor: Samuel Ligon

Description and Interests: High-quality short fiction, creative nonfiction, poetry, and author interviews are sought by this literary journal. Published twice each year, it welcomes new, as well as established writers. Circ: 1,400.
Website: http://willowsprings.ewu.edu

Freelance Potential: 100% written by nonstaff writers. Publishes 60 freelance submissions yearly; 20% by unpublished writers, 80% by authors who are new to the magazine. Receives 415 unsolicited mss monthly.

Submissions and Payment: Sample copy available. Guidelines and submission periods available at website. Send complete ms. Accepts electronic submissions via online submissions manager, and simultaneous submissions if identified. Responds in 2–4 months. One-time rights. Written material, word lengths vary. No payment. Provides 2 contributor's copies.

Windspeaker

13245-146 Street NW
Edmonton, Alberta T5L 4S8
Canada

Editor: Debora Steel

Description and Interests: Since 1983, *Windspeaker* has been reaching Canada's Aboriginal people with news of current events and issues affecting their communities, as well as with reports on sports, arts, and entertainment. Published monthly, it also features profiles of Aboriginal individuals and groups. Circ: 24,000+.
Website: www.ammsa.com

Freelance Potential: 40% written by nonstaff writers.

Submissions and Payment: Sample articles and guidelines available at website. Query or send complete ms. Accepts email to dsteel@ammsa.com. Response time varies. All rights. Articles, 500–800 words; $3.60 per published inch for single-source article; $4.15 per published inch for multi-source article. Digital images at 200 dpi; payment rates vary. Kill fee, 50%. Pays on publication.

Wine Enthusiast

333 North Bedford Road
Mount Kisco, NY 10549

Managing Editor: Joe Czerwinski

Description and Interests: The mission of this monthly wine and spirits magazine is to educate and entertain readers in the most accessible and user-friendly way, as part of an active, upscale, and fulfilling lifestyle. New writers have the most success with the front-of-the-book sections, including wine region news, short profiles, creative food and drink recipes, trend pieces, and travel updates. Circ: 180,000.
Website: www.winemag.com

Freelance Potential: 50% written by nonstaff writers. Accepts 20% of submissions received.

Submissions and Payment: Sample articles and guidelines available at website. Query with résumé or clips. Accepts email to appropriate editor. Response time varies. Written material, word lengths vary. All rights. Written material, $.50–$1 per word. Kill fee, 25%. Pays upon publication.

Wine X Magazine

5139 Dry Creek Road
Healdsburg, CA 95448

Associate Editor: Jenna Corwin

Description and Interests: With an editorial mission to inform, entertain, and enlighten a new generation of wine consumers, this ezine takes a cutting-edge approach that appeals to its hip, young adult readership. It seeks articles about wine, food, and the young adult lifestyle that might not fit in with the style of any other wine magazine. It is updated regularly. Hits per month: Unavailable.
Website: www.winexmagazine.com

Freelance Potential: 90% written by nonstaff writers. Publishes 100 freelance submissions yearly; 1% by authors who are new to the magazine.

Submissions and Payment: Sample copy and guidelines available at website. Query or send complete ms. Accepts submissions via website and email to jenna@winexmagazine.com. Responds if interested. All rights. Articles, 1,000–2,000 words; payment rates vary. Payment policy varies.

Wisconsin Review

800 Algoma Boulevard
Oshkosh, WI 54901

Senior Editor: Nicholas Williams

Description and Interests: This literary journal from the University of Wisconsin-Oshkosh is published once each year. It offers a collection of high-quality writing in the form of fiction, essays, poetry, and translations. It is no longer accepting reviews. Circ: 2,000.
Website: www.uwosh.edu/wisconsinreview

Freelance Potential: 100% written by nonstaff writers. Of the freelance submissions published yearly, 10% are by unpublished writers, 60% are by authors who are new to the magazine. Receives 30 unsolicited mss monthly.

Submissions and Payment: Sample copy available. Guidelines and deadlines available at website. Send complete ms with cover letter and brief author bio. Accepts hard copy. SASE. Also accepts submissions via online submissions manager. Responds in 2–6 months. First North American serial rights. Fiction and essays, to 5,000 words, 15 pages, double-spaced. Poetry, 3–5 poems per submission. No payment. Provides 2 contributor's copies.

Woman's Life

P.O. Box 5020
Port Huron, MI 48061-5020

Managing Editor: Wendy L. Krabach

Description and Interests: Dedicated to helping women care for themselves and their families, *Woman's Life* seeks articles that address health and fitness, emotional well-being, financial planning, life insurance needs, and career achievement. It is published quarterly by the Woman's Life Insurance Society. Circ: 34,000.
Website: www.womanslife.org

Freelance Potential: 95% written by nonstaff writers. Publishes 6–10 freelance submissions yearly; 70% by unpublished writers, 25% by authors who are new to the magazine, 5% by experts. Receives 10 queries monthly.

Submissions and Payment: Sample copy and guidelines available. Query. Accepts email queries to wkrabach@womanslife.org. Responds in 1 day. Rights vary. Articles, 1,000–1,500 words; payment rates vary. Pays on publication. Provides 3 contributor's copies.

Women with Wheels

1885 Willowview Terrace
Northfield, IL 60093

Editor: Susan Frissell

Description and Interests: Geared especially for women, this online magazine offers expert-written articles about cars and trucks, on topics such as test-driving, buying and leasing, and basic maintenance. It also features new product information, personal experience pieces, and profiles and interviews. It is updated quarterly. Hits per month: Unavailable.
Website: www.womenwithwheels.com

Freelance Potential: 99% written by nonstaff writers. Publishes 1–2 freelance submissions yearly; 1% by unpublished writers, 1% by authors who are new to the magazine, 98% by experts.

Submissions and Payment: Guidelines available at website. Send complete ms. Accepts email submissions to editor@womenwithwheels.com. Responds in 1–4 weeks. Rights vary. Articles, 350–700 words. Depts/columns, word lengths vary. No payment.

Woodcraft Magazine

P.O. Box 7020
Parkersburg, WV 26102-7020

Editor: Jim Harrold

Description and Interests: Woodworkers find plenty of projects, techniques, and products in this magazine that is published six times each year. Circ: 100,581.
Website: www.woodcraftmagazine.com

Freelance Potential: 85% written by nonstaff writers. Publishes 100 freelance submissions yearly; 10% by unpublished writers, 50% by new authors, 10% by experts. Receives 15–30 queries, few unsolicited mss monthly.

Submissions and Payment: Sample copy, guidelines, and theme list available. Query with outline and samples; or send complete ms with photo thumbnails. Accepts hard copy and email to editor@woodcraftmagazine.com. No simultaneous submissions. SASE. Responds in 1 month. First serial rights. Articles, 1,200-2,500 words. Depts/columns, word lengths vary. Written material, $175 per published page. Pays on publication.

The Worcester Review

1 Ekman Street
Worcester, MA 01607

Managing Editor: Diane Mulligan

Description and Interests: Appearing annually, *The Worcester Review* celebrates the rich literary history of central New England through works of fiction, poetry, and literary criticism. Circ: 750.
Website: www.theworcesterreview.org

Freelance Potential: 95% written by nonstaff writers. Publishes 40 freelance submissions yearly; 75% by authors who are new to the magazine. Receives 50 unsolicited mss monthly.

Submissions and Payment: Sample copy available. Guidelines available at website. Send complete ms with cover letter and brief author bio. Accepts hard copy and simultaneous submissions if identified. SASE. Responds in 9 months. First rights. Articles and fiction, to 4,000 words. Poetry, 3–5 poems per submission. Provides 2 contributor's copies and a subscription.

Workers Write!

P.O. Box 250382
Plano, TX 75025-0382

Editor: David LaBounty

Description and Interests: This annual literary journal gives voice to writers who are making a living doing something other than writing. Themed issues feature fiction and poetry about a particular workplace setting. Circ: 1,200.
Website: www.workerswritejournal.com

Freelance Potential: 95% written by nonstaff writers. Publishes 10 freelance submissions yearly; 50% by unpublished writers, 90% by authors who are new to the magazine. Receives 50 unsolicited mss monthly.

Submissions and Payment: Sample copy available. Guidelines and editorial calendar available at website. Send complete ms. Will consider reprints. Accepts email submissions to address at website. Responds in 2 months. First North American serial and reprint rights. Fiction, 500–5,000 words; $5–$50. Pays on acceptance. Provides 1 contributor's copy.

Working Money

4757 California Avenue SW
Seattle, WA 98116–4499

Editor: Jayanthi Gopalakrishnan

Description and Interests: This online magazine, updated frequently, targets market newcomers. It offers information on the global financial trading world, investing, world markets, and trend analysis. Hits per month: Unavailable.
Website: www.traders.com

Freelance Potential: 95% written by nonstaff writers. Publishes 80–90 freelance submissions yearly; 60–70% by unpublished writers, 50% by authors who are new to the magazine, 60% by experts. Receives 10 queries, 10 unsolicited mss monthly.

Submissions and Payment: Sample copy and guidelines available at website. Query with outline; or send complete ms. Prefers email to editor@traders.com (Word attachments); will accept hard copy, disk submissions, and simultaneous submissions if identified. SASE. Responds in 3–4 months. All rights. Articles, to 2,000 words; $180. Pays upon posting.

World Art Glass Quarterly

P.O. Box 321168
Los Gatos, CA 95032

Editor in Chief: Curt Walton

Description and Interests: This arts magazine covers the architectural and art glass world in quarterly issues. It features profiles of some of the finest art glass artists in the world, providing a peek into their studios, inspirations, and techniques. It also covers exhibits, events, and noteworthy collections. It seeks writers who are well versed in the art and can communicate its intricacies. Circ: 20,000.
Website: www.artglassquarterly.com

Freelance Potential: 25% written by nonstaff writers. Publishes 10 freelance submissions yearly; 50% by unpublished writers, 50% by experts. Receives 5 queries monthly.

Submissions and Payment: Sample copy and guidelines available. Query. Accepts hard copy and email queries to cdwalton@artglassquarterly.com. SASE. Responds in 6 weeks. All rights. Articles, 1,000–2,000 words; $300–$350. Pays on publication.

World Policy Journal

220 Fifth Avenue, 9th Floor
New York, NY 10001

Managing Editor: Christopher Shay

Description and Interests: *World Policy Journal* covers pressing issues in global affairs and is known for lively, intelligent writing that challenges conventional wisdom on world news and analysis. Published quarterly, it seeks illuminating articles set on foreign soil. Circ: 10,000.
Website: www.worldpolicy.org

Freelance Potential: 95% written by nonstaff writers. Publishes 20–30 freelance submissions yearly; 10% by unpublished writers, 50% by authors who are new to the magazine, 30% by experts. Receives 30–50 queries monthly.

Submissions and Payment: Sample copy and guidelines available at website. Query with synopsis and clips. Accepts email to shay@worldpolicy.org (Word or PDF attachments) and simultaneous submissions. Responds in 1–2 months. Rights vary. Articles, to 5,000 words; $500. Kill fee, $50. Pays on publication. Provides 2 contributor's copies.

World Pulse Magazine

Lovejoy Center
909 NW 19th Avenue, Suite C
Portland, OR 97209

Editor: Jensine Larsen

Description and Interests: Covering global issues from a woman's perspective, this quarterly magazine accepts articles that are solution-oriented and timely and that demonstrate the collective power of women globally. Writers are encouraged to first post to *PulseWire*, the magazine's online community. The editors favor writers who are from the regions on which they are reporting. Circ: 100,000.
Website: www.worldpulse.com

Freelance Potential: 50% written by nonstaff writers; most by authors who are new to the magazine. Receives 2 queries monthly.

Submissions and Payment: Sample articles, guidelines, and theme lists available at website. Query. Accepts email queries to editor@worldpulse.com. Response time varies. Non-exclusive rights. Articles and depts/columns, word lengths and payment rates vary. Payment policy varies. Provides 1 contributor's copy.

The WREN Magazine

2312 Carey Avenue
Cheyenne, WY 82001

Editor: Cara Eastwood

Description and Interests: Published 11 times each year by the Wyoming Rural Electric Association, this magazine features regional lifestyle pieces, profiles, historical reports, and practical pieces of interest to a general readership. It wants personal, localized articles that put a human face on larger issues. Circ: 41,000.
Website: http://wyomingrea.org

Freelance Potential: 60% written by nonstaff writers. Publishes 22–33 freelance submissions yearly; 50% by unpublished writers, 50% by authors who are new to the magazine, 20% by experts. Receives 2 unsolicited mss monthly.

Submissions and Payment: Sample copy and guidelines available. Send complete ms. Accepts hard copy. SASE. Responds in 3 months. First serial rights. Articles, 500–1,000 words; $50–$100. Depts/columns, 500–850 words; $50. Payment policy varies. Provides contributor's copies.

The Yale Review 

P.O. Box 208243
New Haven, CT 06520-8243

Editor: J. D. McClatchy

Description and Interests: *The Yale Review* recently celebrated its 100th anniversary. This university-affiliated literary journal publishes fiction, poetry, and essays four times each year. Circ: 8,000.
Website: www.yale.edu/yalereview

Freelance Potential: 100% written by nonstaff writers. Publishes 120 freelance submissions yearly; 10% by unpublished writers, 10% by authors who are new to the magazine. Receives 400 unsolicited mss monthly.

Submissions and Payment: Sample copy available. Accepts hard copy. No simultaneous submissions. SASE. Responds in 2 months. First rights. Articles and fiction, word lengths vary. Poetry, no line limits. Written material, payment rates vary. Pays on publication. Provides 2 contributor's copies.

Yankee

P.O. Box 520
1121 Main Street
Dublin, NH 03444

Assistant Editor: Debbie Despres

Description and Interests: This magazine offers a look at the people, places, and culture of New England. Published six times each year, it appeals to both tourists and natives. Circ: 350,000.
Website: www.yankeemagazine.com

Freelance Potential: 40% written by nonstaff writers. Publishes 30 freelance submissions yearly; 1% by authors who are new to the magazine, 2% by experts. Receives 80 queries and mss monthly.

Submissions and Payment: Sample copy available. Guidelines available at website. Query or send complete ms with cover letter, clips, and brief author bio. Accepts hard copy and email to editors@yankeepub.com. SASE. Responds in 4–6 weeks. All rights. Articles, 500–2,000 words; $1 per word. Depts/columns, word lengths and payment rates vary. Written material, payment rates vary. Pays on acceptance. Provides contributor's copies.

Your Teen

23214 Ranch Road
Beachwood, OH 44122

Editor in Chief: Susan Borison

Description and Interests: *Your Teen* magazine addresses the challenges inherent in raising teens and helps parents to continue the journey toward successful parenting. Its articles and departments/columns offer the perspectives of professionals, parents, and teenagers themselves on relevant topics. Published quarterly, it tackles the topics of teen substance abuse, bullying, driving, relationships, education, technology, health, and sexuality. Circ: 25,000.
Website: www.yourteenmag.com

Freelance Potential: 50% written by nonstaff writers. Of the freelance submissions published yearly, most are by unpublished writers.

Submissions and Payment: Sample copy available. Guidelines available at website. Query. Accepts email queries to editor@yourteenmag.com. Response time varies. Rights vary. Articles and depts/columns, word lengths vary. Written material, no payment.

YourTango

236 West 27th Street, 8th Floor
New York, NY 10001

Senior Editor: Genevieve Lill

Description and Interests: *YourTango* is a daily updated website for women ages 18–54 who want to "live their best love lives." It offers informative articles on marital and other romantic relationships, sex, parenting, fitness and health, finances, and dating. Profiles of couples and personal experience pieces are also featured. Hits per month: 2.9 million.
Website: www.yourtango.com

Freelance Potential: 50% written by nonstaff writers. Publishes 120–180 freelance submissions yearly; 2% by unpublished writers, 65% by authors who are new to the magazine.

Submissions and Payment: Query. Guidelines available on website. Accepts email queries to editor@yourtango.com. Response time varies. First North American serial rights. Articles and depts/columns, word lengths and payment rates vary. Pays 1 month after publication.

Trade & Professional Magazines

Acupuncture Today

P.O. Box 4139
Huntington Beach, CA 92605–4139

Senior Associate Editor: Brenda Duran

Description and Interests

The profession of acupuncture and Eastern medicine is covered in this professional magazine for practitioners. It features industry news, opinion pieces, case reports, and articles on trends, techniques, and research. As a rule, the magazine accepts material only from professional practitioners of acupuncture and Oriental medicine. Circ: 23,600.

Contents: 60% articles; 30% depts/columns; 10% other
Frequency: Monthly
Website: www.acupuncturetoday.com

Freelance Potential

70% written by nonstaff writers. Publishes 10–12 freelance submissions yearly; 15% by unpublished writers, 10% by authors who are new to the magazine, 75% by experts. Receives 4–5 unsolicited mss monthly.

Submissions

Accepts email queries. Send complete ms with resume or brief bio and relevant links to sources. Prefers email to editorial@acupuncturetoday.com; will accept disk submissions with hard copy. No simultaneous submissions. SASE. Responds in 6 weeks.

- Articles: 750–1,200 words. Informational and how-to articles; profiles; interviews; and opinion and personal experience pieces. Topics include health, alternative medicine, nutrition, technology, sports, and fitness.
- Depts/columns: 600–900 words. Herbs, supplements, business issues, opinion pieces.
- Artwork: High-resolution digital images; 300 dpi, 450x600 pixels or higher, JPEG or TIFF format.

Sample Issue

48 pages. Advertising. Sample copy, guidelines, article submission deadlines, and theme list available at website.

- "Ancient Medicine, Modern Gadgets: A Guide for Your Practice." Apps and other technology to help practitioners get organized.
- "The Psychobiology of Pain." Understanding the experience of pain, along with its neurological and biochemical underpinnings.

Rights and Payment

All rights. No payment.

Ag Weekly

P.O. Box 918
Bismark, ND 58501

Editor: Mark Conlon

Description and Interests

Focusing on Idaho, Montana, and Wyoming, *Ag Weekly* features news and updates that affect livestock, agriculture, farming trends, and technology. The publication was started in 1991 and includes farmers, dairymen, cattlemen, and agricultural businesses among its readers. *Ag Weekly* is currently looking for in-state freelancers. At this time, it will not consider submissions from writers outside the Pacific Northwest area. Circ: 13,000.

Contents: 75% articles; 25% depts/columns
Frequency: Print: Monthly; Website: Weekly
Website: www.agweekly.com

Freelance Potential

80–90% written by nonstaff writers. Publishes 325 freelance submissions yearly; 5–10% by authors who are new to the magazine, 2% by experts. Receives 20 queries monthly.

Submissions

Query. Accepts hard copy and email queries to mark.conlon@lee.net. SASE. Responds in 6 weeks.

- Articles: 700–1,100 words. Informational articles and opinion pieces. Topics include regional and local agricultural issues, weather, irrigation, livestock, environmental issues, gardening, computers, new products, and technology.
- Depts/columns: Word lengths vary. Producer reports; market reports; and livestock, dairy, and equine issues.

Sample Issue

40 pages. Advertising. Sample copy and guidelines available. Editorial calendar available at website.

- "Environmental Views: Pesticide Adventures at Triangle Lake." A "pitchfork rebellion" against pesticides in a small Oregon town has some worried they'll lose the ability to control invasives like Russian knapweed.
- "Child Drownings in Irrigation Canals Target of Safety Campaign." Idaho's high ranking in number of child drownings triggers bilingual television safety campaign warning residents of the danger, which peaks in summer.

Rights and Payment

One-time and second rights. Written material, payment rates vary. Pays on publication.

Airbrush Action

3209 Atlantic Avenue
P.O. Box 438
Allenwood, NJ 08720

Publisher/Executive Editor: Cliff Stieglitz

Description and Interests

This magazine is for those who employ the art of airbrush painting on any type of media. Editorial includes coverage of stencils, airbrush makeup, airbrush tanning, body art, paint brands and colors, kits, airbrush sets, brushes, and models. It welcomes new stories on artists, techniques, industry news, new products, and events. Stories should have a practical or how-to slant that readers can apply to their own art. Circ: 40,000+.

Contents: 60% articles; 30% depts/columns; 10% other
Frequency: 6 times each year
Website: www.airbrushaction.com

Freelance Potential

90% written by nonstaff writers. Publishes 24 freelance submissions yearly; 50% by authors who are new to the magazine, 50% by experts. Receives 25 queries, 5 unsolicited mss monthly.

Submissions

Query with clips; or send complete ms. Accepts email submissions to ceo@airbrushaction.com and simultaneous submissions if identified. Responds in 10 days.

- Articles: Word lengths vary. Informational and how-to articles; profiles; interviews; personal experience pieces; and new product information. Topics include airbrushing techniques, tools, and artists, trends; automotive and motorcycle customizing; T-shirt design; body art; nail art; comic-book art; sign production; murals; and fine art.
- Depts/columns: Staff-written.
- Artwork: Digital images, 5x7 and 300 dpi, saved as JPEGs and submitted on disc by mail.

Sample Issue

82 pages. Advertising. Sample copy available.

- "Stencils, Up-Selling & Walk-Aways." The advantages of using stencils to boost t-shirt sales.
- "Pinstriping a Mailbox with Flames." A new way to decorate plastic motorcycle tank mail boxes at an upcoming bike show.

Rights and Payment

One-time rights. Written material, payment rates vary. Payment policy varies. Provides 6 contributor's copies.

American Drycleaner

566 West Lake Street
Chicago, IL 60661

Editorial Director: Bruce Beggs

Description and Interests

This trade magazine of the drycleaning industry targets retail drycleaners with the latest information on market trends, equipment, and business practices. For the retail drycleaners out in the field, it looks to provide practical information to help increase retailers' business and provide best-quality service to their customers. Circ: 25,000.

Contents: 60% articles; 40% depts/columns
Frequency: Monthly
Website: www.americandrycleaner.com

Freelance Potential

75% written by nonstaff writers. Publishes 120 freelance submissions yearly; 10% by unpublished writers, 15% by authors who are new to the magazine, 75% by experts. Receives 5 queries monthly.

Submissions

Query. Accepts hard copy and email queries to bbeggs@americantrademagazines.com. SASE. Responds in 1–2 months.

- Articles: 1,200–1,800 words. Informational and how-to articles; personal experience pieces; expert advice; profiles; interviews; and new product information (to 300 words). Topics include drycleaning, management, marketing, production equipment and supplies, and associations.
- Depts/columns: 1,200–1,800 words. Marketing, point-of-sale systems, plant operations, and industry news.
- Artwork: B/W or color prints or slides.

Sample Issue

132 pages. Advertising. Sample copy and editorial calendar available.

- "Rather Switch than Fight?" Alternatives to perc, a dry cleaning chemical.
- "Plant Design Awards: Merit Award, Pride Cleaners & TIDE Dry Cleaners." A skating rink-turned processing plant that serves dry cleaners in the Kansas City metro area.

Rights and Payment

Exclusive first and reprint rights. Written material, $50–$500. Artwork, $100–$300. Kill fee, 10%. Pays on publication. Provides 3–5 contributor's copies.

American Fitness

15250 Ventura Boulevard, Suite 200
Sherman Oaks, CA 91403

Editor: Meg Jordan, Ph.D., RN

Description and Interests

American Fitness, the publication of the Aerobics and Fitness Association of America, is written for trainers, health club owners, and other fitness professionals. It seeks to inform them of the latest news in science, exercise, health, nutrition, and the fitness industry. Articles should contain an advanced level of knowledge and credible sources. Circ: 100,000.

Contents: 60% articles; 40% depts/columns
Frequency: 6 times each year
Website: www.americanfitness.com

Freelance Potential

50% written by nonstaff writers. Publishes 36 freelance submissions yearly; 30% by unpublished writers, 30% by authors who are new to the magazine, 30% by experts. Receives 30 queries, 10 unsolicited mss monthly.

Submissions

Accepts queries with clips or complete ms with bio. Accepts hard copy and disk or email to americanfitness@afaa.com. SASE. No simultaneous submissions. Responds in 3–12 months.

- Articles: 800–1,500 words. Informational and how-to articles; profiles; and interviews. Topics include exercise, nutrition, health, innovations and trends, physiology, women's health, sports medicine, teaching exercise, fitness motivation, fitness trends, and marketing.
- Depts/columns: 800–1,000 words. Research reports, news, and nutrition.
- Artwork: Color slides, transparencies, or high resolution 300 dpi TIF, PDF, or JPG files.
- Other: CEU Corner 1,500–2,500 words, plus 15 multiple choice questions, diagrams, sidebars.

Sample Issue

70 pages. Advertising. Sample articles, guidelines and editorial calendar available at website.

- "Shiva Rea: Giving Us More Daily Energy." Yoga teacher/author seeks balance in life.
- "Anna Kournikova: Moving Forward and Continuing to Make a Difference." Russian tennis player found meaning in volunteer work.

Rights and Payment

First rights. Written material, $100–$200. Pays following publication. Provides 6 contributor's copies.

American School Board Journal

1680 Duke Street
Alexandria, VA 22314

Editor in Chief: Glenn Cook

Description and Interests

Founded in 1891, this professional journal covers emerging education trends, issues, and solutions for school board members, superintendents, and other education administrators. It looks for a mix of practical, thought-provoking, and timely articles on every educational topic, including policy making, student achievement, legislation, and the art of school leadership, with special emphasis on district-level leadership. Circ: 50,000.

Contents: 50% articles; 50% depts/columns
Frequency: Monthly
Website: www.asbj.com

Freelance Potential

55% written by nonstaff writers. Publishes 20–25 freelance submissions yearly; 15% by unpublished writers, 15% by authors who are new to the magazine, 70% by experts. Receives 10–12 queries, 10–12 unsolicited mss monthly.

Submissions

Prefers query with clips and author bio; will accept complete ms. Accepts hard copy on disk (MS Word). No simultaneous submissions. Responds in 6–8 weeks.

- Articles: 1,250–2,500 words. Informational and how-to articles. Topics include emerging education trends and solutions, policy management, technology, and fundraising.
- Depts/columns: 1,000–1,200 words. News analysis, research findings, book reviews, communications, school law, finance, school governance, facilities, technology, and professional advice.

Sample Issue

52 pages. Advertising. Sample copy and guidelines available at website.

- "Humble School Leaders." An often overlooked quality can boost student achievement and enhance district morale.
- "Keep Public School Public." Makes the case for governance of public schools by education pros, not citizens.

Rights and Payment

All rights. Solicited articles, $800+. Unsolicited articles, no payment. Depts/columns, payment rates vary. Pays on publication. Provides 3 contributor's copies.

American String Teacher

4155 Chain Bridge Road
Fairfax, VA 22030

Articles Editor: Mary Wagner

Description and Interests

Published by the American String Teachers Association, this magazine serves as a teaching aid for those instructing students in violin, viola, cello, bass, guitar, and harp. It also presents news pertinent to the profession and association updates. It contains some music history features as well. Many articles are written by members of the association. A firsthand knowledge of teaching string instruments in an educational setting is extremely helpful if one wishes to write for the magazine. Articles must be well researched. Circ: 11,500.

Contents: Articles; depts/columns
Frequency: Quarterly
Website: www.astaweb.com

Freelance Potential

100% written by nonstaff writers. Publishes 30 freelance submissions yearly; 5% by unpublished writers, 50% by authors who are new to the magazine. Receives 4 queries monthly.

Submissions

Accepts queries and complete ms. Prefers email queries to ASTarticles@astaweb.com (Word attachments); will accept hard copy (5 copies) directed to Editor Mary Jane Dye. Include title page, contact information, and brief bio. Response time varies.

- Articles: 1,500–3,000 words. Informational and factual articles; profiles; and association news. Topics include teaching, methodology, techniques, competitions, and auditions.
- Depts/columns: Word lengths vary. Teaching tips, opinion pieces, and industry news.

Sample Issue

96 pages. Advertising. Sample articles and guidelines available at website.

- "Here Comes the Judge." Article discusses ways in which teachers can self-assess at the start of each new school year.
- "Learning by Teaching/Addressing a Need: Peer Tutoring in Your Orchestra Program." Article explains how students benefit from the different expertises and insights of private tutors.

Rights and Payment

All rights. No payment. Provides 5 contributor's copies.

American Theatre

520 Eighth Avenue, 24th Floor
New York, NY 10018–4156

Editor in Chief: Jim O'Quinn

Description and Interests

The main focus of this magazine is professional, nonprofit theater. It covers trends and events in the theater world, artists, and recent economic and legislative developments that affect the arts. *American Theatre* does not normally run articles or features on academic or community theater. Significant productions are sometimes showcased in the Critic's Notebook section, however no reviews are published. Circ: 45,000.

Contents: 50% articles; 50% depts/columns
Frequency: 10 times each year
Website: www.tcg.org

Freelance Potential

40% written by nonstaff writers. Publishes 100–150 freelance submissions yearly; 5% by unpublished writers, 30% by authors who are new to the magazine, 60% by experts. Receives 40 queries monthly.

Submissions

Query with résumé and clips. Accepts email to jim@tcg.org and hard copy. SASE. Responds in 2 months.

- Articles: 1,500–3,000 words. Informational articles; profiles; interviews; criticism; and opinion pieces. Topics include professional, nonprofit theater, and theater productions and troupes around the world.
- Depts/columns: 500–2,500 words. News, short profiles, and critical analysis.

Sample Issue

88 pages. Advertising. Sample articles and guidelines available at website.

- "Bridging the Two Solitudes." The love/hate relationship between two dominant cultural and linguistic groups: Canada's Francophone and Anglophone theatre communities.
- "A Tale of 2 Festivals." A look at two very different towns that host the Stratford Shakespeare Festival and the Shaw Festival each spring.

Rights and Payment

Rights negotiable. Feature articles, $350. Shorter articles, payment rates vary. Depts/columns, $150–$250. Kill fee, 50%. Pays on publication. Provides 2 contributor's copies.

Area Development

Site & Facility Planning

Halcyon Business Publications
400 Post Avenue
Westbury, NY 11590

Editor: Geraldine Gambale

Description and Interests

Corporate decision makers responsible for choosing sites and planning facilities for expansion or relocation are the target audience of this magazine. Writers should not use promotional material. They should also avoid negative comments or comparisons of areas. Circ: 45,000.

Contents: 80% articles; 20% depts/columns
Frequency: 6 times each year
Website: www.areadevelopment.com

Freelance Potential

80% written by nonstaff writers. Publishes 25 freelance submissions yearly; 10% by authors who are new to the magazine, 20% by experts. Receives 6 queries, 1 unsolicited ms monthly.

Submissions

Query or send complete ms. Accepts hard copy and email to gerri@areadevelopment.com. SASE. Responds in 1 month.

- Articles: 1,200–2,400 words. Informational articles. Topics include labor costs, infrastructure, community relations, security, financing, government controls, legislation, and operating costs—all as they relate to relocating or expanding corporate facilities.
- Depts/columns: Word lengths vary. News, industry updates, and opinions.
- Artwork: JPEG or TIFF images at 300 dpi.

Sample Issue

88 pages. Advertising. Sample articles available at website. Writers' guidelines and editorial calendar available.

- "Finding a Strategic Location for Shared Services Operations." Risk management strategies to reduce uncertainty amid operational innovations.
- "An Urban Enterprise Zones Primer." The beneficial cost savings that accrue from locating in an enterprise zone.

Rights and Payment

Two-time rights. All material, payment rates vary. Pays after publication. Provides 1 contributor's copy.

Army Magazine

2425 Wilson Boulevard
Arlington, VA 22201

Editor in Chief: Mary Blake French

Description and Interests

Published by the Association of the United States Army, this magazine runs features about current and past military operations and aims to foster support for programs and personnel, both active and retired. It's interested in seeing photographs or artwork that may enhance the writer's article. The writer should also include headline suggestions. Circ: 80,000.

Contents: 60% articles; 40% depts/columns
Frequency: Monthly
Website: www.ausa.org

Freelance Potential

80% written by nonstaff writers. Publishes 50 freelance submissions yearly; 10% by unpublished writers, 30% by authors who are new to the magazine, 60% by experts. Receives 10 unsolicited mss monthly.

Submissions

Send complete ms with author bio. (Query for book reviews.) Accepts hard copy and email to armymag@ausa.org. No simultaneous submissions. Responds in 3 months.

- Articles: 1,000–1,500 words. Informational and how-to articles; photo essays; and personal experience and opinion pieces. Topics include the U.S. military, army history, weapons, and battles.
- Depts/columns: 750–1,000 words. Weapons, legislation, book reviews, and history.
- Artwork: EPS, TIFF, or JPEG images at 300 dpi.

Sample Issue

88 pages. Advertising. Sample articles and guidelines available at website.

- "Mission Command: Reflections from the Combined Arms Center Commander." How experience in Iraq and Afghanistan has changed mission command.
- "Toxic Leadership: What Are We Talking About?" Identifying and removing toxic leaders from the Army.

Rights and Payment

All rights. Written material, \$.12–\$.18 per word. Pays on publication. Provides 3 contributor's copies.

Art Education

1806 Robert Fulton Drive
Suite 300, Reston, VA 20191

Editor: Robert Sweeney

Description and Interests

Art Education is filled with an array of resources and ideas for art teachers working with students of all ages, in both school and community settings. It is published by the National Art Education Association. It seeks submissions that are relevant to everyday practice—whether in the classroom, museum, or community arts center. Circ: 23,000.

Contents: 100% articles; 0% depts/columns
Frequency: 6 times each year
Website: www.arteducators.org/research/art-education

Freelance Potential

90% written by nonstaff writers. Publishes 36 freelance submissions yearly; 40% by unpublished writers, 40% by authors who are new to the magazine. Receives 15 mss monthly.

Submissions

Accepts email to arteducationjournal@gmail.com. Include cover letter, title and information page. Restrict contact information to a separate sheet. No simultaneous submissions. Responds in 3+ months.

- Articles: To 3,000 words. Research-based informational articles; personal experience pieces; profiles; and interviews. Topics include education, the visual arts, curriculum planning, art history, and art criticism.
- Depts/columns: To 2,750 words. Instructional resources and lesson plans.
- Artwork: Photo file sizes of 50–100K and 72 dpi resolution.

Sample Issue

54 pages. Advertising. Guidelines available at website.

- "Seeking and Collecting at Home: Sharing Personal Histories in the Art Room." An installation project instills a sense of personal history and the ways that these histories can be used in a classroom setting.
- "Beyond Art Waitressing: Meaningful Engagement in Interactive Online Galleries." Interactive websites and galleries promote numerous platforms through which educators can convey their messages.

Rights and Payment

All rights. No payment. Provides 2 contributor's copies.

The Artist's Magazine

4700 East Galbraith Road
Cincinnati, OH 45220

Editor: Maureen Bloomfield

Description and Interests

Showcasing the best work in all media and styles, this magazine celebrates the artist as well as the art. It features informative and encouraging articles containing practical lessons in technique, along with interviews and news of exhibitions and events. The goal of the magazine is not that readers will be able to copy the work, but that they might learn something from other artists' techniques and strategies to improve their own art. Circ: 120,000.

Contents: 60% articles; 40% depts/columns
Frequency: 10 times each year
Website: www.artistsnetwork.com

Freelance Potential

70% written by nonstaff writers. Of the freelance submissions published yearly, 5% are by unpublished writers, 5% are by authors who are new to the magazine, 50% are by experts. Receives 50 queries monthly.

Submissions

Query with clips and slides or disk images of artist's work. Accepts hard copy. SASE. Responds in 6 months.

- Articles: 800–1,200 words. Informational and how-to articles; profiles; interviews; and new product information. Topics include the visual arts and artists.
- Depts/columns: Word lengths vary. Instructional pieces, business, marketing, art industry news, and opinion pieces.

Sample Issue

80 pages. Advertising. Sample articles and guidelines available at website. Theme list/editorial calendar available by calling 888-419-0421.

- "How to Draw People Using the Block-in Method." Achieving accurate proportions and realistic figures by using the block-in method and gridding.
- "Palette Knife Painting Techniques for 3D Objects." Representing three-dimensional objects using the knife-painting technique.

Rights and Payment

All rights. Articles, $400–$600. Depts/columns, payment rates vary. Kill fee, 25%. Pays on publication. Provides 2 contributor's copies.

Authorship

National Writers Association
10940 South Parker Road, #508
Parker, CO 80134

Editor: Sandy Whelchel

Description and Interests

This online magazine of the National Writers Association is read by members for its practical information on all aspects of the business of writing. Each issue features how-to articles, industry updates, and humor pieces. Poetry is accepted if it has a writing theme. Authors should not submit inspirational, "how I became a successful writer" pieces. What gets its attention are articles slanted toward aspects of fiction—creating characters and setting scenes, for example. Hits per month: 3,000+.

Contents: 60% articles; 39% depts/columns; 1% other
Frequency: Quarterly
Website: www.nationalwriters.com

Freelance Potential

90% written by nonstaff writers. Publishes 35 freelance submissions yearly; 35% by unpublished writers, 40% by authors who are new to the magazine, 30% by experts. Receives 15 unsolicited mss monthly.

Submissions

Send complete ms. Accepts hard copy, disk submissions (Word files), and simultaneous submissions if identified. SASE. Responds in 3 months.

- Articles: 800 words. Informational and how-to articles; profiles; and interviews. Topics include writing, editing, publishing, marketing, and business opportunities.
- Depts/columns: Staff-written.

Sample Issue

Sample copy and guidelines available.

- "Literary Agents in Love." Humorous article compares the methods editors use for rejecting manuscripts to turning down dates.
- "Stop Spending Your Promo Dollars on Throw-Away Marketing!" Article explores more effective marketing programs that utilize social networking.

Rights and Payment

First serial rights. Written material, $10. Pays on publication.

Aviation Maintenance

Aerospace & Security Media Ltd
5590 North Diversey Blvd, Apt. 209
Milwaukee,WI 53217

Editor in Chief: Joy Finnegan

Description and Interests

This industry magazine covers the news and changing landscape of aviation maintenance issues. It also publishes profiles of international aviation maintenance companies and industry trends. Its readers are professionals in the field, from aviation technicians to company leaders. *Aviation Maintenance* seeks writers who know their way around the topics and also have experience covering an international industry. Circ: 27,800.

Contents: 80% articles; 20% depts/columns
Frequency: 6 times each year
Website: www.avmain-mag.com

Freelance Potential

50% written by nonstaff writers. Publishes 35 freelance submissions yearly; 15% by authors who are new to the magazine, 85% by experts. Receives 3 queries monthly.

Submissions

Accepts email queries to news@avmain-mag.com. Responds in 1 week.

- Articles: Word lengths vary. Informational and how-to articles; technical reports; profiles; interviews; and new product information. Topics include aviation and aircraft maintenance and management.
- Depts/columns: Word lengths vary. News, government updates, safety, and tools.

Sample Issue

42 pages. Advertising. Sample articles and editorial calendar available at website. Writers' guidelines available.

- "New Promises in Paint." An automobile paint coating process lends efficiency, durability and weight reduction to the aerospace industry.
- "Aging Gracefully." Challenges of keeping older aircraft in the air.

Rights and Payment

All rights. Written material, $.35 per word. Pays on publication. Provides 3 contributor's copies.

AXS Longboard Retailer Magazine

1136 Center Street, Suite 293
Thornhill, Ontario L4J 3M8.

Editors/Publishers: Rick Tetz and Michael Brooke

Description and Interests

AXS Longboard Retailer was created to share valuable information about longboarding products; new ideas about the skateboard marketplace; and best practices with retailers, business owners, and managers. The readership is both in Canada and the U.S. Circ: 5,000.

Contents: 80% articles; 20% depts/columns
Frequency: Quarterly
Website: www.axsgear.com

Freelance Potential

Open to articles on longboards/skateboards.

Submissions

Guidelines available. Accepts articles through the website from registered users.

- Articles: Informational articles; how-to's and profiles. Topics include skateboard retailer business practices, marketing, management, new technology, and design.
- Depts/columns: Product reviews, news.

Sample Issue

Advertising. Sample articles available at website.

- "Xylan Longboards Light the Way." Discussion about the super-reflective technology behind the Xylan longboards.
- "Overcoming the Fear of Succeeding: Become an Entrepreneur." A conversation about entrepreneurship, including means stepping outside one's comfort zone and examining the many possibilities.

Rights and Payment

Rights, unavailable. Written material, payment rates and policy, unavailable.

Bankers Digest

P.O. Box 743006
Dallas, TX 75374-3006

Publisher & Editor: Bonnie Jamison Blackman

Description and Interests

News of the banking industry in the southwestern region of the U.S., including personnel changes, charter activities, and industry news, is covered in this publication. It focuses on the banking industry in Arizona, Arkansas, Louisiana, Mississippi, New Mexico, Oklahoma, and Texas. All material should be localized to these regions. Circ: 2,600.

Contents: 40% depts/columns; 30% articles; 30% other
Frequency: Weekly
Website: www.bankersdigest.com

Freelance Potential

90% written by nonstaff writers. Publishes 50 freelance submissions yearly; 10% by authors who are new to the magazine, 100% by experts. Receives 10 queries monthly.

Submissions

Send complete ms and accompanying photos. Accepts hard copy, disk submissions, and email submissions to bankersdigest@bankersdigest.com. SASE. Responds in 1 month.

- Articles: 200–400 words. Informational and how-to articles; profiles; interviews; opinion pieces; and new product information. Topics include banking management, technology, financial industry news, and bank association meetings and events.
- Depts/columns: Word lengths vary. Regional news, charter activity, and personal reports.
- Artwork: Digital images at 300 dpi.

Sample Issue

12 pages. Advertising. Sample article and guidelines available at website.

- "Safe Deposit." An accounting of safe deposit vaults that became fiery infernos after accidental fires.
- Sample dept/column: "News Highlights" reports on personnel changes in the region's banks.

Rights and Payment

All rights. No payment.

Bartender

P.O. Box 158
Liberty Corner, NJ 07938

Publisher & Editor: Ray Foley

Description and Interests

This magazine covers the behind-the-bar scene with features on cocktail creation and bartender how-to's. Unusual products and bar humor are also a big part of its content. Articles are fairly short, very tightly focused, and written in a light and fun style. It's always looking for cartoons and humor. Circ: 105,000.

Contents: 25% articles; 20% depts/columns; 31% recipes; 24% other
Frequency: Quarterly
Website: www.bartender.com

Freelance Potential

70% written by nonstaff writers. Publishes 6 freelance submissions yearly; 40% by unpublished writers, 30% by authors who are new to the magazine, 30% by experts. Receives 6 queries monthly.

Submissions

Query. Accepts queries via email form at website. Accepts hard copy. SASE. Responds in 1 month.

- Articles: To 1,000 words. Informational, self-help, and how-to articles; profiles; personal experience pieces; humor; and new product information. Topics include bartending, cocktails, wine, beer, and related news.
- Depts/columns: To 1,000 words. Cooking with spirits, drink recipes, bar tricks, new products, and trivia.
- Other: Cartoons, jokes, quotes, horoscopes.

Sample Issue

34 pages. Advertising. Sample issue and editorial calendar available.

- "In Tribute to LeRoy Neiman." Article shares the author's memories of this artist who recently passed.
- Sample dept/column: "LiBARy" reviews new books about bartending and liquor.

Rights and Payment

First rights. Written material, payment rates vary. Pays on publication. Provides contributor's copies.

BedTimes

501 Wythe Street
Alexandria, VA 22314-1917

Editor in Chief: Julie A. Palm

Description and Interests

BedTimes focuses on news, trends, management issues, and general business stories of interest to mattress manufacturers and their suppliers. It seeks contributors experienced in trade journalism, ideally with the bedding industry. It is particularly interested in articles that show mattress manufacturers ways to reduce costs and operate more efficiently. *BedTimes* is not a consumer or retail magazine. Circ: 4,000.

Contents: 75% articles; 25% depts/columns
Frequency: Monthly
Website: www.bedtimesmagazine.com

Freelance Potential

20–30% written by nonstaff writers. Publishes 25–40 freelance submissions yearly; 10–20% by authors who are new to the magazine, 30% by experts. Receives 10 queries monthly.

Submissions

Query with résumé and clips. Accepts email queries to jpalm@sleepproducts.org. Responds in 3 weeks.

- Articles: Word lengths vary. Informational articles; profiles; and interviews. Topics include mattress and bedding manufacturing, marketing, factory worker safety, mattress disposal and recycling, federal regulations, sleep research, and business management.
- Depts/columns: Word lengths vary. Plant Management, Marketing Report, Regulatory Update, Management Issues, Cost Management and Employee Relations, Sustainability Report.

Sample Issue

78 pages. Advertising. Sample copy, guidelines, and editorial calendar available at website.

- "Jamison Bedding." How a luxury consumer products marketer applied lessons learned to a new industry.
- "A New Way of Thinking: Strategies for Having Your Cake and Eating It, Too." Change unhealthy thought patterns to move forward.

Rights and Payment

All rights. Written material, payment rates vary. Pays on acceptance. Provides 1–3 author's copies.

Better Buildings 

120 Broadway
New York, NY 10271

Content Director: John Salustri

Description and Interests
The iconic magazine that defined best practices for the building operations industry in the New York tristate region in the 1980s has returned as a national publication. Included as a supplement in *Real Estate Forum*, its content focuses on energy management, capital improvements, engineering advancements, property upgrades, and design/construction innovations. Circ: 53,927.

Contents: Articles
Frequency: Quarterly
Website: www.reforum.com/betterbuildings/

Freelance Potential
Receives many freelance submissions monthly.

Submissions
Query or send complete ms. Accepts hard copy. SASE. Response time varies.

- Articles: Word lengths vary. Informational and how-to articles, profiles, and interviews. Topics include energy management, capital improvements, engineering advancements, property upgrades, design/construction innovations, property upgrades, adaptive reuse trends, and maintenance solutions.

Sample Issue
100 pages. Advertising. Sample copy available at website.

- "Getting Creative in the Lodging Space." Article discusses the pitfalls that face lodging companies including funding and the Euro crisis.
- "BOMA International: Advocates for the Private Sector." Article shares the company's viewpoint on government incentives for making commercial properties more efficient.
- "What Tenants Want." Article discusses the new tenant demands that have surfaced in today's competitive market.

Rights and Payment
Rights vary. Payment rates and policy vary.

Bicycle Retailer and Industry News

25431 Cabot Road, Suite 204
Laguna Hills, CA 92653

Editor: Lynette Carpiet

Description and Interests
Providing analysis and reporting on all aspects of the bicycle industry, this tabloid is read by manufacturers, distributors, and retailers alike. It covers industry trends, pricing, and new developments. It welcomes queries from journalists with experience covering an industry. It needs reporters who are capable of reporting trends and other news. Circ: 7,400.

Contents: 90% articles; 10% depts/columns
Frequency: 18 times each year
Website: www.bicycleretailer.com

Freelance Potential
10% written by nonstaff writers. Publishes 25–30 freelance submissions yearly; 5% by unpublished writers, 5% by industry experts. Receives 5 mss monthly.

Submissions
Accepts complete ms through form at website. Response time varies.

- Articles: 500–750 words. Informational articles; profiles; interviews; opinion pieces; and new product information. Topics include bicycle sales, business management, biking accessories and apparel, industry news, and new product development.
- Depts/columns: Staff-written.

Sample Issue
86 pages. Advertising. Sample articles available to view at website.

- "Events' Massive Popularity in Europe Bolsters Industry, Local Economies." Wiggle's expanding line-up of non-competitive, multi-distance rides.
- "Pedro's Emerges Leaner." The bike care and tool brand gets resuscitated with new inventory and more capital.

Rights and Payment
All rights. Written material, $.35 per word. Pays on acceptance. Provides 2 author's copies.

Biotechnology Healthcare

780 Township Line Road
Yardley, PA 19067

Managing Editor: Katherine T. Adams

Description and Interests

Biotechnology Healthcare reports on how biopharmaceuticals and molecular diagnostics are managed and used, and on their value to third-party payers and employer purchasers. Also features pieces on research. It welcomes articles by freelance business and medical writers within their subject areas. While many of its feature articles are commissioned, it is eager to receive pitches from bona fide experts in the field. Circ: 35,000.

Contents: 75% articles; 25% depts/columns
Frequency: 4 times each year
Website: www.biotechnologyhealthcare.com

Freelance Potential

80% written by nonstaff writers. Publishes 40 freelance submissions yearly; 5–10% by unpublished writers, 15% by new authors, 10% by experts. Receives 15 queries monthly.

Submissions

Query with bio or send complete ms. Accepts hard copy and email queries to kadams@medimedia.com (Word attachments). SASE. Responds in 2 weeks.

- Articles: 1,500–3,000 words. Informational articles; profiles; and interviews. Topics include medical services, cost management, benefit design, molecular diagnostics, late-stage drug development, health economics, and public policy.
- Depts/columns: Staff-written.

Sample Issue

50 pages. Advertising. Sample articles available at website.

- "Connecting Patients with Speciality Products," by Jack McCain. Distribuiton models for specialty pharmaceuticals.
- "Biologics and the Principles of Health Insurance." A review of basic insurance concepts and how they relate to coverage of biologics.

Rights and Payment

All rights. Written material, \$.75–\$.85 per word. Kill fee, \$300. Pays on acceptance. Provides 1+ contributor's copies.

BizTech

300 North Milwaukee Avenue
Vernon Hills, IL 60061

Editor in Chief: Ryan Peterson

Description and Interests

This magazine helps IT leaders and business managers leverage technology to reduce costs and increase business productivity. Each issue is filled with product reviews, tips, trend information, and case studies. Queries should only cover topics that are highly relevant to business. Writers should have a strong background in technology and have the ability to offer solutions and best practices. Circ: Unavailable.

Contents: 50% articles; 50% depts/columns
Frequency: Quarterly
Website: www.biztechmagazine.com

Freelance Potential

80% written by nonstaff writers. Publishes 65 freelance submissions yearly; 5% by authors who are new to the magazine, 75% by industry experts. Receives 8 queries monthly.

Submissions

Query. Accepts email queries to ryanpet@cdw.com. Responds in 1 month.

- Articles: 1,000–1,500 words. Informational and how-to articles; profiles; and interviews. Topics include technology, software, and business issues.
- Depts/columns: To 1,000 words. Trends, industry news, product reviews, case studies.

Sample Issue

48 pages. Sample copy available at website. Guidelines and editorial calendar available.

- "Businesses Save Money with New Technologies and Reinvest in Other Areas." Discussion of cloud computing, managed networking and managed print services.
- "Virtual Savings Equal Real Dollars." Cost savings to be had from virtualizing technologies.

Rights and Payment

First rights. Written material, payment rates vary. Kill fee varies. Pays on publication.

BOMB

80 Hanson Place, Suite 703
Brooklyn, NY 11217

Managing Editor: Sabine Russ

Description and Interests

This magazine of art and culture is about artists and written by artists. Interviews between artists of all genres, reviews of music, writing, film, and theater result in ongoing conversations between actors, directors, writers, musicians, and artists. Most of the material is by contract artists and writers, but submissions of poetry and fiction are welcome for *First Proof*, the magazine's annual literary supplement. Circ: 60,000.

Contents: 65% articles; 25% fiction and poetry; 10% depts/columns
Frequency: Quarterly
Website: www.bombsite.com

Freelance Potential

70% written by nonstaff writers. Publishes roughly 10 freelance submissions yearly. Receives 100 unsolicited mss monthly.

Submissions

The only unsolicited submissions accepted are for poetry and prose in its literary supplement, *First Proof*, from January 1 to August 31. Accepts hard copy only. SASE. Accepts simultaneous submissions. Responds in 4–6 months.

- Articles: Not accepting submissions.
- Fiction: To 20 pages. Literary, contemporary, and experimental fiction.
- Depts/columns: Not accepting submissions.
- Other: Poetry, no line limits.

Sample Issue

96 pages. Sample copy and guidelines available at website.

- "Louise Belcourt." A conversation with the painter.
- "Chris Andrews." Interview with the translator and poet.

Rights and Payment

All rights. Articles and depts/columns, payment rates vary. Fiction, $100. Poetry, payment rates vary. Pays on publication.

Book Dealers World

P.O. Box 606
Cottage Grove, OR 97424

Submissions Editor: Al Galasso

Description and Interests

For 30+ years, the mission of this magazine has been to help independent publishers market their books more cost effectively. Published by the National Association of Book Entrepreneurs, it is read by mail-order dealers, bookstores, publishers, libraries, teachers, and gift shops in the U.S., Canada, and abroad. It features articles on authors and publishers, and marketing strategies. All articles should offer solid information or insight into marketing books. Circ: 10,000+.

Contents: 50% articles; 25% depts/columns; 25% other
Frequency: 3 times a year
Website: www.bookmarketingprofits.com

Freelance Potential

80% written by nonstaff writers. Publishes 10 freelance submissions yearly; 30% by unpublished writers, 60% by authors who are new to the magazine, 10% by experts. Receives 6 queries, 3 unsolicited mss monthly.

Submissions

Query with clips or writing samples; or send complete ms. Accepts hard copy. SASE. Responds in 1 month.

- Articles: 1,000–1,500 words. Informational, how-to, and self-help articles; new product information; and interviews. Topics include writing, publishing, and marketing.
- Depts/columns: 500 words. Publisher profiles, book reviews, new product information, news, and events.
- Artwork: B/W prints.

Sample Issue

32 pages. Little advertising. Sample copy available at website.

- "Top 7 Ways to Market Your Book from the Comfort of Home." Leveraging Amazon, writing news releases and blogs and using social marketing tools to promote books.
- "How Self-Published Books Create Highly Profitable Businesses." Three examples of how self-publishing led to further business opportunities.

Rights and Payment

First rights. Articles, $25–$40. Depts/columns, $20. Artwork, payment rates vary. Pays on publication. Provides 1 contributor's copy.

California Lawyer

44 Montgomery Street, Suite 500
San Francisco, CA 94104

Editor: Martin Lasden

Description and Interests
Covering law-related topics of interest to lawyers in California, this journal keeps its readers abreast of regional and national trends. It also profiles leading personalities on the bench and bar, and combines pressing legal news with entertaining features. It seeks lively writing and in-depth reporting that goes beyond the headlines. It assigns an average three feature articles each month. Circ: 140,000.

Contents: 70% depts/columns; 30% articles
Frequency: Monthly
Website: www.callawyer.com

Freelance Potential
75% written by nonstaff writers. Publishes 80–90 freelance submissions yearly; 5% by unpublished writers, 15% by authors who are new to the magazine, 10% by experts. Receives 20 queries, 10 unsolicited mss monthly.

Submissions
Prefers query with clips; will accept complete ms with sources. Accepts email to martin_lasden@dailyjournal.com. Responds in 2–4 weeks.

- Articles: 1,500–4,000 words. Investigative and narrative features; profiles; and interviews. Topics include politics, legal affairs, legislation, government, social issues, legal technology, and corporate counsel trends.
- Depts/columns: 400–800 words. News items, current case law, case studies, essays, and reviews. Topics include the effect of technology on the practice of law, state and national politics, and business strategies.

Sample Issue
64 pages. Advertising. Sample copy available at website. Editorial calendar and writers' guidelines available at website.

- "Skirting Morrison." Discussion of the U.S. Supreme Court case ruling that federal securities laws don't apply to transactions on foreign exchanges.
- "Social Media: Clear and Current User Policies." Three settled FTC cases involving electronic privacy policies.

Rights and Payment
All rights. Articles, $1,500–$3,000. Depts/columns, $150–$450. Kill fee, 33%. Pays on acceptance. Provides 3 contributor's copies.

CBA Retailers + Resources

9240 Explorer Drive, Suite 200
Colorado Springs, CO 80920

Publications Director: Kathleen Samuelson

Description and Interests
Published by the Christian Bookseller's Association, this magazine is read by Christian retailers and suppliers as an information source for business ideas and strategies, marketing and merchandising techniques, new products, and human resource management. Its goal is to equip readers for business success and ministry. Most of the articles it publishes are written by experienced Christian retailers. Circ: 6,000.

Contents: 50% articles; 50% depts/columns
Frequency: Monthly
Website: www.cbaonline.org

Freelance Potential
40% written by nonstaff writers. Publishes 200 freelance submissions yearly; 1% by unpublished writers, 5% by authors who are new to the magazine, 80% by experts. Receives 3 queries monthly.

Submissions
Query with clips or writing samples. Accepts email queries to ksamuelson@cbaonline.org. Responds in 2 months.

- Articles: Word lengths vary. Informational and how-to articles; profiles; interviews; personal experience pieces; and new product information. Topics include Christian products, stores, and merchandising.
- Depts/columns: Word lengths vary. Book and product reviews, sales and marketing tips, merchandising, human resources, and technology.

Sample Issue
56 pages. Advertising. Sample copy available at website. Guidelines and theme list available.

- "Get a Flying Leap Over the Competition." Article provides an overview of topics and resources to be featured at CBA's upcoming conference for Christian retailers.
- Sample dept/column: "Entrepreneurs" reports on Christian bookstores that run side-by-side businesses that complement each other.

Rights and Payment
Worldwide print and electronic rights. Written material, $.30 per word. Pays on publication. Provides 1 contributor's copy.

CFO 

6 West 48th Street, 7th Floor
New York, NY 10036

Editorial Director: Kate O'Sullivan

Description and Interests

This magazine is designed to help today's CFOs stay on top of their ever-increasing responsibilities. The major content areas covered in each issue are accounting and tax, banking and capital markets, risk and compliance, human capital and careers, growth companies, strategy, and technology. Profiles and interviews round out the mix. At this time, most of its articles are written by staff or frequent contributors, but queries for white papers are being accepted. Circ: Unavailable.

Contents: 40% articles; 60% depts/columns
Frequency: Monthly
Website: www3.cfo.com

Freelance Potential

Open to white papers.

Submissions

Query. Accepts queries via website. Response time varies.

- Articles: Word lengths vary. Informational and how-to articles, profiles, and interviews. Topics include accounting, banking, capital markets, and risk and compliance.
- Depts/columns: Word lengths vary. Technology, strategies, risk management, company growth.

Sample Issue

Advertising. Sample articles available at website.

- "Whose Company Is It?" Article discusses a controversial book that has rekindled the debate over shareholder value and the purpose of the public corporation.
- "Latin America: A Sunnier Outlook." Article reveals results from a recent global business outlook survey of Latin American and Brazilian CFOs.
- Sample dept/column: Capital Markets discusses the increase in alternative lending for companies rejected by traditional banks.

Rights and Payment

Rights vary. Payment rates and policy.

Chief Executive

One Sound Shore Drive, Suite 100
Greenwich, CT 06830

Editor in Chief: J. P. Donlon

Description and Interests

This magazine and its ChiefExecutive.net website provide CEOs and business owners perspective of the strategic issues facing company CEOs, presidents, and chairmen. Articles address business strategy, trends, management, and finance, and also features profiles of CEOs. It welcomes articles from recognized experts, and strive to offer clear-eyed reporting of CEOs' successes and failures in ways that illuminate, educate, entertain, and inspire business leaders. Circ: 42,000.

Contents: 75% articles; 20% depts/columns; 5% other
Frequency: 6 times each year
Website: www.chiefexecutive.net

Freelance Potential

85% written by nonstaff writers. Publishes 50 freelance submissions yearly; 15% by authors who are new to the magazine, 25% by experts. Receives 720 queries yearly.

Submissions

Query with author background and relevant data and research to be used to illustrate key points. Include charts and graphs, where applicable. Accepts email to editorial@chiefexecutive.net. Responds in 2–3 weeks.

- Articles: To 2,000 words. Informational articles; profiles; interviews; and opinion pieces. Topics include business strategy and management, trends and developments in technology, marketing, and finance.
- Depts/columns: 600 words. Profiles, product reviews, industry news, and opinion pieces.
- Artwork: Digital images at 300 dpi.

Sample Issue

64 pages. Advertising. Guidelines and editorial calendar available at website.

- "Skilled Executive or Psychopath?" Psychopathic characteristics in the workplace.
- "Goldman Sachs: A Cautionary Tale in Branding." The gap between Goldman Sachs' image and reality.

Rights and Payment

First North American serial rights. Written material, payment rates vary. Payment policy varies. Provides 2 contributor's copies.

Children's Ministry

1515 Cascade Avenue
Loveland, CO 80539

Managing Editor: Jennifer Hooks

Description and Interests
Youth ministers, Sunday School teachers, and others who work to bring the Christian faith to children read this magazine for insights, ideas, and inspiration. It strives to offer its readers new ways to bring Jesus Christ's teaching to children, whether in the classroom, at home, or in the wider community. Circ: 65,000.

Contents: Articles; depts/columns
Frequency: 6 times each year
Website: www.childrensministry.com

Freelance Potential
60–80% written by nonstaff writers. Publishes 25–35 freelance submissions yearly; 60% by unpublished writers, 60% by authors who are new to the magazine. Receives 200 unsolicited mss monthly.

Submissions
Query or send complete ms. Prefers email to PuorgBus@group.com; will accept hard copy. SASE. Responds in 2–3 months.

- Articles: 500–1,700 words. Informational and how-to articles; and personal experience pieces. Topics include Christian education, family issues, child development, and faith.
- Depts/columns: 50–300 words. Educational issues, activities, devotionals, family ministry, parenting, crafts, and resources.
- Other: Activities, games, and tips. Submit seasonal material 6–8 months in advance.

Sample Issue
122 pages. Advertising. Sample articles available at website. Guidelines available.

- "Big Church Hurts." Big-church practices that encourage kids to self-distract and tune out.
- "Taking on the Child Sex Trade." The global epidemic of child sex trafficking.

Rights and Payment
All rights. Articles, 1,000–2,200 words, $75–$400. Depts/columns, $40–$75. Pays on acceptance. Provides 1 contributor's copy.

The Christian Ranchman

3011 FM 718
Newark, TX 76071

Editor: Dave Harvey

Description and Interests
Published by "Cowboys for Christ," this free tabloid-style newspaper is filled with religious inspiration and articles on faith that relate directly to those who live the life of a rancher. It also features poetry and personal essays on Christian themes. The publication reports on recent news and current programs of the organization, and provides chapter updates. It welcomes stories that relate the word of God to everyday cowboy life. Short features as well as poetry with a Christian theme are always needed. Circ: 15,000.

Contents: 35% articles; 20% depts/columns; 45% other
Frequency: 6 times a year
Website: www.cowboysforchrist.net

Freelance Potential
30% written by nonstaff writers. Publishes 25 freelance submissions yearly; 60% by unpublished writers, 45% by experts.

Submissions
Query or send complete ms. Accepts hard copy and email to ranchman@cowboysforchrist.net. SASE. Response time varies.

- Articles: Word lengths vary. Informational and inspirational articles; and personal experience pieces. Topics include Christianity, raising livestock, and the ranching life.
- Depts/columns: Word lengths vary. Chapter updates, prayers, and the Bible.
- Other: Poetry with Christian themes.

Sample Issue
16 pages. No advertising. Sample copy available at website.

- "The Cowboy and the Cross." The origins of the cowboy and cross logo.
- "A Beautiful Spirit." The loving spirit of a stallion named Pretty Boy.

Rights and Payment
All rights. No payment.

Claims Journal 

Wells Publishing Inc.
3570 Camino del Rio North, Suite 200
San Diego, CA 92108

Editor in Chief: Andrea Ortego-Wells

Description and Interests

Professionals in the property/casualty insurance industry read this magazine for its detailed coverage of fraud research and investigation, coverage analysis, management advice, and industry statistics and trends. Circ: 20,000.

Contents: Articles; depts/columns
Frequency: Quarterly
Website: www.claimsjournal.com

Freelance Potential

Receives many freelance submissions monthly.

Submissions

Query with outline. Accepts email to awells@insurancejournal.com. Queries should include details on why the reader needs to know about the proposed topic. Response time varies.

- Articles: Word lengths vary. Informational and how-to articles. Topics include property and casualty insurance, fraud research and investigations, coverage analysis for claims personnel, management advice, and industry statistics and trends.
- Depts/columns: Word lengths vary. Industry news, events calendar, reviews.

Sample Issue

Advertising. Sample copy available at website.

- "Study Finds Drivers Unaware of Their Texting Habits." Article discusses research that shows most drivers don't realize they are texting while driving.
- "Timing Crucial in Product Failure Liability Investigations." Article stresses the importance of hiring a cause and origin expert early in the process of a product failure liability investigation.
- "Navigating the Rental Car Insurance Industry." Article explains the different insurance options for various situations.

Rights and Payment

Rights vary. Payment rates and policy vary.

Classical Singer

P.O. Box 1710
Draper, UT 84020-1710

Editor: Sara Thomas

Description and Interests

Professional singers and those hoping to become vocal artists look to *Classical Singer* for career advice and inspiration. Its goal is to give emerging artists and those who teach them the latest news and trends in the arts. Circ: 8,000.

Contents: 65% articles; 35% depts/columns
Frequency: 10 times a year
Website: www.classicalsinger.com

Freelance Potential

90% written by nonstaff writers. Of the freelance submissions yearly, 15% are by unpublished writers, 30% are by authors who are new to the magazine, 40% are by experts. Receives 10 unsolicited mss monthly.

Submissions

Send complete ms with 3-line biography. Availability of artwork improves chance of acceptance. Accepts email to sara@classicalsinger.com (Word attachments). Responds in 1 month.

- Articles: Cover stories to 3,300–3,800 words. Features, 1,500–2,000 words. Informational articles; profiles; and interviews. Topics include singers, conductors, and stage directors; singing; auditioning; voice coaching and teaching; music; opera; theater; and laryngology.
- Depts/columns: Word lengths vary. Auditioning, travel tips, singers from the past.
- Artwork: Color JPEGs at 300 dpi.

Sample Issue

52–134 pages. Advertising. Sample copy and editorial calendar available at website. Writers' guidelines available.

- "Early and Often." Gregory Spears' *Requiem* amid the context of early and contemporary music.
- "The Entrepreneurial Career: Fundraising 2.0." Raising money online.

Rights and Payment

All rights. Written material, $.05 per word; $50 minimum. Pays on publication. Provides 5 contributor's copies.

Cloud Computing Magazine

800 Connecticut Avenue, 1st Floor East
Norwalk, CT 06854

Group Editorial Director: Erik Linask

Description and Interests

Cloud Computing Magazine aims to be the IT industry's definitive source for all things cloud—from public, community, hybrid, and private cloud resources, to security and the business continuity, and everything in between. Each issue covers the latest advances and the leaders at the forefront of this technology. The magazine analyzes innovative tactics, critical information technology, and proven techniques. Circ: Unavailable.

Contents: Articles; depts/columns
Frequency: Quarterly
Website: www.cloud-computing.tmcnet.com

Freelance Potential

Freelance percentage not currently available.

Submissions

Query. Accepts email to elinask@tmcnet.com. Response time varies.

- Articles: Word lengths vary. Informational and how-to articles. Topics include cloud computing developments, technology, IT leaders, analysis of tactics, critical information technology, challenges and solutions.
- Depts/columns: Word lengths vary. Cloud security, management, integration, and compliance.

Sample Issue

Advertising. Sample copy available at website.

- "The Future of Mobile Cloud." Article discusses the transition of cloud services as more mobile enterprises adopt them.
- "Prevailing Against the Challenges of PCI Compliance in the Cloud." Article explains how to select and deploy PCI security controls for cloud server environments.
- Sample dept/column: Cloud Security reveals the 7 deadly sins that will jeapordize security.

Rights and Payment

Rights vary. Payment rates and policy vary.

Club & Resort Business

175 Strafford Avenue, Suite 1
Wayne, PA 19087

Editor: Joe Barks

Description and Interests

This business magazine targets the operations and management staff of private clubs and resorts, delivering articles on issues relating to running a successful, efficient business. Topics include design, technology, grounds, and food and beverage service. The best articles will offer useful ideas and creative solutions to the challenges faced by the publication's readers. Circ: 23,000.

Contents: 60% articles; 40% depts/columns
Website: www.clubandresortbusiness.com

Freelance Potential

40% written by nonstaff writers. Publishes 25 freelance submissions yearly; 5% by authors who are new to the magazine. Receives 2 queries monthly.

Submissions

Query with résumé and clips. Accepts hard copy and email to jbarks@clubandresortbusiness.com. SASE. Responds in 1–3 months.

- Articles: 1,200–1,700 words. Informational articles; profiles; and interviews. Topics include management, environmental issues, and recreation—as it relates to resorts.
- Depts/columns: Staff-written.

Sample Issue

64 pages. Advertising. Sample articles available. Editorial calendar available at website.

- "View from the Top." Article shares best practices from some of the leading-edge properties across the country.
- "Finer with Age" Article profiles the recent clubhouse renovations at the Monroe Golf Club.

Rights and Payment

All rights; rights relinquished after 6 months if material is not published. Written material, $500. Kill fee, 25%. Pays on acceptance. Provides 1 contributor's copy.

CM Cleanfax

19 British American Boulevard West
Latham, NY 12110-1405

Senior Editor: Jeff Cross

Description and Interests

This magazine publishes practical advice and solutions that will help those in the upholstery cleaning and restoration professions. Its content is focused on business management and technical know-how with the aim of increasing readers' profits and efficiency. It prefers to work with consultants and experts within the industry. Circ: 25,000+.

Contents: 30% articles; 20% depts/columns; 50% other
Frequency: Monthly
Website: www.cleanfax.com

Freelance Potential

70% written by nonstaff writers. Publishes 100 freelance submissions yearly; 5% by unpublished writers, 50% by authors who are new to the magazine, 65% by experts. Receives 1 unsolicited ms monthly.

Submissions

Send complete ms. Accepts hard copy and email submissions to jcross@ntpmedia.com (Word attachments). SASE. Responds in 2 weeks.

- Articles: To 1,000 words. Informational and how-to articles. Topics include professional carpet and upholstery cleaning, fire and water damage restoration, equipment, technology, and business management issues.
- Depts/columns: 800 words. News and trends, trade association updates.
- Artwork: B/W or color prints, slides, or transparencies; high-resolution digital images. Tables and diagrams.

Sample Issue

48 pages. Advertising. Sample copy available at website. Guidelines and theme list available.

- "Profitability Disasters." How personal beliefs and decision-making affect profitability.
- "Commercial Carpet Maintenance." Three encapsulation techniques that produce better results.

Rights and Payment

All rights. All material, payment rates vary. Payment policy varies. Provides up to 10 contributor's copies.

Coal People Magazine

P.O. Box 6247
Charleston, WV 25362

Managing Editor: Christina Karawan

Description and Interests

This magazine's focus is on the worldwide coal and energy industry and its people. Its content blends human interest stories with business management, news, and technology. It is always interested in hearing about specific mining practices and sites. Different aspects of the industry are highlighted each month. It appreciates articles written in the first person. Circ: 14,500.

Contents: 40% articles; 30% depts/columns; 20% fiction; 10% other
Frequency: 10 times each year
Website: www.coalpeople.com

Freelance Potential

50% written by nonstaff writers. Publishes 30 freelance submissions yearly; 20% by unpublished writers, 50% by authors who are new to the magazine, 60% by experts. Receives 15 queries monthly.

Submissions

Send complete ms (MS Word) with identified and captioned images, if available, contact details, and brief bio. Accepts email to cpm@ntelos.net. Responds in 3 months.

- Articles: 2,500 words. Informational articles; personal experience and opinion pieces; profiles; interviews; and humor. Topics include coal mining and the energy industry.
- Fiction: To 2,500 words. Stories with coal mining themes.
- Depts/columns: 500 words. News, coal mining industry personalities, event reports, new product information.

Sample Issue

62 pages. Advertising. Sample copy and editorial calendar available at website.

- "Shale Gas Operations: Freshwater Impoundments Under Scrutiny." Legal issues raised by horizontal well drilling in shale gas operations.
- "Arch Coal Leer Mine Will be a World-Class Mining Complex." Arch Coal's plans to develop a metallurgical coal mine and prep plant complex in north-central West Virginia.

Rights and Payment

First rights. Written material, $150–$250. Pays on publication. Provides 1 copy.

Comstock's

1006 Fourth Street, 3rd Floor
Sacramento, CA 95814

Editor in Chief: Douglas Curley

Description and Interests

Business leaders in the Capital Region of California turn to this publication for an in-depth look at business practices, opportunities, and personalities. It also covers local government and pertinent legal issues. While it doesn't want opinion pieces, it does like articles to have a specific angle and to make some sort of case. It strives for accurate, intelligent writing that is not overly technical. Circ: 18,000.

Contents: 30% articles; 10% depts/columns; 60% other
Frequency: Monthly
Website: www.comstocksmag.com

Freelance Potential

80% written by nonstaff writers. Publishes 120 freelance submissions yearly; 10% by unpublished writers, 25% by authors who are new to the magazine, 10% by experts. Receives 1 query monthly.

Submissions

Query. Accepts hard copy and email queries to dcurley@comstocksbusiness.com. SASE. Response time varies.

- Articles: Word lengths vary. Informational articles; profiles; interviews; and personal experience pieces. Topics include business issues and leaders in California's Capital Region.
- Depts/columns: Word lengths vary. News; profiles; and financial, legal, and medical issues.

Sample Issue

82 pages. Advertising. Sample copy and editorial calendar available at website. Guidelines available.

- "Picking Up Speed." The rebound in auto sales.
- Curd Your Enthusiasm." Cheesemaking caters to consumers' growing taste for artisanal cheeses.

Rights and Payment

First serial rights. Written material, payment rates vary. Pays 30 days after publication. Provides 1 contributor's copy.

Convenience Distribution

2750 Prosperity Avenue, Suite 530
Fairfax, VA 22031

Editor & Associate Publisher: Joan R. Fay

Description and Interests

This trade journal targets distributors of convenience goods (tobacco, snacks, candy, beverages) with industry news, market trends, management topics, and new product information. Writers must have experience covering this industry in order to be considered for assignments. Circ: 11,000.

Contents: 80% articles; 20% depts/columns
Frequency: 10 times each year
Website: www.conveniencedistribution-magazine.com

Freelance Potential

75% written by nonstaff writers. Publishes 50 freelance submissions yearly; 5% by authors who are new to the magazine.

Submissions

All articles are assigned. Send résumé with 2 writing samples and list of references. Accepts hard copy or email to joanf@awmanet.org. SASE. Responds in 1 month.

- Articles: 150–3,600 words. Informational and how-to articles; profiles; and new product information. Topics include the marketing and distribution of candy, tobacco, groceries, food services, and general merchandise; wholesalers; convenience stores; equipment; industry trends; customer relations; legislation; and association news and events.
- Depts/columns: Most are staff-written. Word lengths vary. Business and association news, management advice, supplier profiles, technology updates, and product reports.

Sample Issue

90 pages. Advertising. Sample copy, guidelines and editorial calendar available at website.

- "Tobacco Policy Update." A look at how roll-your-own machines threaten convenience store business, tobacco tax increases, and the future of dissolvables.
- "GAO Issues Report on Tobacco Taxes." Report on a GAO recommendation to equalize taxes on tobacco products.

Rights and Payment

All rights. Written material, $.50 per word. Kill fee, 50%. Pays on acceptance. Provides contributor's copies upon request.

Convention South

P.O. Box 2267
Gulf Shores, AL 36547

Editor: Mariane Bundock

Description and Interests

Convention South serves the meetings industry with information that keeps planners abreast of convention opportunities in the southeastern region of the U.S. City profiles and management issues are also included. How-to's and articles that can help readers with site selection are its biggest needs. Circ: 18,000.

Contents: 70% articles; 30% depts/columns
Frequency: Monthly
Website: www.conventionsouth.com

Freelance Potential

75% written by nonstaff writers. Publishes 75 freelance submissions yearly; 10% by authors who are new to the magazine, 90% by industry experts. Receives 4 queries, 4 unsolicited mss monthly.

Submissions

Query or send complete ms. Accepts hard copy, disk submissions, and email queries to info@conventionsouth.com. SASE. Responds in 1 month.

- Articles: Word lengths vary. Informational and how-to articles; profiles; and new product information. Topics include meeting planning, meeting sites, convention bureaus, civic centers, theme parties, recreation, and business issues.
- Depts/columns: Word lengths vary. Industry news, destination spotlights.
- Artwork: B/W or color prints, or color transparencies.

Sample Issue

50 pages. Advertising. Sample copy available at website. Editorial calendar available at website.

- "Riveting Resorts: X Factors that Seal the Deal." Some of the unique traits of full-service resorts that set them apart from one another.
- "Spark Interest & Pin It: How the Social Media Site Pinterest Builds a Buzz for Meetings." How Pinterest can be used to enhance exposure as part of your marketing strategies.

Rights and Payment

All rights. Written material, payment rates vary. Pays on publication. Provides 2 copies.

Corn & Soybean Digest

7900 International Drive, Suite 650
Minneapolis, MN 55425

Editor: Kurt Lawton

Description and Interests

This magazine covers issues of importance to the profitability of corn and soybean farmers. Many articles cover farm and business management, agronomy, related trends, pricing, and production techniques. Its ideal writer is experienced in row-crop agriculture and is a strong photographer and writer. It looks for any topic that will help its readers increase production and profit. Circ: 147,000.

Contents: 80% articles; 20% depts/columns
Frequency: 11 times each year
Website: www.cornandsoybeandigest.com

Freelance Potential

50% written by nonstaff writers. Publishes 50 freelance submissions yearly; 10% by authors who are new to the magazine, 5% by experts. Receives 5 queries monthly.

Submissions

Query. Accepts hard copy and email queries to klawton@csdigest.com. SASE. Responds in 2 weeks.

- Articles: 500–1,000 words. Informational and how-to articles; profiles; and interviews. Topics include corn and soybean production, agricultural techniques, farm management, and crop marketing.
- Depts/columns: Word lengths vary.

Sample Issue

56 pages. Sample articles available at website. Guidelines and editorial calendar available.

- "Eye on Crops." A review of current weather conditions, activity in corn and soybean fields, and local closing bids.
- "Are Nematodes Causing Stunted, Yellowing or White Corn?" Discussion of symptoms of nematode damage to corn crops, how to conduct field sampling, and management options.

Rights and Payment

All rights. Written material, $1 per edited word. Pays on acceptance. Provides 1 contributor's copy.

Country Folks

6113 State Highway 5
P.O. Box 121
Palatine Bridge, NY 13428

Editor: Joan Kark-Wren

Description and Interests

This regional publication offers farmers articles on farm management, crops, livestock, and farm family life. It publishes 4 regional editions that cover the east coast from North Carolina to Maine. Because this newspaper is its readers' weekly connection to agriculture, it wants submissions that reflect the most current regional news, concerns, and events. Circ: 14,000.

Contents: 80% articles; 20% depts/columns
Frequency: Weekly
Website: www.countryfolks.com

Freelance Potential

75% written by nonstaff writers. Publishes 50 freelance submissions yearly; 5% by unpublished writers, 5% by authors who are new to the magazine, 5% by experts. Receives 5 queries monthly.

Submissions

Query with résumé and writing samples. Accepts hard copy and email to jkarkwren@leepub.com. SASE. Responds in 2–4 weeks.

- Articles: Word lengths vary. Informational and how-to articles; personal experience pieces; profiles; and interviews. Topics include family farming, agriculture, and livestock.
- Depts/columns: Word lengths vary. Futures, dairy farming, and beef production.

Sample Issue

32 pages. Advertising. Sample copy, guidelines, and editorial calendar available.

- "Raising Premium Pork at Foosteps Farm." Profile of the Certified Humane producer of grass-fed pork, heirloom beef, and poulty in Stonington, Connecticut.
- "Older vs. Better Cows: Age May Not Trump Herd Improvement." Why cross-breeding to make reproductive improvements may not be the best choice.

Rights and Payment

First rights. Written material, $2.50 per column inch. Pays on publication. Provides 1 contributor's copy.

Country Folks Grower

6113 State Highway 5
P.O. Box 121
Palatine Bridge, NY 13428

Editor: Joan Kark-Wren

Description and Interests

This trade newspaper is published in 3 regional editions, Eastern, Midwest, and West. It covers topics for greenhouses, nurseries, fruit and vegetable growers, direct marketers, and gardening centers. It wants articles that reflect the most current news, products, and events in this field. It also expects material to relate to the region. Circ: 35,000.

Contents: 80% articles; 20% depts/columns
Frequency: Monthly
Website: www.cfgrower.com

Freelance Potential

75% written by nonstaff writers. Publishes 50 freelance submissions yearly; 5% by unpublished writers, 5% by authors who are new to the magazine, 5% by experts. Receives 5 queries monthly.

Submissions

Query or send complete ms. Accepts hard copy and email to jkarkwren@leepub.com. SASE. Responds in 2–4 weeks.

- Articles: Word lengths vary. Informational and how-to articles; profiles; and interviews. Topics include fruit and vegetable equipment, irrigation, pest control, packaging, specialty crops, and greenhouses.
- Depts/columns: Word lengths vary. New products and supplies, trade shows.

Sample Issue

60 pages. Advertising. Sample copy, editorial calendar, and guidelines available at website.

- "Winter Greenhouse Thrives in the Northwoods of Wisconsin." A look at the greenhouse's hardy perennials, display gardens and miniature gardens.
- "Food Modernization Act Implemented." Mandated safety standards for production of fresh produce in Ohio.

Rights and Payment

First rights. Written material, payment rates vary. Pays upon publication. Provides 1 contributor's copy.

Credit Today

P.O. Box 20091
Roanoke, VA 24018

Publisher: Rob Lawson

Description and Interests

Providing "tomorrow's tools for today's credit professionals," *Credit Today* is a subscriber-based, business-to-business website that features in-depth reporting on the issues, news, and trends that affect the industry. It seeks articles that educate and empower its readers to excel in the credit, customer service, and business industries. Circ: Unavailable.

Contents: 80% articles; 10% depts/columns; 10% other
Frequency: Monthly
Website: www.credittoday.net

Freelance Potential

80% written by nonstaff writers. Publishes 60 freelance submissions yearly; 10% by unpublished writers, 10% by authors who are new to the magazine, 10% by industry experts. Receives 2 queries monthly.

Submissions

Query. Accepts email to editor@credittoday.net. Responds in 1 month.

- Articles: 700–1,400 words. Informational and how-to articles; new product information; personal experience pieces; profiles; and interviews. Topics include credit management, sales, risk, debt collection, payment policies, legal issues, technology, staffing issues, and industry news and trends.
- Depts/columns: Staff-written.

Sample Issue

16 pages. No advertising. Sample articles and guidelines available at website.

- "2012 Credit Group Survey, Part 3: Relating the Extraordinary Value of Credit Groups." A look at the value of credit group participation and how to motivate a non-group member to participate.
- "Energizing a Credit Staff's Potential." A new manager helps a credit staff reach its full potential.

Rights and Payment

All rights. Written material, payment rates vary. Pays on acceptance. Provides 2–3 author's copies.

Cutting Tool Engineering

40 Skokie Boulevard, Suite 450
Northbrook, IL 60062-1698

Editor: Alan Richter

Description and Interests

This magazine's emphasis is on the purchase, use, and maintenance of cutting and grinding equipment, tools, and related accessories. Most of its readers are in the automotive, aerospace, or medical industries. It likes articles with a narrow focus that provide relevant technical detail and a complete explanation of a subject. Mentioning a specific product is acceptable, as long as it is not in a promotional sense. Circ: 40,000.

Contents: 60% articles; 30% depts/columns; 10% other
Frequency: Monthly
Website: www.ctemag.com

Freelance Potential

40% written by nonstaff writers. Publishes 10 freelance submissions yearly; 10% by authors who are new to the magazine, 90% by experts. Receives 5 queries, 3 unsolicited mss monthly.

Submissions

Query with outline or abstract. Accepts email submissions to alanr@jwr.com (Word or RTF). Availability of artwork improves chance of acceptance. Responds in 1 month.

- Articles: 1,500–2,000 words. Informational and how-to articles; and new product information. Topics include management, maintenance, technology, and tools.
- Depts/columns: Staff-written.
- Artwork: B/W or color JPEG, TIFF, or EPS images at 260–300 dpi.

Sample Issue

84 pages. Advertising. Sample copy and editorial calendar available at website. Guidelines available.

- "Quality Countdown." An industry veteran identifies the top 10 factors in maintaining and improving quality control in parts manufacturing.
- "Linear Motion via Ballscrew Drives." Discussion of the screw-and-ballnut design used in machine tool axes.

Rights and Payment

All rights. Written material with artwork, $.50 per word. Kill fee, $100. Pays on publication. Provides 3 contributor's copies.

Dairy Goat Journal

145 Industrial Drive
Medford, WI 54451

Editor: Jennifer Stultz

Description and Interests

Dairy Goat Journal provides news, information, and instructional articles about the dairy industry for dairy goat owners around the world. Raising, breeding, and caring for dairy goats are covered here, and successful goat farmers are profiled. Writers with experience in the industry are preferred. It seeks articles that tell them something new and interesting about dairy goat farming. Interviews and profiles are always of interest. Circ: 10,000.

Contents: 70% articles; 30% depts/columns
Frequency: 6 times each year
Website: www.dairygoatjournal.com

Freelance Potential

45% written by nonstaff writers. Publishes 100+ freelance submissions yearly; 10% by unpublished writers, 20% by authors who are new to the magazine, 50% by experts. Receives 10 queries monthly.

Submissions

Query or send complete ms. Accepts hard copy and email to csyeditorial@tds.net. SASE. Responds in 2 weeks.

- Articles: 750–2,500 words. Informational, how-to, and self-help articles; profiles; and interviews. Topics include farming, agriculture, cheesemaking, dairying, feeding, cooking, herd health and safety, business management, and goat herd ownership.
- Depts/columns: Word lengths vary. Veterinary issues and news.

Sample Issue

58 pages. Advertising. Sample articles available for view at website.

- "Cheese Maker Loves Flavor." Kansas couple experiments with cheese using both cow and goat milk.
- "Fish Oil Makes Goat Cheese Healthier." Adding fish oil to goat cheese doesn't compromise taste or shelf life.

Rights and Payment

First rights. Written material, $50–$100. Pays on publication.

Data Center Management

742 East Chapman Avenue
Orange, CA 92866

Managing Editor: Karen Riccio

Description and Interests

Written for data center management professionals and members of AFCOM, this professional trade magazine keeps readers abreast of news and trends in the industry. In addition, it offers profiles of industry leaders and articles on the latest strategies in data storage and center management. It looks for writers who have experience in the field of data storage, and can cover the issues and technology with authority. Circ: 4.500.

Contents: 50% articles; 50% depts/columns
Frequency: 6 times each year
Website: www.afcom.com

Freelance Potential

80% written by nonstaff writers. Publishes 40 freelance submissions yearly; 10% by authors who are new to the magazine, 70–80% by industry experts. Receives 25 queries monthly.

Submissions

Query with abstract. Accepts email queries to editor@afcom.com. Responds in 1 month.

- Articles: 2,000 words. Informational and how-to articles; personal experience and opinion pieces; profiles; and interviews. Topics include data center technology, management, security, and troubleshooting.
- Depts/columns: 800 words.

Sample Issue

52 pages. Advertising. Sample articles available at website. Guidelines and editorial calendar available.

- "Courting Disaster: Denial is NOT an Option." Disaster recovery and busines continuity in the face of physical disasters, cyber-attacks, or data breach.
- "Defraying Costs with Energy Rebates." Understanding the eligibility requirements for state and federal energy efficiency incentives and rebates.

Rights and Payment

All rights. Written material, $.50–$.75 per word. Pays on publication. Provides 2–3 author's copies.

Dermascope

310 East Interstate 30, Suite B107
Garland, TX 75043

Editor: Amy McKay

Description and Interests

Dermascope Magazine, the publication of the Aesthetics International Association, refers to itself as "the encyclopedia of aesthetics and spa therapy." It strives to keep readers informed on all aspects of the industry, including trends, research, and new products. Articles should be educational and thorough, but not promote specific products or procedures. Circ: 16,000.

Contents: 70% depts/columns; 30% articles
Frequency: Monthly
Website: www.dermascope.com

Freelance Potential

75% written by nonstaff writers. Publishes 70 freelance submissions yearly; 5% by unpublished writers, 20% by authors who are new to the magazine, 90% by experts. Receives 8 queries monthly.

Submissions

Send complete ms with brief author bio, professional color head shot, one- or two-sentence quote/tease about the article, three to five review questions, signed copyright waiver agreement, and artwork. Accepts email submissions to amckay@dermascope.com. Responds in 2 months. No simultaneous submissions or reprints.

- Articles: 1,500–2,500 words. Informational and how-to articles; profiles; interviews; media reviews; and new product information. Topics include medical procedures, diet, skin care, massage, makeup, health, fitness, careers, and education.
- Depts/columns: 180–1,200 words. Financial advice, book reviews, makeup, new products, and salons.
- Artwork: Color high-resolution digital images at 300 dpi; JPEG, TIFF, PSD, or EPS format.

Sample Issue

130 pages. Advertising. Sample articles, guidelines, and editorial calendar available at website.

- "Annette Hanson, Aesthetician, Author, Educator, and Entrepreneur. Profile of a New York skin care expert.
- "Do Not Let the Sun Go to Your Head!" A primer on sun care protection and brands.

Rights and Payment

All rights. No payment. Provides 1 contributor's copy.

Desktop Engineering

1283 Main Street
P.O. Box 1039
Dublin, NH 03444

Managing Editor: Jamie Gooch

Description and Interests

This professional magazine targets design engineering teams with information on design, simulation, and prototyping technologies. It features application stories, product reviews and reports on news and trends affecting the computer design industry. Its readers are not necessarily computer geeks, but they are very tech savvy and need to be kept abreast of the computer-based tools and technology they must use in their jobs. Circ: 60,000.

Contents: 75% articles; 25% depts/columns
Frequency: Monthly
Website: www.deskeng.com

Freelance Potential

85% written by nonstaff writers. Publishes 60 freelance submissions yearly; 10% by unpublished writers, 10–15% by authors who are new to the magazine, 80% by industry experts. Receives 10 queries monthly.

Submissions

Query with detailed outline that includes: working title, summary, graphic elements, and short author bio. Accepts email queries to jgoochs@deskeng.com. Responds in 2 weeks if interested.

- Articles: 800–1,200 words. Informational and how-to articles; case studies; profiles; interviews; and new product information. Topics include leading-edge computer technologies, computer platforms, operating systems, applications, engineering software, and peripherals.
- Depts/columns: 500–1,000 words. Short news items, commentaries, and product reviews.

Sample Issue

48 pages. Advertising. Sample copy and guidelines available at website.

- "Opting for Optimization, Part 2." A formidable concept can boost analysis tools.
- "Support for Women in Engineering." Encouraging young adults to pursue careers in STEM.

Rights and Payment

First North American serial rights. Written material, payment rates vary. Kill fee, 30–40%. Pays on publication. Provides 2 author's copies.

Distributed Energy

P.O. Box 3100
Santa Barbara, CA 93130

Editor: Elizabeth Cutright

Description and Interests

Distributed Energy is "the journal of energy efficiency and reliability." It is written to help professionals address concerns regarding power interruptions and to explore solutions for increasing energy self-reliance. How-to articles, interviews, opinion pieces, and new product information are all featured. Its readers are responsible for evaluating, planning, engineering, maintaining, and developing their company's local, onsite power capabilities. Circ: 20,000+.

Contents: Articles; depts/columns
Frequency: 7 times each year
Website: www.distributedenergy.com

Freelance Potential

90% written by nonstaff writers. Publishes 50 freelance submissions yearly; 25% by authors who are new to the magazine, 10% by industry experts. Receives 5 queries, 1 unsolicited ms each month.

Submissions

Query or send complete ms. Accepts submissions via website. Include description, word count, and photos, if available. Graphics enhance submissions. Response time varies.

- Articles: Word lengths vary. Informational and how-to articles; interviews; new product information; and opinion pieces. Topics include distributed energy, onsite power generation-related activities, engineering, construction, maintenance, management, technology, business, and conservation.
- Depts/columns: Word lengths vary. New product reviews.

Sample Issue

66 pages. Advertising. Sample copy and guidelines available at website.

- "Signed, Sealed, Delivered." Improving energy efficiency by creating a better sealed building envelope.
- "Missing Link." The importance of energy storage when it comes to efficiency, the grid and renewable energy.

Rights and Payment

All rights. Written material, payment rates vary. Payment policy varies.

DOTmed Business News

29 Broadway, Suite 2500
New York, NY 10006

Editor in Chief: Sean Ruck

Description and Interests

This trade magazine is written for CEOs, directors, and other decision makers in the hospital and healthcare fields. It offers industry news, technological advances, medical issues, economics, and other concerns of upper management in the healthcare field. A background in medical writing is preferred, but not required, for this magazine. Circ: 37,500.

Contents: 60% articles; 40% depts/columns
Frequency: Monthly
Website: www.dotmed.com

Freelance Potential

20% written by nonstaff writers. Publishes 30 freelance submissions yearly; 5% by unpublished writers, 5% by authors who are new to the magazine, 5% by experts. Receives 20 queries, 5 unsolicited mss monthly.

Submissions

Query. Accepts email queries to news@dotmed.com. Responds in 2 months.

- Articles: 1,500–3,000 words. Informational and how-to articles; profiles; interviews; personal experience; opinion pieces; and new product information. Topics include business, science and technology, medical services and care, health management, education, equipment, and maintenance.
- Depts/columns: 500–1,200 words. News briefs, business, legal updates, medical history, and product reviews.

Sample Issue

66 pages. Advertising. Sample copy available at website. Guidelines and editorial calendar available.

- "After a Rough Year, PET Stands to Shine." PET rubidium generators, used to detect coronary artery disease, emerge from recall.
- "Expert Tips for Getting the Most Out of SPECT Equipment." Extending the lifespan of expensive SPECT equipment.

Rights and Payment

First rights. Articles, $150–$250. Depts/columns, $100–$150. Kill fee, $50. Pays on publication. Provides 1–5 contributor's copies.

Ed Tech: Focus on Higher Education

230 North Milwaukee Avenue
Vernon Hills, IL 60061

Editor in Chief: Ryan Petersen

Description and Interests

College and university employees responsible for maximizing technology for educational purposes are the audience of this magazine. It features trends and their practical applications, real-life solutions, and product reviews—all designed to help IT professionals and tech educators in their jobs. It needs writers who are technology experts and can show their readers practical ways to utilize the latest products in their higher education settings. Circ: Unavailable.

Contents: 50% articles; 50% depts/columns
Frequency: Quarterly
Website: www.edtechmag.com

Freelance Potential

90% written by nonstaff writers. Publishes 50 freelance submissions yearly; 20% by authors who are new to the magazine, 80% by experts. Receives 10 queries monthly.

Submissions

Query. Accepts email to ryanpet@cdw.com. Responds in 1 month.

- Articles: 1,000–2,500 words. Informational and how-to articles; media reviews; and new product information. Topics include information management in higher education, best practices, case studies, and technology implementation.
- Depts/columns: 1,000 words. Opinion pieces, business cases, project management, and security issues.

Sample Issue

48 pages. Sample articles and editorial calendar available at website.

- "Q&A with Must-Read Blogger Andreas Brockhaus of the University of Washington Bothell." Discussion of cloud computing, learning analytics, and online learning.
- "How to Establish a Process for Patch Management." Tips for streamlining the process of patch management and minimzing risks.

Rights and Payment

First rights. Written material, payment rates vary. Pays on publication. Provides 1 author's copy.

Ed Tech: Focus on K–12

230 North Milwaukee Avenue
Vernon Hills, IL 60061

Editor in Chief: Ryan Petersen

Description and Interests

This magazine explores the myriad ways technology can be used in classrooms. Focusing on elementary and secondary education, it keeps teachers and administrators informed on innovations and trends, while also discussing best practices and offering case studies and product reviews. It always welcomes submissions from educators and others who have a strong grasp of how technology can be effectively used to advance student achievement. Circ: Unavailable.

Contents: 50% articles; 50% depts/columns
Frequency: Quarterly
Website: www.edtechmag.com

Freelance Potential

90% written by nonstaff writers. Publishes 70 freelance submissions yearly; 20% by unpublished writers, 80% by experts. Receives 10 queries each month.

Submissions

Query. Accepts email queries to ryanpet@cdw.com. Responds in 1 month.

- Articles: 1,000–2,500 words. Informational and how-to articles. Topics include technology and information management in educational settings, using technology to supplement school curricula, professional development, and funding sources.
- Depts/columns: 1,000 words. Technology news, case studies, and how-to's.

Sample Issue

48 pages. Sample articles and editorial calendar available at website.

- "No Facebook or Twitter in Class? Try These Teaching Work-Arounds." How to maximize social media's learning potential without actually having access to the tools.
- "How Do Technology and Professional Development Shape Student Performance?" The impact of professional development programs on teachers and their students in rural Missouri schools.

Rights and Payment

Exclusive rights. Written material, payment rates vary. Pays on publication. Provides 1 author's copy.

Educational Horizons

Pi Lambda Theta
P.O. Box 7888
Bloomington, IN 47407-7888

Managing Editor

Description and Interests

Educational Horizons is the official magazine of Pi Lambda Theta. It was revamped to focus on the professional needs of teacher candidates, graduate education students, and early career teachers. It accepts submissions for two regular features, as described below. It seeks articles that will meet the professional needs of aspiring teachers and those already in service. Authors' experiences as teachers can help others just starting their careers. The publication places a strong emphasis on providing practical information that new teachers who are within the first five years of their careers can use. Circ: 11,000.

Contents: Articles; depts/columns
Frequency: Quarterly
Website: www.pilambda.org

Freelance Potential

95% written by nonstaff writers. Publishes 10–15 freelance submissions yearly; 75% by authors who are new to the magazine. Receives 60 queries, 12 unsolicited mss monthly.

Submissions

Accepts complete ms. Accepts email submissions to edhorizons@pdkintl.org (Word attachments). Response time varies.

- Articles: "Why I Teach." 300-word essay about why you chose to become a teacher. It can be personal, inspirational, or humorous. Your personal motivations should be included.
- Depts/columns: "I Wish I Had Known." A few sentences on what you wish you had known when you were a new teacher. Tips can be practical, inspirational, or humorous.

Sample Issue

68 pages. Little advertising. Sample articles, editorial calendar, and guidelines available at website.

- "*Not* Teaching Ethics." Emphasizing process as much as content when teaching ethics.
- Why I Teach." Reflections on becoming an educator.

Rights and Payment

First rights. No payment. Provides 5 copies.

Educational Leadership

ASCD
1703 North Beauregard Street
Alexandria, VA 22311-1714

Editor in Chief: Marge Scherer

Description and Interests

Educators and administrators of students in pre-K through grade 12 turn to *Educational Leadership* for articles addressing the practical realities of a contemporary classroom. It features conversational, research-based articles on teaching techniques, curriculum development, and leadership. All articles must relate to its themes. Access them at the website under "Write for ASCD." Circ: 170,000.

Contents: 80% articles; 20% depts/columns
Frequency: Monthly
Website: www.ascd.org

Freelance Potential

95% written by nonstaff writers. Publishes 130 freelance submissions yearly; 75% from unsolicited submissions, 50% by unpublished writers, 50% by authors who are new to the magazine. Receives 75 unsolicited mss each month.

Submissions

Send complete ms. Prefers email to elsubmissions@ascd.org (Word attachments) with "Educational Leadership manuscript submission" in subject line; will accept hard copy (send 2 copies). Responds in 1–2 months. No simultaneous submissions.

- Articles: 1,500–2,500 words. Informational and how-to articles; profiles; interviews; opinion and personal experience pieces; research, online resources. Topics include preparing students for college, beginning teachers, reading, grading practices.
- Depts/columns: Staff-written.
- Artwork: Digital photos, 300 dpi.

Sample Issue

96 pages. Advertising. Sample copy, guidelines, and theme list available at website.

- "Reading a Garden." Creative use of gardens to strengthen literacy.
- "Summarize to Get the Gist." The value of summarizing complex texts to develop reading comprehension and argument-writing skills.

Rights and Payment

All or first rights. No payment. Provides 5 contributor's copies.

The Engravers Journal

P.O. Box 318
Brighton, MI 48116

Senior Editor: Jackie Zack

Description and Interests

This trade magazine is focused solely on the engraving and award industry. It offers articles about both the technical and business aspects of the industry. Its stamp of approval goes to well-written articles that provide the latest and most pertinent industry information, especially those written by experts in the field. Circ: 33,000.

Contents: 75% articles; 25% depts/columns
Frequency: Monthly
Website: www.engraversjournal.com

Freelance Potential

100% written by nonstaff writers. Publishes 60–70 freelance submissions yearly; 10% by unpublished writers, 30% by authors who are new to the magazine, 20% by experts. Receives 3–4 queries, 2–3 unsolicited mss monthly.

Submissions

Query or send complete ms. Accepts hard copy, disk submissions (Word or WordPerfect files), and email to editor@engraversjournal.com. SASE. Responds to queries in 1 month, to mss in 3 months.

- Articles: To 1,000 words. Informational and how-to articles; product reviews, how-to; and humor pieces. Topics include audio, video, management, marketing, industry news, maintenance, media, software, business, computers, law, and communications—all as they pertain to the engraving and award industry.
- Depts/columns: Word lengths vary. Industry resources and supplies.

Sample Issue

53 pages. Advertising. Sample copy available at website.

- “"A Look at Award Resins." Learning about resin awards.
- "Laser Sources Explained." Understanding the differences between various types of lasers can lead to a well-informed buying decision.

Rights and Payment

Semi-exclusive rights. Written material, $100–$500. Pays on acceptance. Provides 1 author's copy.

Enrichment Journal

1445 North Boonville Avenue
Springfield, MO 65802

Managing Editor: Rick Knoth

Description and Interests

Assemblies of God ministers and other Pentecostal/charismatic leaders rely on this magazine for support, inspiration, and advice. The magazine exists for the purpose of enriching and encouraging Pentecostal ministers to equip and empower spirit-filled believers for effective ministry. Circ: 33,000.

Contents: 76% articles; 24% depts/columns; 1% fiction
Frequency: Quarterly
Website: www.enrichmentjournal.ag.org

Freelance Potential

95% written by nonstaff writers. Publishes 25 freelance submissions yearly; 2% by unpublished writers, 18% by authors who are new to the magazine, 80% by experts. Receives 10 unsolicited mss monthly.

Submissions

Send complete ms. Accepts email submissions to enrichmentjournal@ag.org and hard copy. SASE. Responds in 3 months.

- Articles: 1,200–2,100 words. Informational; profiles; interviews; and ministry tips. Topics include pastoral practice, preaching, program and ministry ideas, sermon illustrations and outlines.
- Depts/columns: How-to's on program and ministry ideas for ministers/church leaders, 200–500 words. News, book reviews, theology, and medical ethics, 1,200–2,100 words.

Sample Issue

128–144 pages. Advertising. Sample copy available at website. Guidelines available.

- "Is the Old Testament God Evil?" Rebutting New Atheist assertions about the Old Testament God.
- "Once Saved, Always Saved?" Where the Scripture stands on the claim by some that once salvation is gained, it cannot be lost.

Rights and Payment

First rights. Written material, to $.10 per word. Kill fee, 50%. Pays on publication. Provides 1 contributor's copy.

Entrepreneur

2445 McCabe Way, Suite 400
Irvine, CA 92614

Editor in Chief: Amy Cosper

Description and Interests

Marketing, sales, management, technology, business issues and strategies, and finances are some of the topics covered in this magazine for entrepreneurs. It's looking for timely articles that not only inform but also motivate readers, most of whom are running small- to mid-sized businesses. Short profiles of, and interviews with, successful entrepreneurs are always sought. Circ: 600,000.

Contents: 75% depts/columns; 25% articles
Frequency: Monthly
Website: www.entrepreneur.com

Freelance Potential

85% written by nonstaff writers. Publishes 36 freelance submissions yearly; 15% by authors who are new to the magazine. Receives 120 queries each month.

Submissions

Query with clips and writing samples. Accepts email queries for website only to pitches@entrepreneur.com. Accepts email queries for magazine to queries@entrepreneur.com. Responds to queries in 6 weeks.

- Articles: To 2,000 words. Informational and how-to articles; interviews, and short profiles. Topics include business issues, entrepreneurship, marketing, and sales.
- Depts/columns: 300–600 words. Money management, insurance and tax issues, legal topics, and the Internet.

Sample Issue

116 pages. Advertising. Sample copy and guidelines available at website.

- "Telltale Signs You Have a Workplace Bully." Identifying four different types of bullies and how to handle them.
- "Barter Kings' Guide to Building a Business Without Cash." Getting what you need to grow your business without paying for it.

Rights and Payment

First worldwide and electronic rights. Written material, payment rates vary. Kill fee, 20%. Pays on acceptance.

Exchange

17725 NE 65th Street, Unit B-275
Redmond, WA 98052

Associate Editor: Donna Rafanello

Description and Interests

Exchange addresses the day-to-day issues faced by childcare professionals. The publication is a forum for center administrators in childcare management to exchange ideas and share their challenges and successes. Exchange's Writing Project recruits early childhood educators as new writers and offers mentoring from a writing coach to help guide them through the process of writing and submitting articles. Circ: 27,000.

Contents: 70% articles; 30% depts/columns
Frequency: 6 times each year
Website: www.childcareexchange.com

Freelance Potential

85% written by nonstaff writers. Publishes 120 freelance submissions yearly; 50% by unpublished writers, 20–33% by authors who are new to the magazine. Receives 12 queries and mss monthly.

Submissions

Query or send complete ms with author bio and photo, and references. Accepts email to submission@childcareexchange.com. Accompanying illustrations or photos; email to scott@childcareexchange.com or by mail. Responds in 1 week.

- Articles: 1,800 words. Informational, how-to, and self-help articles. Topics include staff recruitment, motivation, and training; leadership; working with parents; evaluation; brain research; creativity and play; child development; multicultural education; financial management; legal issues; policy matters; reading; advocacy and rights; and school-age care.
- Depts/columns: Word lengths vary. Staff development and training, curriculum topics, and parent perspectives.

Sample Issue

96 pages. Sample articles and guidelines available at website.

- "Creating a Video Tour to Market Your Center." Leveraging technology to promote your workplace.
- "Growing Your Business by Adapting Employer Child Care Practices." Nontraditonal options for child care.

Rights and Payment

All rights. Articles, $300. Depts/columns, payment rates vary. Pays on publication. Provides 2 copies.

Executive Housekeeping Today

1001 Eastwind Drive, Suite 301
Westerville, OH 43081-3361

Editor: Leah Driscoll

Description and Interests

This official publication of the International Executive Housekeepers Association offers expert advice as well as industry and member news. It seeks to help readers achieve personal and professional growth. It looks for authoritative articles that will inform executive housekeepers about the latest developments in the industry. Circ: 4,000+. (Digital version: 8,000+)

Contents: 65% articles; 25% depts/columns; 10% other
Frequency: Monthly
Website: www.ieha.org

Freelance Potential

80% written by nonstaff writers. Publishes 36 freelance submissions yearly; 5% by unpublished writers, 5% by authors who are new to the magazine, 90% by industry experts. Receives 6 unsolicited mss monthly.

Submissions

Send complete ms with artwork. Accepts email queries and submissions to ldriscoll@ieha.org (Word attachments). Responds in 2 months.

- Articles: 1,500–2,000 words. How-to articles; profiles; interviews; personal experience pieces; and new product information. Topics include association news, consumer interests, current trends, maintenance, management, environmental services, regulations and laws, employee recognition, training and development, and safety issues.
- Depts/columns: 800 words. Environmental issues, personal growth, and industry news.
- Artwork: Color prints; high-resolution JPEG, PDF, or TIFF images.

Sample Issue

32 pages. Advertising. Sample articles, guidelines, and editorial calendar available at website.

- "Innovations in Pest Control." The newest options for pest control treatments and technologies.
- "Translating Effective Leadership: It's Greek to Me!" Tips for managing others.

Rights and Payment

First world and reprint rights. No payment.

Expo Magazine

10 Norden Place
Norwalk, CT 06855

Executive Editor: Lee Barney

Description and Interests

Targeting managers of trade and consumer shows, this magazine focuses on effective strategies and solutions for organizing successful events. Each issue provides destination profiles, case studies, ideas, and practical how-to advice. The editorial focus is based on its editorial calendar. Please refer to that before submitting an idea or article. *Expo* is always interested in industry trends and practical how-to advice. Circ: 8,500.

Contents: 70% depts/columns; 30% articles
Frequency: 9 times each year
Website: www.expoweb.com

Freelance Potential

75% written by nonstaff writers. Publishes 40 freelance submissions yearly; 20% by authors who are new to the magazine, 10% by experts. Receives 5 queries monthly.

Submissions

Query with outline and source list. Accepts hard copy and email to lbarney@red7media.com. SASE. Responds in 2 months.

- Articles: 1,800 words. Informational and how-to articles. Topics include business, retail, event planning, marketing, and current events.
- Depts/columns: 650 words. Industry news briefs, interviews, trends, best practices, and site selection.

Sample Issue

72 pages. Advertising. Sample articles and editorial calendar available at website.

- "The Pulse of an Industry: Examining Medical Meetings." Unique needs of medical trade shows and conferences and a conversation with four event planners.
- "Destination and Convention Center Trend Survey: The Northeast and Mid-Atlantic." Revealing results of the annual survey show venue is an important consideration, along with exhibit hall size, cost, and availability.

Rights and Payment

First North American serial rights. Written material, $.50 per word. Pays on acceptance.

Fancy Food & Culinary Products

233 North Michigan Avenue, Suite 1780
Chicago, IL 60601

Editor: Barbara Wujcik

Description and Interests

This magazine is geared specifically toward retailers and buyers of gourmet food and drink products, housewares, and culinary accessories. It offers product reviews, retailing and marketing advice, and coverage of trade shows. Although most of its editorial content is generated by staff writers, freelance writers who know the business of food retailing are welcome to query with their fresh ideas. Circ: 22,000.

Contents: 60% articles; 40% depts/columns
Frequency: 11 times a year
Website: www.fancyfoodmagazine.com

Freelance Potential

10% written by nonstaff writers. Publishes 24 freelance submissions yearly; 10% by unpublished writers, 30% by experts. Receives 3 queries each month.

Submissions

Query with résumé and clips. Accepts hard copy and email to bwujcik@talcott.com. SASE. Responds in 1 month.

- Articles: 1,500 words. Informational and how-to articles; profiles; interviews; industry news; marketing; and new product information. Topics include food, dining, nutrition, and diet.
- Depts/columns: 800–1,000 words. News and product reviews.

Sample Issue

26 pages. Advertising. Sample copy available. Editorial calendar available at website.

- "Homemade Appetizers: Delicious Finger Foods in No Time." The new niche of cheese balls and dip mixes.
- "It's Easy Being Green." How to throw a "green" dinner party with eco-friendly products.

Rights and Payment

All rights. Articles, $350–$600. Depts/columns, payment rates vary. Kill fee, $50. Pays on publication. Provides 3 contributor's copies.

Federal Construction

P.O. Box 3908
Suwanee, GA 30024

Editor: Michael J. Pallerino

Description and Interests

Federal Construction Magazine is a comprehensive resource for commercial construction executives. The ezine helps them build businesses, remain competitive, and succeed in federal construction projecs. The audience consists of government administrators, contractors, architects, engineers, suppliers, and others. Circ: Unavailable.

Contents: 50% articles; 50% depts/columns
Frequency: 6 times each year
Website: www:federalconstruction magazine.com

Freelance Potential

Receives several queries monthly.

Submissions

Query. Accepts email to mikep@fc-mag.com. Response time varies.

- Articles: Word lengths vary. Informational and how-to articles, and profiles. Topics include business strategies, communications, innovations, industry tips, and business leaders.
- Depts/columns: Word lengths vary. Environment, legal reviews, new products, and industry news.

Sample Issue

Advertising. Sample copy available at website.

- "Steel Isn't Just for the Bars." Article explains how stainless steel drainage made a difference at the Orleans Parish Correctional facility.
- "Guarding Against the Unknown." Article discusses the cost-efficiency of fenestration testing in building safety.
- Sample dept/column: The Perspective column discusses strategic planning versus strategic thinking.

Rights and Payment

Rights vary. Payment rates and policy vary.

Fed Tech

230 North Milwaukee Avenue
Vernon Hills, IL 60061

Editor in Chief: Ryan Petersen

Description and Interests

This magazine presents information technology innovations for federal government employees responsible for data management. Articles include the latest trends and tools that aid in cost cutting and security. Writers need to provide cutting-edge technology information in an accessible way and be well-versed in federal government agency environments, needs, and practices. Circ: 70,000.

Contents: 50% articles; 50% depts/columns
Frequency: Quarterly
Website: www.fedtechmagazine.com

Freelance Potential

90% written by nonstaff writers. Publishes 60 freelance submissions yearly; 20% by authors who are new to the magazine, 80% by industry experts. Receives 10 queries monthly.

Submissions

Query. Accepts email to ryanpet@cdw.com. Responds in 1 month.

- Articles: 1,000–2,500 words. Informational and how-to articles; profiles; interviews; media reviews; and new product information. Topics include information management, technology, computers, the federal government, management, politics, and public affairs.
- Depts/columns: 1,000 words. Network security, procurement strategies, data storage, and human resource issues.

Sample Issue

48 pages. Advertising. Sample articles at website.

- "Telework Thrives as Mobility Grows." How federal agencies help employees work from home, saving millions in the process and contributing to happier workers.
- "Voice and Video Chat Help Teleworkers Simulate the Water Cooler." Facilitating team-building and trust among telework employees using voice- and video-conferencing, along with collaboration software so everyone remains engaged.

Rights and Payment

Exclusive rights. Written material, payment rates vary. Pays on publication. Provides 1 copy.

Fine Woodworking

The Taunton Press
63 South Main Street
P.O. Box 5506
Newtown, CT 06470-5506

Managing Editor: Mark Schofield

Description and Interests

With a mission to help experienced and weekend hobbyists become better woodworkers, this magazine features how-to articles regarding furniture-making and other fine woodworking projects. It is a reader-written magazine, and relies on skilled woodworkers to share their practical experience and knowledge. Circ: 275,000.

Contents: 75% articles; 25% depts/columns
Frequency: 7 times each year
Website: www.finewoodworking.com

Freelance Potential

90% written by nonstaff writers. Publishes 70 freelance submissions yearly; 10% by unpublished writers, 10% by authors who are new to the magazine, 100% by experts. Receives 20 queries, 3 unsolicited mss monthly.

Submissions

Accepts queries at fw@taunton.com. Query with a proposal or outline; include artwork and brief author bio. Accepts hard copy, email to tmckenna@taunton.com, and simultaneous submissions if identified. SASE. Responds in 1–2 months.

- Articles: Word lengths vary. Informational and how-to articles. Topics include furniture making, woodworking projects, power and hand tools, joinery, design, and finishing.
- Depts/columns: Word lengths vary. Woodworking and wood finishing techniques, reviews of new woodworking tools and gadgets.
- Artwork: Photographs. Line drawings.

Sample Issue

98 pages. Advertising. Sample articles and guidelines available at website. Editorial theme list available.

- "Got Rust?" New products prove vastly superior to old prevention techniques.
- Shaker-Inspired Hall Table." Classic design adds balance and grace.

Rights and Payment

Exclusive First North American serial rights and other medium rights. Articles, $150 per page. Depts/columns, $50–$150 per page. Kill fee, $150. Pays on acceptance. Provides 2 author's copies.

Fire Engineering

21-00 Route 208 South
Fair Lawn, NJ 07410-2602

Executive Editor: Diane Feldman

Description and Interests

Launched in 1877, *Fire Engineering* magazine provides training, education, and management information for fire and emergency services personnel. All authors must be experts in the fire services. It accepts articles on any topic that concerns the firefighting community. All material should have a focus on lessons learned from which others can benefit. Circ: Unavailable.

Contents: 50% articles; 50% depts/columns
Frequency: Monthly
Website: www.fireengineering.com

Freelance Potential

100% written by nonstaff writers. Publishes 150–200 freelance submissions yearly.

Submissions

Send complete ms with author information and photos. Accepts CD or email submissions to dianef@pennwell.com (Word and JPEG attachments only). No simultaneous submissions. Responds in 2–3 months.

- Articles: 1,000+ words. Informational and how-to articles; and opinion and personal experience pieces. Topics include firefighter training and management, technology, communications, rescue techniques, and emergency response strategies.
- Depts/columns: 850–1,000+ words. New product information, technology, personal experiences, and volunteer management and recruitment.
- Artwork: JPEG images at 300 dpi.

Sample Issue

188 pages. Sample articles and guidelines available at website. Editorial calendar available.

- "Construction Concerns for Firefighters: Reinforcing Stars on Buildings." Decorative reinforcing plates used to stabilize aging buildings can fail in a fire and accelerate collapse of the structure.
- "Training Days: Fire Location and Nozzle Evolution." A drill uses a thermal imaging camera.

Rights and Payment

Rights vary. Written material, payment rates vary. Pays on publication. Provides 3 author's copies.

Fishing Tackle Retailer

42 South Washington Avenue, 2nd Floor
Brownsville, TN 38012

Managing Editor: Ken Cook

Description and Interests

As "the business magazine of the sportfishing industry," *Fishing Tackle Retailer* offers manufacturers and purveyors of sportfishing tackle information on trade shows and the latest industry trends, new product reviews, and sales tips. Its goal is to help retailers, wholesalers, and manufacturers sell more fishing tackle. Since this is a trade magazine, it does not publish articles for the casual angler. It invites new writers with experience in the industry to submit queries. Circ: 18,000.

Contents: 50% articles; 50% depts/columns
Frequency: 7 times each year
Website: www.fishingtackleretailer.com

Freelance Potential

80% written by nonstaff writers. Publishes 75+ freelance submissions yearly; 20% by authors who are new to the magazine, 10% by experts. Receives 1 query monthly.

Submissions

Query with clips. Accepts hard copy. SASE. Responds in 2 weeks if interested.

- Articles: 1,000–2,000 words. Informational and how-to articles; profiles; interviews; and new product information. Topics include sportfishing, retail trends, tournaments and competitions, business management, and sportfishing destinations.
- Depts/columns: Staff-written.

Sample Issue

68 pages. Advertising. Sample copy available at website.

- "If Your Store Sales are Flat or Down, Here's Why!" Addresses a series of missteps and how to fix them.
- "The Who, What, and Where on Rods, Reels, and Combos." Discussion of the $2.2 billion rod, reel, and combo category and what brands they're buying.

Rights and Payment

First-time publishing rights. Written material, payment rates vary. Pays on publication. Provides 1 contributor's copy.

ForeWord Reviews

425 Boardman Avenue, Suite B
Traverse City, MI 49684

Editor in Chief: Julie Eakin

Description and Interests

"Good Books Independently Published" is the motto for this magazine, which supplies reviews for booksellers, book buyers, publishing insiders, and librarians. It focuses on books from independent publishers. It also publishes articles on publishing trends and other book-related topics. Many of its freelancers teach at universities or work at libraries. Circ: 8,000.

Contents: 70% articles; 30% depts/columns
Frequency: 6 times each year
Website: www.forewordreviews.com

Freelance Potential

70% written by nonstaff writers. Publishes 600 freelance submissions yearly; 15% by authors who are new to the magazine, 30% by experts. Receives 10 queries monthly.

Submissions

Query with prospective interviews and clips. No unsolicited mss. Accepts email queries to julie@forewordmagazine.com. Responds in 1 month.

- Articles: 450–1,600 words. Informational and how-to articles; profiles; interviews; opinion pieces; and reviews. Topics include current publishing trends, bookselling associations, public affairs, writing, and multicultural and ethnic issues.
- Depts/columns: 375–450 words. Reviews, essays.

Sample Issue

64 pages. Advertising. Sample copy available at website. Guidelines and editorial calendar available.

- "*All Cry Chaos.*" Review of the mystery book by Leonard Rosen.
- "*Walking Made My Path.*" Review of the autobiography and memior of Judith Laikin Elkin.

Rights and Payment

All rights. Written material, $25–$200. Pays 2 months after publication. Provides 3 contributor's copies.

Form

Pioneering Design

512 East Wilson Avenue, Suite 213
Glendale, CA 91206

Editor in Chief: Caren Kurlander

Description and Interests

Interior and commercial designers as well as architects read this trade journal for inspiration and industry news. It showcases contemporary spaces, profiles design professionals, and offers information on products and events that are of interest to those in the design field. Writers should read several back issues to get a sense of its tone and the topics they cover. Circ: 18,000.

Contents: 50% articles; 50% depts/columns
Frequency: 6 times each year
Website: www.formmag.net

Freelance Potential

95% written by nonstaff writers. Publishes 30 freelance submissions yearly; 10% by authors who are new to the magazine, 100% by experts. Receives 10 queries monthly.

Submissions

Query with résumé, writing samples, and artwork. Accepts email queries to edit@formmag.net. Availability of artwork improves chance of acceptance. Responds in 1 week.

- Articles: Word lengths vary. Informational articles; profiles; interviews; and opinion pieces. Topics include architecture, design, sustainable buildings, and architects.
- Depts/columns: Word lengths vary. Products, materials, trends, techniques, projects, events, and book reviews.
- Artwork: High-resolution digital images.

Sample Issue

40 pages. Advertising. Sample articles at website. Guidelines available. Editorial calendar available at website.

- "Infinity Bridge by 10 Design and Buro Happol Wins Competition." Winning design features a triangular, ribbon-like structure and a double-eight figure, a symbol of prosperity in China, where it will be located.
- "AIA LA Jury Announces Nominees in the Restaurant Design Awards Competition." Details of the eighth annual design awards contest.

Rights and Payment

First North American serial rights. All material, payment rates vary. Pays on publication. Provides 5 contributor's copies.

The Franchise Handbook

5555 North Port Washington Road, Suite 305
Milwaukee, WI 53217

Editor in Chief: Maria Lahm

Description and Interests

This magazine targets people who are exploring business ownership through franchising, as well as those who are in the early stages of franchise ownership. The emphasis here is on expert advice. Contributors should have expertise in, or experience with, topics relevant to franchising, such as marketing, finance, and legal issues. Circ: 60,000.

Contents: 20% articles; 20% depts/columns; 60% other
Frequency: Quarterly
Website: www.franchisehandbook.com

Freelance Potential

80% written by nonstaff writers. Publishes 15 freelance submissions yearly; 20% by unpublished writers, 50% by authors who are new to the magazine, 80% by experts. Receives 8 queries monthly.

Submissions

Query. Accepts email queries to maria@franchisehandbook.com. Responds in 1 month.

- Articles: 1,400 words. Informational and how-to articles; profiles; interviews; and personal experience pieces. Topics include franchise opportunities, marketing, and networking.
- Depts/columns: Word lengths vary. Personal experience pieces, services, and franchise show schedules.

Sample Issue

180 pages. Advertising. Sample copy available at website. Writers' guidelines and editorial calendar available.

- "Spending on Children Continues Apace in All Types of Economic Conditions." Discussion of the economic influence children exert on parents and the tenfold increase in child care spending over the past five decades.
- "A Goal-Oriented Franchisee Makes it Work." Laid-off sales and marketing pro turns to an auto protection services franchise to stage his second act.

Rights and Payment

Second and electronic rights. No payment. Provides 2 contributor's copies.

Good Fruit Grower

105 South 18th Street, Suite 217
Yakima, WA 98901

Editor: Geraldine Warner

Description and Interests

Targeting orchardists and vineyardists, *Good Fruit Grower* covers the ins and outs of growing tree fruits, as well as producing juice and wine. It provides timely and in-depth reporting on key industry issues. It welcomes science-based articles on the growing, packing, handling, marketing, and promotion of all tree fruits. Circ: 12,000.

Contents: Articles; depts/columns
Frequency: 17 times each year
Website: www.goodfruit.com

Freelance Potential

10% written by nonstaff writers. Publishes 30 freelance submissions yearly; 5% by authors who are new to the magazine, 5% by experts. Receives 5 queries monthly.

Submissions

Query with author biography. Accepts hard copy and email queries to getit@goodfruit.com. SASE. Responds in 1 month.

- Articles: 1,500 words. Informational and how-to articles; profiles; interviews; and opinion pieces. Topics include growing, packing, handling, marketing, and promotion of tree fruits and wine grapes.
- Depts/columns: 1,000 words. Industry profiles, research reports, opinions, environmental practices, industry events, news briefs, and new product information.

Sample Issue

62 pages. Advertising. Sample copy and editorial calendar available at website. Writers' guidelines available.

- "Finding the Ideal Peach Orchard." Changes in labor efficiency methods could change the peach growing business in Pennsylvania.
- "Later and Later Cherries." Late season varieties are fueling a growing trend in late-season shipments.

Rights and Payment

One-time rights. Written material, $.50 per word. Pays on publication. Provides contributor's copies upon request.

Government Computer News

8609 Westwood Center Drive, Suite 500
Vienna, VA 22182-2215

Editor in Chief: Paul McCloskey

Description and Interests

Launched in 1982, this magazine bills itself as the "online authority for government IT professionals." Through its print version and online presence, it covers technologies, designs, and IT management for government offices. Freelancers should be aware that only about 45 percent of its editorial content is in print. The majority of its material is posted directly on its website as daily updates. Accepted submissions will likely be published online. Circ: 100,000.

Contents: 85% articles; 15% depts/columns
Frequency: 16 times each year
Website: http://gcn.com

Freelance Potential

10% written by nonstaff writers. Publishes 15–20 freelance submissions yearly; 2% by authors who are new to the magazine, 8% by industry experts. Receives 10 queries monthly.

Submissions

Query. Accepts email queries to pmccloskey@1105govinfo.com. Responds in 2 weeks.

- Articles: 500–2,000 words. Informational articles; profiles; interviews; and new product information. Topics include computers, technology, electronics, management, and science—all as they relate to government IT issues.
- Depts/columns: 300–600 words. Opinion pieces, product reviews, and industry news.

Sample Issue

36 pages. Advertising. Sample articles available at website. Guidelines available.

- "Domestic Drones: What are They Good For?" Discussion of the use of pilotless aircraft for use by federal, state, and local agencies.
- "Make Your Browser Invincible." A review of Invincea Enterprise Edition, a malware-trapping software useful for those who work from home.

Rights and Payment

All rights. Written material, $1 per word. Kill fee, 25–50%. Pays on acceptance. Provides 3 contributor's copies.

Grading & Excavation Contractor

Forester Media Inc.
P.O. Box 3100
Santa Barbara, CA 93130

Editor: John Trotti

Description and Interests

This magazine offers practical business advice for all kinds of earthmoving contractors. Articles cover productivity, management issues, equipment, technology, day-to-day responsibilities, and safety. Writers need to aim high in their expectations of the reader's knowledge and expertise and focus on technical aspects. If the article is too basic, the magazine can't use it. Circ: 29,000.

Contents: 90% articles; 10% depts/columns
Frequency: 7 times each year
Website: www.gradingandexcavating.com

Freelance Potential

90% written by nonstaff writers. Publishes 45 freelance submissions yearly; 20% by authors who are new to the magazine, 20% by industry experts. Receives 10 queries, 2 unsolicited mss each month.

Submissions

Query or send complete ms. Accepts disk submissions (Word files) with hard copy, and electronic submissions through the website. SASE. Responds in 6–8 months.

- Articles: 2,000–3,500 words. Informational and how-to articles; profiles; and new product information. Topics include grading and excavation issues, equipment and machinery, and business management.
- Depts/columns: 500 words. Technology, safety, new products, and project profiles.

Sample Issue

58 pages. Advertising. Sample copy, guidelines, and editorial calendar available at website.

- "Rolling Out the Fabric of the Road." The use of geosynthetics in paving operations gets a boost from Congress.
- "Green Highways." Extending the lifespan of roads depends in part on the type of surfacing treatments used.

Rights and Payment

All rights. Written material, payment rates vary. Pays on publication. Provides 1 copy.

Hard Hat News

6113 State Highway 5
P.O. Box 121
Palatine Bridge, NY 13428

Editor: John Casey

Description and Interests

This business news tabloid covers seven northeastern states and serves professionals in the construction business. It covers news and products related to all aspects of big construction, including private and public projects—both residential and commercial. It also reports on financial matters, bidding processes, and industry trends, particularly those relating to the northeastern region of the U.S. It prefers to work with writers who know the industry and have some journalistic experience. Circ: 21,000.

Contents: 50% articles; 50% depts/columns
Frequency: Monthly
Website: www.hardhat.com

Freelance Potential

65% written by nonstaff writers. Publishes 25 freelance submissions yearly; 20% by unpublished writers, 5% by authors who are new to the magazine, 20% by experts.

Submissions

Query. Accepts email to jcasey@leepub.com. Responds in 1 day.

- Articles: 800–2,500 words. Informational and how-to articles; company profiles; and jobsite stories. Topics include construction, land clearing; excavation; paving; road, bridge, and underground construction; and demolition.
- Depts/columns: Word lengths vary. Industry news and equipment information.
- Artwork: High-resolution digital images.

Sample Issue

32 pages. Advertising. Sample copy available at website. Editorial calendar available.

- "Tips for Doing a Better Paving Job." Production and placement of hot mix asphalt contributes to better results.
- "Bergkamp's M212 Paver Carries More." Profile of a mounted slurry seal and micro surfacing paver that can extend pavement life by 7 years and minimize greenhouse gas emissions.

Rights and Payment

All or first rights. Written material, $2.50 per column inch. Pays on acceptance. Provides 3 contributor's copies.

Hart's E&P

1616 South Voss, Suite 1000
Houston, TX 77057–2627

Executive Editor: Rhonda Duey

Description and Interests

Reaching an audience of oil and gas professionals, this magazine presents clear and concise information that helps readers make informed decisions regarding operations. Topics include seismic exploration, geology, geophysics, drilling, and information technology. Please use its editorial calendar as a basis for deciding on a topic. Circ: 51,000.

Contents: 70% articles; 30% depts/columns
Frequency: Monthly
Website: www.epmag.com

Freelance Potential

50% written by nonstaff writers. Publishes 70–80 freelance submissions yearly; 35% by unpublished writers, 25% by authors who are new to the magazine, 50% by experts. Receives 5 queries monthly.

Submissions

Query with abstract. Accepts email queries to rduey@hartenergy.com. Responds in 1 month.

- Articles: To 1,200 words. Informational articles; opinion pieces; and new product information. Topics include business, current events, machinery, maintenance, management, marine exploration, technology, and politics—all as they relate to the oil and gas production industries.
- Depts/columns: Word lengths vary. News analysis, exploration, technology, and politics.

Sample Issue

80 pages. Advertising. Sample copy and editorial calendar available at website. Writers' guidelines available.

- "Escape from the Unconventional Treadmill." Unconventional plays have their drawbacks and a less predictable production profile.
- "Mirroring Opportunities across the Atlantic." The search for the next big thing in offshore oil and gas drilling.

Rights and Payment

All rights. Written material, $300–$350 per 1,200-word page. Pays on publication. Provides 2 contributor's copies.

Hispanic Business

475 Pine Avenue
Santa Barbara, CA 93117-3709

Associate Editor: Joshua Molina

Description and Interests

This magazine focuses on significant trends and news affecting the U.S. Hispanic business market. Read by business owners, executives, and professionals, it also profiles successful entrepreneurs. Its editorial content is also useful to media and marketing professionals with an interest in trends in the Hispanic marketplace. Circ: 225,000.

Contents: 65% articles; 35% depts/columns
Frequency: Monthly
Website: www.hispanicbusiness.com

Freelance Potential

20% written by nonstaff writers. Publishes 40 freelance submissions yearly; 10% by authors who are new to the magazine, 10% by experts. Receives 30 queries monthly.

Submissions

Query with outline, résumé and clips. Accepts queries via submission form at website (Word attachments) only. Select option "editorial." Responds in 6 weeks.

- Articles: Word lengths vary. Informational and how-to articles; profiles; interviews; and opinion pieces. Topics include Hispanic entrepreneurs, economic trends, business news and events, government procurement, workplace diversity, politics, advertising, the media, technology, education, and entertainment.
- Depts/columns: Word lengths vary. Economic news, financial advice, technology, legal advice, regional reports, careers, and travel.

Sample Issue

64 pages. Advertising. Sample articles, guidelines, and editorial calendar available at website.

- "Finance in the Blood: Citi's Maria G. Hackley is Woman of the Year." Profile of the global banking whiz.
- "Succeeding Everywhere: Hispanic Women Making Inroads." A look at truly remarkable Hispanic business leaders, who rank among the elite Hispanic women nominated for the magazine's 2012 award.

Rights and Payment

All rights. Written material, $.50 per word. Kill fee, 25%. Pays on publication. Provides 2 copies.

Hoard's Dairyman

28 Milwaukee Avenue West
P.O. Box 801
Fort Atkinson, WI 53538

Managing Editor: Steve A. Larson

Description and Interests

The dairy industry and rural life are covered in detail in this magazine for dairy farmers. It looks at business issues, feeding and breeding, herd health, and industry people, places, and events. About 75 percent of its readers are U.S. dairy farmers. The rest of its audience is made up of veterinarians, breeding industry representatives, university researchers, agricultural and health department officials, private consultants, and commercial company representatives. Circ: 68,621.

Contents: 50% articles; 50% depts/columns
Frequency: 20 times each year
Website: www.hoards.com

Freelance Potential

70% written by nonstaff writers. Publishes 100+ freelance submissions yearly; 5% by unpublished writers, 5% by authors who are new to the magazine, 60% by experts. Receives 5 queries monthly.

Submissions

Query with detailed proposal. Accepts email to editors@hoards.com. Responds in 2 weeks.

- Articles: 1,300–1,500 words. Informational and how-to articles; and profiles. Topics include milk production, equipment and technology, feeding, breeding, herd health, silage crops, business, and dairymen.
- Depts/columns: 900–1,100 words. Dairy industry news.

Sample Issue

46 pages. Advertising. Sample articles available at website. Guidelines available.

- "How Low Could Milk Prices Go?" A look at historical milk pricing as a means of predicting future trends.
- "Can Buying Local Food Really Save the Planet?" Analyzing the claims of the local food movement.

Rights and Payment

All rights. Articles, $300–$600. Pays on acceptance. Provides 6 contributor's copies.

Home Business Connection

1595 South Mount Joy Street
Elizabethtown, PA 17022

Editor

Description and Interests

Home Business Connection is focused on helping readers start a profitable home business. It features articles on business models and opportunities, and it also profiles successful home-based businesses. It is always interested in receiving success stories that can inspire its readers. Circ: 125,000.

Contents: 75% articles; 5% depts/columns; 20% other
Frequency: Monthly
Website: www.CEMPublications.com

Freelance Potential

30% written by nonstaff writers. Publishes 50+ freelance submissions yearly; 10% by authors who are new to the magazine, 30% by experts. Receives 10 queries monthly.

Submissions

Query. Accepts email queries to editor@homebusinessconnection.com. Responds in 2 weeks.

- Articles: 900 words. Informational articles; profiles; and interviews. Topics include network and multi-level marketing; franchises; online businesses; travel opportunities; women-friendly businesses; legal, real estate, and financial home businesses; start-ups; small business grants; and successful home-based business people.
- Depts/columns: Staff-written.

Sample Issue

48 pages. Advertising. Sample copy available at website. Writers' guidelines and editorial calendar available.

- "Meat Cutter to Money Maker." Former meat-cutter discovers success through network marketing.
- Sample dept/column: "MLM Company of the Month" profiles Morinda Bioactives.

Rights and Payment

Exclusive rights. Articles, $150. Pays on publication. Provides 5 contributor's copies.

Home Energy

1250 Addison Street, Suite 211B
Berkeley, CA 94702

Editor: Jim Gunshinan

Description and Interests

Home Energy focuses on advancing home energy performance. Articles cover residential energy efficiency, comfort, safety, and green building issues for builders and contractors. Most of its writers are experts in the building science field. It is always on the lookout for objective and practical information on energy efficiency. Circ: 5,500.

Contents: 70% articles; 30% depts/columns
Frequency: 6 times each year
Website: www.homeenergy.org

Freelance Potential

80% written by nonstaff writers. Publishes 4–6 freelance submissions yearly; 10% by unpublished writers, 50% by authors who are new to the magazine, 80% by industry experts. Receives 10 queries monthly.

Submissions

Send complete ms. Accepts email submissions to contact@homeenergy.org (MS Word, RTF, or text documents) and simultaneous submissions if identified. Responds in 1 month.

- Articles: 1,800–3,500 words. Informational and how-to articles; profiles; interviews; personal experience pieces; and new product information. Topics include business, residential construction and design, energy conservation, house and home, science, and technology.
- Depts/columns: *Trends* (short news stories, 400–1,800 words); *Field Notes* (first-person testimonials, 1,500–3,000 words); and columns (reader Q&A, 400–1,500 words).
- Artwork: Digital images as TIFFs or JPEGs; color or B/W prints. Line drawings.

Sample Issue

64 pages. Advertising. Sample copy, guidelines and editorial calendar available at website.

- "Pimp My Blower Door Kit: Blower Door Makeover." Retrofitting a 15-year-old blower door kit.
- "Wasting Energy or Catching Fire." The implications of sprinkler systems for the thermal building envelope.

Rights and Payment

All rights. Written material, $.20 per word; maximum $500. Pays on publication. Provides 1 contributor's copy.

The Horse

P.O. Box 919003
Lexington, KY 40591-9003

Editor in Chief: Stephanie L. Church

Description and Interests
Professional, hands-on horse owners read this magazine for the latest news and developments on equine health care and management. It features how-to information, technical articles, and interviews. It likes technical and how-to articles that are informative and educational. It also likes topical interviews, but accepts no first-person experiences unless they are from professionals. Circ: 40,000.

Contents: 65% articles; 35% depts/columns
Frequency: Monthly
Website: www.thehorse.com

Freelance Potential
80% written by nonstaff writers. Publishes 1,400 freelance submissions yearly; 20% by authors who are new to the magazine, 20% by industry experts. Receives 5–10 queries monthly.

Submissions
Query with résumé and clips. Prefers email queries to schurch@thehorse.com; will accept hard copy. SASE. Responds in 1–2 months.

- Articles: 250–4,000 words. Informational and how-to articles; profiles; and interviews. Topics include equine health, breeding, barn management, and horse behavior.
- Depts/columns: 250–1,800 words. Opinions, research, and new products. "Behavior," 300–1,500 words.
- Artwork: Digital images at 300 dpi or higher; prints or slides (upon request).

Sample Issue
58 pages. Advertising. Sample articles, guidelines, and editorial calendar available at website.

- "New York Offers Discounts for Vaccinating Horses against EEE." Legislators allocated funding to combat an increase in eastern equine encephalitis in humans and horses.
- "Navigating Natural Disasters with Horses." Planning in advance can speed response time during widifires and other natural disasters.

Rights and Payment
First and electronic rights for written material; one-time rights for artwork. Written material, payment rates vary. Artwork, $40–$350. Pays on acceptance.

Independent Banker

1615 L Street NW, Suite 900
Washington, DC 20036

Senior Vice President, Publications: Timothy Cook

Description and Interests
Published by the Independent Community Bankers of America, this trade magazine publishes news and analysis of the banking industry. It also covers the professional and financial issues that affect community bankers. Though its editorial calendar lays out its upcoming issues, it will find a place for all articles that are relevant to its readers. Circ: 13,500.

Contents: 60% articles; 40% depts/columns
Frequency: Monthly
Website: www.independentbanker.org

Freelance Potential
50% written by nonstaff writers. Publishes 45 freelance submissions yearly; 2% by unpublished writers, 10% by authors who are new to the magazine, 20% by industry experts. Receives 4 queries, 10 unsolicited mss monthly.

Submissions
Query or send complete ms. Accepts ms with certification of original work (see guidelines for wording) and text pasted in body of email to magazine@icba.org. Responds if interested. Responds in 1 month.

- Articles: To 1,000 words. Informational and how-to articles; and profiles. Topics include banking, management, finance, business, government, and computers.
- Depts/columns: 800 words. Technological issues, portfolio management, and agricultural banking.
- Artwork: Digital images at 300 dpi or higher. Prefers JPEG format.

Sample Issue
88 pages. Advertising. Sample copy, writers' guidelines, and editorial calendar available at website.

- "Safe and Sound." Fraud-prevention tools like ACH block services, ACH filters, and positive pay can help commerical customers.
- "Mapping the Future." Unconventional results in the 2011 rankings of the 400 top-performing community banks.

Rights and Payment
North American first serial rights, electronic rights, and second serial and electronic rights. Written material, $600. Pays on acceptance.

Infinite Energy

New Energy Foundation
P.O. Box 2816
Concord, NH 03302-2816

Managing Editor: Christy Frazier

Description and Interests

Infinite Energy magazine combines highly technical articles and non-technical pieces on new energy and new science; and analyzes the political, social, and economic implications of these changes. Articles must be impeccably researched, yet written for lay readers as well as scientists. Most of its content comes from scientists, engineers, and journalists. Circ: 5,000.

Contents: 85% articles; 15% depts/columns
Frequency: 6 times each year
Website: www.infinite-energy.com

Freelance Potential

90% written by nonstaff writers. Publishes 30 freelance submissions yearly; 25% by unpublished writers, 25% by authors who are new to the magazine, 25% by industry experts. Receives 10 unsolicited mss monthly.

Submissions

Send complete ms with author biography. Prefers email submissions to staff@infinite-energy.com (Word or PDF attachments); will accept CD submissions with hard copy. SASE. Responds in 3 months.

- Articles: Word lengths vary. Informational articles and opinion pieces. Topics include experimental results in cold fusion and new energy, theoretical ideas related to new science, science history, technology, and conventional and alternative energy advances.
- Depts/columns: Word lengths vary. Book reviews and opinion pieces.

Sample Issue

72 pages. Little advertising. Sample articles and guidelines available at website.

- "Potential Advantages and Impacts of LENR Generators of Thermal and Electrical Power and Energy." Positive features and future use of LENR generators of power and energy.
- "Unexpected End to First Trial for Gene Mallove's Murder." Update on the investigation into the murder of *Infinite Energy* founder, Dr. Eugene Mallove.

Rights and Payment

Second rights. No payment. Provides 4 contributor's copies.

Inside Counsel

222 South Riverside Plaza, Suite 620
Chicago, IL 60606

Editor in Chief: Cathleen Flahardy

Description and Interests

Inside Counsel offers in-depth coverage of the legal issues and concerns facing general counsels and in-house legal professionals. It does this through articles, essays, opinions, profiles, and interviews. Law firm news and circuit updates are also regularly provided. It usually assigns most freelance work, but will consider queries from experienced writers working as general corporate or in-house counsels. Circ: 40,000.

Contents: Articles; depts/columns
Frequency: Monthly
Website: www.insidecounsel.com

Freelance Potential

25% written by nonstaff writers. Receives 10 queries monthly.

Submissions

Query with detailed proposal and credentials. Accepts email to cflahardy@insidecounsel.com. Responds in 1 month.

- Articles: 2,100 words. Informational articles. Topics include contemporary legal issues in the corporate world.
- Depts/columns: 1,100 words. Profiles, essays, opinions, litigation, technology, intellectual property, regulatory issues, labor and employment, global legal issues, product reviews, court rulings, and career news.

Sample Issue

75 pages. Advertising. Sample copy available at website.

- "3 Cases Help Shape How Lawyers Conduct and Pay for e-Discovery." Several electronic discovery-centric cases and lessons to be learned from them.
- "Transformative Leadership Awards Honors Women in Corporate Law." Coverage of the Chicago awards program which honors law firms committed to diversity and advancing women.

Rights and Payment

All rights. Written material, payment rates vary. Pays on publication. Provides 1 author's copy.

InSite

P.O. Box 62189
Colorado Springs, CO 80962-2189

Editor: Jackie Johnson

Description and Interests

Published by the Christian Camp and Conference Association, *InSite* features practical information for event coordinators and administrators along with association news and the perspectives of those in the field. Practical tips and articles on running a camp or conference effectively are always needed. Profiles/interviews are the best bet for freelancers new to the publication. It is crucial to study a sample copy before querying. Circ: 8,500.

Contents: Articles; depts/columns
Frequency: 6 times each year
Website: www.ccca.org

Freelance Potential

90% written by nonstaff writers. Of the freelance submissions published yearly, 15% are by unpublished writers, 22% are by authors who are new to the magazine, and 63% are by industry experts. Receives 1–2 queries, 2 unsolicited mss monthly.

Submissions

Prefers query; will accept complete ms. Accepts email submissions to editor@ccca.org. Responds in 1 month. Submit seasonal material queries six months in advance.

- Articles: 1,000–1,500 words. Informational and how-to articles; profiles; interviews; and personal experience pieces. Topics include administration, personnel development, camper/guest needs, programming, health and safety, operations, fundraising, marketing, fundraising, and public relations.
- Depts/columns: Staff-written.

Sample Issue

50 pages. Advertising. Sample copy, guidelines, and editorial calendar available at website.

- "Intelligent Design." Article focuses on the keys to planning and executing successful facilities improvements.
- "Freshening Up." Article offers creative suggestions for improving a camp's appearance.

Rights and Payment

First rights. Written material, $.20 per word. Pays on publication. Provides 1 contributor's copy.

Instructor

P.O. Box 713
New York, NY 10013

Managing Editor: Chris Borris

Description and Interests

Filled with ideas, information, and resources for classroom success, *Instructor* is written for teachers of kindergarten through grade eight. It also offers articles on learning processes, classroom management, trends, personal development, and hands-on activities and lesson plans. Information that can be translated into hands-on, successful projects in the classroom is especially sought. Circ: 100,000.

Contents: 50% articles; 50% depts/columns
Frequency: 6 times each year
Website: www.scholastic.com/instructor

Freelance Potential

90% written by nonstaff writers. Publishes 55 freelance submissions yearly; 10% by unpublished writers, 80–90% by experts. Receives 10 queries, 20 unsolicited mss monthly.

Submissions

Query or send complete ms. Include your school, location and grade/subject you teach, and indicate section to which you're submitting. Accepts hard copy. SASE. Responds in 2–3 months.

- Articles: 800–1,200 words. Informational and how-to articles; profiles; interviews; personal experience pieces; media reviews; and new product information. Topics include educational issues and trends, classroom management and practice, teaching strategies, and career development.
- Depts/columns: Activities & Classroom Tips, to 250 words. Theme Units, 400–800 words. Curriculum lesson plans. Include color photos or students' work samples.

Sample Issue

64 pages. Advertising. Sample copy available.

- "Common Core: Victory is Yours." Article includes hands-on activities for meeting the new standards.
- "Lessons from the Teaher of the Year." Article presents an interview with the teacher of the year.

Rights and Payment

One-time and Internet rights. Written material, $.80–$1.00 per word. Kill fee, 50%. Pays on acceptance. Provides 2 contributor's copies.

JAZZed

21 Highland Circle, Suite 1
Needham, MA 02494

Executive Editor: Christian Wissmuller

Description and Interests

School and independent music teachers specializing in jazz read this magazine for its articles on how best to teach this complicated musical form. In addition to articles on techniques and teaching strategies, it features interviews with musicians and teachers. It prefers articles that present practical, hands-on information that will help teachers instruct their students. It likes subjects that will help perpetuate and grow the jazz culture. Circ: 13,000+.

Contents: Articles; depts/columns
Frequency: 6 times each year
Website: www.jazzedmagazine.com

Freelance Potential

40% written by nonstaff writers. Publishes 26 freelance submissions yearly; 60% by authors who are new to the magazine.

Submissions

Query. Accepts hard copy and email queries to cwissmuller@symphonypublishing.com. SASE. Response time varies.

- Articles: Word lengths vary. Informational and how-to articles; interviews; and new product information. Topics include jazz, music, and music education, festivals.
- Depts/columns: Word lengths vary. Profiles, reviews, and new product information.

Sample Issue

68 pages. Advertising. Sample copy available at website.

- "I Hear Freedom in That Sound," by Kevin M. Mitchell. Grammy nominee Kate McGarry's cultural exchange activities.
- "Notes on Lyric Writing and Song Conception." The author discusses how she finds inspiration for writing lyrics and music in her surroundings and transforms that on paper.
- Sample dept/column: "Noteworthy: Roy Haynes Honored by Peabody Conservatory" reports on the legendary drummer/bandleader's award for his musical contributions.

Rights and Payment

First rights. Written material, payment rates vary. Pays on publication. Provides 2 author's copies.

JEMS

Journal of Emergency Medical Services

525 B Street, Suite 1800
San Diego, CA 92101

Editor in Chief: A. J. Heightman

Description and Interests

Targeting emergency medical responders and doctors/nurses, JEMS provides information on best practices, treatment, and gear. How-to's and tips for the field are also offered here. All writers must have experience in the emergency medical services. Circ: 45,000.

Contents: 60% articles; 40% depts/columns
Frequency: Monthly
Website: www.jems.com

Freelance Potential

70% written by nonstaff writers. Publishes 40–44 freelance submissions yearly; 100% by unpublished writers, 30% by authors who are new to the magazine, 70% by industry experts. Receives 10–20 queries monthly.

Submissions

Prefers query with outline and cover letter that includes author qualifications, main point, and supporting documentation for proposed article; will accept complete ms. Accepts online submissions only via http://ees.elsevier.com/jems. No simultaneous submissions. Responds in 3–6 months.

- Articles: 1,500–2,500 words. Informational articles; profiles; interviews; opinion pieces; and new product information. Topics include clinical developments and controversies in pre-hospital care, provider health, professional development, innovative applications of EMS, and EMS equipment and technology.
- Depts/columns: 750 words. News, research findings, gear and gadgets, media reviews, humor, and "Case of the Month."

Sample Issue

116 pages. Advertising. Sample articles, editorial calendar, and guidelines available at website.

- "'Time Is Brain' in Prehospital Stroke Treatment." Tips on recognizing and responding to stroke.
- "Richmond Ambulance Authority Creates EMS Safety Culture." Best practices to prevent patient safety incidents.

Rights and Payment

All rights. Articles, $200–$400. Depts/columns, $100–$200. News items, $25. Pays on publication.

Journal of Christian Nursing

P.O. Box 7895
Madison, WI 53707-7825

Editor in Chief: Kathy Schoonover-Shoffner

Description and Interests

The target audience of this publication is Christian nurses and nursing educators whose faith is an integral part of their practice. It addresses current health issues and trends with a focus on improved patient care. The journal is written by and for nurses. It addresses a large and varied audience, from nursing students to veteran practitioners and educators. Articles should be inspiring, encouraging and contain a biblical, Christian perspective. Circ: 6,000.

Contents: 65% articles; 25% depts/columns; 10% other
Frequency: Quarterly (monthly online)
Website: www.ncf-jcn.org

Freelance Potential

95% written by nonstaff writers. Publishes 50 freelance submissions yearly; 20% by unpublished writers, 25% by authors who are new to the magazine, 5% by experts. Receives 3 queries monthly.

Submissions

Prefers complete ms. Accepts electronic submissions through website only at http://ncf–jcn.edmgr.com. No simultaneous submissions. Responds in 3 months.

- Articles: 1,400–4,900 words. Informational, how-to articles and personal experience pieces. Topics include nursing issues and trends, spiritual care, ethics, values, healing, parish or faith community nursing, and education.
- Depts/columns: To 700 words. Ethics, spiritual care, medical news, and education.

Sample Issue

57 pages. Little advertising. Sample copy and guidelines available at website.

- "Unhappy? Low Morale? Try the 5 Languages of Appreciation in the Workplace." How to show your appreciation and encourage co-workers.
- "When the Topic is Sex: Facilitating Parent Child Communication in the Faith Community." Learn how to foster healthy family discussions between parents and children about a sensitive topic.

Rights and Payment

All rights. Pays for solicited articles only. Provides 2 contributor's copies.

Journal of Court Reporting

8224 Old Courthouse Road
Vienna, VA 22180

Editor: Jacqueline Schmidt

Description and Interests

A professional journal for court reporters, this magazine covers the issues and news of the field, along with information about the activities of the National Court Reporters Association. It is always looking for well-reasoned articles on various aspects of the profession. Articles may be based on personal experience or involve research into the topic. Circ: 18,000.

Contents: 50% depts/columns; 10% articles; 40% other
Frequency: 10 times each year
Website: www.ncraonline.org

Freelance Potential

90% written by nonstaff writers. Publishes 200 freelance submissions yearly; 90% by unpublished writers, 40% by authors who are new to the magazine, 90% by experts in the field. Receives 1 query monthly.

Submissions

Query or send complete ms on CD. Prefers email submissions (MS Word) with signed article contract (found at website) to jschmidt@ncrahq.org; accepts hard copy. Responds in 4–6 weeks.

- Articles: 1,500–2,000 words. Informational and how-to articles. Topics include careers, working relationships, technology, and ethical issues.
- Depts/columns: 500–1,200 words. NCRA and industry news; stenography techniques, training, and exams; captioning; new products; technology; humor; and opinion.
- Artwork: High-resolution digital images.

Sample Issue

98 pages. Advertising. Guidelines and style manual available at website.

- "Portrait of a Killer." Profile of a Paducah, Kentucky boy who shot and killed his classmates.
- "Onsite CART: Then and Now." Author's experience with his first pro bono onsite CART assignment.

Rights and Payment

North American print and electronic rights. Written material, payment rates vary. Pays on acceptance.

Journal of Information Ethics

P.O. Box 32
West Wardsboro, VT 05360

Editor: Robert Hauptman

Description and Interests

This scholarly journal of information and opinion tackles the ethical issues surrounding the ever-changing world of information technology and communication. All submissions must deal with some aspect of information ethics. Scholarship does not have to be mind-numbing, tedious, or pedantic—it should be stimulating, controversial, and enticing. Circ: Unavailable.

Contents: 75% articles; 5% depts/columns; 20% other
Frequency: Twice each year
Website: www.mcfarlandbooks.com

Freelance Potential

90% written by nonstaff writers. Publishes 10 freelance submissions yearly; 75% by authors who are new to the magazine. Receives 1–2 unsolicited mss monthly.

Submissions

Query or send complete ms with 75-word author bio on separate page. Accepts hard copy (2 copies) with disk or email submissions to hauptman@stcloudstate.edu. SASE. Responds immediately.

- Articles: 10–25 pages. Informational articles and opinion pieces. Topics include business, government, libraries, computers, education, public affairs, science and technology, privacy, censorship, cyberspace and social issues.
- Depts/columns: "Academics," "Current Issues," and "Web Briefs," 4–6 pages. Reviews, word lengths vary.

Sample Issue

120 pages. Little advertising. Sample copy available. Guidelines available at website.

- "Written for the Moment." Author argues that disclosure and publication of text messages and emails is immoral.
- "For the Sake of One Child." Balancing free Internet access in public libraries against the chance that library resources could be used to commit a crime.

Rights and Payment

Rights vary. Articles, $50. Depts/columns and reviews, $25. Pays on publication. Provides 2 contributor's copies.

Kids' Ministry Ideas

55 West Oak Ridge Drive
Hagerstown, MD 21740

Editor: Candace Graves DeVore

Description and Interests

Church leaders who work with children are the primary audience for this Seventh-day Adventist publication. It aims to be a valuable resource filled with practical information, helpful tips, and program ideas. All its articles contain practical ideas and easy-to-understand instructions that readers can implement. Creative activities for leaders to use with children are especially needed. Use of sidebars, boxes, and lists of information is encouraged. Circ: 3,500.

Contents: Articles; depts/columns
Frequency: Quarterly
Website: www.kidsministryideas.com

Freelance Potential

50% written by nonstaff writers. Publishes 15 freelance submissions yearly; 10% by authors who are new to the magazine.

Submissions

Query or send complete ms with brief bio. Accepts hard copy and email (MS Word) submissions to kidsmin@rhpa.org. Response time varies.

- Articles: 300–800 words. Informational and how-to articles. Topics include religious education programs, family involvement, youth ministry, education resources, help for small churches, nurturing volunteers, Vacation Bible School ideas, faith, prayer, and spirituality.
- Depts/columns: Word lengths vary. Teaching strategies, advice, crafts and activities, and leadership training.

Sample Issue

30 pages. Advertising. Sample articles and guidelines available at website.

- "Help! I'm Being Followed." Commitment and faithfulness are essential for effective Christian leadership.
- "Vacation Bible School: Making God Real." Favorite summertime memories from childhood.

Rights and Payment

First North American serial rights. Written material, $20–$100. Pays 5–6 weeks after acceptance. Provides 1 contributor's copy.

Latin Trade

Latin Trade Group
1001 Brickell Bay Drive, Suite 2700
Brickell Bay Office Tower
Miami, FL 33131

Managing Editor: Elida Bustos

Description and Interests

Corporate and government leaders turn to this magazine for news and information about trade, business development, and corporations in Latin America. It is published in Spanish, Portuguese, and English. It looks for writing that appeals to sophisticated business professionals, corporate executives, and government officials. Experience in writing international business news is a plus. Circ: 164,000.

Contents: 80% articles; 20% depts/columns
Frequency: 6 times each year
Website: www.latintrade.com

Freelance Potential

50% written by nonstaff writers. Publishes 60–80 freelance submissions yearly; 25% by authors who are new to the magazine. Receives 5 queries each month.

Submissions

Query with author biography and clips. Accepts email queries to jbamrud@latintrade.com. Responds in 1 month.

- Articles: 700 words. Informational articles; profiles; and interviews. Topics include Latin American companies, commodities, industries, economics, business trends, technology, executives, and officials.
- Depts/columns: *The Scene, Tech Trends,* and *Made In* (leading exports). Word lengths vary. News briefs, Q&As, destinations, book reviews, and economic indicators.

Sample Issue

68 pages. Advertising. Sample copy, writers' guidelines, and editorial calendar available at website.

- "Brazil Consumer Fever: and Some Headache." Brazilian consumers wield formidable purchasing power.
- "The Evolution of Hotel Security in Bogota." Colombian success in making hotel security more stringent, but less visible, has boosted foreign tourism.

Rights and Payment

All rights. Written material, $.50 per word. Pays after publication.

Leadership Journal

465 Gundersen Drive
Carol Stream, IL 60188

Editor: Marshall Shelley

Description and Interests

Tools for leadership of Christian churches are found in this publication. Written for pastors, church staff, and lay leaders from a range of denominations, it provides practical and inspirational help for ministering to Christians in a complex world. It strives to offer spiritual wisdom and hard-won insight for effectively living the gospel. Circ: 50,000.

Contents: 60% articles; 40% depts/columns
Frequency: Quarterly
Website: www.christianitytoday.com

Freelance Potential

80% written by nonstaff writers. Publishes 30–35 freelance submissions yearly; 20% by unpublished writers, 97% by authors who are new to the magazine, 50% by experts. Receives 30 queries monthly.

Submissions

Query with brief outline and contact information for you and your church. Accepts queries via form at website. Responds in 2 weeks.

- Articles: 3,000 words. Informational and how-to articles; profiles; interviews; and personal experience pieces. Topics include church administration, stewardship, leadership, ethics, long-range planning, conflict resolution, team building, preaching, soul care, pastoral theology, innovation, neighborhood involvement and home life.
- Depts/columns: 250 words. Ministry tools and pastoral resources.
- Other: Blog posts, current events and cultural trends.

Sample Issue

98 pages. Advertising. Sample articles, guidelines and theme list available at website.

- "My Unsought Calling." A pastor's experience with a parishioner who hears voices threatening to do her harm.
- "Engaging the Enemy." Church leaders describe spiritual warfare.

Rights and Payment

First non-exclusive rights. Written material, $.15 per word. Kill fee, 33%. Pays on acceptance. Provides 1 contributor's copy.

The Leather Crafters & Saddlers Journal

222 Blackburn Street
Rhinelander, WI 54501-2902

Publisher: Dot Reis

Description and Interests

Each issue of this magazine features a large and varied selection of leatherwork projects for all skill levels. Also included are industry and guild news, as well as trade show reports. It is always interested in hearing about new projects. Sub missions should include a list of materials and tools, step-by-step instructions, patterns, and photos. Circ: 7,000.

Contents: 70% articles; 20% depts/columns; 10% other
Frequency: 6 times each year
Website: www.leathercraftersjournal.com

Freelance Potential

10% written by nonstaff writers. Publishes 80 freelance submissions yearly; 5% by authors who are new to the magazine. Receives 3 unsolicited mss monthly.

Submissions

Send complete ms with patterns and author biography. Accepts disk submissions with hard copy and email (make text and photos separate attachments) to journal@newnorth.net. Availability of artwork improves chance of acceptance. SASE. Response time varies.

- Articles: 700 words. Informational and how-to articles; and profiles. Topics include leatherwork and saddlery techniques, tools, materials, projects, marketing, and artists.
- Depts/columns: Word lengths vary. Industry and guild news, events, contests, and profiles.
- Artwork: Digital images in PDF, JPEG, or TIFF format at 300 dpi.

Sample Issue

100 pages. Advertising. Writers' guidelines available at website.

- "Checkbook Cover Part 4: A Project for Beginners." Step-by-step instructions.
- "How to Make a 12-Strand Round & Flat-Braided Leather Bracelet." Directions for creating leather jewelry.

Rights and Payment

First North American serial rights. Written material, $20–$250. Artwork, payment rates vary. Pays on publication. Provides 2 copies.

Managed Care

780 Township Line Road
Yardley, PA 19067

Editor: John Marcille

Description and Interests

Original research, analysis, and commentary about the health care industry are found in *Managed Care*. Its readers include physicians, medical directors, and HMO administrators. This publication accepts peer-reviewed academic papers only and submissions should demonstrate scientific studies. Circ: 44,000.

Contents: 40% articles; 60% depts/columns
Frequency: Monthly
Website: www.managedcaremag.com

Freelance Potential

75% written by nonstaff writers. Publishes 20 freelance submissions yearly; 5% by unpublished writers, 5% by authors who are new to the magazine, 20% by experts. Receives 5 queries, 5 unsolicited mss monthly.

Submissions

Accepts complete ms. Accepts hard copy and email submissions to Editors@ManagedCareMag.com (Word attachments); include disclosure form found at website. Response time varies.

- Articles: To 4,200 words. Academic pieces. Topics include cost and effectiveness of programs, products, and procedures in health care financing and delivery including physician payment mechanisms, risk arrangements, contracting issues, practice guidelines, pharmacy and formulary issues, legal and antitrust matters, and ethics.
- Depts/columns: Staff-written.

Sample Issue

54 pages. Advertising. Sample copy and guidelines available at website.

- "Health Plans Won't Sit Out While Docs, Hospitals Dance." Article explains how insurers are cautiously accepting accountable care organizations.
- "Health Care Reform in England—Commercial Opportunity Or Another False Dawn." Article discusses the possibility of U.K.'s health reforms generating commerical opportunities for US companies.

Rights and Payment

All rights. Written material, $.75 per word. Kill fee, 20%. Pays 45 days after acceptance. Provides 1+ contributor's copies.

Marine Corps Gazette

715 Broadway Street
Quantico, VA 22134

Editor: Col. John Keenan

Description and Interests

This magazine is written especially for members of the United States Marine Corps, both active and retired. It offers articles focusing on leadership, tactics, training, logistics, marksmanship, recruiting, and other military topics with the goal of providing an open forum and a free exchange of ideas relating to the U.S. Marines and military capabilities. Circ: 30,000.

Contents: 98% articles; 2% depts/columns
Frequency: Monthly
Website: www.mca-marines.org/gazette

Freelance Potential

99% written by nonstaff writers. Publishes 300 freelance submissions yearly; 10% by unpublished writers, 30% by authors who are new to the magazine, 90% by experts. Receives 30–50 unsolicited mss monthly.

Submissions

Send complete ms with artwork. Accepts hard copy and email to gazette@mca-marines.org (Word and photo file attachments), disk submissions with hard copy. SASE. Responds in 1 month.

- Articles: 2,000–3,000 words. Informational articles and essays. Topics include military history, personnel, weaponry, and military operations.
- Depts/columns: Book reviews and essays, 300–750 words. "Ideas and Issues," 750–1,500 words.
- Artwork: TIFF, JPEG, or EPS images at 300 dpi.

Sample Issue

92 pages. Advertising. Sample copy and guidelines available at website.

- "Expeditionary Medical Care." Article details a typical day in the life of the medical corps personnel who treat wounded soldiers from Afghanistan.
- "One Battalion's Efforts to Prevent Mishaps and Save Lives." Article explains how a force preservation plan of attack is necessary in preventing accidents and injuries.

Rights and Payment

All rights. No payment.

Marking Industry Magazine

136 West Vallette Street, Suite 6
Elmhurst, IL 60126-4377

Managing Editor: Anne Shadis

Description and Interests

This magazine is read by rubber stamp retailers and marking device manufacturers for its expert-written articles, profiles and interviews, industry news, and product reviews. It publishes unbiased articles on the industry, individual companies, and products. Timeliness and impartiality are important. Circ: 1,300.

Contents: 80% articles; 15% depts/columns; 5% other
Frequency: Monthly
Website: www.markingdevices.com

Freelance Potential

55% written by nonstaff writers. Publishes 24 freelance submissions yearly; 5% by unpublished writers, 10% by authors who are new to the magazine, 85% by experts. Receives 20 queries monthly.

Submissions

Query. Accepts email queries to editor@markingdevices.com (Word attachments). Responds in 3 months.

- Articles: 900–1,500 words. Informational and how-to articles. Topics include industry trends, marketing, and business issues.
- Depts/columns: Word lengths vary. Industry trends, news, and resources.
- Artwork: B/W and color prints; TIFF or JPEG images at 300 dpi (color) or 150 dpi (B/W).

Sample Issue

30 pages. Advertising. Sample articles and guidelines available at website.

- "Stamp Shop Web: Step by Step." Article provides instructions for creating and editing custom attributes and font set definitions.
- "CorelDRAW Applied: Understanding and Using the Object Manager." Article discusses the features of the Object Manager and its uses in artwork preparation.

Rights and Payment

Rights negotiable. No payment. Provides contributor's copies.

Massage & Bodywork

25188 Genesee Trail Road, Suite 200
Golden, CO 80401

Editor in Chief: Leslie A. Young

Description and Interests

Professional practitioners of massage, bodywork, and related therapies turn to this magazine for its coverage of current modalities and techniques, research, profiles of professionals, and practice-building strategies. It welcomes interesting and tightly focused articles relating to the business side of massage as well as the techniques and spirituality of bodywork therapies. Circ: 95,000.

Contents: 30% articles; 70% depts/columns
Frequency: 6 times each year
Website: www.massageandbodywork.com

Freelance Potential

90% written by nonstaff writers. Publishes 6 freelance submissions yearly; 15% by authors who are new to the magazine, 85% by experts. Receives 20 queries, 30 unsolicited mss monthly.

Submissions

Query or send complete ms. Accepts email submissions to editor@abmp.com (Word attachments). Responds in 2 months.

- Articles: 1,000–3,000 words. Informational, self-help, and how-to articles; profiles; interviews; and personal experience pieces. Topics include health, fitness, diet, nutrition, alternative therapies, technology, and social issues—all as they pertain to massage, bodywork, and somatic therapies.
- Depts/columns: Word lengths vary. News briefs, business issues, research, and product reviews.

Sample Issue

128 pages. Advertising. Sample articles and guidelines available at website.

- "Make your Appointments Stick." Article provides tips for preventing same-day cancellations.
- "Over-Manipulation Syndrome." Article explains how massage can help clients who continually crack fingers, necks, or backs.

Rights and Payment

First North American serial and electronic rights. Written material, payment rates vary. Pays on acceptance. Provides 2 contributor's copies.

Material Handling Wholesaler

P.O. Box 725
Dubuque, IA 52004-0725

Publisher: Dean Millius

Description and Interests

This specialty journal has been serving the material handling industry for more than 30 years. News and issues, suppliers, management strategies, and notable people within the industry are all covered here. Writers should be familiar with the industry and experienced in covering business issues. Circ: 7,800.

Contents: 60% articles; 40% depts/columns
Frequency: Monthly
Website: www.mhwmag.com

Freelance Potential

99% written by nonstaff writers. Publishes 120 freelance submissions yearly; 2% by authors who are new to the magazine, 98% by industry experts. Receives 50 unsolicited mss monthly.

Submissions

Send complete ms. Accepts email submissions to editorial@mhwmag.com. Responds in 1 week.

- Articles: 1,500–2,000 words. Informational, how-to, and self-help articles; profiles; interviews; new product information; and opinion pieces. Topics include business strategies, technology, economics, and staffing.
- Depts/columns: 500–1,000 words. Business and financial advice, market trends, industry news, customer service issues, new product information, and media reviews.
- Artwork: Color digital images at 300 dpi.

Sample Issue

44 pages. Advertising. Sample copy available at website. Writer's guidelines and editorial calendar available.

- "West Point Rack's Customer First Philosophy Pays Off." Article profiles this company and the reasons for its success.
- "More Tax Complications." Article looks at changes to the Internal Revenue Code due to the latest Supreme Court decision on Obamacare.

Rights and Payment

Rights vary. All material, payment rates vary. Payment policy varies. Provides 1 author's copy.

Medical Economics

641 Lexington Avenue, 8th Floor
New York, NY 10022

Director of Editorial: Tara Schwartz

Description and Interests

Medical Economics is read by physicians working in practices outside hospital settings. It offers informative articles on financial, legal, and medical issues, as well as personal experience pieces. It does not publish research papers or theoretical works; rather its readers want practical advice on how to run their practices. Circ: 178,341.

Contents: 60% articles; 40% depts/columns
Frequency: 24 times each year
Website: www.modernmedicine.com

Freelance Potential

30% written by nonstaff writers. Publishes 40 freelance submissions yearly; 4% by authors who are new to the magazine, 30% by experts. Receives 10 queries monthly.

Submissions

Query with clips or writing samples. Accepts email queries to tschwartz@advanstar.com. Responds in 2–4 weeks.

- Articles: 1,000–2,000 words. Informational articles and personal experience pieces. Topics include practice management, personal finance, career development, medical/legal issues, managed care, professional ethics, malpractice, third-party payers, and relations with patients and colleagues.
- Depts/columns: Staff-written.

Sample Issue

98 pages. Advertising. Sample copy and guidelines available.

- "FDA Approves New Treatment for a Type of Late-Stage Prostate Cancer." Article announces a drug approval aimed for prostate cancer patients in which other drugs failed.
- "Retinal Disease Research Gets $2.4 million Boost." Article discusses the retinal degenerative disease causes and treatments that will be explored through eight new research projects.

Rights and Payment

First world rights. Articles, $600. Kill fee, 25% for assigned articles only. Pays on acceptance. Provides 2 contributor's copies.

Midwifery Today

P.O. Box 2672
Eugene, OR 97402-0223

Editor-in-Chief: Jan Tritten

Description and Interests

This publication offers a mix of scientific articles and personal experience pieces about midwifery, pregnancy, and childbirth. It also includes information on labor support and childbirth education. Its goal is to foster communication between childbirth educators and to promote responsible midwifery and childbirth education around the world. Circ: 3,000.

Contents: 70% articles; 20% depts/columns; 10% other
Frequency: Quarterly
Website: www.midwiferytoday.com

Freelance Potential

60% written by nonstaff writers. Publishes 150 freelance submissions yearly; 10% by unpublished writers, 20% by authors who are new to the magazine, 90% by experts. Receives 8 queries monthly.

Submissions

Query or send complete ms with short author bio. Accepts email to editorial@midwiferytoday.com (Word and RTF attachments). No simultaneous submissions. Responds in 1 month.

- Articles: 800–1,500 words. Informational and how-to articles; profiles; interviews; and personal experience pieces. Topics include pregnancy, childbirth, midwifery, health, fitness, nutrition, and family life.
- Depts/columns: Word lengths vary. News briefs, media reviews, and Q&As.
- Other: Poetry.

Sample Issue

72 pages. Advertising. Sample articles, guidelines, and editorial calendar available at website.

- "26 Ways to Change Birth Globally." Article discusses small things all midwives can do to change societal attitudes to birth and to promote midwifery.
- "A Bermuda Story." Article describes the trials of a first-time mother having a homebirth in Bermuda.

Rights and Payment

First rights. Written material, no payment. Artwork, $15–$50. Provides 2 contributor's copies and a 1-year subscription.

Mini-Storage Messenger

2531 West Dunlap Avenue
Phoenix, AZ 85021

Publisher: Poppy Behrens

Description and Interests

A mix of storage business news, research data, and interviews attracts self-storage operators to this magazine. It also reports on development, management, and marketing issues within the industry. Writers with new ideas and fresh voices are encouraged to send a query. Circ: 20,000.

Contents: 60% articles; 40% depts/columns
Frequency: Monthly
Website: www.ministoragemessenger.com

Freelance Potential

90% written by nonstaff writers. Publishes 100 freelance submissions yearly; 10% by unpublished writers, 25% by new authors, 20% by experts. Receives 2–3 queries monthly.

Submissions

All articles are assigned. To be considered, query with résumé and writing samples. Accepts hard copy and email to pbehrens@minico.com. SASE. Responds in 2 weeks.

- Articles: 2,500+ words. Informational articles; profiles; interviews; and product information. Topics include facility operations, investment and finance, location studies, traffic counts, rental and occupancy rates, legal issues, case studies, business management, construction, and development.
- Depts/columns: 1,200–1,600 words. Products, legal issues, industry news, and market watch.

Sample Issue

80 pages. Advertising. Sample copy, guidelines, and editorial calendar available.

- "Technology Makes Its Mark." Article highlights the recent technology upgrades that are happening throughout the storage industry.
- "Retail Merchandising As Easy As 1,2,3." Article discusses how the ease and convenience of displaying storage and moving supplies draw customers in.

Rights and Payment

First and reprint rights. Articles, $275–$400. Depts/columns, payment rates vary. Pays on acceptance. Provides 3 contributor's copies.

Ministry Today

600 Rinehart Road
Lake Mary, FL 32746

Editorial Director: Marcus Yoars

Description and Interests

Ministry Today offers evangelical Christian pastors and church leaders in-depth articles on the practical side of ministering. Applicable advice, rather than theory, is the mainstay of this publication. It also features profiles and interviews. New writers are encouraged to look to the magazine's departments for the best chance at publication. It does not publish sermons, poetry, or fiction. Circ: 25,000.

Contents: 50% articles; 50% depts/columns
Frequency: 6 times each year
Website: www.ministrytodaymag.com

Freelance Potential

70% written by nonstaff writers. Publishes 60 freelance submissions yearly.

Submissions

Query with outline, word count, and possible sources; or send complete ms. Accepts hard copy and email to ministrytoday@charismamedia.com. Responds in 2 weeks.

- Articles: To 2,500 words. Informational and how-to articles; profiles; interviews; and new product information. Topics include church leadership and management, miracles and healing, and people who are living Christian lives.
- Depts/columns: To 700 words. "Ministry Life," "Ministry Leadership," "Ministry Outreach," "Ministry Facilities."

Sample Issue

62 pages. Advertising. Sample articles and guidelines available at website.

- "She Practices What She Preaches." Article features a profile of Joyce Meyer, founder of Hand of Hope Ministries.
- "Living Radically Generous." Article describes the need for others to aggressively look for ways in which to help others.

Rights and Payment

All North American serial rights. Written material, payment rates vary. Pays on publication.

Mobile Self-Storage Magazine

2531 West Dunlap Avenue
Phoenix, AZ 85021

Publisher: Poppy Behrens

Description and Interests
Mobile self-storage owners and operators read this magazine for its comprehensive coverage of management issues, marketing strategies, new products, and industry news and trends. It is published by the Mobile Self-Storage Association. All articles are assigned but new ideas and a unique outlook on this fast-moving industry are always welcome. Circ: 20,000.

Contents: 35% articles; 65% depts/columns
Frequency: Quarterly
Website: www.mobileselfstoragemagazine.com

Freelance Potential
90% written by nonstaff writers. Publishes 20–25 freelance submissions yearly; 20% by authors who are new to the magazine, 25% by industry experts. Receives 1 query monthly.

Submissions
All articles are assigned. Query with résumé and writing samples. Accepts hard copy and email queries to pbehrens@minico.com. SASE. Responds in 2 weeks.

- Articles: 2,500+ words. Informational articles; profiles; interviews; and new product information. Topics include occupancy, marketing, customer service, lien sales, property maintenance, security, and management tools.
- Depts/columns: 1,200–1,600 words. New products, legal issues, and industry news.

Sample Issue
96 pages. Advertising. Sample articles and editorial calendar available at website. Writers' guidelines available.

- "Cyber Loan Workouts." Article offers options and strategies for borrowers who are struggling to meet loan obligations.
- "Auctions as Grab Bags." Article discusses the recent curiosity about storage auctions due to the popularity of the tv show, "Storage Wars."

Rights and Payment
First and reprint rights. Articles, $275–$400. Depts/columns, payment rates vary. Pays on acceptance. Provides 3 contributor's copies.

Momentum

National Catholic Educational Association
1005 North Glebe Road, Suite 525
Arlington, VA 22201-5792

Editor: Brian E. Gray

Description and Interests
Catholic educators working at the elementary through college levels subscribe to *Momentum* for updates on education trends, information on ways to support and promote Catholic education, and news from the National Catholic Education Association. Practical, easy-to-replicate ideas for schools and parishes, as well as new information on technology are always of interest. Circ: 23,000.

Contents: 80% articles; 20% depts/columns
Frequency: Quarterly
Website: www.ncea.org

Freelance Potential
95% written by nonstaff writers. Publishes 90 freelance submissions yearly; 20% by unpublished writers, 65% by authors who are new to the magazine, 25% by experts. Receives 10 queries each month.

Submissions
Query or send complete ms. Accepts email to momentum@ncea.org (Word attachments) and hard copy with CD. No simultaneous submissions. Responds in 1–3 months.

- Articles: Features, 1,500 words. Research pieces, 3,500–5,000 words. Informational and how-to articles; profiles; and interviews. Topics include educational trends, methodology, financial development, and catechism.
- Depts/columns: "From the Field," opinions and essays, 700–1,000 words. Book reviews, 500–750 words.

Sample Issue
80 pages. Guidelines, and editorial calendar available at website.

- "Listening: A Pathway to Civility." Article proclaims the benefits of going beyond paying attention politely to active listening as a pathway to promoting civil discourse.
- "Battling Bullying." Article discusses anti-bullying actions being taken by Catholic schools.

Rights and Payment
First North American serial rights. Payment rates vary. Pays on publication. Provides 2 copies.

Mortgage Banking

1717 Rhode Island Avenue NW, Suite 400
Washington, DC 20036

Editor in Chief: Janet Reilley Hewitt

Description and Interests

This magazine analyzes the critical issues and trends that affect the real estate finance industry. It is read by financial services executives, mortgage bankers, and brokers. Its content is written by leading industry CEOs and veteran mortgage journalists who truly understand the business and can interpret it for readers. Circ: 10,000.

Contents: 40% articles; 55% depts/columns; 5% other
Frequency: Monthly
Website: www.mortgagebankingmagazine.com

Freelance Potential

90% written by nonstaff writers. Publishes 175 freelance submissions yearly; 10% by unpublished writers, 10% by authors who are new to the magazine, 80% by experts. Receives 20 queries each month.

Submissions

Query with outline. Accepts email to jhewitt@mortgagebankers.org. Responds in 1 week.

- Articles: 2,500 words. Informational and how-to articles; profiles; and interviews. Topics include real estate trends, mortgage origination strategies, financial legislation, sales management, fraud, financial education, and commercial and multifamily real estate.
- Depts/columns: 1,000 words. Industry news, executive essays, Q&As, legislative reports, diversity training, technology, commercial real estate, mortgage servicing advice, broker business, and conference coverage.

Sample Issue

114 pages. Advertising. Sample copy, guidelines, and editorial calendar available at website.

- "The Distressed Property Dilemma." Article reveals how housing servicers are trying to manage their foreclosures and real estate-owned properties.
- "Has Tucson Hit Bottom?." Article discusses the the foreclosure problem in this Arizona city.

Rights and Payment

First and reprint rights. Written material, payment rates vary. Pays on acceptance. Provides 2+ contributor's copies.

MovieMaker

8328 De Soto Avenue
Canoga Park, CA 91304

Editor in Chief: Timothy Rhys

Description and Interests

MovieMaker is the leading resource on the art and business of making movies. It offers articles of interest to both film aficionados and filmmakers. Profiles of influential members of the movie-making community and reports on industry news and festivals are featured. Submissions should reflect knowledge of the movie industry while inspiring and educating readers. Circ: 44,000.

Contents: Articles; depts/columns
Frequency: 6 times each year
Website: www.moviemaker.com

Freelance Potential

90% written by nonstaff writers. Publishes 75–100 freelance submissions yearly; 5% by unpublished writers, 25% by authors who are new to the magazine, 50% by experts. Receives 50 queries each month.

Submissions

Query with résumé and clips. Prefers email queries to trhys@moviemaker.com (no attachments); will accept hard copy. SASE. Responds in 2 months.

- Articles: 800–1,000 words. Informational and how-to articles; profiles; interviews; and creative nonfiction. Topics include the art and business of making movies.
- Depts/columns: 250–1,500 words. Media reviews, new product information, event coverage, and industry news.

Sample Issue

96 pages. Advertising. Sample articles available at website. Guidelines and theme list available.

- "Greta Gerwig, Inside Outsider." Article features a profile of this actress who has quickly risen to fame.
- "Lights, Camera, Social Action." Article explains the concept of "crowdfunding" and how it is helping get movies produced in the current economy.

Rights and Payment

Rights vary. Articles, $75–$500. Depts/columns, payment rates vary. Kill fee varies. Pays within 30 days of publication. Provides 3 author's copies.

MSW Management

Forester Media
P.O. Box 3100
Santa Barbara, CA 93130

Editor: John Trotti

Description and Interests

MSW Management presents informative and engaging articles about the public-sector municipal waste industry, including source reduction, composting, recycling, and landfills. Articles should be readable even when dealing with a highly technical subject. Assume readers have a high level of expertise. Circ: 25,000.

Contents: Articles; depts/columns
Frequency: 7 times each year
Website: www.forester.net

Freelance Potential

90% written by nonstaff writers. Publishes 45–50 freelance submissions yearly; 20% by unpublished writers, 30% by authors who are new to the magazine, 40% by industry experts. Receives 10 queries, 2 unsolicited mss monthly.

Submissions

Send complete ms with artwork. Accepts submissions via website. Responds in 1 month.

- Articles: 3,000 words. Informational and how-to articles; profiles; interviews; and opinion pieces. Topics include environmental compliance, landfill management, source reduction, waste collection and transfer, composting, recycling, incineration, public and private projects, and odor management.
- Depts/columns: 1,000 words. Opinions, news, products, and project profiles.

Sample Issue

78 pages. Advertising. Sample copy, guidelines, and editorial calendar available at website.

- "Profits Under the ADC." Article details the winning formula for landfill profitability.
- "When Green Turns to Gold." Article explains how converting organic waste into raw materials creates jobs and builds more competitive manufacturing industries.
- "Staying Power." Article highlights how one landfill solved its erosion problem with the right combination of seed.

Rights and Payment

All rights. Written material, payment rates vary. Pays 30 days after acceptance. Provides 1 contributor's copy.

Nailpro

7628 Densmore Avenue
Van Nuys, CA 91406

Executive Editor: Stephanie Yaggy

Description and Interests

Nailpro is a professional trade magazine for those who own, manage, or work in nail salons. In addition to articles on techniques and products, it also gives readers advice on running a business and serving clients. The best query is one that shows the writer's experience in the industry as well as the kind of information it will share with readers. Circ: 65,000.

Contents: 50% articles; 42% depts/columns; 8% other
Frequency: Monthly
Website: www.nailpro.com

Freelance Potential

80% written by nonstaff writers. Publishes 60 freelance submissions yearly; 30% by unpublished writers, 20% by authors who are new to the magazine, 80% by experts. Receives 5–6 queries, 3 unsolicited mss monthly.

Submissions

Prefers query; will accept complete ms. Prefers email to syaggy@creativeage.com; will accept hard copy. SASE. Responds in 1 month.

- Articles: 1,500–2,000 words. Informational, technical, and how-to articles; profiles; and interviews. Topics include artistic nail techniques, salon management, business issues, and health issues.
- Depts/columns: 1,000–2,000 words. News, technical tips, and new product information.

Sample Issue

210 pages. Advertising. Sample copy available at website. Guidelines available.

- "The Art of Interviewing." Article discusses how to best fulfill staffing needs by asking smart interview questions.
- "In Any Event." Article describes which nail art fashions best match different holidays.

Rights and Payment

All rights. Articles, $300–$400. Depts/columns, $250. Pays on acceptance. Provides 1 contributor's copy.

Networking Times

11418 Kokopeli Place
Chatsworth, CA 91311

Editor: Josephine M. Gross, Ph.D

Description and Interests
Networking Times targets network marketers, direct sales people, home business owners, and others who practice relationship marketing. Each issue features personal and professional development strategies for networking, marketing, leadership, goal-setting, team building, and communication, with an emphasis on acquiring skills and building the right mindset in order to build a profitable networking business. Circ: 25,000.
Contents: 60% articles; 40% depts/columns
Frequency: 6 times each year
Website: www.networkingtimes.com

Freelance Potential
40% written by nonstaff writers. Publishes 50 freelance submissions yearly; 5% by unpublished writers, 5% by authors who are new to the magazine, 20% by experts. Receives several queries monthly.

Submissions
Query or send complete ms with clips, brief author bio, and headshot. Accepts email queries to editors@networkingtimes.com (Word attachments). Responds in 1 week.

- Articles: 1,000 words. Informational and how-to articles; profiles; interviews; and opinion pieces. Topics include networking, careers, business issues, Internet marketing, finance, and entrepreneurship.
- Depts/columns: 1,000 words. Opinion pieces, book reviews.

Sample Issue
72 pages. No advertising. Sample copy and guidelines available at website.

- "The Education of Jack Canfield." Article features a profile of the originator and coauthor of the Chicken Soup for the Soul books.
- "The Professor of Network Marketing." Article presents an interview with Charles King, the creator of a popular video presentation.
- Sample dept/column: "Internet Marketing" offers ten tips for using Pinterest to grow business and increase one's circle of influence.

Rights and Payment
All rights. No payment. Provides 3 author's copies.

The Network Journal
Black Professionals and Small Business Magazine

39 Broadway, Suite 2430
New York, NY 10006

Executive Editor: Rosalind McLymont

Description and Interests
Black businessmen and women and entrepreneurs turn to *The Network Journal* as a resource for professional and business growth. Its award-winning content includes news, trends, technology, and profiles of professionals who reveal their strategies for success. Its editorial content is meant to educate and empower readers. Articles must be well researched and written with insight. Circ: 66,000.
Contents: Articles; depts/columns
Frequency: 6 times each year
Website: www.tnj.com

Freelance Potential
30% written by nonstaff writers. Publishes 70–80 freelance submissions yearly; 25% by authors who are new to the magazine, 15% by industry experts.

Submissions
Query with résumé and 3 writing samples. Accepts hard copy and email to editors@tnj.com. SASE. Responds in 1 month.

- Articles: Cover stories, 1,200–1,500 words. In-depth profiles of black professionals. Features, 600–800 words. Informational, self-help, and how-to articles; interviews; opinion pieces; and new product information. Topics include business news and trends, entrepreneurs, career strategies, and success stories.
- Depts/columns: 600 words. Finance, economics, book reviews, and technology.

Sample Issue
52 pages. Advertising. Sample articles available at website. Guidelines and theme list available.

- "Jamaica Introduces Garveyism in Classrooms." Article discusses the controversial decision to introduce Marcus Garvey to Jamaican classrooms.
- "Sample Dept/Column: "Pesonal Finance" provides 10 tips for breaking bad money habits.

Rights and Payment
All rights. Written material, $100–$300. Pays on publication. Provides 1 contributor's copy.

Network Marketing Business Journal

20636 Burl Court, Unit E
Joliet, IL 60433

Editorial Manager: Brenda Follmer

Description and Interests

This international newspaper emphasizes the how-to's of network marketing and includes authoritative articles on home office technology, direct selling, and direct marketing. It accepts work from new writers as long as they are professionals familiar with the network marketing industry. Submissions should include a short biography and a list of available photos, charts, or drawings. Circ: 200,000.

Contents: 60% articles; 30% depts/columns; 10% other
Frequency: Monthly
Website: www.nmbj.com

Freelance Potential

70% written by nonstaff writers. Publishes 60 freelance submissions yearly; 40% by authors who are new to the magazine, 100% by experts. Receives 16 unsolicited mss monthly.

Submissions

Send complete ms with author bio. Accepts hard copy, disk submissions, email submissions to editors@nmbj.com, and fax submissions to 815-726-5550. SASE. Responds in 1 month.

- Articles: To 2,000 words. Informational and how-to articles; opinion and personal experience pieces; profiles; and interviews. Topics include home office technology, marketing, direct selling, and networking.
- Depts/columns: To 2,000 words. Industry news, legal issues, company profiles.

Sample Issue

20 pages. Advertising. Sample articles available at website. Guideliness available.

- "Internet Coach, Along with Evolv Opportunity, Can Help Take You to the Next Level." Article discusses the direct marketing strategies that made one company successful.
- "Solavei." Article explains why this company is shifting its advertising focus to its customers and social networking.

Rights and Payment

All rights. No payment. Provides 2 contributor's copies.

Nevada Business

375 North Stephanie Street, Building 23
Henderson, NV 89014

Managing Editor: Tarah Figueroa

Description and Interests

This regional business magazine covers the business scene in Nevada, including what's new in gaming, media, manufacturing, health care, real estate, financial services, and tourism. It also profiles businesses and civic leaders. Articles may be specific to one company or industry, or may be a trend or analysis piece. Whatever the topic, it must be tailored specifically to Nevada businesses and business people. Circ: 20,000.

Contents: 50% articles; 50% depts/columns
Frequency: Monthly
Website: www.nevadabusiness.com

Freelance Potential

98% written by nonstaff writers. Publishes 60 freelance submissions yearly; 10% by unpublished writers, 10% by authors who are new to the magazine, 25% by experts. Receives 10 queries monthly.

Submissions

Query. Accepts email queries to tarah@nevadabusiness.com. Responds in 1 month.

- Articles: To 2,500 words. Informational articles and profiles. Topics include Nevada businesses, careers, government, law, management, and politics.
- Depts/columns: 600–1,000 words. Nevada news briefs, profiles, and technology.
- Artwork: B/W or color digital images at 300 dpi.

Sample Issue

40 pages. Advertising. Sample issue and editorial calendar available at website. Guidelines available.

- "Wealth Management." Article discusses the need to diversify investments when planning for retirement.
- "Building Nevada: Rural Nevada." Article highlights unique business opportunities in unique communities around the state.
- Sample dept/column: "Free Market Watch" discusses how state policymakers are affected by recent Obamacare decisions.

Rights and Payment

All rights. Written material, $.20. Kill fee, 50%. Pays on publication. Provides 5 contributor's copies.

The New Physician

45610 Woodland Road, Suite 300
Sterling, VA 20166

Editor: Pete Thomson

Description and Interests
Medical students and residents read this magazine for its progressive coverage of issues that are not covered by more traditional medical journals. It seeks articles that raise critical questions about medical education and medicine. Many of its departments are written by reader contributors. Most of the feature articles fit in with each issue's theme, and should be written in long-form, magazine-style journalism. Circ: 34,000.

Contents: Articles; depts/columns
Frequency: 6 times each year
Website: www.amsa.org/tnp

Freelance Potential
75% written by nonstaff writers. Publishes 10 freelance submissions yearly; 30% by unpublished writers, 30% by authors who are new to the magazine, 20% by experts. Receives 5 queries, 10 unsolicited mss monthly.

Submissions
Prefers query with outline and writing samples; will accept complete ms. Accepts hard copy, email to tnp@amsa.org, and simultaneous submissions if identified. Does not return unsolicited mss. Responds in 10–12 weeks.

- Articles: 1,200–2,500 words. Informational articles and personal experience pieces. Topics include medical education, practicing medicine, healthcare policies, and activism.
- Depts/columns: 500–1,200 words. Opinions, news items, case studies, advice, finance, careers, and reviews.

Sample Issue
34 pages. Advertising. Sample articles and guidelines available at website. Theme list available.

- "The Kindest Specialty." Article details the differences between palliative care and hospice.
- Sample dept/column: "Academic Tactics" offers advice when making the decision to take a gap year.

Rights and Payment
All rights. Written material, $.50 per word. Pays on acceptance. Provides 2 author's copies.

Occupational Health & Safety

14901 Quorum Drive, Suite 425
Dallas, TX 75254

Editor: Jerry Laws

Description and Interests
This magazine provides in-depth information on the techniques and applications to assess and control workplace health and safety hazards, as well as the latest legislation and trends affecting it. Its audience ranges from health and safety managers and engineers to occupational nurses and therapists. Circ: 80,000.

Contents: 90% articles; 10% depts/columns
Frequency: Monthly
Website: www.ohsonline.com

Freelance Potential
80% written by nonstaff writers. Publishes 100 freelance submissions yearly; 5% by unpublished writers, 10% by authors who are new to the magazine, 80% by experts. Receives 3–4 unsolicited mss monthly.

Submissions
Query or send complete ms. Accepts email to jlaws@1105media.com. No simultaneous submissions. Responds in 1 week.

- Articles: 1,500 words. Informational and how-to articles. Topics include health and safety management, training, techniques, and applications; legislation; first responders; leadership; careers; and worker productivity.
- Depts/columns: 900 words. New products, news, trends, and management issues.

Sample Issue
68 pages. Advertising. Sample articles, guidelines, and editorial calendar available at website.

- "Stepping Up the Pace." Article outlines the health insurance exchange deadline that will affect all states.
- "OSHA's Stance on Safety Incentive Programs." Article discusses the validity of these programs or whether they discourage employees from reporting injuries.

Rights and Payment
All rights. No payment. Provides 4 contributor's copies.

OfficePro

P.O. Box 20404
Kansas City, MO 64195-0404

Managing Editor: Emily Allen

Description and Interests

Written for those in the administrative field, *OfficePro* provides its readers with the latest information and tips to help them excel at their jobs. Published by the International Association of Administrative Professionals, it also features product reviews and industry news. Its editors seek new, up-to-date information that offers a fresh perspective on office life and the issues that matter to today's office professional. All submissions must include sources. Circ: 35,000.

Contents: 60% articles; 25% depts/columns; 15% other
Frequency: 7 times each year
Website: www.iaap-hq.org

Freelance Potential

90% written by nonstaff writers. Publishes 36 freelance submissions yearly; 10% by unpublished writers, 20% by authors who are new to the magazine, 10% by experts. Receives 5 queries monthly.

Submissions

Query with outline and writing samples. Accepts email queries only to eallen@iaap-hq.org. Responds in 2 weeks.

- Articles: 1,200–1,500 words. Informational articles; personal experience pieces; and new product information. Topics include business, computers, education, feminism, management, and writing.
- Depts/columns: 700–800 words. Industry news, fitness tips, resources, case studies.

Sample Issue

44 pages. Advertising. Sample articles, guidelines, and editorial calendar available at website.

- "Karlena Rannals: Be The One." Article profiles the newest president of IAAP.
- "The Sandwich Generation." Article provides strategies for those who find themselves raising children while caring for an aging parent.

Rights and Payment

Exclusive rights. Written material, payment rates vary. Pay on acceptance. Kill fee. Provides 2 contributor's copies.

Outreach

2231 Faraday Avenue, Suite 120
Carlsbad, CA 92008-7728

Editor

Description and Interests

This magazine shares outreach ideas from churches across the country in an effort to inspire, challenge, and inform outreach mission leaders. Its articles aim to inspire volunteerism, provide effective leadership strategies, and help people from various communities connect with God. Submissions without previously published writing samples will not be considered. Circ: 30,000.

Contents: Articles; depts/columns
Frequency: 7 times each year
Website: www.outreachmagazine.com

Freelance Potential

65% written by nonstaff writers. Publishes 30 freelance submissions yearly; 15% by authors who are new to the magazine, 40% by experts. Receives 10 queries monthly.

Submissions

Query or send complete ms with clips, résumé, and cover letter explaining the reader take-away for your idea. Will also consider work for hire. Accepts hard copy and email to TellUs@outreachmagazine.com. SASE. Responds in 8 weeks.

- Articles: 1,500–2,500 word features. Informational and how-to articles; profiles; and interviews. Topics include Christian outreach, evangelism, ministry, church leadership, and contemporary issues.
- Depts/columns: 200–600 words. News and trends, opinion pieces, outreach ideas, and media reviews.

Sample Issue

130 pages. Sample articles and guidelines available at website.

- "Catalyst for Growth: The Outreach Interview." Article presents interview with Andy Stanley, author of "Deep and Wide: Creating Churches Unchurched People Love to Attend."
- "The Leadership Investment." Article discusses 5 elements to help build and lead a network of visionary church leaders.

Rights and Payment

First serial rights. Written material, payment rates vary. Pays on publication.

Pallet Enterprise

10244 Timber Ridge Drive
Ashland, VA 23005

Assistant Publisher: Chaille Brindley

Description and Interests

This trade magazine covers the pallet construction and wood processing industries. In addition to profiling the companies and leaders that are moving the industry, it reports on new products and designs and also covers related news. Writers with knowledge of the pallet industry who are capable of investigating the issues, not just writing profiles, are preferred. Circ: 10,000.

Contents: 45% articles; 55% depts/columns
Frequency: Monthly
Website: www.palletenterprise.com

Freelance Potential

35% written by nonstaff writers. Publishes 24 freelance submissions yearly; 80% by industry experts. Receives 1 query monthly.

Submissions

Query. Accepts email to chaille@ireporting.com. Responds in 1 week.

- Articles: 1,800 words. Informational and how-to articles; profiles; and new product information. Topics include pallet standards, pallet companies, manufacturing techniques, sawmills, recycling, and materials.
- Depts/columns: Staff-written.
- Artwork: Color prints.

Sample Issue

70 pages. Advertising. Sample copy available at website. Writers' guidelines and editorial calendar available.

- "Resawing for Pallet Lumber." Article provides an overview of the models and characteristics of resaw suppliers.
- "Lovett Family Adjusts to Meet Changes in the Pallet Industry." Article profiles Lovett Pallet company and its focus on quality and professional development to provide superior customer service.
- "A Comparison of Pallet Cants and Grade Lumber Price Trends." Article offers an economist's view on the factors that influence availability and prices of pallet cants.

Rights and Payment

Worldwide publication rights. Articles, $250–$300. Artwork, $50–$100. Pays on acceptance. Provides 2–5 contributor's copies.

Pest Management Professional

600 Superior Avenue East, Suite 1100
Cleveland, OH 44114

Editor in Chief: Marty Whitford

Description and Interests

A mix of technical, how-to, and informational articles are found in this magazine about the pest control industry. Topics include business management, new equipment, methods and products, innovative solutions, and industry news. It welcomes case studies and profiles of successful people and companies. Circ: 21,000+.

Contents: Articles; depts/columns
Frequency: Monthly
Website: www.mypmp.net

Freelance Potential

40% written by nonstaff writers. Publishes 50 freelance submissions yearly; 10% by unpublished writers, 10% by authors who are new to the magazine, 60% by experts. Receives 25 queries, 3 unsolicited mss monthly.

Submissions

Query with outline; or send complete ms with author biography. Accepts hard copy and email to mwhitford@questex.com (Word attachments). SASE. Response time varies.

- Articles: Word lengths vary. Informational and how-to articles; profiles; and new product information. Topics include pest control technology and equipment, pesticides, business issues, industry news, and problem solving strategies.
- Depts/columns: Word lengths vary. Trends, business advice, technology updates, and pest-control community news and profiles.

Sample Issue

126 pages. Sample articles available at website. Editorial calendar available.

- "Syngenta Professional Products: Spider Tips." Article details the integrated approach that will effectively control spiders.
- Sample dept/column: "News/Products" describes the new website for Termimesh, LLC.

Rights and Payment

Rights vary. Written material, payment rates vary. Payment policy varies.

Pet Age

18 South Michigan Avenue, Suite 1100
Chicago, IL 60603-3233

Managing Editor: Cathy Foster

Description and Interests

Read by owners and managers of retail pet stores, *Pet Age* offers practical ideas and solutions for everyday issues. Managing, purchasing, selling, and maintenance are some of the issues covered. It is looking for fresh insights on industry topics and practical business advice, not information on the care of pets. Circ: 23,700.

Contents: 30% articles; 70% depts/columns
Frequency: Monthly
Website: www.petage.com

Freelance Potential

45% written by nonstaff writers. Publishes 85 freelance submissions yearly; 1% by unpublished writers, 25% by authors who are new to the magazine, 5% by experts. Receives 10 queries monthly.

Submissions

Query with résumé and clips. Accepts email queries to cfoster@hhbacker.com. Responds in 2–3 months.

- Articles: 1,500–2,000 words. Informational and how-to articles; and opinion pieces. Topics include animals, associations, business, retail, computers, government and law, management issues, media, communications, and environmental issues.
- Depts/columns: Staff-written.

Sample Issue

64 pages. Advertising. Sample articles and editorial calendar available at website. Guidelines available.

- "The New Pet Med Market." Article explains how independent pet retailers can compete with big stores and vet offices for a piece of the pet medication market.
- "Pet Supplies Segment Up Just 2% in 2011." Article discusses survey results about the shopping patterns for nonfood pet supplies.

Rights and Payment

First North American serial rights. Written material, payment rates vary. Pays on acceptance. Provides 1 contributor's copy.

Pet Business

333 Seventh Avenue, 11th Floor
New York, NY 10001

Editor in Chief: Mark Kalaygian

Description and Interests

This trade magazine targets specialty pet store owners and managers with information on retail strategies and management issues in addition to articles on pets, pet care, and new products. A knowledge of retail business strategies is imperative here. The ideal writer has a background in reporting on industry issues. Circ: 24,000+.

Contents: 25% articles; 75% depts/columns
Frequency: Monthly
Website: www.petbusiness.com

Freelance Potential

60% written by nonstaff writers. Publishes 100 freelance submissions yearly; 20% by authors who are new to the magazine, 80% by industry experts. Receives 10 queries monthly.

Submissions

Query with synopsis and clips. Prefers email queries to mkalaygian@petbusiness.com; will accept hard copy. SASE. Responds in 1 month.

- Articles: 1,000–2,000 words. Informational and how-to articles; profiles; interviews; and opinion pieces. Topics include pets, animals, business, careers, computers, management, media, the environment, public affairs, and retailing.
- Depts/columns: Staff-written.
- Artwork: Color transparencies or prints; JPEG or TIFF images.

Sample Issue

156 pages. Advertising. Sample copy and editorial calendar available at website.

- "Welcome to the Club." Article offers a profile of the Arizona-based Pet Club which has seen rapid growth.
- "A Positive Social Print." Article describes examples of pet product manufacturers making a difference in the lives of needy pets.
- "Identifying a Profit Center." Article discusses how retailers can increase profits by offering fashionable and high-tech ID tags.

Rights and Payment

All rights. Articles, $300. Kill fee, 50%. Pays on acceptance. Provides 5 contributor's copies.

P. I. Magazine

4400 Route 9 South, Suite 1000
Freehold, NJ 07728–7198

Editor: Grace Elting Castle

Description and Interests

This trade magazine provides the latest in technology, surveillance tips, and legal and law enforcement news to help private investigators be more successful. New writers must be familiar with *P. I. Magazine* before submitting, and be able to write for an audience of professional investigators. Circ: 10,000.

Contents: 60% articles; 20% depts/columns; 20% other
Frequency: 6 times each year
Website: www.pimagazine.com

Freelance Potential

90% written by nonstaff writers. Publishes 50 freelance submissions yearly; 40% by unpublished writers, 40% by authors who are new to the magazine, 20% by industry experts. Receives 10 queries monthly.

Submissions

Send complete ms for material under 750 words; query for longer articles. Accepts email to editor@pimagazine.com (Word attachments). No simultaneous submissions. Responds in 1 month.

- Articles: 750–2,000 words. Informational and how-to articles; profiles; and new product information. Topics include audio and video surveillance, software, the Internet, law enforcement, legal issues, forensics, security, fraud, business management, media, communications, psychology, and training.
- Depts/columns: To 600 words. Crime detection, fugitive recovery, tips, surveillance, Internet tools, networking, profiles, news, gadgets, legislative reports, and book reviews.

Sample Issue

88 pages. Advertising. Sample articles and guidelines available at website.

- "Dead Men Don't Talk, But the Packing Slip Will." Article shares details on creating a plan for investigating business theft and fraud.
- "Criminal Profiling." Article explains the debate about the usefulness of criminal profiling.

Rights and Payment

First-time rights. Written material, $.20–$.25 per word. Pays on publication.

Ping! Zine

1814 South Range Avenue, Suite D
P.O. Box 516
Denham Springs, LA 70726

Editor in Chief/Publisher: Keith Duncan

Description and Interests

Ping! Zine features news and information regarding computer servers and Web hosting. Its articles and how-to's provide information on computer security, code, and maintenance for professionals and those in charge of maintaining websites. All articles must be vendor-neutral in tone. Nothing with a self-promoting tone will be accepted. Circ: 45,000.

Contents: 50% articles; 40% depts/columns; 10% other
Frequency: 6 times each year
Website: www.pingzine.com

Freelance Potential

70% written by nonstaff writers. Publishes 100 freelance submissions yearly; 80% by unpublished writers, 70% by authors who are new to the magazine, 90% by industry experts. Receives 10 queries monthly.

Submissions

Query with working title and summary. Accepts email queries to info@pingzine.com (no attachments). Responds in 1 month.

- Articles: To 3,500 words. Informational and how-to articles; profiles; and interviews. Topics include business, computers, science, and technology—all as they relate to the Web hosting industry.
- Depts/columns: 1,500 words. Media reviews and new product information.

Sample Issue

66 pages. Advertising. Sample articles and writers' guidelines available at website. Editorial calendar available.

- "Best Way to Run PHP in Shared Hosting." Article explains the performance, stability, and security trade-offs for the different ways to run PHP on the server.
- "Something Useful About Server Security." Article discusses the latest information on server security.

Rights and Payment

First world rights. Written material, payment rates vary. Pays on publication. Provides 10 contributor's copies.

Pizza Today

908 South 8th Street, #200
Louisville, KY 40203

Editor in Chief: Jeremy White

Description and Interests

Information and advice to help pizza restaurants be more efficient, profitable, and popular is the editorial focus of this business magazine. Published by the National Association of Pizzeria Operators, it targets owners of independent and franchised pizzerias. All articles must be solutions-based and offer readers information on either making a better product or running their pizzeria more efficiently. Writers with experience covering the restaurant industry are preferred. Circ: 42,000.

Contents: 50% articles; 50% depts/columns
Frequency: Monthly
Website: www.pizzatoday.com

Freelance Potential

30% written by nonstaff writers. Publishes 120 freelance submissions yearly; 1% by unpublished writers, 5% by authors who are new to the magazine, 25% by experts. Receives 20 queries monthly.

Submissions

Query with clips. Accepts email queries to jwhite@pizzatoday.com. Responds in 1 month.

- Articles: 1,000 words. Informational articles; profiles; interviews; and photo-essays. Topics include staff training and management; food preparation and presentation; food service marketing, promotion, and delivery; pizza ingredients; beverages; safety; security; cleaning and maintenance; and customer retention.
- Depts/columns: Staff-written.

Sample Issue

98 pages. Advertising. Sample copy, guidelines, and editorial calendar available at website.

- "Cash Only." Article discusses the financial risks of being a cash-only business.
- "Rocky Mountain High." Article profiles the Borriello Brothers on their New York-style pizzerias based in Colorado.
- "Listen, Learn, Earn." Article shares marketing ideas that were successful generating business on an otherwise slow day.

Rights and Payment

First rights. Articles, $500. Pays on acceptance.

Planning

American Planning Association
205 North Michigan Avenue, Suite 1200
Chicago, IL 60601

Editor & Publisher: Sylvia Lewis

Description and Interests

The focus of this magazine for members of the American Planning Association is urban, suburban, rural, and small town planning; environmental and social planning; neighborhood revitalization; and economic development. It prefers writers with professional experience in planning or environmental concerns. Circ: 45,000.

Contents: 40% articles; 30% depts/columns; 30% other
Frequency: 10 times each year
Website: www.planning.org

Freelance Potential

75% written by nonstaff writers. Publishes 40 freelance submissions yearly; 5% by unpublished writers, 15% by authors who are new to the magazine, 85% by experts. Receives 50 queries monthly.

Submissions

Query with author biography, sources, and available artwork. Accepts hard copy and email queries to slewis@planning.org. Availability of artwork improves chance of acceptance. SASE. Responds in 6 weeks.

- Articles: 2,500 words. Informational articles and case studies. Topics include urban design, suburban and rural planning, environmental and social planning, neighborhood revitalization, and economic development.
- Depts/columns: News, to 500 words. Book reviews, 500–700 words. Opinion pieces, 600 words.
- Artwork: Digital images at 300 dpi or higher in JPEG, EPS, TIFF, or PDF formats.

Sample Issue

56 pages. Advertising. Sample copy, guidelines, and editorial calendar available at website.

- "Water War, Southern Style." Article explains the 20-year battle over water between Georgia, Alabama, and Florida.
- "What's Next for Quebec's Northern Frontier?" Article examines the ambitious plan for the resource-rich northern territory.

Rights and Payment

All rights. Written material, $100–$1,500. Artwork, $50–$300. Pays on publication. Provides 2 contributor's copies.

Plate

1415 North Dayton Street
Chicago, IL 60642

Editor: Chandra Ram

Description and Interests

Plate is a culinary magazine that reports on both traditional and innovative topics in each of its themed issues. Geared to professional chefs and those in the food industry, it features more than 60 recipes and interviews with industry leaders and up-and-coming chefs. The editors seek writers with a broad range of contacts and who are obsessed with food and always curious about new flavors and cuisines. Circ: 35,000.

Contents: Articles; depts/columns
Frequency: 6 times each year
Website: www.plateonline.com

Freelance Potential

70% written by nonstaff writers.

Submissions

Query with clips and bio. Accepts email to cram@plateonline.com. Response time varies.

- Articles: 500–1,800 words. Informational and how-to articles, and interviews. Topics include food, cooking, professional chefs, and recipes.
- Depts/columns: Word lengths vary. Industry news.

Sample Issue

Advertising. Sample articles available at website.

- "Pichet Ong Reveals His Sweet Side." Article includes an interview with the owner of a New York City bakery on his culinary influences.
- "Gluten Intolerance 101." Article discusses this common ailment and innovative ways to make gluten-free meals.

Rights and Payment

All rights. Written material, $1 per word. Pays on publication.

Podiatry Management

P.O. Box 750129
Forest Hills, NY 11375

Editor: Barry H. Block, DPM, JD

Description and Interests

Business and practice issues are tackled in this magazine for podiatrists. It covers topics such as office management, technology, finance, and marketing. There is an increased need for freelance writers and for articles on practice management that provide valuable tips and solutions. All articles should include quotes from podiatrists. Circ: 16,500.

Contents: 70% articles; 20% depts/columns; 10% other
Frequency: 9 times each year
Website: www.podiatrym.com

Freelance Potential

50% written by nonstaff writers. Publishes 30 freelance submissions yearly; 5% by unpublished writers, 10% by authors who are new to the magazine, 20% by experts. Receives 10 queries, 5 unsolicited mss monthly.

Submissions

Query or send complete ms. Accepts email to bblock@prodigy.net. Responds in 10 days.

- Articles: 1,500–2,500 words. Informational and how-to articles; profiles; and interviews. Topics include health, marketing, office efficiency, money matters, staff management, legal issues, and business.
- Depts/columns: 600–750 words. News and product reviews.

Sample Issue

218 pages. Advertising. Sample copy and guidelines available.

- "Autologous Platelets for Treatment of Tendonopathy of the Foot and Ankle." Article reviews recent studies and available systems for platelet concentrates in the treatment of tendonopathy.
- "Textbook of Bunion Surgery." Article discusses the fourth edition of this book.

Rights and Payment

First North American serial rights. Written material, payment rates vary. Pays on publication. Provides 2 contributor's copies.

Poets & Writers Magazine

90 Broad Street, Suite 2100
New York, NY 10004

Editor: Kevin Larimer

Description and Interests

Poets & Writers Magazine features news for and about the contemporary literary community within the U.S. Each issue includes how-to articles on the business of creative writing, essays, interviews with contemporary writers, and information about literary grants and awards. Its readership includes students and faculty of creative writing programs, professional writers, and those who write as a hobby. Circ: 60,000.

Contents: 50% articles; 50% depts/columns
Frequency: 6 times each year
Website: www.pw.org

Freelance Potential

75% written by nonstaff writers. Publishes 75 freelance submissions yearly; 5% by unpublished writers, 25% by new authors, 30% by experts. Receives 30–50 queries monthly.

Submissions

Query or send complete ms with 2 clips. Accepts hard copy and email to editor@pw.org. SASE. Responds in 4–6 weeks.

- Articles: 1,500–3,000 words. Informational articles; profiles; interviews; and opinion pieces. Topics include contemporary writers, writers' conferences and residencies, small presses, and regional writing.
- Depts/columns: Word lengths vary. Personal essays, practical tips, how-to's, news briefs, and industry trends.

Sample Issue

144 pages. Advertising. Sample articles and writers' guidelines available at website.

- "Emma Straub's Life in Letters (So Far)." Article profiles this author about her early struggles and her debut novel.
- Sample dept/column: "The Literary Life" discusses the recent history and upcoming changes in the publishing landscape.

Rights and Payment

Exclusive worldwide and non-exclusive reprint rights. Written material, $200–$300. Pays on publication. Provides 2 contributor's copies.

Police and Security News

1208 Juniper Street
Quakertown, PA 18951-1520

Managing Editor: James Devery

Description and Interests

A mix of educational and entertaining information for professionals in the law enforcement field can be found in this magazine. Its articles cover day-to-day issues as well as technology, news, products, training, and services. It is read by law enforcement professionals at all levels of government. Circ: 24,000.

Contents: 40% articles; 60% depts/columns
Frequency: 6 times each year
Website: www.policeandsecuritynews.com

Freelance Potential

100% written by nonstaff writers. Publishes 60 freelance submissions yearly; 10% by authors who are new to the magazine, 100% by industry experts. Receives 10 queries monthly.

Submissions

Query. Prefers email queries to jdevery@policeandsecuritynews.com; will accept hard copy. SASE. Responds in 2 weeks.

- Articles: Word lengths vary. Informational and how-to articles; and personal experience pieces. Topics include law enforcement, homeland security, forensics, weapons, ammunition, community relations, recruitment, technology, speed control, and motor vehicle pursuit.
- Depts/columns: Word lengths vary. Industry news, technology, training, legal Q&As.
- Artwork: B/W or color prints or slides.

Sample Issue

68 pages. Advertising. Sample copy and editorial calendar available at website. Writers' guidelines available.

- "Micro-Nine: The Snubs of the 21st Century." Article explains the new options available on the market for service pistols.
- "Training to Avoid Handgun-ECD Confusion." Article discusses training tips for avoiding a potentially deadly incident.

Rights and Payment

First North American serial rights. Written material, $.10 per word. Artwork, $10–$20. Pays on publication. Provides 6 author's copies.

Powersports Business

3300 Fernbrook Lane North, Suite 200
Minneapolis, MN 55447

Senior Editor: Dave McMahon

Description and Interests

Breaking news, market analysis, and industry trends regarding the powersports industry are covered here for manufacturers, dealers, and distributors of powersports vehicles. *Powersports Business* also reports on successful companies and business strategies. It puts an emphasis on breaking news and analysis, so writers with a business journalism background are preferred. Circ: 12,000.

Contents: Articles; depts/columns
Frequency: 16 times each year
Website: www.powersportsbusiness.com

Freelance Potential

30% written by nonstaff writers. Publishes 80 freelance submissions yearly. Receives 10–15 queries monthly.

Submissions

Query. Accepts email queries to dmcmahon@powersportsbusiness.com. Responds in 1 month.

- Articles: 1,000 words. Informational and how-to articles; profiles; interviews; and new product information. Topics include business issues relating to the sale of motorcycles, snowmobiles, personal watercraft, and all-terrain vehicles.
- Depts/columns: Word lengths vary. Company and dealer profiles, marketing and hiring advice, new product information, opinions, and trade association news.

Sample Issue

46 pages. Advertising. Sample articles and theme list/editorial calendar available at website.

- "PSB Q2 Survey Shows Service Departments Stay Busy." Article shares results from a survey measuring the success of service departments.
- "Dealer Races Forward with Speed Shop at Track." Article discusses the grand opening of the Transportation Revolution's Speed Shop in New Orleans.

Rights and Payment

First rights. Written material, payment rates vary. Pays on publication. Provides 3 copies.

Practice Link

415 Second Avenue
P.O. Box 100
Hinton, WV 25951

Editor: Laura Hammond

Description and Interests

This magazine, formerly *Unique Opportunties*, is designed to inform physicians of the practice opportunities available that are best suited to their personal and professional needs. It also features articles on career planning and career development issues. It welcomes queries from writers on economic, business, and career-related issues that would interest physicians who are planning to relocate or change practices. Circ: 80,000.

Contents: 40% articles; 60% depts/columns
Frequency: Quarterly
Website: www.practicelink.com/magazine

Freelance Potential

90% written by nonstaff writers. Publishes 4 freelance submissions yearly; 10% by authors who are new to the magazine, 100% by experts. Receives 20 queries monthly.

Submissions

Query with clips. Accepts hard copy and email queries to laura.hammond@practicelink.com. No simultaneous submissions. SASE. Responds in 2–3 months.

- Articles: 1,500–3,500 words. Informational and how-to articles. Topics include economic, business, legal, and other career-related issues of interest to physicians.
- Depts/columns: 1,000–1,500 words. Legal matters, practice operations, and opinions.

Sample Issue

80 pages. Advertising. Sample copy at website. Guidelines available.

- "What Employers Want." Article provides tips for getting a job in the midst of an economic downturn and office downsizing.
- "Love Where You Land." Article discusses the best ways to research locations and employers to avoid future disappointment.

Rights and Payment

First North American serial and electronic rights. Written material, \$.50–\$.75 per word. Pays 30 days after acceptance. Provides 5 copies.

Preaching

402 BNA Drive, Suite 400
Nashville, TN 37217-2509

Executive Editor: Dr. Michael Duduit

Description and Interests

This publication is written for, and largely by, preachers, particularly those of the Evangelical, Baptist, and Presbyterian denominations. Its articles seek to inspire, teach, and encourage pastors while providing practical information they can use on the pulpit or in the congregation. Because the articles reflect preaching experiences and offer homiletical techniques, writers should be active/retired pastors or college/seminary faculty. Circ: 10,000.

Contents: 80% articles; 20% depts/columns
Frequency: 6 times each year
Website: www.preaching.com

Freelance Potential

80% written by nonstaff writers. Publishes 50–60 freelance submissions yearly; 10% by unpublished writers, 20% by authors who are new to the magazine, 50% by experts. Receives 10 queries, 25 unsolicited mss monthly.

Submissions

Query for articles. Send complete ms for sermons. Accepts hard copy and email to editor@preaching.com. SASE. Responds to queries in 2 months, to mss in 4–6 months.

- Articles: 1,750–2,000 words. Informational and how-to articles; and interviews. Topics include Christian leadership, pastoral guidance, homiletical resources, and worship.
- Depts/columns: Word lengths vary. Resources, book reviews, and opinion pieces.
- Other: Sermons, 1,250–1,500 words. Children's sermons, 250–300 words.

Sample Issue

56 pages. Advertising. Sample articles available at website. Guidelines and theme list available.

- "You're Not a Dog, So Break the Chains." Article sermonizes on moving forward in one's life to live out God's plan.
- "Managing Multiple Priorities Effectively." Article shares tips in keeping life and the ministry's priorities in balance.

Rights and Payment

First and second rights. Written material, $35–$50. Pays on publication. Provides 1 contributor's copy.

Preservation

National Trust for Historic Preservation
1785 Massachusetts Avenue NW
Washington, DC 20036

Editor in Chief: Dennis Hockman

Description and Interests

Focusing on the preservation and protection of historic places, the articles here offer information and reporting on preservation, as well as profiles of efforts to preserve buildings. Coverage is not limited to residential or historic buildings—all preservation issues are welcome, from train depots and theaters to battlefields. Circ: 270,000.

Contents: 50% articles; 10% depts/columns; 40% other
Frequency: Quarterly
Website: www.preservationnation.org/magazine

Freelance Potential

60% written by nonstaff writers. Publishes 16 freelance submissions yearly; 10% by authors who are new to the magazine, 10% by experts. Receives 25 queries monthly.

Submissions

Query only with clips. Accepts email queries to preservation@savingplaces.org. Responds in 1 month.

- Articles: To 2,000 words. Informational articles; profiles; interviews; and personal experience and opinion pieces. Topics include architecture, history, art, antiques, nature, the environment, public affairs, travel, tourism, and people.
- Depts/columns: 1,500 words. News, places, travel, and books.

Sample Issue

76 pages. Advertising. Sample copy and guidelines available at website.

- "Encore Performance." Article describes the renovations of several theaters that once catered to African Americans before integration.
- "Sangre De Cristo." Article profiles this national heritage area in Colorado where the history of three cultures converge.

Rights and Payment

Rights revert back to author after 90 days. Written material, payment rates vary. Pays on publication. Provides 2 contributor's copies.

Primary Care Optometry News

6900 Grove Road
Thorofare, NJ 08086-9447

Editor: Michael D. DePaolis, OD, FAAO

Description and Interests

Focusing on the latest research and news on eye health and vision issues, this tabloid targets optometrists in the United States. It also covers legal issues and patient care. Writers should have a thorough knowledge of the optometry field to write for the publication; many of its authors are doctors. Circ: 40,000.

Contents: 60% articles; 40% depts/columns
Frequency: Monthly
Website: www.healio.com/optometry

Freelance Potential

5% written by nonstaff writers. Publishes 5 freelance submissions yearly; 1% by authors who are new to the magazine, 5% by experts. Receives 5 queries monthly.

Submissions

Query with outline. Accepts email queries to optometry@healio.com. Responds in 3 days.

- Articles: 500–1,500 words. Informational and how-to articles; new product information; and opinion pieces. Topics include optometry research, practice, and legislation; practice management; disease diagnosis; and treatment options.
- Depts/columns: 1,200–1,500 words. Case presentations, legislative developments, practice management, new product information, and industry news.
- Artwork: B/W and color digital images at 300 dpi.

Sample Issue

30 pages. Advertising. Sample copy available at website. Writers' guidelines and editorial calendar available.

- "Consider Sleep Apnea in Patients with Normal Tension Glaucoma." Article discusses the reduced risk of early myocardial infarction when sleep apnea is diagnosed and treated.
- "Know What Signs Will Resolve on Their Own After Cataract Surgery." Article discusses what to expect after a patient's surgery and what poses a potential problem.

Rights and Payment

First worldwide rights. All material, payment rates vary. Kill fee varies. Pays on publication. Provides 3 contributor's copies.

Principal

1615 Duke Street
Alexandria, VA 22314

Managing Editor: Kaylen Tucker

Description and Interests

Elementary and middle school principals read this magazine for "in-the-trenches" features about all aspects of school administration. Articles cover current education issues and interfacing with parents and school staff. It seeks practical, jargon-free articles that address a variety of educational issues from the principal's perspective. Principals with a rewarding, insightful, or humorous experience to share are welcome to send a submission. Circ: 23,000.

Contents: 50% articles; 50% depts/columns
Frequency: 5 times each year
Website: www.naesp.org

Freelance Potential

90% written by nonstaff writers. Publishes 20 freelance submissions yearly; 80% by authors who are new to the magazine. Receives 10 queries, 8 unsolicited mss monthly.

Submissions

Query or send complete ms with a list of relevant Web resources. Accepts email to publications@naesp.org (Word attachments). No simultaneous submissions. Responds in 2–3 months.

- Articles: 1,500–2,000 words. Informational and how-to articles. Topics include K–8 education, special and gifted education, early intervention, career stages, school culture, managing and supporting teachers, working with parents, and principal autonomy.
- Depts/columns: 800–1,000 words. "Practitioner's Corner," "Reflective Principal," "Ten to Teen," "Raising the Bar," and "Speaking Out."

Sample Issue

72 pages. Advertising. Sample articles, guidelines, and editorial calendar available at website.

- "Early Career Principals." Article recommends strategies for dealing with difficult and resistant employees.
- Sample dept/column: "Speaking Out" debates the perils of pay for performance.

Rights and Payment

Rights negotiable. No payment. Provides 3 contributor's copies.

Proceedings

U.S. Naval Institute
291 Wood Road
Annapolis, MD 21402-5034

Editor in Chief: Paul Merzlak

Description and Interests
Proceedings is the magazine of the U.S. Naval Institute that aims to stimulate, illuminate, provoke, and when appropriate, entertain its readers. It deals with national defense issues, primarily from a naval viewpoint. Articles should have a strong national defense but also encourage constructive debate. Most submissions are from active or retired service personnel. Circ: 70,000.

Contents: 60% articles; 40% depts/columns
Frequency: Monthly
Website: www.usni.org

Freelance Potential
100% written by nonstaff writers. Publishes 150 freelance submissions yearly; 75% by authors who are new to the magazine. Receives 30–40 queries each month.

Submissions
Query with 2- to 3-line bio; or send complete ms with word count and bio. Prefers email submissions to articlesubmission@usni.org (attach files); will accept disk submissions. SASE. Responds to queries in 1 month, to mss in 2–3 months.

- Articles: To 3,000 words. Informational articles. Topics include national security, terrorism, military history, vessels, aircraft, weaponry, military tactics, and leadership.
- Depts/columns: Commentaries, to 700 words. How-to's, to 1,500 words. Book reviews, to 650 words. Anecdotes, to 300 words.

Sample Issue
96 pages. Advertising. Sample articles and guidelines available at website and in each issue.

- "A 'Leap Ahead' for the 21st-Century Navy." Article reports on the new Gerald R. Ford-class aircraft carriers.
- "Time to Fly Right." Article discusses the need to develop crew criteria for unmanned aerial systems.

Rights and Payment
All rights. Written material, payment rates vary. Pays on publication. Provides 2 contributor's copies and a 1-year USNI membership.

Professional Pilot

30 South Quaker Lane, Suite 300
Alexandria, VA 22314

Managing Editor: Phil Rose

Description and Interests
Professional pilots read this publication for industry news, FAA updates, and piloting techniques. Weather, aviation hazards, and other safety issues are also covered. Most of its writers are aviation professionals. Circ: 30,000.

Contents: 60% articles; 40% depts/columns
Frequency: Monthly
Website: www.propilotmag.com

Freelance Potential
75% written by nonstaff writers. Publishes 40 freelance submissions yearly; 2% by unpublished writers, 10% by authors who are new to the magazine, 75% by experts. Receives 10 queries, 6 unsolicited mss monthly.

Submissions
Query or send complete ms. Accepts hard copy, disk submissions, and email submissions to prose@propilotmag.com. SASE. Responds in 2 months.

- Articles: To 2,500 words. Informational and how-to articles; profiles; interviews; and new product information. Topics include aircraft, airlines, piloting techniques, aviation technology, airline maintenance, airshows, FAA regulations, law enforcement tactics, international operations, and weather.
- Depts/columns: Word lengths vary. Accident recaps, aviation hazards, and business and helicopter news.
- Other: Quizzes and cartoons.

Sample Issue
152 pages. Advertising. Sample articles and editorial calendar available at website. Writers' guidelines available.

- "Airport Access." Article reports on the changes in daily operations at DCA since 9/11.
- "Martin Resource Management Builds Petroleum Business with Diverse Fleet." Article features a profile of this aviation company that has a diverse fleet to meet its travel needs.

Rights and Payment
All rights. Articles, $500+. Depts/columns, payment rates vary. Pays on publication. Provides contributor's copies upon request.

Profit

1 Mount Pleasant Road, 11th Floor
Toronto, Ontario M4Y 2Y5
Canada

Editor: Ian Portsmouth

Description and Interests
Canadian entrepreneurs and corporate leaders read *Profit* for up-to-date business news and strategies for company growth. Expert advice, marketing trends, technology, and profiles of successful businessmen and women make up its editorial content. Writers must be familiar with the Canadian business scene and Best Management Practices. Circ: 88,982.

Contents: 80% articles; 20% depts/columns
Frequency: 6 times each year
Website: www.profitguide.com

Freelance Potential
75% written by nonstaff writers. Publishes 60 freelance submissions yearly; 10% by authors who are new to the magazine, 5% by experts. Receives 5 queries monthly.

Submissions
Query with writing samples. Accepts email queries to profit@profit.rogers.com (attach samples). Responds in 1 month.

- Articles: 500–3,000 words. Informational and how-to articles; profiles; interviews; and opinion pieces. Topics include Canadian firms, entrepreneurs, start-ups, and business management issues.
- Depts/columns: 600–1,100 words. Capital, profiles, post-mortem analysis, marketing, finance, labor and hiring, health, leisure pursuits, and new product information.

Sample Issue
88 pages. Advertising. Sample copy and editorial calendar available at website. Writers' guidelines available.

- "Money for Your Maternity Leave." Article explains the new law which allows self-employed people to buy into the Employment Insurance program.
- "Private Business Bucks Trends." Article discusses the projected growth rate of Canadian businesses despite a weak economy.

Rights and Payment
First publication and non-exclusive electronic rights. Written material, \$.60–\$.80 Canadian per word. Kill fee varies. Pays on acceptance. Provides 3 contributor's copies.

P3 Update

5419 Hollywood Boulevard, Suite C227
Hollywood, CA 90027

Editor: James Thompson

Description and Interests
Filmmakers, producers, and other entertainment industry professionals look to *P3 Update* for news on the latest technology for film and video production. Now exclusively online, it covers locations, pre- and postproduction, editing, and new product information. It is always in need of postproduction articles. Writers familiar with Web 2.0 are welcome to submit. Circ: 34,000.

Contents: 70% articles; 15% depts/columns; 15% other
Frequency: Monthly
Website: www.p3update.com

Freelance Potential
90% written by nonstaff writers. Publishes 90 freelance submissions yearly; 1% by unpublished writers, 1% by authors who are new to the magazine, 98% by industry experts. Receives 500 queries monthly.

Submissions
Query with outline. Accepts email to jt@p3update.com. Responds in 1–2 weeks.

- Articles: 1,000–1,500 words. Informational and how-to articles; profiles; interviews; and personal experience pieces. Topics include film and video production, equipment and tech nology, lighting, and postproduction.
- Depts/columns: 500 words. Industry news, technology, and new products.

Sample Issue
Advertising. Sample copy and editorial calendar available at website. Guidelines available.

- "The Rocky Mountain Region." Article details the benefits of filming in Montana, Idaho, Colorado, Wyoming, and Utah.
- "New ASC President Stephen Lighthill Talks Cinematography." Article profiles the new ASC president and his background.
- Sample dept/column: "Technology News" reviews the new JVC ProHD Camcorder.

Rights and Payment
First North American serial rights. Articles, \$450. Depts/columns, \$200. Kill fee, 20%. Pays on publication.

Public Power

American Public Power Association
1875 Connecticut Avenue NW, Suite 1200
Washington, DC 20009-5715

Editor: David L. Blaylock

Description and Interests
Targeting upper-level management and policy makers of municipally owned electric companies, this publication offers the latest on operations and technology. It also covers utility news and legislative issues. Writers should have a strong knowledge of the electric utility industry and the technological language associated with it is extremely helpful. Circ: 20,000.
Contents: 50% articles; 50% depts/columns
Frequency: 8 times each year
Website: www.publicpower.org

Freelance Potential
60% written by nonstaff writers. Publishes 50 freelance submissions yearly; 5% by unpublished writers, 5% by authors who are new to the magazine, 85% by industry experts. Receives 2–3 queries monthly.

Submissions
Query. Accepts email queries to dblaylock@publicpower.org. Responds in 2+ weeks.

- Articles: 1,000–2,500 words. Informational articles; profiles; and interviews. Topics include public utility management, operations, regulations, business, technology, law, politics, and science.
- Depts/columns: Word lengths vary. Q&A interviews with public officials; engineering advice; broadband policies and trends; research updates; and safety, human resource, and customer service issues.

Sample Issue
36 pages. Advertising. Sample copy and editorial calendar available at website. Guidelines available.

- "An Ever-Greening Vision." Article discusses Washington's Snohomish County's commitment to renewable energy and efficiency.
- "Enhancing the Customer Experience." Article reports on First Quartile Consulting's annual study of public utilities.

Rights and Payment
First North American serial rights. Written material, $500–$2,500. Pays on acceptance. Provides 2–6 contributor's copies.

QSR 

Editor: Sam Oches

Description and Interests:
QSR (Quick Service Restaurant) aims to be the leading source of news and information about the $257 billion limited-service restaurant industry. This includes fast food, fast-casual dining, concessions, and convenience stores. Each issue focuses on food and beverage, operations, technology, and expansion. Circ: Unavailable.
Contents Articles; depts/columns
Frequency: Monthly
Website: www.qsrmagazine.com

Freelance Potential
Receives many freelance submissions monthly.

Submissions
Query. Accepts hard copy and email to sam@qsrmagazine.com. SASE. Response time varies.

- Articles: Word lengths vary. Informational and how-to articles, and research reports. Topics include food and beverage, operations, tech nology, and expansion.
- Depts/columns: Word lengths vary. Events, and industry news.

Sample Issue
Advertising. Sample articles available at website.

- "Fancy Fast Food." Article describes quick service restaurants that are upgrading interiors and menu items for a sophisticated feel.
- "The Evolution of Food Safety." Article reveals the need for more stringent food safety efforts due to the increased use of raw products.
- "Turn Sustainability into Profitability." Article describes how one franchise is using broad sustainable practices to attract eco-conscious consumers.

Rights and Payment
Rights vary. Payment rates and policy vary.

Quilting Arts Magazine

Interweave
490 Boston Post Road, Suite 15
Sudbury, MA 01776

Editor: Vivika Hansen DeNegre

Description and Interests

This publication explores all aspects of quilting. It features articles that appeal to a wide range of skill levels, covering such diverse areas as wearable art, contemporary quilting, and embellished quilting. It is interested in quick and stylish projects with modern-day appeal. Projects and ideas that stretch the creative limits of readers and inspire them to try something new are needed. Circ: Unknown.

Contents: 45% depts/columns; 35% articles; 20% other
Frequency: 6 times each year
Website: www.quiltingdaily.com

Freelance Potential

Unavailable.

Submissions

Query with artwork. Accepts hard copy and email submissions to submissions@quiltingarts.com. SASE. Responds in 3 months.

- Articles: Word lengths vary. Informational and how-to articles. Topics include contemporary textile works, surface design, embellishments, and motifs.
- Depts/columns: Word lengths vary. "Spotlight," News.
- Artwork: Low-resolution digital images for query purposes only.

Sample Issue

Advertising. Sample copy available. Guidelines and theme calendar available at website.

- "Explore Over-the-Top Embellishments." Article describes how to use such embellishments as beads, paint, ink, and felting.
- Sample dept/column: "Spotlight" profiles the beaded quilts and hand stitched artistry of Lisa Binkley.

Rights and Payment

First rights. Written material, payment rates vary. Payment policy varies.

Rangefinder

6255 Sunset Boulevard, 20th Floor
Los Angeles, CA 90028

Editor: Bill Hurter

Description and Interests

This magazine is written for, and often by, professional photographers. It seeks to inspire and educate with features on equipment, marketing, technique, computer technology, and creative photographers. All photos submitted with articles must include model releases. Circ: 61,000.

Contents: 75% articles; 25% depts/columns
Frequency: Monthly
Website: www.rangefinderonline.com

Freelance Potential

90% written by nonstaff writers. Publishes 145 freelance submissions yearly; 15% by authors who are new to the magazine, 100% by industry experts. Receives 15 queries monthly.

Submissions

Send complete ms. Accepts email to bhurter@rfpublishing.com (Word attachments) and disk submissions with artwork. Availability of artwork improves chance of acceptance. No simultaneous submissions. Responds in 2 weeks.

- Articles: Profiles, 1,200–1,800 words. How-to and informational articles, 1,000–1,500 words. Topics include the work of professional photographers, photographic techniques and equipment, marketing, and business.
- Depts/columns: "Rf Cookbook," 350–600 words. "First Exposure" and "Field Test," 1,200–1,500 words.
- Artwork: Prefers digital image files at 300 dpi on CD; will accept 8x10 to 11x14 glossy or satin prints, unsigned.

Sample Issue

146 pages. Advertising. Sample articles, guidelines, and editorial calendar available at website.

- "Going Mobile." Article presents 10 applications that can benefit the photography business.
- "Saying No..." Article explains the best ways to refuse a crazy client request.

Rights and Payment

One-time and electronic rights. All material, payment rates vary. Pays on publication. Provides contributor's copies.

Referee

2017 Lathrop Avenue
Racine, WI 53405

Managing Editor: Julie Sternberg

Description and Interests

Sports officiating is the name of the game here. Each issue features articles that help readers improve their officiating, as well as profiles, interviews, news, health and legal features, and investigative reports. It seeks information on rules, mechanics, or officiating philosophies for the sports-specific columns on basketball, football, soccer, baseball, and softball. *Referee* serves an audience of sports officials from youth to professional levels. Circ: 88,000.

Contents: 60% articles; 40% depts/columns
Frequency: Monthly
Website: www.referee.com

Freelance Potential

70% written by nonstaff writers. Publishes 45 freelance submissions yearly; 5% by unpublished writers, 5% by authors who are new to the magazine, 90% by experts. Receives 5 queries, 5 unsolicited mss monthly.

Submissions

Query or send complete ms. Accepts hard copy and email to submissions@referee.com. SASE. Responds in 1–2 weeks.

- Articles: 1,500–3,500 words. Informational, self-help, and how-to articles; profiles; interviews; humor; news reports; and personal experience pieces. Topics include all aspects of sports officiating.
- Depts/columns: Sports-specific articles, 500–1,000 words. "Law," "Getting It Right," "Profiles," "Last Call" (a first person experience), reviews, profiles, legal issues, tips, news, and essays; word lengths vary.

Sample Issue

72 pages. Advertising. Sample copy and guidelines available at website.

- "The Replay Trap." Article discusses whether expanded replay in the MLB is a good thing.
- "Art McNally: What He Means to NFL Officiating." Article profiles this NFL legend.

Rights and Payment

All rights. Written material, $.04+ per word. Pays on acceptance. Provides 1+ author's copies.

Reiki News Magazine

21421 Hilltop Street, Suite 28
Southfield, MI 48033-4009

Editor in Chief: William Lee Rand

Description and Interests

Teachers and practitioners read this magazine for information that will inspire them and show them how to use Reiki more effectively. First-person pieces about people who have been healed, articles about Reiki history, and recent research projects are also featured. Whether inspirational or informational, articles need to be truly useful and helpful to the reader while showing how Reiki can improve one's life. Circ: 20,000.

Contents: Articles; depts/columns
Frequency: Quarterly
Website: www.reiki.org

Freelance Potential

90% written by nonstaff writers. Publishes 40 freelance submissions yearly; 50% by unpublished writers, 50% by authors who are new to the magazine, 50% by experts. Receives 4 queries monthly.

Submissions

Query with outline, sample paragraphs or general description, and clips. Accepts email queries to lemurio@aol.com (Word attachments). Responds in 1 month.

- Articles: 1,500–3,000 words. Informational, how-to, and inspirational articles; and personal experience pieces. Topics include Reiki techniques, history, and practice.
- Depts/columns: Word lengths vary. Reiki stories, training, and programs.

Sample Issue

80 pages. Sample articles and guidelines available at website.

- "World Peace is Coming." Article discusses the process of peace, what is needed to get there, and how one can help.
- "Reiki for Women." Article discusses how women can benefit from Reiki as a form of spirituality, prayer, and meditation.
- "A Heeler's 11 Year Journey with Reiki." Article describes a woman's experiences caring for a dog she adopted from the shelter.

Rights and Payment

All rights. No payment. Provides 5–10 contributor's copies.

REM

2255-B Queen Street East, Suite 1178
Toronto, Ontario M4E 1G3
Canada

Managing Editor: Jim Adair

Description and Interests

This tabloid helps realtors keep their fingers on the pulse of the Canadian real estate scene, with news about market trends, legal issues, and home financing options, as well as profiles of successful realtors. News and sales tips for those working in the Canadian real estate market are needed. Circ: 38,000.

Contents: 70% articles; 30% depts/columns
Frequency: Monthly
Website: www.remonline.com

Freelance Potential

50% written by nonstaff writers. Publishes 50 freelance submissions yearly; 20% by authors who are new to the magazine, 80% by industry experts. Receives 4 queries monthly.

Submissions

Query with author qualifications and writing samples. Accepts email to jim@remonline.com. Responds in 1 month.

- Articles: 800–1,000 words. Informational, how-to, and self-help articles; profiles; interviews; humor; new product information; and personal experience and opinion pieces. Topics include Canadian real estate markets, trends, news, and real estate agents.
- Depts/columns: Word lengths vary. Industry news, agent profiles, legal issues, humor, business advice, and book reviews.
- Artwork: High-resolution color digital images.

Sample Issue

48 pages. Advertising. Sample articles at website.

- "How to Make a Million in 5 Years." Article shares the secrets of success from Canada's top sales representative for the last seven years.
- "Watch Out: It's the Fear Monster." Article explains how to break out of one's shell when brainstorming and let the ideas flow.

Rights and Payment

First Canadian print rights. Written material, $200–$300 Canadian. Pays on acceptance. Provides 1 contributor's copy.

RetailerNOW

500 Giuseppe Court, Suite 6
Roseville, CA 95678

Editor: Melissa Dressler

Description and Interests

Launched in 2012 by the National and Western Home Furnishings Associations, RetailerNOW seeks to challenge conventional thinking by engaging home furnishing professionals in a meaningful dialogue about trends, strategies, and current issues affecting the industry. It also provides ideas that readers can use to increase profits and customer service. It relies heavily on industry experts for its articles. It requires freelancers to have specific knowledge of the industry and extensive experience writing about it. Circ: 12,000/Digital: 6,000.

Contents: 80% articles; 20% depts/columns
Frequency: 10 times each year
Website: www.retailernowmag.com

Freelance Potential

75% written by nonstaff writers. Publishes 20–25 freelance submissions yearly; 5% by unpublished writers, 10% by authors who are new to the magazine, 25% by industry experts. Receives 3 queries each month.

Submissions

Query with résumé, writing samples, and credentials. Accepts hard copy and email queries to info@nhfa.org. SASE. Responds in 1–2 months.

- Articles: 3,000–5,000 words. Informational and how-to articles; and business profiles. Topics include family businesses, customer satisfaction, employee relations, design, the Internet, business strategies, and management issues.
- Depts/columns: 1,500–2,000 words. Operations, advertising, marketing, training, creative leadership, legal news, and finance.

Sample Issue

52 pages. Advertising. Sample copy, editorial calendar, and guidelines available at website.

- "Stop the Madness," by John Albanese. Discussion of the paradigm shift in consumer purchasing habit and an argument for embracing e-commerce.
- "Scan & Scram," by Martin Roberts. "Showrooming" by smartphone users, the latest challenge to brick-and-mortar retail stores.

Rights and Payment

First North American serial rights. Articles, $500–$800. Depts/columns, $250–$350. Pays on acceptance. Provides 1 contributor's copy.

SchoolArts

50 Portland Street
Worcester, MA 01608

Editor: Nancy Walkup

Description and Interests

The mission of this professional journal is to provide inspiration, information, and ideas to art educators at all grade levels. It invites art education professionals to share their successful lessons, areas of concern, and approaches to teaching art. Circ: 20,000.

Contents: 60% articles; 40% depts/columns
Frequency: 9 times each year
Website: www.davisart.com

Freelance Potential

75% written by nonstaff writers. Publishes 200 freelance submissions yearly; 60% by unpublished writers, 60% by authors who are new to the magazine. Receives 10 unsolicited mss each month.

Submissions

Send complete ms with artwork and signed permission form. Accepts CD with text and photographs. No simultaneous submissions. SASE. Responds in 1–2 months.

- Articles: To 800 words. Informational and how-to articles; profiles; and personal experience pieces. Topics include the arts, education, art history, new applications of art techniques, and curriculum development.
- Depts/columns: 500–1,200. New product information, profiles, and fresh ideas.
- Artwork: Photographs and slides; digital images at 300 dpi. Line art.

Sample Issue

54 pages. Advertising. Sample copy, guidelines, and theme list available at website.

- "Kindergarten Animation." Article explores engaging approaches to teaching animation to young students.
- "Fall Leaf Portraits." Article describes a lesson using nature to transform the self portrait.
- Sample dept/column: "Design Thinking" offers information on transfiguration in design.

Rights and Payment

All rights. Written material, payment rates vary. Pays on publication. Provides 6 contributor's copies.

Self-Storage Now!

2531 West Dunlap Avenue
Phoenix, AZ 85021

Editor: Tammy LeRoy

Description and Interests

Professional self-storage managers turn to this publication for its timely coverage of marketing, sales, service, and management issues. Each article is written to help self-storage companies operate more efficiently and increase profits. Particular attention is given to space rental sales techniques and methods of increasing revenues through retail and ancillary sales to tenants and other customers. Circ: 31,000.

Contents: 60% articles; 40% depts/columns
Frequency: Quarterly
Website: www.selfstoragenow.com

Freelance Potential

90% written by nonstaff writers. Publishes 100 freelance submissions yearly; 10% by unpublished writers, 10% by authors who are new to the magazine, 40% by industry experts. Receives 5–6 queries monthly.

Submissions

Query with résumé and writing samples. Accepts hard copy and email to ssnow@minico.com. SASE. Responds in 2 weeks.

- Articles: 2,500+ words. Informational articles; profiles; interviews; and new product information. Topics include occupancy, marketing, customer service, lien sales, property maintenance, security, insurance, and management tools.
- Depts/columns: 1,200–1,600 words. New products, legal issues, and industry news.

Sample Issue

26 pages. Advertising. Sample articles available at website. Writers' guidelines and editorial calendar available.

- "Managers and Technology." Article discusses technology options that can help cut costs, increase efficiency, and simplify processes.
- Networking at Trade Shows and Expos." Article offers tips for maximizing networking opportunities at trade shows.

Rights and Payment

First and reprint rights. Articles, $250–$300. Depts/columns, payment rates vary. Payment policy varies. Provides 1 contributor's copy.

Sheep!

145 Industrial Drive
Medford, WI 54451

Editor: Nathan Griffith

Description and Interests

Sheep farmers, ranchers, and wool crafters read this magazine for its timely and informative updates on farm management and other industry news, as well as its profiles of successful flockmasters. It is interested in articles that offer creative suggestions for flockmasters selling wool and pelts to craft users. Circ: 10,000.

Contents: 60% articles; 40% depts/columns
Frequency: 6 times each year
Website: www.sheepmagazine.com

Freelance Potential

65% written by nonstaff writers. Publishes 20–25 freelance submissions yearly; 10% by unpublished writers, 40% by authors who are new to the magazine, 10% by experts. Receives 5 queries monthly.

Submissions

Query. Prefers email to sheepmag@tds.net; will accept hard copy and simultaneous submissions if identified. SASE. Responds in 2 weeks.

- Articles: 600–3,000 words. Informational and how-to articles; profiles; interviews; and new product information. Topics include sheep production and products, wool crafts, pasture management, sheep forage, shearing methods and equipment, and ovine health.
- Depts/columns: 50–1,000 words. Veterinary issues, market reports, book reviews, and breeding.

Sample Issue

66 pages. Advertising. Sample articles available at website. Guidelines available.

- "Cache Valley Virus: Next Lambing-Time's Losses Caused in Autumn." Article explains this disease and some steps for prevention.
- "Team-Building the Fun Way: Blending Recreation, Discovery and Flock Profit." Article describes a team-building program for business excecutives that takes them away from desks and onto farms.

Rights and Payment

First North American serial and/or all rights. Articles, $30–$200. Depts/columns, payment rates vary. Pays on publication. Provides contributor's copies.

Shot Business

2 Park Avenue
New York, NY 10016-5695

Editor: Slaton White

Description and Interests

This magazine provides new product and business management information for business people working in the fields of shooting, hunting, and outdoor trades. The official publication of the National Shooting Sports Foundation, it is read by manufacturers, retailers, and sales representatives who need ideas for keeping their hunting- and shooting-related businesses profitable. Because more pieces are now staff-written, it is using less freelance material. Circ: 21,000.

Contents: 55% articles; 45% depts/columns
Frequency: 7 times each year
Website: www.shotbusiness.com

Freelance Potential

30% written by nonstaff writers. Publishes 10 freelance submissions yearly; 1% by authors who are new to the magazine, 2% by industry experts.

Submissions

Query. Accepts email queries to slaton.white@bonniercorp.com. Responds in 2 weeks.

- Articles: 1,500–2,000 words. Informational articles. Topics include the manufacturing, marketing, and retailing of shooting and hunting products.
- Depts/columns: Staff-written.

Sample Issue

60 pages. Advertising. Sample copy available at website. Guidelines available.

- "SHOT Show University." Article reports on the upcoming day-long seminars scheduled for hunting and shooting retailers.
- "Gear Up." Article gives tips for selling accessories such as gun cleaners and holsters.
- "Compliance Center." Article covers online resources that provide information on the lastest regulations.

Rights and Payment

All rights. Written material, payment rates vary. Pays on acceptance.

Skin Inc.

336 Gundersen Drive, Suite A
Carol Stream, IL 60188-2403

Associate Editor: Cathy Christensen

Description and Interests
Focusing on the business side of the skin care and day spa industries, this journal shares the latest news and issues with its audience of skin-care professionals and spa owners and managers. Writers are welcome to submit information on cutting-edge treatments and formulations, and government regulations. Circ: 30,000+.

Contents: 60% articles; 40% depts/columns
Frequency: Monthly
Website: www.skininc.com

Freelance Potential
30% written by nonstaff writers. Publishes 40 freelance submissions yearly; 5% by unpublished writers, 45% by authors who are new to the magazine, 50% by experts. Receives 5 queries monthly.

Submissions
Query with outline. Accepts email to cchristensen @allured.com. No simultaneous submissions. Responds in 2 weeks.

- Articles: 750–1,500 words. Informational and how-to articles; profiles; interviews; personal experience pieces; and new product information. Topics include skin-care science and treatments, makeup, dermatology, plastic surgery, spas, estheticians, and regulations.
- Depts/columns: Word lengths vary. Industry news, career advice, spa management, spa cuisine, new product information, supplier profiles, and interviews with estheticians.

Sample Issue
84 pages. Advertising. Sample copy, guidelines, and editorial calendar available at website.

- "Is It Time to Raise Your Prices?" Article discusses which factors to analyze in order to determine whether its time to raise prices.
- "Understanding the Psyche of the Male Client." Article explains the differences of male clients in order to attract and retain them as customers.

Rights and Payment
Exclusive rights. Written material, $100–$250. Pays on acceptance. Provides 2 author's copies.

Small Farm Today

3903 West Ridge Trail Road
Clark, MO 65243-9525

Editor: Ron Macher

Description and Interests
Small Farm Today is dedicated to the preservation and promotion of small farming, rural living, sustainability, and agripreneurship. It includes articles about growing crops, raising livestock, and diversifying products. It uses a "can-do," upbeat approach, and all submissions should reflect this attitude. Articles that explain how to do something from start to finish, citing specific examples involved in the process, are needed. Circ: 7,000.

Contents: 60% articles; 35% depts/columns; 5% other
Frequency: 6 times each year
Website: www.smallfarmtoday.com

Freelance Potential
90% written by nonstaff writers. Publishes 30 freelance submissions yearly; 5% by unpublished writers, 20% by authors who are new to the magazine. Receives 4 queries monthly.

Submissions
Prefers query; will accept complete ms and reprints. Accepts hard copy and email queries to smallfarm@socket.net. SASE. Responds in 2 months.

- Articles: 1,400–2,600 words. Informational and how-to articles; personal experience pieces; profiles; and interviews. Topics include farming, agriculture, gardening, animals, and technology.
- Depts/columns: 800–1,500 words. Book reviews, new product information, agriculture news, and farm management.

Sample Issue
36 pages. Advertising. Sample copy available. Writers' guidelines and editorial calendar available at website.

- "Modern Marketing of Colored Mohair." Article discusses the attractiveness of this fiber and ways to best market it to consumers.
- "Breeding Alpacas for Fun and Fiber." Article offers a primer on raising alpacas and the uses of alpaca fleece for fiber arts.

Rights and Payment
First serial and non-exclusive second rights. Original written material, $.035 per word, reprints, $.02 per word. Pays 2 months after publication. Provides 1 contributor's copy.

Smart Retailer

707 Kautz Road
St. Charles, IL 60174

Editor: Susan Wagner

Description and Interests

Smart Retailer originally started out as *Country Business* and targeted the country gift market. In 2012, the magazine broadened its scope to cover all popular gift and home-decor styles. Practical articles provide ideas on retail and marketing strategies, information on finance and technology, and suggestions for increasing store traffic and revenue. It is always seeking profiles of successful retailers and vendors that contain tips readers can use in their own stores. Articles should be written in a clear, concise style. Circ: 30,000.

Contents: 60% depts/columns; 40% articles
Frequency: 6 times each year
Website: www.smart-retailer.com.

Freelance Potential

65% written by nonstaff writers. Publishes 20–30 freelance submissions yearly; 20% by authors who are new to the magazine, 50% by experts. Receives 5–10 queries monthly.

Submissions

Query with résumé and published clips. Accepts email queries to cbiz@sampler.emmis.com (subject line: Writer's Query). Responds if interested.

- Articles: 1,500–1,800 words. Informational and how-to articles; and profiles. Topics include marketing, technology, finance, legal issues, retailing, small business, new products, and niche markets.
- Depts/columns: 1,200–1,500 words. Industry news and trends, vendor profiles, business and marketing tips, and employee issues.

Sample Issue

64 pages. Advertising. Sample articles, guidelines, and editorial calendar available at website.

- "How to Prosper in Turbulent Times," by Rich Kizer and Georganne Bender. Straightforward advice for retail management.
- "Meeting Madness," by Shirley Bednarz. Improving meeting effectiveness.

Rights and Payment

All rights. Written material, payment rates vary. Kill fee, 50%. Pays 45 days after acceptance. Provides 1 contributor's copy.

Solar Power World

WTWH Media
2019 Center Street, Suite 300
Cleveland, OH 44113

Editor: Paul Dvorak

Description and Interests

Positioned as a leading information source for the solar power industry, this publication reports on technological developments as well as industry trends. The magazine was founded in 2011, and is read by power purchasers, manufacturers, and technical professionals involved in the design and installation of solar power projects. Circ: Unknown.

Contents: 80% articles; 20% depts/columns
Frequency: Bimonthly
Website: www.solarpowerworldonline.com

Freelance Potential

Won an ASBPE Azbee Award of Excellence in 2012 for work by full-time and freelance editors, writers, art directors, and designers.

Submissions

Accepts email to pdvorak@wtwhmedia.com.

- Articles: Informational and how-to's. Topics include solar power development and manufacturing, installation, new technology.
- Depts/columns: Projects, product reviews, business, contractor tips.

Sample Issue

65 pages. Advertising. Sample copy and guidelines available at website.

- "Test and Verify." A primer for testing rooftop solar arrays to see how they will stand up to heavy winds.
- Sample dept/column: Project Review examines the Crescent Dune Solar Energy Project, which will provide power without intermittency.

Rights and Payment

Rights and payment policy information is unavailable.

Souvenirs, Gifts & Novelties

10 East Athens Avenue, Suite 208
Ardmore, PA 19003

President and Executive Editor: Scott C. Borowsky

Description and Interests

Marketing and management techniques that help souvenir and gift shop owners run more profitable businesses are found in this publication. Many of its readers operate shops at resort and vacation destinations. It seeks articles that will help readers sell more merchandise in their gift and souvenir stores. Writers should send features that include strategies for success. Circ: 43,085.

Contents: 75% articles; 15% depts/columns; 10% other
Frequency: 8 times each year
Website: www.sgnmag.com

Freelance Potential

80% written by nonstaff writers. Publishes 40 freelance submissions yearly; 10% by authors who are new to the magazine, 10% by industry experts. Receives 12 queries monthly.

Submissions

Query. Accepts email queries to editorsgnmag@kanec.com and simultaneous submissions if identified. Responds in 1 week.

- Articles: 1,000 words. Informational and how-to articles; profiles; interviews; and new product information. Topics include novelties and gifts, souvenirs, business management, marketing and merchandising, industry trends, and promotional ideas.
- Depts/columns: Word lengths vary. Product news, trade show reports, and news briefs.

Sample Issue

138 pages. Advertising. Sample articles and editorial calendar available at website. Guidelines available.

- "Getting the Details Right." Article provides strategies for stocking popular apparel sizes and colors.
- Sample dept/column: "Commentary" explains why the end of the season is a good time to take stock of successes and failures.

Rights and Payment

All rights. Written material, payment rates vary. Payment policy varies.

State Tech

300 North Milwaukee Avenue
Vernon Hills, IL 60061

Editor in Chief: Ryan Petersen

Description and Interests

This magazine targets IT and other communications/technical support professionals working for local and state municipalities. It covers trends in information management, new technology, applied technology, management systems, malware threats, and other ways in which technology can aid government operations. Material is only accepted from professionals within the IT field as it relates to government operations. Every article must give readers information or an idea that promotes doing their job better. Circ: Unavailable.

Contents: 50% articles; 50% depts/columns
Frequency: Quarterly
Website: www.statetechmagazine.com

Freelance Potential

90% written by nonstaff writers. Publishes 50 freelance submissions yearly; 20% by authors who are new to the magazine, 80% by industry experts. Receives 10 queries monthly.

Submissions

Query. Accepts email queries to ryanpet@cdw.com. Responds in 1 month.

- Articles: 1,000–2,500 words. Informational and how-to articles; profiles; interviews; media reviews; and new product information. Topics include information management, technology, computers, government, management, politics, and public affairs.
- Depts/columns: 1,000 words. Emerging technologies, case studies, technology, new products, and insights from CIOs.

Sample Issue

48 pages. Sample copy and editorial calendar available at website.

- "The Future of Public Safety." Article details the new technologies that help police departments focus on proactive crime prevention.
- Sample dept/column: "Tech Watch" discusses the benefits of mobile video conferencing.

Rights and Payment

Exclusive rights. Written material, payment rates vary. Pays on publication. Provides 1 contributor's copy.

Student Lawyer

American Bar Association
321 North Clark Street
Chicago, IL 60654

Editor: Angela Gwizdala

Description and Interests

Published by the law student division of the American Bar Association, this magazine looks for practical, how-to articles from experts on careers and job searching. It also offers discussions on legal education issues and the legal profession. It is a legal affairs features magazine, not a legal journal. Articles must be informative, lively, well researched, and good reads. Circ: 32,000.

Contents: 50% articles; 50% depts/columns
Frequency: 9 times each year
Website: www.americanbar.org

Freelance Potential

100% written by nonstaff writers. Publishes 30 freelance submissions yearly; 5% by unpublished writers, 5% by authors who are new to the magazine, 2% by experts. Receives 5 queries, 8 unsolicited mss monthly.

Submissions

Query with 3 clips or send ms. Accepts email to studentlawyer@americanbar.org (Word attachments). Responds in 1 month.

- Articles: 1,500–2,000 words. Informational, how-to, and self-help articles; profiles; interviews; and personal experience pieces. Topics include legal trends, practicing law, education, careers, legal issues, and social issues affecting law students.
- Depts/columns: 1,000 words. Ethics, law school, professionalism, communication skills, and career trends. Opinions, 600 words. Reviews, 600–1,000 words.

Sample Issue

48 pages. Advertising. Sample articles and guidelines available at website.

- "Occupy Law Street: Lawyers and Students Band Together to Tackle Complex Issues." Article reviews this movement and its effects one year later.
- Sample dept/column: "In Session" profiles a law student who is also a chess champion.

Rights and Payment

First rights. Written material, payment rates vary. Pays on acceptance. Provides 5 copies.

The Tasting Panel

17203 Ventura Boulevard, Suite 5
Encino, CA 91316

Managing Editor: David Gadd

Description and Interests

This beverage industry publication is read by buyers and distributors of wine, beer, and spirits, and by other industry professionals. It covers industry trends and news, profiles those who make the industry tick, and spotlights new ideas. It is always interested in hearing from writers with experience covering the alcohol beverage markets. Story ideas from wine and spirits producers are also accepted. Circ: 50,000.

Contents: 50% articles; 50% depts/columns
Frequency: Monthly
Website: www.tastingpanelmag.com

Freelance Potential

80% written by nonstaff writers. Publishes 60 freelance submissions yearly; 5% by authors who are new to the magazine, 90% by industry experts. Receives 10 queries monthly.

Submissions

Query with writing sample. Accepts email to dgadd@tastingpanelmag.com (Word attachments). Responds in 1 week.

- Articles: 300 words. Informational and how-to articles; profiles; interviews; humor; and new product information. Topics include wine, spirits, vintners, producers, and sommeliers.
- Depts/columns: Word lengths vary. New product reviews.

Sample Issue

132 pages. Advertising. Sample copy and editorial calendar available at website.

- "Going for the Gold." Article profiles Karlsson's Gold, a small-batch artisanal vodka.
- "Reposado Rhythm." Article reports on the availability and differences of reposado tequilas available on the market.
- Sample dept/column: "Alternative Beverages" reviews wines with style and substance.

Rights and Payment

Rights vary. Articles, $150–$400. Depts/columns, $100. Pays 1 month after receipt of invoice. Provides up to 10 contributor's copies.

Tea & Coffee Trade Journal

26 Broadway, Floor 9M
New York, NY 10004

Editor in Chief: Vanessa Facenda

Description and Interests

Since 1901, this magazine has been an international and trusted voice of the tea and coffee industry. Its news, trends, and market analysis are geared toward growers, importers/exporters, wholesalers, and specialty retailers. Freelance writers must have both a strong understanding of the tea and coffee industry and a good feel for the types of topics that its readers will find informative. Circ: 13,000.

Contents: 60% articles; 40% depts/columns
Frequency: Monthly
Website: www.teaandcoffee.net

Freelance Potential

40% written by nonstaff writers. Publishes 40 freelance submissions yearly; 5% by authors who are new to the magazine, 25% by industry experts. Receives 10 queries monthly.

Submissions

Query. Accepts email to editor@teaandcoffee.net and simultaneous submissions if identified. Response time varies.

- Articles: 1,200 words. Informational and how-to articles; and personal experience and opinion pieces. Topics include varieties of coffee and tea, coffee and tea growing and growers, processing and marketing coffee and tea, and industry trends.
- Depts/columns: 300 words. Industry news, equipment, and packaging.

Sample Issue

54 pages. Advertising. Sample copy available at website. Editorial calendar available.

- "Brazil Maintains Its Coffee Dominance." Article analyzes Brazil's coffee industry and its effects on the market and future crops.
- "Sipping Through Time." Article discusses the history and legends associated with rare Chinese pu-erh teas.

Rights and Payment

One-time rights. Written material, $.20 per word. Pays 3 months after publication.

Teachers & Writers

520 Eighth Avenue, Suite 2020
New York, NY 10018

Editor: Susan Karwoska

Description and Interests

Teachers & Writers is all about teaching the art of writing—from the kindergarten classroom through college—as well as in non-classroom settings. The magazine publishes both practical and theoretical material geared toward a general audience of teachers. Material should present lively explorations of its stated mission: "educating the imagination." Articles that present innovative techniques and ideas, or shine a new light on a familiar subject matter are welcome. Circ: 3,000.

Contents: Articles; depts/columns
Frequency: Quarterly
Website: www.twc.org/magazine

Freelance Potential

60% written by nonstaff writers. Publishes 8 freelance submissions yearly; 5% by unpublished writers, 50% by authors who are new to the magazine. Receives 10 queries monthly.

Submissions

Query. Prefers email to editors@twc.org (Word attachments); will accept hard copy. SASE. Response time varies.

- Articles: 500–2,500 words. Informational articles; profiles; interviews; reviews; and opinion pieces. Topics include education, writing, creativity, and nurturing the imagination.
- Depts/columns: Staff-written.

Sample Issue

48 pages. Sample articles available at website. Guidelines available at website.

- "Teaching Artist Snapshots." Article profiles the works of Gary Earl Ross and Celia White.
- "A Kid Named A." Article shares a teacher/student experience of persuading the student to think for himself.
- "Creating a Poem to Celebrate Your Community." Article shares ideas and exercises for creating a community poem project.

Rights and Payment

One-time rights. Written material, $20 per printed column. Pays on publication. Provides 2 contributor's copies.

Teachers of Vision

Christian Educators Association International
227 North Magnolia Avenue, Suite 2
Anaheim, CA 92801

Contributing Editor: Judy Turpen

Description and Interests

This magazine offers Christian educators guidance, encouragement, and dialogue about issues in public and private education. Writters should keep in mind that articles need a distinctively Christian viewpoint but without preaching. Circ: 8,000.

Contents: 50% articles; 40% depts/columns; 10% other
Frequency: Quarterly
Website: www.ceai.org

Freelance Potential

60% written by nonstaff writers. Publishes 50–65 freelance submissions yearly; 30% by unpublished writers, 60% by authors who are new to the magazine, 10% by experts. Receives 8–10 queries, 6–8 unsolicited mss monthly.

Submissions

Query or send complete ms with brief bio. Accepts reprints. Prefers email submissions to tov@ceai.org (RTF files); will accept hard copy. SASE. Responds in 2 months.

- Articles: Features, 1,000–2,500 words. Informational and how-to articles; personal experience and inspirational pieces; and research reports. Topics include educational philosophy and methodology. Mini-features, 400–750 words. Topics include holidays, special events, teaching techniques, education news.
- Depts/columns: Staff-written.
- Other: Poetry. Submit seasonal material at least 4 months in advance.

Sample Issue

32 pages. Sample copy and guidelines available at website.

- "When Your Student Announces 'I'm Gay!'" Article offers readers suggestions for dealing with this subject.
- "Stand By Me: Finding the Tools to Address Bullying and Teasing." Article provides strategies for dealing with this growing problem.

Rights and Payment

First. limited reprint, and electronic rights. Written material, payment rates vary. Pays on publication. Provides 3 contributor's copies.

Tech Directions

P.O. Box 8623
Ann Arbor, MI 48107

Managing Editor: Susanne Peckham

Description and Interests

This professional magazine gives technology and technical career educators articles on teaching techniques, classroom projects, and lab procedures. It also covers the issues facing the technology and applied science education fields. It is open to any idea or project that will help tech teachers in the classroom or lab. Circ: 40,000.

Contents: 65% articles; 35% depts/columns
Frequency: 10 times each year
Website: www.techdirections.com

Freelance Potential

90% written by nonstaff writers. Publishes 40 freelance submissions yearly; 40% by authors who are new to the magazine. Receives 5 queries, 10 mss monthly.

Submissions

Query or send complete ms. Accepts hard copy, disk submissions, and email to susanne@techdirections.com. No simultaneous submissions. SASE. Responds to queries in 1 week, to mss in 6–8 weeks.

- Articles: To 2,000 words. Informational and how-to articles; opinion pieces; and new product information. Topics include computers, software, technology, electronics, machinery, automotive subjects, design, engineering, woodworking, metalworking, careers, and education.
- Depts/columns: Staff-written.
- Other: Word games, puzzles, brainteasers, cartoons, and jokes.

Sample Issue

30 pages. Advertising. Sample copy, guidelines, and editorial calendar available at website.

- "Revitalize Electrical Program with Renewable Energy Focus." Article explains easy strategies for starting a renewable energy technology program.
- "Green Technology Resources." Article reviews green products that educators can incorporate into the curriculum.

Rights and Payment

All rights. Articles, $25. Puzzles and brainteasers, $5–$25. Pays on publication. Provides 3 copies.

Technical Analysis of Stocks & Commodities

4757 California Avenue SW
Seattle, WA 98116

Editor: Jayanthi Gopalakrishnan

Description and Interests

Filled with news, trends, and stock market analysis, this financial magazine is focused on giving traders and traders-to-be current information to stay on top of their trading game. All writers should have professional experience in the financial markets and be able to report, analyze, and predict for readers, many of whom are trading novices. Circ: 65,000.

Contents: 80% articles; 20% depts/columns
Frequency: 13 times each year
Website: www.traders.com

Freelance Potential

90% written by nonstaff writers. Publishes 100 freelance submissions yearly; 20% by unpublished writers, 20% by authors who are new to the magazine, 80% by experts. Receives 10 queries, 15 unsolicited mss monthly.

Submissions

Query with outline; or send complete ms. Accepts email to editor@traders.com, hard copy, disk submissions, and simultaneous submissions if identified. SASE. Responds in 2–3 weeks.

- Articles: To 2,000 words. Informational and how-to articles; interviews; and personal experience pieces. Topics include trading tecniques, statistics, artificial intelligence, and trading psychology.
- Depts/columns: Word lengths vary. Reviews of websites, software, and books; traders' tips; news, and futures liquidity.

Sample Issue

98 pages. Advertising. Sample articles, guidelines, and editorial calendar available at website.

- "The Markets Through Time." Article features an interview with stock market expert Mark Chaikin.
- "Trading the Trend." Article explains a strategy that can identify a major reversal.

Rights and Payment

All rights. Written material, payment rates vary. Pays on publication. Provides 2 contributor's copies.

TimberWest

P.O. Box 610
Edmonds, WA 98020

Managing Editor: Diane Mettler

Description and Interests

Since 1975, *TimberWest* has reported on all aspects of mechanized harvesting and wood processing technology in the forestry markets of the western United States. In addition to news of the industry, it publishes articles on trends, new technology, business strategies, legislation, products, people, and company profiles. It prefers to work with writers who are familiar with the issues surrounding the logging and sawmilling industries. Circ: 11,000+.

Contents: Articles; depts/columns
Frequency: 6 times each year
Website: www.forestnet.com

Freelance Potential

80% written by nonstaff writers. Publishes 25 freelance submissions yearly; 15% by authors who are new to the magazine, 5% by industry experts. Receives 1–2 queries monthly.

Submissions

Query with clips and artwork availability. Accepts hard copy and email queries to diane@forestnet.com. SASE. Responds in 3 weeks.

- Articles: Features, 1,000–1,200 words. News, 500–800 words. Informational articles; company profiles; and opinion pieces. Topics include logging, sawmills, the environment, forestry, wildfire management, legislation, machinery, technology, logging and lumber companies, and industry news.
- Depts/columns: Staff-written.
- Artwork: Prints; digital images.

Sample Issue

42 pages. Sample articles available at website. Guidelines available.

- "The Little Sawmill That Could." Article discusses the successful strategies of a Montana-based lumber company that has kept it competitive.
- "Biomass Removal." Article profiles a logging company and its foray into biomass removal.

Rights and Payment

First rights. Feature articles, $350. News articles, $250. Cover photos, $200. Pays on acceptance.

Today's Catholic Teacher

2621 Dryden Road, Suite 300
Dayton, OH 45439

Editor: Betsy Shepard

Description and Interests

Filled with practical information and classroom activities for Catholic school educators, this magazine addresses today's educational issues and covers the latest national trends. It is written for teachers and administrators from kindergarten through grade eight. The style is direct, concise, informative, and accurate. Writing should be enjoyable to read and free of educational jargon. Circ: 50,000.

Contents: 60% articles; 40% depts/columns
Frequency: 6 times each year
Website: www.catholicteacher.com

Freelance Potential

80% written by nonstaff writers. Publishes 25 freelance submissions yearly; 20% by unpublished writers, 20% by authors who are new to the magazine, 25% by experts. Receives 20 queries, 20 unsolicited mss monthly.

Submissions

Query or send complete ms. Accepts hard copy and email to bshepard@peterli.com. SASE. Responds to queries in 1 month, to mss in 3 months.

- Articles: 600–1,500 words. Informational and how-to articles; and personal experience pieces. Topics include curriculum, testing, technology, creative teaching, classroom management, and national education trends.
- Depts/columns: Staff-written.
- Artwork: Digital images at 300 dpi

Sample Issue

76 pages. Advertising. Sample articles and writers' guidelines available at website. Editorial calendar available.

- "St. Damien of Molokai." Article provides a lesson plan for a prayer service honoring this saint.
- "Parents as Partners: Effective Strategies for Catholic Teachers." Article offers tips for maintaining a healthy relationship with parents.

Rights and Payment

First serial rights. Articles, \$100–\$250. Pays on publication. Provides 3 contributor's copies.

Today's Photographer

American Image Press
P.O. Box 42
Hamptonville, NC 27020-0042

Editor in Chief: Vonda H. Blackburn

Description and Interests

Read by members of the International Freelance Photographers Organization, *Today's Photographer* is loaded with tips on how to make money with one's camera. Articles should include technical information, as the magazine's readers are professional photographers seeking to expand their skill sets. Circ: 78,000.

Contents: 70% articles; 30% depts/columns
Frequency: Quarterly
Website: www.aipress.com

Freelance Potential

90% written by nonstaff writers. Publishes 40 freelance submissions yearly; 60% by unpublished writers, 40% by authors who are new to the magazine. Receives 20 unsolicited mss monthly.

Submissions

IFPO member authors only. Send complete ms with artwork. Prefers disk submissions; will accept hard copy and simultaneous submissions if identified. SASE. Responds in 3–6 months.

- Articles: Word lengths vary. Informational and how-to articles; personal experience pieces; and new product information. Topics include event photography, business management, working with clients, and finding assignments.
- Depts/columns: Word lengths vary. Book reviews and "On Assignment" briefs.
- Artwork: B/W and color prints; 35mm or larger color transparencies.

Sample Issue

52 pages. Advertising. Sample copy available at website. Guidelines available.

- "A Turn of Events Tuf." Article shares a photographer's first experience working an NFL game.
- "Greatest Color" Article describes the photographic opportunities at the world's largest ballooning event.

Rights and Payment

One-time rights. No payment. Provides contributor's copies upon request.

Tourist Attractions & Parks

10 East Athens Avenue, Suite 208
Ardmore, PA 19003

President/Executive Editor: Scott Borowsky

Description and Interests

This industry publication covers the business of running amusement and water parks, stadiums, festivals, museums, and all other tourist and leisure attractions. Among its topics are industry trends, news, management issues, and food service. It prefers to work with journalists who know how to cover an industry. Circ: 31,483.

Contents: 95% articles; 5% depts/columns
Frequency: 7 times each year
Website: www.tapmag.com

Freelance Potential

75% written by nonstaff writers. Publishes 50+ freelance submissions yearly; 10% by authors who are new to the magazine. Receives 1–10 queries, 10–20 unsolicited mss monthly.

Submissions

Query or send complete ms. Accepts hard copy, disk submissions, and simultaneous submissions if identified. SASE. Responds in 1 month.

- Articles: 1,000–2,000 words. Informational and how-to articles; and profiles. Topics include theme parks, water parks, amusement parks, campgrounds, fairs, carnivals, food service, recreational activities, light and sound attractions, park management, and the entertainment industry.
- Depts/columns: Word lengths vary. News briefs and new product information.

Sample Issue

98 pages. Advertising. Sample articles, theme list/editorial calendar available at website.

- "What Does the Guest Hear?" Article discusses the importance of customer service.
- "The Garbage Details." Article discusses useful garbage handling tactics for every entertainment facility.

Rights and Payment

First serial rights. Written material, payment rates vary. Payment policy varies. Provides 3–4 contributor's copies.

The Trapper & Predator Caller

700 East State Street
Iola, WI 54990-0001

Managing Editor: Jared Blohm

Description and Interests

Founded in 1975, *Trapper & Predator Caller* serves as a source of practical information and industry trends for North American fur harvesters and animal-control workers. It seeks stories focused on methods and equipment used in trapping, calling, or hunting. Circ: 43,000.

Contents: 70% articles; 20% depts/columns; 10% other
Frequency: 10 times each year
Website: www.trapperpredatorcaller.com

Freelance Potential

95% written by nonstaff writers. Publishes 60 freelance submissions yearly; 20% by unpublished writers, 50% by authors who are new to the magazine, 50% by experts. Receives 30 queries, 20 unsolicited mss monthly.

Submissions

Prefers query; will accept complete ms. Accepts email submissions to jared.blohm@fwmedia.com (Word attachments). Artwork improves chance of acceptance. Responds in 2–3 weeks.

- Articles: 1,500–2,500 words. Informational articles; profiles; interviews; and personal experience pieces. Topics include trapping, predator calling, muzzleloader hunting, conservation, history, and nature.
- Depts/columns: 800–1,200 words. Market reports, association news, and new product information.
- Artwork: Prefers high-resolution digital images, 300 pixels per square inch in TIFF or JPEG file formats; will accept prints.

Sample Issue

64 pages. Advertising. Sample articles and guidelines available at website.

- "Is Birth Control the Future of Coyote Management." Article reports on an experimental study using chemical contraception.
- "Fur Handling 101." Article offers instruction on proper skinning.

Rights and Payment

All rights. All material, payment rates vary. Pays 45 days after publication. Provides 1 author's copy.

TravelAge West

11400 West Olympic Boulevard, Suite 325
Los Angeles, CA 90064

Editor in Chief: Ken Shapiro

Description and Interests

Written for travel agents in the western United States, this magazine has been reporting on popular and unusual travel destinations around the world for 40 years. Its purpose is to provide timely, practical material to help agents better serve their clients. Information on cruising and the latest travel trends and products is also featured. Submissions must address the needs and interests of Western US-based travel agents. Circ: 26,000.

Contents: 80% articles; 20% depts/columns
Frequency: 26 times each year
Website: www.travelagewest.com/Magazine/

Freelance Potential

45% written by nonstaff writers. Publishes 100 freelance submissions yearly; 10% by authors who are new to the magazine, 10% by industry experts. Receives 20 queries monthly.

Submissions

Query with résumé and clips. Accepts email queries to letters@travelagewest.com. Response time varies.

- Articles: 500–700 words. Informational and how-to articles; profiles; and interviews. Topics include U.S. and international travel destinations, lodging, cruises, tour operators, and industry news and trends.
- Depts/columns: Word lengths vary. Short industry updates; opinion pieces.

Sample Issue

40 pages. Advertising. Sample articles and editorial calendar at website. Theme list available.

- "What to Do in Kingston." Article reports on the history and attractions of Jamaica's capital.
- "Tequila Tasting in Los Cabos." Article discusses the rise in popularity of tequila tastings in this Mexican resort.
- "Wind Star Refreshes." Article describes the renovations of Windstar Cruises yachts.

Rights and Payment

All rights. Written material, payment rates vary. Pays on publication. Provides 1 contributor's copy.

Tree Care Industry Magazine

136 Harvey Road, Suite 101
Londonderry, NH 03053

Editor: Don Staruk

Description and Interests

This magazine of the Tree Care Industry Association strives to be the definitive resource for commercial, residential, and municipal arborists. It is packed with information on regulations, standards, safety issues, and new products. Circ: 24,000.

Contents: 45% articles; 55% depts/columns
Frequency: Monthly
Website: http://tcia.org

Freelance Potential

80% written by nonstaff writers. Publishes 60 freelance submissions yearly; 5% by unpublished writers, 20% by authors who are new to the magazine, 75% by industry experts. Receives 8–10 queries monthly.

Submissions

Query. Accepts email queries to editor@tcia.org. Availability of artwork improves chance of acceptance. Response time varies.

- Articles: 1,200–3,000 words. Informational and how-to articles; and new product information. Topics include trees, business, maintenance, machinery, nature, and the environment.
- Depts/columns: 600–1,200 words. Industry news and business issues.
- Artwork: B/W or color prints; JPEG, TIFF, EPS, or PDF files. Line drawings and graphs.

Sample Issue

68 pages. Advertising. Sample copy available at website. Guidelines and theme list available.

- "How is Your Business Coping with Fleet Technology Advancements?" Article discusses factors to consider when purchasing new equipment.
- "Biochar for Arborists." Article reports on how tree care professionals are developing applications for biochar.

Rights and Payment

All rights. Articles, $200–$350. Depts/columns, $50–$150. Stand-alone artwork, $25. Pays on publication. Provides 2 contributor's copies.

Underground Construction

P.O. Box 941669
Houston, TX 77094-8669

Editor: Robert Carpenter

Description and Interests

Underground construction and rehabilitation in the water, sewer, gas, and telecommunications industries are covered in this magazine. It focuses on projects, issues, and answers for a management audience. Circ: 38,000.

Contents: 40% articles; 60% depts/columns
Frequency: Monthly
Website: www.uconline.com

Freelance Potential

40% written by nonstaff writers. Publishes 40 freelance submissions yearly; 5% by authors who are new to the magazine, 10% by industry experts. Receives 2 queries monthly.

Submissions

Query. Accepts hard copy and email queries to rcarpenter@oildom.com. SASE. Responds in 2 months.

- Articles: 750–2,500 words. Informational articles and new product information. Topics include tools, techniques, and regulations for the underground construction, rehabilitation, and remediation of oil and gas pipelines; telecommunications services; and electric, water, and sewer utilities.
- Depts/columns: Word lengths vary. Rehabilitation technology, news, and products.
- Artwork: High-resolution digital images.

Sample Issue

68 pages. Advertising. Sample copy and editorial calendar available at website. Guidelines available.

- "Tackling the Big Jobs." Article describes the world's largest boring machine and the Canadian company that owns it.
- "Energy Growth Fuels Large HDD Rig Boom." Article discusses the new energy projects in development using HDD rigs.

Rights and Payment

One-time exclusive rights. Articles, $400–$800. Depts/columns and artwork, payment rates vary. Kill fee varies. Pays on acceptance. Provides 4 contributor's copies.

Veterinary Economics

8033 Flint Street
Lenexa, KS 66214

Editor: Brendan Howard

Description and Interests

The primary focus of this magazine is the business of running a veterinary practice. Its articles cover management issues, client relations, design, finances, and personnel issues. It also highlights industry news impacting veterinary practices, such as changes in vaccine protocols. Most articles include interviews with practicing veterinarians or case study examples. Circ: 55,000+.

Contents: 60% articles; 40% depts/columns
Frequency: Monthly
Website: www.dvm360.com

Freelance Potential

70% written by nonstaff writers. Publishes 60 freelance submissions yearly; 2% by unpublished writers, 5% by authors who are new to the magazine, 66% by experts. Receives 8 queries, 5 unsolicited mss monthly.

Submissions

Query. Accepts hard copy and email to ve@advanstar.com. SASE. Responds in 12–16 weeks.

- Articles: 800–2,000 words. Informational and how-to articles; profiles; interviews; and creative nonfiction. Topics include veterinary business, careers, computers, and practice management issues.
- Depts/columns: Word lengths vary. "Practice Tips," "Growth Center," Building the Bond," "Hot Button," and "Product News."

Sample Issue

64 pages. Advertising. Sample articles, writers' guidelines, and theme list/editorial calendar available at website.

- "Know What You Want—Be Ready to Fight for Your New Veterinary Practice." Article profiles a Maryland veterinarian who opened his dream hospital.
- "One Size Doesns't Fit All." Article discusses the importance of catering healthcare options to each patient.
- Sample dept/column: "Hot Button" details three steps to getting one's career back on track.

Rights and Payment

All rights. Written material, payment rates vary. Pays on publication. Provides 5 tearsheets.

Vineyard & Winery Management

P.O. Box 14459
Santa Rosa, CA 95402-6459

Editor in Chief: Tina Caputo

Description and Interests

This trade publication has been covering the wine industry of North America for 35 years. It offers industry professionals a resource for keeping up with new trends in marketing, production technology, management strategies, and news from across the industry. Writers must be well-versed in the wine industry and vineyard management. Any topic that will keep readers informed about the industry and give them tools to increase their quality and efficiency is of interest. Circ: 7,500.

Contents: 60% articles; 40% depts/columns
Frequency: 6 times each year
Website: www.vwm-online.com

Freelance Potential

70% written by nonstaff writers. Publishes 30 freelance submissions yearly; 5% by unpublished writers, 5% by authors who are new to the magazine, 90% by experts. Receives 10 queries monthly.

Submissions

Query. Accepts email queries to tcaputo@vwm-online.com and simultaneous submissions if identified. Responds in 1 month.

- Articles: 2,000 words. Informational and how-to articles. Topics include wine technology, marketing, public relations, compliance, and viticulture.
- Depts/columns: 1,200–1,500 words. Business management issues.

Sample Issue

130 pages. Advertising. Sample articles available at website. Guidelines available.

- "Vigilant About Lake County." Article profiles California-based Vigilance Winery.
- "Q&A: Paul Mabray." Article features an interview with VinTank's chief strategy officer on using technology to connect wineries with their customers.
- "Video Marketing Goes Viral." Article offers tips for conceptualizing and creating effective winery videos.

Rights and Payment

All rights. Written material, payment rates vary. Pays on publication. Provides contributor's copies.

Watercolor Artist

10151 Carver Road, Suite 200
Blue Ash, OH 45242

Editor: Kelly Kane

Description and Interests

Watercolor Artist is designed to inform, instruct, and inspire watermedia painters of all levels. Each issue is packed with ideas and tips that will improve skills and build or maintain a successful painting career. Its voice is conversational, engaging, and informative. Articles should emphasize the creative process and important or unique techniques must be fully explained or demonstrated. Circ: 52,000.

Contents: Articles; depts/columns
Frequency: 6 times each year
Website: www.artistsnetwork.com

Freelance Potential

Publishes numerous freelance submissions each year.

Submissions

Query with outline, résumé, clips, and at least 10 images of watermedia work. Prefers hard copy; will accept email to WCAMAG@fwmedia.com (attach images). Availability of artwork improves chance of acceptance. SASE. Responds in 3 months.

- Articles: 500–2,000 words. Informational and how-to articles; profiles; interviews; and personal experience pieces. Topics include watercolor techniques, tools, and artists.
- Depts/columns: Word lengths vary. "Making a Splash," "Creativity Workshop," "Meet the Masters," and "Studio Staples."
- Artwork: Color slides or transparencies; high-resolution digital images.

Sample Issue

72 pages. Sample articles and guidelines available at website.

- "Josy Britton's Mosaic Techniques for Watercolor Painting." Article describes this artist's mosaic techniques that she invented from her love of impressionism.
- "Everyday Tropical Life Watercolor Paintings." Article highlights the watercolor paintings featured at a Bahamas gallery.

Rights and Payment

First world serial rights. Written material, to $600. Artwork, no payment. Pays on acceptance. Provides 2 contributor's copies.

Wines & Vines

65 Mitchell Boulevard, Suite A
San Rafael, CA 94903

Editor: Jim Gordon

Description and Interests

This trade magazine serves the entire wine and grape industry with coverage of news, trends, techniques, and products. In addition to its how-to's and market coverage, it reports on the boutique winery industry and growing regions in America. It does not accept any submission without first receiving a query. All prospective writers must demonstrate a thorough understanding of the industry. Circ: 8,400.

Contents: 50% articles; 50% depts/columns
Frequency: Monthly
Website: www.winesandvines.com

Freelance Potential

50% written by nonstaff writers. Publishes 60 freelance submissions yearly; 10% by authors who are new to the magazine, 30% by industry experts. Receives 15 queries monthly.

Submissions

Query. Accepts email to edit@winesandvines.com. Responds if interested.

- Articles: 1,500 words. Informational, how-to, and self-help articles; interviews; new product information; and personal experience and opinion pieces. Topics include grape growing, winemaking, marketing, winemaking technology, and boutique wineries.
- Depts/columns: 1,000 words. News, business trends, and opinion pieces.

Sample Issue

68 pages. Advertising. Sample articles available at website. Guidelines and theme list/editorial calendar available.

- "Hidden Deductions." Article outlines the savings available despite pending tax increases.
- "New Teaching Winery." Article reveals an architect's plan for Yavapai College's new winery program.
- Sample dept/column: "Event Preview" includes information on the upcoming Hong Kong Wine & Spirits Fair.

Rights and Payment

First North American serial rights. Written material, $500. Pays on acceptance. Provides up to 3 contributor's copies.

WorkBoat

121 Free Street
Portland, ME 04101

Editor in Chief: David Krapf

Description and Interests

This trade magazine covers the inland and coastal waterways and the news, products, trends, and innovations of the commercial vessels that are in those waters. It is read by operators of commercial vessels. The magazine's geographical coverage includes inland river systems, intercoastal waterways, ports, harbors, and the offshore oilfields. Circ: 25,413.

Contents: 75% articles; 25% depts/columns
Frequency: Monthly
Website: www.workboat.com

Freelance Potential

50% written by nonstaff writers. Publishes 50 freelance submissions yearly; 5% by unpublished writers, 10% by authors who are new to the magazine, 10% by experts. Receives 5 queries monthly.

Submissions

Query. Accepts email to dkrapf@divcom.com (Word attachments). Responds in 1–3 days.

- Articles: 800–1,200 words. Informational and how-to articles; opinion pieces; and new product information. Topics include inland and coastal tugs and barges, the offshore oil industry, second-tier boat yards, passenger vessels, the U.S. Coast Guard, the Army Corps of Engineers, boatbuilding, industry meetings, legislation, and regulation.
- Depts/columns: "News Log," 200–500 words.
- Artwork: High-resolution digital images.

Sample Issue

84 pages. Advertising. Sample issue and editorial calendar available at website. Writer's guidelines available.

- "Rolling On." Article reports on new ATB's coming onto the market.
- "Ocean View." Article highlights the five new deepwater structures due for installation in the Gulf of Mexico.

Rights and Payment

First and limited second rights. Articles, $250–$1,200. Depts/columns, $200. Artwork, $50–$300. Pays on publication. Provides 1 copy.

WOW! Women on Writing

P.O. Box 41104
Long Beach, CA 90853

Editor in Chief: Angela Mackintosh

Description and Interests

In service to the sisterhood of female writers, this website is dedicated to sharing insights, experiences, and lessons learned regarding the craft of writing. Topics include writing techniques, genre trends, and getting published. It seeks queries that have a fully fleshed-out idea, a rough breakdown of the content, and sources, if applicable. Hits per month: 1 million.

Contents: Articles; depts/columns
Frequency: Monthly
Website: www.wow-womenonwriting.com

Freelance Potential

100% written by nonstaff writers. Publishes 170 freelance submissions yearly; 5% by unpublished writers, 25% by new authors.

Submissions

Query or send complete ms with author biography and writing samples. Accepts email to submissions@wow-womenonwriting.com (with "Query" or "Submission" in subject line; no attachments). Responds only if interested.

- Articles: To 3,000 words. Informational articles; profiles; interviews; and personal experience pieces. Topics include writing, publishing, and book marketing.
- Depts/columns: "How2" and "Inspiration," 1,500–2,000 words. "20 Questions," word lengths vary.

Sample Issue

Sample copy and guidelines available at website. Theme list available.

- "Tagline—What It Is and Why You Need One." Article discusses the importance of a tagline and some ideas in choosing one to best sell one's work.
- "Phrases We Need to Find and Kill." Article shares the author's list of oft-used phrases she would like to eliminate.

Rights and Payment

First electronic and archival rights. Articles, $75–$150. Depts/columns, $50–$75. Pays on publication.

The Writer

85 Quincy Avenue, Suite 2
Quincy, MA 02169

Editor: Jeff Reich

Description and Interests

Focusing on the craft of writing and getting published, *The Writer* covers publishing trends, the steps to good writing, and the changing markets for writers. Practical solutions for writing problems, literary magazine profiles, and tips from famous authors round out the mix. Circ: 30,000.

Contents: 60% articles; 40% depts/columns
Frequency: Monthly
Website: www.writermag.com

Freelance Potential

95% written by nonstaff writers. Publishes 120 freelance submissions yearly; 5% by unpublished writers, 30–40% by authors who are new to the magazine, 65% by industry experts. Receives 100 queries monthly.

Submissions

Query. Email to tweditorial@madavor.com. Usually responds in 1–2 months.

- Articles: 600–3,500 words. Informational and how-to articles; profiles; interviews; personal essays; and new product information. Topics include writing techniques, freelancing, market trends, language and grammar, literary agents, and publishers.
- Depts/columns: 600–1,600 words. News, reviews, markets, and personal experience pieces.

Sample Issue

58 pages. Advertising. Sample copy available at website.

- "First Person Plural Gives 'Us,' A Role." Article explains why the rarely used first-person plural achieves effects that can't be replicated with any other POV.
- "Set Your Writing Free." Article offers an entertaining look at confronting and conquering the demons that hinder one's creativity.
- Sample dept/column: "How I Write" shares suggestions for character development from *Silver Sparrow* author Tayari Jones.

Rights and Payment

First North American serial rights. Articles and depts/columns, $100–$400. Book reviews, $40–$80. Pays on acceptance. Provides 2 contributor's copies.

Writer's Digest

10151 Carver Road, Suite 200
Cincinnati, OH 45242

Senior Managing Editor: Zachary Petit

Description and Interests

Writer's Digest helps writers improve their skills, get published, stay on top of industry trends, and maintain a thriving career. Its articles are written by bestselling authors, up-and-coming writers, and seasoned editors. The interviews are all written in-house but queries are accepted for profiles, as long as they have not been submitted to the magazine's annual competition. Circ: 80,000.

Contents: 50% articles; 50% depts/columns
Frequency: 8 times each year
Website: www.writersdigest.com

Freelance Potential

75% written by nonstaff writers. Publishes 40 freelance submissions yearly; 20% by unpublished writers, 10% by authors who are new to the magazine, 70% by industry experts. Receives 80+ queries monthly.

Submissions

Query with outline or send complete ms; include list of publishing credits. Accepts email to wdsubmissions@fwmedia.com (no attachments). Responds in 2–3 months.

- Articles: Author profiles, 800–2,000 words. Writing technique articles, 1,000–1,500 words. Topics include writing techniques, working with an agent, marketing one's work, and publishing trends.
- Depts/columns: "Inkwell," to 800 words.

Sample Issue

76 pages. Advertising. Sample articles, guidelines, and editorial calendar available at website.

- "Write the Perfect Query Letter." Article shares a real-life novel pitch that led to a book deal and details how to query one's own work.
- "Your Agent Wish List." Article provides information on agents looking for new clients and tips on writing in each genre.

Rights and Payment

First North American print and perpetual world digital rights. Written material, $.30–$.50 per word. Kill fee, 25%. Pays on acceptance. Provides contributor's copies.

Written By

7000 West Third Street
Los Angeles, CA 90048

Managing Editor: Christina McBride

Description and Interests

As the member publication of the Writers Guild of America West, *Written By* is all about the craft of screenwriting. It features articles and essays on techniques, market trends, and successful screenwriters. All freelancers must be TV/film writers or journalists covering the industry. Circ: 18,000.

Contents: 50% articles; 50% depts/columns
Frequency: 6 times each year
Website: www.wga.org/writtenby

Freelance Potential

50% written by nonstaff writers. Publishes 10–15 freelance submissions yearly; 10% by unpublished writers, 30% by authors who are new to the magazine, 70% by experts. Receives 15 queries monthly.

Submissions

Prefers query with résumé and 3 clips; will accept complete ms. Accepts hard copy, email to writtenby@wga.org, and simultaneous submissions if identified. SASE. Response time varies.

- Articles: 2,000–3,000 words. Informational articles; profiles; and interviews. Topics include screeenwriters, screenwriting, legal issues, trends, and Hollywood history.
- Depts/columns: Word lengths vary. Opinion pieces, writers' tools, new media, electronic scripting, business and legal issues, how-to's, writer spotlights, and personal essays.

Sample Issue

60 pages. Sample copy and writers' guidelines available at website.

- "The Good Doctor." Article profiles Neal Baer, best known for his work on *ER* and *Law & Order SVU*, and his personal commitment to illuminating the hidden worlds of medicine, disease, and poverty.
- "Speaking Their Language." Article highlights the new teen drama, *Switched at Birth*, as the industry's first to include several deaf or hard-of-hearing characters.
- Sample dept/column: "Altscreen" discusses whether censorship resulted in the cancellation of *The 99* comic series.

Rights and Payment

Exclusive one-time rights. Articles, $1,000–$3,000. Depts/columns, $500. Pays on acceptance. Provides 2 contributor's copies.

Youth and Discipleship Leadership

1080 Montgomery Avenue Northeast
Cleveland, TN 37311

Editor: Shelia Stewart

Description and Interests

Christian educators and youth ministry workers find useful tips and inspiring stories in each issue of this magazine. Its focus is on discipling readers and instructing them on ways to incorporate acts of Christian living into everyday life. Profiles of individuals or groups who are advancing Christian education with distinctive ministries and practical how-to articles are particularly welcome. Circ: 10,000.

Contents: Articles; depts/columns
Frequency: Quarterly
Website: www.pathwaypress.org

Freelance Potential

10% written by nonstaff writers. Publishes 10 freelance submissions yearly; 90% by previously unpublished authors; 10% by authors new to the magazine. Receives 2–3 queries, 2 unsolicited manuscripts monthly.

Submissions

Guidelines available at website. Send complete ms. Accepts hard copy and email to Editorial Assistant at tammy_hatfield@pathwaypress.org (Word attachments). SASE. Responds in 3 weeks.

- Articles: 500–1,000 words. Informational, inspirational, how-to, profiles, interviews, humor, personal experience. Topics include Christian ministry, programming ideas, discipleship, Christian education.
- Depts/columns: Staff-written.

Sample Issue

32 pages. Advertising. Sample copy available at website.

- "Integrity...Yours, Mine, Ours," by J. David Stephens. Article discusses the meaning of integrity and questions of conduct.
- "Keeping-It-Real Leadership," by Tony P. Lane. Article provides suggestions for living an authentic life.

Rights and Payment

First rights. Written material, $25–$50. Kill fee, 50%. Pays on publication. Provides 1–10 contributor's copies.

YouthWorker Journal

YWJ/Salem Publishing/CCM Communications
402 BNA Drive, Suite 400
Nashville, TN 37217–2509

Managing Editor: Amy L. Lee

Description and Interests

YouthWorker Journal strives to be a source of information and inspiration for those working within youth ministries. Along with curriculum reviews and interviews with youth ministers, it publishes articles that provide ideas, spiritual support, and fundraising tools. Each issue contains numerous articles focusing on a single theme. A digital version features additional content. Circ: 10,000.

Contents: 50% articles; 50% depts/columns
Frequency: 6 times each year
Website: www.youthworker.com

Freelance Potential

100% written by nonstaff writers. Publishes 50+ freelance submissions yearly; 15% by unpublished writers, 25% by new authors, 30% by experts. Receives 60 queries monthly.

Submissions

Query with outline, introduction, short bio, and clips. Accepts email queries to ALee@Salem Publishing.com (include "Query" in subject line). Response time varies.

- Articles: 200–3,000 words. Informational and how-to articles; profiles; and interviews. Topics include Christian youth ministry and mission work, theology in youth ministry, successful programs, encouragement of youth workers.
- Depts/columns: Word lengths vary. "10 Minutes in God's Word," 1,000–1,200 words. "Worldview," 800–900 words. Media reviews, 200–600 words.

Sample Issue

64 pages. Advertising. Sample copy available. Guidelines and theme list available at website under "Help."

- "Talking About Sports: Competition and Character." Article suggests dicussion starters to use with students that compare sports to life.
- "Fundraising 101." Article offers tips for making fundraising seem less daunting.

Rights and Payment

All rights. Written material, payment policy varies. Pays 30–45 days after acceptance. Provides 1 contributor's copy.

Additional Trade Magazines

Animation World Magazine

Digital publication

6525 Sunset Boulevard, Garden Suite 10
Hollywood, CA 90028

Contributing Editor: Bill Desowitz

Whom to contact

Description and Interests: Cutting-edge technology and industry news are the focus of this web-based magazine for professional animators. Updated daily, it strives to provide a single source of up-to-the-minute information on all aspects of this field for animators across the globe. Hits per month: 150,000.
Website: www.awn.com

Gives brief characterization of the magazine, its frequency, the types and topics of articles and stories it publishes and needs, and its readers; gives website address.

Freelance Potential: 80–90% written by nonstaff writers. Publishes 170–180 freelance submissions yearly.

Indicates openness to freelance submissions, including how many are published yearly and the percentage by unpublished writers, when provided by the publisher.

Submissions and Payment: Sample articles available on website. Query or send complete ms with résumé and brief author biography. Accepts email submissions to editor@awn.com. Response time varies. Rights vary. Articles, 1,200 words. Written material, word lengths and payment rates vary. Pays on acceptance.

Provides guidelines for submitting material; indicates typical rights and payment.

Icon Key

 New Listing

 Epublisher

 Not currently accepting submissions

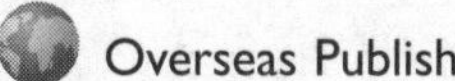

 Fiction makes up at least 10% of magazine editorial content

Acres U.S.A.

P.O. Box 91299
Austin, TX 78709-1299

Editor

Description and Interests: The focus of *Acres U.S.A.* is sustainable and organic agricultural practices. Each monthly issue presents articles of interest to farmers and ranchers on topics such as soil management, raising livestock, and new technologies in this field. Circ: 17,000.
Website: www.acresusa.com

Freelance Potential: 70% written by nonstaff writers. Publishes 70 freelance submissions yearly. Receives 10 unsolicited mss monthly.

Submissions and Payment: Sample articles available at website. Guidelines available. Send complete ms with Social Security number. Prefers email submissions to editor@acresusa.com; accepts hard copy. SASE. Responds in 3 months. Rights negotiable. Articles, 2,000 words; $.10 per word. Depts/columns, word lengths and payment rates vary. B/W or color prints, slides, or digital images at 300 dpi; $5 per photo. Pays on publication.

Adverse Event Reporting News

19-B Wirt Street SW
Leesburg, VA 20175

Editor/Publisher: Ken Reid

Description and Interests: The focus of this newsletter is on the adverse effects and safety issues of drugs as they pertain to FDA and European Union Regulatory standards. It covers drug-related clinical trials, recalls, and litigation in 26 issues each year. Circ: Unavailable.
Website: www.fdainfo.com

Freelance Potential: 20% written by nonstaff writers. Publishes 30–40 freelance submissions yearly; 10% by authors who are new to the magazine, 30% by experts.

Submissions and Payment: Sample copy, guidelines, and theme list/editorial calendar available. Query with writing samples. Accepts email to kreid@fdainfo.com. Responds in 1 week. Second rights. Articles, 600–1,000 words; $250. Depts/columns, 800–1,200 words; payment rates vary. Pays on publication.

AfterCapture

6255 Sunset Boulevard, 20th floor
Los Angeles, CA 90028-742

Editor: Bill Hurter

Description and Interests: Available through iTunes, this magazine for photographers and digital imaging professionals covers "everything after the image is taken." Writers must submit a bio that reflects a deep knowledge of imagemaking and image-manipulation technologies. *AfterCapture* is affiliated with *RangeFinder*. Circ: 40,000.
Website: www.rangefinderonline.com/AfterCapture.shtml

Freelance Potential: 10% written by nonstaff writers. Publishes 70 freelance submissions yearly; 30% by authors who are new to the magazine.

Submissions and Payment: Sample copy at website. Send email queries to Bill Hurter at bhurter@rfpublishing.com. Responds in 2 weeks. First serial and electronic rights. Written material, payment rates vary. Pays on publication.

Against the Grain

Linking Publishers, Vendors, and Librarians

MSC 98, The Citadel
209 Richardson Avenue
Charleston, SC 29409

Submissions: Leah Hinds

Description and Interests: *Against the Grain* addresses topics relevant to the scholarly publishing industry. Appearing six times a year, it covers mergers, acquisitions, and marketing in the publishing information chain, as well as legal issues and new technologies. Circ: 2,500.
Website: www.against-the-grain.com

Freelance Potential: 6% written by nonstaff writers. Publishes 30 freelance submissions yearly; 10% by unpublished writers, 20% by authors who are new to the magazine; 60% by experts.

Submissions and Payment: Sample copy, guidelines, and editorial calendar available. Query. Accepts email queries to Leah Hinds at leah@katina.info. Responds immediately. All rights. Articles, 2,000–3,000 words. Fiction and depts/columns, to 2,500 words. JPEG or EPS files. No payment. Provides up to 5 contributor's copies.

Agweek

P.O. Box 6008
Grand Forks, ND 58206-6008

Editor: Lisa Gibson

Description and Interests: A weekly tabloid for agricultural professionals, *Agweek* covers farming in the northwestern U.S. and southern Canada. It targets crop growers as well as cattle and dairy farmers, and features news and articles on agricultural policy and programs. Circ: 30,000.
Website: www.agweek.com

Freelance Potential: Publishes few freelance submissions yearly; 10% by unpublished writers, 98% by authors who are new to the magazine. Receives 1–2 queries, 1–2 unsolicited mss each month.

Submissions and Payment: Sample copy and guidelines available. Query or send complete ms. Accepts hard copy and email to lgibson@agweek.com. SASE. Response time varies. One-time rights. Articles, 1,500 words. Depts/columns, 750 words. Written material, payment rates vary. Payment policy varies.

Airport Improvement

3780 Chapel Road
Brookfield, WI 53045

Editor: Rebecca Douglas

Description and Interests: Devoted exclusively to covering airport operations, this magazine appears six times each year. Topics of interest to its professional readers include improvements to terminals, baggage handling, security, parking, and ground support. Stories about specific projects are featured, with details on how challenges were overcome. Circ: 5,200.
Website: www.airportimprovement.com

Freelance Potential: 100% written by nonstaff writers. Publishes 66 freelance submissions yearly; 100% by authors who are new to the magazine.

Submissions and Payment: Sample copy available at website. Guidelines available. Query or send complete ms. Accepts hard copy and email submissions to rebeccadouglas@airportimprovement.com. SASE. Responds in 1 month. All rights. Articles, 1,000+ words. Written material, payment rates vary. Pays 1 month after invoice.

American Salesman

320 Valley Street
Burlington, IA 52601

Editor: Todd Darnall

Description and Interests: This monthly publication targets sales professionals seeking timely, expert advice for success. With a national audience and its content spanning across fields, it addresses sales productivity, staff motivation, goal setting, and more. Circ: Unavailable.
Website: www.salestrainingandtechniques.com

Freelance Potential: 100% written by nonstaff writers. Publishes 40–50 freelance submissions yearly; 30% by authors who are new to the magazine, 70% by experts. Receives 12 unsolicited mss monthly.

Submissions and Payment: Sample copy and guidelines available at website. Send complete ms with résumé and word count. Accepts email to articles@salestrainingandtechniques.com. (Word attachments). Responds in 1 week. All rights. Articles, 500–1,000 words; $.04 per word. Pays on publication. Provides 2 contributor's copies.

American Secondary Education

Ashland University, Dwight Schar COE, Room 231
401 College Avenue
Ashland, OH 44805

Editor: Dr. James A. Rycik

Description and Interests: Three times each year, *American Secondary Education* offers practical and theoretical articles about secondary education. The focus is on curriculum, instruction, assessment, and fostering academic achievement. The magazine is widely distributed to university and high school libraries throughout the U.S. and Canada. Circ: 450.
Website: www.ashland.edu/ase

Freelance Potential: 99% written by nonstaff writers. Publishes 20 freelance submissions yearly; 75% by new authors. Receives 3–5 mss monthly.

Submissions and Payment: Sample copy available. Send complete ms to asejournal@ashland.edu. No simultaneous submissions. Response time varies. All rights. Articles, 10–30 double-spaced pages. Depts/columns, word lengths vary. No payment. Provides 1 contributor's copy.

American Songwriter

1303 16th Avenue South, 2nd Floor
Nashville, TN 37212

Attention: Freelance

Description and Interests: Practical information and inspiration for songwriters appear in this magazine, published six times each year. It features in-depth interviews with up-and-coming and established songwriters, publishers, producers, and other industry insiders. All genres of music are covered—from hip-hop to classical. Circ: 45,000+.
Website: www.americansongwriter.com

Freelance Potential: 90% written by nonstaff writers. Publishes 20 freelance submissions yearly.

Submissions and Payment: Sample copy and guidelines available. Seeks resume and clips before making freelance assignments; email to info@americansongwriter.com or submit hard copy to the address above. First North American serial rights. Articles, 300–1,200 words; $25–$60. Kill fee, 25%. Pays on publication. Provides 2 contributor's copies.

Angus Beef Bulletin

American Angus Association
3201 Frederick Avenue
St. Joseph, MO 64506-2997

Editor: Shauna Rose Hermel

Description and Interests: *Angus Beef Bulletin* is read by commercial cattlemen who seek information on the angus beef industry. Articles cover trends and association news, and topics such as herd health, production, management, and breeding. In addition to the print edition, which appears five times each year, there is a monthly electronic supplement. Writers must know the industry thoroughly. Circ: 70,000.
Website: www.angusbeefbulletin.com

Freelance Potential: 70% written by nonstaff writers.

Submissions and Payment: Sample articles available at website. Guidelines available. Send complete ms. Accepts email submissions to shermel@angusjournal.com. Responds in 3 months. Rights vary. Articles, 1,500–2,200 words. Depts/columns, 750 words. Written material, payment rates vary. Pays on publication.

Angus Journal

American Angus Association
3201 Frederick Avenue
St. Joseph, MO 64506-2997

Editor: Shauna Rose Hermel

Description and Interests: *Angus Journal* is a monthly magazine specifically for beef industry seedstock producers. Informative articles on all aspects of seedstock production appear alongside interviews and profiles, industry news items, and new product reviews. Association news also is provided. It is expected that all submissions be authored by experienced writers who know the beef industry well. Circ: 14,000.
Website: www.angusjournal.com

Freelance Potential: 70% written by nonstaff writers.

Submissions and Payment: Sample articles available at website. Guidelines and theme list/editorial calendar available. Send complete ms. Accepts email submissions to shermel@angusjournal.com. Responds in 3 months. Rights vary. Articles, 1,500–2,200 words. Depts/columns, 750 words. Written material, payment rates vary. Pays on publication.

Animation World Magazine

6525 Sunset Boulevard, Garden Suite 10
Hollywood, CA 90028

Contributing Editor: Bill Desowitz

Description and Interests: Cutting-edge technology and industry news are the focus of this web-based magazine for professional animators. Updated daily, it strives to provide a single source of up-to-the-minute information on all aspects of this field for animators across the globe. Hits per month: 150,000.
Website: www.awn.com

Freelance Potential: 80–90% written by nonstaff writers. Publishes 170–180 freelance submissions yearly.

Submissions and Payment: Sample articles available on website. Query or send complete ms with résumé and brief author biography. Accepts email submissions to editor@awn.com. Response time varies. Rights vary. Articles, 1,200 words. Written material, word lengths and payment rates vary. Pays on acceptance.

Apparel

801 Gervais Street, Suite 101
Columbia, SC 29201

Editor in Chief: Jordan Speer

Description and Interests: *Apparel* is aimed at professionals in the clothing and soft goods industry. Its monthly issues provide readers with updates on industry news and trends, informative articles on technology, expert marketing advice, and new product reviews. It also publishes profiles of industry leaders. Circ: 18,000.
Website: www.apparelmag.com

Freelance Potential: 40% written by nonstaff writers. Publishes 40 freelance submissions yearly; 10% by unpublished writers, 10% by authors who are new to the magazine, 50% by experts. Receives 3 queries monthly.

Submissions and Payment: Sample copy available at website. Query with outline. Accepts email queries to jspeer@apparelmag.com. Response time varies. All rights. Articles, 1,200 words. Written material, payment rates vary. Pays on acceptance. Provides 1 contributor's copy.

The Appraisers Standard

New England Appraisers Association
6973 Crestridge Road
Memphis, TN 38119

Editor: Edward T. Tuten

Description and Interests: Under new ownership, this quarterly of the New England Appraisers Association targets personal property appraisers and antique dealers. It covers appraisal, art, off-beat collections, and interesting finds. Circ: 350.
Website: www.newenglandappraisers.org

Freelance Potential: 70% written by nonstaff writers. Publishes 4 freelance submissions yearly; 25% by authors who are new to the magazine, 75% by experts. Receives 1 query monthly.

Submissions and Payment: Sample copy and guidelines available. Query or send complete ms with author bio and credentials. Accepts hard copy and email submissions to etuten551@aol.com. SASE. Responds in 1 month. Rights vary. Articles, 700 words; $60. B/W prints contributor's copies.

ArrowTrade Magazine

3479 409th Avenue NW
Braham, MN 55006

Editor: Tim Dehn

Description and Interests: *ArrowTrade Magazine* is written specifically for businesspeople involved in the selling, distributing, and manufacturing of archery and bowhunting gear. Published six times a year, it helps readers stay updated on industry trends and new products. Circ: 10,000.
Website: www.ezflipmags.com/Magazines/ArrowTrade_Magazine

Freelance Potential: 70% written by nonstaff writers. Publishes 35–45 freelance submissions yearly; 5% by authors who are new to the magazine.

Submissions and Payment: Sample copy available at website. Query or send complete ms. Accepts hard copy and email to arrowtrade@northlc.com. SASE. Response time varies. First print and electronic rights. Written material, word lengths vary. Articles, $400–$575. Depts/columns, $175–$250. Payment policy varies.

Bench & Bar of Minnesota

600 Nicollet Mall, Suite 380
Minneapolis, MN 55402

Editor: Judson Haverkamp

Description and Interests: Read and written by attorneys practicing law in Minnesota, this magazine offers articles that advance the education, competence, ethical practice, and public responsibility of the state's lawyers. It appears 11 times each year. Circ: 17,500.
Website: www.mnbenchbar.com

Freelance Potential: 75% written by nonstaff writers. Publishes 30+ submissions yearly; 10% by unpublished writers, 60% by authors who are new to the magazine. Receives 5–6 queries and unsolicited mss monthly.

Submissions and Payment: Sample articles and guidelines available at website. Query or send ms with short bio and recent photo. Accepts hard copy and email submissions to jhaverkamp@mnbar.org. Response time varies. First serial rights. Articles, to 3,500 words; payment rates vary. Pays on acceptance. Provides 2 contributor's copies.

Bowling Center Management

122 South Michigan Avenue, Suite 1506
Chicago, IL 60603

Editor: Michael Mazek

Description and Interests: Devoted exclusively to bowling center operations, this monthly magazine publishes articles on facilities management, marketing and promotions, technology, finances, and human resources, in order to help center managers operate more effectively and profitably. Circ: 6,000.
Website: www.bcmmag.com

Freelance Potential: 60% written by nonstaff writers. Publishes 40–50 freelance submissions yearly; 2–4% by authors who are new to the magazine. Receives 2–3 queries monthly.

Submissions and Payment: Sample copy and editorial calendar available at website. Query. Accepts hard copy and email queries to bcmmagazine@gmail.com. SASE. Response time varies. First rights. Articles, word lengths vary; $150–$200. Pays on acceptance. Provides 2 contributor's copies.

BSD Magazine

1521 Concord Pike, Suite 301
Wilmington, DE 19803

Editor in Chief: Michal Gladecki

Description and Interests: A professional publication founded in 2008, *BSD Magazine* targets BSD users, enthusiasts, and communities, including programmers, administrators, and other IT professionals. Each monthly issue features articles and opinion pieces from computer professionals and BSD gurus. It also publishes technology reports, user tutorials, and practical information to show that BSD systems are reliable, secure, and user-friendly. Circ: 5,000.
Website: www.bsdmag.org

Freelance Potential: 85% written by nonstaff writers. Publishes 40 freelance submissions yearly; 45% by authors who are new to the magazine.

Submissions and Payment: Sample copy available at website. Query with outline. Accepts email queries to editors@bsdmag.org. Response time varies. Exclusive rights. Articles, word lengths vary; $30 per page. Payment policy varies.

Business Today

Foundation for Student Communication
48 University Place, Room 305
Princeton, NJ 08544

Editor in Chief: Sam Heffernan

Description and Interests: One of the most widely circulated student-run magazines in the country, *Business Today* targets college students with articles on business and economic issues, executive interviews, and student opinion pieces. It is published twice each year. Circ: 200,000.
Website: www.businesstoday.org

Freelance Potential: 60% written by nonstaff writers. Publishes 5–10 freelance submissions yearly; 20% by unpublished writers, 60% by authors who are new to the magazine, 20% by experts.

Submissions and Payment: Sample copy, guidelines, and theme list/editorial calendar available at website. Query with outline, word count, and sources. Accepts email queries to magazine@businesstoday.org. Responds in 1 week. All rights. Articles and depts/columns, 1,000+ words. 5x7 B/W or color prints. No payment. Provides 3 copies.

Called Magazine

P.O. Box 822514
Pembroke Pines, FL 33082

Publisher: Marsha DuCille

Description and Interests: Female pastors and women in Christian ministry read this publication for its practical articles on ministerial finances, marketing, and outreach, as well as for its inspirational articles on spiritual growth, relationships, and wellbeing. The Bible is the primary source of all content. Appearing quarterly, *Called Magazine* aims to cover 360 degrees of a Christian woman's needs in a sophisitcated and practical way. Circ: 25,000+.
Website: www.calledmagazine.com

Freelance Potential: Publishes 85–100 freelance submissions yearly; 75% by authors who are new to the magazine.

Submissions and Payment: Sample copy and guidelines available at website. Send complete ms. Prefers email to articles@calledmagazine.com; will accept hard copy. SASE. Responds if interested. First world rights. Articles and depts/columns, word lengths and payment rates vary. Pays on publication.

Camping Magazine

American Camp Association
5000 State Road 67 North
Martinsville, IN 46151-7902

Editor in Chief: Harriet Lowe

Description and Interests: *Camping Magazine* presents new programming ideas, the latest trends, current legislative and risk management issues, and other topics relevant to owning, administering, or directing youth camps. It is published six times each year. Circ: 7,000.
Website: www.acacamps.org

Freelance Potential: 90% written by nonstaff writers. Publishes 30–35 freelance submissions yearly; 50% by unpublished writers, 30% by authors new to the magazine, 90% by industry experts.

Submissions and Payment: Sample copy and guidelines available at website. Send complete ms with bio and photos. Accepts email to magazine@acacamps.org (Word documents). Responds in 3 months. All rights. Articles, 1,500–2,500 words. Research columns, 1,200–1,600 words. Color prints, digital images. No payment. Provides 3 copies.

Canadian Screenwriter

366 Adelaide Street West, Suite 401
Toronto, Ontario M5V 1R9
Canada

Editor: David Kinahan

Description and Interests: Through in-depth interviews and articles, the inner workings of the Canadian film and television industries are revealed in this trade magazine. Its content focuses on the business, art, and craft of screenwriting. All articles are assigned; but pitches are welcome. It is published three times each year. Circ: 3,200–5,000.
Website: www.wgc.ca

Freelance Potential: 60% written by nonstaff writers. Publishes 9–12 freelance articles yearly; 10–15% by authors who are new to the magazine. Receives 4–6 queries monthly.

Submissions and Payment: Sample copy available. Query. Accepts hard copy. SAE/IRC. Response time varies. First print and electronic rights. Written material, word lengths vary; $.60 per word. Pays on acceptance.

Canadian Writer's Journal

Box 1178
New Liskeard, Ontario P0J 1P0
Canada

Editor: Deborah Ranchuk

Description and Interests: Writers looking to improve their skills and get published look to this magazine for practical advice and encouragement. Published six times each year, it offers how-to articles for both emerging and established authors, with an emphasis on the Canadian market. Circ: 350.
Website: www.cwj.ca

Freelance Potential: Receives 60 mss monthly.

Submissions and Payment: Sample copy available. Guidelines available at website. Send complete ms with short bio. Accepts email to editor@cwj.ca (no attachments; write "Submission" in subject line), and simultaneous submissions if identified. Responds in 3 months. One-time rights. Articles, 400–2,500 words; $7.50 CA per page. Pays on publication. Provides 1 contributor's copy.

Catholic Library World

141 Middleton Library
LSU Libraries
Baton Rouge, LA 70803

Editor: Sigrid Kelsey

Description and Interests: Library professionals are the target audience for this publication of the Catholic Library Association. Each quarterly issue is filled with book and media reviews, in addition to articles on library science, librarianship, and association news. Circ: 1,100.
Website: www.cathla.org

Freelance Potential: 90% written by nonstaff writers. Publishes 12–16 freelance submissions yearly. Receives 20 queries, 1–2 unsolicited mss monthly.

Submissions and Payment: Sample copy and guidelines available. Query or send complete ms. Accepts email to skelsey@lsu.edu. Response time varies. Author retains copyright. Articles, word lengths vary. Depts/columns, 150–300 words. Reviews, 150–300 words. No payment. Provides 1 contributor's copy.

The Cattleman

1301 West 7th Street, Suite 201
Fort Worth, TX 76102

Editor: Ellen Humphries Brisendine

Description and Interests: Articles of interest to ranchers and those in related businesses fill this monthly magazine. Published by the Texas and Southwestern Cattle Raisers Association, its content helps readers make informed business decisions regarding raising cattle and improving profits.
Circ: 16,310.
Website: www.thecattlemanmagazine.com

Freelance Potential: 25% written by nonstaff writers. Publishes 20 freelance submissions yearly; 10% by authors who are new to the magazine, 90% by experts. Receives 2 queries monthly.

Submissions and Payment: Sample articles and guidelines available at website. Query with clips. Accepts email to ehbrisendine@tscra.org (Word attachments). Responds in 2 months. First rights. Articles, 1,500–2,000 words. Depts/columns, 500–900 words. Written material, payment rates vary. Pays on acceptance. Provides 1 contributor's copy.

Chef

233 North Michigan Avenue, Suite 1780
Chicago, IL 60601

Acting Managing Editor: Brent Frei

Description and Interests: Articles offering practical advice on topics ranging from picking ingredients to preparing delicacies are published in this magazine for commercial and noncommercial chefs alike. Product reviews, industry news, and interviews are also featured in issues appearing eight times each year. Circ: 39,000.
Website: www.chefmagazine.com

Freelance Potential: 25% written by nonstaff writers. Of the freelance submissions published yearly, 100% are by experts. Receives 10+ queries monthly.

Submissions and Payment: Sample copy and editorial calendar available at website. Query with clips. Accepts hard copy and email to btfrei@aol.com. SASE. Response time varies. First serial rights. Articles, 1,200–1,800 words. Depts/columns, 800–1,200 words. Written material, payment rates vary. Payment policy varies.

Chile Pepper

12829 Trinity Street
Stafford, TX 77477

Editor in Chief: Rick McMillen

Description and Interests: Appearing six times each year, *Chile Pepper* covers the spicy food industry, including picking and preparing the best peppers, and profiling the hottest chefs and restaurants.
Circ: 150,000.
Website: www.chilepepper.com

Freelance Potential: 65% written by nonstaff writers. Publishes 15 freelance submissions yearly; 5% by unpublished writers, 10% by authors who are new to the magazine, 25% by experts. Receives 50 queries monthly.

Submissions and Payment: Sample copy available at website. Guidelines and editorial calendar available. Query. Accepts email queries to editor@chilepepper.com. Responds in 1 month. All rights. Articles, 400–800 words. Depts/columns, 200–400 words. Written material, payment rates vary. Pays on publication. Provides 2 contributor's copies.

Cleaning Business

3693 East Marginal Way South
Seattle, WA 98134

Submissions: William R. Griffin

Description and Interests: Written for self-employed and small-business cleaning professionals, this online trade magazine provides expert business advice, product reviews, and coverage of industry news and trends. It is updated quarterly. Hits per month: Unavailable.
Website: www.cleaningbusiness.com

Freelance Potential: 30% written by nonstaff writers. Publishes 20 freelance submissions yearly; 60% by unpublished writers, 20% by experts. Receives 20 queries, 10 unsolicited mss each month.

Submissions and Payment: Sample copy available at website. Guidelines available. Query or send complete ms. Accepts hard copy and email to wgriffin@cleaningconsultants.com. SASE. Responds in 1 month. All rights. Articles, 1,000–1,500 words; $50–$150. Depts/columns, word lengths and payment rates vary. Pays on publication.

Closing the Gap

526 Main Street
P.O. Box 68
Henderson, MN 56044

Managing Editor: Megan Turek

Description and Interests: This publication focuses on the use of assistive technology to enhance the education, rehabilitation, mobility, and recreation of adults and children with special needs. It offers expert-written informative articles in issues appearing six times each year. Circ: 10,000.
Website: www.closingthegap.com

Freelance Potential: 100% written by nonstaff writers. Publishes 30–35 freelance submissions yearly; 50% by unpublished writers, 70% by authors who are new to the magazine, 50% by experts. Receives 3 queries monthly.

Submissions and Payment: Sample copy available. Guidelines available at website. Send complete ms. Accepts email to mturek@closingthegap.com (Word attachments). Responds in 6 weeks. All rights. All articles, 2,000 words. No payment. Provides 1 contributor's copy.

The College Store

500 East Lorain Street
Oberlin, OH 44074

Editor: Michael von Glahn

Description and Interests: The National Association of College Stores publishes this magazine six times each year. *The College Store* keeps NACS members abreast of association news and events. It also publishes articles on all aspects of the operation of collegiate retail, including business and legal issues. Circ: 11,000.
Website: www.nacs.org

Freelance Potential: 40% written by nonstaff writers. Publishes 12–18 freelance submissions yearly; 5% by authors who are new to the magazine.

Submissions and Payment: Sample copy available. Guidelines available at website. Send query or complete ms to thecollegestore@nacs.org (Word attachments). Response time varies. One-time print and electronic rights. Articles, 1,200–2,000 words. Payment rates vary. JPEG images at 300 dpi. Pays on acceptance. Provides 2 contributor's copies.

Community College Week

P.O. Box 1305
Fairfax, VA 22038

Publisher: Pam Barrett

Description and Interests: Reaching faculty and administrators of two-year colleges across the country, this publication covers academic issues, technology, and career training. It appears twice each month. Circ: 18,000.
Website: www.ccweek.com

Freelance Potential: 75% written by nonstaff writers. Publishes 75 freelance submissions yearly; 40% by authors who are new to the magazine, 10% by experts. Receives 5 queries monthly.

Submissions and Payment: Sample articles and guidelines available at website. Send complete ms. Prefers email to pbarrett@ccweek.com (Word documents). Responds in 1 month. First serial rights. Articles, 600–1,200 words. Depts/columns, word lengths vary. JPEG images at 300 dpi. Written material, $.35 per word. Kill fee, $.15 per word. Pays on publication. Provides 6 contributor's copies.

Composting News

9815 Hazelwood Avenue
Strongsville, OH 44149

Editor: Ken McEntee

Description and Interests: *Composting News*, an industry newsletter published monthly since 1992, covers the latest news and issues of concern to the producers, marketers, and end-users of compost, mulch, and other organic waste-based products. Its articles track pricing; cover new technology, research, and equipment; and analyze the latest legislation and regulation. Circ: 2,000.
Website: www.compostingnews.com

Freelance Potential: 30% written by nonstaff writers. Publishes 15 freelance submissions yearly.

Submissions and Payment: Sample copy and editorial calendar available. Query or send complete ms. Accepts email submissions to ken@recycle.cc. Response time varies. Rights vary. Articles, word lengths and payment rates vary. Payment policy varies.

Concrete Openings Magazine

13577 Feather Sound Drive, Suite 560
Clearwater, FL 33762

Associate Editor: Russell Hitchen

Description and Interests: This trade magazine is read not only by concrete cutting contractors but also by the specifiers of concrete cutting services, such as architects, engineers, general contractors, and government agencies. Quarterly issues cover topics including business, technology, insurance, and safety. Circ: 17,000.
Website: www.concreteopenings.com

Freelance Potential: 10% written by nonstaff writers. Publishes 12 freelance submissions yearly. Receives 10 queries and unsolicited mss monthly.

Submissions and Payment: Sample copy and guidelines available at website. Query or send complete ms. Accepts email submissions with submission form at website; email to rhitchen@concreteopenings.com (Word or PDF attachments). Response time varies. First rights. Written material, word lengths vary. No payment. Provides 2 contributor's copies.

The Concrete Producer

8725 West Higgins Road, Suite 600
Chicago, IL 60631

Editor: Tom Bagsarian

Description and Interests: This magazine, appearing seven times each year, seeks articles that emphasize new ideas behind the faces, introduce new ways for concrete producers to be more profitable, and explain how new technology is applied. Circ: 20,000.
Website: www.theconcreteproducer.com

Freelance Potential: 30% written by nonstaff writers. Publishes 10 freelance submissions yearly; 5% by unpublished writers, 10% by authors who are new to the magazine, 25% by experts. Receives 5 queries, 3 mss monthly.

Submissions and Payment: Sample articles available at website. Editorial calendar available. Query or send complete ms. Accepts email submissions to tbagsarian@hanleywood.com. Response time varies. Rights vary. Articles, 1,200 words. Depts/columns, 600 words. Written material, payment rates vary. Payment policy varies.

Diesel Tech

360 B Street
Idaho Falls, ID 83402

Editor: Brady Kay

Description and Interests: Diesel truck owners, racers, makers, and enthusiasts turn to this photo-filled magazine for the very latest on diesel technology, modifications, and how-to information. It appears seven times each year. Circ: 18,449.
Website: www.dieseltechmag.com

Freelance Potential: 50% written by nonstaff writers. Publishes 15 freelance submissions yearly; 5% by unpublished writers, 10% by authors who are new to the magazine, 85% by industry experts. Receives 5 queries, 2 unsolicited mss monthly.

Submissions and Payment: Sample copy and guidelines available. Editorial calendar available at website. Query or send complete ms. Accepts email to dteditor@harrispublishing.com. Responds to queries in 1–2 weeks, to mss in 1–2 months. First North American serial rights. Articles, 800–2,500 words; $250–$350. Depts/columns, 800–2,000 words; $100–$300. Color digital images at 300 dpi. Pays on publication. Provides 3–5 contributor's copies.

Direct Selling News

200 Swisher Road
Lake Dallas, TX 75065

Editorial Director: Teresa Day

Description and Interests: The monthly *Direct Selling News* targets executives in sales and marketing. Its aim is to help readers manage, improve, and increase their businesses around the world. Its features cover legal and regulatory issues, financial trends, entrepreneurship, and corporate philanthropy. Circ: 6,500.
Website: www.directsellingnews.com

Freelance Potential: 20% written by nonstaff writers.

Submissions and Payment: Sample articles available at website. Email queries via the website. Responds in 3 weeks. Work-for-hire. Articles, 800–2,500 words. Depts/columns, 1,500–3,000 words. Written material, $.50-$1 per word. Pays on acceptance. Provides 2 contributor's copies.

Diverse

Issues in Higher Education

10520 Warwick Avenue, Suite B-8
Fairfax, VA 22030

Editor: Toni Coleman

Description and Interests: *Diverse* is a newsmagazine focusing exclusively on matters of access and opportunity for all in higher education. It covers news and issues relating to the needs and opportunities for black, Asian, Hispanic, and Native American students. It is published twice each month. Circ: 40,000.
Website: www.diverseeducation.com

Freelance Potential: 50% written by nonstaff writers. Publishes 50 freelance submissions yearly; 5% by authors who are new to the magazine, 5% by experts. Receives 60 queries monthly.

Submissions and Payment: Sample articles and editorial calendar available at website. Query with outline. Accepts email queries to editor@diverseeducation.com. Responds in 1 month. All rights. Articles, 800–2,500 words. Depts/columns, 600–1,000 words. Written material, $.35 per word. Pays on publication. Provides 2 contributor's copies.

Earth

4220 King Street
Alexandria, VA 22302

Editor: Dr. Christopher Keane

Description and Interests: Aimed at scientists and educated members of the public, this monthly magazine of the American Geological Institute runs articles about the Earth and the solar system. It takes readers behind the headlines for in-depth analysis of science topics. Circ: 15,000.
Website: www.earthmagazine.org

Freelance Potential: 30–50% written by nonstaff writers. Publishes 50 freelance submissions yearly; 50% by unpublished writers, 15% by authors who are new to the magazine, 15% by experts. Receives 5 queries monthly.

Submissions and Payment: Sample articles available at website. Guidelines available. Query. Accepts email queries to earth@earthmagazine.org. Responds in 1–2 weeks. All rights. Articles, 500–2,500 words. Depts/columns, 800 words. Written material, payment rates vary. Pays on acceptance. Provides 3 contributor's copies.

Domainer's Magazine

103 Pennsylvania Avenue
Matamoras, PA 18336

Editor in Chief: Jerry J. Nolte, Jr.

Description and Interests: Launched in 2007 and now exclusively online, this magazine targets domain name owners and Internet marketers. Updated regularly, it reviews online tools and hardware, features expert interviews, and discusses the latest industry news and trends. Circ: 15,000.
Website: www.domainersmagazine.com

Freelance Potential: 70% written by nonstaff writers. Publishes 20 freelance submissions yearly; 35% by unpublished writers, 25% by authors who are new to the magazine, 50% by experts. Receives 9 queries monthly.

Submissions and Payment: Sample copy available at website. Query with résumé and clips. Accepts email to editor@domainersmagazine.com. Responds in 1–2 months. All rights. Articles, 2,000–3,500 words. Depts/columns, 800–1,750 words. Written material, $100–$250. Pays on publication.

EDC

2401 West Big Beaver Road, Suite 700
Troy, MI 48084

Editor: Derrick Teal

Description and Interests: This monthly magazine has merged with its sister publication, *Sustainable Facility*. Published monthly, it provides information and resources for designing, constructing, remodeling, operating, and maintaining the sustainable built environment. Published monthly, it is not accepting freelance submissions at this time. Check the website for updates to this policy. Circ: 43,000.
Website: www.EDCmag.com

Freelance Potential: 75% written by nonstaff writers. Publishes 10–14 freelance submissions yearly.

Submissions and Payment: Sample articles, guidelines, and editorial calendar available at website. Not accepting freelance submissions at this time. Query. Accepts email to teald@bnpmedia.com. Response time varies. One-time rights. Articles, 500–1,000 words. Depts/columns, word lengths vary. No payment. Provides 1 contributor's copy.

Eddies

Reflections on Fisheries Conservation

USFWAS Fisheries RM 9100D
500 Gold Avenue SW
Albuquerque, NM 87103

Editor: Craig Springer

Description and Interests: The U.S. Fish & Wildlife Service publishes *Eddies* quarterly for readers interested in its current fisheries conservation efforts. Articles are scientifically accurate but highly readable by a general audience. Informative articles on American fish species are sought. Circ: 20,000.
Website: www.fws.gov/eddies

Freelance Potential: 25% written by nonstaff writers. Publishes 10 freelance submissions yearly; 30% by unpublished writers, 60% by authors who are new to the magazine, 70% by experts.

Submissions and Payment: Sample copy available at website. Guidelines available. Query with explanation of article's relevance. Accepts email queries to craig_springer@fws.gov. Response time varies. Rights vary. Articles, 900 words. Depts/columns, word lengths vary. Written material, payment rates vary. Payment policy varies.

Electronic Green Journal

University of California–Los Angeles
Charles E. Young Research Library
Box 951575
Los Angeles, CA 90095-1575

General Editor: Maria A. Jankowska

Description and Interests: This electronic professional journal on international environmental information welcomes articles and research from all fields of environmental study and conservation. It is updated semiannually. Hits per month: 30,000.
Website: www.escholarship.org/uc/uclalib_egj

Freelance Potential: 90% written by nonstaff writers. Publishes 50 freelance submissions yearly; 90% by authors who are new to the magazine, 15% by experts. Receives 1 unsolicited ms monthly.

Submissions and Payment: Guidelines available at website. Send complete ms (use APA style; include abstract). Accepts submissions through website only. No simultaneous submissions. Responds in 2–3 months. Electronic rights. Articles, word lengths vary. Digital artwork. No payment.

El Restaurante Mexicano

P.O. Box 2249
Oak Park, IL 60303

Editor: Kathleen Furore

Description and Interests: Read by owners and operators of Mexican and Latin eating establishments, this quarterly publication offers articles on industry trends, new products, business basics, and management. Recipes are also offered in each issue. All stories are assigned. Circ: 21,000.
Website: www.restmex.com

Freelance Potential: 15–20% written by nonstaff writers. Publishes 6–8 freelance submissions yearly; 10% by authors who are new to the magazine, 20% by industry experts. Receives 5–10 queries monthly.

Submissions and Payment: Sample copy and editorial calendar available at website. Query with clips. Accepts email queries to kfurore@restmex.com. Responds in 1–2 months. First North American serial rights. Articles, 1,000–1,500 words; $250–$300. Kill fee, 50%. Pays on publication. Provides 1–2 contributor's copies.

Emergency Medicine News

333 Seventh Avenue, 19th Floor
New York, NY 10001

Editor: Lisa Hoffman

Description and Interests: *Emergency Medicine News* reports on the breaking news and trends in emergency medicine. It offer news and profiles and regular columns on toxicology, ultrasound, and technology. All material is written with an eye on the rapid developments at the forefront of emergency medicine. It also publishes a twice-monthly enewsletter with all original material. Circ: 34,000.
Website: www.em-news.com

Freelance Potential: 99% written by nonstaff writers, most by experts. Publishes 20 freelance submissions yearly; very few by new authors.

Submissions and Payment: Sample articles available at website. Query. Accepts email queries to emn@lww.com. Responds in 1–2 weeks. First North American serial rights. Articles and depts/columns, word lengths and payment rates vary. Pays on acceptance.

EnergyBiz

2821 South Parker Road, Suite 1105
Aurora, CO 80014

Editor in Chief: Martin Rosenberg

Description and Interests: *Energy Biz* provides industry leaders in the energy business with new marketing ideas, answers to marketing challenges, and more effective and creative ways to grow their businesses. Each issue examines formative trends, techniques, and strategies as well as the people behind them. It is published six times each year. Circ: 22,000.
Website: www.energybiz.com

Freelance Potential: 50% written by nonstaff writers. Of the freelance submissions yearly, 40% are by industry experts.

Submissions and Payment: Sample copy, guidelines, and editorial calendar available at website. Query. Accepts email to editor@energycentral.com. Response time varies. Rights vary. Articles and depts/columns, word lengths and payment rates vary. Payment policy varies.

Engineering News-Record

2 Penn Plaza, 9th Floor
New York, NY 10121

Projects Editor: Scott Lewis

Description and Interests: This weekly news magazine covers the entire construction industry, with the exception of homebuilding. It covers the design and construction of high-rise buildings, stadiums, airports, long-span bridges, tunnels, and power plants. Features about innovative construction projects are needed. Accepted material may appear on the website or in both online and print versions. Circ: 60,000.
Website: www.enr.com

Freelance Potential: 40% written by nonstaff writers. Publishes 400 freelance submissions yearly.

Submissions and Payment: Sample copy, guidelines, and editorial calendar available at website. Query. Accepts email to scott_lewis@mcgraw-hill.com and phone queries to 212-904-3507. Response time varies. All rights. Articles, word lengths and payment rates vary. Payment policy varies.

Faith & Form

47 Grandview Terrace
Essex, CT 06426

Editor: Michael J. Crosbie

Description and Interests: This quarterly publication is devoted to studying the interrelationship of faith, architecture, and art. Its readership includes those who design, create, and furnish places of worship. Circ: 4,500.
Website: www.faithandform.com

Freelance Potential: 90% written by nonstaff writers. Publishes 15 freelance submissions yearly; 50% by unpublished writers, 50% by authors who are new to the magazine. Receives 6–12 queries and unsolicited mss monthly.

Submissions and Payment: Sample articles and editorial calendar available at website. Query or send complete ms. Prefers email submissions to mcrosbie@faithandform.com (Word or RTF attachments); will accept hard copy. SASE. Response time varies. First rights. Written material, word lengths vary. No payment. Provides 2 contributor's copies.

Farmers' Markets Today

120 West Fourth Street, Suite A
Cedar Falls, IA 50613-2864

Editor: Mary Shepherd

Description and Interests: Published six times each year, this is "the business journal for direct-to-customer marketers" of locally grown foods. Each issue offers growers informative articles on the business side of their farming enterprise as well as profiles and interviews, opinion pieces, and product reviews. Circ: 5,000.
Website: www.farmersmarketstoday.com

Freelance Potential: 25% written by nonstaff writers. Publishes 15–20 freelance submissions yearly; 5% by unpublished writers, 10% by authors who are new to the magazine, 10% by experts. Receives 4 queries monthly.

Submissions and Payment: Sample articles available at website. Query. Accepts hard copy and email to info@farmersmarketstoday.com. SASE. Response time varies. First North American serial rights. Articles and depts/columns, word lengths vary. Written material, $75–$150. Pays on publication.

Feedlot

116 East Long
P.O. Box 850
Dighton, KS 67839

Editor: Jill Dunkel

Description and Interests: Appearing seven times each year, *Feedlot* provides practical information that can be used in the day-to-day operation of cattle farms. Articles on herd management, breeding, and health are found along with industry news. Circ: 11,500.
Website: www.feedlotmagazine.com

Freelance Potential: 80% written by nonstaff writers. Publishes 20 freelance submissions yearly; 20% by unpublished writers, 20% by authors who are new to the magazine, 60% by experts. Receives 1 query, 1 unsolicited ms monthly.

Submissions and Payment: Sample copy and editorial calendar available at website. Guidelines available. Query or send complete ms. Accepts hard copy. SASE. Responds in 1 month. All rights. Articles, to 680 words; payment rates vary. Pays on publication. Provides 2 contributor's copies.

Filmmaker

68 Jay Street, Suite 425
Brooklyn, NY 11201

Managing Editor: Nick Dawson

Description and Interests: Subtitled "The Magazine of Independent Film," this quarterly seeks to make information on filmmaking accessible to a broad audience. It includes articles on the production process and interviews with directors. Circ: 35,000.
Website: www.filmmakermagazine.com

Freelance Potential: 40% written by nonstaff writers. Publishes 80 freelance submissions yearly; 5% by unpublished writers, 35% by authors who are new to the magazine, 80% by experts. Receives 40+ queries monthly.

Submissions and Payment: Sample copy and guidelines available. Query with writing samples. Accepts email to nick@filmmakermagazine.com. Responds in 1 month. All rights. Articles, 2,000 words. Depts/columns, 1,000 words. Written material, payment rates vary. Payment policy varies.

Floor Covering News

550 West Old Country Road, Suite 204
Hicksville, NY 11801

Senior Executive Editor: Matthew Spieler

Description and Interests: Known as "the publication more retailers prefer," *Floor Covering News* provides information on industry trends, new products, building business, and technology developments. Up-to-date content is offered in 26 issues each year. Circ: 16,000.
Website: www.fcnews.net

Freelance Potential: 20% written by nonstaff writers. Of the freelance submissions published yearly, 10% are by authors who are new to the magazine. Receives 30+ queries monthly.

Submissions and Payment: Sample copy and editorial calendar available at website. Query. Accepts email queries to fcnews@optonline.net. Response time varies. First rights. Articles and depts/columns, word lengths and payment rates vary. Payment policy varies.

Floral Management

1601 Duke Street
Alexandria, VA 22314-3406

Editor in Chief: Kate F. Penn

Description and Interests: Considered "The Floral Business Authority," this monthly presents practical information to help floral shop owners and operators succeed. Topics such as marketing, floral design, new products, and industry news are covered. It also features profiles of industry leaders. Circ: 16,000.
Website: www.safnow.org

Freelance Potential: 10% written by nonstaff writers. Publishes 6–10 freelance submissions yearly; 20% by authors who are new to the magazine, 80% by industry experts. Receives 7–10 queries monthly.

Submissions and Payment: Sample copy, guidelines, and theme list available. Editorial calendar available at website. Query. Accepts email queries to kpenn@safnow.org. Responds in 2–3 months. All rights. Articles, 1,000–3,000 words. Depts/columns, 700–900 words. Written material, payment rates vary. Pays on publication.

Footwear Plus

36 Cooper Square, 4th floor
New York, NY 10003

Associate Editor: Lyndsey McGregor

Description and Interests: Published 10 times each year, *Footwear Plus* magazine provides footwear retailers with the industry information they need to stay competitive, and retail strategies that will help them remain profitable. Its business to business–oriented articles cover the designers, brands, and trends of the industry, and provide comprehensive retailing and management tips. Circ: 20,000.
Website: www.footwearplusmagazine.com

Freelance Potential: 90% written by nonstaff writers. Publishes 10 freelance submissions yearly. Receives 10 queries monthly.

Submissions and Payment: Sample copy and editorial calendar available at website. Guidelines available. Query. Accepts hard copy. SASE. Response time varies. First rights. Articles and depts/columns, word lengths and payment rates vary. Payment policy varies.

The Forensic Teacher Magazine

P.O. Box 5263
Wilmington, DE 19808

Editor: Mark Feil

Description and Interests: *The Forensic Teacher* aims to help forensic teachers at every level educate their students. Published three times each year, it seeks effective classroom strategies, tips, and techniques. Most of the articles published are classroom-tested exercises and lessons. Circ: 30,000.
Website: www.theforensicteacher.com

Freelance Potential: 50% written by nonstaff writers. Publishes 18 freelance submissions yearly; 85% by unpublished writers, 70% by new authors. Receives 2 queries, 2 unsolicited mss monthly.

Submissions and Payment: Sample copy and guidelines available. Query or send complete ms. Accepts email to admin@theforensicteacher.com. Responds to queries in 2 weeks, mss in 2 months. First world, electronic, and reprint rights. Articles, 400–3,000 words; filler, 50–200 words. Written material, $.02 per word. Pays 90 days after publication.

Freelance Market News

8–10 Dutton Street
Manchester, M3 1LE
England

Editor: Angela Cox

Description and Interests: This newsletter is a source for information about the publishing industry in the U.K. and abroad, including markets, new publications, and advice for writers hoping to get published. It appears 11 times each year. Circ: Unavailable.
Website: www.freelancemarketnews.com

Freelance Potential: 40% written by nonstaff writers. Publishes 11 freelance submissions yearly; 15% by unpublished writers, 15% by authors who are new to the magazine, 70% by experts. Receives 5 unsolicited mss monthly.

Submissions and Payment: Sample copy and guidelines available at website. Send complete ms. Accepts email to fmn@writersbureau.com (Word attachments). Responds in 2–4 weeks. First British serial rights. Articles, 700–1,500 words. Depts/columns, 40–200 words. Written material, £40–£50 per 1,000 words. Pays on acceptance. Provides 1 author's copy.

Freelance Writer's Report

P.O. Box A
North Stratford, NH 03590

Executive Director: Dana K. Cassell

Description and Interests: This monthly newsletter provides tips on writing and getting published, and it looks at trends in the magazine and book publishing industries. It targets members of the Writers-Editors Network, an association dedicated to supporting writers. Circ: 500.
Website: www.writers-editors.com

Freelance Potential: 30% written by nonstaff writers. Publishes 70–75 freelance submissions yearly; 10% by authors who are new to the magazine, 100% by experts. Receives 6 unsolicited mss monthly.

Submissions and Payment: Sample copy and guidelines available at website. Send complete ms. Prefers email to submissions@writers-editors.com; will accept hard copy. SASE. Responds in 2–3 days. One-time rights. Articles, 750 words; $.10 per word. Pays on publication. Provides 1 contributor's copy.

General Aviation News

P.O. Box 39099
Lakewood, WA 98496-0099

Editor: Janice Wood

Description and Interests: Covering general aviation for more than 60 years, this magazine provides news and features on aircraft and aircraft maintenance, as well as coverage of aviation events. Appealing primarily to an audience of pilots and aircraft owners, it is published 24 times each year. Circ: 50,000.
Website: www.generalaviationnews.com

Freelance Potential: 25% written by nonstaff writers. Publishes few freelance submissions yearly. Receives 5 queries monthly.

Submissions and Payment: Sample copy and guidelines available at website. Query. Accepts email queries to janice@generalaviationnews.com. Responds in 3 weeks. First North American serial rights. Articles, 7,00–1,000 words. Depts/columns, word lengths vary. Artwork, JPEG images at 300 dpi. Written material, $75–$500. Pays on publication. Provides 1 contributor's copy.

The Gourmet Retailer

570 Lake Cook Road, Suite 310
Deerfield, IL 60015

Editor in Chief: Anna Wolfe

Description and Interests: Purveyors of gourmet kitchenware and specialty foods turn to this magazine for information on the latest products and how to market and merchandise them. This quarterly also includes practical articles on how to manage a successful gourmet retail operation. Circ: 32,000.
Website: www.gourmetretailer.com

Freelance Potential: 5–10% written by nonstaff writers. Publishes 12 freelance submissions yearly; 1% by authors who are new to the magazine, 10% by experts.

Submissions and Payment: Sample copy available at website. Theme list/editorial calendar available. Query with writing samples and biography. Accepts email queries to awolfe@stagnitomedia.com. Responds in 1 month. All rights. Articles, to 2,000 words. Depts/columns, to 1,000 words. Written material, payment rates vary. Pays 60 days after publication.

Green Profit

P.O. Box 1660
West Chicago, IL 60186

Editor: Chris Beytes

Description and Interests: *Green Profit* publishes articles and columns that offer practical advice to owners and managers of garden centers. Appearing monthly, it focuses on ways to boost sales and build profits. Circ: 27,000.
Website: www.greenprofit.com

Freelance Potential: 50% written by nonstaff writers. Publishes 45 freelance submissions yearly; 10% by unpublished writers, 10% by authors who are new to the magazine, 80% by experts. Receives 2 unsolicited mss monthly.

Submissions and Payment: Sample copy available at website. Guidelines available. Query or send complete ms with photos. Accepts email to cbeytes@ballpublishing.com and simultaneous submissions if identified. Responds in 3 weeks. First North American serial rights. Articles, 800 words. Depts/columns, word lengths vary. Written material, to $250. Pays on publication. Provides 1 copy.

GrowerTalks Magazine

P.O. Box 1660
West Chicago, IL 60186

Editor: Chris Beytes

Description and Interests: *GrowerTalks Magazine* combines information on growing flowers and plants with practical advice on operating a profitable commercial greenhouse. It includes articles on increasing sales, predicting market trends, and new products and technologies. Published monthly, it also features profiles of greenhouse owners. Circ: 27,000.
Website: www.growertalks.com

Freelance Potential: 50% written by nonstaff writers. Publishes 10 freelance submissions yearly; 3% by authors who are new to the magazine.

Submissions and Payment: Sample copy available at website. Query. Send email to cbeytes@ballpublishing.com. Accepts hard copy. SASE. Response time varies. First North American serial rights. Articles and depts/columns, word lengths vary; $100–$300. Payment policy varies.

Highway News and Good News

P.O. Box 117
Marietta, PA 17547-0117

Editor: Inge Koenig

Description and Interests: The mission of *Highway News and Good News* is to lead truckers to Jesus Christ and help them grow in their faith. Published monthly, it offers human interest pieces, personal experiences, and testimonials that truckers and their families will find edifying and helpful. Circ: 23,000.
Website: www.transportforchrist.org/highway

Freelance Potential: 20% written by nonstaff writers. Publishes 12–15 freelance submissions yearly; 50% by unpublished writers, 5% by experts.

Submissions and Payment: Sample copy available at website. Guidelines available by email request. Send complete ms. Accepts email to editor@transportforchrist.org. Responds in 2–4 months. Rights vary. Articles, to 800 words. Depts/columns, 300 words. B/W or color prints. No payment.

Home Builder

4819 St. Charles Boulevard
Pierrefonds, Quebec H9H 3C7
Canada

Editor: Judy Penz Sheluk

Description and Interests: As the official publication of the Canadian Home Builders' Association, *Home Builder* covers all aspects of residential building and ways to make it profitable. It includes pieces on home-building products and techniques, as well as perspectives on the current market for single-family dwellings. Appearing six times each year, it's read by builders, contractors, and remodelers. Though it accepts submissions, most of its content is staff-written. Circ: 26,000.
Website: www.homebuildercanada.com

Submissions and Payment: Sample articles and editorial calendar available at website. Query or send complete ms with artwork. Accepts email to editor@work4.ca. SAE/IRC. Response time varies. Rights vary. Articles, 700–1,200 words. Depts/columns, 750 words. High-resolution digital images. All material, payment rates vary. Provides 5 copies.

Impressions

1145 Sanctuary Parkway, Suite 355
Alpharetta, GA 30009-4772

Editor in Chief: Marcia Derryberry

Description and Interests: *Impressions* is a trade journal for people who make their living in the screen-printing and embroidery industry. In addition to practical articles about business management, it includes instructional articles on design, techniques, and alternative decorating in eight issues a year. Circ: 40,000.
Website: www.impressionsmag.com

Freelance Potential: 40% written by nonstaff writers. Publishes 60–80 freelance submissions yearly; 5% by authors who are new to the magazine, 40% by industry experts. Receives 2 queries monthly.

Submissions and Payment: Sample copy available at website. Editorial calendar available. Query with outline, résumé, and clips. Accepts email queries to mderryberry@impressionsmag.com. Responds in 3 months. All rights. Articles, 2,000 words; $350. Depts/columns, to 1,000 words; $250. Pays on publication.

Incentive

100 Lighting Way
Secaucus, NJ 07094-3626

Editor in Chief: Vincent Alonzo

Description and Interests: This magazine focuses on running employee recognition and incentive packages. It primarily covers incentive program strategies, and the travel and merchandise that are offered as part of the programs. Monthly issues include how-to pieces, case studies, and do's and don'ts for operating recognition and incentive programs. Circ: 65,000.
Website: www.incentivemag.com

Freelance Potential: 50% written by nonstaff writers. Of the freelance submissions published yearly, 10% are by unpublished writers, 30% are by authors who are new to the magazine, and 60% are by experts. Receives 10 queries monthly.

Submissions and Payment: Sample copy, guidelines, and editorial calendar available. Query with writing samples. Accepts hard copy. SASE. Response time varies. Rights vary. Articles, 750 words. Depts/columns, 300 words. No payment.

The Insurance Record

9601 White Rock Trail, #213
Dallas, TX 75238-2588

Editor: Glen E. Hargis

Description and Interests: This newsmagazine appears 26 times each year with the latest news, trends, and analysis regarding the Texas insurance industry. It is seeking articles about business strategies, particularly those that utilize social networking. Circ: 2,800.
Website: www.insrecord.com

Freelance Potential: 20% written by nonstaff writers. Publishes 50 freelance submissions yearly; 3% by unpublished writers, 2% by authors who are new to the magazine, 95% by experts. Receives 4 queries monthly.

Submissions and Payment: Sample articles available at website. Guidelines and editorial calendar available. Query. Accepts email to insrecrd@swbell.net (Word attachments). Responds in 2 months. Rights vary. Articles, word lengths vary. Photoshop digital images at 300 dpi. No payment. Provides 1 contributor's copy.

InTents

1801 County Road B West
Roseville, MN 55113

Associate Editor: Sigrid Tornquist

Description and Interests: People involved in the tent rental and special events industry find information about effective marketing and business operations here. Appearing five times each year, the magazine showcases successful businesses and their owners. Circ: 10,000.
Website: www.intentsmag.com

Freelance Potential: 60% written by nonstaff writers. Publishes 18–24 freelance submissions yearly; 5% by unpublished writers, 50–60% by authors who are new to the magazine, 25% by industry experts. Receives 2 queries monthly.

Submissions and Payment: Sample articles and editorial calendar available at website. Guidelines available. Query with résumé and ideas. Accepts email queries to editorial@ifai.com. Responds in 1 month. Full reprint rights. Articles, 1,250–1,500 words; $500. Depts/columns, 750–1,000 words; $300. Pays 30 days from invoice date. Provides 1 copy.

International Bluegrass

International Bluegrass Music Association
2 Music Circle South, Suite 100
Nashville, TN 37203

Editor: Nancy Cardwell

Description and Interests: *International Bluegrass* was created especially for professional bluegrass musicians. It covers events of interest to members of the International Bluegrass Music Association as well as organization news. Published monthly, it looks for contributions from writers who understand the bluegrass scene and can write well-researched articles. It is not a fan magazine. Circ: 3,000.
Website: www.ibma.org

Freelance Potential: 5% written by nonstaff writers. Publishes 6 freelance submissions each year.

Submissions and Payment: Sample articles available at website. Query. Accepts email queries to info@ibma.org (Word attachments). Responds in 2 weeks. Print and electronic rights. Articles, 1,000–1,200 words; $150. Pays on publication. Provides contributor's copies upon request.

Interval World

P.O. Box 431920
Miami, FL 33243-1920

Editors

Description and Interests: This magazine is published three times each year exclusively for members of Interval International, a timeshare exchange network. It provides coverage of destinations and includes travel tips and articles on ways to save money while seeing the world. Circ: 2 million.
Website: www.resortdeveloper.com

Freelance Potential: 35% written by nonstaff writers. Publishes 12–15 freelance submissions yearly; 20% by authors who are new to the magazine. Receives 3 queries, 1 unsolicited ms each month.

Submissions and Payment: Sample copy available at website. Query or send complete ms. Accepts email submissions to IntervalEditors@intervalintl.com (Word attachments). Response time varies. All rights. Articles, 1,500–2,000 words. Depts/columns, 1,000 words. Written material, $.33 per word. Pays on acceptance. Provides 1 contributor's copy.

Journal of Insurance Operations

881 Alma Real Drive, Suite 205
Pacific Palisades, CA 90272

Editor in Chief: Rob Berg

Description and Interests: This digital professional journal provides executives at insurance companies with in-depth coverage of innovations in management strategies, organizational designs, and operations technology. Writers should be insurance industry professionals with something to share. It is updated regularly. Hits per month: Unavailable.
Website: www.jiops.com

Freelance Potential: 85% written by nonstaff writers. Publishes 20+ freelance submissions yearly; 50% by unpublished writers, 75% by authors who are new to the magazine, 100% by industry experts. Receives 30–40 queries monthly.

Submissions and Payment: Sample articles and guidelines available at website. Query. Accepts online queries at website. Responds in 1 month. Rights vary. Articles, 700–2,000 words. No payment. Provides 2 contributor's copies.

Kashrus Magazine

P.O. Box 204
Brooklyn, NY 11204

Editor in Chief: Rabbi Yosef Wikler

Description and Interests: *Kashrus Magazine* provides information about the kosher food trade to a readership that includes both industry professionals and consumers. Published five times each year, it features articles on kosher food suppliers and their products, restaurants, and travel, as well as consumer alerts and first-person pieces. Circ: 10,000.
Website: www.kashrusmagazine.com

Freelance Potential: 45% written by nonstaff writers. Publishes 15 freelance submissions yearly; 5% by unpublished writers, 14% by authors who are new to the magazine, 10% by experts. Receives 5 queries monthly.

Submissions and Payment: Sample articles available at website. Guidelines and editorial calendar available. Query with clips or writing samples. Accepts hard copy. SASE. Responds in 1 week. One-time rights.

Know

The Magazine for Paralegals

44-489 Town Center Way D436
Palm Desert, CA 92260-2723

Editor in Chief: Chere Estrin

Description and Interests: A professional trade magazine for paralegals, this magazine, which is now completely digital, is a source of information regarding career advancement, job performance, and industry trends. Appearing six times each year, it accepts work only from experts in the field. Circ: 10,000.
Website: www.paralegalknowledge.com

Freelance Potential: 40% written by nonstaff writers. Of the freelance submissions published yearly, 100% are by experts. Receives 10–20 queries monthly.

Submissions and Payment: Sample copy available at website. Guidelines available. Query. Accepts email queries to info@paralegalknowledge.com (Word attachments). Responds in 1 month. Rights vary. Articles, 1,500–2,500 words; $100–$300. Depts/columns, 750–1,000 words; $100–$200. Kill fee varies. Pays on publication. Provides 2 contributor's copies.

Law Enforcement Technology

1233 Janesville Avenue
Fort Atkinson, WI 53538

Editor: Jonathan Kozlowski

Description and Interests: *Law Enforcement Technology* is a monthly publication with a target audience of police chiefs, sheriffs, and other law enforcement supervisors. Topics include new products, management issues, emerging technology, and trends in training. Its focus is on apprehending criminals safely and efficiently and utilizing technology to secure evidence. Circ: 30,097.
Website: www.officer.com

Freelance Potential: 30% written by nonstaff writers. Publishes 50 freelance submissions yearly; 5% by authors who are new to the magazine. Receives 50 queries monthly.

Submissions and Payment: Sample copy available at website. Guidelines available. Accepts email queries to Jonathan.Kozlowski@cygnusb2b.com. Responds in 2–4 weeks. All rights. Articles, 1,800–2,400 words; $300. Pays 1 month after publication.

Make-Up Artist Magazine

12808 NE 95th St.
Vancouver, WA 98682

Managing Editor: Heather Wisner

Description and Interests: Written for make-up artists in film, fashion, television, theater, and retail, this publication covers news, trends, behind-the-scenes articles, techniques, products, and profiles in its six annual issues. It also has a digital edition in addition to print. Circ: 16,000.
Website: www.makeupmag.com

Freelance Potential: 60% of total content written by nonstaff writers.

Submissions and Payment: Sample copy available at website. Guidelines and editorial calendar available. Query. Email queries to heather_w@makeupmag.com. Responds in 1 week. First rights. Articles: $.20–$.50 per word. Depts/columns, word lengths vary; $100. Kill fee, 25%. Pays on publication. Provides 2 contributor's copies.

Markee 2.0

506 Roswell Street
Suite 220
Marietta, GA 30060

Editor: Cory Sekine-Pettite

Description and Interests: This magazine covers the techniques, trends, news, and views of film and video production and post-production. All of its editorial content is written by experts in the industry. Published monthly, its articles range from selecting equipment and postproduction techniques to independent filmmaking. Circ: 20,000.
Website: www.markeemag.com

Freelance Potential: 100% written by nonstaff writers. Publishes many freelance submissions yearly, 100% by industry experts. Receives 1 query monthly.

Submissions and Payment: Sample articles available at website. Send résumé for consideration for freelance assignments. Response time varies. All rights. Articles and depts/columns, word lengths and payment rates vary. Pays on publication. Provides 2 contributor's copies.

MedEsthetics

7628 Densmore Avenue
Van Nuys, CA 91406-2042

Executive Editor: Inga Hansen

Description and Interests: This magazine was created to provide practical business information for practitioners of noninvasive cosmetic procedures. Published six times each year, it includes reports on new technologies, techniques, and products, as well as information on practice management. Circ: 21,000.
Website: www.medestheticsmagazine.com

Freelance Potential: 50% written by nonstaff writers. Publishes 12–15 freelance submissions yearly; 30% by authors who are new to the magazine, 50% by experts.

Submissions and Payment: Sample copy available at website. Query with résumé. Accepts hard copy and email queries to ihansen@creativeage.com. SASE. Responds in 2 months. First North American serial rights. Articles, 2,000 words; $500. Depts/columns, 1,200 words; $400. Pays on acceptance. Provides 1 contributor's copy.

MetalClay Artist

115 River Road, RR#3, Unit #2
Merrickville, Ontario K0G 1N0
Canada

Editor in Chief: Jeannette Froese LeBlanc

Description and Interests: This magazine bills itself as the first created by and for serious metal artists. Published quarterly both in print and digitally, it boasts editorial contributions from the most noted metal clay artists in North America and beyond. With articles tailored to all levels of experience, it welcomes submissions for step-by-step projects, tips, best practices, and sources of inspirations. Circ: Unavailable.
Website: www.metalclayartistmag.com

Freelance Potential: Receives many freelance submissions monthly.

Submissions and Payment: Sample articles and guidelines available at website. Query or send complete ms with photos of artwork or project. Accepts hard copy, or contact editor via form at website.

Metal Roofing Magazine

700 East State Street
Iola, WI 54990-0001

Editor: Jim Austin

Description and Interests: This business management magazine targets professional builders, contractors, and suppliers in the metal roofing industry. It offers comprehensive coverage of new products, industry and supplier news, and research and development, seven times each year. Due to budget cuts, the need for freelance writers has decreased.
Circ: 26,000.
Website: www.constructionmagnet.com

Freelance Potential: 5% written by nonstaff writers. Publishes 6–8 freelance submissions yearly, 10% by experts. Receives 8–14 queries each month.

Submissions and Payment: Sample articles available at website. Query. Accepts hard copy and email queries to jim.austin@fwmedia.com. SASE. Response time varies. All rights. Written material, and payment rates vary.

Minority Engineer

Equal Opportunity Publications
445 Broad Hollow Road, Suite 425
Melville, NY 11747

Director, Editorial & Production: James Schneider

Description and Interests: Three times each year, this magazine provides minority engineering students and professionals with expert-written articles on career opportunities, development, and advancement. Circ: 18,000.
Website: www.eop.com

Freelance Potential: 50% written by nonstaff writers. Publishes 15 freelance submissions yearly; 25% by unpublished writers, 25% by authors who are new to the magazine, 50% by experts. Receives 10 queries, 5 mss monthly.

Submissions and Payment: Sample articles and editorial calendar available at website. Query with article outline. Send complete ms for filler. Accepts hard copy, disk submissions, and email to jschneider@eop.com. SASE. Responds in 1 month. First rights. Articles, 1,500 words. Depts/columns, 800 words. Written material, $.10 per word. Pays on publication. Provides 1+ contributor's copies.

Mobile Developer Magazine

Calgary, Alberta
Canada

Publisher: Fabrizio Pilato

Description and Interests: A publication created for and by mobile developers, this digital magazine is a resource for industry news, technology development, and product, and business development. Updated six times each year, it accepts submissions from mobile communications and software development experts. Hits per month: Unavailable.
Website: www.mobiledevmag.com

Freelance Potential: Publishes several freelance submissions yearly.

Submissions and Payment: Guidelines available at website. Query. Accepts email queries to writers@mobiledevmag.com. Articles, 1,000–3,000 words; product reviews, 500–1,500 words; Sneak App-Eek column, 600–3,000 words; and how-to's, 500–3,000 words. No payment.

MPVHub Audio Magazine

Station D, P.O. Box 46837
Vancouver, BC V6J 5M4
Canada

Editor: Rounik Sethi

Description and Interests: This quarterly aims to be the place that professional music makers go to learn more about their craft. *MPVHub Audio* focuses on software education and features music software tutorials, reviews, and interviews with music production experts. It seeks nonlinear editors (audio, video, 3D or related areas) who write well. Circ: 200,000.
Website: www.mpvhub.com

Freelance Potential: New writers must first contribute to macProVideo.com's Online Hub.

Submissions and Payment: Sample copy and guidelines available at website. Query. Accepts queries at website (PDF format only); include brief description of article. Response time varies. Written material, word lengths vary. Rights vary. Payment rates and policy vary.

The Music & Sound Retailer

25 Willowdale Avenue
Port Washington, NY 11050

Editor: Dan Ferrisi

Description and Interests: Writers who play or have a vast knowledge of musical instruments are welcome to query this magazine. Distributed to music stores throughout the U.S., *The Music & Sound Retailer* features corporate profiles and covers business and marketing issues, trends, and industry news. It is published monthly. Circ: 11,000.
Website: www.msretailer.com

Freelance Potential: 12% written by nonstaff writers. Publishes 20 freelance submissions yearly; 5% by unpublished writers, 10% by authors who are new to the magazine, 10% by experts. Receives 5 queries monthly.

Submissions and Payment: Sample articles at website. Query with 2–5 clips. Accepts email to dferrisi@testa.com. First rights. Articles, word lengths vary; $300+. Kill fee, $100. Pays on publication.

My Safety

P.O. Box 1080
Geneva, NY 14456

Publisher: Eric Giguere

Description and Interests: After a near-death accident on the job, Publisher Eric Giguere started this publication in 2012 to educate and promote safety awareness. It is read by both managers and employees. Many articles come directly from workers with personal safety experiences of consequence—accidents, survival stories, details of best and worst practices. *My Safety* also includes profiles of regular workers performing their daily jobs. Circ: 6,700.
Website: www.mysafetymagazine.com

Freelance Potential: Freelance percentages not yet available. "Real people in the field" provide many of the features and columns.

Submissions and Payment: Sample copy and editorial calendar available at website. Query to giguere@localnet.com. Rights and payment information unavailable.

National Petroleum News

1030 West Higgins Road, Suite 230
Park Ridge, IL 60068

Editor in Chief: Keith Reid

Description and Interests: Appearing nine times each year, *National Petroleum News* covers the retail side of the petroleum industry. Its wide readership includes single-site gas station and convenience store owners, as well as oil company executives. It offers informative articles, opinion pieces, new product information, and industry news and trends.
Circ: 22,500.
Website: www.npnweb.com

Freelance Potential: 50% written by nonstaff writers. Publishes 36 freelance submissions yearly; 10% by authors who are new to the magazine.

Submissions and Payment: Sample articles and guidelines available at website. Query. Accepts email queries to kreid@m2media360.com. Response time varies. All rights. Articles, 1,200–1,800 words. "Industry Voices," 800–1,000 words. No payment.

New Holland News

P.O. Box 1895
New Holland, PA 17557-0903

Editor: Gary Martin

Description and Interests: Now published four times each year, *New Holland News* offers full-color coverage of farming and agriculture in North America. The farmers and ranchers who read it are looking for ideas to help them overcome challenges and prosper. Circ: Unavailable.
Website: www.agriculture.newholland.com/us

Freelance Potential: 80% written by nonstaff writers. Publishes 35–40 freelance submissions yearly; 10% by authors who are new to the magazine. Receives 30 queries, 2 unsolicited mss each month.

Submissions and Payment: Sample articles available at website. Guidelines available. Query or send complete ms. Accepts hard copy. SASE. Responds in 2 months. First North American serial rights. Articles, 1,200–1,500 words; $800+. Pays on acceptance. Provides 3 contributor's copies.

NRB Today

National Religious Broadcasters
9510 Technology Drive
Manassas, VA 20110

Director of Communications: Kenneth Chan

Description and Interests: Now found exclusively online, *NRB Today* provides Christian broadcasters and other industry leaders with news and opinions on all types of religious broadcasting. It is updated weekly. Hits per month: 10,000.
Website: www.nrb.org

Freelance Potential: 2% written by nonstaff writers. Publishes 40 freelance submissions yearly; 15% by unpublished writers, 35% by authors who are new to the magazine, 50% by experts. Receives 4 unsolicited mss monthly.

Submissions and Payment: Guidelines and editorial calendar available. Send complete ms with artwork. Accepts hard copy, disk submissions with hard copy, and email to kchan@nrb.org. SASE. Responds in 1 month. First and second rights. Written material, 1,000–2,000 words; $100–$500. Digital images at 300 dpi. Payment policy varies.

O&A Marketing News

559 South Harbor Boulevard, Suite A
Anaheim, CA 92805-4525

Editor: Kathy Laderman

Description and Interests: This magazine targets the people involved in the supplying and marketing of petroleum products, such as oil and alternative fuel. Operators of carwash businesses and service stations also find pertinent information in its pages. Focusing on 13 western states, it covers industry news, trade shows, and new products. Published seven times each year, it is always in search of regional news. Circ: 4,000+.
Website: www.kalpub.com

Freelance Potential: 10% written by nonstaff writers. Publishes 20 freelance submissions yearly; 1% by authors new to the magazine, 1% by experts. Receives 100 queries monthly.

Submissions and Payment: Sample copy available. Editorial calendar available at website. Query. Accepts hard copy. SASE. Response time varies. One-time and electronic rights. Articles, 4–10 column inches; $1.25 per column inch. Payment policy varies.

One +

3030 LBJ Freeway, Suite 1700
Dallas, TX 75234

Asssociate Managing Editor: Blair Potter

Description and Interests: The target readers of this monthly trade magazine are those who plan meetings and vendors who offer services for meetings. *One +* provides how-to information and destination reviews. Circ: 31,500.
Website: www.mpiweb.org

Freelance Potential: 80% written by nonstaff writers. Publishes several freelance submissions yearly; 5% by unpublished writers, 50% by authors who are new to the magazine, 40% by experts. Receives 3 queries monthly.

Submissions and Payment: Sample articles and guidelines available at website. Editorial calendar available. Query. Accepts email queries to bpotter@mpiweb.org. Responds in 1 month. Print and electronic global unlimited rights. Articles, 4,000–5,000 words. Depts/columns, 600–1,000 words. Written material, $.50 per word. Kill fee varies. Pays on publication. Provides 2 contributor's copies.

Onion World

8405 Ahtanum Road
Yakima, WA 98903

Editor: D. Brent Clement

Description and Interests: This magazine is designed to help commercial onion growers improve their production and marketing capabilities. It is published eight times each year. Circ: 5,100.
Website: www.columbiapublications.com/onionworld

Freelance Potential: 50% written by nonstaff writers. Publishes 20 freelance submissions yearly; 10% by authors who are new to the magazine, 35% by experts.

Submissions and Payment: Sample copy and editorial calendar available at website. Query or send complete ms. Accepts hard copy and email submissions to dbrent@columbiapublications.com. SASE. Responds in 1 month. First rights. Articles, 1,200–1,500 words; $250. Color JPEG images; payment rates vary. Pays on publication. Provides up to 5 contributor's copies.

Ornamental & Miscellaneous Metal Fabricator

805 South Glynn Street, Suite 127 #311
Fayetteville, GA 30214

Editor: Todd Daniel

Description and Interests: Industry news, project updates, business tips, and profiles can be found in each of the six issues per year. It is published by the National Ornamental & Miscellaneous Metals Association. Circ: 8,000.
Website: www.nomma.org

Freelance Potential: 50% written by nonstaff writers. Publishes 30 freelance submissions yearly; 10% by unpublished writers, 10% by authors who are new to the magazine, 50% by experts. Receives 6 queries monthly.

Submissions and Payment: Sample copy available at website. Guidelines available. Query. Accepts hard copy and email queries to editor@nomma.org. SASE. Response time varies. One-time rights. Articles, 1,500 words; $250–$400. Depts/columns, 900 words; $100–$150. Kill fee, 50%. Pays on acceptance.

The Paper Stock Report

9815 Hazelwood Avenue
Strongsville, OH 44149-2305

Publisher/Editor: Ken McEntee

Description and Interests: People working in the paper recycling market read this newsletter for updates on the latest industry trends. It reports on global markets and environmental issues, and provides price quotations. Published 24 times each year for the past 21 years, it looks for writers who have expertise in this field. Circ: 2,000.
Website: www.recycle.cc

Freelance Potential: 20% written by nonstaff writers. Receives few queries and unsolicited mss monthly.

Submissions and Payment: Sample copy and editorial calendar available. Query or send complete ms. Accepts email submissions to ken@recycle.cc. Response time varies. Rights vary. Articles, word lengths vary; $.20 per word. B/W prints. Payment policy varies.

Party & Paper Retailer

Great American Publishing
P.O. Box 128
Sparta, MI 49345

Managing Editor: Abby Heugel

Description and Interests: Owners and managers of party supply and stationery stores read this monthly trade magazine for the latest marketing trends and strategies for increasing business. It also covers practical matters like staff relations and store layout. Circ: 25,000.
Website: www.partypaper.com

Freelance Potential: 20% written by nonstaff writers. Publishes 10–15 freelance submissions yearly. Receives 5 queries monthly.

Submissions and Payment: Sample articles available at website. Query with clips. Accepts hard copy and email queries to ppredit@partypaper.com. SASE. Responds in 1 month. Articles, 800–1,200 words. Depts/columns, 700 words. Written material, payment rates vary. Pays on publication. Provides 2 copies.

PeerSphere

The CMO Council
4151 Middlefield Road
Palo Alto, CA 94303

Managing Editor: Mary Anne Flowers

Description and Interests: This quarterly journal of the Chief Marketing Officer (CMO) Council is peer-driven, drawing from the vast range of insight and experience that its members possess. Articles are aimed at providing best practices and commentary to senior client-side marketing executives. *PeerSphere* is produced in digital and print formats. The fall issue included articles on social media analytics of the customer experience, and a feature on Tupperware's entrance into the market in India. Circ: 6,000.
Website: www.cmocouncil.org

Freelance Potential: As a peer-produced professional journal, open to submissions with relevant marketing experience.

Submissions and Payment: Sample articles available at website. Accepts email to mflowers@cmocouncil.org. Rights and payment policies, unavailable.

Photo District News 

770 Broadway, 8th Floor
New York, NY 10003

Editor: Holly Stuart Hughes

Description and Interests: Each month this magazine, in publication just over a year, brings professional photographers everything they need to succeed in a competitive business. Its editorial consists of news, profiles, and features on the photo industry, photography techniques, digital imaging, and new products, as well as marketing and legal advice. Photo essays and galleries showcase the work of photography legends and emerging talent. *PDN* is affiliated with *RangeFinder*. Circ: 20,000.
Website: www.pdnonline.com

Freelance Potential: Freelance percentages not yet available.

Submissions and Payment: Sample articles and editorial calendar available at website. Accepts email to hhughes@pdnonline.com. Rights and payment policies unavailable.

Physician's Practice

5523 Research Park Drive, Suite 220
Baltimore, MD 21228-9942

Managing Editor: Keith Martin

Description and Interests: Providing doctors with information and advice on managing their practices more efficiently, It seeks articles from physicians on their experiences practicing medicine and from practice management experts on office management topics. *Physician's Practice* is published 10 times per year. Circ: 150,000.
Website: www.physicianspractice.com

Freelance Potential: 33% written by nonstaff writers. Publishes 20–30 freelance submissions yearly; 5% by unpublished writers, 10% by authors who are new to the magazine, 20% by experts. Receives 10 queries monthly.

Submissions and Payment: Sample copy, guidelines, and editorial calendar available at website. Query. Email queries to keith.martin@ubm.com. Articles, 1,000–1,250 words, $250.

Playground Magazine

360 B Street
Idaho Falls, ID 83402

Editor: Lane Lindstrom

Description and Interests: Focusing on design trends and topics of interest to those who manage or build playgrounds, this magazine is published quarterly. Circ: 10.740.
Website: www.playgroundmag.com

Freelance Potential: 70% written by nonstaff writers. Publishes 6–8 freelance submissions yearly; 5% by unpublished writers, 5% by authors who are new to the magazine, 90% by experts. Receives 2 queries monthly.

Submissions and Payment: Sample articles available at website. Guidelines and theme list/editorial calendar available. Query. Accepts email queries to lindstrm@playgroundmag.com. Responds in 1–2 months. First North American serial rights. Articles, 1,500 words. Depts/columns, 400–800 words. High-resolution digital images at 300 dpi. Written material, payment rates vary. Pays on publication. Provides 3 contributor's copies.

Police Times

6350 Horizon Drive
Titusville, FL 32780

Executive Editor: Jim Gordon

Description and Interests: Published quarterly by the American Federation of Police and Concerned Citizens, *Police Times* features articles on police training, new products and services, and techno logical advances that assist law enforcement. It puts an emphasis on profiles of smaller departments or people who made a mark in law enforcement. Circ: Unavailable.
Website: www.aphf.org/pt.html

Freelance Potential: 60% written by nonstaff writers. Publishes 30 freelance submissions yearly.

Submissions and Payment: Guidelines available at website. Query or send complete ms. Accepts disk submissions wth hard copy (short queries may also be faxed to 321-264-0033). SASE. Response time varies. All rights. Articles, to 2,500 words; $25–100. B/W or color prints. Pays on acceptance. Provides 1 contributor's copy.

Produce Business

P.O. Box 810425
Boca Raton, FL 33481-0425

Editorial Director: Ken Whitacre

Description and Interests: All the latest news and marketing trends for produce purveyors and providers can be found in this monthly trade magazine. Interviews with store owners and restauranteurs, as well as informative articles on specific produce sectors and news affecting this industry, are included. Prospective writers should have previous business writing experience and clips to be considered for this magazine. Circ: 15,000.
Website: www.producebusiness.com

Freelance Potential: 95% written by nonstaff writers. Publishes 160 freelance submissions yearly; 5% by authors who are new to the magazine.

Submissions and Payment: Sample copy available at website. Guidelines available. Query. Accepts hard copy. SASE. Response time varies. All rights. Articles and depts/columns, word lengths vary; $.20 per word. Payment policy varies.

Professional Artist

Turnstile Publishing
1500 Park Center Drive
Orlando, FL 32835

Editor: Kim Hall

Description and Interests: In addition to providing information on juried competitions, this publication offers visual artists career advice, including tips on marketing, financing, and legal issues. Formerly titled *Art Calendar*, it is published 10 times each year. Circ: 20,000+.
Website: www.ProfessionalArtistMag.com

Freelance Potential: 80% written by nonstaff writers. Publishes 150 freelance submissions yearly; 5% by unpublished writers, 10% by authors who are new to the magazine, 90% by experts. Receives 10 queries monthly.

Submissions and Payment: Sample copy and guidelines available at website. Query. Accepts email queries to khall@professionalartistmag.com. Res-ponse time varies. First North American serial rights. Articles, word lengths vary; $250. Pays 30 days after publication. Reprint master upon request.

Quick Frozen Foods International

2125 Center Avenue, Suite 305
Fort Lee, NJ 07024-5898

Editor & Publisher: John M. Saulnier

Description and Interests: All aspects of the global frozen foods industry are covered in this quarterly. It includes articles on products, packaging, warehousing, and retailing of frozen foods throughout the world. Circ: 15,000.
Website: www.qffintl.com

Freelance Potential: 25% written by nonstaff writers. Publishes 20 freelance submissions yearly; 30% by authors who are new to the magazine, 10% by experts. Receives 5 queries, 10 unsolicited mss monthly.

Submissions and Payment: Sample articles and editorial calendar available at website. Query or send complete ms. Accepts hard copy and Macintosh disk submissions (Word files). SASE. Responds in 1 month. First world rights. Written material, word lengths and payment rates vary. Pays on publication. Provides 1 contributor's copy.

Ratchet + Wrench

1043 Grand Avenue, #372
St. Paul, MN 55105

Editor: Jake Weyer

Description and Interests: *Ratchet + Wrench* is written for owners and managers of mechanical auto care centers and collision shop operators who also service mechanical issues. Its subtitle is "Strategies and Inspiration for Auto Care Success." Each monthly edition features profiles of leaders in the field, case studies, and valuable advice on how to improve business through financial decisions, employee management, marketing, customer service, training, and technology. Circ: 100,000.
Website: www.ratchetandwrench.com

Freelance Potential: Receives many freelance submissions monthly.

Submissions and Payment: Sample copy at website. Query. Accepts email to news@ratchetandwrench.com. Response time varies. Written material, word lengths vary. Rights vary. Payment rates and policy vary.

Recording

5408 Idylwild Trail
Boulder, CO 80301

Editor: Lorenz Rychner

Description and Interests: Written by and for professionals in the audio recording industry, this monthly magazine provides in-depth coverage of topics relevant to the industry. It features timely and authoritative articles, how-to columns, profiles, interviews, and reviews. Circ: 15,000.
Website: www.recordingmag.com

Freelance Potential: 50% written by nonstaff writers. Of the freelance submissions published yearly, 5% are by auuthors who are new to the magazine.

Submissions and Payment: Sample articles available at website. Guidelines and theme list available. Query. Accepts email to lorenz@recordingmag.com. Responds in 1 month. Rights vary. Articles and depts/columns, word lengths and payment rates vary. Payment policy varies.

Remodeling

One Thomas Circle NW, Suite 600
Washington, DC 20005

Editorial Director: Sal Alfano

Description and Interests: *Remodeling* is a monthly trade magazine for professionals who own or manage remodeling businesses. It offers the latest market trends and new products, practical information on company management and client relations, and profiles of successful remodelers. Circ: 85,704.
Website: www.remodelingmagazine.com

Freelance Potential: 10% written by nonstaff writers. Publishes 12 freelance submissions yearly; 5% by authors who are new to the magazine, 25% by industry experts. Receives 3 queries monthly.

Submissions and Payment: Sample articles and editorial calendar available at website. Query. Accepts hard copy. SASE. Response time varies. Rights vary. Articles and depts/columns, 250–3,000 words; $.75–$1 per word. Pays on acceptance. Provides 2 contributor's copies.

Restaurant Development & Design ★

Zoomba Group
110 Schiller, Suite 312
Elmhurst, IL 60126

Editor in Chief: Joseph M. Carbonara

Description and Interests: The mission of this start-up magazine is to help facilitate a conversation and exchange of ideas among restaurant development executives at the corporate and franchisee levels, design consultants, and construction providers. It covers design trends, project profiles, and best practices. Launched in 2012, *Restaurant Development & Design* published two issues in its first year. Circ: 15,000.
Website : www.rddmag.com

Freelance Potential: Receives many queries monthly.

Submissions and Payment:: Sample copy at website. Query. Accepts email to joe@zoombagroup.com. Response time varies. Written material, word lengths vary. Rights vary. Payment rates and policy vary.

Retail Traffic

249 West 17th Street, 3rd Floor
New York, NY 10011

Editorial Director: David Bodamer

Description and Interests: This magazine is considered the go-to source for retail real estate trends and information. It serves developers, owners, retailers, brokers, architects, lenders, and other real estate services with market profiles, case studies, and analysis. In addition, it features articles on property management, marketing, leasing, financial deals, security, and technology. It is published monthly. Circ: 35,000.
Website: www.retailtrafficmag.com

Freelance Potential: 30% written by nonstaff writers. Publishes 20 freelance submissions yearly. Receives 30 queries monthly.

Submissions and Payment: Sample articles available at website. Query. Accepts hard copy. SASE. Responds in 2–3 months. All rights. Articles, 1,200–2,000 words. Depts/columns, word lengths vary. Written material, payment rates vary. Pays on publication. Provides 2 contributor's copies.

Road King

Parthenon Publishing
102 Woodmont Boulevard, Suite 450
Nashville, TN 37205

Editor: Nancy Henderson

Description and Interests: *Road King* is published six times each year for long-haul truck drivers and focuses on trends, technology, and owner-operator practices as well as lifestyle pieces on the outside interests of truckers. Topics must be geared to the truck driver, not the general reader. Circ: 260,000.
Website: www.roadking.com

Freelance Potential: 30% written by nonstaff writers. Publishes 15 freelance submissions yearly; less than 5% by unpublished writers, 70% by industry experts. Receives 25 queries monthly.

Submissions and Payment: Sample articles and guidelines available at website. Query with résumé and writing samples. Accepts email to submissions@roadking.com. Responds in 1–2 months. First and electronic rights. Articles, 300–1,000 words. Depts/columns, to 600 words. Digital images. Payment rates vary. Pays on acceptance.

Roundup Magazine

Western Writers of America
271 CR 219
Encampment, WY 82325

Editor: Johnny D. Boggs

Description and Interests: This magazine for members of the Western Writers of America offers organization news, member profiles, and articles on issues that pertain to literature of the American West. It appears six times each year. Circ: 1,000.
Website: www.westernwriters.org

Freelance Potential: 80% written by nonstaff writers. Publishes 30 freelance submissions yearly; 5% by unpublished writers, 5% by authors who are new to the magazine, 100% by experts. Receives 1–2 unsolicited mss monthly.

Submissions and Payment: Sample articles at website. Guidelines available. Send complete ms. Prefers email to candywwa@aol.com (no attachments); will accept hard copy and disk submissions. SASE. Responds in 2–4 months. First rights. Articles, 750–2,000 words. B/W or color prints or slides. No payment. Provides 2 author's copies.

St. Louis Construction News & Real Estate

1038 Walnut Terrace
Byrnes Mill, MO 63049

Editor: Peter Downs

Description and Interests: Published six times each year, this magazine is read by construction and real estate professionals working in the St. Louis area. It covers the latest industry trends, local business activities, and new products. Circ: 3,500.
Website: www.stlouiscnr.com

Freelance Potential: 10% written by nonstaff writers. Publishes 12 freelance submissions yearly; 5% by authors who are new to the magazine, 100% by experts. Receives 2 queries each month.

Submissions and Payment: Sample articles and editorial calendar available at website. Query with résumé. Accepts email queries via website or to peter@stlouiscnr.com. Responds in 1 month. First North American serial rights. Articles, 1,400 words; $400. Depts/columns, 300 words; $50+. Pays on publication. Provides 2 contributor's copies.

Santé

On-Premise Communications
100 South Street
Bennington, VT 05211

Publisher and Editor: Mark Vaughan

Description and Interests: *Santé* covers food, wine, and spirits for restauranteurs and those working in the hospitality industry. Published quarterly, it offers advice, business news, and useful information that promotes business. The style is professional—no consumer topics—and accessible. Circ: 40,000.
Website: www.santemagazine.com

Freelance Potential: 75% written by nonstaff writers. Purchases 95 manuscripts each year.

Submissions and Payment: Sample copy available at website. Query with 3 clips, 2 or 3 strong ideas, résumé, and brief description of your qualifications. Accepts email to mvaughan@santemagazine.com. Articles, 650–1,800 words. Depts/columns, word lengths vary. Written material, $300-$800. Payment policy varies.

Scrap

1615 L Street NW, Suite 600
Washington, DC 20036-5610

Publisher & Editor in Chief: Kent Kiser

Description and Interests: Recycling industry professionals and members of the Institute of Scrap Recycling Industries read *Scrap* for articles on management, legislation, equipment, safety, and industry trends such as the green movement. Most articles are assigned. It appears six times each year. Circ: 8,601.
Website: www.scrap.org

Freelance Potential: 50% written by nonstaff writers. Publishes 30 freelance submissions yearly; 10% by authors who are new to the magazine. Receives 4 queries monthly.

Submissions and Payment: Sample articles, guidelines, and editorial calendar available at website. For assignment consideration, query with letter of introduction and 2 feature clips. Accepts hard copy. Responds in 2 months. All rights. Articles, 2,000–3,000 words; $600–$1,000. Depts/columns, 500–1,000 words; payment rates vary. Pays on acceptance. Provides 2 contributor's copies.

Signal

4400 Fair Lakes Court
Fairfax, VA 22033-3899

Submissions: Maryann Lawlor

Description and Interests: *Signal* serves an international audience of government, industry, and military leaders in the information security, intelligence, and research and development industries. Published monthly by the Armed Forces Communications and Electronics Association, it provides news and updates on the technologies, concepts, trends, and applications in those fields. Circ: 34,000.
Website: www.afcea.org/signal

Freelance Potential: 40% written by nonstaff writers. Publishes 5 freelance submissions each year.

Submissions and Payment: Sample articles and guidelines available at website. Query. Accepts hard copy and email via website. Response time varies. First rights. Articles, 1,500–1,800 words. Payment rates vary. Payment policy varies.

Ski Area Management

84 Cross Brook Road
PO Box 644
Woodbury, CT 06798

Editor: Rick Kahl

Description and Interests: Appearing six times each year, this magazine provides expert advice on the business and technical issues of mountain resort operations. Circ: 3,500.
Website: www.saminfo.com

Freelance Potential: 80% written by nonstaff writers. Publishes 25 freelance submissions yearly; 20% by unpublished writers, 20% by authors who are new to the magazine, 50% by experts. Receives 8 queries monthly.

Submissions and Payment: Sample articles and editorial calendar available at website. Guidelines available. Query with outline and 2 paragraphs. Accepts email queries to rick@saminfo.com. Responds in 1 month. All world periodical and limited electronic rights. Articles, 800–1,600 words. Depts/columns, 100–1,000 words. Written material, $350–$500. Pays on publication. Provides 1 contributor's copy.

Small Business Advisor

11 Franklin Avenue
Hewlett, NY 11557

Submissions: Barbara Dere

Description and Interests: This monthly newsletter was created to help small businesses achieve their goals. Article topics include taxes, sales strategies, and employee hiring/compensation. Circ: 1,000.
Website: www.smallbusinessadvice.com/newsletter

Freelance Potential: 30% written by nonstaff writers. Publishes 50 freelance submissions yearly; 10% by unpublished writers, 10% by authors who are new to the magazine, 80% by experts. Receives 150 queries, 30 unsolicited mss each month.

Submissions and Payment: Sample articles available at website. Guidelines available. Query or send complete ms. Accepts hard copy, disk submissions, and simultaneous submissions if identified. SASE. Responds in 1–4 months. Two-time rights. Articles, to 900 words. Depts/columns, to 100 words. No payment. Provides 2 contributor's copies.

Smallholder Magazine

Hook House, Hook Road
Wimblington March, Cambs PE15 0QL
United Kingdom

Editor: Liz Wright

Description and Interests: Owners of small agricultural or livestock farms are the audience for this magazine, published 13 times each year. It covers raising livestock, growing organic foods, and other rural lifestyle topics. Circ: 20,000.
Website: www.smallholder.co.uk

Freelance Potential: 90% written by nonstaff writers. Of the freelance submissions published yearly; 10% are by authors who are new to the magazine.

Submissions and Payment: Sample articles available at website. Guidelines and theme list/editorial calendar available. Query. Accepts email queries to liz.wright1@btconnect.com. Responds in 1 week. First British rights. Articles, 700–1,400 words; payment rates vary. Digital images at 300 dpi; £5 per photo. Pays within 6 months of publication.

SOMA Magazine

888 O'Farrell Street, Suite 103
San Francisco, CA 94109

Editor in Chief: Ali Ghanbarian

Description and Interests: *SOMA* is an avant-garde arts, fashion, design, and culture publication with a hip, trendsetting readership of creative professionals. Published six times each year, it presents articles on culture icons, as well as current events, social issues, the arts, and music. Circ: 125,000.
Website: www.somamagazine.com

Freelance Potential: 70% written by nonstaff writers. Publishes 2 freelance submissions yearly; 10% by authors who are new to the magazine. Receives 20 queries monthly.

Submissions and Payment: Sample copy available at website. Query. Accepts email queries to editorial@somamagazine.com. Responds in 3 months. Rights vary. Articles, 800–2,000 words. Depts/columns, 500–800 words. Written material, payment rates vary. Pays on publication. Provides 1 contributor's copy.

Strings

P.O. Box 767
San Anselmo, CA 94979

Editorial Director: Greg Cahill

Description and Interests: This monthly publication targets advanced string musicians and teachers. It offers how-to articles on technique, instrument care for experienced players, and teaching tips. *Strings* also covers the professional string concert scene with reviews and profiles. Circ: 17,000.
Website: www.allthingsstrings.com

Freelance Potential: 75% written by nonstaff writers. Publishes 50–60 freelance submissions yearly. Receives 30 queries monthly.

Submissions and Payment: Sample articles available at website. Query. Accepts email queries to editors.st@stringletter.com. Responds in 1 month. World rights. Articles, 750–3,000 words. Depts/columns, 750–900 words. Reviews and news items, 200 words. Written material, payment rates vary. Kill fee, 50%. Pays on acceptance. Provides 2 contributor's copies.

Successful Farming

1716 Locust Street
Des Moines, IA 50309

Editor: Dave Kurns

Description and Interests: With an editorial mission to serve the diverse business, production, and information needs of families that make farming and ranching their primary livelihood, *Successful Farming* features articles on harvesting, crop choice, farm management, and equipment. It is published 13 times each year. Circ: 442,000.
Website: www.agriculture.com/successful-farming

Freelance Potential: 3% written by nonstaff writers. Publishes 10–20 freelance submissions yearly; 1% by unpublished writers, 1% by authors who are new to the magazine, 1% by industry experts. Receives 5 queries monthly.

Submissions and Payment: Sample articles available on website. Guidelines available. Query. Accepts hard copy. SASE. Responds in 1 month. All rights. Articles and depts/columns, word lengths and payment rates vary. Pays on acceptance. Provides 2 contributor's copies.

Supervision

320 Valley Street
Burlington, IA 52601

Editor: Todd Darnall

Description and Interests: Articles that help business supervisors and managers perform at their best are found in this monthly magazine. It covers issues such as effective leadership and managing and motivating employees. Circ: 500+.
Website: www.supervisionmagazine.com

Freelance Potential: 80% written by nonstaff writers. Publishes 25 freelance submissions yearly; 10% by unpublished writers, 25% by authors who are new to the magazine, 20% by experts. Receives 5 unsolicited mss monthly.

Submissions and Payment: Sample copy and guidelines available at website. Send complete ms with word count and résumé. Accepts email submissions to articles@supervisionmagazine.com (Word attachments). Responds in 1 week. All rights. Articles, 1,500–2,000 words; $.04 per word. Pays on publication. Provides 1 contributor's copy.

Sustainable Farmer

1500 Sandhill Road
Mason, MI 48854

Editor: Bonnie Bucqueroux

Description and Interests: *Sustainable Farmer* is an ezine dedicated to building an online community in which people can exchange ideas and innovations about how to produce food and fiber with respect for the future of all living things. It is updated weekly and provides the latest research, techniques, and tips on sustainable agriculture, as well as profiles of people involved in this movement. Hits per month: 15,000.
Website: www.sustainablefarmer.com

Freelance Potential: 10% written by nonstaff writers. Publishes 10 freelance submissions yearly; 10% by authors who are new to the magazine.

Submissions and Payment: Sample copy available at website. Query or send complete ms. Accepts hard copy and email to info@sustainablefarmer.com. SASE. Response time varies. First worldwide electronic rights. Articles and depts/columns, word lengths and payment rates vary. Payment policy varies.

Symphony

33 West 60th Street, 5th Floor
New York, NY 10023

Managing Editor: Jennifer Melick

Description and Interests: *Symphony*, read by orchestra members and decision makers, covers trends, developments, new music, and profiles. Published quarterly, it welcomes new writers who have a clear command of classical music and the arts-related fields. Circ: 20,000.
Website: www.americanorchestras.org

Freelance Potential: 50% written by nonstaff writers. Publishes 18 freelance submissions yearly; 20% by authors who are new to the magazine, 80% by industry experts. Receives 15 queries monthly.

Submissions and Payment: Sample copy available at website. Guidelines available. Query with clips. Accepts hard copy and email queries to jmelick@americanorchestras.org. SASE. Responds in 1 month. First print and electronic rights. Articles, 2,500 words. Depts/columns, 1,500 words. Written material, payment rates vary. Pays on acceptance. Provides 1 contributor's copy.

Tanning Trends

3101 Page Avenue
P.O. Box 1630
Jackson, MI 49203-2254

Editor: Ashley Laabs

Description and Interests: Published monthly by the International Smart Tan Network, this magazine is written for indoor tanning salon owners and managers. Freelance writers with an expert knowledge of the industry are welcome to submit ideas on trends, new products, and techniques for increasing business. Circ: 20,000.
Website: www.smarttan.com

Freelance Potential: 10% written by nonstaff writers. Publishes 12 freelance submissions yearly; 5% by unpublished writers, 5% by authors who are new to the magazine, 90% by industry experts.

Submissions and Payment: Sample copy available at website. Query or send complete ms. Accepts email to editor@smarttan.com. Response time varies. Rights vary. Articles and depts/columns, word lengths and payment rates vary. Payment policy varies.

3x3

The Magazine of Contemporary Illustration

244 Fifth Avenue, Suite F269
New York, NY 10001

Publisher & Design Director: Charles Hively

Description and Interests: Focused exclusively on the art of contemporary illustration, this publication appears three times each year in the U.S., Canada, the United Kingdom, and Europe. Each issue features the works of three well-known artists and interviews by fellow illustrators. New talent is also showcased. Circ: 4,300.
Website: www.3x3mag.com

Freelance Potential: 90% written by nonstaff writers. Publishes 12 freelance submissions yearly; 50% by unpublished writers, 90% by authors who are new to the magazine.

Submissions and Payment: Sample copy available at website. Guidelines available. Query. Accepts hard copy and email queries to chively@3x3mag.com. SASE. Response time varies. One-time print and electronic rights. Articles, to 1,000 words; $300. Pays on publication. Provides 3 contributor's copies.

Travel Goods Showcase

301 North Harrison Street, #412
Princeton, NJ 08540-3512

President/CEO: Michele Marini Pittenger

Description and Interests: Published by the Travel Goods Association, this quarterly is one of the largest trade magazines for retailers of travel products and accessories. It features product reviews, market trends, and trade show events. It also covers association news. Circ: 5,000.
Website: www.travel-goods.org

Freelance Potential: 95% written by nonstaff writers. Publishes 8–12 freelance submissions yearly; 50% by authors who are new to the magazine.

Submissions and Payment: Sample articles and editorial calendar available at website. Query. Accepts email queries to info@travel-goods.org. Response time varies. First and electronic rights. Articles, 1,500–2,500 words; payment rates vary. Pays on publication. Provides 2 contributor's copies.

Today's Facility Manager

44 Apple Street, Suite 3
Tinton Falls, NJ 07724

Editor: Anne Vazquez

Description and Interests: Targeting facility managers of commercial and industrial buildings, this monthly trade magazine has information on management and maintenance issues, trends, and new products. Circ: 50,000.
Website: www.todaysfacilitymanager.com

Freelance Potential: 50% written by nonstaff writers. Publishes 25 freelance submissions yearly; 10% by unpublished writers, 10% by new authors. Receives 5–10 unsolicited mss monthly.

Submissions and Payment: Sample articles at website. Send complete ms with artwork. Accepts hard copy and email submissions to vazquez@groupc.com. SASE. Response time varies. Written material, 1,000–2,000 words; payment rates vary. Kill fee, 20%. Pays 1 month after publication. Provides 2 contributor's copies.

Trucker's Connection Magazine

1123 South University Avenue, Suite 320
Little Rock, AR 72204

Editor: Lyndon Finney

Description and Interests: This monthly publication for truck drivers aims to inform and entertain. It features articles on the industry, safety, and destinations. Circ: 100,000.
Website: www.thetrucker.com

Freelance Potential: 33% written by nonstaff writers. Publishes 100 freelance submissions yearly; 5% by unpublished writers, 10% by authors who are new to the magazine, 15% by industry experts. Receives 1 query monthly.

Submissions and Payment: Sample articles at website. Editorial calendar available. Accepts hard copy, email submissions to news@thetrucker.com (Word attachments) and fax to 501-666-0700. SASE. Responds in 2–3 weeks. First North American serial rights. Articles, 1,000–1,500 words. Depts/columns, 200–400 words. Written material, $.35 per word. Pays on publication.

University Business

488 Main Avenue
Norwalk, CT 06851

Editor in Chief: Tim Goral

Description and Interests: This monthly publication is written for presidents and upper-level managers of two- and four-year colleges and universities. It covers the latest education trends as well as the current issues involving enrollment, academic affairs, technology, and legislation. Circ: 46,000.
Website: www.universitybusiness.com

Freelance Potential: 30% written by nonstaff writers. Publishes 30–40 freelance submissions yearly; 10% by authors who are new to the magazine.

Submissions and Payment: Sample articles and guidelines available at website. Query. Accepts email queries to tgoral@universitybusiness.com (Word documents). Responds in 2–3 weeks. All rights for 90 days. Articles, to 2,500 words. Depts/columns, to 1,400 words. Payment rates and policy vary.

Validation Times

19-B Wirt Street SW
Leesburg, VA 20175

Managing Editor: Melissa Winn

Description and Interests: *Validation Times* is a monthly newsletter focusing on pharmaceutical and biotech quality assurance and manufacturing issues as well as issues relating to the research sector. It also covers FDA compliance and GMP validation. Circ: Unavailable.
Website: www.fdainfo.com

Freelance Potential: 20% written by nonstaff writers. Publishes 30–40 freelance submissions yearly; 20% by authors who are new to the magazine, 30% by experts. Receives 3 queries each month.

Submissions and Payment: Sample articles available at website. Guidelines and theme list/editorial calendar available. Query with writing samples. Accepts email queries to mwinn@fdainfo.com. Responds in 1 week. Second rights. Articles, 600–1,000 words; $250. Depts/columns, 800–1,200 words; payment rates vary. Pays on publication.

VentureBeat

50 California Street, Suite 3270
San Francisco, CA 94111

Executive Editor: Dylan Tweney

Description and Interests: The target audience for this online publication is entrepreneurs pursuing technology start-ups. It covers venture capital, innovation in the technology sector—currently, that particularly means the cloud—and mobile applications. It also covers industry events. Hits per month: 6 million.
Website: http://venturebeat.com

Freelance Potential: 10–20% written by nonstaff writers.

Submissions and Payment: Sample postings available on the website. Submit your credentials before querying with an idea to dylan@venturebeat.com. Features, 500–1,000 words. Contributing writers with contracts may write 15–20 300-word postings a week. License relationship with *VentureBeat*. Pay varies; $20–$50 plus traffic bonus per posting. Pays within 30 days.

Venues Today

P.O. Box 2540
Huntington Beach, CA 92647

Assignment Editor: Dave Brooks

Description and Interests: *Venues Today* shares "the news behind the headlines" in music, family shows, conventions, and fairs. Published monthly, it targets managers, owners, operators, and bookers of sports and live entertainment venues. It accepts how-to and informational articles, and profiles of performers and industry personalities. Circ: 10,000.
Website: www.venuestoday.com

Freelance Potential: 60% written by nonstaff writers. Publishes 20–40 freelance submissions yearly; 15% by authors who are new to the magazine. Receives 2 queries, 1 unsolicited ms each month.

Submissions and Payment: Sample articles and editorial calendar available at website. Query. Accepts email queries to dave@venuestoday.com. Responds in 1–2 days. All rights. Articles, 800–1,200 words; $100–$250. Kill fee varies. Pays on publication. Provides 2 contributor's copies.

Watch Journal

Houston, TX

Editorial Director: Marie A. Picon

Description and Interests: This is a luxury magazine built around watches and read by affluent watch enthusiasts. It utilizes a visually stunning format to focus on design and technology. Prospective freelancers must have knowledge of the watch industry and/or luxury products in general. It appears six times each year. Circ: Unavailable.
Website: www.watchjournal.com

Freelance Potential: 40% written by nonstaff writers. Publishes 10 freelance submissions yearly; 5% by unpublished writers, 5% by authors who are new to the magazine, 90% by industry experts. Receives 1 query monthly.

Submissions and Payment: Query with detailed proposal. Accepts email queries to mpicon@watchjournal.com. Responds in 1 month. All rights. Articles, 800–1,200 words. Depts/columns, 300–500 words. Written material, $.50 per word. Pays on publication. Provides 1 contributor's copy.

Water & Wastewater News

1105 Media Inc.
14901 Quorum Drive, Suite 425
Dallas, TX 75254

Submissions: L. K. Williams

Description and Interests: This twice-weekly electronic newsletter is read by professionals in the environment industries, including water, waste, air, and energy. It seeks information on current issues in the water industry. Hits per month: 40,000.
Website: http://eponline.com/portals/water.aspx

Freelance Potential: 15% written by nonstaff writers. Publishes 12+ freelance submissions yearly; 8% by unpublished writers, 50% by authors who are new to the magazine, 30% by experts. Receives 3 queries monthly.

Submissions and Payment: Sample articles available at website. Accepts mail or email queries to lwilliams@1105media.com or smahoney@1105media.com. First rights or assign copyright. Articles and depts/columns, 1,000 words. Guest blog posts, 300–400 words. No payment.

Watercolor

133 West 19th Street, 7th Floor
New York, NY 10011

Associate Editor: Naomi Ekperigin

Description and Interests: This quarterly arts magazine is written for professional or advanced amateur artists who want to learn about and from other artists. The majority of its articles profile an accomplished watermedia artist and provide step-by-step instructions in the use of his or her technique. It also publishes articles on recent exhibitions and historical articles on a particular medium or technique. Circ: 40,000.
Website: www.artistdaily.com

Freelance Potential: 60% written by nonstaff writers. Publishes many freelance submissions yearly.

Submissions and Payment: Sample copy and guidelines available at website. Query with résumé, clips, and 10 digital images of artist's work on CD. Responds in 6–8 weeks. All rights. Articles, 1,500–2,000 words; $500. Kill fee, $75. Pays on publication.

Woman Engineer

445 Broad Hollow Road, Suite 425
Melville, NY 11747

Editor: Jim Schneider

Description and Interests: *Woman Engineer* is a career guidance and recruitment magazine for female engineering, computer science, and IT students and professionals. Its articles cover such issues as finding employment, career trends, career planning, employers, and career development—at all stages of a career. It is published three times each year. Circ: 56,000.
Website: www.eop.com

Freelance Potential: 75% written by nonstaff writers. Publishes 15 freelance submissions yearly.

Submissions and Payment: Sample articles available at website. Guidelines available. Query with résumé and clips. Prefers email to jschneider@eop.com; will accept hard copy. SASE. Response time varies. First North American serial rights. Written material, word lengths vary; $.10 per word. Pays 4–6 weeks after publication.

Women in Business

American Business Women's Association
11050 Roe Avenue, Suite 200
Overland Park, KS 66211

Editor

Description and Interests: Career development and workplace skills are the focus of this publication for working women. It is published six times each year, and is available both in print and as a digital magazine. Circ: 20,000.
Website: www.abwa.org

Freelance Potential: 15% written by nonstaff writers. Publishes 16 freelance submissions yearly; 5% by authors who are new to the magazine, 4% by experts. Receives 5 queries, 10–15 unsolicited mss each month.

Submissions and Payment: Query or send complete ms with writing samples and résumé. Prefers email to mkatz@abwa.org; will accept hard copy. SASE. Response time varies. First North American serial rights. Articles, 500-1,500 words. Depts/columns, word lengths vary. Written material, $100 per 500 words. Kill fee, 50%. Pays on acceptance. Provides 2 copies.

Work Your Way

Editor: Mary Cummings

Description and Interests: *Work Your Way* is an online resource for working mothers everywhere. Its core audience is well-educated, entrepreneurial-minded women. It provides advice on flexible working, freelancing, franchising, direct selling, and working smarter and more profitably. It features interviews with business leaders and inspirational, entrepreneurial women. All articles are contributed by female business owners, freelancers, direct sellers, and work-at-home mothers. while *Work Your Way* is based in the U.K., it is open to submissions internationally. Hits per month 2,000.
Website: www.workyourway.co.uk

Freelance Potential: 100% written by nonstaff writers.

Submissions and Payment: Sample articles available at the website. Contact the publication via the online Contact Us page. Rights vary. Written material, payment rates vary. Pays on publication.

The World of Welding

Hobart Institute
400 Trade Square East
Troy, OH 45373

Editor: Marty Baker

Description and Interests: As the official publication of the Hobart Institute of Welding Technology, this quarterly keeps students and alumni abreast of school news and activities, and also features articles on industry trends, welding advice, and product information. Circ: 6,500.
Website: www.welding.org

Freelance Potential: 10% written by nonstaff writers. Publishes 6 freelance submissions yearly; 9% by unpublished writers, 1% by authors who are new to the magazine, 90% by experts. Receives 1 unsolicited ms monthly.

Submissions and Payment: Sample copy available at website. Send complete ms. Prefers email submissions to hiwt@welding.org (Word or PDF attachments); will accept hard copy and PC disk submissions. SASE. Responds in 1 week. All rights. Articles, 750–1,000 words. Depts/columns, 500–750 words. No payment. Provides 3 contributor's copies.

World Trade 100

Editor in Chief: Martha L. Walz

Description and Interests: Articles in this monthly magazine are of interest to the executives at manufacturers, wholesalers, and retailers involved in domestic and international trade. Its informational features and profiles cover the supply chain, global trends, transportation, warehousing, shipping, finance, markets, economics, technology, law, and risk and compliance. *WT100* is available in print, digital, and iPad editions. Circ: 75,000.
Website: www.worldtradewt100.com

Freelance Potential: 50% written by nonstaff writers. Buys 50 mss a year.

Submissions and Payment: Sample articles available at website. Query with clips to walzm@bnpmedia.com. Also accepts hard copy. Articles, 450–1,000 words. Depts/columns, 800 words. All rights. Pays $.50 a word, on publication.

Worship Leader Magazine

32234 Paseo Adelanto, Suite A
San Juan Capistrano, CA 92675

Managing Editor: Jeremy Armstrong

Description and Interests: Eight times each year this magazine reaches ministry leaders who are looking for information and inspiration to sharpen their skills in the worship arts. Writers will first be considered for online publication before contributing to the magazine. Circ: 30,000.
Website: www.worshipleader.com

Freelance Potential: 60% written by nonstaff writers. Publishes 20 freelance submissions yearly; 1% by authors who are new to the magazine, 90% by experts. Receives 5 queries monthly.

Submissions and Payment: Sample articles available at website. Guidelines and editorial calendar available. Query. Accepts hard copy and email via the website. Responds in 3–6 months. All rights. Articles, 2,000 words; $200–$800. Depts/columns, 800–1,000 words; $.25 per word. Kill fee, 50%. Pays on publication. Provides 3 contributor's copies.

Writing on the Edge

University of California at Davis
1 Shields Avenue
Davis, CA 95616

Editor: David Masiel

Description and Interests: Articles and essays about writing and teaching writing are provided in this magazine read by university-level educators. Interviews with established authors and educators are also featured as well as stories, poems, and cartoons. *Writing on the Edge* is published twice each year. Circ: 2,000..
Website: http://woe.ucdavis.edu

Freelance Potential: 97% written by nonstaff writers. Publishes 20 freelance submissions yearly; 20% by unpublished writers, 80% by new authors, 90% by experts. Receives 10 mss monthly.

Submissions and Payment: Sample articles and guidelines available at website. Send complete ms to drmasiel@ucdavis.edu (Word attachment) or 3 hard copies. SASE. Articles: To 5,000 words. Responds in 3 months. First rights. Written material, word lengths vary. No payment. Provides 2 contributor's copies.

Z-Life

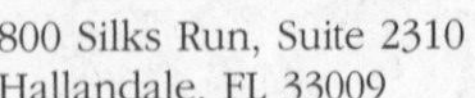

800 Silks Run, Suite 2310
Hallandale, FL 33009

Editor in Chief: Andrea Carneiro

Description and Interests: *Z* stands for *Zumba* in this quarterly, launched in 2010 to cover the high-profile exercise dance craze. The audience is fitness instructors, and the magazine is also sold at Whole Foods grocery stores. The topics covered in *Z-Life* are the music, dance, and fitness associated with Zumba "parties," but more generally, the focus is on nutrition, health, beauty, and fashion. Circ: 155,000.
Website: http://zlife.zumba.com

Description and Interests:85% written by nonstaff writers. Open to developing ongoing relationships with writers.

Submissions and Payment: Sample articles available on the website. Email queries to andrea.carniero@zumba.com. Features, 1,500–2,500 words. Articles on trends, 500–750 words. All rights. Pays $.65 per word. Kill fee, 25%. Pays within 60 days of publication.

Zoning Practice

American Planning Association
205 N. Michigan Ave., Suite 1200
Chicago IL 60601

Editors

Description and Interests: A publication of the American Planning Association, *Zoning Practice* targets professional planners and others about such topics as zoning enforcement of noise and odor, historic preservation, land use, zoning law, and land-use regulations. Circ: 2,000.
Website: www.planning.org

Description and Interests: 90% written by nonstaff writers. Interested in finding new authors.

Submissions and Payment: Sample article and contributors' guidelines availables at website. Email to zoningpractice@planning.org. Feature articles, 3,000 words. Query with 1-page outline, bio, and an explanation of the suitability of the topic proposed. All rights. News Briefs, 500–750 words. Articles, $300–$500. News Briefs, $150. Pays on publication.

Regional Magazines

AAA Midwest Traveler

12901 North Forty Drive
St. Louis, MO 63141

Managing Editor: Deborah Reinhardt

Description and Interests: Appearing six times each year, this regional membership magazine publishes informative articles on travel and automobile safety for members in Missouri, southern Illinois, southern Indiana, and eastern Kansas. Circ: 520,195.
Website: www.aaa.com/traveler

Freelance Potential: 55% written by nonstaff writers. Publishes 20–30 freelance submissions yearly; 1% by unpublished writers, 5% by authors who are new to the magazine. Receives 100 queries monthly.

Submissions and Payment: Sample copy, guidelines, and editorial calendar available at website. Query between January and April. Accepts email to dreinhardt@aaamissouri.com, hard copy, simultaneous submissions if identified, and reprints. SASE. Responds in 4 weeks. One-time, non-exclusive North American serial and electronic rights. Articles, 1,200 words; $400–$550. Digital images at 300 dpi; payment varies. Pays on acceptance.

AAA Southern Traveler

12901 North Forty Drive
St. Louis, MO 63141

Managing Editor: Deborah Reinhardt

Description and Interests: Read by AAA members in Arkansas, Louisiana, and Mississippi, this publication offers informative articles on travel and automobile safety and maintenance. It appears six times each year. Circ: 230,000.
Website: www.aaa.com/traveler

Freelance Potential: 55% written by nonstaff writers. Publishes 10 freelance submissions yearly; 1% by unpublished writers, 5% by authors who are new to the magazine. Receives 100 queries monthly.

Submissions and Payment: Sample copy, guidelines, and editorial calendar available at website. Query between January and April. Accepts email to dreinhardt@aaamissouri.com, hard copy, simultaneous submissions if identified, and reprints. SASE. Responds in 4 weeks. One-time, non-exclusive North American serial and electronic rights. Articles, 1,200 words; $400–$550. Digital images at 300 dpi; payment varies. Pays on acceptance.

About Families

P.O. Box 840
Lebanon, PA 17042

Editor: Mari Conners

Description and Interests: Serving Pennsylvania's Berks and Lebanon counties, *About Families* aims to be a central resource of information for the entertainment, cultural, and educational offerings within the community. It is published monthly both digitally and in print. Circ: Unavailable.
Website: www.aboutfamiliespa.com

Freelance Potential: Receives several freelance submissions monthly.

Submissions and Payment: Sample copy available at website. Send complete ms. Accepts hard copy. Submissions not returned. Response time varies. Rights vary. Payment rates and policy vary.

Act Two

P.O. Box 12
Fairfield, CT 06824-0012

Editor: Rosemary Cass

Description and Interests: Calling itself "a magazine for the second half of life," this new publication focuses on what comes next for those who have worked long and hard and now have the time and energy (plus the financial freedom) to enjoy themselves. It accepts proposals for features and fiction. Circ: Unavailable.
Website: www.acttwomagazine.com/

Freelance Potential: Unavailable.

Submissions and Payment: Sample copy available. Query. Accepts email to submissions@acttwomagazine.com. Rights and payment information unavailable.

Adirondack Life

P.O. Box 410
Jay, NY 12941

Editor: Annie Stoltie

Description and Interests: The natural beauty of New York State's Adirondack Park is depicted in this magazine, which appears eight times each year. It also profiles the region's people and explores its culture, history, recreation, wildlife, and public issues. Circ: 45,000.
Website: www.adirondacklife.com

Freelance Potential: 80–90% written by nonstaff writers. Publishes 35 freelance submissions yearly; 10% by unpublished writers, 10% by authors who are new to the magazine. Receives 20 queries monthly.

Submissions and Payment: Sample articles and guidelines available at website. Query with clips. Prefers email queries to astoltie@adirondacklife.com; will accept hard copy. SASE. Responds in 1 month. First North American serial rights. Articles, 1,500–3,500 words. Depts/columns, 1,000–1,800 words. Written material, $.30 per word. Pays 1 month after publication. Provides 2 contributor's copies.

Adventures NW

4130 Angela Court
Bellingham, WA 98229

Editor: John D'Onofrio

Description and Interests: Rooted in Cascadia, *Adventures NW* has been the region's leading source of outdoors information—and inspiration—since 2006. Hiking, climbing, running, cycling, paddling, sailing, surfing, skiing, boarding, 'shoeing: it's all here in a glossy, full-color quarterly. Circ: 60,000.
Website: www.adventuresnw.com

Freelance Potential: Unavailable.

Submissions and Payment: Sample articles and guidelines available at website. Send detailed query with topic, length, images, and writing sample to editor@adventuresnw.com. Payment rates vary. Pays 30 days after publication.

Akron Life

1653 Merriman Road, Suite 116
Akron, OH 44313

Editor: Georgina Carson

Description and Interests: This lifestyle publication provides information designed to enhance and enrich the experience of living in or visiting Akron and its surrounding areas. The places, personalities, and events in the arts, entertainment, business, politics, and social scene are covered. It appears monthly. Circ: 15,000.
Website: www.akronlife.com

Freelance Potential: 10% written by nonstaff writers.

Submissions and Payment: Sample articles available at website. Query with published clips. Accepts email to editor@bakermediagroup.com. Responds only if interested. All rights. Written material, 300–2,000 words. Payment rates vary. Kill fee, 50%. Pays on publication.

Alabama Heritage

P.O. Box 870342
Tuscaloosa, AL 35487-0342

Editor in Chief: Donna Cox-Baker

Description and Interests: The people, places, and culture that make Alabama unique are the focus of this quarterly. Published by the Alabama Department of Archives and History, it favors pieces that make connections between the past and the present. Circ: 10,000.
Website: www.alabamaheritage.com

Freelance Potential: 80% written by nonstaff writers. Publishes 20 freelance submissions yearly; 10% by unpublished writers, 60% by authors who are new to the magazine, 50% by experts. Receives 15 queries, 10–15 mss monthly.

Submissions and Payment: Sample articles and guidelines available at website. Query with writing samples. Accepts hard copy and email to heritage@bama.ua.edu. SASE. Response time varies. All rights. Articles, 2,000–4,500 words. Depts/columns, 250–1,200 words. Written material, $50–$350. Pays on publication. Provides 10 contributor's copies.

Alabama Living

340 TechnaCenter Drive
Montgomery, AL 36117-6031

Editor: Lenore Vickrey

Description and Interests: Published monthly by an electric cooperative, *Alabama Living* includes articles about the state's recreation and outdoor opportunities, as well as lifestyle topics of interest to those who live or work in the region. Circ: 400,000.
Website: www.alabamaliving.com

Freelance Potential: 90% written by nonstaff writers. Publishes 20 freelance submissions yearly; 5% by unpublished writers, 10% by authors who are new to the magazine. Receives 4 queries monthly.

Submissions and Payment: Sample copy available at website. Guidelines and editorial calendar available. Query. Accepts email queries to lvickrey@areapower.com (Word attachments). Responds in 1 month. All rights. Articles, 500–600 words; $100 ($150 with photos). Pays on acceptance. Provides 3–4 contributor's copies.

Alaska Business Monthly

501 West Northern Lights Boulevard, Suite 100
Anchorage, AK 99503

Managing Editor: Susan Harrington

Description and Interests: Business owners and residents of Alaska read this monthly magazine. It covers a variety of topics, from the environment to entrepreneurship, fisheries to finance, and tourism to technology. Circ: 12,000.
Website: www.akbizmag.com

Freelance Potential: 80% written by nonstaff writers. Publishes 300+ freelance submissions yearly; 5% by unpublished writers, 10% by authors who are new to the magazine, 10% by experts. Receives 30–50 queries monthly.

Submissions and Payment: Sample copy available. Guidelines and editorial calendar available at website. Query with 3 clips or send complete ms. Prefers email to editor@akbizmag. com (Word or RTF attachments); accepts hard copy. Responds in 1–2 months. All rights. Articles, 500–2,500 words; $125–$300. Kill fee, $50. Pays on publication. Provides 2 contributor's copies.

Alaska Magazine

301 Arctic Slope Avenue, Suite 300
Anchorage, AK 99518

Senior Editor: Debbie Cutler

Description and Interests: *Alaska* brings superlative writing on Alaskan topics to readers 10 times each year. It works with established and new writers. Topics include the issues facing Alaska, its history, people, travel, natural history, adventure, and sports. Circ: 200,000.
Website: www.alaskamagazine.com

Freelance Potential: 70% written by nonstaff writers. 90% of the sportsman section is freelance written. Publishes 40 freelance submissions yearly.

Submissions and Payment: Sample copy and guidelines available at website. Query. Accepts email to debbie.cutler@alaskamagazine.com. Responds in 4–6 weeks. Work must be original and unpublished. Articles, 700–1,500 words. First or one-time and electronic rights. Written material, $200–$700; maximum $1,500 for written material with photos. Pays on publication.

Albemarle Magazine

375 Greenbrier Drive, Suite 100
Charlottesville, VA 22901

Publisher: Alison Dickie

Description and Interests: This magazine showcases all there is to see and do in Central Virginia and the Albemarle County region. Published six times each year, it visits the area's homes and gardens, covers local history, and profiles personalities. Circ: 10,000.
Website: www.albemarlemagazine.com

Freelance Potential: 30% written by nonstaff writers. Publishes 12 freelance submissions yearly; 5% by unpublished writers, 25% by authors who are new to the magazine. Receives 20 queries monthly.

Submissions and Payment: Guidelines available. Query with author bio, résumé, and clips. Accepts email to editorial@albemarlemagazine.com. Response time varies. First North American serial rights. Articles, 900–3,500 words; payment rates vary. Pays on publication. Provides 2 contributor's copies.

Alberta Venture

10259–105 Street
Edmonton, Alberta T5J 1E3
Canada

Editor in Chief: Ruth Kelly

Description and Interests: The key issues and players in Alberta, Canada's business scene are the focus of this monthly. It offers readers insight into the region's economic trends and the issues that affect its growth. Circ: 28,000.
Website: www.albertaventure.com

Freelance Potential: 70% written by nonstaff writers. Publishes 120 freelance submissions yearly; 5% by unpublished writers, 20% by authors who are new to the magazine, 5% by experts. Receives 5 queries monthly.

Submissions and Payment: Sample copy available at website. Query. Accepts email queries to admin@albertaventure.com. Responds in 2 weeks. First Canadian print and electronic rights. Articles, 1,200–3,000 words. Depts/columns, 600–1,200 words. Written material, $.50 per word. Kill fee, 30%. Pays on publication. Provides 1 contributor's copy.

AMC Outdoors

5 Joy Street
Boston, MA 02108

Features: Heather Stephenson
Departments: Marc Chalufour

Description and Interests: The Appalachian Mountain Club publishes this magazine six times each year. It focuses on hiking and recreation on and near the Appalachian Trail, while also addressing preservation of the mountains, rivers, and trails of the Northeast outdoors. Circ: 90,000.
Website: www.outdoors.org

Freelance Potential: 40% written by nonstaff writers. Publishes 24 freelance submissions yearly; 15% by authors who are new to the magazine, 5% by experts. Receives 10 queries monthly.

Submissions and Payment: Sample articles and guidelines available at website. Query. Accepts email to amcpublications@outdoors.org. For assignments, email résumé and clips. Responds in 2-4 weeks. All rights. Articles, 2,000–2,500 words; $500–$700. Depts/columns, 300–750 words; $150–$400. Pays on publication. Provides 5 contributor's copies.

Ann Arbor Observer

2390 Winewood
Ann Arbor, MI 48103

Editor: John Hilton

Description and Interests: This monthly magazine covers news and entertainment, with articles on Ann Arbor's government, business, and education, along with pieces on the city's dining, arts, and culture. Circ: 60,000.
Website: www.annarborobserver.com

Freelance Potential: 50% written by nonstaff writers. Publishes 100 freelance submissions yearly; 10% by unpublished writers, 25% by authors who are new to the magazine.

Submissions and Payment: Sample articles available at website. Prefers query; will accept complete ms. Accepts email to hilton@aaobserver.com. Response time varies. Unlimited, non-exclusive rights. Articles, 1,000–3,500 words; $500–$1,000. Depts/columns, 150–2,500 words; $75–$550. Kill fee varies. Pays on publication. Provides 2 contributor's copies.

Appalachian Heritage 

Berea College
C. P. O. Box 2166
Berea, KY 40404

Editor: George Brosi

Description and Interests: This quarterly literary magazine of the Southern Appalachians publishes fiction, creative nonfiction, reviews, opinion pieces, and poetry about the region or written by authors from the region. Work may be historical or contemporary in nature. Circ: 900.
Website: www.berea.edu/appalachianheritage

Freelance Potential: 95% written by nonstaff writers. Publishes 100 freelance submissions yearly; 10% by unpublished writers, 75% by authors who are new to the magazine. Receives 100 unsolicited mss monthly.

Submissions and Payment: Sample articles and guidelines available at website. Send complete ms. Accepts hard copy. SASE. Responds in 3–6 months. First rights. Articles and fiction, 3,500 words. Book reviews, 500 words. Poetry, to 84 lines. No payment. Provides 3 contributor's copies.

Arizona Foothills Magazine

8132 North 87th Place
Scottsdale, AZ 85258

Executive Editor: Elizabeth Smith

Description and Interests: This monthly is a lifestyle magazine for the sophisticated and affluent residents of Arizona's valley regions. It publishes personality profiles and articles on the area's leisure activities, fashion, travel, arts scene, dining, and home topics. Circ: 60,000+.
Website: www.arizonafoothillsmagazine.com

Freelance Potential: 15% written by nonstaff writers. Publishes 12–36 freelance submissions yearly; 3% by authors who are new to the magazine. Receives 3 queries monthly.

Submissions and Payment: Sample articles, editorial calendar available at website. Query with résumé and clips. Accepts electronic queries through website only. Responds in 1 month. All rights. Articles, 600–2,000 words. Depts/columns, 600 words. Written material, payment varies. Kill fee, 25%. Pays 2 months after publication. Provides 1 contributor's copy.

Arizona Highways

Arizona Department of Transportation
2039 West Lewis Avenue
Phoenix, AZ 85009

Editor: Robert Stieve

Description and Interests: *Arizona Highways* celebrates the natural beauty and attractions of the Grand Canyon State. Monthly issues offer articles on scenic routes, travel, outdoor adventures, and state history and culture. Personality profiles are also featured. All published material is assigned. Circ: 200,000.
Website: www.arizonahighways.com

Freelance Potential: 10% written by nonstaff writers. Receives 50 queries monthly.

Submissions and Payment: All work is assigned. Check website for submissions calendar. Query with clips. No unsolicited mss. Accepts email queries to kkramer@arizonahighways.com. Responds in 1 month. First North American serial rights. Articles and travel pieces, 1,500-4,000. Depts/columns, word lengths vary. Payment rates vary. Pays on acceptance. Provides 2 contributor's copies.

Arizona Networking News

P.O. Box 5477
Scottsdale, AZ 85261

Editor: Joanne Henning Tedesco

Description and Interests: Six times each year, this newsletter offers readers in Arizona informative articles on many topics, all from a holistic perspective. Circ: 50,000.
Website: www.aznetnews.com

Freelance Potential: 80% written by nonstaff writers. Publishes 500 freelance submissions yearly; 60% by unpublished writers, 20% by authors who are new to the magazine, 20% by experts. Receives 5 queries, 10 unsolicited mss monthly.

Submissions and Payment: Sample copy and guidelines available. Query or send complete ms. Accepts disk submissions (Word) and email to editor@aznetnews.com. SASE. Responds to queries in 2 weeks, to mss in 2 months. First rights. Articles, 350–500 words. No payment. Provides contributor's copies upon request.

Arkansas Review 

A Journal of Delta Studies

P.O. Box 1890
Arkansas State University
State University, AR 72467

General Editor: Janelle Collins

Description and Interests: *Arkansas Review* explores the Mississippi Delta region through fiction, poetry, essays, creative nonfiction, and visual art. It also publishes reviews of books related to the Delta. This journal appears three times each year. Circ: 900.
Website: http://altweb.astate.edu/arkreview

Freelance Potential: 95% written by nonstaff writers. Publishes 12–15 freelance submissions yearly; 10% by unpublished writers, 80% by authors who are new to the magazine. Receives 20 unsolicited mss monthly.

Submissions and Payment: Sample copy available. Guidelines available at website. Send complete ms. Accepts hard copy, email to arkansasreview@astate.edu, and simultaneous submissions. SASE. Responds in 4 months. First North American serial rights. Written material, word lengths vary. B/W prints. No payment. Provides 3 contributor's copies and a subscription.

Arlington Magazine

1319 North Greenbrier St.
Arlington, VA 22205

Editor: Jenny Sullivan

Description and Interests: The bimonthly *Arlington Magazine* premiered in late 2011. It reports on the people, businesses, and lifestyle surrounding the affluent communities of Arlington, McLean, and Falls Church, Virginia. The magazine targets readers who are "smart and sophisticated, but don't take themselves too seriously." Writers need not shy away from the "thornier" issues, as well. Articles that address these matters in a serious way and provide helpful information on how to deal with them are always welcome. Circ: 25,000.
Website: www.arlingtonmagazine.com

Freelance Potential: Receives numerous submissions monthly.

Submissions and Payment: Sample articles available at website. Query. Accepts email queries to editorial@arlingtonmagazine.com. Response time varies. Articles and depts/columns, word lengths vary. Rights and payment vary.

Aruba Nights

1751 Richardson Street, Suite 5530
Montreal, Quebec H3K 1G6
Canada

Editor: Jennifer McMorran

Description and Interests: This annual magazine serves as the tourist's guide to Aruba. Its articles describe the events, destinations, and entertainment awaiting visitors to the island. It also features shopping and dining reviews and profiles of local personalities. Circ: 245,000.
Website: www.nightspublications.com

Freelance Potential: 90% written by nonstaff writers. Publishes 20 freelance submissions yearly; 25% by authors who are new to the magazine, 75% by experts. Receives 5 queries monthly.

Submissions and Payment: Sample copy available. Query with writing sample. Accepts email queries to editor@nightspublications.com. Responds in 1–2 months. Exclusive or first Caribbean and North American rights. Articles, 250–700 words; \$100–\$300. Depts/columns, 250–500 words; payment rates vary. Pays on acceptance.

Aspen Magazine

720 East Durant Avenue, Suite E8
Aspen, CO 81611

Editor in Chief: Janet O'Grady

Description and Interests: Founded in 1974, and recently acquired by Modern Luxury, this lifestyle magazine focuses on the culture, fashion, cuisine, nightlife, boundless recreational opportunities, nature, and local personalities of Aspen. It appears eight times each year. Circ: 180,000.
Website: www.aspenmagazine.com

Freelance Potential: 50% written by nonstaff writers. Publishes 20–25 freelance submissions yearly; 5% by unpublished writers, 30% by experts. Receives 8–10 queries monthly.

Submissions and Payment: Sample articles available at website. Guidelines available. Query. Accepts email to janran@aspenmagazine.com. Responds in 1–2 months. First North American serial rights. Articles, 1,500–3,000 words. Depts/columns, 500–1,000 words. Written material, payment rates vary. Kill fee, 10%. Payment policy varies. Provides 1 conributor's copy.

Athens Parent

P.O. Box 465
Watkinsville, GA 30677

Editor in Chief: Shannon Howell Baker

Description and Interests: Targeting parents, grandparents, educators, and others interested in the well-being of children and families, this publication is distributed in Athens, Georgia, and the surrounding area. Fun, informative articles on family activities, summer camps, and birthday parties appear alongside deeper discussions of education, health, social issues, teens, single parenting, and discipline. It appears six times each year. Circ: 13,000.
Website: www.athensparent.com

Freelance Potential: 85% written by nonstaff writers. Publishes 40 freelance submissions yearly. Receives 25 queries monthly.

Submissions and Payment: Guidelines, theme list, and sample articles at website. Query. Accepts hard copy and email queries to editor@athensparent.com. SASE. Response time varies. All rights. Articles and depts/columns, word lengths and payment rates vary. Payment policy varies.

At Home Tennessee 

671 North Ericson Road, Suite 200
Cordova, TN 38018

Editor: Janna Herbison

Description and Interests: From decor, design, fashion, and beauty to cuisine, entertaining, travel, and health, *At Home Tennessee* covers it all. Published monthly, it doesn't accept unsolicited manuscripts. Instead, new writers should send a résumé and clips. Circ: 107,000.
Website: www.athometn.com

Freelance Potential: Receives many queries monthly.

Submissions and Payment: Sample copy available. Query with résumé and 3 writing samples/clips. Accepts hard copy. SASE. Rights vary. Written material, 400–900 words; $50–$200. Kill fee, 50%. Pays on publication.

AT Journeys

P.O. Box 807
Harpers Ferry, WV 25425

Managing Editor: Wendy K. Probst

Description and Interests: This membership magazine of the Appalachian Trail Conservancy focuses on people, places, and events pertaining to the Appalachian Trail, as well as on nature and conservation issues. It is published six times each year. Circ: 38,000.
Website: www.appalachiantrail.org

Freelance Potential: 30% written by nonstaff writers. Publishes 10 freelance submissions yearly; 60% by unpublished writers, 5% by authors who are new to the magazine, 60% by experts. Receives 30 queries, 15 unsolicited mss monthly.

Submissions and Payment: Guidelines and sample articles available at website. Query or send complete ms. Accepts email to editor@appalachiantrail.org (Word or RTF attachments) and hard copy. Responds in 6 months. Rights vary. Articles, 800–1,500 words. Depts/columns, 200–500 words. Written material, payment rates vary. Pays on publication. Provides 10–15 contributor's copies.

Atlanta Parent

2346 Perimeter Park Drive
Atlanta, GA 30341

Editor: Julie Bookman

Description and Interests: This monthly publication for families in the Atlanta area looks for down-to-earth, practical, activity-based pieces on topics important to parents. Articles on education, children's health, and family recreation should include quotes from experts in Atlanta and across the country. Circ: 100,000.
Website: www.atlantaparent.com

Freelance Potential: 40% written by nonstaff writers. Publishes 20 freelance submissions yearly.

Submissions and Payment: Sample articles and guidelines available at website. Send complete ms. Prefers email submissions to editor@atlantaparent.com (Word attachments); will accept hard copy. Response time varies. One-time print electronic rights. Articles, 800–1,200 words. Payment rates vary. Pays on publication. Provides 1 tearsheet.

Austin Woman

1213 West 49th Street
Austin, TX 78756

Executive Editor: Deborah Hamilton-Lynne

Description and Interests: This monthly celebrates the women of the greater Austin, Texas, area with profiles of successful women and articles on health, style, entertainment, food, and all things Austin. AW Media also publishes *ATX Man*, a brother publication to *Austin Woman* that offers the same type of editorial geared toward men. Both are available in print, as a digital ezine, or as a mobile app. Circ: 27,000+.
Website: www.austinwomanmagazine.com

Freelance Potential: The editors report they have opportunities for freelance writers who wish to work on an assignment basis.

Submissions and Payment: Sample copy and editorial calendar at website. To be considered for freelance assignments, send an email to editor@awmediainc.com. Rights and payment rates vary.

Back Porch View

Aguilar Publishing
P.O. Box 8085
Bigfork, MT 59911

Editor: Chris Friar

Description and Interests: This small Montana lifestyle quarterly first published in summer 2011. It focuses on those who live in Flathead Valley and covers topics such as frugal living, self-reliance, rural life, home-based businesses, and families. *Back Porch View* also publishes fiction, memoirs of the region, and humor. Circ: Unavailable.
Website: www.backporchmagazine.com/

Freelance Potential: Open to short stories, essays, illustrations, and music.

Submissions and Payment: Sample copy and guidelines available on the website. Send complete ms. Accepts email to apibooks@yahoo.com. Articles and fiction, 500–1,000 words. No payment. Provided contributor's copies.

Baltimore

100 Lancaster Street, Suite 400
Baltimore, MD 21202

Managing Editor: Max Weiss

Description and Interests: Dating back to 1907, *Baltimore* is America's oldest city magazine. Whether it's an article on which crabhouse has the best hard-shells or a profile on a local prominent person, the magazine features widespread coverage of the city. New writers have the best chance of acceptance with the front-of-the-book sections and departments. Send a query that demonstrates character, dramatic narrative, and factual analysis. *Baltimore* is published monthly. Circ: 53,145.
Website: www.baltimoremagazine.net

Freelance Potential: Unavailable.

Submissions and Payment: Sample articles and guidelines available at website. Query with clips. Prefers email to appropriate editor; will accept hard copy. SASE. Rights vary. Articles, 1,600–2,500 words. Depts/columns, 300–2,000 words. Payment rates and policy vary.

Bask

1400 Newport Centre Drive, Suite 100
Newport Beach, CA 92660

Editor in Chief: Amy Adams

Description and Interests: Targeting affluent adults, ages 35 to 60, in coastal Orange County, Los Angeles, and San Diego, California, *Bask* is a lifestyle magazine. Published quarterly, it features articles that celebrate the finer things in life, such as fashion, food, golf, decor, entertaining, and gala fundraising events, as well as prominent people in the area. Circ: 45,000.
Website: www.baskmagazine.com

Freelance Potential: Open to submissions on home design, wellness, men's style, culture and the arts, people and events, and charitable causes. All pieces should be delivered "with a sense of balance, wit, and timeless style."

Submissions and Payment: Sample articles available at website. For submission information, contact the editors via form at website. Written material, word lengths and payment rates vary.

Bay Nature

1328 6th Street, Suite 2
Berkeley, CA 94710

Editorial Director: Dan Rademacher

Description and Interests: This quarterly publication features articles about the natural history, plants, and wildlife of the San Francisco Bay and its surrounding land with the goal of conserving and restoring the area. Circ: 8,000.
Website: www.baynature.org

Freelance Potential: 90% written by nonstaff writers. Publishes 30–40 freelance submissions yearly; 20% by unpublished writers, 20% by authors who are new to the magazine.

Submissions and Payment: Sample articles and guidelines available at website. Query with résumé or send complete ms. Prefers email queries to dan@baynature.org; accepts hard copy. SASE. Responds in 3 months. First-time print and electronic rights. Articles, 700–3,000 words. Depts/columns, word lengths vary. Written material, payment rate varies. Kill fee, 25%. Pays 30 days after publication. Provides 4 contributor's copies.

Bay State Parent

101 Water Street
Worcester, MA 01604

Editor: Jennifer Lucarelli

Description and Interests: This monthly magazine is read by parents living in eastern and central Massachusetts for its articles on topics ranging from relationships and recreation, to family finance and health issues. Circ: 42,000.
Website: www.baystateparent.com

Freelance Potential: 95% written by nonstaff writers. Publishes 72–144 freelance submissions yearly; 5% by unpublished writers, 30% by authors who are new to the magazine. Receives 10 queries monthly.

Submissions and Payment: Sample copy available at website. Guidelines available. Query. Accepts email queries to editor@baystateparent.com (Word attachments). Responds in 1 month. First Massachusetts and electronic rights. Articles, to 2,000 words; $50–$85. Depts/columns, to 1,500 words; no payment. Kill fee varies. Pays on publication. Provides 1 contributor's copy.

Bend of the River

The Magazine of the Historic Maumee Valley for 40 Years

P.O. Box 859
Maumee, OH 43537

Publisher: R. Lee Raizk

Description and Interests: This magazine chronicles life in the Maumee Valley of northwestern Ohio and southeastern Michigan. Appearing 10 times each year, it presents readers with a variety of history articles, nostalgia, and personal experience pieces about this region of the U.S. Photographs depicting life in the valley are featured prominently. Circ: 6,500.
Website: www.bendoftherivermagazine.com

Freelance Potential: 75% written by nonstaff writers. Publishes 100 freelance submissions yearly; 50% by unpublished writers, 50% by authors who are new to the magazine. Receives 10 queries, 50 unsolicited mss monthly.

Submissions and Payment: Sample copy available. Query or send complete ms. Accepts hard copy. SASE. Responds in 1 month. One-time rights. Articles, 1,500 words; $25–$50. Pays on publication. Provides 1 contributor's copy.

Birmingham Parent

700–C Southgate Drive
Pelham, AL 35124

Editor and Publisher: Carol Muse Evans

Description and Interests: This monthly magazine seeks fresh, well-researched articles on parenting and family topics. It seeks to be an indispensable local resource for its readers. Articles must have a local focus to be considered. Circ: 35,000.
Website: www.birminghamparent.com

Freelance Potential: 60% written by nonstaff writers. Publishes 36 freelance submissions yearly; 2% by unpublished writers, 10% by authors who are new to the magazine, 5% by experts. Receives 50+ queries, 25 unsolicited mss monthly.

Submissions and Payment: Sample copy available at website. Query with résumé, clips, and availability of artwork; or send complete ms. Accepts email submissions to editor@birminghamparent.com (include "Query" in subject line). Responds in 1 month. First North American serial and electronic rights. Articles, 700–1,500 words; payment rates vary. Kill fee, 20%. Pays on publication. Provides 2 contributor's copies.

Bonaire Nights

1751 Richardson Street, Suite 5530
Montreal, Quebec H3K 1G6
Canada

Editor: Jennifer McMorran

Description and Interests: This digest-size magazine is published annually for visitors to Bonaire, an island in the Caribbean. It provides a guide to the island's activities, beaches, entertainment, nightlife, shopping, lodging, and dining. Circ: 80,000.
Website: www.nightspublications.com

Freelance Potential: 90% written by nonstaff writers. Publishes 5–10 freelance submissions yearly; 25% by authors who are new to the magazine, 75% by experts. Receives 5 queries monthly.

Submissions and Payment: Sample copy and guidelines available. Query with clips or writing samples. Accepts email queries to editor@nightspublications.com. Responds in 1–2 months. Exclusive or first Caribbean and North American serial rights. Articles, 250–700 words. Depts/columns, 250–500 words. Written material, $100–$300. Pays on acceptance.

Boston Magazine

300 Massachusetts Avenue
Boston, MA 02115

Editor: John Wolfson

Description and Interests: Expository features, narratives, profiles, and investigative journalism come together with sophisticated style in this monthly magazine to cover the multi-faceted city of Boston. It also publishes articles on dining, entertainment, real estate, and business. Circ: 94,301.
Website: www.bostonmagazine.com

Freelance Potential: 20% written by nonstaff writers. Publishes 120 freelance submissions yearly; 5% by authors who are new to the magazine. Receives 90 queries monthly.

Submissions and Payment: Sample articles and editorial calendar available at website. Query. Accepts email queries to editor@bostonmagazine.com. Responds in 2 weeks. First North American serial rights. Articles, 1,500–3,500 words. Depts/columns, 1,500–1,800 words. Written material, payment rates vary. Pays on publication. Provides 1–2 contributor's copies.

The Boundary Waters Journal

9396 Rocky Ledge Road
Ely, MN 55731

Editor/Publisher: Stu Osthoff

Description and Interests: Helping readers enjoy recreational activities such as hiking, canoeing, fishing, and camping in the Boundary Waters Canoe Area Wilderness is the mission of this quarterly magazine. Stories, not dry reports, are preferred. Circ: 30,000.
Website: www.boundarywatersjournal.com

Freelance Potential: 80% written by nonstaff writers. Publishes 20 freelance submissions yearly; 30% by unpublished writers, 30% by authors who are new to the magazine, 50% by experts. Receives 20 unsolicited mss monthly.

Submissions and Payment: Sample articles and guidelines available at website. Send complete ms. Accepts email to stu@boundarywatersjournal.com (Word attachments). Responds in 1 month. First North American serial rights. Articles and fiction, 2,000–5,000 words; $200–$500. Pays on publication.

Brava

951 Kimball Lane, Suite 104
Verona, WI 53593

Associate Editor: Meagan Parrish

Description and Interests: *Brava* targets Madison-area women of style and substance and delivers to them local information on fashion, home, health, and family trends. It also features profiles of inspiring local women and businesses. Published monthly, it prefers to work with writers living in the Madison region of Wisconsin. Circ: 60,000.
Website: www.bravamagazine.com

Freelance Potential: 10–20% written by nonstaff writers. Publishes 10–20 freelance submissions yearly; 25% by authors new to the magazine, 25% by experts. Receives 10+ unsolicited mss monthly.

Submissions and Payment: Sample copy and guidelines available at website. Query or send complete ms with clips. Accepts email to meagan@bravaenterprises.com. Response time varies. First rights. Articles and depts/columns, word lengths and payment rates vary. Pays on publication. Provides 2 contributor's copies.

Brooklyn Parent

1440 Broadway, Suite 501
New York, NY 10018

Editorial Director: Dawn Roode

Description and Interests: Keeping Brooklyn, New York, parents up to date with area news and happenings, this tabloid appears monthly. *Brooklyn Parent* highlights life in Brooklyn and provides articles on topics such as family finances, health and safety, and education issues. A calendar of events and summer camp guide is published as well. Circ: 400,000.
Website: www.nymetroparents.com

Freelance Potential: 50% written by nonstaff writers. Publishes 300 freelance submissions yearly. Receives 1 query, 3 unsolicited mss each month.

Submissions and Payment: Sample articles available at website. Query or send complete ms with 2 writing samples. Accepts email to droode@davlermedia.com. Responds if interested. First New York area rights. Articles, 800–900 words. Depts/columns, to 600 words. No payment. Provides 2 contributor's copies.

California Northern

P.O. Box 2268
Sacramento, CA 95812

Editor in Chief: Casey Mills

Description and Interests: *California Northern* is dedicated to showcasing the region's cultures, environments, histories, and identities. It provides a rare place for long-form regional journalism, essays, and fiction. Authors from the Northern California region are preferred. It appears twice each year. Circ: 500.
Website: www.calnorthern.net

Freelance Potential: Of the freelance submissions published yearly, most are by authors who are new to the magazine.

Submissions and Payment: Sample copy and guidelines available at website. Query for nonfiction. Send complete ms for fiction. Accepts hard copy and email to submissions@calnorthern.net. SASE. Response time varies. Rights vary. Articles, 2,500–12,000 words. Fiction, word lengths vary. Notes from the Field essays, 500–750 words. Poetry, up to 5 poems. Written material, payment rates vary. Payment policy varies.

California Territorial Quarterly

6848 U Skyway
Paradise, CA 95969

Editors/Publishers: Bill & Penny Anderson

Description and Interests: The editors of *California Territorial Quarterly* seek meticulously researched articles covering all aspects of California history from the early 1800s through the turn of the twentieth century. Submissions should be interesting to a general readership and include photo suggestions. Circ: 3,000.
Website: www.californiahistory.com

Freelance Potential: 90% written by nonstaff writers. Publishes 10–12 freelance submissions yearly; 10% by unpublished writers, 20% by authors who are new to the magazine, 70% by experts. Receives 3–4 queries, 2–3 mss monthly.

Submissions and Payment: Sample articles and guidelines available at website. Send complete ms. Accepts hard copy and email submissions to info@californiahistory.com. Responds in 2–4 weeks. One-time rights. No payment. Provides 25 contributor's copies.

Capital Style

34 South Third Street
Columbus, OH 43215

Editor: Kristy Eckert

Description and Interests: This upscale women's magazine covers life in Central Ohio. It is published six times each year as a print magazine and has a complementary website that is updated daily. It covers beauty and fashion, the home, shopping, entertaining, food and dining, and regional charities and events. Profiles of successful women are also regularly published. Circ: 35,000.
Website: www.capital-style.com

Freelance Potential: Open to pitches on all topics listed above. The editors note that while they give consideration to every pitch, competition is fierce due to the number of submissions received.

Submissions and Payment: Sample articles available at website. Query. Accepts email queries to keckert@capital-style.com. Response time varies. Written material, word lengths vary.

Carolina Gardener

P.O. Box 13070
Ruston, LA 71273

Editor: Karen Alley

Description and Interests: This magazine focuses on planning and planting gardens in North and South Carolina and the southeastern U.S. Published nine times each year, it presents vibrantly illustrated articles about growing flowers, vegetables, and herbs, as well as garden design. Article submissions that include photographs are especially welcome. Circ: 13,000.
Website: www.carolinagardener.com

Freelance Potential: 70% written by nonstaff writers. Publishes 70 freelance submissions yearly; 25% by authors who are new to the magazine. Receives 5–10 queries monthly.

Submissions and Payment: Sample copy available. Query with writing samples. Accepts hard copy and email queries to editor@carolinagardener.com. SASE. Responds in 2 weeks. One-time rights. Articles, 300–1,000 words; $75–$175. Pays on publication.

Carolina Homes & Interiors

P.O. Box 22617
Charleston, SC 29413

Publisher/Editor: Bill Macchio

Description and Interests: This lifestyle magazine puts North and South Carolina real estate and attractions in the spotlight. Its photo-filled issues are published quarterly. Circ: 30,000.
Website: www.carolinahomesandinteriors.com

Freelance Potential: 40% written by nonstaff writers. Publishes 35–40 freelance submissions yearly; 10% by unpublished writers, 20% by authors who are new to the magazine, 10% by experts. Receives 1–2 queries monthly.

Submissions and Payment: Sample copy available at website. Query. Accepts hard copy and email queries to publisher@mediaservices1.com. SASE. Responds in 1 month. Rights vary. Articles, 800–1,200 words. Depts/columns, 350–450 words. Written material, $.15 per word. High-resolution digital images. Pays on publication. Provides 1–2 contributor's copies.

Carolina Parent

5716 Fayetteville Road, Suite 201
Durham, NC 27713

Editor: Crickett Gibbons

Description and Interests: This monthly magazine covers a wide range of well-researched and locally relevant parenting topics. It publishes several annual guides for parents and families and also uses freelancers for its website content. Circ: 44,000.
Website: www.carolinaparent.com

Freelance Potential: 60% written by nonstaff writers. Publishes 150 freelance submissions yearly; 2% by unpublished writers, 5% by authors who are new to the magazine, 20% by experts. Receives 600 queries, 480 unsolicited mss monthly.

Submissions and Payment: Sample copy, guidelines, and editorial calendar available at website. Query with clips. Accepts email to cgibbons@carolinaparent.com (Word attachments) and reprints. Response time varies. One-time print, first, and electronic rights. Articles, 650–1,300 words. Depts/columns, 650–900 words. Written material, payment rates vary. Pays on publication. Provides 1 tearsheet.

Carologue

South Carolina Historical Society
100 Meeting Street
Charleston, SC 29401-2215

Editor: Hope Hornsby

Description and Interests: The South Carolina Historical Society publishes this quarterly magazine for its members and the general public. Issues highlight the organization's collections, as well as articles on little-known episodes in the state's past and profiles of current and historical figures. Circ: 3,000.
Website: www.southcarolinahistoricalsociety.org

Freelance Potential: 30% written by nonstaff writers. Publishes 8–10 freelance submissions yearly. Receives 4 unsolicited mss monthly.

Submissions and Payment: Sample copy available. Guidelines available at website. Send complete ms with artwork or suggestions for artwork. Prefers email to hope.hornsby@schsonline.org (Word attachments); will accept hard copy. Responds in 6–10 weeks. One-time rights. Articles, 1,500–3,000 words. Digital images at 300 dpi. No payment. Provides 10 contributor's copies.

Cary Magazine

301 Cascade Pointe Lane
Cary, NC 27513

Co-Editors: Emily Uhland & Tara Croft

Description and Interests: Fine dining, gardening, golfing, and fitness are among the many lifestyle topics covered in this magazine for residents of North Carolina's Wake County. It is published six times each year. Circ: 25,000.
Website: www.carymagazine.com

Freelance Potential: 75% written by nonstaff writers. Publishes 75 freelance submissions yearly; 25% by authors who are new to the magazine, 40% by experts. Receives 15 queries each month.

Submissions and Payment: Sample articles available at website. Guidelines and editorial calendar available. Query with résumé and writing samples. Accepts email queries via the website. Responds in 1 month. First rights. Articles, to 1,500 words. Depts/columns, to 1,000 words. Written material, $.30 per word. Pays on publication. Provides 1–2 contributor's copies.

Charleston Magazine

P.O. Box 1794
Mt. Pleasant, SC 29465-1794

Editor in Chief: Darcy Shankland

Description and Interests: This glossy monthly highlights life in Charleston from its local arts scene to regional cuisine. All content has a Carolina connection. Circ: 35,000.
Website: www.charlestonmag.com

Freelance Potential: 65% written by nonstaff writers. Publishes 50 freelance submissions yearly; 2% by unpublished writers, 10% by authors who are new to the magazine. Receives 40 queries, 2 unsolicited mss monthly.

Submissions and Payment: Sample articles available at website. Query or send complete ms, with clips. Accepts hard copy or email submissions to dshankland@charlestonmag.com. SASE. Response time varies. First serial rights. Articles, 1,500 words. Depts/columns, 1,200 words. Written material, payment rates vary. Pays 1 month after publication. Provides contributor's copies.

Charlotte Parent

214 West Tremont Avenue, Suite 302
Charlotte, NC 28203

Editor: Eve White

Description and Interests: The joys and challenges of parenthood are the focus of this monthly publication. It provides local resources and guides to area events. Circ: 52,000.
Website: www.charlotteparent.com

Freelance Potential: 50% written by nonstaff writers. Publishes 45 freelance submissions yearly; 15% by unpublished writers, 25% by authors who are new to the magazine. Receives 80–85 queries, 60–65 unsolicited mss monthly.

Submissions and Payment: Sample copy, guidelines, and theme list available at website. Query or send complete ms or reprint with résumé and word count. Accepts email to editorial@charlotteparent.com (Word attachments). Response time varies. One-time print and electronic rights. Articles, 500–1,200 words. Depts/columns, word lengths vary. Assigned articles, \$45–\$125; reprints, \$15–\$35. Pays on publication. Provides tearsheets.

Charlotte Viewpoint

P.O. Box 31113
Charlotte, NC 28231-1113

Editor in Chief: Christina Ritchie Rogers

Description and Interests: Commentary, essays, fiction, poetry, and articles about Charlotte's city life, arts, and culture are presented in this web-based journal of creative expression. Written for an informed and literate audience, it was created to showcase the talent of the city's citizens and spark conversation about the growth and future of the city. Hits per month: Unavailable.
Website: www.charlotteviewpoint.org

Freelance Potential: Opportunities exist here for writing "that explores our creative life as citizens in the broadest terms." The editors are not interested in political commentary.

Submissions and Payment: Guidelines available at website. Send complete ms. Accepts email via the website (Word attachments). Responds in 10 days. Author retains rights. Written material, to 1,500 words; payment rates vary. Payment policy varies.

Chesapeake Bay Magazine

1819 Bay Ridge Avenue
Annapolis, MD 21403

Managing Editor: Ann Levelle

Description and Interests: This monthly focuses on boating on the Chesapeake Bay and its tributaries. It covers powerboating, sailing, fishing, and the people, places, history, and natural history of the region. Circ: 40,000.
Website: www.chesapeakeboating.net

Freelance Potential: 60% written by nonstaff writers. Publishes 150 freelance submissions yearly; 5% by unpublished writers, 10% by authors who are new to the magazine, 85% by experts. Receives 15 queries monthly.

Submissions and Payment: Sample articles available at website. Query. Prefers email queries to editor@chesapeakeboating.net; will accept hard copy. SASE. Responds in 6 weeks. First rights. Articles, 900–2,400 words; \$200–\$1,000. Depts/columns, word lengths vary; \$75–\$400. Pays on acceptance. Provides 3 contributor's copies.

Chesapeake Family

929 West Street, Suite 210
Annapolis, MD 21401

Editor: Betsey Stein

Description and Interests: If it's of interest to parents living in Maryland's Chesapeake Bay area, it's likely to be covered in this monthly magazine. Articles that focus on education, health issues, local travel and fun, and include local sources, are always of interest. Circ: 40,000.
Website: www.chesapeakefamily.com

Freelance Potential: 80% written by nonstaff writers. Publishes 40 freelance submissions yearly; 10% by unpublished writers, 40% by new authors, 20% by experts. Receives 40 unsolicited mss monthly.

Submissions and Payment: Sample copy, guidelines, and editorial calendar available at website. Query with author credits and clips or send complete ms. Prefers email to editor@chesapeakefamily.com (Word attachments). Response time varies. One-time print rights and electronic rights. Articles, 1,000 words; \$75–\$200. Depts/columns, 750 words; \$50. Reprints, \$35. Kill fee, \$25. Payment policy varies.

Chicago Magazine

435 North Michigan Avenue, Suite 1100
Chicago, IL 60611

Editor: Esther Kang

Description and Interests: The Windy City's affluent residents and visitors read this monthly lifestyle magazine for its up-to-date coverage of local people, places, and events. Articles on the city's political, cultural, and social history are also featured in this publication. Circ: 155,000.
Website: www.chicagomag.com

Freelance Potential: 50% written by nonstaff writers. Publishes 150 freelance submissions yearly; 1% by unpublished writers, 10% by authors who are new to the magazine. Receives 50 queries monthly.

Submissions and Payment: Sample copy and guidelines available. Query with clips or writing samples. Accepts email to appropriate editor (see website). Responds if interested. All rights. Articles and depts/columns, word lengths and payment rates vary. Pays on publication. Provides 1 contributor's copy.

Chicago Reader

350 North Orleans Street
Chicago, IL 60654

Editor: Mara Shalhoup

Description and Interests: Commentary and criticism can be found in this weekly regional news magazine covering Chicago's urban scene. It is known for its in-depth reporting on the city's politics and culture. Circ: 90,000.
Website: www.chicagoreader.com

Freelance Potential: 50% written by nonstaff writers. Publishes 25 freelance submissions yearly; 50% by authors who are new to the magazine. Receives dozens of queries and unsolicited mss monthly.

Submissions and Payment: Sample articles and guidelines available at website. Query or send complete ms. Accepts email to mail@chicagoreader.com (no attachments) and simultaneous submissions if identified. Response time varies. First serial and nonexclusive web rights. Short features, 250–1,200 words. Features, 2,500+ words. Reviews, 600–1,200 words. Payment rate varies. Kill fee, 25%. Pays on publication. Provides 1+ contributor's copies.

Cincinnati

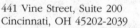

441 Vine Street, Suite 200
Cincinnati, OH 45202-2039

Editor: Jay Stowe

Description and Interests: *Cincinnati Magazine* blends humor, reviews, narratives, personal essays, and in-depth reports about life in the city. Topics include food, travel, shopping, history, neighborhoods, and schools. Circ: 38,000.
Website: www.cincinnatimagazine.com

Freelance Potential: Publishes 25 unsolicited mss each year.

Submissions and Payment: Sample articles available at website. Send SASE for writers' guidelines. Query with clips. Accepts hard copy and email to jstowe@cincinnatimagazine.com. SASE. All rights. Articles, 2,500–3,500 words; \$500–\$1,000. Depts/columns, 1,000–1,500 words; \$200–\$400. Pays on publication.

Cincinnati Family Magazine

10945 Reed Hartman Highway, Suite 221
Cincinnati, OH 45242

Editor: Sherry Hang

Description and Interests: Parents in Cincinnati read this monthly magazine for local news and regional event coverage. Articles on parenting and family issues are also regularly featured. Circ: 30,000.
Website: www.cincinnatifamilymagazine.com

Freelance Potential: 25% written by nonstaff writers. Publishes 12–24 freelance submissions yearly; 25% by new authors. Receives 8–12 queries, 4–8 unsolicited mss monthly.

Submissions and Payment: Guidelines and editorial calendar available. Sample copy available on website. Query or send complete ms. Accepts hard copy and email to sherryh@daycommail. com. SASE. Response time varies. First rights, plus electronic rights for 60 days. Articles, word lengths vary; $75–$125. Depts/columns, word lengths and payment rates vary. Pays 30 days after publication.

City & Shore Magazine

500 East Broward Boulevard, 9th Floor
Fort Lauderdale, FL 33394

Editor: Mark Gauert

Description and Interests: People who enjoy the good life in South Florida read *City & Shore Magazine*. Published six times each year, it covers upscale lifestyle topics, including house and home, cars, entertainment, food, fashion, and dining. Travel pieces and profiles offer the best opportunities for new writers. Circ: 46,000.
Website: www.cityandshore.com

Freelance Potential: 85% written by nonstaff writers. Publishes 6–10 freelance submissions yearly; 10% by authors who are new to the magazine. Receives 30 queries monthly.

Submissions and Payment: Sample copy available at website. Query. Accepts hard copy. Responds in 2 weeks. First-time rights. Articles, word lengths vary. Depts/columns, 175–250 words. Written material, payment rates vary. Kill fee, 50%. Pays on publication. Provides 1 contributor's copy.

City Parent

447 Speers Road, Suite 4
Oakville, Ontario L6K 3S4
Canada

Editor in Chief: Jane Muller

Description and Interests: From child development to nutrition, and teen issues to summer camps, *City Parent* articles reflect events and resources in the greater Toronto area. It is published monthly. Circ: 70,000.
Website: www.cityparent.com

Freelance Potential: 60% written by nonstaff writers. Publishes 24–30 freelance submissions yearly; 10% by authors who are new to the magazine. Receives 300+ unsolicited mss monthly.

Submissions and Payment: Sample copy at website. Editorial calendar available. Send complete ms. Accepts email to cityparent@haltonsearch.com. Availability of artwork improves chance of acceptance. Responds if interested. First rights. Articles, 500–1,000 words. Depts/columns, word lengths vary. Color prints or transparencies. Written material, $50–$100. Pays on publication. Provides 1 contributor's copy.

Coastal Family 

P.O. Box 15847
Savannah, GA 31416

Editor/Publisher: Louise D. Phelps

Description and Interests: Education, health and fitness, travel, and recreation are covered in this monthly magazine for coastal Georgia and the South Carolina Lowcountry. It is not accepting submissions at this time. Circ: 18,000.
Website: www.coastalfamily.com

Freelance Potential: 10% written by nonstaff writers. Publishes 5–10 freelance submissions yearly; 10% by authors who are new to the magazine. Receives 8–12 queries monthly.

Submissions and Payment: Guidelines available. Sample articles and editorial calendar available on website. Not accepting freelance submissions at this time. Check website for updates to this policy.

ColoradoBiz

6160 South Syracuse Way, Suite 300
Greenwood Village, CO 80111

Editor: Mike Cote

Description and Interests: This monthly, which appears in print and as an ezine, covers the people and issues that dominate the business scene in Colorado. The best way to break in is through the "State of the State" news section. Circ: 21,000+, print; 27,500, online.
Website: www.cobizmag.com

Freelance Potential: 70% written by nonstaff writers. Publishes 100–120 freelance submissions yearly; 10% by authors who are new to the magazine, 20% by experts. Receives 3–6 queries monthly.

Submissions and Payment: Sample articles available at website. Guidelines available. Query with clips. Accepts email queries to mcote@cobizmag.com (Word attachments). Response time varies. First North American serial rights. Articles, 500–3,000 words. Depts/columns, 250–650 words. Written material, $.40 per word. Pays on publication.

Columbus Parent

34 South 3rd Street
Columbus, OH 43215

Editor: Jane Hawes

Description and Interests: Timely and practical information about raising children in the Columbus, Ohio, area is the focus of this monthly magazine. Topics include education, health, child development, and local entertainment and recreation. All work is assigned to local writers. Circ: 47,000.
Website: www.columbusparent.com

Freelance Potential: 25% written by nonstaff writers. Publishes 35 freelance submissions yearly; 10% by authors who are new to the magazine. Receives 1,000 queries monthly.

Submissions and Payment: Local writers only. Sample articles available at website. All work is assigned. To be considered for assignments, submit résumé and 3 writing samples. Accepts hard copy. No unsolicited manuscripts. Response time varies. Rights vary. Articles, 250–700 words. Depts/columns and fiction, 300 words. Written material, payment rates vary. Pays on publication.

CommonCall

P.O. Box 259019
Plano, TX 75025-9019

Editor: Marv Knox

Description and Interests: Focusing on inspiring stories about people living out their faith, *CommonCall* is a new monthly magazine for Christians living in Texas. It also includes informative and thought-provoking articles about missions, evangelism, leadership, best practices, and family life. The first issue was published in January 2013. Circ: Unavailable.
Website: www.baptiststandard.com

Freelance Potential: Receives many freelance submissions monthly.

Submissions and Payment: Sample articles available at website. Query. Accepts email to marvknox@baptiststandard.com. Response time varies. Written material, word lengths vary. Rights vary. Payment rates and policies vary.

Community Observer

2390 Winewood
Ann Arbor, MI 48104

Editor: John Hilton

Description and Interests: *Community Observer* takes a close look at the Michigan towns of Chelsea, Dexter, Manchester, and Saline. Quarterly issues cover local civic issues, arts, entertainment, and personalities. Compelling anecdotes are also featured. Circ: 21,000.
Website: www.arborweb.com

Freelance Potential: 50% written by nonstaff writers. Publishes 100 freelance submissions yearly; 10% by unpublished writers, 25% by authors who are new to the magazine.

Submissions and Payment: Sample copy available. Prefers query; will accept complete ms. Accepts email submissions to editor@arborweb.com. Response time varies. First North American serial rights. Articles, 1,000– 3,500 words; $300–$500. Depts/columns, word lengths and payment rates vary. Kill fee varies. Pays on publication. Provides 2 contributor's copies.

Connecticut Magazine

40 Sargent Drive
New Haven, CT 06511

Editor: Charles Monagan

Description and Interests: Showcasing the best Connecticut has to offer, this monthly magazine features articles on the state's arts and entertainment, travel, and restaurants. Politics and business are also covered. Circ: 90,000.
Website: www.connecticutmag.com

Freelance Potential: 60% written by nonstaff writers. Publishes 100 freelance submissions yearly; 2% by unpublished writers, 5% by authors new to the magazine. Receives 40 queries monthly.

Submissions and Payment: Sample articles and guidelines available at website. Query with writing samples. Accepts hard copy and email to cmonagan@connecticutmag.com. SASE. Responds in 1–2 months. Exclusive rights for 90 days. Articles, 3,000+ words. Depts/columns, to 1,800 words. Payment rates vary. Kill fee varies, maximum 20%. Pays on publication. Provides 1 contributor's copy.

Connecticut Parent

420 East Main Street, Suite 18
Branford, CT 06405

Associate Publisher: Joe Zibell

Description and Interests: This monthly magazine offers articles on topics of interest to parents. It also spotlights local resources for education, entertainment, and recreation. All material must have a Connecticut tie-in. Circ: 60,000.
Website: www.ctparent.com

Freelance Potential: 55% written by nonstaff writers. Publishes 12–24 freelance submissions yearly; 10% by unpublished writers, 10% by authors who are new to the magazine, 25% by experts. Receives 10–20 unsolicited mss monthly.

Submissions and Payment: Sample copy available at website. Send complete ms. Accepts email submissions to editorial@ctparent.com (Word attachments). Response time varies. Exclusive Connecticut rights. Written material, 1,000–1,500 words; $40. B/W or color JPEG images. Pays on publication. Provides 1 tearsheet.

Cooperative Living

P.O. Box 2340
Glen Allen, VA 23058-2340

Editor: Bill Sherrod

Description and Interests: This magazine provides customers of Virginia, Maryland, and Delaware, electric cooperatives with tips on electrical safety and energy conservation, as well as features on local personalities and area attractions. It appears 10 times each year. Circ: 490,000.
Website: www.co-opliving.com

Freelance Potential: 80% written by nonstaff writers. Publishes 30 freelance submissions yearly; 1% by unpublished writers, 2% by authors who are new to the magazine, 10% by experts. Receives 2 unsolicited mss monthly.

Submissions and Payment: Sample copy and editorial calendar available at website. Query or send complete ms. Accepts disk submissions and email queries to bsherrod@odec.com. SASE. Responds in 3 months. Rights vary. Articles, 500–1,500 words; $200. Depts/columns, word lengths and payment rates vary. Pays on publication. Provides 10 contributor's copies.

The Cooperator

102 Madison Avenue, 5th Floor
New York, NY 10016

Editor: Debra A. Estock

Description and Interests: Appearing monthly in tabloid format, *The Cooperator* reports on the co-op and condominium markets in New York City and New Jersey. It seeks experienced business writers to provide up-to-date information on news and trends. Circ: 50,000.
Website: www.cooperator.com

Freelance Potential: 85% written by nonstaff writers. Publishes 120+ freelance submissions yearly; 10% by unpublished writers, 15% by authors who are new to the magazine, 25% by experts. Receives 2 queries monthly.

Submissions and Payment: Sample articles available at website. Query with outline. Accepts hard copy and email queries to editorial@cooperator.com. SASE. Responds in 2 weeks. All rights. Articles, 1,500–1,700 words; $400. Depts/columns, to 800 words; payment rates vary. Pays on publication. Provides 5 contributor's copies.

Country Line Magazine

9508 Chisholm Trail
Austin, TX 78748

Editor: T. J. Greaney

Description and Interests: This monthly presents the sights, sounds, and flavors of Texas, from the prairie dog lands in the Panhandle to the Padre Island seashore. All material is based on Christian values. Circ: 25,000.
Website: www.countrylinemagazine.com

Freelance Potential: 95% written by nonstaff writers. Publishes 50 freelance submissions yearly; 25% by unpublished writers, 20% by authors who are new to the magazine. Receives 8–10 queries monthly.

Submissions and Payment: Sample copy available at website. Query. Accepts email queries to tj@countrylinemagazine.com (no attachments). Responds in 1 month. First North American serial rights. Articles, 750–1,500 words; $50–$75. B/W and color prints, payment rates vary. Pays on publication. Provides 3 contributor's copies.

Curaçao Nights

1751 Richardson Street, Suite 5530
Montreal, Quebec H3K 1G6
Canada

Editor: Jennifer McMorran

Description and Interests: Curaçao's lifestyle, particularly its nightlife, is celebrated in this photo-filled publication designed for visitors to the island nation. Articles on travel, shopping, dining, and entertainment are offered in annual issues. Circ: 165,000.
Website: www.nightspublications.com

Freelance Potential: 90% written by nonstaff writers. Publishes 15 freelance submissions yearly; 25% by authors who are new to the magazine, 75% by experts. Receives 5 queries monthly.

Submissions and Payment: Sample copy available. Query with clips or writing samples. Accepts email queries to editor@nightspublications.com. Responds in 1–2 months. Exclusive or first Caribbean and North American rights. Articles, 250–700 words; $100–$300. Depts/columns, 250–500 words; payment rates vary. Pays on acceptance.

DAC News Magazine

241 Madison Avenue
Detroit, MI 48226

Editor and Publisher: Kenneth Voyles

Description and Interests: *DAC News Magazine* is written for and about members of the Detroit Athletic Club. It regularly features articles about the city's businesses, as well as its history and culture, sporting events, dining establishments, and entertainment scene. Monthly issues focus on topics including travel and leisure, education and technology, and automobiles. Circ: 4,000.
Website: www.thedac.com

Freelance Potential: 20% written by nonstaff writers. Publishes 8–10 freelance submissions yearly.

Submissions and Payment: Editorial calendar available at website. Query. Accepts hard copy. SASE. Response time varies. First rights. Articles and depts/columns, word lengths and payment rates vary. Payment policy varies.

Delaware Beach Life

P.O. Box 417
Rehoboth Beach, DE 19971

Editor: Terry Plowman

Description and Interests: Appearing eight times each year, this photo-filled magazine celebrates the history, culture, lifestyle, and people of coastal Delaware. It publishes in-depth articles on topics particular to the region, as well as profiles of local personalities. Circ: 16,000.
Website: www.delawarebeachlife.com

Freelance Potential: 95% written by nonstaff writers. Publishes 75 freelance submissions yearly; 5% by authors who are new to the magazine. Receives 5 queries monthly.

Submissions and Payment: Sample copy available at website. Guidelines available. Query. Accepts email queries to info@delawarebeachlife.com. Responds in 1 month. First North American serial rights. Articles, 1,500–3,000 words; $500–$750. Fiction, to 1,500 words; $200–$300. Depts/columns, 1,000–1,200 words; $150–$250. Kill fee, 50%. Pays on publication. Provides 2 contributor's copies.

Design NJ

83 South Street
Freehold, NJ 07728

Editor: Ren Miller

Description and Interests: Appearing seven times each year, this magazine focuses on the interior and landscape design and architecture of New Jersey homes. It includes renovation and design ideas, as well as landscaping ideas. Circ: 25,000.
Website: www.designnewjersey.com

Freelance Potential: 25% written by nonstaff writers. Publishes 30 freelance submissions yearly; 5% by authors who are new to the magazine. Receives 5 queries monthly.

Submissions and Payment: Guidelines and editorial calendar available at website. Sample articles available at website. Query with artwork. Prefers hard copy; accepts email queries to rmiller@designnewjersey.com. SASE. Responds in 1 month. First rights. Written material, word lengths vary. Professional digital images at 300 dpi. All material, payment rates vary. Payment policy varies. Provides up to 5 contributor's copies.

Detroit News

615 West Lafayette Boulevard
Detroit, MI 48226

Op-Ed Editor: James Dickson

Description and Interests: State and local news relevant to readers in southeastern Michigan is the focus of this daily publication. Also offered are feature articles on topics ranging from business to education, and technology to entertainment, all with a regional angle. Opinion pieces and commentary on local issues are considered. Circ: 300,000.
Website: www.detnews.com/editorial

Freelance Potential: 99% written by nonstaff writers. Publishes 340 freelance submissions yearly; 15% by authors who are new to the magazine, 85% by experts.

Submissions and Payment: Sample copy available at website. Send complete ms. Accepts hard copy, email submissions to letters@detnews.com or comment@detnews.com. Accepts simultaneous submissions if identified. Responds in 1–2 weeks. Exclusive Michigan rights. Letters, 250–300 words. Commentaries, 600–750 words; $75. Pays on publication. Provides 1 contributor's copy.

Diablo Magazine

2520 Camino Diablo
Walnut Creek, CA 94597

Editor: Susan Dowdney Safipour

Description and Interests: This San Francisco East Bay regional prefers writers familiar with the areas of Contra Costa and southern Alameda counties, Oakland, and Berkeley. The monthly covers lifestyle, food, design, travel, education, parenting, and regional politics. It also includes profiles of local personalities. Circ: 43,500.
Website: www.diablomag.com

Freelance Potential: 50% written by nonstaff writers. Publishes 60 freelance submissions yearly.

Submissions and Payment: Sample copy available. Query with cover letter and writing samples. Accepts email queries to d-mail@maildiablo.com and hard copy. SASE. Response time varies. Articles, 2,000 words. Depts/columns, 75–300 words. First rights. Payment rates vary. Pays on publication.

Discover Maine Magazine

10 Exchange Street, Suite 208
Portland, ME 04101

Editor/Publisher: Jim Burch

Description and Interests: Appearing in eight themed issues a year, each focusing on a different region, *Discover Maine Magazine* offers a fond look at the state's past. From sports to shipbuilding, business tycoons to conservationists, this magazine covers the events and people, both well- and little-known, that made their mark on Maine. Circ: 12,000.
Website: www.discovermainemagazine.com

Freelance Potential: 100% written by nonstaff writers. Publishes 180 freelance submissions yearly; 75% by unpublished writers, 10% by authors who are new to the magazine.

Submissions and Payment: Sample copy available at website. Query. Accepts hard copy and submissions via website. SASE. Responds in 2 weeks. Rights vary. Articles, 1,000+ words; $25.

Downtown Phoenix Journal

Urban Affair
365 North 4th Avenue
Phoenix, AZ 85003

Publisher: Catrina Kahler

Description and Interests: The urban center and offerings of Phoenix are the subject of this regional, appearing quarterly in print and as a blog-centered website. All content has a "hyper local" focus, offering community news and information, profiles of Phoenix's movers and shakers, and coverage of everything and anything happening downtown. Circ: 20,000.
Website: www.downtownphoenixjournal.com

Freelance Potential: Open to submissions from experienced news or feature writers who are extremely familiar with Phoenix.

Submissions and Payment: Sample articles available at website. Query or send complete ms. Accepts email queries to editor@dphxj.com. Written material, word lengths vary. Rights and payment, unknown.

Drink Me Magazine

2017 Mission Street, Second Floor
San Francisco, CA 94110

Editor: Daniel Yaffe

Description and Interests: Appearing six times each year and distributed throughout the San Francisco region, this is a pocket-sized, lifestyle magazine created for the alcohol enthusiast. It publishes articles that celebrate the art and culture of alcohol. Circ: 35,000.
Website: www.drinkmemag.com

Freelance Potential: 40% written by nonstaff writers. Publishes 15 freelance submissions yearly; 15% by unpublished writers, 50% by authors who are new to the magazine. Receives 20 queries and unsolicited mss monthly.

Submissions and Payment: Sample copy available at website. Query or send complete ms. Accepts email submissions to info@drinkmemag.com. Response time varies. First and electronic rights. Written material, word lengths and payment rates vary. Pays on publication. Provides 2 contributor's copies.

East Texas Historical Journal

P.O. Box 6223 SFA Station
Nacogdoches, TX 75962-6223

Editor: M. Scott Sosebee

Description and Interests: The Lone Star State, especially the East Texas region, is the focus of this journal published by the East Texas Historical Association. Appearing twice yearly, issues offer articles, often in the form of letters and diaries, as well as book reviews. Circ: 500–600.
Website: www.easttexashistorical.org

Freelance Potential: 90% written by nonstaff writers. Publishes 10–12 freelance submissions yearly; 50% by unpublished writers, 50% by authors who are new to the magazine. Receives 3 queries monthly.

Submissions and Payment: Sample copy available. Send complete ms. Requires hard copy and email submission (Word attachment) to sosebeem@sfasu.edu (Word attachments). SASE. Responds in 1 week. All rights. Articles, to 25 typed pages. No payment. Provides 1 contributor's copy.

El Paso Magazine 

416 North Stanton, Suite 300
El Paso, TX 79901

Publisher: Luigi Bozzo

Description and Interests: El Paso's cosmopolitan side is highlighted in this online magazine, featuring in-depth articles, personality profiles, and reviews. Coverage of local businesses and community organizations also is provided. *El Paso* is updated regularly. Hits per month: Unavailable.
Website: www.elpasomagazine.com

Freelance Potential: 15% written by nonstaff writers. Publishes 60 freelance submissions yearly; 20% by new authors, 5% by experts. Receives 10 queries monthly.

Submissions and Payment: Query with sample paragraphs and/or specific, angled story idea. Accepts email queries to luigi@fourbnetworks.com (Word attachments). Responds in 1 month. Rights vary. Articles and depts/columns, word lengths vary; $.20 per word. Digital images, $150. Kill fee, 50%. Pays on publication.

Emerald Coast Magazine

1932 Miccosukee Road
Tallahassee, FL 32308

Editor: Zandra Wolfgram

Description and Interests: The best of Florida's Emerald Coast is given the spotlight in this magazine, published six times each year. Personality profiles are combined with news and articles on local entertainment and culture. Circ: 23,000.
Website: www.emeraldcoastmagazine.com

Freelance Potential: 30% written by nonstaff writers. Publishes 10 freelance submissions yearly; 10% by unpublished writers, 20% by authors who are new to the magazine, 5% by experts. Receives 4 queries, 1 unsolicited ms monthly.

Submissions and Payment: Sample copy available at website. Guidelines available. Query or send complete ms. Accepts submissions via website. Responds if interested. One-time rights. Articles, 1,500–3,000 words; $100–$250. Depts/columns, 500–1,200 words; $100–$150. Pays on publication.

Emerge

753 Main Street, #3
Danville, VA 24540

Content Editor: Selena Lipscomb

Description and Interests: *Emerge* is a quarterly publication serving as the voice of the African American community in Danville, Virginia, and surrounding regions. Its mission is to build community, effect change, and include "views from across the social spectrum." Regular editorial content includes the latest in the arts, entertainment, business, and health. Circ: Unavailable.
Website: http://emergeva.com

Freelance Potential: Receives numerous submissions monthly.

Submissions and Payment: Sample copy available. Query or send complete ms. Accepts email to infor@emergeva.com. Response time varies. Articles, word lengths vary. Rights and payment vary.

Empire State Report

P.O. Box 9001
Mount Vernon, NY 10552-9001

Publisher: Stephen Acunto

Description and Interests: New York State politics, public policy, and governance are covered in *Empire State Report*. It appears monthly and is read by state, county, and town officials, as well as politicians and business leaders. It looks for objective writing by people who understand state government. Circ: 7,500.
Website: www.empirestatereport.com

Freelance Potential: 80% written by nonstaff writers. Publishes 24 freelance submissions yearly. Receives many queries monthly.

Submissions and Payment: Sample copy available. Guidelines and editorial calendar available. Query with list of interests. Accepts faxes to 914-966-3264. Responds in 2 months. First serial rights. Articles, 1,000–3,000 words. Depts/columns, 700–1,000 words. Written material, payment rates vary. Pays within 2 months of publication. Provides 25 contributor's copies.

Evansville Business

223 NW Second Street, Suite 200
Evansville, IN 47708

Editor: Kristen Tucker

Description and Interests: Profiles of successful businesspeople, as well as local industry news and trends, appear in this publication. It zeroes in on the Evansville, Indiana, business community six times each year. Circ: 13,000.
Website: www.evansvilleliving.com/business

Freelance Potential: 50% written by nonstaff writers. Publishes 40–50 freelance submissions yearly; 50% by authors who are new to the magazine. Receives 10-12 queries monthly.

Submissions and Payment: Sample articles available at website. Query with résumé and clips. Accepts hard copy and email queries to ktucker@evansvilleliving.com (Word attachments). SASE. Responds in 1 month. All rights. Articles, 500–5,000 words. Depts/columns, 800–1,200 words. Articles and depts/columns, $125–$500. Kill fee varies. Pays after publication. Provides 2 contributor's copies.

Evansville Living

223 NW Second Street, Suite 200
Evansville, IN 47708

Editor: Kristen Tucker

Description and Interests: Everything that appears in *Evansville Living* has a southern Indiana angle. This full-color lifestyle magazine appears six times each year. Circ: 13,000.
Website: www.evansvilleliving.com

Freelance Potential: 35% written by nonstaff writers. Publishes 50 freelance submissions yearly; 5% by unpublished writers, 10% by authors who are new to the magazine, 5% by experts. Receives 30 queries monthly.

Submissions and Payment: Sample articles available at website. Query with résumé and clips. Accepts hard copy and email queries to ktucker@evansvilleliving.com (Word attachments). SASE. Responds in 1 month. All rights. Articles, 500–5,000 words. Depts/columns, 800–1,200 words. Articles and depts/columns, $125–$500. Kill fee varies. Pays after publication. Provides 2 contributor's copies.

Evince 

753 Main Street, #3
Danville, VA 24541

Editor: Joyce Wilburn

Description and Interests: *Evince* is a monthly news magazine covering the arts, entertainment, education, economic development, and lifestyle in the Danville, Virginia area. It issues include informational articles, profiles, and personal experience pieces. Circ: Unavailable.
Website: www.evincemagazine.com

Freelance Potential: Receives many freelance submissions monthly.

Submissions and Payment: Sample copy available at website. Query. Accepts email to info@evincemagazine.com. Response time varies. Written material, word lengths vary. Rights vary. Payment rates and policies vary.

Fairfield County Business Journal

3 Gannett Drive
White Plains, NY 10604-3407

Managing Editor: Bob Rozycki

Description and Interests: People who live and work in Fairfield County, Connecticut, read this magazine for news about local businesses and industry. This weekly also offers advice and information about marketing, personnel, and management issues. Circ: 18,000.
Website: www.westfaironline.com

Freelance Potential: 10% written by nonstaff writers. Publishes 300 freelance submissions yearly; 60% by unpublished writers, 5% by authors who are new to the magazine, 35% by experts. Receives 200 queries monthly.

Submissions and Payment: Sample copy and guidelines available. Query. Accepts email queries to jgolden@westfairinc.com. Responds in 3–5 days. Rights vary. Articles, word lengths and payment rates vary. Depts/columns, 700 words; no payment. Pays on publication.

Fairfield Living

205 Main Street
Westport, CT 06880

Editor: Diane Sembrot

Description and Interests: A companion magazine to other at-home publications in Fairfield County, such as *Greenwich, Stamford,* and *Westport, Fairfield Living* debuted in 2011. The magazines cover subjects of interest to those living on the Gold Coast of Connecticut, including dining, homes and gardens, businesses, style, healthy living, entertainment, and people. Circ: 6,500.
Website: www.mofflymedia.com

Freelance Potential: Receives numerous submissions monthly.

Submissions and Payment: Sample copy available. Query. Accepts email to DianeS@mofflymedia.com. Response time varies. Articles and dept/columns, word lengths vary. Rights and payment vary.

Families on the Go

Life Media
P.O. Box 55445
St. Petersburg, FL 33732

Founder/Publisher: Barbara Doyle

Description and Interests: Appealing to busy Tampa Bay area families who want practical information, *Families on the Go* offers real-life advice on topics, such as education, health, parenting, and relationships. It appears in both print and electronic form, with updates six times each year. Circ: 120,000.
Website: www.familiesonthego.org

Freelance Potential: 80% written by nonstaff writers. Publishes 50 freelance submissions yearly; 25% by unpublished writers.

Submissions and Payment: Sample copy and guidelines available at website. Query or send complete ms. Accepts email submissions to editor@familiesonthego.org (Word attachments). Responds only if interested. Exclusive regional rights. Articles, 350–750 words. Depts/columns, word lengths vary. Written material, payment rates vary. Pays on publication. Provides 2 contributor's copies.

5280

The Denver Magazine

1515 Wazee Street, Suite 400
Denver, CO 80202

Editor and Publisher: Daniel Brogan

Description and Interests: Targeting a savvy and sophisticated readership, *5280* offers an inside view of what's happening in Colorado's capital, with a focus on culture, architecture, restaurants, fashion, and entertainment. It appears monthly. Circ: 85,000.
Website: www.5280.com

Freelance Potential: 65% written by nonstaff writers. Publishes 80 freelance submissions yearly; 5% by unpublished writers, 30% by authors who are new to the magazine. Receives 50 queries monthly.

Submissions and Payment: Sample copy and guidelines available at website. Query with outline and source list. Accepts email queries through the website. Response time varies. First North American serial rights. Articles, to 6,000 words. Depts/columns, 800–1,200 words. Payment rates vary. Pays 40 days after publication. Provides 1 contributor's copy.

Fish Alaska

The Magazine of Fishing the Greatland

P.O. Box 113403
Anchorage, AK 99511

Editor: Troy Letherman

Description and Interests: Read by professional and recreational fishermen alike, this magazine seeks to provide accurate, timely, and in-depth analysis of Alaska's many fishing opportunities. It appears 10 times each year. Circ: 35,000.
Website: www.fishalaskamagazine.com

Freelance Potential: 75% written by nonstaff writers. Publishes 100 freelance submissions yearly; 10% by unpublished writers, 20% by authors who are new to the magazine, 70% by experts. Receives 10 queries monthly.

Submissions and Payment: Sample articles available at website. Query. Accepts email to tletherman@fishalaskamagazine.com. Responds in 1 month. First and electronic rights. Articles, 2,500 words; $200–$500. Depts/columns, 1,000 words; payment rates vary. Pays on publication. Provides 2 contributor's copies.

Fitness Plus Magazine

4474 East 5th Street
Tucson, AZ 85711

Editor: Brenda Lee Kozuch

Description and Interests: Aimed specifically at active residents of Arizona, this specialty publication focuses on the health and well-being of its readers. Monthly issues offer informative articles on nutrition and diet, fitness and exercise, product reviews, regional wellness events, and travel. Circ: 100,000.
Website: www.fitplusmag.com

Freelance Potential: 90% written by nonstaff writers. Publishes 25 freelance submissions yearly; 25% by unpublished writers, 10% by authors who are new to the magazine. Receives 10 queries monthly.

Submissions and Payment: Sample articles available at website. Guidelines available. Query. Accepts email queries via website to editor@fitplusmag.com. Response time varies. First North American serial rights. Articles, word lengths vary; $.10 per word. Pays on the 15th of the month of publication.

FLW Outdoors

30 Gamble Lane
Benton, KY 42054

Editor: Colin Moore

Description and Interests: Catering to the serious angler, *FLW Outdoors* fills its eight issues with cutting-edge tips and techniques, destination features, tournaments, and new product reviews. This tournament organization's publication emphasizes entertaining and educational pieces that will help its readers catch more and bigger fish. Circ: 100,000.
Website: www.flwoutdoors.com

Freelance Potential: 50% written by nonstaff writers. Publishes 100 freelance submissions yearly; 10% by authors who are new to the magazine. Receives 25 queries monthly.

Submissions and Payment: Sample articles available at website. Guidelines and editorial calendar available. Query. Accepts email queries to cmoore@flwoutdoors.com. Responds in 1 week. First North American serial rights. Articles, 200 words; $500. Depts/columns, word lengths and payment rates vary. Pays on acceptance.

Ft. Myers Magazine

15880 Summerlin Road, Suite 189
Ft. Myers, FL 33908

Editorial Director: Pat Simms-Elias

Description and Interests: This magazine celebrates the arts and living in southwest Florida. Published six times each year, it is targeted to the creative, active residents of the area and their guests and offers lifestyle and leisure features. Circ: 20,000.
Website: www.ftmyersmagazine.com

Freelance Potential: 90% written by nonstaff writers. Publishes 10–15 freelance submissions yearly; 25% by unpublished writers, 10% by authors who are new to the magazine, 5% by experts. Receives 10 unsolicited mss monthly.

Submissions and Payment: Sample articles, guidelines, and editorial calendar available at website. Query with writing samples; or send complete ms. Accepts email submissions to ftmyers@optonline.net (Word attachments). Responds in 6–12 weeks. One-time rights. Articles, 500–1,500 words; $.10 per word. Pays within 30 days of publication. Provides 1 contributor's copy.

Frederick Gorilla

P.O. Box 259019
Plano, TX 75025-9019

Editor in Chief: Mike Clem

Description and Interests: Published six times each year, *Frederick Gorilla* is a current events magazine that spotlights business, life, and politics in the community of Frederick, Virginia. Each issue offers stories designed to evoke relevant discussions among residents and highlight not only the sophistication of the area, but also the grit, the controversy, and the contention that is often ignored by the mainstream media. Circ: 40,000.
Website: www.frederickgorilla.com

Freelance Potential: Receives many freelance submissions monthly.

Submissions and Payment: Sample articles available at website. Send query via website (About section). Response time varies. Written material, word lengths vary. Rights vary. Payment rates and policies vary.

Gateway

Missouri History Museum
P.O. Box 11940
St. Louis, MO 63112-0040

Editor: Victoria Monks

Description and Interests: Annual issues of this membership magazine offer essays that delve into the people, places, and events that have shaped—and are shaping—St. Louis and Missouri. Circ: 11,000.
Website: www.mohistory.org

Freelance Potential: 75% written by nonstaff writers. Publishes 6 freelance submissions yearly; 10% by unpublished writers, 10% by authors who are new to the magazine, 60% by experts. Receives 5 unsolicited mss monthly.

Submissions and Payment: Sample copy available. Guidelines available at website. Query with writing samples; or send complete ms. Accepts email to vwmonks@mohistory.org (Word attachments) and hard copy. SASE. Responds in 1–2 months. First rights. Long essays, 3,500–5,000 words; $300–$400. Short essays, 2,000–2,500 words; $250–$300. Pays on publication. Provides 3 contributor's copies.

Georgia Backroads

P.O. Box 585
Armuchee, GA 30105-0585

Publisher: Dan Roper

Description and Interests: Georgia history, nature, travel, and lifestyles are the focus of this quarterly. It has been in publication for more than 25 years. Circ: 16,500.
Website: www.georgiabackroads.com

Freelance Potential: 75% written by nonstaff writers. Publishes 40 freelance submissions yearly; 20% by authors who are new to the magazine, 15% by experts. Receives 5–10 queries and unsolicited mss monthly.

Submissions and Payment: Sample articles available at website. Query with illustration ideas; or send complete ms. Accepts hard copy and email to georgiabackroads@comcast.net. SASE. Responds in 1 month. Rights negotiable. Articles, 1,500–3,000 words; $.15–$.20 per word. B/W or color digital photos, 5x7, 300 dpi; $5. Pays on publication. Provides up to 5 contributor's copies.

Georgia Magazine

P.O. Box 1707
2100 East Exchange Place
Tucker, GA 30085

Editor: Ann Orowski

Description and Interests: Electric co-ops in Georgia use this monthly to communicate the importance of energy efficiency and to update readers on the electric industry. It also includes lifestyle pieces with broad appeal, written in a conversational style. Circ: 500,800.
Website: www.georgiamagazine.com

Freelance Potential: 85% written by nonstaff writers. Publishes 12 freelance submissions yearly; 20% by authors who are new to the magazine, 80% by experts.

Submissions and Payment: Sample copy and guidelines available at website. Query. Accepts hard copy and email to ann.orowski@georgiaemc.com, and simultaneous submissions if identified. Responds in 2–3 months. First North American serial rights. Articles, 1,200 words; $500 and up. Depts/columns, 500–800 words; $300–$500. Pays on publication.

Goldenseal

The Culture Center
1900 Kanawha Boulevard East
Charleston, WV 25305

Editor: John Lilly

Description and Interests: Published quarterly, *Goldenseal* documents West Virginia's cultural background and recent history. Topics covered range from folklife to politics, religion, crafts, music, and farming. Circ: 15,000.
Website: www.wvculture.org/goldenseal

Freelance Potential: 95% written by nonstaff writers. Publishes 30 freelance submissions yearly; 20% by unpublished writers, 50% by authors who are new to the magazine, 1% by experts. Receives 10 queries monthly.

Submissions and Payment: Sample articles and guidelines available at website. Query or send complete ms. Accepts hard copy. SASE. Responds in 6–9 months. One-time rights. Articles, 500–3,000 words; $.10 per word. High-resolution digital images or 8x10 prints; $25. Pays on publication. Provides 3 contributor's copies.

The Growler

Beer Dabbler Publications
095 West 7th Street
St. Paul, MN 5504

Editor: Jason Zabel

Description and Interests: *The Growler* is a bimonthly magazine focusing on craft beer and the culture surrounding it in and around the Twin Cities. Its mission is to educate and entertain a wide spectrum of craft beer drinkers. The magazine highlights the latest news in the industry, features brewer profiles, and lists area events. Additional content can be found at the website. Circ: Unavailable.
Website: www.growlermag.com

Freelance Potential: Receives many freelance submissions monthly.

Submissions and Payment: Sample copy available at website. Query. Accepts email to ideas@growlermag.com. Response time varies. Written material, word lengths vary. Rights vary. Payment rates and policies vary.

Gulfshore Life

3560 Kraft Road, Suite 301
Naples, FL 34105

Submissions

Description and Interests: *Gulfshore Life* portrays the upscale lifestyle of Florida's Gulf Coast. Appearing monthly in glossy, full-color format, it shows the best the region has to offer in restaurants, recreation, entertainment, real estate, and outdoor living. Circ: 23,500.
Website: www.gulfshorelife.com

Freelance Potential: 50% written by nonstaff writers. Publishes 60 freelance submissions yearly; 5% by unpublished writers, 10% by authors who are new to the magazine, 5% by experts. Receives 10 queries monthly.

Submissions and Payment: Sample articles available at website. Guidelines available. Query with clips or writing samples. Accepts hard copy. SASE. Responds in 2–6 weeks. First North American serial rights. Articles, word lengths vary; $300–$500. Depts/columns, 800–2,000 words; $200. Pays on publication. Provides 1 contributor's copy.

Hampton Roads Magazine

1264 Perimeter Parkway
Virginia Beach, VA 23454

Editor in Chief: Melissa M. Stewart

Description and Interests: This magazine is dedicated to Hampton Roads, Virginia. Its articles cover lifestyle topics, including home and garden, recreation, travel, and dining. Profiles of local personalities and coverage of the arts and entertainment scene are featured. It appears eight times each year. Circ: 40,000.
Website: www.hamptonroadsmagazine.com

Freelance Potential: 90% written by nonstaff writers. Publishes many freelance submissions yearly; 10% by authors who are new to the magazine.

Submissions and Payment: Sample articles available at website. Guidelines available. Query with résumé and at least 3 clips. Accepts hard copy and email queries to melissa@hrmag.com. SASE. Responds in 2 months. First North American serial rights. Articles, 2,500–4,000 words. Depts/columns, 600–800 words. Written material, $.25 per word. Kill fee, 30%. Pays on publication.

Harrisburg Magazine

3400 North Sixth Street
Harrisburg, PA 17110

Publisher & Editor in Chief: Patti Boccassini

Description and Interests: Harrisburg residents and visitors read this monthly magazine for its articles on topics ranging from education to regional recreation. It also provides coverage of the city's arts and entertainment scene and features profiles of local people. Circ: 21,000.
Website: www.harrisburgmagazine.com

Freelance Potential: 80% written by nonstaff writers. Publishes 50–100 freelance submissions yearly; 10% by unpublished writers, 10% by authors who are new to the magazine. Receives 5–10 queries monthly.

Submissions and Payment: Sample articles available at website. Query. Accepts hard copy and email queries to pboccassini@harrisburgmagazine.com. SASE. Responds in 2 months. All rights. Articles, 1,200–5,000 words; $100–$300. Depts/columns, word lengths and payment rates vary. Payment policy varies. Provides 2 contributor's copies.

Healthcare Journal of New Orleans

17732 Highland Road, Suite G-137
Baton Rouge, LA 70810

Editors: Smith Hartley and Karen Stassi

Description and Interests: Each issue of this magazine provides important information and analysis for local health-care professionals, including medical news, administrative guidance, quality measures, interviews, and legal issues. Circ: 83,000.
Website: www.healthcarejournalno.com

Freelance Potential: Receives many freelance submissions monthly.

Submissions and Payment: Sample copy available at website. Query or send complete ms. Accepts email to editor@healthcarejournalno.com. Response time varies. Written material, word lengths vary. Rights vary. Payment rates and policies vary.

Healthy & Fit

P.O. Box 26
Mason, MI 48854

Publisher: Tim Kissman

Description and Interests: Aimed specifically at readers living in and around mid-Michigan, *Healthy & Fit* publishes expert-written articles on topics such as nutrition, exercise, and healthy living. Traditional and holistic approaches, preventive care, and integrative medicine are covered in this monthly magazine. All content should have a regional angle. Circ: 14,000.
Website: www.healthyandfitmagazine.com

Freelance Potential: 90% written by nonstaff writers. Publishes 24 freelance submissions yearly; 50% by unpublished writers, 50% by authors who are new to the magazine, 100% by experts. Receives 12 queries monthly.

Submissions and Payment: Sample articles available at website. Query or send complete ms. Accepts email to tim@healthyandfitmagazine.com. Responds in 2 months. Rights vary. Articles, word lengths and payment rates vary. Pays on publication. Provides 2 contributor's copies.

O. Henry  

145 West Pennsylvania Avenue
Southern Pines, NC 28387

Editor: Jim Dodson

Description and Interests: This bimonthly regional is named for American short story writer William Sydey Porter, who wrote under the pen name O. Henry. It offers a unique blend of lifestyle articles and, honoring its namesake, a selection of fiction, poetry, and creative nonfiction from North Carolina writers in every issue. Other topics include regional food and wine, local homes and gardens, the area's arts scene, and profiles of notable residents. Circ: 18,000.
Website: www.ohenrymag.com

Freelance Potential: Issues regularly include articles from contributing writers.

Submissions and Payment: Sample copy available at website. Query. Accepts email queries to jim@ohenrymag.com. Rights and payment information unknown.

HM

The Magazine of HistoryMiami

101C West Flagler Street
Miami, FL 33130

Managing Editor: Victoria Cervantes

Description and Interests: Formerly *South Florida History,* this publication is for readers with a love of history, with a particular interest in southern Florida and the Caribbean. Appearing annually, its articles celebrate the people, places, and events that have shaped the region. Writers are encouraged to submit relevant visuals. Circ: 3,000.
Website: www.historymiami.org

Freelance Potential: 80% written by nonstaff writers. Publishes 3 freelance submissions yearly; 50% by unpublished writers, 75% by authors new to the magazine, 30% by experts.

Submissions and Payment: Sample copy available. Guidelines available at website. Query or send complete ms with photographs and author bio. Prefers email to publications@historymiami.org; accepts disk submissions. SASE. Response time varies. Rights vary. Articles, 2,500–3,500 words. Book reviews, 300 words. No payment. Provides 3 contributor's copies.

The 'Hood

4609 South Baja Avenue, #201
Sioux Falls, SD 57106

Editor: Taryn Sonnenfeld

Description and Interests: *The 'Hood* is short for parenthood, childhood, fatherhood, or motherhood, and this magazine covers all those stages of family life. It features articles on child development, parenting issues, education, and family health. It prides itself on featuring only information relevant to families in the Sioux Falls region, and it will only work with local writers. It appears nine times each year. Circ: 10,000.
Website: www.thehoodmagazine.com

Freelance Potential: 80% written by nonstaff writers. Publishes 30 freelance submissions yearly; 80% by unpublished writers, 10% by authors who are new to the magazine.

Submissions and Payment: Sample copy available at website. Query or send complete ms. Accepts electronic submissions through the website. Response time varies. All rights. Articles and depts/columns, word lengths vary. No payment.

Horses All

1666 Dublin Avenue
Winnipeg, Manitoba R3H OH1
Canada

Editor: Craig Couillard

Description and Interests: Each month, *Horses All* reports on equine news and events of interest to horse enthusiasts living in Alberta and western Canada. It focuses on training, health, and product updates. Circ: 6,000.
Website: www.horsesall.com

Freelance Potential: 90% written by nonstaff writers. Publishes 36 freelance submissions yearly; 20% by unpublished writers, 30% by authors who are new to the magazine, 50% by experts. Receives 5 queries monthly.

Submissions and Payment: Sample articles available at website. Guidelines available. Query with writing sample. Accepts email queries to craig.couillard@fbcpublishing.com. Responds in 1 month. First Canadian rights. Articles, to 700 words; $100 Canadian. 4x6 B/W or color prints or digital images at 300 dpi. Pays on publication. Provides 1 contributor's copy.

H Texas

12829 Trinity Street
Stafford, TX 77477

Editor

Description and Interests: Geared to a slightly upscale audience, *H Texas* is focused on covering culture, lifestyles, business, entertainment, politics, and personalities in the city of Houston. Published quarterly, it is always interested in celebrity profiles. Circ: 55,000.
Website: www.htexas.com

Freelance Potential: 30% written by nonstaff writers. Publishes 12–20 freelance submissions yearly; 5% by authors who are new to the magazine. Receives 50 queries, 10 unsolicited mss each month.

Submissions and Payment: Sample issue available at website. Theme list/editorial calendar available. Query or send complete ms. Accepts email to editor@htexas.com. Responds to queries in 10 days, to mss in 1 month. Rights vary. Articles, to 1,500 words. Depts/columns, word lengths vary. No payment. Provides 5 contributor's copies.

Hudson Valley

2678 South Road, Suite 202
Poughkeepsie, NY 12601

Editor in Chief: Olivia J. Abel

Description and Interests: The best that New York's scenic Hudson Valley has to offer can be found in this monthly. It provides a sophisticated slant on the region's events, issues, destinations, and people. Circ: 32,000.
Website: www.hvmag.com

Freelance Potential: 70% written by nonstaff writers. Publishes 20+ freelance submissions yearly; 5% by unpublished writers, 30% by authors who are new to the magazine, 10% by experts. Receives 30 queries, 10 mss monthly.

Submissions and Payment: Sample articles and editorial calendar available at website. Guidelines available. Prefers query with clips; will accept complete ms. Accepts hard copy. SASE. Responds in 1–3 months. First rights. Articles, 1,200–4,000 words. Depts/columns, 800–1,800 words. Articles and depts/columns, payment rates vary. Pays on publication. Provides 1 contributor's copy.

The Improper Bostonian

142 Berkeley Street, 3rd Floor
Boston, MA 02116

Managing Editor: Nick Altschuller

Description and Interests: This biweekly takes an irreverent tone in presenting the city's latest trends and happenings. It features profiles and articles on dining, entertainment, travel, fashion, and lifestyle for Boston's affluent 20s–40s group. Circ: 86,500.
Website: www.improper.com

Freelance Potential: 25% written by nonstaff writers. Publishes 15–20 freelance submissions yearly; 30% by unpublished writers, 30% by new authors, 80% by experts. Receives 8 queries monthly.

Submissions and Payment: Sample articles and editorial calendar available at website. Query with clips. Prefers email to nick@improper.com. First and electronic rights. Written material, payment rates vary, up to $1 a word. Kill fee, 30%. Pays on publication.

Indianapolis Monthly

1 Emmis Plaza
40 Monument Circle, Suite 100
Indianapolis, IN 46204

Editor: Amanda Heckert

Description and Interests: Indianapolis area residents find regional information about dining hot spots, decorating, and events in this monthly. It also includes longer, in-depth articles on more substantive issues, crime pieces, first-person essays, and long-form narrative. Circ: 45,000.
Website: www.indianapolismonthly.com

Freelance Potential: 55% written by nonstaff writers. Publishes 12 freelance submissions yearly; 5% by unpublished writers, 10% by authors who are new to the magazine. Receives 5 queries monthly.

Submissions and Payment: Sample articles available at website. Query. Accepts hard copy. SASE. Response time varies. First North American serial rights. Articles, 2,000–3,000 words; $500–$1,000. Depts/columns, 1,500–2,000 words; $350–$700. Kill fee, 25%. Pays on publication. Provides 1 contributor's copy.

Inland NW

P.O. Box 4250
5790 West Van Giesen Street
West Richland, WA 99353

Editor in Chief: Wil Byers

Description and Interests: Formerly titled *Mid-Colmbian Magazine, Inland NW* showcases Washington State's central region in words and images. It appears six times each year with articles covering topics ranging from the local art scene to the business community, and home life to the great outdoors. Circ: 27,000+.
Website: www.inlandnw.com

Freelance Potential: 40% written by nonstaff writers. Publishes 40 freelance submissions yearly; 30% by unpublished writers, 30% by authors who are new to the magazine, 40% by experts. Receives 10 queries monthly.

Submissions and Payment: Sample articles available at website. Query with writing samples. Accepts email queries to editor@kionapublishing.com. Responds in 1 month. Rights vary. Articles, 500–1,500 words; $.12 per word. Color digital images; $15 per photo. Pays on publication.

Inside Jersey

One Star Ledger Plaza
Newark, NJ 07102-1200

Editor: Rosemary Parrillo

Description and Interests: This monthly magazine is all about living in New Jersey. Published by *The Star-Ledger*, New Jersey's daily newspaper, it is a blend of lifestyle articles, profiles, and dining and local entertainment reviews. Added to that blend are hard-hitting articles on the state's politics, business climate, sports, and current events. Circ: 100,000.
Website: www.nj.com/insidejersey

Freelance Potential: 65% written by nonstaff writers. Publishes 300 freelance submissions yearly; 50% by authors who are new to the magazine.

Submissions and Payment: Sample articles available at website. Query with clips and writing samples. Accepts email queries to rparrillo@starledger.com. Response time varies. First rights. Articles and depts/columns, word lengths vary; $.35–$.50 per word. Pays on publication. Provides 2 contributor's copies.

Inside Pennsylvania Magazine

200 Market Street
Sunbury, PA 17801

Managing Editor: Joanne Arbogast

Description and Interests: This quarterly magazine shows all that Central Pennsylvania has to offer. It explores the region's parks, scenery, homes, gardens, and distinctive destinations. An original short story or poem is featured in each issue. Circ: 17,000.
Website: www.insidepamagazine.com

Freelance Potential: 75% written by nonstaff writers. Publishes 60+ freelance submissions yearly; 2% by unpublished writers, 5% by new authors.

Submissions and Payment: Central Pennsylvania authors only. Sample articles available at website. Query. Accepts email queries to jarbogast@insidepamagazine.com. Fiction and poems to jzaktansky@dailyitem.com. Responds in 6 weeks. Exclusive first rights. Articles, word lengths vary; $100. Fiction, to 750 words. Depts/columns, word lengths and payment rates vary. Pays on publication.

Inside Wisconsin Sports

2901 International Lane, Suite 100
Madison, WI 53704

Managing Editor: Emily Attwood

Description and Interests: Written for athletes, players, coaches, and fans, this monthly magazine covers all types of sports in the state of Wisconsin at all levels, from high school through the major leagues. It seeks writers who can provide engaging coverage of athletic events and profiles of local sports personalities. Circ: 20,000.
Website: www.insidewisconsinsports.com

Freelance Potential: 75% written by nonstaff writers. Publishes 120 freelance submissions yearly; 90% by experts. Receives 10 queries each month.

Submissions and Payment: Sample articles available at website. Guidelines available. Query with outline. Accepts email queries through website. Responds in 1 month. All rights. Articles, 1,200 words; $250. Kill fee, $50. Pays on publication. Provides 2 contributor's copies.

Insite Magazine

123 East William J. Bryan Parkway
Bryan, TX 77803

Publisher: Angelique Gammon

Description and Interests: Local people and places are the focus of this community monthly, which details life in Texas's Brazos Valley. *Insite* profiles interesting personalities and businesses, reports on the issues of the region, and provides entertainment and dining reviews and local event info. Prospective writers must have access to local sources to be considered. Circ: 8,000.
Website: www.insitebrazosvalley.com

Freelance Potential: 25–30% written by nonstaff writers. Publishes 15–20 freelance submissions yearly; 5–10% by unpublished writers, 5–10% by authors who are new to the magazine.

Submissions and Payment: Sample copy available at website. Guidelines available. Query. Accepts hard copy and email to agammon@insitegroup.com. SASE. Response time varies. One-time rights. Articles and depts/columns, word lengths vary; $.10 per word. Pays on publication. Provides 1 contributor's copy.

Invitation Tupelo

P.O. Box 3192
Tupelo, MS 38802

Managing Editor: Emily Welly

Description and Interests: This regional publication about communities in north Mississippi covers the events, people, lifestyles, and issues of the region. Additional articles cover health, food and wine, charitable events, regional celebrations, and more from the area. It is published 10 times each year. Circ: 45,000.
Website: www.invitationtupelo.com

Freelance Potential: Open to freelancers who are familiar with the issues of the region.

Submissions and Payment: Sample articles available at website. Query. Accepts email queries to erwelly@gmail.com. Response time varies. Written material, word lengths vary.

The Iowan

Pioneer Communications, Inc.
300 Walnut Street, Suite 6
Des Moines, IA 50309

Editor: Beth Wilson

Description and Interests: *The Iowan*, published six times each year, explores everything Iowa has to offer. Each issue travels into diverse pockets of the state to discover the sights, meet the people, learn the history, taste the cuisine, and experience the culture. Circ: 20,000.
Website: www.iowan.com

Freelance Potential: 75% written by nonstaff writers. Accepts 36 unsolicited queries yearly.

Submissions and Payment: Sample copy available. Guidelines available at website. Query with proposal, an explanation of where, when, and why it fits into the magazine, suggested images, and published clips. Accepts hard copy and email to editor@iowan.com. Materials are not returned. One-time rights. Articles, 1,000–1,500 words; $150–$450. Depts/columns, 500–750 words; $100. Kill fee, $100. Pays on publicaton.

Island Gourmet

1751 Richardson Street, Suite 5530
Montreal, Quebec H3K 1G6
Canada

Editor: Jennifer McMorran

Description and Interests: This annual gourmet food and lifestyle magazine brings the food and dining, culture, nightlife, and entertainment of the Caribbean island of Aruba to readers everywhere—but particularly to tourists and those planning to visit soon. Circ: 165,000.
Website: www.nightspublications.com

Freelance Potential: 90% written by nonstaff writers. Publishes 15 freelance submissions yearly; 25% by authors who are new to the magazine, 75% by experts. Receives 5 queries monthly.

Submissions and Payment: Sample copy available. Query with writing samples. Accepts email queries to editor@nightspublications.com. Responds in 1–2 months. Exclusive or first Caribbean and North American rights. Articles, 300–900 words. Depts/columns, 300–600 words. Written material, $125–$375. Pays on acceptance.

Jacksonville

1261 King Street
Jacksonville, FL 32204

Publisher/Editor: Joseph White

Description and Interests: This monthly magazine offers Jacksonville residents and visitors coverage of regional news and events, profiles of local personalities, and articles on the lifestyle unique to the area. Circ: 22,000.
Website: www.jacksonvillemag.com

Freelance Potential: 15% written by nonstaff writers. Publishes 40–50 freelance submissions yearly; 5% by authors who are new to the magazine, 10% by experts. Receives 15–20 queries each month.

Submissions and Payment: Sample copy and guidelines available at website. Query. Accepts email to joe@jacksonvillemag.com and hard copy. Responds if interested. First North American serial rights. Articles, 1,000–2,000 words; $200–$500. Depts/columns, 1,000–2,000 words; $150–$300. Pays on publication. Provides 1–3 contributor's copies.

JerseyMan Magazine

7025 Central Highway
Pennsauken, NJ 08109

Publisher: Ken Dunek

Description and Interests: Dubbed "the thinking man's guide to an active Jersey life," this lifestyle magazine covers subjects of interest to men, such as regional sports, family, relationships, health, technology, dining, and entertainment. Circ: 25,000.
Website: www.jerseymanmagazine.com

Freelance Potential: The editors report that while they are open to the usual men's lifestyle topics, they are on the lookout for content that readers will find nowhere else. The more Jersey-centric the piece, the better it will be received.

Submissions and Payment: Sample articles available at website. Query. Accepts email queries to ken@jerseymanmagazine.com. Response time varies. Written material, word lengths vary.

Journal Plus

The Magazine of the Central Coast

654 Osos Street
San Luis Obispo, CA 93401

Publisher: Steve Owens

Description and Interests: This community magazine is written by and for the people of the central coast of California. It features a mix of profiles of notable people and places, coverage of local businesses, feature articles on leisure activities, historical pieces, and health and fitness information. It works only with writers who live in or hail from the region. It is published monthly. Circ: 25,000.
Website: www.slojournal.com

Freelance Potential: 50% written by nonstaff writers. Publishes 50–60 freelance submissions yearly. Receives 50 queries monthly.

Submissions and Payment: Sample copy and guidelines available at website. Query or send complete manuscript. Accepts hard copy. SASE. Responds in 1 month. Local market and first rights. Articles, 600–1,400 words; $50–$75. Pays on publication. Provides 1 contributor's copy.

Just Out

P.O. Box 10609
Portland, OR 97296

Editor in Chief: Alley Hector

Description and Interests: *Just Out* is the longest published LGBTQ publication in the Portland, Oregon, metro area. Though it started as a newspaper, it is now a monthly glossy magazine, featuring character-driven editorial and entertainment, sports, and politics highlights. Circ: 700,000.
Website: www.justout.com

Freelance Potential: Receives many freelance submissions monthly.

Submissions and Payment: Sample articles available at website. Query with brief bio and writing sample. Accepts email to editor@justout.com. Response time varies. Written material, word lengths vary. Rights vary. Payment rates and policy vary.

Kalamazoo Parent

P.O. Box 580
Portage, MI 49081

Editor: Vicky Girard

Description and Interests: The monthly *Kalamazoo Parent* was launched in 2011 with the goal of helping readers find family-friendly activities every day of the year. It covers child- and family-oriented events, destinations, and activities throughout southwest Michigan. It also offers articles on family fun and parenting issues. Local is the key word for all submissions. Circ: 10,000.
Website: www.kalamazooparent.com

Freelance Potential: Receives several submissions monthly.

Submissions and Payment: Sample copy available at website. Guidelines available. Query or send complete ms. Accepts hard copy and email to editor@kalamazooparent.com. SASE. Response time varies. Articles and depts/columns, word lengths vary. Rights and payment vary.

Kansas!

Kansas Department of Commerce
1000 South West Jackson Street, Suite 100
Topeka, KS 66612-1354

Editor

Description and Interests: The Sunflower State comes alive in words and images in this Kansas Department of Commerce publication. Each quarterly issue features travel pieces, articles on the state's history, and coverage of the events and attractions in each of six specified tourism regions. Circ: 45,000.
Website: www.kansasmag.com

Freelance Potential: 90% written by nonstaff writers. Publishes 40 freelance submissions yearly; 10% by unpublished writers, 20% by authors who are new to the magazine, 70% by experts. Receives 12 queries monthly.

Submissions and Payment: Sample articles and guidelines available at website. Query with outline, photo suggestions, résumé, clips or writing samples. Accepts hard copy and email to kansas.mag@travelks.com. SASE. Response time varies. One time rights. Articles, 800–1,000 words; payment rates vary. Pays on acceptance. Provides 6 contributor's copies.

Kansas City Prime Magazine

7275 West 162nd Street, Suite 107
Overland Park, KS 66085

Publisher: Lindsay Aydelotte

Description and Interests: Focusing on the active and ageless lifestyle, *Prime Magazine* is geared to people over 50. Among the many topics included are health and fitness, food, personal finance, travel, and relationships. Circ: 700,000.
Website: www.primemagkc.com

Freelance Potential: Unavailable.

Submissions and Payment: Sample copy available at website. Query with brief bio and writing sample. Accepts email to editor@justout.com. Response time varies. Written material, word lengths vary. Rights vary. Payment rates and policy vary.

Kansas City Voices 

Whispering Prairie Press
P.O. Box 410661
Kansas City, MO 64141

Prose or Poetry Editor

Description and Interests: Appearing in November each year, this annual journal offers an eclectic mix of previously unpublished fiction, essays, and poetry, as well as visual art. Established and emerging writers alike are represented in its pages. Circ: 1,000.
Website: wwwwppress.org

Freelance Potential: 100% written by nonstaff writers. Publishes 30–50 freelance submissions yearly; 30% by unpublished writers, 70% by authors who are new to the magazine.

Submissions and Payment: Sample copy available. Guidelines available at website. Send complete ms from December 15 to March 15. Accepts electronic submissions via website only. Accepts simultaneous submissions if identified. Responds if interested. First rights. Essays and fiction, to 2,500 words; $30. Poetry, to 35 lines, to 3 poems per submission; $20. Pays on publication. Provides 1 contributor's copy.

Kearsarge Magazine

P.O. Box 1482
Grantham, NH 03753

Editor: Laura Jean Whitcomb

Description and Interests: The articles of *Kearsarge Magazine* report on what's happening in the Sunapee/Kearsarge region of New Hampshire in a way that interests residents, visitors, and tourists. The magazine covers arts and entertainment, culture and heritage, and lifestyle topics, as well as local news and personalities. It is published quarterly. Circ: 20,000.
Website: www.kearsargemagazine.com

Freelance Potential: 50–75% written by nonstaff writers. Publishes 16–20 freelance submissions yearly; 10% by unpublished writers, 50% by authors who are new to the magazine.

Submissions and Payment: Sample articles available at website. Query. Accepts email to laurajean@kearsargemagazine.com. Response time varies. First North American serial and electronic rights. Written material, word lengths and payment rates vary. Pays on publication.

Kentucky Living

P.O. Box 32170
Louisville, KY 40232

Editor: Paul Wesslund

Description and Interests: Filled with articles that celebrate the people, culture, and history of Kentucky, this lifestyle magazine is published monthly. It has some themed issues; see website for editorial calendar. Circ: 500,000.
Website: www.kentuckyliving.com

Freelance Potential: 50% written by nonstaff writers. Publishes 40–42 freelance submissions yearly; 10% by unpublished writers, 5% by authors who are new to the magazine, 5% by experts. Receives 20 queries, 20 unsolicited mss each month.

Submissions and Payment: Sample copy and guidelines available at website. Prefers query with writing samples; will accept complete ms. Accepts hard copy and email to e-mail@kentuckyliving.com (Word attachments), and simultaneous submissions if identified. SASE. Responds in 2 months. Full rights. Articles, 500–1,500 words; $75–$935. Pays on acceptance. Provides 1 contributor's copy.

Kentucky Monthly

P.O. Box 559
Frankfort, KY 40601-0559

Executive Editor: Kim Butterweck

Description and Interests: This colorful magazine highlights the state of Kentucky and its people, events, and culture. Articles, profiles, photo-essays, and reviews are all aimed at a general readership. It is published 10 times each year. Circ: 40,000.
Website: www.kentuckymonthly.com

Freelance Potential: 30% written by nonstaff writers. Publishes 30–40 freelance submissions yearly; 20% by unpublished writers, 30% by authors new to the magazine, 20% by experts. Receives 10 queries and unsolicited mss monthly.

Submissions and Payment: Sample articles and guidelines available at website. Query or send complete ms with résumé and 2 clips. Accepts email queries only (put "Query" in the subject line) to kim@kentuckymonthly.com. Responds in 3 weeks. All rights. Articles, 1,000–2,500 words. Depts/columns, 800 words. Written material, $.15 a word. Pays on publication.

Khabar

3790 Holcomb Bridge Road, Suite 101
Norcross, GA 30092

Editor: Parthiv Parekh

Description and Interests: New and second-generation Indian and South Asian immigrants living in Georgia, Alabama, Tennessee, and South Carolina, are the target audience of this monthly publication. It offers articles on assimilation and culture clashes and features on current events, entertainment, and business. Circ: 27,000.
Website: www.khabar.com

Freelance Potential: 70% written by nonstaff writers. Publishes 100 freelance submissions yearly; 25% by unpublished writers, 40% by authors who are new to the magazine.

Submissions and Payment: Sample articles available at website. Guidelines available. Query. Accepts email to parthiv@khabar.com (Word attachments). Responds if interested. Limited exclusive rights. Written material, word lengths and payment rates vary. Pays on publication. Provides 1 contributor's copy.

Know Atlanta

450 Northridge Parkway, Suite 202
Atlanta, GA 30350

Editor: Gwyn Herbein

Description and Interests: *Know Atlanta* was created to serve as a guide for individuals and businesses that are considering relocating to the Atlanta metropolitan area. Published quarterly, it offers full-color coverage of the region's real estate, recreation, education, and job markets. Circ: 48,000.
Website: www.knowatlanta.com

Freelance Potential: 20% written by nonstaff writers. Publishes 10 freelance submissions yearly; 5% by authors who are new to the magazine, 1% by industry experts. Receives 10 queries monthly.

Submissions and Payment: Sample copy available at website. Guidelines and editorial calendar available. Query. Accepts hard copy and email queries to gwyn@knowatlanta.com. SASE. Responds in 1 month. All rights. Articles, 300–1,800 words; payment rates vary. Pays on publication. Provides 1 contributor's copy.

Lake Country Journal

P.O. Box 978
Brainerd, MN 56401
Editor: Jodi Schwen

Description and Interests: *Lake Country Journal* captures the essence of why residents work, play, and live in one of the fastest growing areas in the midwest. Through a blend of articles from features and fiction, to recreation, recipes, gardening, and nature, this lifestyle magazine, appearing six times each year, showcases local natural and cultural resources. Circ: 14,500.
Website: www.lakecountryjournal.com

Freelance Potential: 90% written by nonstaff writers. Publishes 95+ freelance submissions yearly.

Submissions and Payment: Sample copy available. Guidelines available at website. Query with clips. Accepts hard copy and email queries to jodi@lakecountryjournal.com. Responds in 2–3 months. One-time rights. Prose, 100–1,500 words. Poetry, to 4 poems. Payment varies. Kill fee, 25%. Pays on publication.

Lake Superior Magazine

310 East Superior Street
Duluth, MN 55802

Managing Editor: Bob Berg

Description and Interests: Lake Superior's history, events, and tourism are this magazine's focus. The bimonthly seeks contemporary nonfiction about the region and historical stories with a modern tie, and covers nature, education, science, and regional events. The editors like unexpected slants. Circ: 20,000.
Website: www.lakesuperior.com

Freelance Potential: 70% written by nonstaff writers. Publishes 30 freelance submissions yearly; 10% by unpublished writers, 25% by authors who are new to the magazine, 5% by experts. Receives 5–10 unsolicited mss monthly.

Submissions and Payment: Sample articles and guidelines available at website. Prefers complete ms with photos; accepts queries. Accepts hard copy and CD. SASE. Responds in 4 months. First and electronic rights. Articles, 1,600–2,200 words. Fiction and depts/columns, 900–1,400 words. Written material, to $600. Pays on publication. Provides 1 contributor's copy.

The Lane Report

201 East Main Street, 14th Floor
Lexington, KY 40507

Editorial Director: Mark Green

Description and Interests: For more than 25 years, *The Lane Report* has been covering important business and economic development stories in Kentucky. Each monthly issue is read by the state's business leaders and policymakers. Circ: 15,000.
Website: www.lanereport.com

Freelance Potential: 60% written by nonstaff writers. Publishes 40 freelance submissions yearly; 1% by unpublished writers, 10% by authors who are new to the magazine, 5–10% by experts. Receives 3–4 queries monthly.

Submissions and Payment: Sample articles, guidelines, and editorial calendar available at website. Query with résumé and 2–3 clips. Accepts hard copy and email to markgreen@lanereport.com. Responds in 1 week. Rights vary. Articles, 750–3,000 words. Depts/columns, 100–750 words. Written material, $.15–$.20 per word. Pays on acceptance.

L.A. Parent

443 East Irving Drive, Suite A
Burbank, CA 91504

Submissions: Christina Elston

Description and Interests: This monthly publication is a go-to resource for Los Angeles county families. It features articles on education, parenting, and unique activities in the area. It also offers guides to learning centers. Almost all writers live within the magazine's coverage area. Circ: 120,000.
Website: www.losangeles.parenthood.com

Freelance Potential: 50% written by nonstaff writers. Publishes 10–15 freelance submissions yearly; 5% by unpublished writers, 10% by authors who are new to the magazine, 10% by experts. Receives 6–10 queries monthly.

Submissions and Payment: Sample articles and guidelines available at website. Query. Accepts email queries to christina.elston@parenthood.com (Word attachments). No simultaneous submissions. Responds in 6 months. First serial rights. Articles, 800–1,500 words; payment rates vary. Pays on publication. Provides contributor's copies.

Lexington Family Magazine

138 East Reynolds Road, Suite 201
Lexington, KY 40517

Editor: John Lynch

Description and Interests: This family tabloid for residents of central Kentucky features events calendars, as well as ideas for family recreation, entertainment, and travel. Appearing monthly, it also offers articles that tackle a wide range of parenting issues. Circ: 30,000.
Website: www.lexingtonfamily.com

Freelance Potential: 45% written by nonstaff writers. Publishes 100 freelance submissions yearly; 5% by authors who are new to the magazine, 10% by experts. Receives 30 queries, 30 unsolicited mss monthly.

Submissions and Payment: Sample copy available at website. Query. Accepts queries through website and to info@lexingtonfamily.com. Response time varies. All rights. Articles, 500–1,500 words. Depts/columns, 800 words. Written material, payment rates vary. Pays on publication. Provides 25 contributor's copies.

Life in the Finger Lakes

P.O. Box 1080
Geneva, NY 14456

Editor: Mark Stash

Description and Interests: This quarterly publication celebrates life in the Finger Lakes region of New York. It reflects the past, present, and future of the region in every season by focusing on the natural beauty, history, and culture of the area with informational and first-person articles. Circ: Unknown.
Website: www.lifeinthefingerlakes.com

Freelance Potential: Unavailable.

Submissions and Payment: Sample articles and guidelines at website. Query with outline or send complete ms (prefers Word documents). Accepts email to mark@lifeinthefingerlakes.com and hard copy. Rights unknown. Written material, $.12 a word. Pays on publication. Provides 1 contributor's copy.

Litchfield Magazine

386 Main Street
Ridgefield, CT 06877

Editor in Chief: Geoffrey Morris

Description and Interests: Written for full-time and weekend residents of northwestern Connecticut, this publication features lifestyle articles and features on area attractions and services. It appears six times each year. Circ: 10,000.
Website: www.townvibe.com

Freelance Potential: 90% written by nonstaff writers. Publishes 20 freelance submissions yearly; 1% by unpublished writers, 20% by authors who are new to the magazine, 2% by experts. Receives 250 queries monthly.

Submissions and Payment: Sample articles available at website. Accepts email queries to gmorris@morrismediagroup.com. Responds in 1 week. First print and simultaneous publication rights. Articles, 400–1,000 words. Depts/columns, 200–300 words. Written material, payment rates vary. Pays on publication. Provides 1 contributor's copy.

The L Magazine

45 Main Street, Suite 806
Brooklyn, NY 11201

Editor in Chief: Jonny Diamond

Description and Interests: *L Magazine* describes itself as combining the methodology of an alternative weekly with the hard content of an event/city guide in a unique publication model. It is distributed free every two weeks to readers in the heart of the New York metropolitan area, from Brooklyn to Manhattan. Topics range from local cosmoplitan events to fashion, the arts, books, sex, dance, and reviews. Circ: 107,000.
Website: www.thelmagazine.com

Freelance Potential: 30–40% written by nonstaff writers. Accepts 10% of freelance submissions.

Submissions and Payment: Sample articles available at website. Accepts email queries with links to clips to jonny@thelmagazine.com. Exclusive rights. Articles, 1,000–2,500 words; short fiction (for annual literary contest), to 1,500 words. Pays up to $.25 per word. Kill fee, up to 33%. Pays within 1 week of publication.

Long Island Woman

P.O. Box 176
Malverne, NY 11565

Editor: Arie Nadboy

Description and Interests: Women who live on Long Island, New York, read this monthly tabloid for its coverage of regional events and activities, as well as profiles of local personalities. Articles on parenting, relationships, home and garden, family travel, and personal finance are regularly offered. Book reviews are also published. Circ: 40,000.
Website: www.liwomanonline.com

Freelance Potential: 25% written by nonstaff writers. Publishes 25 freelance submissions yearly. Receives 100 queries and mss monthly.

Submissions and Payment: Sample copy available. Writers' guidelines available at website. Query or send complete ms. Accepts email only to editor@liwomanonline.com. Responds if interested. One-time rights. Articles, 500–2,250 words; $70–$200. Kill fee, 20%. Pays within 1 month of publication. Provides 1 tearsheet.

Louisiana Conservationist

P.O. Box 98000
Baton Rouge, LA 70898

Editor: Gabe Giffin

Description and Interests: Dedicated to the conservation and restoration of Louisiana's natural resources, this quarterly is published by the state's Department of Wildlife and Fisheries. It offers informational and first-person articles on wildlife and habitats. Circ: 16,000.
Website: www.louisianaconservationist.org

Freelance Potential: 45% written by nonstaff writers. Publishes 12 freelance submissions yearly; 5% by unpublished writers, 15% by authors who are new to the magazine, 80% by experts. Receives 3 unsolicited mss monthly.

Submissions and Payment: Sample copy available at website. Use contact form at website. Responds in 3 months. All rights. Articles, 1,200–1,500 words; $175. Digital images at 300 dpi. Pays on publication. Provides 1 contributor's copy.

Louisiana Cookin'

3803 Cleveland Avenue
New Orleans, LA 70179

Editor in Chief: Daniel Schumacher

Description and Interests: Six times each year lovers of Louisiana food and drink gobble up this magazine's delicious combination of recipes and culinary insights. Circ: 45,000.
Website: www.louisianacookin.com

Freelance Potential: 75% written by nonstaff writers. Publishes 20 freelance submissions yearly; 25% by authors who are new to the magazine, 75% by experts. Receives 12 queries each month.

Submissions and Payment: Sample copy and guidelines available. Editorial calendar available at website. Query with résumé and 3 clips. Accepts email queries to daniel@louisianacookin.com. Responds only if interested. First North American serial rights. Articles, 1,000–2,000 words, plus recipes; $350. Depts/columns, word lengths vary; $250. Kill fee, 20%. Pays on publication. Provides 3 contributor's copies.

Louisiana Literature

SLU Box 10792
Southeastern Louisiana University
Hammond, LA 70402

Editor: Jack Bedell

Description and Interests: *Louisiana Literature* is always looking to publish the finest poetry and fiction available whether it's by a local writer or a nationally recognized author. Published twice each year, it seeks poetry that shows firm control and craft and is sophisticated, yet accessible to a broad readership. It accepts literary, mainstream, and regional fiction. Circ: Unavailable.
Website: www.louisianaliterature.org

Freelance Potential: Receives 100 unsolicited mss monthly.

Submissions and Payment: Sample copy available. Guidelines available at website. Send complete ms with author bio. Accepts hard copy. No simultaneous submissions. SASE. Responds in 3 months. Fiction, 1,000–6,000 words. Poetry, 3–5 poems per submission. One-time rights. No payment. Provides contributor's copies.

Louisville

137 West Muhammad Ali Boulevard, Suite 101
Louisville, KY 40202-1438

Editor: Kane Webb

Description and Interests: Residents of metropolitan Louisville turn to this monthly for insightful articles on local personalities, business news, entertainment, lifestyle, and regional travel features. It also serves as a guide to upcoming events and attractions and includes reviews of books, restaurants, movies, plays, and musical performances. Circ: 30,000.
Website: www.loumag.com

Freelance Potential: 50% written by nonstaff writers. Publishes 75 freelance submissions yearly; 10% by unpublished writers, 10% by authors who are new to the magazine.

Submissions and Payment: Sample copy available at website. Guidelines available. Query. Accepts email queries to editorial@loumag.com. Responds in 2 months. First North American serial rights. Articles, to 3,000 words; $50–$500+. Pays on acceptance. Provides 3 contributor's copies.

Madison Magazine

7025 Raymond Road
Madison, WI 53719

Editor: Brennan Nardi

Description and Interests: For 30 years, this monthly magazine has covered the arts, entertainment, and businesses that are a part of Madison, Wisconsin. Circ: 20,583.
Website: www.madisonmagazine.com

Freelance Potential: 30% written by nonstaff writers. Publishes 24 freelance submissions yearly; 2% by unpublished writers, 10% by authors who are new to the magazine, 5% by experts. Receives 8–10 queries monthly.

Submissions and Payment: Sample copy and guidelines available. Editorial calendar available at website. Query with résumé and clips. Accepts hard copy and email to bnardi@madisonmagazine.com. SASE. Responds in 1 month. First North American serial rights. Articles, 300–2,500 words. Depts/columns, to 800 words. Written material, payment rates vary. Kill fee, 33%. Pays on publication. Provides 2 contributor's copies upon request.

Maine

Thomas Reid Publishing LLC
75 Market Street, Suite 203
Portland, ME 04101

Editor in Chief: Susan Grisanti

Description and Interests: This monthly shines the spotlight on the people, places, and culture that make Maine a unique place. Read by residents and visitors alike, it publishes articles on destinations of interest, the arts, and the shopping and dining of the region, as well as essays and profiles regarding the personalities and lifestyle of Maine. There is even a little poetry included in the mix. Circ: Unavailable.
Website: www.themainemag.com

Freelance Potential: Open to submissions, as long as they are in keeping with the magazine's vibrant style and upscale readership.

Submissions and Payment: Sample articles available at website. Query. Accepts electronic queries via form at website only. Response time varies. Articles and depts/columns, word lengths vary. Payment policy varies.

Manhattan

7 West 51st Street, 5th Floor
New York, NY 10019

Editor in Chief: Cristina Cuomo

Description and Interests: Catering to the interests, sensibilities, and 24/7 lifestyle of New York City's most affluent and influential readers, the monthly *Manhattan* delivers the absolute best this unarguably international city has to offer. Whether a special feature on design trends, cutting-edge fashion spreads, in-depth reviews of the city's hot spots, or a revealing celebrity profile, the magazine features and departments aim to cover it all. Circ: 60,000.
Website: www.modernluxury.com/manhattan

Freelance Potential: 90% written by nonstaff writers.

Submissions and Payment: Accepts email queries with bio to ccuomo@modernluxury.com. 60-day exclusive rights. Articles, to 2,000 words. Depts/columns, 50–700 words. Fiction, to 3,000 words. Pays $.50+ per word. Pays 1 month after publication.

The Mariner

601 Bridge Street
Elkton, MD 21921

Editor: Wendy Gilbert

Description and Interests: Dedicated to boating on the Upper Chesapeake Bay, *The Mariner* celebrates the people and pleasures of the region. It is published 10 times each year. Circ: 25,000.
Website: www.themariner.net

Freelance Potential: 70% written by nonstaff writers. Publishes 25 freelance submissions yearly; 5% by unpublished writers, 20% by authors who are new to the magazine, 20% by experts. Receives 3 queries, 2 mss monthly.

Submissions and Payment: Sample copy available. Queries. Accepts submissions through the website. Responds in 1 week. Rights vary. Articles, 800 words; $80. JPEG images at 200 dpi; $10. Pays on publication.

Marin Magazine

One Harbor Drive, Suite 208
Sausalito, CA 94965

Editorial Director: Nikki Wood

Description and Interests: Marin County is the smallest of the San Francisco Bay Area counties in size and population, but what it lacks in acreage it compensates for in visual appeal. It is home to redwood forests, the Golden Gate Bridge, wine country, and the communities of Tiburon and Sausalito. *Marin Magazine* is the only city and regional magazine that covers this area, and is published monthly. Circ: 36,000.
Website: www.marinmagazine.com

Freelance Potential: Unavailable.

Submissions and Payment: Samples articles and editorial calendar available at website. Query. Accepts email to editorial@marinmagazine.com. Rights and payment policy unknown.

Martha's Vineyard Arts & Ideas

P.O. Box 1410
West Tisbury, MA 02575

Publisher and Executive Editor: Patrick Phillips

Description and Interests: This quarterly magazine highlights local arts, entertainment, and events. In print and digitally, it promotes the island's creative community and the businesses and organizations that support it. Each submission should bring an awareness of where and who the reader is—part of an island community, as well as part of a much larger world. Circ: Unavailable.
Website: www.mvartsandideas.com

Freelance Potential: Receives numerous submissions monthly.

Submissions and Payment: Sample articles available at website. Send complete ms. Accepts electronic submissions via website. Response time varies. Articles, depts/columns, poetry, and short stories; word lengths vary. Rights and payment rates and policy vary.

Martha's Vineyard Magazine

P.O. Box 66
Edgartown, MA 02539

Editor: Nicole M. Miller

Description and Interests: This regional explores life on Martha's Vineyard through articles, interviews, profiles, humor, and personal experience pieces. Article topics include Vineyard history, nature, home and garden, boating, antiques, and recreation. Local issues and trends are also explored. *Martha's Vineyard Magazine* appears locally eight times each year. Circ: Unavailable.
Website: www.mvmagazine.com

Freelance Potential: 90% written by nonstaff writers.

Submissions and Payment: Sample articles available at website. Sample copy and guidelines available. Contact the editor through form at website. Response time varies. Rights vary. Articles and depts/columns, word lengths and payment rates vary. Payment policy varies.

Metro

550 South First Street
San Jose, CA 95113-2806

Managing Editor: Michael S. Gant

Description and Interests: Known as "Silicon Valley's Weekly Newspaper," *Metro* offers news, views, and reviews from an alternative perspective. Technology, politics, and business are among the topics covered. Profiles of local personalities also are published. Circ: 65,000+.
Website: www.metrosiliconvalley; www.metroactive.com

Freelance Potential: 50% written by nonstaff writers. Publishes 200 freelance submissions yearly; 20% by unpublished writers, 30% by authors who are new to the magazine, 10% by experts. Receives 20 queries monthly.

Submissions and Payment: Sample copy available at metropdf.com. Guidelines available. Accepts email to editor@metronews.com or submissions through form at website only. Response time varies. First rights. Written material, word lengths and payment rates vary. Pays on publication. Provides 1 contributor's copy.

Metro Parent Magazine

22041 Woodward Avenue
Ferndale, MI 48220-2520

Executive Editor: Julia Elliott

Description and Interests: *Metro Parent* is published monthly and read by families in southeastern Michigan. Articles cover all aspects of family relationships, child health, education, sports and activities, new products, and consumer information. Circ: 70,000.
Website: www.metroparent.com

Freelance Potential: 75% written by nonstaff writers. Publishes 250 freelance submissions yearly; 35% by authors new to the magazine. Receives 500 queries and unsolicited mss monthly.

Submissions and Payment: Sample articles and guidelines available at website. Query or send complete ms. Accepts email to jelliot@metroparent.com and simultaneous submissions if identified. Responds in one month if interested. First rights. Articles, 1,000–2,500 words; $100–$350. Depts/columns, 500–700 words; $50–$75. Parent Pipeline reviews, 300–600 words; $35–$50. Pays on publication.

Michigan Historical Review

Central Michigan University
250 Preston Street
Mount Pleasant, MI 48859

Editor: Lane T. Demas

Description and Interests: Twice a year, this publication offers expert-written articles covering the political, social, cultural, and economic aspects of Michigan and the Great Lakes Region. It also explores American, Canadian, and Midwestern history. Circ: 2,500.
Website: http://clarke.cmich.edu/michigan_historical_review_tab

Freelance Potential: 100% written by nonstaff writers. Publishes 10 freelance submissions yearly; 50% by unpublished writers, 75% by authors who are new to the magazine, 100% by experts. Receives 3 unsolicited mss monthly.

Submissions and Payment: Sample copy available. Guidelines available at website. Send 2 copies of complete ms. Accepts hard copy and email to mihisrev@cmich.edu. SASE. All rights. Articles, to 10,000 words. No payment. Provides 2 contributor's copies.

Michigan Out-of-Doors

Michigan United Conservation Clubs
P.O. Box 30235
Lansing, MI 48912-3785

Editor: Tony Hansen

Description and Interests: Michigan's outdoor recreational opportunities, particularly hunting and fishing, are covered in this photo-filled magazine. Articles on conservation efforts in the state are also included. Circ: 85,000.
Website: www.michiganoutofdoors.com/magazine/

Freelance Potential: 90% written by nonstaff writers. Publishes 75 freelance submissions yearly; 5% by unpublished writers, 15% by authors who are new to the magazine, 25% by experts. Receives 25 queries monthly.

Submissions and Payment: Sample copy, guidelines available. Query with outline. Accepts email to thansen@mucc.org. Responds in 1 month. First North American serial rights. Articles, 1,500–2,000 words; $75–$200. Depts/columns, 750–1,000 words; $60–$90. Pays on acceptance. Provides 3 contributor's copies.

Midwest Living

1716 Locust Street
Des Moines, IA 50309

Query Editor

Description and Interests: This magazine celebrates the midwestern lifestyle with articles on food, decorating, gardening, and entertaining. It also features regional travel and recreation ideas. *Midwest Living* is published six times each year. Circ: 925,000.
Website: www.midwestliving.com

Freelance Potential: Works with freelancers mainly as scouts of travel locations, with reliable contributors receiving steady assignments. Assignments limited to 4–5 articles annually. Some short, front-of-book assignments are available. Mostly open to pitches for short items about restaurants, lodging, and attractions.

Submissions and Payment: Sample articles and guidelines available at website. Query with clips. Accepts hard copy. Responds if interested. All rights. Articles, 100–1,000 words. Depts/columns, 200–500 words. Written material, payment rate varies. Pays on acceptance. Provides 1 contributor's copy.

Milwaukee Magazine

126 North Jefferson Street, Suite 100
Milwaukee, WI 53202

Editor: Cristina Daglas

Description and Interests: This monthly magazine covers the people, places, and issues of Milwaukee and southeastern Wisconsin through profiles of local personalities, and informative articles on topics from sports and politics to education and entertainment. Circ: 35,000.
Website: www.milwaukeemagazine.com

Freelance Potential: 50% written by nonstaff writers. Publishes 25 freelance submissions yearly; 5% by unpublished writers, 5% by authors who are new to the magazine. Receives 15 queries monthly.

Submissions and Payment: Sample articles and guidelines available at website. Query with clips. Prefers email to cristina.daglas@milwaukeemag.com; accepts hard copy and simultaneous submissions. SASE. First North American serial rights. Articles, 2,500–5,000 words. Depts/columns, 150–700 words. Written material, payment rates vary. Pays on publication. Provides 2 contributor's copies.

Minnesota Conservation Volunteer

500 Lafayette Road
St. Paul, MN 55155-4046

Managing Editor: Keith Goetzman

Description and Interests: This magazine explores the natural ecosystems found in Minnesota. It is published six times each year and focuses on understanding and protecting the state's natural resources. Circ: 165,000.
Website: www.dnr.state.mn.us

Freelance Potential: 60% written by nonstaff writers. Publishes 25 freelance submissions yearly; 5% by unpublished writers, 10% by authors who are new to the magazine, 60% by experts. Receives 24+ queries monthly.

Submissions and Payment: Sample copy, guidelines available at website. Query. Accepts hard copy, email to keith.goetzman@state.mn.us. SASE. Responds in 1 month. First serial rights. Articles, 1,200–1,800 words. Essays, 800–1,200 words. Field notes, 200–500 words. Written material, $.05 a word; $100 for e-rights. Pays on publication. Provides 5 contributor copies.

Minnesota Parent

Minnesota Premier Publications
1115 Hennepin Avenue South
Minneapolis, MN 55403

Editor: Kathleen Stoehr

Description and Interests: Minnesota parents of babies through tweens turn to this monthly publication for relevant activities and resources for families in their state. Contained in its pages are articles, reviews, and profiles that focus on such topics as education, health, relationships, and money. Circ: 52,500.
Website: www.mnparent.com

Freelance Potential: 50% written by nonstaff writers. Publishes 24 freelance submissions yearly.

Submissions and Payment: Sample copy available at website. For freelance consideration, submit letter to the editor. Accepts email via website or to kstoehr@mnpubs.com. Response time varies. First North American serial and electronic rights. Articles and depts/columns, word lengths vary; $50–$350. Pays on publication.

Mississippi Magazine

5 Lakeland Circle
Jackson, MS 39216

Editor: Melanie Ward

Description and Interests: *Mississippi Magazine* celebrates the people, places, culture, and history of the Magnolia State. Upbeat articles, profiles of local personalities, and nostalgic essays fill six issues each year. Circ: 42,000.
Website: www.mississippimagazine.com

Freelance Potential: 15% written by nonstaff writers. Publishes 10–20 freelance submissions yearly; 25% by unpublished writers, 25% by new authors, 50% by experts. Receives 30+ queries monthly.

Submissions and Payment: Sample copy and guidelines available at website. Query with brief bio and clips. Send complete ms for On Being Southern essay only. Prefers hard copy; will accept email to editor@mismag.com (no attachments). No simultaneous submissions. SASE. Responds in 2 months. First rights. Articles, 800–1,200 words; $250–$350. Depts/columns, 100–1,200 words; $25–$250. Pays on publication. Provides 6 copies.

Missouri Conservationist

2901 West Truman Boulevard
P.O. Box 180
Jefferson City, MO 65102

Editor in Chief: Ara Clark

Description and Interests: *Missouri Conservationist* reports monthly on the fish, forest, and wildlife resources of the state and on what is being done to preserve them. The magazine also gives readers information on outdoor activities and ideas for enjoying nature. Circ: 480,000.
Website: www.mdc.mo.gov/conmag

Freelance Potential: 20% written by nonstaff writers. Publishes 6 freelance submissions yearly; 5% by unpublished writers, 5% by authors who are new to the magazine, 90% by experts. Receives 6 queries monthly.

Submissions and Payment: Sample copy available at website. Guidelines available. Query with writing samples. Contact through website. Responds in 1–2 months. First, reprint, and electronic rights. Articles, 1,400–1,700 words; $400–$600. Pays on acceptance. Provides 10 copies.

Missouri Life

501 High Street, Suite A
Boonville, MO 65233

Editor in Chief: Danita Allen Wood

Description and Interests: Missouri residents and visitors can discover the state's people and places in this magazine's articles and images. Published six times each year, *Missouri Life* provides information on everything from history to restaurants to recreation. Circ: 22,000.
Website: www.missourilife.com

Freelance Potential: 75% written by nonstaff writers. Publishes 40 freelance submissions yearly; 5% by unpublished writers, 30% by authors who are new to the magazine, 10% by experts. Receives 30 queries monthly.

Submissions and Payment: Sample copy and guidelines available at website. Query with photo or art ideas. Accepts email to info@missourilife.com. Response time varies. Rights vary. Articles, 1,500 words. Depts/columns, 600 words. Written material, payment rates vary, $50 minimum. Payment policy varies.

Mobile Bay Parents

Watson Media
555 Farmington Road
Montgomery, AL 36109

Publisher & Editor in Chief: Lynn Knighton

Description and Interests: This monthly magazine for parents along Alabama's Gulf Coast launched in 2011. It features parenting information, local resources for family entertainment, and guides for camps, after-school activities, and summer fun. The editorial is a mix of child development advice from local experts and practical tips for busy families. Circ: 25,000.
Website: www.mobilebayparents.com

Freelance Potential: Receives numerous submissions monthly.

Submissions and Payment: Sample articles available at website. Query. Accepts email to info@mobilebayparents.com. Response time varies. Articles and depts/columns, word lengths vary. Rights and payment rates unknown.

Moms & Dads Today

P.O. Box 3617
Duluth, MN 55803-3617

Publisher: Tracy Mangan

Description and Interests: Created in 2012, *Moms & Dads Today* offers parenting articles and resources for families on the shores of Lake Superior. It prefers articles that can be localized to the region, but will consider general family-related topics. Each of the six issues focuses on a specific theme. Circ: 23,000.
Website: www.momsanddadstoday.com

Freelance Potential: Open to freelance submissions.

Submissions and Payment: Guidelines and editorial calendar available at website. Send complete ms. Accepts hard copy or email submissions (in Word) to tracy@momsanddads-today.com. Include contact details, word count, source list, and brief bio. Responds only if interested. First North American print and electronic rights. Payment varies. Pays for articles for use in print and online; does not pay for filler.

Montana

The Magazine of Western History

225 North Roberts Street
P.O. Box 201201
Helena, MT 59620-1201

Editor: Molly Holz

Description and Interests: The Montana Historical Society publishes this quarterly magazine featuring peer-reviewed articles on significant people, places, and events in the history of the state and of the American and Canadian Wests. Suggestions for illustrations enhance submissions. Circ: 9,000.
Website: www.montanahistoricalsociety.org

Freelance Potential: 95% written by nonstaff writers. Publishes 20 freelance submissions yearly; 30% by unpublished writers, 75% by authors who are new to the magazine. Receives 20 mss monthly.

Submissions and Payment: Sample copy available. Guidelines available at website. Send complete ms. Prefers email submissions to mholz@mt.gov; will accept hard copy. SASE. Responds in 6–8 weeks. All rights. Articles, to 6,000 words. Depts/columns, word lengths vary. B/W prints. No payment.

The Monthly

1416 Park Avenue
Alameda, CA 94501

Co-Editor: Sarah Weld

Description and Interests: Issues of this monthly magazine delve into Northern California's East Bay area through essays, articles, profiles, and reviews. Topics include: food, health, science, the environment, and entertainment. Circ: 60,000.
Website: www.themonthly.com

Freelance Potential: 95% written by nonstaff writers. Of the freelance submissions published yearly, 25% are by authors who are new to the magazine. Receives 20 queries, 10 unsolicited mss monthly.

Submissions and Payment: Sample copy available at website. Guidelines and editorial calendar available. Query with clips. Accepts email to editorial@themonthly.com (Word attachments). Responds to queries in 1 month, to mss in 2 months. First North American serial rights. Articles, to 4,000 words; $50–$800. Depts/columns, to 1,500 words; $50–$350. Kill fee, 100%. Pays on publication. Provides 2 contributor's copies.

Mpls.St.Paul

220 South 6th Street, Suite 500
Minneapolis, MN 55402-4507

Executive Editor: Adam Platt

Description and Interests: Minneapolis–St. Paul residents and visitors alike turn to this monthly magazine for information on where to shop, dine, and be entertained in the area. Interviews with local personalities, regional event coverage, and articles on the area's culture, history, and lifestyle are also featured. Circ: 72,000.
Website: www.mspmag.com

Freelance Potential: 25% written by nonstaff writers. Publishes 100 freelance submissions yearly; 5% by authors who are new to the magazine.

Submissions and Payment: Sample articles available at website. Guidelines available. Query with résumé, outline, and clips; or send complete ms. Accepts email to edit@mspmag.com or to specific editors via the website. Responds in 6 weeks. All rights. Articles, 500–4,000 words. Depts/columns, 400–1,000 words. Written material, $.50 per word. Pays on acceptance. Provides 1 contributor's copy.

Naperville Dog

P.O. Box 4915
Naperville, IL 60567

Editor: Brooke Keane

Description and Interests: This magazine premiered in 2011 covering the local canine community. Published six times each year in print and digitally, it includes profiles of dogs and owners, trainer tips, businesses, veterinary advice, and reviews. It seeks nonfiction topics from local writers that relate to the Naperville canine community. Circ: 6,000.
Website: www.napervilledog.com

Freelance Potential: Receives numerous submissions monthly.

Submissions and Payment: Sample articles and guidelines available at website. Send complete ms. Accepts hard copy (include Article submission form from website) and electronic submissions via website. SASE. Response time varies. Articles and depts/columns, word lengths vary. Print and electronic rights. Written material, $25. Provides 1 contributor's copy.

Nebraska History

Nebraska State Historical Society
P.O. Box 82554
Lincoln, NE 68501-2544

Editor: David Bristow

Description and Interests: Nebraska history is vividly portrayed in this quarterly. It offers well-researched pieces that are written to appeal to a general audience. Circ: 3,500.
Website: www.nebraskahistory.org

Freelance Potential: 90% written by nonstaff writers. Publishes 12 freelance submissions yearly; 10% by unpublished writers, 50% by authors who are new to the magazine, 90% by experts. Receives 4 queries and unsolicited mss monthly.

Submissions and Payment: Sample articles and guidelines available at website. Query or send complete ms with photos and author bio. Accepts submissions of hard copy and CD, or email to david.bristow@nebraska.gov (Word or RTF attachments). SASE. Responds in 2 months. All rights. Articles, 3,000–7,500 words; short articles, 1,000–2,000 words. No payment. Provides 6 contributor's copies.

NebraskaLand

Nebraska Game and Parks Commission
P.O. Box 30370
Lincoln, NE 68503-0370

Editor: Doug Carroll

Description and Interests: Published 10 times each year, this magazine focuses on Nebraska's great outdoors, with colorfully illustrated articles about hiking, fishing, wildlife, and natural history. Circ: 30,000.
Website: www.outdoornebraska.ne.gov

Freelance Potential: 10% written by nonstaff writers. Publishes 10 freelance submissions yearly; 2% by unpublished writers, 5% by authors who are new to the magazine, 8% by experts. Receives 5 queries monthly.

Submissions and Payment: Guidelines available at website. Query with résumé, outline, and writing samples; or send complete ms. Accepts hard copy with disk submissions and email to doug.carroll@nebraska.gov. SASE. Responds in 6 months. First serial rights. Articles, 800–4,000 words. Depts/columns, to 1,000 words. Written material, $.15 per word. Payment policy varies. Provides 10 author's copies.

Nevada Magazine

401 North Carson Street
Carson City, NV 89701

Editor: Matthew B. Brown

Description and Interests: *Nevada Magazine* offers informative and entertaining features on the state. Published six times each year, it covers city and rural destinations, new restaurants, personality profiles, history, upcoming events, and the gaming industry. Circ: 20,000.
Website: www.nevadamagazine.com

Freelance Potential: 25% written by nonstaff writers. Publishes 20–25 freelance submissions yearly; 20% by unpublished writers, 20% by authors who are new to the magazine, 10% by experts. Receives 5–10 queries monthly.

Submissions and Payment: Sample copy available. Guidelines available at website. Prefers query; will accept complete ms. Prefers email to editor@nevadamagazine.com or phone call to 775-687-0602. Response time varies. First North American serial rights. Articles, 500–1,500 words; $.25–$.35 per word or flat rate up to $250. Pays on publication.

New England Entertainment Digest

P.O. Box 88
Burlington, MA 01803

Owner/Editor: JulieAnn Charest Govang

Description and Interests: Updated daily, this ezine provides timely information on the region's arts and entertainment scene. It covers everything from casting calls to opening night reviews, as well as workshops for industry professionals. All content pertains to New England and New York. Hits per month: 10,000.
Website: www.jacneed.com

Freelance Potential: 100% written by nonstaff writers. Publishes 120 freelance submissions yearly; 2% by authors who are new to the magazine. Receives 5 queries monthly.

Submissions and Payment: Sample articles available at website. Query or send complete ms. Accepts email queries to submissions@jacneed.com and hard copy. Rights vary. Written material, word lengths and payment rates vary. Pays on publication.

New Hampshire Magazine

150 Dow Street
Manchester, NH 03101

Executive Editor: Rick Broussard

Description and Interests: *New Hampshire Magazine* provides the latest information on what's new and newsworthy in the state. Its monthly issues also feature articles on interesting personalities, destinations, events, restaurants, shopping, and home decor. Circ: 30,000.
Website: www.nhmagazine.com

Freelance Potential: 40% written by nonstaff writers. Publishes 100 freelance submissions yearly; 10% by authors who are new to the magazine.

Submissions and Payment: Sample articles and editorial calendar available at website. Guidelines available. Query or send complete ms. Accepts hard copy and email to editor@nhmagazine.com. SASE. Response time varies. First and electronic rights. Articles and depts/columns, word lengths vary; $50–$500. Pays on publication. Provides 2 copies.

New Haven Magazine

20 Grand Avenue
New Haven, CT 06513

Editor: Michael C. Bingham

Description and Interests: This monthly magazine publishes articles about newsworthy happenings in and around New Haven, Connecticut. Topics include local politics, culture, and business. Comprehensive regional events coverage and profiles of local personalities are featured as well. Circ: 13,000.
Website: www.newhavenmagazine.com

Freelance Potential: 75% written by nonstaff writers. Publishes 60 freelance submissions yearly; 10% by unpublished writers, 10% by authors who are new to the magazine, 10% by experts. Receives 10 queries monthly.

Submissions and Payment: Sample issue available at website. Guidelines available. Query with clips. Accepts email queries to mbingham@conntact.com. Responds in 1 week. All rights. Articles, 500–2,000 words; payment rates vary. Kill fee varies. Pays on publication. Provides 3–5 contributor's copies.

New Jersey Family

480 Morris Avenue
Summit, NJ 07901

Editor: Judy Grover

Description and Interests: With an emphasis on northern and central New Jersey, this parenting publication is distributed free on a monthly basis. Features and departments cover child development, education, health, family finance, and kids' activities. The editors prefer to work with New Jersey writers. All material must have a local angle. Circ: 126,000.
Website: www.njfamily.com

Freelance Potential: 60% written by nonstaff writers. Publishes 150 freelance submissions yearly; 33% by unpublished writers, 33% by authors who are new to the magazine. Receives 20 queries monthly.

Submissions and Payment: Sample articles and guidelines available at website. Query. Accepts email to njfamilyeditor@njfamily.com and simultaneous submissions if identified. Response time varies. First serial rights. Articles, 600–1,200 words; $.10 per word; $25–$50 for reprints; web-only posts, $5–$15. Pays on publication. Provides tearsheet.

New Mexico Magazine

Lew Wallace Building
495 Old Santa Fe Trail
Santa Fe, NM 87505-2750

Editor in Chief: Dave Herndon

Description and Interests: This monthly travel and lifestyle magazine spotlights the culture, people, history, arts, and recreational opportunities of the Land of Enchantment. Its editorial mix covers the down-home with the upscale for state residents and visitors. The Going Places section provides the best chance of acceptance for new writers. Circ: 93,408.
Website: www.nmmagazine.com

Freelance Potential: 60% written by nonstaff writers. Publishes 180 freelance submissions yearly; 20% by authors who are new to the magazine.

Submissions and Payment: Sample articles and guidelines available at website. Query with clips. Accepts hard copy and email queries to queries@nmmagazine.com (embed pitch, add clips as attachments). No unsolicited mss. Response time varies. First publication and exclusive worldwide rights. Articles, 500–1,500 words; $.35–$.40 per word. Pays on acceptance. Provides 2 contributor's copies.

Newport Life Magazine

101 Malbone Road
Newport, RI 02840

Managing Editor: Annie Sherman

Description and Interests: *Newport Life Magazine* is just that—a magazine about life in Newport, Rhode Island. Appearing seven times each year, it covers local politics, education, and environmental issues. Local personality profiles and interviews, event coverage, and articles on Newport's history are regularly featured. Circ: 10,000.
Website: www.newportlifemagazine.com

Freelance Potential: 15% written by nonstaff writers. Publishes 10 freelance submissions yearly; 5% by authors who are new to the magazine. Receives 5 queries monthly.

Submissions and Payment: Sample articles, guidelines, and editorial calendar available at website. Query with clips. Accepts hard copy and email to asherman@newportri.com. SASE. Responds in 1 month. First North American serial rights. Written material, word lengths and payment rates vary. Kill fee, 25%. Pays on publication.

New York Family

79 Madison Avenue, 16th Floor
New York, NY 10016

Editor: Eric Messinger

Description and Interests: *New York Family* is an upscale monthly publication with a hip tone that targets Manhattan parents. It features articles on health, relationships, education, fashion, and travel. It also offers profiles on parent business and charity ventures, usually run by parents and families, and the occasional essay. Circ: 40,000+.
Website: www.newyorkfamily.com

Freelance Potential: 50% written by nonstaff writers. Publishes 40 freelance submissions yearly; 40% by authors who are new to the magazine. Receives 10–12 queries monthly.

Submissions and Payment: Sample copy available at website. Query. Accepts email queries to emessinger@manhattanmedia.com. Response time varies. First rights. Articles, 800–1,200 words. Depts/columns, 400–800 words. Written material, $25–$300. Pays on publication. Provides 3 contributor's copies.

New York Runner

New York Road Runners
9 East 89th Street
New York, NY 10128

Editorial Director: Gordon Bakoulis

Description and Interests: This member magazine for the New York Road Runners appears five times a year. In addition to articles on health and nutrition, it offers expert training tips and profiles of athletes, teams, and coaches. It also publishes organization news and activities, as well as event and race coverage. Circ: 45,000.
Website: www.nyrr.org

Freelance Potential: 50% written by nonstaff writers. Publishes 10–20 freelance submissions yearly; 25% by authors who are new to the magazine, 25% by experts. Receives 5–10 queries monthly.

Submissions and Payment: Sample copy and guidelines available. Query. Accepts hard copy. SASE. Responds in 1 month. First North American serial rights. Articles, 750–1,000 words; $50–$250. 8x10 B/W prints; $35–$300. Pays on publication.

New York Sportscene

2090 Fifth Avenue, Suite 2
Ronkonkoma, NY 11779

Editor in Chief: Mike Cutino

Description and Interests: Whether it's the Yankees, Giants, Rangers, or Nets, *New York Sportscene* provides avid sports fans the most comprehensive coverage on all sports in the tri-state area. Published monthly, it features interviews and articles on athletes, coaches, management personnel, and other personalities. Circ: 40,000.
Website: www.nysportscene.com

Freelance Potential: 20% written by nonstaff writers. Publishes 25 freelance submissions yearly; 5% by unpublished writers, 10% by authors who are new to the magazine, 5% by experts. Receives 2 queries monthly.

Submissions and Payment: Sample copy and guidelines available. Query. Accepts email queries to mike@nysportscene.com. Responds in 2 months. One-time rights. Articles, 1,000 words; $.075 per word. Payment policy varies.

New York State Conservationist

625 Broadway, 4th Floor
Albany, NY 12233-4502

Assistant Editor: Eileen Stegemann

Description and Interests: Published six times each year by the New York State Department of Environmental Conservation, this magazine targets a general audience with articles that relate to the state's natural, environmental, cultural, and historic resources. News from the DEC is also included. Circ: 80,000.
Website: www.theconservationist.org

Freelance Potential: 67% written by nonstaff writers. Publishes 20 freelance submissions yearly; 5% by unpublished writers, 10% by authors who are new to the magazine, 15% by experts. Receives 20+ queries monthly.

Submissions and Payment: Sample copy and guidelines available at website. Query. Accepts hard copy. SASE. Response time varies. All rights. Articles, to 2,000 words; $50–$100. Pays after publication. Provides contributor's copies.

New York Tennis

United Sports Publications
1220 Wantagh Avenue
Wantagh, NY 11793

Editor in Chief: Eric C. Peck

Description and Interests: This magazine promotes tennis on every level in the New York community, from professional to amateur tennis players, businesses that support the sport, and youth players and their families. It is the official publication of the U.S. Tennis Association Eastern-Metro Region. Freelance writers should know the sport well and focus on local topics only. Circ: 20,000.
Website: www.newyrktennismagazine.com

Freelance Potential: Receives numerous submissions monthly.

Submissions and Payment: Sample articles available at website. Query. Accepts email to info@usptennis.com. Response time varies. Articles and depts/columns, word lengths vary. Rights and payment rates and policy vary.

Niagara Escarpment Views

50 Ann Street
Georgetown, Ontario L7G 2V2
Canada

Editor: Gloria Hildebrandt

Description and Interests: This quarterly covers all life along Canada's Niagara Escarpment, including tourist destinations, homes, gardens, local culture, nature, history, and outdoor activities. Circ: 25,000.
Website: www.neviews.ca

Freelance Potential: 70% written by nonstaff writers. Publishes 8–12 freelance submissions yearly; 5% by unpublished writers, 5% by authors who are new to the magazine, 10% by experts. Receives 1 query monthly.

Submissions and Payment: Sample copy available. Query with clips. Accepts email queries through the website. Responds in 1 day. First Canadian serial and electronic rights. Articles, 1,000 words. Depts/columns, 750 words. Written material, $.40 per word. Kill fee, 50%. Pays on acceptance. Provides copies.

NNY Business

260 Washington Street
Watertown, NY 13601

Editor: Kenneth J. Eysaman

Description and Interests: Small business owners, corporate executives, and others who play a key role in the business community in and around Watertown, New York, are the target audience of this monthly. It reports on local business news, and covers economic development, regional trends in manufacturing, the retail and service industries, and entrepreneurship in Lewis, St. Lawrence, and Jefferson counties. Circ: 3,000.
Website: www.nnybizmag.com

Freelance Potential: 50% written by nonstaff writers. Publishes 30–40 freelance submissions yearly; 20% by unpublished writers, 20% by authors who are new to the magazine, 10% by experts.

Submissions and Payment: Query. Accepts email to nnybusiness@wdt.net. Accepts hard copy. SASE. Response time varies. All rights. Articles, word lengths and payment rates vary. Pays on acceptance. Provides 2 contributor's copies.

North Dakota Horizons

1605 East Capitol Avenue, Suite 101
P.O. Box 1091
Bismarck, ND 58502

Editor: Andrea Winkler Collin

Description and Interests: The articles in this quarterly magazine focus on the people, places, and events that make North Dakota worth visiting. Submissions should include high-quality photographs whenever possible. Circ: 10.000.
Website: www.ndhorizons.com

Freelance Potential: 25% written by nonstaff writers. Publishes 6 freelance submissions yearly; 10% by unpublished writers, 20% by authors who are new to the magazine, 10% by experts. Receives 10 queries, 3 unsolicited mss each month.

Submissions and Payment: Sample articles and guidelines available at website. Prefers queries, accepts complete ms. Prefers email to ndhorizons@btinet.net; will accept hard copy. SASE. Response time varies. First rights. Features, to 1,500–2,000 words; short articles, essays, 1,000–1,200; $.20 per word. Slides, 5x7 prints, or digital images at 300 dpi; $125–$300. Pays on publication. Provides 3 copies.

Northeast Flavor

1 Government Street, Suite 1
Kittery, ME 03904

Editor in Chief: Jean Kerr

Description and Interests: This regional food, wine, and dining magazine celebrates the tastes and flavors of the northeastern region of the United States. Published quarterly, it offers articles on chefs and restaurants of the region, along with cooking tips and techniques and recipes for home cooks. Circ: 20,000.
Website: www.northeastflavor.com

Freelance Potential: Open to submissions in each of its six sections: food and cooking, chefs and restaurants, "In the Glass," local farms and markets, and Northeast traditions.

Submissions and Payment: Sample articles available at website. For submission information, contact the editor at editor@northeastflavor.com. Response time varies. Written material, word lengths vary. Rights and payment rates unknown.

Northern Breezes Sailing Magazine

3949 Winnetka Avenue North
Minneapolis, MN 55427

Editor: Alan Kretzschmar

Description and Interests: Sailing on the Great Lakes and the lakes of the Midwest is the focus of this magazine, which appears nine times each year. Technical and general interest articles, personality profiles and interviews, event coverage, and destination pieces are featured, as well as book, boat, and product reviews. Circ: 17,500.
Website: www.sailingbreezes.com

Freelance Potential: 90% written by nonstaff writers. Publishes 50 freelance submissions yearly; 25% by authors who are new to the magazine.

Submissions and Payment: Sample copy and guidelines available at website. Query or send complete ms. Accepts email to alan@sailingbreezes.com and hard copy. Response time varies. First serial and electronic rights. Articles, 1,000–3,000 words; $50–$150. Book reviews, $25. Pays on publication.

Northern Woodlands

P.O. Box 471
Corinth, VT 05039

Assistant Editor: Meghan Oliver

Description and Interests: Scientifically accurate, highly readable articles distinguish this quarterly magazine about forestry and woodlands preservation in New England and New York State. It is open to working with new writers. Circ: 15,000.
Website: www.northernwoodlands.org

Freelance Potential: 60% written by nonstaff writers. Publishes 50 freelance submissions yearly; 1% by unpublished writers, 5% by authors who are new to the magazine, 20% by experts. Receives 30 queries, 15 unsolicited mss monthly.

Submissions and Payment: Sample copy and guidelines available at website. Query with clips. Send complete ms for Knots and Bolts. Accepts email to meghan@northernwoodlands.org. Responds in 2–4 weeks. One-time rights. Articles, 1,000–3,000 words; $.10 per word. Depts/columns, 200–700 words; payment rates vary. Pays on publication. Provides 1–2 contributor's copies.

Northwest Travel

P.O. Box 1370
Gig Harbor, WA 98335

Editor in Chief: Allen Cox

Description and Interests: *Northwest Travel* seeks to promote travel to the northwest region of the U.S. with its focus on nature, history, unique events, and restaurants. It is published six times each year. Circ: 50,000.
Website: www.nwtravelmag.com

Freelance Potential: 70% written by nonstaff writers. Publishes 75 freelance submissions yearly; 10% by unpublished writers, 15% by authors who are new to the magazine, 70% by experts. Receives 30+ queries monthly.

Submissions and Payment: Sample articles available at website. Guidelines available. Query with location, seasonal information, and artwork if available. Accepts email to editor@nwtravelmag.com. Responds in 2–3 months. First North American serial rights. Articles and depts/columns, 350–3,000 words. Payment rates vary. Slides or digital images. Pays on publication. Provides 3 contributor's copies.

Not Born Yesterday!

P.O. Box 722
Brea, CA 92822

Publisher/Editor: Amanda Blake Secola

Description and Interests: Published monthly, *Not Born Yesterday!* caters to the senior citizens of Southern California with news on activities, health and fitness issues, the arts, and financial issues. It is especially open to articles pertaining to the habits and lifestyles of people between the ages of 80 and 100. Circ: 100,000+.
Website: www.nbynews.com

Freelance Potential: 60% written by nonstaff writers. Publishes 20 freelance submissions yearly; 25% by unpublished writers, 25% by authors who are new to the magazine, 50% by experts. Receives 15 queries monthly.

Submissions and Payment: Sample copy available. Query with outline. Accepts email queries to nbynews@juno.com. Responds in 1 month. All rights. Articles, 750 words. Depts/columns, 200 words. No payment. Provides 2 contributor's copies.

Now

189 Church Street
Toronto, Ontario M5B 1Y7
Canada

Editor/Publisher: Michael Hollett

Description and Interests: Toronto-based news, events, and entertainment are the focus of this weekly tabloid, written for young, urban professionals. Each issue offers the latest information on the city's arts, music scene, dining, and fashion. Profiles of local residents are also featured. Circ: 411,000.
Website: www.nowtoronto.com

Freelance Potential: 35% written by nonstaff writers. Publishes 52 freelance submissions yearly; 3% by unpublished writers, 3% by authors who are new to the magazine, 10% by experts. Receives 30 queries monthly.

Submissions and Payment: Sample articles and editorial calendar available at website. Query. Prefers email queries (see website for appropriate editor). Responds in 2 weeks. Rights vary. Written material, word lengths and payment rates vary. Payment policy varies.

Now & Then 

The Appalachian Magazine

Center for Appalachian Studies and Services
East Tennessee State University
P.O. Box 70556
Johnson City, TN 37614-1707

Managing Editor: Randy Sanders

Description and Interests: Fiction, features, personal essays, and poems are found in this magazine about life in Appalachia. Themed issues are published twice each year. Circ: 500–1,000.
Website: www.etsu.edu/cass/nowandthen

Freelance Potential: 80% written by nonstaff writers. Publishes 40–50 freelance submissions yearly; 15% by unpublished writers, 20% by new authors. Receives 10 queries, 10 mss monthly.

Submissions and Payment: Guidelines and sample articles at website. Prefers original work; will accept reprints. Send complete ms. with cover letter. Accepts email to nowandthen@etsu.edu (Word attachments); hard copy, simultaneous submissions if identified. SASE. First North American serial rights. Written material, to 1,500 words. Offers an honorarium and 1 copy.

NYMetro Parents 

1440 Broadway, Suite 501
New York, NY 10018

Managing Editor: Dawn Roode

Description and Interests: *NYMetro Parents* publishes eight award-winning monthly magazines that serve families in New York City and its Long Island and Connecticut suburbs. While it does not accept poetry, fiction, travel pieces, and rarely essays, it welcomes articles on a range of parenting and family issues. Circ: 400,000.
Website: www.nymetroparents.com

Freelance Potential: Receives many freelance submissions monthly.

Submissions and Payment: Sample copy and guidelines available at website. Query or send complete ms with 2 writing samples, a sidebar, and contact information for sources. Accepts email to DRoode@davlermedia. com. Responds only if interested. Articles, 800–900 words. Depts/columns, 600 words. Rights vary. Payment rates and policy vary.

OC Family Magazine

1451 Quail Street, Suite 201
Newport Beach, CA 92660

Editor: Susan Belknapp

Description and Interests: This monthly magazine for parents in Orange County, California, features regional issues and sources. It also has general articles that would be found in national parenting publications. Topics include relationships, health, and school. Circ: 55,000.
Website: www.ocfamily.com

Freelance Potential: 82% written by nonstaff writers. Publishes 50 freelance submissions yearly; 1% by unpublished writers, 1% by authors who are new to the magazine, 5% by experts. Receives 15 queries monthly.

Submissions and Payment: Sample copy available at website. Guidelines, theme list, editorial calendar available. Query. Accepts email queries to sbelknapp@churmmedia.com. Responds in 1 month. One- time rights. Articles, 800–2,500 words; $100–$500. B/W and color prints; $90. Kill fee, $50. Pays 45 days after publication. Provides 3 contributor's copies.

Official Virginia Wine Lover

P.O. Box 1110
Forest, VA 24551

Editor: June Britt

Description and Interests: This e-newsletter is known as "your source for the latest Virginia wine news." It covers the wines, vineyards, and winery events and festivals throughout the state in regularly updated issues. Restaurant reviews, detailed information about wine trails, and other destination pieces are featured. Hits per month: 50,000+.
Website: www.vawinelover.com

Freelance Potential: 20% written by nonstaff writers. Publishes 10–20 freelance submissions yearly; 10% by authors who are new to the magazine.

Submissions and Payment: Sample copy available at website. Query. Accepts hard copy. SASE. Response time varies. First North American serial rights. Articles and depts/columns, word lengths and payment rates vary. Payment policy varies.

Ohio

1422 Euclid Avenue, Suite 730
Cleveland, OH 44115

Executive Editor: Vivian Pospisil

Description and Interests: This monthly magazine showcases all things offered by the state of Ohio, including its culture, history, outdoor life, dining, and homes. Circ: 80,000.
Website: www.ohiomagazine.com

Freelance Potential: 40% written by nonstaff writers. Publishes 48 freelance submissions yearly; 10% by authors who are new to the magazine. Receives 30 queries monthly.

Submissions and Payment: Sample copy, guidelines, and editorial calendar available at website. Query with résumé and 3 clips. Accepts hard copy and email queries to vspospisil@ohiomagazine.com. SASE. Responds in 6–8 weeks. First North American serial rights. Articles, to 2,000 words. Depts/columns, 1,000–1,300 words. Front-of-book pieces, 250 words. Written material, payment rates vary. Pays on publication. Provides 2 contributor's copies.

Oklahoma Today

120 North Robinson, Suite 600
Oklahoma City, OK 73102

Editor: Steffie Corcoran

Description and Interests: Oklahoma's hot spots and hidden corners are explored in this glossy, colorful magazine. Published six times each year, it strives to capture the state's essence through engaging writing about distinctive people and places. Circ: 38,000.
Website: www.oklahomatoday.com

Freelance Potential: 80% written by nonstaff writers. Publishes 40 freelance submissions yearly; 5% by unpublished writers, 10% by authors who are new to the magazine, 20% by experts. Receives 30 queries monthly.

Submissions and Payment: Sample articles and guidelines available at website. Query with clips or send complete ms. Prefers email to steffie@oklahomatoday.com; accepts hard copy. Response time varies. First rights. Articles, to 3,500 words. Depts/columns, 250–800 words. Written material, $.25 per word. Pays on publication. Provides 1 copy.

Orange Appeal

903 Lake Lily Drive, B359
Maitland, FL 32751

Editor and Publisher: Christi Ashby

Description and Interests: Educated, active, and affluent women in Central Florida make up the target audience of this community magazine, appearing six times each year. It covers the region's events, fashion, and philanthropy, and offers profiles of successful and interesting women. Coverage of family events and issues, and shopping destinations are also featured. Circ: 13,000+.
Website: www.orangeappeal.com

Freelance Potential: Open to submissions from writers who are familiar with Central Florida and can offer well-written articles that will appeal to the readership.

Submissions and Payment: Sample articles available at website. For submission information, contact the editor at christi@orangeappeal.com. Response time varies. Written material, word lengths vary. Payment rates and policy unknown.

Orange Magazine

40 Mulberry Street
P.O. Box 2046
Middletown, NY 10940

Editor: Brenda Gilhooly

Description and Interests: From the Hudson Valley Media Group, *Orange Magazine* is filled with information on and articles about Orange County, New York. Personality profiles, county issues, and lifestyle pieces are all featured here. It is published six times each year. It is a sister publication of the recently launched *Ulster Magazine*, which offers similar content geared for residents of nearby Ulster County. Circ: Unavailable.
Website: www.orangemagazineny.com

Freelance Potential: Freelance submissions are accepted for both *Orange* and *Ulster* magazines. Writers from the region are preferred.

Submissions and Payment: Sample copy available at website. Query for submission information. Accepts hard copy. Response time varies. Articles and depts/columns, word lengths vary. Payment information unknown.

Oregon Business

715 SW Morrison, Suite 800
Portland, OR 97205

Editor: Robin Doussard

Description and Interests: *Oregon Business* is about the state's businesses, the policies that shape them, and the people who run them. Published monthly, it profiles not only dynamic businessmen and women but also successful partnerships and collaborations. Circ: 20,000.
Website: www.oregonbusiness.com

Freelance Potential: 20% written by nonstaff writers. Publishes 15–20 freelance submissions yearly; 10–20% by authors who are new to the magazine, 10–20% by experts. Receives 10–20 queries monthly.

Submissions and Payment: Sample articles and guidelines available at website. Query with résumé and clips. Accepts email queries to editor@oregonbusiness.com (attach files). Responds in 2 weeks. First North American serial rights. Articles, 700–3,000 words. Depts/columns, 100–600 words. Written material, $.50 per word. Pays on publication. Provides 3 contributor's copies.

Oregon Coast

4969 Highway 101, Suite 2
Florence, OR 97439

Editor: Alicia Spooner

Description and Interests: The Oregon coast's beauty, history, and attractions are showcased in this magazine that appears six times each year. It prefers vivid articles that motivate readers to follow in the author's footsteps. Circ: 40,000.
Website: www.northwestmagazines.com

Freelance Potential: 70% written by nonstaff writers. Publishes 20–60 freelance submissions yearly; 10% by unpublished writers, 15% by authors who are new to the magazine, 50% by experts. Receives 20–30 queries monthly.

Submissions and Payment: Sample copy and guidelines available at website. Query with location, source info, and clips, or send complete ms. Accepts email to edit@nwmags.com, hard copy, and simultaneous submissions if identified. SASE. Responds in 3 months. First North American serial rights. Written material, 450–3,000 words; $100–$650. Kill fee, 33%. Pays on publication. Provides 2 contributor's copies.

Ottawa Family Living

Coyle Publishing
67 Neil Avenue
Stittsville, Ontario K2S 1B9
Canada

Editor: Pat den Boer

Description and Interests: Targeting Ottawa families with young children, *Ottawa Family Living* covers education, recreation, health, child-rearing, and child development. Published quarterly, it is geared to families at all stages and aims to be a valuable resource for making the best of family life in Ottawa. Circ: 40,000.
Website: www.ottawafamilyliving.com

Freelance Potential: Receives numerous submissions monthly.

Submissions and Payment: Sample articles available at website. Query. Accepts email to Pam@coylepublishing.com. Response time varies. Articles, word lengths vary. Rights and payment rates and policy vary.

Our State

Down Home in North Carolina

P.O. Box 4552
Greensboro, NC 27404

Editor: Elizabeth Hudson

Description and Interests: If it's about North Carolina, it's covered here. *Our State* celebrates the people, places, history, and culture of the state for readers who are passionate about where they live. It is published monthly. Circ: 150,000+.
Website: www.ourstate.com

Freelance Potential: 100% written by nonstaff writers. Publishes 15–20 freelance submissions yearly; 5% by unpublished writers, 15% by authors who are new to the magazine.

Submissions and Payment: Sample articles, guidelines, and editorial calendar available at website. Query with résumé and writing samples. Accepts hard copy and email to editorial@ourstate.com. SASE. Responds in 6–8 weeks. First North American serial and electronic rights. Articles, 1,500 words. Written material, payment rates vary. Pays on publication. Provides 1 contributor's copy.

Out & About

307 A Street
Wilmington, DE 19801

Contributing Editor: Bob Yearick

Description and Interests: *Out & About* covers Delaware's entertainment offerings with articles on dining, music, movies, nightlife, and area events. Published monthly, the magazine always welcomes in-depth profile queries. Circ: 28,000.
Website: www.outandabout.com

Freelance Potential: 30% written by nonstaff writers. Publishes 60–75 freelance submissions yearly; 10% by unpublished writers, 40% by authors who are new to the magazine, 5% by experts. Receives 5–10 queries monthly.

Submissions and Payment: Sample copy available at website. Guidelines, and editorial calendar available. Query with outline. Accepts email queries via the website. Responds in 1 week. All rights. Articles, 800–2,500 words. Fiction, to 2,000 words. Depts/columns, to 1,000 words. Written material, payment rates vary. Pays on publication.

Out Smart

3406 Audubon Place
Houston, TX 77006

Senior Editor: Nancy Ford

Description and Interests: Serving the gay, lesbian, bisexual, and transgender community of the Houston area, *Out Smart* focuses on regional and national news and local events, entertainment, and culture. Published monthly, it also has select distribution in other Texas cities. Circ: 60,000.
Website: www.outsmartmagazine.com

Freelance Potential: 65% written by nonstaff writers. Publishes 20 freelance submissions yearly; 50% by unpublished writers, 10% by authors who are new to the magazine, 10% by experts. Receives 10 queries monthly.

Submissions and Payment: Sample copy and guidelines available at website. Query through submission form on website or email nancy@outsmartmagazine.com. SASE. Responds in 6 weeks. First North American serial rights. Articles, 800–2,500 words. Depts/columns, 50–1,200 words. Written material, \$.05–\$.08 per word. Pays on publication.

The Ozarks Mountaineer

815 Lee Street
Branson, MO 65616

Editor: Fred R. Pfister

Description and Interests: The history, culture, people, and natural beauty of the Ozark Mountains are portrayed in this magazine, published six times each year. Circ: 18,000.
Website: www.ozarksmountaineer.com

Freelance Potential: 90% written by nonstaff writers. Publishes 50 freelance submissions yearly; 20% by unpublished writers, 20% by new authors. Receives 45 unsolicited mss monthly.

Submissions and Payment: Sample articles and guidelines available at website. Send complete ms with photos. Prefers email to frpfister@suddenlink.net (Word or Quark attachments); will accept hard copy and disk submissions. SASE. Response time varies. First and electronic rights. Articles, 200–1,500 words; $30 per published page. Depts/columns, word lengths vary; $45. Pays on publication. Provides 3 contributor's copies.

Palm Beach Woman 

39 West 37th Street, 15th Floor
New York, NY 10018

Senior Staff Writer: Deborah Welky

Description and Interests: Aimed at Florida's Palm Beach County's professional women, specifically midlevel and executive management, entrepreneurs, and the self employed, this publication provides career, business, and lifestyle features. Published quarterly, it also showcases women of achievement in the local businessworld. Circ: 40,000.
Website: www.palmbeachwoman.com

Freelance Potential: Unavailable.

Submissions and Payment: Sample copy available at website. Query. Accepts email queries to deb@palmbeachwoman.com. Rights and payment rates unavailable.

Palm Springs Life

303 North Indian Canyon Drive
Palm Springs, CA 92262

Editor in Chief: Steven Biller

Description and Interests: This magazine showcases the lifestyle of its affluent readership, which includes residents of Palm Springs, and of tourists to the area. Coverage of local events, entertainment, and the arts rounds out each issue. It is published monthly. Circ: 50,000.
Website: www.palmspringslife.com

Freelance Potential: 85% written by nonstaff writers. Publishes 25–30 freelance submissions yearly; 15% by authors who are new to the magazine, 5% by experts. Receives 8 queries, 8 unsolicited mss monthly.

Submissions and Payment: Sample copy and editorial calendar available. Query or send complete ms. Accepts hard copy and email submissions to steven@palmspringslife.com. SASE. Responds in 2 months. First rights. Written material, word lengths vary; $250–$500. Pays on publication. Provides 2 contributor's copies.

Panama Days

1751 Richardson Street, Suite 5530
Montreal, Quebec H3K 1G6
Canada

Editor: Jennifer McMorran

Description and Interests: *Panama Days* is published annually and distributed to hotel rooms to inform and entertain guests about Panama's history, culture, entertainment, and recreational activities. Circ: Unavailable.
Website: www.nightspublications.com

Freelance Potential: 90% written by nonstaff writers. Publishes 15 freelance submissions yearly; 25% by authors who are new to the magazine, 75% by experts. Receives 5 queries monthly.

Submissions and Payment: Sample copy and guidelines available. Query with writing sample. Accepts email queries to editor@nightspublications.com. Responds in 1–2 months. Exclusive or first Caribbean and North American rights. Articles, 250–900 words. Depts/columns, 250–500 words. Written material, $100–$375. Pays on acceptance.

Parenting New Hampshire

150 Dow Street
Manchester, NH 03101

Editor: Melanie Hitchcock

Description and Interests: This monthly tabloid is packed with articles, essays, profiles, activities, reviews and poetry aimed at New Hampshire parents. It features practical information for all ages. Preference given to local writers. Circ: 27,000.
Website: www.parentingnh.com

Freelance Potential: 85% written by nonstaff writers. Publishes 25–35 freelance submissions yearly; 20% by unpublished writers, 50% by authors who are new to the magazine. Receives 1,200 queries, 12–24 unsolicited mss monthly.

Submissions and Payment: Sample copy and guidelines available at website. Query with writing samples or send complete ms. Accepts hard copy, and email to editor@parentingnh.com. SASE. Response time varies. All rights. Articles and depts/columns, 500–800 words. Written material, $30. Pays on acceptance. Provides 3 contributor's copies.

Patch.com

Chief Content Officer: Rachel Feddersen

Description and Interests: This innovative addition to the digital publishing field is all about local news. It seeks editors and writers who are passionate about where they live to report on the people, issues, and events that are currently impacting their town and community. Each town's multi-media site is interactive with residents being able to post events, opinions, and photos. Circ: Varies.
Website: www.patch.com

Freelance Potential: Varies from site to site.

Submissions and Payment: Sample sites and job opportunities available at website. Fill out form on website to edit a particular region or contact editor of a specific town for freelance writing. Rights unknown. Written material, word length varies. Payment rates vary. Payment policy unknown.

Pennsylvania Game News

2001 Elmerton Avenue
Harrisburg, PA 17110-9797

Submissions: Patricia Monk

Description and Interests: As the official voice of the Pennsylvania Game Commission, this magazine highlights outdoor sports opportunities in the state. Published monthly, it covers hunting, conservation, wildlife, and natural history. Circ: 75,000.
Website: www.penngamenews.com

Freelance Potential: 70% written by nonstaff writers. Publishes 60 freelance submissions yearly; 15% by unpublished writers, 25% by authors who are new to the magazine. Receives 60 unsolicited mss monthly.

Submissions and Payment: Sample copy available at website. Guidelines available. Send complete ms. Accepts hard copy and hard copy submissions, with disk (Word). SASE. Responds in 6–8 weeks. All rights. Articles, 1,500–2,500; $.06 per word. Color prints and illustrations; $15. Pays on acceptance. Provides 3 contributor's copies.

Pennsylvania Heritage

Commonwealth Keystone Building
400 North Street, Plaza Level
Harrisburg, PA 17120-0053

Editor: Michael J. O'Malley III

Description and Interests: This quarterly introduces a general readership to Pennsylvania's rich culture and historic legacy. Topics covered include travel, historic sites, oral history, science, industry, and the arts. Circ: 5,000+.
Website: www.paheritage.org

Freelance Potential: 60% written by nonstaff writers. Publishes 8–12 freelance submissions yearly; 20% by unpublished writers, 20% by authors who are new to the magazine.

Submissions and Payment: Sample copy and guidelines available. Send complete ms with author bio, list of 6–12 books for further reading, credits, sources, and artwork. Accepts disk submissions with hard copy and email submissions to miomalley@pa.gov (Word attachments). Response time varies. First and electronic rights. Articles, 2,000–3,500 words; $100–$500. Pays on publication.

Pennsylvania Magazine

P.O. Box 755
Camp Hill, PA 17001-0755

Editor: Matthew K. Holliday

Description and Interests: *Pennsylvania Magazine,* published six times each year, features engaging articles on the state's history, people, places, and events. Circ: 26,400.
Website: www.pa-mag.com

Freelance Potential: 100% written by nonstaff writers. Publishes 90 freelance submissions yearly; 15% by unpublished writers, 30% by authors who are new to the magazine. Receives 15 queries monthly.

Submissions and Payment: Sample copy available. Query with outline and artwork. Accepts hard copy and email queries to editor@pa-mag.com. SASE. Responds in 1 month. One-time, first-use rights. Articles, 1,000–2,500 words, $200–$410; shorts, 100–800 words, $60–$150. Photographs, 4x6 or larger color prints, slides, or digital files; $25–$35. Pays on acceptance. Provides 5 contributor's copies.

Philadelphia City Paper

123 Chestnut Street, 3rd Floor
Philadelphia, PA 19106

Editor in Chief: Theresa Everline

Description and Interests: *Philadelphia City Paper* covers the politics, current events, business, and social issues happening in the city. It also publishes profiles of the city's personalities, and reports on its active arts, entertainment, an dining scene. It is published weekly. Circ: 85,000.
Website: www.citypaper.net

Freelance Potential: 50% written by nonstaff writers. Publishes 20 freelance submissions yearly; 10% by unpublished writers, 10% by authors who are new to the magazine. Receives 10 queries monthly.

Submissions and Payment: Sample copy and theme list/editorial calendar available at website. Accepts email queries to editorial@citypaper.net (Word attachments). Responds in 1 month. Rights vary. Articles, 500–3,000 words; $.10 per word. Kill fee, 50%. Pays on publication. Provides 5 contributor's copies.

Philadelphia Magazine

1818 Market Street, 36th Floor
Philadelphia, PA 19103

Managing Editor: Bridget Salmons

Description and Interests: *Philadelphia Magazine* offers an in-depth look at the people, places, and news of the City of Brotherly Love. Published monthly, it is a guide to the city's food, fashions, events, and arts. Circ: 116,706.
Website: www.phillymag.com

Freelance Potential: 5% written by nonstaff writers. Publishes 10 freelance submissions yearly; 20% by unpublished writers, 20% by authors who are new to the magazine, 20% by experts. Receives 10 queries monthly.

Submissions and Payment: Sample copy available at website. Query with résumé and clips. Accepts hard copy, faxes to 215-656-3502, and email to bsalmons@phillymag.com. SASE. Response time varies. First North American serial rights. Articles, 3,000–6,000 words. Depts/columns, 1,000–4,000 words. Written material, payment rates vary. Pays on publication. Provides 2 contributor's copies.

Phoenix Magazine

15169 North Scottsdale Road, Suite C310
Scottsdale, AZ 85254

Managing Editor: Adam Klawonn

Description and Interests: *Phoenix Magazine* features the ins and outs of the city's entertainment, events, dining options, and recreational activities. Read by tourists and residents alike, it also publishes historical articles. It appears monthly. Circ: 73,000.
Website: www.phoenixmag.com

Freelance Potential: 50% written by nonstaff writers. Publishes 30 freelance submissions yearly; 25% by authors who are new to the magazine. Receives 10 queries monthly.

Submissions and Payment: Sample copy available. Guidelines and editorial calendar available at website. Query with résumé and credentials. Prefers email to aklawonn@citieswestpub.com; accepts hard copy. SASE. Responds in 6 weeks. First North American serial rights. Articles, 600–1,500 words. Depts/columns, 150–500 words. Payment varies. Pays on publication. Provides 1 contributor's copy.

PineStraw

145 West Pennsylvania Avenue
Southern Pines, NC 28387

Editor: Jim Dodson

Description and Interests: Celebrating the people, places, and culture of the Sandhills is the purpose of this publication. Each month it features articles on local arts, food, and outdoor recreation as well as significant personalities who have shaped the past and will impact the future of the region. Fiction, poetry, and creative nonfiction are also included. Circ: 15,000.
Website: www.pinestrawmag.com

Freelance Potential: Unavailable.

Submissions and Payment: Sample copy available at website. Query. Accepts email queries to jim@pinestrawmag.com. Rights and payment information unknown.

The Pitch

1701 Main Street
Kansas City, MO 64108

Editor: Scott Wilson

Description and Interests: A sister publication to New York City's *Village Voice*, *The Pitch* provides high-energy, progressive coverage of what's happening in Kansas City. It profiles the city's vibrant arts, entertainment, and culture scenes, including music reviews. It also provides investigative coverage of the city's political, educational, and social issues. It is published weekly. Circ: 90,000.
Website: www.pitch.com

Freelance Potential: 20% written by nonstaff writers. Publishes 20 freelance submissions yearly. Receives 6 queries monthly.

Submissions and Payment: Sample copy available at website. Guidelines available. Query with 3 clips. Accepts hard copy. SASE. Responds in 1 month. First North American serial rights. Written material, word lengths and payment rates vary. Pays on publication. Provides 2 contributor's copies.

Pitt Magazine

University of Pittsburgh
400 Craig Hall
Pittsburgh, PA 15260

Editor in Chief: Cindy Gill

Description and Interests: Although focused on the stories of students, alumni, and staff at the University of Pittsburgh, this quarterly strives to find angles that are entertaining and worthwhile to any reader. Circ: 240,000.
Website: www.pittmag.pitt.edu

Freelance Potential: 20% written by nonstaff writers. Publishes 25 freelance submissions yearly; 1% by unpublished writers, 10% by authors who are new to the magazine. Receives 20 queries monthly.

Submissions and Payment: Sample copy available at website. Query with writing samples. Accepts hard copy and email queries to pittmag@pitt.edu. SASE. Responds in 1 month. First North American serial rights. Articles, 2,000–2,500 words. Depts/columns, 150–750 words. Written material, $75–$1,250. Kill fee, 25%. Pays on acceptance. Provides 5 contributor's copies.

Pittsburgh Parent

P.O. Box 374
Bakerstown, PA 15007

Editor: Patricia Poshard

Description and Interests: Local information and resources on topics relating to raising a family in the Pittsburgh area are the focus of this monthly parenting magazine. Circ: 43,000.
Website: www.pittsburghparent.com

Freelance Potential: 80% written by nonstaff writers. Publishes 120 freelance submissions yearly; 20% by authors who are new to the magazine. Receives 100–120 queries and unsolicited mss monthly.

Submissions and Payment: Sample copy and guidelines available at website. Editorial calendar, available. Query or send complete ms. Accepts email to editor@pittsburghparent.com. Responds if interested. First serial rights. Articles, to 950 words. Cover feature, 2,500–2,750 words. Depts/columns, word lengths vary. Fiction, to 1,000 words. Written material, payment rates vary. Pays 45 days after publication.

Points North

568 Peachtree Parkway
Cumming, GA 30041

Senior Editor: Heather Brown

Description and Interests: The target audience of this upscale, monthly publication is comprised of the residents of "Atlanta's stylish northside." Articles showcase the best entertainment, shopping, restaurants, and experiences the area has to offer. It also features prominent personalities and business leaders, as well as home, fashion, and lifestyle pieces applicable to its affluent readership. Circ: 70,000.
Website: www.ptsnorth.com

Freelance Potential: 10% written by nonstaff writers. Publishes 25+ freelance submissions yearly; 10% by new authors. Receives 10+ queries monthly.

Submissions and Payment: Sample copy available at website. Query with clips, author qualifications, and photo ideas. Accepts email queries to editorial@ptsnorth.com (Word attachments). Responds in 6–8 weeks. First serial and electronic rights. Written material, word lengths vary; $250–$500. Pays on publication.

Portland Monthly

165 State Street
Portland, ME 04101

Editor & Publisher: Colin Sargent

Description and Interests: Appearing 10 times each year, this magazine features trends, personalities, and unique offerings in Portland and Maine's coastal communities. It also publishes short fiction in every issue. Circ: 100,000+.
Website: www.portlandmonthly.com

Freelance Potential: 75% written by nonstaff writers. Publishes 50 freelance submissions yearly; 5% by unpublished writers, 10% by authors who are new to the magazine, 20% by experts. Receives 50 queries, 100 unsolicited mss monthly.

Submissions and Payment: Sample articles and guidelines available at website. Query with clips and author bio. Accepts email queries to staff@portlandmonthly.com (no attachments) and hard copy. Response time varies. First serial and electronic rights. Articles, to 2,000 words. Fiction, to 1,000 words. Depts/columns, to 1,000 words. Written material, $100–$600. Pays on publication. Provides 1 copy.

PQ Monthly

P.O. Box 306
Portland, OR 97207

Editor in Chief: Julie Cortez

Description and Interests: Targeting the gay, lesbian, and transgender population, *PQ Monthly* covers all lifestyle topics in and around Portland, Oregon. Interviews and essays appear alongside arts and culture news and regional events. Circ: 200,000.
Website: www.pqmonthly.com

Freelance Potential: Receives many freelance submissions monthly.

Submissions and Payment: Sample copy available at website. Query. Accepts email queries to info@pqmonthly.com. Response time varies. Written material, word lengths vary. Rights vary. Payment rates and policy vary.

Prairie Business

P.O. Box 6008
Grand Forks, ND 58206-6008

Editor: Kris Bevill

Description and Interests: Featuring the most up-to-date business news and trends for the Northern Plains, *Prairie Business* covers financial services, agriculture, energy, and technology, among other topics. It is published monthly. Circ: 15,000+.
Website: www.prairiebizmag.com

Freelance Potential: 30% written by nonstaff writers. Publishes 35–40 freelance submissions yearly; 5% by unpublished writers, 5–10% by authors who are new to the magazine, 5% by experts. Receives 1–2 queries monthly.

Submissions and Payment: Sample copy and theme list/editorial calendar available at website. Query with author biography. Accepts email queries to kbevill@prairiebizmag.com and hard copy. SASE. Responds in 1–2 months. Rights vary. Articles, 700–900 words; $.15 per word. Pays on publication. Provides 2 contributor's copies.

Prairie Messenger

Box 190
Muenster, Saskatchewan S0K 2Y0
Canada

News Editor: Maureen Weber

Description and Interests: *Prairie Messenger* is a tabloid newspaper that covers local, national, and international news and current affairs from a Catholic perspective. Published 45 times each year, it seldom accepts submissions from non-Canadian writers. Circ: 5,300.
Website: www.prairiemessenger.ca

Freelance Potential: 50% written by nonstaff writers. Publishes 12 freelance submissions yearly; 10% by unpublished writers, 10% by authors who are new to the magazine. Receives 1 unsolicited ms monthly.

Submissions and Payment: Sample articles and guidelines available at website. Query or send complete ms. Accepts email submissions to pm.canadian@stpeterspress.ca. Responds in 2 months. Rights vary. Articles and depts/columns, to 950 words. Comment and features, $60; poetry $25. Pays at the end of each month. Provides 2–4 copies.

Provincetown Arts 

650 Commercial Street
Provincetown, MA 02657

Editor: Christopher Busa

Description and Interests: Once each year, *Provincetown Arts* compiles a collection of articles, stories, and poetry that showcase the work of Cape Cod's creative community. Circ: 10,000.
Website: www.provincetownarts.org

Freelance Potential: 90% written by nonstaff writers. Publishes 80 freelance submissions yearly.

Submissions and Payment: Sample articles and guidelines available at website. Send complete ms with biographical paragraph between September and December only. Accepts email to cbusa@comcast.net. Responds in 2 months. One-time and second rights. Articles, 1,500–4,000 words; $100+. Fiction, 500–5,000 words; $100+. Poetry, no line limits, to 3 poems per submission; $25–$50. 8x10 B/W or color prints; $20–$100. Pays on publication. Provides 3 contributor's copies.

Raising Arizona Kids

5229 North 7th Avenue, #B202
Phoenix, AZ 85254-5257

Editor & Publisher: Karen Davis Barr

Description and Interests: This Arizona parenting magazine focuses on issues that affect the health and well being of children from birth through high school. Arts, education, community outreach, parenting tips, local events, food, and crafts are among the topics covered in this monthly. It only works with Arizona-based writers. Circ: 35,000.
Website: www.raisingarizonakids.com

Freelance Potential: 35% written by nonstaff writers. Publishes up to 50 freelance pieces yearly; 10% by unpublished writers, 20% by authors who are new to the magazine. Receives 4 queries monthly.

Submissions and Payment: Sample articles and guidelines available at website. Accepts email queries to editorial@raisingarizonakids.com. Include links to published articles, if available. No simultaneous submissions. Responds in 30 days. All rights. Articles, 1,000–3,000 words; $150 and up. Depts/columns, 250-750 words; $25 and up. Pays on publication.

Random Lengths News

P.O. Box 731
San Pedro, CA 90733-0731

Managing Editor: Terelle Jerricks

Description and Interests: This tabloid bills itself as an alternative paper, reporting news not available in the mainstream media. Published 27 times each year, it runs features about people and events in San Pedro, Wilmington, Long Beach, and their surrounding areas in California. Circ: 22,500.
Website: www.randomlengthsnews.com

Freelance Potential: 60% written by nonstaff writers. Of the freelance submissions published yearly, 5% are by authors who are new to the magazine. Receives 2 queries monthly.

Submissions and Payment: Sample copy and editorial calendar available at website. Query or send complete ms. Accepts email submisions to editor@randomlengthsnews.com (RTF attachments). Response time varies. First North American serial rights. Articles, to 1,500 words; $.05 per word. Kill fee for regular contributors only. Pays on publication. Provides contributor's copies upon request.

Recreation News

1713 Grafton Ridge Court
Forest Hill, MD 21050

Editor: Marvin Bond

Description and Interests: Governmental and corporate employees working in the Baltimore and Capital area read this monthly travel magazine. Pieces on little-known destinations and activities are sought. Circ: 100,000+.
Website: www.recreationnews.com

Freelance Potential: 75% written by nonstaff writers. Publishes 150 freelance submissions yearly; 15% by authors new to the magazine, 5% by experts. Receives 20 queries monthly.

Submissions and Payment: Sample copy, guidelines, and editorial calendar available at website. Query with clips. Prefers email submissions to editor@ recreationnews.com (Word attachments). Accepts reprints. Responds in 1 month if interested. One-time and electronic rights. Articles, 600–1,000 words. Depts/columns, 300–600 words. Written material, $50–$300. JPEG images at 150 dpi minimum. Pays on publication.

Red River Family Magazine

P.O. Box 7654
Lawton, OK 73506

Executive Editor: Laura Clevenger

Description and Interests: This monthly targets families in southwestern Oklahoma and northern Texas with articles on health, relationships, education, military families, and area events. It is open to working with new writers with fresh ideas. Circ: 20,000.
Website: www.redriverfamily.com

Freelance Potential: 70% written by nonstaff writers. Publishes 100 freelance submissions yearly; 10% by unpublished writers, 80% by authors who are new to the magazine.

Submissions and Payment: Sample copy available at website. Query with clips or writing samples. Accepts email submissions and guideline requests to laura@redriverfamily.com. Response time varies. One-time print and electronic rights. Articles and depts/columns, word lengths vary; $20–$50. Pays on acceptance. Provides 2 contributor's copies.

Reign

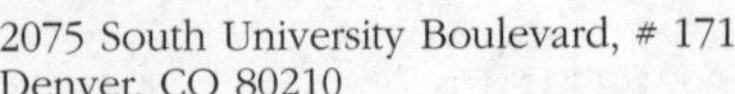

2075 South University Boulevard, # 171
Denver, CO 80210

Publisher and Editor in Chief: Betsy Martin

Description and Interests: "Denver's authority on fabulous," this new digital lifestyle magazine covers everything the mile-high city has to offer young women, from culture to dining and style. Readers are "self-professed girly girls," who are educated and affluent. Circ: 9,000.
Website: www.denverreign.com

Freelance Potential: Receives numerous submissions monthly.

Submissions and Payment: Sample copy available at website. Query. Accepts email to betsy@ denverreign.com. Response time varies. Articles and depts/columns, word lengths vary. Rights and payment rates and policy vary.

Reverb Monthly

1008 Western Ave., Suite 300
Seattle, WA 98104

Editor: Chris Kornelis

Description and Interests: From the *Seattle Weekly,* this monthly print magazine covers the music scene in and around Seattle. It aims to provide a snapshot of the Seattle sound and put that scene into perspective. Each issue uses a different theme as a starting point for conversations about the audible and cultural implications of the sounds, institutions, and personalities of the local music scene. Circ: 77,500.
Website: www.microapp.seattleweekly.com/reverb/reverbymonthly

Freelance Potential: Receives numerous queries monthly.

Submissions and Payment: Sample copy available at website. Query. Accepts email to music@ seattleweekly.com. Response time varies. Articles and depts/columns, word lengths vary. First North American serial rights. Written material, $50–$800.

Reverie

Midwest African American Literature

P.O. Box 23096
Detroit, MI 48223

Editors: Qiana Towns & Randall Horton

Description and Interests: *Reverie* is an annual literary journal featuring fiction, essays, and poetry by African American writers with ties to the American Midwest. It appears in print and online. Circ: 1,000.
Website: www.aquariuspressbookseller.net/reverie midwestafricanamericanliterature.html

Freelance Potential: 100% written by nonstaff writers. Publishes 75 freelance submissions yearly; 75% by unpublished writers, 25% by authors who are new to the magazine. Receives 10–20 unsolicited mss monthly.

Submissions and Payment: Sample copy at website. Send ms. Accepts email only to reverie.journal@gmail.com (Word or RTF attachments with "Reverie" in subject line). See website for deadline. Fiction and essays, to 3,000 words. Reviews, to 500 words. Poetry, to 50 lines; to 3 poems per submission. No payment. Provides 1 contributor's copy.

Rio Grande Family

P.O. Box 7654
Lawton, OK 73506

Executive Editor: Laura Clevenger

Description and Interests: This monthly publication is written for families in central New Mexico. It features articles on health, relationships, education and military families, and also serves as a guide to the region's family events. The editors are open to working with new writers who have fresh ideas. Circ: 25,000.
Website: www.riograndefamily.com

Freelance Potential: 70% written by nonstaff writers. Publishes 100 freelance submissions yearly; 10% by unpublished writers, 80% by authors who are new to the magazine.

Submissions and Payment: Sample copy available at website. Query with clips or writing samples. Accepts email submissions and guidelines requests to laura@riograndefamily.com. Response time varies. One-time print and electronic rights. Articles and depts/columns, word lengths vary; $20–$50. Pays on acceptance. Provides 2 contributor's copies.

River Hills Traveler

P.O. Box 245
St. Clair, MO 63077-0245

Editor: Emery Styron

Description and Interests: *River Hills Traveler* is a tabloid that helps readers explore Missouri's great outdoors. Its features cover topics such as hunting, fishing, camping, hiking, and birding in the state. Published 11 times each year, it is most open to articles about traditional and nontraditional outdoor activities in specific place settings in Missouri. Circ: 5,000.
Website: www.riverhillstraveler.com

Freelance Potential: 90% written by nonstaff writers. Publishes 11 freelance submissions yearly by authors who are new to the magazine. Receives 3 unsolicited mss monthly.

Submissions and Payment: Guidelines available at website. Send complete ms. Accepts email to estyron@rhtrav.com (no attachments) and simultaneous submissions. Availability of photos improves change of acceptance. Responds in 1 month. One-time rights. Articles, to 1,000 words; $15–$50. Pays on publication. Provides a 1-year subscription.

The Roanoker

3424 Brambleton Avenue
Roanoke, VA 24018

Editor: Kurt Rheinheimer

Description and Interests: This magazine covers the metropolitan Roanoke lifestyle with articles on dining, home design, entertainment, and business. It is published six times each year. Circ: 15,000.
Website: www.theroanoker.com

Freelance Potential: 50% written by nonstaff writers. Publishes 12–18 freelance submissions yearly; 10% by writers who are new to the magazine. Receives 6 queries, 6 unsolicited mss monthly.

Submissions and Payment: Sample articles and editorial calendar available at website. Query or send complete ms. Accepts disk submissions (Word) and email to jwood@leisurepublishing.com. SASE. Responds in 1–2 months. First North American serial rights. Articles, 800–2,000 words. Depts/columns, 400 words. Written material, payment rates vary. Pays on publication. Provides 2 contributor's copies.

Roanoke Valley Woman

Daily Herald
916 Roanoke Ave., P.O. Box 520
Roanoke Rapids, NC 27870

Executive Editor: Stephen Hemelt
Editor: Kris Smith

Description and Interests: *Roanoke Valley Woman* is a quarterly magazine from the *Daily Herald*. It offers women of all ages and stages information on careers, family, the single life, and retirement. All stories must have a local angle. Circ: 6,000.
Website: www.microapp.seattleweekly.com/reverb/reverbymonthly

Freelance Potential: Receives numerous queries monthly.

Submissions and Payment: Sample articles available at website. Query. Accepts email to ksmith@rrdailyherald.com or shemelt@rrdailyherald.com. Response time varies. Articles, word lengths vary. Rights vary. Payment rates and policy vary.

Rocky Mountain Rider

P.O. Box 995
Hamilton, MT 59840

Editor: Natalie Riehl

Description and Interests: Positive human interest stories that appeal to "horsepeople" living in the American West appear in this monthly magazine. Profiles, historical pieces, regional event coverage, and new product information make up its editorial content. Circ: 14,000.
Website: www.rockymountainrider.com

Freelance Potential: 90% written by nonstaff writers. Publishes 100 freelance submissions yearly; 50% by authors who are new to the magazine. Receives 5 queries, 20 unsolicited mss monthly.

Submissions and Payment: Sample copy and guidelines available at website. Query or send complete ms. Accepts hard copy. SASE. Responds to queries in 1 month, to mss in 2 months. Rights vary. Articles, 500–2,000 words. Filler, 100–500 words. Written material, about $30 per 1,000 words. B/W or color prints, $5. Pays on publication.

Rural Missouri

P.O. Box 1645
Jefferson City, MO 65102

Associate Editor: Heather Berry

Description and Interests: Published by a Missouri electric cooperative, this monthly celebrates rural life. It features articles on a broad spectrum of regional topics. Circ: 540,000+.
Website: www.ruralmissouri.coop

Freelance Potential: 15% written by nonstaff writers. Publishes 60 freelance submissions yearly; 50% by unpublished writers, 50% by authors who are new to the magazine. Receives 15 unsolicited mss monthly.

Submissions and Payment: Sample copy, guidelines at website. Prefers query with clips; accepts complete ms. Prefers email submissions to hberry@ruralmissouri.coop (RTF attachments). Accepts hard copy. SASE. Availability of artwork improves chance of acceptance. Responds in 6–8 weeks. First and electronic rights. Articles, 1,000–1,100 words. JPEG images at 300 dpi. All material, payment rates vary. Pays on acceptance. Provides 3–6 copies.

Sacramento News & Review

1124 Del Paso Boulevard
Sacramento, CA 95815

Co-Editors: Rachel Leibrock, Nick Miller

Description and Interests: From hard-hitting investigative pieces to wacky stories, this weekly newspaper covers the news of Sacramento and its environs. Circ: 85,000.
Website: www.newsreview.com/sacramento/home

Freelance Potential: 50% written by nonstaff writers. Publishes 1,000 freelance submissions yearly; 5% by unpublished writers, 20% by authors who are new to the magazine. Receives 21 queries monthly.

Submissions and Payment: Local writers only. Sample copy and guidelines available. Query with résumé and clips. Accepts hard copy and email queries to melinda@newsreview.com. SASE. Responds in 2 weeks. First North American serial and electronic rights. Articles, 1,200 words. Reviews, 600 words. Essays and op-eds, 900 words. Written material, payment rates vary. Pays on publication. Provides 2 contributor's copies.

St. Louis Family

SLM Media Group
1600 South Brentwood Boulevard, #550
St. Louis, MO 63144

Editor in Chief: Christy Marshall

Description and Interests: Launched in 2012, *St. Louis Family* is published monthly along with *St. Louis Magazine,* and the website stlmag.com. They bring the best of St. Louis to families living in the city, including information about education, health care, sports, entertainment, and shopping. It features affordable family activities, and articles on schools, daycare facilities, and more. Circ: 200,000.
Website: www.stlmag.com/St-Louis-Magazine/StL-Family

Freelance Potential: Unknown.

Submissions and Payment: Sample articles available at website. Submit story ideas via the online form at http://corp.stlmag.com/submit-story-idea. Rights and payment information unavailable.

St. Maarten Nights

1751 Richardson Street, Suite 5530
Montreal, Quebec H3K 1G6
Canada

Editor: Jennifer McMorran

Description and Interests: Writers who are familiar with St. Maarten are needed for this annual magazine. It publishes profiles of the island's personalities, hot spots, tourist attractions, and dining and shopping districts. It also publishes pieces on the island's culture. Circ: 225,000.
Website: www.nightspublications.com

Freelance Potential: 90% written by nonstaff writers. Publishes 15 freelance submissions yearly; 25% by authors who are new to the magazine, 75% by experts. Receives 5 queries monthly.

Submissions and Payment: Sample copy and guidelines available. Query with writing samples. Accepts email queries to editor@nightspublications.com. Responds in 1–2 months. Exclusive or first Caribbean and North American rights. Articles, 250–700 words. Depts/columns, 250–500 words. Written material, \$100–\$300. Pays on acceptance.

San Antonio

121 Interpark Boulevard, Suite 407
San Antonio, TX 78216

Editor in Chief: Rebecca Fontenot

Description and Interests: This monthly lifestyle publication brings the latest trends in dining, travel, home and garden, the arts, and style in San Antonio to readers, along with profiles of notable residents. It strives to appeal to both a mature, affluent audience as well as young up and comers. Circ: 35,000.
Website: www.sanantoniomag.com

Freelance Potential: 65–70% written by nonstaff writers.

Submissions and Payment: Sample articles available at website. Query with clips. Accepts email to rebecca@sanantoniomag.com and hard copy. Response time varies. FIrst North American rights. Articles, 1,000–1,200 words. Depts/columns, 200–800 words. Written material, \$.35–\$.50 a word. Kill fee, 25%. Pays on acceptance.

San Diego Family Magazine

P.O. Box 23960
San Diego, CA 92193-3960

Editor: Kirsten Flournoy

Description and Interests: *San Diego Family Magazine* gives parents an insider view of places and personalities of interest in this part of California. Published monthly, it also offers essays and informative articles on social issues, as well as book, product, and dining reviews, and craft ideas. Circ: 120,000.
Website: www.sandiegofamily.com

Freelance Potential: 90% written by nonstaff writers. Publishes 120–200 freelance submissions yearly; 10% by authors who are new to the magazine. Receives 10 mss monthly.

Submissions and Payment: Sample copy and guidelines available at website. Query or send complete ms. Accepts email submissions to Kirsten@sandiegofamily.com (put "Article Submission or Query" as subject). Responds in 1 month. First and electronic rights. Articles, 400-1,000 words; \$1.25 per column inch. Pays on publication. Provides 1 copy.

Sandlapper

The Magazine of South Carolina

3007 Millwood Avenue
Columbia, SC 29205

Editor: Elaine Gillespie

Description and Interests: This quarterly regional focuses on the very best that South Carolina has to offer, from its natural beauty to its rich heritage. *Sandlapper* is always interested in putting the spotlight on individuals who are making a positive difference. Circ: 60,000.
Website: www.sandlapper.org/magazine

Freelance Potential: 60% written by nonstaff writers. Publishes 32 freelance submissions yearly; 15% by authors who are new to the magazine. Receives 25 queries, 2 unsolicited mss each month.

Submissions and Payment: Sample articles and guidelines available at website. Query or send complete ms. Accepts hard copy and email submissions to elaine@sandlapper.org. SASE. No simultaneous submissions. Responds in 1–2 months. First and second rights. Articles, 400–2,400 words; $50–$100 per published page. Pays 1 month after publication.

San Francisco

243 Vallejo Street
San Francisco, CA 94111

Editor in Chief: Bruce Kelley

Description and Interests: This monthly covers the people, places, and happenings of "the city by the Bay" through articles, profiles, and reviews. Its content is provided by experienced writers who thoroughly know the city's political, business, social, and cultural scenes. Circ: 115,000.
Website: www.sanfranmag.com

Freelance Potential: 50% written by nonstaff writers. Publishes 60 freelance submissions yearly; 5% by unpublished writers, 30% by authors who are new to the magazine. Receives 100 queries monthly.

Submissions and Payment: Sample copy available. Query with clips. Accepts hard copy. SASE. Responds in 1–2 months. First North American serial rights. Articles and depts/columns, word lengths vary; $1 per word. Kill fee, 25%. Pays on acceptance.

Santa Barbara Family Life

P.O. Box 4867
Santa Barbara, CA 93140

Editor: Nansie Chapman

Description and Interests: This monthly tabloid informs those living in Santa Barbara about the area's educational, recreational, arts and entertainment happenings. It also offers readers articles on health and relationships and connects them with businesses, volunteer opportunities, and community resources. Circ: 60,000.
Website: www.sbfamilylife.com

Freelance Potential: 5% written by nonstaff writers. Publishes 10 freelance submissions yearly; 5% by unpublished writers, 10% by authors who are new to the magazine. Receives 20 queries and unsolicited mss monthly.

Submissions and Payment: Sample copy available at website. Query or send complete ms. Accepts email to nansie@sbfamilylife.com. Responds if interested. Rights vary. Articles, 500–1,100 words. Depts/columns, word lengths vary. Written material, $25–$35. Payment policy varies.

Savannah Magazine

P.O. Box 1088
Savannah, GA 31405

Editor: Linda Wittish

Description and Interests: Six times each year, this magazine publishes articles on regional travel, history, and lifestyle, as well as topics of general interest. It also profiles local personalities and places. Circ: 15,000.
Website: www.savannahmagazine.com

Freelance Potential: 90% written by nonstaff writers. Publishes 60 freelance submissions yearly; 10% by authors who are new to the magazine. Receives 200 queries, 10 unsolicited mss monthly.

Submissions and Payment: Sample copy and guidelines available. Editorial calendar available at website. Query with outline or send complete ms. Accepts email to editor@savannahmagazine.com. Responds in 1 month. First rights. Articles, 500–1,000 words. Depts/columns, 250–500 words. Written material, payment rates vary. Kill fee, 20%. Pays on publication. Provides 1 contributor's copy.

Scene Magazine

P.O. Box 489
Fort Collins, CO 80522

Editor: Amy Schakel

Description and Interests: *Scene Magazine* is an entertainment and lifestyle publication for the Northern Colorado region. Written solely by students, it offers in-depth coverage of the region's arts, local events, music, theater, restaurants, and after-hours entertainment. It is published monthly. Articles addressing the area's cultural trends are always of interest. Circ: 20,000.
Website: www.scenemagazine.info

Freelance Potential: Of the freelance submissions published yearly, 20% are by authors who are new to the magazine, 20% are by experts. Receives 4–8 queries monthly.

Submissions and Payment: Sample articles available at website. Query with résumé and writing samples. Accepts email to editor@scenemagazine.info. Responds in 2 months. All rights. Articles, 500–1,200 words; $35–$80. Kill fee, 50%. Pays on publication. Provides 10 contributor's copies.

Seattle Magazine

Tiger Oak Publications, Inc.
1518 First Avenue South, Suite 500
Seattle, WA 98134

Editorial Director: Rachel Hart

Description and Interests: This monthly regional magazine offers residents and visitors an inside look at the city and region, from its arts and entertainment scene to business and politics to its natural beauty and recreation opportunities. Circ: 49,425.
Website: www.seattlemag.com

Freelance Potential: 75% written by nonstaff writers. Publishes 100 freelance submissions yearly; 5% by unpublished writers, 5% by authors who are new to the magazine. Receives 20 queries monthly.

Submissions and Payment: Local writers only. Sample articles and guidelines available at website. Query with résumé, outline, and clips. Accepts email queries to appropriate editor for your subject matter (see website). Responds if interested. One-time and electronic rights. Articles, 1,500–3,500 words, $400–$1,000. Depts/ columns, 1,200 words; $350. Pays 3 months after publication. Provides 2+ copies.

Serendipity

Fairfield & Westchester Counties

Unger Publishing
1 Dock Street
Stamford, CT 06902

Submissions Editor

Description and Interests: Covering family living in Fairfield County, Connecticut, and nearby Westchester County, New York, *Serendipity* offers lifestyle articles on living, health and fitness, food and drink, entertaining, home design, and travel. The magazine also publishes media reviews and coverage of the region's arts scene. It is published 10 times a year. Circ: 12,500.
Website: www.serendipitysocial.com

Freelance Potential: The editors state they are always happy to hear editorial pitches from readers and qualified writers. The best pitches are those that offer smart editorial infused with humor and fun.

Submissions and Payment: Sample articles available at website. Query. Accepts email queries to editorial@UngerPublishing.com. Response time varies. Articles and depts/columns, word lengths vary.

Simply Buckhead

P.O. Box 11633
Atlanta, GA 30355

Editor: Allison Weiss Entrekin

Description and Interests: With the tagline, "Your Guide to Living Well in Atlanta," *Simply Buckhead* is an upscale lifestyle magazine distributed 6 times each year through Buckhead and the surrounding areas of Decatur, Vinings, Sandy Springs, Brookhaven, and Highland. It strives to be the authority on who to know and where to go in the region, focusing on the neighborhoods' best and brightest people and places. Circ: 22,000.
Website: www.simplybuckhead.com

Freelance Potential: Open to submissions from writers who are familiar with the region. It looks for a writing tone that is sophisticated yet approachable.

Submissions and Payment: Sample copy and editorial calendar available at website. Query with pitch. Accepts email queries to editor@simplybuckhead.com. Response time varies. Articles and depts/columns, word lengths vary.

SJ Magazine

1223 North Church Street
Moorestown, NJ 08057

Editor: Marianne Aleardi

Description and Interests: Southern New Jersey is the focus of this magazine. Monthly issues address lifestyle topics including health, fitness, and relationships, along with other topics ranging from politics and the economy to arts and entertainment. Regional family-friendly events and recreation are also covered. Circ: 63,000.
Website: www.sjmagazine.net

Freelance Potential: 75% written by nonstaff writers. Publishes 120 freelance submissions yearly; 15% by unpublished writers, 15% by authors who are new to the magazine, 2% by experts. Receives 40 queries monthly.

Submissions and Payment: Sample articles available at website. Query with 1 clip. Accepts email queries to info@sjmagazine.net. Response time varies. All rights. Articles and depts/columns, word lengths and payment rates vary. Pays 45 days after publication. Provides contributor's copies.

Slice

729 West Sheridan Avenue, Suite 101
Oklahoma City, OK 73102

Editor in Chief: Elizabeth Meares

Description and Interests: People who live in Central Oklahoma get an behind the scenes look at the offering of their region through this monthly publication. Lifestyle pieces, regional news, and profiles of local personalities make up its editorial content. Circ: 146,250.
Website: www.sliceok.com

Freelance Potential: Unavailable.

Submissions and Payment: Sample copy available and guidelines available at website. Query with detailed pitch or send complete ms. Prefers email to editor@sliceok.com. Rights unknown. Articles, word lengths vary. Depts/columns, word lengths vary. Payment rates and policy vary.

Society Charlotte

209 Delburg Street, Suite 209
Davidson, NC 28036

Publisher: Paige Roselle

Description and Interests: A free monthly magazine, *Society Charlotte* spotlights the philanthropic activities of this city. It offers articles on events, programs, and profiles of supporters. Also included are columns on local businesses, dining, fashion, design, and wine. Circ: Unknown.
Website: www.societycharlotte.com

Freelance Potential: Unavailable.

Submissions and Payment: Sample articles available at website. Query. Accepts email to proselle@societycharlotte.com. Rights, unknown. Written material, payment rates and payment policy unknown.

The South

116 Bull Street
Savannah, GA 31401

Associate Editor: Sarah Jones

Description and Interests: Appearing six times each year, the "new" South is explored in articles, profiles, interviews, and reviews. *The South* reflects a blend of traditional and contemporary perspectives. Circ: 20,000.
Website: www.thesouthmag.com

Freelance Potential: 75% written by nonstaff writers. Of the freelance submissions published yearly, 10% are by unpublished writers, 20% are by authors who are new to the magazine, 15% are by experts. Receives 15 queries monthly.

Submissions and Payment: Sample copy available at website. Query with résumé and writing samples. Accepts email to editor@thesouthmag.com. Responds in 1 month. First North American serial rights. Articles, 2,000–3,000 words. Depts/columns, 1,200–1,700 words. Written material, payment rates vary. Kill fee, 20%. Pays on publication. Provides 1 contributor's copy.

South Carolina Historical Magazine

100 Meeting Street
Charleston, SC 29401

Editor: Matthew Lockhart

Description and Interests: *South Carolina Historical Magazine* features scholarly articles each quarter that are annotated and offer insight into historic events and personalities of the state. Circ: 4,000.
Website: www.southcarolinahistoricalsociety.org/?page_id=23

Freelance Potential: 90% written by nonstaff writers. Publishes 12 freelance submissions yearly; 25% by unpublished writers, 50% by authors who are new to the magazine, 50% by experts. Receives 5 queries, 5 unsolicited mss each month.

Submissions and Payment: Sample copy available. Guidelines available at website. Prefers email submissions with brief bio to matthew.lockhart@schsonline@ org. Accepts hard copy. First North American serial rights. Articles, 25–30 pages. No payment. Provides 5+ copies.

South Carolina Wildlife

1000 Assembly Street
P.O. Box 167
Columbia, SC 29202-0167

Editor in Chief: David Lucas

Description and Interests: Published six times each year, this magazine focuses on conservation of the state's wildlife and natural habitats. It features articles on outdoor activities, scenic areas, and environmental issues. Humorous outdoor stories are appreciated. Circ: 55,000.
Website: www.scwildlife.com

Freelance Potential: 85% written by nonstaff writers. Publishes 30 freelance submissions yearly; 5–10% by authors who are new to the magazine. Receives 15–20 queries monthly.

Submissions and Payment: Sample articles and guidelines available at website. Accepts hard copy, email queries, and submissions with clips and bio to lucasd@dnr.sc.gov. SASE. Responds in 8–10 weeks. First North American serial rights. Articles, 500–2,000 words. Written material, $.20 per word. Pays on acceptance.

South Dakota Magazine

P.O. Box 175
Yankton, SD 57078

Managing Editor: Kate Hunhoff

Description and Interests: Six times a year, *South Dakota Magazine* contains articles and photographs that capture the state's history, geography, culture, and personalities. Circ: 45,000+.
Website: www.southdakotamagazine.com

Freelance Potential: 50% written by nonstaff writers. Publishes 20 freelance submissions yearly; 20% by unpublished writers, 20% by authors who are new to the magazine, 20% by experts. Receives 30 queries monthly.

Submissions and Payment: Sample articles available at website. Query or send complete ms with photos if available. Availability of photos increases chance of acceptance. Accepts hard copy, email to submissions@southdakotamagazine.com and electronic submissions via website. Responds in 1 month. First serial rights. Articles and fiction, 500–2,500 words; $25–$200. B/W or color prints or slides; payment rates vary. Pays on publication.

Southern Boating

330 North Andrews Avenue
Fort Lauderdale, FL 33301

Executive Editor: Liz Pasch

Description and Interests: This monthly magazine covers the boating lifestyle in the southeastern waters of the United States to the Bahamas with both destinations and how-to pieces. It includes shorter articles featuring family-oriented boating topics and new gear reviews. Circ: 47,000.
Website: www.southernboating.com

Freelance Potential: 40% written by nonstaff writers. Publishes 45 freelance submissions yearly; 10% by unpublished writers, 15% by authors who are new to the magazine, 80% by experts. Receives 3 queries monthly.

Submissions and Payment: Sample articles available at website. Query. Accepts email queries to liz@southernboating.com. Availability of artwork improves chance of acceptance. Responds in 3–4 weeks. One-time rights. Articles, 600–1,000 words; $400–$650. High-resolution digital images. Pays on publication.

South Florida Parenting

1701 Green Road, Suite B
Deerfield Beach, FL 33064

Editor: Kyara Lomer Camarena

Description and Interests: Articles on a variety of parenting topics fill the pages of this regional monthly magazine. It also provides readers with info on local events, new products, health and safety. Preference given to local writers and topics. Circ: 90,000.
Website: www.sun-sentinel.com

Freelance Potential: 85% written by nonstaff writers. Publishes 90 freelance submissions yearly; 5% by authors who are new to the magazine, 10% by experts. Receives 10 queries, 150–200 unsolicited mss monthly.

Submissions and Payment: Sample copy and guidelines available at website. Query with clips, or send complete ms. Accepts email submissions only to klcamarena@tribune. com. Responds in 2 months if interested. One-time and electronic rights. Articles, 800–1,500 words. Depts/columns, to 750 words. Written material, $25–$115. Provides contributor's copies upon request.

South Jersey Mom

P.O. Box 268
Wenonah, NJ 08090

Executive Editor: M.B. Sanok

Description and Interests: Real stories from real moms are what readers will find in this monthly magazine. Each issue features inspiring stories, parenting trends, and local opinions about national issues. The editors prefers to work with local writers. Circ: 40,000+.
Website: www.southjerseymom.com

Freelance Potential: 2% written by nonstaff writers. Publishes 50–75 freelance submissions yearly; 40% by unpublished writers, 10% by authors who are new to the magazine, 20% by experts.

Submissions and Payment: Sample copy, guidelines, and editorial calendar available at website. Query with bio and two clips or writing samples. Accepts email to michelle@superiogx.com. Response time varies. Rights vary. Articles and depts/columns, word lengths vary. No payment. Provides 2 contributor's copies.

Southwestern Historical Quarterly

1155 Union Circle, #311580
Denton, TX 76203-5017

Editor: Randolph B. "Mike" Campbell

Description and Interests: The Texas State Historical Association brings this peer-reviewed, quarterly journal of authoritative research about Texas and its surrounding states to members, history lovers, and scholars. Circ: 3,000.
Website: www.tshaonline.org

Freelance Potential: 85% written by nonstaff writers. Publishes 4–12 freelance submissions yearly; 30% by unpublished writers, 65% by authors who are new to the magazine. Receives 2 unsolicited mss monthly.

Submissions and Payment: Sample copy and guidelines available at website. Send 3 copies of the complete ms and illustration idea. Accepts hard copy. Responds in 3 months. All rights. Articles, to 40 pages. Digital images at 300 dpi. No payment. Provides 5 contributor's copies.

Spacing

720 Bathurst Street, Suite 309
Toronto, ON M5S 2R4

Managing Editor: Todd Harrison

Description and Interests: Presenting creative examples, solutions, and celebrations of city public spaces is the aim of this publication that appears quarterly. Articles focus on events, organizations, issues, people, and projects related to public space in Toronto and beyond. An awareness of the social implications and the politics of public space is helpful. Circ: 30,000.
Website: www.spacing.ca

Freelance Potential: Unknown.

Submissions and Payment: Query with writing sample. Accepts email queries to toddharrison@ spacing.ca. Accepts simultaneous submissions if identified. Rights unknown. Payment rates vary. Payment policy unknown.

Spark

The Huntsville Times
2317 Memorial Parkway SW
Huntsville, AL 35801

Editor: Anna Claire Vollers

Description and Interests: *The Huntsville Times* launched *Spark* in 2011. The northern Alabama lifestyle magazine is published bi-monthly. It covers the arts and culture, food, fashion, home, decorating, travel, and community events and people. *Spark* promotes itself as upscale, covering "beautiful people and the swankiest soirees," stylish businesses, and the good life. Circ: 30,000.
Website: www.al.com/spark

Freelance Potential: 90% written by nonstaff writers. Publishes 40 freelance submissions yearly; 25% by authors who are new to the magazine. Receives 10 queries monthly.

Submissions and Payment: Sample copy available at website. Query. Accepts email to anna.vollers@htimes.com. Response time varies. Articles and depts/columns, word lengths vary. Rights vary. Payment rates and policy vary.

Suncoast Transformation

242 South Washington Boulevard, #193
Sarasota, FL 34236

Editor

Description and Interests: *Suncoast Transformation* serves readers in Florida's Suncoast area with articles designed to inspire and empower them to improve their lives through a healthy lifestyle, positive spirituality, and a focus on personal growth. It is available each month in print, online, and also for the Kindle. Circ: 20,000.
Website: www.suncoasttransformation.com

Freelance Potential: Open to submissions by local authors as well as leaders in the spiritual growth arena. Article topics may be in line with upcoming themes, or of the author's choosing.

Submissions and Payment: Sample articles, guidelines, and theme list available at website. Send complete ms with author bio. Accepts electronic submissions via website. Response time varies. Author retains rights. Articles, 250–1,000 words.

Sunset

80 Willow Road
Menlo Park, CA 94205

Executive Editor: Christine Ryan

Description and Interests: Started over 100 years ago, this monthly magazine showcases all that is wonderful about the West from food, to home design, to travel and recreational activities.The Weekend Guide section offers the best opportunity for writers new to the magazine. Circ: 1.2 million.
Website: www.sunset.com

Freelance Potential: 60% written by nonstaff writers. 95% of its freelancers live in the region they are writing about.

Submissions and Payment: Sample articles and guidelines available at website. Query with clips. Prefers email to appropriate editor. Responds in one month if interested. All rights. Articles, word lengths vary. Written material, $1–$1.50 a word. Pays on acceptance.

Susquehanna Life

Central Pennsylvania's Lifestyle Magazine

637 Market Street
Lewisburg, PA 17837

Publisher/Editor: Erica Shames

Description and Interests: This regional publication accepts submissions on all lifestyle topics as long as they are interesting, positive, and centered in or around Central Pennsylvania. It is published quarterly. Circ: 45,000+.
Website: www.susquehannalife.com

Freelance Potential: 80% written by nonstaff writers. Publishes 20 freelance submissions yearly; 10% by unpublished writers, 40% by authors who are new to the magazine, 20% by experts. Receives 20 queries, 5 unsolicited mss monthly.

Submissions and Payment: Sample copy available at website. Query or send complete ms. Accepts hard copy and email submissions to susquehannalife@gmail.com. SASE. Responds in 1–3 months. One-time and electronic rights. Articles, to 1,000 words; $75–$125. Pays on publication. Provides 1 contributor's copy.

Syracuse New Times

1415 West Genesee Street
Syracuse, NY 13204-2156

Editor: Molly English

Description and Interests: A diverse range of topics that appeal to residents in the Syracuse region appear in this weekly tabloid. Articles feature interviews with local personalities, event coverage, politics, current events, and regional sports news. Circ: 46,000.
Website: www.syracusenewtimes.com

Freelance Potential: 25% written by nonstaff writers. Publishes 100 freelance submissions yearly; 10% by unpublished writers. Receives 10 queries monthly.

Submissions and Payment: Sample copy available at website. Query with résumé and outline. Accepts hard copy and simultaneous submissions if identified. SASE. Responds in 6 weeks. One-time rights. Articles, to 2,000 words; $50–$200. Depts/columns, 800–1,000 words; $20–$70. B/W negatives or line art; $25–$100. Pays on publication. Provides 2 contributor's copies.

Tallahassee Magazine

1932 Miccosukee Road
Tallahassee, FL 32308

Editor: Rosanne Dunkelberger

Description and Interests: Tallahassee is in the spotlight in this lifestyle magazine. Articles cover local personalities, places, and happenings in glossy issues appearing bimonthly. Circ: 17,500.
Website: www.tallahasseemagazine.com

Freelance Potential: 25% written by nonstaff writers. Of the freelance submissions published yearly, 20% are by unpublished writers, 5% are by authors who are new to the magazine.

Submissions and Payment: Sample articles available at website. Guidelines available. Query or send complete ms with artwork. Prefers email to rdunkelberger@rowlandpublishing.com; will accept hard copy and Macintosh disk submissions. SASE. Responds in 6 weeks. One-time rights. Articles, 1,000–3,500 words. Depts/columns, 150–500 words. Written material, $100–$400. Pays on acceptance. Provides 2 contributor's copies.

Tampa Bay Wellness

275551 Cashford Circle, #102
Wesley Chapel, FL 33544

Publisher: Keith Matter

Description and Interests: This newsprint magazine is one of Tampa Bay's oldest holistic and alternative health magazines. Published monthly, its pages are filled with natural methods for dealing with physical and emotional ailments and lifestyle issues. Circ: 17,000.
Website: www.tampabaywellness.com

Freelance Potential: 80% written by nonstaff writers. Publishes 125 freelance submissions yearly; 60% by unpublished writers, 30% by authors who are new to the magazine. Receives 30 queries monthly.

Submissions and Payment: Sample copy available at website. Guidelines and theme list available. Query. Accepts hard copy and email to angela@tampabaywellness.com. SASE. Responds in 1 month. Rights vary. Articles, 750–950 words. Depts/columns, to 1,000 words. No payment. Provides 1 contributor's copy.

Texas Gardener

10566 North River Crossing
P.O. Box 9005
Waco, TX 76714

Editor/Publisher: Chris S. Corby

Description and Interests: A mix of technical, how-to, informational articles, and profiles fill this magazine, but they all share the same focus: growing a successful garden in Texas. It is published six times a year. Circ: 25,000.
Website: www.texasgardener.com

Freelance Potential: 60% written by nonstaff writers. Publishes 40–50 freelance submissions yearly; 10% by unpublished writers, 10% by authors who are new to the magazine, 50% by experts. Receives 10 queries monthly.

Submissions and Payment: Sample articles and guidelines available at website. Query with outline and clips or send complete ms. Accepts hard copy, disk, and email submissions to info@texasgardener.com. No simultaneous submissions. Responds in 6 weeks. One-time rights. Articles, 700–1,750 words; $50–$200. "Between Neighbors," 2 typed pages; $25. Pays on publication. Provides 2 contributor's copies.

Texas Highways

P.O. Box 141009
Austin, TX 78714-1009

Contact: Editorial Query

Description and Interests: "The official travel magazine of Texas" is published monthly by the Texas Department of Transportation. It showcases the historical, unusual, and noteworthy destinations in the state. It also features articles on events and entertainment coming to the area. Circ: 225,000.
Website: www.texashighways.com

Freelance Potential: 50% written by nonstaff writers. Publishes 30–40 freelance submissions yearly; 20% by unpublished writers, 10% by authors who are new to the magazine. Receives 30+ queries monthly.

Submissions and Payment: Sample articles and guidelines available at website. Prefers concise query with clips to letters05@texashighways.com; will accept hard copy. SASE. Responds in 1+ months. First North American serial rights. Articles, 1,200–1,800 words; $.50 per word. Pays on acceptance. Provides 3 contributor's copies.

Texas Home & Living

13552 Highway 183 North, Suite A
Austin, TX 78750

Associate Publisher: Brona Stockton

Description and Interests: This glossy interior design magazine is published six times each year and caters to affluent Texas homeowners with features on extraordinary traditional and contemporary homes, and lifestyle articles. Circ: 50,000.
Website: www.texashomeandliving

Freelance Potential: 50% written by nonstaff writers. Publishes 24 freelance submissions yearly; 10% by unpublished writers, 20% by authors who are new to the magazine, 10% by experts. Receives 6 queries monthly.

Submissions and Payment: Sample copy, guidelines, and theme list/editorial calendar available at website. Accepts email queries to ideas@ texashomeandliving.com. Responds in 2 months. All rights. Articles, 1,200 words. Depts/columns, 1,000 words. Written material, $200. Pays on publication.

Texas Monthly

P.O. Box 1569
Austin, TX 78767

Editor: Jack Silverstein

Description and Interests: *Texas Monthly* is a monthly about state culture that reminds natives of their proud heritage and is a journalistic road map for others of the state, its history, and people. The best way to break in is to pitch a great Texas story, know the subject matter, and have a keen sense of the magazine. Circ: 300,000.
Website: www.texasmonthly.com

Freelance Potential: 15% written by nonstaff writers.

Submissions and Payment: Sample articles available at website. Query with clips. Accepts hard copy and email to jsilverstein@ texasmonthly.com. SASE. Response time varies. Articles, word lengths vary. Depts/columns, 2,000– 2,500 words. First North American serial rights and nonexclusive reprint rights. Written material, $1 per word. Kill fee negotiable. Pays on acceptance.

Texas Music

P.O. Box 50273
Austin, TX 78763

Publisher/Editor: Stewart Ramser

Description and Interests: This quarterly magazine seeks to give readers a look "inside the music of Texas." Featuring in-depth interviews with the state's prominent recording artists and up-and-coming musicians, it includes retrospective articles on past music legends. It also serves as a guide to music events. Circ: 35,000.
Website: www.txmusic.com

Freelance Potential: 80% written by nonstaff writers. Publishes 25 freelance submissions yearly. Receives 20 queries monthly.

Submissions and Payment: Sample articles available at website. Query with published clips. Accepts hard copy and email queries to editor@txmusic.com. SASE. Response time varies. All rights. Articles, 1,500–5,000 words. Depts/columns, 1,000–2,000 words. Written material, payment rates vary. Pays on publication.

Texas Parks & Wildlife

4200 Smith School Road, Building D
Austin, TX 78744

Editor: Louie Bond

Description and Interests: A monthly magazine, *Texas Parks & Wildlife* covers all aspects of the Texas outdoors including fishing, hunting, camping, bicycling, and hiking. Articles also discuss state park destinations and conservation issues. Circ: 125,000.
Website: www.tpwmagazine.com/editorial/

Freelance Potential: 10% written by nonstaff writers. Publishes 10 freelance submissions yearly; 10% by unpublished writers, 10% by authors who are new to the magazine, 40% by experts. Receives 20 queries monthly.

Submissions and Payment: Sample articles and guidelines available at website. Query. Accepts email queries to louie.bond@tpwd.state.tx.us. Responds in 2 months. First North American serial rights. Articles, 1,200–2,000 words;. depts/columns, 100–1,000 words; $.50 per word. Digital images (JPEG or TIFF format), high resolution transparencies to brandon.jakobeit@tpwd.state.tx.us; $40–$500. Pays on publication.

Texas Town & City

1821 Rutherford Lane, Suite 400
Austin, TX 78754-5128

Editor: Karla Vining

Description and Interests: Published by the Texas Municipal League, this magazine gives municipal leaders the information they need to be more effective in their jobs. It covers such topics as municipal regulations and legislation, public finances, employee management, and city issues. It appears 11 times each year. Circ: 13,000.
Website: www.tml.org/pub_ttc.asp

Freelance Potential: 40% written by nonstaff writers. Publishes 22 freelance submissions yearly; 50% by authors who are new to the magazine, 5% by experts. Receives 2–3 queries each month.

Submissions and Payment: Sample copy and editorial calendar available at website. Query with outline. Accepts email queries to kvining@tml.org. Responds in 3 weeks. Rights vary. Articles, 1,200 words. Prints, charts, graphs, line art. No payment.

Times of the Islands 

P.O. Box 234
Providenciales, Turks and Caicos Islands
British West Indies

Managing Editor: Kathy Borsuk

Description and Interests: This quarterly magazine captures the heart and soul of the Turks and Caicos Islands through its articles and photography. Articles cover the island's history, culture, and lifestyle. Circ: 10,000.
Website: www.timespub.tc

Freelance Potential: 25% written by nonstaff writers. Publishes 3 freelance submissions yearly; 20% by unpublished writers, 20% by authors new to the magazine, 60% by experts. Receives 2 queries, 1 unsolicited ms monthly.

Submissions and Payment: Sample copy available at website. Prefers query; will accept complete ms. Accepts hard copy and email to timespub@tciway.tc. SAE/IRC. Responds in 2 months. Articles, fiction, and depts/columns, word lengths vary. Written material, $.30 per word. Pays on publication.

Today's Chicago Woman

150 East Huron Street, Suite 1011
Chicago, IL 60613

Managing Editor: Carrie Williams

Description and Interests: For women in Chicago, this monthly magazine offers career, health, fashion, and beauty articles. Published monthly, it also highlights the city's current events, attractions, and dining options. Circ: 50,000.
Website: www.tcwmag.com

Freelance Potential: 60% written by nonstaff writers. Publishes 100+ freelance submissions yearly; 5% by unpublished writers, 10% by authors who are new to the magazine, 25% by experts. Receives 15 queries monthly.

Submissions and Payment: Sample articles available at website. Accepts hard copy and email queries with résumé and clips to minute.mentor@tcwmag.com. Response time varies. First North American serial rights. Written material, word lengths and payment rates vary. Pays on publication. Provides 1 contributor's copy.

Toledo City Paper

1120 Adams Street
Toledo, OH 43604

Editor in Chief: Collette Jacobs

Description and Interests: The news, politics, arts, and social issues of Toledo are covered here biweekly, with a progressive perspective. Also featured are articles on dining, entertainment, and nightlife. Most of the articles are assigned. Circ: 36,000.
Website: www.toledocitypaper.com

Freelance Potential: 5% written by nonstaff writers. Publishes 25–30 freelance submissions yearly; 20% by unpublished writers, 20% by authors who are new to the magazine, 20% by experts. Receives 20 unsolicited mss monthly.

Submissions and Payment: Sample articles available at website. Guidelines available. Send email query with cover letter, resume, and clips to editor@toledocitypaper.com. Responds in 2 months. All rights. Articles, 600–800 words; $10–$350. 3x5 prints or 35mm slides or transparencies; payment rates vary. Pays on publication.

Tops

Top Marketing Group
465 East High Street, Suite 201
Lexington, KY 40507-1938

President/Editor: Keith Yarber

Description and Interests: "See and be seen" is the theme of this regional magazine that covers nonprofit fundraising galas, city-sponsored events, and other noteworthy gatherings in the Lexington area. Published every month, it also runs features on fashion, home decorating, and entertaining. Circ: 30,000.
Website: www.topsinlex.com

Freelance Potential: 10% written by nonstaff writers. Publishes 5–10 freelance submissions yearly; 5% by authors who are new to the magazine.

Submissions and Payment: Sample copy available at website. Guidelines available. Send complete ms. Accepts email submissions to info@topsinlex.com. Response time varies. First or reprint rights. Articles and depts/columns, word lengths and payment rates vary. Pays on publication. Provides 2 contributor's copies.

Tucson Woman

Wick Communications
3280 East Hemisphere Loop, Suite 174
Tucson, AZ 85706

Editor: Linda Ray

Description and Interests: This quarterly publication is written for women living in Tucson, Arizona. It features articles on food, health, history, beauty, and lifestyle, all with a Tucson slant. Circ: 40,000.
Website: tucsonwoman.com

Freelance Potential: Unavailable.

Submissions and Payment: Sample articles available at website. Query. Accepts email to linda@tucsonwoman.com. Rights, unknown. Written material, word lengths vary. Payment rates and payment policy, unknown.

Ulster Magazine

40 Mulberry Street
Middletown, NY 10940

Editor: Brenda Gilhooly

Description and Interests: Active baby boomers who live, work, play, and shop in Ulster County, New York are the target audience of this publication, published 6 times a year. It highlights what there is to see and do in Ulster County and also features profiles of area residents and business owners. Circ: 10,000.
Website: www.ulstermagazine.com

Freelance Potential: Freelance submissions are accepted for both *Orange* and *Ulster* magazines. Writers from the region are preferred.

Submissions and Payment: Sample copy available at website. For submission information, send email to bgilholly@th-record.com. Rights, unknown. Written material, payment rates vary. Payment policy, unknown.

Utah Boomers

145 West Crystal Avenue
Salt Lake City, UT 84115

Managing Editor: Teresa Glenn

Description and Interests: Catering to the specific needs of 46- to 64-year-olds living in Utah, this magazine addresses such issues as retirement, financial planning, caring for aging parents, raising children, and menopause. Originally launched as a print magazine, *Utah Boomers* now appears exclusively as a quarterly digital. Hits per month: Unavailable.
Website: www.utahboomersmagazine.com

Freelance Potential: Accepts freelance submissions on topics such as home and lifestyle, health and fitness, financial issues, and leisure activities. All material must relate to Utah Baby Boomers.

Submissions and Payment: Sample copy available at website. For information on submissions, contact the editor via the website or by email to teresa.glenn@utboomer.com. Response time varies. Written material, word lengths vary.

Vermont Business Magazine

365 Dorset Street
South Burlington, VT 05403

Editor: Timothy McQuiston

Description and Interests: This monthly magazine features timely and in-depth reporting of business and economic issues in the state of Vermont. Legislative news, industry trends, and profiles of prominent businesspeople are also covered. Circ: 7,000.
Website: www.vermontbiz.com/magazine

Freelance Potential: 80% written by nonstaff writers. Publishes 100 freelance submissions yearly; 5% by authors who are new to the magazine, 5% by experts. Receives 10 queries monthly.

Submissions and Payment: Sample articles and editorial calendar available at website. Query. Accepts email queries to mcq@vermontbiz.com. Responds if interested. First North American serial rights. Articles, 1,000–2,000 words; $.10 per word. Pays on publication. Provides 2 contributor's copies.

Vermont Life Magazine

One National Life Drive, 6th Floor
Montpelier, VT 05620

Editor: Mary Hegarty Nowlan

Description and Interests: This sophisticated regional magazine is published quarterly. Articles about personalities, destinations, and issues within the state are well researched and journalistic in tone. Circ: 52,097.
Website: www.vermontlife.com

Freelance Potential: 95% written by nonstaff writers. Publishes 35–40 freelance submissions yearly; 1% by unpublished writers, 1% by authors who are new to the magazine. Receives 45–50 queries monthly.

Submissions and Payment: Sample articles and guidelines available at website. Prefers query with résumé and writing samples; accepts complete ms. Accepts hard copy and email queries to editors@vtlife.com. Responds within 1 month if interested. First North American serial rights. Articles, to 2,000 words; $600–$800. Pays on acceptance. Provides 1 contributor's copy.

Via

3055 Oak Road
Mailstop W510
Walnut Creek, CA 94597

Editor: Anne McSilver

Description and Interests: *Via* is AAA's magazine for members living in Northern California, Nevada, Utah, Oregon, southern Idaho, Montana, Wyoming, and Alaska. It offers a mix of how-to articles and tips on travel along with features on destinations that are up the road, and sometimes across the globe. New writers have the best chance of acceptance with the front-of-the-book sections. Circ: 3 million.
Website: www.viamagazine.com

Freelance Potential: Receives 125 queries monthly.

Submissions and Payment: Sample articles available at website. Query with relevant clips. Accepts email to viamail@viamagazine.com. Responds in 3 months. Written material, word lengths vary; $1 per word. Rights vary. Kill fee 30%. Pays on acceptance.

Village Profile

33 North Geneva Street
Elgin, IL 60120

Staff Writer/Editor: Becky Hogan

Description and Interests: *Village Profile* lifestyle magazines highlight specific aspects of over 1,000 communities across the U.S., including schools, parks and recreation, events, green practices, and public affairs. A local connection by the writer is preferred but not required. Issues appear annually. Circ: Not available.
Website: www.villageprofile.com

Freelance Potential: 20% written by nonstaff writers. Publishes a limited number of freelance submissions yearly; but welcomes new writers, both published and unpublished. Receives 1 query monthly.

Submissions and Payment: Sample copy available at website. Query with unedited writing samples. Accepts email to bhogan@villageprofilemail. com. Responds in 1 day. Rights vary. Articles, 650–800 words; $75. Pays on acceptance. Provides up to 3 contributor's copies.

Virginia Living

109 East Cary Street
Richmond, VA 23219

Editor: Erin Parkhurst

Description and Interests: An upscale lifestyle magazine that is written just for Virginians, this magazine covers the arts, dining, travel, and leisure opportunities of the state. It also publishes articles on the region's interesting history, places, and personalities. It is published six times a year. Circ: 30,000.
Website: www.virginialiving.com

Freelance Potential: 75% written by nonstaff writers. Publishes 60 freelance submissions yearly; 5% by unpublished writers, 10% by authors who are new to the magazine. Receives 10 unsolicited mss monthly.

Submissions and Payment: Sample articles available at website. Guidelines available. Send complete ms. Accepts email submissions to editor@ capefear.com. Responds in 1 month. First North American serial rights. Articles, 2,000 words. Depts/ columns, 800 words. Written material, $100–$500. Pays on publication.

Virginia Wine Lover

1264 Perimeter Parkway
Virginia Beach, VA 23454

Executive Editor: Patrick Evans-Hylton

Description and Interests: Fifth in wine production in the United States, the Virginia wine industry is thriving, along with "the good life" that surrounds it. This magazine, published twice each year, celebrates that fact with articles about the region's wineries and wines, its personalities and events, and the food and upscale lifestyle that accompanies them. Circ: 40,000.
Website: www.virginiawinelover.com

Freelance Potential: 20% written by nonstaff writers. Publishes 10–20 freelance submissions yearly; 10% by authors who are new to the magazine.

Submissions and Payment: Sample copy available at website. Query. Accepts hard copy and email to patrick@virginiawinelover.com. SASE. Response time varies. First North American serial rights. Articles and depts/columns, word lengths and payment rates vary. Payment policy varies.

Voyageur

Northeast Wisconsin's Historical Review

P.O. Box 8085
Green Bay, WI 54308-8085

Editor: Victoria Goff

Description and Interests: Historians and history enthusiasts interested in Northeast Wisconsin are the audience of this magazine, published twice each year. Personalities, events, and places of the past are all explored in its pages. Circ: 5,000.
Website: www.voyageurmagazine.org

Freelance Potential: 85% written by nonstaff writers. Publishes 12 freelance submissions yearly; 25% by unpublished writers, 80% by authors who are new to the magazine, 50% by experts. Receives 1 query, 1 unsolicited ms monthly.

Submissions and Payment: Sample articles available at website. Guidelines available. Send complete ms on disk with scanned or photocopied images, a 150-word abstract, and one hard copy. Accepts simultaneous submissions. Responds in 2 weeks. All rights. Articles, to 5,000 words. Depts/columns, to 2,000 words. No payment.

Wake Living

189 Wind Chime Court, Suite 104
Raleigh, NC 27615

Editor: Danielle Jackson

Description and Interests: Articles that focus on the lifestyle and culture of North Carolina's Wake County are found in this quarterly magazine. Circ: 35,000.
Website: www.wakeliving.com

Freelance Potential: 50% written by nonstaff writers. Publishes 30–50 freelance submissions yearly; 30% by unpublished writers, 20% by authors who are new to the magazine, 20% by experts. Receives 20 queries monthly.

Submissions and Payment: Local writers only. Sample articles available at website. Guidelines and editorial calendar available. Query with outline. Accepts email queries to djackson@whmags.com. Responds in 1–3 months. All rights. Articles, 600–1,000 words. Depts/columns, 400–600 words. Written material, $150–$350. Kill fee, 25%. Pays within 1 month of publication. Provides 2 contributor's copies.

Washington City Paper

2390 Champlain Street NW
Washington, DC 20009

Editor: Mike Madden

Description and Interests: A variety of journalistic genres including investigative pieces, essays, and profiles of local institutions fills this weekly newspaper. Its editors value writers with a fresh, dynamic style. Circ: 73,000+.
Website: www.washingtoncitypaper.com

Freelance Potential: 50% written by nonstaff writers. Publishes 50 freelance submissions yearly; 5% by unpublished writers, 10% by authors who are new to the magazine. Receives 8 queries, 5–10 mss monthly.

Submissions and Payment: Sample articles and guidelines available at website. Prefers complete ms; accepts queries with clips. Prefers email submissions to mail@washingtoncitypaper.com (Word attachments). Accepts hard copy. Responds in 1 week. First rights. Articles, 2,500–5,000 words; depts/columns, 150–500 words. Written material, $15–$2,000.

Washington Family Magazine

485 Spring Park Place, Suite 500
Herndon, VA 20170

Editor: Marae Leggs

Description and Interests: This monthly publication is written for families in the Washington, DC, area. It features articles on pregnancy, tips on parenting infants through teens, and information on regional activities. Circ: 70,000.
Website: www.washingtonfamilymagazine.com

Freelance Potential: 75% written by nonstaff writers. Publishes 90 freelance submissions yearly; 50% by unpublished writers, 50% by authors who are new to the magazine. Receives 1,200 queries and unsolicited mss monthly.

Submissions and Payment: Sample copy available at website. Query with clips, or send complete ms. Accepts Macintosh disk submissions and email to editor@thefamilymagazine.com. SASE. Response time varies. Regional rights. Articles, 500–700 words; $35–$50. Depts/columns, word lengths and payment rates vary. Pays on publication. Provides 1 copy.

Washington Flyer

1129 20th Street, NW
Washington, DC 20036

Editor in Chief: Michael McCarthy

Description and Interests: Published bimonthly by the Metropolitan Washington Airports Authority, this magazine offers destination information for travelers and residents flying in and out of Washington DC. Circ: 130,306.
Website: www.washingtonflyer.com

Freelance Potential: 75% written by nonstaff writers. Publishes 35 freelance submissions yearly; 5% by unpublished writers, 25% by authors who are new to the magazine, 10% by experts. Receives 50–100 queries monthly.

Submissions and Payment: Sample articles and editorial calendar available at website. Guidelines available. Query with clips or writing samples. Accepts email queries to mmccarthy@tmgcustommedia.com. Responds in 2 months. All rights. Articles, 500–1,200 words; $400–$900. Depts/columns, 300–400 words; $150–$300. Pays on publication. Provides 3–5 contributor's copies.

Washington Gardener

826 Philadelphia Avenue
Silver Spring, MD 20910

Editor: Kathy Jentz

Description and Interests: Avid gardeners living in and around the nation's capital turn to this magazine for ideas, inspiration, and tips for growing flowers and plants in this region. Published six times each year, it includes a color photograph with each article. Circ: 5,000.
Website: www.washingtongardener.com

Freelance Potential: 50% written by nonstaff writers. Publishes 10 freelance submissions yearly; 10% by unpublished writers, 10% by authors who are new to the magazine, 80% by experts. Receives 10 queries monthly.

Submissions and Payment: Sample copy available. Guidelines available at website. Prefers email queries to washingtongardener@rcn.com with "Query" in subject line. Response time varies. First rights. Articles, 700–1,000 words. Written material, $25–$100. Pays on publication.

Washingtonian 

1828 L Street NW, Suite 22
Washington, DC 20036

Features Editor: Denise Wills

Description and Interests: This monthly magazine gives residents of the nation's capitol and the surrounding metropolitan area including Maryland and Northern Virginia, the latest scoop on local dining, shopping, and entertainment. Also features are personality profiles, lifestyle pieces, and essays–all with a Washington slant. Circ: 150,000.
Website: washingtonian.com

Freelance Potential: Unavailable.

Submissions and Payment: Sample articles and guidelines available at website. Query with clips. Prefers email to editorial@washingtonian.com. First North American serial and electronic rights. Feature articles, 3,000–5,000 words. Service articles, 500–2,000 words. Written material, $.75 per word. Kill fee, 33%. Pays on publication.

Washington Trails

705 2nd Avenue, Suite 300
Seattle, WA 98104

Editor: Eli Boschetto

Description and Interests: The Washington Trails Association works to enhance and promote hiking opportunities in Washington State. Its magazine contains WTA news and views, and articles on public lands and the environment. It is published six times each year. Circ: 10,000.
Website: www.wta.org

Freelance Potential: 80% written by nonstaff writers. Publishes 30 freelance submissions yearly; 60% by unpublished writers, 15% by authors who are new to the magazine, 5% by experts. Receives 10 queries monthly.

Submissions and Payment: Sample articles and guidelines available at website. Prefers email queries with clips and area of interest/expertise to editor@wta.org. Accepts hard copy. Responds in 2–4 weeks. One-time rights. Articles, 1,000–2,000 words; dept/columns, 100–500 words. No payment. Provides 1 contributor's copy.

Westchester Magazine

2 Clinton Avenue
Rye, NY 10580

Editor in Chief: Esther Davidowitz

Description and Interests: Serving an upscale, affluent readership, this monthly lifestyle magazine explores the people, arts, restaurants, real estate, and lifestyle of the county. It also offers essays and features on issues affecting the area. Circ: 58,000.
Website: www.westchestermagazine.com

Freelance Potential: 33% written by nonstaff writers. Publishes 75 freelance submissions yearly; 3% by unpublished writers, 25% by authors who are new to the magazine, 1% by experts. Receives 20 queries monthly.

Submissions and Payment: Sample copy available at website. Guidelines available. Query with outline and clips. Prefers email queries to edavidowitz@westchestermagazine.com; will accept hard copy and simultaneous submissions if identified. SASE. Responds in 1 month. All or first rights. Written material, word lengths vary; $50–$1,000.

West Coast Families

1215-C56 Street
P.O. Box 18057
Delta, British Columbia V4L 2M4
Canada

Managing Editor: Andrea Vance

Description and Interests: This lifestyle magazine is for metropolitan Vancouver parents and families. Its readers are well-educated and affluent. It covers topics such as green living, healthy choices, parenting, education, and local current events. It appears 9 times each year. Circ: 50,000.
Website: www.westcoastfamilies.com

Freelance Potential: 80% written by nonstaff writers. Publishes 12–40 freelance submissions yearly; 25% by authors who are new to the magazine. Receives 33–67 queries monthly.

Submissions and Payment: Sample copy, editorial calendar, and guidelines available at website. Accepts email queries with writing samples to editor@westcoastfamilies.com. Responds in 6–8 weeks. First and electronic rights. Articles, 600–1,200 words; payment rates vary. Kill fee, 50%. Pays on publication.

Western Living

2608 Granville Street, Suite 560
Vancouver, BC V6H 3V3

Editor: Neal McLennan

Description and Interests: Published 10 times a year, this magazine focuses on homes, food and wine, travel, and lifestyle for the people of Western Canada. It publishes regional editions in the different provinces of Canada, all aimed at upscale, well educated readers. Circ: 165,000.
Website: www.westernlivingmagazine.com

Freelance Potential: Unavailable.

Submissions and Payment: Sample articles, guidelines, and editorial calendar available at website. Accepts email queries to neal.mclennan@westernlivingmagazine.com. Articles, 750–1,000 words.. Depts/columns, 400–800 words. Rights, unknown. Written material, payment rates vary. Payment policy, unknown.

Western New York Family Magazine

3147 Delaware Avenue, Suite B
Buffalo, NY 14217

Editor/Publisher: Michele Miller

Description and Interests: This monthly print and online regional publication offers families in the Buffalo, New York, area a source of information on local issues, as well as articles on parenting and family matters. Circ: 25,000.
Website: www.wnyfamilymagazine.com

Freelance Potential: 90% written by nonstaff writers. Publishes 150 freelance submissions yearly; 30% by unpublished writers, 30% by authors who are new to the magazine, 40% by experts. Receives 100 unsolicited mss monthly.

Submissions and Payment: Sample articles, guidelines, and editorial calendar available at website. Send complete ms with brief author bio. Accepts email only to michele@wnyfamilymagazine.com. No simultaneous submissions to local publications. Response time varies. First and online rights. Articles, to 3,000 words. Pays $35–$200. Pays on publication.

Where Toronto

111 Queen Street East, Suite 320
Toronto, Ontario M5C 1S2
Canada

Editor in Chief: Linda Luong

Description and Interests: This magazine offers "Timely Information for Travellers" to the city of Toronto. It provides extensive coverage of the city's nightlife, dining, entertainment, and arts scene; as well as articles on tours and attractions. It prefers articles from local authors. Circ: 64,000.
Website: www.where.ca/toronto

Freelance Potential: 10% written by nonstaff writers. Publishes 8–10 freelance submissions yearly; 10% by new authors, 10% by experts. Receives 10 queries each month.

Submissions and Payment: Sample copy available at website. Query. Accepts hard copy and email queries to lluong@where.ca. SAE/IRC. Responds in 2 months. First North American serial rights. Articles, 800 words; $.50 per word. Kill fee, 50%. Pays on publication. Provides 3 contributor's copies.

Windy City Times

5315 North Clark Street, #192
Chicago, IL 60640

Executive Editor: Tracy Baim

Description and Interests: Online and in print, this weekly newspaper serves Chicago's GLBT community with coverage of news and issues of interest. Circ: 15,000.
Website: www.windycitymediagroup.com

Freelance Potential: 50% written by nonstaff writers. Publishes hundreds of freelance submissions yearly; 10% by unpublished writers, 10% by authors who are new to the magazine. Receives 100 unsolicited mss monthly.

Submissions and Payment: Sample articles available at website. Editorial calendar available. Send complete ms. Accepts email submissions only to editor@windycitymediagroup.com. Responds in 1 month. Exclusive rights in local market. Articles, 800–1,500 words; $25–$50. 5x7 B/W prints; payment rates vary. Payment policy varies. Provides 1 contributor's copy.

Wisconsin Natural Resources

Wisconsin Department of Natural Resources
P.O. Box 7921
Madison, WI 53707

Editor: Natasha Kassulke

Description and Interests: This magazine welcomes contributions on Wisconsin's resources and environmental concerns. Published six times each year, it includes topics such as outdoor activities, profiles, how-to's, seasonal articles, and natural resources observation and research. Circ: 85,000+.
Website: http://dnr.wi.gov/wnrmag

Freelance Potential: 30% written by nonstaff writers.

Submissions and Payment: Sample articles and guidelines available at website. Query. Send email to natasha.kassulke@wisconsin.gov. Prefers articles to be both emailed and mailed. Photos increase chance of acceptance. Digital images, 300 dpi, minimum (JPEG). Articles, 500–2,500 words. No payment. Provides contributor copies on request.

Wisconsin West

2905 Seymour Road
Eau Claire, WI 54703

Publisher: Wayne Turnquist

Description and Interests: This regional publication celebrates the personalities, recreation, history, arts, lifestyle, and events of western Wisconsin. It relies heavily on the work of freelancers, and prefers articles that are area-specific. Circ: 3,000.
Website: www.wisconsinwest.com

Freelance Potential: 95% written by nonstaff writers. Publishes 39–43 freelance submissions yearly; 30% by authors who are new to the magazine. Receives 1 query monthly.

Submissions and Payment: Sample copy and guidelines available at website. Prefers complete ms; accepts queries with writing samples. Prefers email to wisconsinwestmagazine@ymail.com; accepts hard copy. SASE. Photos increase chance of acceptance. Responds in 6–8 weeks. First rights. Articles, 800–5,000 words. Written material, $75–$150. Pays on publication. Provides 2 contributor's copies.

Zone 4 Magazine

P.O. Box 3208
Bozeman, MT 59772

Chief Editor: Dan Spurr

Description and Interests: Practical articles about high-altitude gardening appear in this quarterly. It targets an audience of gardeners and landscapers living in Colorado, Utah, Montana, Wyoming, and Idaho. Circ: 5,000.
Website: www.zone4magazine.com

Freelance Potential: 90% written by nonstaff writers. Publishes 35–40 freelance submissions yearly; 15% by unpublished writers, 5% by authors who are new to the magazine, 25% by experts. Receives 5–10 queries monthly.

Submissions and Payment: Sample articles and guidelines available at website. Query. Prefers email queries to dan@zone4magazine.com (Word attachments). Accepts hard copy. SASE. First North American serial rights. Feature articles, 2,000 words. Non-feature articles, 750–1,200 words. Depts/columns, 500–800 words. Payment rates vary. Payment policy, unknown.

Contests & Awards

Selected Contests & Awards

One way to have your work read by editors and other writers is to enter writing contests. Winning or placing in a contest can open the door to publication and recognition, but in some contests a read is as good as a win. At the very least you are acquiring writing experience and clips. Be completely clear about the quality of clips you are acquiring as you approach your next market.

If you do not win a contest, you are still refining your craft, and increasing your submissions. Read published winning entries to gain insight into how your work compares with the competition. Find readers in critique groups and honest writing companions to help improve your writing skills and ideas.

Contests generate excitement. For editors, contests are a way to discover new writers. Entries are especially focused because of a contest guidelines, and therefore closely target an editor's current needs. For writers, the benefit is that every contest entry is read, often by more than one editor. Submissions are not relegated to an untouched slush pile. And you don't have to be the grand-prize winner to benefit—non-winning manuscripts are often purchased by the publication for future issues.

To be considered for the contests and awards that follow, fulfill all of the requirements carefully. For each listing, we have included the address, a description, the entry requirements, the deadline, and the prize. In some cases, the 2013 deadlines were not available at press time. We close *Best of the Magazine Markets* late fall, early winter and contests may not establish their criteria until spring or summer. We recommend that you write to the addresses provided or visit the websites to request an entry form and the contest guidelines, which usually specify the current deadline.

Abilene Writers Guild Annual Contest

Sharon Ellison
1025 Grand Avenue
Abilene, TX 79605

Description: This contest awards prizes for original, unpublished work in 10 categories, including adult fiction, flash fiction, inspiration, memoir, novels, children's stories, and poetry. It is open to all writers.
Website: www.abilenewritersguild.org/contests.cfm

Length: Poetry, to 50 lines; children's stories, to 750 words; other short works, to 1,200 words. Novels, first 10 pages and one-page synopsis.

Requirements: Entry fee, $10 for short pieces; $15 for novels. Accepts hard copy. Author's name and contact information must appear only on a cover sheet. SASE. Visit website for details and entry form.

Prize: First prize in each category, $100; second prize, $65; third prize, $35.

Deadline: Submissions are accepted between October 1 and November 30.

Alligator Juniper National Writing Contest

Prescott College
220 Grove Avenue
Prescott, AZ 86301

Description: Writers of all levels, especially emerging or early-career writers, are encouraged to submit work to this contest. Entries may be in the categories of fiction, creative nonfiction, or poetry.
Website: www.prescott.edu/experience/publications/alligatorjuniper/writing-contest-guidelines.html

Length: Prose, to 30 pages. Poetry, to 5 poems.

Requirements: Entry fee, $15. Accepts hard copy and simultaneous submissions, if identified. All entries must include specific acknowledgement that your work may be published in the magazine *Alligator Juniper*, even if it does not win the contest. SASE. Visit the website for complete guidelines.

Prize: First prize in each category, $1,000. Winning entries are published in *Alligator Juniper*.

Deadline: October 1. Contest opens August 15.

American Kennel Club Family Dog Fiction Writing Contest ★

260 Madison Avenue
New York, NY 10016

Description: This annual contest accepts entries of original, unpublished stories that feature purebred or mixed breed dogs—no stories with talking dogs, however. It is open to anyone except employees of the AKC and their immediate families.
Website: www.akc.org/pubs/fictioncontest

Length: To 2,000 words.

Requirements: One entry per author. Author's name, address, and phone number must appear on the first page; name and page number on successive pages. No entry fee. Accepts hard copy. No simultaneous submissions.

Prize: First place, $500; second place, $250; third place, $100. Winning stories will be published in the AKC's *Family Dog,* as space allows.

Deadline: Postmarked by January 31, 2013.

American Literary Review Contest

P.O. Box 311307
University of North Texas
Denton, TX 76203-1307

Description: This annual contest awards prizes in three categories: short story, essay, and poetry.
Website: www.english.unt.edu/alr/contest.html

Length: Fiction, to 8,000 words. Creative nonfiction, to 6,500 words. Poetry, no length restrictions, limit 3 poems per entry.

Requirements: Entry fee, $15 per story or essay, or up to 3 poems. Accepts submissions via the online submission manager, or mailed hard copy; no emails. Include a cover sheet with name, contact information, and title. Author's name should not appear on the manuscript. Enclose a $15 reading fee (includes subscription) for multiple entries, and SASE for contest results. Review guidelines before submitting.

Prize: Winner in each category receives $1,000 and publication in *American Literary Review*.

Deadline: October 1.

American Short Fiction Contest

Jill Gerard/Department of Creative Writing
UNCW/601 South College Road
Wilmington, NC 28403

Description: This contest, sponsored by *American Short Fiction*, accepts unpublished short fiction on any theme. All entries will be considered for publication. Note that *American Short Fiction* is on hiatus, but expects to "resume full operations as soon as possible." Stories published in this journal have been reprinted in the annual *Best American Short Stories,* and authors have won the Pushcart Prize.
Website: www.americanshortfiction.org

Length: To 6,000 words.

Requirements: Entry fee, $20, payable via PayPal. Accepts electronic submissions at the website. Accepts multiple and simultaneous submissions. Entrant's name must not appear in the file itself.

Prize: $1,000 and publication; second prize, $500.

Deadline: December.

Sherwood Anderson Fiction Award

Mid-American Review
Department of English
Bowling Green State University
Bowling Green, OH 43403

Description: This award is given annually to a short story of strong literary merit. Original, previously unpublished stories of any genre are eligible.
Website: www.bgsu.edu/studentlife/organizations/midamericanreview

Length: To 6,000 words.

Requirements: Entry fee, $10. Accepts hard copy. All participants receive the issue of *Mid-American Review* in which the winning entries are published. SASE for early results; manuscripts are not returned. Visit the website for details.

Prize: First prize, $1,000 and publication in *Mid-American Review*. Four finalists receive notations and are also considered for publication.

Deadline: November 15.

Arizona Authors Association Literary Contest

AZ Authors Contest Coordinator
6145 West Echo Lane
Glendale, AZ 85302

Description: Short stories, essays, articles, true stories, poetry, novels, and children's literature are accepted in this annual contest. All writers may enter. The contest has separate categories for published and unpublished works.
Website: www.azauthors.com/contest_index.html

Length: Essays and short stories, to 15 pages. Unpublished novels, first 25 pages and synopsis.

Requirements: Entry fee, $20. Send 3 copies, with submission form. Do not put author name on the manuscript, only on the entry form.

Prize: Category winners, $100, publication in *Arizona Literary Magazine*. Second prize, $50 and publication; third prize, $25 and publication.

Deadline: July 1.

Art Affair Writing Contests

P.O. Box 54302
Oklahoma City, OK 73154

Description: This competition is open to poets and writers of original, unpublished work. Categories are Western short fiction, short story, and poetry.
Website: www.shadetreecreations.com

Length: Western fiction and short stories, to 5,000 words. Poetry, to 60 lines.

Requirements: Entry fee, $5 for Westerns and short fiction; $3 for each poem. Include a cover page with contact information and title. Entries will not be returned. Visit the website for complete details.

Prize: Western short stories and short fiction: first prize, $50; second prize, $25; third prize, $15. Poetry: First prize, $40; second prize, $25; third prize, $15.

Deadline: October 1.

Arts & Letters Prizes Competition

Campus Box 891
Georgia College & State University
Milledgeville, GA 31061

Description: This annual contest accepts entries in four categories: short fiction, poetry, creative nonfiction, and drama.
Website: http://al.gcsu.edu/prizes.php

Length: Short stories and creative nonfiction, to 25 pages. Poetry, to 8 pages. Drama, one-act plays.

Requirements: Entry fee, $17 per uploaded submission via online submissions manager, or $15 for hard copy. Submission fee pays for one-year subscription. Note genre on envelope. Submit only one entry per genre at a time. Include a cover sheet with author's name, contact information, and title of work. Author's name must not appear on manuscript. Visit website for more information.

Prize: Winners in each category receive $1,000, and publication in *Arts & Letters.*

Deadline: February 1 to March 18.

Atlantic Writing Competition

Writers' Federation of Nova Scotia
1113 Marginal Road
Halifax, Nova Scotia B3H 4P7
Canada

Description: Open to writers living in Atlantic Canada, this annual competition accepts unpublished short stories, poetry, magazine articles or essays, plays, writing for children, and YA novels. Published authors may not enter the competition in the genre in which they have been published.
Website: http://writers.ns.ca/competitions.html

Length: Short stories, creative nonfiction, to 3,000 words. Poems, to 6 per entry. Other categories vary.

Requirements: Entry fees: $25 ($20 for members, students, or seniors); $35 for novels ($30 for members, students, or seniors). One entry per category. Use pseudonym on manuscript.

Prize: First- through third-place winners in each category receive awards ranging from $200 to $50.

Deadline: November 9.

AWP Award Series

The Association of Writers & Writing Programs
Carty House, Mail Stop 1E3
George Mason University
Fairfax, VA 22030-4444

Description: Annual awards are given for book-length works of prose, creative nonfiction, collections of short stories, and poetry.
Website: www.awpwriter.org/contests/series.htm

Length: Novels, 60,000-word minimum. Short story collections and creative nonfiction, 150–300 pages. Poetry, 48-page minimum.

Requirements: Entry fee, $20 for AWP members; $30 for nonmembers. Accepts electronic submissions via Submittable. Visit the website for complete guidelines and entry form.

Prize: Poetry and short fiction winners receive $5,500 and publication. Creative nonfiction and novel winners receive $2,500 and publication.

Deadline: January 1 through February 28.

Doris Bakwin Award for Writing

Carolina Wren Press
120 Morris Street
Durham, NC 27701

Description: This biennial contest, held in odd-numbered years, seeks collections of short stories written by women. It encourages submissions from new and established writers. The publisher also runs the Carolina Wren Press Poetry Series, a contest for a full-length book of poetry.
Website: http://carolinawrenpress.org/submissions/contests

Length: 50–60 pages.

Requirements: Entry fee, $20. Accepts hard copy with disk. Accepts simultaneous submissions, if identified. Complete guidelines are posted on the website in late summer.

Prize: Prizes range from $150 to $600.

Deadline: January 1 through March 31.

Baltimore Review Contest

P.O. Box 529
Fork, MD 21051

Description: The staff of the *Baltimore Review* awards prizes to original, unpublished poetry, fiction, and nonfiction of all styles and forms. Contests have two reading periods. Each has a different theme, announced on the blog, Facebook page, and on a contest page during the submission period.
Website: www.baltimorereview.org

Length: To 6,000 words. Poetry, up to 3 poems.

Requirements: Entry fee, $10. Accepts submissions through online system with brief bio and simultaneous submissions (notify editors if entry is accepted elsewhere). SASE for list of winners.

Prize: First prize, $300. Second prize, $200; third prize, $100. Winning entries will be published in the *Baltimore Review*.

Deadline: August 1 to November 30 or February 1 to May 30.

Bartleby Snopes Annual Writing Contest

Guild Complex
P.O. Box 478880
Chicago, IL 60647-9998

Description: Unpublished short stories composed entirely of dialogue are eligible for this annual prize. There are no limits on characters, but the submission cannot use any narration.
Website: www.bartlebysnopes.com

Length: Fiction, to 2,000 words.

Requirements: Entry fee, $10. Accepts electronic submissions via website. Accepts multiple submissions (one per entry). No simultaneous submissions.

Prize: First place, $250 and publication in *Bartleby Snopes*; 4 honorable mentions, $10 and publication.

Deadline: September 15.

Bechtel Prize

Teachers and Writers Collaborative
520 Eighth Avenue, Suite 2020
New York, NY 10018

Description: This prize is awarded annually to an exemplary unpublished article or essay related to creative writing education or literary studies. Entries should "offer compelling portraits of the work done in creative writing classrooms, address important issues in creative writing education, and/or explore the nature of the writing life."
Website: www.twc.org/publications/bechtel-prize

Length: To 2,500 words.

Requirements: No entry fee. Accepts hard copy and multiple entries. Submit two copies of entry, one with a cover sheet with name, contact information, and title, and the second cover sheet with the title only. Send SASE or visit the website for complete guidelines. Entries that do not conform to the guidelines will be disqualified.

Prize: First prize, publication in *Teachers & Writers Magazine*.

Deadline: July1.

Black Orchid Novella Award

Jane K. Cleland
P.O. Box 3233
New York, NY 10163-3233

Description: Traditional mystery novellas compete annually for this award. All work must be previously unpublished. The award is sponsored by the Wolfe Pack, an organization of fans of fictional detective Nero Wolfe, and *Alfred Hitchcock's Mystery Magazine*.
Website: www.nerowolfe.org/htm/neroaward/black_orchid_award/BO_award_intro.htm

Length: 15,000–20,000 words.

Requirements: No entry fee. Multiple entries are accepted under separate cover. Accepts hard copy. SASE. Visit the website for complete competition guidelines.

Prize: Winner receives a cash award of $1,000 and publication in the December issue of *Alfred Hitchcock's Mystery Magazine*.

Deadline: May 31.

Boulevard Poetry Contest for Emerging Poets

6614 Clayton Road, Box 325
Richmond Heights, MO 63117

Description: Poets who have not yet published a book of poetry with a national press are invited to submit their work for this annual competition.

Website: www.boulevardmagazine.org/poetry-contest.html

Length: Three poems per entry.

Requirements: Entry fee, $15 per group of 3 poems and $15 for each additional group. Entry fee includes a one-year subscription. Accepts entries via website submissions manager, or hard copy. Accepts multiple entries, and simultaneous submissions. Author information and title should appear on page one. Enclose a self-addressed, stampled postcard for acknowledgment of receipt.

Prize: Winner receives $1,000 and publication in *Boulevard*.

Deadline: June 1.

Boulevard Short Fiction Contest for Emerging Writers

6614 Clayton Road, Box 325
Richmond Heights, MO 63117

Description: Writers who have not yet published a book of fiction, poetry, or creative nonfiction with a national press are invited to submit short stories for this annual competition.

Website: www.boulevardmagazine.org/partners.html

Length: To 8,000 words.

Requirements: Entry fee, $15 per group of 3 poems and $15 for each additional group. Entry fee includes a one-year subscription. Accepts entries via website submissions manager, or hard copy. Accepts multiple entries, and simultaneous submissions. Author information and title should appear on page one. Enclose a self-addressed, stampled postcard for acknowledgment of receipt.

Prize: Winner receives $1,500 and publication.

Deadline: December 31.

Briar Cliff Review Writing Competition

Fiction, Poetry, and Creative Nonfiction Contest
3303 Rebecca Street
Sioux City, IA 51104-2100

Description: Each year this competition awards prizes for a short story, a poem, and an essay or creative nonfiction piece. Entries are judged by the editors of the *Briar Cliff Review*.

Website: www.briarcliff.edu/campus/bc_review/bcreview_new/contest_new.aspx

Length: Fiction and creative nonfiction, to 6,000 words. Poetry, 3 poems, 1 per page.

Requirements: Entry fee, $20. Accepts hard copy. Accepts simultaneous submissions, if identified. Enclose a bio and cover sheet with identifying and contact information; name should not appear on manuscript. SASE for list of winners. All participants receive an issue of the *Briar Cliff Review* in which the contest winners are published.

Prize: First prize in each category, $1,000 and publication in the *Briar Cliff Review*.

Deadline: November 1.

Burnside Review Fiction Chapbook Competition

P.O. Box 1782
Portland, OR 97207

Description: This annual chapbook contest is in its sixth year. It accepts entries of one longer story or multiple shorter pieces. *Burnside Review* likes "work that breaks the heart. That leaves us in a place that we don't expect to be. We like the lyric. We like the narrative. We like when the two merge."

Website: www.burnsidereview.org/contests.php

Length: Fiction, to 10,000 words.

Requirements: Entry fee, $15. Accepts hard copy or email to contests@burnsidereview.org. Email submissions must pay $16 entry fee through PayPal to sid@burnsidereview.org. Include two cover sheets; one with author's name and contact information and one with title of entry only.

Prize: Winning author receives $200, and 10 copies of the printed chapbook.

Deadline: September 15 through January 31.

Burnside Review Poetry Chapbook Competition

P.O. Box 1782
Portland, OR 97207

Description: This annual chapbook contest accepts poetry entries. *Burnside Review* is a nonprofit, independent journal of poetry and fiction that favors lyrical writing.
Website: www.burnsidereview.org/contests.php

Length: 19–24 pages.

Requirements: Entry fee, $15. Accepts hard copy and email to contests@burnsidereview.org. Email submissions must pay the entry fee through PayPal to sid@burnsidereview.org. Include two cover sheets; one with author's name and contact information and one with title of entry only.

Prize: Winning author receives $200, publication in *Burnside Review*, and 10 copies of the printed chapbook.

Deadline: March 15 to June 30.

Canadian Writer's Journal Short Fiction Contest

Box 1178
New Liskeard, Ontario POJ 1PO
Canada

Description: For Canadian citizens or landed immigrants, this contest accepts entries of original, unpublished short stories of any genre.
Website: www.cwj.ca/04-00fiction.htm

Length: To 2,500 words.

Requirements: Entry fee, $5 per story. Accepts hard copy. Author name, contact information, and 200-word bio should be submitted on a cover sheet; author identification may not appear on the manuscript itself. SAE/IRC for list of contest winners; manuscripts are not returned.

Prize: First prize, $150; second prize, $100; third prize, $50. Winners also receive a copy of the *Journal*. Winning entries are published in the *Journal* and in *Choice Works*, a chapbook.

Deadline: April 30.

CAPA Jerry Labriola/ Brian Jud Contest

Connecticut Authors and Publishers Association
223 Buckingham Street
Oakville, CT 06779

Description: Short stories, personal essays, poetry, and children's stories may be entered into this annual contest, which is open to all authors and not just Connecticut residents. Entries must be original and unpublished.
Website: www.aboutcapa.com/writing_contest.htm

Length: Short stories and children's fiction, to 2,000 words; essays, to 1,500 words; poetry, to 30 lines.

Requirements: Entry fee, $10 per story or essay, and up to 3 poems. Each must be accompanied by a separate entry form. Submit four copies. Manuscripts must have no identifying information.

Prize: First prize, $100; second prize, $50. Winners are published in *The Authority*, CAPA's monthly newsletter. An ebook anthology of all winners will be published through Amazon for Kindle.

Deadline: December 24.

CCW Spring Writing Contest

P.O. Box 997
Pacific Grove, CA 93950

Description: Sponsored by the Central Coast Writers branch of the California Writers Club, this competition accepts previously unpublished short stories and poems.
Website: www.centralcoastwriters.org

Length: Short stories, to 2,500 words. Poetry, to 50 lines.

Requirements: Entry fee, $10 per short story, $8 for members; $5 per poem, $3 for members. Accepts hard copy and simultaneous submissions. Entries will not be returned. Visit the website for complete submission guidelines.

Prize: First prize in each category, $250 and publication in *Homestead Review*.

Deadline: September 1 and January 31.

Jane Chambers Playwriting Contest

Georgetown University
108 Davis Performing Arts Center
Box 571063, 37 & O Street NW
Washington, DC 20057-1063

Description: Feminist "plays and performance texts written by women and presenting significant opportunities for female performers" are sought for this award. Experimentation in form and subject matter is welcome.
Website: www.athe.org/displaycommon.cfm?an=1&subarticlenbr=25

Length: No length limits.

Requirements: No entry fee. Limit one entry per playwright annually; send three copies with résumé. Accepts hard copy. Complete guidelines and application forms are available at the website.

Prize: Winner receives $1,000 and a rehearsed reading at ATHE's annual midsummer conference.

Deadline: February 15.

The Chariton Review Short Fiction Prize

Truman State University Press
100 East Normal Avenue
Kirksville, MO 63501-4221

Description: This annual contest sponsored by the literary journal *The Chariton Review* welcomes unpublished entries in short fiction, on any theme. Entries must be written in English.
Website: http://tsup.truman.edu

Length: To 5,000 words.

Requirements: Entry fee, $20. Accepts hard copy. Accepts multiple and simultaneous submissions. Include two title pages: one with the manuscript title and author's contact information, and the other with only the manuscript title. Include an SASE for confirmation of receipt. Manuscripts will not be returned. All entrants receive the prize issue of *The Chariton Review*.

Prize: $1,000 and publication. Three finalists are published in the spring issue.

Deadline: September 30.

Chautauqua Literary Journal Contest

Jill Gerard, Department of Creative Writing
UNCW/601 South College Road
Wilmington, NC 28403

Description: This contest is held annually to honor a poem or group of poems, a short story, or an essay on a particular theme. Each year it focuses on a different literary form. The most recent contest was open to poets, and the theme was journeys and pilgrimages.
Website: www.ciweb.org/contest-information

Length: To 3 poems and up to 5 pages; no line limits.

Requirements: Entry fee, $20. Accepts electronic submissions via the website. Accepts multiple entries with separate entry fees. Accepts simultaneous submissions, if identified. Include a cover sheet with contact information and poem titles. Author's name must not appear on the manuscript.

Prize: $1,000 and publication in *Chautauqua*.

Deadline: November 1.

The Chautauqua Prize

Jordan Steves, Department of Education
Chautauqua Institution
1 Ames Avenue
P.O. Box 28,
Chautauqua, NY 14722

Description: This prize from a renowned lifelong learning institution is awarded to a book of original fiction or narrative nonfiction first published in English in the U.S. in the previous year. All submissions must be nominated, whether by publishers, agents, authors, or readers.
Website:www.ciweb.org/prize

Length: No length restrictions.

Requirements: Entry fee, $60. Accepts hard copy. Enclose entry form, 8 copies of book in bound or galley form, and SASE for receipt confirmation. Entries cannot be returned. Full eligibility and submission guidelines available at website.

Prize: Winner will receive $7,5,00 and an all expenses paid, one-week summer residency at Chautauqua Institution in western New York.

Deadline: September 4 to December 31.

Crab Creek Review Fiction Contest

7315 34th Avenue NW
Seattle, WA 98117

Description: This contest accepts entries of original, unpublished short stories on any subject. It is sponsored annually by the *Crab Creek Review*.
Website: www.crabcreekreview.org/contest.htm

Length: To 3,000 words.

Requirements: Entry fee, $10. Accepts email submissions only to crabcreekcontest@gmail.com. The entry should be a Word attachment named with the author's full name and "Fiction Contest." Include a cover letter in the body of the email, with name, contact information, title, and a brief bio. Author's name should not appear on the manuscript. Accepts simultaneous submissions, if identified.

Prize: Winner receives $200 and publication in *Crab Creek Review*.

Deadline: September 15 to December 15.

Crazyhorse Fiction Prize

Department of English
College of Charleston
66 George Street
Charleston, SC 29424

Description: This annual competition awards a prize for an original, previously unpublished short story or poetry. All entries are considered for publication in the literary journal.
Website: www.crazyhorsejournal.org

Length: Fiction, to 20 pages. Poetry, to 3 poems (10 pages maximum).

Requirements: Entry fee, $20, which includes a journal subscription. Accepts online submissions through the website only. Include cover page with author information and title of entry. Author name may not appear on manuscript. SASE for list of winners only.

Prize: Winner receives $2,000 and publication in *Crazyhorse*.

Deadline: Submit during the month of January.

Creative Nonfiction Writing Contests

Creative Nonfiction Foundation
5501 Walnut Street, Suite 202
Pittsburgh, PA 15232

Description: These contests are open to all writers of unpublished creative nonfiction. Topics vary and range from essays for book collections to special journal issues. One recent subject was sustainability. Pieces should be vivid and dramatic, with a strong narrative. *Creative Nonfiction* also sponsors daily Twitter micro-essay contests.
Website: www.creativenonfiction.org/thejournal/submittocnf.htm#truecrime

Length: Word lengths vary; see guidelines.

Requirements: Entry fees vary by contest; see website for details. Accepts multiple submissions and electronic submissions.

Prize: Multiple cash awards vary by contest, and awards include publication in *Creative Nonfiction*; see website for details.

Deadline: Varies by contest; see website for details.

Crossquarter Short Science Fiction Contest

P.O. Box 23749
Santa Fe, NM 87502

Description: Science fiction, fantasy, and urban fantasy stories are judged in this annual competition held by Crossquarter Publishing. Stories should depict a balancing of body, mind, heart, and the best of the human spirit. Entries must be original and unpublished.
Website: www.crossquarter.com/contest.html

Length: To 7,500 words.

Requirements: Entry fee, $15 for first story; $10 for additional entries. Submit electronically by CD or email attachment, saving the file in RTF format. Entries should be accompanied by an official entry form.

Prize: First place, $250; additional prizes range from $125 to $50. Winners are published in an anthology from Crossquarter Publishing.

Deadline: March 15.

Sheldon Currie Fiction Prize

The Antigonish Review
P.O. Box 5000, St. Francis Xavier University
Antigonish, Nova Scotia B2G 2W5
Canada

Description: Prizes are awarded by the literary journal *The Antigonish Review* for original, unpublished short stories on any subject. The journal also holds the Great Blue Heron Poetry Contest.
Website: www.antigonishreview.com

Length: To 20 pages.

Requirements: Entry fee, $25 from Canada; $30 in the U.S.; $40 outside of North America. Accepts hard copy. All entries must include a cover sheet with author's name and contact information and title of story; author's name may not appear on subsequent pages. No simultaneous submissions. Guidelines are available at website.

Prize: First prize, $600; second prize, $400; third prize, $200. All three winning entries are published in *The Antigonish Review*.

Deadline: July 31.

Danahy Fiction Prize

Tampa Review
University of Tampa Press
401 West Kennedy Boulevard
Tampa, FL 33606-1490

Description: This contest is open to all unpublished short stories. Entries are judged by the editors of *Tampa Review* and are considered for publication. The literary journal also gives an annual prize for poetry.
Website: www.ut.edu/tampareview

Length: 500–5,000 words.

Requirements: Entry fee, $20 (includes a one-year subscription). Accepts hard copy and submissions via the website. Multiple entries and simultaneous submissions are permitted. Include a cover letter with author's name and contact information, and word count. Current University of Tampa students and faculty are not eligible.

Prize: Winner receives $1,000 and publication in *Tampa Review*.

Deadline: November 1.

The Amanda Davis Highwire Fiction Award ★

849 Valencia Street
San Francisco, CA 94110

Description: Created in honor of author Amanda Davis, who died in a plane crash, this award from McSweeney's honors a woman writer younger than 32 who embodies Amanda's personal strengths and needs some time to finish a book in progress.
Website: www.mcsweeeneys.net/pages/the-amanda-davis-highwire-fiction-award

Length: 5,000–40,000 words.

Requirements: Entry fee, $20. Accepts electronic submissions via www.amandadavis.submittable.com, or hard copy. Include a brief explanation of financial status with submission. SASE.

Prize: $2,500.

Deadline: December 15.

Annie Dillard Award for Creative Nonfiction

Bellingham Review
Mail Stop 9004, Old Main 245
Western Washington University
Bellingham, WA 98225-9004

Description: This award, offered by the *Bellingham Review*, goes to a previously unpublished work of creative nonfiction. 2013 is a transitional year, as the contest moves to online submissions only.
Website: www.bhreview.org

Length: To 6,000 words.

Requirements: Entry fee, $20 for first entry; $10 for each additional entry. Prefers electronic submissions via website; 2013 is the last year hard copy is accepted. Author's name should not appear on manuscript. Simultaneous submissions accepted, if identified.

Prize: First prize, $1,000 and publication in the *Bellingham Review*. Second- and third-place winners are considered for publication.

Deadline: December 1 to March 15.

Jack Dyer Fiction Prize

Crab Orchard Review
Dept. of English, Faner Hall 2380, Mail Code 4503
Southern Illinois University Carbondale
Carbondale, IL 62901

Description: This prize is awarded to a previously unpublished work of fiction written in English by a U.S. citizen or permanent U.S. resident.
Website: www.craborchardreview.siuc.edu/dyer.html

Length: To 6,000 words.

Requirements: Entry fee, $20 per piece ($22.50 for online submissions); limit 3 entries. Accepts hard copy (indicate genre on envelope) and online submissions via Submittable. Author's name, contact information, and title of story must appear on a cover sheet only; no name on subsequent pages. Manuscripts are not returned; enclose SASE for list of winners only.

Prize: Winner receives $2,000 and publication in the winter/spring issue of *Crab Orchard Review*. Two finalists are also chosen.

Deadline: March 1 to May 4.

Eaton Literary Awards

Eaton Literary Agency
P.O. Box 49795
Sarasota, FL 34230-6795

Description: The Eaton Literary Agency gives these awards annually to book-length manuscripts of fiction or nonfiction, short stories, and articles. The work must be previously unpublished. All submissions to the agency are automatically entered into the awards program.
Website: www.eatonliterary.com/submissions.htm

Length: Book-length fiction and nonfiction, 10,000+ words. Articles and short stories, to 10,000 words.

Requirements: No entry fee. Accepts hard copy and email submissions to info@eatonliterary.com. SASE. Guidelines available at website.

Prize: Book-length winner, $2,500; short story/article winner, $500.

Deadline: Book-length entries, August 31. Short story/article entries, March 31.

Arthur Ellis Awards

4C-240 Westwood Road
Guelph, Ontario N1H 7W9
Canada

Description: The best in Canadian mysteries and crime writing is honored by these awards from Crime Writers of Canada. The categories are first crime novel, crime novel, crime novella, crime short story, French crime book (fiction and nonfiction), juvenile or YA crime book (fiction and nonfiction), and nonfiction crime book.
Website: www.crimewriterscanada.com/awards

Length: Varies by category. Novel, minimum 50,000 words. Novella, 8,000–20,000 words. Short story, to 8,000 words.

Requirements: Fee, $15 for short stories; $35 for books. Crime, detective, espionage, mystery, suspense, and thriller writing are welcome. Writers must be Canadian citizens regardless of place of residence. See website for detailed guidelines.

Prize: A statue, given at an annual awards dinner.

Deadline: December 15.

Aura Estrada Short Story Contest

P.O. Box 425786
Cambridge, MA 02142

Description: This annual contest was named for a Mexican-born writer and scholar in New York who drowned at age 30. Her writing had appeared in the *Boston Review*, which sponsors the contest. It seeks submissions of original, unpublished short stories of any type.
Website: http://bostonreview.net/about/contest/index.php

Length: To 5,000 words.

Requirements: Entry fee, $20 (includes half-year subscription). Encourages online submissions; will accept hard copy. Include cover page with author information, word count, and title; and title page with title only. Author name should not appear on manuscript. No simultaneous submissions. Submissions are not returned.

Prize: Winning author receives $1,500 and publication in the summer issue of the *Boston Review*.

Deadline: October 1.

Event Creative Nonfiction Contest

The Douglas College Review
P.O. Box 2503
New Westminster, British Columbia V3L 5B2
Canada

Description: Manuscripts exploring the creative nonfiction form are sought for this annual competition. All work must be previously unpublished. Check back issues of *Event* to see past winners of the contest.
Website: www.douglas.bc.ca/visitors/event-magazine/contestdetails.html

Length: To 5,000 words.

Requirements: Entry fee, $34.95 (includes one-year subscription to *Event*). Multiple entries are accepted under separate cover. Accepts hard copy. No simultaneous submissions. SASE. Visit website for more information.

Prize: Two or three prizes; two at $750 or three at $500, plus payment for publication in *Event*.

Deadline: April 23.

Family Circle Fiction Contest

Family Circle
805 Third Avenue, 22nd Floor
New York, NY 10022

Description: This contest accepts unique, unpublished short stories, which are judged based on writing ability, topic creativity, originality, and overall excellence. Entries must not have previously won any prize or award.
Website: www.familycircle.com/family-fun/fiction

Length: To 2,500 words.

Requirements: Entry fee, $20. Accepts up to two entries per person. Include name and contact information on each page. Entries will not be returned or acknowledged. See website for detailed guidelines.

Prize: Grand prize, $750; second place, $250; third place, $250.

Deadline: Postmarked by September 7.

William Faulkner–William Wisdom Competition

624 Pirate's Alley
New Orleans, LA 70116

Description: The New Orleans and Southern U.S. storytelling tradition is recognized in this annual competition. Categories include unpublished short story, essay, novel, novella, novel-in-progress, poetry, and short story by a high school student.
Website: www.wordsandmusic.org/competition.html

Length: Novel and narrative nonfiction, 100,000–225,000+ words. Novella, to 25,000 words. Short story, to 10,000 words. Novel-in-progress, to 12,500 words.

Requirements: Fees, $10–$75, depending on category. Include an entry form; details and form are available on website. Multiple submissions allowed.

Prize: Prizes range from $750 to $7,500, and publication in *The Double Dealer*. Award presented at the annual meeting of the Faulkner Society.

Deadline: January 1 to April 1.

Fineline Competition for Prose Poems, Short Shorts

Department of English
Bowling Green State University
Bowling Green, OH 43403

Description: This contest awards prizes for literary-quality prose poems and short, short stories. Entries must be original and unpublished.
Website: www.bgsu.edu/studentlife/organizations/midamericanreview

Length: To 500 words. Submit a set of three prose poems or stories.

Requirements: Entry fee, $10. Poems in verse will be automatically disqualified. Accepts hard copy. Send SASE for results. Submissions are not returned. Guidelines are posted on the website in late summer.

Prize: First prize, $1,000 and publication in *Mid-American Review*.

Deadline: June 1.

H. E. Francis Award

Department of English
University of Alabama
Morton Hall 222
Huntsville, AL 35899

Description: The University of Alabama English Department and the Ruth Hindman Foundation present this award to the best original, unpublished short stories.
Website: www.uah.edu/la/departments/english

Length: To 5,000 words.

Requirements: Entry fee, $15 per entry. Accepts hard copy. Accepts simultaneous submissions, if identified. Include a cover sheet, three copies of the manuscript, and an SASE for an announcement of the winner. The contest is judged by a panel of award-winning authors, literary journal editors, directors of creative writing programs, and "an eclectic collection of accomplished professionals" from many fields.

Prize: $1,000.

Deadline: December 31.

FreeFall Prose and Poetry Contest

922 9th Avenue SE
Calgary, Alberta T2G 0S4
Canada

Description: This competition is open to authors of original, unpublished prose and poetry. It is sponsored by *FreeFall*, "Canada's Magazine of Exquisite Writing."
Website: www.freefallmagazine.ca/contest.html

Length: Prose, to 3,000 words. Poetry, to 5 poems.

Requirements: Entry fee, $21 (includes a one-year subscription; outside Canada, participants receive a digital subscription). Alexandra Writers' Centre Society members, $10; $5 for additional entries. Accepts hard copy and website submissions, with entry form. No author's name on entry. No simultaneous submissions. Visit the website for complete details.

Prize: First prize, $300 in each category; second prize, $150; third prize, $75; honorable mention, $25. All winning pieces are published in *FreeFall*.

Deadline: December 31.

Fugue Annual Prose and Poetry Contest

200 Brink Hall, University of Idaho
P.O. Box 441102
Moscow, ID 83844

Description: Original and previously unpublished works of fiction, nonfiction, and poetry are eligible for entry in this competition, sponsored by *Fugue*, "a journal of new literature."
Website: www.fuguejournal.org

Length: Prose, to 10,000 words. Poetry, to 5 pages (3 poems maximum).

Requirements: Entry fee, $15 (includes a one-year subscription). Accepts submissions via an online submissions manager, or emails to fugue-prosesubmissions@uidaho.edu or fugue-poetrysubmissions@uidaho.edu.

Prize: First-place winners in each category receive $750 and publication in *Fugue*. Second- and third-place winners are also published.

Deadline: January 1 to May 1.

John Gardner Memorial Prize

Harpur Palate
English Department, Binghamton University
Box 6000
Binghamton, NY 13902-6000

Description: Author and creative writing teacher John Gardner is remembered through this contest for unpublished short stories.
Website: www.harpurpalate.blogspot.com/p/contests/html

Length: To 8,000 words.

Requirements: Entry fee, $15 per story. Multiple entries are allowed. Include a cover letter with name, address, phone, email address, and story title. Do not include author's name on manuscript. Prefers online submissions; will accept hard copy. Send SASE for contest results.

Prize: $500, publication in the summer issue of *Harpur Palate*; and a one-year subscription to the literary journal.

Deadline: February 1 to April 15.

Glimmer Train Family Matters Contest

Glimmer Train Press
4763 SW Maplewood
P.O. Box 80430
Portland, OR 97280-1430

Description: Short stories about family of all configurations are sought for this contest, which is held twice each year. No children's stories. Work must be original and previously unpublished.
Website: www.glimmertrain.com/familymatters.html

Length: To 12,000 words.

Requirements: Entry fee, $15. Accepts electronic submissions through the website. Accepts multiple entries. If they qualify, stories may be entered in other *Glimmer Train*-sponsored contests. Send SASE or visit the website for guidelines.

Prize: First prize, $1,500; publication in *Glimmer Train Stories*; and 20 copies of the issue in which the story appears. Second prize, $500; third prize, $300.

Deadline: April 1 to April 30; October 1 to October 31.

Glimmer Train Fiction Open

Glimmer Train Press
4763 SW Maplewood
P.O. Box 80430
Portland, OR 97280-1430

Description: This fiction contest is open to all writers, all themes and to previously published or unpublished work. It is held four times a year.
Website: www.glimmertrain.com/fictionopen.html

Length: 2,000–20,000 words.

Requirements: Entry fee, $19. Accepts up to three entries, submitted via the website. Novel excerpts are eligible, as long as they read like complete stories. Stories may be entered in more than one *Glimmer Train* contest.

Prize: First prize, $2,500; publication in *Glimmer Train*; and 20 copies of the issue in which the story appears. Second prize, $1,000; third prize, $600.

Deadline: March 1–30; June 1–30; September 1–30; December 1–January 2.

Glimmer Train Short Story Award for New Writers

Glimmer Train Press
4763 SW Maplewood
P.O. Box 80430
Portland, OR 97280-1430

Description: Held four times each year, this award from the literary journal *Glimmer Train* is for writers whose work has not appeared in a publication with a circulation over 5,000.
Website: www.glimmertrain.com/newwriters.html

Length: To 12,000 words.

Requirements: Entry fee, $15. Accepts up to three entries, submitted via the website. Stories may be entered in other *Glimmer Train* contests. Guidelines available at website.

Prize: First prize, $1,500; publication in *Glimmer Train*; and 20 copies of the issue in which the story is published. Second prize, $500; third prize, $300.

Deadline: February 1–28; May 1–30; August 1–31; November 1–30.

Glimmer Train Very Short Fiction Award

Glimmer Train Press
4763 SW Maplewood
P.O. Box 80430
Portland, OR 97280-1430

Description: Very short works of previously unpublished fiction are eligible for entry in this contest, which is held twice each year by *Glimmer Train*.
Website: www.glimmertrain.stores.yahoo.net/veryshort.html

Length: To 3,000 words.

Requirements: Entry fee, $15. Accepts up to three entries, submitted via the website. Stories may be entered in other *Glimmer Train* contests. Guidelines available at website.

Prize: First prize, $1,500; publication in *Glimmer Train*; and 20 copies of the issue in which the story is published. Second prize, $500; third prize, $300.

Deadline: January 1–31; July 1–31.

Good Housekeeping Short Story Contest

Editorial Offices
300 West 57th Street, 28th Floor
New York, NY 10019

Description: Original, unpublished works of fiction that reflect an aspect of women's lives today are eligible for entry in the *Good Housekeeping* fiction competition.

Website: www.goodhousekeeping.com/sweeps/fiction-contest

Length: To 3,500 words.

Requirements: No entry fee. Accepts electronic submissions at fictioncontest@goodhousekeeping.com. Include the story title in the subject line. Entries are not returned or acknowledged.

Prize: Grand prize, $3,000 and possible publication in the May issue of *Good Housekeeping*. Two runners-up will each receive $750 and possible publication at www.goodhousekeeping.com.

Deadline: July 1 to September 1.

Grey Sparrow Journal Flash Fiction Contest

P.O. Box 211664
St. Paul, MN 55121

Description: This contest was created in 2012 to recognize high-caliber work in flash fiction that is unpublished. The response in its inaugural year was beyond expectations and entries came from as far away as the Netherlands and Australia.

Website: http://greysparrowpress.sharepoint.com/Pages/winter2012FlashCompetition.aspx

Length: To 500 words.

Requirements: $5 entry fee. Accepts multiple entries under separate cover. Accepts simultaneous submissions, if identified. Submit to dsdianefuller@gmail.com. No contact information allowed on manuscript. Submissions not returned.

Prize: Grand prize, $100 and publication in *Grey Sparrow Journal*; four honorable mentions. All contest entries are considered for regular inclusion in the journal.

Deadline: June 15.

The Guild Literary Complex Prose Awards

Guild Complex
P.O. Box 478880
Chicago, IL 60647-9998

Description: Short works of nonfiction and fiction written by Illinois residents over the age of 21 are accepted for this annual contest. The Guild Literary Complex is a community-based literary group that encourages literary contributions to society.

Website: www.guildcomplex.org

Length: To 1,000 words.

Requirements: Entry fee, $5. Accepts email submissions to contest@guildcomplex.org. Write "Prose Awards" in the subject line; attach document. Also accepts hard copy. Name should not appear on the manuscript. SASE. Visit website for detailed guidelines.

Prize: First place in each category, $250 and a reading at an October event.

Deadline: Check guidelines.

The Gulf Coast Writer's Association Let's Write Contest

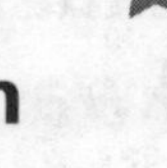

P.O. Box 10294
Gulfport, MS 39505

Description: Open to all writers, whether published or not, this contest accepts fiction, nonfiction, and poetry. Entries must be original and unpublished. Most genres are accepted, with the exception of graphic violence, horror, erotica, pornography, or writing with a moral, racial, or religious bias.

Website: www.gcwriters.org

Length: Fiction and nonfiction, to 2,500 words; poetry, to 50 lines.

Requirements: Entry fee, $8 for fiction, nonfiction, or up to 3 entries. Mail all entries. Include cover page, but no identifying information on any manuscript page. See website for cover page details.

Prize: First place in each category, $100 and publication in the *Magnolia Quarterly*. Second place, $60; third place, $25.

Deadline: April 15.

John Guyon Literary Nonfiction Prize

Crab Orchard Review
Dept. of English, Faner Hall 2380, Mail Code 4503
Southern Illinois University Carbondale
1000 Faner Drive
Carbondale, IL 62901

Description: The John Guyon Prize honors excellence in original, unpublished literary nonfiction, also called creative nonfiction or literary journalism. It is conferred by the literary journal, *Crab Orchard Review*.
Website: www.craborchardreview.siuc.edu/dyer.html

Length: To 6,500 words.

Requirements: Entry fee, $20 per piece ($22.50 for online submissions). Include contact information and title on a cover sheet. Do not include author's name anywhere on the manuscript.

Prize: $2,000, plus publication in *Crab Orchard Review*.

Deadline: March to May. Check guidelines for specific dates.

Wilda Hearne Flash Fiction Contest

Southeast Missouri State University Press
One University Plaza, MS 2650
Cape Girardeau, MO 63701

Description: Short-short stories on any theme are accepted for this annual contest sponsored by Southeast Missouri State University Press. All entries must be previously unpublished.
Website: www6.semo.edu/universitypress/hearne.htm

Length: To 500 words.

Requirements: Entry fee, $10. Accepts hard copy. Include separate cover sheet with title and contact information. There must be no identifying name on the pages. Send SASE for results. Visit the website for complete details.

Prize: First place, $300 and publication in *Big Muddy: A Journal of the Mississippi River Valley*.

Deadline: October 1.

Heart of the Rockies Contest

Colorado Romance Writers
P.O. Box 448
Eastlake, CO 80614-0448

Description: Unpublished romance writers are welcome to enter this competition for awards in categories that include short contemporary romance, romantic suspense, historical romance, paranormal/time travel, young adult, and others. Only the first 215 entries are considered.
Website: www.crw-rwa.ning.com/page/heart-of-the-rockies

Length: To 35 pages.

Requirements: Entry fee, $25 for members of Colorado Romance Writers; $30 for nonmembers. Accepts electronic submissions through the website. Each contestant receives a written critique and two evaluations. See website for category descriptions, complete rules, and entry form.

Prize: First-place winner in each category, $25. Finalists receive certificates.

Deadline: June 1 to August 17.

Lorian Hemingway Short Story Competition

P.O. Box 993
Key West, FL 33041

Description: New writers of short fiction whose work has not been published in a magazine with a circulation over 5,000 are encouraged to submit entries, on any theme. The final judge is the granddaughter of Ernest Hemingway.
Website: www.shortstorycompetition.com

Length: To 3,500 words.

Requirements: Entry fee, $15 for stories postmarked by May 1; $20, if postmarked by May 15. Author's name should not appear on manuscript; contact information, title, and word count is to be included on a separate cover sheet only. Accepts hard copy and electronic submissions at website.

Prize: First prize, $2,500, and publication in *Cutthroat: A Journal of the Arts*. Second and third prizes, $500 each. Honorable mentions are also awarded.

Deadline: May 15.

The Eric Hoffer Award for Short Prose

Hopewell Publications
P.O. Box 11
Titusville, NJ 08560

Description: This award is given to unpublished works of fiction and creative nonfiction. Judges are on the editorial board of a literary anthology. The award honors the memory of a famous American philosopher. Another annual contest is held to honor independent books.
Website: www.hofferaward.com

Length: To 10,000 words.

Requirements: No entry fee. Accepts electronic submissions at www.bestnewwriting.com/BNWsubmit.html. Limit one entry per author each quarter. Author name and title of work must appear on all pages of the manuscript. Entries are not returned. Independent books are judged as a separate category; visit website for more information, fees, and categories.

Prize: First prize, $250 and publication in *Best New Writing* anthology.

Deadline: March 31.

Hunger Mountain Creative Nonfiction Prize

Vermont College of Fine Arts
36 College Street
Montpelier, VT 05602

Description: Original and previously unpublished works of creative nonfiction written in English are sought for this annual contest, sponsored by the arts journal *Hunger Mountain*.
Website: www.hungermtn.org/contests

Length: To 10,000 words.

Requirements: Entry fee, $20. Accepts hard copy or entries via the submissions manager. Accepts multiple entries, and simultaneous submissions, if identified. Author's name should not appear on the manuscript; enclose an index card with story title, author's name, and contact information. All entries are considered for publication in *Hunger Mountain*.

Prize: First prize, $1,000 and publication in *Hunger Mountain*. Two honorable mentions receive $100.

Deadline: September 10.

Hunger Mountain Howard Frank Mosher Short Fiction Prize

Vermont College of Fine Arts
36 College Street
Montpelier, VT 05602

Description: Original and previously unpublished works of short fiction written in English are sought for this annual contest, sponsored by the arts journal *Hunger Mountain*.
Website: www.hungermtn.org/contests/

Length: To 10,000 words.

Requirements: Entry fee, $20. Accepts hard copy or entries via the submissions manager. Accepts multiple entries, and simultaneous submissions, if identified. Author's name should not appear on the manuscript; enclose an index card with story title, author's name, and contact information. All entries are considered for publication in *Hunger Mountain*.

Prize: First prize, $1,000 and publication in *Hunger Mountain*. Two honorable mentions receive $100.

Deadline: June 30.

The Iowa Review Award

The Iowa Review
308 EPB
Iowa City, IA 52242

Description: *The Iowa Review* awards prizes in the categories of fiction, nonfiction, and poetry. All work must be previously unpublished.
Website: www.iowareview.org

Length: Prose, to 25 pages; Poetry, to 10 pages; one poem per page.

Requirements: Entry fee, $20. Accepts hard copy and electronic submissions at website. No identification may appear on the manuscript; name, contact information, and title of work are to be noted only on cover sheet. Label envelope "Contest entry" and state category of competition. Enclose SAS postcard for confirmation of receipt of entry and SASE for final word on your work.

Prize: Winners in each category receive $1,500; first runners-up receive $750. Winners and runners-up are published in the December issue of *The Iowa Review*.

Deadline: Postmarked between January 1 and January 31.

E. M. Koeppel $1,100 Short Fiction Contest

Writecorner Press
P.O. Box 140310
Gainesville, FL 32614

Description: This annual contest, held since 2004, presents awards for previously unpublished fiction in any style and with any theme.
Website: www.writecorner.com

Length: To 3,000 words.

Requirements: Entry fee, $15; $10 for each additional entry. Accepts hard copy. Submit one copy with two title pages; one copy should be devoid of author's name and contact information. Manuscripts will not be returned. Guidelines available at website.

Prize: Winner receives $1,100. Editor's Choice winners receive $100.

Deadline: Entries are accepted between October 1 and April 30.

David J. Langum Sr. Prizes in American Historical Fiction and American Legal History

The Langum Charitable Trust
2809 Berkeley Drive
Birmingham, AL 35242

Description: These contests encourages quality historical writing geared to the general public. One is awarded for teh best American historical fiction, and the other for the best in American legal history or biography. The contests are open to books published the preceding year. Self-published or subsidized books are not accepted.
Website: www.langumtrust.org

Length: No word limit.

Requirements: Accepts hard copy. Refer to website for specific guidelines.

Prize: First place, $1,000.

Deadline: December 1.

Literary Juice Flash Fiction Contest

Description: Flash fiction that is risky, witty, highly creative, and even a little bizzare is eligible for this contest by the new online journal *Literary Juice*. Submissions must be original, unpublished, and in any genre except novel excerpts.
Website: www.literaryjuice.com

Length: To 700 words.

Requirements: Entry fee, $5. Accepts electronic submissions via website. Accepts multiple and simultaenous submissions, if identified.

Prize: First place, $200 and publication in *Literary Juice*. Runner-up, $50 and publication in *Literary Juice*.

Deadline: February 15.

Literary Laundry Competitions

Description: The editorial team behind this contest encourages writers to submit their unpublished poetry, short stories, or one-act dramas. Other genres are also accepted. Each issue of *Literary Laundry* is accompanied by a writing competition. It is a journal "edited by devoted writers and ardent critics."
Website: www.literarylaundry.com

Length: Fiction, to 6,000 words. One-act plays, to 15 pages. Poetry, to 2 pages.

Requirements: No entry fee. Accepts electronic submissions at website. Include cover letter with bio and an abstract explaining why the submission is of interest to a contemporary audience. One work per category is accepted during each review cycle, but multiple submissions in multiple categories are accepted. No simultaneous submissions.

Prize: First place, $500 for best poem and best short story; $250 for best one-act drama.

Deadline: December 15.

Many Mountains Moving Poetry & Flash Fiction Contests

1705 Lombard Street
Philadelphia, PA 19146

Description: Open to all poets and writers whose work is in English. Submissions may not be previously published.
Website: www.mmminc.org

Length: Flash fiction, to 1,500 words. Poetry, to 5 poems; 10 pages total.

Requirements: Entry fee, $15 for up to 2 flash fiction stories or 5 poems. Accepts hard copy and electronic submissions to editors@mmminc.org. No name should appear on submission; enclose a cover letter with name and contact information, title, and genre. Writers competing in both categories are asked to send entries in separate envelopes.

Prize: First-place winners receive $500 and publication in *Many Mountains Moving*.

Deadline: December 10.

Many Mountains Moving Press Poetry Book Prize

1705 Lombard Street
Philadelphia, PA 19146

Description: Open to all poets and writers whose work is in English. Submissions may not be previously published. The most recent winner is being published by MMMPress in 2013.
Website: www.mmminc.org

Length: 50–100 pages of original poetry.

Requirements: Entry fee, $25. Accepts hard copy and electronic submissions to editors@mmminc.org. No name should appear on submission itself; enclose a cover letter with name and contact information, title of submission, and genre. Include SASE for list of winners; manuscript will not be returned. Guidelines at website.

Prize: First-place winners in each category receive $1,000 and publication in *Many Mountains Moving*.

Deadline: December.

Marguerite McGlinn Prize for Fiction

93 Old York Road, Suite 1/#1-753
Jenkintown, PA 19046

Description: This annual short fiction contest of previously unpublished works is open to writers residing in or originally from the United States.
Website: www.philadelphiastories.org/margueritemcglinn-prize/fiction-0

Length: To 8,000 words.

Requirements: Entry fee, $10. Accepts electronic submissions at website. Multiple and simultaneous submissions accepted. All entrants receive a one-year subscription to *Philadelphia Stories*. Visit website for more information.

Prize: $2,000 and an invitation to an awards dinner in October, plus publication in the print and online editions of *Philadelphia Stories*.

Deadline: June 15.

Memoir Prize

Memoir Journal
1316 67th Street #8
Emeryville, CA 94608

Description: This competition, with two yearly submission periods, honors traditional and nontraditional forms of nonfiction memoirs. All work must be original and previously unpublished.
Website: www.memoirjournal. net/submit

Length: Prose, to 10,000 words. Poetry, maximum 5 poems.

Requirements: No entry fee. Accepts hard copy and electronic submissions via the website. Accepts simultaneous submissions, if identified. Name, contact information, and title of work should appear on cover page; title of work must appear on every page of manuscript. Manuscripts are not returned.

Prize: Grand prize, $500; runners-up will receive $250 or $100. All winners will be published in the print and digital editions of the *Memoir Journal* website and receive 3 complimentary copies.

Deadline: May 1–August 16; November 1–February 16.

Memoirs Ink Writing Contest

10866 Washington Boulevard, Suite 518
Culver City, CA 90232

Description: *Memoirs Ink* runs a half-yearly as well as an annual contest for the best personal essays, memoirs, or autobiographical stories. Entries can be serious, humorous, or artsy.
Website: www.memoirsink.com/contests

Length: Half-yearly, to 1,500 words. Annual, to 3,000 words.

Requirements: Entry fee, $17; previous entrants, $15. Late entries require additional $5 fee. All entries must be written in the first-person. Accepts hard copy. Accepts multiple submissions. Include your name only on the submission form, available on the website. Guidelines available at website.

Prize: First prize, $1,000; pecond prize, $500; third prize, $250.

Deadline: Half-yearly: February 15; late deadline March 1. Annual: August 1; late entries, August 15.

Meridian Editors' Prize

University of Virginia
P.O. Box 400145
Charlottesville, VA 22904-4145

Description: Works of fiction and poetry are considered for this annual contest. *Meridian* is a semi-annual literary journal from the University of Virginia and its Masters of Fine Arts program. UVA students and alumni, faculty and staff, are not eligible.
Website: www.readmeridian.org

Length: Fiction, to 10,000 words. Poetry, to 4 poems and to 10 pages per entry.

Requirements: Entry fee, $8 (includes a one-year electronic subscription to Meridian). Limit of two entries per genre. Accepts electronic submissions through ManuscriptHub.com, which is accessible via the online guidelines. Visit the website for complete instructions.

Prize: First-place winners in each category receive $1,000 and publication in *Meridian.*

Deadline: January 8.

Micro Award

Alan Presley
PSC 817, Box 23
FPO AE 09622-0023

Description: This contest recognizes published English prose fiction under 1,000 words, otherwise known as flash fiction.
Website: www.microaward.org

Length: To 1,000 words.

Requirements: Submissions must be prose fiction published either in print or electronically in the year preceding the award. Self-published fiction is eligible. Authors may submit one story; editors may submit two stories from their publications. Accepts email to admin@microaward.org. Cover letter should indicate venue and date of publication, word count, and author's name and contact information.

Prize: First prize, $500.

Deadline: Entries are accepted between October 1 and December 31.

Mississippi Review Prize

The University of Southern Mississippi
118 College Drive, #5144
Hattiesburg, MS 39406-0001

Description: Open to all works written in English, this competition awards prizes for fiction and poetry. Students or employees of the University of Southern Mississippi are ineligible.
Website: www.usm.edu/mississippi-review/mrcontest.html

Length: Fiction, 1,000–8,000 words. Poetry, 3 poems, to 10 pages.

Requirements: Entry fee, $15. Accepts hard copy. All entries must include author's name and contact information, title of work, and "MR Prize" on page one. Manuscripts are not returned.

Prize: Winners in each category receive $1,000. Winners and finalists are published in the *Mississippi Review.*

Deadline: August 1 through December 1.

The Missouri Review Jeffrey E. Smith Editors' Prize

357 McReynolds Hall
The University of Missouri–Columbia
Columbia, MO 65211

Description: *The Missouri Review* sponsors this annual competition and presents awards for original, unpublished fiction, essays, and poetry submitted.
Website: www.missourireview.com/contest

Length: Fiction and essays, to 25 pages. Poetry, any number of poems, to 10 pages.

Requirements: Entry fee, $20 (includes a one-year subscription to *The Missouri Review*). Multiple entries must be submitted separately. Accepts electronic submissions, or hard copy. Accepts simultaneous submissions, if identified. Mark envelope "Fiction," "Essay," or "Poetry."

Prize: Winners in each category receive $5,000 and publication in the *Best American* series. Finalists receive $100+ and are considered for publication.

Deadline: October 1.

Monkey Puzzle Press Flash Fiction Contest

P.O. Box 20804
Boulder, CO 80308

Description: This contest welcomes flash fiction on any theme. Monkey Puzzle Press publishes novels, poetry collections, short story collections, hybrid works, fiction, and nonfiction, by new and established writers.
Website: www.monkeypuzzlepress.com/literary events/monkey-puzzles

Length: To 1,000 words.

Requirements: Entry fee, $10. Accepts hard copy, multiple submissions, and electronic submissions to monkeypuzzlepress.prose@gmail.com; put "Flash Fiction Contest" in the subject line. Author name, address, phone number, and email address must appear on first page. SASE for receipt confirmation.

Prize: First place, $300; second place: $150; third place, $50.

Deadline: Check website.

Narrative Story Contest

Description: Previously unpublished fiction and nonfiction works with a strong narrative drive are considered for this annual competition. Short shorts, short stories, essays, memoirs, photo essays, graphic fiction, literary nonfiction, and excerpts are all accepted. Entries cannot have been chosen as finalists or received honorable mention in other contests. *Narrative* is a digital publication "dedicated to storytelling in the digital age."
Website: www.narrativemagazine.com

Length: Short stories, 500–2,000 words. Longer fiction and literary nonfiction, 2,000–40,000 words. Poetry, to 5 poems.

Requirements: Entry fee, $22 (includes free access to Narrative Backstage). Accepts electronic submissions through the website. Accepts simultaneous submissions. Complete guidelines and category information available at the website.

Prize: Winners receive prizes from $2,500 to $100, depending on category.

Deadline: November 30.

Nelligan Prize for Short Fiction

Colorado Review
9105 Campus Delivery, Department of English
Colorado State University
Fort Collins, CO 80523-9105

Description: This annual contest is for previously unpublished short stories of any theme. It is sponsored by the Center for Literary Publishing at Colorado State University.
Website: http://coloradoreview.colostate.edu/nell/sub.htm

Length: To 50 pages.

Requirements: Entry fee, $15; $17 for electronic submissions. Accepts hard copy and electronic submissions. Accepts multiple entries. Include two cover pages; one with author information, word count, and title of entry, and one with title only. Include SASE for results. Manuscripts are not returned.

Prize: Winner receives $2,000 and publication in the fall/winter issue of *Colorado Review*.

Deadline: January 1 to March 14.

The New Guard

P.O. Box 10612
Portland, ME 04104

Description: The finalists and semifinalists of the Machigonne Fiction and Knightville Poetry contests are published in the annual issue of *The New Guard,* an independent literary review. Entries to these contests in 2012 were double the year before.
Website: www.newguard review.

Length: Literary and experimental fiction, to 7,500 words. Poetry, to 300 lines and 3 poems per entry.

Requirements: Entry fee, $15. Accepts electronic submissions via website. Check website for additional guidelines.

Prize: $1,000 each for fiction and poetry and publication in *The New Guard.*

Deadline: July.

New Letters Literary Awards

University of Missouri–Kansas City
University House, 5101 Rockhill Road
Kansas City, MO 64110–2499

Description: Originally established to encourage new writers, and expand new genres by established writers, this annual competition accepts essays, fiction, and poetry.
Website: www.newletters.org/awards.asp

Length: Essays and fiction, to 8,000 words. Poetry, to 6 poems per entry.

Requirements: Entry fee, $15 for first entry (includes one-year subscription to *New Letters*); $10 for each additional entry. Accepts hard copy, online submissions. Accepts simultaneous submissions, if identified. Include two cover sheets, one with identifying and contact information, category, and title of work; one with title and category only.

Prize: First-place winners in each category receive $1,500.

Deadline: May 18.

New Millennium Writings Award

Room M2
P.O. Box 2463
Knoxville, TN 37901

Description: The literary journal *New Millennium Writings* has conferred awards for fiction, nonfiction, and poetry for more than 35 years.
Website: www.newmillenniumwritings.com/awards.php

Length: Short-short fiction, to 1,000 words. Fiction or nonfiction, to 6,000 words. Up to 3 poems per entry, to 5 pages total.

Requirements: Entry fee, $17 ($20 for electronic submissions). Accepts hard copy, electronic submissions via website, multiple submissions, and simultaneous submissions if identified. Include a cover sheet or cover letter.

Prize: $1,000 each in the categories of fiction, short-short fiction, nonfiction, and poetry. Winners are showcased in *New Millennium Writings.*

Deadline: January 31.

Newport Review Flash Fiction Contest

P.O. Box 65
Warren, RI 02885

Description: Works of the brief but demanding genre of flash fiction are awarded prizes in this annual competition, sponsored by the online arts journal *Newport Review.*
Website: www.newportreview.org

Length: To 1,000 words.

Requirements: Entry fee, $8 per story; $21 for 3 for entries. Limit 6 entries per competition. Accepts electronic submissions via the website. Manuscript should include writer's name and contact information.

Prize: First prize, $250 and publication. Second-prize winner receives $150 and publication, and third-prize winner receives $100 and publication. Honorable mention receives publication.

Deadline: October.

Flannery O'Connor Award for Short Fiction

University of Georgia Press
Main Library, 3rd Floor
320 South Jackson Street
Athens, GA 30602

Description: This competition welcomes short story or novella collections. Stories may have been published singly but should not have appeared in a book-length collection of the author's own work.
Website: www.ugapress.org/index.php/series/FOC

Length: 40,000–75,000 words.

Requirements: Entry fee, $25. Accepts electronic submissions via website. Accepts multiple submissions, and simultaneous submissions, if identified. Title, author's name, and contact information should appear on a top cover sheet only. Include a table of contents. All submissions and announcement of winners and finalists will be confirmed via email.

Prize: Two winners receive $1,000 and book contracts from the University of Georgia Press.

Deadline: April 2 to June 1.

Ohio State University Prize in Short Fiction

Ohio State University Press
180 Pressey Hall
1070 Carmack Road
Columbus, OH 43210-1002

Description: Ohio State University conveys an annual award for a collection of short stories or novellas, or a combination of the two. They may have been previously published or unpublished.
Website: www.ohiostatepress.org

Length: 150–300 pages. Individual stories or novellas in the collection may not exceed 125 pages.

Requirements: Entry fee, $20. Accepts hard copy. Include a cover sheet, title page with word count, and table of contents. Send SASE for results; manuscripts are not returned.

Prize: Publication, with a $1,500 advance against royalties.

Deadline: Submissions must be postmarked in January.

The Seán Ó Faoláin Short Story Competition

The Munster Literature Centre, Frank O'Connor House
84 Douglas Street
Cork, Ireland

Description: In honor of one of Ireland's most accomplished story writers and theorists, this annual competition is open to writers from around the world.
Website: www.munsterlit.ie/SOFPage.html

Length: Word lengths vary.

Requirements: $20 entry fee, for U.S. entrants. Accepts online submissions via website. Check guidelines for complete submission information.

Prize: Grand prize, €2,000 (about $2,700), publication in the literary journal, *Southword,* and a week-long stay at Anam Cara Writer's and Artist Retreat. Second prize, €500 and publication. Four honorable mentions, €120, and publication.

Deadline: May to July.

On-the-Verge Emerging Voices Award

Society of Children's Book Writers and Illustrators
8271 Beverly Boulevard
Los Angeles, CA 90048

Description: This award was created "to foster the emergence of diverse voices in children's books" and honor writers and illustrators from traditionally under-represented cultures in American juvenile literature. Manuscripts must be unpublished, unagented, and not under contract.
Website: www.scbwi.org

Length: Word lengths vary.

Requirements: Accepts email to voices@scbwi.org; include author bio, synopsis, and explanation why entry will bring forward an under-represented voice. See guidelines for additional details.

Prize: All-expenses paid trip to the SCBWI winter conference, a year's membership, and an SCBWI mentor for a year.

Deadline: November 15.

Pacific Northwest Writers Association Literary Contest

PMB 2712, 1420 NW Gilman Boulevard, Suite 2
Issaquah, WA 98027

Description: This contest features 12 categories, including short story, poetry, and short topics (articles, essays, memoir). Book-length categories include mainstream, historical, romance, mystery, and science fiction and fantasy.
Website: www.pnwa.org

Length: Short stories, to 14 pages. Short nonfiction, to 10 pages. Other categories, word lengths vary.

Requirements: Entry fee, $35 for PNWA members; $50 for nonmembers. Accepts hard copy with registration form. Include SASE. All pages must have category number (see Category Definitions on the website), title, and page number. Entries receive two critiques.

Prize: First place, $700 and the Zola Award. Second place, $300.

Deadline: February 22.

Palooka Press Chapbook Contest

Editor: Jonathan Starke

Description: This new literary magazine accepts submissions of fiction, poetry, nonfiction, drama, graphic narrative, and mixed genre for its contest as well as for possible publication
Website: www.palookamag.com/palookapress.htm

Length: 35–50 pages.

Requirements: $10 entry fee. Accepts online entries via the Submishmash submissions manager. Accepts multiple submissions, and simultaneous submissions, if identifed. Include cover letter with title, word count, and author contact information. No identifying information should appear anywhere on manuscript.

Prize: Publication in Palooka Press, 20 copies, $100, and bio and photo featured on website.

Deadline: December 1.

The Katherine Paterson Prize for Young Adult and Children's Writing

Hunger Mountain, Vermont College of Fine Arts
36 College Street
Montpelier, VT 05602

Description: Books, short stories, and excerpts geared to children and young adults are accepted. The contest is named for the author of *The Bridge to Terabithia* and other well-respected fiction.
Website: www.hungermtn.org

Length: To 10,000 words.

Requirements: Entry fee, $20. Accepts electronic submissions via the website, or hard copy. Author's name should not appear on the manuscript. SASE for list of winners. Visit website for guidelines.

Prize: First place, $1,000 and publication in *Hunger Mountain*. Two honorable mentions, $100 each and possible publication.

Deadline: June 30.

Pearl Short Story Prize

3030 East Second Street
Long Beach, CA 90803

Description: Open to all types of fiction, this contest is sponsored by the literary magazine *Pearl*. Entries should be well-crafted narratives with interesting, believable characters and meaningful situations. Previously unpublished stories only.
Website: www.pearlmag.com/contests.html

Length: To 4,000 words.

Requirements: Entry fee, $10. Accepts hard copy. Accepts simultaneous submissions, if identified. Author name and address should appear on the first page of the manuscript. Complete contest guidelines are posted at the website. Include SASE for return of the manuscript.

Prize: $250, publication in *Pearl*, and 10 copies of the issue in which the story appears.

Deadline: April 1 to May 31.

PEN Center USA Literary Awards

269 South Beverly Drive, #1163
Beverly Hills, CA 90212

Description: This competition is open to authors who live west of the Mississippi River. It calls for works produced or published in the preceding calendar year in the categories of fiction, creative nonfiction, research nonfiction, poetry, children's literature, translation, journalism, drama, teleplay, and screenplay.
Website: www.penusa.org/awards

Length: No length restrictions.

Requirements: Entry fee, $35. Accepts hard copy. Submit four published copies of entry, with entry form available on the website.

Prize: First prize in each category, $1,000 and an invitation to the annual Literary Awards Festival in Los Angeles. Include SASE for confirmation of receipt.

Deadline: December 31 for book category; January 31 for non-book categories.

Phoebe Fiction Contest

Phoebe
MSN 2C5
George Mason University
4400 University Drive
Fairfax, VA 22030

Description: The literary magazine *Phoebe* holds this annual contest, which accepts entries of previously unpublished short fiction. Novel excerpts will not be considered.
Website: www.phoebejournal.com

Length: To 7,500 words.

Requirements: Entry fee, $15. Accepts submissions via the website. Accepts simultaneous submissions, if identified. Include name, contact information, and title of story in a cover letter. No identifying information may appear on the manuscript itself.

Prize: Winner receives $1,000 and publication in *Phoebe.*

Deadline: December 15.

Phoebe Nonfiction Contest

Phoebe
MSN 2C5
George Mason University
4400 University Drive
Fairfax, VA 22030

Description: This annual contest accepts entries of previously unpublished nonfiction. Narrative work with a research component is encouraged.
Website: www.phoebejournal.com

Length: To 5,000 words.

Requirements: Entry fee, $12. Accepts submissions via the website. Accepts simultaneous submissions, if identified. Include name, contact information, and title of work in a cover letter. No identifying information may appear on the manuscript itself.

Prize: Winner receives $500 and publication in *Phoebe.*

Deadline: December 15.

Pikes Peak Writers Fiction Contest 

P.O. Box 64273
Colorado Springs, CO 80962

Description: After many successful years, the organizers have decided to revamp this contest with an announcement made in time for the 2014 Pikes Peak Writers Conference. Please check the website regularly for an announcement.
Website: www.ppwc.net/html/contest.html

Length: Short stories.

Requirements: Information on entry fees and submission requirements will be posted in time for the 2014 Pikes Peak Writers Conference.

Deadline: Check website.

Prairie Fire Press Creative Nonfiction Contest

423-100 Arthur Street
Winnipeg, Manitoba R3B 1H3
Canada

Description: Original, previously unpublished works of creative nonfiction are eligible for entry in this annual competition, sponsored by the literary magazine *Prairie Fire*.
Website: www.prairiefire.ca

Length: To 5,000 words.

Requirements: Entry fee, $32 (includes a one-year subscription to *Prairie Fire*). One article per entry. Accepts hard copy. No simultaneous submissions. Author's name and contact information on cover sheet only. Visit the website for complete guidelines.

Prize: First prize, $1,250; second prize, $500; third prize, $250. All winning entries are published in *Prairie Fire*; authors receive payment for publication in addition to prize money.

Deadline: November 30.

Prairie Fire Press Short Fiction Contest

423-100 Arthur Street
Winnipeg, Manitoba R3B 1H3
Canada

Description: This annual contest from *Prairie Fire* awards prizes for previously unpublished short fiction.
Website: www.prairiefire.ca

Length: To 10,000 words.

Requirements: Entry fee, $32 (includes a one-year subscription to *Prairie Fire*). One article per entry. Accepts hard copy. No simultaneous submissions. Author's name and contact information on cover sheet only. Visit the website for complete guidelines.

Prize: First prize, $1,250; second prize, $500; third prize, $250. All winning pieces are published in *Prairie Fire* and authors receive payment for publication in addition to prize money.

Deadline: November 30.

Prism International Literary Nonfiction Contest

Buchanan E462, 1866 Main Mall
Vancouver, British Columbia V6T 1Z1
Canada

Description: Authors around the world are eligible to submit to this contest sponsored by the University of British Columbia and literary magazine *Prism International*.
Website: www.prismmagazine.ca/contests

Length: To 6,000 words.

Requirements: Entry fee, $35 for Canadian entries; $40 for U.S. entries; $5 for each additional entry. All submissions include a one-year subscription to *Prism International*. Accepts hard copy and electronic submissions. Include entry form and a cover page with author's name and address, and title of manuscript. Include title only on each manuscript page.

Prize: Grand prize, $1,500 and publication in the winter issue of *Prism International*.

Deadline: November.

Prism International Short Fiction Contest

Buchanan E462, 1866 Main Mall
Vancouver, British Columbia V6T 1Z1
Canada

Description: Original, unpublished short stories compete for prizes in this competition from the University of British Columbia and *Prism International*. Works of translation are eligible.
Website: www.prismmagazine.ca/contests

Length: To 6,000 words.

Requirements: Entry fee, $35 for Canadian entries; $40 for U.S. entries; $5 for each additional entry. All submissions include a one-year subscription to *Prism International*. Accepts hard copy and electronic submissions. Include entry form and a cover page with author's name and address, and title of manuscript. Include title only on each manuscript page.

Prize: Grand prize, $2,000 and publication in *Prism International*. Two runner-up prizes, $300 and $200.

Deadline: January 25.

Reader's Digest Writing Contest

P.O. Box 50005
Prescott, AZ 86301-5005

Description: This contest is about the theme of "Your Life" and accepts original, unpublished stories that share a life lesson, simple advice, a funny moment, or other story from your life.
Website: www.facebook.com/ReadersDigest

Length: To 150 words.

Requirements: There is no entry fee. Accepts multiple entries on different topics. Submit via the *Reader's Digest* Facebook page. Essays may be supported with a photo or video. Visit the page for complete details.

Prize: Grand prize, $25,000; 10 runner-ups will win $2,500. The 11 honorees will also be published on Readersdigest.com. The most popular Facebook entry will receive $2,500.

Deadline: November 1.

Roanoke Review Fiction Contest

221 College Lane
Salem, VA 24153

Description: This annual contest is open to works of creative short fiction. It is sponsored by the literary magazine of Roanoke College.
Website: www.roanokereview.wordpress.com

Length: To 5,000 words.

Requirements: Entry fee, $15 for each story submitted. Multiple entries are accepted. Accepts hard copy or electronic submissions at website. Complete submission guidelines available at website.

Prize: First prize, $1,000; second prize, $500. Winning entries and finalists are published in the spring issue of the *Roanoke Review*.

Deadline: November 1.

San Antonio Writers Guild Contests

P.O. Box 100717
San Antonio, TX 78201-8717

Description: Fiction, nonfiction, and poetry are the divisions of this annual contest for unpublished work.
Website: www.sawritersguild.com

Length: Short story, to 4,000 words. Flash fiction, to 1,000 words. Novel, first chapter or up to 5,000 words. Nonfiction, to 2,500 words. Poetry, to 3 poems of up to 40 lines.

Requirements: Entry fee, $10 for members; $20, nonmembers. Accepts hard copy. Accepts multiple entries, in up to three categories. Refer to the website for specific guidelines. The annual Louise Stewart Writing Contest also looks for nonfiction and poems on a different topic each year.

Prize: First place, $150; second place, $75; third place, $50.

Deadline: October.

Mona Schreiber Prize

3940 Laurel Canyon Boulevard, #566
Studio City, CA 91604

Description: Writers of comedic essays, articles, short stories, poetry, shopping lists, and any other forms of writing are invited to submit for this annual competition, named for a popular humor writer and creative writing teacher in San Mateo County.
Website: www.brashcyber.com/mona.htm

Length: To 750 words.

Requirements: Entry fee, $5. Multiple entries are accepted under separate cover. Accepts hard copy. Manuscripts are not returned. Include email address for list of winners. Visit the website for complete competition guidelines.

Prize: First-place winner receives $500 and publication on the website. Second place receives $250; third place, $100.

Deadline: December 1.

The A. David Schwartz Fiction Prize

Cream City Review
University of Wisconsin–Milwaukee
P.O. Box 413
Milwaukee, WI 53201

Description: This annual contest is open to previously unpublished works of fiction. It is sponsored by the nonprofit literary magazine *Cream City Review* and Harry W. Schwartz Bookshops.
Website: www.creamcityreview.org/submit

Length: To 20 pages.

Requirements: Entry fee, $15 per story. Accepts hard copy. Simultaneous submissions are eligible as long as author discloses acceptance of the work elsewhere.

Prize: Winner receives $1,000 and publication in *Cream City Review*.

Deadline: December 31.

Seven Hills Literary Contest

Tallahassee Writers Association
P.O. Box 3428
Tallahassee, FL 32315

Description: The *Seven Hills Review*, an annual journal from the Tallahassee Writers Association, holds this contest for the genres of short story, creative nonfiction, flash fiction, and writing for children.
Website: www.twaonline.org

Length: Short story, to 2,500 words, any genre. Creative nonfiction, to 2,500 words. Flash fiction, to 500 words. Children's stories (for ages 6–12), to 2,500 words.

Requirements: Entry fee, $12, TWA members; $17, nonmembers. Accepts electronic submissions via website only. Author's name should not appear on the manuscript.

Prize: First place, $100; second place, $75; third place, $50. Winners are published in the *Seven Hills Review*.

Deadline: August 31.

The Mary Shelley Award for Imaginative Fiction

c/o *Rosebud* Magazine
N3310 Asje Road
Cambridge, WI 53523

Description: This competition seeks original, unpublished works of fantasy, fiction, mystery, and horror. The editors of the sponsoring nonprofit publication, *Rosebud*, are also open to stories that reach beyond the boundaries of those genres and take literary and creative risks.
Website: www.rsbd.net

Length: 1,000–3,500 words.

Requirements: Entry fee, $10. Accepts hard copy. Accepts multiple entries. Complete guidelines are posted at the website. For information, query to jrodclark@rsbd.net.

Prize: First prize, $1,000 and publication in *Rosebud*. Four runners-up, $100 each and publication in *Rosebud*.

Deadline: October.

Kay Snow Writing Contest

Willamette Writers
2108 Buck Street
West Linn, OR 97068

Description: Named for the founder of the Williamette Writers, one of the largest writers' organizations in the U.S., the annual Kay Snow contest includes categories for fiction, nonfiction, poetry, screenwriting, juvenile writing, and student writers (18 and under).
Website: www.willamettewriters.com

Length: Fiction and nonfiction, to 2,500 words. Screenwriting, to 10 pages. Poetry, 2 poems to a total of 5 pages.

Requirements: Entry fee, $10, members; $15, nonmembers. Detailed submission guidelines are available at the website.

Prize: First prize, $300; second prize, $150; third prize, $50.

Deadline: April 19.

So to Speak Contests

George Mason University, MSN 2C5
4400 University Drive
Fairfax, VA 22030

Description: *So to Speak,* a feminist journal of language and art, awards prizes in the categories of fiction; and nonfiction, including memoirs and vignettes; and poetry.
Website: www.sotospeakjournal.org/contests

Length: Fiction and nonfiction, to 4,500 words. Poetry, to 5 poems per submission, not to exceed 10 pages.

Requirements: Entry fee, $15. Accepts electronic submissions via the website, with a cover letter.

Prize: First-place winner in each category receives $500 and publication in *So to Speak.* Three finalists are also published in the journal.

Deadline: Fiction, March 15. Nonfiction and poetry, October 15.

Southwest Writers Writing Contest

3721 Morris NE, Suite A
Albuquerque, NM 87111-3611

Description: This annual contest is open to original, unpublished works of fiction, nonfiction, screenplays, and poetry in 12 categories, including mainstream novel, mystery/suspense, science fiction, historical novel, YA, mainstream short story, memoir, essay, and nonfiction book.
Website: www.southwestwriters.com/contestRules.php

Length: Fiction and screenplay, first 20 pages. Mainstream short story, 4,000–6,000 words. Poetry, to 3 pages, or 3 haiku on one page.

Requirements: Entry fee, $20; $35 for nonmembers. Entry fee for poetry, $10; $20 for nonmembers. Critique available for additional fee. Accepts hard copy. Visit website for more information.

Prize: First place, $150; second place, $100; third place, $50. First-place winner competes for the $1,000 Storyteller Award.

Deadline: May 1. Late entries, May 15, with $10 fee.

The Ruth Stone Poetry Prize

RSPP
Hunger Mountain
Vermont College of Fine Arts
36 College Street
Montpelier, VT 05602

Description: The literary journal *Hunger Mountain* holds this annual poetry contest, which is judged by the journal's editors and guest authors.
Website: www.hungermtn.org/ruth-stone-poetry-prize

Length: To 3 poems.

Requirements: Entry fee, $20. Accepts electronic submissions via website submissions manager, or hard copy. Accepts multiple submissions. Name should not appear on the manuscript. SASE for list of winners.

Prize: First place, $1,000 and publication in *Hunger Mountain* online. Two honorable mentions, $100 each and possible publication.

Deadline: December 10.

Tickled by Thunder Fiction Magazine Contests

14076-86A Avenue
Surrey, British Columbia V3W 0V9
Canada

Description: This publication offers several contests throughout the year. It offers prizes in the categories of fiction, articles, and poetry. The quarterly *Tickled by Thunder*'s mission is to help new writers succeed. It sponsors nine yearly contests.
Website: www.tickledbythunder.com

Length: Fiction and articles, to 2,000 words. Poetry, no line limit.

Requirements: Entry fees vary and are waived or reduced for subscribers. Accepts electronic submissions via website. See website for detailed guidelines.

Prize: Winners receive $150 Canadian for fiction; $75 for poetry; $5 for articles. Winners receive publication in *Tickled by Thunder,* a contributor's copy, and a one-year subscription.

Deadline: See website for various deadlines.

Toasted Cheese Writing Contests

Description: *Toasted Cheese* is a literary journal and runs three contest categories a year. Three Cheers and a Tiger is held in the spring and fall; it is a 48-hour short story contest on a mystery or science fiction/fantasy topic. A Midsummer Tale accepts creative nonfiction on a summer theme. Dead of Winter accepts themed horror fiction set in winter.
Website: www.tclj.toasted-cheese.com/contest.htm

Length: Varies for each contest.

Requirements: No entry fee. Accepts electronic entries pasted into the body of an email. See individual contest guidelines for specific submission addresses, which vary. Include a bio and word count. One entry per person per contest. Complete guidelines available at website.

Prize: Winners receive Amazon gift cards ranging from $10–$50 and publication in *Toasted Cheese*. Honorable mentions may be awarded.

Deadline: Approximately March 21, June 21, September 21, and December 21.

Utah Original Writing Competition

617 East South Temple
Salt Lake City, UT 84102

Description: Open to all Utah residents, this annual contest has honored distinguished unpublished work in a variety of categories since 1958. Categories include novel, short story, short nonfiction, personal essay, book-length nonfiction, children's book, screenplay, and poetry.
Website: http://arts.utah.gov/opportunities/competitions/writing.html

Length: Word lengths vary for each category. Check the website for complete information.

Requirements: No entry fee.

Prize: First prize for novel, bio/history, story collection, YA book, $1,000. First prize for poetry, short story, narrative nonfiction/ essay. $500. Second prize ranges from $500 to $150.

Deadline: April 15 to June 28.

Herman Voaden Playwriting Competition

Queens University Drama Department
Kingston, Ontario K7L 3N6
Canada

Description: The purpose of this annual competition is to develop a distinctly Canadian voice in the theater and to encourage the writing of Canadian drama. It is open to Canadian citizens and landed immigrants. Unpublished and unproduced works in English are eligible.
Website: www.queensu.ca/drama/Voaden-Playwriting-Contest

Length: Full-length plays.

Requirements: Entry fee, $45. Email one PDF copy, with entry form, available online. Author's name should only appear on the entry form. See website for complete details.

Prize: First prize, $3,000; second prize, $2,000. Both winners receive a one-week workshop and public reading with a professional director and cast. Eight honorable mentions receive short written critiques.

Deadline: January 15.

The Robert Watson Literary Prizes

The Greensboro Review
MFA Writing Program, 3302 MHRA Building
University of North Carolina–Greensboro
Greensboro, NC 27402-6170

Description: Previously unpublished poetry and works of short fiction compete annually for these prizes, sponsored by *The Greensboro Review* at the University of North Carolina.
Website: www.greensbororeview.org/contests

Length: Fiction, to 25 pages. Poetry, to 10 pages.

Requirements: Entry fee, $14 (includes one-year subscription to *The Greensboro Review*). Accepts hard copy, and entries via the website submissions manager. Accepts simultaneous submissions, if identified. Mark envelopes with "Fiction" or "Poetry." SASE for receipt confirmation.

Prize: First-place winners in each category receive $1,000 and publication in the spring issue of *The Greensboro Review*.

Deadline: September 15.

Whispering Prairie Press Writing Contest

P.O. Box 410661
Kansas City, MO 64141

Description: This contest accepts original, unpublished entries of flash fiction, and nonfiction personal essays, and poetry in any style and on any theme. It is open to writers nationwide. Whispering Prairie Press publishes the journal *Kansas City Voices*.
Website: www.wppress.org

Length: Flash fiction and essays, to 1,000 words. Poetry, up to 1 page single spaced.

Requirements: Entry fee, $10; two entries for $18; three entries for $25. Accepts electronic entries via the website submissions manager. Author contact information must not be on manuscript pages.

Prize: First place, $100; second place: $50; third place, $25, plus one honorable mention for every 10 entries. Winners are not published, and the contest retains no right to the works submitted.

Deadline: June 30.

Willow Springs Fiction Prize

Willow Springs
501 North Riverpoint Boulevard, Suite 425
Spokane, WA 99202

Description: Sponsored by the semiannual *Willow Springs* literary journal, this annual contest accepts short stories on any subject. All entries must be previously unpublished.
Website: http://willowsprings.ewu.edu/contests.php

Length: No word limit.

Requirements: Entry fee, $20 (includes one-year subscription). Accepts hard copy or electronic submission via website. Accepts multiple submissions. Include a cover letter with author's name, contact information, and short bio. Author's name should not appear on manuscript.

Prize: Winner receives $2,000 and publication in *Willow Springs*.

Deadline: November 15.

Thomas Wolfe Fiction Prize

Professor Anthony S. Abbott
P.O. Box 7096
Davidson College
Davidson, NC 28035

Description: This annual competition, sponsored by North Carolina's Writers' Network, is open to all fiction "writers regardless of geographical region or previous publication." Work submitted must be previously unpublished.
Website: www.ncwriters.org

Length: To 12 double-spaced pages.

Requirements: Entry fee, $15 for members; $25 for nonmembers. Accepts hard copy. Accepts multiple entries. Submit two copies and a cover sheet with title, author name, contact information, and word count. Author's name should not appear on manuscript.

Prize: Winner receives $1,000 and possible publication in the *Thomas Wolfe Review*.

Deadline: January 30.

Tobias Wolff Award for Fiction

Bellingham Review
Cashier's Office, Mail Stop 9004
Old Main 245
Western Washington University
Bellingham, WA 98225-9004

Description: Short fiction and novel excerpts are sought for this annual competition, named for the author regarded as a master of memoir and short stories. Only unpublished works are eligible.
Website: www.bhreview.org

Length: To 6,000 words.

Requirements: Entry fee, $20 for first entry; $10 for each additional entry. Prefers electronic submissions via the website submissions manager; will accept hard copy. Accepts simultaneous submissions, if identified. Author's name should not appear on manuscript.

Prize: First prize, $1,000 and publication in the *Bellingham Review*. Second- and third-place winners and finalists may be considered for publication.

Deadline: March 15.

Wow! Women on Writing Contests

P.O.Box 41104
Long Beach, CA 90853

Description: Flash fiction contests offered quarterly by this ezine emphasize creativity and originality. Entries may be of any style and must be written in English. Each contest is limited to 300 entries.

Website: www.wow-womenonwriting.com/contest.php

Length: 250–750 words.

Requirements: Entry fee, $10. Accepts email submissions to contest@wow-womenonwriting.com (no attachments; include "Submission" with date of contest in subject line). Include your name, contact information, and word count at the end of your story. Critiques are available for an additional $10.

Prize: First prize, $350, publication in *Wow!* and an interview on the *Wow!* blog, Second- and third-prize winners receive $250 and $150, respectively, and publication in *Wow!*

Deadline: February 28, May 31, August 31, and November 30.

Writers @ Work Fellowship Competition

P.O. Box 711191
North Salt Lake, UT 84171-1191

Description: Writers @ Work, a nonprofit literary arts organization, sponsors this annual contest that recognizes emerging writers of fiction, literary nonfiction, and poetry. Writers not yet published in the category of their entry are eligible to submit original work.

Website: www.writersatwork.org

Length: To 7,500 words.

Requirements: Reading fee, $20. Accepts electronic submissions via the website's submissions manager.

Prize: First prize, $1,000, publication in *Quarterly West*, a featured reading, and tuition for the organization's annual conference. Two honorable mentions, $250.

Deadline: January 1 to March 1.

Writer's Digest Crime Short Story Competition

4700 East Galbraith Road
Cincinnati, OH 45236

Description: This *Writer's Digest* magazine contest accepts original, unpublished crime stories. Entries must be written in English; no other restrictions apply.

Website: www.writersdigest.com/competitions/writing-competitions

Length: To 4,000 words.

Requirements: Entry fee, $20. Accepts hard copy and electronic submissions via website. Include entry form. Visit website for more information.

Prize: First prize, $500 and promotion in *Writer's Digest* and the *2013 Novel & Short Story Writer's Market*.

Deadline: October.

Writer's Digest Horror Short Story Competition

4700 East Galbraith Road
Cincinnati, OH 45236

Description: This contest accepts entries of horror-themed short stories. Entries must be in English and previously unpublished.

Website: www.writersdigest.com/competitions/writing-competitions

Length: To 4,000 words.

Requirements: Entry fee, $20. Accepts hard copy and electronic submissions via website. Include entry form. Visit website for more information.

Prize: First prize, $500 and promotion in *Writer's Digest* and the *2013 Novel & Short Story Writer's Market*.

Deadline: October.

Writer's Digest Romance Short Story Competition

4700 East Galbraith Road
Cincinnati, OH 45236

Description: This *Writer's Digest* contest accepts romance short stories that are written in English and previously unpublished.
Website: www.writersdigest.com/competitions/writing-competitions

Length: To 4,000 words.

Requirements: Entry fee, $20. Accepts hard copy and electronic submissions via website. Include entry form. Visit website for more information.

Prize: First prize, $500 and promotion in *Writer's Digest* and the *2013 Novel & Short Story Writer's Market*.

Deadline: October.

Writer's Digest Writing Competition

4700 East Galbraith Road
Cincinnati, OH 45236

Description: This annual competition calls for entries in 10 different categories, including children's and YA fiction, short stories, screenplays, magazine articles, and plays. It accepts previously unpublished work only.
Website: www.writersdigest.com/competitions

Length: Word lengths vary by category. See website for details.

Requirements: Entry fee, $20 for the first poem entry) and $15 for each additional poem; all other entries, $30 for the first manuscript and $20 for each additional manuscript submitted in the same online session. Accepts submissions via website only.

Prize: Grand prize, $3,000, a trip to the *Writer's Digest* Conference, and individual attention from four editors or agents.

Deadline: June.

Writers-Editors Network Competition

P.O. Box A
North Stratford, NH 03590

Description: This contest offers prizes in the categories of nonfiction, fiction, children's literature, and poetry. It is sponsored by the Writers-Editors Network and accepts a mix of published and unpublished work.
Website: www.writers-editors.com

Length: To 5,000 words.

Requirements: Entry fees vary for each category; members pay up to 50% less. Accepts hard copy and email submissions to contestentry@writers-editors.com. Visit the website for more information, including the breakdown of divisions and categories, rules, and requirements.

Prize: First-, second-, and third-place winners in each category receive $100, $75, and $50 respectively, plus certificates. Honorable mention certificates are also awarded in each category.

Deadline: March 15.

Zoetrope All-Story Short Fiction Contest

916 Kearny Street
San Francisco, CA 94133

Description: Each year literary stories of all genres are sought for this competition, which has been held for 17 years. Entries must be previously unpublished.
Website: www.all-story.com/contests.cgi

Length: To 5,000 words.

Requirements: Entry fee, $15. Register online, then upload your entry; also accepts hard copy. Accepts multiple entries. Name and address may appear on the first page or in a separate cover letter only. Write "Short Fiction Contest" on the envelope, and on the story. Include SASE for contest results.

Prize: First prize, $1,000; second prize, $500; third prize, $250. Winners and seven finalists are considered for representation by literary agents.

Deadline: July–October.

Indexes

2013 Market News: New Listings ★

About.com
About Families
Act Two
Adventures NW
Akron Life
American Car Collector
American Fine Art
Amethyst Arsenic
Amp It Up!
Apple
AskMen
At Home Tennessee
Austin Man
AXS Longboard Retailer
Babble.com
Back Porch View
Backstagemouse.com
Baltimore
Bards and Sages Quarterly
Bartleby Snopes
Bartleby Snopes Writing Contest
Bead Trends
Best in Travel Magazine
Better Buildings
The Brooklyner
Catamaran Literary Reader
CFO
Cigar & Spirits
Cincinnati
Claims Journal
Cloud Computing Magazine
Collier's
CommonCall
Connecting: Solo Travel Network
Cosign Magazine
Cosmopolitan
Cosmopolitan for Latinas
Crosswalk.com
The Amanda Davis Highwire Fiction Award
Desert Ashram
Diabetes Forecast
Dirt Toys Magazine
Elk Hunter
Entra
ESPN The Magazine
Ever
Evince
The Fader
The Fiscal Times
Fitness
Frederick Gorilla
Fried Fiction
GQ
Grandparents.com
Grantland Quarterly
The Growler
The Guild Literary Complex Prose Awards
The Gulf Coast Writer's Association Let's Write Contest
Gumshoe
HBCU Connect On Campus
Healthcare Journal of New Orleans
Hemispheres
O. Henry
HM
Home School Enrichment
The Improper Bostonian
The Intelligent Optimist
The Iowan
Jet
Joy of Kosher with Jamie Geller
Just Out
Kansas City Prime Magazine
The Knot
Ladies Home Journal
Lake Country Journal
David J. Langum Sr. Prizes in American Historical Fiction and American Legal History
Life in the Finger Lakes
Literary Juice
Literary Juice Flash Fiction Contest
Literary Laundry
The L Magazine
Louisiana Kitchen
Louisiana Literature
Makeshift
Manhattan
Marin Magazine
Men's Health
Mirror Moms
M Magazine
Moms & Dads Today
Mother Earth Living
MPVHub Audio Magazine
My Safety
Narrative
NNY Business
NYMetro Parents
The Sean O Faolain Short Story Competition
Off Track Planet
On-the-Verge Emerging Voices Award
Outside
Pacific Standard
Palm Beach Woman
Palooka Press Chapbook Contest
Parenting Children with Special Needs
Patch.com
The Katherine Paterson Prize for Young Adult and Children's Writing
PeerSphere
Peloton
Photo District News
PineStraw
Plate
The Pointing Dog Journal
PQ Monthly
Praxis
QSR
Ratchet + Wrench
Real Simple
Redbook
Restaurant Development & Design
Revolver
Ryse
St. Louis Family
San Antonio
Scuba Sport
SFRevu
Shelf Unbound
Skirt!
Slice
Smart Retailer
Society Charlotte
The Society Diaries
Solar Power World
Spacing
Spin
The Ruth Stone Poetry Prize
Strange Horizons
Sunset
TechRevu
Tell Magazine
Texas Monthly
Thriving Family
TQR, Total Quality Reading
Tucson Woman
Ulster Magazine
VentureBeat
Via
Washingtonian
Western Hunter
Western Living
Where Women Cook
Wine Enthusiast
Work Your Way
World Trade 100
Z-Life
Zoning Practice

2013 Market News: Deletions

Abaco Life
Absent Willow Review
Absolutely Business
Acres
African Voices
AHP Perspective
Américas
Ancestry
ANSOM
Collectors News and Antiques
Aquarium Fish International
artsee
Automated Builder
Baja Life
Balloons & Parties Magazine
Bellowing Ark
The Big Ugly Review
Bird Talk
The Black Boot
BuilderNews
Cabling Business Magazine
CareerFOCUS
Chic Mom Magazine
The Christian Response
Chronos
Cleveland Family
Collectible Automobile
Colorado Explorer
The Common Review
Contempora Magazine
Courier Magazine
Craft
The Deal
The Diamond Registry Bulletin
Directed By Magazine
The Dirty Goat
Doll Reader
Fiction Fix
Field Trial Magazine
Filipinas
Foster City International Writer's Contest
Get Married Magazine
Glass Craftsman
Global Woman Magazine
Good Dog
Ella T. Grasso Literary Award
The Greyhound Review
The Growing Edge
Hearts of the Country
The Herb Companion
Homemakers
Horizons (NY)
I Do for Brides
Illumen
Inside Kung-Fu
In the Snake
Journal America
Journal of Asian Martial Arts
The Labor Paper
Latitudes & Attitudes
Leving's Divorce Magazine
Light of Consciousness
Living Aboard
Lompoc Valley Magazine
Marine Business Journal
Massive Online Gamer
Mindflights
MultiCultural Review
New York Trend
NJ Savvy Living
Nutrition Health Review
Office Solutions
Omega Directory
Our House
Paradoxism
Pine Magazine
Reach Out Magazine
Riverwind
Russia! Magazine
David B. Saunders Creative Nonfiction Prize
The Sensible Sound
Southern New England Woman
Spa Magazine
Sports Northwest
Sue Magazine
SweetMama
Teddy Bear Review
thinkBIG Magazine
13th Moon
3/GO Triathlon
270inc Business Magazine
Wascana Review
Waste Reduction Tips
Whole Living
Wisconsin Trails Magazine
Woman's Day Special Interest Publications
Writers' Journal
Writer's Journal Fiction Contest
Xavier Review
The Yalobusha Review
Yemassee Journal
Zahir
Zakar

Best for First-Time Writers

Some magazines are more receptive to freelancers they have not worked with before than others. We have compiled a list of magazines where at least 50 percent of their freelance material is written by previously published writers who are new to those magazines. If you approach these publications with well-written, appropriate material, you can increase your odds of publication.

Absinthe
Adoptive Families
Aethlon
African American Golfer's Digest
AGNI
Airbrush Action
Airport Improvement
Alabama Heritage
Alaska Quarterly Review
Alternative Harmonies
The American Interest
American Libraries
American Literary Review
American School & University
American Secondary Education Journal
American String Teacher
America's Civil War
Amoskeag
Angels on Earth
Animal Sheltering Magazine
Antiques & Fine Art
Apogee Photo Magazine
Appalachian Heritage
Aquarius
Arkansas Review
Artful Dodge
Art Jewelry
Arts & Activities
Ascent Aspirations Magazine
Autism Asperger's Digest
Backwoods Home Magazine
Bellingham Review
Bench & Bar of Minnesota
Bend of the River
Berkeley Fiction Review
Best New Writing
Bibliotheca Sacra
Big World
Bitch Magazine
Blackbird
BlackFlash
Black Warrior Review
Blue Mesa Review
Bluestem
Bogg
Book Dealers World
Boulevard
The Briar Cliff Review
Briarpatch
Bull Spec
Business Today
Button
Callaloo
Called Magazine
Calyx
Canadian Woodworking & Home Improvement
Capper's
Carolina Quarterly
The Chaffin Journal
Chattahoochee Review
Chicago Reader
Children's Ministry
Chrysalis Reader
The Cincinnati Review
Clavier Companion
Closing the Gap
CM Cleanfax
Coal People Magazine
Colorado Review
Columbia: A Journal
Conceit Magazine
Concho River Review
Conduit
Conscience
Conscious Dancer
Coping with Cancer
Crab Orchard Review
The Cream City Review
Creations Magazine
Creative Nonfiction
Creative With Words
Cultural Survival Quarterly
Curve
CutBank
Deer & Deer Hunting
Democracy
Descant
Desert Ashram
Devozine
Dimensions
Dimensions of Early Childhood
Disciple Magazine
The Dollar Stretcher
Dossier
Downstate Story
The Drama Review
Drink Me Magazine
Earth Island Journal
East Texas Historical Journal
Eddies
Educational Horizons
Educational Leadership
Electronic Green Journal
The Elks Magazine
Ellipsis...Literature and Art
Espace
Euphony Journal
Evansville Business
Evansville Review
Faith & Form
Farm and Ranch Living
Fate
Feminist Studies
Fifth Wednesday Journal
Financial History
Fine Gardening
The First Line
Flint Hills Review
The Florida Review
Folio
The Forensic Teacher Magazine
Forge
Fourteen Hills: The SFSU Review
The Franchise Handbook
Frigg
Gas Engine Magazine
A Gathering of the Tribes
Georgetown Review
The Gettysburg Review
Gifted Education Press Quarterly
Glimmer Train
Goldenseal
Good Life Living Green Magazine
Gray Areas
Greatest Uncommon Denominator
The Green Hills Literary Lantern
Green Mountains Review
GreenPrints
Grit
Group
Gulf Coast
Gulf Stream
The G.W. Review
Hanging Loose
Hardboiled
Harpur Palate
Hawai'i Review
Hayden's Ferry Review
Healthy & Fit
HM
Home Energy
The Humanist
Hunger Mountain
Image
India Currents
Indiana Review
Inns Magazine
Inside Jersey
Insight
InTents
International Gymnast
Iowa Review
Irreantum
Island
Italian Americana
Jabberwock Review
Jazzed
Jersey Devil Press
J Journal
The Journal
Journal of Information Ethics
Journal of Insurance Operations
Kaleidoscope
Kansas City Voices
Kearsarge Magazine
Kelsey Review
Kerem
Kestrel
Krave Magazine
Lapham's Quarterly
Leadership Journal
Leading Edge Magazine

Best for First-Time Writers

Lighthouse Digest
Limestone
Literary Mama
The Long Story
The Louisville Review
Lullwater Review
The Madison Review
Make
Massachusetts Review
Mature Years
The Maynard
Memoir Journal
Michigan Historical Review
Michigan History
Mid-American Review
Miniature Horse World
The Minnesota Review
Mobius
Modernism
Momentum
Mom Magazine
Montana
Ms. Fitness
Mystery Readers Journal
Nano Fiction
Natural Bridge
Naval History
Nebraska History
Necrology Shorts
Neo-opsis Science Fiction Magazine
New Delta Review
New Orleans Review
The New Orphic Review
NewsUSA
Nimrod International Journal
Nineteenth Century
North Atlantic Review
North Carolina Literary Review
Nostalgia Magazine
Notre Dame Review
Obsidian
OnEarth
One Story
On The Premises
Parabola
Parameters
Parenting New Hampshire
Passages North
Pearl
Pediatrics for Parents
Peregrine
Phoebe
Ping! Zine
The Pink Chameleon
Plain Spoke
Pleiades
Ploughshares
Porchlight
Portland Review
Prairie Journal
Praxis
Principal
PRISM
Prism International
Proceedings
Psychology Today
P31 Woman
Quaker Life
Quest
Rack
Rambunctious Review
Raven Chronicles
Red Cedar Review
Red River Family Magazine
Red Rock Review
Red Wheelbarrow
Reed Magazine
Reiki News Magazine
Response
Reunions
Review
Rio Grande Family
River HIlls Traveler
RiverSedge
Road King
Roanoke Review
Rockford Review
Rocky Mountain Rider
Rose & Thorn Journal
Rosebud
Rugby Magazine
Rural Missouri
Sacred Fire
Sacred Journey
Salt Hill
Salvo Magazine
Sanskrit
Saudi Aramco World
The Savage Kick
Scandinavian Review
SchoolArts
Sea History
Seeing the Everyday
Single Again
Sinister Wisdom
Small Boats
Snowy Egret
SN Review
Social Forces
Soft Dolls & Animals
So To Speak
South American Explorers
South Carolina Historical Magazine
The South Carolina Review
The Southeast Review
Southern Humanities Review
The Southern Review
South Loop Review
Southwestern Historical Quarterly
Southwest Review
SpeciaLiving
Spin-Off
Spirit of Change
The Splinter Generation
StarDate
Stone's Throw Magazine
StoryQuarterly
The Storyteller
sub-Terrain
Sycamore Review
Tampa Review
Tea
Teachers & Writers
Teachers of Vision
Telemark Skier
Texas Town & City
TheatreForum
Thema
Third Coast
Threads
Tikkun Magazine
Timber Home Living
Toward Freedom
The Trapper & Predator Caller
Travel Goods Showcase
Tropical Fish Hobbyist
UMM
Verbatim
Vermont Ink
Vestal Review
Vibrant Life
Vietnam
Washington Square
Water & Wastewater News
West Branch
The Western Historical Quarterly
Westview
Where Women Create
Whiskey Island Magazine
Whitefish Review
The William and Mary Review
Willow Review
Willow Springs
Woodcraft Magazine
WoodenBoat
The Worcester Review
Workers Write!
Working Money
World Policy Journal
The WREN Magazine
The Writer's Chronicle
Writing on the Edge
YourTango
Zoetrope: All Story

Best for Unpublished Writers

You can improve your chances of breaking into the market by submitting your work to periodicals that are receptive to unpublished writers. The majority of the publications listed in this directory consider material from unpublished writers; however, some are more receptive than others.

Below is a list of magazines that acquire more than half of their freelance material from previously unpublished writers. There aren't any guarantees, but if you approach these magazines with well-written, appropriate material, you can increase your odds.

African Violet Magazine
The Allegheny Review
Alternative Harmonies
American Legion Auxiliary
Angels on Earth
Annals of Improbable Research
Arizona Networking News
Arts & Activities
AT Journeys
BackHome
The Backwoodsman
Bead & Button
Bend of the River
Best New Writing
Camping Magazine
Capper's
Chattahoochee Review
Children's Ministry
Christian Home & School
The Christian Ranchman
Classic Toy Trains
Cleaning Business
Closing the Gap
Columbia: A Journal
Conceit Magazine
Coonhound Bloodlines
Creating Keepsakes
Creative With Words
Curious Parents
Dimensions of Early Childhood
Disciple Magazine
Discover Maine Magazine
Downstate Story
Earth
East Texas Historical Journal
Educational Leadership
EFCA Today
Ellipsis...Literature and Art
Espace
Exchange
Fairfield County Business Journal
Faith & Form
Farm and Ranch Living
Fibre Focus
The Forensic Teacher Magazine
4 Wheel Drive & Sports Utility Magazine
The Free Press
Gas Engine Magazine
German Life
Glimmer Train
Grain
Greatest Uncommon Denominator
Group
Hawai'i Review
Healthy & Fit
Highway News and Good News
HM
The 'Hood
Indiana Review
Inkwell
Insight
International Gymnast
In the Wind
JEMS
The Journal
Journal of Court Reporting
Journal of Insurance Operations
Kelsey Review
Leading Edge Magazine
The Maynard
Michigan Historical Review
Military
Military History
Military Review
Mom Magazine
Ms. Fitness
Nano Fiction
The New Orphic Review
Nostalgia Magazine
Obsidian
Out Smart
Pediatrics for Parents
Phoebe
Ping! Zine
Pointed Circle
Purpose
The Quilter Magazine
Rack
Railroad Evangelist
Red Cedar Review
Reiki News Magazine
Reptiles
Reunions
Reverie
Rugby Magazine
Rug Hooking
Rural Missouri
Sanskrit
SchoolArts
Seeing the Everyday
Sinister Wisdom
Skeet Shooting Review
South American Explorers
Spin-Off
Tampa Bay Wellness
Texas Runner & Triathlete
Today's Photographer
Tropical Fish Hobbyist
Vista
Washington Square
Whispering Wind
Woman's Life
Workers Write!
Working Money
World Art Glass Quarterly
The WREN Magazine
Youth & Discipleship Leadership Journal

Category Index

Associations

Beauty & Fashion

Business

Current Events

Education

Entertainment

Environment

Family

Historical

Horror

Humor

Inspirational

Literary

Mainstream

Multicultural

Mystery

Regional

Romance

Science Fiction

Western

Finances

Food

Gardening

Gay, Lesbian, Transgender

Government

Health & Fitness

History

Hobbies & Crafts

House & Home

How-to

Humor, Nonfiction

Hunting & Fishing

Inspirational Nonfiction

Lifestyle

Machinery & Maintenance

Management

Marine

Marketing

Media Reviews

Medical

Men's

Military

Multicultural Nonfiction

Music

Nature & the Outdoors

New Age

New Products

Nostalgia

Nutrition

Opinion

Parenting

Personal Experience

Poetry

Politics

Pop Culture

Profiles

Psychology

Public Affairs

Recreation

Relationships

Religion

Science

Self-help

Seniors

Sexuality

Social Issues

Sports

Technology

Travel

Vehicles

Women's

Writing

Magazine Index

 indicates a new listing

B

C